Symbols Used in This Book

α [alpha] = ad valorem tax (or tariff) rate

Δ [capital delta] = change in the following variable (for example, the change in p between Periods 1 and 2 is $\Delta p = p_2 - p_1$, where p_2 is the value of p in Period 2 and p_1 is the value in Period 1)

ε [epsilon] = the price elasticity of demand

η [eta] = the price elasticity of supply

ι [iota] = incidence of a tax that falls on consumers

$\mathcal{L}$ = lump-sum tax

π [pi] = profit = revenue – total cost = $R - C$

ρ [rho] = profit tax rate

τ [tau] = specific or unit tax (or tariff)

θ [theta] = probability or share

ξ [xi] = the income elasticity of demand

Abbreviations, Variables, and Function Names

AFC = average fixed cost = fixed cost divided by output = F/q

AVC = average variable cost = variable cost divided by output = VC/q

AC = average cost = total cost divided by output = C/q

AP_Z= average product of input Z (for example, AP_L is the average product of labor)

C = total cost = variable cost + fixed cost = $VC + F$

CRS = constant returns to scale

CS = consumer surplus

CV = compensating variation

$D(q)$ = market demand function

$D_r(q)$ = residual demand function

DRS = decreasing returns to scale

DWL = deadweight loss

EV = equivalent variation

F = fixed cost

i = interest rate

I = indifference curve

IRS = increasing returns to scale

K = capital

L = labor

LR = long run

m = constant marginal cost

M = materials

MC = marginal cost = $\Delta C/\Delta q$

MP_Z = marginal (physical) product of input Z (for example, MP_L is the marginal product of labor)

MR = marginal revenue = $\Delta R/\Delta q$

MRS = marginal rate of substitution

MRT = marginal rate of transformation

$MRTS$ = marginal rate of technical substitution

n = number of firms in an industry

p = price

PPF = production possibility frontier

PS = producer surplus = revenues minus variable costs = $R - VC$

Q = market (or monopoly) output

$\bar{Q}$ = output quota

q = firm output

R = revenue = pq

r = price of capital services

s = per-unit subsidy

$S(q)$ = market supply function

$S_o(q)$ = supply of all the other firms in the industry

SC = a measure of economies of scope

SR = short run

T = tax revenues (αpQ, τQ, $\rho\pi$)

U = utility

U_z = marginal utility of good Z

VC = variable cost

w = wage

W = welfare

Y = income or budget

Microeconomics

Jeffrey M. Perloff

University of California, Berkeley

ADDISON-WESLEY

An imprint of Addison Wesley Longman, Inc.

Reading, Massachusetts • Menlo Park, California • New York • Harlow, England
Don Mills, Ontario • Sydney • Mexico City • Madrid • Amsterdam

To my mother, Mimi Perloff

Executive Editor: Denise Clinton
Senior Development Manager: Sylvia Mallory
Development Editors: Jane Tufts, Sylvia Mallory
Senior Administrative Assistant: Jennifer Vito
Supplements Editor: Deborah Kiernan
Copy Editor: Barbara Willette
Senior Production Supervisors: Mary Sanger, Nancy Fenton
Marketing Manager: Amy Cronin
Associate New Media Editor: Wendy Wong
Text and Cover Designer: Regina Hagen
Art Editing Supervisor: Meredith Nightingale
Senior Technical Art Specialist: Joe Vetere
Electronic Production Administrator: Sally Simpson
Print Buyer: Sheila Spinney
Art Editor: Sandra Scholten
Illustrator: Jim McLaughlin
Cover Photo: © Hideki Kuwajima/Photonica

Photo credits appear on page A–48, which constitutes a continuation of the copyright page.

Library of Congress Cataloging-in-Publication Data

Perloff, Jeffrey M.,
Microeconomics/Jeffrey M. Perloff.
p. cm.
Includes index.
ISBN 0-201-59137-5
I. Microeconomics. II. Title.
HB172.P39 1998
338.5—dc21 98-23043
CIP

1 2 3 4 5 6 7 8 9 10—RNT—0201009998

CONTENTS

PREFACE

When I was a student, I fell in love with microeconomics because it cleared up many mysteries about the world and provided the means to answer new questions. I wrote this book to show students that economic theory has practical, problem-solving uses and is not an empty academic exercise.

This book shows how individuals, policymakers, and firms can use microeconomic tools to analyze and resolve problems. For example, students learn that

- individuals can draw on microeconomic theories when deciding about issues such as whether to invest and whether to sign a contract that pegs prices to the government's measure of inflation;
- policymakers (and voters) can employ microeconomics to predict the impact of government taxes, regulations, and other measures before they are enacted;
- lawyers and judges use microeconomics in antitrust, discrimination, and contract cases;
- firms apply microeconomic principles to produce at least cost and maximize profit, select strategies, decide whether to buy from a market or to produce internally, and write contracts to provide optimal incentives for employees.

My experience in teaching microeconomics for the departments of economics at MIT, the University of Pennsylvania, and the University of California, Berkeley; the Department of Agricultural and Resource Economics at Berkeley; and the Wharton Business School has convinced me that students prefer this emphasis on real-world issues.

FEATURES

This book differs from other microeconomics texts in three main ways. First, it integrates real-world examples throughout, not just in isolated applications. Second, it places greater emphasis than other texts on modern theories—such as industrial organization theories, game theory, transaction cost theory, information theory, and contract theory—that are useful in analyzing actual markets. Third, it employs a step-by-step approach to demonstrate how to use microeconomic theory to solve problems and analyze policy issues.

Widget-Free Economics

To convince students that economics is practical and useful, not just a textbook exercise, this text presents theories using real-world examples rather than made-up analyses of widgets, those nonexistent products beloved by earlier generations of textbook writers. These real economic "stories" are integrated into the formal presentation of many economic theories, discussed in featured Applications, and analyzed in what-if policy discussions.

Integrated Real-World Examples. The book uses real-world examples throughout the narrative to illustrate many basic theories of microeconomics. Students learn the basic model of supply and demand using estimated supply and demand curves for Canadian processed pork. They analyze consumer choice employing typical consumers' estimated indifference curves between beer and wine and mill workers' indifference curves between income and leisure. Students examine the effects of income taxes for estimated labor supply curves from several countries. They learn about production and cost functions using evidence from a Norwegian printing firm. Students see monopoly theory applied to a patented pharmaceutical, Tagamet. They use oligopoly theories to analyze the rivalry between United Airlines and American Airlines on the Chicago–Los Angeles route and between Coke and Pepsi in the cola industry. They investigate whether it pays to go to college at various interest rates. They examine why some lawyers charge by the hour while others share the trial award with their clients.

Applications. The text also includes many featured Applications to illustrate the versatility of microeconomic theory. One such application derives an isoquant for semiconductors using actual data. Other applications look at measures of the pleasure consumers get from television, and the amount by which recipients value Christmas presents relative to the cost to gift givers. Applications analyze the impact of government subsidies on the rivalry between Boeing and Airbus and the effects of the coverage of the O. J. Simpson trial on television advertising. One application investigates whether buying flight insurance makes sense. Another examines the financial benefits Michael Jordan provides to basketball teams other than his own, the Chicago Bulls.

What-If Policy Analysis. In addition, the book uses economic models to probe the likely outcomes of changes in public policies. Students learn how to conduct what-if analyses of policies such as taxes, subsidies, barriers to entry, price floors and ceilings, quotas and tariffs, zoning, laws limiting diversification, pollution controls, licensing laws, and laws governing pensions. For example, the text analyzes the effects of taxes on virtually every type of market.

The book also reveals the limits of economic theory for policy analysis. For example, to illustrate why attention to actual institutions is important, the text uses three different models to show how the effects of minimum wages vary across types of markets and institutions. Similarly, the text illustrates that a minimum wage law that is harmful in a competitive market may be desirable in certain noncompetitive markets.

Modern Theories

The first half of this text comprehensively treats the perfect competition model. The second half concentrates on imperfectly competitive markets, in which firms have market power, firms and consumers are uncertain about the future and have limited information, and there are externalities and public goods.

The book goes beyond basic microeconomic theory to look at theories and applications from many important contemporary fields of economics. Extensive coverage of problems from resource economics, labor economics, international trade, public finance, and industrial organization is featured throughout. Individual chapters examine special topics such as exhaustible and renewable resources, labor supply, tariffs and quotas, risk bearing under uncertainty, vertical integration, and strategies about entry.

This book differs from other microeconomics texts by using game theory throughout the second half rather than isolating the topic in a single chapter. Game theory and decision trees are used to study oligopoly quantity and price setting, strategic trade policy, strategic behavior in multiperiod games (such as collusion and preventing entry), strategic advertising, investing when there's uncertainty about the future, and pollution (the Coase Theorem). Unlike most texts, this book covers pure and mixed strategies and analyzes both normal-form and extensive-form games.

The last two chapters draw from modern contract theory to analyze adverse selection and moral hazard extensively, instead of (as other texts do) mentioning these topics only in passing, if at all. The text covers lemons markets, signaling, preventing shirking, and the revelation of information (including through contract choice).

Solved Problems

Many professors report that their biggest challenge in teaching microeconomics is helping students learn to solve new problems. This book is based on the belief that the best way to teach this important skill is to demonstrate problem solving repeatedly and then to give students exercises to do on their own. Each chapter (except Chapter 1) provides several Solved Problems showing students how to answer qualitative and quantitative problems using a step-by-step approach. Rather than empty arithmetic exercises demanding no more of students than to employ algebra or a memorized mathematical formula, the Solved Problems focus on important economic issues such as analyzing government policies and determining firms' optimal strategies.

One Solved Problem uses game theory to examine the competition between Netscape and Microsoft in the Internet browser market. Another shows how a monopolistically competitive airline equilibrium would change if fixed costs (such as fees for landing slots) rise. Others examine how an ad valorem tax affects a competitive market with an inelastic supply curve, why firms charge different prices at factory stores than elsewhere, and when markets for lemons exist, among many other topics.

The Solved Problems illustrate how to approach the two sets of formal end-of-chapter problems. The first set of problems poses questions that students can solve using graphs or verbal arguments; the second set requires the use of math. The answers to selected end-of-chapter problems appear at the end of the book, and the solutions to the remaining problems may be found in the Instructor's Manual.

CONTENTS AND ORGANIZATION

The first half of the book (Chapters 1–10) examines markets in which many firms compete. It emphasizes that such competition has very desirable properties. The second half (Chapters 11–20) considers what happens in the real world when various conditions of the ideal perfect competition model do not hold, so that there are few firms, few buyers, uncertainty, and pollution.

Following Chapter 1's introduction to the study of microeconomics, Chapters 2 and 3 use the supply-and-demand model to analyze a competitive market with many firms. These chapters show that the amount of goods consumers want and how many units firms are willing to sell at each possible price jointly determine the market price.

Chapters 4 and 5 examine how individual consumers decide on the amount of each good and service to buy based on market prices, income, government regulations, and other factors. Chapters 6 and 7 apply the theory of the firm to investigate how the amount that firms can produce depends on the resources available and on technology, and how firms use their knowledge of various technologies and the prices of various inputs to pick the technology that allows them to produce in the least costly manner.

Chapters 8–10 deal with perfect competition. Chapter 8 shows how firms use their knowledge about costs to decide how much output to produce at any given price so as to maximize their profits. Chapters 9 and 10 investigate how consumers and firms gain or lose from government actions and events that affect market prices.

Chapters 11–14 focus on market power and market structure. Chapter 11 shows that a monopoly sets a price above marginal cost. Chapter 12 uses game theory to analyze oligopolistic firms' behavior and shows that an oligopoly charges a price that is usually above the competitive price and below the monopoly price.

Chapter 13 shows that if firms produce differentiated products, the prices they charge differ and the average price is higher than if consumers view the products as identical. The chapter also examines how monopolistic and oligopolistic firms price discriminate across customers. Chapter 14 uses game theory to explore how firms act to drive competitors out of the market or to keep them from entering the market in the first place. It also examines how firms use advertising strategically.

Chapters 15 and 16 cover input markets. Chapter 15 looks at equilibrium in input markets and observes that a firm produces an input itself (rather than buying it from other firms) if it is less expensive to produce that input. Chapter 16 examines how firms take the interest rate into account in deciding whether it pays to make sizable capital investments to build manufacturing plants or to buy machinery. It also discusses how prices in markets for exhaustible resources such as oil and coal depend on interest rates.

Chapters 17–20 turn to the role of uncertainty, missing markets, and limited information. Chapter 17 considers how firms and individuals make decisions when there is uncertainty about future prices or events such as floods and earthquakes. Chapter 18 discusses the serious social problems that arise when there is no price for a good because there is no market, or there is no price for a bad such as pollution. This chapter uses game theory to illustrate the Coase Theorem and to explain why bargaining usually cannot solve externality problems. The chapter ends with an analysis of public goods.

Chapters 19 and 20 examine how limited or unequal information between buyers and sellers affects prices, output, and product quality. Chapter 19 analyzes the effects of varying information between parties in a transaction on market price and product quality. For example, firms are likely to charge higher prices if consumers do not know the prices that each firm in the market sets. Finally, Chapter 20 shows how people try to solve problems created by asymmetric information through the use of individualized contracts rather than markets.

ALTERNATIVE ORGANIZATIONS

Because instructors differ as to the order in which they cover material, this text has been designed for maximum flexibility. The most common approach to teaching microeconomics is to follow the sequence of the chapters in the first half of this book: supply and demand (Chapters 2 and 3), consumer theory (Chapters 4 and 5), the theory of the firm (Chapters 6 and 7), and the competitive model (Chapters 8 and 9). Many instructors then cover monopoly (Chapter 11), oligopoly (Chapter 12 and possibly Section 13.1), price discrimination (Sections 13.2 through 13.5), input markets (Chapter 15), uncertainty (Chapter 17), and externalities (Chapter 18).

A common variant is to present uncertainty (Sections 17.1 through 17.3) immediately after consumer theory. Some instructors may want to cover the material on price discrimination (Sections 13.2 through 13.7) immediately after monopoly (Chapter 11). Many instructors like to take up welfare issues between discussions of the competitive model and noncompetitive models, as Chapter 10, on general equilibrium and economic welfare, does. Alternatively, that chapter may be covered at the end of the course. Faculty can assign material on factor markets earlier (Section 15.1 could follow the chapters on competition, and the remaining section could follow Chapter 11). The material in Chapters 14–20 can be presented in a variety of orders, though Chapter 20 should follow Chapter 19 if both are covered, and Section 17.4 should follow Chapter 16.

Many business school courses skip consumer theory (and possibly some aspects of supply and demand, such as Chapter 3) to allow more time for consideration of the topics covered in the second half of this book. Business school faculty may want to place particular emphasis on strategies (Chapter 14), vertical integration (Section 15.4), capital markets (Chapter 16), and modern contract theory (Chapters 19 and 20).

Technically demanding sections are marked with a star. Subsequent sections and chapters can be understood even if these sections are skipped.

SUPPLEMENTS TO ACCOMPANY *Microeconomics*

Excellent supplements for this textbook are available for students and faculty. The **Study Guide,** by Charles F. Mason of the University of Wyoming and Robert Whaples of Wake Forest University, provides students with a quick guide to Key Concepts and Formulas, as well as additional Applications, and it walks them through the solution of many problems. Students can then work through a large number of Practice Problems on their own and check their answers against those in the Guide. At the end of each Study Guide chapter is a set of Exercises suitable for homework assignments.

Instructors may choose from a wealth of supplements. The **Instructor's Manual,** by Peter von Allmen of Moravian College, has many useful and creative teaching ideas. It also offers an additional Application in each chapter, as well as extra problems and answers, and it provides solutions for the end-of-chapter text problems for which answers are not given at the end of this book. Peter Zaleski of Villanova University developed a **Test Bank** featuring many different types of problems of varying levels of complexity, suitable for homework assignments and exams. A computerized testing program for Windows users, **TestGen-EQ,** provides the same questions as the print Test Bank in a versatile electronic format.

Additionally for instructors, all the text figures are available both as full-color **PowerPoint Presentation** slides and as separately bound black-and-white **Transparency Masters.** The perforated and three-hole-punched book containing the masters also includes convenient **Student Graph Worksheets** reproducing all the text figures; these may be photocopied and distributed to students for class note taking.

I am pleased to announce, too, that *Microeconomics* will be supported by a dedicated **Web Site** (**http://hepg.awl.com/** then use keyword **Perloff**) with extensive resources for professors and students. Finally, we have developed a set of original **Microeconomics Experiments** for instructors who opt to use active classroom learning to help their students grasp key principles.

ACKNOWLEDGMENTS

My greatest debt is to my students and to the two best development editors in the business, Jane Tufts and Sylvia Mallory. My students at MIT, the University of Pennsylvania, and the University of California, Berkeley, patiently dealt with my various approaches to teaching them microeconomics and made useful (and generally polite) suggestions. I received constructive student and faculty comments on early versions of this book when it was used by faculty members at Berkeley and by Jerome Culp at the Duke University Law School.

Jane Tufts reviewed drafts of this book for content and presentation. By showing me how to present the material as clearly, orderly, and thoroughly as possible, she greatly strengthened this text. Sylvia Mallory worked valiantly to improve my writing style and helped to shape and improve every aspect of the book's contents and appearance. In addition, Jane and Sylvia collected the views and advice of many reviewers from around the world.

My excellent research assistants—Hayley Chouinard, R. Scott Hacker, Nancy McCarthy, Enrico Moretti, Asa Sajise, Gautam Sethi, Zhihua Shen and Klaas van't Veld—worked hard to collect facts, develop examples, and check material. I am particularly grateful to Klaas, Scott, and Zhihua for helping to produce many of the best examples in the book. Nancy, Enrico, and Asa showed flair in collecting facts. Hayley and Gautam carefully checked the final version of the book and made very helpful suggestions.

Many people were very generous in providing me with data, models, and examples, including the following: Peter Berck, University of California, Berkeley: exhaustible resources and investments; James Brander, University of British Columbia: American Airlines and United Airlines; Richard Garbaccio, Brandeis University: China; Farid Gasmi, Université des Sciences Sociales, Toulouse: Coke and Pepsi; Claudia Goldin, Harvard University: income distribution; Rachel Goodhue, University of California, Davis: incentives; William Greene, New York University: power plants; Nile Hatch, University of Illinois: semiconductors and learning by doing; Gloria Helfand, University of Michigan: ozone example; Charles Hyde, University of Melbourne: demand estimates; Fahad Khalil, University of Washington: contract theory; Jean-Jacques Laffont, Université des Sciences Sociales, Toulouse: Coke and Pepsi; Karl D. Meilke, University of Guelph: pork; Giancarlo Moschini, Iowa State University: pork; Michael Roberts, University of California, Berkeley: exhaustible resources; Quang Vuong, Université des Sciences Sociales, Toulouse, and University of Southern California: Coke and Pepsi.

Writing a textbook is hard work for everyone involved. I am grateful to the many teachers of microeconomics who spent untold hours reading and commenting on proposals and chapters. Many of the best ideas in this book are due to them. I particularly thank W. Bruce Allen of the Wharton School of Business, who read every single word in the book at least twice (and commented productively on nearly each one). James Brander, University of British Columbia; James Dearden, Lehigh University; Steven Goldman, Berkeley; Charles F. Mason, University of Wyoming; David Reitman, Department of Justice; Nora Underwood, University of California, Davis; and Robert Whaples, Wake Forest University read many chapters and offered particularly insightful comments. Peter Berck made major contributions to Chapter 16. I also thank the following reviewers, who provided valuable comments at various stages:

M. Shahid Alam, Northeastern Univ.
Niels Anthonisen, Univ. of Western Ontario
Vic Brajer, California State Univ., Fullerton
Joni S. Charles, Southwest Texas State Univ.
Dean Croushore, Federal Reserve Bank of Philadelphia
Andrew Daughety, Vanderbilt Univ.
John Edgren, Eastern Michigan Univ.
Roy Gardner, Indiana Univ.
Rod Garratt, Univ. of California, Santa Barbara
J. Fred Giertz, Univ. of Illinois, Urbana–Champaign
Srihari Govindan, Univ. of Western Ontario
Claire Hammond, Wake Forest Univ.
John A. Hansen, State Univ. of New York, Fredonia
L. Dean Hiebert, Illinois State Univ.
Charles Kahn, Univ. of Illinois, Urbana–Champaign
Fred Luk, Univ. of California, Los Angeles
Robert Main, Butler Univ.
David Malueg, Tulane Univ.
Steve Margolis, North Carolina State Univ.
James Meehan, Colby College
Claudio Mezzetti, Univ. of North Carolina, Chapel Hill
Janet Mitchell, Cornell Univ.
Kathryn Nantz, Fairfield Univ.
Patrick B. O'Neil, Univ. of North Dakota
Christos Papahristodoulou, Uppsala Univ.
Sharon Pearson, Univ. of Alberta
Ingrid Peters-Fransen, Wilfrid Laurier Univ.
Sunder Ramaswamy, Middlebury College
S. Abu Turab Rizvi, Univ. of Vermont
Nancy Rose, Sloan School of Business, MIT
Joshua Rosenbloom, Univ. of Kansas
David Sappington, Univ. of Florida
William Doyle Smith, Univ. of Texas at El Paso
Philip Sorenson, Florida State Univ.
Shankar Subramanian, Cornell Univ.
Judith Thornton, Univ. of Washington
Kay Unger, Univ. of Montana
Peter von Allmen, Moravian College
Eleanor T. von Ende, Texas Tech Univ.
Lawrence J. White, New York Univ.
Peter Zaleski, Villanova Univ.
Mark Zupan, Univ. of Arizona

In addition, I thank Bob Solow, the world's finest economics teacher, who showed me how to simplify models without losing their essence. I've also learned a great deal over the years about economics and writing from my coauthors on other projects, especially Dennis Carlton (my coauthor on *Modern Industrial Organization*), Jackie Persons, Steve Salop, Michael Wachter, Larry Karp, Peter Berck, and Dan Rubinfeld (whom I thank for still talking to me despite my decision to write this book).

It was a pleasure to work with the good people at Addison-Wesley, who were incredibly helpful in producing this book. Marjorie Williams and Barbara Rifkin signed me to write it. Denise Clinton, Executive Editor for Economics and Finance, was instrumental in making the entire process work. Mary Sanger and Nancy Fenton supervised the production process and worked hard to eliminate all glitches and bugs. Barbara Willette ably copyedited the book. Sally Simpson did a masterful job of typesetting the book. Gina Hagen designed the handsome interior and cover, and Meredith Nightingale developed the illustrations. Sandra Scholten supervised the drawing of the figures, which took final form under artist Jim McLaughlin's skilled hand. I also want to acknowledge, with gratitude, the efforts of Deborah Kiernan in coordinating the publication of the supplements, Wendy Wong in developing the Web site, and Amy Cronin in marketing the entire program.

Finally, I thank my family, Mimi Perloff, Jackie Persons, and Lisa Perloff (p. 473), for their great patience and support during the nearly endless writing process. And I apologize for misusing their names—and those of my other relatives and friends—in the book!

J. M. P.

CHAPTER 1

Introduction

I've often wondered what goes into a hot dog. Now I know and I wish I didn't. —William Zinsser

If each of us could get all the food, clothing, and toys we want without working, no one would study economics. Unfortunately, most of the good things in life are scarce—we can't all have as much as we want. Thus, scarcity is the mother of economics.

Microeconomics is the study of how individuals and firms make themselves as well off as possible in a world of scarcity, and the consequences of those individual decisions for markets and the entire economy.[1] In studying microeconomics, we examine how individual consumers and firms make decisions and how the interaction of many individual decisions affects markets.

Microeconomics is often called *price theory* to emphasize the important role that prices play. Microeconomics explains how the actions of all buyers and sellers determine prices and how prices influence the decisions and actions of individual buyers and sellers.

In this chapter, we examine three main topics:

1. **Microeconomics: the allocation of scarce resources:** Microeconomics is the study of the allocation of scarce resources.
2. **Models:** Economists use models to make testable predictions.
3. **Uses of microeconomic models:** Individuals, governments, and firms use microeconomic models and predictions in decisionmaking.

1.1 MICROECONOMICS: THE ALLOCATION OF SCARCE RESOURCES

Individuals and firms allocate their limited resources to make themselves as well off as possible. Consumers pick the mix of goods and services that makes them as happy as possible given their limited wealth. Firms decide which goods to produce, where to produce them, how much to produce to maximize their profits, and how to produce those levels of output at the lowest cost by using more or less of various inputs such as labor, capital, materials, and energy. The owners of a depletable natural resource such as oil decide when to use it. Government decisionmakers—to benefit consumers, firms, or government bureaucrats—decide which goods and services the government produces and whether to subsidize, tax, or regulate industries and consumers.

[1]In contrast, *macroeconomics*, the other major field of study in economics, covers the interactions of all the aspects of the economy at once, concentrating on aggregate economic variables, such as total national output and rates of inflation, unemployment, and interest, rather than on individuals. Where a microeconomist may study how an increase in the interest rate on college loans affects students' education decisions, a macroeconomist may study how an increase in the government's money supply affects the interest rate of college loans.

Trade-offs

People make trade-offs because they can't have everything. A society (indeed, the world) faces three key trade-offs:

- **Which goods and services to produce:** If a society produces more cars, it must produce fewer of other goods and services, because there are only so many *resources*—workers, raw materials, capital, and energy—available to produce goods.
- **How to produce:** To produce a given level of output, a firm must use more of one input if it uses less of one input. Cracker and cookie manufacturers switch between palm oil and coconut oil, depending on which is less expensive.
- **Who gets the goods and services:** The more of society's goods and services you get, the less someone else gets.

Who Makes the Decisions

These three allocation decisions may be made explicitly by the government or may reflect the interaction of independent decisions by many individual consumers and firms. In the former Soviet Union, the government told manufacturers how many cars of each type to make and which inputs to use to make them. The government also decided which consumers would get a car.

In most other countries, how many cars of each type are produced and who gets them are determined by how much it costs to make cars of a particular quality in the least expensive way and how much consumers are willing to pay for them. More consumers would own a hand-made Rolls-Royce and fewer would buy a mass-produced Ford Taurus if a Rolls (at $337,100) were not so much more expensive than a Taurus (at $16,000).

APPLICATION

Oregon Decides Which Medical Treatments to Provide

In 1989, to restrain the skyrocketing costs of Medicaid, which provides health care for low-income people, Oregon excluded some previously covered poor people.[2] Almost immediately, state decisionmakers changed their mind. They decided that, rather than reduce the number of poor people who receive aid, the government would further limit the range of services provided.

After a great deal of debate, the new plan went into effect in 1994. The state ranked 688 medical procedures using factors that included a treatment's

---

[2]MacKenzie, Bill, "Rationing Helps Poor in Oregon Get Care," *Newsday*, April 22, 1993:44; "State's Expanded Medicaid Program to Begin with Managed Care Component," *BNA Pension & Benefits Reporter*, 21(7), February 14, 1994:391; "ADA Analyses of the Oregon Health Care Plan," *Issues in Law & Medicine*, March 22, 1994.

medical effectiveness, its cost, and subjective social values about which treatments or conditions are most important to treat.

Medicaid covers only the top 568 of these procedures. Treatments are provided for all major diseases of women and children; all preventive and screening services; some treatments not currently covered by Medicaid requirements, such as dental procedures, hospice services, prescription drugs, most transplants, and routine physicals and mammograms; preventive services such as maternity and newborn care and immunizations; and comfort care and diagnostic services. The plan does not pay to treat conditions that get better on their own, such as a viral sore throat, dizziness, and benign cysts in the eye; conditions for which home treatments are effective; and conditions for which treatment generally is ineffective, such as aggressive medical intervention for advanced cancer.

Thus, Oregon's government makes two of the three main allocation decisions itself rather than leaving these decisions to individuals. The government decides who gets medical care: It provides some care to all poor Oregonians, instead of just to the poorest of the poor. The government also decides which services are provided. ■

Prices Determine Allocations

> An Economist's Theory of Reincarnation: *If you're good, you come back on a higher level. Cats come back as dogs, dogs come back as horses, and people—if they've been real good like George Washington—come back as money.*

Prices link the decisions about *which goods and services to produce*, *how to produce*, and *who gets the goods and services*. Prices influence the decisions of individual consumers and firms, and the interactions of these decisions by consumers, firms, and the government determine price.

Interactions between consumers and firms take place in a **market**, which is an exchange mechanism that allows buyers to trade with sellers. A market may be a town square where people go to trade food and clothing, or it may be an international telecommunications network over which people buy and sell financial securities. Typically, when we talk about a single market, we refer to trade in a single good or group of goods that are highly related, such as various flavors of soft drinks, movies, novels, and brands of automobiles.[3]

---

[3]We use the term *market* loosely to illustrate economic concepts rather than to provide a legal definition of a market. For example, when we say that "an increase in the price of gasoline in the Chicago market affects the price of gasoline in the St. Louis market," we mean that the gasoline prices in the two cities are related. Lawyers use an explicit definition of a market that turns on exactly how closely these prices are related. Whether there are two separate markets or a single combined market is a key issue in many legal cases.

Most of this book concerns how prices are determined within a market. We show that the *number of buyers and sellers* in a market and the amount of *information* they have help to determine whether the price equals the cost of production. We also show that if there is no market—and, hence, no market price—serious problems, such as high levels of pollution, result.

APPLICATION

Tax on Fast-Food Containers

In 1994, the German Federal Administrative Court upheld the right of cities to impose taxes on disposable containers.[4] One city, Kassel, requires snack bars and fast-food restaurants to pay a tax of 30¢ for each paper plate they use, 25¢ for each can or nonreturnable bottle, and 6¢ for each plastic spoon, fork, or knife. Such a large tax changes *how fast-food meals are produced*, as restaurants substitute from the now relatively more expensive disposable products to nondisposable products. After the tax, many fast-food outlets in Kassel began serving cream in reusable metal pitchers, jam in glass jars, and french fries on plates made of edible wafers.

Because the tax raised its costs of production, McDonald's raised its prices. In response to the higher prices and reduced convenience, consumers began eating at home and in regular restaurants more often. As a result, McDonald's may close its outlet in Kassel. Thus, the changes in how fast-food meals are produced and the cost of producing them change the decision as to *what to produce.*

Kassel now produces 500 fewer tons of garbage than it did in the year before the tax was imposed. People who buy from fast-food firms and vending machines bear the cost of cleaning up the environment through higher fast-food prices. Relatively more fast food is consumed in cities that do not tax disposable products and less in cities that do. Thus, this tax affects *who gets the goods.* ■

1.2 MODELS

Everything should be made as simple as possible, but not simpler. —Albert Einstein

To *explain* how individuals and firms allocate resources and how market prices are determined, economists use a **model**: a description of the relationship between two or more economic variables. Economists also use models to *predict* how a change in one variable will affect another.

---

[4]Kinzer, Stephen, "Germany Upholds Tax on Fast-Food Containers," *New York Times*, August 22, 1994.

APPLICATION

Income Threshold Model and China

According to an *income threshold model*, no one who has an income level below a threshold buys a particular consumer durable, which is a good that can be used for long periods of time such as a refrigerator or car. The theory also holds that almost everyone whose income is above the threshold does buy the durable.

If this theory is correct, we predict that, as most people's incomes rise above that threshold in less-developed countries, consumer durable purchases will go from near zero to large numbers virtually overnight. This prediction is consistent with evidence from Malaysia, where the income threshold for buying a car is about $4,000.[5]

Given such evidence from other countries, many firms believe that this model's predictions will apply to China. Incomes are rising rapidly in China and are approaching the threshold levels for many types of durable goods. As a result, these companies are predicting that the greatest consumer durable goods sales boom in history will take place there over the next decade. Anticipating this boom, these companies have greatly increased their investments in durable goods manufacturing plants in China. Annual foreign investments went from $916 million a year in 1983 to more than $4 billion in 1991 to $42 billion in 1996: a 46-fold increase in a decade (*China Statistical Yearbook*, 1997). Anticipating this growth potential, even traditional political opponents of the People's Republic—Taiwan, South Korea, and Russia—have been investing in China. ■

Simplifications by Assumption

We stated the income threshold model verbally, but we could have presented it using graphs or mathematics. Regardless of how the model is described, an economic model is a simplification of reality that contains only its most important features. Without simplifications, it is difficult to make predictions because the real world is too complex to analyze fully.

By analogy, if the manual accompanying your new videocassette recorder (VCR) has a diagram showing the relationships between all the parts in the VCR, the diagram will be overwhelming and useless. In contrast, if it shows a photo of the buttons on the front of the machine with labels describing the purpose of each button, the manual is useful and informative.

---

[5] "Next in Line: Chinese Consumers," *The Economist*, 326(7795), January 23, 1993:66–67; Pelline, Jeff, "U.S. Businesses Pour into China," *San Francisco Chronicle*, May 17, 1994:B1–2.

Economists make many *assumptions* to simplify their models.[6] When using the income threshold model to explain car purchasing behavior in Malaysia, we *assume* that factors other than income, such as the color of cars, are irrelevant to the decision to buy cars. Therefore, we ignore the color of cars that are sold in Malaysia in describing the relationship between average income and the number of cars consumers want. If this assumption is correct, by ignoring color, we make our analysis of the auto market simpler without losing important details. If we're wrong and these ignored issues are important, our predictions may be inaccurate.

Throughout this book, we start with strong assumptions to simplify our models. Later, we add complexities. For example, in most of the book, we assume that consumers know the price each firm charges. In many markets, such as the New York Stock Exchange, this assumption is realistic. It is not realistic in other markets, such as the market for used automobiles, in which consumers do not know the prices each firm charges. To devise an accurate model for markets in which consumers have limited information, we need to add consumer uncertainty about price into the model, as we do in Chapter 19.

Testing Theories

Economic *theory* is the development and use of a model to test *hypotheses*, which are predictions about cause and effect. We are interested in models that make clear, testable predictions, such as "If the price rises, the quantity demanded falls." A theory that said "People's behavior depends on their tastes, and their tastes change randomly at random intervals" is not very useful because it does not lead to testable predictions.

Economists test theories by checking whether predictions are correct.[7] If a prediction does not come true, they may reject the theory.[8] Economists use a model until it is refuted by evidence or until a better model is developed.

A good model makes sharp, clear predictions that are consistent with reality. Some very simple models make sharp predictions that are incorrect, and other more complex models make ambiguous predictions—any outcome is possible—which are untestable. The skill in model building is to chart a middle ground.

The purpose of this book is to teach you how to think like an economist in the sense that you can build testable theories using economic models or apply existing

---

[6]An economist, an engineer, and a physicist are stranded on a desert island with a can of beans but no can opener. How should they open the can? The engineer proposes hitting the can with a rock. The physicist suggests building a fire under it to build up pressure and burst the can open. The economist thinks for a while and then says, "*Assume* that we have a can opener. . . ."

[7]This book cites many empirical studies that test hypotheses; however, it does not present the statistical methodology needed to formally test models. For that, you need to study *econometrics*: the application of statistics to economics.

[8]We can use evidence on whether a theory's predictions are correct to *refute* the theory but not to *prove* it. If a model's prediction is inconsistent with what actually happened, the model must be wrong, so we reject it. Even if the model's prediction is consistent with reality, however, the model's prediction may be correct for the wrong reason. Hence, we cannot prove that the model is correct—we can only fail to reject it.

models to new situations. Just because all well-trained economists think alike in that they develop and use testable models does not mean that they all agree. Quite the contrary. I doubt that you'll be surprised to learn that economists often disagree. One economist presents a logically consistent argument that prices will go up next quarter. Another, using a different but equally logical theory, contends that prices will fall. If the economists are reasonable, they agree that pure logic alone cannot resolve their dispute. Indeed, they agree that they'll have to use empirical evidence—facts about the real world—to find out which prediction is correct.

Although one economist's model may differ from another's, a key assumption in most microeconomic models is that individuals allocate their scarce resources so as to make themselves as well off as possible.[9] Of all affordable combinations of goods, consumers pick the bundle of goods that gives them the most possible enjoyment. Firms try to maximize their profits given limited resources and existing technology. That resources are limited plays a crucial role in these models. Were it not for scarcity, people could consume unlimited amounts of goods and services, and sellers could become rich beyond limit.

As we show throughout this book, the maximizing behavior of individuals and firms determines society's three main allocation decisions: which goods are produced, how these goods are produced, and who gets the goods. For example, diamond-studded pocket combs will be sold only if firms find it profitable to sell them. It will pay for the firms to make and sell these combs only if consumers value the combs as much as or more than it costs the firm to produce them. Consumers will be willing to buy the combs only if they get more pleasure from the combs than they would from the other goods they could buy with the same resources.

Positive Versus Normative

The use of models of maximizing behavior sometimes leads to predictions that seem to be harsh or heartless. For instance, a World Bank economist predicted that, if an African government kept the price of food low during a drought, food shortages would occur and people would starve. The predicted outcome is awful, but the economist was not heartless. The economist was only making a scientific prediction about the relationship between cause and effect: Price controls (cause) lead to food shortages and starvation (effect).

Such a scientific prediction is called a **positive statement:** a testable hypothesis about cause and effect. "Positive" does not mean that we are certain about the truth of our statement—it only indicates that we can test the truth of the statement.

If the World Bank economist is correct, should the government control prices? If the government believes the economist's predictions, it knows that the low prices help those consumers who are lucky enough to be able to buy as much food as they

---

[9]Some people are offended by this approach to economics because it seems to say that everyone is only looking out for number one. However, there is no reason to assume that, just because people maximize, they are selfish. You could, after all, get pleasure from providing your family or neighbors with goods and services.

want, while hurting both the firms that sell food and the people who are unable to buy as much food as they want, some of whom may die. As a result, the government's decision whether to use price controls turns on whether the government cares more about the winners or the losers.[10] That is, to decide on its policy, the government makes a value judgment.

Instead of first making a prediction and testing it and then making a value judgment to decide whether to use price controls, the government could make a value judgment directly. The value judgment could be based on the belief that "because people *should* have prepared for the drought, the government *should* not try to help them by keeping food prices low." Alternatively, the judgment could be based on the view that "people *should* be protected against price gouging during a drought, so the government *should* use price controls."

These two statements are *not* scientific predictions. Each is a value judgment or **normative statement**: a conclusion as to whether something is good or bad. A normative statement cannot be tested because a value judgment cannot be refuted by evidence. It is a prescription rather than a prediction. A normative statement concerns what somebody believes *should* happen; a positive statement concerns what *will* happen.

Although a normative conclusion can be drawn without first conducting a positive analysis, a policy debate will be more informed if positive analyses are conducted first.[11] As was discussed in our application, Oregon's Health Services Commission, in deciding which medical treatments to provide poor people, used both positive analyses—scientific evidence on the cost and effectiveness of treatment—and normative judgments—subjective judgments about which treatments or conditions were more important.

Suppose your normative belief is that the government should help the poor. Should you vote for a candidate who advocates a higher minimum wage (the law says that the wage firms pay cannot be lower than a specified level), a European-style welfare system (guaranteeing health care, housing, and other basic goods and services), an end to our current welfare system, a negative income tax (in which the less income a person has, the more the government gives that person), or job training programs? Positive economic analysis can be used to predict whether these programs will benefit poor people but not whether they are good or bad. Using these predictions and your value judgment, you can decide for whom to vote.

Economists' emphasis on positive analysis has implications for what we study and even our use of language. For example, many economists stress that they study people's *wants* rather than their *needs*. Although people need certain minimum levels

---

[10]The government might want to consider other possible policies at the same time. Other options include importing food from abroad or taxing the rich (including those who make large profits from selling food at high prices) and subsidizing the poor, who could then afford to buy more food.

[11]Some economists draw the normative conclusion that, as social scientists, we economists *should* restrict ourselves to positive analyses. Others argue that we shouldn't give up our right to make value judgments just like the next person (who happens to be biased, prejudiced, and pigheaded, unlike us).

of food, shelter, and clothing to survive, most people in developed economies have enough money to buy goods well in excess of the minimum levels necessary to maintain life. As a result, in wealthy countries, the word *need* is often meant as a value judgment.

You almost certainly have been told by some elder that "you *need* a college education." That person was probably making a value judgment—"you *should* go to college"—rather than a scientific prediction that you will suffer terrible economic deprivation if you do not go to college. We can't test such value judgments, but we can test a hypothesis such as "One-third of the college-age population *wants* to go to college at current prices."

1.3 USES OF MICROECONOMIC MODELS

Have you ever imagined a world without hypothetical situations? —Steven Wright

Because microeconomic models *explain* why economic decisions are made and allow us to make *predictions*, they can be very useful for individuals, governments, and firms in making decisions. Throughout this book, we consider examples of how microeconomics aids in actual decisionmaking. Here, we briefly look at some uses by individuals and governments and then we examine a series of recent decisions by General Motors.

Uses of Microeconomics by Individuals and Governments

Individuals use microeconomics to make purchasing and other decisions. In Chapter 5, we examine how inflation and adjustments for inflation affect individuals. In Chapter 16, we show how to determine whether it pays financially to go to college.

Another use of microeconomics is helping you decide for whom to vote based on candidates' views on economic issues. Does your candidate advocate increasing government spending on education or reducing regulation of businesses to stimulate growth? Will these policies actually stimulate growth? Will they have other desirable or undesirable side effects?

Your government's elected and appointed officials use (or could use) economic models in many ways. Recent administrations have placed increased emphasis on economic analysis. Today, economic and environmental impact studies are required before many projects can commence. The President's Council of Economic Advisors and other federal economists analyze and advise national government agencies on the likely economic effects of all major policies.

Indeed, probably the major use of microeconomic models by governments is to predict the probable impact of a policy before it is adopted. In Chapter 3, we show how to predict the likely impact of a tax on the prices consumers pay and on the tax revenues raised.

In some cases, microeconomic analysis suggests solutions to problems, such as how countries may protect themselves against harmful, coordinated actions of firms. Groups of firms—including many international groups of producers of commodities such as oil, mercury, peppers, and diamonds—try to coordinate their activities to raise prices. Some of these organizations, called *cartels*, keep prices above noncartel levels for years, while others fail miserably. Microeconomic theory predicts which cartels will succeed and which will fail. By using this theory, governments can act to undermine cartels by prohibiting certain actions by firms or by altering their buying behavior, as we discuss in Chapter 12. For example, how governments let firms bid on major projects may determine whether a cartel succeeds or fails.

APPLICATION

Putting Saturn in Orbit

Many firms have staffs of economists to make predictions and evaluate policies. In Chapter 5, we discuss how General Motors (GM) uses a study by one of its staff economists to predict consumer demand for its cars.

Microeconomic analysis was particularly important to GM when it started selling its line of Saturn cars in 1991. GM broke a lot of its old rules.[12] GM built Saturns differently from the way it built its other cars and changed its relationship with its dealers so that they would sell and service the cars in a new way. Did GM's gamble work?

Manufacturing Costs

Starting up the Saturn line was a major risk; GM spent an estimated $5 billion to get Saturn going. (Investment policies are examined in Chapter 16.) To keep manufacturing costs down, GM built a new plant that uses modern technology and a team approach and other Japanese-style management methods to assemble cars. One of these, just-in-time inventories, allows GM to keep its inventory costs down by having suppliers ready to deliver parts almost immediately when needed. The Saturn plant produces relatively few models, and its sharing of engines and other major parts reduces production costs. (We analyze how firms minimize costs in Chapters 6 and 7.)

---

[12]This section is based on Edwards, Martin, "We're Not Dealing: Fixed-Price Sales Find Fans," *Business Journal of North Carolina*, 7(33) November 30, 1992:20; Jedlicka, Dan, "Saturn Becomes a Star; GM's Newest Baby Has Won Buyers' Trust," *Chicago Sun-Times*, December 2, 1992:Auto Times, 3; Pelline, Jeff, "No-Dicker Stickers for New Cars," *San Francisco Chronicle*, April 15, 1993:D1; Pelline, Jeff, "GM Sold on New Pricing," *San Francisco Chronicle*, July 2, 1993:D1; "Automakers Urge Dealers to Quit Haggling," *The Plain Dealer*, February 20, 1994:43K; Glover, Mark, "There's No Haggling over GM Sales Jump," *Sacramento Bee*, February 4, 1994:D1; Martin, Tim, " 'No-Dicker' Sticker Has Mixed Success," *The Nashville Tennessean*, April 12, 1994; Levy, Michael, "Auto Sales Undergoing a Revolution; New Pricing, Mega-Dealerships Change Business," *The Buffalo News*, April 24, 1994:Business, 15.

In building its new plant and designing its new car, GM had to take into account the federal government's emissions standards and other pollution regulations. (In Chapter 18, we analyze how firms react to such regulations and the effects of the regulations.)

Some industry experts believe that GM lost $500 million a year in the first few years because it couldn't make enough cars to cover its investment. Does it make sense to run a plant at a loss for a while? (We first examine this issue in Chapter 8.) In keeping the plant operating, GM may be counting on Saturn managers' and workers' gaining experience in producing cars, which will lower the costs of production in the future. (In Chapter 7, we discuss learning by doing.)

Pricing

GM does not sell Saturns the way it sells its other cars. Knowing consumers' tastes with respect to the cars' features, service, and purchasing negotiations was an essential part of GM's new strategy. (Consumer decisionmaking is analyzed in Chapters 4 and 5.)

Saturn's most striking marketing innovation was the "no-dicker sticker." Saturn dealers charge a fixed price for a car—they don't negotiate with customers as do most dealers. Why? One reason is that, according to a J. D. Power survey, 78% of American car buyers dislike negotiating for a new car. At the very least, this negotiation process is time consuming.

Why do traditional firms want to bargain with customers? It allows them to charge customers different prices. As Chapter 13 shows, such price discrimination can raise a firm's profits.

In the past, some consumers who did not bargain well or had little information about costs and prices paid substantially more than the dealer's cost for a car. One dealer claims that car dealers often marked up their price over cost by 24% in the 1960s. Now, however, Consumers Union and other organizations provide consumers with information about dealers' costs. Using this information, some consumers are able to strike better deals than they could previously. (Chapter 19 discusses the roles of unequal information on the prices consumers pay.) As a result, price markups have fallen; one dealers' group reported that their prices averaged 6.7% over their costs of a car, or about $1,200, in 1993.

Dealers

GM wanted its Saturn dealers not only to charge a fixed price, but also to provide superior service. With superior service, they could compete more effectively with dealers of high-quality imported cars and attract repeat customers. How could GM induce its dealers to provide superior service? (Chapter 20 discusses how one firm gives another incentives to ensure the desired behavior.)

GM ensured that its dealers would earn unusually high profits by limiting the number of Saturn dealers. Initially, GM had only 230 Saturn dealers nationally, compared with 5,000 Chevy dealers. As a result, a Saturn dealer's markup of its price above its costs is greater than it would be if the dealer had to compete with many other local Saturn dealers (see Chapter 12). According to one expert, the typical Saturn price markup is 13% over dealer costs, whereas traditional dealer markups average about half that.

Are higher dealer prices and profits good for GM? On the one hand, the higher retail price cuts current sales of Saturns, which hurts GM. On the other hand, the resulting high profits give dealers an incentive to provide superior service. As one dealer said, "If there were more Saturn dealers, with more competition among ourselves, we couldn't afford to give extra service. The trouble with non-Saturn GM dealers is that they cut their own throats by charging too little and taking most profit out of deals." Extra service should increase the demand for Saturns, which helps GM.

Because its sales staff does not have to spend time negotiating with each customer, Saturn dealers need fewer salespeople. Some dealers calculate that traditional dealers need a 30–40% larger sales staff. Thus, the ratio of labor to capital in traditional dealers is different than that in fixed-price dealers. (Chapters 6 and 7 analyze substitution between inputs.)

At traditional dealerships, a salesperson gets a commission of about a quarter of the markup on a final sale. Because they make money from each extra sale, these salespeople use cold calls (phone calls to strangers) and personal contacts to attract customers. In contrast, Saturn sales staff are paid a salary. As a result, Saturn salespeople have less incentive to pursue customers aggressively than do salespeople who earn a commission (see Chapter 20). To offset this effect, some Saturn dealers boost advertising to generate showroom traffic (see Chapter 14).

Strategy

Why did GM change the way it did business? The reason was that its old approach was not working: GM was losing business and profits to other auto manufacturers.

GM was particularly concerned about its sales in California, where it was losing business to its competitors. As a result, in 1993, GM started using fixed prices on its Pontiacs and Oldsmobiles as well as Saturns in California. GM's California sales jumped 30.6% from October to December, compared with a 2.5% increase for the rest of the California auto industry. Its share of auto sales increased 22% over those three months.

By the very way it designed the Saturn, GM went after a particular type of customer. Only relatively short customers can fit comfortably in a Saturn. Customers who want sporty or other special features are not going to buy a Saturn. Saturn was apparently designed for customers who want to minimize the hassles in their life. A Saturn customer does not have to negotiate over price and is assured a well-built, well-serviced car (with a loaner available if repairs take a long time). (Chapter 13 discusses how firms aim at specific market niches.)

Other dealers and auto manufacturers did not stand still. In picking its strategies, a firm forms beliefs about how its rival will react to its actions (see Chapters 12 and 13). When GM drops its wholesale price, Ford and Honda respond to prevent the loss of sales and profits. When GM started selling Saturns and some of its other cars at fixed prices, Ford began using fixed prices on two of its vehicles. Rival manufacturers have also aimed for the customer profile that Saturn targeted. (Chapters 12–14 examine how large firms compete with each other in setting their prices or quantities. Chapter 13 looks at more complex pricing and investment strategies that firms use to gain at the expense of their competitors.)

Thus, GM made many production, marketing, and strategy decisions based on microeconomic models and predictions. The test that GM uses to determine whether its models and predictions are correct is whether Saturn makes a profit. ■

Summary

1. **Microeconomics: the allocation of scarce resources:** Microeconomics is the study of the allocation of scarce resources. Consumers, firms, and the government must make allocation decisions. The three key trade-offs a society faces are which goods and services to produce, how to produce them, and who gets the goods and services. These decisions are highly interrelated and depend on the prices that consumers and firms face and on government actions. Market prices affect the decisions of individual consumers and firms, and the interaction of the decisions of individual consumers and firms determines market prices. The organization of the market, especially the number of firms in the market and the information consumers and firms have, plays an important role in determining whether the market price is equal to or higher than marginal cost.
2. **Models:** Models based on economic theories are used to predict the future or to answer questions about how some change, such as a tax increase, affects various sectors of the economy. A good theory is simple to use and makes clear, testable predictions that are not refuted by evidence. Most microeconomic models are based on maximizing behavior. Economists use models to construct *positive* hypotheses concerning how a cause leads to an effect. These positive questions can be tested. In contrast, *normative* statements, which are value judgments, cannot be tested.
3. **Uses of microeconomic models:** Individuals, governments, and firms use microeconomic models and predictions to make decisions. For example, to maximize its profits, a firm needs to know consumers' decisionmaking criteria, the trade-offs between various ways of producing and marketing its product, government regulations, and other factors. For large companies, beliefs about how a firm's rivals will react to its actions play a critical role in how it forms its business strategies.

CHAPTER

2

Supply and Demand

Talk is cheap because supply exceeds demand.

When asked, "What is the most important thing you know about economics?" many people reply, "Supply equals demand." This statement is a shorthand description of one of the simplest yet most powerful models of economics. The supply-and-demand model describes how consumers and suppliers interact to determine the *quantity* of a good or service sold in a market and the *price* at which it is sold. To use the model, you need to determine three things: buyers' behavior, sellers' behavior, and how they interact. After reading this chapter, you should be adept enough at using the supply-and-demand model to analyze some of the most important policy questions facing your country today, such as those concerning international trade, minimum wages, and price controls on health care.

After reading that grandiose claim, you may ask, "Is that all there is to economics? Can I become an expert economist that fast?" The answer to both these questions is "no" (of course). You also need to learn the limits of this model and what other models to use when this one does not apply.[1]

Even with its limitations, the supply-and-demand model is the most widely used economic model. It provides a good description of how many markets function, and works particularly well in markets in which there are many buyers and many sellers, such as in most agriculture and labor markets. As with all good theories, the supply-and-demand model can be tested—and, possibly, shown to be false. In those markets where it is applicable, it allows one to make accurate predictions easily.

In this chapter, we examine six main topics:

1. **Demand:** The quantity of a good or service that consumers demand depends on price and other factors such as consumers' incomes and the price of related goods.
2. **Supply:** The quantity of a good or service that firms supply depends on price and other factors such as the cost of inputs firms use to produce the good or service.
3. **Market equilibrium:** The interaction between consumers' demand and firms' supply determines the market price and quantity of a good or service that is bought and sold.
4. **Shocking the equilibrium:** Changes in a factor that affects either demand (such as an increase in the price of related goods) or supply (such as a rise in the price of inputs) or a new government policy (such as a new tax) alter the market price and quantity of a good.
5. **Effects of government interventions:** Government policies may alter the equilibrium and cause the quantity supplied to differ from the quantity demanded.
6. **When to use the supply-and-demand model:** The supply-and-demand model applies to only competitive markets.

---

[1]It is also necessary to learn the economists' secret handshake.

2.1 DEMAND

Potential consumers decide how much of a good or service to buy on the basis of its price and many other factors, including their own tastes, information, prices of other goods, income, and government actions. Before concentrating on the role of price in determining demand, let's look briefly at some of the other factors.

Consumers' *tastes* determine what they are willing to buy. Consumers do not purchase foods they dislike, artwork they hate, or clothes they view as unfashionable or uncomfortable. Advertising may influence peoples' tastes. Perhaps because of advertising, some consumers are willing to spend a substantial premium for brand-name cereals and aspirin or buy the athletic shoes that their favorite athlete endorses.

Similarly, *information* (or misinformation) about the uses of a good affects consumers' decisions. A few years ago when many consumers were convinced that oatmeal could lower their cholesterol level, they rushed to grocery stores and bought large quantities of oatmeal. (They even ate some of it until they remembered that they couldn't stand how it tastes.)

The *prices of other goods* also affect consumers' purchase decisions. Before deciding to buy Levi's jeans, for instance, you might check the prices of other brands. If the price of a close *substitute*—a product that you view as similar or identical to the one you are considering purchasing—is much lower than the price of Levi's jeans, you may buy that brand instead. Similarly, the price of a *complement*—a good that you like to consume at the same time as the product you are considering buying—may affect your decision. If you eat pie only with ice cream, the higher the price of a scoop of ice cream, the less likely you are to buy a piece of pie in a restaurant.

Income plays a major role in determining what and how much to purchase. People who suddenly inherit great wealth may purchase a Rolls Royce or other luxury items and would probably no longer buy do-it-yourself repair kits.

Government rules and regulations affect purchase decisions. Sales taxes increase the price that a consumer must spend for a good, and government-imposed limits on the use of a good may affect demand. If a city's government forbids the use of skateboards on its streets, skateboard sales fall in that city.

Other factors also may affect the demand for specific goods. Consumers are more likely to have telephones if most of their friends have telephones. Carter, Shepard, and Whitney (1991) found that the number of Californians attending thoroughbred racing events (the demand for racing) falls with income, decreases as the number of racing days per year offered by off-track wagering facilities falls, and increases with the ratio of winnings paid back to bettors to the bets placed and with the number of days of racing per year. The demand for small, dead evergreen trees is substantially higher in December than at other times of the year.

Dr. David A. Kessler, former U.S. Commissioner of Food and Drugs, alleged that Brown & Williamson Tobacco Corporation developed a genetically engineered tobacco with more than double the amount of nicotine that some other cigarettes deliver to the smoker.[2] Higher levels of nicotine may increase addiction and thus affect the demand for cigarettes.

Although many factors influence demand, economists usually concentrate on how price affects the quantity demanded. The relationship between price and quantity demanded plays a critical role in determining the market price and quantity in a supply-and-demand analysis. To determine how a change in price affects the quantity demanded, economists must hold constant other factors such as income and tastes that affect demand.

The Demand Curve

The amount of a good that consumers are *willing* to buy at a given price, holding constant the other factors that influence purchases, is the **quantity demanded.** The quantity demanded of a good or service can exceed the quantity *actually* sold. For example, as a promotion, a local store might sell compact disks (CDs) of music for $1 each today only. At that low price, you might want to buy 25 CDs, but, because the store ran out of stock, you can buy only 10 CDs. The quantity you demand is 25—it's the amount you *want*, even though the amount you can *actually* buy is only 10.

We can show the relationship between price and the quantity demanded graphically. A **demand curve** shows the quantity demanded at each possible price, holding constant the other factors that influence purchases. Figure 2.1 shows the estimated demand curve, D^1, for processed pork in Canada (Moschini and Meilke 1992). (Although this demand curve is a straight line, demand curves may also be smooth curves or wavy.) The vertical axis of the graph measures the price, p, per unit of the good—here dollars per kilogram (kg). The horizontal axis measures the quantity, Q, of the good, which is usually expressed in some *physical measure* (million kg of dressed cold pork carcass weight) *per time period* (per year).[3]

The demand curve hits the vertical price axis at $14.30, indicating that no quantity is demanded when the price is $14.30 (or higher). The demand curve hits the horizontal quantity axis at 286 million kg—the amount of pork that consumers want if the price is zero. To find out what quantity is demanded at a price between these extremes, pick that price on the vertical axis—say $3.30 per kg—draw a horizontal line across until you hit the demand curve, then draw a line straight down to the horizontal quantity axis; 220 million kg per year is demanded at that price.

One of the most important things to know about a graph of a demand curve is what is *not* shown. All relevant economic variables that are not explicitly shown on the demand curve graph—tastes, information, prices of other goods (such as beef

[2]Warren E. Leary, "Cigarette Company Developed a Potent Gene-Altered Tobacco," *New York Times*, June 22, 1994:A1, C20. In 1998, a biotechnology firm agreed to plead guilty to conspiring with a major U.S. cigarette manufacturer to raise the nicotine content of tobacco plants. Hall, Carl T., "Oakland Firm Admits Tobacco Plot; High-Nicotine Research for Big Cigarette-Maker," *San Francisco Chronicle*, January 8, 1998:A1.

[3]Economists use the convention that price is on the vertical axis and quantity is on the horizontal axis. There's nothing conceptually wrong with labeling the axes the other way, but if you do that during an exam, your teacher might not notice the switch in axes and think your diagram is wrong.

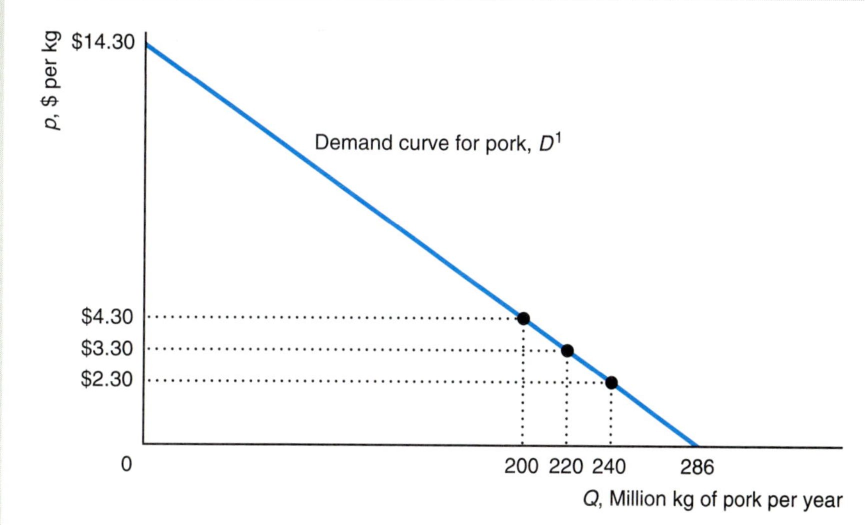

Figure 2.1 A Demand Curve. The estimated demand curve, D^1, for processed pork in Canada (Moschini and Meilke 1992) shows the relationship between the quantity demanded per year and the price per kg. The downward slope of the demand curve shows, holding other factors that influence demand constant, that consumers demand less of a good when its price is high and more when the price is low. A change in price causes a *movement along* the demand curve.

and chicken), income of consumers, and others—are held constant. Thus, the demand curve shows how quantity varies with price but not how quantity varies with tastes, information, the price of substitute goods, or other variables.[4]

Effect of Prices on the Quantity Demanded. Many economists claim that the most important *empirical* finding in economics is the **Law of Demand:** Consumers demand more of a good, the lower the price of a good, holding constant tastes, the prices of other goods, and other factors that influence the amount they consume. According to the Law of Demand, *demand curves slope downward*, as in Figure 2.1.[5]

---

[4]Because prices, quantities, and other factors change simultaneously over time, economists use statistical techniques to hold the effects of factors other than the price of the good constant so that they can determine how price affects the quantity demanded. (See Appendix 2A.) Moschini and Meilke (1992) used such techniques to estimate the pork demand curve in Figure 2.1. As with any estimate, their estimates are probably more accurate in the observed range of prices ($1 to $6 per kg) than at very high or very low prices.

[5]As Chapter 5 notes, an empirical study could find an upward-sloping demand curve in theory. As a practical matter, however, empirical evidence strongly supports the Law of Demand: Virtually every estimated demand curve is downward sloping if we include the extreme cases of vertical (extremely downward-sloping) and horizontal (no slope) demand curves.

A downward-sloping demand curve illustrates that consumers demand more of this good when its price is lower and less when its price is higher. What happens to the quantity of pork demanded if the price of pork drops and all other variables remain constant? If the price of pork falls by a dollar from \$3.30 to \$2.30 in Figure 2.1, the quantity consumers want to buy increases from 220 to 240.[6] Similarly, if the price increases from \$3.30 to \$4.30, the quantity consumers demand decreases from 220 to 200. These changes in the quantity demanded in response to changes in price are *movements along the demand curve*. Thus, the demand curve is a concise summary of the answers to the question "What happens to the quantity demanded as the price changes, when all other factors are held constant?"

Effects of Other Factors on Demand. If a demand curve measures the effects of price changes when all other factors that affect demand are held constant, how can we use demand curves to show the effects of a change in one of these other factors, such as the price of beef? One solution is to draw the demand curve in a three-dimensional diagram with the price of pork on one axis, the price of beef on a second axis, and the quantity of pork on the third axis. But just thinking about drawing such a diagram probably makes your head hurt.

Economists use a simpler approach to show the effect on demand of a change in a factor that affects demand other than the price of the good. A change in any factor other than price of the good itself causes a *shift of the demand curve* rather than a *movement along the demand curve*.

Many people view beef as a close substitute for pork. Thus, at a given price of pork, if the price of beef rises, some people will switch from beef to pork. Figure 2.2 shows how the demand curve for pork shifts to the right from the original demand curve D^1 to a new demand curve D^2 as the price of beef rises from \$4.00 to \$4.60 per kg. (The quantity axis starts at 176 instead of 0 in the figure to emphasize the relevant portion of the demand curve.) On the new demand curve, D^2, more pork is demanded at any given price than on D^1. At a price of pork of \$3.30, the quantity of pork demanded goes from 220 on D^1, before the change in the price of beef, to 232 on D^2, after the price change.

Similarly, a change in information can shift the demand curve. The average number of eggs per year each American eats has fallen steadily since 1955, even though the price of eggs has fallen relative to the price of other goods during this period. Brown and Schrader (1990) found that new information about the link between cholesterol (eggs are high in cholesterol) and heart disease caused the demand curve for eggs to shift to the left. This shift was largely responsible for the per capita decline in fresh egg consumption of 16% to 25% by the first quarter of 1987.

[6]Economists, being lazy, typically do not state the relevant physical and time period measures unless they are particularly useful. They refer to "quantity" rather than something useful such as "metric tons per year" and "price" rather than "cents per pound." Being as lazy as the next economist, I'll follow this sloppy convention when no confusion is likely to arise. To keep from driving us all nuts, from here on, I'll usually refer to the price as \$3.30 (with the "per kg" understood) and the quantity as 220 (with the "million kg per year" understood).

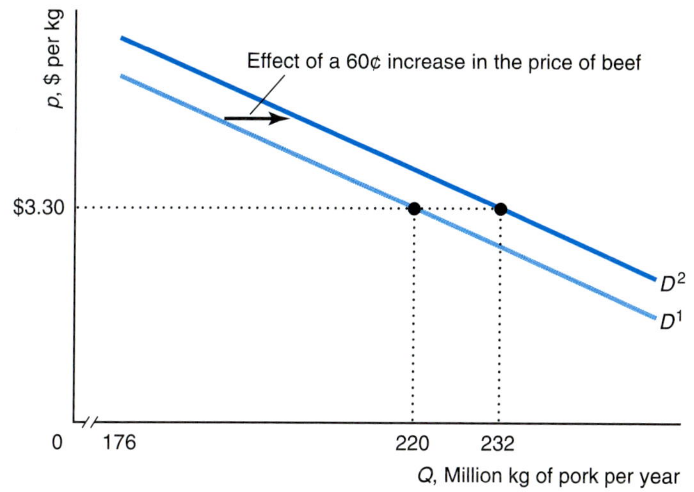

Figure 2.2 A Shift of the Demand Curve. The demand curve for processed pork *shifts* to the right from D^1 to D^2 as the price of beef rises from \$4 to \$4.60. As a result of the increase in beef prices, more pork is demanded at any given price.

To properly analyze the effects of a change in some variable on the quantity demanded, we must distinguish between a *movement along a demand curve* and a *shift of a demand curve*. A change in the *price of a good* causes a *movement along a demand curve*. A change in *any other factor besides the price of the good* causes a *shift of the demand curve*.

The Demand Function

In addition to drawing the demand curve, you can write it as a mathematical relationship called the *demand function*. The processed pork demand function is

$$Q = \tilde{D}(p, p_b, p_c, Y), \tag{2.1}$$

where Q is the quantity of pork demanded, p is the price of pork, p_b is the price of beef, p_c is the price of chicken, and Y is the income of consumers. This expression says that the amount of pork demanded varies with the price of pork, the price of substitutes (beef and chicken), and the income of consumers. Any other factors that are not explicitly listed in the demand function are assumed to be irrelevant (the price of llamas in Peru) or held constant (the price of fish).

By writing the demand function in this general way, we are not explaining exactly how the quantity demanded varies as p, p_b, p_c, or Y changes. Instead, we can rewrite

Equation 2.1 as a specific function:

$$Q = 171 - 20p + 20p_b + 3p_c + 2Y. \tag{2.2}$$

Equation 2.2 is the estimated demand function that underlies the demand curve D^1 in Figures 2.1 and 2.2.[7]

When we drew the demand curve D^1 in Figures 2.1 and 2.2, we held p_b, p_c, and Y at their typical values during the period studied: p_b = \$4 per kg, $p_c = \$3\frac{1}{3}$ per kg, and Y = 12.5 thousand dollars. If we substitute these values for p_b, p_c, and Y in Equation 2.2, we can rewrite the quantity demanded as a function of only the price of pork:

$$\begin{aligned} Q &= 171 - 20p + 20p_b + 3p_c + 2Y \\ &= 171 - 20p + (20 \times 4) + \left(3 \times 3\frac{1}{3}\right) + (2 \times 12.5) \end{aligned}$$

or

$$Q = 286 - 20p. \tag{2.3}$$

The straight-line demand curve D^1 in Figures 2.1 and 2.2—where we hold the price of beef, the price of chicken, and disposable income constant at these typical values —is described by the *linear* demand function in Equation 2.3.

The constant term, 286, in Equation 2.3 is the quantity demanded if the price is zero. Setting the price equal to zero in Equation 2.3, we find that the quantity demanded is $Q = 286 - (20 \times 0) = 286$. Figure 2.1 shows that $Q = 286$ where D^1 hits the quantity axis at a price of zero.

This equation also shows us how quantity demanded changes with a change in price: a movement *along* the demand curve. If the price increases from p_1 to p_2, the change in price, Δp, equals $p_2 - p_1$. (The Δ symbol, the Greek letter "delta," means "change in" the following variable, so Δp means the "change in price.") As Figure 2.1 illustrates, if the price of pork increases by \$1 from p_1 = \$3.30 to p_2 = \$4.30, Δp = \$1 and $\Delta Q = Q_2 - Q_1 = 200 - 220 = -20$ million kg per year.

More generally, the quantity demanded at p_1 is $Q_1 = D(p_1)$, and the quantity demanded at p_2 is $Q_2 = D(p_2)$. The change in the quantity demanded, $\Delta Q = Q_2 - Q_1$, in response to the price change is

$$\begin{aligned} \Delta Q &= Q_2 - Q_1 \\ &= D(p_2) - D(p_1) \\ &= (286 - 20p_2) - (286 - 20p_1) \\ &= -20(p_2 - p_1) \\ &= -20\Delta p. \end{aligned}$$

Thus, the change in the quantity demanded, ΔQ, is -20 times the change in the price, Δp. If Δp = \$1, $\Delta Q = -20\Delta p = -20$.

---

[7]The numbers are rounded slightly from the estimates to simplify the calculation. For example, the estimate of the coefficient on the price of beef is 19.5, not 20, as the equation shows.

The slope of a demand curve is $\Delta p/\Delta Q$, the "rise" (Δp, the change along the vertical axis) divided by the "run" (ΔQ, the change along the horizontal axis). The slope of demand curve D^1 in Figures 2.1 and 2.2 is

$$\text{slope} = \frac{\text{rise}}{\text{run}} = \frac{\Delta p}{\Delta Q} = \frac{1 \text{ dollar per kg}}{-20 \text{ million kg per year}}$$
$$= -0.05 \text{ dollars per million kg per year.}$$

The negative sign of this slope is consistent with the Law of Demand. The slope says that the price rises by \$1 per kg as the quantity demanded falls by 20 million kg per year. Turning that statement around: The quantity demanded falls by 20 million kg per year as the price rises by \$1 per kg.

Thus, we can use the demand curve to answer questions about how a change in price affects the quantity demanded and how a change in the quantity demanded affects price. We can also answer these questions using demand functions.

To answer the question about how a change in quantity affects price, we use algebra to rewrite Equation 2.3 so that price is a function of quantity. We call this rewritten demand curve an *inverse demand curve*. Subtracting Q from both sides of Equation 2.3 and adding $20p$ to both sides, we find that

$$20p = 286 - Q.$$

Then, dividing both sides of the equation by 20, we obtain the expression of p as a function of Q:

$$p = 14.30 - 0.05Q. \tag{2.4}$$

Equation 2.4 shows that if the quantity increases by ΔQ, price falls by $\Delta p = -0.05 \Delta Q$ (where -0.05 is the number multiplied by Q in the equation).[8] For consumers to demand one more million kg of pork per year, price must fall by nearly 5¢ a kg, which is a *movement along the demand curve*.

Summing Demand Curves

If we know the demand curve for each of two consumers, how do we determine the total demand for the two consumers combined? The total quantity demanded *at a given price* is the sum of the quantity each consumer demands at that price.

We can use the demand functions to determine the total demand of several consumers. Suppose the demand function for Consumer 1 is

$$Q_1 = D^1(p),$$

---

[8]Let the quantity increase from Q_1 to Q_2 so that $\Delta Q = Q_2 - Q_1$. The change in price is $\Delta p = p_2 - p_1$:

$$\begin{aligned}\Delta p &= (14.30 - 0.05Q_2) - (14.30 - 0.05Q_1)\\ &= -0.05(Q_2 - Q_1)\\ &= -0.05\Delta Q.\end{aligned}$$

and the demand function for Consumer 2 is

$$Q_2 = D^2(p).$$

At price is p, Consumer 1 demands Q_1 units, Consumer 2 demands Q_2 units, and the total demand of both consumers is the sum of the quantities each demands separately:[9]

$$Q = Q_1 + Q_2 = D^1(p) + D^2(p).$$

It makes sense to add the quantities demanded only when both consumers face the same price. Adding the quantity Consumer 1 demands at one price to the quantity Consumer 2 demands at another price would be like adding apples and oranges.

APPLICATION

Aggregating the Demand for Cling Peaches

We illustrate how to combine individual demand curves to get a total demand curve graphically using estimated demand curves for cling peaches (French and King 1986). Cling peaches are used only for canning. (The fresh peaches you buy in the grocery store are freestone peaches.) The total demand for cling peaches in Figure 2.3 is the sum of the demand for cling peaches for use in cans of peaches and the demand for cling peaches for use in cans of fruit cocktail.

Farmers sold cling peaches for \$183 per ton in 1984. At that price, fruit cocktail canners demanded $Q_f = 4$ tons per 10,000 consumers per year and peach canners demanded $Q_c = 18$, so the total quantity demanded was $Q = Q_f + Q_c = 4 + 18 = 22$. ■

2.2 SUPPLY

Knowing how much consumers want is not enough, by itself, to tell us what price and quantity are observed in a market. To determine the market price and quantity, we also need to know how much firms want to supply. In this section, we look at the factors that affect how much of a good or service a firm wants to supply to the market.

Firms determine how much of a good to supply on the basis of the price of that good and other factors, including the costs of production and government rules and regulations. Usually, we expect firms to supply more at a higher price. Before

---

[9]We can generalize this approach to look at the total demand for three or more consumers. In each case, the total demand is the sum of the individual demands for each consumer at a specific price. For example, at price p, the total demand, Q, for three consumers is

$$Q = Q_1 + Q_2 + Q_3 = D^1(p) + D^2(p) + D^3(p).$$

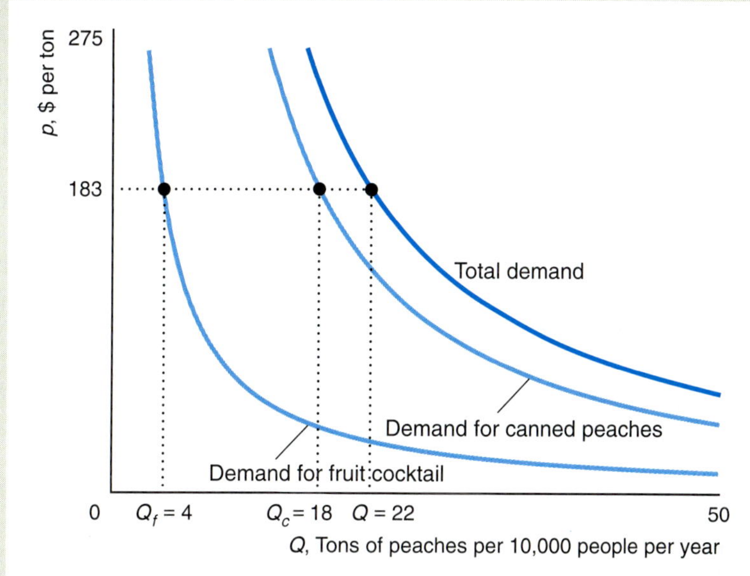

Figure 2.3 Total Demand for Cling Peaches. At any given price, the total quantity demanded of cling peaches is the sum of the quantity demanded by canners of peaches and the quantity demanded by canners of fruit cocktail. The demand curves are based on estimates by French and King (1986).

concentrating on the role of price in determining supply, we'll briefly describe the role of some of the other factors.

Costs of production affect how much a firm wants to sell of a good. As a firm's costs fall, it is willing to supply more, all else the same. If the firm's cost exceeds what it can earn from selling the good, the firm sells nothing. Factors that affect costs, then, also affect supply. A technological advance that allows a firm to produce a good at lower cost leads a firm to supply more of that good, all else the same.

Government rules and regulations also affect how much firms want or are allowed to sell. Taxes and many government regulations—such as those covering pollution, sanitation, and health insurance—affect the costs of production. Other regulations affect when and how the product can be sold. In Germany, retailers may not sell most goods and services on Sundays or during evening hours. In the United States, the sale of cigarettes and liquor to children is prohibited. New York, San Francisco, and many other cities restrict the number of taxicabs.

The Supply Curve

The **quantity supplied** is the amount of a good that firms *want* to sell at a given price, holding constant other factors that influence firms' supply decisions, such as costs and government actions. We can show the relationship between price and the quantity supplied graphically. A **supply curve** shows the quantity supplied at each possible price, holding constant the other factors that influence firms' supply decisions. Figure 2.4 shows the estimated supply curve, S^1, of pork (Moschini and Meilke 1992). This supply curve is a straight line, but other supply curves may be smooth curves or wavy. As with the demand curve, the price on the vertical axis is measured in dollars per physical unit (dollars per kg), and the quantity on the horizontal axis is measured in physical units per time period (millions of kg per year).[10] Because we hold fixed other variables that may affect the supply, such as costs and government rules, the supply curve concisely answers the question "What happens to the quantity supplied as the price changes, holding all other factors constant?"

Effect of Price on Supply. We illustrate how price affects the quantity supplied using the supply curve for processed pork in Figure 2.4. The supply curve for pork is upward sloping. As the price of pork increases, firms supply more. If the price is \$3.30, the market supplies a quantity of 220. If the price rises to \$5.30, the quantity

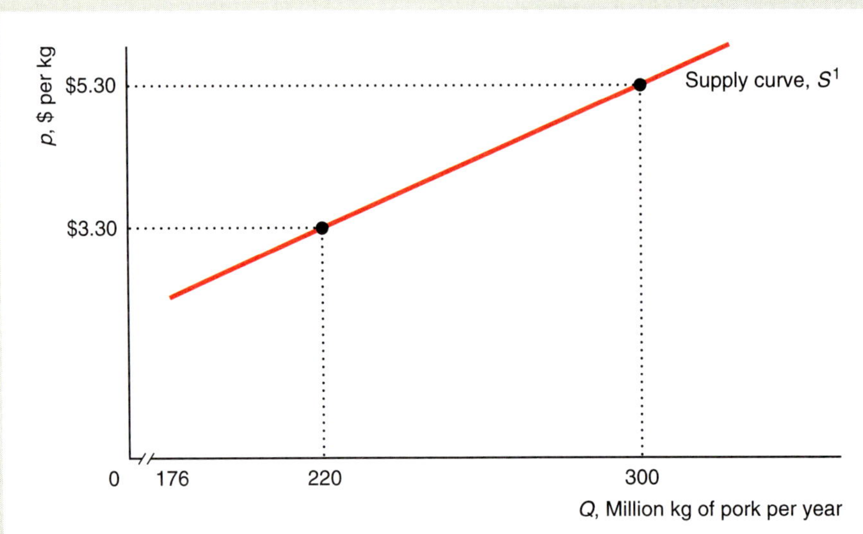

Figure 2.4 A Supply Curve. The estimated supply curve, S^1, of processed pork in Canada (Moschini and Meilke 1992) shows the relationship between the quantity supplied per year and the price per kg, holding cost and other factors that influence supply constant. The upward slope of this supply curve indicates that firms supply more of this good when its price is high and less when the price is low. An increase in the price of pork causes a movement *along the supply curve*, resulting in a larger quantity of pork supplied.

[10]The horizontal axis starts at 176 (rather than 0) for the purposes of scaling so that we can focus on the part of the supply curve that is actually observed.

supplied rises to 300. An increase in the price of pork causes a *movement along the supply curve*, resulting in more pork being supplied.

Although the Law of Demand requires that the demand curve slope down, there is *no* "Law of Supply" that requires the market supply curve to have a particular slope. The market supply curve can be upward sloping, vertical, horizontal, or downward sloping. Many supply curves slope upward, such as the one for pork. Along such supply curves, the higher the price, the more firms are willing to sell, holding costs and government regulations fixed.

Effects of Other Variables on Supply. A change in a variable other than the price of pork causes the entire *supply curve to shift*. Suppose the price, p_h, of hogs—the main factor used to produce processed pork—increases from $1.50 per kg to $1.75 per kg. Because it is now more expensive to produce pork, the supply curve shifts to the left, from S^1 to S^2 in Figure 2.5. Firms want to supply less pork at any given price than before the price of hogs rose. At a price of processed pork of $3.30, the quantity supplied falls from 220 on S^1, before the increase in the hog price, to 205 on S^2, after the increase in the hog price.

Again, it is important to distinguish between a *movement along a supply curve* and a *shift of the supply curve*. When the price of pork changes, the change in the quantity supplied reflects a *movement along the supply curve*. When costs, government rules, or other variables that affect supply change, the entire *supply curve shifts*.

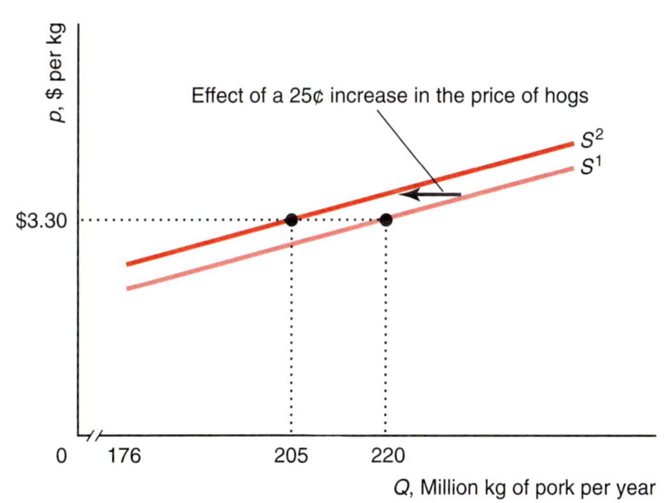

Figure 2.5 A Shift of a Supply Curve. An increase in the price of hogs from $1.50 to $1.75 per kg causes the supply curve for processed pork to shift from S^1 to S^2. At the price of processed pork of $3.30, the quantity supplied falls from 220 on S^1 to 205 on S^2.

The Supply Function

We can write the relationship between the quantity supplied and price and other factors as a mathematical relationship called the *supply function*. Written generally, the processed pork supply function is

$$Q = S(p, p_h), \tag{2.5}$$

where Q is the quantity of processed pork supplied, p is the price of processed pork, and p_h is the price of a hog. The supply function, Equation 2.5, also may be a function of other factors such as wages, but, by leaving them out, we are implicitly holding them constant.

Based on Moschini and Meilke (1992), the linear pork supply function in Canada is

$$Q = 178 + 40p - 60p_h, \tag{2.6}$$

where quantity is in millions of kg per year and the prices are in Canadian dollars per kg. If we hold the price of hogs fixed at its typical value of \$1.50 per kg, we can rewrite the supply function as[11]

$$Q = 88 + 40p. \tag{2.7}$$

What happens to the quantity supplied if the price of processed pork increases by $\Delta p = p_2 - p_1$? Using the same approach as before, we learn from Equation 2.7 that $\Delta Q = 40\Delta p$.[12] A \$1 increase in price ($\Delta p = 1$) causes the quantity supplied to increase by $\Delta Q = 40$ million kg per year. This change in the quantity of pork supplied as p increases is a *movement along the supply curve*.

Summing Supply Curves

The total supply curve shows the total quantity produced by all suppliers at each possible price. For example, the total supply of rice in Japan is the sum of the domestic and foreign supply curves of rice.

Suppose the domestic supply curve (panel a) and foreign supply curve (panel b) of rice in Japan are as Figure 2.6 shows. The total supply curve, S in panel c, is the horizontal sum of the Japanese *domestic* supply curve, S^d, and the *foreign* supply

---

[11]By substituting $p_h = \$1.50$ into Equation 2.6, we find that

$$\begin{aligned} Q &= 178 + 40p - 60p_h \\ &= 178 + 40p - (60 \times 1.50) \\ &= 88 + 40p. \end{aligned}$$

[12]As the price increases from p_1 to p_2, the quantity supplied goes from Q_1 to Q_2, so the change in quantity supplied, $\Delta Q = Q_2 - Q_1$, is

$$\begin{aligned} \Delta Q &= (88 + 40p_2) - (88 + 40p_1) \\ &= 40(p_2 - p_1) \\ &= 40\Delta p. \end{aligned}$$

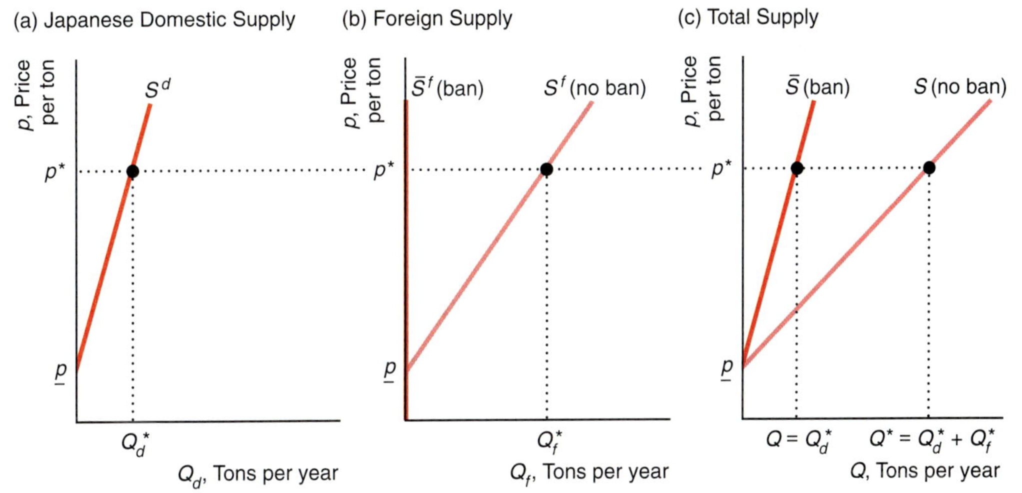

Figure 2.6 Total Supply Is the Sum of Domestic and Foreign Supply. If foreigners may sell their rice in Japan, the total Japanese supply of rice, S, is the horizontal sum of the domestic Japanese supply, S^d, and the imported foreign supply, S^f. With a ban on foreign imports, the foreign supply curve, $\bar{S}^f$, is zero at every price, so the total supply curve, $\bar{S}$, is the same as the domestic supply curve, S^d.

curve, S^f. In the figure, the Japanese and foreign supplies are zero at any price equal to or less than $\underline{p}$, so the total supply is zero. At prices above $\underline{p}$, the Japanese and foreign supplies are positive, so the total supply is positive. For example, when price is p^*, the quantity supplied by Japanese firms is Q_d^* (panel a), the quantity supplied by foreign firms is Q_f^* (panel b), and the total quantity supplied is $Q^* = Q_d^* + Q_f^*$ (panel c). Because the total supply curve is the horizontal sum of the domestic and foreign supply curves, the total supply curve is flatter than either of the other two foreign supply curves.

Effects of Government Import Policies on Supply Curves

We can use this approach for deriving the total supply curve to analyze the effect of government policies on the total supply curve. Traditionally, the Japanese government banned the importation of foreign rice. We want to determine how much less is supplied at any given price to the Japanese market because of this ban.

Without a ban, the foreign supply curve is S^f in panel b of Figure 2.6. A ban on imports eliminates the foreign supply, so the foreign supply curve after the *ban* is imposed, $\bar{S}^f$, is a vertical line at $Q_f = 0$. The import ban has no effect on the domestic supply curve, S^d, so the supply curve is the same as in panel a.

Because the foreign supply with a ban, $\bar{S}^f$, is zero at every price, the total supply with a ban, $\bar{S}$, in panel c is the same as the Japanese domestic supply, S^d, at any given price. The total supply curve with a ban lies to the left of the total supply curve without a ban, S. Thus, the effect of the import ban is to rotate the total supply curve toward the vertical axis.

The limit that a government sets on the quantity of a foreign-produced good that may be imported is called a **quota**. By absolutely banning the importation of rice, the Japanese government sets a quota of zero on rice imports. Sometimes, governments set positive quotas, $\bar{Q} > 0$. The foreign firms may supply as much as they want, Q_f, as long as they supply no more than the quota: $Q_f \le \bar{Q}$.

We investigate the effect of such a quota in Solved Problem 2.1. In most of the solved problems in this book, you are asked to determine how a *change* in a variable or policy *affects* one or more variables. In this problem, the policy *changes* from no quota to a quota, which *affects* the total supply curve.

SOLVED PROBLEM 2.1

How does a quota set by the United States on foreign steel imports of $\bar{Q}$ affect the total American supply curve for steel given the domestic supply, S^d in panel a of Figure 2.7, and foreign supply, S^f in panel b?

Answer

1. *Determine the American supply curve without the quota:* The *no-quota* total supply curve, S in panel c of Figure 2.7, is the horizontal sum of the U.S. domestic supply curve, S^d, and the no-quota foreign supply curve, S^f.

2. *Show the effect of the quota on foreign supply:* At prices less than $\bar{p}$, foreign suppliers want to supply quantities less than the quota, $\bar{Q}$. As a result, the foreign supply curve under the quota, $\bar{S}^f$, is the same as the no-quota foreign supply curve, S^f, for prices less than $\bar{p}$. At prices above $\bar{p}$, foreign suppliers want to supply more but are limited to $\bar{Q}$. Thus, the foreign supply curve with a quota, $\bar{S}^f$, is vertical at $\bar{Q}$ for prices above $\bar{p}$.

3. *Determine the American total supply curve with the quota:* The total supply curve with the quota, $\bar{S}$, is the horizontal sum of S^d and $\bar{S}^f$. At any price above $\bar{p}$, the total supply equals the quota plus the domestic supply. For example at p^*, the domestic supply is Q_d^* and the foreign supply is $\bar{Q}_f$, so the total supply is $Q_d^* + \bar{Q}_f$. Above $\bar{p}$, $\bar{S}$ is the domestic supply curve shifted $\bar{Q}$ units to the right. As a result, the portion of $\bar{S}$ above $\bar{p}$ has the same slope as S^d.

4. *Compare the American total supply curves with and without the quota:* At prices less than or equal to $\bar{p}$, the same quantity is supplied with and without the quota, so $\bar{S}$ is the same as S. At prices above $\bar{p}$, less is supplied with the quota than without one, so $\bar{S}$ is steeper than S, indicating that a given increase in price raises the quantity supplied by less with a quota than without one. ■

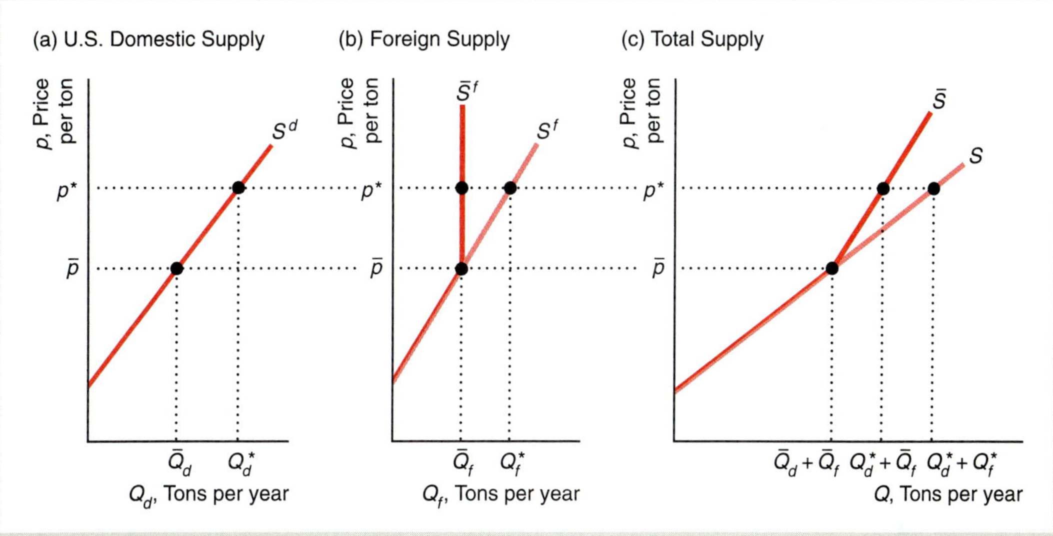

Figure 2.7 Quota on Steel Reduces Total Supply. The U.S. government limits the amount of foreign steel that can be imported to $\bar{Q}$. As a result, the foreign supply curve shifts from S^f to $\bar{S}^f$, which is vertical at $\bar{Q}_f$, at any price above $\bar{p}$. Consequently, the total American supply curve with the quota, $\bar{S}$, is steeper than the no-quota supply, S, at prices above $\bar{p}$.

2.3 MARKET EQUILIBRIUM

The supply and demand curves determine the price and quantity at which goods and services are bought and sold in the market. The demand curve shows the quantities consumers want to buy at various prices, and the supply curve shows the quantities firms want to sell at various prices. Unless the price is set so that consumers want to buy exactly the same amount that suppliers want to sell, either some buyers cannot buy as much as they want or some sellers cannot sell as much as they want.

When all traders are able to buy or sell as much as they want, we say that the market is in **equilibrium**: a situation in which no one wants to change his or her behavior. A price at which consumers can buy as much as they want and sellers can sell as much as they want is called an *equilibrium price*. The quantity that is bought and sold at the equilibrium price is called the *equilibrium quantity*.

Using a Graph to Determine the Equilibrium

This little piggy went to market . . .

To illustrate how supply and demand curves determine the equilibrium price and quantity, we use our old friend, the processed pork example. Figure 2.8 shows the supply, *S*, and demand, *D*, curves for pork. The supply and demand curves intersect at point *e*, the market equilibrium, where the equilibrium price is $3.30 and the equilibrium quantity is 220 million kg per year, which is the quantity firms want to sell *and* the quantity consumers want to buy.

Using Math to Determine the Equilibrium

We can determine the processed pork market equilibrium mathematically, using the supply and demand functions. We use these two functions to solve for the equilibrium price at which the quantity demanded equals the quantity supplied (the equilibrium quantity).

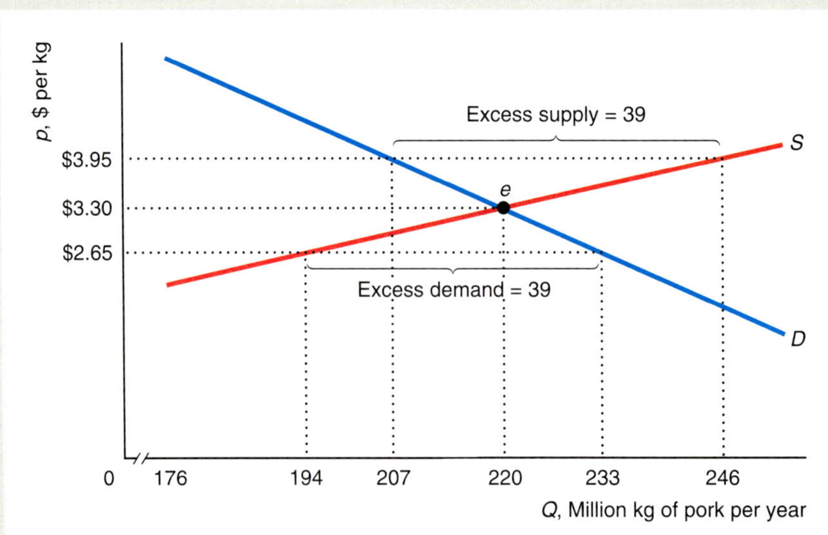

Figure 2.8 Market Equilibrium. The intersection of the processed pork supply curve, *S*, and the demand curve, *D*, determines the market equilibrium point, *e*, where p = $3.30 per kg and Q = 220 million kg per year. At a lower price, p = $2.65, the quantity supplied is only 194, whereas the quantity demanded is 233, so there is excess demand of 39. At p = $3.95, a price higher than the equilibrium price, there is excess supply of 39 because the quantity demanded, 207, is less than the quantity supplied, 246. When there is excess demand or supply, market forces drive the price back to the equilibrium price of $3.30.

The demand function, Equation 2.3, shows the relationship between the quantity demanded, Q_d, and the price:

$$Q_d = 286 - 20p.$$

The supply function, Equation 2.7, tells us the relationship between the quantity supplied, Q_s, and the price:

$$Q_s = 88 + 40p.$$

We want to find the p at which $Q_d = Q_s = Q$, the equilibrium quantity. Because the left-hand sides of the two equations are equal in equilibrium, $Q_s = Q_d$, the right-hand sides of the two equations must be equal:

$$286 - 20p = 88 + 40p.$$

Adding $20p$ to both sides of this expression and subtracting 88 from both sides, we find that $198 = 60p$. Dividing both sides of this last expression by 60, we find that the equilibrium price is $p = \$3.30$. We can determine the equilibrium quantity by substituting this p into either the supply or the demand equation:

$$\begin{aligned} Q_d &= Q_s \\ 286 - (20 \times 3.30) &= 88 + (40 \times 3.30) \\ 220 &= 220. \end{aligned}$$

Thus, the equilibrium quantity is 220.

Market Forces Drive the Market to Equilibrium

A market equilibrium is not just an abstract concept or a theoretical possibility. We observe markets in equilibrium. Indirect evidence that you observe a market in equilibrium is that you can buy as much as you want of the good at the market price. You almost always can buy as much as you want of such common goods as milk and ballpoint pens.

Amazingly, a market equilibrium occurs without any explicit coordination between consumers and firms. In a competitive market such as that for agricultural goods, millions of consumers and thousands of firms make their buying and selling decisions independently. Yet each firm can sell as much as it wants; each consumer can buy as much as he or she wants. It is as though an unseen market force, like an *invisible hand*, directs people to coordinate their activities to achieve a market equilibrium.

What really causes the market to move to an equilibrium? If the price is not at the equilibrium level, consumers or firms have an incentive to change their behavior in a way that will drive the price to the equilibrium level, as we now illustrate.

If the price were initially lower than the equilibrium price, consumers would want to buy more than suppliers want to sell. If the pork price is \$2.65 in Figure 2.8, firms are willing to supply 194 million kg per year but consumers demand 233 million kg. At this price, the market is in *disequilibrium*, at which the quantity demanded is unequal to the quantity supplied. There is **excess demand**—the amount by which the quantity demanded exceeds the quantity supplied at a specified price—of 39 (= 233 – 194) million kg per year at a price of \$2.65.

Some consumers are lucky enough to buy the pork at \$2.65. Other consumers cannot find anyone who is willing to sell them pork at that price. What can they do? Some frustrated consumers may offer to pay suppliers more than \$2.65. Alternatively, suppliers, noticing these disappointed consumers, may raise their prices. Such actions by consumers and producers cause the market price to rise. As the price rises, the quantity that firms want to supply increases and the quantity that consumers want to buy decreases. This upward pressure on price continues until it reaches the equilibrium price, \$3.30, where there is no excess demand.

If, instead, price is initially above the equilibrium level, suppliers want to sell more than consumers want to buy. For example, at a price of pork of \$3.95, suppliers want to sell 246 million kg per year but consumers want to buy only 207 million kg, as the figure shows. At \$3.95, the market is in disequilibrium. There is an **excess supply**—the amount by which the quantity supplied is greater than the quantity demanded at a specified price—of 39 (= 246 – 207) at a price of \$3.95. Not all firms can sell as much as they want. Rather than incur storage costs (and possibly have their unsold pork sit around and spoil), firms lower the price to attract additional customers. As long as price remains above the equilibrium price, some firms have unsold pork and want to lower the price further. The price falls until it reaches the equilibrium level, \$3.30, where there is no excess supply and hence no more pressure to lower the price further.

In summary, at any price other than the equilibrium price, either consumers or suppliers are unable to trade as much as they want. These disappointed people act to change the price, driving the price to the equilibrium level. The equilibrium price is called the *market clearing price* because it removes from the market all frustrated buyers and sellers: There is no excess demand or excess supply at the equilibrium price.

2.4 SHOCKING THE EQUILIBRIUM

Once an equilibrium is achieved, it can persist indefinitely because no one applies pressure to change the price. The equilibrium changes only if a shock occurs that shifts the demand curve or the supply curve. These curves shift if one of the variables we were holding constant changes. If tastes, income, government policies, or costs of production change, the demand curve or the supply curve or both shift, so the equilibrium changes.

Effects of a Shift in the Demand Curve

Suppose that the price of beef increases by 60¢, so consumers substitute pork for beef. As a result, the demand curve for pork shifts outward from D^1 to D^2 in panel a of Figure 2.9. At any given price, consumers want more pork than they did before

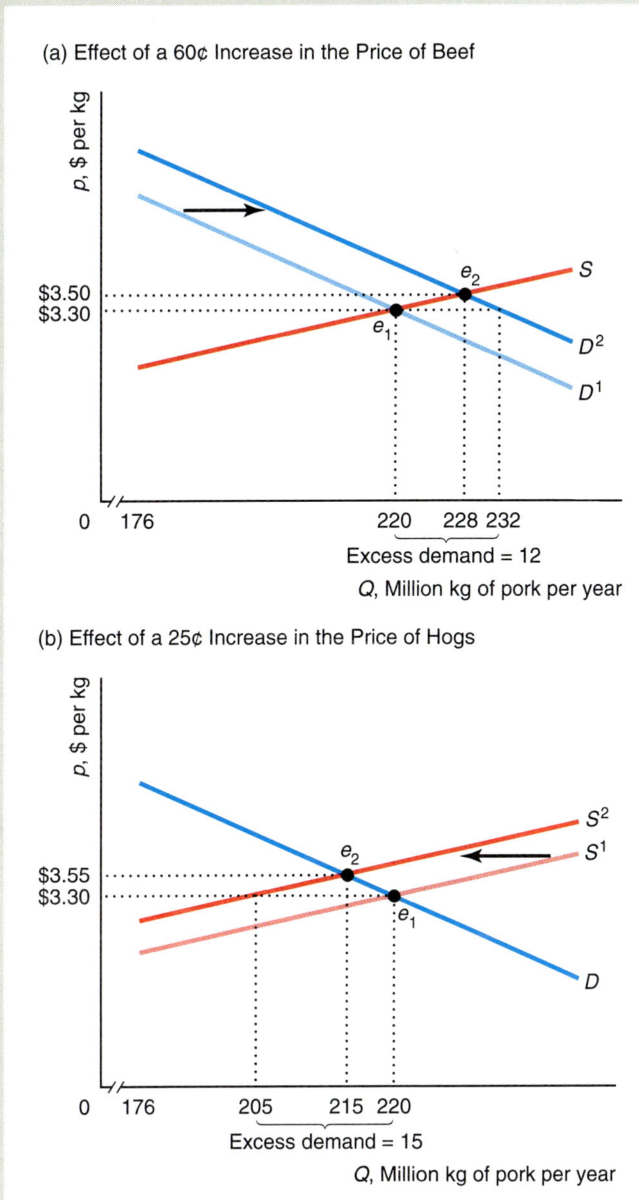

Figure 2.9 Effects of a Shift of the Demand Curve. (a) An increase in the price of beef by 60¢ causes the demand curve for processed pork to shift outward from D^1 to D^2. At the original equilibrium, e_1, price, \$3.30, there is excess demand of 12. Market pressures drive the price up until it reaches \$3.50 at the new equilibrium e_2. (b) An increase in the price of hogs by 25¢ causes the supply curve for processed pork to shift to the left from S^1 to S^2, driving the market equilibrium from e_1 to e_2.

the price of beef rose. In particular, at the original equilibrium price of pork, \$3.30, consumers now want to buy 232 million kg of pork per year. At that price, however, suppliers still want to sell only 220. As a result, there is excess demand of 12. Market pressures drive the price up until it reaches a new equilibrium at \$3.50. At that price, firms want to sell 228 and consumers want to buy 228, the new equilibrium quantity. Thus, the pork equilibrium goes from e_1 to e_2 as a result of the increase in the price of beef. Both the equilibrium price and the equilibrium quantity of pork rise as a result of the outward shift of the pork demand curve. Here, the increase in the price of beef causes a *shift of the demand curve*, causing a *movement along the supply curve*.

Effects of a Shift in the Supply Curve

Now suppose that the price of beef stays constant at its original level but the price of hogs increases by 25¢. It is now more expensive to produce pork because the price of a major input, hogs, has increased. As a result, the supply curve for pork shifts to the left from S^1 to S^2 in panel b of Figure 2.9. At any given price, firms want to supply less pork than they did before the price of hogs increased. At the original equilibrium price of pork of \$3.30, consumers still want 220, but suppliers are now only willing to supply 205, so there is excess demand of 15. Market pressure forces the price of pork up until it reaches a new equilibrium at e_2, where the equilibrium price is \$3.55 and the equilibrium quantity is 215. The increase in the price of hogs causes the equilibrium price to rise but the equilibrium quantity to fall. Here, a *shift of the supply curve* results in a *movement along the demand curve*.

In summary, a change in an underlying factor, such as the price of a substitute or the price of an input, shifts the demand or supply curve. As a result of this shift in the demand or supply curve, the equilibrium changes. To describe the effect of this change in the underlying factor on the market, we compare the original equilibrium price and quantity to the new equilibrium values.

SOLVED PROBLEM 2.2

Mathematically, how does the equilibrium price of pork vary as the price of hogs changes if the variables that affect demand are held constant at their typical values?

Answer:

1. *Solve for the equilibrium price of pork in terms of the price of hogs:* The demand function does not depend on the price of hogs, so we can use Equation 2.3 from before,

$$Q_d = 286 - 20p.$$

To see how the equilibrium depends on the price of hogs, we use supply function Equation 2.6:

$$Q_s = 178 + 40p - 60p_h.$$

The equilibrium is determined by equating the right-hand sides of these demand-and-supply equations:

$$286 - 20p = 178 + 40p - 60p_h.$$

Rearranging terms in this last expression, we find that

$$60p = 108 + 60p_h.$$

Dividing both sides by 60, we have an expression for the equilibrium price of processed pork as a function of the price of hogs:

$$p = 1.8 + p_h. \tag{2.8}$$

(As a check, when p_h equals its typical value, \$1.50, Equation 2.8 says that the equilibrium price of pork is p = \$3.30, which we know is correct from our earlier calculations.)

We find the equilibrium quantity as a function of the price of hogs by substituting this expression for the equilibrium price, Equation 2.8, into the demand equation (though we could use the supply function instead):

$$Q = 286 - 20p = 286 - 20(1.8 + p_h) = 250 - 20p_h.$$

(Again, as a check, if p_h equals its typical value of \$1.50, $Q = 220$, which we know is the original equilibrium quantity.)

2. *Show how the equilibrium price of pork varies with the price of hogs:* Using the same technique that we have applied several times before, we know from Equation 2.8 that $\Delta p = \Delta p_h$. Any increase in the price of hogs causes an equal increase in the price of processed pork. As panel b of Figure 2.9 illustrates, if the price of hogs increases by Δp_h = \$0.25 (from \$1.50 to \$1.75), the price of pork p increases by $\Delta p = \Delta p_h$ = \$0.25 (from \$3.30 to \$3.55). ■

2.5 EFFECTS OF GOVERNMENT INTERVENTIONS

A government can affect a market equilibrium in many ways. Sometimes, government actions cause a shift in either the supply curve or the demand curve, which causes the equilibrium to change. Some government interventions, however, cause the quantity demanded to differ from the quantity supplied.

Policies That Shift Supply Curves

Many government policies cause either the supply curve or the demand curve or both to shift. As we saw earlier, quotas on imports affect the supply curve. We illustrate the effect of quotas on market equilibrium.

The Japanese government's ban on rice imports raised the price of rice in Japan substantially. Figure 2.10 shows the Japanese demand curve for rice, D, and the total supply curve without a ban, S. The intersection of S and D determines the equilibrium, e_1, if rice imports are allowed.

What is the effect of a ban on foreign rice on Japanese demand and supply? The ban has no effect on demand if Japanese consumers do not care whether they eat domestic or foreign rice. The ban causes the total supply curve to rotate toward the origin from S (total supply is the horizontal sum of domestic and foreign supply) to $\bar{S}$ (total supply equals the domestic supply).

The intersection of $\bar{S}$ and D determines the new equilibrium, e_2, which lies above and to the left of e_1. The ban causes a shift of the supply curve and a movement along the demand curve. It leads to a fall in the equilibrium quantity from Q_1 to Q_2 and a rise in the equilibrium price from p_1 to p_2. Because of the Japanese ban on imported rice, the price of rice in Japan has at times been over seven times higher than the price in the rest of the world.

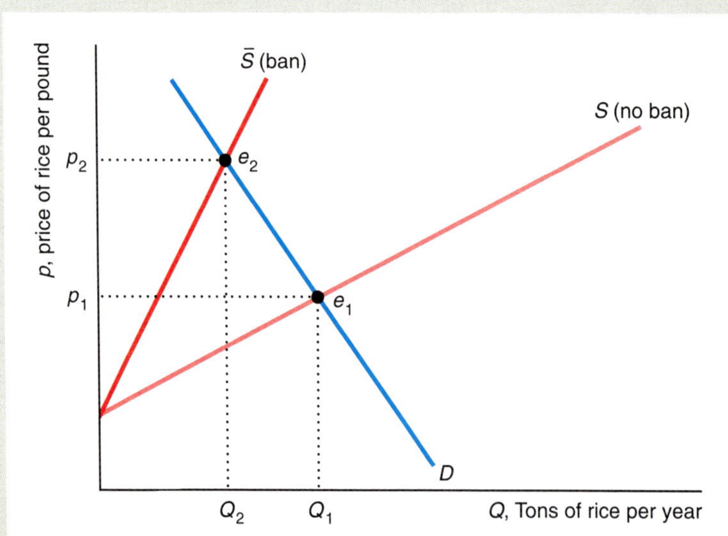

Figure 2.10 A Ban on Rice Imports Raises the Price in Japan. A ban on rice imports shifts the total supply of rice in Japan without a ban, S, to $\bar{S}$, which equals the domestic supply alone. As a result, the equilibrium changes from e_1 to e_2. The ban causes the price to rise from p_1 to p_2 and the equilibrium quantity to fall to Q_1 from Q_2.

A quota of $\bar{Q}$ may have a similar effect to an outright ban; however, a quota may have no effect on the equilibrium if the quota is set so high that it does not limit imports. We investigate this possibility in Solved Problem 2.3 and in the following application.

SOLVED PROBLEM 2.3

What is the effect of a U.S. quota on steel of $\bar{Q}$ on the equilibrium in the United States steel market? *Hint:* The answer depends on whether the quota binds (is low enough to affect the equilibrium).

Answer:

1. *Show how a quota, $\bar{Q}$, affects the total supply of steel in the United States:* Figure 2.11 reproduces the no-quota total American supply curve of steel, S, and the total supply curve under the quota, $\bar{S}$ (which we derived in Figure 2.7). At a price below $\bar{p}$, the two supply curves are identical, because the quota is not binding: It is greater than the quantity foreign firms want to supply. Above $\bar{p}$, $\bar{S}$ lies to the left of S.

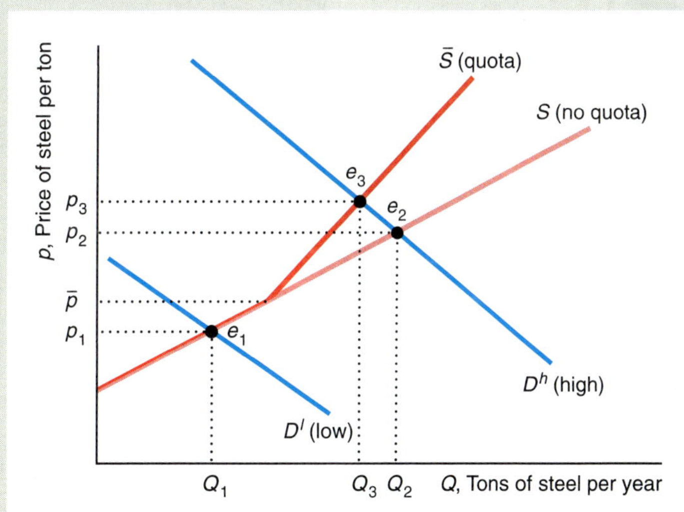

Figure 2.11 A Quota May Not Alter the Equilibrium. The U.S. steel quota, which causes the total supply to shift from S to $\bar{S}$, has no effect on equilibrium at e_1 if the demand curve is D^l. If the demand curve is D^h, the equilibrium changes from e_2 without the quota to e_3 with the quota. The quota drives up the equilibrium price from p_2 to p_3 and reduces the equilibrium quantity from Q_2 to Q_3.

2. *Show the effect of the quota if the original equilibrium quantity is less than the quota so that the quota does not bind:* Suppose the American demand is relatively *low* at any given price so that the demand curve, D^l, intersects both the supply curves at a price below $\bar{p}$. The equilibria both before and after the quota is imposed are at e_1, where the equilibrium price, p_1, is less than $\bar{p}$. Thus, if the demand curve lies near enough to the origin that the quota is not binding, the quota has no effect on the equilibrium.
3. *Show the effect of the quota if the quota binds:* With a relatively *high* demand curve, D^h, the quota affects the equilibrium. The no-quota equilibrium is e_2, where D^h intersects the no-quota total supply curve, S. After the quota is imposed, the equilibrium is e_3, where D^h intersects the total supply curve with the quota, $\bar{S}$. The quota raises the price of steel in the United States from p_2 to p_3 and reduces the quantity from Q_2 to Q_3. ■

APPLICATION

American Steel Quotas

The U.S. government has repeatedly limited imports of steel into the United States.[13] In many different years, the U.S. government negotiated with Japanese and European governments to have those countries limit the amount of steel they sold in the United States. Various agreements were in effect from 1969 through 1974. But in many of those years, the quotas were set so high that they had no effect (as in the equilibrium e_1 on demand curve D^1 in Figure 2.11).

In 1971 and 1972, however, these quotas apparently were binding for most steel products. In those years, the quotas raised average U.S. steel prices between 1.2% and 3.5%. (The equilibrium price with the quota, p_3, is higher than without the quota, p_2, if the demand curve is D^h in Figure 2.11.)

In 1984, President Ronald Reagan announced a new set of *voluntary* quotas, which covered most steel-exporting countries and limited finished steel imports into the United States to 18.5% of the total U.S. sales for 1985–1989. These limits on imports drove up prices above what they would have been without

[13]This section is based on Crandall (1987).

the quotas. In 1979–1980, in the absence of quotas, the average U.S. price of steel (p_2) was approximately the same as the market price in Antwerp, Belgium. In 1984 and 1985, under the Reagan quotas, the average U.S. price (p_3) was about 25% higher than the corresponding price in Antwerp. ■

Policies That Cause Demand to Differ from Supply

Some government policies do more than merely shift the supply or demand curve. For example, governments may control prices directly, a policy that leads to either excess supply or excess demand if the price the government sets differs from the equilibrium price. We illustrate this result with two types of price control programs. When the government sets a *price ceiling* at $\bar{p}$, the price at which goods are sold may be no higher than $\bar{p}$. When the government sets a *price floor* at $\underline{p}$, the price at which goods are sold may not fall below $\underline{p}$.

Price Ceilings. Price ceilings have no effect if they are set above the equilibrium price that would be observed in the absence of the price controls. If the government says that firms may charge no more than $\bar{p}$ = \$5 per gallon of gas and firms are actually charging p = \$1.30, the government's price control policy is irrelevant. However, if the equilibrium price, p, would be above the price ceiling $\bar{p}$, the price that is actually observed in the market is the price ceiling.

To keep prices from rising in wartime, the United States government has used price ceilings. During World War II, for example, the prices of all staples (such as sugar and gasoline) were controlled. To limit inflation, President Richard Nixon instituted wage and price controls on many goods in 1971–1972. Since 1992, there have been periodic debates in Congress about whether to apply price controls to medical services.

The U.S. experience with gasoline illustrates the effects of price controls. In the 1970s, the Organization of Petroleum Exporting Countries (OPEC) reduced supplies of oil to Western countries, where oil is converted into gasoline. As a result, the total supply curve of gasoline in the United States—the horizontal sum of domestic and OPEC supply curves—shifted to the left from S^1 to S^2 in Figure 2.12. Because of this shift, the equilibrium price of gasoline would have risen substantially, from p_1 to p_2. In an attempt to protect consumers by keeping gasoline prices from rising, the U.S. government set price ceilings on gasoline in 1973 and 1979.

The government told gas stations that they could charge no more than $\bar{p} = p_1$. Figure 2.12 shows the price ceiling as a solid horizontal line extending from the price axis at $\bar{p}$. The price control is binding because $p_2 > \bar{p}$. The observed price is the price ceiling. At $\bar{p}$, consumers want to buy $Q_d = Q_1$ gallons of gasoline, which is the equilibrium quantity they bought before OPEC acted. Suppliers, however, sell only Q_s gallons, which is determined by the intersection of the price control line with S^2. As a result of the binding price control, there is excess demand of $Q_d - Q_s$.

Were it not for the price controls, market forces would drive up the market price to p_2, where the excess demand would be eliminated. The government price ceiling prevents this adjustment from occurring. As a result, an enforced price ceiling causes a **shortage**: a persistent excess demand.

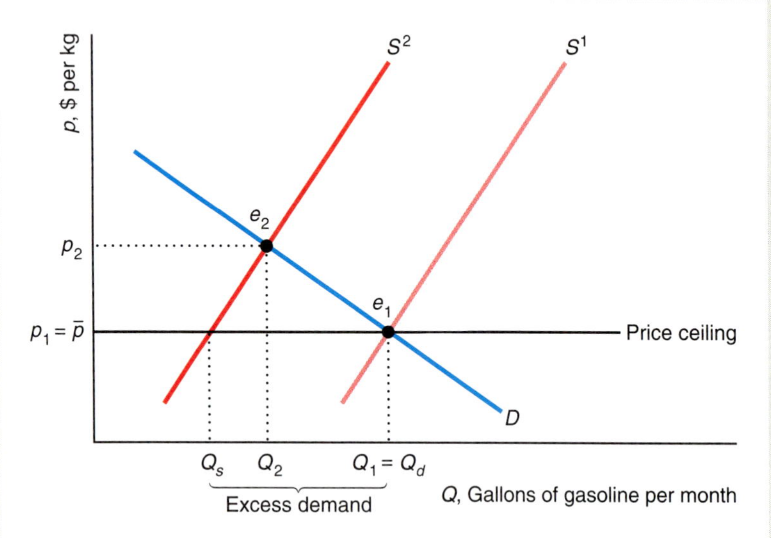

Figure 2.12 Price Ceiling on Gasoline. Supply shifts from S^1 to S^2. Under the government's price control program, gasoline stations may not charge a price above the price ceiling $\bar{p} = p_1$. At that price, producers are only willing to supply Q_s, which is less than the amount $Q_1 = Q_d$ that consumers want to buy. The result is excessive demand or a shortage of $Q_d - Q_s$.

At the time of the controls, some government officials argued that the shortages were caused by OPEC's cutting off its supply of oil to the United States, but that's not true. Without the price controls, the new equilibrium would be e_2. In this equilibrium, the price, p_2, is much higher than before, p_1; however, there is no shortage. Moreover, without controls, the quantity sold, Q_2, is greater than the quantity sold under the control program, Q_s.

With a binding price ceiling, the supply-and-demand model predicts an *equilibrium with a shortage*. In this equilibrium, the quantity demanded does not equal the quantity supplied. The reason that we call this situation an equilibrium, even though a shortage exists, is that no consumers or firms want to act differently, given the law. Without the price controls, consumers faced with a shortage would try to get more output by offering to pay more, or firms would raise prices. With effective government price controls, they know that they can't drive up the price, so they live with the shortage.

So what happens? Some lucky consumers get to buy Q_s units at the low price of $\bar{p}$. Other potential customers are disappointed: They would like to buy the good at that price, but they cannot find anyone willing to sell gas to them.

What determines which consumers are lucky enough to find goods to buy at the low price when there are price controls? With enforced price controls, sellers use criteria other than price to allocate the scarce commodity. Firms may supply their friends, long-term customers, or people of a certain race, gender, age, or religion. They may sell their goods on a first-come-first-served basis. Or they may limit everyone to only a few gallons. Yet another possibility is that firms and customers evade the price controls.

Whether price controls lead to a shortage depends on whether the controls are enforced or evaded. A consumer could go to a gas station owner and say, "Let's not tell anyone, but I'll pay you twice the price the government sets if you'll sell me as much gas as I want." If enough customers and gas station owners behaved that way, no shortage would occur.

APPLICATION

Gas Lines

The 1973 and 1979 price controls on gasoline led to gas shortages and long lines of cars at service stations as consumers waited to buy scarce gasoline.[14] Some stations sold their gas on a first-come-first-served basis. Others rationed the amount of gasoline they would sell to an individual, sometimes to as little as one or two gallons. After selling all their gasoline, stations closed. Few stations opened on weekends or in the evenings.

Customers waited hours in long lines of cars to buy gas. Some lined up as early as 4:00 A.M. on the Saturday of the long Washington's Birthday weekend. Some stations reported lines of over 75 cars by 7:00 A.M. According to Consumers Union, tests showed that a mile-long line of idling six-cylinder cars burns up 150 gallons of gasoline per hour. Thus, the lines worsened the shortage.

The long lines and limits on purchases led to frayed tempers, traffic jams, fights, and worse. In Oxnard, California, a frustrated motorist who tried to cut in ahead of 150 other cars, but whose passage was blocked by the attendant, allegedly tried to run the attendant down.

Some retailers ignored the price controls and raised their prices. Others evaded the controls by using *tie-in sales*, by which customers could buy gasoline if they also purchased another, highly priced item such as a very expensive car wash.

[14] "Saxbe Warns Gas Stations," *Los Angeles Times*, January 8, 1974:(I)16; "Waiting in Line? Gasoline Burns Too," *Los Angeles Times*, February 8, 1974:(I)22; "Psst! Let's Get Tanked at Old Phil's," *Los Angeles Times*, February 11, 1974:(I)21; "Favoritism in Sale of Gasoline Banned," *Los Angeles Times*, February 13, 1974:(I)1; "52 Cities Have No Lines at the Pumps," *Los Angeles Times*, February 13, 1974:(I)15; David Shaw, "Motorists Besiege Open Gas Stations; Fistfights Break Out," *Los Angeles Times*, February 17, 1974:(I)1; "L.A. Cars Sparkle in Fuel Crisis," *Los Angeles Times*, February 17, 1974:(I)30.

U.S. Attorney General William B. Saxbe threatened to bring criminal and civil actions against gas station operators who used either of these approaches to evade the price controls.

Americans respected the price control laws more in some cities than in others. A study of 92 major U.S. cities found no gasoline lines in 52 of them. In cities such as Chicago, Hartford, New York, Portland, and Tucson, however, potential customers waited in line for an hour or more before getting to the pump.

Some stations posted "Out of Gas" signs early every morning. But people who had a dealer-supplied red plastic strip in their window, identifying them as regular customers, could buy gasoline.

In response to this tactic, Federal Energy Director William F. Simon prohibited gas stations from discriminating against buyers by practices such as selling gasoline only to regular customers or to those who purchased large amounts of gasoline in advance. Director Simon was operating under his authority to control prices and allocate motor fuels during this crisis. He urged motorists to contact the Internal Revenue Service immediately if they believed they were being discriminated against in violation of his order. A station owner who was convicted of violating the regulation under the criminal code could be fined up to $5,000, according to the Federal Energy Office.

The price stabilization office of the Internal Revenue Service reported many complaints of price-gouging and illegal selling tactics. One Saturday, more than 300 complaints were phoned in within the first six hours of the day.

In summary, the government acted to protect consumers from having to pay high prices for oil. By so doing, it created shortages and incurred substantial enforcement costs. Deacon and Sonstelie (1989) calculate that for every dollar consumers saved during another episode of gasoline price controls in 1980, they lost $1.16 in waiting time and other factors.

Would you rather pay a relatively high price and be able to buy as much gasoline as you want at that price or pay a low price and have to stand in line to buy a restricted amount? Consumers disagree about the answer to this question. Presumably, consumers who put a relatively low value on their time are more likely to like controls, while higher-income consumers curse the controls. ■

Price Floors. Governments also commonly use price floors. One of the most important examples of a price floor is the minimum wage in labor markets.

The minimum wage law forbids employers from paying less than the minimum wage, $\underline{w}$. Currently, the federal minimum wage is $5.15 an hour. If the minimum wage binds—exceeds the equilibrium wage, w^*—the minimum wage creates *unemployment*, which is a persistent excess supply of labor.[15]

---

[15]Where the minimum wage applies to only a few labor markets (Chapter 10) or where only a single firm hires all the workers in a market (Chapter 15), a minimum wage may not cause unemployment. The U.S. Department of Labor has an extensive history of the minimum wage law, coverage of labor markets over time, state minimum wage laws, and other information at its Web site: www.dol.gov.

For simplicity, suppose that there is a single labor market, in which everyone is paid the same wage. Figure 2.13 shows the supply and demand curves for labor services (hours worked). Firms buy hours of labor service—hire workers. The quantity measure on the horizontal axis is hours worked per year, and the price measure is the wage per hour.

With no government intervention, the market equilibrium is *e*, where the wage is w^* and the number of hours worked is L^*. The minimum wage creates a price floor, a horizontal line, at $\underline{w}$. At that wage, quantity demand falls to L_d and quantity supplied rises to L_s. As a result, there is an excess supply or unemployment of $L_s - L_d$. The minimum wage prevents market forces from eliminating this excess supply, so it leads to an equilibrium with unemployment.

It is ironic that a law designed to help workers by raising their wages may harm some of them by causing them to become unemployed. A minimum wage law benefits only those who remain employed.[16]

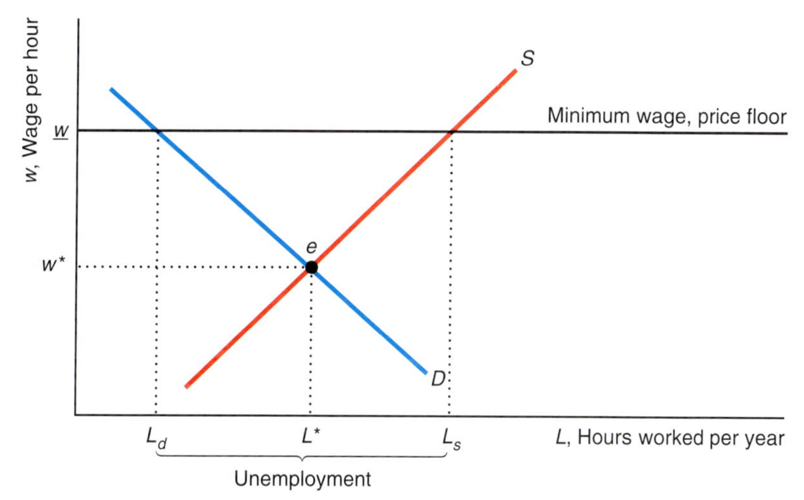

Figure 2.13 Minimum Wage. In the absence of a minimum wage, the equilibrium wage is w^* and the equilibrium number of hours worked is L^*. A minimum wage, $\underline{w}$, set above w^*, leads to unemployment—persistent excess supply—because the quantity demanded, L_d, is less than the quantity supplied, L_s.

[16]The minimum wage could raise the wage enough that total wage payments, wL, rise despite the fall in demand for labor services. Here, if the workers could share the unemployment—so everybody works fewer hours than he or she wants—all workers could benefit from the minimum wage.

APPLICATION

Minimum Wage Law in Puerto Rico

In 1938, the Fair Labor Standards Act established a $\underline{w}$ = 25¢ per hour minimum wage for many U.S. industries engaged in interstate commerce. This rate was at or below the equilibrium wage in most of these industries, so this price floor had little effect. Unfortunately, the same minimum wage was applied to Puerto Rico, where the average wage was much lower: only about 7¢ (= w^* in Figure 2.13) in tobacco and coffee industries, 12¢ in fruit canning, 14¢ in laundries, and 18¢ in apparel industries.[17]

Employers in several important Puerto Rican industries screamed bloody murder. Employers in the tobacco-stemming industry would not comply with the law and practically locked out workers, making them unemployed.

The needlework export industries were decimated. A comparison of 1939–1940 to 1940–1941 shows that exports fell by 61% in cotton manufacturing and linen manufacturing, 71% in silk manufacturing, and 47% in other needlework manufacturing.

This loss of jobs and output devastated Puerto Rico. In response, the U.S. Congress established special minimum wages for specific Puerto Rican industries. For example, by the end of 1940, the rate fell to as low as 12.5¢ in some parts of the needlework industry.

In 1950, the average minimum wage was 20¢ in Puerto Rico compared to 75¢ in the United States. Starting in 1974, the Puerto Rican minimum wage was raised gradually to the U.S. level. By 1983, both minimums were the same, $3.35.

In 1987, the minimum wage was two-thirds (63%) of the average hourly earnings in manufacturing in Puerto Rico but only one-third (34%) on the mainland. Castillo-Freeman and Freeman (1992) estimate that island employment would have been 8–10% higher in 1987 if the minimum wage had been set so that the ratio of the minimum to the average wage were comparable to that in the United States. They find that the change in the minimum wage was responsible for one-third of the drop in the employment rate (the ratio of employment to population) in Puerto Rico from 1975 to 1987. ■

Why Supply Need Not Equal Demand

The price ceiling and price floor examples show that supply does not necessarily equal demand in a supply-and-demand model. Supply need not equal demand because of the way we defined these two terms. We defined the quantity supplied as the amount

[17] Puerto Rico is a self-governing island commonwealth in free association with the United States. Its residents are U.S. citizens. This application is based on Perloff (1950) [my dad]; Reynolds, Gregory, and Torruellas (1965); and Castillo-Freeman and Freeman (1992).

firms *want* to sell at a given price, holding other factors that affect supply, such as the price of inputs, constant. The quantity demanded is the quantity that consumers *want* to buy at a given price, if other factors that affect demand are held constant. The quantity that firms want to sell and the quantity that consumers want to buy at a given price need not equal the *actual* quantity that is bought and sold.

When the government imposes a binding price ceiling of $\bar{p}$ on gasoline, the quantity demanded is greater than the quantity supplied. Despite the lack of equality between the quantity supplied and the quantity demanded, the supply-and-demand model is useful in analyzing this market because it predicts the excess demand that is actually observed.

We could have defined the quantity supplied and the quantity demanded so that they must be equal. If we were to define the quantity supplied as the amount firms *actually* sell at a given price and the quantity demanded as the amount consumers *actually* buy, supply must equal demand in all markets because the quantity demanded and the quantity supplied are *defined* to be the same quantity.

It is worth pointing out this distinction because many people, including politicians and newspaper reporters, are confused on this point. Someone insisting that "demand *must* equal supply" must be defining demand and supply as the *actual* quantities sold.

Because we define the quantities supplied and demanded in terms of people's *wants*—and not *actual* quantities bought and sold—the statement that "supply equals demand" is a theory, not merely a definition. This theory says that the equilibrium price and quantity in a market are determined by the intersection of the supply curve and the demand curve if the government does not intervene. Further, we use the model to predict excess demand or excess supply when a government does control price. The observed gasoline shortages during the period when the U.S. government controlled gasoline prices are consistent with this prediction.

2.6 WHEN TO USE THE SUPPLY-AND-DEMAND MODEL

As we've seen throughout this chapter, the supply-and-demand theory can help us to understand and predict real-world events in many markets. In Chapters 2 through 10, we discuss competitive markets in which the supply-and-demand model is a powerful tool for predicting what will happen to market equilibrium if underlying conditions—tastes, incomes, and prices of inputs—change. The types of markets for which the supply-and-demand model is useful are described at length in these chapters, particularly Chapter 8. Briefly, this model is applicable in markets in which:

- **Everyone is a price taker:** Because no consumer or firm is a very large part of the market, no one can affect the market price. Easy entry of firms into the market, which leads to a large number of firms, is usually necessary to ensure that firms are price takers.
- **Firms sell identical products:** Consumers do not prefer one firm's good to another.

- **Everyone has full information about the price and quality of goods:** Consumers know if a firm is charging a price higher than the price others set, and they know if a firm tries to sell them inferior-quality goods.
- **Costs of trading are low:** It is not time consuming, difficult, or expensive for a buyer to find a seller and make a trade or for a seller to find and trade with a buyer.

Markets with these properties are called *perfect competitive markets*.

Where there are many firms and consumers, no single firm or consumer is a large enough part of the market to affect the price. If you stop buying bread or if one of the many thousands of wheat farmers stops selling the wheat used to make the bread, the price of bread will not change. Consumers and firms are *price takers*: They cannot affect the market price.

In contrast, if there is only one seller of a good or service—a *monopoly* (Chapter 11)—that seller is a *price setter* and can affect the market price. Because demand curves slope down, a monopoly can increase the price it receives by reducing the amount of a good it supplies. Firms are also price setters in an *oligopoly*—a small number of firms in a market—or in markets where they sell differentiated products so that a consumer prefers one product to another (Chapters 12 and 13). In markets with price setters, the market price is usually higher than that predicted by the supply-and-demand model. That doesn't make the supply-and-demand model generally wrong. It means only that the supply-and-demand model does not apply to markets with small number of sellers or buyers. In such markets, we use other models.

If consumers have less information than a firm, the firm can take advantage of consumers by selling them inferior-quality goods or by charging a much higher price than that charged by other firms. In such a market, the observed price is usually higher than that predicted by the supply-and-demand model, the market may not exist at all (consumers and firms cannot reach agreements), or different firms may charge different prices for the same good (see Chapter 19).

The supply-and-demand model also is not fully appropriate in markets in which it is costly to trade with others because the cost of a buyer's finding a seller or of a seller's finding a buyer are high. **Transaction costs** are the expenses of finding a trading partner and making a trade for a good or service other than the price paid for that good or service. These costs include the time and money spent to find someone with whom to trade. For example, you may have to pay to place a newspaper advertisement to sell your gray 1983 Honda with 137,000 miles. Or you may have to go to many stores to find one that sells a shirt in exactly the color you want, so your transaction cost includes transportation cost and your time. The cost of a long-distance call to place an order is a transaction cost. Other transaction costs include the costs of writing and enforcing a contract, such as the cost of lawyers' time. Where transaction costs are high, no trades may occur, or, if they do occur, individual trades may occur at a variety of prices (see Chapters 13 and 19).

Thus, the supply-and-demand model is not appropriate in markets in which there are only one or a few sellers (electricity), firms produce differentiated products (music CDs), consumers know less than sellers about quality or price (used cars), and there are high transaction costs (nuclear turbine engines). The supply-and-demand model has proved to be appropriate and useful in many agricultural, financial, labor, construction, services, wholesale, retail, and other markets.

Summary

1. **Demand:** The quantity demanded of a good or service by consumers depends on their tastes, the price of a good, the price of goods that are substitutes and complements, their income, information, government regulations, and other factors. The *Law of Demand*—which is based on observation—says that *demand curves slope down.* The higher the price, the less of the good is demanded, holding constant other factors that affect demand. A change in price causes a *movement along the demand curve.* A change in income, tastes, or another factor that affects demand other than price causes the entire *demand curve to shift.* To get a total demand curve, we horizontally sum the demand curves of individuals or types of consumers or countries. That is, we add the quantities demanded by each individual at a given price to get the total demanded.
2. **Supply:** The quantity supplied of a good or service by firms depends on the price, costs, government regulations, and other factors. The market supply curve need not slope upward but usually does. A change in price causes a *movement along the supply curve.* A change in the price of an input or government regulation causes the entire *supply curve to shift.* The total supply curve is the horizontal sum of the supply curves for individual firms.
3. **Market equilibrium:** The intersection of the demand curve and the supply curve determines the equilibrium price and quantity in a market. Market forces—actions of consumers and firms—drive the price and quantity to the equilibrium levels if they are initially too low or too high.
4. **Shocking the equilibrium:** A change in an underlying factor other than price causes a shift of the supply curve or the demand curve, which alters the equilibrium. For example, if the price of beef rises, the demand curve for pork shifts outward, causing a movement along the supply curve and leading to a new equilibrium at a higher price and quantity. If changes in these underlying factors follow one after the other, a market that adjusts slowly may stay out of equilibrium for an extended period.
5. **Effects of government interventions:** Some government policies—such as a ban on imports—cause a shift in the supply or demand curves, thereby altering the equilibrium. Other government policies—such as a price control or minimum wage—cause the quantity supplied to be greater or less than the quantity demanded so there are persistent excesses or shortages.
6. **When to use the supply-and-demand model:** The supply-and-demand model is a powerful tool to explain what happens in a market or to make predictions about what will happen if an underlying factor in a market changes. This model, however, is applicable only in markets with many buyers and sellers; identical goods; certainty and full information about price, quantity, quality, incomes, costs, and other market characteristics; and low transaction costs.

Problems[18]

1. What was the effect on the worldwide market for alcoholic beverages of the U.S. Prohibition amendment, which banned the sale or production of alcohol in the United States? Explain what happened to the supply curves, demand curves, and the equilibrium prices and quantities.
2. The U.S. supply of frozen orange juice comes from Florida and Brazil. What is the effect of a freeze

[18]Answers to selected problems appear at the end of the book.

that damages oranges in Florida on the price of frozen orange juice in the United States and on the quantities of orange juice sold by Floridian and Brazilian firms?

3. A tax of \$1 per unit is placed on suppliers of playing cards. What happens to the equilibrium price and quantity?
4. What is the effect of a quota $\bar{Q} > 0$ on equilibrium price and quantity? (*Hint:* Carefully show how the total supply curve shifts.)
5. Usury laws place a ceiling on interest rates that lenders such as banks can charge borrowers. Low-income households in states with usury laws have significantly lower levels of consumer credit (loans) than comparable households in states without usury laws (Villegas, 1989). Why? (*Hint:* The interest rate is the price of a loan and the amount of the loan is the quantity measure.)
6. After a major earthquake struck Los Angeles in January 1994, some stores raised the price of milk to over \$6 a gallon. The local authorities announced that they would investigate and that they would enforce a law prohibiting price increases of more than 10% during an emergency period.[19] What is the likely effect of such a law?
7. Is it possible that an outright ban on foreign imports will have no effect on the equilibrium price? (*Hint:* Suppose that imports occur only at relatively high prices.)
8. If certain jurisdictions ban the use of skateboards on city streets, what is the likely effect on the market for skateboards? How do such laws affect the supply curve, the demand curve, and equilibrium price and quantity?
9. A newspaper article suggests that a crackdown on a cocaine-smuggling ring caused cocaine prices in Manhattan to rise from \$20,000 to \$30,000 a kilo.[20] Illustrate in a supply-and-demand diagram why this happened, and explain in words.
10. A group of American doctors has called for a limit on the number of foreign-trained physicians who are allowed to practice in the United States. What effect would such a limit have on the equilibrium quantity and price of doctor services in the United States? How are American-trained doctors and consumers affected?
11. Suppose cotton is produced only in the United States and China. The U.S. government says that, if an American farmer sells a bale of cotton at the world price p, the government will give the farmer $(p^* - p)$ per bale, where $p^* > p$. What happens to the quantities sold by American and Chinese growers and the world price of cotton?
12. Use a supply-and-demand diagram to explain the statement "Talk is cheap because supply exceeds demand." At what price is this comparison being made?

Math Problems

13. Using the estimated demand function for processed pork in Canada, determine how price changes as the quantity demanded increases by one unit (that is, the quantity demanded increases by one million kg per year). (*Hint:* Rewrite the demand function so that price is a function of quantity.)
14. Using the estimated demand function for processed pork in Canada (Equation 2.2), show how the quantity demanded at a given price changes as per capita income, Y, increases by \$100 a year.
15. Suppose the price of beef, p_b, in Canada increased by 30%, from \$4 to \$5.20. How does the demand curve for processed pork shift?
16. The supply of corn by the United States is $Q_a = a + bp$, and the supply by the rest of the world is $Q_r = c + ep$. What is the world supply?

---

[19] Later, a state law was proposed to prevent price gouging after an earthquake or other disasters. Michael Liedtke, "Post-Disaster, Price-Gouging Bill Draws an Unexpected Foe," *Contra Costa Times*, July 2, 1994:D1.

[20] Wren, Christopher S., "Cocaine's Price Rises Sharply, and Officials Seek Answers," *New York Times*, May 2, 1997:A20.

17. The demand function for a good is $Q = a - bp$, and the supply functions is $Q = c + ep$, where a, b, c, and e are positive constants. Solve for the equilibrium price and quantity in terms of these four constants.

18. Show how the equilibrium quantity of pork varies with income.

19. Using the demand for processed pork (Equation 2.2) and supply (Equation 2.6), solve for the equilibrium price and quantity in terms of the price of hogs (p_h), the price of beef (p_b), the price of chicken (p_c), and income (Y). If p_h = \$1.50 per kg, p_b = \$4 per kg, p_c = \$3$\frac{1}{3}$ per kg, and Y = \$12.5 thousand, what are the equilibrium price and quantity?

CHAPTER 3

Applying the Supply-and-Demand Model

Few of us ever test our powers of deduction, except when filling out an income tax form. —Laurence J. Peter

In 1989, Californians voted to increase the tax on cigarettes from 10¢ to 35¢ per pack. Is a 250% tax increase large enough to discourage a substantial number of people from smoking? We can use supply-and-demand analysis to answer this question.

When a tax rate or another underlying factor that affects the demand or supply curves changes, the equilibrium price and quantity also change. Chapter 2 showed that you can predict the direction of the change—the *qualitative* change—in equilibrium price and quantity even without knowing the exact shape of the demand and supply curves. In the examples in Chapter 2, all you needed to know to give a qualitative answer was the direction in which the supply curve or demand curve shifted when an underlying factor changed.

To determine the exact amount the equilibrium quantity and price change—the *quantitative* change—you can use estimated equations for the demand and supply functions, as we demonstrated using the pork example in the previous chapter. This chapter shows how to use a single number to describe the shape of a demand or supply curve and how to use these summary numbers for the demand and supply curves to obtain quantitative answers to what-if questions.

What determines the shapes of demand and supply curves? To answer this question, we have to examine the decisions made by individual consumers and firms.

In this chapter, we examine five main topics:

1. **How shapes of demand and supply curves matter:** The effect of a shock (such as a new tax or an increase in the price of an input) on market equilibrium depends on the shape of demand and supply curves.
2. **Sensitivity of quantity demanded to price:** The sensitivity of the quantity demanded to price is summarized by a single measure called the price elasticity of demand.
3. **Sensitivity of quantity supplied to price:** The sensitivity of the quantity supplied to price is summarized by a single measure called the price elasticity of supply.
4. **Long run versus short run:** The sensitivity of the quantity demanded or supplied to price varies with time.
5. **Effects of a sales tax:** How a sales tax increase affects the equilibrium price and quantity of a good and whether the tax falls more heavily on consumers or suppliers depend on the shape of the supply and demand curves.

3.1 HOW SHAPES OF DEMAND AND SUPPLY CURVES MATTER

How a shock that shifts the supply curve affects the market equilibrium depends on the shape of the demand curve. Similarly, the effect on equilibrium of a shock that shifts the demand curve depends on the shape of the supply curve.

We illustrate the importance of the shape of the demand curve using the processed pork example (Moschini and Meilke 1992) from Chapter 2. The supply of pork depends on the price of pork and the price of hogs, the major input in producing processed pork. A 25¢ increase in the price of hogs causes the supply curve of pork to shift to the left from S^1 to S^2 in panel a of Figure 3.1. The *shift of the supply curve* causes a *movement along the demand curve*, D^1, which is downward sloping. The equilibrium quantity falls from 220 to 215 million kg per year, and the equilibrium price rises from \$3.30 to \$3.55 per kg.

Thus, this supply shock—an increase in the price of hogs—hurts consumers by raising the equilibrium price 25¢ per kg. Customers buy less (215 instead of 220) but spend more. The amount customers spend, the pork firms' revenue, R, equals price times quantity: $R = pQ$. In the initial equilibrium, e_1, the revenue is

$$R_1 = (\$3.30 \text{ per kg}) \times (220 \text{ million kg per year}) = \$726 \text{ million per year.}$$

After the price of hogs increases, revenue rises to

$$R_2 = (\$3.55 \text{ per kg}) \times (215 \text{ million kg per year}) = \$763.25 \text{ million per year.}$$

Thus, the amount spent by consumers rises by $\Delta R = R_2 - R_1 = \$37.25$ million per year. Table 3.1 summarizes these effects.

A supply shock would have different effects if the demand curve had a different shape. Suppose the quantity demanded were not sensitive to a change in the price, so the same amount is demanded no matter what the price is, as in vertical demand curve D^2 in panel b. A 25¢ increase in the price of hogs again shifts the supply curve from S^1 to S^2. Equilibrium quantity does not change, but the price consumers pay rises to \$3.675. Revenue rises $\Delta R = \$82.5$ million per year from $R_1 = \$726$ million per year to $R_2 = \$808.5$ million per year. Thus, the amount consumers spend rises by more when the demand curve is vertical instead of downward sloping.

Table 3.1 Effect on the Processed Pork Market of a 25¢ Increase in the Price of Hogs Depends on the Shape of the Demand Curve

If Demand is	Change in Price, Δp, cents per kg	Change in Quantity, ΔQ, million kg per year	Change in Revenue, ΔR, million dollars per year
Downward sloping (actual demand)	25	−5	37.25
Vertical	37.5	0	82.5
Horizontal	0	−15	−49.5

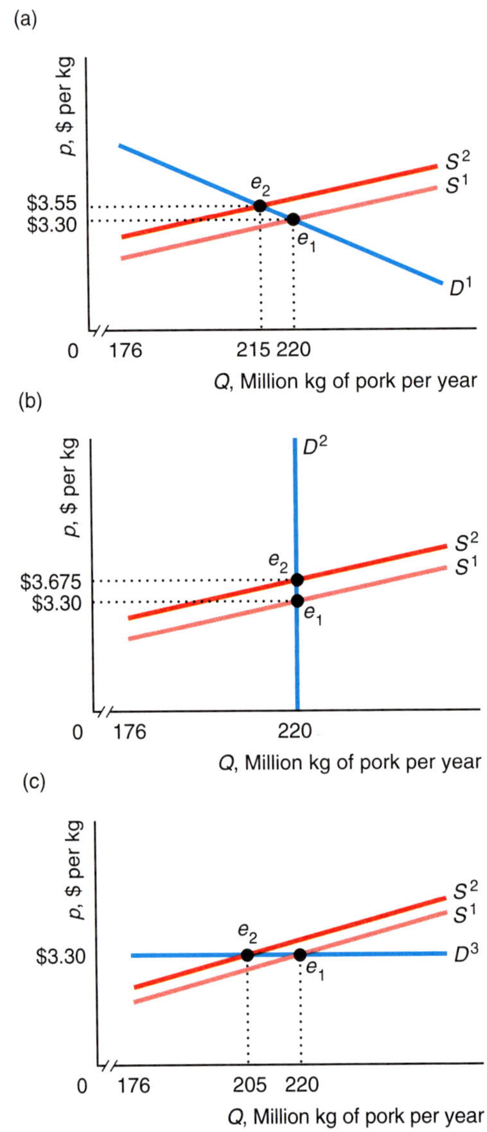

Figure 3.1 Effect of a Supply Shock Depends on the Shape of the Demand Curve. A decrease in the price of hogs shifts the supply of processed pork outward (Moschini and Meilke 1992). (a) Given the actual, downward-sloping, linear demand curve, the equilibrium price rises from $3.30 to $3.55 and the equilibrium quantity falls from 220 to 215. (b) If the demand curve were vertical, the supply shock would cause price to rise to $3.675 while quantity would remain unchanged. (c) If the demand curve were horizontal, the supply shock would not affect price but would cause quantity to fall to 205.

Now suppose that consumers are very sensitive to price: They will buy virtually unlimited quantities of pork at $3.30 per kg (or less), but, if the price rises even slightly, they stop buying pork. The demand curve, D^3 in panel c, is horizontal. Here, an increase in the price of hogs has *no* effect on the price consumers pay; however, the equilibrium quantity drops substantially to 205 million kg per year. Because the equilibrium price is unchanged and quantity falls, revenue falls by $\Delta R = -\$49.50$ to $R_2 = 676.5$ million per year. Thus, how consumer spending changes, how much the equilibrium quantity falls, and how much the equilibrium price of processed pork rises when the price of hogs increases depend on the shape of the demand curve.

3.2 SENSITIVITY OF QUANTITY DEMANDED TO PRICE

Knowing how much quantity demanded falls as the price increases, holding all else constant, is therefore important in predicting the effect of a shock in a supply-and-demand model. We can determine how much quantity demanded falls as the price rises using an accurate drawing of the demand curve or the demand function (the equation that describes the demand curve). It is convenient, however, to be able to summarize the relevant information to answer what-if questions without having to write out an equation or draw a graph. Armed with such a summary statistic, the pork firms can predict the effect on the price of pork and their revenues from a shift in the market supply curve.

In this section, we discuss a summary statistic that describes the shape of a demand curve and show how this information allows us to predict the effect of a shock on the equilibrium quantity and firms' revenues. In the next section, we discuss a similar statistic that summarizes the shape of the supply curve. At the end of the chapter, we show how the government can use these summary measures for demand and supply to predict the effect of a new sales tax on the equilibrium price, firms' revenues, and tax receipts.

Price Elasticity of Demand

The most commonly used measure of the sensitivity of one variable, such as the quantity demanded, to another variable, such as price, is an **elasticity**, which is the percentage change in one variable in response to a given percentage change in another variable. We can use the *price elasticity of demand* (or *elasticity of demand*) to describe the shape of the demand curve. The **price elasticity of demand** is the percentage change in the quantity demanded, Q, in response to a given percentage change in the price, p. The price elasticity of demand (which we call ε, the Greek letter *epsilon*) may be calculated as

$$\varepsilon = \frac{\text{percentage change in quantity demanded}}{\text{percentage change in price}} = \frac{\Delta Q/Q}{\Delta p/p}, \tag{3.1}$$

where the symbol Δ (the Greek letter *delta*) indicates a change, so ΔQ is the change in the quantity demanded, $\Delta Q/Q$ is the percentage change in the quantity demanded, Δp is the change in price, and $\Delta p/p$ is the percentage change in price.[1] For example, if a 1% increase in the price results in the quantity demanded falling by –3%, the elasticity of demand is $\varepsilon = -3\%/1\% = -3$.[2]

It is often more convenient to calculate the elasticity of demand using an equivalent expression,

$$\varepsilon = \frac{\Delta Q/Q}{\Delta p/p} = \frac{\Delta Q}{\Delta p}\frac{p}{Q}, \tag{3.2}$$

where $\Delta Q/\Delta p$ is the ratio of the change in quantity to the change in price.[3]

We can use Equation 3.2 to calculate the elasticity of demand for a linear demand curve, which has a demand function (holding fixed other variables that affect demand) of

$$Q = a - bp,$$

where a is the quantity demanded when price is zero ($Q = a - b \times 0 = a$) and $-b$ is the ratio of the fall in quantity to the rise in price, $\Delta Q/\Delta p$.[4] Thus, for a linear demand curve, the elasticity of demand is

$$\varepsilon = \frac{\Delta Q}{\Delta p}\frac{p}{Q} = -b\frac{p}{Q}. \tag{3.3}$$

As an example, we calculate the elasticity of demand for the linear pork demand curve D in panel a of Figure 3.1. The estimated linear demand function for pork that holds constant other factors that influence demand besides price (Equation 2.3,

---

[1]The elasticity is the percentage change in quantity divided by the percentage change in price. Percentage changes are independent of units. In the pork example from Chapter 2, $\Delta p/p$ is the change in price in dollars per kg divided by the price in dollars per kg, so, roughly speaking, the units of measure, dollars per kg, in the numerator and the denominator cancel. Because the elasticity is the ratio of two percentages, it is a pure number: It has no units of measure.

[2]Because demand curves slope down according to the Law of Demand, the elasticity of demand is a negative number. Realizing that, some economists ignore the negative sign when reporting a demand elasticity. In the example, instead of saying the elasticity is –3, they would say that the elasticity is 3 (with the negative sign understood).

[3]When we use calculus, we use infinitesimally small changes in price (Δp approaches zero), so we write the elasticity as $(\mathrm{d}Q/\mathrm{d}p)(p/Q)$. When discussing elasticities, we assume that the change in price is small.

[4]As the price increases from p_1 to p_2, the quantity demanded goes from Q_1 to Q_2, so the change in quantity demanded is

$$\Delta Q = Q_2 - Q_1 = (a - bp_2) - (a - bp_1) = -b(p_2 - p_1) = -b\Delta p.$$

Thus, $\Delta Q/\Delta p = -b$. Alternatively, using calculus, we know that $\mathrm{d}Q/\mathrm{d}p = \mathrm{d}(a - bp)/\mathrm{d}p = -b$, where $\mathrm{d}Q/\mathrm{d}p = \Delta Q/\Delta p$ for very small changes in price, Δp.

based on Moschini and Meilke 1992) is

$$Q = 286 - 20p,$$

where Q is the quantity of pork demanded in million kg per year and p is the price of pork in dollars per kg. For this demand equation, $a = 286$ and $b = 20$. Using Equation 3.3, we find that the elasticity of demand at the equilibrium e_1 in panel a, where $p = \$3.30$ and $Q = 220$ million kg per year, is

$$\varepsilon = b\frac{p}{Q} = -20 \times \frac{3.30}{220} = -0.3.$$

The negative sign on the elasticity of demand of pork illustrates the Law of Demand: Less quantity is demanded as the price rises. The elasticity of demand concisely answers the question "How much does quantity demanded fall in response to a 1% increase in price?" A 1% increase in price leads to an ε% change in the quantity demanded. At the equilibrium, a 1% increase in the price of pork leads to a –0.3% fall in the quantity of pork demanded: A price increase causes a less than proportionate fall in the quantity of pork demanded.

Elasticity Along the Demand Curve

The elasticity of demand varies along most demand curves. We next show that the elasticity of demand is different at every point along a downward-sloping linear demand curve. Then we point out that the elasticities are constant along horizontal and vertical linear demand curves. Next we discuss how consumers' expenditures and firms' revenues vary with the elasticity along a demand curve.

Downward-Sloping Linear Demand Curve. On strictly downward-sloping linear demand curves—those that are neither vertical nor horizontal—the elasticity of demand is a more negative number the higher the price is.[5] A 1% increase in price causes a larger percentage fall in quantity near the top (left) of the demand curve than near the bottom (right).

The linear pork demand curve in Figure 3.2 illustrates this pattern. Where this demand curve hits the quantity axis ($p = 0$ and $Q = a = 286$ million kg per year), the elasticity of demand is $\varepsilon = -b(0/a) = 0$, according to Equation 3.3. Where the price is zero, a 1% increase in price does not raise the price, so quantity does not change. At a point where the elasticity of demand is zero, the demand curve is said to be *perfectly inelastic*. As a physical analogy, if you try to stretch an inelastic steel rod, the length does not change. The change in the price is the force pulling at

[5]Equation 3.3 shows the elasticity of demand for a linear demand curve is $-bp/Q$. As price rises, the quantity falls, causing p/Q to rise and the elasticity to become more negative. We can give a geometric interpretation. From the demand function, we know that $p = (a - Q)/b$. Substituting this expression for p in the elasticity definition, we obtain $\varepsilon = -bp/Q = -(a - Q)/Q$. Thus, at any given Q, the elasticity of demand is the ratio of the distance from Q to the intercept on the horizontal axis, a, divided by the distance from the origin to Q. As Q increases, $(a - Q)$ becomes smaller, so the elasticity gets closer to zero.

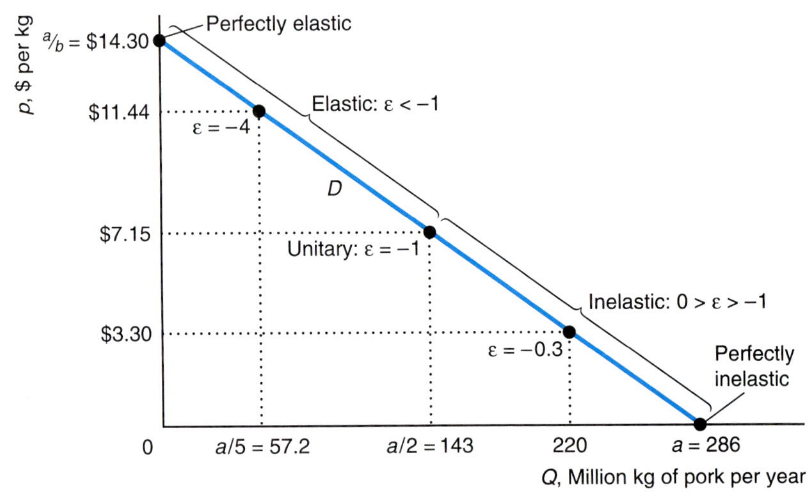

Figure 3.2 Elasticity Along the Pork Demand Curve. With a linear demand curve, such as the pork demand curve, the higher the price, the more elastic (ε is larger in absolute value—a larger negative number) is the demand curve. The demand curve is perfectly inelastic (ε is 0) where the demand curve hits the horizontal axis, is perfectly elastic (ε is −∞) where the demand curve hits the vertical axis, and has unitary elasticity (ε is −1) at the midpoint of the demand curve.

demand; if the quantity demanded does not change in response to this pulling, it is perfectly inelastic.

For quantities between the midpoint of the linear demand curve and the lower end where $Q = a$, the demand elasticity lies between 0 and −1: $0 \ge \varepsilon > -1$. A point along the demand curve where the elasticity is between 0 and −1 is *inelastic* (but not perfectly inelastic). Where the demand curve is inelastic, a 1% increase in price leads to a fall in quantity of less than 1%. For example, at the competitive pork equilibrium, $\varepsilon = -0.3$, so a 1% increase in price causes quantity to fall by −0.3%. A physical analogy is a piece of rope that does not stretch much—is inelastic—when you pull on it: Changing price has relatively little effect on quantity.

At the midpoint of the linear demand curve, $p = \frac{1}{2}(a/b)$ and $Q = a/2$, so $\varepsilon = -bp/Q = -b(\frac{1}{2}[a/b])/(a/2) = -1$.[6] Such an elasticity of demand is called a *unitary elasticity*: A 1% increase in price causes a 1% fall in quantity.

At prices higher than at the midpoint of the demand curve, the elasticity of demand is less than negative one, $\varepsilon < -1$, which is called *elastic*. A physical analogy

[6]The demand curve intersects the horizontal axis at $Q = a - bp = a - b0 = a$ and the vertical axis where $Q = 0 = a - bp$, or $p = a/b$. Thus, at the midpoint of the demand curve, the quantity is $\frac{1}{2}a$ and the price is $\frac{1}{2}(a/b)$.

is a rubber band that stretches substantially when you pull on it. A 1% increase in price causes a more than 1% fall in quantity. The figure shows that the elasticity is –4 where $Q = a/5$: A 1% increase in price causes a 4% drop in quantity.

As the price rises, the elasticity gets more and more negative, approaching negative infinity. Where the demand curve hits the price axis, it is *perfectly elastic.*[7] At the price a/b where $Q = 0$, a 1% decrease in p causes the quantity demanded to become positive, which is an infinite increase in quantity.

The elasticity of demand varies along most demand curves, not just downward-sloping linear ones. Along a special type of demand curve, called a *constant elasticity demand curve*, however, the elasticity is the same at every point along the curve.[8] Two extreme cases of these constant elasticity demand curves are the strictly vertical and the strictly horizontal linear demand curves.

Horizontal Demand Curve. The demand curve that is horizontal at p^* in panel a of Figure 3.3 shows that people are willing to buy as much as firms sell at any price less than or equal to p^*. If the price increases even slightly above p^*, however, demand falls to zero. Thus, a small increase in price causes an infinite drop in quantity, so the demand curve is perfectly elastic.[9]

Why would a demand curve be horizontal? One reason is that consumers view this good as identical to another good and do not care which one they buy. Suppose consumers view Washington apples and Oregon apples as identical. They won't buy Washington apples if these sell for more than apples from Oregon. Similarly, they won't buy Oregon apples if their price is higher than that of Washington apples. If the two prices are equal, consumers do not care which type of apple they buy. Thus, the demand curve for Oregon apples is horizontal at the price of the Washington apples.

Vertical Demand Curve. A vertical demand curve, panel b in Figure 3.3, is perfectly inelastic everywhere. Such a demand curve is an extreme case of the linear demand curve with an infinite (vertical) slope. If the price goes up, the quantity demanded is unchanged, so the elasticity of demand must be zero.[10]

---

[7]The demand curve hits the price axis at $p = a/b$ and $Q = 0$, so the elasticity is $-bp/0$. As the price approaches a/b, the elasticity approaches negative infinity. An intuition for this convention is provided by looking at a sequence, where –1 divided by 1/10 is –10; –1 divided by 1/100 is –100; and so on. The smaller the number we divide by, the more negative is the result, which goes to $-\infty$ (negative infinity) in the limit.

[8]Constant elasticity demand curves all have the form $Q = Ap^{\varepsilon}$, where A is a positive constant and ε is a negative constant, which is the demand elasticity at every point along these demand curves.

[9]As a linear demand curve gets closer to horizontal, the inverse of its slope, $\Delta Q/\Delta p$, approaches negative infinity, $-\infty$. (If a \$1 increase in price causes quantity demanded to fall by 10 units, $\Delta Q/\Delta p = -10$; if quantity falls by 100, $\Delta Q/\Delta p = -100$, and so forth.) Because both p and Q are positive numbers along a horizontal demand curve, as $\Delta Q/\Delta p$ approaches negative infinity, the elasticity, $\varepsilon = (\Delta Q/\Delta p)(p/Q)$, approaches negative infinity.

[10]Because quantity does not change with price, $\Delta Q/\Delta p = 0$. As a consequence, the elasticity is $(\Delta Q/\Delta p)(p/Q) = 0(p/Q) = 0$.

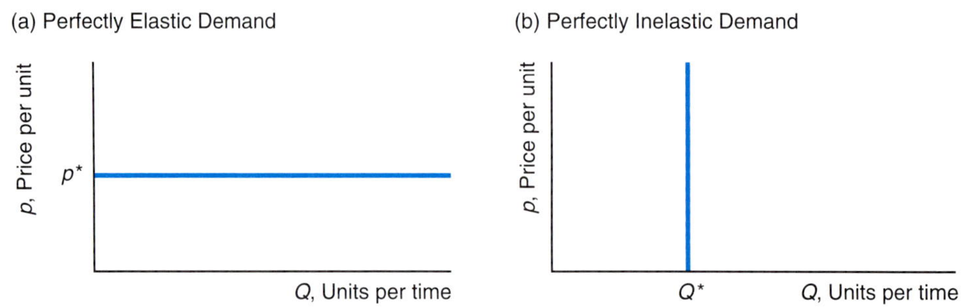

A demand curve is vertical for *essential* goods—goods that people feel they must have and will pay anything to get. Because Jerry is a diabetic, his demand curve for insulin could be vertical at a day's dose, Q^*. More realistically, he may have a demand curve (panel c of Figure 3.3) that is perfectly inelastic only at prices below p^*, the maximum price he can afford to pay. Because he cannot afford to pay more than p^*, he buys nothing at higher prices. As a result, his demand curve is perfectly elastic up to Q^* units at a price of p^*.

Other Demand Elasticities

We refer to the price elasticity of demand as *the* elasticity of demand. There are, however, other demand elasticities that show how the quantity demanded changes in response to changes in variables other than price that affect the quantity demanded. Two such demand elasticities are the income elasticity of demand and the cross-price elasticity of demand.

Income Elasticity. As income increases, the demand curve shifts. If the demand curve shifts to the right, a larger quantity is demanded at any given price. If, instead, the demand curve shifts to the left, a smaller quantity is demanded at any given price.

We can measure how sensitive the quantity demanded at a given price is to income by using an elasticity. The **income elasticity of demand** (or *income elasticity*) is the percentage change in the quantity demanded in response to a given percentage change in income, Y. The income elasticity of demand may be calculated as

$$\xi = \frac{\text{percentage change in quantity demanded}}{\text{percentage change in income}} = \frac{\Delta Q/Q}{\Delta Y/Y} = \frac{\Delta Q}{\Delta Y}\frac{Y}{Q},$$

where ξ is the Greek letter *xi*. If quantity demanded increases as income rises, the income elasticity of demand is positive. If the quantity does not change as income rises, the income elasticity is zero. Finally, if the quantity demanded falls as income rises, the income elasticity is negative.

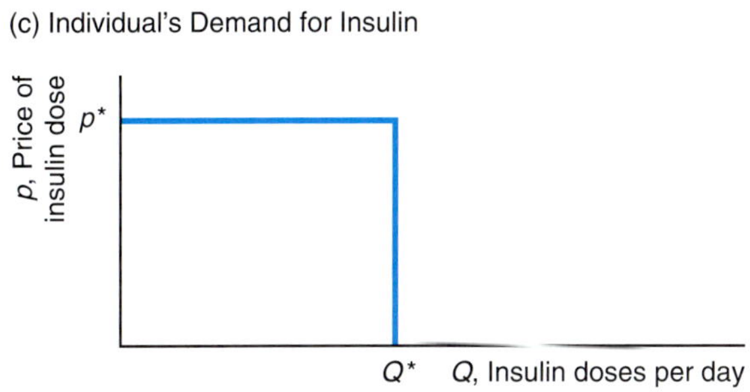

Figure 3.3 Vertical and Horizontal Demand Curves. (a) A horizontal demand curve is perfectly elastic at p^*. (b) A vertical demand curve is perfectly inelastic at every price. (c) The demand curve of an individual who is diabetic is perfectly inelastic below p^* and perfectly elastic at p^*, which is the maximum price the individual can afford to pay.

We calculate the income elasticity for pork using the demand function, Equation 2.2:

$$Q = 171 - 20p + 20p_b + 3p_c + 2Y. \tag{3.4}$$

where p is the price of pork, p_b is the price of beef, p_c is the price of chicken, and Y is the income (in thousands of dollars). Because the change in quantity as income changes is $\Delta Q/\Delta Y = 2$,[11] we can write the income elasticity as

$$\xi = \frac{\Delta Q}{\Delta Y}\frac{Y}{Q} = 2\frac{Y}{Q}.$$

At the equilibrium, quantity $Q = 220$ million kg per year and income is $Y = \$12.5$ thousand, so the income elasticity is $2 \times (12.5/220) \approx 0.114$. The positive income elasticity shows that an increase in income causes the pork demand curve to shift to the right. Holding the price of pork constant at \$3.30 per kg, a 1% increase in income causes the demand curve for pork to shift to the right by 25 ($= \xi \times 220$) million kg, which is about one ninth of one percent of the equilibrium quantity.

Income elasticities play an important role in our analysis of consumer behavior in Chapter 5. Typically, goods that society views as necessities, such as food, have income elasticities near zero. Goods that society considers to be luxuries generally have income elasticities greater than 1.

Cross-Price Elasticity. The **cross-price elasticity of demand** is the percentage change in the quantity demanded in response to a given percentage change in the price of another good, p_o. The cross-price elasticity may be calculated as

$$\frac{\text{percentage change in quantity demanded}}{\text{percentage change in price of another good}} = \frac{\Delta Q/Q}{\Delta p_o/p_o} = \frac{\Delta Q}{\Delta p_o}\frac{p_o}{Q}.$$

[11]At income Y_1, the quantity demanded is $Q_1 = 171 - 20p + 20p_b + 3p_c + 2Y_1$. At income Y_2, $Q_2 = 171 - 20p + 20p_b + 3p_c + 2Y_2$. Thus, $\Delta Q = Q_2 - Q_1 = 2(Y_2 - Y_1) = 2(\Delta Y)$, so $\Delta Q/\Delta Y = 2$.

When the cross-price elasticity is negative, the goods are *complements* (Chapter 2). If the cross-price elasticity is negative, people buy less of the good when the price of the other good increases: The demand curve for this good shifts to the left. For example, if people like cream in their coffee, as the price of cream rises, they consume less coffee, so the cross-price elasticity of the quantity of coffee with respect to the price of cream is negative.

If the cross-price elasticity is positive, the goods are *substitutes* (Chapter 2). As the price of the other good increases, people buy more of this good. For example, the quantity demanded of pork increases when the price of beef, p_b, rises. From Equation 3.4, we know that $\Delta Q/\Delta p_b = 20$. As a result, the cross-price elasticity between the price of beef and the quantity of pork is

$$\frac{\Delta Q}{\Delta p_b}\frac{p_b}{Q} = 20\frac{p_b}{Q}.$$

At the equilibrium where $p = \$3.30$ per kg and $Q = 220$ million kg per year, and $p_b = \$4$ per kg, the cross-price elasticity is $20 \times (4/220) \approx 0.364$. As the price of beef rises by 1%, the quantity of pork demanded rises by a little more than a third of a percent.

Taking account of cross-price elasticities is important in making business and policy decisions. General Motors wants to know how much a change in the price of a Toyota affects the demand for its Chevy.

APPLICATION

Demanding Rail Safety

In 1992, in response to the deaths of four people in rail accidents in the previous year, British Rail spent £215 million ($373 million) on new safety precautions.[12] To cover this expenditure, fares had to increase 7%.

Were these safety expenditures a good idea? Some people argue that saving lives is worth "any price." If we assume that these new safety precautions will save four lives a year, the cost per life saved is $93.25 million. But that expenditure might not be the only cost of this policy.

British Rail's economists estimated the demand for rail travel as a function of the price. They found that a 7% increase in price reduced the number of passenger kilometers traveled by rail by 1 billion kilometers, or roughly 3.5%. Thus, the demand elasticity is

$$\varepsilon = \frac{\text{percentage change in quantity}}{\text{percentage change in price}} = \frac{-3.5\%}{7\%} = -\frac{1}{2}.$$

[12]This discussion is based on "Rail Safety: Costing Lives," *The Economist*, 324(7776) September 12, 1992:66.

In response to the rail price increase, what do these discouraged passengers do instead of taking a train? If they travel the same distance by car, accident statistics suggest that 4.9 of them will die. If so, the expected effect of this extra spending on rail safety is to kill nearly an extra person per year! Therefore, if the estimated demand elasticity and probabilities of accidents are accurate, making the additional safety expenditures was a bad idea.

To conduct this analysis properly, one would want to know the cross-price elasticity of automobile travel with respect to a change in the price of rail travel. An increase in the price of rail travel does not necessarily cause the demand for automobile travel to increase by as much as the demand for rail travel falls.

Not everyone is comfortable with considering such a trade-off between reduced rail deaths and increased deaths by car; however, if one believes this type of cost-benefit analysis is appropriate, elasticities play a crucial role. For example, if the rail travel demand elasticity were close to zero (and not the –0.5 that British Rail estimates), there would be no trade-off of deaths from rail and road accidents from this expenditure. ■

3.3 SENSITIVITY OF QUANTITY SUPPLIED TO PRICE

To answer many what-if questions, we need information about the sensitivity of the quantity supplied to changes in price. For example, to know how a sales tax will affect market price, a government needs to know the sensitivity to price of both the quantity supplied and the quantity demanded.

The Elasticity of Supply

Just as we can use the elasticity of demand to summarize information about the shape of a demand curve, we can use the elasticity of supply to summarize information about the shape of a supply curve. The **price elasticity of supply** (or *elasticity of supply*) is the percentage change in the quantity supplied in response to a given percentage change in the price. The price elasticity of supply (η, the Greek letter *eta*) is

$$\eta = \frac{\text{percentage change in quantity supplied}}{\text{percentage change in price}} = \frac{\Delta Q/Q}{\Delta p/p} = \frac{\Delta Q}{\Delta p}\frac{p}{Q}, \qquad (3.5)$$

where Q is the *quantity supplied*. If $\eta = 2$, a 1% increase in price leads to a 2% increase in the quantity supplied.

The definition of the elasticity of supply, Equation 3.5, is very similar to the definition of the elasticity of demand, Equation 3.1. The key distinction is that the elasticity of supply describes the movement along the supply curve as price changes, whereas the elasticity of demand describes the movement along the demand curve as price changes. That is, in the numerator, the supply elasticity depends on the "percentage change in the *quantity supplied*," whereas the demand elasticity depends on the "percentage change in the *quantity demanded*."

If the supply curve is upward sloping, $\Delta p/\Delta Q > 0$, the supply elasticity is positive: $\eta > 0$. If the supply curve slopes down, the supply elasticity is negative: $\eta < 0$.

To show how to calculate the elasticity of supply, we use the supply function for pork (based on Moschini and Meilke 1992), Equation 2.7,

$$Q = 88 + 40p,$$

where Q is the quantity of pork supplied in million kg per year and p is the price of pork in dollars per kg. This supply function is a straight line in Figure 3.4. (The horizontal axis starts at 176 rather than at the origin.) The number multiplied by p in the supply function, 40, shows how much the quantity supplied rises as the price increases: $\Delta Q/\Delta p = 40$. At the equilibrium where $p = \$3.30$ and $Q = 220$, the elasticity of supply of pork is

$$\eta = \frac{\Delta Q}{\Delta p}\frac{p}{Q} = 40 \times \frac{3.30}{220} = 0.6.$$

As the price of pork increases by 1%, the quantity supplied rises by slightly less than two-thirds of a percent.

We use the terms *inelastic* and *elastic* to describe *upward-sloping* supply curves, just as we did for demand curves. If $\eta = 0$, we say that the supply curve is *perfectly*

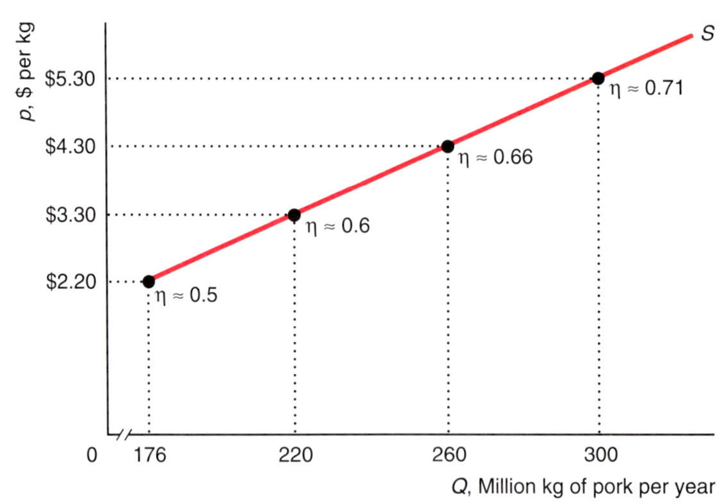

Figure 3.4 Elasticity Along the Pork Supply Curve. The elasticity of supply, η, varies along the pork supply curve. The higher is price, the larger is the supply elasticity.

inelastic: The supply does not change as price rises. If $0 < \eta < 1$, the supply curve is *inelastic* (but not perfectly inelastic): A 1% increase in price causes a less than 1% rise in the quantity supplied. If $\eta = 1$, the supply curve has a *unitary elasticity*: A 1% increase in price causes a 1% increase in quantity. If $\eta > 1$, the supply curve is *elastic*. If η is infinite, the supply curve is *perfectly elastic*.

Elasticity Along the Supply Curve

The elasticity of supply may vary along the supply curve. The elasticity of supply varies along most linear supply curves.

The supply function of a linear supply curve is

$$Q = g + hp,$$

where g and h are constants. By the same reasoning as before, $\Delta Q = h\Delta p$, so $h = \Delta Q/\Delta p$ shows the change in the quantity supplied as price changes.

The supply curve for pork is $Q = 88 + 40p$, so $g = 88$ and $h = 40$. Because $h = 40$ is positive, the quantity of pork supplied increases as the price of pork rises.

The elasticity of supply for a linear supply function is $\eta = h(p/Q)$. The elasticity of supply for the pork is $\eta = 40p/Q$. As the ratio p/Q rises, the supply elasticity rises. Along most linear supply curves, the ratio p/Q changes as p rises.

The pork supply curve, Figure 3.4, is inelastic at each point shown. The elasticity of supply varies along the pork supply curve: It is 0.5 when $p = \$2.20$, 0.6 when $p = \$3.30$, and about 0.71 when $p = \$5.30$.

Only *constant elasticity of supply curves* have the same elasticity at every point along the curve.[13] Two extreme examples of both constant elasticity of supply curves and linear supply curves are the vertical and the horizontal supply curves.

The supply curve that is vertical at a quantity, Q^*, is perfectly inelastic. No matter what the price is, firms supply Q^*. An example of inelastic supply is a perishable item such as fresh fruit. If the perishable good is not sold, it quickly becomes worthless. Thus, the seller accepts any market price for the good.

A supply curve that is horizontal at a price, p^*, is perfectly elastic. Firms supply as much as the market wants—a potentially unlimited amount—if the price is p^* or above. Firms supply nothing at a price below p^*, which does not cover their cost of production.

3.4 LONG RUN VERSUS SHORT RUN

The shapes of demand and supply curves depend on the relevant time period. Short-run elasticities may differ substantially from long-run elasticities. The duration of the *short run* depends on how long it takes consumers or firms to adjust for a particular good.

---

[13]All constant elasticity of supply curves are of the form $Q = Bp^{\eta}$, where B is a constant and η is the constant elasticity of supply at every point along the curve.

Demand Elasticities over Time

Two factors that determine whether short-run demand elasticities are larger or smaller than long-run elasticities are the ease of substitution and storage opportunities. Often, one can substitute between products in the long run but not in the short run.

When oil prices rose rapidly in the 1970s and 1980s because of actions by OPEC, consumers in most Western countries did not greatly alter the amount of oil they demanded. Someone who drove 27 miles to and from work every day in a 1969 Chevy could not easily reduce the amount of gasoline purchased. In the long run, however, this person could buy a new, smaller car, get a job closer to home, join a car pool, or in other ways reduce the amount of gasoline purchased.

Gallini (1983) estimated long-run demand elasticities that are more elastic than the short-run elasticity for gasoline in Canada. She finds that the short-run elasticity is –0.35; the five-year intermediate-run elasticity is nearly twice as elastic, –0.7; and the ten-year, long-run elasticity is approximately –0.8, which is slightly more elastic. A 1% increase in price lowers the quantity demanded by only about a 0.35% in the short run but by more than twice as much, 0.8%, in the long run.

With goods that can be easily stored, short-run demand curves may be more elastic than long-run curves. If frozen orange juice goes on sale this week at your local supermarket, you may buy large quantities and store the extra in your freezer. As a result, you may be more sensitive to price changes for frozen orange juice in the short run than in the long run.

Similarly, Capps and Nayga (1990) found that demand elasticities are more elastic in the short run than in the long run for several types of meat. They also found that the short-run demand for ground beef is elastic, –1.8, but that the long-run elasticity is inelastic, –0.6. Thus, the short-run quantity response for beef to a 1% price change is three times as great in the short run as in the long run.

Supply Elasticities over Time

Supply curves also may have different elasticities in the short run than in the long run. If a manufacturing firm wants to increase production in the short run, it can do so by hiring workers to use its machines around the clock, but how much it can expand its output is limited by the fixed size of its manufacturing plant and the number of machines it has. In the long run, however, the firm can build another plant and buy or build more equipment. Thus, we would expect this firm's long-run supply elasticity to be greater than its short-run elasticity.

Similarly, to produce more hogs, one needs to breed and raise them, a time-consuming process. Moschini and Meilke (1992) found that the elasticity of supply of hogs is almost perfectly inelastic, 0.04, in the short run (a year), whereas the elasticity supply is more elastic, 0.33, in the long run (many years). Thus, a 1% increase in price has almost no effect on the quantity of hogs supplied in the short run but increases the quantity supplied in the long run by one-third of a percent.

Similarly, Adelaja (1991) found that the short-run elasticity of supply of milk is 0.36, whereas the long-run (essentially forever) supply elasticity is 0.51. As a result, the quantity response to a 1% increase in price is about 42% (= [0.51 – 0.36]/0.36) more in the long run than in the short run.

3.5 EFFECTS OF A SALES TAX

Before voting for a new sales tax, legislators want to predict the effect of the tax on prices, quantities, and tax revenues. If the new tax will produce a very large increase in the price consumers pay, legislators who vote for the tax may lose their jobs in the next election. Voters' ire is likely to be even greater if the tax does not raise significant tax revenues.

In this section, we examine three questions about the effects of a sales tax:

1. What effect does a sales tax have on equilibrium prices and quantity?
2. Is it true, as many people claim, that taxes assessed on producers are *passed along* to consumers? That is, do consumers pay for the entire tax?
3. Do the equilibrium price and quantity depend on whether the tax is assessed on consumers or producers?

How much a tax affects the equilibrium price and quantity and how much of the tax falls on consumers depend on the shape of the demand and supply curves, which is summarized by the elasticities. Knowing only the elasticities of demand and supply, we can make accurate predictions about the effects of a new tax and determine how much of the tax falls on consumers.

Two Types of Sales Taxes

Governments use two types of sales taxes. The most common sales tax is called an *ad valorem* tax by economists and *the* sales tax by real people. For every dollar the consumer spends, the government keeps a fraction, α, which is the ad valorem tax rate. As of 1997, Japan's national sales tax was $\alpha = 5\%$. If a Japanese consumer buys a CD player for \$100, the government collects $\alpha \times \$100 = 5\% \times \$100 = \$5$ in taxes, and the seller receives $(1 - \alpha) \times \$100 = \$95$.[14]

The other type of sales tax is a *specific* or *unit* tax, where a specified dollar amount, τ, is collected per unit of output. The federal government collects $\tau = 18.3¢$ on each gallon of gas sold in the United States. Many communities charge a fixed filing fee or tax on every house sold.

Equilibrium Effects of a Specific Tax

To answer our three questions, we must extend the standard supply-and-demand analysis to take taxes into account. Let's start by assuming that the specific tax is assessed on firms at the time of sale. If the consumer pays p for a good, the government takes τ and the seller receives $p - \tau$.

---

[14]For specificity, we assume that the price firms receive is $p = (1 - \alpha)p^*$, where p^* is the price consumers pay and α is the ad valorem tax rate on the price consumers pay. Many governments, however, set the ad valorem sales tax, β, as an amount added on to the price sellers charge, so consumers pay $p^* = (1 + \beta)p$. By setting α and β appropriately, the taxes are equivalent. Here, $p = p^*/(1 + \beta)$, so $(1 - \alpha) = 1/(1 + \beta)$. For example, if $\beta = \frac{1}{3}$, then $\alpha = \frac{1}{4}$.

Specific Tax Effects in the Pork Market. Suppose the government collects a specific tax of τ = \$1.05 per kg of processed pork from pork producers. The original, or pretax, supply curve is S^1 in Figure 3.5. Because of the tax, suppliers keep only $p - \tau$ of price p that consumers pay. Thus, at every possible price paid by consumers, firms are willing to supply less than when they received the full amount consumers paid. Before the tax, the supply curve is S^1, so firms were willing to supply 206 million kg per year at a price of \$2.95. After the tax, firms receive only \$1.90 if consumers pay \$2.95, so they are not willing to supply 206. For firms to be willing to supply 206, they must receive \$2.95 after the tax, so consumers must pay \$4. As a result, the after-tax supply curve, S^2, is τ = 1.05 above the original supply curve S^1 at every quantity, as the figure shows.

We can use this figure to illustrate the answer to our first question concerning the effects of the tax on the equilibrium. *The specific tax causes the price consumers pay to rise, the quantity to fall, and tax revenue to rise.*

The intersection of the pretax pork supply curve S^1 and the pork demand curve D in Figure 3.5 determines the pretax equilibrium, e_1. The equilibrium price is p_1 = \$3.30, and the equilibrium quantity is Q_1 = 220. The tax shifts the supply curve to S^2,

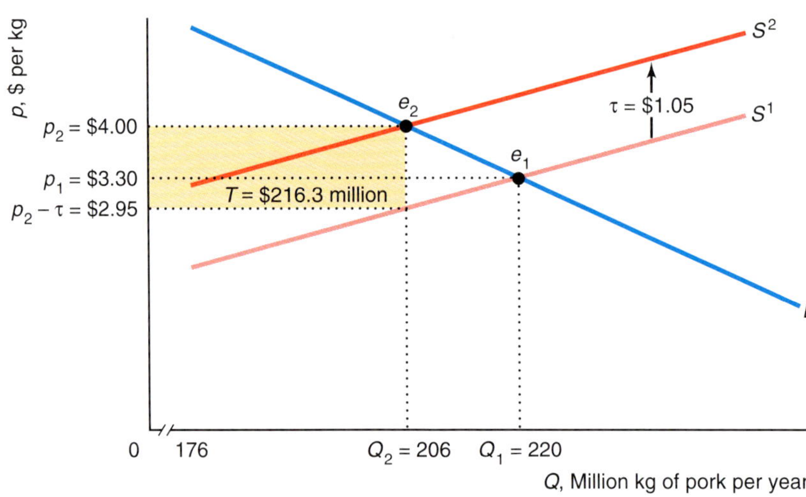

Figure 3.5 Effect of a \$1.05 Specific Tax on the Pork Market Collected from Producers. The specific tax of τ = \$1.05 per kg collected from producers shifts the pretax pork supply curve from S^1 to the posttax supply curve S^2. The tax causes the equilibrium to shift from e_1 (determined by the intersection of S^1 and D) to e_2 (intersection of S^2 with the D). The equilibrium price increases from \$3.30 to \$4.00. Two-thirds of the incidence of the tax falls on consumers, who spend 70¢ more per unit. Producers receive 35¢ less per unit after the tax. The government collects tax revenues of $T = \tau Q_2$ = \$216.3 million per year.

so the after-tax equilibrium is e_2, where consumers pay $p_2 = \$4$, firms receive $p_2 - \$1.05 = \$2.95$, and $Q_2 = 206$. Thus, the price that consumers pay increases by $\Delta p = p_2 - p_1 = \$4 - \$3.30 = 70¢$, and the quantity falls by $\Delta Q = Q_2 - Q_1 = 206 - 220 = -14$ because of the tax.

Although the consumers and producers are worse off because of the tax, the government acquires new tax revenue of $T = \tau Q = \$1.05 \times$ (206 million kg per year) = \$216.3 million per year. The length of the shaded rectangle in the figure is $Q_2 = 206$ million kg per year, and its height is $\tau = \$1.05$ per kg, so the area of the rectangle equals the tax revenue.[15]

Specific Tax Effects Depend on Elasticities. The effects of the tax on the equilibrium prices and quantity depend on the elasticities of supply and demand. The government raises the tax from zero to τ, so the change in the tax is $\Delta\tau = \tau - 0 = \tau$. In response to this change in the tax, the price consumers pay increases by

$$\Delta p = \left(\frac{\eta}{\eta - \varepsilon}\right)\Delta\tau, \tag{3.6}$$

where ε is the demand elasticity and η is the supply elasticity at the equilibrium (see Appendix 3A). As Figure 3.5 shows, the demand elasticity for pork is $\varepsilon = -0.3$, and the supply elasticity is $\eta = 0.6$, so a change in the tax of $\Delta\tau = \$1.05$ causes the price consumers pay to rise by

$$\Delta p = \left(\frac{\eta}{\eta - \varepsilon}\right)\Delta\tau = \frac{0.6}{0.6 - [-0.3]} \times \$1.05 = 70¢.$$

For a given supply elasticity, the more elastic is demand, the less the equilibrium price rises when a tax is imposed. In the pork equilibrium in which the supply elasticity is $\eta = 0.6$, if the demand elasticity were $\varepsilon = -2.4$ instead of -0.3 (that is, the linear demand curve had a less steep slope through the original equilibrium point), the consumer price would rise only $0.6/(0.6 - [-2.4]) \times \$1.05 = 21¢$ instead of $70¢$.

Similarly, for a given demand elasticity, the greater is the supply elasticity, the larger is the increase in the equilibrium price consumers pay when a tax is imposed. In the pork example, in which the demand elasticity is $\varepsilon = -0.3$, if the supply elasticity were $\eta = 1.2$ instead of 0.6, the consumer price would rise $1.2/(1.2 - [-0.3]) \times \$1.05 = 84¢$ instead of $70¢$.

APPLICATION

Discouraging Smoking

Tom Hodgson, chief economist at the National Center for Health Statistics, estimates that smoking adds \$500 billion to the current generation's health

[15]The figure shows only part of the length of the rectangle because the horizontal axis starts at 176.

insurance bill.[16] If the government really wants to stop people, especially teenagers, from smoking, how should it do so? It could spend millions on education programs and public service ads. Alternatively, the government could raise the tax on cigarettes, which would reduce smoking and raise revenues rather than cost money.

The more elastic the demand, the more a tax on cigarettes discourages smoking. Keeler, Hu, Barnett, and Manning (1993) estimate that the short-run demand elasticity for cigarettes is inelastic, between –0.3 and –0.5, but that the long-run elasticity is slightly more elastic, between –0.5 and –0.6. One possible reason for the difference in short-run and long-run elasticities is that cigarettes are addictive. Few addicted users stop smoking when the price rises in the short run; however, some potential smokers do not start if the price rises in the long run. Keeler, Hu, Barnett, and Manning conclude that the 1989 increase in the California cigarette tax from 10¢ to 35¢ per pack reduced cigarette consumption by 10–12%. Other studies show that taxes have a greater impact on teenagers than on older people, so an increase in cigarette prices reduces teenage smoking by twice as much as for the population as a whole.

Thus, a moderate tax that raises the price of cigarettes can reduce smoking significantly. In addition to federal taxes, states add their own taxes. The rates differ substantially across states. In 1997, the tax was 2.5¢ per pack in Virginia, 3¢ in Kentucky, 5¢ in North Carolina, 12¢ in Georgia, 37¢ in California, 44¢ in Illinois and Wisconsin, 65¢ in the District of Columbia, 75¢ in Michigan, 78¢ in Massachusetts, 82.5¢ in Washington, and $1 in Alaska.

---

[16]This application is based on Keeler, Hu, Barnett, and Manning (1993); "A Tax We Can Live With," *University of California at Berkeley Wellness Letter*, 9(9), June 1993:7; Passell, Peter, "Doing Well by Doing Good," *New York Times*, December 24, 1992:C2; Koretz, Gene, "Add $2 to the Cost of a Pack of Cigarettes . . . ," *Business Week*, 3309, March 15, 1993:18; "Tobacco: Armageddon and Appalachia," *The Economist*, 7820, July 17, 1993:25; "In Canada, They're Cutting Sin Taxes," *Business Week*, 3359, February 21, 1994:44; Farrell, Christopher, "This Sin Tax Is Win-Win," *Business Week*, April 11, 1994:31; Marshall, Jonathan, "Smokers Paying Their Way," *San Francisco Chronicle*, August 29, 1994:D1, D3; Marshall, Jonathan, "Life Is Very Good for Silicon Valley Residents," *San Francisco Chronicle*, January 13, 1997:B3.

Because of this difference in rates across states, a tax increase in one state may not lead to a substantial price increase for all consumers in that state. When Michigan raised its cigarette tax from 25¢ to 75¢ on May 1, 1994, taxable cigarette sales fell nearly 27%, while sales over the Indiana border, where the tax is 15.5¢, jumped 40%. According to one estimate, cigarette smuggling grew 250% from 1980 to 1994 as state taxes differentials grew. Cigarettes are smuggled from low-tax states, Mexico, untaxed tribal reservations, and military bases to high-tax states. As a consequence, if one wants to discourage smoking in a given state, a national tax is more effective than high taxes in that state alone.

The U.S. tax rate on tobacco is the lowest of all industrialized countries. In mid-1992, the after-tax price of a pack in Britain, Canada, Germany, Ireland, and Norway ranged from \$4.13 to \$5.80, compared to an average of only \$1.90 in the United States.

Adjusting for inflation, the U.S. federal tax was 45% lower in 1996 than 20 years earlier. The federal specific tax was 8¢ per pack from 1951 through 1982, 16¢ from 1983 to 1989, 20¢ from 1991 to 1992, and 24¢ from 1993 on. As of 1997, it is scheduled to rise to 34¢ by 2000 and to 39¢ by 2002.

In Canada, the price of cigarettes, adjusting for inflation and including taxes, increased 158% from 1979 to 1991, resulting in a drop in teenage smoking by 61% and overall smoking by 38%. The Canadian tax reached \$2.69 per pack but was recently cut to \$1.82, in part to reduce cross-border shopping and smuggling from the United States.

In 1993 and 1997, Congress debated increasing the tax to \$2 per pack. According to the Coalition on Smoking and Health (an advocacy group), an increase in the cigarette tax of \$2 per pack would reduce the number of smokers by 7.6 million, save 1.9 million lives, and raise \$23 billion a year in federal tax revenue. Other estimates, which expect fewer smokers to quit, put the extra tax revenue at up to \$35 billion a year. ■

Tax Incidence of a Specific Tax

We can now answer our second question: Who is hurt by the tax? The **incidence of a tax on consumers**, ι (*iota*), is the share of the tax that falls on consumers. The incidence of the tax that falls on consumers is $\iota = \Delta p/\Delta \tau$, the amount by which the price to consumers rises as a fraction of the amount the tax increases.

In our pork example in Figure 3.5, a $\Delta \tau = \$1.05$ increase in the specific tax causes consumers to pay $\Delta p = 70¢$ more per kg than they would if no tax were assessed. Thus, consumers bear two-thirds of the incidence of the pork tax:

$$\Delta p/\Delta \tau = \$0.70/\$1.05 = \frac{2}{3}.$$

Firms receive $(p_2 - \tau) - p_1 = (\$4 - \$1.05) - \$3.30 = \$2.95 - \$3.30 = -35¢$ less per kg than they would in the absence of the tax. The incidence of the tax on firms—

the amount by which the price to them falls, divided by the tax—is \$0.35/\$1.05 = $\frac{1}{3}$. The sum of the share of the tax on consumers, $\frac{2}{3}$, and that on firms, $\frac{1}{3}$, adds to the entire tax effect, 1. Equivalently, the increase in price to consumers minus the drop in price to firms equals the tax: 70¢ − [−35¢] = \$1.05 = τ.

Tax Incidence Depends on Elasticities. If the demand curve slopes downward and the supply curve slopes upward, as in Figure 3.5, the incidence of the tax *does not* fall solely on consumers. Firms do not pass along the entire tax in higher prices.

Firms can pass along the full cost of the tax only when the demand or supply elasticities take on certain extreme values. To determine the conditions under which firms can pass along the full tax, we need to know how the incidence of the tax depends on the elasticities of demand and supply. By dividing both sides of Equation 3.6 by $\Delta\tau$, we can write the incidence of the tax that falls on consumers as

$$\iota \equiv \frac{\Delta p}{\Delta \tau} = \frac{\eta}{\eta - \varepsilon}. \tag{3.7}$$

Because the demand elasticity for pork is $\varepsilon = -0.3$ and the supply elasticity is $\eta = 0.6$, the incidence of the pork tax that falls on consumers is

$$\iota = 0.6/(0.6 - [-0.3]) = \frac{2}{3}.$$

The more elastic is demand, holding the supply elasticity constant, the less is the burden of the tax on consumers. Similarly, the greater is the supply elasticity, holding the demand elasticity constant, the greater is the burden on consumers. Thus, as the demand curve becomes relatively inelastic (ε approaches zero) or the supply curve becomes relatively elastic (η becomes very large), the incidence of the tax falls mainly on consumers.

SOLVED PROBLEM 3.1

If the supply curve is perfectly elastic and demand is linear and downward sloping, what is the effect of a \$1 specific tax collected from producers on equilibrium price and quantity, and what is the incidence on consumers? Why?

Answer

1. *Determine the equilibrium in the absence of a tax:* Before the tax, the perfectly elastic supply curve, S^1 in Figure 3.6, is horizontal at p_1. The downward-sloping, linear demand curve, D, intersects S^1 at the pretax equilibrium, e_1, where the price is p_1 and the quantity is Q_1.

2. *Show how the tax shifts the supply curve and determine the new equilibrium:* A specific tax of \$1 shifts up the pretax supply curve by \$1 to S^2,

which is horizontal at $p_1 + 1$. The intersection of D and S^2 determines the after-tax equilibrium, e_2, where the price consumers pay is $p_2 = p_1 + 1$, the price firms receive is $p_2 - 1 = p_1$, and the quantity is Q_2.

3. *Compare the before- and after-tax equilibria:* The specific tax causes the equilibrium quantity to fall from Q_1 to Q_2, the price firms receive to remain at p_1, and the equilibrium price consumers pay to rise from p_1 to $p_2 = p_1 + 1$. The entire incidence of the tax falls on consumers:[17]

$$\iota = \Delta p/\Delta\tau = (p_2 - p_1)/\$1 = \$1/\$1 = 1.$$

4. *Explain why:* The reason consumers must absorb the entire tax is that firms will not supply the good at a price that is any lower than they received before the tax, p_1. Thus, the price must rise enough that the price suppliers receive after tax is unchanged. As consumers do not want to consume as much at a higher price, the equilibrium quantity falls. ■

Elasticity, Revenue, and Tax Strategy. Governments often use a sales tax to raise tax revenue. Such a tax, however, harms consumers and producers by reducing the quantity sold and consumed.

Some economists and politicians argue that, all else the same, we should tax more heavily goods with relatively inelastic demands. They argue that a sales tax is less harmful in terms of reduced consumption and raises more revenue, the less elastic demand is.[18] If the demand curve is vertical at Q_1, the quantity demanded is unchanged by a tax τ, and the revenue is τQ_1. With a downward-sloping demand curve, the tax reduces the quantity demanded from the original quantity Q_1 to Q_2, and the tax is only τQ_2, which is less than τQ_1.

Presumably, most voters would agree with the goal of reducing the harm of taxes. Whether they favor increasing tax revenues is less clear. Moreover, the less elastic the demand, the larger is the incidence of the tax that consumers bear. Presumably, few voters would favor taxes that fall mainly on consumers.

---

[17]Equivalently, we can use elasticities. By dividing both the numerator and the denominator of the right-hand side of Equation 3.8 by η, we can rewrite that incidence equation as

$$\iota = \eta/(\eta - \varepsilon) = 1/(1 - \varepsilon/\eta).$$

As η goes to infinity, ε/η goes to zero, so the incidence approaches 1.

[18]The quantity demanded depends on its price, which depends on the specific tax, $Q(p(\tau))$. Differentiating quantity with respect to the specific tax, we learn that the change in quantity as the tax changes is $dQ/d\tau = (dQ/dp)(dp/d\tau)$. By multiplying and dividing this expression by p/Q, we find that the change in quantity as the tax changes is $\varepsilon(Q/p)(dp/d\tau)$. Thus, the closer ε is to zero, the less that quantity falls, all else the same. Revenue is $R = pQ(p(\tau))$. Thus, the tax causes revenue to change by

$$dR/d\tau = [Q + p(dQ/dp)]dp/d\tau = [1 + \varepsilon](dp/d\tau).$$

The closer ε is to zero, the larger the revenue effect.

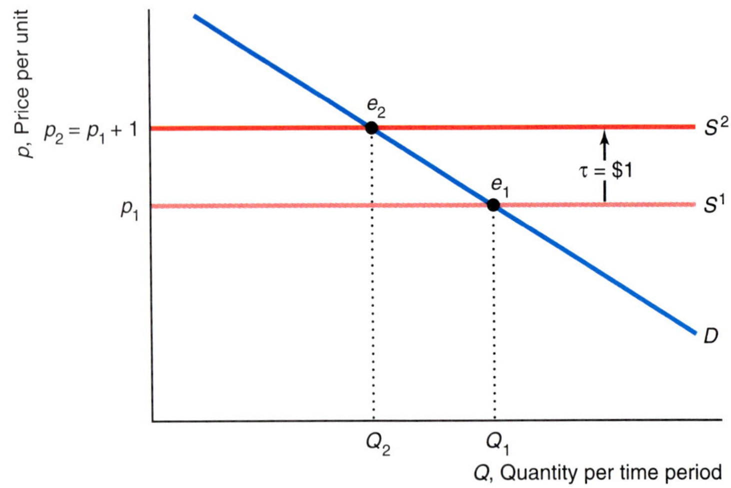

Figure 3.6 Effect of a $1 Specific Tax with a Perfectly Elastic Supply Curve. The perfectly elastic pretax supply curve, S^1, which is horizontal at p_1, intersects the demand curve, D, at e_1. The after-tax supply curve is horizontal at $p_2 = p_1 + \$1$. It intersects D at the after-tax equilibrium, e_2. The tax raises the equilibrium price by \$1, so the full incidence of the tax falls on consumers.

APPLICATION

Gasoline Taxes as a Revenue Source

Many governments rely heavily on gasoline taxes for revenues. Because the demand for gasoline is relatively inelastic, a tax on gasoline falls mainly on consumers and has little effect on the equilibrium quantity of gasoline consumed.[19]

Gallini (1983) estimates that the short-run demand elasticity for gasoline in Canada is about –0.35. Another recent study concludes that the elasticity in Europe is about –0.2. As Umberto Rastelli, an economist in the Italian Foreign Ministry, says, "When the tax goes up again, we can measure a little reduction

[19]This application is based on Gallini (1983); "Energy Taxes: Coming Soon, to a Station Near You," *The Economist*, 326(7793), January 3, 1993:24; and Viviano, Frank, "High Gas Tax a Way of Life in Europe," *San Francisco Chronicle*, January 22, 1993:A1; Hebert, H. Josef, "Examining the Surge in Gas Prices," *Rocky Mountain News*, May 3, 1996:34A; Kessler, Glenn, "Running on Empty," *Newsday*, May 8, 1996:A3.

in traffic for a couple of weeks—but after that, it's back to normal." Because of this relatively inelastic demand, most developed countries (except the United States) apply very large specific taxes to gasoline to raise substantial revenues.

U.S. federal gasoline taxes are 18.3¢ per gallon, and average state and local taxes add another 22¢ per gallon. The U.S. federal government raises less than 1% of its budget from these taxes.

In Japan, the $1.63 tax raises 5% of government revenues. European taxes per gallon average 20 times U.S. federal rates. Turkey charges $1.70 per gallon. The U.K. tax is $2.21 per gallon and produces 17% of the government's budget revenue. Taxes are even higher in Germany ($2.59), France ($2.80), and Italy ($3.65), where these taxes raise 4–5% of the federal budget revenues.

The United States could raise substantially more revenues by increasing its gasoline tax. It is estimated that each extra 1¢ per gallon gasoline tax yields an extra $1 billion in revenues. A 50¢ per gallon increase in the tax would cost American households between $500 and $1,200 a year. ■

Equilibrium Is the Same No Matter Who Is Taxed

Our third question is "Does the equilibrium or the incidence of the tax depend on whether the tax is collected from suppliers or demanders?" Surprisingly, in a supply-and-demand model, the equilibrium and the incidence of the tax are the same regardless of whether the government collects the tax from consumers or producers.

We've already seen that, when the tax is collected from firms, they are able to pass on some or all of the tax to consumers. We now show that, if the tax is collected from consumers, they can pass the producer's share back to the firms.

Suppose the specific tax τ = $1.05 on pork is collected from consumers rather than from sellers. Because the government takes τ from each p consumers spend, sellers receive only $p - \tau$. Thus, the demand curve as seen by firms shifts down by $1.05 from D^1 to D^2 in Figure 3.7.

The intersection of D^2 and the supply curve S determines the after-tax equilibrium, e_2, where the equilibrium quantity is Q_2 and the price received by producers is $p_2 - \tau$. The price paid by consumers, p_2 (on the original demand curve D^1 at Q_2), is τ above the price received by producers.

Comparing Figure 3.7 to Figure 3.5, we see that the after-tax equilibrium is the same regardless of whether the tax is imposed on the consumers or sellers. The price to consumers rises by the same amount, Δp, so the incidence of the tax, $\iota = \Delta p/\Delta\tau$, is also the same.

A specific tax, regardless of whether the tax is collected from consumers or producers, creates a *wedge* equal to the per unit tax of τ between the price consumers pay, p, and the price suppliers receive, $p - \tau$. Indeed, we can insert a wedge—the vertical line τ = $1.05 long in the figure—between the original supply and demand curves to determine the after-tax equilibrium.

In short, regardless of whether firms or consumers pay the tax to the government, you can solve tax problems by shifting the supply curve, shifting the demand curve, or using a wedge. All three approaches give the same answer.

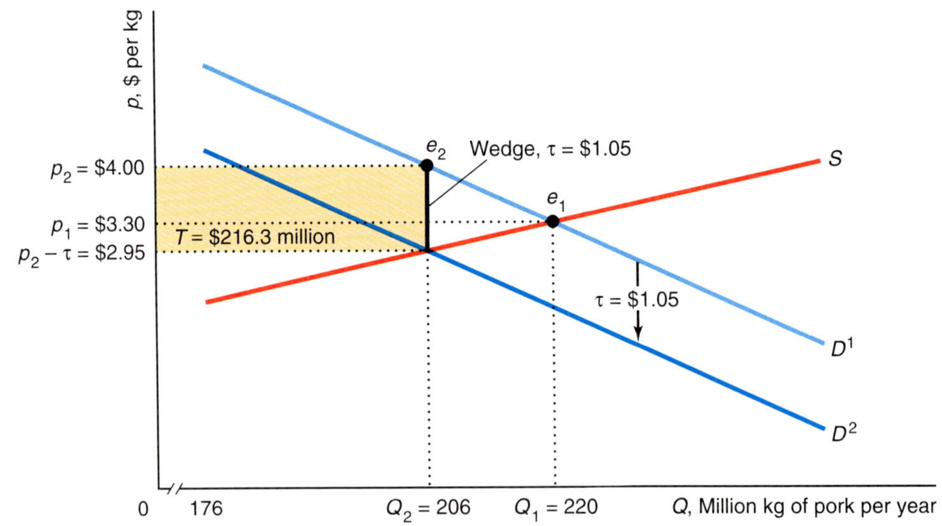

Figure 3.7 Effect of a $1.05 Specific Tax on Pork Collected from Consumers. The tax shifts the demand curve down by τ = $1.05 from D^2 to D^2. The new equilibrium is the same as when the tax is applied to suppliers in Figure 3.6. We can also determine the after-tax equilibrium by sticking a wedge τ = $1.05 long between S and D^1.

Ad Valorem and Specific Taxes Have Similar Effects

In contrast to specific sales taxes, governments levy ad valorem taxes on a wide variety of goods. Most states apply an ad valorem sales tax to most goods and services, exempting a few staples such as food and medicine.

Suppose the government imposes an ad valorem tax of α on the price that consumers pay for processed pork instead of a specific tax. We already know that the equilibrium price is $4 with a specific tax of $1.05 per kg. At that price, an ad valorem tax of α = $1.05/$4 = 26.25% raises the same amount of tax per unit as a $1.05 specific tax.

It is usually easiest to analyze the effects of an ad valorem tax by shifting the demand curve. Figure 3.8 shows how a specific tax and an ad valorem tax shift the processed pork demand curve. The specific tax shifts the pretax demand curve, D, down to D^s, which is parallel to the original curve. The ad valorem tax shifts the demand curve to D^a. At any given price p, the gap between D and D^a is αp, which is greater at high prices than at low prices. The gap is $1.05 (= 0.2625 × $4) per unit when the price is $4, and $2.10 when the price is $8.

Imposing an ad valorem tax causes the after-tax equilibrium quantity, Q_2, to fall below the original quantity, Q_1, and the after-tax price, p_2, to rise above the original price, p_1. The tax collected per unit of output is $\tau = \alpha p_2$. The incidence of the

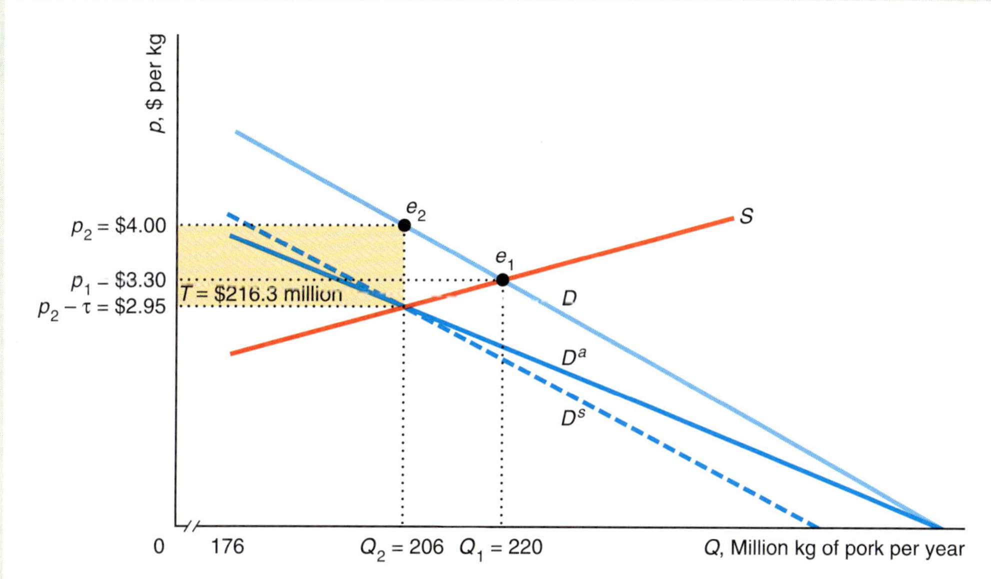

Figure 3.8 A Comparison of an Ad Valorem and a Specific Tax on Pork. Without a tax, the demand curve is D and the supply curve is S. The ad valorem tax of $\alpha = 26.25\%$ shifts the demand curve facing firms to D^a. The gap between D and D^a, the per unit tax, is larger at higher prices. In contrast, the demand curve facing firms given a specific tax of \$1 per kg, D^s, is parallel to D. The after-tax equilibrium is the same with both of these taxes.

tax that falls on consumers is the change in price, $\Delta p = (p_2 - p_1)$, divided by the change in the per unit tax, $\Delta t = \alpha p_2 - 0$, collected:

$$\iota = \Delta p/(\alpha p_2).$$

The incidence of an ad valorem tax is generally shared between consumers and suppliers. Because the ad valorem tax of $\alpha = 26.25\%$ has exactly the same impact on the equilibrium pork price and raises the same amount of tax per unit as the \$1.05 specific tax, the incidence is the same for both types of taxes. (As with specific taxes, the incidence depends on the elasticities of supply and demand, but we'll spare you going through that.)

SOLVED PROBLEM 3.2

If the short-run supply curve for fresh fruit is perfectly inelastic and the demand curve is a downward-sloping straight line, what is the effect of an ad valorem tax on equilibrium price and quantity, and what is the incidence on consumers? Why?

Answer:

1. *Determine the before-tax equilibrium:* The perfectly elastic supply curve, S, is vertical at Q^* in Figure 3.9. The pretax demand curve, D^1, intersects S at e_1, where the equilibrium price to both consumers and producers is p^* and the equilibrium quantity is Q^*.

2. *Show how the tax shifts the demand curve and determine the after-tax equilibrium:* When the government imposes an ad valorem tax with a rate of α, the demand curve as seen by the firms rotates down to D^2, where the gap between the two demand curves is αp. The intersection of D and S^2 determines the after-tax equilibrium, e_2. The equilibrium quantity remains unchanged at Q^*. Consumers continue to pay p^*. The government collects αp^* per unit, so firms receive less, $(1 - \alpha)p^*$, than the p^* they received before the tax.

3. *Determine the incidence of the tax on consumers:* The consumers continue to pay the same price, so $\Delta p = 0$ when the tax increases by αp^* (from 0), and the incidence of the tax that falls on consumers is

$$\iota = \$0/(\alpha p^*) = 0\%.$$

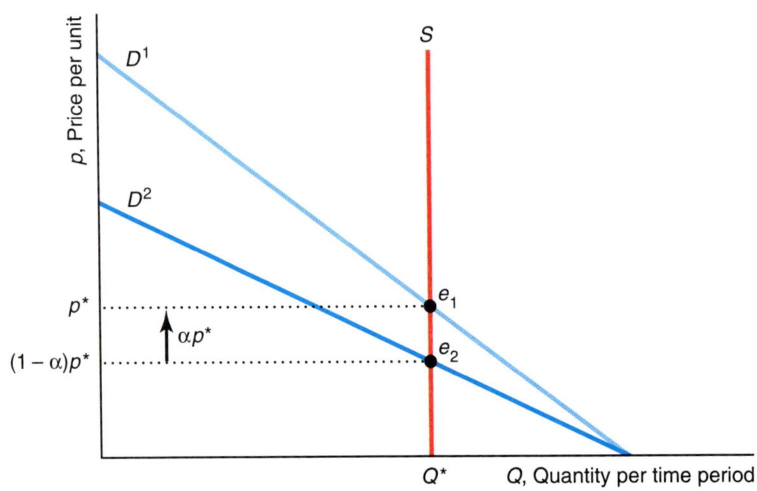

Figure 3.9 Effect of an Ad Valorem Tax with an Inelastic Supply Curve. The intersection of D^1 and the inelastic supply curve S determines the pretax equilibrium at e_1, where the price is p^* and the quantity is Q^*. The ad valorem tax rotates the demand curve to D^2, which intersects S at the same quantity, Q^*. In the posttax equilibrium, e_2, consumers pay p^* and firms receive $(1 - \alpha)p^*$, so the full incidence of the tax falls on firms.

4. *Explain why the incidence of the tax falls entirely on firms:* The reason why firms absorb the entire tax is that firms supply the same amount of fruit, Q^*, no matter what tax the government sets. If firms were to raise the price, consumers would buy less fruit and suppliers would be stuck with the essentially worthless excess quantity, which would spoil quickly. Thus, because suppliers prefer to sell their produce at a positive price rather than a zero price, they absorb any tax-induced drop in price. ■

APPLICATION

Incidence of Federal Ad Valorem Taxes

Thanks to a change in federal law, we have a natural experiment that determines in which markets consumers bear the full incidence of sales taxes. On July 1, 1965, the federal ad valorem taxes on many goods and services were eliminated, and the 10% tax on automobiles was reduced to 7%. By the end of 1965, taxes on admissions to theaters, variety shows, and athletic and racing events, as well as on club dues and initiation fees, were also canceled.

Comparing prices before and after this change, we can determine how much the price fell in response to the tax's elimination. When the tax was in place, the tax per unit on a good that sold for p was αp. If the price fell by αp when the tax was eliminated, consumers must have been bearing the full incidence of the tax. Consequently, consumers got the full benefit of removing the tax from those goods.

Brownlee and Perry (1967) found that the entire amount of the tax cut was passed on to consumers immediately for many commodities. These commodities and services included all those studied for which the taxes were collected at the retail level (except admissions and club dues) and most commodities for which excise taxes were imposed at the manufacturer level. Goods for which consumers got essentially the entire tax cut included face powder, sterling silverware, wristwatches, and handbags. As Solved Problem 3.1 demonstrates, when the supply curve is nearly perfectly elastic, we would expect the full incidence of a tax—and hence the full benefit of the tax cut—to fall on consumers.[20] A perfectly elastic supply curve is likely when all firms have the same costs, as we might expect in retailing. The full incidence of the tax also falls on consumers if the demand curve is completely inelastic (end-of-chapter Problem 3).

Essentially none of the tax savings were passed on for motion picture admissions and club dues. We would expect this result either if the elasticity of demand were perfectly elastic (Problem 4 at the end of this chapter) or if the elasticity of supply were perfectly inelastic (Problem 5 at the end of the chapter).

---

[20]That question looks at a specific tax; however, the analysis with an ad valorem tax is similar. The ad valorem tax shifts the demand curve differently; but both the before-tax and after-tax demand curves intersect the supply curve at the same price because the supply curve is horizontal. As a result, the full incidence of the tax must fall on consumers.

The price decline was less than the amount of the tax cut for many lower-valued items on which manufacturers' taxes were reduced. The 10% reduction in taxes led to only a 6.3% drop in prices for portable TVs, 1.4% for golf clubs, and 0.9% for stereo records and golf balls. Thus, for these goods, neither the demand nor the supply curves were perfectly elastic or perfectly inelastic. ■

Summary

1. **How shapes of the demand and supply curves matter:** The degree to which a shock (such as an increase in the price of a factor) shifts the supply curve and affects the equilibrium price and quantity and firms' revenues depends on the shape of the demand curve. Similarly, the degree to which a shock (such as an increase in the price of a substitute) shifts the demand curve and affects the equilibrium depends on the shape of the supply curve.

2. **Sensitivity of quantity demanded to price:** The price elasticity of demand (or elasticity of demand), ε, summarizes the shape of a demand curve at a particular point. The elasticity of demand is the percentage change in the quantity demanded in response to a given percentage change in price. For example, a 1% increase in price causes the quantity demanded to fall by ε%. Because demand curves slope down by the Law of Demand, the elasticity of demand is always negative.

   The demand curve is perfectly inelastic if $\varepsilon = 0$, inelastic if $0 > \varepsilon > -1$, unitary elastic if $\varepsilon = -1$, elastic if $\varepsilon < -1$, and perfectly elastic when ε approaches negative infinity. A vertical demand curve is perfectly inelastic at every price. A horizontal demand curve is perfectly elastic.

   The income elasticity of demand is the percentage change in the quantity demanded in response to a given percentage change in income. The cross-price elasticity of demand is the percentage change in the quantity demanded of one good when the price of a related good increases by a given percentage.

   How revenue (price times quantity) changes when the price increases depends on the elasticity of demand. Revenue reaches a maximum where the demand elasticity is unitary. If demand is inelastic, an increase in price raises revenue. If demand is elastic, a decrease in price raises revenue.

3. **Sensitivity of quantity supplied to price:** The price elasticity of supply (or elasticity of supply), η, is the percentage change in the quantity supplied in response to a given percentage change in price. The elasticity of supply is positive if the supply curve has an upward slope. A vertical supply curve is perfectly inelastic. A horizontal supply curve is perfectly elastic.

4. **Long run versus short run:** Long-run elasticities of demand and supply may differ from the corresponding short-run elasticities. Where consumers can substitute between goods more readily in the long run, long-run demand curves are more elastic than short-run demand curves. If goods can be stored easily, however, short-run demand curves are more elastic than long-run curves. If producers can increase output at lower extra cost in the long run than in the short run, the long-run elasticity of supply is greater than the short-run elasticity.

5. **Effects of a sales tax:** The two common types of sales taxes are ad valorem taxes, by which the government collects a fixed percent of the price paid per unit, and specific taxes, by which the government collects a fixed amount of money per unit sold. Both types of sales taxes typically raise the equilibrium price and lower the equilibrium quantity. Both usually raise the price consumers pay and lower the price suppliers receive, so consumers do not bear the full burden or incidence of the tax. The effects on quantity, price, and the incidence of the tax that falls on consumers depend on the demand and supply elasticities. In competitive markets, for which supply-and-demand analysis is appropriate, the effect of a tax on equilibrium quantities, prices, and the incidence of the tax is unaffected by whether the tax is collected from consumers or producers.

Problems

1. Give one or more rules for determining the section of a straight-line demand curve that is elastic.
2. The shares of consumers who have cable television service are 59% for people with incomes of \$25,000 or less; 66%, \$25,000–\$34,999; 67%, \$35,000–\$49,999; 71%, \$50,000–\$74,999; and 78%, \$75,000 or more.[21] What can you say about the income elasticity for cable television?
3. What is the effect of a \$1 specific tax on equilibrium price and quantity if demand is perfectly inelastic? What is the incidence on consumers? Explain.
4. What is the effect of a \$1 specific tax on equilibrium price and quantity if demand is perfectly elastic? What is the incidence on consumers? Explain.
5. What is the effect of a \$1 specific tax on equilibrium price and quantity if supply is perfectly inelastic? What is the incidence on consumers? Explain.
6. What is the effect of a \$1 specific tax on equilibrium price and quantity if demand is perfectly elastic and supply is perfectly inelastic? What is the incidence on consumers? Explain.
7. List as many conditions as you can for the incidence of a tax to fall entirely on consumers.
8. Do you care whether a 15¢ tax per gallon of milk is collected from milk producers or from consumers at the store? Why?
9. Give some examples of evidence that would convince you that the demand curve for a given product was inelastic. Similarly, what evidence would convince you that a supply curve was elastic? (*Hint*: Consider shocks caused by changes in factors that affect demand or by taxes.)
10. A rent control law limits the price of an apartment. What is the likely effect of such a law in the short run? What is the likely effect of the law in the long run? Be sure to discuss the quantity and quality of apartments available for rent.
11. Consider the market for labor services. The state collects a tax of α (where $0 < \alpha < 1$) cents of every dollar a worker earns. If the state raises its minimum wage, what happens to the amount of tax revenues it collects? Must tax revenue necessarily rise or fall?

Math Problems

12. Calculate the price and cross-price elasticities of demand for coconut oil. The coconut oil demand function is (Buschena and Perloff 1991)

$$Q = 1{,}200 - 9.5p + 16.2p_p + 0.2Y.$$

where Q is the quantity of coconut oil demanded in thousands of metric tons per year, p is the price of coconut oil in cents per pound, p_p is the price of palm oil per pound, and Y is the income of consumers. Assume that p is initially 45¢ per pound, p_p is 31¢ per pound, and Q is 1,275 thousand metric tons per year.

13. Using the coconut oil demand function from the previous problem, calculate the income elasticity of demand for coconut oil. (If you do not have all the numbers necessary to calculate numerical answers, write your answers in terms of variables.)
14. The supply curve is $Q = g + hp$. Write a formula for the elasticity of supply in terms of p (and not Q). Now give one entirely in terms of Q.
15. A constant elasticity supply curve, $Q = Bp^{\eta}$, intersects a constant elasticity demand curve, $Q = Ap^{\varepsilon}$, where A, B, η, and ε are constants. What is the incidence of a \$1 specific tax? Does your answer depend on where the supply curve intersects the demand curve? Interpret your result.
16. A constant elasticity supply curve, $Q = Bp^{\eta}$, intersects a linear demand curve: $Q = a - bp$. What is the incidence of a \$1 specific tax? Does your answer depend on where the supply curve intersects the demand curve? Interpret your result.

[21] Avalos, George, "TCI, Other Cable Firms Losing Some Favored Customers," *West County Times*, 22(7), January 7, 1997:1A, 12A.

CHAPTER 4

Consumer Choice

If this is coffee, please bring me some tea; but if this is tea, please bring me some coffee. —Abraham Lincoln

Alexx's employer wants to transfer him to the firm's Paris office. Although Alexx likes the idea of living in Paris, he's concerned about the high cost of living there. The firm offers to pay him enough in French francs that he can buy the same combination of goods in Paris that he is buying currently in the United States. In terms of what he can consume, will this higher income undercompensate, fully compensate, or overcompensate Alexx for the higher prices in Paris?

The government gives poor people food stamps, which they may use in retail stores only to buy food. Would the benefit to recipients be greater if they were given cash instead of food stamps? Would they buy less food?

As we saw in Chapters 2 and 3, the supply-and-demand model is useful for analyzing economic questions concerning markets. We could use the supply-and-demand model to examine the market prices of brioches in Paris and New York or the effect of food stamps on the market price of veal. However, the supply-and-demand model cannot be used to answer questions concerning individuals, such as Alexx's problem about whether to move to Paris or whether cash or food stamps are better for an individual.

To answer questions about individual decisionmaking, we need a model of individual behavior. In our model of consumer behavior:

- Individual *tastes* or *preferences* determine the amount of pleasure people derive from the goods and services they consume.
- Consumers face *constraints* or limits on their choices.
- Consumers *maximize* their well-being or pleasure from consumption, subject to the constraints they face.

Consumers spend their money on the products that give them the most pleasure. If you like music and don't have much of a sweet tooth, you spend a lot of your money on concerts, tapes, and CDs and relatively little on candy. On the other hand, your chocoholic friend with the tin ear may spend a great deal on Hershey's Kisses and very little on music.

All consumers must choose which goods to buy because limits on wealth prevent them from buying everything that catches their fancy. In addition, government rules restrict what they may buy: Young consumers cannot buy alcohol or cigarettes legally, and at any age, it is illegal to buy crack and other recreational drugs. Therefore, consumers buy those goods that give them the most pleasure, subject to the constraints that they cannot spend more money than they have and that they cannot spend it in ways that the government forbids.

In economic analyses designed to explain behavior (positive analysis—see Chapter 1) rather than judge it (normative statements), economists assume that *the consumer is the boss*. If your brother gets pleasure from smoking, economists don't argue with him that it is bad for him any more than they'd tell your sister, who likes reading Stephen King, that she should read Adam Smith's *Wealth of Nations* instead. Accepting each consumer's tastes is not the same as condoning the resulting behaviors. Economists want to predict behavior. They want to know, for example, whether your brother will smoke more next year if the price of cigarettes decreases 10%. The prediction is unlikely to be correct if economists say, "He shouldn't smoke; therefore, we predict he'll stop smoking next year." A prediction based on your brother's actual tastes is more likely to be correct: "Given that he likes cigarettes, he is likely to smoke more of them next year if the price falls."

In this chapter, we examine four main topics:

1. **Preferences:** We can use three properties of preferences to predict which combinations, or bundle, of goods an individual prefers to other combinations.
2. **Utility:** Economists summarize a consumer's preferences using a *utility* function, which assigns a numerical value to each possible bundle of goods, reflecting the consumer's relative ranking of these bundles.
3. **Budget constraint:** Prices, income, and government restrictions limit a consumer's ability to make purchases by determining the rate at which a consumer can trade one good for another.
4. **Consumer's constrained choice:** Consumers maximize their pleasure from consuming various possible bundles of goods given their income, which limits the amount of goods they can purchase.

4.1 PREFERENCES

We start our analysis of consumer behavior by examining consumer preferences. Using three basic assumptions, we can predict a great deal about preferences. Once we know about consumers' preferences, we can add information about the constraints consumers face, so we can answer many questions, such as the ones posed at the beginning of the chapter, or derive demand curves, as is done in the next chapter.

As a consumer, you choose among many goods. Should you get ice cream or cake for dessert? Should you spend most of your money on a large apartment or rent a single room and use the savings to pay for trips and concerts? In short, you must allocate your money to buy a *bundle* (*market basket* or combination) of goods.

How do consumers choose the bundle of goods they buy? One possibility is that consumers behave randomly and blindly choose one or another good without any thought; consumers appear to make systematic choices. For example, you probably buy more or less the same items each time you go to the grocery store.

To explain consumer behavior, economists *assume* that consumers have a set of tastes or preferences that they use to guide them in choosing between goods. These tastes differ substantially across individuals. Three out of four European men prefer colored underwear, while three out of four American men prefer white underwear.[1] Some people, such as President Bill Clinton, like broccoli, whereas others, among them former President George Bush, hate it.[2] To put all our cards on the table, let's start by specifying the underlying assumptions in the economist's model of consumer behavior.

Properties of Consumer Preferences

Economists make three critical assumptions about the properties of consumers' preferences. For brevity, these properties are referred to as *completeness*, *transitivity*, and *more is better*.

Completeness. The completeness property is that, when faced with a choice between any two bundles of goods, a consumer can rank them so that one and only one of the following relationships is true: The consumer prefers the first bundle to the second, prefers the second to the first, or is indifferent between them. This property rules out the possibility that the consumer cannot decide which bundle is preferable.

It would be very difficult to predict behavior if consumers' rankings of bundles were not logically consistent. The next property eliminates the possibility of certain types of illogical behavior.

Transitivity. The transitivity (or what some people refer to as *rationality*) property is that a consumer's preferences over bundles is consistent in the sense that if the consumer *weakly prefers* Bundle z to Bundle y (likes z at least as much as y), and weakly prefers Bundle y to Bundle x, then the consumer weakly prefers Bundle z to Bundle x.

If your sister told you she preferred a scoop of ice cream to a piece of cake, a piece of cake to a bar of candy, and a bar of candy to a scoop of ice cream, you'd probably think she'd lost her mind. At the very least, you wouldn't know which of these desserts to serve her.

More Is Better. The more-is-better property holds that, all else the same, more of a commodity is better than less of it. That is, consumers are not *satiated*. Indeed, economists define a **good** as a commodity for which more is preferred to less, at least at some levels of consumption. In contrast, a **bad** is something for which less is preferred to more, such as pollution. We now concentrate on goods.

Although the completeness and transitivity properties are crucial to the analysis that follows, the more-is-better property is included to simplify the analysis—our most important results would follow even without this property.

---

[1] L. M. Boyd, "The Grab Bag," *San Francisco Examiner*, September 11, 1994:5.

[2] Sometimes, it is difficult to distinguish taste differences from knowledge. For example, one is unlikely to buy a food one has never tasted. In the western United States, 56.2% of people have eaten artichokes, whereas only 27.8% have tried them nationally, and only 18.9% in the Midwest (Schreiner, Tim, "What Westerners Are Likely to Like," *San Francisco Chronicle*, October 30, 1986:2).

So why do economists assume that the more-is-better property holds? The most compelling reason is that it appears to be true about most people.[3] A second reason is that, if consumers can freely dispose of excess goods, a consumer can be no worse off with extra goods. (We examine a third reason later in the chapter: Consumers buy goods only when this condition is met.)

Preference Maps

Surprisingly enough, with just these three properties, we can tell a lot about a consumer's preferences. One of the simplest ways to summarize information about a consumer's preferences is to create a graphical interpretation—a map—of a consumer's preferences. Throughout this chapter, we concentrate on choices between only two goods for graphical simplicity, but the model can be generalized to handle any number of goods.

To illustrate, let's consider a choice between only two goods. For example, each semester, Lisa, who lives for fast food, decides how many pizzas and burritos to eat. The various bundles of pizzas and burritos she might consume are shown in panel a of Figure 4.1, with (individual-size) pizzas per semester on the horizontal axis and burritos per semester on the vertical axis.

At Bundle *e*, for example, Lisa consumes 25 pizzas and 15 burritos per semester. By the more-is-better property, all the bundles that lie above and to the right (area *A*) are preferred to Bundle *e* because they contain at least as much of both pizza and burritos as Bundle *e*. Thus, Bundle *f* (30 pizzas and 20 burritos) in that region is preferred to *e*. By the same reasoning, Lisa likes all the bundles that lie in area *B*, below and to the left of *e*, such as Bundle *d* (15 pizzas and 10 burritos), less than *e*.

Bundles such as *b* (30 pizzas and 10 burritos), in the region below and to the right of *e*, or *c* (15 pizzas and 25 burritos), in the region above and to the left, may or may not be preferred to *e*. We can't use the more-is-better property to determine which bundle is preferred because these bundles each contain more of one good and less of the other than does *e*.

Indifference Curves. Suppose we asked Lisa to identify all the bundles that gave her the same amount of pleasure as consuming Bundle *e*. Using her answers, we draw curve *I* in panel b of Figure 4.1 through all bundles she likes as much as *e*. Curve *I* is an **indifference curve**: the set of all bundles of goods that a consumer views as being equally desirable.

---

[3]When teaching microeconomics to Wharton MBAs, I told them about a cousin of mine who had just joined a commune in Oregon. His worldly possessions consisted of a tent, a Franklin stove, enough food to live on, and a few clothes. He said that he didn't need any other goods—that he was satiated. A few years later, one of these students bumped into me on the street and said, "Professor, I don't remember your name or much of anything you taught me in your course, but I can't stop thinking about your cousin. Is it really true that he doesn't want *anything* else? His very existence is a repudiation of my whole way of life." Actually, my cousin had given up his ascetic life and was engaged in telemarketing, but I, for noble pedagogical reasons, responded, "Of course he still lives that way—you can't expect everyone to have the tastes of an MBA."

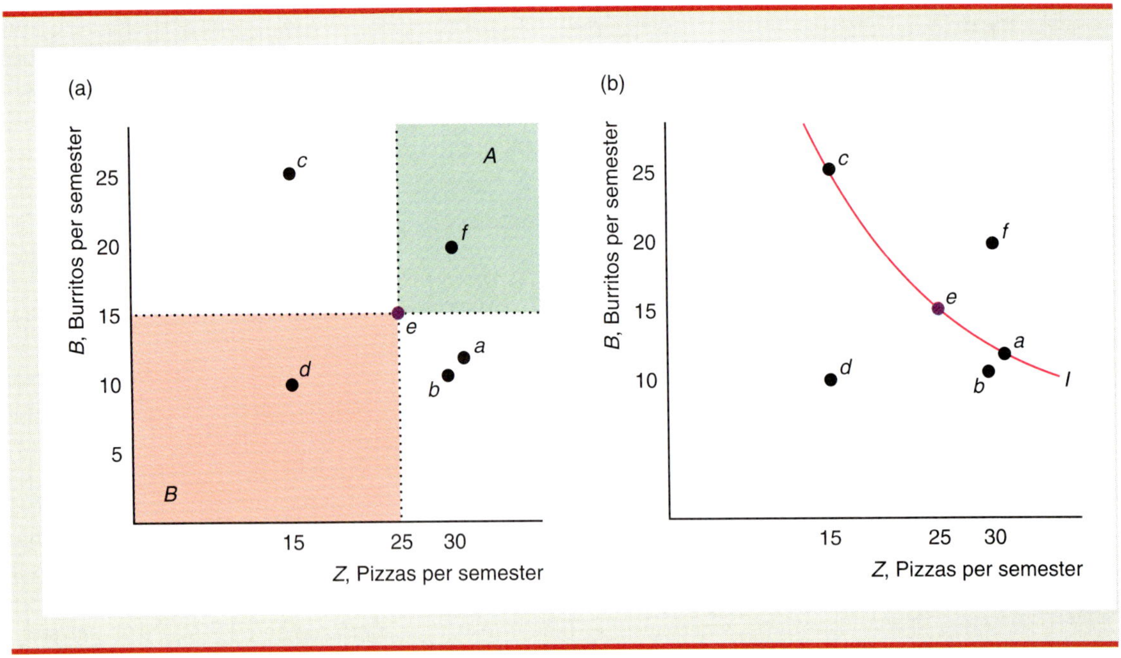

Indifference curve I includes Bundles c, e, and a, so Lisa is indifferent between consuming Bundles c, e, and a. From this indifference curve, we also know that Lisa prefers e (25 pizzas and 15 burritos) to b (30 pizzas and 10 burritos). How do we know that? Bundle b lies below and to the left of Bundle a, so Bundle a is preferred to Bundle b by the more-is-better property. Both Bundle a and Bundle e are on indifference curve I, so Lisa likes Bundle e as much as Bundle a. Because Lisa is indifferent between e and a and she prefers a to b, she must prefer e to b by transitivity.

If we asked Lisa many, many questions, in principle, we could draw an entire set of indifference curves through every possible bundle of burritos and pizzas. Lisa's preferences are summarized in an **indifference map** or *preference map*, which is a complete set of indifference curves that summarize a consumer's tastes. Panel c of Figure 4.1 shows three of Lisa's indifference curves, I^0, I^1, and I^2.

We assume that indifference curves are continuous—have no gaps—as the figure shows. The indifference curves are parallel in the figure, but they need not be. All indifference curve maps must have four important properties:

1. Bundles on indifference curves farther from the origin are preferred to those on indifference curves closer to the origin.
2. There is an indifference curve through every possible bundle.
3. Indifference curves cannot cross.
4. Indifference curves slope down.

First, we show that bundles on indifference curves farther from the origin (zero units of both goods) are preferred to those on indifference curves closer to the origin. By the more-is-better property, Lisa prefers Bundle f to Bundle e in panel c of Figure 4.1. She is indifferent among all the bundles on indifference curve I^2 and

(c)

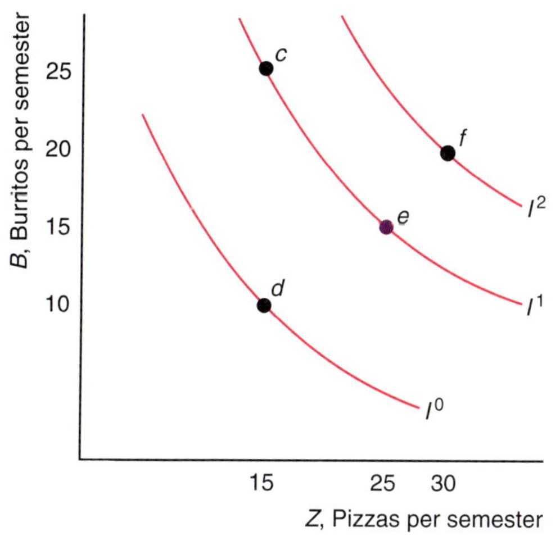

Figure 4.1 Bundles of Pizzas and Burritos Lisa Might Consume. Pizzas per semester are on the horizontal axis, and burritos per semester are on the vertical axis. (a) Lisa prefers more to less, so she prefers Bundle *e* to any bundle in area *B*, including *d*. Similarly, she prefers any bundle in area *A*, including *f*, to *e*. (b) The indifference curve, I^1, shows a set of bundles (including *c*, *e*, and *a*) among which she is indifferent. (c) Three indifference curves, I^0, I^1, and I^2 summarize Lisa's preferences.

Bundle *f*, just as she is indifferent among all the bundles, such as Bundle *c*, on indifference curve I^1 and Bundle *e*. By the transitivity property, she prefers Bundle *f* to Bundle *e*, which she likes as much as Bundle *c*, so she prefers Bundle *f* to Bundle *c*. By this type of reasoning, she prefers all bundles on I^2 to all bundles on I^1.

Second, we show that there is an indifference curve through every possible bundle as a consequence of the completeness property: The consumer can compare any bundle to another. Compared to a given bundle, some bundles are preferred, some are enjoyed equally, and some are inferior. Connecting the bundles that give the same pleasure produces an indifference curve that includes the given bundle.

Third, we show that indifference curves cannot cross: A given bundle cannot be on two indifference curves. Suppose that two indifference curves crossed at Bundle *e* as in panel a of Figure 4.2. Because Bundles *e* and *a* lie on the same indifference curve I^0, Lisa is indifferent between *e* and *a*. Similarly, she is indifferent between *e* and *b* because both are on I^1. By transitivity, if Lisa is indifferent between *e* and *a* and she is indifferent between *e* and *b*, she must be indifferent between *a* and *b*. But that's impossible! Bundle *b* is above and to the right of bundle *a*, so Lisa *must* prefer *b* to *a* by the more-is-better property. Thus, because preferences are transitive and more is better than less, indifference curves cannot cross.

Fourth, we show that indifference curves must be downward sloping. Suppose to the contrary that an indifference curve sloped up, as in panel b of Figure 4.2. The consumer is indifferent between Bundles *a* and *b* because both lie on the same indifference curve, *I*. But the consumer prefers *b* to *a* by the more-is-better property: Bundle *a* lies strictly below and to the left of Bundle *b*. Because of this contradiction—the consumer cannot both be indifferent between *a* and *b* and strictly prefer *b* to *a*—indifference curves cannot be upward sloping.

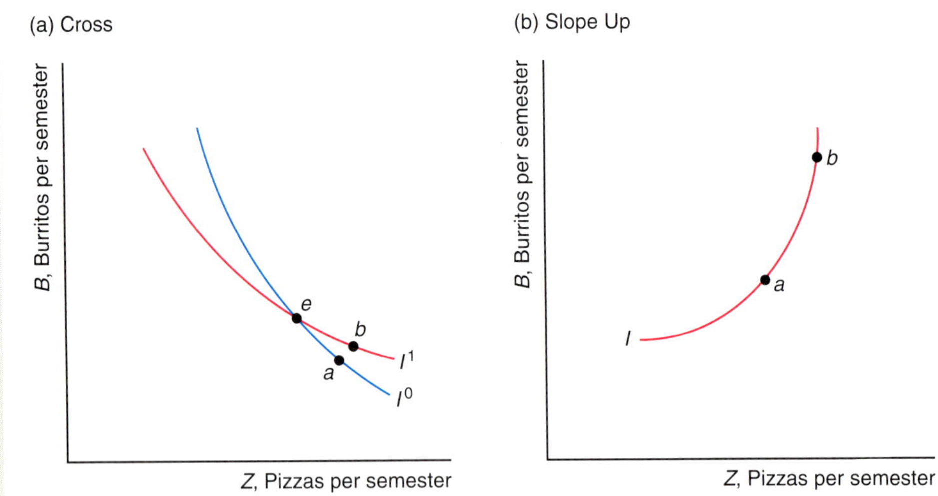

SOLVED PROBLEM 4.1

Can indifference curves be thick?

Answer

Draw an indifference curve that is at least two bundles thick, and show that a preference property is violated: Panel c of Figure 4.2 shows a thick indifference curve, *I*, with two bundles, *a* and *b*, identified. Bundle *b* lies above and to the right of *a*: Bundle *b* has more of both burritos and pizza. Thus, by the more-is-better property, Bundle *b* must be strictly preferred to Bundle *a*. But the consumer must be indifferent between *a* and *b* because both bundles are on the same indifference curve. Because both relationships between *a* and *b* cannot be true, there is a contradiction. Consequently, indifference curves cannot be thick. (We emphasize this point by drawing indifference curves with very thin lines in our figures.) ■

Willingness to Substitute Between Goods. Lisa is willing to make some trades between goods. The downward slope of her indifference curves shows that Lisa is willing to give up some burritos for more pizza or vice versa. She is indifferent between Bundles *a* and *b* on her indifference curve *I* in panel a of Figure 4.3. If she initially has Bundle *a* (eight burritos and three pizzas), she could get to Bundle *b*

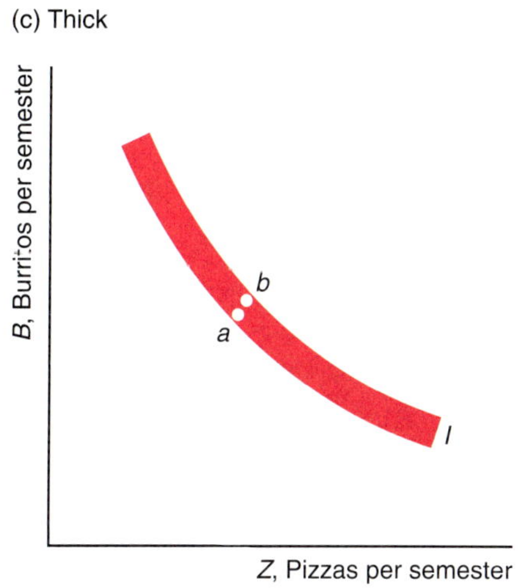

Figure 4.2 Impossible Indifference Curves. (a) Suppose the indifference curves cross at Bundle *e*. Lisa is indifferent between *e* and *a* on indifference curve I^0 and between *e* and *b* on I^1. If Lisa is indifferent between *e* and *a* and she is indifferent between *e* and *b*, she must be indifferent between *a* and *b* by transitivity. But *b* has more of both pizzas and burritos than *a*, so she *must* prefer *a* to *b*. Because of this contradiction, indifference curves cannot cross. (b) Suppose indifference curve *I* slopes up. The consumer is indifferent between *b* and *a* because they lie on *I* but prefers *b* to *a* by the more-is-better assumption. Because of this contradiction, indifference curves cannot be upward sloping. (c) Suppose indifference curve *I* is thick enough to contain both *a* and *b*. The consumer is indifferent between *a* and *b* because both are on *I* but prefers *b* to *a* by the more-is-better assumption because *b* lies above and to the right of *a*. Because of this contradiction, indifference curves cannot be thick.

(five burritos and four pizzas) by trading three burritos for one more pizza. She is indifferent whether she makes this trade of not.

Lisa's willingness to trade one good for another is measured by her **marginal rate of substitution** (*MRS*): the maximum amount of one good a consumer will sacrifice to obtain one more unit of another good. The marginal rate of substitution refers to the trade-off (rate of substitution) of burritos for a marginal (small, additional or incremental) change in the number of pizzas. Lisa's marginal rate of substitution of burritos for pizza is

$$MRS = \frac{\Delta B}{\Delta Z},$$

where ΔZ is the number of pizzas Lisa will give up to get ΔB more burritos or vice versa. *The marginal rate of substitution is the slope of the indifference curve.*[4]

Moving from Bundle *a* to Bundle *b*, Lisa will give up three burritos, $\Delta B = -3$, to obtain one more pizza, $\Delta Z = 1$, so her marginal rate of substitution is $-3/1 = -3$. That is, the marginal rate of substitution is the slope of the indifference curve. The negative sign shows that Lisa is willing to give up one good to get the other (her indifference curve slopes down).

[4]The slope is "the rise over the run": how much we move along the vertical axis (rise) as we move along the horizontal axis (run). Technically, by the marginal rate of substitution, we mean the slope at a particular bundle. That is, we want to know what the slope is as ΔZ gets very small. In calculus terms, the relevant slope is a derivative. See Appendix 4A.

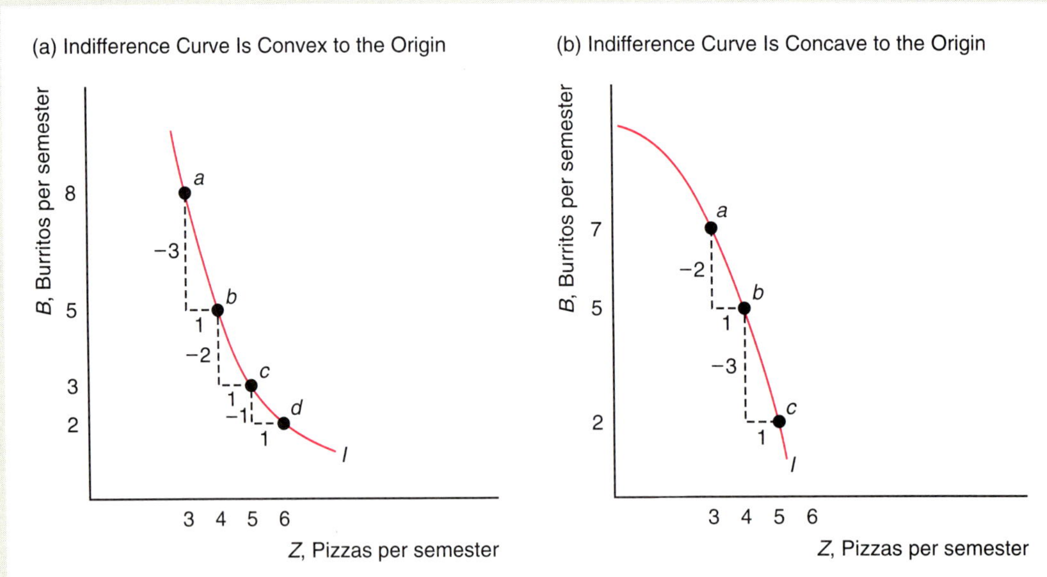

Figure 4.3 Marginal Rate of Substitution. (a) At Bundle *a*, Lisa is willing to give up three burritos for one more pizza; whereas at *b*, she is willing to give only two burritos to obtain another pizza. That is, the relatively more burritos she has, the more she is willing to trade for another pizza. Bundles *a* and *b* are on her indifference curve *I*, so she is indifferent between them. (b) An indifference curve of this shape is unlikely to be observed. Lisa would be willing to give up more burritos to get one more pizza, the fewer the burritos she has. Moving from Bundle *c* to *b*, she will trade one pizza for three burritos, whereas moving from *b* to *a*, she will trade one pizza for two burritos, even though she now has relatively more burritos to pizzas.

Curvature of Indifference Curves. Must indifference curves be curved like *I* in panel a of Figure 4.3, which is *convex* to the origin (the middle of each indifference curve is closer to the origin than if the indifference curve were a straight line)? They don't have to be convex, but casual observation suggests that most people's indifference curves are convex. Most people, when they have a lot of one good, are willing to give up a relatively large amount of it to get a good of which they have very little. After that first trade, however, they are willing to give up less of the first good to get the same amount more of the second good.

Lisa is willing to give up three burritos to obtain one more pizza when she is at *a* in panel a of Figure 4.3. At *b*, she is willing to trade only two burritos for a pizza. At *c*, she is even less willing to trade; she will give up only one burrito for another pizza. This willingness to trade fewer burritos for one more pizza as we move down and to the right along the indifference curve reflects a *diminishing marginal rate of substitution*: The marginal rate of substitution approaches zero as we move down and to the right along an indifference curve. That is, the indifference curve becomes flatter (less sloped) as we move down and to the right.

It is hard to imagine that Lisa's indifference curves are *concave*, as in panel b, rather than *convex*, as in panel a. If her indifference curve is concave, Lisa would be willing to give up more burritos to get one more pizza, the fewer the burritos she has. In panel b, she trades one pizza for three burritos moving from Bundle *c* to *b*, and she trades one pizza for only two burritos moving from *b* to *a*, even though her ratio of burritos to pizza is greater. Though it is difficult to imagine concave indifference curves, two extreme versions of downward-sloping, convex indifference curves are plausible: straight-line or right-angle indifference curves.

One extreme case is **perfect substitutes**: goods that a consumer is completely indifferent as to which to consume. Because Bill cannot taste any difference between Coca-Cola and Pepsi-Cola, he views them as perfect substitutes: He is indifferent between one can of Coke and one can of Pepsi. His indifference curves for these two goods are straight, parallel lines with a slope of –1 everywhere along the curve in panel a of Figure 4.4.

Bill's marginal rate of substitution is –1 at every point along these indifference curves. The slope of indifference curves of perfect substitutes need not always be –1; it can be any constant rate.

For example, Charles knows from reading the labels that Clorox bleach is twice as strong as a generic brand. As a result, Charles is indifferent between one cup of Clorox and two cups of the generic bleach. The slope of his indifference curve is –2 (where the generic bleach is on the vertical axis).[5]

The other extreme case is **perfect complements**: goods that a consumer is interested in consuming only simultaneously. Grace doesn't like pie by itself or ice cream by itself but loves pie à la mode: a slice of pie with a scoop of vanilla ice cream on top. Her indifference curves have right angles in panel b of Figure 4.4. If she has only one piece of pie, she gets as much pleasure from it and one scoop of ice cream, Bundle *a*, as from it and two scoops, Bundle *d*, or as from it and three scoops, Bundle *e*. That is, she won't eat the extra scoops because she does not have pieces of pie to go with the ice cream. Therefore, she consumes only bundles like *a*, *b*, and *c* in which pie and ice cream are in equal proportions.

At a bundle like *a*, *b*, or *c*, she will not substitute a piece of pie for an extra scoop of ice cream. For example, if she were at *b*, she would be unwilling to give up an extra slice of pie to get, say, two extra scoops of ice cream, as at point *e*. Indeed, she wouldn't give up the slice of pie for a virtually unlimited amount of extra ice cream because the extra ice cream is worthless to her. That is, her marginal rate of substitution is zero.[6]

---

[5]Sometimes it is difficult to guess what goods are close substitutes. According to Harper's Index (reproduced in *San Francisco Examiner*, May 22, 1994, This World:6), flowers, perfume, and fire extinguishers rank 1, 2, and 3 among Mother's Day gifts that Americans consider "very appropriate."

[6]Except in this limiting case of perfect complements, if a consumer can choose between only two goods, they must be substitutes. If the consumer may choose among three or more goods, however, any pair may be substitutes or complements. If Lisa were choosing among pizza, burritos, and a cola, she might view a cola as a complement to both pizza and burritos and view pizza and burritos as substitutes for each other. The cola might not be a perfect complement. She may be willing to eat pizza without also consuming a cola, but she would be happier if she had both.

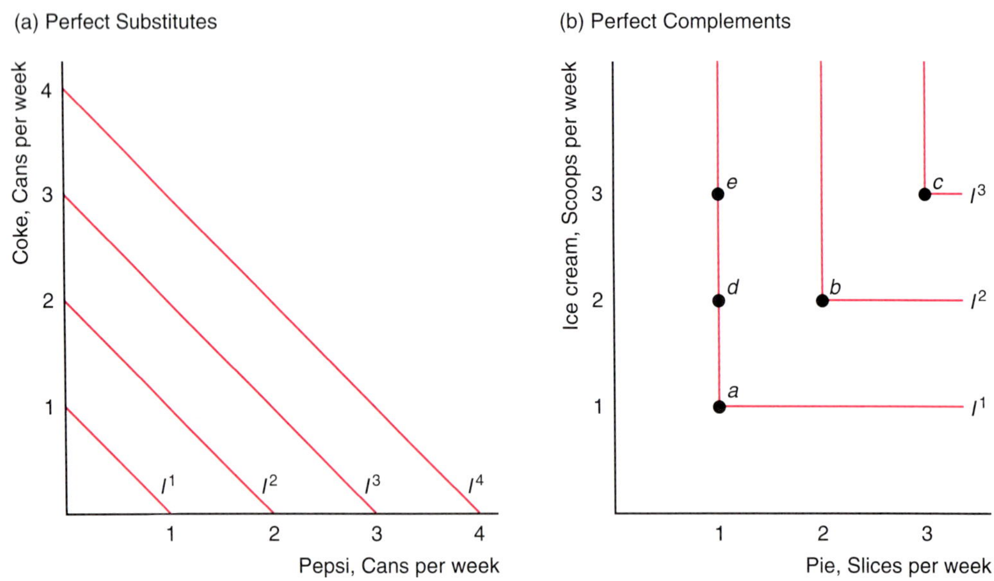

The standard-shaped, convex indifference curve in panel c of Figure 4.4 lies between these two extreme examples. Convex indifference curves show that a consumer views two goods as imperfect substitutes.

APPLICATION

Indifference Curves Between Food and Clothing

On the basis of the estimates of Eastwood and Craven (1981) using U.S. data, we draw the indifference curves of the average consumer between food consumed at home and clothing in Figure 4.5. The food and clothing measures are weighted averages of various different goods. At relatively low quantities of food and clothing, the indifference curves, such as I^1, are nearly right angles: perfect complements. As we move away from the origin, the indifference curves become flatter: closer to perfect substitutes.

One interpretation of these indifference curves is that there are minimum levels of food and clothing necessary to support life. The consumer cannot trade one good for the other if it means having less than these critical levels. As the consumer has more of both goods, however, the consumer is increas-

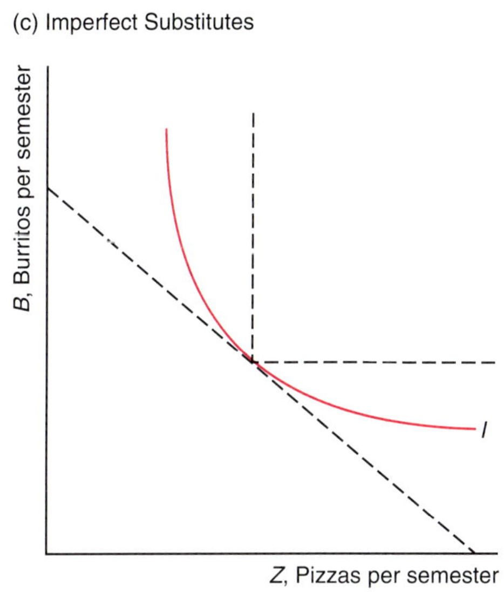

Figure 4.4 Perfect Substitutes, Perfect Complements, Imperfect Substitutes. (a) Bill views Coke and Pepsi as perfect substitutes. His indifference curves are straight, parallel lines with a marginal rate of substitution (slope) of –1. Bill is willing to exchange one can of Coke for one can of Pepsi. (b) Grace likes pie à la mode but does not like pie or ice cream by itself: She views ice cream and pie as perfect complements. She will not substitute between the two; she consumes them only in equal quantities. (c) Lisa views burritos and pizza as imperfect substitutes. Her indifference curve lies between the extreme cases of perfect substitutes and perfect complements.

ingly willing to trade between the two goods. According to these estimates, food and clothing are perfect complements when the consumer has little of either good, and perfect substitutes when the consumer has large quantities of both goods. ■

4.2 UTILITY

Underlying our model of consumer behavior is the belief that consumers can compare various bundles of goods and decide which gives them the greatest pleasure. We can summarize a consumer's preferences by assigning a numerical value to each possible bundle reflecting the consumer's relative ranking of these bundles.

Following Jeremy Bentham, John Stuart Mill, and other nineteenth-century British economist-philosophers, economists call this numerical value that reflects the relative rankings of various bundles of goods **utility**. The statement that "Bonnie prefers Bundle x to Bundle y" is equivalent to the statement that "consuming Bundle x gives Bonnie more utility than consuming Bundle y." Bonnie prefers x to y if Bundle x gives Bonnie 10 *utils* (the name given to a unit of utility) and Bundle y gives her 8 utils.

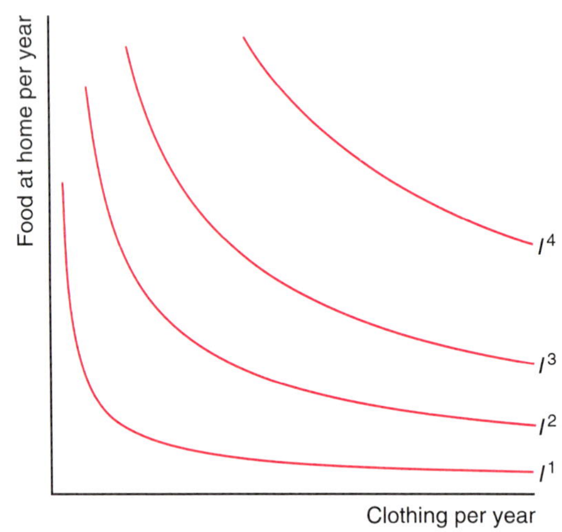

Figure 4.5 Indifference Curves Between Food and Clothing. Eastwood and Craven (1981) estimate the indifference curves of the average American consumer between food consumed at home and clothing. Near the origin, indifference curves such as I^1 are nearly right angles—nearly perfect complements. Away from the origin, the indifference curves become flatter—closer to perfect substitutes.

Utility Function

If we knew the **utility function**—the relationship between this utility measure and every possible bundle of goods—we could summarize the information in indifference maps succinctly. Suppose for example that the utility, U, that Lisa gets from burritos and pizzas is

$$U = \sqrt{BZ}.$$

From this function, we know that the more she consumes of either good, the greater is the utility, U, that Lisa receives. Using this function, we can determine whether she would be happier if she had Bundle x with 9 burritos and 16 pizzas or Bundle y with 13 of each. The utility she gets from x is 12 $(= \sqrt{9 \times 16})$ utils. The utility she gets from y is 13 $(= \sqrt{13 \times 13})$ utils. Therefore, she prefers y to x.

The utility function is a concept that economists use to help them think about consumer behavior; utility functions do not exist in any fundamental sense. If you ask your mother what her utility function is, she would be puzzled—unless, of course, she is an economist. On the other hand, if you asked her enough questions about choices of bundles of goods, you could construct a function that accurately summarizes her preferences. For example, by questioning people, Rousseas and Hart (1951) constructed indifference curves between eggs and bacon, and MacCrimmon and Toda (1969) constructed indifference curves between money and pens and between money and French pastries.

Typically, consumers can easily answer questions about whether they prefer one bundle to another, such as "Do you prefer a bundle with one scoop of ice cream and two pieces of cake to another bundle with two scoops of ice cream and one piece of cake?" But they have difficulty answering questions about how much more they prefer one bundle to another because they don't have a measure to describe how their pleasure from two goods or bundles differs. Therefore, we may know a consumer's rank-ordering of bundles, but we are unlikely to know by how much more that consumer prefers one bundle to another.

Ordinal Preferences

If we know only consumers' relative rankings of bundles, our measure of pleasure is *ordinal* rather than *cardinal*. An ordinal measure is one that tells us the relative ranking of two things but not how much more one rank is than another.

If a professor assigns only letter grades to an exam, we know that a student who receives a grade of A did better than a student who received a B, but we can't say how much better from that ordinal scale. Nor can we tell whether the difference in performance between an A student and a B student is greater or less than the difference between a B student and a C student.

A cardinal measure is one by which absolute comparisons between ranks may be made. Money is a cardinal measure. If you have \$100 and your brother has \$50, we know not only that you have more money than your brother, but also that you have exactly twice as much money as he does.

Because utility is an ordinal measure, we should not put any weight on the absolute differences between the utility associated with one bundle and another.[7] We care only about the relative utility or ranking of the two bundles.

Utility and Indifference Curves

We can use Lisa's utility function to construct a three-dimensional diagram that shows how utility varies with changes in the consumption of B and Z. Imagine that you are standing with your back against a corner of a room. Walking away from the corner along the wall to your left, you are tracing out the B axis: The farther you

[7]Let $U(B, Z)$ be the original utility function and $V(B, Z)$ be the new utility function after we have applied a *positive monotonic transformation*: a change that increases the value of the function at every point. These two utility functions give the same ordinal ranking to any bundle of goods. (Economists often express this idea by saying that a *utility function is unique only up to a positive monotonic transformation*.) Suppose, for example, that $V(B, Z) = \alpha + \beta U(B, Z)$, where $\beta > 0$. The rank ordering is the same for these utility functions because $V(B, Z) = \alpha + \beta U(B, Z) > V(B^*, Z^*) = \alpha + \beta U(B^*, Z^*)$ if and only if $U(B, Z) > U(B^*, Z^*)$.

get from the corner, the more burritos Lisa has. Similarly, starting back at the corner and walking along the wall to your right, you are moving along the Z axis. When you stand in the corner, you are leaning against the utility axis, where the two walls meet. The higher the point along your back, the greater is Lisa's utility. Because her utility is increasing (more is preferred to less) in both B and Z, her utility rises as you walk away from the corner (origin) along either wall or into the room, where Lisa has more B or Z or both. Lisa's utility or *hill of happiness* rises as you move away from the corner.

What is the relationship between Lisa's utility and one of her indifference curves: those combinations of B and Z that give Lisa a particular level of utility? Imagine that the hill of happiness is made of clay. If you were to cut the hill parallel to the floor at a particular height on the wall—a given level of utility—you'd get a smaller hill above the cut. Now suppose that you place that smaller hill directly on the floor and trace the outside edge of the hill. Looking down at the floor, the traced outer edge of the hill represents an indifference curve on the two-dimensional floor. Making other parallel cuts in the hill of happiness, placing the smaller hills on the floor, and tracing their outside edges, you could obtain a mapping of indifference curves, where each indifference curve reflects a different level of utility.

Utility and Marginal Utility

Using Lisa's utility function over burritos and pizza, we can show how her utility changes if she gets to consume more of one of the goods. We now suppose that Lisa has the utility function in Figure 4.6. The curve in panel a shows how Lisa's utility rises as she consumes more pizzas while we hold her consumption of burritos fixed at 10. Because pizza is a *good*, Lisa's utility rises as she consumes more pizza.

If her consumption of pizzas increases from $Z = 4$ to 5, $\Delta Z = 5 - 4 = 1$, her utility increases from $U = 230$ to 250, $\Delta U = 250 - 230 = 20$. The extra utility ($\Delta U$) that she gets from consuming the last unit of a good ($\Delta Z = 1$) is the **marginal utility** from that good. Thus, marginal utility is the slope of the utility function (Appendix 4A):

$$MU_Z = \Delta U/\Delta Z.$$

Lisa's marginal utility from increasing her consumption of pizza from 4 to 5 is

$$MU_Z = \Delta U/\Delta Z = 20/1 = 20.$$

Panel b shows that Lisa's marginal utility from consuming one more pizza varies with the number of pizzas she consumes, holding her consumption of burritos constant. Her marginal utility of pizza curve falls as her consumption of pizza increases, but the marginal utility remains positive: Each extra pizza gives Lisa pleasure, but it gives her less pleasure than the previous pizza relative to other goods.

Utility and Marginal Rates of Substitution

Earlier, we learned that the marginal rate of substitution (MRS) is the slope of the indifference curve. The marginal rate of substitution also can be expressed in terms

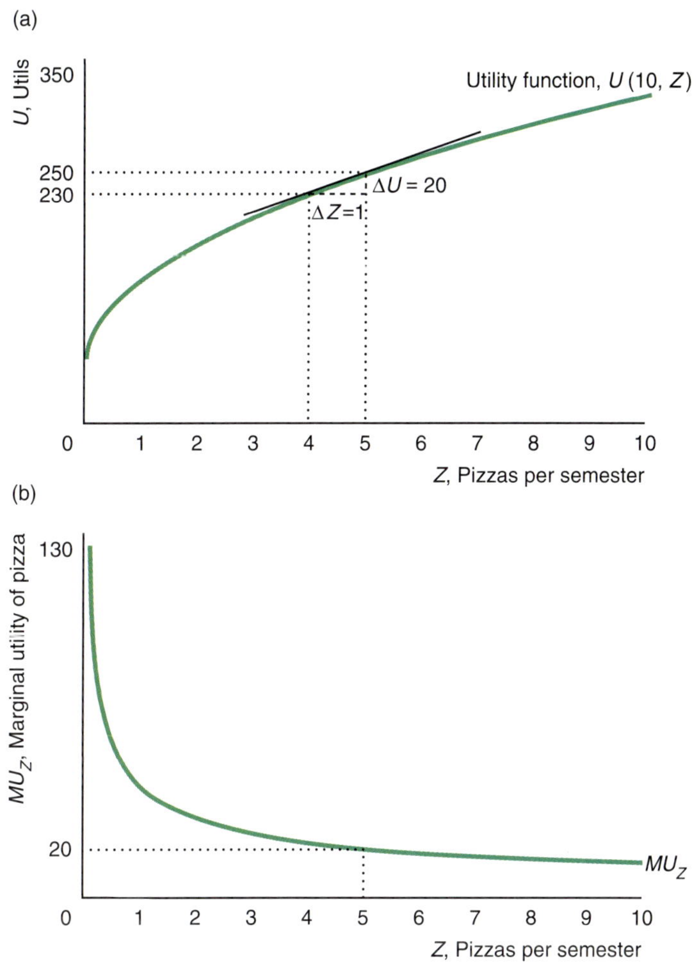

Figure 4.6 Utility and Marginal Utility. As Lisa consumes more pizza, holding her consumption of burritos constant at 10, her total utility, U, increases and her marginal utility of pizza, MU_Z, decreases (though it remains positive).

of marginal utilities. If Lisa has 10 burritos and 4 pizzas in a semester and gets one more pizza, her utility rises. That extra utility is the marginal utility from the last pizza, MU_Z. Similarly, if she received one extra burrito instead, her marginal utility from the last burrito is MU_B.

Suppose that Lisa trades from one bundle on an indifference curve to another by giving up some burritos to gain more pizza. She gains marginal utility from the extra pizza but loses marginal utility from fewer burritos. As Appendix 4A shows, the marginal rate of substitution can be written as

$$MRS = \frac{\Delta B}{\Delta Z} = -\frac{MU_Z}{MU_B}. \tag{4.1}$$

The *MRS* is the negative of the ratio of the marginal utility from another pizza to the marginal utility from another burrito.

4.3 BUDGET CONSTRAINT

You can't have everything. . . . Where would you put it? —Steven Wright

Knowing an individual's preferences is only the first step in analyzing that person's consumption behavior. Consumers maximize their well-being subject to constraints. The most important constraint most of us face in deciding what to consume is our personal budget constraint.

If we cannot save and borrow, our budget is the income we receive in a given period. If we can save and borrow, we can save money early in life to consume later, such as when we retire; or we can borrow money when we are young and repay these sums later in life. Savings is, in effect, a "good" that consumers can buy. For simplicity, we assume that each consumer has a fixed amount of money to spend now, so we can use the terms *budget* and *income* interchangeably.

For graphical simplicity, we assume that consumers spend their money on only two goods. If Lisa spends all her budget, Y, on pizza and burritos, then

$$p_B B + p_Z Z = Y, \tag{4.2}$$

where $p_B B$ is the amount she spends on burritos and $p_Z Z$ is the amount she spends on pizzas. Equation 4.2 is her budget constraint. It shows that her expenditures on burritos and pizza use up her entire budget.

How many burritos can Lisa buy? We can solve Equation 4.2 for the number of burritos Lisa can buy as a function of the prices, income, and pizza she buys. Subtracting $p_Z Z$ from both sides of Equation 4.2 and dividing both sides by p_B, we learn that

$$B = \frac{Y - p_Z Z}{p_B}. \tag{4.3}$$

According to Equation 4.3, she can buy more burritos with a higher income, a lower price of burritos or pizza, or the purchase of fewer pizzas.[8] For example, if she has one more dollar of income (Y), she can buy $1/p_B$ more burritos.

[8]By using calculus, we find that $dB/dY = 1/p_B > 0$, $dB/dZ = -p_Z/p_B < 0$, $dB/dp_Z = -Z/p_B < 0$, and $dB/dp_B = -(Y - p_Z Z)/(p_B)^2 = -B/p_B < 0$.

Table 4.1 Allocations of a \$50 Budget Between Burritos and Pizza

Bundle	Burritos	Pizza
a	25	0
b	20	10
c	10	30
d	0	50

If $p_Z = \$1$, $p_B = \$2$, and $Y = \$50$, Equation 4.2 is

$$B = \frac{\$50 - \$1 \times Z}{\$2} = 25 - \frac{1}{2}Z. \tag{4.4}$$

As the equation shows, every two pizzas cost Lisa one burrito. How many burritos can she buy if she spends all her money on burritos? By setting $Z = 0$ in Equation 4.3, we find that $B = Y/p_B = \$50/\$2 = 25$. Similarly, if she spends all her money on pizza, $B = 0$ and $Z = Y/p_Z = \$50/\$1 = 50$.

Instead of spending all her money on pizza or all on burritos, she can buy some of each. Table 4.1 shows four possible bundles she could buy. For example, she can buy 20 burritos and 10 pizzas with \$50.

Equation 4.4 is plotted in panel a of Figure 4.7. This line is called a **budget line** (or *budget constraint*): the bundles of goods that can be bought if the entire budget is spent on those goods at given prices. This budget line shows the combinations of burritos and pizzas that Lisa can buy if she spends all of her \$50 on these two goods. The four bundles in Table 4.1 are labeled on this line.

Lisa could, of course, buy any bundle that cost less than \$50. The **opportunity set** is all the bundles a consumer can buy, including all the bundles inside the budget constraint and on the budget constraint.[9] Lisa's opportunity set is the shaded area in the figure. She could buy 10 burritos and 15 pieces of pizza for \$35, which falls inside the constraint. Unless she wants to spend the other \$15 on something else, though, she may as well spend all of it on the food she loves and pick a bundle on the budget constraint rather than inside it.

Slope of the Budget Constraint

Every extra unit of Z that Lisa purchases reduces B by $-p_Z/p_B$, according to Equation 4.3, so the slope of the budget line is $\Delta B/\Delta Z = -p_Z/p_B$. The slope of the budget line is called the **marginal rate of transformation** (*MRT*): the trade-off the market imposes on the consumer in terms of the amount of one good the consumer must give up to obtain more of the other good. The marginal rate of transformation

[9]The opportunity set is all those bundles of positive Z and B such that $p_B B + p_Z Z \le Y$.

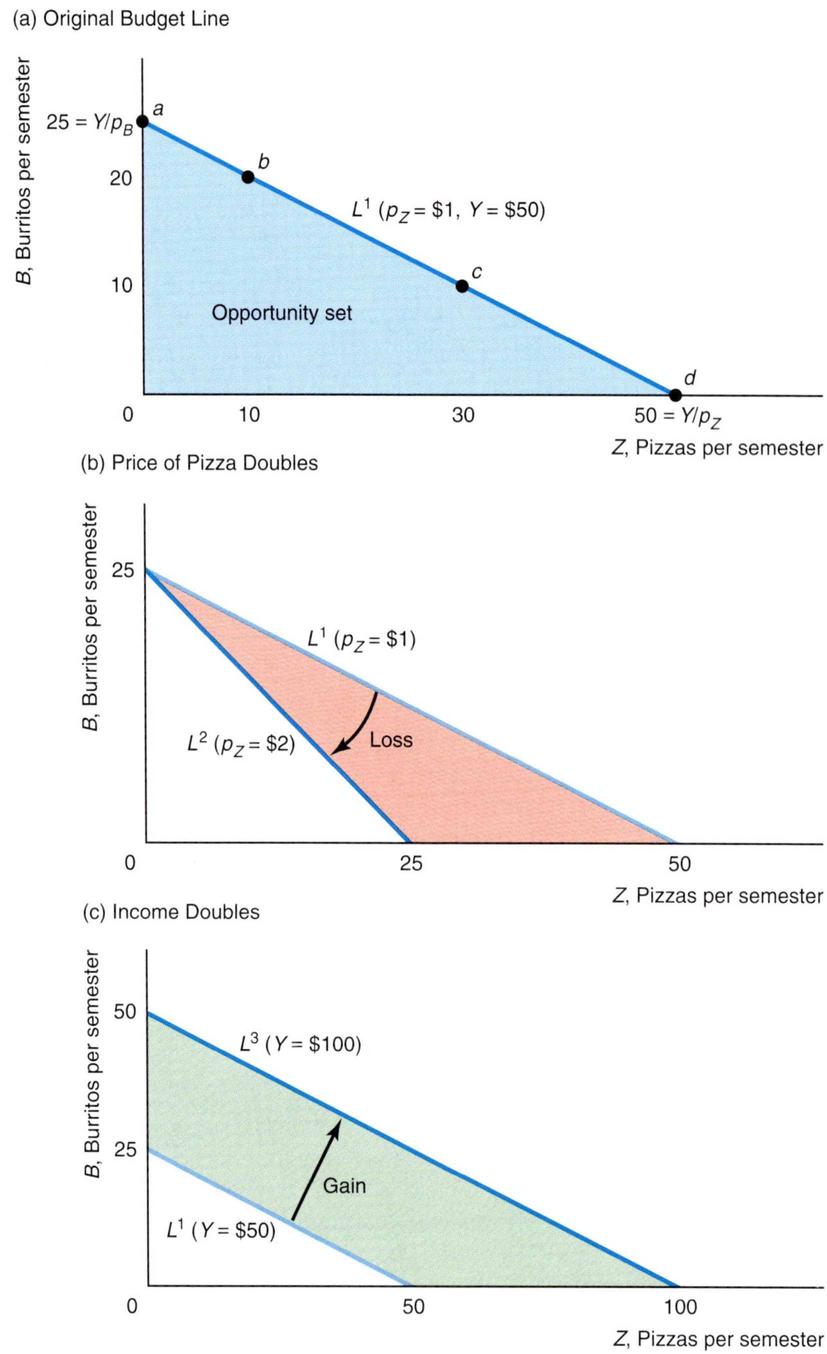
(a) Original Budget Line
B, Burritos per semester
25 = Y/p_B
20
10
a
b
c
d
L^1 (p_Z = $1, Y = $50)
Opportunity set
0
10
30
50 = Y/p_Z
Z, Pizzas per semester
(b) Price of Pizza Doubles
B, Burritos per semester
25
L^1 (p_Z = $1)
L^2 (p_Z = $2)
Loss
0
25
50
Z, Pizzas per semester
(c) Income Doubles
B, Burritos per semester
50
25
L^3 (Y = $100)
Gain
L^1 (Y = $50)
0
50
100
Z, Pizzas per semester

Figure 4.7 Budget Constraint. (a) If $Y = \$50$, $p_Z = \$1$, and $p_B = \$2$, Lisa can buy any bundle in the opportunity set, the shaded area, including points on the *budget line*, L^1, which has a slope of $-\frac{1}{2}$. (b) If the price of pizza increases from \$1 to \$2 a slice, her budget constraint rotates from L^1 to L^2 around the intercept on the burrito axis. The slope of the new budget line, L^2, is -1. The shaded area shows the combinations of pizza and burritos that she can no longer afford. (c) At the original prices, her new budget constraint moves from L^1 to L^2 if Lisa's income increases by \$50. This shift is parallel: Both budget lines have the same slope of $-\frac{1}{2}$. The new opportunity set is larger by the shaded area.

is the rate at which Lisa can trade burritos for pizza in the marketplace:

$$MRT = \frac{\Delta B}{\Delta Z} = -\frac{p_Z}{p_B}. \tag{4.5}$$

Because the price of pizza is half that of a burrito ($p_Z = \$1$ and $p_B = \$2$), the marginal rate of transformation facing Lisa is

$$MRT = -\frac{p_Z}{p_B} = \frac{\$1}{\$2} = -\frac{1}{2}.$$

An extra pizza costs her half an extra burrito—or, equivalently, an extra burrito costs her two pizzas.

Purchasing Fractional Quantities

The budget constraint in panel a in Figure 4.7 is a smooth, continuous line, and the opportunity set includes all the points inside that constraint. Implicitly, this drawing implies that Lisa can buy fractional numbers of burritos and pizzas. Is that true? Do you know of a restaurant that will sell you a quarter of a burrito? Probably not.

Why then don't we draw the opportunity set and the budget constraint as points (bundles) of whole numbers of burritos and pizzas? The reason is that Lisa can buy a burrito at a *rate* of one-half per time period. If Lisa buys one burrito every other week, she buys an average of one-half a burrito every week. Thus, it is plausible that she could purchase fractional amounts over time, and this diagram concerns her behavior over a semester.

Effect of a Change in Price on Consumption

If the price of pizza doubles but the price of burritos is unchanged, the budget constraint swings in toward the origin in panel b of Figure 4.7. If Lisa spends all her money on burritos, she can buy as many burritos as before, so the budget line still hits the burrito axis at 25. If she spends all her money on pizza, however, she can now buy only half as many pizzas as before, so the budget line intercepts the pizza axis at 25 instead of at 50.

The new budget constraint is steeper and lies inside the original one. As the price of pizza increases, the slope of the budget line, *MRT*, changes. On the original line, L^1, the $MRT = -\frac{1}{2}$. On the new line, L^2, the $MRT = p_Z/p_B = -\$2/\$2 = -1$. Lisa is unambiguously worse off (unless she wants to eat burritos only), because she no longer can afford the combinations of pizza and burritos in the shaded area.

A decrease in the price of pizza would have the opposite effect: The budget line would rotate outward around the intercept of the line and the burrito axis. As a result, the opportunity set would increase.

Effect of a Change in Income on Consumption

If the consumer's income increases, the consumer can buy more of all goods. Suppose Lisa's income increases by \$50 per semester to $Y = \$100$. Her budget constraint shifts outward—away from the origin—and is parallel to the original constraint in panel c. Why is the new constraint parallel to the original one? The intercept of the budget line on the burrito axis is Y/p_B, and the intercept on the pizza axis is Y/p_Z. Thus, holding prices constant, the intercepts shift outward in proportion to the change in income. Originally, if she spent all her money on pizza, Lisa could buy 50 = \$50/\$1 pizzas; now she can buy 100 = \$100/\$1. Similarly, the burrito axis intercept goes from 25 = \$50/\$2 to 50 = \$100/\$2.

A change in income affects only the position and not the slope of the budget line. The slope is determined by only the relative prices of pizza and burritos. If the prices of both pizza and burritos fall by half, Lisa can buy twice as much as previously with the same budget. The budget line shifts outward parallel by the same amount as if her income doubled. Thus, her opportunity set is identical if both prices drop by half *or* her budget doubles.

SOLVED PROBLEM 4.2

During World War II, the U.S. government rationed gasoline, setting a quota on how much a consumer could purchase. If a consumer could afford to buy 12 gallons a week but the government restricted purchases to no more than 10 gallons a week, what happened to the consumer's opportunity set?

Answer

1. *Draw the original opportunity set using a budget line between gasoline and all other goods*: In Figure 4.8, the consumer can afford to buy up to 12 gallons of gasoline a week if not constrained. The opportunity set, areas *A* and *B*, is bounded by the axes and the budget line.
2. *Add a line to the figure showing the quota, and determine the new opportunity set*: A vertical line at 10 on the gasoline axis indicates the quota.

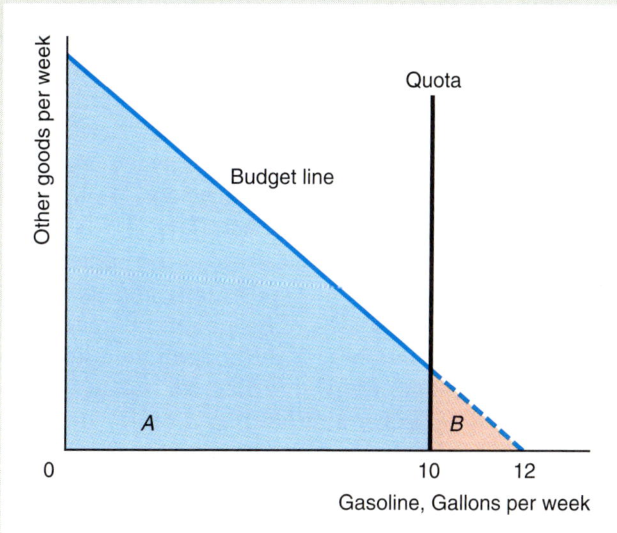

Figure 4.8 Effect of a Quota on the Opportunity Set. Without a quota, the consumer can buy up to 12 gallons of gasoline per week. The opportunity set is area $A + B$. With a quota of 10 gallons, the opportunity set is only area A: area B is lost.

The new opportunity set, area *A*, is bounded by the axes, the budget line, and the quota line.

3. *Compare the two opportunity sets*: Because of the rationing, the consumer loses part of the original opportunity set: the triangle *B* to the right of the 10 gallons line. The consumer has fewer opportunities because of rationing. ■

4.4 CONSUMER'S CONSTRAINED CHOICE

My problem lies in reconciling my gross habits with my net income. —Errol Flynn

Were it not for the budget constraint, consumers who prefer more to less would consume unlimited amounts of all goods. Well, they can't have it all! Instead, consumers maximize their well-being subject to their budget constraints. To complete our analysis of consumer behavior, we have to determine the bundle of goods that maximizes well-being subject to the budget constraint.

The Consumer's Optimum Bundle

To determine which of the points on the budget constraint gives Lisa the highest level of pleasure, we use her indifference curves in panel a of Figure 4.9.[10] We will show that her optimal bundle lies on an indifference curve that touches the budget constraint at only one point (*e* on I^2)—hence the indifference curve does not cross the constraint. We show this result by rejecting the possibility that the optimal bundle could be located off the budget constraint or that it lies on an indifference curve that intersects the budget constraint.

The optimal bundle must be on the budget constraint. Bundles that lie on indifference curves above the constraint, such as those on I^3, are not in the opportunity set. Thus, though Lisa prefers *f* on indifference curve I^3 to *e* on I^2, *f* is too expensive and she can't purchase it. Although Lisa could buy a bundle inside the budget constraint, she does not want to do so, because more is better than less: For any bundle inside the constraint (such as *d* on I^1), there is another bundle on the constraint with more of at least one of the two goods, and hence she prefers that bundle. Therefore, the optimal bundle must lie on the budget constraint.

Bundles that lie on indifference curves that cross the budget constraint (such as I^1, which crosses the constraint at *a* and *c*) are less desirable than certain other bundles on the constraint. Only some of the bundles on indifference curve I^1 lie within the opportunity set: Bundles *a* and *c* and all the points on I^1 between them, such as *d*, can be purchased. Because I^1 crosses the budget constraint, the bundles between *a* and *c* on I^1 lie strictly inside the constraint, so there are bundles in the opportunity set (area $A + B$) that are preferable to these bundles on I^1 and affordable. By the more-is-better property, Lisa prefers *e* to *d* because *e* has more of both pizza and burritos than *d*. By transitivity, *e* is preferred to *a*, *c*, and all the other points on I^1—even those, like *g*, that Lisa can't afford. Because indifference curve I^1 crosses the budget constraint, area *B* contains at least one bundle that is preferred to—lies above and to the right of—at least one bundle on the indifference curve.

Thus, the optimal bundle must lie on the budget constraint and be on an indifference curve that does not cross it. Such a bundle is the *consumer's equilibrium*. If Lisa is consuming this bundle, she has no incentive to change her behavior by substituting one good for another.

So far, we've shown that the optimal bundle must lie on an indifference curve that touches the budget constraint but does not cross it. There are two ways that outcome can be reached. The first is an *interior solution*, in which the optimal bundle has positive quantities of both goods: The optimal bundle is on the budget line other than at one end or the other. The other possibility is called a *corner solution*, where the optimal bundle is at one end or the other of the budget line: It is at a corner with one of the axes.

Interior Solution. In panel a of Figure 4.9, bundle *e* on indifference curve I^2 is the equilibrium bundle. It lies in the interior of the budget line away from the corners.

---

[10]Appendix 4B uses calculus to determine the bundle that maximizes utility subject to the budget constraint.

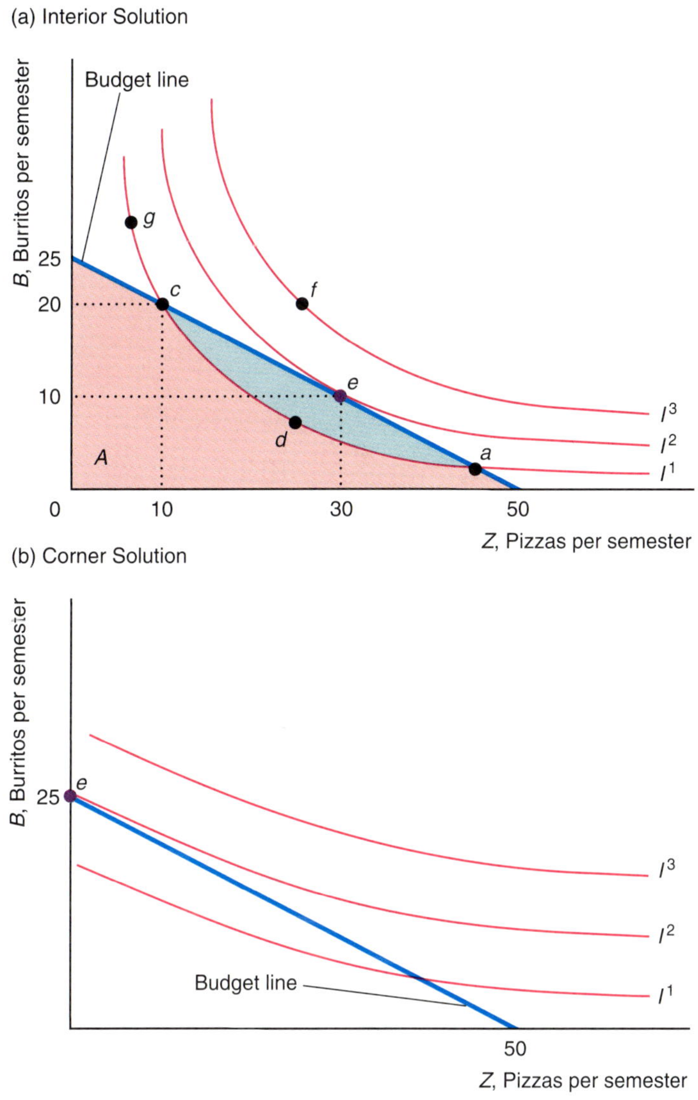

Figure 4.9 Consumer Maximization. (a) Interior solution: Lisa's optimal bundle is *e* (10 burritos and 30 slices of pizza) on indifference curve I^2. Any bundle that is preferred to *e* (such as points on indifference curve I^3) lies outside of the opportunity set—it can't be purchased. Bundles inside the opportunity set, such as *d*, are less desirable than *e*. (b) Corner solution: Spenser's indifference curves are relatively flat (he'll give up many pizzas for one more burrito), so his optimal bundle occurs at a corner of the opportunity set at Bundle *e*: 25 burritos and 0 pizzas.

Lisa prefers consuming a balanced diet, e, of 10 burritos and 30 pizzas, to eating only one type of food or the other.

For the indifference curve I^2 to touch the budget constraint but not cross it, it must be *tangent* to the budget constraint: The budget constraint and the indifference curve have the same slope at the point e where they touch. The slope of the indifference curve, the marginal rate of substitution, measures the rate at which Lisa is *willing* to trade burritos for pizza: $MRS = -MU_Z/MU_B$, Equation 4.1. The slope of the budget line, the marginal rate of transformation, measures the rate at which Lisa *can* trade her money for burritos or pizza in the market: $MRT = -p_Z/p_B$, Equation 4.5. Thus, Lisa's utility is maximized at the bundle where the rate at which she is willing to trade burritos for pizza equals the rate at which she can trade:

$$MRS = -\frac{MU_Z}{MU_B} = -\frac{p_Z}{p_B} = MRT.$$

By rearranging terms, this condition is equivalent to

$$\frac{MU_Z}{p_Z} = \frac{MU_B}{p_B}. \tag{4.6}$$

Equation 4.6 says that the marginal utility of pizza divided by the price of a pizza (the amount of extra utility from pizza per dollar spent on pizza), MU_Z/p_Z, equals the marginal utility of burritos divided by the price of a burrito, MU_B/p_B. Thus, Lisa's utility is maximized if the last dollar she spends on pizza gets her as much extra utility as the last dollar she spends on burritos. If the last dollar spent on pizza gave Lisa more extra utility than the last dollar spent on burritos, Lisa could increase her happiness by spending more on pizza and less on burritos.

Corner Solution. Spenser's indifference curves in panel b of Figure 4.9 are flatter than Lisa's. His optimal bundle lies on an indifference curve that touches the opportunity set only once, at the upper-left corner of the opportunity set, e, where he buys only burritos (25 burritos and 0 pizzas).

Bundle e is the optimal bundle because the indifference curve does not cross the constraint into the opportunity set. If it did, another bundle would give Spenser more pleasure.

Spenser's indifference curve is not tangent to his budget line. It would cross the budget line if both the indifference curve and the budget line were continued into the "negative pizza" region of the diagram, on the other side of the burrito axis.

SOLVED PROBLEM 4.3

Previously, gasoline was less expensive in the United States than in Canada, but now gasoline costs less in Canada than in the United States. How will the gasoline-purchasing behavior of a consumer who lives equally close to gas stations in both countries change?

Answer

1. *Describe the indifference curves of the consumer for Canadian and American gasoline*: Presumably, the consumer views American gasoline and Canadian gasoline as perfect substitutes, so the indifference curves are straight lines with a slope of –1 in Figure 4.10.

2. *Draw the initial budget line where prices are relatively low in the United States, and show the equilibrium*: For specificity, we assume that, initially, a gasoline budget of Y bought 15 gallons of gasoline in the United States but only 10 gallons in Canada: budget line L^1. The consumer picks the highest indifference curve, I^2, that touches this budget constraint. The equilibrium, e_1, is a corner solution: The consumer buys gasoline only in the United States. More generally, as long as the budget line is flatter than the indifference curve, the consumer buys only American gasoline. If we let p_a be the American price and p_c be the Canadian price, the slope of the budget line, $-p_a/p_c$, is greater (closer to zero) than the slope of the indifference curves, –1, because $p_a < p_c$.

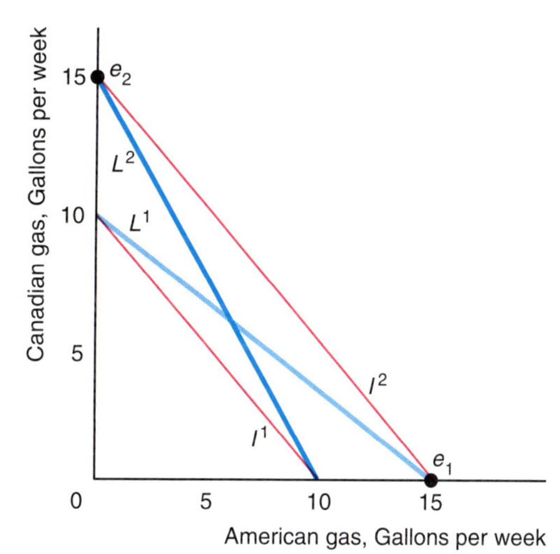

Figure 4.10 Effect of Price Change on Where to Buy Gasoline. A consumer views Canadian and American gasoline as identical. When prices are relatively low in the United States, budget line L^1, the consumer buys only in the United States, e_1. After a change in the relative prices, the consumer's budget line is L^2, so that consumer buys only Canadian gasoline, e_2.

3. *Draw the new budget line where prices are relatively low in Canada and show the new equilibrium*: After the price change, $-p_a/p_c < -1$, so the consumer buys only Canadian gasoline. In the figure, after the price change, Y buys 15 gallons in Canada and only 10 gallons in the United States: budget line L^1. As a result, the consumer buys only in Canada at e_2, where I^2 hits L^2. Thus, the consumer buys in whichever country the gasoline is cheapest: a corner solution. ■

APPLICATION

Substitution Effects in Canada

In 1991, the after-tax prices of most products were higher in Canada than in the United States.[11] As a result, many Canadians who lived near the border shopped in the United States for food, clothing, gasoline, electronics, appliances, and other goods. Particularly attractive for Canadian shoppers were items that had much higher sales taxes in Canada—such as gasoline, tobacco, and alcoholic beverages—that cost more than twice as much in Canada as in the United States. Many stores sprang up just over the border to accommodate Canadians on lightning-fast shopping trips.

A relative drop in the value of the Canadian dollar changed the behavior of many Canadians. A Canadian dollar, which was worth 90¢ in U.S. currency in late 1991, was worth only 78¢ in American currency by the end of 1992. As the price differential shrank between Canadian and American goods, Canadians increasingly bought from Canadian stores.

Most Canadians incur greater transportation costs by shopping in the United States rather than in Canada. (Buying many goods in one trip would help, but Ottawa enforced the rule that one can bring in only $20 duty free on a single-day trip to the United States.) The effective price that Canadians pay in the United States is the price of the good plus the extra transportation costs. The farther a Canadian lives from the border, the less likely that it pays to shop in the United States.

In November 1991, gasoline cost about 25¢ Canadian more per liter in Canada, whereas the difference was only about 16¢ Canadian a year later. As gasoline became less of a bargain in the United States, the number of Canadians who entered the United States by auto and returned to Canada the same day dropped by about 1 million, which was about a fifth of those who had formerly shopped in the United States. Overall, business in Bellingham, Washington (near the border), was down about 18–20% during the 1992 Christmas shopping season from the previous year. Canadian retailers benefitted substantially from this change. ■

[11]Farnsworth, C. H., "Canada's Shoppers Snubbing U.S.," *New York Times*, January 18, 1993:C1.

Optimal Bundles Are on Convex Sections of Indifference Curves

Earlier, we argued, on the basis of introspection, that most indifference curves are convex to the origin. Now that we know how to determine a consumer's optimal or equilibrium bundle, we can give a more compelling explanation about why we assume that indifference curves are convex. We can show that, if indifference curves are smooth, optimal bundles lie either on convex sections of indifference curves or at the point where the budget constraint hits an axis.

Suppose that indifference curves were strictly concave to the origin as in panel a of Figure 4.11. Indifference curve I^1 is tangent to the budget line at *d*, but that bundle is not optimal. Bundle *e* on the corner between the budget constraint and the burrito axis is on a higher indifference curve, I^2, than is *d*. Thus, if a consumer had strictly concave indifference curves, the consumer would buy only one good—here, burritos. Similarly, as we saw in Figure 4.10, consumers with straight-line indifference curves buy only the cheapest good. Because we do not see consumers buying only one good, indifference curves must have convex sections.

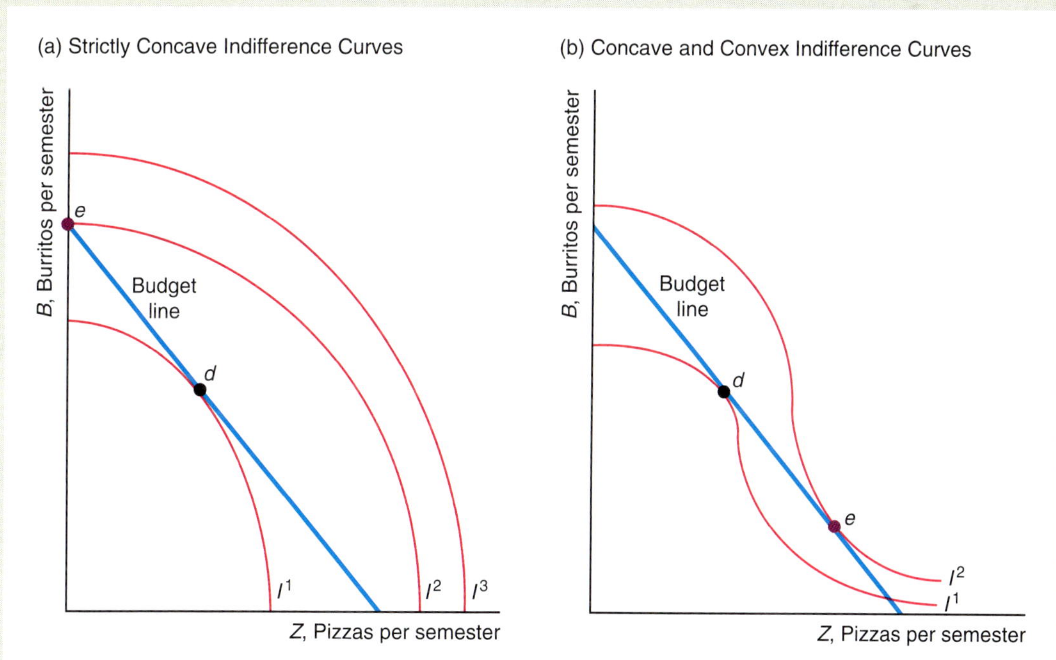

Figure 4.11 Optimal Bundles Are on Convex Sections of Indifference Curves. (a) Indifference curve I^1 is tangent to the budget line at Bundle *d*, but Bundle *e* is superior because it lies on a higher indifference curve, I^2. If indifference curves are strictly concave to the origin, the optimal bundle, *e*, is at a corner. (b) If indifference curves have both concave and convex sections, a bundle such as *d*, which is tangent to the budget line in the concave portion of indifference curve I^1, cannot be an optimum bundle because there must a preferable bundle in the convex portion of a higher indifference curve, *e* on I^2 (or at a corner).

If indifference curves have both concave and convex sections as in panel b of Figure 4.11, the optimal bundle lies in a convex section or at a corner. Bundle *d*, where a concave section of indifference curve I^1 is tangent to the budget line, cannot be an optimum bundle. Here, *e* is the optimal bundle and is tangent to the budget constraint in the convex portion of the higher indifference curve I^2. *If a consumer buys positive quantities of two goods, the indifference curve is convex and tangent to the budget line at that optimal bundle.*

Buy Where More Is Better

A key assumption in our analysis of consumer behavior is that more is preferred to less: Consumers are not satiated. We now show that, if both goods are consumed in positive quantities and their prices are positive, more of either good must be preferred to less. Suppose that the opposite were true and that Lisa prefers fewer burritos to more. Because burritos cost her money, she could increase her well-being by reducing the amount of burritos she consumes until she consumes no burritos—a scenario that violates our assumption that she consumes positive quantities of both goods.[12] Though it is possible that consumers prefer less to more at some large quantities, we do not observe consumers making purchases where that occurs.

In summary, we do not observe consumer equilibria at bundles where indifference curves are concave or consumers are satiated. Thus, we can safely assume that indifference curves are convex and that consumers prefer more to less in the ranges of goods that we actually observe.

SOLVED PROBLEM 4.4

Alexx doesn't care about where he lives, but he does care about what he eats. Alexx spends all his money on restaurant meals at either American or French restaurants. His firm offers to transfer him from its Miami office to its Paris office, where he will face different prices. The firm will pay him a salary in French francs such that he can buy the same bundle of goods in Paris that he is currently buying in Miami.[13] Will Alexx benefit by moving to Paris?

---

[12]Similarly, at her optimal bundle, Lisa cannot be *satiated*: indifferent between consuming more or fewer burritos. Suppose that her budget is obtained by working and that Lisa does not like working at the margin. Were it not for the goods she can buy with what she earns, she would not work as many hours as she does. Thus, if she were satiated and did not care if she consumed fewer burritos, she would reduce the number of hours she worked, thereby lowering her income, until her optimal bundle occurred at a point where more was preferred to less or she consumed none.

[13]In a survey of 649 firms, 77% of the Asian firms, 86% of the North American firms, and 69% of the European firms said that they provide their employees sent abroad equivalent purchasing power to maintain their home lifestyle (*1997–1998 Worldwide Survey of International Assignment Policies and Practices*, N.Y.: Organization Resources Counselors, Inc., 1997).

Answer

1. *Show Alexx's equilibrium in the United States*: Alexx's optimal bundle a in the United States is determined by the tangency of his indifference curve I^1 and his American budget constraint L^A in Figure 4.12.
2. *Discuss what happens if prices are higher in France but the relative prices between American and French meals are the same*: If the prices of both French and American meals are x times higher in France than in the United States, the relative cost of French and American meals are the same. If the firm raises Alexx's income x times, his budget line does not change. Thus, if relative prices are the same in Miami and Paris, his budget line and optimal bundle are unchanged, so his level of utility is unchanged.
3. *Show the new equilibrium if relative prices in France differ from those in the United States*: Alexx's firm adjusts his income so that Alexx can buy the same bundle, a, as in the United States, so his new budget line in France, L^F, must go through a. Suppose, as seems reasonable, that French meals are relatively less expensive than American meals in Paris. If Alexx

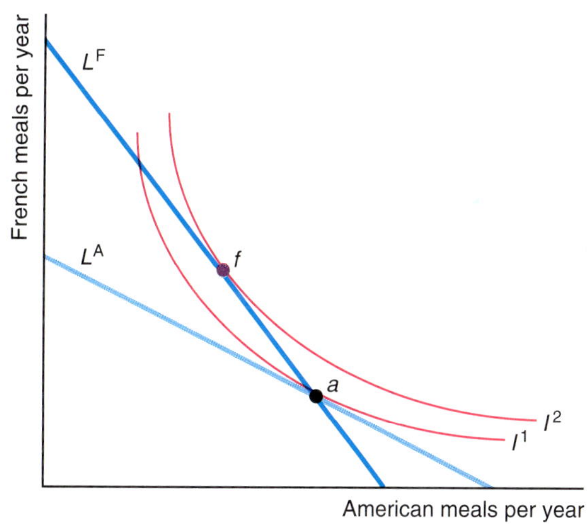

Figure 4.12 Substituting Toward Less Expensive Meals. Alexx's optimal bundle is a in the United States where his indifference curve I^1 is tangent to his budget constraint L^A. In France, where French meals are relatively inexpensive, he substitutes toward French meals and away from American meals. His new optimal bundle is f, where I^2 is tangent to L^F. Because I^2 is above I^1, he is better off in France.

spends all his money on French meals, he can buy more in Paris than in the United States; and if he spends all his money on American meals, he can buy fewer in Paris than in the United States. As a result, L^F hits the vertical axis at a higher point than the L^A line and cuts the L^A line at Bundle *a*. Alexx's new optimal bundle, *f*, is determined by the tangency of I^2 and L^F. Thus, if relative prices are different in Paris than in Miami, Alexx is better off with the transfer. He was on I^1 and is now on I^2. Alexx could buy his original bundle, *a*, but chooses to substitute toward French meals, which are relatively inexpensive in France, thereby raising his utility.[14] ■

Food Stamps

I've known what it is to be hungry, but I always went right to a restaurant.
—Ring Lardner

We can use the theory of consumer choice to analyze whether poor people are better off receiving food stamps or a comparable amount of cash. Currently, federal, state, and local governments work together to provide a food subsidy for poor Americans. Households that meet income, asset, and employment eligibility requirements receive coupons that can be used to purchase only food from retail stores. The Food Stamps Program is one of the nation's largest social welfare programs with expenditures of $26.3 billion for nearly 23 million people in 1997.[15]

Since the food stamp programs started in the early 1960s, economists, nutritionists, and policymakers have debated "cashing out" food stamps by providing checks or cash instead of coupons that can be spent only on food. Legally, food stamps may not be sold, though a black market does exist for food stamps. Because of technological advances in electronic fund transfers, switching from food stamps to a cash program should substantially lower administrative costs and reduce losses due to fraud and theft.

Would a switch to a comparable cash subsidy increase the well-being of food stamp recipients? Would the recipients spend less on food and more on other goods?

Cash Gives Greater Choice Than Food Stamps. Poor people who receive cash have more choices than do those who receive a comparable amount of food stamps. With food stamps, only extra food can be obtained. With cash, either food or other goods can be purchased. As a result, a cash grant raises a recipient's opportunity set by more than do food stamps of the same value, as we now show.

In Figure 4.13, the price of a unit of food and the price of all other goods are both $1 per unit with an appropriate choice of units. A person with a monthly income of

---

[14]If French meals were relatively more expensive than American meals in Paris, the L^F budget line would cut the L^A budget line from below rather than from above as shown. The analysis, however, would be essentially unchanged. Whether both prices, one price, or neither price is higher than in the United States is irrelevant to our analysis.

[15]http://www.usda.gov/fcs/stamps/fspfor~1.htm.

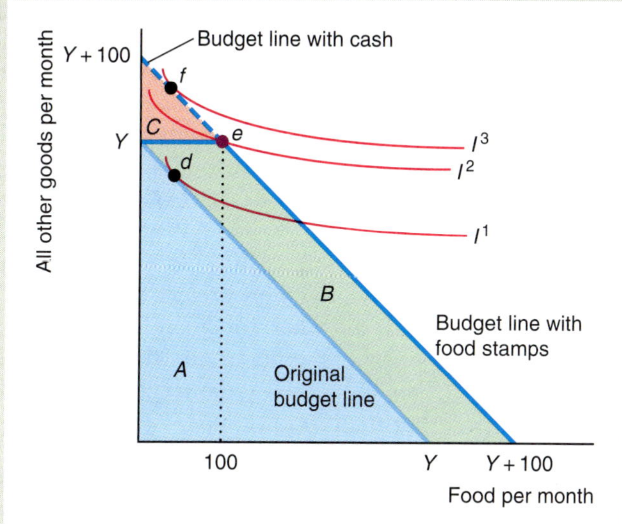

Figure 4.13 Food Stamps Versus Cash. The lighter line shows the original budget line of an individual with *Y* income per month. The heavier line shows the budget constraint with \$100 worth of food stamps. The budget constraint with a grant of \$100 in cash is a line between *Y* + 100 on both axes. The opportunity set increases by area *B* with food stamps but by *B* + *C* with cash. An individual with these indifference curves consumes Bundle *d* (with less than 100 units of food) with no subsidy, *e* (*Y* units of all other goods and 100 units of food) with food stamps, and *f* (more than *Y* units of all other goods and less than 100 units of food) with a cash subsidy. This individual's utility is greater with a cash subsidy than with food stamps.

Y has a budget line that hits both axes at *Y*: The person can buy *Y* units of food per month, *Y* units of all other goods, or any linear combination. The opportunity set is area *A*.

If that person receives a subsidy of \$100 in cash per month, the person's new monthly income is *Y* + \$100. The budget constraint with cash hits both axes at *Y* + 100 and is parallel to the original budget constraint. The opportunity set increases by *B* + *C* to *A* + *B* + *C*.

If the person receives \$100 worth of food stamps, the food stamps budget constraint has a kink. Because the food stamps can be spent only on food, the budget constraint shifts 100 units to the right for any quantity of other goods up to *Y* units. For example, if the recipient buys only food, now *Y* + 100 units of food can be purchased. If the recipient buys only other goods with the original *Y* income, that person can get *Y* units of other goods plus 100 units of food. However, the food stamps cannot be turned into other goods, so the recipient can't buy $Y + 100$ units of other goods, as can be done under the cash transfer program. The food stamps opportunity set is areas $A + B$, which is larger than the presubsidy opportunity set by B. The opportunity set with food stamps is smaller than that with the cash transfer program by C.

A recipient benefits as much from cash or an equivalent amount of food stamps if the recipient would have spent at least $100 on food if given cash. In other words, the individual is indifferent between cash and food stamps if that person's indifference curve is tangent to the downward-sloping section of the food stamps budget constraint.

On the other hand, if the recipient would not spend at least $100 on food if given cash, the recipient prefers receiving cash to food stamps. Figure 4.13 shows the indifference curves of an individual who prefers cash to food stamps. This person chooses Bundle *e* (Y units of all other goods and 100 units of food) if given food stamps but Bundle *f* (more than Y units of all other goods and less than 100 units of food) if given cash. This individual is on a higher indifference curve, I^2 rather than I^1, if given cash rather than food stamps.

APPLICATION

Food Stamp Experiments

There are four effects of giving recipients cash instead of food stamps: (1) Some individuals consume less food and more of other goods, (2) some individuals consume fewer nutrients, (3) the administrative costs of these welfare programs fall, and (4) each recipient's utility stays the same or rises.

According to Fraker's (1990) review of many statistical analyses, an additional dollar of income causes an average low-income household to increase its food expenditures by 5–10¢, and an additional dollar of food stamps leads to a 20–45¢ increase in food expenditures. Five experiments (Moffitt 1989; Fasciano, Hall, and Beebout 1993; Carlson 1993) show that responses to cashing out vary by area and demographic group. In Puerto Rico, giving cash instead of stamps had no detectable influence on food expenditures; however, black market trafficking in food stamps was apparently widespread. In three out of four studies in the United States, researchers found that giving cash reduces household food expenditures, but the magnitude of the effect varies widely, from zero to 17%.

Three studies of the nutrition effects of substituting cash for food stamps found no effect in Alabama, a 5% drop in San Diego, and a 6–11% decline in nutrients in Washington State. Even in Washington, however, cash recipients consumed far in excess of the recommended daily allowance of most nutrients.

A 1980 experiment involving elderly recipients in nine sites around the United States and a 1982 experiment in Puerto Rico show that the administrative costs and losses due to fraud and theft could be substantially reduced by switching to cash. Administrative costs fell from $2.05 to $1.03 per case per month in Alabama when checks were used in the pure study. The government replaces lost or stolen checks but not clients' coupons that are lost or stolen, an additional benefit to recipients under the cash program.

If recipients spend less on food under the cash program, presumably they achieve higher utility from that program. Recipients report preferring cash. Of recipients in San Diego and Alabama's pure experiments, 4 out of 10 mentioned the greater choice of goods with cash. Other reported advantages of the cash program were more choice of stores and fewer feelings of embarrassment. Indeed, it is possible that the stigma of using food stamps may discourage participation in food stamp programs. ■

Why We Give Food Stamps. Two groups in particular object to giving cash instead of food stamps: some policymakers, because they fear that cash might be spent on booze or drugs, and some nutritionists, who worry that poor people will spend the money on housing or other goods and get too little nutrition.

In response, many economists argue that poor people are the best judges of how to spend their scarce resources. The question of whether it is desirable to let poor people choose what to consume is normative (a question of values), and economic theory cannot answer it. How poor people will change their behavior, however, is a positive (scientific) question, which we can analyze. Experiments to date find that cash recipients consume slightly lower levels of food but receive at least adequate levels of nutrients and that they prefer receiving cash.

Given that recipients are as well off or better off receiving cash than food stamps, why do we have food stamps programs instead of providing cash? The introduction to Fasciano, Hall, and Beebout (1993, p. 6)—a report by the U.S. Department of Agriculture's Food and Nutrition Service, which administers the food stamp program—offers this explanation:

> From the perspective of recipient households, cash is more efficient than coupons in that it permits each household to allocate its resources as it sees fit. . . . But in a more general sense, recipients' welfare clearly depends on public support for the program. And what evidence we have suggests that taxpayers are more comfortable providing in-kind, rather than cash, benefits and may consequently be more generous in their support of a coupon-based program. The question of which benefit form best promotes the welfare of financially needy households is thus more complex than it might appear.

Summary

Consumers maximize their utility (well-being) subject to constraints based on their income and the prices of goods.

1. **Preferences:** To predict consumers' responses to changes in these constraints, economists use a theory about individuals' preferences. One way of summarizing consumers' preferences is with a family of indifference curves. An indifference curve consists of all those bundles of goods that give the consumer a particular level of utility. On the basis of observations of consumers' behavior, economists assume that consumers' preferences have three properties: completeness, transitivity, and more is better. Given these three assumptions,

indifference curves have the following properties:

- Consumers get more pleasure from bundles on indifference curves the farther from the origin the curves are.
- Indifference curves cannot cross.
- There is an indifference curve through any given bundle.
- Indifference curves have no thickness.
- Indifference curves slope downward.
- Consumers are observed purchasing positive quantities of goods only where their indifference curves are convex to the origin.

2. **Utility:** Economists call the relative rankings of bundles of goods *utility*. Utility is an ordinal measure: By comparing the utility a consumer gets from each of two bundles, we know that the consumer prefers the bundle with the higher utility, but we can't tell by how much the consumer prefers that bundle. The marginal utility from a good is the extra utility a person gets from consuming one more unit of that good, holding the consumption of all other goods constant. The rate at which a consumer is willing to substitute Good 1 for Good 2, the marginal rate of substitution, *MRS*, depends on the relative amounts of marginal utility the consumer gets from each of the two goods.

3. **Budget constraint:** The amount of goods consumers can buy at given prices is limited by their income. As a result, the greater their income and the lower the prices of goods, the better off they are. The rate at which they can exchange Good 1 for Good 2 in the market, the marginal rate of transformation, *MRT*, depends on the relative prices of the two goods.

4. **Consumer's constrained choice:** Each person picks an affordable bundle of goods to consume so as to maximize his or her pleasure. If an individual consumes both Good 1 and Good 2 (an interior solution), the individual's utility is maximized when the following four equivalent conditions hold:
   - The indifference curve between the two goods is tangent to the budget constraint.
   - The consumer buys the bundle of goods that is on the highest obtainable indifference curve.
   - The consumer's marginal rate of substitution (the slope of the indifference curve) equals the marginal rate of transformation (the slope of the budget line).
   - The last dollar spent on Good 1 gives the consumer as much extra utility as the last dollar spent on Good 2.

   However, consumers do not buy some of all possible goods (corner solutions). The last dollar spent on a good that is actually purchased gives more extra utility than would a dollar's worth of a good the consumer chose not to buy.

Problems

1. Lori loves ice cream but dislikes lima beans (to her, lima beans are a *bad*). Draw Lori's indifference curves between ice cream and lima beans. Does your answer depend on whether there's free disposal? That is, can she throw the beans away, or must she eat them if she has them? Do her indifference curves slope up? If so, how do you reconcile that slope with the more-is-better assumption?

2. Give as many reasons as you can why we believe that indifference curves are convex.

3. Mary has *lexicographic* preferences: She prefers one good absolutely over another (as in a dictionary, in which words that start with *a* always come before those that start with *b*). Mary strictly prefers bagels to muffins. She is unwilling to give up any amount of bagels for some muffins. However, she is willing to eat muffins if bagels are not available. Can you draw her indifference curves?

4. What happens to a consumer's equilibrium if all prices and income double? (*Hint:* What happens to the intercepts of the budget line?)

5. Draw indifference curves with a good on one axis and a *neutral* product—one that the consumer is indifferent about whether or not to consume—on the other axis.

6. Show the optimal bundle if an individual has straight-line indifference curves with a different slope than the budget line. What happens if the straight-line indifference curves have exactly the same slope as the budget line?

7. In Spenser's state, a sales tax of 10% is applied to clothing but not to food. Show the effect of this tax on Spenser's choice between food and clothing using indifference curves.
8. What happens to the budget line if the government applies a specific tax of $1 per gallon on gasoline but does not tax other goods? What happens to the budget line if the tax applies only to purchases of gasoline in excess of 10 gallons per week?
9. What is the effect of a 50% income tax on a consumer's budget line and opportunity set?
10. A poor person who has an income of $1,000 receives $100 worth of food stamps. Draw the budget constraint if the food stamp recipient can sell these coupons on the black market for less than their face value.
11. Is a poor person more likely to benefit from $100 a month worth of food stamps (that can be used only to buy food) or $100 a month worth of clothing stamps (that can be used only to buy clothing)? Why?
12. Since 1979, recipients have been given food stamps. Before 1979, however, people bought food stamps at a subsidized rate. For example, to get $1 worth of food stamps, a household paid about 15¢ (the exact amount varied by household characteristics and other factors). What is the budget constraint facing an individual if that individual may buy up to $100 per month in food stamps at 15¢ per each $1 coupon?
13. Show how much an individual's opportunity set increases if the government gives food stamps rather than sells them at subsidized rates.

Math Problems

14. A consumer's utility function is $U = 10X^2Y$. The price of X is $p_X = \$10$, the price of Y is $p_Y = \$5$, and his income is $Y = \$150$. What is his optimal consumption bundle? Show in a graph.
15. Suppose a consumer has a utility function $U(B, Z) = AB^{\alpha}Z^{\beta}$, where A, α, and β are constants, B is burritos, and Z is pizzas. If the price of burritos, p_B, is $2 and the price of pizzas, p_Z, is $1, what is the consumer's optimal bundle?
16. If a consumer's utility function is $U(B, Z) = B + AB^{\alpha}Z^{\beta} + Z$, what is that individual's marginal utility of Z? What is the individual's marginal rate of substitution between these two goods?
17. ★ A consumer requires a minimum level of consumption, a *threshold*, to derive additional utility: $U(X, Y)$ is 0 if $X + Y \le 5$ and is $X + Y$ otherwise. Draw the indifference curves for this consumer. Which of our usual assumptions are violated by this example?

CHAPTER 5

Applying Consumer Theory

Median annual income Americans believe they would need to fulfill their "dreams": $102,000. —*Harper's Index*, 1995

We used consumer theory in Chapter 4 to show how a consumer chooses a bundle of goods, subject to a budget constraint, so as to maximize happiness. Here we apply consumer theory to derive demand curves and examine their properties.

We start by using consumer theory to show how to determine the shape of a demand curve for a good by varying the price of a good, holding other prices and income constant. Firms use information about the shape of demand curves when setting prices. Governments apply this information in predicting the impact of policies such as taxes and price controls.

We then use consumer theory to show how an increase in income causes the demand curve to shift. Firms use information about the relationship between income and demand to predict which less-developed countries will substantially increase their demand for the firms' products.

Next, we show that an increase in the price of a good has two effects on demand. First, consumers would buy less of the now relatively more expensive good even if they were compensated with cash for the price increase. Second, consumers' incomes can't buy as much as before because of the higher price, so consumers buy less of at least some goods.

We use this analysis of these two demand effects of a price increase to show why the government's measure of inflation, the Consumer Price Index (CPI), overestimates the amount of inflation. Because of this bias in the CPI, some people gain and some lose from contracts that adjust payment on the basis of the government's inflation index. You may have signed a long-term lease for an apartment in which your rent payments increase over time in proportion to the change in the CPI. If so, you lose and your landlord gains from this bias.

Finally, we show how we can use our consumer theory of demand to determine an individual's labor *supply* curve. Knowing the shape of workers' labor supply curves is important in analyzing the effect of income tax rates on work and on tax collections. When he first ran for President, Ronald Reagan argued that if the income tax rates were cut, workers would work so many more hours that tax revenues would increase. If he was right, everyone could be made better off by a tax cut. If he was wrong, the deficit could grow to record levels. Before Congress adopted his tax cut, economists used empirical studies based on consumer theory to predict the effect of the tax rate cut on tax collections, as we discuss at the end of this chapter.

In this chapter, we examine five main topics:

1. **Deriving demand curves:** We use consumer theory to derive demand curves, showing how a change in price causes a shift along a demand curve.
2. **How income changes shift demand curves:** We use consumer theory to determine how a demand curve shifts because of a change in income.
3. **Effects of a price change:** A change in price has two effects on demand, one having to do with a change in relative prices and the other concerning a change in the consumer's opportunities.
4. **Cost-of-living adjustments:** Using this analysis of the two effects of price changes, we show that the CPI overestimates the rate of inflation.
5. **Deriving labor supply curves:** Using consumer theory to derive the demand curve for leisure, we can derive workers' labor supply curves and use them to determine how a reduction in the income tax rate affects labor supply and tax revenues.

5.1 DERIVING DEMAND CURVES

We use consumer theory to show by how much the quantity demanded of a good falls as its price rises. An individual chooses an optimal or equilibrium bundle of goods by picking the point on the highest indifference curve that touches the budget line (Chapter 4). When a price changes, the budget constraint facing the consumer shifts, so the consumer chooses a new optimal bundle. By varying one price, holding other prices and income constant, we determine how the quantity demanded changes as the price changes, which is the information we need to draw the demand curve. After deriving an individual's demand curve, we show the relationship between consumer tastes and the shape of the demand curve, which is summarized by the elasticity of demand (Chapter 3).

We derive a demand curve using the information about tastes from indifference curves.[1] To illustrate how to construct a demand curve, we estimated a set of indifference curves between wine and beer, using data for American consumers. Panel a of Figure 5.1 shows three of the estimated indifference curves for a typical U.S. consumer, whom we call Mimi.[2] These indifference curves are convex to the origin: Mimi views beer and wine as imperfect substitutes (Chapter 4). We can construct Mimi's demand curve for beer by holding her budget, her tastes, and the price of wine constant at their initial levels and varying the price of beer.

The vertical axis in panel a measures the number of gallons of wine Mimi consumes each year, and the horizontal axis measures the number of gallons of beer she drinks per year. Mimi spends $Y = \$419$ per year on beer and wine. The price of beer, p_b, is \$12 per unit, and the price of wine, p_w, is \$35 per unit.[3] The slope of her budget line, L^1, is $-p_b/p_w = -12/35 \approx -\frac{1}{3}$. At those prices, Mimi consumes bundle e_1, 26.7

[1]Appendix 4B uses math to derive the demand curves of a consumer who has a Cobb-Douglas utility function.

[2]My mother, Mimi, wanted the most degenerate character in the book named after her. She and I both hope that you do not consume as much beer or wine as the typical American in this example.

[3]To ensure that the prices are whole numbers, we state the prices using an unusual unit of measure (not gallons).

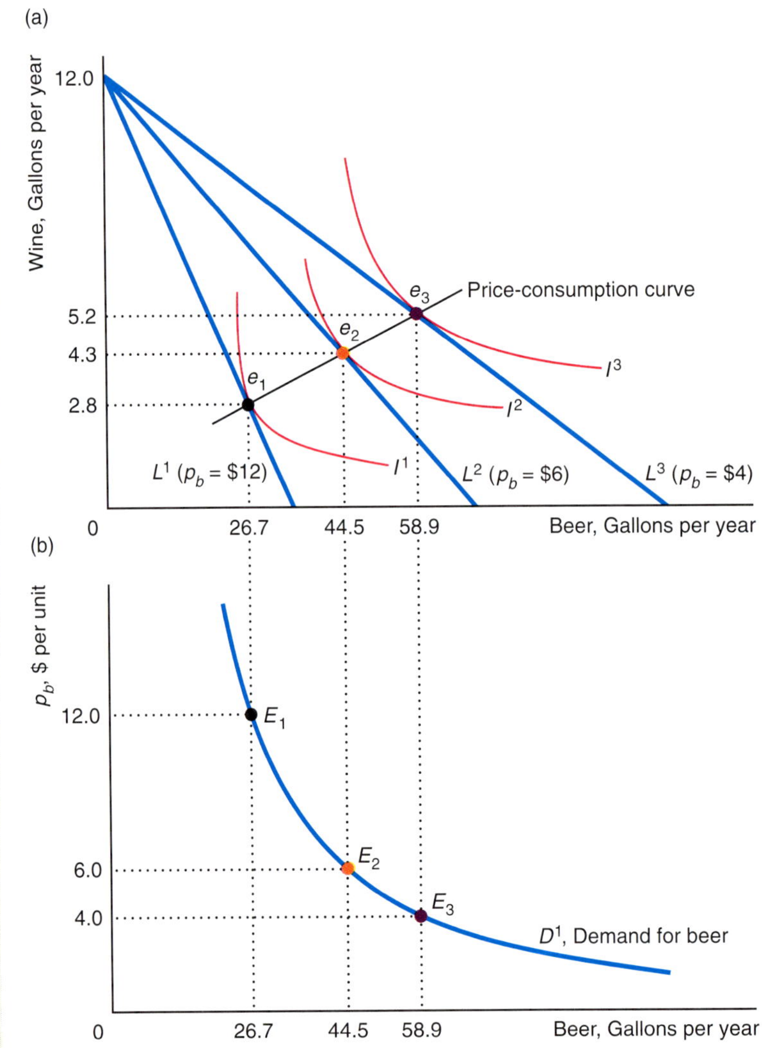

Figure 5.1 Deriving an Individual's Demand Curve. If the price of beer falls, holding the price of wine, the budget, and tastes constant, the typical American consumer buys more beer, according to my estimates. (a) At the actual budget line, L^1, where the price of beer is $12 per unit and the price of wine is $35 per unit, the average consumer's indifference curve I^1 is tangent at Bundle e_1, 26.7 gallons of beer per year and 2.8 gallons of wine per year. If the price of beer falls to $6 per unit, the new budget constraint is L^2, and the average consumer buys 44.5 gallons of beer per year and 4.3 gallons of wine per year. (b) By varying the price of beer, we trace out the individual's demand curve, D_1. The beer price-quantity combinations E_1, E_2, and E_3 on the demand curve for beer in panel b correspond to optimal Bundles e_1, e_2, and e_3 in panel a.

gallons of beer per year and 2.8 gallons of wine per year, a combination that is determined by the tangency of indifference curve I^1 and budget line L^1.[4]

If the price of beer falls in half to $6 per unit, while the price of wine and her budget remain constant, Mimi's budget line rotates outward to L^2. If she were to spend all her money on wine, she could buy the same 12 (≈ 419/35) gallons of wine per year as before, so the intercept on the vertical axis of L^2 is the same as for L^1. However, if she were to spend all her money on beer, she could buy twice as much, 70 gallons instead of 35 gallons of beer, as before, so L^2 hits the horizontal axis twice as far from the origin as L^1. As a result, L^2 has a flatter slope, about $-\frac{1}{6}$ (≈ −6/35), than L^1. The slope is flatter because the price of beer has fallen relative to the price of wine.

Because beer is now relatively less expensive, Mimi drinks relatively more beer. She chooses bundle e_2, 44.5 gallons of beer per year and 4.3 gallons of wine per year, where her indifference curve I^2 is tangent to L^2. If the price of beer falls again, say to $4 per unit, Mimi consumes bundle e_3, 58.9 gallons of beer per year and 5.2 gallons of wine per year.[5] The lower the price of beer, the happier Mimi is because she can consume more on the same budget: She is on a higher indifference curve (or perhaps just plain higher).

Panel a also shows the *price-consumption curve*, which is the line through the equilibrium bundles, such as e_1, e_2, and e_3, that Mimi would consume at each price of beer, when the price of wine and Mimi's budget are held constant. Because the price-consumption curve is upward sloping, we know that Mimi's consumption of both beer and wine increases as the price of beer falls.

We can use the same information in the price-consumption curve to draw Mimi's demand curve for beer, D^1, in panel b. Corresponding to each possible price of beer on the vertical axis of panel b, we record on the horizontal axis the quantity of beer demanded by Mimi from the price-consumption curve.

Points E_1, E_2, and E_3 on the demand curve in panel b correspond to bundles e_1, e_2, and e_3 on the price-consumption curve in panel a. Both e_1 and E_1 show that, when the price of beer is $12, Mimi demands 26.7 gallons of beer per year. When the price falls to $6 per unit, Mimi increases her consumption of beer to 44.5 gallons of beer, point E_2. The demand curve, D^1, is downward sloping as predicted by the Law of Demand.

We can use the relationship between the points in panels a and b to show that Mimi's utility is lower at point E_1 on D^1 than at point E_2. Point E_1 corresponds to

---

[4]These figures reflect the average annual per capita consumption of wine and beer. These numbers seem ridiculously high, given how many teetotalers are included in the average, but they've been checked in several sources. Apparently, some heavy drinkers are really skewing the average. The residents of greater Los Angeles drink enough beer, wine, and liquor annually to float 22 aircraft carriers (L. M. Boyd, "The Grab Bag," *San Francisco Examiner*, November 7, 1993:World 5). The French consume 45% more and the British 20% less alcohol per person than Americans. Czechs consume 45 gallons per person (*U.S. News & World Report*, December 22, 1997:16).

[5]These quantity numbers are probably higher than they would be in reality because we are assuming that Mimi continues to spend the same total amount of money on beer and wine as the price of beer drops.

bundle e_1 on indifference curve I^1, whereas E_2 corresponds to bundle e_2 on indifference curve I^2, which is farther from the origin than I^1, so Mimi's utility is higher at E_2 than at E_1. Mimi is better off at E_2 than at E_1 because the price of beer is lower at E_2, so she can buy more goods with the same budget.

5.2 HOW INCOME CHANGES SHIFT DEMAND CURVES

To trace out the demand curve, we looked at how an increase in the good's price—holding income, tastes, and other prices constant—causes a downward *movement along* the demand curve. Now we examine how an increase in income, when all prices are held constant, causes a *shift of* the demand curve.

Businesses routinely use information on the relationship between income and the quantity demanded. For example, in deciding where to market its products, Whirlpool wants to know which countries are likely to spend a relatively large percentage of any extra income on refrigerators and washing machines.

A Rise in Income Shifts the Demand Curve

We illustrate the relationship between the quantity demanded and income by examining how Mimi's behavior changes when her income rises, while the prices of beer and wine remain constant. Figure 5.2 shows three ways of looking at the relationship between income and the quantity demanded. All three diagrams have the same horizontal axis: the quantity of beer consumed per year. In the consumer theory diagram, panel a, the vertical axis is the quantity of wine consumed per year. In the demand curve diagram, panel b, the vertical axis is the price of beer per unit. Finally, in panel c, which shows the relationship between income and quantity directly, the vertical axis is Mimi's budget, Y.

A rise in Mimi's income causes the budget constraint to shift outward in panel a, which increases Mimi's opportunities. Her budget constraint L^1 at her original income $Y = \$419$, is tangent to her indifference curve I^1 at e_1.

As before, Mimi's demand curve for beer is D^1 in panel b. Point E_1 on D^1, which corresponds to point e_1 in panel a, shows how much beer, 26.7 gallons per year, Mimi consumes when the price of beer is \$12 per unit (and the price of wine is \$35 per unit).

Now suppose that Mimi's beer and wine budget, Y, increases by roughly 50% to \$628 per year. Her new budget line, L^2 in panel a, is farther from the origin but

Figure 5.2 Effect of a Budget Increase on an Individual's Demand Curve. As the annual budget for wine and beer, Y, increases from \$419 to \$628 and then to \$837, holding prices constant, the typical consumer buys more of both products, as shown by the upward slope of the income-consumption curve (a). That the typical consumer buys more beer as income increases is shown by the outward shift of the demand curve for beer (b) and the upward slope of the Engel curve for beer (c).

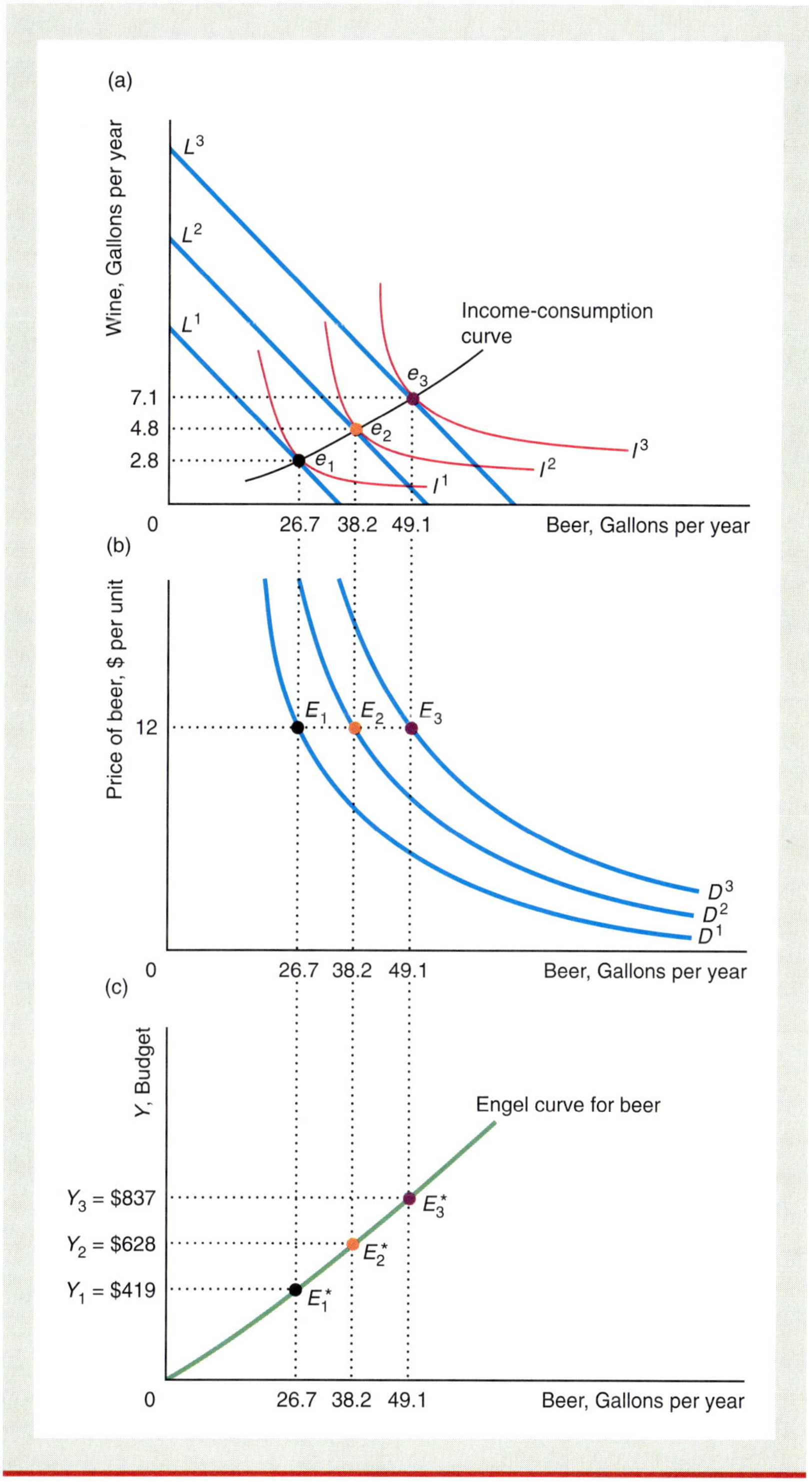
(a)
Wine, Gallons per year
L^3
L^2
L^1
Income-consumption curve
e_3
e_2
e_1
7.1
4.8
2.8
I^3
I^2
I^1
0
26.7 38.2 49.1
Beer, Gallons per year
(b)
Price of beer, $ per unit
12
E_1 E_2 E_3
D^3
D^2
D^1
0
26.7 38.2 49.1
Beer, Gallons per year
(c)
Y, Budget
Engel curve for beer
Y_3 = $837
Y_2 = $628
Y_1 = $419
E_3^*
E_2^*
E_1^*
0
26.7 38.2 49.1
Beer, Gallons per year

parallel to her original budget constraint, L^1, because the prices of beer and wine are unchanged. Given this larger budget, Mimi chooses bundle e_2. The increase in her income causes her demand curve to shift to D^2, in panel b. Holding Y at \$628, we can derive D^2 by varying the price of beer, in the same way as we derived D^1 in Figure 5.1. When the price of beer is \$12 per unit, she buys 38.2 gallons of beer per year, E_2 on D^2. Similarly, if Mimi's income increases to \$837 per year, her demand curve shifts to D^3.

The *income-consumption curve* through bundles e_1, e_2, and e_3 in panel a shows how Mimi's consumption of beer and wine increases as her income rises. As Mimi's income goes up, her consumption of both wine and beer increases.

We can show the relationship between the quantity demanded and income directly rather than by shifting demand curves to illustrate the effect. In panel c, we plot an **Engel curve**: the relationship between the quantity demanded of a single good and income, holding prices constant. Income is on the vertical axis, and the quantity of beer demanded is on the horizontal axis. On Mimi's Engel curve for beer, points E_1^*, E_2^*, and E_3^* correspond to points E_1, E_2, and E_3 in panel b and to e_1, e_2, and e_3 in panel a.

SOLVED PROBLEM 5.1

Mahdu views Cragmont and Canada Dry ginger ales as perfect substitutes: He is indifferent as to which one he drinks. The price of a 12-ounce can of Cragmont, p, is less than the price of a 12-ounce can of Canada Dry, p^*. What does Mahdu's Engel curve for Cragmont ginger ale look like? How much does his weekly ginger ale budget have to rise for Mahdu to buy one more can of Cragmont ginger ale per week?

Answer

1. *Use indifference curves to derive Mahdu's equilibrium choice*: Because Mahdu views the two brands as perfect substitutes, his indifference curves, such as I^1 and I^2 in panel a of Figure 5.3, are straight lines with a slope of −1 (Chapter 4). When his income is Y_1, his budget line hits the Canada Dry axis at Y_1/p^* and his Cragmont axis at Y_1/p. Mahdu maximizes his utility by consuming Y_1/p cans of the less expensive Cragmont ginger ale and no Canada Dry (corner solution). As his income rises, say to Y_2, his budget line shifts outward and is parallel to the original one, with the same slope of $-p/p^*$. Thus, at each income level, his budget lines are flatter than his indifference curves, so his equilibria lie along the Cragmont axis.

2. *Use the first figure to derive his Engel curve*: Because his entire budget, Y, goes to buying Cragmont, Mahdu buys $q = Y/p$ cans of Cragmont ginger ale. This expression, which shows the relationship between his income and the

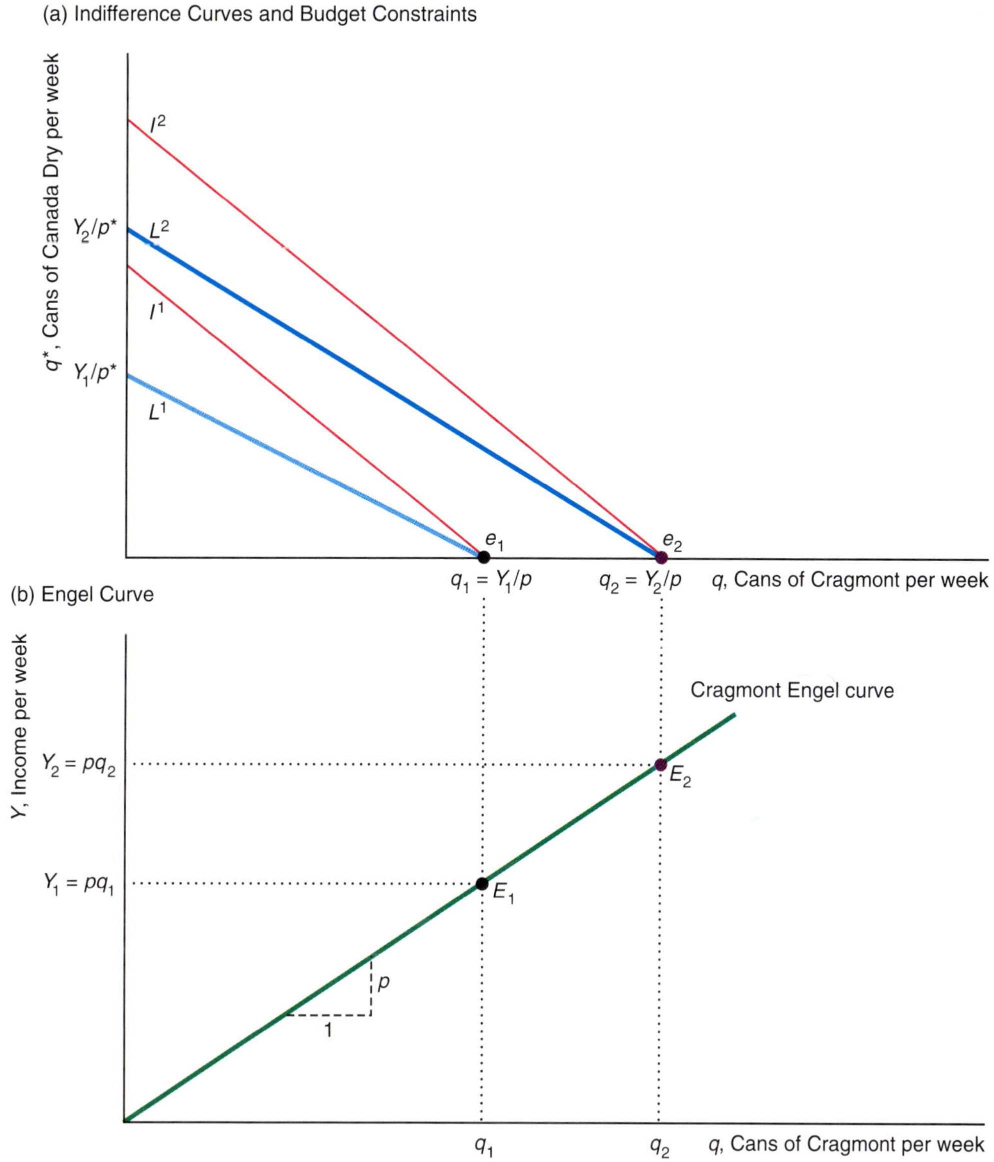

Figure 5.3 Engel Curve for Perfect Substitutes. The price of Cragmont ginger ale, p, is less than the price of Canada Dry ginger ale, p^*. (a) Because Mahdu views the brands as perfect substitutes—he's indifferent between them—he buys only the less expensive brand. (b) As a result, his Engel curve is a straight line with a slope of p.

quantity of Cragmont ginger ale he buys, is Mahdu's Engel curve for Cragmont. The points E_1 and E_2 on the Engel curve in panel b correspond to e_1 and e_2 in panel a. We can rewrite this expression for his Engel curve as $Y = pq$. This relationship is drawn in panel b as a straight line with a slope of p. As q increases by one can ("run"), Y increases by p ("rise"). Because all his ginger ale budget goes to buying Cragmont, his income needs to rise by only p for him to buy one more can of Cragmont per week. ■

Consumer Theory and Income Elasticities

Income elasticities tell us how much the quantity demanded changes as income increases. We can use income elasticities to summarize the shape of the Engel curve, the shape of the income-consumption curve, or the movement of the demand curves when income increases. For example, firms use income elasticities to predict the impact of income taxes on consumption. We first discuss the definition of income elasticities and then show how they are related to the income-consumption curve.

Income Elasticities. We defined the income elasticity of demand in Equation 3.5 as

$$\xi = \frac{\text{percentage change in quantity demanded}}{\text{percentage change in income}} = \frac{\Delta Q/Q}{\Delta Y/Y}.$$

Mimi's income elasticity of beer, ξ_b, is 0.88, and that of wine, ξ_w, is 1.38 (based on our estimates for the average American consumer). When her income goes up by 1%, she consumes 0.88% more beer and 1.38% more wine. Thus, according to these estimates, as income falls, consumption of beer and wine by the average American falls—contrary to frequent (unsubstantiated) claims in the media that people drink more as their incomes fall during recessions.

Most goods, like beer and wine, have positive income elasticities. A good is called a **normal good** if as much or more of it is demanded as income rises. Thus, a good is a normal good if its income elasticity is greater than or equal to zero: $\xi \geq 0$.

Some goods, however, have negative income elasticities: $\xi < 0$. A good is called an **inferior good** if less of it is demanded as income rises. No value judgment is intended by the use of the term *inferior*. An inferior good need not be defective or of low quality. Some of the better-known examples of inferior goods are foods, such as starches like potatoes and cassava, that very poor people typically eat in large quantities. Some economists—apparently seriously—claim that human meat is an inferior good: Only when the price of other foods is very high and people are starving will they turn to cannibalism.

A good that is inferior for some people may be superior for others. One strange example concerns treating children as a consumption good. Even though they can't buy children in a market, people can decide how many children to have. Willis (1973) estimated the income elasticity for the number of children in a family. He found that children are an inferior good, $\xi = -0.18$, if the wife has relatively little education and the family has average income: These families have fewer children as their income increases. In contrast, children are a normal good, $\xi = 0.044$, in families in which the wife is relatively well educated. For both types of families, the income elasticities are close to zero, so the number of children is not very sensitive to income.

Income-Consumption Curves and Income Elasticities. The shape of the income-consumption curve for two goods tells us the sign of the income elasticities: whether the income elasticities for those goods are positive or negative. We know that Mimi's income elasticities of beer and wine are positive because the income-consumption curve in panel a of Figure 5.2 is upward sloping. As income rises, the budget line shifts outward and hits the upward-sloping income-consumption line at higher levels of both goods. Thus, as her income rises, Mimi demands more beer and wine, so her income elasticities for beer and wine are positive. Because the income elasticity for beer is positive, the demand curve for beer shifts to the right in panel b of Figure 5.2 as income increases.

To illustrate the relationship between the slope of the income-consumption curve and the sign of income elasticities, we examine Peter's choices of food and housing. Peter purchases bundle *e* in Figure 5.4 when his budget constraint is L^1. When his income increases, so his budget constraint is L^2, he selects a bundle on L^2. Which bundle he buys depends on his tastes: his indifference curves.

The horizontal and vertical dotted lines through *e* divide the new budget line, L^2, into three sections. In which of these three sections the new optimal bundle is located determines Peter's income elasticities of food and clothing.

Suppose Peter's indifference curve is tangent to L^2 at a point in the upper-left section of L^2 (to the left of the vertical dotted line that goes through *e*) such as *a*. If Peter's income-consumption curve is ICC^1, which goes from *e* through *a*, he buys more housing and less food as his income rises.[6] Housing is a normal good, and food is an inferior good.

If, instead, the new optimal bundle is located in the middle section of L^2 (above the horizontal dotted line and to the right of the vertical dotted line), such as at *b*, his income-consumption curve ICC^2 through *e* and *b* is upward sloping. He buys more of both goods as his income rises, so both food and housing are normal goods.

Third, suppose his new optimal bundle is in the bottom-right segment of L^2 (below the horizontal dotted line). If his new optimal bundle is *c*, his income-consumption curve ICC^3 slopes downward from *e* through *c*. As his income rises, Peter consumes more food and less housing, so food is a normal good and housing is an inferior good.

Some Goods Must Be Normal. It is impossible for all goods to be inferior. We illustrate this point using Figure 5.4. At his original income, Peter faced budget constraint L^1 and bought the combination of food and housing *e*. When his income goes up, his budget constraint shifts outward to L^2. Depending on his tastes (the shape of his indifference curves), he may buy more housing and less food, such as Bundle *a*; more of both, such as *b*; or more food and less housing, such as *c*. Therefore, either both goods are normal or one good is normal and the other is inferior.

---

[6]We draw the possible *ICC* curves as straight lines for simplicity. In general, they may curve.

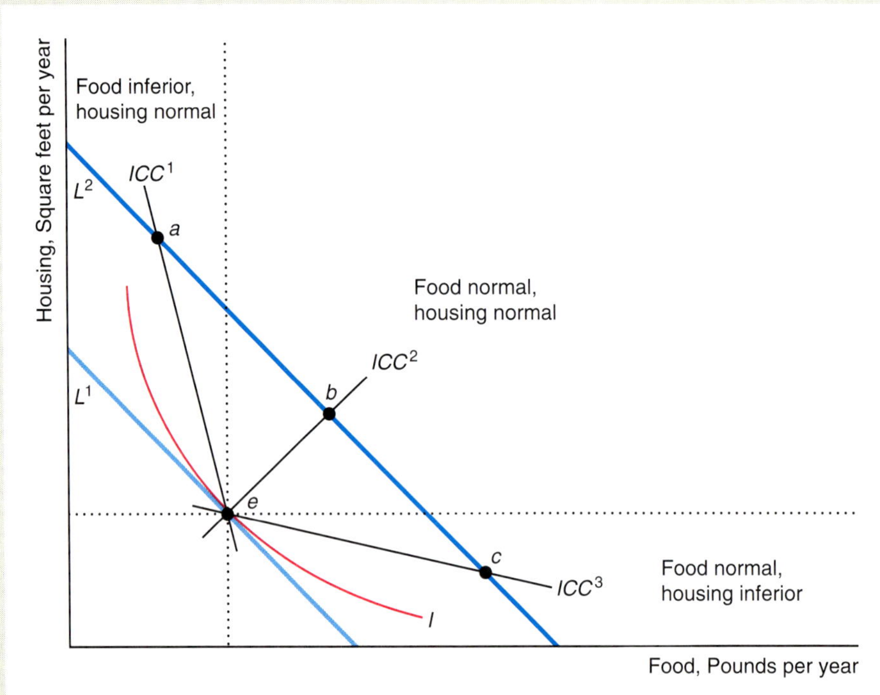

Figure 5.4 Income-Consumption Curves and Income Elasticities. At the initial income, the budget constraint is L^1 and the optimal bundle is *e*. After income rises, the new constraint is L^2. With an upward-sloping income-consumption curve such as ICC^2, both goods are normal. With an income-consumption curve, such as ICC^1, that goes through the upper-left section of L^2 (to the left of the vertical dotted line through *e*), housing is normal and food is inferior. With an income-consumption curve, such as ICC^3, that cuts L^2 in the lower-right section (below the horizontal dotted line through *e*), food is normal and housing is inferior.

If both goods were inferior, Peter would buy less of both goods as his income rises—which makes no sense. Were he to buy less of both, he would be buying a bundle that lies inside his original budget constraint L^1. Even at his original, relatively low income, he could have purchased that bundle but chose not to, buying *e* instead. By the more-is-better assumption of Chapter 4, there is a bundle on the budget constraint that gives Peter more utility than any given bundle inside the constraint.

Even if an individual does not buy more of the usual goods and services, that person may put the extra money into savings. Empirical studies find that savings is a normal good.

Income Elasticities May Vary with Income. A good may be normal at some income levels and inferior at others. When Gail was poor and her income increased slightly, she ate meat more frequently, and her meat of choice was hamburger. Thus, when her income was low, hamburger was a normal good. As her income increased further, however, she switched from hamburgers to steak. Thus, at higher incomes, hamburger is an inferior good.

We show Gail's choice between hamburger (horizontal axis) and all other goods (vertical axis) in panel a of Figure 5.5. As Gail's income increases, her budget line shifts outward, from L^1 to L^2, and she buys more hamburger: Bundle e_2 lies to the right of e_1. As her income increases further, shifting her budget line outward to L^3, Gail reduces her consumption of hamburger: Bundle e_3 lies to the left of e_2.

Gail's Engel curve in panel b captures the same relationship. At low incomes, her Engel curve is upward sloping, indicating that she buys more hamburger as her income rises. At higher incomes, her Engel curve is backward bending.

As their incomes rise, many consumers switch between lower-quality (hamburger) and higher-quality (steak) versions of the same good. This switching behavior explains the pattern of income elasticities across different-quality cars.

APPLICATION

Income Elasticities of Demand for Cars

As their incomes rise, some consumers buy their first car or an additional car, but others trade in their plain old car for a new sports car or luxury car. We expect that consumers will buy relatively more fancy cars than plain ones as incomes rise. In economic jargon, the income elasticity of demand is higher for sports car and luxury cars than for other cars.

Bordley and McDonald (1993) estimate the income elasticity of demand for various types of cars. The income elasticity of demand is 1.8 on average across all cars, 1.5 for an economy car, 1.6 for small cars, 1.8 for compact and midsize cars, 1.9 for large and sporty cars, and 2.5 for luxury cars. Thus, as expected, purchases of all types of cars rise faster than incomes, and purchases of large and sporty cars or luxury cars rise by more than purchases of economy, small, and compact and midsize cars.

Table 5.1 shows the income elasticities for various cars. If average incomes increase by 1%, demand for small, utilitarian Chevettes grows by about the same amount (1.2%), but demand for sporty Corvettes grows more than three times as much (3.2%).

Knowing these income elasticities, an auto manufacturer expects the demand for its fancy cars to rise more rapidly than demand for other cars during boom periods, when incomes are rising, and the demand for fancy cars to plummet more rapidly than the demand for other cars during busts, when incomes fall.

Do auto manufacturers really care about this information? Definitely. One of the authors of this study is employed by the General Motors Research Labs. ■

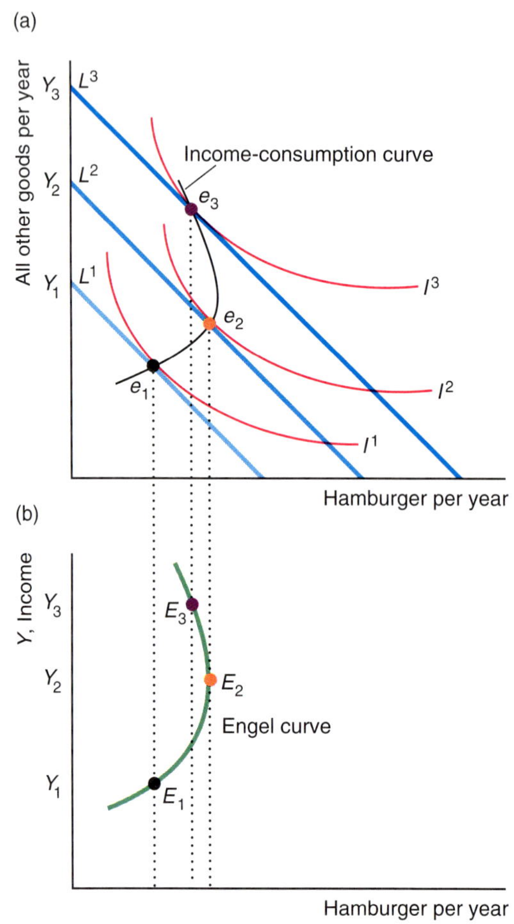

Figure 5.5 A Good That Is Inferior and Normal. When she was poor and her income increased, Gail bought more hamburger; however, when she became wealthier and her income rose, she bought less hamburger (she switched to steak). (a) The forward slope of the income-consumption curve from e_1 to e_2 and the backward bend from e_2 to e_3 show this pattern. (b) The forward slope of the Engel curve at low incomes, E_1 to E_2, and the backward bend at higher incomes, E_2 to E_3, also show this pattern.

Table 5.1 Estimated Income Elasticities of Demand for Various Cars

Car Model	Income Elasticity	Car Model	Income Elasticity
Accord	2.2	Maxima	2.5
BMW 700 Series	4.4	Mercedes 56	4.4
Camry	2.3	Mustang	1.9
Chevette	1.2	Nova 85	1.6
Civic	2.6	Olds 98	2.4
Corvette	3.2	Porsche 923	4.2
Eagle	1.7	Riviera	2.8
Festiva	1.4	Sprint	1.3
Grand Am	1.8	Taurus	2.1
Jaguar XJS	4.5	Volvo 760	3.4
Jetta	2.1	VW Fox	1.8
Mark VII	3.3	Yugo GV	1.2

Source: Bordley and McDonald (1993).

5.3 EFFECTS OF A PRICE CHANGE

An increase in a price of a good, holding other prices and income constant, has two effects on an individual's demand. One is the *substitution effect*: If their utility is held constant, as the price of the good increases, consumers *substitute* other, now relatively cheaper, goods for that one. The other is the *income effect*: An increase in price reduces a consumer's buying power, effectively reducing the consumer's *income*, causing the consumer to buy less of at least some goods. A doubling of the price of all the goods the consumer buys is equivalent to a drop in income to half its original level (Chapter 4). Even a rise in the price of only one good reduces a consumer's ability to buy the same amount of all goods as before. For example, if the price of food increases in China, the effective purchasing power of a Chinese consumer falls substantially because 55% of Chinese consumers' income is spent on food.[7]

When a price goes up, the total change in the quantity purchased is the sum of the substitution and income effects. When estimating the effects of a price change on the quantity an individual demands, economists decompose this combined effect into the two separate components. By decomposing the change in demand into two effects, economists gain extra information that they can use to answer questions about whether inflation measures are accurate and whether an increase in tax rates will raise tax revenue, as we demonstrate at the end of this chapter.

[7]State Statistical Bureau, *Statistical Yearbook of China*. Beijing, China: State Statistical Bureau Publishing House, 1992.

Income and Substitution Effects with a Normal Good

We illustrate the substitution and income effects in Figure 5.6, which shows how Mimi changes her allocation of income when the price of beer falls from \$12 to \$4 per unit. With this decrease, Mimi's budget constraint rotates outward from L^1 to L^2. The new budget constraint is flatter, $-p_b/p_w = -4/35 \approx -\frac{1}{9}$, than is L^1, $-12/35 \approx -\frac{1}{3}$, because beer is now less expensive relative to wine.

Mimi can choose between more wine-beer bundles than she could at the higher price. The area between the two budget constraints is the increase in her opportunity set (Chapter 4) from the drop in the price of beer.

At the original price of beer and with a budget of \$419, Mimi chooses Bundle e_1 (26.7 gallons of beer and 2.8 gallons of wine per year), where her indifference curve

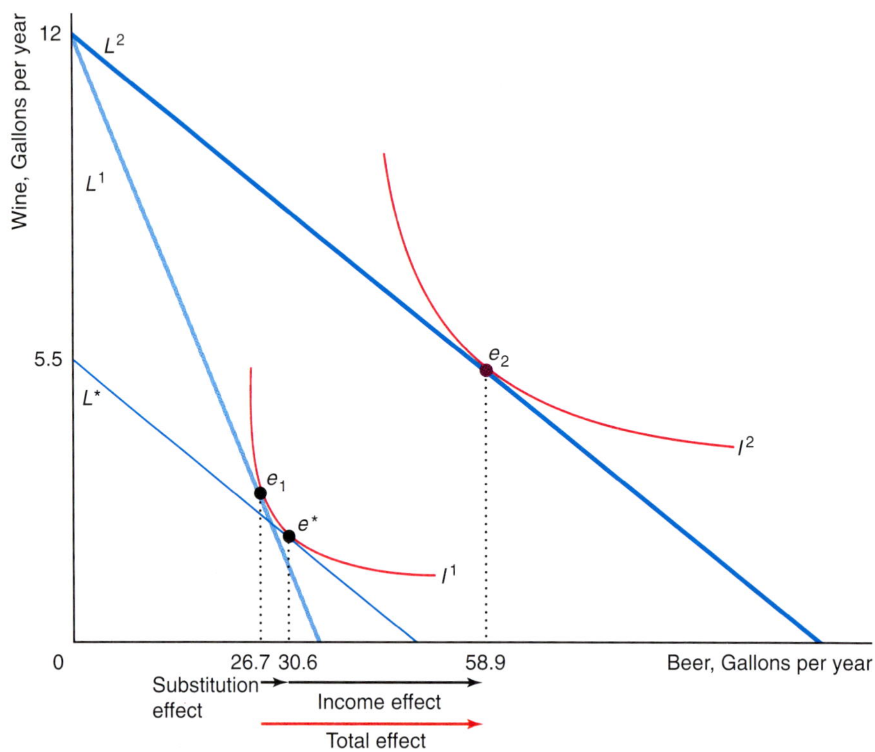

Figure 5.6 Substitution and Income Effects with Normal Goods. A decrease in the price of beer causes Mimi's budget line to rotate from L^1 to L^2. The imaginary budget line L^* has the same slope as L^2 and is tangent to indifference curve I^1. The shift of the optimal bundle from e_1 to e_2 is the *total effect* of the price change. The total effect can be decomposed into the *substitution effect*—movement from e_1 to e^*—and the *income effect*—the movement from e^* to e_2.

I^1 is tangent to her budget constraint L^1. When the price of beer drops, Mimi's new equilibrium bundle is e_2 (where she buys 58.9 gallons of beer), which occurs where her indifference curve I^2 is tangent to L^2.

The movement from e_1 to e_2 is the total change in her consumption owing to the fall in the price of beer. In particular, the *total effect* on Mimi's consumption of beer from the drop in the price of beer is that she now drinks 32.2 (= 58.9 – 26.7) more gallons of beer per year. In the figure, the arrow pointing to the right and labeled "Total effect" shows this increase in beer consumption. We can break the total effect into a substitution and an income effect.

The **substitution effect** is the change in the quantity of a good that a consumer demands when the good's price changes, holding other prices and the consumer's *utility* constant. That is, the substitution effect is the change in the quantity demanded from a *compensated change in the price* of beer, when we decrease Mimi's income by enough to offset the drop in the price of beer so that her utility stays constant. To determine the substitution effect, we draw an imaginary budget constraint, L^*, that is parallel to L^2 and tangent to Mimi's original indifference curve, I^1. This imaginary budget constraint, L^*, has the same slope, $-\frac{1}{9}$, as L^2 because both curves are based on the lower price of beer. For L^* to be tangent to I^1, we need to reduce Mimi's budget from \$419 to \$194 to offset the benefit of the lower price of beer. If Mimi's budget constraint were L^*, she would choose bundle e^*, where she consumes 30.6 gallons of beer.

Thus, if the price of beer falls relative to that of wine and Mimi's utility is held constant by lowering her income, Mimi's optimal bundle shifts from e_1 to e^*, which is the substitution effect. She buys 3.9 (= 30.6 – 26.7) gallons more beer per year, as the arrow pointing to the right labeled "Substitution effect" shows.

The **income effect** is the change in the quantity of a good a consumer demands because of a change in income, holding prices constant. The change in income is due to the change in the price of beer, which allows Mimi to buy more with her same budget. The parallel shift of the budget constraint from L^* to L^2 captures this effective increase in income. The movement from e^* to e_2 is the income effect, as the arrow pointing to the right labeled "Income effect" shows. As her budget increases from \$194 to \$419, Mimi consumes 28.3 (= 58.9 – 30.6) more gallons of beer per year.

The *total effect from the price change is the sum of the substitution and income effects*, as the arrows show. Mimi's total effect (in gallons of beer per year) from a drop in the price of beer is

$$\begin{aligned} \text{total effect} &= \text{substitution effect} + \text{income effect} \\ 32.2 &= 3.9 + 28.3. \end{aligned}$$

Because indifference curves are convex to the origin, *the substitution effect is unambiguous:* More of a good is consumed when its price falls. A consumer always substitutes a less expensive good for a more expensive one, holding utility constant.

The direction of the income effect depends on the income elasticity. Because beer is a normal good for Mimi, her income effect is positive. Thus, both Mimi's substitution effect and her income effect go in the same direction.

Income and Substitution Effect with an Inferior Good

If a good is inferior, the income effect goes in the opposite direction from the substitution effect. For most inferior goods, the income effect is smaller than the substitution effect. As a result, the total effect moves in the same direction as the substitution effect, but the total effect is smaller. However, the income effect can more than offset the substitution effect in extreme cases. We now examine such a case.

Dennis chooses between spending his money on Chicago Bulls basketball games and on movies, as Figure 5.7 shows. When the price of movies falls, Dennis's budget line shifts from L^1 to L^2. The total effect of the price fall is the movement from e_1 to e_2. We can break this total movement into an income and a substitution effect.

Dennis's income effect, the movement to the left from bundle e^* to e_2, is negative, as the arrow pointing left labeled "Income effect" shows. The income effect is negative because Dennis views movies as an inferior good.

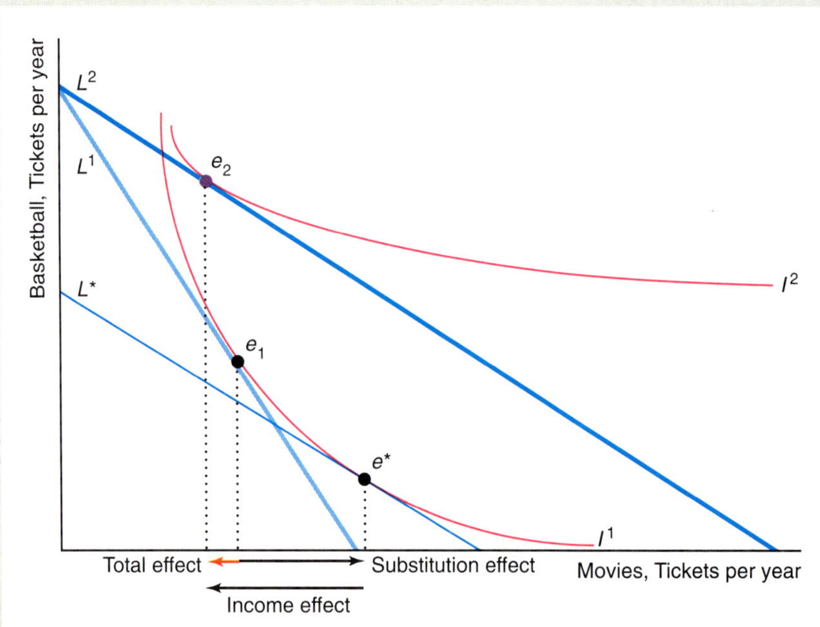

Figure 5.7 Giffen Good. Because a movie ticket is an inferior good for Dennis, the income effect, the movement from e^* to e_2, from a drop in the price of movies is negative. This negative income effect more than offsets the positive substitution effect, the movement from e_1 to e^*, so the total effect, the movement from e_1 to e_2, is negative. Thus, a movie ticket is a Giffen good because as its price drops, Dennis consumes less of it.

Dennis's substitution effect for movies is positive because movies are now less expensive than they were before the price change. The substitution effect is the movement to the right from e_1 to e^*.

The total effect of a price change, then, depends on which effect is larger. Because Dennis's negative income effect for movies more than offsets his positive substitution effect, the total effect of a drop in the price of movies is negative.

A good is called a **Giffen good** if a decrease in its price causes the quantity demanded to fall.[8] Thus, going to the movies is a Giffen good for Dennis. The price decrease has an effect that is similar to an income increase: His opportunity set increases as the price of movies drops. Dennis spends the money he saves on movies to buy more basketball tickets. Indeed, he decides to increase his purchase of basketball tickets even further by reducing his purchase of movie tickets.

The demand curve for a Giffen good has an upward slope! Dennis's demand curve for movies is upward sloping because he goes to more movies at the high price, e_1, than at the low price, e_2.

The Law of Demand (Chapter 2), however, says that demand curves slope downward. You're no doubt wondering, how I'm going to try to worm my way out this apparent contradiction. The answer is that I claimed that the Law of Demand was an empirical regularity, not a theoretical necessity. Although it's theoretically possible for a demand curve to slope upward, economists have found few, if any, real-world examples of a Giffen good.[9]

★**Measuring the Substitution and Income Effects.** By decomposing the total effect of a price change into substitution and income effects, we can address several issues. We can determine how likely it is that a good is a Giffen good. Further, we can determine the effect of government policies that compensate some consumers. President Jimmy Carter, when advocating a tax on gasoline, and President Bill Clinton, when calling for an energy tax, proposed providing an income compensation for poor consumers. To evaluate the effect of these policies, we want to know the substitution and income effects of a price change of energy.

The price elasticity of demand, ε, captures the total effect of a price change. We can decompose the price elasticity of demand into two terms involving elasticities that capture the substitution and income effects. We measure the substitution effect using the *substitution elasticity of demand*, ε^*, which is the percentage that quantity demanded falls for a given percentage increase in price if we compensate the consumer to keep the consumer's utility constant. The income effect depends on the income elasticity, ξ, and the share of the budget spent on that good.

---

[8]A nineteenth-century British economist, Robert Giffen, argued that poor people in Ireland increased their consumption of potatoes when the price rose because of a blight. More recent studies of the Irish potato famine dispute this observation, however.

[9]Battalio, Kagel, and Kogut (1991), however, showed in an experiment that quinine water is a Giffen good for lab rats!

The relationship among the price elasticity of demand, ε, the substitution elasticity of demand, ε^*, and the income elasticity of demand, ξ, is the *Slutsky equation* (named after its discoverer, the Russian economist Eugene Slutsky):[10]

$$\begin{aligned} \text{total effect} &= \text{substitution effect} + \text{income effect} \\ \varepsilon &= \varepsilon^* + (-\theta\xi), \end{aligned} \tag{5.1}$$

where θ is the budget share of this good: the amount spent on this good divided by the total budget.

If a consumer spends little on a good, a price change does not affect the consumer's total budget significantly. For example, your purchasing power is hardly affected if the price you have to pay for garlic triples. The total effect, ε, for garlic hardly differs from the substitution effect, ε^*, because the price change has—at best—a negligible effect on income.

In Mimi's original equilibrium, e_1, in which the price of beer was \$12 and Mimi bought 26.7 gallons of beer per year, Mimi spent about three-quarters of her \$419 budget on beer: $0.76 = (12 \times 26.7)/419$. Thus, Mimi's Slutsky equation is

$$\begin{aligned} \varepsilon &= \varepsilon^* - \theta\xi \\ -0.76 &\approx -0.09 - (0.76 \times 0.88). \end{aligned}$$

The total effect of a price change—the price elasticity of demand—is $\varepsilon = -0.76$. Because beer is a normal good for Mimi, the income effect reinforces the substitution effect. Indeed, the size of the total change is due more to the income effect, $-\theta\xi = -0.67$, than to the substitution effect, $\varepsilon^* = -0.09$. If the price of beer rises by 1% but Mimi is given extra income so that her utility remains constant, Mimi reduces her consumption of beer by less than a tenth of a percent (substitution effect). Without compensation, Mimi reduces her consumption of beer by about three-quarters of a percent (total effect).

For a Giffen good to have an upward-sloping demand curve, ε must be positive. The substitution elasticity, ε^*, is always negative: Consumers buy less of a good as its price goes up, holding utility constant. Thus, for a good to have an upward-sloping demand curve, the income effect, $-\theta\xi$, must be positive and large relative to the substitution effect. For the income effect to be positive, the good must be inferior, $\xi < 0$.[11]

For the income effect, $-\xi\theta$, to be a large positive number, either the good is very inferior (ξ is a very negative number, which is not common) or the budget share, θ, is closer to 1 than to 0, or both. One reason why we don't see upward-sloping demand curves is that the goods on which consumers spend a large share of their budget, such as housing, are usually normal goods.

---

[10]Appendix 5B sketches the derivation of this relation.

[11]Vandermeulen (1972) argues that both inferiority and satiability—the consumer is near the point where more of this good is not better—are necessary for a positive price effect.

APPLICATION

International Comparison of Substitution and Income Effects

Economists in many countries estimate the substitution and income effects using data on how consumer purchases change over time as prices and incomes change. Table 5.2 shows estimated substitution and income effects for various basic goods for four countries.

By comparing these estimates, we determine whether tastes are similar across countries. The substitution elasticities of demand, ε^*, are fairly similar across countries, but there are some notable differences. The substitution elasticity of demand for clothing is almost completely inelastic in Greece ($\varepsilon^* = -0.14$) but fairly close to unitary elasticity in the other three countries. If the price of clothes rises by 1% in each country, Greeks buy almost the same

Table 5.2 Estimated Compensated Price and Income Demand Elasticities

	Canada, 1947–1979	Greece, 1960–1986	United Kingdom, 1954–1974	United States, 1967–1982
Substitution elasticities, ε^*				
Food	–0.54	–0.31	0.00[a]	–0.87[b]
Clothing	–0.81	–0.14	–0.94	–1.31
Housing	NA	–0.57[c]	–0.30	–0.39
Fuel	–0.61	NA	–0.08	–0.54
Transportation and communications	–0.71	–0.74	–1.17	–0.67[d]
Durables	NA	–0.67	NA	–0.93
Income elasticities, ξ				
Food	0.27	0.91	0.17[a]	0.95[b]
Clothing	0.04	1.40	2.92	1.34
Housing	NA	0.84[c]	–0.02	0.76
Fuel	1.64	NA	0.86	1.21
Transportation and communications	1.57	0.98	1.05	1.35[d]
Durables	NA	1.17	NA	1.48

[a]Excludes beverages and tobacco.
[b]Excludes alcohol and tobacco.
[c]Includes fuel.
[d]Excludes communications.

Sources: United States: Taube and MacDonald (1991); Canada: Anderson and Blundell (1983); Greece: Mergos and Donatos (1989); United Kingdom: Deaton and Muelbauer (1980).

amount of clothes as before, but Britons, Americans, and Canadians decrease the quantity they buy by about 1%.

Some of the income elasticities vary substantially across countries. The estimated income elasticities for clothing vary from near 0 in Canada to nearly 3 in the United Kingdom. Although Canadians don't increase the amount they spend on clothes as their incomes rise, Britons increase their spending on clothing three times as much as their incomes rise. ■

SOLVED PROBLEM 5.2

Next to its plant, a manufacturer of dinner plates has an outlet store that sells plates of both first quality (perfect plates) and second quality (plates with slight blemishes). The outlet store sells a relatively large share of seconds. At its outlet stores elsewhere, the firm sells many more first-quality plates than second-quality plates. Why? (Assume that consumers' tastes with respect to plates are the same everywhere and that there is a cost, *s*, of shipping each plate from the factory to the firm's other stores.)

Answer

1. *Determine how the relative prices of plates differ between the two types of stores*: The slope of the budget line facing consumers at the factory outlet store is $-p_1/p_2$, where p_1 is the price of first-quality plates and p_2 is the price of the seconds. It costs the same, s, to ship a first-quality plate as a second because they weigh the same and have to be handled in the same way. At all other stores, the firm adds the cost of shipping to the price it charges at its factory outlet store, so the price of a first-quality plate is $p_1 + s$ and the price of a second is $p_2 + s$. As a result, the slope of the budget line facing consumers at the other retail stores is $-(p_1 + s)/(p_2 + s)$. The seconds are relatively less expensive at the factory outlet than at other stores. For example, if p_1 = \$2 and p_2 = \$1, and s = \$1 per plate, the slope of the budget line is –2 at the outlet store and –3/2 elsewhere. Thus, the first-quality plate costs twice as much as a second at the outlet store but only 1.5 times as much elsewhere.

2. *Use the relative price difference to explain why relatively more seconds are bought at the factory outlet*: Holding a consumer's income and tastes fixed, if the price of seconds rises relative to that of firsts (as we go from the factory outlet to other retail shops), most consumers will buy relatively more firsts. The substitution effect is unambiguous: Were they compensated so that their utilities were held constant, consumers would unambiguously substitute firsts for seconds. It is possible that the income effect

could go in the other direction; however, as most consumers spend relatively little of their total budget on plates, the income effect is presumably small relative to the substitution effect. Thus, we expect relatively fewer seconds to be bought at the retail stores than at the factory outlet. (Problem 9 at the end of the chapter asks you to illustrate this answer using graphs.) ■

5.4 COST-OF-LIVING ADJUSTMENTS

By knowing both the substitution and income effects, we can answer questions that we could not if we knew only the total effect. For example, if they have an estimate of the income effect, firms can predict the impact of a negative income tax (a gift of money from the government) on the consumption of their products. Similarly, if we know the size of both the substitution and income effects, we can determine how accurately the government measures inflation.

Many long-term contracts and government programs include cost-of-living adjustments (COLAs), which raise prices or incomes in proportion to an index of inflation. Not only business contracts but also rental contracts, alimony payments, salaries, pensions, and Social Security payments are frequently adjusted in this manner over time. In this section, we use consumer theory to show that a cost-of-living measure that governments commonly use overestimates how the true cost of living changes over time. Because of this overestimate, you overpay your landlord if the rent on your apartment rises with this measure.

Inflation Indexes

The prices of most goods rise over time. We call the increase in the overall price level *inflation.*

Real Versus Nominal Prices. The actual price of a good in each year is called the *nominal price*. The price adjusted for inflation is the *real price*.

Because the overall level of prices rise over time, nominal prices usually increase more rapidly than real prices. For example, the nominal price of a McDonald's hamburger rose from 15¢ in 1955 to 75¢ in 1998, nearly a fourfold increase.[12] However, the real price of a burger fell because the prices of other goods rose more rapidly than that of a burger.

How do we adjust for inflation to calculate such a real price? The U.S. government and many other governments measure the cost of a standard bundle of goods for use in comparing prices over time. This measure is called the Consumer Price Index (CPI). Each month, the government reports how much it costs to buy the

[12]"Is The Price Still Right?" *Consumer Reports*, 59(8), August 1994:495.

bundle of goods that an average consumer purchased in a *base* year (with the base year changing every few years).

By comparing the cost of buying this bundle over time, we can determine how much the overall price level has increased. In the United States, the CPI was 26.8 in 1955 and 162.2 in March 1998.[13] The cost of buying the bundle of goods increased 605% (≈162.2/26.8) from 1955 to 1998.

We can use the CPI to calculate the real price of a hamburger over time. In terms of 1998 dollars, the real price of a hamburger in 1955 was

$$\frac{\text{CPI for 1998}}{\text{CPI for 1955}} \times \text{ price of a burger} = \frac{162.2}{26.8} \times 15¢ \approx 91¢.$$

If you could have purchased the hamburger in 1955 with 1998 dollars—which are worth less than 1955 dollars—the hamburger would have cost 91¢. The real price in 1998 dollars (and the nominal price) of a hamburger in 1998 was only 75¢. Thus, the real price of a hamburger fell by about a fourth. If we compared the real prices in both years using 1955 dollars, we would reach the same conclusion that the real price of hamburgers fell by about a fourth.

Calculating Inflation Indexes. The government collects data on the quantities and prices of 364 individual goods and services, such as housing, dental services, watch and jewelry repairs, college tuition fees, taxi fares, women's hairpieces and wigs, hearing aids, slipcovers and decorative pillows, bananas, pork sausage, and funeral expenses. These prices rise at different rates. If the government merely reported all these price increases separately, most of us would find this information overwhelming. It is much more convenient to use a single summary statistic, the CPI, which tells us how prices rose *on average*.

We can use an example with only two goods, clothing and food, to show how the CPI is calculated. In the first year, consumers buy C_1 units of clothing and F_1 units of food at prices p_C^1 and p_F^1. We use this bundle of goods, C_1 and F_1, as our base bundle for comparison. In the second year, consumers buy C_2 and F_2 units at prices p_C^2 and p_F^2.

The government knows, from its survey of prices each year, that the price of clothing in the second year is p_C^2/p_C^1 times as large as the price the previous year and the price of food is p_F^2/p_F^1 times as large. If the price of clothing was \$1 in the first year and \$2 in the second year, the price of clothing in the second year is $\frac{2}{1} = 2$ times, or 100%, larger than in the first year.

One way we can average the price increases of each good is to weight them equally. But do we really want to do that? Do we want to give as much weight to the price increase of skateboards as to the price increase of automobiles? An alternative approach is to give a larger weight to the price change of a good as we spend

[13]The number 162.2 is not an actual dollar amount. Rather, it is the actual dollar cost of buying the bundle divided by a constant. That constant was chosen so that the average expenditure in the period 1982–1984 was 100.

more of our income on that good, its budget share. The CPI takes this approach of weighting using budget shares.[14]

The CPI for the first year is the amount of income it takes to buy the market basket actually purchased that year:

$$Y_1 = p_C^1 C_1 + p_F^1 F_1. \tag{5.2}$$

The cost of buying the first year's bundle in the second year is

$$Y_2 = p_C^2 C_1 + p_F^2 F_1. \tag{5.3}$$

To calculate the rate of inflation, we determine how much more income it would take to buy the first year's bundle in the second year, which is the ratio of Equation 5.2 to Equation 5.3:

$$\frac{Y_2}{Y_1} = \frac{p_C^2 C_1 + p_F^2 F_1}{p_C^1 C_1 + p_F^1 F_1}.$$

For example, from 1996 to 1997, the U.S. CPI rose by $1.023 \approx Y_2/Y_1$ from $Y_1 = 156.9$ to $Y_2 = 160.5$. Thus, it cost 2.3% more in 1997 than in 1996 to buy the same bundle of goods.

The ratio Y_2/Y_1 reflects how much prices rise on average. By multiplying and dividing the first term in the numerator by p_C^1 and multiplying and dividing the second term by p_F^1, we find that this index is equivalent to

$$\frac{Y_2}{Y_1} = \frac{\left(\frac{p_C^2}{p_C^1}\right) p_C^1 C_1 + \left(\frac{p_F^2}{p_F^1}\right) p_F^1 F_1}{Y_1} = \left(\frac{p_C^2}{p_C^1}\right)\theta_C + \left(\frac{p_F^2}{p_F^1}\right)\theta_F,$$

where $\theta_C = p_C^1 C_1/Y_1$ and $\theta_F = p_F^1 F_1/Y_1$ are the budget shares of clothing and food in the first or base year. The CPI is a *weighted average* of the price increase of each good, p_C^2/p_C^1 and p_F^2/p_F^1, where the weights are each good's budget share in the base year, θ_C and θ_F.

Effects of Inflation Adjustments

A CPI adjustment of prices in a long-term contract overcompensates for inflation. We use an example involving an employment contract to illustrate the difference between using the CPI to adjust a long-term contract and using a true cost-of-living adjustment, which holds utility constant.

---

[14]This discussion of the CPI is simplified in a number of ways. A number of sophisticated adjustments are made to the CPI that are ignored here, including repeated updating of the base year (chaining). For a much more complete discussion of the CPI, see Pollak (1989) and Diewert and Nakamura (1993).

CPI Adjustment. Klaas signed a long-term contract when he was hired. According to the COLA clause in his contract, his employer increases his salary each year by the same percentage as that at which the CPI increases. If the CPI this year is 5% higher than the CPI last year, Klaas's salary rises automatically by 5% over last year's.

Klaas spends all his money on clothing and food. His budget constraint in the first year is $Y_1 = p_C^1 C + p_F^1 F$, which we rewrite as

$$C = \frac{Y_1}{p_C^1} - \frac{p_F^1}{p_C^1} F.$$

The intercept of the budget constraint, L^1, on the vertical, clothing axis in Figure 5.8 is Y_1/p_C^1 and the slope of the constraint is $-p_F^1/p_C^1$. The tangency of his indifference curve I^1 and the budget constraint L^1 determine his equilibrium consumption bundle in the first year, e_1, where he purchases C_1 and F_1.

In the second year, his salary rises with the CPI to Y_2, so his budget constraint, L^2, in that year is

$$C = \frac{Y_2}{p_C^2} - \frac{p_F^2}{p_C^2} F.$$

The new constraint L^2 has a flatter slope, $-p_F^2/p_C^2$, than L^1 because the price of clothing rose more than the price of food. The new constraint goes through the original equilibrium bundle e_1 because, by increasing his salary using the CPI, the firm ensures that Klaas can buy the same bundle of goods in the second year that he chose in the first year.

He *can* buy the same bundle, but *does* he? The answer is no! His optimal bundle in the second year is e_2, where indifference curve I^2 is tangent to his new budget constraint L^2. The movement from e_1 to e_2 is the *total effect* from the changes in the real prices of clothing and food. *This adjustment to his income does not keep him on his original indifference curve*, I^1.

Indeed, Klaas is better off in the second year than in the first year. The CPI adjustment *overcompensates* him for the change in inflation in the sense that his utility increases.

Klaas is better off because the prices of clothing and food did *not* increase by the same amount. Suppose that the price of clothing and food had both increased by *exactly* the same amount. After a CPI adjustment, Klaas's budget constraint in the second year, L^2, would be exactly the same as that in the first year, L^1, so he would choose exactly the same bundle, e_1, in the second year as in the first year.

Because the price of food rose by less than the price of clothing, L^2 is not the same as L^1. Food became cheaper relative to clothing. Thus, by consuming more food and less clothing, Klaas has higher utility in the second year.

Had clothing become relatively less expensive, Klaas would have raised his utility in the second year by consuming relatively more clothing. Thus, it doesn't matter which good becomes relatively less expensive over time—it's only necessary for one of them to become a relative bargain for Klaas to benefit from the CPI compensation.

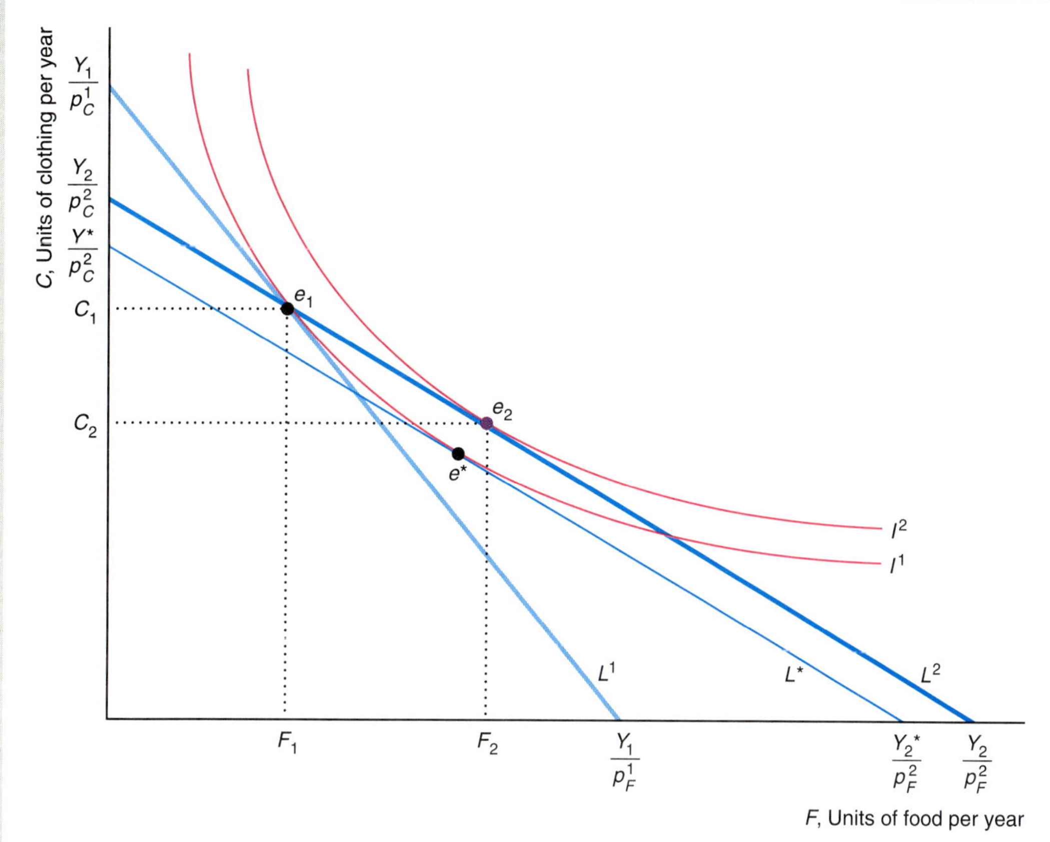

Figure 5.8 The Consumer Price Index. In the first year, when Klaas has an income of Y_1, his optimal bundle is e_1, where indifference curve I^1 is tangent to his budget constraint L^1. In the second year, the price of clothing rises more than the price of food. Because his salary increases in proportion to the CPI, his second-year budget constraint L^2 goes through e_1, so he can buy the same bundle as in the first year. His new optimal bundle, however, is e_2, where I^2 is tangent to L^2. The CPI adjustment overcompensates him for the increase in prices: Klaas is better off in the second year because his utility is greater on I^2 than on I^1. With a smaller, true cost-of-living adjustment, Klaas's budget constraint L^* is tangent to I^1 at e^*.

True Cost-of-Living Adjustment. We now know that a CPI adjustment overcompensates for inflation. What we want is a *true cost-of-living index*: an inflation index that holds utility constant over time.

How big an increase in Klaas's salary would leave him exactly as well off in the second year as in the first? We can answer this question applying the same technique we use to identify the substitution and income effects. We draw an imaginary budget line, L^* in Figure 5.8, that is tangent to I^1, so that Klaas's utility remains constant, but that has the same slope as L^2. The income, Y^*, corresponding to that imaginary budget constraint is the amount that leaves Klaas's utility constant. Had Klaas received Y^* in the second year instead of Y_2, he would have chosen bundle e^* instead of e_2. Because e^* is on the same indifference curve, I^1, as e_1, Klaas's utility would be the same in both years.

The numerical example in Table 5.3 illustrates how the CPI overcompensates Klaas.[15] Suppose p_C^1 is \$1, p_C^2 is \$2, p_F^1 is \$4, and p_F^2 is \$5. In the first year, Klaas spends his income, Y_1, of \$400 on $C_1 = 200$ units of clothing and $F_1 = 50$ units of food and has a utility of 2,000, which is the level of utility on I^1. If his income did not increase in the second year, he would substitute toward the relatively inexpensive food, cutting his consumption of clothing in half but reducing his consumption of food by only a fifth. His utility would fall to 1,265.

If his second-year income increases in proportion to the CPI, he can buy the same bundle, e_1, in the second year as in the first. His second-year income is $Y_2 = \$650$ $(= p_C^2 C_1 + p_F^2 F_1 = \$2 \times 200 + \$5 \times 50)$. Klaas is better off if his budget increases to Y_2. He substitutes toward the relatively inexpensive food, buying less clothing than in the first year but more food, e_2. His utility rises from 2,000 to approximately 2,055 (the level of utility on I^2).

How much would his income have to rise to leave him only as well off as he was in the first year? If his second-year income is $Y^* \approx \$632.50$, by appropriate substitution toward food, e^*, he can achieve the same level of utility, 2,000, as in the first year.

We can use the income that just compensates Klaas, Y^*, to construct a true cost-of-living index. In our numerical example, the true cost-of-living index rose 58.1% $(\approx [632.50 - 400]/400)$, while the CPI rose 62.5% $(= [650 - 400]/400)$.

Size of the CPI Substitution Bias. We have just demonstrated that the CPI has an *upward bias* in the sense that an individual's utility rises if we increase that person's income by the same percentage as that at which the CPI rises. If we make the CPI adjustment, we are implicitly assuming—incorrectly—that consumers do not substitute toward relatively inexpensive goods when prices change but keep buying the same bundle of goods over time. We call this overcompensation a *substitution bias*.

Table 5.3 Cost-of-Living Adjustments

	p_C	p_F	Income, Y	Clothing	Food	Utility, U
First year	\$1	\$4	$Y_1 = \$400$	200	50	2,000
Second year	\$2	\$5				
No adjustment			$Y_1 = \$400$	100	40	≈1,265
CPI adjustment			$Y_2 = \$650$	162.5	65	≈2,055
True COLA			$Y^* \approx \$632.50$	≈158.1	≈63.2	2,000

[15]We assume that Klaas has a utility function $U = 20\sqrt{CF}$, which we use to draw Figure 5.8.

There is no substitution bias if all prices increase at the same rate, so that relative prices remain constant. The faster some prices rise relative to others, the more pronounced is the upward bias caused by substitution to now less expensive goods.

Economists estimate how large the substitution bias is for the typical household. By most estimates, the upward bias is not very large per year. Using an index of 101 goods, Manser and McDonald (1988) estimate that the substitution bias was about a fifth of a percent (0.18%) per year for the period 1959–1985. As the following application discusses, a national commission concludes that the current substitution bias is larger: 0.4%.

APPLICATION

The Total CPI Bias

Since 1995, members of both parties in Congress have proposed changing the CPI. They argue that the upward bias in the CPI has been largely to blame for the rapid increases in costs for various government programs. The Senate Finance Committee commissioned a group of economists to determine how biased the CPI is. The commission (Boskin et al. 1997) concluded that the CPI overstated inflation by about 1.1 percentage points per year owing to

- the *substitution bias*: 0.4 percentage point a year;
- failure to take proper account of the *spread of discount stores*, so that the wrong prices are used in the calculation: 0.1 percentage point; and
- failure to account adequately for *quality improvements* or *new products*—particularly in drugs and computers—so that prices are overstated: 0.6 percentage point.[16]

They concluded that for 1983–1986, the overestimate of the annual change in the CPI is 0.25% for housing (compared to an annual change of 4.20%), 1.00% for nonprescription drugs and medical supplies (annual change, 3.68%), 0.30% for furniture (0.72%), 0.30% for food (3.60%), 5.60% for computers (–2.39%), 1.00% for clothing (2.15%), and 0.59% for new cars (2.60%).

Although a 1.1 percentage point bias might sound small, the cumulative bias can be substantial over a number of years. Moreover, even small annual biases may matter to some firms. For example, the United States Postal Service (USPS) has a COLA based on the CPI in its union contracts. In 1995, a typical union employee earned $45,000 a year, including benefits.[17] A bias of 1.1% a year costs the USPS $495 extra per employee. Because the USPS has

[16]For example, Hausman (1994) calculates that, by ignoring the introduction of 190 new cereals in the 1980–1993 period, the CPI may overstate inflation of cereal prices by as much as 25%.

[17]*Statistical Abstract of the United States*, 1996.

about 875,000 employees, the bias costs the USPS over $433 million per year—and benefits its employees by the same amount.

According to the commission's final report, the CPI bias alone makes it the fourth-largest "federal program" after Social Security, health care, and defense. The commission calculated that $634 billion of the national debt would be eliminated in five years if the CPI rose 1% less rapidly per year. Offsetting the gain to the government is the loss to Social Security recipients and others who receive government funds, who would get smaller cost-of-living increases with an adjusted CPI. ■

5.5 DERIVING LABOR SUPPLY CURVES

Throughout this chapter, we've used consumer theory to examine consumers' *demand* behavior. Perhaps surprisingly, we can use the consumer theory model to derive the *supply curve* of labor. We are going to do that by deriving a demand curve for time spent *not* working and then use that demand curve to draw the supply curve of hours spent working.

Labor-Leisure Choice

People choose between working to earn money to buy goods and services and consuming *leisure*: all time spent not working. In addition to sleeping, eating, and playing, leisure includes time spent cooking meals and fixing things around the house. The number of hours worked per day, H, equals 24 minus the hours of leisure or nonwork, N, in a day:

$$H = 24 - N.$$

Using consumer theory, we can determine the demand curve for leisure once we know the price of leisure. What does it cost you to watch TV or go to school or do anything for an hour other than work? It costs you the wage, w, you could have earned from an hour's work: The price of leisure is forgone earnings. The higher your wage, the more an hour of leisure costs you. For this reason, taking an afternoon off costs a lawyer who earns $250 an hour much more than it costs someone who earns the minimum wage.

We use an example to show how the number of hours of leisure and work depends on the wage, unearned income (such as inheritances and gifts from parents), and tastes. Jackie spends her total income, Y, on various goods. For simplicity, we assume that the price of these goods is $1 per unit, so she buys Y goods. Her utility, U, depends on how many goods and how much leisure she consumes:

$$U = U(Y, N).$$

Initially, we assume that Jackie can choose to work as many or as few hours as she wants for an hourly wage of w. Jackie's earned income equals her wage times the number of hours she works, wH. Her total income, Y, is her earned income plus her unearned income, Y^*:

$$Y = wH + Y^*.$$

Panel a of Figure 5.9 shows Jackie's choice between leisure and goods. The vertical axis shows how many goods, Y, Jackie buys. The horizontal axis shows both hours of leisure, N, which are measured from left to right, and hours of work, H, which are measured from right to left. Jackie maximizes her utility given the *two* constraints she faces. First, she faces a time constraint, which is a vertical line at 24 hours of leisure. There are only 24 hours in a day; all the money in the world won't buy her more hours in a day. Second, Jackie faces a budget constraint. Because Jackie has no unearned income, her initial budget constraint, L^1, is $Y = w_1H = w_1(24 - N)$. The slope of her budget constraint is $-w_1$, because each extra hour of leisure she consumes costs her w_1 goods.

Jackie picks her optimal hours of leisure, $N_1 = 16$, so that she is on the highest indifference curve, I^1, that touches her budget constraint. She works $H_1 = 24 - N_1 = 8$ hours per day and earns an income of $Y_1 = w_1H_1 = 8w_1$.

We derive Jackie's demand curve for leisure using the same method that we used to derive Mimi's demand curve for beer. We raise the price of leisure—the wage—in panel a of Figure 5.9 to trace out Jackie's demand curve for leisure in panel b. As the wage increases from w_1 to w_2, leisure becomes more expensive and Jackie demands less of it.

By subtracting her demand for leisure at each wage—her demand curve for leisure in panel a of Figure 5.10—from the 24, we construct her labor supply curve—the hours she is willing to work as a function of the wage—in panel b.[18] Her supply curve of hours worked is the mirror image of the demand curve for leisure: For every extra hour of leisure that Jackie consumes, she works one fewer hour.

Income and Substitution Effects

An increase in the wage causes both income and substitution effects, which alter an individual's demand for leisure and supply of hours worked. The *total effect* of an increase in Jackie's wage from w_1 to w_2 is the movement from e_1 to e_2 in Figure 5.11. Jackie works $H_2 - H_1$ fewer hours and consumes $N_2 - N_1$ more hours of leisure.

By drawing an imaginary budget constraint, L^*, that is tangent to her original indifference curve with the slope of the new wage, we can divide the total effect into substitution and income effects. The *substitution effect*, the movement from e_1 to e^*, must be negative: A compensated wage increase causes Jackie to consume fewer hours of leisure, N^*, and work more hours, H^*.

As the wage rises, if Jackie works the same number of hours as before, she has a higher income. The *income effect* is the movement from e^* to e_2. Because leisure is a normal good for Jackie, as her income rises, she consumes more leisure. When

[18]Appendix 5A shows how to derive the labor supply curve using calculus.

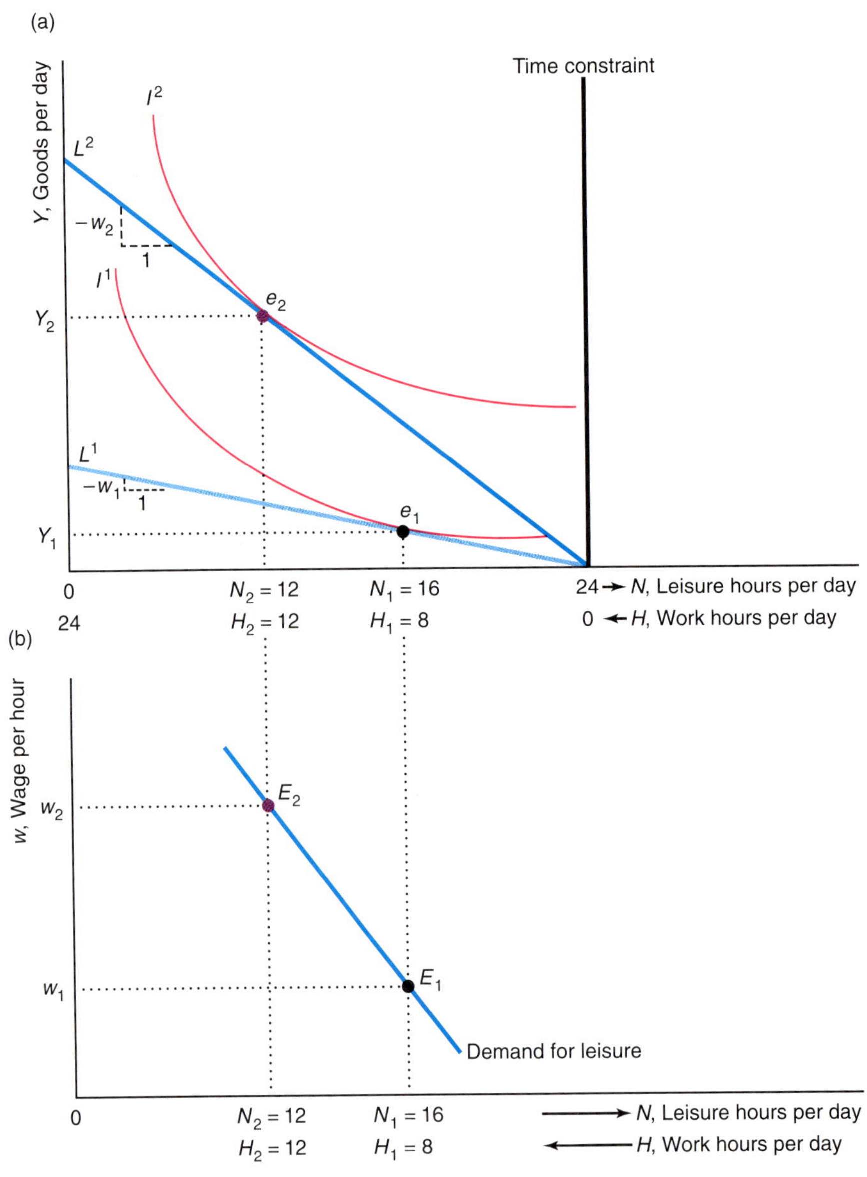

Figure 5.9 Demand for Leisure. (a) Jackie chooses between leisure, N, and other goods, Y, subject to a time constraint (vertical line at 24 hours) and a budget constraint L^1, which is $Y = w_1 H = w_1(24 - N)$, with a slope of $-w_1$. The tangency of her indifference curve I^1 with her budget constraint L^1 determines her optimal bundle e_1, where she has $N_1 = 16$ hours of leisure and works $H_1 = 24 - N_1 = 8$ hours. If her wage rises from w_1 to w_2, Jackie shifts from optimal bundle e_1 to e_2. (b) The bundles e_1 and e_2 correspond to E_1 and E_2 on her leisure demand curve.

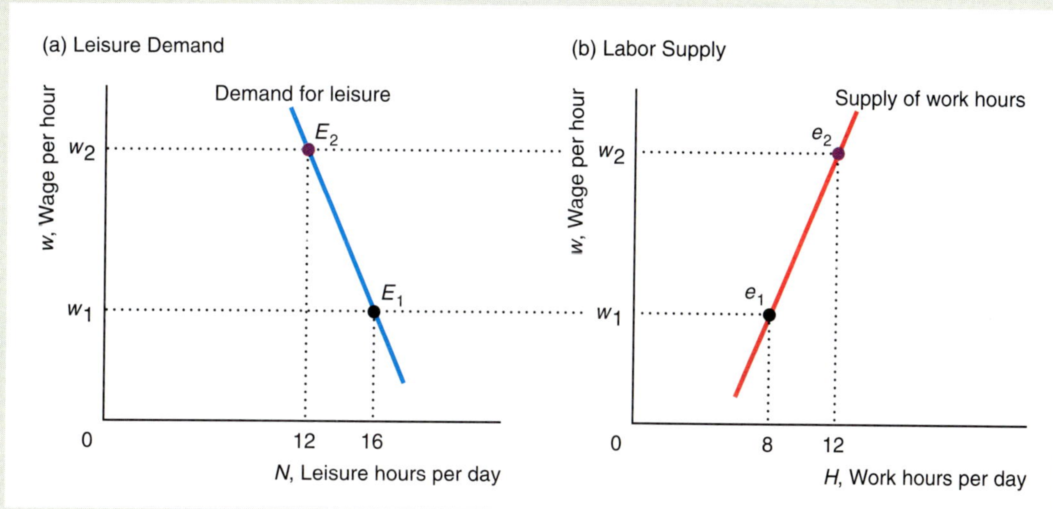

Figure 5.10 Supply Curve of Labor. (a) Jackie's demand for leisure is downward sloping. (b) At any given wage, the number of hours that Jackie works, H, and the number of hours of leisure, N, that she consumes add to 24. Thus, her supply curve of hours worked, which equals 24 hours minus the number of hours of leisure she demands, is upward sloping.

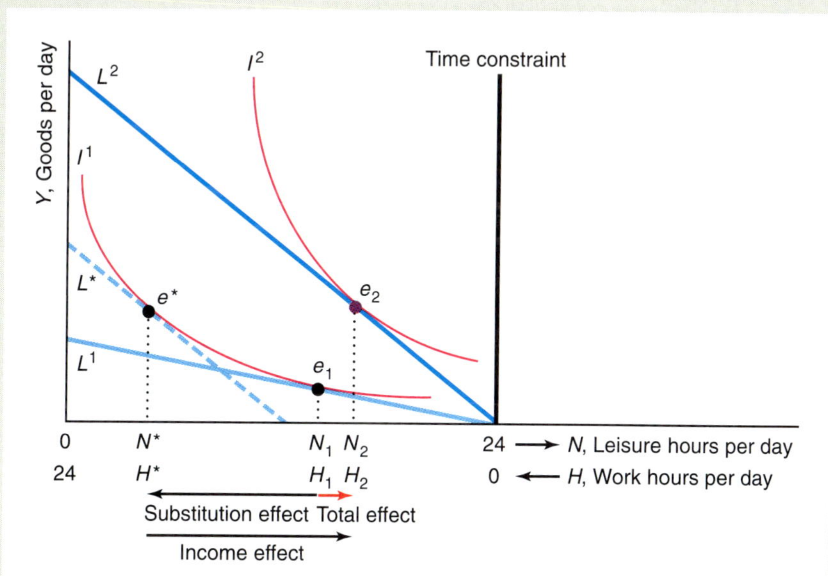

Figure 5.11 Income and Substitution Effects of a Wage Change. A wage change causes both a substitution and an income effect. The movement from e_1 to e^* is the substitution effect, the movement from e^* to e_2 is the income effect, and the movement from e_1 to e_2 is the total effect.

leisure is a normal good, the substitution and income effects work in opposite directions, so whether leisure demand increases or not depends on which effect is larger. Jackie's income effect dominates the substitution effect, so the total effect for leisure is positive: $N_2 > N_1$. Jackie works fewer hours as the wage rises, so her labor supply curve is backward bending.

If leisure is an inferior good, both the substitution effect and the income effect work in the same direction, and hours of leisure definitely fall. As a result, if leisure is an inferior good, a wage increase unambiguously causes the hours worked to rise.

SOLVED PROBLEM 5.3

Enrico receives a no-strings-attached scholarship that pays him an extra Y^* per day. How does this scholarship affect the number of hours he wants to work? Does his utility increase?

Answer:

1. *Show his consumer equilibrium without unearned income:* When Enrico had no unearned income, his budget constraint, L^1 in Figure 5.12, hit the hours-leisure axis at 0 hours and had a slope of $-w$.

2. *Show how the unearned income affects his budget constraint:* The extra income causes a parallel, upward shift of Y^*. His new budget constraint, L^2, has the same slope as before because his wage does not change. The extra income cannot buy Enrico more time, of course, so L^2 cannot extend to the right of the time constraint. As a result, L^2 is vertical at 0 hours up to Y^*: His income is Y^* if he works no hours. Above Y^*, L^2 slants toward the goods axis with a slope of $-w$.

3. *Show that the relative position of the new to the original equilibrium depends on his tastes:* The change in the number of hours he works depends on Enrico's tastes. Panels a and b show two possible sets of indifference curves. In both diagrams, when facing budget constraint L^1, Enrico chooses to work H_1 hours. In panel a, leisure is a normal good, so, as his income rises, Enrico consumes more leisure than originally: He moves from Bundle e_1 to Bundle e_2. In panel b, he views leisure as an inferior good and consumes fewer hours of leisure than originally: He moves from e_1 to e_3. (Another possibility is that the number of hours he works is unaffected by the extra unearned income.)

3. *Discuss how his utility changes:* Regardless of his tastes, Enrico has more income in the new equilibrium and is on a higher indifference curve after receiving the scholarship. In short, he feels that more money is better than less. ■

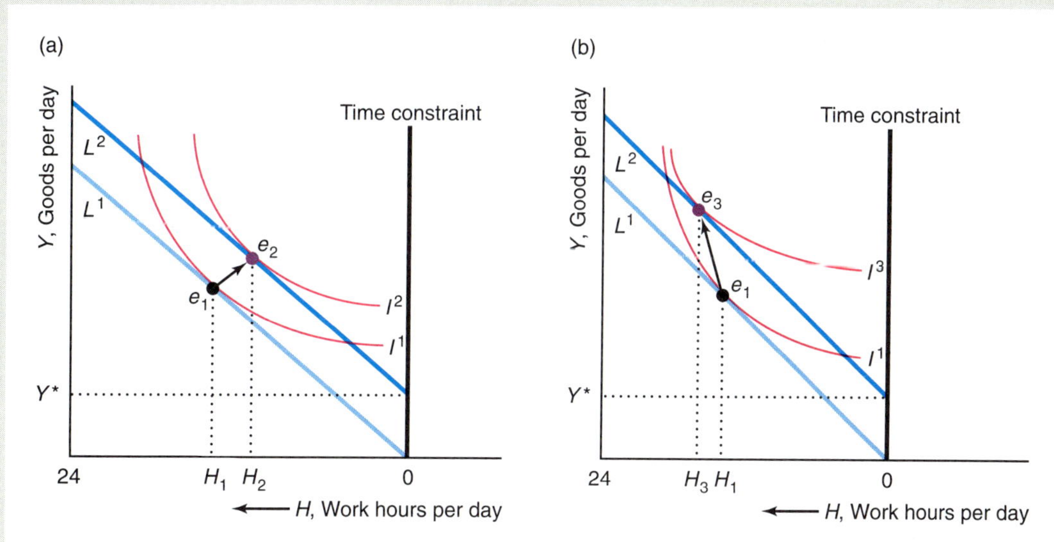

Figure 5.12 Effect on Work Hours of an Increase in Unearned Income. Receiving a scholarship for Y^* per day shifts the budget constraint upward from L^1 to L^2. Hours worked may (a) decrease, move from e_1 to e_2, or (b) increase, move from e_1 to e_3, depending on the shape of the indifference curves. Utility must rise: Both I^2 and I^3 are above I^1.

APPLICATION

Leisure-Income Choices of Textile Workers

Dunn (1977, 1978, 1979), using data obtained by questioning Southern cotton mill workers and examining their behavior, determined their indifference curves, which we can use to examine income and substitution effects. A typical worker's indifference curves are close to right angles (Figure 5.13), indicating that leisure and all other goods are nearly perfect complements: The worker is relatively unwilling to substitute goods for leisure. (Workers' indifference curves vary only slightly by race and gender.)

At the original wage, \$2.09/hour, the budget constraint is L^1 and a typical worker chooses to work 42.4 hours/week (assuming that there are 100 total hours to be allocated between work and leisure), Bundle e_1. An increase in the wage of \$1 per hour causes the budget constraint to rotate outward to L^2. An uncompensated increase in the wage increases the demand for leisure and reduces the hours worked to 29.5 per week, Bundle e_2. Thus, workers' labor supply curves are backward bending: Workers decrease their hours as their wage rises. An increase in the wage from \$2.09 to \$3.09 leads to weekly earnings rising only from \$88.69 to \$91.18 because of the offsetting reduction in the hours worked.

What would happen if, when the wage increased, workers' incomes were reduced so that they remained on the original indifference curve, I^1? That is, what is the substitution effect for this \$1 wage increase? The imaginary budget

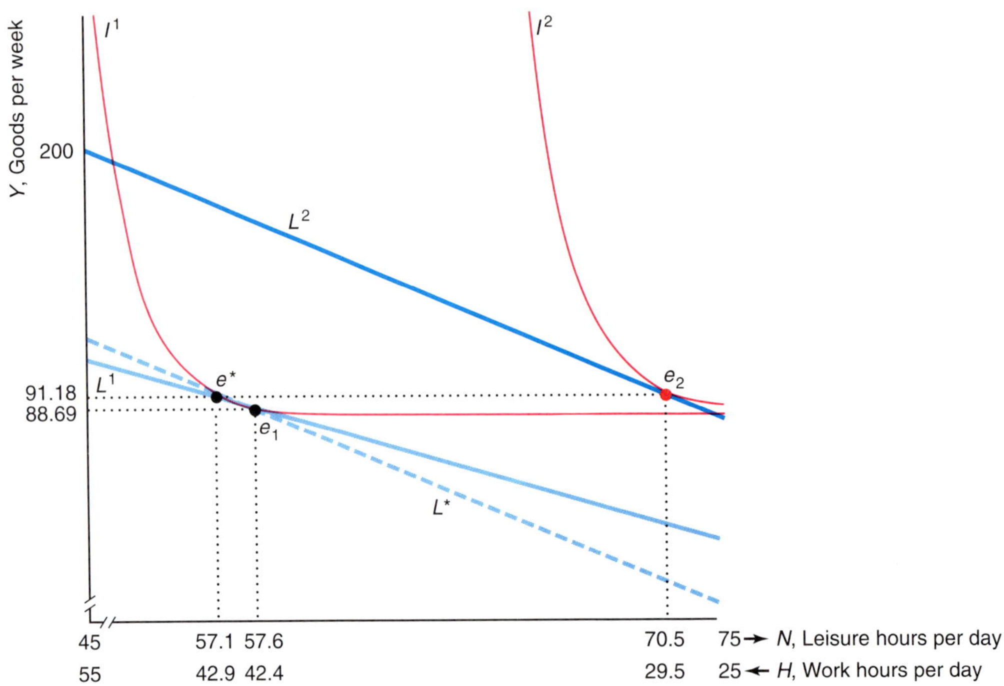

Figure 5.13 Effect of a Wage Increase for Textile Workers. The budget constraint at the original wage of \$2.09 per hour is L^1, where individuals work 42.4 hours/week and have 57.6 hours of leisure (assuming that there are 100 total hours to be allocated between work and leisure), Bundle e_1. When the wage rises from \$2.09 to \$3.09, the substitution effect is an increase in work hours of one-half hour a week: the movement from e_1 to e^*. The income effect, the movement from e_1 to e_2, causes work hours to fall by 13.4 hours a week. Thus, the total effect of a wage increase, the movement from e_1 to e_2, is a drop of 12.9 hours per week.

constraint L^* is parallel to L^2 but tangent to indifference curve I^1 at e^*. Thus, the substitution effect—the movement from e_1 to e^*—due to a compensated wage increase is an increase in weekly hours by half an hour a week to 42.9 hours. The income effect (the movement from e^* to e_2) is to work 13.4 (= 29.5 – 42.9) fewer hours a week. ■

Shape of the Labor Supply Curve

Whether the labor supply curve is upward sloping, is backward bending, or has sections that are upward sloping and others that are backward bending depends on the income elasticity of leisure. Suppose a worker views leisure as an inferior good at low wages and a normal good at high wages. As the wage increases, the demand for leisure first falls and then rises, and the hours supplied to the market first rise and then fall.

The budget line rotates upward from L^1 to L^2 as the wage rises in panel a of Figure 5.14. Because leisure is an inferior good at low incomes, in the new optimal bundle, e_2, this worker consumes less leisure and more goods than at the original bundle, e_1.

At higher incomes, however, leisure is a normal good. At an even higher wage, the new equilibrium is e_3, on budget line L^3, where the quantity of leisure demanded is higher and the number of hours worked is lower. Thus, the corresponding supply

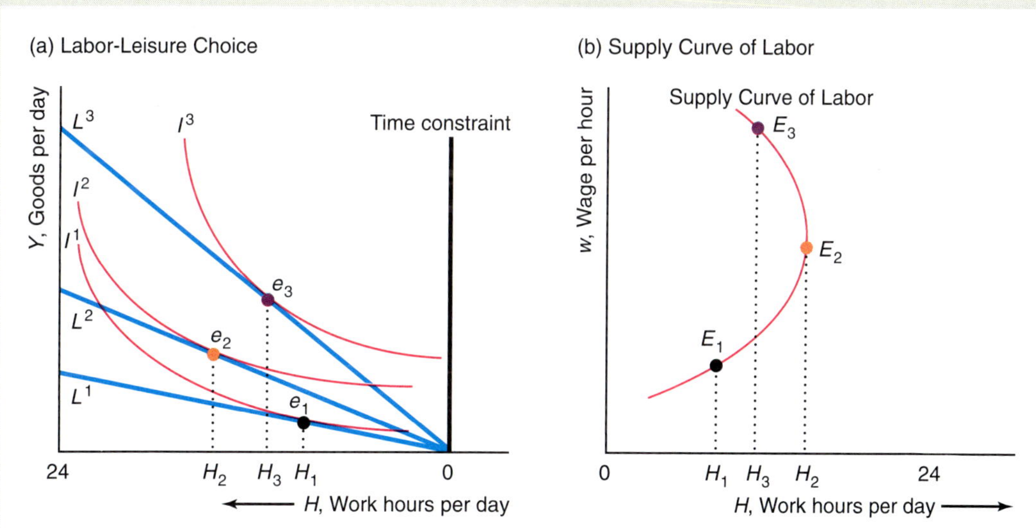

Figure 5.14 Labor Supply Curve That Is Upward Sloping and Then Backward Bending. At low incomes, an increase in the wage causes the worker to work more: the movement from e_1 to e_2 in (a) or from E_1 to E_2 in (b). At higher incomes, an increase in the wage causes the worker to work fewer hours: the movement from e_2 to e_3 or from E_2 to E_3.

curve of labor slopes upward at low wages and bends backward at higher wages in panel b.

Do labor supply curves slope upward or backward? Economic theory alone cannot answer this question: Both forward-sloping and backward-bending supply curves are *theoretically* possible. Empirical research is necessary to resolve this question.

APPLICATION

Estimated Labor Supply Curves

Empirical studies (many of which are surveyed in Killingsworth 1983) find that the slopes of labor supply curves vary across demographic groups. Most studies find that the labor supply curves for British and American men are virtually vertical because the income and substitution effects offset each other almost exactly.

Studies find that the typical British man has a slightly backward-sloping supply of labor, with an estimated elasticity of supply ranging between –0.2 and –0.05. That is, as the wage rises by 1%, the number of hours these men work falls by at most –0.2%.

Most studies find that American male workers have virtually vertical supply curves, with estimated elasticities of supply ranging between –0.2 and 0.15. A very careful, relatively recent study of prime-age American males (MaCurdy, Green, and Paarsch 1990), which controlled for income taxes, found that both substitution and income effects are essentially zero, so the total effect is zero and the labor supply curve is vertical.

Most studies report that female labor supply curves are upward sloping, averaging across married and unmarried women. Depending on the group and the country, the elasticities of supply range from 0 to relatively large positive numbers such as 4.0 and even higher for a few age groups of unmarried women. A number of studies of wives have found only that their supply curves are virtually vertical: slightly backward bending in Canada and the United States and slightly forward sloping in the United Kingdom and Germany.

Thus, most studies conclude that the hours worked by typical men and married women are not sensitive to wages. Typical single women, however, work more hours when their wage rises. ■

Income Tax Rates and Labor Supply

Why do we care about the shape of labor supply curves? One reason is that we can tell from the shape of the labor supply curve whether an increase in the income tax rate—a percent of earnings—will cause a substantial reduction in the hours of work. Taxes on earnings are a particularly unattractive way of collecting money for the government if supply curves are upward sloping because the taxes cause people to work fewer hours, reducing the amount of goods society produces and raising less tax revenue than would result if the supply curve were vertical or backward bending. On the other hand, if supply curves are backward bending, a small increase in the tax rate increases tax revenue *and* boosts total production (but reduces leisure).

Presidents John Kennedy and Ronald Reagan argued that cutting the marginal tax rate (the percentage of the last dollar earned that the government takes in taxes) would stimulate people to work longer and produce more, desirable effects. President Reagan claimed that tax receipts would increase due to the additional work.[19]

Because tax rates have changed substantially over time, we have a natural experiment to test this hypothesis. The Kennedy tax cuts lowered the top personal marginal tax rate from 91% to 70%. The rate fell over the next couple of decades, and under the Reagan Tax Reform Act of 1986, the top rate for the highest income group dropped to 28%, effective in 1988.

The effect of a tax rate of $\tau = 0.28$ is to reduce the effective wage from w to $(1 - \tau)w = 0.72w$.[20] The tax reduces the after-tax wage by 28%, so a worker's budget constraint rotates downward. If $w_1 = 0.72w_2$ in panel a of Figure 5.14, then the effect of a 28% tax rate on someone who earned w_2 before the tax would be to rotate the budget constraint downward from L^2 to L^1.

As we discussed, if the budget constraint rotates downward, the hours of work may increase or decrease, depending on whether leisure is a normal or an inferior good. The worker in panel b has a labor supply curve that is first upward sloping and then backward bending as in panel b. If the worker's wage is very high, the worker is in the backward-bending section of the labor supply curve.

If so, the relationship between the marginal tax rate, τ, and tax revenue, τwH, is bell shaped as in Figure 5.15.[21] At a zero tax rate, a small increase in the tax rate *must*

---

[19]President Reagan (*Time*, April 14, 1980) gave an even stronger reason to want to cut taxes: "History shows that when the taxes of a nation approach about 20 percent of the people's income, there begins to be a lack of respect for government. . . . When it reaches 25 percent, there comes an increase in lawlessness." According to the Organization for Economic Co-operation and Development (OECD), in 1993, Japan, at 29%, and the United States, at 30%, had the lowest share of tax receipts as a percentage of gross domestic product (GDP) of the industrial nations. The share was 34% in the United Kingdom, 39% in Germany, and 44% in France.

[20]Under a progressive income tax system the marginal tax rate increases with income. The average tax rate differs from the marginal tax rate. Suppose that the marginal tax rate is 20% on the first \$10,000 earned and 30% on the second \$10,000. Someone who earned \$20,000 would pay \$2,000 (= 0.2 × \$10,000) on the first \$10,000 of earnings and \$3,000 on the next \$10,000. That taxpayer's average tax rate is 25% (= [\$2,000 + \$3,000]/\$20,000). For simplicity in the following analysis, we assume that the marginal tax rate is a constant, τ, so that the average tax rate is also τ.

[21]We are assuming that the demand curve for labor is horizontal (the elasticity of demand is infinite), so the effect of the tax depends only on the elasticity of supply. In general, the effect of a tax on the labor market depends on both the elasticity of demand and the elasticity of supply. See Barlow and Sparks (1964), Head (1966), Allingham (1972), and Fullerton (1982) for a formal theoretical analysis on the necessary and sufficient conditions for a tax cut to increase hours worked and tax revenues.

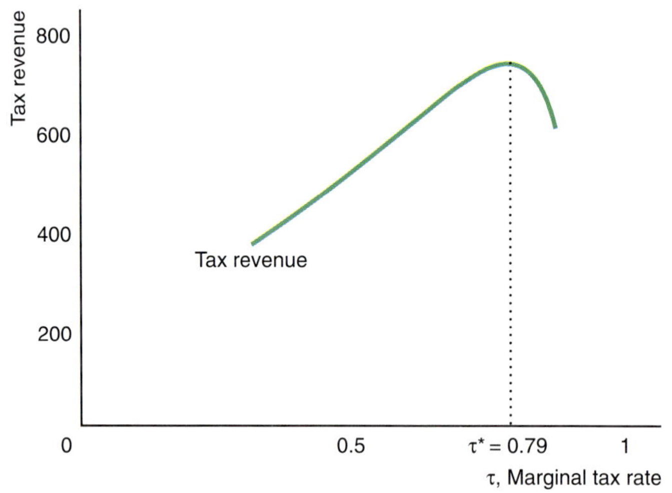

Figure 5.15 Relationship of Tax Revenue to Tax Rates. At marginal tax rates below τ^*, an increase in the rate leads to larger tax collections. At rates above τ^*, however, an increase in the marginal rate decreases tax revenue. These calculations (Fullerton 1982, Table 1, p. 15) are based on the assumption that the labor supply elasticity with respect to the after-tax wage is 0.15.

increase the tax revenue, because no revenue was collected when the tax rate was zero. If the tax rate rises a little more, however, tax revenue must rise even higher for two reasons. First, the government collects a larger percent of every dollar earned because the tax rate is higher. Second, employees work more hours as the tax rate rises because workers are in the backward-bending section of their labor supply curves.

As the tax rate rises far enough, however, the workers are in the upward-sloping section of their labor supply curves. In this section, an increase in the tax rate reduces the number of hours worked. When the tax rate rises high enough, the reduction in hours worked more than offsets the gain from the higher rate, so tax revenue falls.

It makes little sense for a government to operate at very high marginal tax rates in the downward-sloping portion of this bell-shaped curve. The government could get more output *and* more tax revenue by cutting the marginal tax rate. Therefore, the question facing Congress when Reagan took office was whether we were on the downward-sloping section of the curve, where a tax cut would increase revenue. To answer this question, we need to know whether the tax rate before the cut was greater or less than the tax rate τ^* at the peak of the curve.

APPLICATION

Effects of Tax Cuts

Economists have estimated the effects of tax cuts in many countries. As marginal tax rates vary substantially across countries, the effect of a tax cut on tax revenue also differs across counties.

Fullerton (1982) concluded that the marginal tax rate, τ^*, that maximizes tax revenue is very high for the United States. He calculated that $\tau^* = 79\%$ if the labor supply elasticity with respect to after-tax wages is 0.15. Stuart (1984) calculated that τ^* is close to 85%. Given that the American τ^* is between 79% and 85%, the Kennedy era tax cut (from 91% to 70%) raised tax revenue and increased the work effort of top-income-bracket workers, but a Reagan era tax cut (in which the actual rate was about half as big as τ^*) had the opposite effects.

In European countries with higher tax rates, a cut in the marginal tax rate is more likely to raise tax revenues. Stuart (1981) argued that Sweden's 80% marginal tax rate is greater than that country's τ^*. Van Ravenstein and Vijlbrief (1988) calculated that, in the Netherlands, τ^* is approximately 70%, which is close to the actual rate of 67.4% in 1985. ■

Summary

1. **Deriving demand curves:** Individual demand curves can be derived by using the information about tastes contained in a consumer's indifference curve map. Varying the price of one good, holding other prices and income constant, we find how the quantity demanded varies with that price, which is the information we need to draw the demand curve. Consumers' tastes, which are captured by the indifference curves, determine the shape of the demand curve (the elasticity of demand).

2. **How income changes shift demand curves:** Using consumer theory, we can show how the entire demand curve shifts as a consumer's income rises. By varying income, holding prices constant, we see how quantity demanded shifts with income. An Engel curve summarizes the relationship between income and quantity demanded, holding prices constant.

3. **Effects of a price change:** An increase in the price of a good causes both a substitution effect and an income effect. The *substitution effect* is the amount by which a consumer's demand for the good changes as a result of a price increase when we compensate the consumer for the price increase by raising the individual's income by enough that his or her utility does not change. The substitution effect is unambiguous: A compensated rise in a good's price always causes consumers to buy less of that good. The *income effect* shows how a consumer's demand for a good changes as the consumer's income falls. The price rise effectively lowers the consumer's opportunities, because the consumer can now buy less than before with the same income. The income effect can be positive or negative. If a good is normal (the income elasticity is positive), the income effect is negative.

4. **Cost-of-living adjustments:** The government's major index of inflation, the Consumer Price Index, overestimates inflation by ignoring the substitution effect. Though on average small, the substitution bias may be substantial for particular individuals or firms.

5. **Deriving labor supply curves:** Using consumer theory, we can derive the daily demand curve for leisure, which is time spent on activities other than work. By subtracting the demand curve for leisure from 24 hours, we obtain the labor supply curve, which shows how the number of hours worked varies with the wage. Depending on whether leisure is an inferior good or a normal good, the supply curve of labor may be upward sloping or backward bending. Knowing the shape of the supply of labor is important in determining the effects of tax cuts. Empirical evidence based on this theory shows why tax cuts in the 1980s did not increase the tax revenue of individuals as predicted by the Reagan administration.

Problems

1. Derive the demand curve for Coke for a person who views Coke and Pepsi as perfect substitutes.
2. Derive the demand curve for pie for a person who eats pie only à la mode and does not eat either pie or ice cream alone (pie and ice cream are complements).
3. Michael views doughnuts and coffee as perfect complements: He always eats one doughnut with a cup of coffee and will not eat a doughnut without coffee or drink coffee without a doughnut. What does Michael's Engel curve for doughnuts look like? How much does his weekly budget have to rise for Michael to buy one more doughnut per week?
4. Under what conditions does the income effect reinforce the substitution effect? Under what conditions does it have an offsetting effect? If the income effect more than offsets the substitution effect for a good, what do we call that good?
5. Cora spends all her money on food and clothing. When the price of clothing decreases, she buys more clothing. (Note: In the following questions, if the direction of the effect is ambiguous, say so.)
   A. Does the substitution effect cause her to buy more or less clothing? Explain.
   B. Does the income effect cause her to buy more or less clothing? Explain.
6. Suppose Bessie consumes only coffee and coffee cake and consumes them only together (they are complements). By how much will a CPI over these two goods differ from the true cost-of-living index?
7. Do you expect that relatively more high-quality navel oranges are sold in California or New York? Why?
8. Draw a figure to illustrate the verbal answer given in Solved Problem 5.2.
9. Under a welfare plan, poor people are given a lump-sum payment of $\$L$. If they accept this welfare payment, they must pay a high tax, $\tau = \frac{1}{2}$, on anything they earn. If they do not accept the welfare payment, they do not have to pay a tax on their earnings. Show that whether an individual accepts welfare depends on the individual's tastes.
10. If an individual's labor supply curve is forward sloping at low wages and backward bending at high wages, is leisure a Giffen good? If so, at high or low wage rates?
11. Suppose Roy could choose how many hours to work at a wage of w and chose to work seven hours a day. The employer now offers him time-and-a-half wages ($1.5w$) for every hour he works beyond a minimum of eight hours per day. Show how his budget constraint changes. Will he choose to work more than seven hours a day?
12. Jerome moonlights: He holds down two jobs. The higher-paying job pays w, but he can work at most eight hours. The other job pays w^*, but he can work as many hours as he wants. Show how Jerome determines how many hours to work.
13. Suppose that the job in Problem 12 that had no hours restriction was the higher-paying job. How do Jerome's budget constraint and behavior change?
14. Paul and Janice have a child. Both can earn the same wage in the market and choose how many hours they work. They feel that one of them should stay home with their child at least half of the working day, but they do not think it matters which one of them stays home. How many hours should each of them work?
15. If, in Problem 14, Janice's wage, w, is higher than Paul's wage, w^*, how does your answer change?
16. Suppose Howard's wage varies with the hours he works: $w(H) = \alpha H$, $\alpha 70$. Show how the number of hours he chooses to work depends on his tastes.

Math Problems

17. Bill's utility function is Cobb-Douglas, $U = B^{1/4}Z^{3/4}$, his income is Y, the price of B is p_B, and the price of Z is p_Z. Derive his demand curves. (*Hint*: See Appendix 4B.)

18. Derive Bill's Engel curve for B for the utility given in Problem 1.

★19. Using calculus, show that not all goods can be inferior.

20. Using calculus, show the effect of a change in the wage on the amount of leisure an individual wants to consume. (*Hint*: See Appendix 5A.)

21. Answer the same question as in Problem 20 when the utility function is $U = Y^{\alpha}L^{1-\alpha}$.

CHAPTER 6

Firms and Production

Hard work never killed anybody, but why take a chance?
—Charlie McCarthy

The Ghirardelli Chocolate Company converts chocolate and other inputs into an output of 144,000 wrapped chocolate bars and 340,000 wrapped chocolate squares a day. The *material inputs* include chocolate, other food products, and various paper goods for wrapping and boxing the candy. The *labor inputs* include chefs, assembly line workers, and various mechanics and other technicians. The *capital inputs* are the manufacturing plant, the land on which the plant is located, conveyor belts, molds, wrapping machines, and various other types of equipment.

Over time, Ghirardelli has changed how it produces its finished product, increasing the ratio of machines to workers. Several years ago, to minimize employees' risk of repetitive motion injuries, the company spent $300,000 on robots, which pack the wrapped chocolate and put it on pallets.[1] The use of robotic arms resulted in greatly reduced downtime, increased production, and improved working conditions.

This chapter looks at the type of decisions that the owners of firms have to make. First, a decision must be made as to how a firm is owned and managed. Ghirardelli, for example, is a corporation—it is not owned by an individual or partnership—and is run by professional managers. Second, the firm must decide how to produce. Ghirardelli now uses relatively more machines and robots and fewer workers than in the past. Third, if a firm wants to expand output, it must decide how to do that in both the short run and the long run. In the short run, Ghirardelli can expand output by extending the work week to six or seven days and using extra materials. To expand output more, Ghirardelli would have to install more equipment, such as extra robotic arms, hire more workers, and eventually build a new plant, all of which take time. Fourth, given its ability to change its output level, a firm must determine how large to grow. Ghirardelli determines its current investments on the basis of its beliefs about demand and costs in the future.

In this chapter, we examine how a firm chooses its inputs so as to produce efficiently. In Chapter 7, we examine how the firm chooses the least costly among all possible efficient production processes. In Chapter 8, we combine this information about costs with information about revenues to determine how a firm picks the output level that maximizes profit.

The main lesson of this chapter and the next is that firms are not black boxes that mysteriously transform inputs (such as labor, capital, and material) into outputs.

[1]Peter Sinton, "Faster, Flexible Robots Tackle the Job," *San Francisco Chronicle*, May 15, 1995:B1, and the Ghirardelli Chocolate Company.

By using robotic equipment to pack finished, wrapped chocolate, the Ghirardelli Chocolate Company benefits from reduced downtime and increased production.

Economic theory explains how firms make decisions about production processes, types of inputs to use, and the volume of output to produce.

In this chapter, we examine six main topics:

1. **The ownership and management of firms:** Decisions must be made as to how a firm is owned and run.
2. **Production:** A firm converts inputs into outputs using one of possibly many available technologies.
3. **Short-run production: One variable and one fixed input:** In the short run, only some inputs can be varied, so the firm changes its output by adjusting its variable inputs.
4. **Long-run production: Two variable inputs:** The firm has more flexibility in how it produces and how it changes its output level in the long run when all factors can be varied.
5. **Returns to scale:** How the ratio of output to input varies with the size of the firm is an important factor in determining the size of a firm.
6. **Productivity and technical change:** The amount of output that can be produced with a given amount of inputs varies across firms and over time.

6.1 THE OWNERSHIP AND MANAGEMENT OF FIRMS

A **firm** is an organization that converts *inputs* such as labor, materials, and capital into *outputs*, the goods and services that it sells. U.S. Steel combines iron ore, machinery, and labor to create steel. A local restaurant buys raw food, cooks it, and serves it. A landscape designer hires gardeners and machines, buys trees and shrubs, transports them to a customer's home, and supervises the work.

Most goods and services produced in Western countries are produced by firms. In the United States, firms produce 84% of national production, the government produces 12%, nonprofit institutions (such as some universities and hospitals), 4%, and private households, less than 0.2%.[2] In developing countries, the government's share of total national production can be much higher, reaching 37% in Ghana, 38% in Zambia, 40% in Sudan, and 90% in Algeria, though it is as low as 3% in Bangladesh, Paraguay, and Nepal.[3] In this book, we focus on production by for-profit firms rather than by nonprofit organizations and governments.

Ownership of Firms

In most countries, for-profit firms have one of three legal forms: sole proprietorships, partnerships, and corporations. *Sole proprietorships* are firms owned and run by a single individual.

Partnerships are businesses jointly owned and controlled by two or more people. The owners operate under a partnership agreement. If any partner leaves, the partnership agreement ends. For the firm to continue to operate, a new partnership agreement must be written.

Corporations are owned by *shareholders* in proportion to the numbers of shares of stock they hold. The shareholders elect a board of directors who run the firm. In turn, the board of directors usually hires managers who make short-term decisions and long-term plans.

Corporations differ from the other two forms of ownership in terms of personal liability for the debts of the firm. Sole proprietors and partners are personally responsible for the debts of their firms. All of an owner's personal wealth—not just that invested in the firm—is at risk if the business becomes bankrupt and is unable to pay its bills. Even the assets of partners who are not responsible for the failure can be taken to cover the firm's debts.

In contrast to sole proprietorships or partnerships, owners of corporations have **limited liability**: The personal assets of the corporation owners cannot be taken to pay a corporation's debts if it goes into bankruptcy. If the corporation fails, the shares become worthless. Because of the limited liability of corporations, the most

[2]These are shares of the U.S. gross domestic product for 1996 from the *Survey of Current Business*, Table 1.7, 77(3), March 1997. These figures exclude nonmarketed output of private households such as meal production.

[3]Fraction of gross domestic product or gross national product. United Nations Industrial Development Organization, *Industry and Development: Global Report 1992/93*, Vienna, 1992.

shareholders can lose if the firm goes bankrupt is the amount they paid for their stock. As a result, people are more willing to buy shares than they would be if they faced full liability.

In the United States, 90% of business sales are made by corporations, even though fewer than 20% of all firms are corporations. Nearly 73% of all firms are sole proprietorships. Sole proprietorships tend to be small, however, so they are responsible for only 6% of all sales. Partnerships are 7% of all firms and make 5% of sales.[4]

The Management of Firms

In a small firm, the owner usually manages the firm's operations. In larger firms, typically corporations and larger partnerships, a manager or team of managers usually run the company. In such firms, owners, managers, and lower-level supervisors are all decisionmakers.

The various decisionmakers may have conflicting objectives. What is in the best interest of the owners may not be the same as what is in the best interest of managers or other employees. For example, a manager may want a fancy office, a company car, a company jet, and other perks, but the owner would likely oppose these drains on profit.

The owner replaces the manager if the manager pursues personal objectives rather than the firm's objectives. In a corporation, the board of directors is supposed to ensure that managers do not stray. If the manager and the board of directors run the firm badly, the shareholders can fire both or directly change some policies through votes at the corporation's annual meeting for shareholders. Until Chapter 20, we'll ignore the potential conflict between managers and owners and assume that the owner *is* the manager of the firm and makes all the decisions.

What Owners Want

Economists usually assume that a firm's owners try to maximize profit. Presumably, most people invest in a firm to make money—lots of money, they hope. They want the firm to earn a positive profit rather than make a loss (a negative profit). A firm's **profit**, π, is the difference between its revenue, R, which is what it earns from selling the good, and its cost, C, which is what it pays for labor, materials, and other inputs:

$$\pi = R - C.$$

Revenue is p, the price, times q, the firm's quantity: $R = pq$.

In reality, some owners have other objectives, such as having as big a firm as possible or a fancy office or keeping risks low. In Chapter 8, however, we show that a competitive firm is likely to be driven out of business if it doesn't maximize profits.

To maximize profits, a firm must produce as efficiently as possible. A firm engages in **efficient production** (achieves **technological efficiency**) if it cannot

---

[4]Data for 1995 from the *Statistical Abstract of the United States*, Table 834, 1997:537. The numbers add to more than 100% because of rounding.

produce its current level of output with fewer inputs, given existing knowledge about technology and the organization of production. Equivalently, the firm produces efficiently if, given the quantity of inputs used, no more output could be produced using existing knowledge.

If the firm does not produce efficiently, it cannot be profit maximizing—so efficient production is a *necessary condition* for profit maximization. Even if a firm produces a given level of output efficiently, however, it may not be profit maximizing if that output level is too high or too low or if it is using excessively expensive inputs. Thus, efficient production alone is not a *sufficient condition* to ensure that a firm's profit is maximized.

A firm may use engineers and other experts to determine the most efficient ways to produce with a known method or technology. This knowledge, however, does not indicate which of the many technologies, each of which uses different combinations of inputs, allows for production at the lowest cost or with the highest possible profit. How to produce at the lowest cost is an economic decision, typically made by the firm's manager.

6.2 PRODUCTION

A firm uses a *technology* or *production process* to transform *inputs* or *factors of production* into *outputs*. Firms use many types of inputs. Most of these inputs can be grouped into three broad categories:

- **Capital (K):** long-lived inputs such as land, buildings (factories, stores), and equipment (machines, trucks).
- **Labor (L):** human services such as those provided by managers, skilled or white-collar workers (architects, economists, engineers, plumbers), and less-skilled or blue-collar workers (custodians, construction laborers, assembly-line workers).
- **Materials (M):** raw goods (oil, water, wheat) and processed products (aluminum, plastic, paper, steel).

The output can be a *service*, such as an automobile tune-up by a mechanic, or a *physical product*, such as a computer chip or potato chip.

Production Functions

Firms can transform inputs into outputs in many different ways. Candy-manufacturing companies differ in the skills of their work force and the amount of equipment they use. While all employ a chef, a manager, and relatively unskilled workers, some candy firms also use skilled technicians and modern equipment. In small candy companies, the relatively unskilled workers shape the candy, decorate it, package it, and box it by hand. In other, slightly larger firms, the relatively unskilled workers use conveyor belts and other equipment that was invented decades ago. In modern, large-scale plants, the relatively unskilled laborers work with robots and other state-of-the art machines, which are maintained by skilled technicians. Before deciding which production process to use, a firm needs to consider its various options.

The various ways inputs can be transformed into output are summarized in the **production function**: the relationship between the quantities of inputs used and the *maximum* quantity of output that can be produced, given current knowledge about technology and organization. The production function for a firm that uses only labor and capital is

$$q = f(L, K), \tag{6.1}$$

where q units of output (wrapped candy bars) are produced using L units of labor services (days of work by relatively unskilled assembly-line workers) and K units of capital (the number of conveyor belts).

The production function shows only the *maximum* amount of output that can be produced from given levels of labor and capital, because the production function includes only efficient production processes. A profit-maximizing firm is not interested in production processes that are inefficient and waste inputs: Firms do not want to use two workers to do a job that can be done as quickly by one worker.

Time and the Variability of Inputs

A firm can more easily adjust its inputs in the long run than in the short run. Typically, a firm can vary the amount of materials and of relatively unskilled labor it uses comparatively quickly. However, it needs more time to find and hire skilled workers, order new equipment, or build a new manufacturing plant.

The longer a firm has to adjust its inputs, the more factors of production it can alter. The **short run** is a period of time so brief that at least one factor of production cannot be varied practically. A factor that cannot be varied practically in the short run is called a **fixed input**. In contrast, a **variable input** is a factor of production whose quantity can be changed readily by the firm during the relevant time period. The **long run** is a lengthy enough period of time that all inputs can be varied. There are no fixed inputs in the long run—all factors of production are variable inputs.

Suppose that a painting company gets more work than usual one day. Even if it wanted to do so, the firm does not have time to buy or rent an extra truck and buy another compressor to run a power sprayer; these inputs are fixed in the short run. To get the work done that afternoon, the firm uses the company's one truck to drop off a temporary worker, equipped with only a brush and a can of paint, at the last job. In the long run, however, the firm can adjust all its inputs. If the firm wants to paint more houses every day, it hires more full-time workers, gets a second truck, purchases more compressors to run the power sprayers, and buys a computer to keep track of all its projects.

How long it takes for all inputs to be variable depends on the factors a firm uses. For a janitorial service whose only major input is workers, the long run is a very brief period of time. In contrast, an automobile manufacturer may need many years to build a new manufacturing plant or to design and construct a new type of machine. A pistachio farmer needs the better part of a decade before newly planted trees bear a substantial amount of nuts.

For many firms over, say, a month, materials and often labor are variable inputs. Labor is not always a variable input, however. Finding additional highly skilled workers may take substantial time. Similarly, capital may be a variable or fixed input. Some smaller capital assets (trucks and personal computers) can be rented relatively quickly, whereas larger capital assets (buildings and large, specialized pieces of equipment) take years to adjust.

To illustrate the greater flexibility that a firm has in the long run than in the short run, we examine the production function in Equation 6.1, in which output is a function of only labor and capital. We look at first the short-run and then the long-run production process.

6.3 SHORT-RUN PRODUCTION: ONE VARIABLE AND ONE FIXED INPUT

In the short run, we assume that capital is a fixed input and labor is a variable input, so the firm can increase output only by increasing the amount of labor it uses. In the short run, the firm's production function is

$$q = f(L, \bar{K}), \tag{6.2}$$

where q is output, L is workers, and $\bar{K}$ is the fixed number of units of capital.

To illustrate the short-run production process, we consider a firm that assembles computers for a manufacturing firm that supplies it with the necessary parts, such as computer chips and disk drives. The assembly firm cannot increase its capital—eight workbenches fully equipped with tools, electronic probes, and other equipment for testing computers—in the short run, but it can hire extra workers or pay current workers extra to work overtime so as to increase production.

Total Product

The exact relationship between *output* or *total product* and *labor* can be illustrated by using a particular function, Equation 6.2, a table, or a figure. Table 6.1 shows the relationship between output and labor when capital is fixed for a firm. The first column lists the fixed amount of capital: eight fully equipped workbenches. As the number of workers, the amount of labor (second column), increases, total output, the number of computers assembled in a day (third column), first increases and then decreases.

With zero workers, no computers are assembled. One worker with access to the firm's equipment assembles five computers in a day. As the number of workers increases, so does output: 1 worker assembles 5 computers in a day, 2 workers assemble 18, 3 workers assemble 36, and so forth. The maximum number of computers that can be assembled with the capital on hand, however, is limited at 110 per day. That maximum can be produced with 10 or 11 workers. Adding extra workers beyond 11 lowers production as workers get in each other's way. The

Table 6.1 Total Product, Marginal Product, and Average Product of Labor with Fixed Capital

Capital, $\bar{K}$	Labor, L	Output, Total Product of Labor, Q	Marginal Product of Labor, $MP_L = \Delta Q/\Delta L$	Average Product of Labor, $AP_L = Q/L$
8	0	0		
8	1	5	5	5
8	2	18	13	9
8	3	36	18	12
8	4	56	20	14
8	5	75	19	15
8	6	90	15	15
8	7	98	8	14
8	8	104	6	13
8	9	108	4	12
8	10	110	2	11
8	11	110	0	10
8	12	108	–2	9
8	13	104	–4	8

dashed line in the table indicates that a firm would not use more than 11 workers, as to do so would be inefficient. We can show how extra workers affect the total product by using two additional concepts: the marginal product of labor and the average product of labor.

Marginal Product of Labor

Before deciding whether to hire one more worker, a manager wants to determine how much this extra worker, $\Delta L = 1$, will increase output, Δq. That is, the manager wants to know the **marginal product of labor** (MP_L): the change in total output resulting from using an extra unit of labor, holding other factors (capital) constant. If output changes by Δq when the number of workers increases by ΔL, the change in output per worker is[5]

$$MP_L = \Delta q/\Delta L.$$

As Table 6.1 shows, if the number of workers increases from 1 to 2, $\Delta L = 1$, output rises by $\Delta q = 13 = 18 - 5$, so the marginal product of labor is 13.

[5]The formal definition of the marginal product of labor requires that, holding capital fixed at $\bar{K}$, the change in labor be small:

$$MP_L = \partial q/\partial L = \partial f(L, \bar{K})/\partial L.$$

Average Product of Labor

Before hiring extra workers, a manager may also want to know whether output will rise in proportion to this extra labor. To answer this question, the firm determines how extra workers affect the **average product of labor** (AP_L): the ratio of output to the number of workers used to produce that output,

$$AP_L = q/L.$$

Table 6.1 shows that 10 workers can assemble 110 computers in a day, so the average product of labor for 10 workers is 11 computers. The average product of labor for 9 workers is 12 computers per day; thus, increasing from 9 to 10 workers lowers the average product per worker.

Graphing the Product Curves

Figure 6.1 and Table 6.1 show how output, the average product of labor, and the marginal product of labor vary with the number of workers. (The figures are smooth curves because the firm can hire a "fraction of a worker" by employing a worker for a fraction of a day.) The curve in panel a of Figure 6.1 shows how a change in labor affects the **total product of labor**—the amount of output (or *total product*) that can be produced by a given amount of labor. Output rises with labor until it reaches its maximum of 110 computers at 11 workers, point *C*, and thereafter, the number of computers assembled falls with extra workers.

Panel b of the figure shows how the average product of labor and marginal product of labor vary with the number of workers. We can line up the figures in panels a and b vertically because the units along the horizontal axes of both figures, the number of workers per day, are the same. The vertical axes differ, however. The vertical axis is total product in panel a and the average or marginal product of labor—measures of output per unit of labor—in panel b.

Effect of Extra Labor. In most production processes, the average product of labor first rises and then falls as labor increases. One reason the AP_L curve initially rises in Figure 6.1 is that it helps to have more than two hands when assembling a computer. One worker holds a part in place while another one bolts it down. As a result, output increases more than in proportion to labor, so the average product of labor rises. Doubling the number of workers from one to two more than doubles the

Figure 6.1 Production Relationships with Variable Labor. (a) The total product of labor curve shows how many computers, q, can be assembled with eight fully equipped workbenches and a varying number of workers, L, who work an eight-hour day (see columns two and three in Table 6.1). Where extra workers reduce the number of computers assembled, the total product curve is a dashed line, which indicates that such production is inefficient production and not part of the production function. The slope of the line from the origin to point *B* is the average product of labor for six workers. (b) The marginal product of labor ($MP_L = \Delta q/\Delta L$, column four of Table 6.1) equals the average product of labor ($AP_L = q/L$, column five of Table 6.1) at the peak of the average product curve.

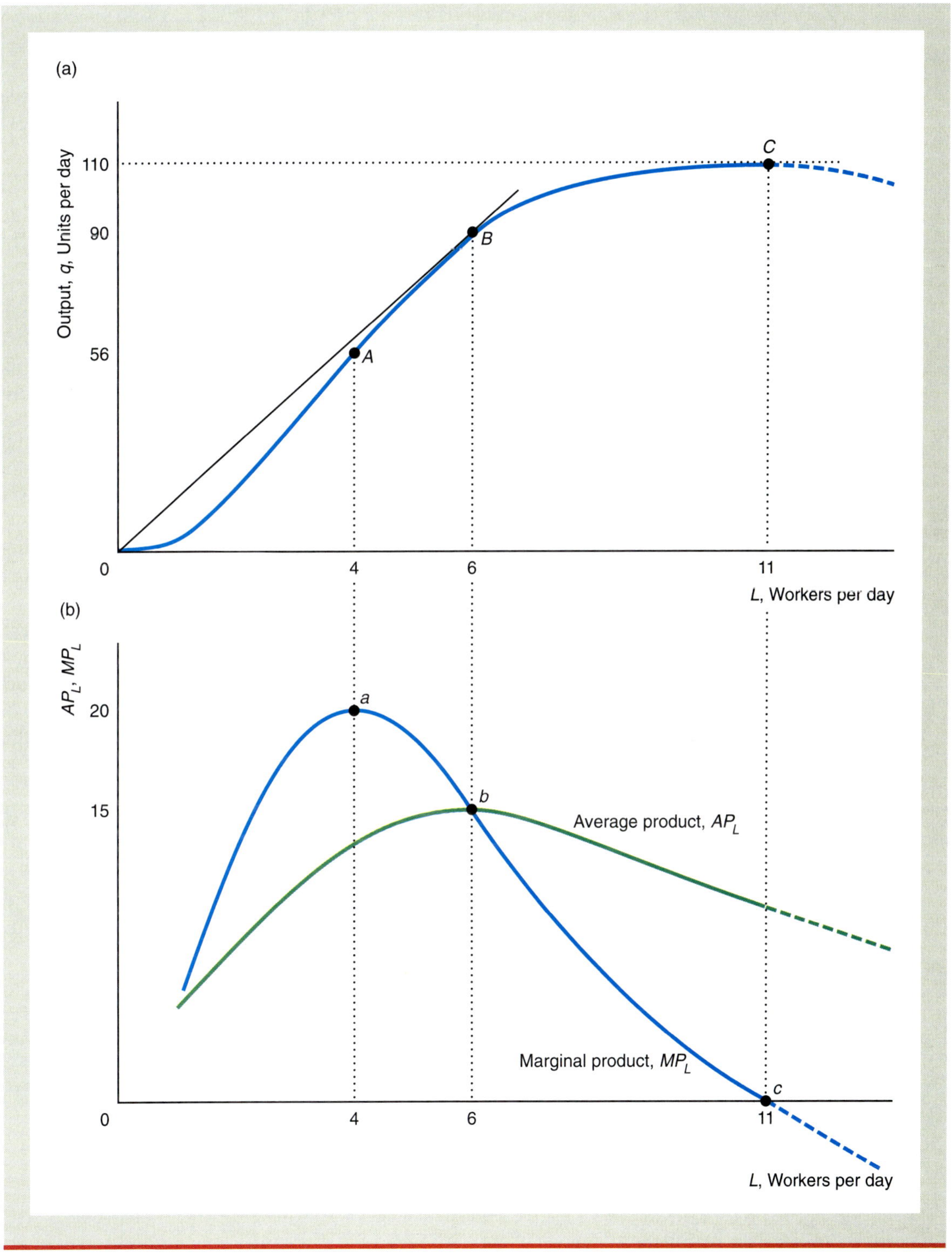
(a)
Output, q, Units per day
110
90
56
0
A
B
C
4
6
11
L, Workers per day
(b)
AP_L, MP_L
20
15
0
a
b
c
Average product, AP_L
Marginal product, MP_L
4
6
11
L, Workers per day

output from 5 to 18 and causes the average product of labor to rise from 5 to 9, as Table 6.1 shows.

Similarly, output initially may rise more than in proportion to labor because of greater specialization of activities. With greater specialization, workers are assigned to tasks at which they are particularly adept, and time is saved by not having workers move from task to task.

As the number of workers rises further, however, output may not increase by as much per worker as they have to wait to use a particular piece of equipment or get in each other's way. In Figure 6.1, as the number of workers exceeds 6, total output increases less than in proportion to labor, so the average product falls.

If more than 11 workers are used, the total product curve falls with each extra worker as the crowding of workers gets worse. Because that much labor is not efficient, that section of the curve is drawn with a dashed line to indicate that it is not part of the production function. Similarly, the dashed portions of the average and marginal product curves are irrelevant because no firm would produce with that many workers.

Relationship of the Product Curves. The three curves are geometrically related. First we use panel b to illustrate the relationship between the average and marginal product of labor curves. Then we use panels a and b to show the relationship between the total product of labor curve and the other two curves.

The average product of labor curve slopes upward where the marginal product of labor curve is above it and slopes downward where the marginal product curve is below it. If an extra worker adds more output—that worker's marginal product—than the average product of the initial workers, the extra worker raises the average product. As Table 6.1 shows, the average product of 2 workers is 9. The marginal product for a third worker is 18—which is above the average product for two workers—so the average product rises from 9 to 12. As panel b shows, when there are fewer than six workers, the marginal product curve is above the average product curve, so the average product curve is upward sloping.

Similarly, if the marginal product of labor for a new worker is less than the former average product of labor, the average product of labor falls. In the figure, the average product of labor falls beyond 6 workers. Because the average product of labor curve rises when the marginal product of labor curve is above it and the average product of labor falls when the marginal product of labor is below it, the average product of labor curve reaches a peak, point *b* in panel b, where the marginal product of labor curve crosses it.[6]

---

[6]We can use calculus to show that the MP_L curve crosses the AP_L curve at its peak. Because capital is fixed, we can write the production function solely in terms of labor: $q = f(L)$. In the figure, $\mathrm{d}f/\mathrm{d}L > 0$ and $\mathrm{d}^2f/\mathrm{d}L^2 < 0$. Thus, $MP_L = \mathrm{d}q/\mathrm{d}L = \mathrm{d}f/\mathrm{d}L > 0$ and $AP_L = q/L = f(L)/L > 0$. A necessary condition for the AP_L curve to reach a peak is that the first-order condition that the derivative of AP_L with respect to L equals zero:

$$\frac{\mathrm{d}AP_L}{\mathrm{d}L} = \left(\frac{\mathrm{d}q}{\mathrm{d}L} - \frac{q}{L}\right)\frac{1}{L} = 0.$$

(At the L determined by the first-order condition, AP_L is maximized if the second-order condition is negative: $\mathrm{d}^2AP_L/\mathrm{d}L^2 = \mathrm{d}^2f/\mathrm{d}L^2 < 0$.) From the first-order condition, $MP_L = \mathrm{d}q/\mathrm{d}L = q/L = AP_L$ at the peak of the AP_L curve.

The geometric relationship between the total product curve and the average and marginal product curves is illustrated in panels a and b of Figure 6.1. We can determine the average product of labor using the total product of labor curve. The average product of labor for L workers equals the slope of a straight line from the origin to a point on the total product of labor curve for L workers in panel a. The slope of this line equals output divided by the number of workers, which is the definition of the average product of labor. For example, the slope of the straight line drawn from the origin to point B ($L = 6$, $q = 90$) is 15, which equals the "rise" of $q = 90$ divided by the "run" of $L = 6$. As panel b shows, the average product of labor for 6 workers at point b is 15.

The marginal product of labor also has a geometric interpretation in terms of the total product curve. The slope of the total product curve at a given point, $\Delta q/\Delta L$, equals the marginal product of labor. That is, the marginal product of labor equals the slope of a straight line that is tangent to the total output curve at a given point. For example, at point C in panel a where there are 11 workers, the line tangent to the total product curve is flat, so the marginal product of labor is zero: A little extra labor has no effect on output. The total product curve is upward sloping when there are fewer than 11 workers, so the marginal product of labor is positive. If the firm is foolish enough to hire more than 11 workers, the total product curve slopes down (dashed line), so the MP_L is negative: Extra workers lower output. Again, this portion of the MP_L curve is not part of the production function.

When there are six workers, the average product of labor equals the marginal product of labor. The reason is that the line from the origin to point B in panel a is tangent to the total product curve, so the slope of that line, 15, is the marginal product of labor and the average product of labor at point b in panel b.

Law of Diminishing Marginal Returns

Next to "supply equals demand," probably the most commonly used phrase of economic jargon is the "law of diminishing marginal returns." This law determines the shapes of the total product and marginal product of labor curves as the firm uses more and more labor.

The *law of diminishing marginal returns* (or diminishing marginal product) holds that, *if a firm keeps increasing an input, holding all other inputs and technology constant, the corresponding increases in output will become smaller eventually.* That is, if only one input is increased, *the marginal product of that input will diminish eventually.*

In Table 6.1, if the firm goes from 1 to 2 workers, the marginal product of labor is 13. If 1 or 2 more workers are used, the marginal product rises: The marginal product for 3 workers is 18, and the marginal product for 4 workers is 20. However, if the firm increases the number of workers beyond 4, the marginal product falls: The marginal product of 5 workers is 19, and that for 6 workers is 15. That is, beyond 4 workers, each extra worker adds less and less extra output, so the total product of labor curve rises by smaller increments. At 11 workers, the marginal product is zero. In short, the law of diminishing marginal returns says that if a firm keeps adding one more unit of an input, the extra output it gets grows smaller and smaller. This diminishing return to extra labor may be due to too many workers sharing too few machines or to crowding, as workers get in each other's way. Thus, as the amount of labor used grows large enough, the marginal product curve approaches zero and the corresponding total product of labor curve becomes nearly flat.

Unfortunately, many people, when attempting to cite this empirical regularity, overstate it. Instead of talking about "diminishing *marginal* returns," they talk about "diminishing returns." The two phrases have different meanings. Where there are "diminishing marginal returns," the MP_L curve is falling—beyond 4 workers in panel b of Figure 6.1—but it may be positive, as the solid MP_L curve between 4 and 11 workers shows. With "diminishing returns," extra labor causes *output* to fall. There are diminishing (total) returns for more than 11 workers—a dashed MP_L line in panel b.

Thus, saying that there are diminishing returns is much stronger than saying that there are diminishing marginal returns. We often observe firms producing where there are diminishing marginal returns to labor, but we rarely see firms operating where there are diminishing total returns. Only a firm that is willing to lose money would operate so inefficiently that it has diminishing returns. Such a firm could produce more output by using fewer inputs.

A second common misinterpretation of this law is to claim that marginal products must fall as we increase an input without requiring that technology and other inputs stay constant. If we increase labor while simultaneously increasing other factors or adopting superior technologies, the marginal product of labor may rise indefinitely. Thomas Malthus provided the most famous example of this fallacy.

APPLICATION

Malthus and Mass Starvation

In 1798, Thomas Malthus—a clergyman and professor of modern history and political economy—predicted that (unchecked) population would grow more rapidly than food production because the quantity of land was fixed.[7] The problem, he believed, was that the fixed amount of land would lead to diminishing marginal product of labor, so output would rise less than in proportion to the increase in farm workers. Malthus grimly concluded that there would be mass starvation.

World population has increased nearly 800% from 1750 to today. Why aren't we all dead from starvation? The simple explanation is that fewer workers using less land can produce much more food today than was possible when

[7]Evidence for this application comes from the *U.S. Statistical Abstract*, 1995 (Table 1401); *FAO Quarterly Bulletin of Statistics*, 6(3), 1993; Donald N. Duvick, "Genetic Contributions to Advances in Yield of U.S. Maize," *Maydica*, 37(1), 1992:69–79; Tweeten (1989); Crossette, "How to Fix a Crowded World: Add People," *New York Times*, November 2, 1997:§4, 1 and 3.

Malthus wrote.[8] Two hundred years ago, most of the population had to work in agriculture to prevent starvation. Today, less than 3% of the U.S. population works in agriculture, and the share of land devoted to agriculture is constantly falling. Yet U.S. food production continues to grow faster than does U.S. population. Similarly, from 1951 to 1992, world food production per capita increased 34%.

Two key factors (in addition to birth control) are responsible for the rapid increase in food production per capita in most countries. First, agricultural technology—such as disease-resistant seeds and better land management practices—has substantially improved, so more output can be produced with the same inputs. Second, although the amounts of land and labor used have remained constant or fallen in most countries in recent years, the use of other inputs such as fertilizer and tractors has increased substantially, so output per acre of land has risen.

For example, from the 1930s to the 1980s, U.S. corn yields increased from 20 bushels per acre to 120 bushels per acre. Roughly half the improvement is due to genetic improvements in seeds, and the rest to technological innovations and new equipment.

Indeed, as developing countries adopt new seeds and pesticides, expand their use of fertilizers and equipment, and change to better farming techniques, they benefit from rapid growth of food production per capita. From 1980 to 1990, the rate of growth of per capita food production was 14% in developing countries, compared to only 5% in developed countries and 7% across all countries.

Parts of Africa, however, have severe problems. Per capita food production has fallen in Africa over the last two decades. Worse, in several recent years, mass starvation has plagued some African countries. Although droughts have contributed, these tragedies appear to be primarily due to political problems such as wars and a breakdown of economic production and distribution systems. If these political problems cannot be solved, Malthus may prove to be right for the wrong reason. ■

6.4 LONG-RUN PRODUCTION: TWO VARIABLE INPUTS

"Eternity is a terrible thought. I mean, where's it going to end?" —Tom Stoppard

We started our analysis of production functions by looking at a short-run production function in which one input, capital, was fixed, and the other, labor, was variable. In the long run, however, both of these inputs are variable. With both factors variable, a firm can usually produce a given level of output by using a great deal of labor and very little capital, a great deal of capital and very little labor, or moderate amounts of both. That is, the firm can substitute one input for another while

[8] Also, 44% of the world's population lives in countries that have fertility rates at or below replacement levels in 1997, and it is thought that this share will rise to 67% by 2015.

continuing to produce the same level of output, in much the same way that a consumer can maintain a given level of utility by substituting one good for another.

Typically, a firm can produce in a number of different ways—some of which require more labor than others. For example, a lumberyard can produce 200 planks an hour with 10 workers using hand saws, with 4 workers using hand-held power saws, or with 2 workers using bench power saws.

We illustrate a firm's ability to substitute between inputs in Table 6.2, which shows the amount of output per day the firm produces with various combinations of labor per day and capital per day. The labor inputs are along the top of the table, and the capital inputs are in the first column. The table shows four combinations of labor and capital that the firm may use to produce 24 units of output. The firm may employ (a) 1 worker and 6 units of capital, (b) 2 workers and 3 units of capital, (c) 3 workers and 2 units of capital, or (d) 6 workers and 1 unit of capital.

Isoquants

These four combinations of labor and capital are labeled *a*, *b*, *c*, and *d* on the "q = 24" curve in Figure 6.2. We call such a curve an **isoquant**, which is a curve that shows the efficient combinations of labor and capital that can produce a single (*iso*) level of output (*quant*ity).[9] An isoquant shows the flexibility that a firm has in producing a given level of output. Figure 6.2 shows three isoquants corresponding to three levels of output. These isoquants are smooth curves because the firm can use fractional units of each input.

We can use these isoquants to illustrate what happens in the short run when capital is fixed and only labor varies. As Table 6.2 shows, if capital is constant at 2 units, 1 worker produces 14 units of output (point *e* in Figure 6.2), 3 workers produce 24 units (point *c*), and 6 workers produce 35 units (point *f*). Thus, if the firm holds one factor constant and varies another factor, it moves from one isoquant to another. In contrast, if the firm increases one input while lowering the other appropriately, the firm stays on a single isoquant.

Table 6.2 Output Produced with Two Variable Inputs

	Labor, L					
Capital, K	1	2	3	4	5	6
1	10	14	17	20	22	**24**
2	14	20	**24**	28	32	35
3	17	**24**	30	35	39	42
4	20	28	35	40	45	49
5	22	32	39	45	50	55
6	**24**	35	42	49	55	60

[9]If the production function is $q = f(L, K)$, then the equation for an isoquant where output is held constant at $\bar{q}$ is $\bar{q} = f(L, K)$.

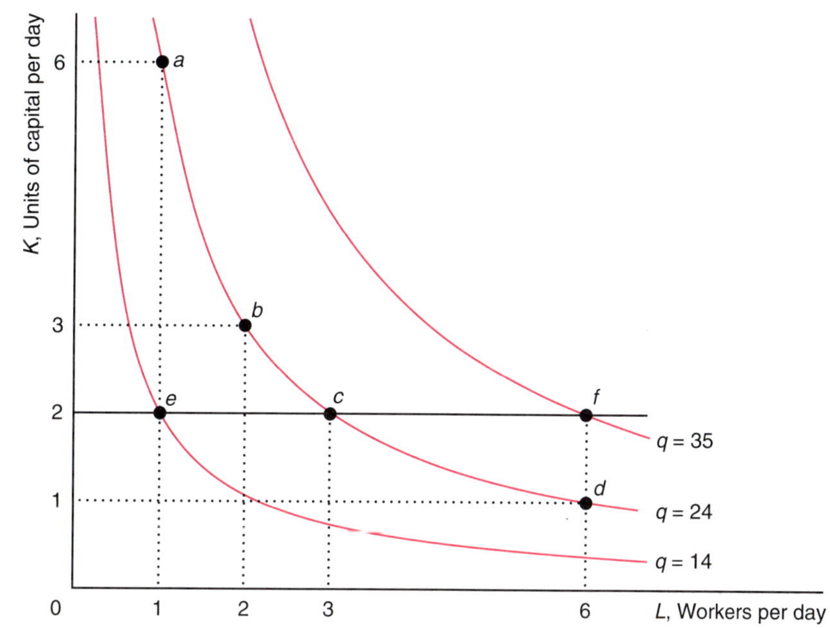

Figure 6.2 Family of Isoquants. These isoquants show the combinations of labor and capital that produce various levels of output (written next to the isoquants). Isoquants farther from the origin correspond to higher levels of output. Points a, b, c, and d are various combinations of labor and capital the firm can use to produce $q = 24$ units of output. If the firm holds capital constant at 2 and increases labor from 1 (point e) to 3 (c) to 6 (f), it shifts from the $q = 14$ isoquant to the $q = 24$ isoquant and then to the $q = 35$ isoquant.

Properties of Isoquants. Isoquants have most of the same properties as indifference curves. The biggest difference between indifference curves and isoquants is that an isoquant holds quantity constant, whereas an indifference curve holds utility constant. We now discuss three major properties of isoquants. Most of these properties result from firms' producing efficiently.

First, *the farther an isoquant is from the origin, the greater is the level of output.* That is, the more inputs a firm uses, the more output it gets if it produces efficiently. At point e in Figure 6.2, the firm is producing 14 units of output with 1 worker and 2 units of capital. If the firm holds capital constant and adds 2 more workers, it produces at point c. Point c must be on an isoquant with a higher level of output—here 24 units—if the firm is producing efficiently and not wasting the extra labor.

Second, *isoquants do not cross.* Such intersections are inconsistent with the requirement that the firm always produces efficiently. For example, if the $q = 15$ and

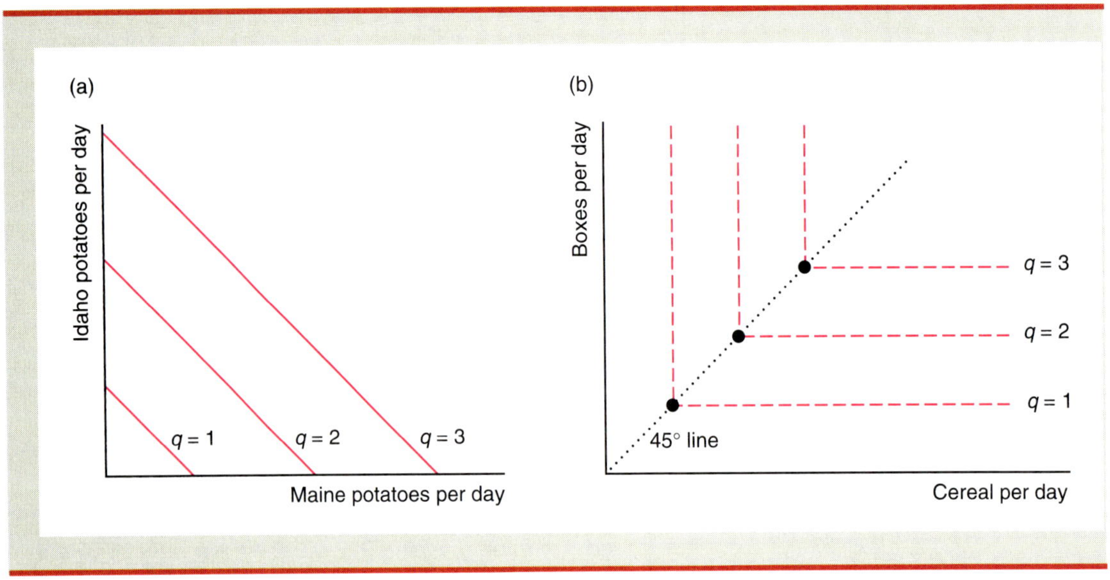

$q = 20$ isoquants crossed, the firm could produce at either output level with the same combination of labor and capital. The firm must be producing inefficiently if it produces $q = 15$ when it could produce $q = 20$. Thus, that labor-capital combination should not lie on the $q = 15$ isoquant, which should include only efficient combinations of inputs. Thus, efficiency requires that isoquants do not cross.

Third, *isoquants slope downward*. If an isoquant sloped upward, then the firm could produce the same level of output with relatively few inputs or relatively many inputs. Producing with relatively many inputs would be inefficient. Thus, because isoquants show only efficient production, an upward-sloping isoquant is impossible. Virtually the same argument can be used to show that isoquants must be thin, as you are asked to do in Problem 4 at the end of this chapter.

Shape of Isoquants. The curvature of an isoquant shows how readily a firm can substitute one input for another. The two extreme cases are production processes in which inputs are perfect substitutes or in which they cannot be substituted for each other.

If the inputs are perfect substitutes, each isoquant is a straight line. Suppose either potatoes from Maine, x, or potatoes from Idaho, y, both of which are measured in pounds per day, can be used to produce potato salad, q, measured in pounds. The production function is

$$q = x + y.$$

One pound of potato salad can be produced by using one pound of Idaho potatoes and no Maine potatoes, one pound of Maine potatoes and no Idahoes, or one-half pound of each type of potato. Panel a of Figure 6.3 shows the $q = 1$, 2,

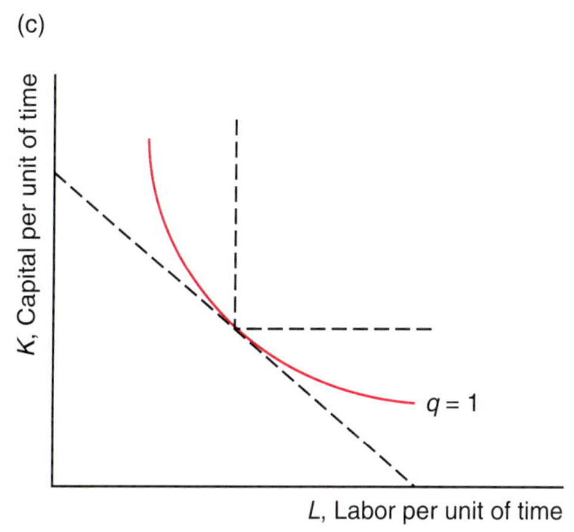

Figure 6.3 Substitutability of Inputs. (a) If the inputs are perfect substitutes, each isoquant is a straight line. (b) If the inputs cannot be substituted at all, the isoquants are right angles (the dashed lines show that the isoquants would be right angles if we included inefficient production). (c) Typical isoquants lie between the extreme cases of straight lines and right angles. Along a curved isoquant, the ability to substitute one input for another varies.

and 3 isoquants. These isoquants are straight lines with a slope of –1 because we need to use an extra pound of Maine potatoes for every pound fewer of Idaho potatoes used.[10]

Sometimes it is impossible to substitute one input for the other: Inputs must be used in fixed proportions. For example, the inputs to produce a 12-ounce (oz) box of cereal, q, are cereal (in 12-oz units per day) and cardboard boxes (boxes per day). If the firm has one unit of cereal and one box, it can produce one box of cereal. If it has one unit of cereal and two boxes, it can still make only one box of cereal. Thus, in panel b, the only efficient points of production are the large dots along the 45° line.[11] Dashed lines show that the isoquants would be right angles if isoquants could include inefficient production processes.

Other production processes allow imperfect substitution between inputs. The isoquants are convex (so the middle of the isoquant is closer to the origin than it would be if the isoquant were a straight line). They do not have the same slope at every point, unlike the straight-line isoquants. Most isoquants are smooth, are downward sloping, curve away from the origin, and lie between the extreme cases of straight lines (perfect substitutes) and right angles (nonsubstitutes) as panel c illustrates.

---

[10]The isoquant for $\bar{q} = 1$ pound of potato salad is $1 = x + y$, or $y = 1 - x$. This equation shows that the isoquant is a straight line with a slope of –1.

[11]This fixed-proportions production function is $q = \min(g, b)$, where g is the number of 12-oz measures of cereal, b is the number of boxes used in a day, and the min function means "take the minimum number of g or b." For example, if g is 4 and b is 3, q is 3.

APPLICATION

A Semiconductor Integrated Circuit Isoquant

We can show why isoquants curve away from the origin by deriving an isoquant for semiconductor integrated circuits (ICs, or "chips").[12] ICs—the "brains" of computers and other electronic devices—are made by building up layers of conductive and insulating materials on silicon wafers. Each wafer contains many ICs, which are subsequently cut into individual chips, called dice.

Semiconductor manufacturers ("fabs") buy the silicon wafers and then use labor and capital to produce the chips. A semiconductor IC's several layers of conductive and insulating materials are arranged in patterns that define the function of the chip.

During the manufacture of ICs, a track moves a wafer into a machine where it is spun and a light-sensitive liquid called photoresist is applied to its whole surface; the photoresist is then hardened. The wafer advances along the track to a point where photolithography is used to define patterns in the photoresist. In photolithography, light transfers a pattern from a template, called a photomask, to the photoresist, which is then "developed" like film, creating a pattern by removing the resist from certain areas. A subsequent process then can either add to or etch away those areas not protected by the resist.

In a repetition of this entire procedure, additional layers are created on the wafer. Because the conducting and insulating patterns in each layer interact with those in the previous layers, the patterns must line up correctly.

To align layers properly, firms use combinations of labor and equipment. In the least capital-intensive technology, employees use machines called *aligners*. Operators look through microscopes and line up the layers by hand and then expose the entire surface. An operator running an aligner can produce 250 layers a day, or 25 ten-layer chips.

A second, more capital-intensive technology uses machines called *steppers*. The stepper picks a spot on the wafer, automatically aligns the layers, and then exposes that area to light. Then the machine moves—*steps* to other sections—lining up and exposing each area in turn until the entire surface has been aligned and exposed. This technology requires less labor: A single worker can run two steppers and produce 500 layers, or 50 ten-layer chips, per day.

A third, even more capital-intensive technology uses a stepper with wafer-handling equipment, which reduces the amount of labor used even more. By linking the tracks directly to a stepper and automating the chip transfer process, human handling can be greatly reduced. A single worker can run 4 steppers with wafer-handling equipment and produce 1,000 layers, or 100 ten-layer chips, per day.

---

[12]This section is based on discussions with Nile Hatch, who analyzed data based on surveys of semiconductor plants around the world. Roy Mallory provided additional input.

Only steppers can be used if the chip requires line widths of 1 micrometer or less.[13] We'll draw an isoquant for producing 200 ten-layer chips that have lines that are more than 1 micrometer wide, for which any of the three technologies can be used.

All three technologies use labor and capital in fixed proportions. To produce 200 chips takes 8 workers and 8 aligners, 3 workers and 6 steppers, or 1 worker and 4 steppers with wafer-handling capabilities. Figure 6.4 shows the three right-angle isoquants corresponding to each of these three technologies.

Some fabs, however, employ a combination of these technologies; some workers use one type of machine while others use different types.[14] By doing so, the fabs can produce using intermediate combinations of labor and capital,

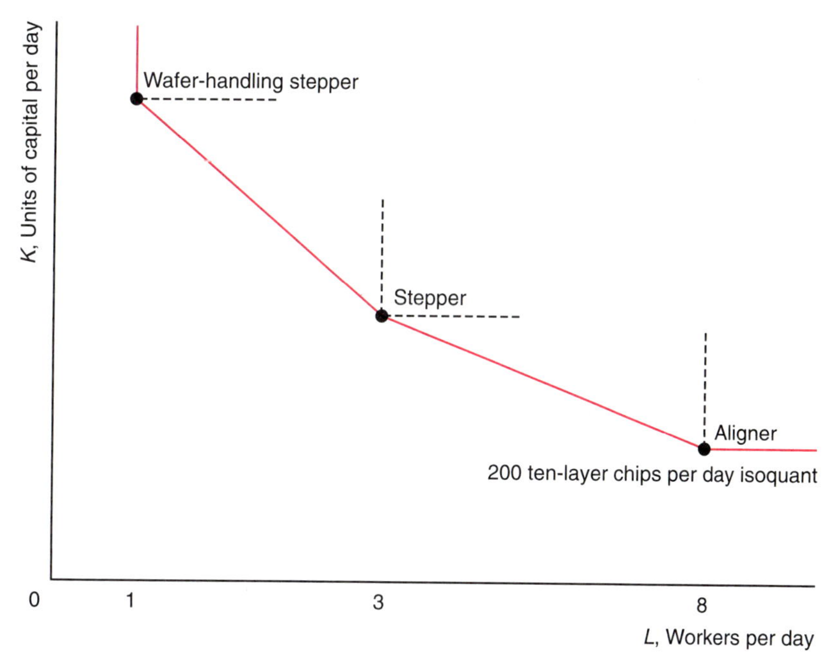

Figure 6.4 Semiconductor Isoquant. To produce semiconductors, any one of three fixed-proportion technologies (dotted line, right-angle isoquants) can be used. The fab's solid line isoquant includes combinations of pairs of these fixed-proportions technologies.

[13]Older generations of personal computers used 386 chips, with 1.5-micrometer pathways. A Pentium II has 0.35-micrometer pathways.

[14]Usually, aligners are used for the layers with relatively wide lines, and steppers are employed for the layers with finer lines. Here, however, either type of machine can be used, because all the lines are relatively wide.

as the solid-line, kinked isoquant in the figure illustrates. The firm does *not* use a combination of the aligner and the wafer-handling stepper technologies because those combinations are less efficient than using the plain stepper (the line connecting the aligner and wafer-handling stepper technologies is farther from the origin than the lines between those technologies and the plain stepper technology).

New processes are constantly being invented. As they are introduced, the isoquant will have more and more kinks (one for each new process) and will begin to resemble the smooth, usual-shaped isoquants we've been drawing. ■

Substituting Inputs

The slope of an isoquant shows the ability of a firm to replace one input with another while holding output constant. Figure 6.5 illustrates this substitution using an isoquant for a Norwegian printing firm, which uses labor, L, and capital, K, to print its output, Q.[15] The isoquant shows various combinations of L and K that the firm can use to produce 10 units of output.

The firm can produce 10 units of output using the combination of inputs at *a* or *b*. At point *a*, the firm uses 2 workers and 39 units of capital. The firm could produce the same amount of output using $\Delta K = -18$ fewer units of capital if it used one more worker, $\Delta L = 1$, point *b*. If we drew a straight line from *a* to *b*, its slope would be $\Delta K/\Delta L = -18$. Thus, this slope tells us how many fewer units of capital (18) the firm can use if it hires one more worker.[16]

The absolute value of the slope of an isoquant is called the *marginal rate of technical substitution* (*MRTS*):[17]

$$MRTS = -\frac{\text{change in capital}}{\text{change in labor}} = -\frac{\Delta K}{\Delta L},$$

The marginal rate of technical substitution tells us how many units of capital the firm can replace with an extra unit of labor while holding output constant.

---

[15]This isoquant is based on the estimated production function $q = 1.52L^{0.6}K^{0.4}$ (Griliches and Ringstad 1971) where different units of measure are used than in the original. A unit of labor, L, is a worker year (2,000 hours of work). Because capital, K, includes various types of machines, and output, q, reflects different types of printed matter, their units cannot be described by any common terms. This production function is an example of a Cobb-Douglas production function: $q = AL^{\alpha}K^{\beta}$, where A, α, and β are constants. We used this same mathematical function earlier as an example of a utility function. Appendix 6A examines the properties of Cobb-Douglas production functions. The isoquant in the figure is for 10 units of output: $10 = 1.52L^{0.6}K^{0.4}$.

[16]The slope of the isoquant at a point equals the slope of a straight line that is tangent to the isoquant at that point. Thus, the straight line between two points on an isoquant has nearly the same slope as the isoquant if the points are close together.

[17]Because isoquants slope downward, we know that the slope of the isoquant is negative. By putting a negative sign in front of the slope, we ensure that the *MRTS* is positive and equals the absolute value of the slope.

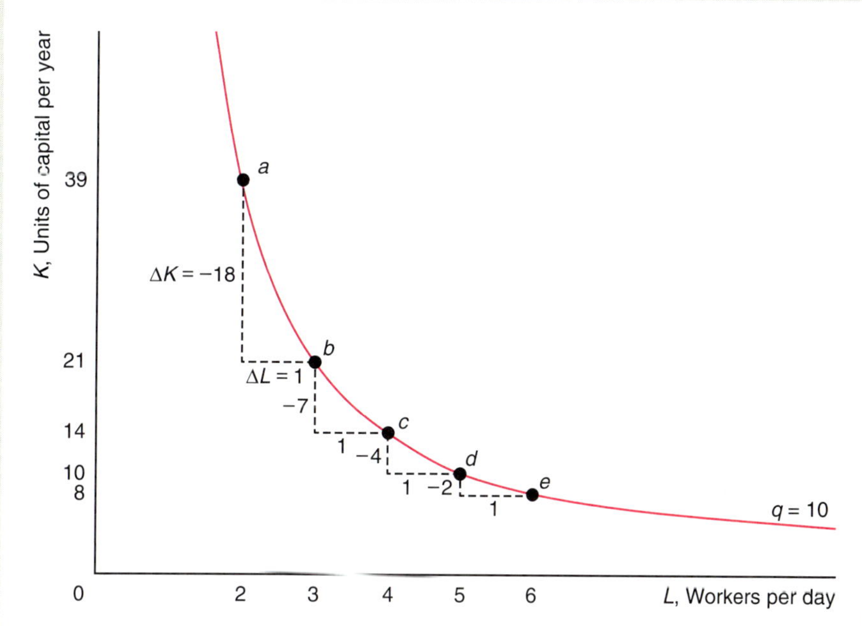

Figure 6.5 The Marginal Rate of Technical Substitution Varies Along an Isoquant. Moving from point a to b, a Norwegian printing firm (Griliches and Ringstad 1971) can produce the same amount of output, $q = 10$, using 18 fewer units of capital, $\Delta K = -18$, if it uses 1 more worker, $\Delta L = 1$. Thus, its $MRTS = -\Delta K/\Delta L = 18$. Moving from point b to c, its $MRTS$ is 7. If it adds yet another worker, moving from point c to d, its $MRTS$ falls to 4. If it adds one more worker, moving from d to e, its $MRTS$ falls to 2. Thus, because it curves away from the origin, this isoquant exhibits a diminishing marginal rate of technical substitution. That is, each extra worker allows the firm to reduce capital by smaller and smaller amounts as the ratio of capital to labor falls.

Substitutability of Inputs Varies Along an Isoquant. The marginal rate of technical substitution varies along a curved isoquant, as in Figure 6.5 for the printing firm. If the firm is initially at point a and it hires one more worker, the firm gives up 18 units of capital and yet remains on the same isoquant at point b, so the $MRTS$ is 18. If the firm hires another worker, the firm can reduce its capital by 7 units and yet stay on the same isoquant, moving from point b to c, so the $MRTS$ is 7. If the firm moves from point c to d, the $MRTS$ is 4; and if it moves from point d to e, the $MRTS$ is 2. This decline in the $MRTS$ along an isoquant as the firm increases labor illustrates *diminishing marginal rates of technical substitution*.

The curvature of the isoquant away from the origin reflects diminishing marginal rates of technical substitution. The more labor the firm has, the harder it is to replace the remaining capital with labor, so the $MRTS$ falls as the isoquant becomes flatter.

In the special case in which isoquants are straight lines, isoquants do not exhibit diminishing marginal rates of technical substitution because neither input becomes more valuable in the production process: The inputs remain perfect substitutes. Solved Problem 6.1 illustrates this result.

SOLVED PROBLEM 6.1

Does the marginal rate of technical substitution vary along the isoquant for the firm that produced potato salad using Idaho and Maine potatoes? What is the *MRTS* at each point along the isoquant?

Answer

1. *Determine the shape of the isoquant.* As Figure 6.3 illustrates, the potato salad isoquants are straight lines because the two types of potatoes are perfect substitutes.
2. *On the basis of the shape, conclude whether the MRTS is constant along the isoquant.* Because the isoquant is a straight line, the slope is the same at every point, so the *MRTS* is constant.
3. *Determine the MRTS at each point.* Earlier, we showed that the slope of this isoquant was –1, so the *MRTS* is 1 at each point along the isoquant. That is, because the two inputs are perfect substitutes, one pound of Idaho potatoes can be replaced by one pound of Maine potatoes. ■

Substitutability of Inputs and Marginal Products. The marginal rate of technical substitution—the degree to which inputs can be substituted for each other—equals the ratio of the marginal products of labor to the marginal product of capital, as we now show. The marginal rate of technical substitution tells us how much a firm can increase one input and lower the other while still staying on the same isoquant. Knowing the marginal products of labor and capital, we can determine how much one input must increase to offset a reduction in the other.

Because the marginal product of labor, $MP_L = \Delta q/\Delta L$, is the increase in output per extra unit of labor, if the firm hires ΔL more workers, its output increases by $MP_L \times \Delta L$. For example, if the MP_L is 2 and the firm hires one extra worker, its output rises by two units.

A decrease in capital alone causes output to fall by $MP_K \times \Delta K$, where $MP_K = \Delta q/\Delta K$ is the marginal product of capital: the output the firm loses from decreasing capital by one unit, holding all other factors fixed. To keep output constant, $\Delta q = 0$, this fall in output from reducing capital must exactly equal the increase in output from increasing labor:

$$MP_L \times \Delta L + MP_K \times \Delta K = 0.$$

By rearranging these terms, we find that[18]

$$\frac{MP_L}{MP_K} = -\frac{\Delta K}{\Delta L} = MRTS. \qquad (6.3)$$

That is, the marginal rate of technical substitution, which is the absolute value of the change in capital relative to the change in labor, equals the ratio of the marginal products.

We can use Equation 6.3 to explain why marginal rates of technical substitution diminish as we move to the right along the isoquant in Figure 6.5. As we replace capital with labor (shift downward and to the right along the isoquant), the marginal product of capital increases—when there are few pieces of equipment per worker, each remaining piece is more useful—and the marginal product of labor falls, so the $MRTS = MP_L/MP_K$ falls.[19]

6.5 RETURNS TO SCALE

So far, we have examined the effects of increasing one input while holding the other input constant (the shift from one isoquant to another) or decreasing the other input by an offsetting amount (the shift along an isoquant). We now turn to the question of *how much output changes if a firm increases all its inputs proportionately*. The answer to this question helps a firm to determine its *scale* or size in the long run.

In the long run, a firm can increase its output by building a second plant and staffing it with the same number of workers as in the first one. Whether the firm chooses to do so turns in part on whether its output increases less than in proportion, in proportion, or more than in proportion to its inputs.

Constant, Increasing, and Decreasing Returns to Scale

If, when all inputs are increased by a certain percentage, output increases by that same percentage, the production function is said to exhibit **constant returns to scale**

---

[18]We can derive this result directly by totally differentiating an isoquant, $\bar{q} = f(L, K)$. As we change labor and capital, the output doesn't change, so

$$\mathrm{d}\bar{q} = 0 = \frac{\partial f}{\partial L}\mathrm{d}L + \frac{\partial f}{\partial K}\mathrm{d}K \equiv MP_L\,\mathrm{d}L + MP_K\,\mathrm{d}K.$$

Rearranging this expression, we find that $MP_L/MP_K = -\mathrm{d}K/\mathrm{d}L = MRTS$.

[19]Figure 6.5 shows the effects of fairly large changes in labor and capital along a printing firm's isoquant. Calculated exactly for small changes (Appendix 6A), the printing firm's $MRTS = 1.5K/L$. As we move to the right along this isoquant, the amount of capital decreases and the amount of labor increases, so the capital/labor ratio falls, causing the $MRTS$ to fall.

(*CRS*). A firm's production process has constant returns to scale if, when the firm doubles its inputs—builds an identical second plant and uses the same amount of labor and equipment as in the first plant—it doubles its output: $f(2L, 2K) = 2f(L, K)$.

We can check whether the potato salad production function has constant returns to scale. If a firm uses x_1 pounds of Idaho potatoes and y_1 pounds of Maine potatoes, it produces $q_1 = x_1 + y_1$ pounds of potato salad. If it doubles both inputs, using $x_2 = 2x_1$ Idaho and $y_2 = 2y_1$ Maine potatoes, it doubles its output:

$$\begin{aligned} q_2 &= x_2 + y_2 \\ &= 2x_1 + 2y_1 = 2q_1. \end{aligned}$$

Thus, the potato salad production function exhibits constant returns to scale.

If output rises more than in proportion to an equal percentage increase in all inputs, the production function is said to exhibit **increasing returns to scale** (*IRS*). A technology exhibits increasing returns to scale if doubling inputs more than doubles the output: $f(2L, 2K) > 2f(L, K)$.

Why might a production function have increasing returns to scale? One reason is that, although it could duplicate a small factory and double its output, the firm might be able to more than double its output by building a single large plant, allowing for greater specialization of labor or capital. In the two smaller plants, workers have to perform many unrelated tasks such as operating, maintaining, and fixing the machines they use. In the large plant, some workers may specialize in maintaining and fixing machines, thereby increasing efficiency. Similarly, a firm may use specialized equipment in a large plant but not in a small one.

If output rises less than in proportion to an equal percentage increase in all inputs, the production function exhibits **decreasing returns to scale** (*DRS*). A technology exhibits decreasing returns to scale if doubling inputs causes output to rise less than in proportion: $f(2L, 2K) < 2f(L, K)$.

One reason for decreasing returns to scale is that the difficulty of organizing, coordinating, and integrating activities increases with firm size. An owner may be able to manage one plant well but may have trouble running two plants.[20] Another reason is that large teams of workers may not function as well as small teams, in which each individual takes greater personal responsibility.

One of the most widely estimated production functions is the Cobb-Douglas (Appendix 6A):

$$q = AL^{\alpha}K^{\beta}, \tag{6.4}$$

where A, α, and β are all positive constants. Solved Problem 6.2 shows that $\gamma = \alpha + \beta$ determines the returns to scale in a Cobb-Douglas production function.

[20] In some sense, the owner's difficulties in running a larger firm may reflect our failure to take into account some factor such as management in our production function. When the firm increases the various inputs, it does not increase the management input in proportion. If so, the "decreasing returns to scale" is really due to a fixed input.

SOLVED PROBLEM 6.2

Under what conditions does a Cobb-Douglas production function, Equation 6.4, exhibit decreasing, constant, or increasing returns to scale?

Answer

1. *Show how output changes if both inputs are doubled*: If the firm initially uses L and K amounts of inputs, it produces

$$q_1 = AL^{\alpha}K^{\beta}.$$

When the firm doubles the amount of both labor and capital it uses, it produces

$$q_2 = A(2L)^{\alpha}(2K)^{\beta} = 2^{\alpha+\beta}AL^{\alpha}K^{\beta}.$$

Thus, its output increases by

$$\frac{q_2}{q_1} = \frac{2^{\alpha+\beta}\,AL^{\alpha}K^{\beta}}{AL^{\alpha}K^{\beta}} = 2^{\alpha+\beta} \equiv 2^{\gamma}, \qquad (6.5)$$

where $\gamma \equiv \alpha + \beta$.

2. *Give a rule for determining the returns to scale*: The Cobb-Douglas production function has decreasing, constant, or increasing returns to scale as γ is less than, equal to, or greater than 1. For example, if $\gamma = 1$, doubling inputs doubles output, $q_2/q_1 = 2^{\gamma} = 2^1 = 2$, so the production function exhibits constant returns to scale. ■

APPLICATION

Returns to Scale in Manufacturing

Increasing, constant, and decreasing returns to scale are commonly observed. Table 6.3 shows estimates of Cobb-Douglas production functions and rates of returns in various Canadian manufacturing industries (Baldwin and Gorecki 1986). The returns to scale measure in the table, γ, is an elasticity. It represents the percentage change in output for a 1% increase in all the inputs. Because the estimated returns to scale measures for a shoe firm is 1, a 1% increase in the inputs causes a 1% increase in output. Thus, a shoe firm's production function exhibits constant returns to scale.

The estimated returns to scale measure for a thread mill is 0.82: A 1% increase in the inputs causes output to rise by 0.82%. Because output rises less than in proportion to the inputs, the thread mill production function exhibits

Table 6.3 Estimated Cobb-Douglas Production Functions for Several Canadian Industries

	Labor α	Capital β	Scale $\gamma = \alpha + \beta$
Decreasing Returns to Scale			
Thread mill	0.64	0.18	0.82
Knitted fabrics	0.55	0.36	0.90
Lime manufacturers	0.60	0.25	0.84
Constant Returns to Scale			
Shoe factories	0.82	0.18	1.00
Hosiery mills	0.55	0.46	1.01
Jewelry and silverware	0.60	0.41	1.01
Increasing Returns to Scale			
Concrete blocks and bricks	0.93	0.40	1.33
Paint	0.71	0.61	1.32
Orthopedic and surgical appliances	0.30	0.99	1.30

Source: Baldwin and Gorecki (1986).

decreasing returns to scale. In contrast, firms that make concrete blocks and bricks have increasing returns to scale production functions, in which a 1% increase in all inputs causes output to rise by 1.33%.

Figure 6.6 uses isoquants to illustrate the returns to scale for the thread mill, shoe factory, and concrete block and bricks firm. We measure the units of labor, capital, and output so that, for all three firms, 100 units of labor and 100 units of capital produce 100 units of output on the $q = 100$ isoquant in the three panels of Figure 6.6. For the constant returns to scale shoe factory, panel b, if both labor and capital are doubled from 100 to 200 units, output doubles to 200 ($= 100 \times 2^1$, multiplying the original output by the rate of increase using Equation 6.5).

That same doubling of inputs causes output to rise to only 177 ($\approx 100 \times 2^{0.82}$) for the thread mill, panel a. Because output rises less than in proportion to inputs, the production function has decreasing returns to scale. If the concrete block and brick firm doubles its inputs, panel c, its output more than doubles, to 251 ($\approx 100 \times 2^{1.33}$), so the production function has increasing returns to scale.

These figures illustrate that the spacing of the isoquant determines the returns to scale. The closer together the $q = 100$ and $q = 200$ isoquants, the greater are the returns to scale.

The returns to scale in these industries are estimated to be the same at all levels of output. A production function's returns to scale may vary, however, as the scale of the firm changes. ■

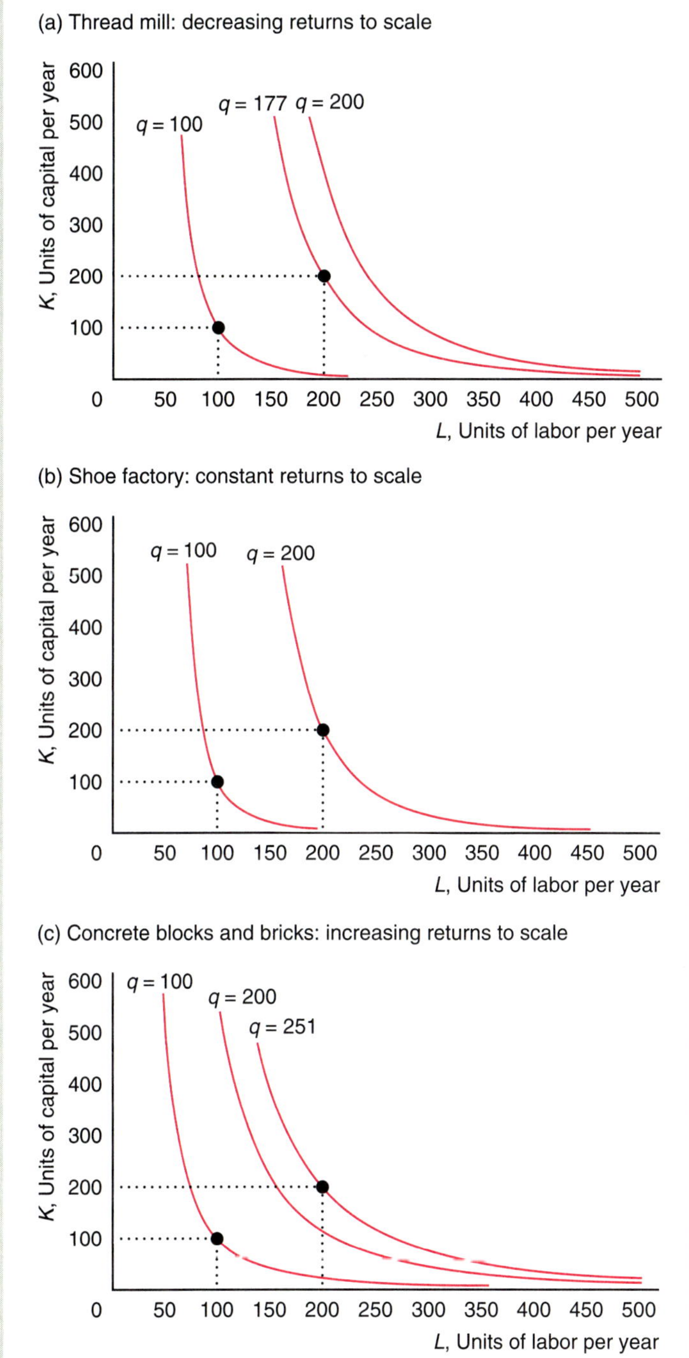

Figure 6.6 Examples of Scale Economies. Isoquants from three Canadian industries illustrate scale economies. In (a), there are decreasing returns to scale; in (b), constant returns; and in (c), increasing returns.

Varying Returns to Scale

Many production functions have increasing returns to scale for small amounts of output, constant returns for moderate amounts of output, and decreasing returns for large amounts of output. When a firm is small, increasing labor and capital allows for gains from cooperation between workers and greater specialization of workers and equipment—*returns to specialization*—so there are increasing returns to scale. As the firm grows, returns to scale are eventually exhausted. There are no more returns to specialization, so the production process has constant returns to scale. If the firm continues to grow, the owner starts having difficulty managing everyone, so the firm suffers from decreasing returns to scale.

We show such a pattern in Figure 6.7. Again, the spacing of the isoquants reflects the returns to scale. Initially, the firm has one worker and one piece of equipment, point a, and produces 1 unit of output on the $q = 1$ isoquant. If the firm doubles its inputs, it produces at b, where $L = 2$ and $K = 2$, which lies on the dashed line through the origin and point a. Output more than doubles to $q = 3$, so the production function exhibits increasing returns to scale in this range. Another

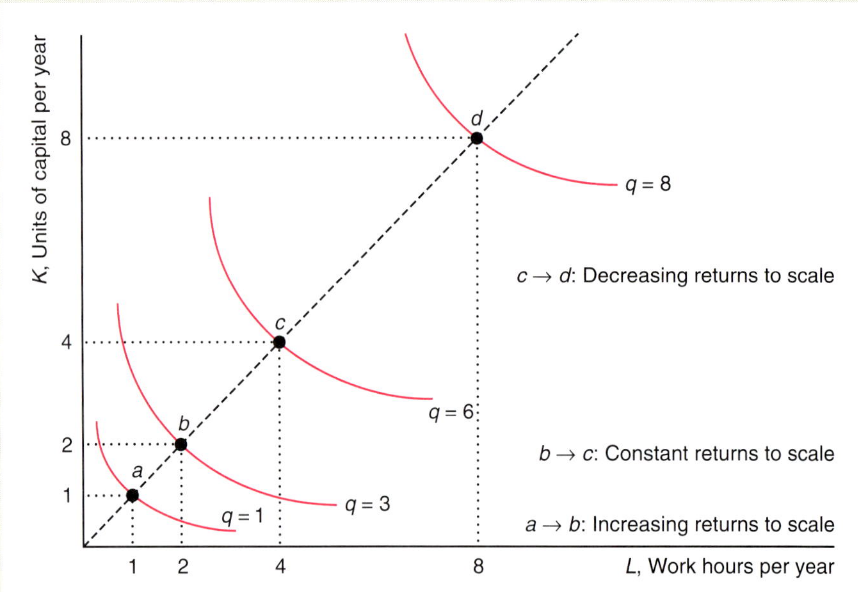

Figure 6.7 Varying Scale Economies. This production function exhibits varying returns to scale. Initially, the firm uses one worker and one unit of capital, point a. It repeatedly doubles these inputs to points b, c, and d, which lie along the dashed line. The first time the inputs are doubled, a to b, output more than doubles from $q = 1$ to $q = 3$, so the production function has increasing returns to scale. The next doubling, b to c, causes a proportionate increase in output, constant returns to scale. At the last doubling, from c to d, the production function exhibits decreasing returns to scale.

doubling of inputs to c causes output to double to six units, so the production function has constant returns to scale in this range. Another doubling of inputs to d causes output to increase by only a third, to $q = 8$, so the production function has decreasing returns to scale in this range.

6.6 PRODUCTIVITY AND TECHNICAL CHANGE

Because firms may use different technologies and different methods of organizing production, the amount of output that one firm produces from a given amount of inputs may differ from that produced by another firm. Moreover, after a technical or managerial innovation, a firm can produce more today from a given amount of inputs than it could in the past.

Relative Productivity

Throughout this chapter, we've assumed that firms produce efficiently. A firm must produce efficiently if it is to maximize its profit. Even if each firm in a market produces as efficiently as possible, however, firms may not be equally *productive*, in the sense that one firm can produce more than another from a given amount of inputs.

A firm may be more productive than others if its manager knows a better way to organize production or if it is the only firm with access to a new invention. Union-mandated work rules, government regulations, other institutional restrictions, or racial or gender discrimination that affect only some firms may lower the relative productivity of those firms.

We can measure the *relative productivity* of a firm by expressing the firm's actual output, q, as a percentage of the output that the most productive firm in the industry could have produced, q^*, from the same amount of inputs: $100q/q^*$. The most productive firm in an industry has a relative productivity measure of 100% (= $100q^*/q^*$ percent).

Caves and Barton (1990) report that the average productivity of firms across U.S. manufacturing industries ranges from 63% to 99%. That is, in the manufacturing industry with the most diverse firms, the average firm produces slightly less than two-thirds as much as the most productive firm, whereas in the manufacturing industry with the most homogeneous firms, all firms are nearly equally productive.

Differences in productivity across markets may be due to differences in the degree of competition. In competitive markets, in which many firms can enter and exit the market easily, less productive firms lose money and are driven out of business, so the firms that are actually producing are equally productive (as Chapter 8 shows). In a less competitive oligopoly market, with few firms and no possibility of entry by new firms, a less productive firm may be able to survive, so firms with varying levels of productivity are observed.

Similarly, in communist and other government-managed economies, in which firms are not required to maximize profits, inefficient firms may survive. For example, a study of productivity in 48 medium-size, machine-building state enterprises in China (Kalirajan and Obwona, 1994) found that the productivity measure ranges from 21% to 100%, with an average of 55%.

APPLICATION

German Versus British Productivity

Even within a single company, a plant in one country may be more productive than a plant in another country operating under different institutional rules and with a different work force. The Ford Motor Company has virtually identical plants in Saarlouis, Germany, and Halewood, England.[21] Each plant manufactures Escorts on production lines equipped with robot welders and automated presses that punch out parts.

Although the plants appear to be identical, the German plant was much more productive in 1981. Whereas the German plant produced 1,200 cars a day (more than the 1,015 that Ford planners predicted) using 7,762 workers, the British plant manufactured only 800 cars a day using 10,040 workers. Equivalently stated, it took only about 21 hours of labor ($L/q = 1/AP_L$) to produce an Escort in Germany compared to about 40 hours in Britain.

Moreover, the German plant turned out the highest-quality cars of any Ford plant. The German Escorts averaged only half as many demerits from quality inspectors as British- or American-made Escorts.

According to Ford officials, the difference was due to the attitudes of the workers. In Britain, under pressure from labor, management used two daily shifts so that no one worked on Friday nights; in Germany, there was no such pressure. Labor unrest was more common in Britain. There were 20 strikes throughout Britain in the first nine months of 1981—though that was considerably less than the 300 strikes in 1976—whereas no strikes occurred in Germany.

British labor leaders argued that the German plant was unsafe. The British union summoned a company doctor to rule, for example, that two workers were required to lift the hood onto a body—a job that a single worker performed at the German plant. Rejecting this claim, a reporter contended that one worker lifted and the other merely watched at the British plant.

Because the British plant is less productive than its German counterpart, we could conclude that the British plant is operating inefficiently. An alternative interpretation is that the British plant is operating as efficiently as possible given the institutional and union rules. ■

---

[21]Rattner, Steven, "A Tale of Two Ford Plants," *New York Times*, October 13, 1981:D1, D4.

Innovations

In its production process, a firm tries to use the best available technological and managerial knowledge. An advance in knowledge that allows more output to be produced with the same level of inputs is called **technical progress.**[22] The use of robotic arms increases the number of automobiles produced with a given amount of labor and raw materials. Better *management or organization of the production process* similarly allows the firm to produce more output from given levels of inputs.

Technical Progress. A technological innovation changes the production process. Last year a firm produced

$$q_1 = f(L, K)$$

units of output using L units of labor services and K units of capital service. Due to a new invention that the firm uses, this year's production function differs from last year's, so the firm produces 10% more output with the same inputs:

$$q_2 = 1.1f(L, K).$$

This firm has experienced *neutral technical change*, in which it can produce more output using the same ratio of inputs. For example, a technical innovation in the form of a new printing press allows more output to be produced by using the same ratio of inputs as before: one worker to one printing press.

Nonneutral technical changes are innovations that alter the proportion in which inputs are used. If a printing press that required two people to operate is replaced by one that can be run by a single worker, then the technical change is *labor saving*. The ratio of labor to other inputs used to produce a given level of output falls after the innovation. Similarly, the ratio of output to labor, the average product of labor, rises.

In our neutral technical change example, the firm's rate of growth of output was 10% (= $\Delta q/q_1$ = (110 – 100)/100) in one year due to the technical change. Table 6.4 shows estimates of the annual rate at which output grew for given levels of inputs in the United States and Poland. The rates of productivity growth differ across industries within a country and across countries for a particular industry. The faster growth in Poland is due to playing catch-up: Starting with antiquated technology and little capital, Poland invested heavily in modern technologies and capital during this period.

[22]The invention of new products is another form of technical innovation.

Table 6.4 Annual Rate of Productivity Growth

United States, 1949–1983[a]		Poland, 1962–1983[b]	
Industry	*Growth Rate (%)*	*Industry*	*Growth Rate (%)*
Food and kindred products	0.7	Food and tobacco	4.9
Tobacco manufactures	0.2		
Lumber and wood products	1.3	Wood and paper	2.5
Paper and allied products	0.9		
Chemicals and allied products	1.5	Chemicals	8.0
Total manufacturing	1.1	Light industry	1.3

[a]Gullickson and Harper (1987) calculated the annual percentage change in output for various U.S. manufacturing industries, holding labor, capital, energy, material, and business service inputs constant.
[b]Terrell (1993) estimated the annual percentage change in output for various Polish industries, holding labor, domestic capital, and Western capital constant.

APPLICATION

Nonneutral Technical Change in Pin Manufacturing

The history of the humble pin illustrates how nonneutral technological change caused the average product of labor to rise over several centuries (Pratten 1980). According to Adam Smith, a factory of 10 highly specialized workers using only hand-held tools could produce 48,000 pins per day in 1776, so the average product of labor was 4,800 pins per day.

In 1824, Samuel W. Wright patented a solid-head pin machine in England. In 1830, this machines produced 45 pins a minute. Machines were substituted for workers. As a consequence of this mechanization, the average product of labor rose 70%.

Because of additional technical advances, machines in 1900 produced 180 pins a minute, and current machines can turn out over 500 per minute. The number of machines a single worker can control has also increased. Currently, one worker can control as many as 24 machines. As a consequence, 50 people are now employed in Britain producing more pins than thousands of workers could manufacture in the early 1800s. By 1980, the average product of labor at one plant in Britain was 800,000 pins per day, an increase of 167 times over the average product in Adam Smith's day. Stated another way, the average product of labor has increased by nearly 2.7% a year for two centuries. ■

Organizational Change. Organizational changes may also change the production function and increase the amount of output produced by a given amount of inputs. Organizational innovations have been very important in automobile manufacturing.

APPLICATION

Automobile Manufacturing Innovations

The automobile industry has experienced a sequence of major technological and organizational innovations. The first, and probably most important, innovations were due to the genius of Henry Ford. In recent years, Japanese manufacturers have made important organizational innovations.

In the early 1900s, Henry Ford revolutionized mass production through two organizational innovations. First, he introduced interchangeable parts, which cut the time required to install parts because workers no longer had to file or machine (adjust by hand) individually made parts to get them to fit.

Second, Ford introduced a conveyor belt and an assembly line to his production process. Before Ford, workers walked around the car, and each worker performed many assembly activities. In Ford's plant, each worker specialized in a single activity such as attaching the right rear of a fender to the chassis. A conveyor belt moved the car at a constant speed from worker to worker along the assembly line. Because his workers gained proficiency from specializing in only a few activities and because the conveyor belts reduced the number of movements workers had to make, Ford could produce more automobiles with the same number of workers. By the early 1920s, Ford had cut the cost of buying a car by more than two-thirds and had increased production from fewer than a thousand cars per year to two million per year.

Organizational innovations continue in auto manufacturing. In recent years, Japanese auto manufacturers have introduced many new approaches. The Toyota production system uses teamwork, just-in-time delivery of parts, and great attention to detail. Each production worker is a "customer" of the previous worker in the assembly line. The worker takes only what is needed, and the previous worker replaces what was taken. Parts are delivered just in time for use, so the firm avoids the cost of maintaining large inventories. For example, the German car maker Porsche, employing Japanese techniques, reduced its manufacturing time per car from 120 to 72 hours, reduced the number of managers it needs by 31%, and cut manufacturing flaws in half.[23] ■

[23]Nash, Nathaniel C., "Putting Porsche in the Pink," *New York Times*, January 1, 1996:17.

Summary

1. **The ownership and management of firms:** Firms are either sole proprietorships, partnerships, or corporations. In smaller firms (particularly sole proprietorships and partnerships), the owners usually run the company. In large firms (such as most corporations), the owners hire managers to run the firms. Owners want to maximize profits. If managers have different objectives than owners, owners must keep a close watch over managers to ensure that profits are maximized.

2. **Production:** Inputs, or factors of production—labor, capital, and materials—are combined to produce output using the current state of knowledge about technology and management. To maximize profits, a firm must produce as efficiently as possible: It must get the maximum amount of output from the inputs it uses, given existing knowledge. A firm may have access to many efficient production processes that use different combinations of inputs to produce a given level of output. New technologies or new forms of organization can increase the amount of output that can be produced from a given combination of inputs. A production function shows how much output can be efficiently produced from various levels of inputs. A firm can vary all its inputs in the long run but only some of them in the short run.

3. **Short-run production: one variable and one fixed input:** In the short run, a firm cannot adjust the quantity of some inputs, such as capital. The firm varies its output by adjusting its variable inputs, such as labor. If all factors are fixed except labor, and a firm that was using very little labor increases its use of labor, its output may rise more than in proportion to the increase in labor because of greater specialization of workers. Eventually, however, as more workers are hired, the workers get in each other's way or wait to share equipment, so output increases by smaller and smaller amounts. This latter phenomenon is described by the law of diminishing marginal returns: The marginal product of an input—the extra output from the last unit of input—eventually decreases as more of that input is used holding other inputs fixed.

4. **Long-run production: two variable inputs:** In the long run, when all inputs are variable, firms can substitute between inputs. An isoquant shows the combinations of inputs that can produce a given level of output. The marginal rate of technical substitution is the absolute value of the slope of the isoquant. Usually, the more of one input the firm uses, the more difficult it is to substitute that input for another input. That is, there are diminishing marginal rates of technical substitution as the firm uses more of one input.

5. **Returns to scale:** If, when a firm increases all inputs in proportion, its output increases by the same proportion, the production process is said to exhibit constant returns to scale. If output increases less than in proportion to inputs, the production process has decreasing returns to scale; if it increases more than in proportion, it has increasing returns to scale. All three types of returns to scale are commonly seen in actual industries. Many production processes exhibit first increasing, then constant, and finally decreasing returns to scale as the size of the firm increases.

6. **Productivity and technical change:** Although all firms in an industry produce efficiently, given what they know and the institutional and other constraints they face, some firms may be more productive than other firms: They can produce more output from a given bundle of inputs. Due to innovations such as technical progress or new means of organizing production, a firm can produce more today than it could in the past from the same bundle of inputs. Such innovations change the production function.

Problems

1. If each extra worker produces an extra unit of output, how do the total product of labor, average product of labor, and marginal product of labor vary with labor?

2. Each extra worker produces an extra unit of output up to six workers. After six, no additional output is produced. Draw the total product of labor, average product of labor, and marginal product of labor curves.

3. What is the difference between an isoquant and an indifference curve?

4. Why must isoquants be thin? (*Hint*: See the explanation of why indifference curves must be thin in Chapter 4.)

5. Suppose a firm has a fixed-proportions production function, in which one unit of output is produced using one worker and two units of capital. If the firm has an extra worker and no more capital, it still can produce only one unit of output. Similarly, one more unit of capital does the firm no good.
   A. Draw the isoquants for this production function.
   B. Draw the total product, average product, and marginal product of labor curves (you probably want to use two diagrams to do so) for this production function.

6. Draw a circle in a diagram with labor services on one axis and capital services on the other. This circle represents all the combinations of labor and capital that produce 100 units of output. Now draw the isoquant for 100 units of output. (*Hint*: Remember that the isoquant includes only the efficient combinations of labor and capital.)

★7. If we plot the profit of a firm against the number of vacation days the owner takes, we find that profit first rises with vacation days (a few days of vacation improve the owner's effectiveness as a manager the rest of the year) but eventually falls as the owner takes more vacation days. If the owner has usual-shaped indifference curves between profit and vacation days, will the manager take the number of vacation days that maximizes profit? If so, why? If not, what will the owner do, and why?

8. In a manufacturing plant, workers use a specialized machine to produce belts. A new machine is invented that is "labor saving." With the new machine, the firm can use fewer workers and still produce the same number of belts as it did using the old machine. In the long run, both labor and capital (the machine) are variable. From what you know, what is the effect of this invention on the AP_L, MP_L, and returns to scale? If you require more information to answer this question, specify what you need to know.

9. Show in a diagram that a production function can have diminishing marginal returns to a factor and constant returns to scale.

10. If a firm lays off workers during a recession, how will the firm's marginal product of labor change?

11. During recessions, American firms lay off a larger proportion of their workers than Japanese firms do. (It has been claimed that Japanese firms continue to produce at high levels and store the output or sell it at relatively low prices during the recession.) Assuming that the production function remains unchanged over a period that is long enough to include many recessions and expansions, would you expect the average product of labor to be higher in Japan or the United States? Why?

12. Does it follow that, because we observe that the average product of labor is higher for Firm 1 than for Firm 2, Firm 1 is more productive in the sense that it can produce more output from a given amount of inputs?

Math Problems

13. Suppose the production function is $q = L^{3/4}K^{1/4}$.
    A. What is the average product of labor, holding capital fixed at $\bar{K}$?
    B. What is the marginal product of labor? (*Hint*: Calculate how much q changes as L increases by one unit, or use calculus.)
    C. Does this production function have increasing, constant, or decreasing returns to scale?

14. What is the production function if L and K are perfect substitutes and each unit of q requires one unit of L or one unit of K (or a combination of these inputs that adds to 1)?

15. At $L = 4$, $K = 4$, the marginal product of labor is 2 and the marginal product of capital is 3. What is the marginal rate of technical substitution?

16. In the short run, a firm cannot vary its capital, $K = 2$, but can vary its labor, L. It produces output q. Explain why the firm will or will not experience diminishing marginal returns to labor in the short run if its production function is
    A. $q = 10L + K$.
    B. $q = L^{1/2}K^{1/2}$.
17. Under what conditions do the following production functions exhibit decreasing, constant, or increasing returns to scale?
    A. $q = L + K$.
    B. $q = L^{\alpha}K^{\beta}$.
    C. $q = L + L^{\alpha}K^{\beta} + K$.
18. Firm 1 and Firm 2 use the same type of production function, but Firm 1 is only 90% as productive as Firm 2. That is, the production function of Firm 2 is $q_2 = f(L, K)$, and the production function of Firm 1 is $q_1 = 0.9f(L, K)$. At a particular level of inputs, how does the marginal product of labor differ between the firms?

CHAPTER 7

Costs

An economist is a person who, when invited to give a talk at a banquet, tells the audience there's no such thing as a free lunch.

A semiconductor manufacturer can produce a chip using many pieces of equipment and relatively few workers' labor or many workers and relatively few machines. How does the firm make its choice?

The firm uses a two-step procedure in determining how to produce a certain amount of output efficiently. It first determines which production processes are *technologically efficient* so that it can produce the desired level of output with the least amount of inputs. As we saw in Chapter 6, the firm uses engineering and other information to determine its production function, which summarizes the many technologically efficient production processes available.

The firm's second step is to pick from these technologically efficient production processes the one that is also **economically efficient**, minimizing the cost of producing a specified amount of output. To determine which process minimizes its cost of production, the firm uses information about the production function and the cost of inputs.

By reducing its cost of producing a given level of output, a firm can increase its profit. Thus, any profit-maximizing competitive, monopolistic, or oligopolistic firm minimizes its cost of production.

In this chapter, we examine five main topics:

1. Measuring costs: Economists count both explicit costs and implicit (opportunity) costs.
2. Short-run costs: In the short run, because only some inputs can be adjusted, some costs (such as labor costs) are variable, while other costs (such as capital costs) are fixed.
3. Long-run costs: In the long run, when all inputs are variable, the firm chooses its mix of inputs so as to minimize its long-run cost.
4. Lower costs in the long run: Long-run cost is as low as or lower than short-run cost because the firm has more flexibility in the long run, technological progress occurs, and workers and managers learn from experience.
5. Cost of producing multiple goods: If the firm produces several goods simultaneously, the cost of each may depend on the quantity of all the goods produced.

Businesspeople and economists need to understand the relationship between costs of inputs and production to determine the least costly way to produce. Economists have an additional reason for wanting to know about costs. As we'll see in later chapters, the relationship between output and costs plays an important role in determining the nature of a market—how many firms are in the market and how high price is relative to cost.

7.1 MEASURING COSTS

To show how a firm's cost varies with its output, we first have to measure costs. Businesspeople and economists often measure costs differently.

Economic Cost

Economists include all relevant costs. To run a firm profitably, a good manager acts like an economist and considers all relevant costs. This same manager, however, may direct the firm's accountant or bookkeeper to measure cost in ways that are consistent with tax and other laws to make the firm's financial statement look good to stockholders or to minimize the firm's taxes this year.

Economists consider both explicit costs and implicit costs. *Explicit costs* are a firm's direct, out-of-pocket payments for inputs to its production process during a given time period such as a year. These costs include production workers' wages, managers' salaries, and payments for materials. However, firms use inputs that may not have an explicit price. These *implicit costs* include the value of the working time of the firm's owner and the value of other resources used but not purchased in a given period.

The **economic cost** or **opportunity cost** is the value of the best alternative use of a resource. The economic or opportunity cost includes both explicit and implicit costs. If a firm purchases and uses an input immediately, that input's opportunity cost is the amount the firm pays for it. If the firm uses an input from its inventory, its opportunity cost is not necessarily the price it paid for the input years ago. Rather, the opportunity cost is what it could buy or sell that input for today.

The classic example of an implicit opportunity cost is captured in the phrase "There's no such thing as a free lunch." Suppose your parents offer to take you to lunch tomorrow. You know that they'll pay for the meal, but you also know that this lunch is not free for you. Your opportunity cost for the lunch is the best alternative use of your time. Presumably, the best alternative use of your time is studying this textbook, but other possible alternatives include what you could earn at a job or the value you place on watching TV. Often, such opportunity costs are a substantial portion of total costs.

If you start your own firm, you should be very concerned about opportunity costs. Suppose your explicit cost is $40,000, including the rent for your work space, the cost of materials, and the wage payments to your employees. Because you do not pay yourself a salary—instead, you keep any profit at the end of the year—the explicit cost does not include the value of your time. According to an economist, your firm's full, economic cost is the sum of the explicit cost plus the opportunity value of your time. If the highest wage you could have earned working for some other firm is $25,000, your full, economic cost is $65,000.

In deciding whether to continue running your firm or to work for someone else, you must consider both the explicit and opportunity costs. If your annual revenue is $60,000, after you pay your explicit cost of $40,000, you keep $20,000 at the end of the year. The opportunity cost of your time, \$25,000, exceeds \$20,000, so you can earn more working for someone else.

APPLICATION

Opportunity Cost of Waiting Time

Canadian taxes pay for public health care. However, taxes do not cover the full cost of medical care. To contain costs, health care is rationed in part by having patients wait for treatment. People who are forced to wait are less likely to request treatment, some diseases clear up on their own during the wait, and some patients die while waiting. Are these additional waiting-time opportunity costs large?

Most Canadian patients remain on a waiting list less than two months. In one province, two-thirds of all inpatients and three-quarters of all outpatients reported waiting less than eight weeks for elective surgery. But 20% of inpatients and 14% of outpatients waited more than 12 weeks.

Many patients suffer or cannot work while waiting for treatment. Doctors estimate that 41% of all patients and 88% of cardiology patients have difficulty in carrying on their work or daily duties as a result of their medical conditions.

As a proxy for the opportunity cost of waiting time for the 41% of people who experience difficulty while waiting, Globerman (1991) used average earnings. (Such a cost measure is an underestimate because it ignores pain and suffering.) He calculated that waiting time cost was approximately \$132 million in 1989 in British Columbia, which is 0.2% of that province's gross domestic product and about 8% of its total health cost. ■

Capital Costs

Determining the opportunity cost of capital, such as land or equipment, requires special considerations. Capital is a **durable good**: a product that is usable for years. Two problems may arise in measuring the cost of capital. The first is how to allocate the initial purchase cost over time. The second is what to do if the value of the capital changes over time.

Allocating Capital Costs over Time. Capital may be rented or purchased. For example, a firm may rent a truck for \$200 a month or buy it outright for \$18,000.

If the firm rents the truck, the rental payment is the relevant opportunity cost. By using the rental rate, we avoid the two measurement problems. The truck is rented period by period, so the firm does not have to worry about how to allocate the purchase cost of a truck over time. Moreover, the rental rate adjusts if the cost of a new truck changes over time.

Suppose, however, that the firm buys the truck. The firm's bookkeeper may *expense* the cost by recording the full \$18,000 when it's made or may *amortize* the cost by spreading the \$18,000 over the life of the truck according to an arbitrary rule set by the relevant government authority, such as the Internal Revenue Service (IRS). Where the IRS approves of several approaches to amortizing expenses, a bookkeeper or an accountant may use whichever arbitrary rule minimizes the firm's taxes.

An economist amortizes the cost of the truck on the basis of its opportunity cost at each moment of time, which is the amount that the firm could charge others to rent the truck. That is, regardless of whether the firm buys or rents the truck, an economist views the opportunity cost of this capital good as a rent per time period: the amount the firm will receive if it rents its truck to others at the going rental rate.[1] If the value of an older truck is less than that of a newer one, the rental rate for the truck falls over time.

Actual and Historical Costs. Not only may the rental rate for a piece of capital fall over time as the capital ages, but it may change because of shifts in supply and demand in the market for capital goods or for other reasons. A piece of capital may be worth much more or much less today than it was when it was purchased.

To maximize its profit, a firm must properly measure the cost of a piece of capital—its current opportunity cost of the capital good—and not what the firm paid for it—its historical cost. Suppose a firm paid \$30,000 for a piece of land that it can resell for only \$20,000. Also suppose that it uses the land itself and the current value of the land to the firm is only \$19,000. Should the firm use the land or sell it? As any child can tell the firm, there's no point in crying over spilt milk. The firm should ignore how much it paid for the land in making its decision. As the value of the land to the firm, \$19,000, is less than the opportunity cost of the land, \$20,000, the firm can make more by selling the land.

The firm's current, opportunity cost of capital may be less than what it paid if the firm cannot resell the capital. A firm that bought a specialized piece of equipment with no alternative use cannot resell the equipment. Because the equipment has no alternative use, the historical cost of buying that capital is a **sunk cost**: an expenditure that cannot be recovered. Because this equipment has no alternative use, the current or opportunity cost of the capital is zero. In short, when determining the rental value of capital, economists use the opportunity value and ignore the historical price.

---

[1]If there is no rental market for a capital good, an economist may calculate an implicit rental rate. To calculate the rental rate for a turbine generator, for which there is no rental market, an economist includes both explicit and implicit opportunity costs. If the firm could sell the generator for \$10,000, the opportunity cost of keeping the generator this year is the interest that could be earned on \$10,000 (see Chapter 16). In addition, the firm incurs direct maintenance costs to keep the generator functioning. Even with good care, the generator will *depreciate* as it becomes less valuable over time due to wear and tear. This depreciation is an additional opportunity cost that the economist includes in determining the rental price of the machine.

APPLICATION

Swarthmore College's Cost of Capital

Many nonprofit institutions such as universities and governmental agencies are notorious for ignoring the implicit cost of their capital. When setting tuition and making other plans, Swarthmore College in Pennsylvania estimates its annual cost at $40,000 per student, based on the cost of salaries, academic and general institutional support, food, maintenance and additions to the physical plant, and other annual expenses such as student aid. This cost calculation is a gross underestimate, however, because it ignores the opportunity cost of the campus—the amount the college could earn by renting out its land and buildings. Including that opportunity cost of its land and buildings raises its true economic cost to about $50,000 annually per student.[2] ■

7.2 SHORT-RUN COSTS

To make profit-maximizing decisions, a firm needs to know how its cost varies with output. A firm's cost rises as it increases its output. A firm cannot vary some of its inputs, such as capital, in the short run (Chapter 6). As a result, it is usually more costly for a firm to increase output in the short run (SR) than in the long run (LR), when all inputs can be varied. In this section, we look at the cost of increasing output in the short run.

SR Cost Measures

We start by using a numeric example to illustrate the basic cost concepts. We then examine the graphic relationship between these concepts.

Cost Levels. To produce a given level of output in the short run, a firm incurs costs for both its fixed and variable inputs. A firm's **fixed cost** (F) is its production expense that does not vary with output. The fixed cost includes the cost of inputs that the firm cannot practically adjust in the short run, such as land, a plant, large machines, and other capital goods. The fixed cost for a capital good a firm owns and uses is the opportunity cost of not renting it to someone else. The fixed cost is $48 per day for the firm in Table 7.1.

A firm's **variable cost** (VC) is the production expense that changes with the quantity of output produced. The variable cost is the cost of the variable inputs: the inputs the firm can adjust to alter its output level, such as labor and materials. Table

---

[2]Passell, Peter, "One Top College's Price Tag: Why So Low, and So High?" *New York Times*, July 27, 1994:A1.

Table 7.1 Variation of SR Cost with Output

Output, q	Fixed Cost, F	Variable Cost, VC	Total Cost, C	Marginal Cost, MC	Average Fixed Cost, $AFC = F/q$	Average Variable Cost, $AVC = VC/q$	Average Cost, $AC = C/q$
0	48	0	48				
1	48	25	73	25	48	25	73
2	48	46	94	21	24	23	47
3	48	66	114	20	16	22	38
4	48	82	130	16	12	20.5	32.5
5	48	100	148	18	9.6	20	29.6
6	48	120	168	20	8	20	28
7	48	141	189	21	6.9	20.1	27
8	48	168	216	27	6	21	27
9	48	198	246	30	5.3	22	27.3
10	48	230	278	32	4.8	23	27.8
11	48	272	320	42	4.4	24.7	29.1
12	48	321	369	49	4.0	26.8	30.8

7.1 shows that the firm's variable cost changes with output. Variable cost goes from \$25 a day when one unit is produced to \$46 a day when two units are produced.

A firm's **cost** (or **total cost**, C) is the sum of a firm's variable cost and fixed cost:

$$C = VC + F.$$

The firm's total cost of producing two units of output per day is \$94 per day, which is the sum of the fixed cost, \$48, and the variable cost, \$46. Because variable cost changes with the level of output, total cost also varies with the level of output, as the table illustrates.

To decide how much to produce, a firm uses several measures of how its cost varies with the level of output. Table 7.1 shows four such measures that we derive using the fixed cost, the variable cost, and the total cost.

Marginal Cost. A firm's **marginal cost** (MC) is the amount by which a firm's cost changes if the firm produces one more unit of output. The marginal cost is[3]

$$MC = \frac{\Delta C}{\Delta q},$$

[3]If we use calculus, the marginal cost is $MC = dC(q)/dq$, where $C(q)$ is the cost function that shows how cost varies with output. The calculus definition says how cost changes for an infinitesimal change in output. To illustrate the idea, however, we use larger changes in the table.

where ΔC is the change in cost when output changes by Δq. Table 7.1 shows that, if the firm increases its output from two to three units, $\Delta q = 1$, its total cost rises from \$94 to \$114, $\Delta C = \$20$, so its marginal cost is $\$20 = \Delta C/\Delta q$.

Because only variable cost changes with output, we can also define marginal cost as the change in variable cost from a one-unit increase in output:

$$MC = \frac{\Delta VC}{\Delta q}.$$

As the firm increases output from two to three units, its variable cost increases by $\Delta VC = \$20 = \$66 - \$46$, so its marginal cost is $MC = \Delta VC/\Delta q = \$20$. A firm uses marginal cost in deciding whether it pays to change its output level.

Average Costs. Firms use three average cost measures. The **average fixed cost** (AFC) is the fixed cost divided by the units of output produced: $AFC = F/q$. The average fixed cost falls as output rises because the fixed cost is spread over more units. The average fixed cost falls from \$48 for 1 unit of output to \$4 for 12 units of output in Table 7.1.

The **average variable cost** (AVC) is the variable cost divided by the units of output produced: $AVC = VC/q$. Because the variable cost increases with output, the average variable cost may either increase or decrease as output rises. The average variable cost is \$25 at one unit, falls until it reaches a minimum of \$20 at six units, and then rises. As we show in Chapter 8, a firm uses the average variable cost to determine whether to shut down operations when demand is low.

The **average cost** (AC)—or *average total cost*—is the total cost divided by the units of output produced: $AC = C/q$. The average cost is the sum of the average fixed cost and the average variable cost:[4]

$$AC = AFC + AVC.$$

In Table 7.1, as output increases, average cost falls until output is eight units and then rises. The firm makes a profit if its average cost is below its price, which is the firm's average revenue.

SR Cost Curves

We illustrate the relationship between output and the various cost measures using curves in Figure 7.1. Panel a shows the variable cost, fixed cost, and total cost curves that correspond to Table 7.1. The fixed cost, which does not vary with output, is a horizontal line at \$48. The variable cost curve is zero at zero units of output and rises with output. The total cost curve, which is the vertical sum of the variable cost curve and the fixed cost line, is \$48 higher than the variable cost curve at every output level, so the variable cost and total cost curves are parallel.

Panel b shows the average fixed cost, average variable cost, average cost, and marginal cost curves. The average fixed cost curve falls as output increases. It

---

[4]Because $C = VC + F$, if we divide both sides of the equation by q, we obtain

$$AC = C/q = F/q + VC/q = AFC + AVC.$$

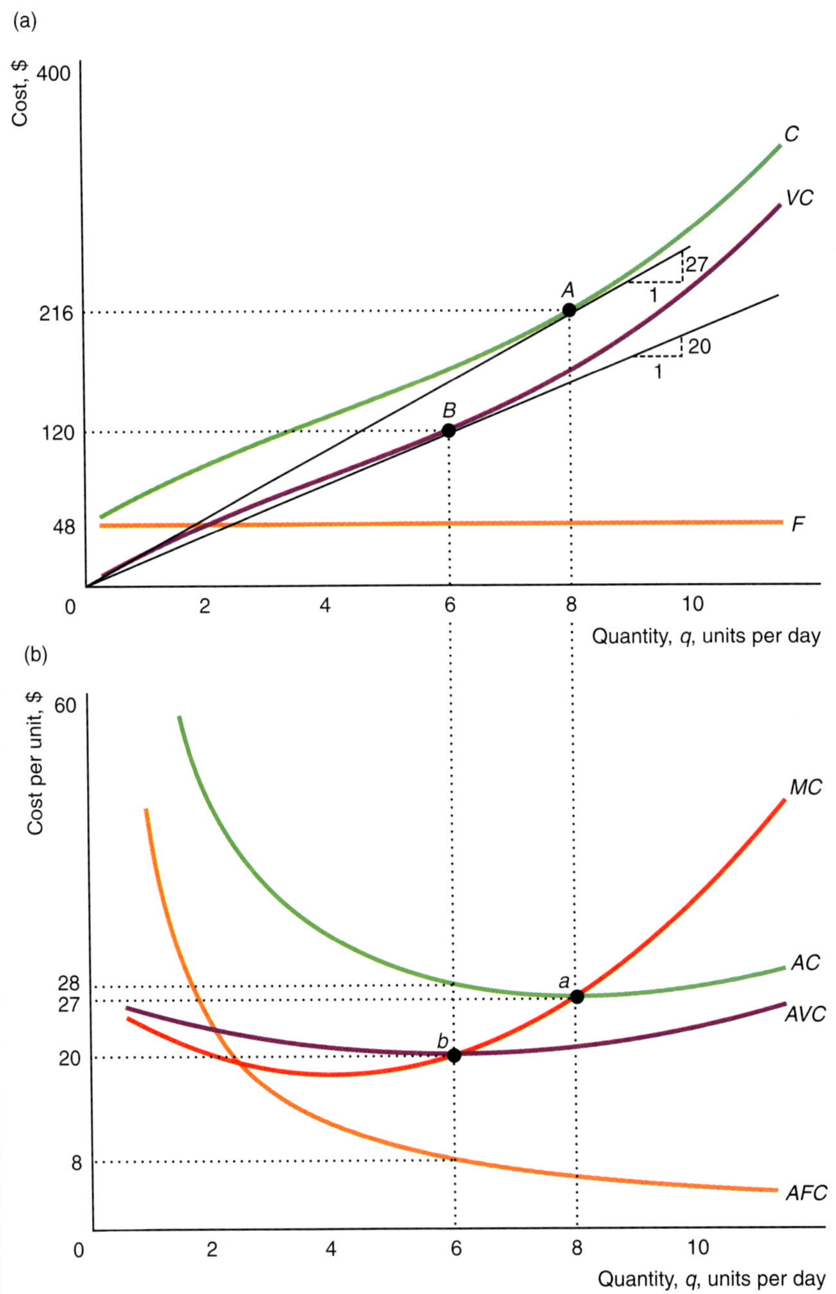
(a)
Cost, $
400
216
120
48
0
2
4
6
8
10
Quantity, q, units per day
C
VC
A
B
27
1
20
1
F
(b)
Cost per unit, $
60
28
27
20
8
0
2
4
6
8
10
Quantity, q, units per day
MC
AC
AVC
AFC
a
b

Figure 7.1 SR Cost Curves. (a) Because the total cost differs from the variable cost by the fixed cost, F, of \$48, the total cost curve, C, is parallel to the variable cost curve, VC. (b) The marginal cost curve, MC, cuts the average variable cost, AVC, and average cost, AC, curves at their minimums. The height of the AC curve at point a equals the slope of the line from the origin to the cost curve at A. The height of the AVC at b equals the slope of the line from the origin to the variable cost curve at B. The height of the marginal cost is the slope of either the C or VC curve at that quantity.

approaches zero as output gets large, because the fixed cost is spread over many units of output. The average cost curve is the vertical sum of the average fixed cost and average variable cost curves. For example, at six units of output, the average variable cost is 20 and the average fixed cost is 8, so the average cost is 28.

The relationships between the average and marginal curves to the total curves are similar to those between the total product, marginal product, and average product curves, which we discussed in Chapter 6. The average cost at a particular output level is the slope of a line from the origin to the corresponding point on the cost curve. The slope of that line is the rise—the cost at that output level—divided by the run—the output level—which is the definition of the average cost. In panel a, the slope of the line from the origin to point A is the average cost for eight units of output. The height of the cost curve at A is 216, so the slope is 216/8 = 27, which is the height of the average cost curve at the corresponding point a in panel b.

Similarly, the average variable cost is the slope of a line from the origin to a point on the variable cost curve. The slope of the dashed line from the origin to B in panel a is 20—the height of the variable cost curve, 120, divided by the number of units of output, 6—which is the height of the average variable cost at six units of output, point b in panel b.

The marginal cost is the slope of either the cost curve or the variable cost curve at a given output level. As the cost and variable cost curves are parallel, they have the same slope at any given output. The difference between cost and variable cost is fixed cost, which does not affect marginal cost.

The dashed line from the origin is tangent to the cost curve at A in panel a. Thus, the slope of the dashed line equals both the average cost and the marginal cost at eight units of output. This equality occurs at the corresponding point a in panel b, where the marginal cost curve intersects the average cost.[5]

[5]To find at which output level q the average cost curve, $AC(q)$, reaches its minimum, we set the derivative of average cost with respect to q equal to zero:

$$\frac{\mathrm{d}AC(q)}{\mathrm{d}q} = \frac{\mathrm{d}\left(\frac{C(q)}{q}\right)}{\mathrm{d}q} = \left(\frac{\mathrm{d}C(q)}{\mathrm{d}q} - \frac{C(q)}{q}\right)\frac{1}{q} = 0.$$

This condition holds at the output q, where $\mathrm{d}C(q)/\mathrm{d}q = C(q)/q$ or $MC = AC$. If the second-order condition holds at that q, the average cost curve reaches its minimum at that quantity. The second-order condition requires that the average cost curve be falling to the left of this q and rising to the right.

Where the marginal cost curve is below the average cost, the average cost curve declines with output. Because the average cost of 47 for two units is greater than the marginal cost of the third unit, 20, the average cost for three units falls to 38. Where the marginal cost is above the average cost, the average cost curve rises with output. At eight units, the marginal cost equals the average cost, so the average is unchanging, which is the minimum point, *a*, of the average cost curve.

We can show the same results using the graph. Because the dashed line from the origin is tangent to the variable cost curve at *B* in panel a, the marginal cost equals the average variable cost at the corresponding point *b* in panel b. Again, where marginal cost is above average variable cost, the average variable cost curve rises with output; and where marginal cost is below average variable cost, the average variable cost curve falls with output. Because the average cost curve is everywhere above the average variable cost curve and the marginal cost curve is rising where it crosses both average curves, the minimum of the average variable cost curve, *b*, is at a lower output level than the minimum of the average cost curve, *a*.

Production Functions and the Shapes of Cost Curves

The production function determines the shapes of a firm's cost curves. The production function shows the amount of inputs needed to produce a given level of output. The firm calculates its cost by multiplying the quantity of each input by its price and summing.

If a firm produces output using capital and labor and its capital is fixed in the short run, the firm's variable cost is its cost of labor. Its labor cost is the wage per hour, w, times the number of hours of labor, L, employed by the firm: $VC = wL$.

In the short run, when the firm's capital is fixed, the only way the firm can increase its output is to use more labor. If the firm increases its labor enough, it reaches the point of *diminishing marginal return to labor*, at which each extra worker increases output by a smaller amount. We can use this information about the relationship between labor and output—the production function—to determine the shape of the variable cost curve and its related curves.

Shape of the Variable Cost Curve. If input prices are constant, the production function determines the shape of the variable cost curve. We illustrate this relationship for the firm in Figure 7.2. The firm faces a constant input price for labor, the wage, of \$5 per hour.

The total product of labor curve in Figure 7.2 shows the firm's short-run production function relationship between output and labor when capital is held fixed. For example, it takes 24 hours of labor to produce six units of output. Nearly doubling labor to 46 hours causes output to increase by only two-thirds to 10 units of output. As labor increases, the total product of labor curve increases less than in proportion. This flattening of the total product of labor curve at higher levels of labor reflects the diminishing marginal return to labor.

This curve shows both the production relation of output to labor and the variable cost relation of output to cost. Because each hour of work costs the firm \$5, we can relabel the horizontal axis in Figure 7.2 to show the firm's variable cost,

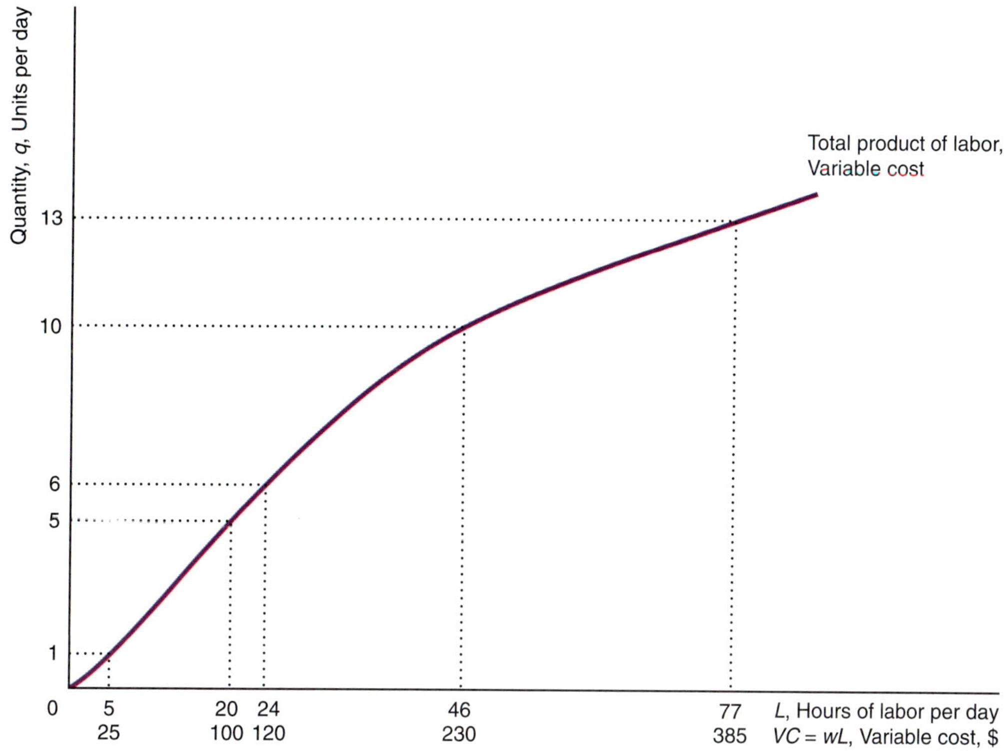

Figure 7.2 Variable Cost and Total Product of Labor. The firm's short-run variable cost curve and its total product of labor curve have the same shape. The total product of labor curve uses the horizontal axis measuring hours of work. The variable cost curve uses the horizontal axis measuring labor cost, which is the only variable cost.

which is its cost of labor. To produce six units of output takes 24 hours of labor, so the firm's variable cost is \$120. By using the variable cost labels on the horizontal axis, the total product of labor curve becomes the variable cost curve, where each worker costs the firm \$120 per day in wages. The variable cost curve in Figure 7.2 is the same as the one in panel a of Figure 7.1 in which the output and cost axes are reversed. For example, the variable cost of producing six units is \$120 in both figures.

Diminishing marginal returns in the production function cause the variable cost to rise more than in proportion as output increases. Because the production function determines the shape of the variable cost curve, it also determines the shape of the marginal, average variable, and average cost curves. We now examine the shape of each of these cost curves in detail because firms rely more on these per unit cost measures than on total variable cost in making decisions.

Shape of the Marginal Cost Curve. The marginal cost is the change in variable cost as output increases by one unit: $MC = \Delta VC/\Delta q$. In the short run, capital is fixed, so the only way the firm can produce more output is to use extra labor. The extra labor required to produce one more unit of output is $\Delta L/\Delta q$. The extra labor costs the firm w per unit, so the firm's cost rises by $w\Delta L/\Delta q$. As a result, the firm's marginal cost is

$$MC = \frac{\Delta VC}{\Delta q} = w\frac{\Delta L}{\Delta q}.$$

The marginal cost equals the wage times the extra labor necessary to produce one more unit of output. To increase output by one unit from five to six units takes four extra workers in Figure 7.2. If the wage is \$5 per hour, the marginal cost is \$20.

How do we know how much extra labor we need to produce one more unit of output? That information comes from the production function. The marginal product of labor—the amount of extra output produced by another unit of labor, holding other inputs fixed—is $MP_L = \Delta q/\Delta L$. Thus, the extra labor we need to produce one more unit of output, $\Delta L/\Delta q$, is $1/MP_L$, so the firm's marginal cost is

$$MC = \frac{w}{MP_L}. \tag{7.1}$$

Equation 7.1 says that the marginal cost equals the wage divided by the marginal product of labor. If the firm is producing five units of output, it takes four extra hours of labor to produce one more unit of output in Figure 7.2, so the marginal product of an hour of labor is $\frac{1}{4}$. Given a wage of \$5 an hour, the marginal cost of the sixth unit is \$5 divided by $\frac{1}{4}$, or \$20, as panel b of Figure 7.1 shows.

Equation 7.1 shows that the marginal cost moves in the direction opposite that of the marginal product of labor. At low levels of labor, the marginal product of labor commonly rises with additional labor because extra workers help the original workers and they can collectively make better use of the firm's equipment (Chapter 6). As the marginal product of labor rises, the marginal cost falls.

Eventually, however, as the number of workers increases, workers must share the fixed amount of equipment and may get in each other's way, so the marginal cost curve slopes upward because of diminishing marginal returns to labor. Thus, the marginal cost first falls and then rises, as panel b of Figure 7.1 illustrates.

Shapes of the Average Cost Curves. Diminishing marginal returns to labor, by determining the shape of the variable cost curve, also determine the shape of the average variable cost curve. The average variable cost is the variable cost divided by output: $AVC = VC/q$. For the firm we've been examining, whose only variable input is labor, variable cost is wL, so average variable cost is

$$AVC = VC/q = wL/q.$$

Because the average product of labor is q/L, average variable cost is the wage divided by the average product of labor:

$$AVC = \frac{w}{AP_L}. \tag{7.2}$$

In Figure 7.2, at six units of output, the average product of labor is $\frac{1}{4}$ (= q/L = 6/24) so the average variable cost is \$20, which is the wage, \$5, divided by the average product of labor, $\frac{1}{4}$.

With a constant wage, the average variable cost moves in the opposite direction of the average product of labor in Equation 7.2. As we discussed in Chapter 6, the average product of labor tends to rise and then fall, so the average cost tends to fall and then rise, as in panel b of Figure 7.1.

The average cost curve is the vertical sum of the average variable cost curve and the average fixed cost curve, as in panel b. If the average variable cost curve is U-shaped, adding the strictly falling average fixed cost makes the average cost fall more steeply than the average variable cost curve at low output levels. At high output levels, the average cost and average variable cost curves differ by ever smaller amounts, as the average fixed cost, F/q, approaches zero. Thus, the average cost curve is also U-shaped.

APPLICATION

SR Cost Curves of a Printing Firm

The short-run average cost curve of a typical Norwegian printing firm (Chapter 6) is U-shaped, even though its average variable cost is strictly upward sloping. Figure 7.3 (based on the estimates of Griliches and Ringstad 1971) shows the firm's various short-run cost curves, where the firm's capital is fixed at $\overline{K} = 100$. Appendix 7A derives the firm's short-run cost curves using math.

The firm's average fixed cost, as always, falls as output increases. The firm's average variable cost curve is strictly increasing. The average cost curve is the vertical sum of the average variable cost and average fixed cost curves. Because the average fixed cost curve falls with output and the average variable cost curve rises with output, the average cost curve is U-shaped. The firm's marginal cost lies above the rising average variable cost curve for all positive quantities of output and cuts the average cost curve at its minimum. ■

Effects of Taxes on Costs

Taxes applied to a firm shift some or all of the marginal and average cost curves. For example, suppose the government collects a specific tax of \$10 per unit of output from the firm. This tax, which varies with output, affects the firm's variable cost but not its fixed cost. As a result, it affects the firm's average cost, average variable cost, and marginal cost curves, but not its average fixed cost curve.

At every quantity, the average variable cost and the average cost rise by the full amount of the tax. The second column of Table 7.2 shows the firm's average variable cost before the tax, AVC^b. For example, if it sells six units of output, its average variable cost is \$20. After the tax, the firm must pay the

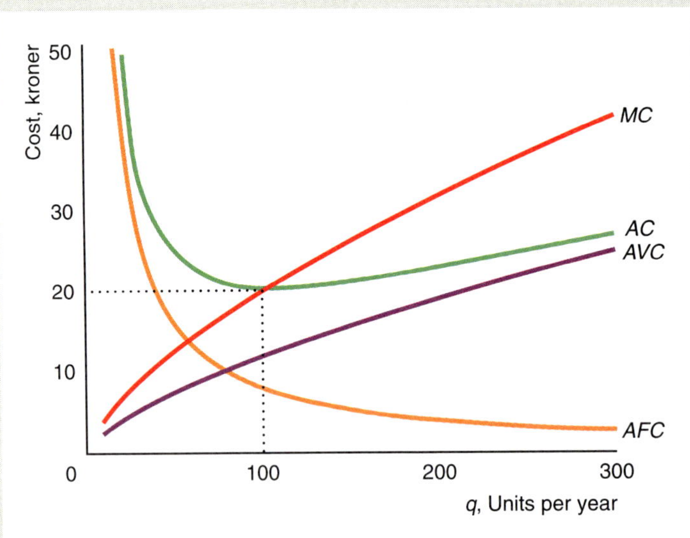

Figure 7.3 Norwegian Printing Company. According to the production function estimated by Griliches and Ringstad (1971), the firm's marginal cost and average variable cost curves rise with output. Because average fixed cost falls with output, average cost, which equals average variable cost plus average fixed cost, is U-shaped. The average cost curve reaches its minimum of 20 kr at 100 units of output.

government \$10 per unit, so the firm's after-tax average variable cost rises to \$30. More generally, the firm's after-tax average variable cost, AVC^a, is its average

Table 7.2 Effect of a Specific Tax of \$10 per unit on SR Costs

Q	AVC^b	$AVC^a = AVC^b + \$10$	$AC^b = C/q$	$AC^a = C/q + \$10$	MC^b	$MC^a = MC^b + \$10$
1	25	35	73	83	25	35
2	23	33	47	57	21	31
3	22	32	38	48	20	30
4	20.5	30.5	32.5	42.5	16	26
5	20	30	29.6	39.6	18	28
6	20	30	28	38	20	30
7	20.1	30.1	27	37	21	31
8	21	31	27	37	27	37
9	22	32	27.3	37.3	30	40
10	23	33	27.8	37.8	32	42
11	24.7	34.7	29.1	39.1	42	52
12	26.8	36.8	30.8	40.8	49	59

variable cost of production—the before-tax average variable cost—plus the tax per unit, \$10: $AVC^a = AVC^b + \$10$.

The average cost equals the average variable cost plus the average fixed cost. Because the tax increases average variable cost by \$10 and does not affect the average fixed cost, the tax increases average cost by \$10.

The tax also increases the firm's marginal cost. Suppose the firm wants to increase output from seven to eight units. The firm's actual cost of producing the third unit—its before-tax marginal cost, MC^b—is \$27. To produce an extra unit of output, the cost to the firm is the marginal cost of producing the extra unit plus \$10, so its after-tax marginal cost is $MC^a = MC^b + \$10$. In particular, its after-tax marginal cost of producing the eighth unit is \$37.

A specific tax shifts the marginal cost and the average cost curves upward in panel a of Figure 7.4 by the amount of the tax, \$10 per unit. The after-tax marginal cost intersects the after-tax average cost at its minimum. Because both the marginal and average cost curves shift upward by exactly the same amount, the after-tax average cost curve reaches its minimum at the same level of output, eight units, as does the before-tax average cost, as both panel a and Table 7.2 show. At eight units, the minimum of the before-tax average cost curve is \$27 and that of the after-tax average cost curve is \$37. Thus, although a specific tax increases a firm's average cost, it does not affect the output at which average cost is minimized.

Similarly, we can analyze the effect of a franchise tax on costs (Solved Problem 7.1). A franchise tax—also called a business license fee—is a lump-sum amount of money that a firm pays for the right to operate a business. An \$800-per-year tax is levied "for the privilege of doing business in California." A three-year license to sell hot dogs in front of New York City's Metropolitan Museum of Art costs \$900,600. These taxes do not vary with output, so they affect firms' fixed costs only—not their variable costs.

SOLVED PROBLEM 7.1

What is the effect of a lump-sum, franchise tax $\mathcal{L}$ on the quantity at which a firm's after-tax average cost curve reaches its minimum? (Assume that the firm's before-tax average cost curve is U-shaped.)

Answer

1. *Determine the average tax per unit of output*: Because the franchise tax is a lump-sum payment that does not vary with output, the more the firm produces, the less tax it pays per unit. The tax per unit is $\mathcal{L}/q$. If the firm sells only one unit, its cost is $\mathcal{L}$; however, if it sells 100 units, its tax payment per unit is only $\mathcal{L}/100$.

2. *Show how the tax per unit affects the average cost*: The firm's after-tax average cost, AC^a, is the sum of its before-tax average cost, AC^b, and its average tax payment per unit, $\mathcal{L}/q$. Because the average tax payment per unit falls

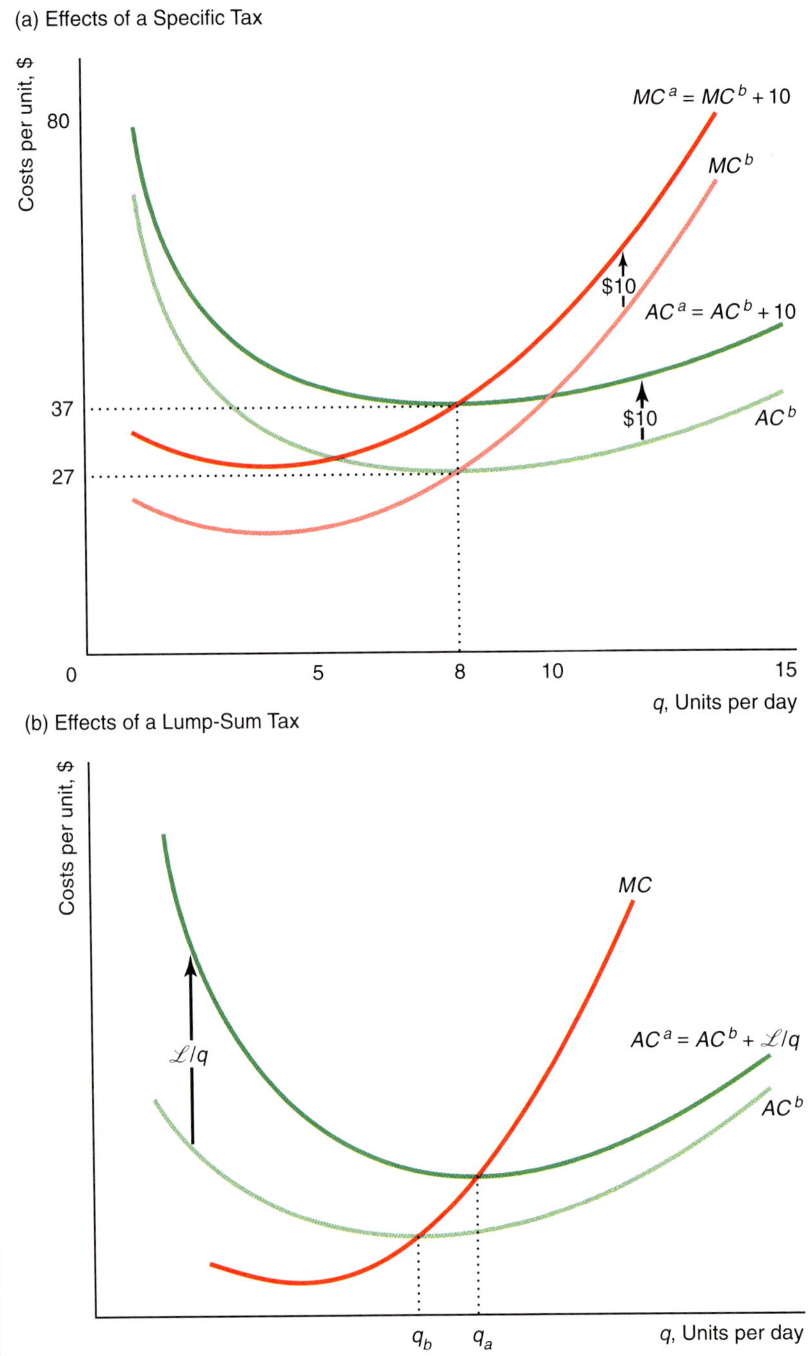

(a) Effects of a Specific Tax
Costs per unit, $
80
37
27
$MC^a = MC^b + 10$
MC^b
\$10
$AC^a = AC^b + 10$
\$10
AC^b
0
5
8
10
15
q, Units per day
(b) Effects of a Lump-Sum Tax
Costs per unit, $
MC
$\mathcal{L}/q$
$AC^a = AC^b + \mathcal{L}/q$
AC^b
q_b
q_a
q, Units per day

Figure 7.4 Effect of Taxes on Cost Curves. (a) A specific tax of \$10 per unit shifts both the marginal cost and average cost curves upward by \$10. Because of the parallel upward shift of the average cost curve, the minimum of both the before-tax average cost curve, AC^b, and the after-tax average cost curve, AC^a, occurs at the same output, eight units. (b) A lump-sum tax, $\mathcal{L}$, shifts the average cost curve upward by $\mathcal{L}/q$ at output q. As a result, the gap between the after-tax and before-tax average cost curve diminishes as output increases. The minimum of the after-tax average cost curve, AC^a, occurs at a larger output, q_a, than the minimum of the before-tax average cost curve, AC^b, which occurs at q_b.

with output, the gap between the after-tax average cost curve and the before-tax average cost curve also falls with output in panel b of Figure 7.4.

3. *Determine the effect of the tax on the marginal cost curve*: Because the franchise tax does not vary with output, it does not affect the marginal cost curve.
4. *Compare the minimum points of the two average cost curves*: The marginal cost curve crosses from below both average cost curves at their minimum points. Because the after-tax average cost lies above the before-tax average cost curve, the quantity at which the after-tax average cost curve reaches its minimum, q_a, is larger than the quantity, q_b, at which the before-tax average cost curve achieves a minimum. ■

SR Cost Summary

We discussed three cost-level curves—total cost, fixed cost, and variable cost—and four cost-per-unit curves—average cost, average fixed cost, average variable cost, and marginal cost. Understanding the shapes of these curves and the relationship between them is crucial to understanding the analysis of firm behavior in the rest of this book. Fortunately, we can derive most of what we need to know about the shapes and the relationship between the curves using four basic concepts:

- In the short run, the cost associated with inputs that cannot be adjusted is fixed, while the cost from inputs that can be adjusted is variable.
- Given that input prices are constant, the shapes of the variable cost and cost curves are determined by the production function.
- Where there are diminishing marginal returns to a variable input, the variable cost and cost curves become relatively steep as output increases, so the average cost, average variable, and marginal cost curves rise with output.
- Because of the relationship between marginals and averages, both the average cost and average variable cost curves fall when marginal cost is below them and rise when marginal cost is above them, so the marginal cost cuts both these average cost curves at their minimum points.

7.3 LONG-RUN COSTS

In the long run, the firm adjusts all its inputs so that its cost of production is as low as possible. The firm can change its plant size, design and build new machines, and otherwise adjust inputs that were fixed in the short run. In our example, there are no long-run fixed costs ($F = 0$) because capital can be varied.

There may, however, be other fixed costs in the long run. For example, the government may collect a lump-sum, franchise tax (which does not depend on output) from the firm every year. For simplicity, we assume that a firm has no fixed cost in the long run (unless we note otherwise).

The long-run total cost equals the long-run variable cost: $C = VC$. Thus, our firm is concerned about only three cost concepts in the long run—total cost, average cost, and marginal cost—instead of the seven cost concepts that it considers in the short run.

To produce a given quantity of output at minimum cost, our firm uses information about the production function and the price of labor and capital. The firm chooses how much labor and capital to use in the long run, whereas the firm chooses only how much labor to use in the short run when capital is fixed. As a consequence, the firm's long-run cost is lower than its short-run cost of production if it has to use the "wrong" level of capital in the short run. In this section, we show how a firm picks the cost-minimizing combinations of inputs in the long run.

Input Choice

A firm can produce a given level of output using many different *technologically efficient* combinations of inputs, as summarized by an isoquant (Chapter 6). From among the technologically efficient combinations of inputs, a firm wants to choose the particular bundle with the lowest cost of production, which is the *economically efficient* combination of inputs. To do so, the firm combines information about technology from the isoquant with information about the cost of labor and capital.

We now show how information about cost can be summarized in an *isocost line*. Then we show how a firm can combine the information in an isoquant and isocost lines to pick the economically efficient combination of inputs.

Isocost Line. The cost of producing a given level of output depends on the price of labor and capital. The firm hires L hours of labor services at a wage of w per hour, so its labor cost is wL. The firm rents K hours of machine services r per hour, so its capital cost is rK. (If the firm owns the capital, r is the implicit rental rate.) The firm's total cost is the sum of its labor and capital costs:

$$C = wL + rK. \tag{7.3}$$

The firm can hire as much labor and capital as it wants at these constant input prices.

The firm can use many combinations of labor and capital that cost the same amount. Suppose the wage rate, w, is \$5 an hour and the rental rate of capital, r, is \$10. Five of the many combinations of labor and capital that the firm can use that

Table 7.3 Bundles of Labor and Capital That Cost the Firm $100

	Labor, L	Capital, K	Labor Cost, $wL = \$5L$	Capital Cost, $rK = \$10K$	Total Cost, $wL + rK$
a	20	0	$100	$0	$100
b	14	3	$70	$30	$100
c	10	5	$50	$50	$100
d	6	7	$30	$70	$100
e	0	10	$0	$10	$100

cost $100 are listed in Table 7.3. These combinations of labor and capital are plotted on an **isocost line**, which is all the combinations of inputs that require the same (*iso*) total expenditure (*cost*). Figure 7.5 shows three isocost lines. The $100 isocost line represents all the combinations of labor and capital that the firm can buy for $100, including the combinations *a* through *e* in Table 7.3.

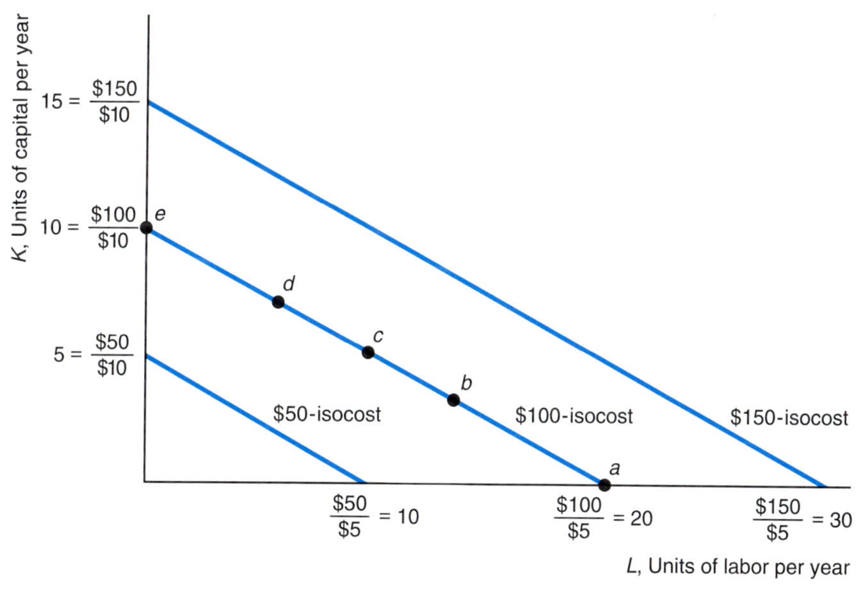

Figure 7.5 A Family of Isocost Lines. An isocost line shows all the combinations of labor and capital that cost the firm the same amount. The greater the total cost, the further from the origin is the isocost. All the isocosts have the same slope, $-w/r = -\frac{1}{2}$. The slope shows the rate at which the firm can substitute capital for labor holding total cost constant: For each extra unit of capital it uses, the firm must use two fewer units of labor to hold its cost constant.

Along an isocost line, cost is fixed at a particular level, $\overline{C}$, so by setting cost at $\overline{C}$ in Equation 7.3, we can write the equation for the $\overline{C}$-isocost line as

$$\overline{C} = wL + rK.$$

Using algebra, we can rewrite this equation to show how much capital the firm can buy if it spends a total of $\overline{C}$ and purchases L units of labor:

$$K = \frac{\overline{C}}{r} - \frac{w}{r}L. \tag{7.4}$$

By substituting $\overline{C}$ = \$100, w = \$5, and r = \$10 in Equation 7.4, we find that the \$100 isocost line is $K = 10 - \frac{1}{2}L$. We can use Equation 7.4 to derive three properties of isocost lines.

First, where the isocost lines hit the capital and labor axes depends on the firm's cost, $\overline{C}$, and on the input prices. The $\overline{C}$ isocost line intersects the capital axis where the firm is using only capital. Setting $L = 0$ in Equation 7.4, we find that the firm buys $K = \overline{C}/r$ units of capital. In the figure, the \$100 isocost line intersects the capital axis at \$100/\$10 = 10 units of capital. Similarly, the intersection of the isocost line with the labor axis is at $\overline{C}/w$, which is the amount of labor the firm hires if it uses only labor. In the figure the intersection of the \$100 isocost line with the labor axis occurs at $L = 20$, where $K = 10 - \frac{1}{2} \times 20 = 0$.

Second, isocosts that are farther from the origin have higher costs than those that are closer to the origin. Because the isocost lines intersect the capital axis at $\overline{C}/r$ and the labor axis at $\overline{C}/w$, an increase in the cost shifts out these intersections with the axes proportionately. The \$50 isocost line hits the capital axis at 5 and the labor axis at 10, whereas the \$100 isocost line intersects at 10 and 20.

Third, the slope of each isocost line is the same. From Equation 7.4, if the firm increases labor by ΔL, it must decrease capital:

$$\Delta K = -(w/r)\Delta L.$$

By dividing both sides of this expression by ΔL, we find that the slope of an isocost line, $\Delta K/\Delta L$, is $-w/r$. Thus, the slope of the isocost line depends on the relative prices of the inputs. The slope of the isocost lines in the figure is $-w/r = -\$5/\$10 = -\frac{1}{2}$. If the firm uses two more units of labor, $\Delta L = 2$, it must reduce capital by one unit, $\Delta K = -\frac{1}{2}\Delta L = -1$, to keep its total cost constant. Because all isocost lines are based on the same relative prices, they all have the same slope, so they are parallel.

The isocost line plays a similar role in the firm's decision making as the budget line does in consumer decision making. Both an isocost line and a budget line are straight lines whose slopes depend on relative prices. There is an important difference between them, however. The consumer has a single budget line determined by the consumer's income. The firm faces many isocost lines, each of which corresponds to a different level of expenditures the firm might make. A firm may incur a relatively low cost by producing relatively little output with few inputs, or it may incur a relatively high cost by producing a relatively large quantity.

Combining Cost and Production Information. By combining the information about costs contained in the isocost lines with information about efficient production summarized by an isoquant, a firm chooses the lowest-cost way to produce a given level of output. We examine how a Norwegian printing firm picks the combination of labor and capital that minimizes its cost of producing 100 units of output. Figure 7.6 shows the isoquant for 100 units of output (based on Griliches and Ringstad 1971) and the isocost lines where the rental rate of a unit of capital is 8 kroner (or kr, a Norwegian monetary unit) and the wage rate is 24 kr.

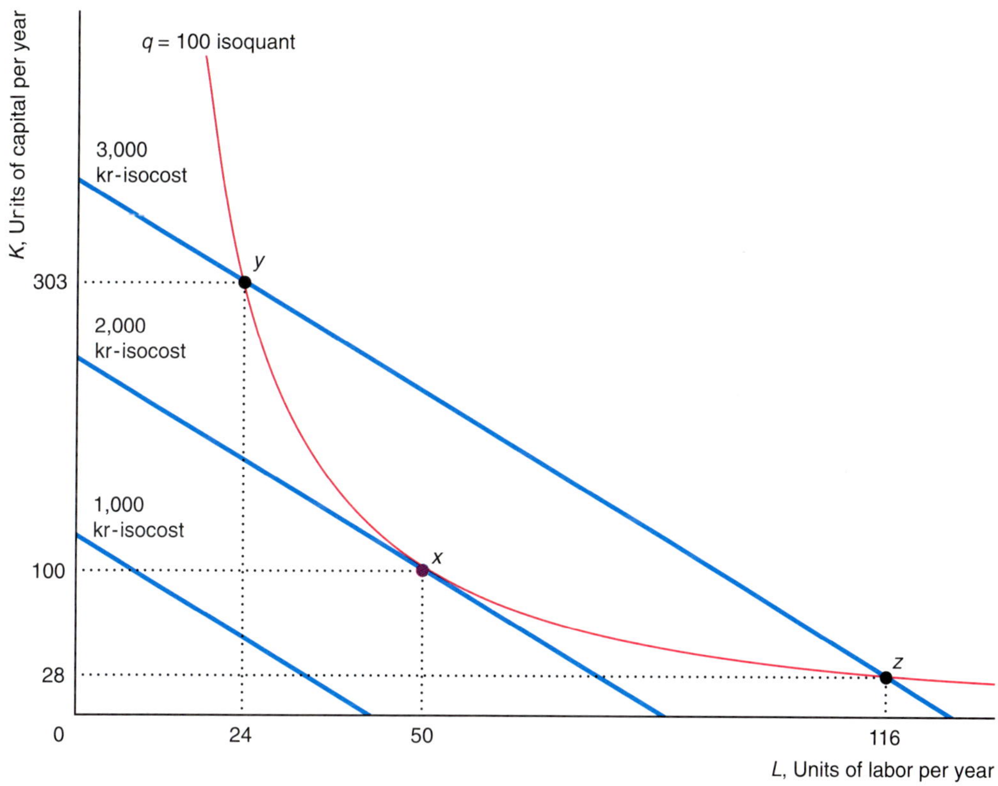

Figure 7.6 Cost Minimization. The Norwegian printing firm minimizes its cost of producing 100 units of output by producing at x ($L = 50$ and $K = 100$). This cost-minimizing combination of inputs is determined by the tangency between the $q = 100$ isoquant and the lowest isocost line, 2,000 kr, that touches that isoquant. At x, the isocost is tangent to the isoquant, so the slope of the isocost, $-w/r = -3$, equals the slope of the isoquant, which is the negative of the marginal rate of technical substitution. That is, the rate at which the firm can trade capital for labor in the input markets equals the rate at which it can substitute capital for labor in the production process.

The firm can choose any of three equivalent approaches. The first is the *lowest-isocost rule*: *The firm minimizes its cost by using the combination of inputs on the isoquant that is on the lowest isocost line that touches the isoquant.* The lowest possible isoquant that will allow the printing firm to produce 100 units of output is the 2,000-kr isocost line. This isocost line touches the isoquant at the bundle of inputs x, where the firm uses $L = 50$ workers and $K = 100$ units of capital.

How do we know that x is the least costly way to produce 100 units of output? We need to demonstrate that other practical combinations of input produce less than 100 units or produce 100 units at greater cost.

If the firm spent less than 2,000 kr, it could not produce 100 units of output. Each combination of inputs on the 1,000-kr isocost line lies below the isoquant, so the firm cannot produce 100 units of output for 1,000 kr.

The firm can produce 100 units of output using other combinations of inputs beside x; however, using these other bundles of inputs is more expensive. For example, the firm can produce 100 units of output using the combinations y ($L = 24$, $K = 303$) or z ($L = 116$, $K = 28$). Both these combinations, however, cost the firm 3,000 kr.

If an isocost line crosses the isoquant twice, as does the 3,000-kr isocost line, there must be another, lower isocost line that also touches the isoquant. The lowest possible isocost line that touches the isoquant, the 2,000-kr isocost line, is tangent to the isoquant at a single bundle, x. Thus, the firm may use the *tangency rule*: *The firm chooses the input bundle where the relevant isoquant is tangent to an isocost line to produce a given level of output at the lowest cost.*

We can interpret this tangency or cost minimization condition in two ways. At the point of tangency, the slope of the isoquant equals the slope of the isocost. As we showed in Chapter 6, the slope of the isoquant is the negative of the marginal rate of technical substitution ($MRTS$). The slope of the isocost is the negative of the ratio of the wage to the cost of capital, $-w/r$. Thus, to minimize its cost of producing a given level of output, a firm chooses its inputs so that the marginal rate of technical substitution equals the relative input prices:

$$MRTS = w/r. \tag{7.5}$$

The firm picks inputs so that the rate at which it can substitute capital for labor in the production process, the $MRTS$, exactly equals the rate at which it can trade capital for labor in input markets, w/r.

The printing company's marginal rate of technical substitution is $1.5K/L$. At $K = 100$ and $L = 50$, its $MRTS$ is 3, which equals the ratio of the input prices it faces, $w/r = 24/8 = 3$. In contrast, at y, the isocost cuts the isoquant so the slopes are not equal. At y, the $MRTS$ is 18.9375, which is greater than the ratio of the input price, 3. Because the slopes are not equal at y, the firm can produce the same output at lower cost. As the figure shows, the cost of producing at y is 3,000 kr, whereas the cost of producing at x is only 2,000 kr.

We can interpret the condition in Equation 7.5 in another way. We showed in Chapter 6 that the marginal rate of technical substitution equals the ratio of the marginal product of labor to that of capital: $MRTS = MP_L/MP_K$. Thus, the cost-minimizing condition in Equation 7.5 is

$$\frac{MP_L}{MP_K} = \frac{w}{r}. \tag{7.6}$$

This expression may be rewritten as

$$\frac{MP_L}{w} = \frac{MP_K}{r}. \tag{7.7}$$

Equation 7.7 states the *last-dollar rule*: *Cost is minimized if inputs are chosen so that the last dollar spent on labor adds as much extra output as the last dollar spent on capital.*

The printing firm's marginal product of labor is[6]

$$MP_L = 0.6q/L,$$

and its marginal product of capital is

$$MP_K = 0.4q/K.$$

At bundle x, the printing firm's marginal product of labor is 1.2 (= 0.6 × 100/50) and its marginal product of capital is 0.4. The last krone (singular of kroner) spent on labor gets the firm

$$MP_L/w = 1.2/24 = 0.05$$

more output. The last krone spent on capital also gets the firm

$$MP_K/r = 0.4/8 = 0.05$$

extra output. Thus, spending one more krone on labor at x gets the firm as much extra output as does spending the same amount on capital. Equation 7.6 holds, so the firm is minimizing its cost of producing 100 units of output.

If instead the firm produced at y, where it is using more capital and less labor, its MP_L is 2.5 (= 0.6 × 100/24) and the MP_K is approximately 0.13 (≈ 0.4 × 100/303). As a result, the last krone spent on labor gets $MP_L/w \approx 0.1$ more unit of output, whereas the last krone spent on capital gets only a fourth as much extra output, $MP_K/r \approx 0.017$. At y, if the firm shifts one krone from capital to labor, output falls by 0.017 because there is less capital and increases by 0.1 because there is more labor for a net gain of 0.983 more output at the same cost. The firm should shift even more resources from capital to labor—which increases the marginal product of capital and decrease the marginal product of labor—until Equation 7.6 holds with equality at x.

---

[6]The printing firm's production function, $q = 1.52L^{0.6}K^{0.4}$, is a Cobb-Douglas production function. Appendix 6A derives the marginal product formula for Cobb-Douglas production functions.

To summarize, we demonstrated that there are three equivalent rules that the firm can use to pick the lowest-cost combination of inputs to produce a given level of output when isoquants are smooth:

- **Lowest-isocost rule:** Pick the bundle of inputs for which the lowest isocost line touches the isoquant.
- **Tangency rule:** Pick the bundle of inputs for which the isoquant is tangent to the isocost line, so the marginal rate of technical substitution equals the ratio of the input prices (Equation 7.5).
- **Last-dollar rule:** Pick the bundle of inputs for which the last dollar spent on one input gives as much extra output as the last dollar spent on any other input (Equation 7.6).

If the isoquant is not smooth, the lowest-cost method of production cannot be determined by using the tangency rule or the last-dollar rule. The lowest-isocost rule always works—even when isoquants are not smooth—as we now illustrate.

APPLICATION

Rice Milling in Java

A dramatic change occurred in the process used for milling rice in Java in the early 1970s (Timmer 1984). Experts believe that about 80% of that country's rice crop was hand-pounded in 1971. By 1973, less than 50%, and perhaps as little as 10%, was hand-pounded. During that period, thousands of new small, mechanical rice mills had been built. What prompted this change in technique? The change was due to a fall in the cost of capital, which increased the factor price of labor relative to capital.

Rice may be milled in five ways: by (1) hand pounding, (2) small-mill processing, (3) large-mill processing, (4) using a small bulk facility, or (5) using a large bulk facility. These methods vary in the amounts of labor and capital services required. Hand pounding, a technique that is at least a millennium old, is labor intensive: Workers use only a wooden pounding pole and pestle. Small-mill processing employs equipment to hull and polish the rice but relies on sun drying rather than mechanical drying equipment. Large mills (which are rare) hull, polish, and dry using a combination of machines and sunlight. Small and large bulk facilities mill and store high-quality rice; these were used in other countries but not in Java.

What was the least expensive way to process rice in Java? The least-cost combination of laborers and capital is determined by finding the lowest isocost that touches the relevant isoquant.

The isoquant for 10 million rupees' worth of processed rice, Figure 7.7, has kinks. The point at each kink represents one of the five milling processes. The straight line connecting a pair of points shows how the same output could be produced by using a combination of those two processes. For example, at the

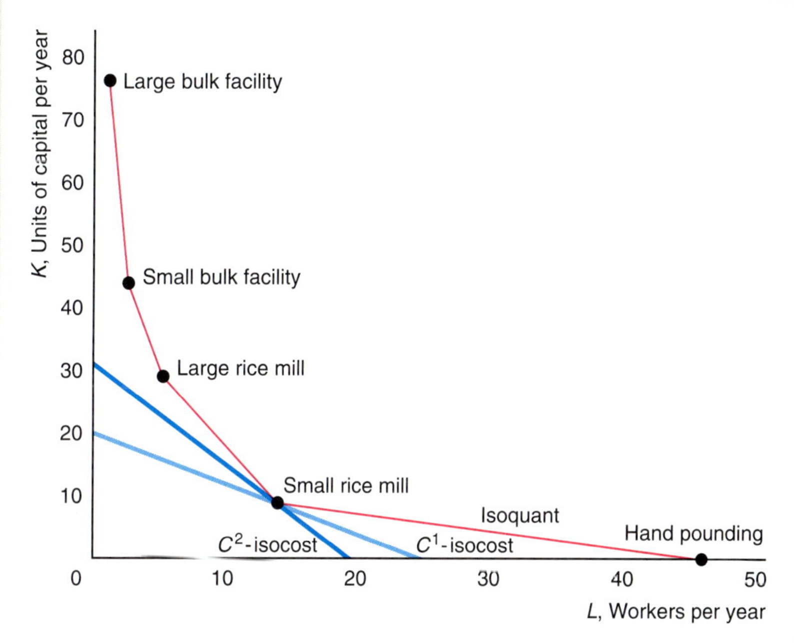

Figure 7.7 Rice Milling in Java. The isoquant for 10 million rupees' worth of processed rice has five kinks in it (Timmer 1984). Each kink represents one of the milling processes. The straight line connecting a pair of dots shows how the same output could be produced by using a combination of those two processes.

midpoint of the line between hand pounding and small mills, half the rice is produced by hand pounding and half by the small mill.

Because the isoquant has kinks, small changes in the relative cost of the two inputs do not necessarily lead to a change in technique. Two different sloped isocost lines C^1 and C^2 (which reflect the range of relative factor prices in 1973) touch the isoquant at the same point: The small rice mill is the least expensive technique. The isocost line must be steeper than C^2 (the price of capital must fall relative to that of labor) for a more capital-intensive technique to be used. ■

Factor Price Changes. Once the Norwegian printing firm determines the lowest-cost combination of inputs to produce a given level of output, it uses that method as long as the input prices remain constant. How should the firm change its behavior if the cost of one of the factors changes? Suppose the wage falls by one-third from 24 kr to 8 kr but the rental rate of capital stays constant at 8 kr.

The firm minimizes its new cost by substituting away from the now relatively more expensive input, capital, toward the now relatively less expensive input, labor. The change in the wage does not affect technological efficiency, so it does not affect the isoquant in Figure 7.8. Because of the wage decrease, the new isocost lines have a flatter slope, $-w/r = -8/8 = -1$, than do the original isoquant lines, $-w/r = -24/8 = -3$.

The relatively steep original isocost line is tangent to the 100 unit isoquant at bundle x ($L = 50$, $K = 100$). The new flatter isocost line is tangent to the isoquant at bundle v ($L = 77$, $K = 52$). Thus, the firm uses more labor and less capital as labor becomes relatively less expensive. Moreover, the firm's cost of producing 100 units falls from 2,000 kr to 1,032 kr because of the fall in the wage.

This example illustrates that a change in the relative prices of inputs affects the mix of inputs that a firm uses. In contrast, if all prices increase by the same amount, so the relative prices do not change, the firm continues to produce any given amount of output using the same input combination as it did originally, as we now show.

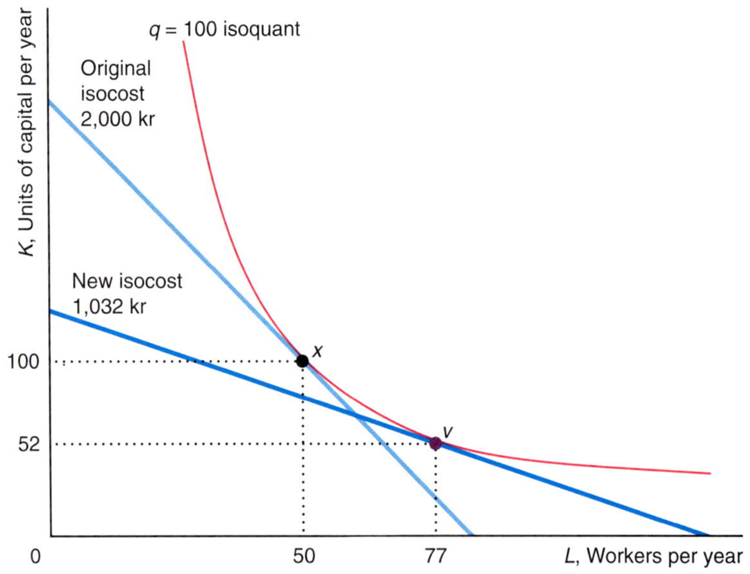

Figure 7.8 Change in Factor Price. Originally, the wage was 24 kr and the rental rate of capital was 8 kr, so the lowest isocost line (2,000 kr) was tangent to the $q = 100$ isoquant at x ($L = 50$, $K = 100$). When the wage falls to 8 kr, the isocost lines became flatter: Labor became relatively less expensive than capital. The slope of the isocost lines falls from $-w/r = -24/8 = -3$ to $-8/8 = -1$. The new lowest isocost line (1,032 kr) is tangent at v ($L = 77$, $K = 52$). Thus, when the wage falls the firm uses more labor and less capital to produce a given level of output, and the cost of production falls from 2,000 kr to 1,032 kr.

SOLVED PROBLEM 7.2

When the input prices were $\hat{w}$ and $\hat{r}$, a firm produced $\hat{q}$ units of output using $\hat{L}$ units of labor and $\hat{K}$ units of capital. Suppose the prices of both its inputs doubles. If the firm continues to produce $\hat{q}$ units of output, will it change the amount of labor and capital it uses? What happens to its cost of producing $\hat{q}$?

Answer

1. *Determine whether the change affects the slopes of the isoquant or the isocost lines*: A change in input prices does not affect the isoquant, which depends only on technology (the production function). Moreover, the doubling of the input prices does not affect the slope of the isocost lines. The original slope was $-\hat{w}/\hat{r}$, and the new slope is $-(2\hat{w})/(2\hat{r}) = -\hat{w}/\hat{r}$.

2. *Using a rule for cost minimization, determine whether the firm changes its input mix*: A firm minimizes its cost by producing where its isoquant is tangent to the lowest possible isocost line. That is, the firm produces where the slope of its isoquant, $-MRTS$, equals the slope of its isocost line, $-w/r$. Because the slopes of the isoquant and the isocost lines are unchanged after input prices doubled, the firm continues to produce $\hat{q}$ using the same amount of labor, $\hat{L}$, and capital, $\hat{K}$, as originally.

3. *Calculate the original cost and the new cost and compare them*: The firm's original cost of producing $\hat{q}$ units of output was $\hat{w}\hat{L} + \hat{r}\hat{K} = \hat{C}$. Its new cost of producing the same amount of output is $(2\hat{w})\hat{L} + (2\hat{r})\hat{K} = 2\hat{C}$. Thus, its cost of producing $\hat{q}$ doubled when the input prices doubled. The isocost lines have the same slope as before, but the cost associated with each isocost line has doubled. ■

How LR Cost Varies with Output

We now know how a firm determines the cost-minimizing output for any given level of output. By repeating this analysis for different output levels, the firm determines how its cost varies with output.

Panel a of Figure 7.9 shows the relationship between the lowest-cost factor combinations and various levels of output for the printing firm when input prices are held constant at w = 24 kr and r = 8 kr. The curve through the tangency points is the long-run **expansion path**: the cost-minimizing combination of labor and capital for each output level. The lowest-cost way to produce 100 units of output is to use the labor and capital combination x (L = 50 and K = 100), which lies on the 2,000-kr isocost line. Similarly, the lowest-cost way to produce 200 units is to use z, which is on the 4,000-kr isocost line. The expansion path goes through x and z.

The expansion path of the printing firm in the figure is a straight line through the origin with a slope of 2: At any given output level, the firm uses twice as much

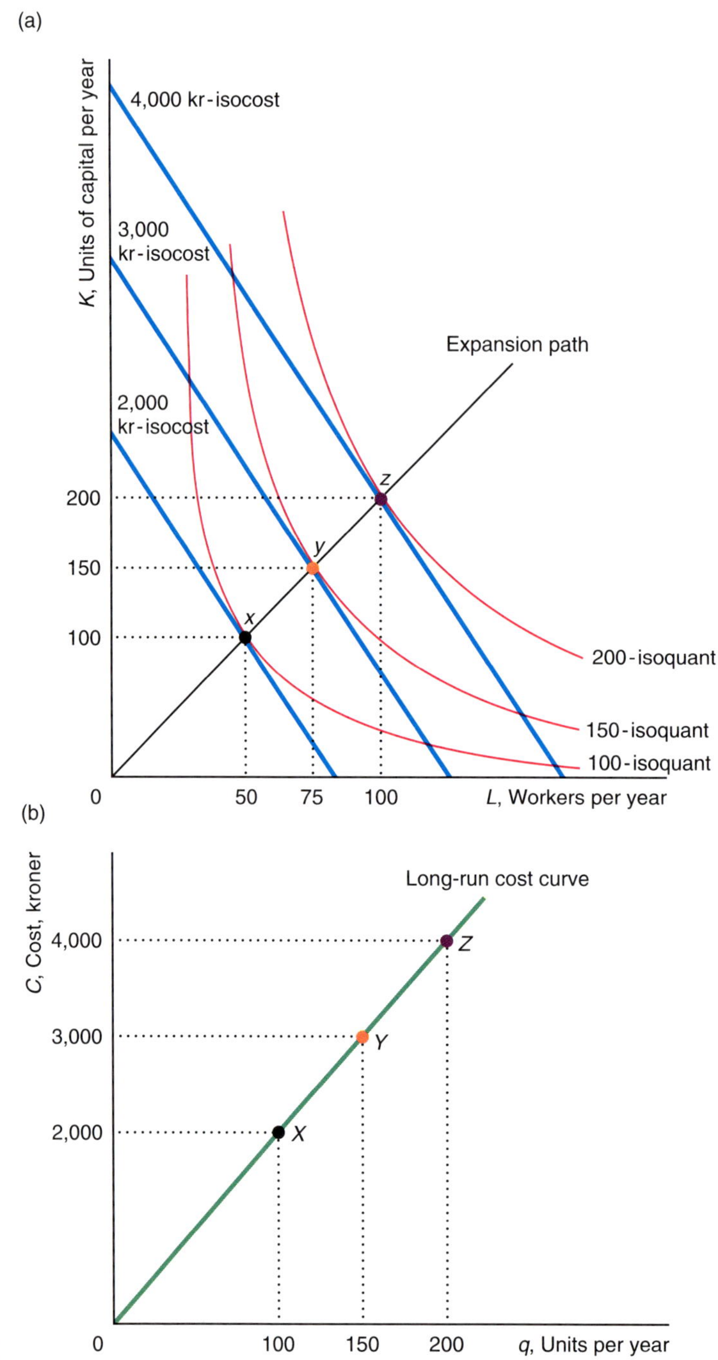
(a)
K, Units of capital per year
4,000 kr-isocost
3,000
kr-isocost
2,000
kr-isocost
Expansion path
z
y
x
200
150
100
200-isoquant
150-isoquant
100-isoquant
0
50
75
100
L, Workers per year
(b)
C, Cost, kroner
Long-run cost curve
4,000
3,000
2,000
Z
Y
X
0
100
150
200
q, Units per year

Figure 7.9 Expansion Path and LR Cost Curve. (a) The curve through the tangency points between isocost lines and isoquants, such as x, y, and z, is called the expansion path. The points on the expansion path are the cost-minimizing combinations of labor and capital for each output level. (b) The expansion path shows the same relationship between long-run cost and output as does the long-run cost curve.

capital as labor.[7] To double its output from 100 to 200 units, the firm doubles the amount of labor from 50 to 100 workers and doubles the amount of capital from 100 to 200 units. Because both inputs double when output doubles from 100 to 200, cost also doubles.

The printing firm's expansion path contains the same information as its long-run cost function, $C(q)$, which shows the relationship between the cost of production and output. From inspection of the expansion path, to produce q units of output takes $K = q$ units of capital and $L = q/2$ units of labor. Thus, the long-run cost of producing q units of output is

$$C(q) = wL + rK = wq/2 + rq = (w/2 + r)q = (24/2 + 8)q = 20q.$$

That is, the long-run cost function corresponding to this expansion path is $C(q) = 20q$. This cost function is consistent with the expansion path in panel a: $C(100) = 2{,}000$ kr at x on the expansion path, $C(150) = 3{,}000$ kr at y, and $C(200) = 4{,}000$ kr at z.

Panel b plots this long-run cost curve. Points X, Y, and Z on the cost curve correspond to points x, y, and z on the expansion path. For example, the 2,000-kr isocost line goes through x, which is the lowest-cost combination of labor and capital that can produce 100 units of output. Similarly, X on the long-run cost curve is at 2,000 kr and 100 units of output. Consistent with the expansion path, the cost curve shows that as output doubles, cost doubles.

SOLVED PROBLEM 7.3

What is the long-run cost function for a fixed-proportions production function (Chapter 6) when it takes one unit of labor and one unit of capital to produce one unit of output? Describe the long-run cost curve.

Answer

Multiply the inputs by their prices and sum to determine total cost. The long-run cost of producing q units of output is $C(q) = wL + rK = wq + rq = (w + r)q$. Cost rises in proportion to output. The long-run cost curve is a straight line with a slope of $w + r$. ■

[7] In Appendix 7B, we show that the expansion path for a Cobb-Douglas production function is $K = [\beta w/(\alpha r)]L$. The expansion path for the printing firm is $K = [0.4 \times 24/(0.6 \times 8)]L = 2L$.

The Shape of LR Cost Curves

The shapes of the average cost and marginal cost curves depend on the shape of the long-run cost curve. To illustrate these relationships, we examine the long-run cost curves of a typical firm that has a U-shaped long-run average cost curve.

The long-run cost curve in panel a of Figure 7.10 corresponds to the long-run average and marginal cost curves in panel b. Unlike the straight-line long-run cost curves of the printing firm and the firm with fixed proportions production, the long-run cost curve of this firm rises less than in proportion to output at outputs below q^* and then rises more rapidly.

We can apply the same type of analysis that we used to study short-run curves to look at the geometric relationship between long-run total, average, and marginal curves. A line from the origin is tangent to the long-run cost curve at q^*, where the marginal cost curve crosses the average cost curve, because the slope of that line equals the marginal and average costs at that output. The long-run average cost curve falls when the long-run marginal cost curve is below it and rises when the long-run marginal cost curve is above it. Thus, the marginal cost crosses the average cost curve at the lowest point on the average cost curve.

Why does the average cost curve first fall and then rise, as in panel b? The explanation differs from those given for why short-run average cost curves are U-shaped.

A key reason why the short-run average cost is initially downward sloping is that the average fixed cost curve is downward sloping: Spreading the fixed cost over more units of output lowers the average fixed cost per unit. There are no fixed costs in the long run, however, so fixed costs cannot explain the initial downward slope of the long-run average cost curve.

A major reason why the short-run average cost curve slopes up at higher levels of output is diminishing marginal returns. In the long run, however, all factors can be varied, so diminishing marginal returns do not explain the upward slope of a long-run average cost curve.

Ultimately, as with the short-run curves, the shape of the long-run curves is determined by the production function relationship between output and inputs. In the long run, returns to scale play a major role in determining the shape of the average cost curve and other cost curves. As we discussed in Chapter 6, increasing all inputs in proportion may cause output to increase more than in proportion (increasing returns to scale) at low levels of output, in proportion (constant returns to scale) at intermediate levels of output, and less than in proportion (decreasing returns to scale) at high levels of output. If a production function has this returns-to-scale pattern and the prices of inputs are constant, long-run average cost must be U-shaped.

To illustrate the relationship between returns to scale and long-run average cost, we use the returns-to-scale example in Figure 6.7, which is reproduced in Table 7.4. The firm produces one unit of output using a unit each of labor and capital. Given a wage and rental cost of capital of \$6 per unit, the total cost and average cost of producing this unit are both \$12. Doubling both inputs causes output to increase more than in proportion to three units, reflecting increasing returns to scale. Because cost only doubles and output triples, the average cost falls. A cost function is said to exhibit **economies of scale** if the average cost of production falls as output expands.

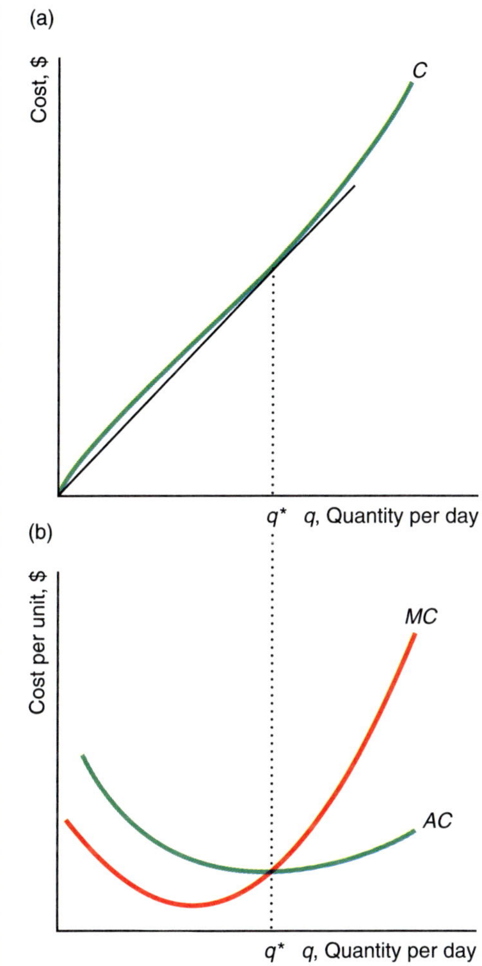

Figure 7.10 LR Cost Curves. (a) The long-run cost curve rises less rapidly than output at output levels below q^* and more rapidly at higher output levels. (b) As a consequence, the marginal cost and average cost curves are U-shaped. The marginal cost crosses the average cost at its minimum at q^*.

Doubling the inputs again causes output to double as well—constant returns to scale—so the average cost remains constant. If an increase in output has no effect on average cost—the average cost curve is flat—there are *no economies of scale*.

Table 7.4 Returns to Scale and LR Costs

Output, Q	Labor, L	Capital, K	Cost, $C = wL + rK$	Average Cost, $AC = C/q$	Returns to Scale
1	1	1	12	12	
3	2	2	24	8	Increasing
6	4	4	48	8	Constant
8	8	8	96	12	Decreasing

$w = r = \$6$ per unit.

Doubling the inputs once more causes only a small increase in output—decreasing returns to scale—so average cost increases. A firm suffers from **diseconomies of scale** if average cost rises when output increases.

Returns to scale in the production function are a sufficient but not necessary condition for economies of scale in the average cost curve. In the long run, a firm may change the ratio of capital to labor that it uses as it expands output. As a result, the firm could have economies of scale in costs without increasing returns to scale in production or could have diseconomies of scale in costs without decreasing returns to scale in production.

Consider a firm that has constant returns to scale in production at every output level. At small levels of output, the firm uses lots of labor and commonly available tools. At large levels of output, the firm designs and builds its own specialized equipment and uses relatively few workers, thereby lowering its average cost. Such a firm has economies of scale in cost despite having constant returns to scale in production.

Average cost curves can have many different shapes. Competitive firms typically have U-shaped average cost curves. Average cost curves in noncompetitive markets may be U-shaped, L-shaped (average cost at first falls rapidly and then levels off as output increases), everywhere downward sloping, or everywhere upward sloping or have other shapes. The shapes of the average cost curves indicate whether the production process has economies or diseconomies of scale.

Table 7.5 Shape of Average Cost Curves in Canadian Manufacturing

Scale Economies	Share of Manufacturing Industries (%)	
Economies of scale: initially downward-sloping *AC*	57	
Everywhere downward-sloping *AC*		18
L-shaped *AC* (downward-sloping, then flat)		31
U-shaped *AC*		8
No economies of scale: flat *AC*	23	
Diseconomies of scale: upward-sloping *AC*	14	

Source: Robidoux and Lester (1992).

Table 7.5 summarizes the shapes of average cost curves of firms in various Canadian manufacturing industries (as estimated by Robidoux and Lester 1992). The table shows that U-shaped average cost curves are the exception rather than the rule in Canadian manufacturing and that nearly one-third of these average cost curves are L-shaped.

Some of these apparently L-shaped average cost curves may be part of a U-shaped curve with long, flat bottoms, where we don't observe any firm producing enough to exhibit diseconomies of scale. Cement firms provide an example of such a cost curve.

APPLICATION

Average Cost of Cement Firms

Cement producers enjoy substantial economies of scale. The average cost curve for a British cement firm in Figure 7.11 (based on data from Norman

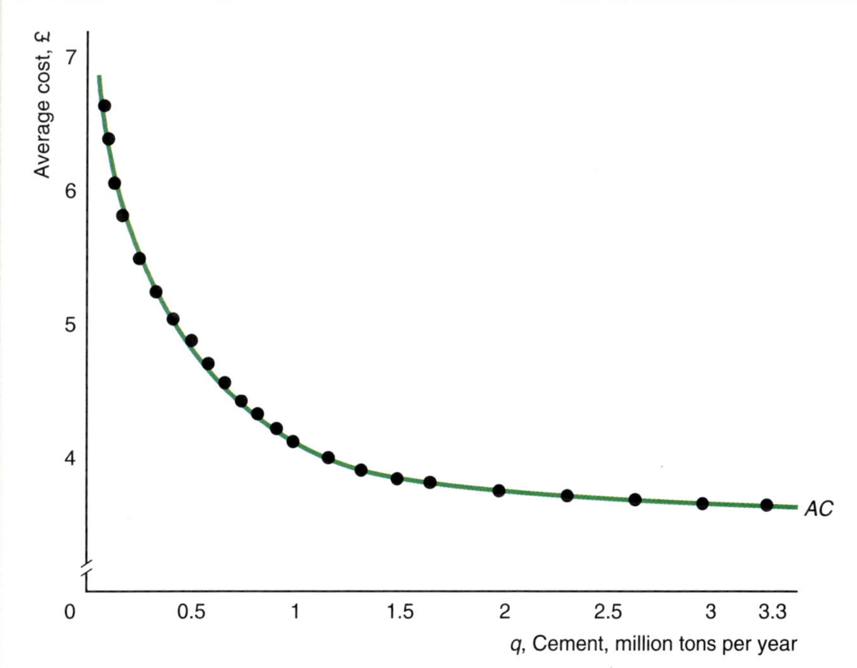

Figure 7.11 Cement Average Cost Curve. The average cost curve for a typical British cement firm is L-shaped, showing that there are economies of scale at every observed output up to about 1,600 tons and little or no economies of scale thereafter. The dots show the average costs for actual plants (Norman 1979), and the line is a curve fitted through these observed points.

1979) is L-shaped: Average cost falls rapidly at first and then more slowly. Norman presented evidence that average cost curves have similar shapes in the United States and West Germany. Jha, Murty, Paul, and Sahni (1991) also found economies of scale in Indian cement, lime, and plaster plants. They estimated that a 1% increase in a plant's output lowers its average cost by 0.14%. Thus, the long-run average cost in India is also L-shaped. ■

Estimating Cost Curves Versus Introspection

Economists use statistical methods to estimate a cost function. Sometimes, however, we can infer the shape by casual observation and deductive reasoning.

As an example, in the good old days, the Good Humor company sent out fleets of ice cream trucks to purvey its products. It seems likely that the company's production process had fixed proportions and constant returns to scale: If it wanted to sell more, Good Humor dispatched one more truck and one more driver. Drivers and trucks are almost certainly nonsubstitutable inputs (the isoquants are right angles). If the cost of a driver is w per day, the rental cost is r per day, and q quantity of ice cream is sold in a day, then the cost function is $C = (w + r)q$.

Such deductive reasoning can lead one astray, as I once discovered. A water heater manufacturing firm provided me with many years of data on the inputs it used and the amount of output it produced. I also talked to the company's engineers about the production process and toured the plant (which resembled a scene from Dante's *Inferno*, with staggering noise levels and flames everywhere).

A water heater consists of an outside cylinder of metal, a liner, an electronic control unit, hundreds of tiny parts (screws, washers, etc.), and a couple of rods that slow corrosion. Workers cut out the metal for the cylinder, weld it together, and add the other parts. "OK," I said to myself, "this production process must be one of fixed proportions because the firm needs one of everything to produce a water heater. How could you substitute a cylinder for an electronic control unit? Or how can you substitute labor for metal?"

I then used statistical techniques to estimate the production and cost functions. Following the usual procedure, however, I did not assume that I knew the exact functional form of the functions. Rather, I allowed the data to "tell" me the type of production and cost functions. To my surprise, the estimates indicated that the production process was not one of fixed proportions. Rather, the firm could readily substitute between labor and capital.

"Surely I've made a mistake," I said to the plant manager after describing these results. "No," he said, "that's correct. There's a great deal of substitutability between labor and metal."

"How can they be substitutes?"

"Easy," he said. "We can use a lot of labor and waste very little metal by cutting out exactly what we want and being very careful. Or we can use relatively little labor, cut quickly, and waste more metal. When the cost of labor is relatively high, we waste more metal. When the cost of metal is relatively high, we cut more carefully." This practice minimizes the firm's cost.

7.4 LOWER COSTS IN THE LONG RUN

In its long-run planning, a firm chooses a plant size and makes other investments so as to minimize its long-run cost on the basis of how many units it produces. Once it chooses its plant size and equipment, these inputs are fixed in the short run. Thus, the firm's long-run decision determines its short run cost. Because the firm cannot vary its capital in the short run but can vary it in the long run, short-run cost is at least as high as long-run cost and is higher if the "wrong" level of capital is used in the short run.

LR Average Cost as the Envelope of SR Average Cost Curves

As a result, the long-run average cost is always equal to or below the short-run average cost. Suppose, initially, that the firm in Figure 7.12 has only three possible plant sizes. The firm's short-run average cost curve is $SRAC^1$ for the smallest possible plant. The average cost of producing q_1 units of output using this plant, point *a* on $SRAC^1$, is \$10. If, instead, the plant used the next larger plant size, its cost of producing q_1 units of output, point *b* on $SRAC^2$, would be \$12. Thus, if the firm knows that it will produce only q_1 units of output, it minimizes its average cost by

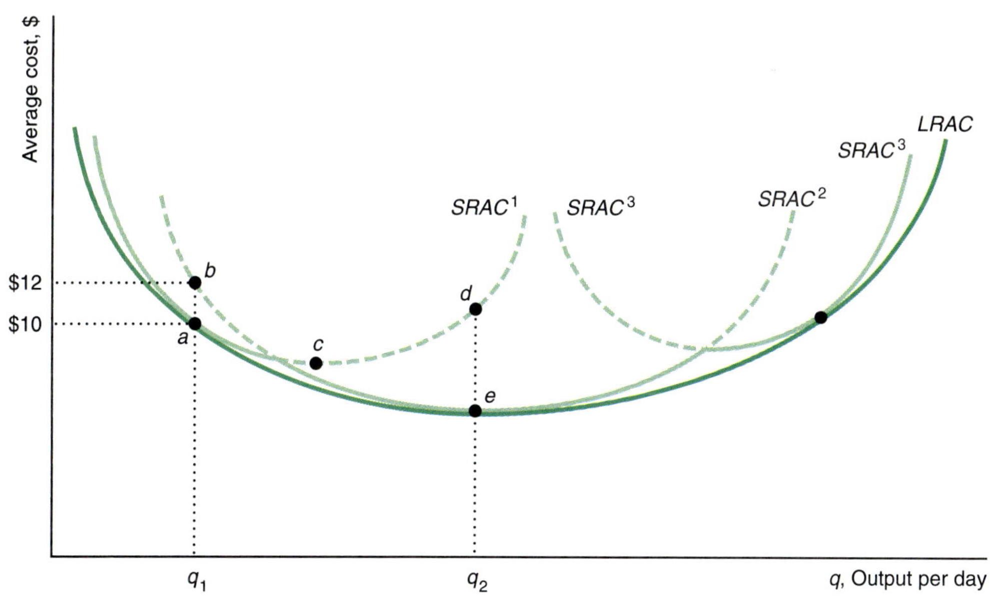

Figure 7.12 LR Average Cost Is the Envelope of SR Average Cost Curves. If there are only three possible plant sizes, with short-run average costs $SRAC^1$, $SRAC^2$, and $SRAC^3$, the long-run average cost curve is the solid, scalloped portion of the three short-run curves. *LRAC* is the smooth and U-shaped long-run average cost curve if there are many possible short-run average cost curves.

using the smaller plant size. On the other hand, if it expects to be producing q_2, its average cost is lower on the $SRAC^2$ curve, point *e*, than on the $SRAC^1$ curve, point *d*.

In the long run, the firm chooses the plant size that minimizes its cost of production, so it picks the plant size that has the lowest average cost for each possible output level. At q_1, it opts for the small plant size, whereas at q_2, it uses the medium plant size. Thus, the long-run average cost curve is the solid, scalloped section of the three short-run cost curves.

If there are many possible plant sizes, the long-run average curve, *LRAC*, is smooth and U-shaped. The *LRAC* includes one point from each possible short-run average cost curve. This point, however, is not necessarily the minimum point from a short-run curve. For example, the *LRAC* includes *a* on $SRAC^1$ and not its minimum point, *c*. A small plant operating at minimum average cost cannot produce at as low an average cost as a slightly larger plant that is taking advantage of economies of scale.

APPLICATION

LR Cost Curves in Printing and Oil Pipelines

We illustrate the relationship between long-run and short-run cost curves for a Norwegian printing firm and for oil pipelines. In the following application, we show the long-run cost when you or a firm chooses between a laser printer and an ink-jet printer, depending on how many pages will be printed.

Printing Firm

Panel a of Figure 7.13 shows the relationship between short-run and long-run average cost curves for the Norwegian printing firm. Because this production function has constant returns to scale, doubling both inputs doubles output, so the long-run average cost, *LRAC*, is constant at 20 kr, as we saw earlier. If capital is fixed at 200 units, the firm's short-run average cost curve is $SRAC^1$.

Figure 7.13 Actual SR and LR Average Cost Curves. (a) Because its production function has constant returns to scale, the Norwegian printing firm's long-run average cost and marginal cost curves are horizontal at 20 kr. The short-run average cost curve is $SRAC^1$ when $K = 200$ and $SRAC^2$ when $K = 600$. The corresponding short-run marginal cost curves are $SRMC^1$ and $SRMC^2$. (b) Oil companies have tremendous economies of scale in the long run, so the long-run average cost falls with output, even though the short-run average cost curves are U-shaped. *Source:* Exxon Company, U.S.A., *Competition in the Petroleum Industry*, 1975, p. 30. Reprinted with permission.

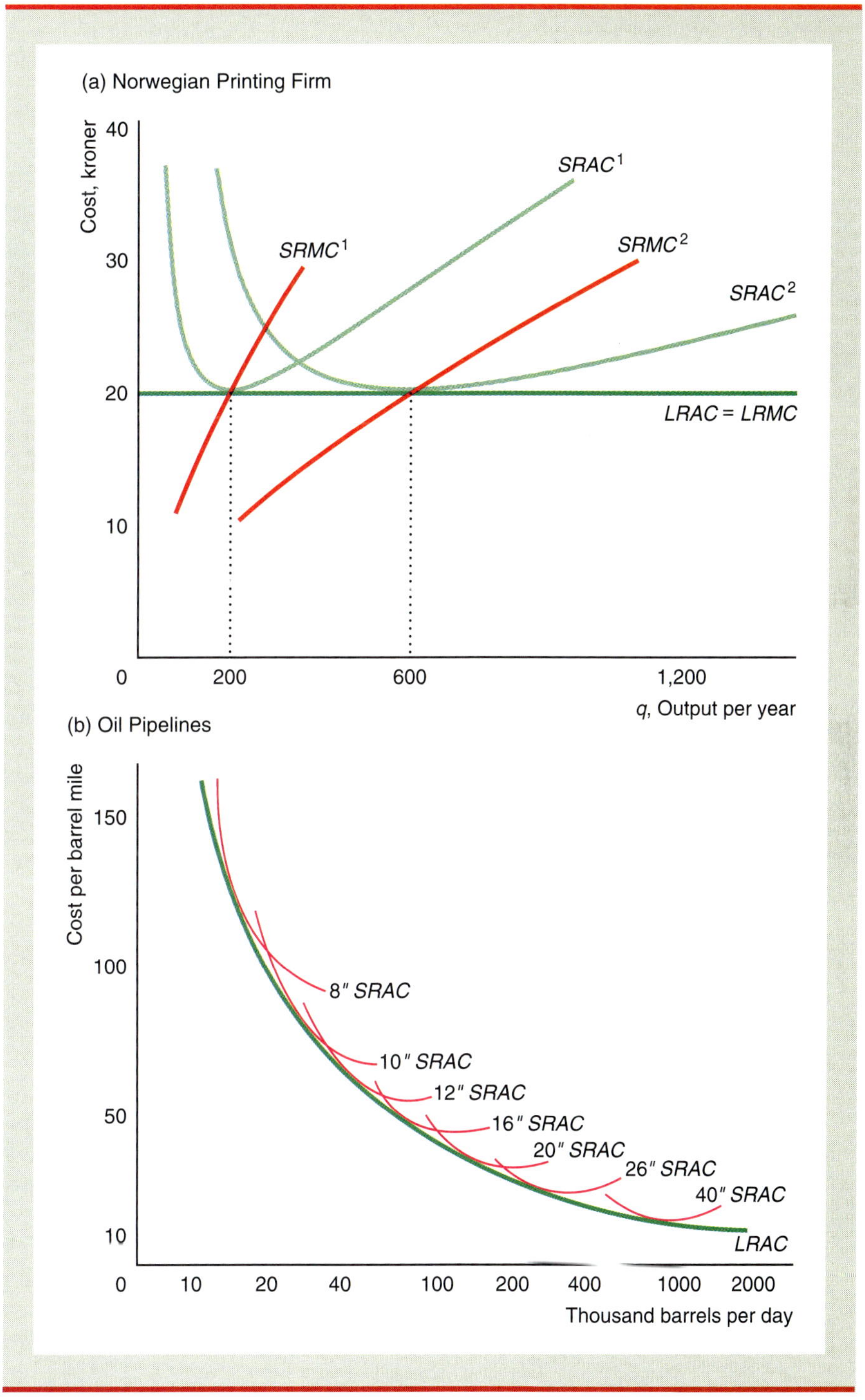
(a) Norwegian Printing Firm
Cost, kroner
40
30
20
10
0
200
600
1,200
q, Output per year
SRAC1
SRMC1
SRMC2
SRAC2
LRAC = LRMC
(b) Oil Pipelines
Cost per barrel mile
150
100
50
10
0
10
20
40
100
200
400
1000
2000
Thousand barrels per day
8" SRAC
10" SRAC
12" SRAC
16" SRAC
20" SRAC
26" SRAC
40" SRAC
LRAC

If the firm produces 200 units of output, its short-run and long-run average costs are equal. At any other output, its short-run cost is higher than its long-run cost.

The short-run marginal cost curves, $SRMC^1$ and $SRMC^2$, in the figure are upward sloping and equal the corresponding U-shaped short-run average cost curves, $SRAC^1$ and $SRAC^2$, only at their minimum points, 20 kr. In contrast, because the long-run average cost is horizontal at 20 kr, the long-run marginal cost curve, *SRMC*, is horizontal at 20 kr. Thus, the long-run marginal cost curve is *not* the envelope of the short-run marginal cost curves.

Oil Pipelines

Oil companies use the information in panel b of Figure 7.13 (based on Exxon 1975, p. 30) to choose what size pipe to use to deliver oil. In the figure, the 8" *SRAC* is the short-run average cost of a pipe with an 8-inch diameter. The long-run average cost curve, *LRAC*, is the envelope of all possible short-run average cost curves. It is more expensive to lay larger pipes than smaller ones, so a firm does not want to install unnecessarily large pipes. The average cost of sending a substantial quantity through a single large pipe is lower than that of sending it through two smaller pipes. For example, the average cost per barrel of sending 200,000 barrels per day through two 16-inch pipes is 1.67 (= \$50/\$30) greater than through a single 26-inch pipe.

Because the company incurs large fixed costs in laying miles and miles of pipelines and because pipes last for years, it does not vary the size of pipes in the short run. In the long run, the oil company installs the ideal pipe size to handle its "throughput" of oil. As Exxon (1975, p. 16) notes, several oil companies share interstate pipelines because of the large economies of scale. ■

APPLICATION

Choosing an Ink-Jet or a Laser Printer

In deciding which piece of capital equipment to buy, firms take a long-run view. Suppose you start a small firm and want to send nice-looking letters to your customers. You can buy a personal laser printer for \$550 or an ink-jet printer for \$285

If you buy the ink-jet, you'll save \$265 right off the bat. The laser costs less per page to operate, however. The cost of ink and paper is about 3.5¢ per page for a laser compared to 4.3¢ per page for an ink-jet. That means that the average cost per page of operating a laser (\$550/q + 0.035, where q is the number of pages) is less than that of an ink-jet (\$285/q + 0.043) after q reaches about 33,000 pages.

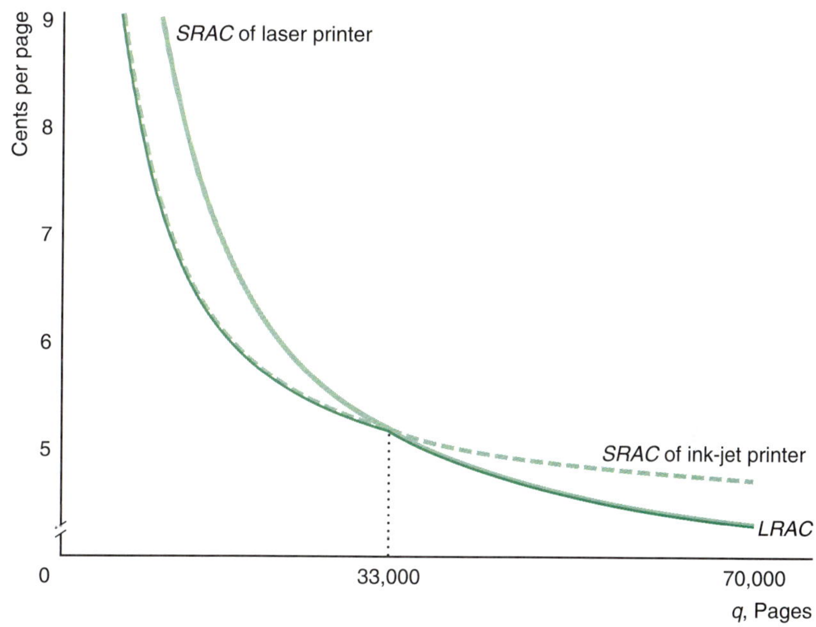

Figure 7.14 Average Cost of Printing. The average cost of printing is less with an ink-jet printer if you print fewer than 33,000 pages and a laser printer if you print more than that.

So should you buy the laser? Well, the typical ink-jet user averages only 15 pages per work week. At that rate, to print 33,000 pages will take about 44 years (assuming that the ink-jet would last that long). Thus, if you print only a few pages per week, buy the ink-jet. To print 33,000 pages in about two years would take an average of about 330 pages per week (assuming 50 business weeks per year), or about 66 pages per business day. Thus, if you print 66 or more pages per day, the laser is cost effective (assuming that it lasts at least two years at this level of use).

Figure 7.14 shows the short-run average cost curves for the laser printer and the ink-jet printer. In the long run, the low-cost choice is the ink-jet if you will be printing fewer than 33,000 pages and the laser if you will be printing more. ■

SR and LR Expansion Paths

Long-run cost is lower than short-run cost because the firm has more flexibility in the long run. To show the advantage of flexibility, we can compare the short-run and long-run expansion paths, which correspond to the short-run and long-run cost curves.

The Norwegian printing firm has greater long-run flexibility. The tangency of the firm's isoquants and isocost lines determines the long-run expansion path in Figure 7.15. The firm expands output by increasing both its labor and capital, so its long-run expansion path is upward sloping. To increase its output from 100 to 200 units (move from x to z), it doubles its capital from 100 to 200 units and its labor from 50 to 100 workers. Its cost increases from 2,000 kr to 4,000 kr.

In the short run, the firm cannot increase its capital, which is fixed at 100 units. The firm can increase its output only by using more labor, so its short-run expansion path is horizontal at $K = 100$. To expand its output from 100 to 200 units (move from x to y), the firm must increase its labor from 50 to 159 workers, and its cost rises from 2,000 kr to 4,616 kr. Doubling output increases long-run cost 2 times and short-run cost approximately 2.3 times.

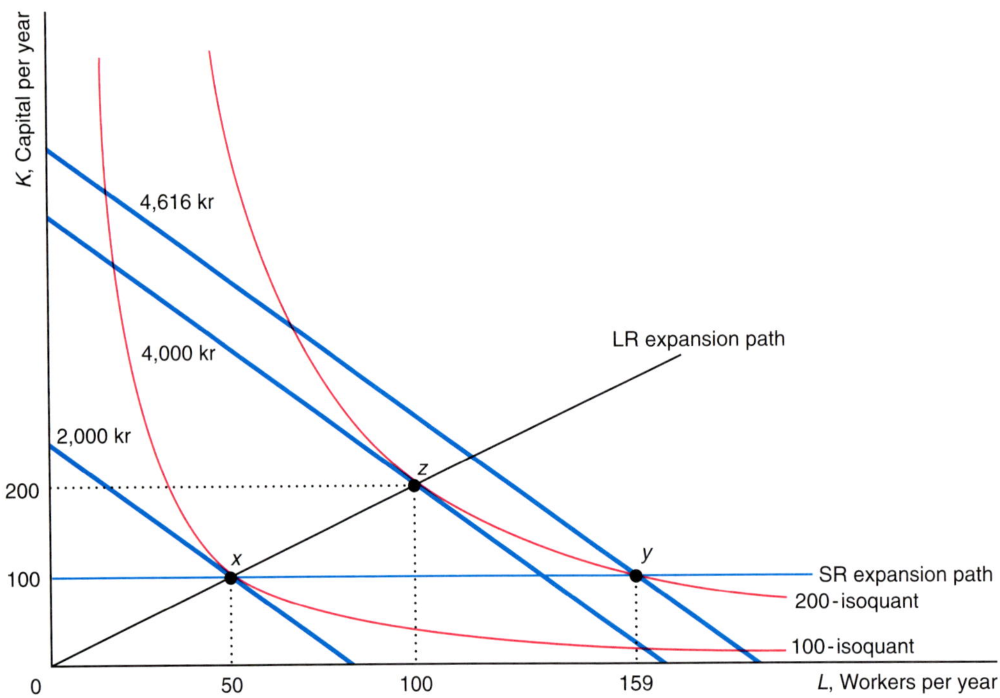

Figure 7.15 LR and SR Expansion Paths. In the long run, the Norwegian printing firm increases its output by using more of both inputs, so its long-run expansion path is upward sloping. In the short run, the firm cannot vary its capital, so its short-run expansion path is horizontal at the fixed level of output. That is, it increases its output by increasing the amount of labor it uses. Expanding output from 100 to 200 raises the printing firm's long-run cost from 2,000 kr to 4,000 kr but raises its short-run cost from 2,000 kr to 4,616 kr.

How Learning by Doing Lowers Costs

Two reasons why long-run cost is lower than short-run cost are that firms have more flexibility in the long run and technical progress (Chapter 6) may lower cost over time. A third reason is **learning by doing:** the productive skills and knowledge of better ways to produce that workers and managers gain from experience.

In some firms, learning by doing is a function of the time since the product was introduced. In others, learning by doing is a function of *cumulative output*: the total number of units of output produced since the product was introduced. Learning is connected to cumulative output if workers become increasingly adept the more times they perform a task. As a consequence, workers become more productive if they make many units over a short period than if they produce a few units over a longer period. For example, the average labor cost of producing a C-141 plane, panel a of Figure 7.16, fell with cumulative output (based on Womer and Patterson 1983).

If a firm is operating in the economies of scale section of its average cost curve, expanding output lowers its cost for two reasons. Its average cost falls today because of economies of scale, and for any given level of output, its average cost is lower in the next period due to learning by doing.

In panel b of Figure 7.16, the firm is currently producing q_1 units of output at point A on average cost curve AC^1. If it expands its output to q_2, its average cost falls in this period to B because of economies of scale. The learning by doing in this period results in a lower average cost, AC^2, in the next period. If the firm continues to produce q_2 units of output in the next period, its average cost falls to b on AC^2.

If instead of expanding output to q_2 in this period, the firm expands to q_3, its average cost is even lower in this period (C on AC^1) due to even more economies of scale. Moreover, its average cost in the next period is even lower, AC^3, due to the extra experience in this period. If the firm continues to produce q_3 in the next period, its average cost is c on AC^3. Thus, all else the same, if learning by doing depends on cumulative output, firms have an incentive to produce more in the short run than they otherwise would to lower their costs in the future.

APPLICATION

Learning by Doing in Computer Chips

The cost of producing a computer memory chip falls substantially due to learning by doing. There are several different types of MOS (metal oxide on silicon) memory chips: EPROM (erasable programmable read-only memory), DRAM (dynamic random-access memory), and fast SRAM (static random-access memory). From one generation to another, EPROM's storage capacity doubles, whereas the storage capacity of DRAM and SRAM increases by a factor of 4. Like clockwork, a new EPROM generation appears every 18 months; a new DRAM every 3 years.

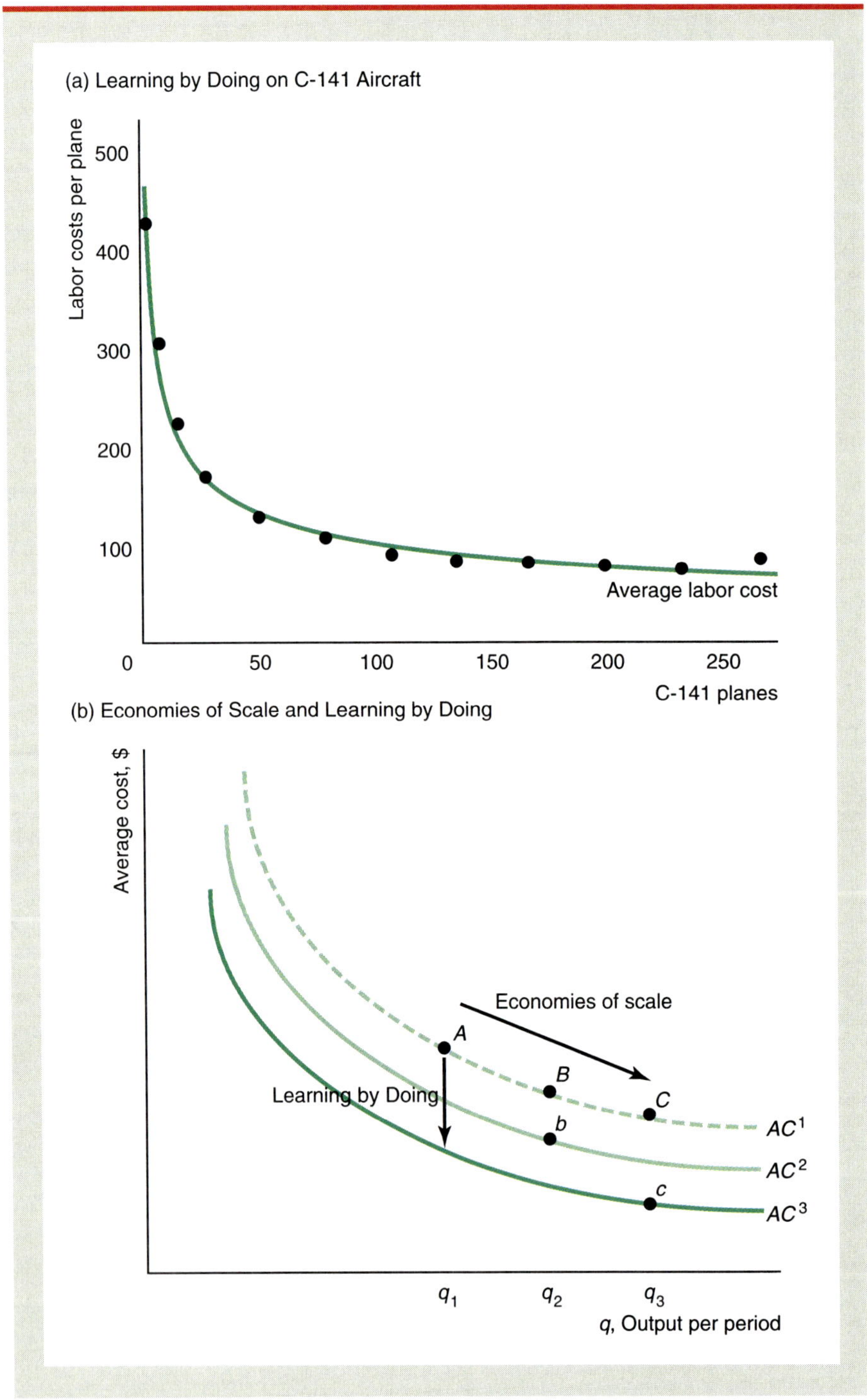
(a) Learning by Doing on C-141 Aircraft
Labor costs per plane
500
400
300
200
100
0
50
100
150
200
250
C-141 planes
Average labor cost
(b) Economies of Scale and Learning by Doing
Average cost, $
Economies of scale
Learning by Doing
A
B
C
b
c
AC1
AC2
AC3
q1
q2
q3
q, Output per period

Figure 7.16 Learning by Doing. (a) As more C-141 aircraft were produced, the average labor cost per plane fell (Womer and Patterson 1983). The horizontal axis shows the cumulative number of planes produced over time. (b) In the short run, extra production reduces a firm's average cost owing to economies of scale: Because $q_1 < q_2 < q_3$, A is higher than B, which is higher than C. In the long run, extra production reduces average cost because of learning by doing. To produce q_2 this period costs B on AC^1 but to produce that same output in the next period would cost only b on AC^2. If the firm produces q_3 instead of q_2 in this period, its average cost in the next period is AC^3 instead of AC^2 because of additional learning by doing. Thus, extra output in this period lowers the firm's cost in two ways: It lowers average cost in this period due to economies of scale and lowers average cost for any given output level in the next period due to learning by doing.

Gruber (1992) finds that the average cost of EPROM chips falls with cumulative output but does not decrease over time or with the scale of production. With each doubling in the cumulative output of an EPROM chip, its average cost falls by 22%. This effect may encourage firms to produce more EPROM chips in the first few months after a new generation is introduced than they would without learning. By doing so, the firm gains experience more rapidly, which causes its average cost to fall more rapidly.

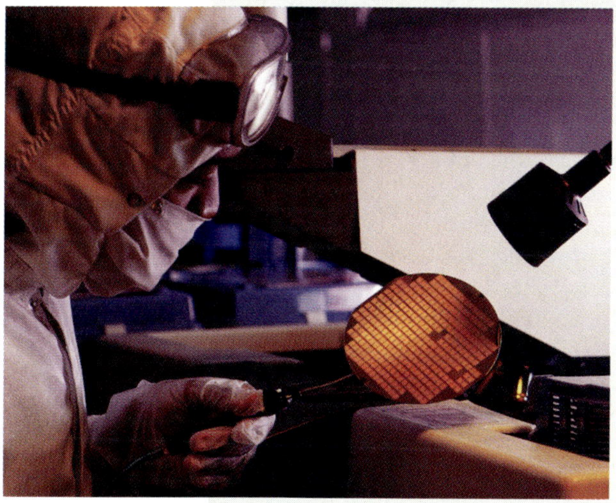

In contrast, the average cost of a DRAM chip does not fall with cumulative output but does fall with the time since introduction and exhibits economies of scale. With fast SRAM chips, only generation age affects average cost.

Although the type and speed of learning by doing vary across chips, they are the same across generations of the same chip. Thus, firms know that they can count on their costs falling and build these predictable cost reductions into their planning over time. ■

7.5 COST OF PRODUCING MULTIPLE GOODS

Few firms produce only a single good. We discuss single-output firms for simplicity. If a firm produces two or more goods, the cost of one good may depend on the output level of the other.

Outputs are linked if a single input is used to produce both of them. For example, mutton and wool both come from sheep; cattle provide beef and hides; and oil supplies both heating fuel and gasoline. It is less expensive to produce beef and hides together than separately. If the goods are produced together, a single steer yields one unit of beef and one hide. If beef and hides are produced separately (throwing away the unused good), the same amount of output requires two steers and more labor.

We say that there are **economies of scope** if it is less expensive to produce goods jointly than separately (Panzar and Willig 1977, 1981). A measure of the degree to which there are economies of *sc*ope (*SC*) is

$$SC = \frac{C(q_1, 0) + C(0, q_2) - C(q_1, q_2)}{C(q_1, q_2)},$$

where $C(q_1, 0)$ is the cost of producing q_1 units of the first good by itself, $C(0, q_2)$ is the cost of producing q_2 units of the second good, and $C(q_1, q_2)$ is the cost of producing both goods together. If the cost of producing the two goods separately, $C(q_1, 0) + C(0, q_2)$, is the same as producing them together, $C(q_1, q_2)$, then SC is zero. If it is cheaper to produce the goods jointly, SC is positive. If SC is negative, so there are diseconomies of scope, the two goods should be produced separately.

To illustrate this idea, suppose that Laura spends one day collecting mushrooms and wild strawberries in the woods. Her **production possibility frontier**—the maximum amounts of outputs (mushrooms and strawberries) that can be produced from a fixed amount of input (Laura's effort during one day)—is PPF^1 in Figure 7.17. The production possibility frontier summarizes the trade-off Laura faces: She picks fewer mushrooms if she collects more strawberries in a day.

If Laura spends all day collecting only mushrooms, she picks 8 pints; if she spends all day picking strawberries, she collects 6 pints. If she picks some of each, however, she can harvest more total pints: 6 pints of mushrooms and 4 pints of strawberries. The product possibility frontier is concave (the middle of the curve is farther from the origin than it would be if it were a straight line) because of the diminishing marginal returns to collecting only one of the two goods. If she collects only mushrooms, she must walk past wild strawberries without picking them. As a result, she has to walk farther if she collects only mushrooms than if she picks both. Thus, there are economies of scope in jointly collecting mushrooms and strawberries.

If, instead, the production possibility frontier were a straight line, the cost of producing the two goods jointly would not be lower. Suppose, for example, that mushrooms grow in one section of the woods and strawberries in another section. In that case, Laura can collect only mushrooms without passing any strawberries. That production possibility frontier is a straight line, PPF^2 in Figure 7.17. By allocating her time between the two sections of the woods, Laura can collect any combination of mushrooms and strawberries by spending part of her day in one section of the woods and part in the other.

A number of empirical studies show that some processes have economies of scope, others have none, and some have diseconomies of scope. Shoesmith (1988) found that there are economies of scope in refining. It is less expensive to produce

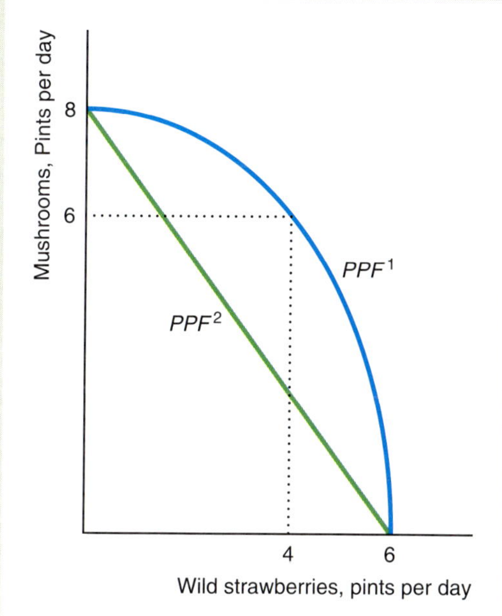

Figure 7.17 Joint Production. If there are economies of scope, the production possibility frontier is bowed away from the origin, PPF^1. If, instead, the production possibility frontier is a straight line, PPF^2, the cost of producing both goods does not fall if they are produced together.

motor gasoline, distillate fuels, and other refined products together than separately. Akridge and Hertel (1986) observed large economies of scope in producing various fertilizers together.

Friedlaender, Winston, and Wang (1983) found that, for four American automobile manufacturers, it is 25% less expensive ($SC = 0.25$) to produce large cars together with small cars and trucks than to produce large cars separately and small cars and trucks together. However, there are no economies of scope from producing trucks together with small and large cars. Producing trucks separately from cars is efficient.

Kim (1987) found substantial diseconomies of scope in using railroads to transport freight and passengers together. It is 41% less expensive ($SC = \ 0.41$) to transport passengers and freight separately than together. In the early 1970s, passenger service was transferred from the private railroad companies to Amtrak, and the services are separate. Kim's estimates suggest that this separation is cost effective.

Summary

From all technologically efficient production processes, a firm chooses the one that is economically efficient. The economically efficient production process is the technologically efficient process for which the cost of producing a given quantity of output is lowest, or the one that produces the most output for a given cost.

1. **Measuring costs:** The economic or opportunity cost of a good is the value of its next best alternative use. Economic cost includes both explicit costs and implicit costs.
2. **Short-run costs:** In the short run, the firm can vary the costs of the factors that it can adjust, but the costs of other factors are fixed. The firm's average fixed cost falls as its output rises. If a firm has a short-run average cost curve that is U-shaped, its marginal cost curve is below the average cost curve when average cost is falling and above average cost when it's rising, so the marginal cost curve cuts the average cost curve at its minimum.
3. **Long-run costs:** In the long run, all factors can be varied, so all costs are variable. As a result, average cost and average variable cost are identical. The firm chooses the combination of inputs it uses to minimize its cost. To produce a given output level, it chooses the lowest isocost that touches the relevant isoquant, which is tangent to the isoquant. Equivalently, to minimize cost, the firm adjusts inputs until the last dollar spent on any input increases output by as much as the last dollar spent on any other input. If the firm calculates the cost of producing every possible output level given current input prices, then it knows its cost function: Cost is a function of the input prices and the output level. If the firm's average cost falls as output expands, it has economies of scale. If its average cost rises as output expands, there are diseconomies of scale.
4. **Lower costs in the long run:** The firm can always do in the long run what it does in the short run, so its long-run cost can never be greater than its short-run cost. Because some factors are fixed in the short run, to expand output, the firm must greatly increase its use of other factors, which is relatively costly. In the long run, the firm can adjust all factors, a process that keeps its cost down. Long-run cost may also be lower than short-run cost if there is technological progress or learning by doing.
5. **Cost of producing multiple goods:** If it is less expensive for a firm to produce two goods jointly rather than separately, there are economies of scope. If there are diseconomies of scope, it is less expensive to produce the goods separately.

Problems

1. Discuss:

   "There are certain fixed costs when you own a plane," [Andre] Agassi explained last week during a break in the action at the Volvo/San Francisco tennis tournament, "so the more you fly it, the more economic sense it makes. . . . The first flight after I bought it, I took some friends to Palm Springs for lunch."[8]

2. The only variable input a janitorial service firm uses to clean offices is workers who are paid a wage, w, of \$8 an hour. Each worker can clean four offices in an hour. Use math to determine the variable cost, the average variable cost, and the marginal cost of cleaning one more office. Draw a diagram like Figure 7.1 to show the variable cost, average variable cost, and marginal cost curves.
3. Using the information in Table 7.1, construct another table showing how a lump-sum franchise tax of \$30 affects the various average cost curves of the firm.
4. A firm builds shipping crates out of wood. How does the cost of producing a 1-cubic-foot cubic crate (each side is 1 foot square) compare to the cost of building an 8-cubic-foot crate if wood costs

[8]Ostler, Scott, "Andre Even Flies Like a Champ," *San Francisco Chronicle*, February 8, 1993:C1.

$1 a square foot and the firm has no labor or other costs? More generally, how does cost vary with volume?

5. You have 60 minutes to take an exam with two questions. You want to maximize your score. Toward the end of the exam, the more time you spend on either question, the fewer extra points per minute you get for that question. How should you allocate your time between the two questions? (*Hint*: Think about producing an output of a score on the exam using inputs of time spent on each of the problems. Then use Equation 7.6.)
6. Boxes of cereal are produced by using a fixed-proportion production function: One box and one unit (8 oz) of cereal produce one box of cereal. What is the expansion path?
7. What is the expansion path if the production function has constant returns to scale?
8. How does the expansion path change if the wage increases while the rental rate of capital stays the same?
9. A U-shaped long-run average cost curve is the envelope of U-shaped short-run average cost curves. On what part of the curve (downward sloping, flat, or upward sloping) does a short-run curve touch the long-run curve? (*Hint*: Your answer should depend on where on the long-run curve the two curves touch.)
10. Suppose the government subsidizes the cost of workers by paying for 25% of the wage (the rate offered by the U.S. government in the late 1970s under the New Jobs Tax Credit program). What effect will this subsidy have on the firm's choice of labor and capital to produce a given level of output?
11. Suppose in Solved Problem 7.1 that the government charges the firm a franchise tax each year (instead of only once). Describe the effect of this tax on the marginal cost, average variable cost, short-run average cost, and long-run average cost curves.
12. What can you say about Laura's economies of scope if her time is valued at $5 an hour and her production possibility frontier is PPF^1 in Figure 7.17?

Math Problems

13. Give the formulas for and plot *AFC*, *MC*, *AVC*, and *AC* if the cost function is:
    A. $C = 10 + 10q$.
    B. $C = 10 + q^2$.
    C. $C = 10 + 10q - 4q^2 + q^3$.
14. What is the long-run cost function if the production function is $q = L + K$?
15. Gail works in a flower shop, where she produces 10 floral arrangements per hour. She is paid $10 an hour for the first 8 hours she works and $15 an hour for each additional hour she works. What is the firm's cost function? What are its *AC*, *AVC*, and *MC* functions? Draw the *AC*, *AVC*, and *MC* curves.
16. A firm's cost curve is $C = F + 10q - bq^2 + q^3$, where $b > 0$.
    A. For what values of b are cost, average cost, and average variable cost positive? (From now on, assume that all these measures of cost are positive at every output level.)
    B. What is the shape of the *AC* curve? At what output level is the *AC* minimized?
    C. At what output levels does the *MC* curve cross the *AC* and the *AVC* curves?
    D. Use calculus to show that the *MC* curve must cross the *AVC* at its minimum point.
18. A firm has two plants that produce identical output. The cost functions are $C_1 = 10q - 4q^2 + q^3$ and $C_2 = 10q - 2q^2 + q^3$.
    A. At what output levels does the average cost curve of each plant reach its minimum?
    B. If the firm wants to produce 4 units of output, how much should it produce in each plant?
19. For a Cobb-Douglas production function, how does the expansion path change if the wage increases while the rental rate of capital stays the same? (*Hint*: See Appendix 7B.)
20. A firm has a Cobb-Douglas production function, $Q = AL^{\alpha}K^{\beta}$, where $\alpha + \beta < 1$. On the basis of this information, what properties does its cost function have?
21. A firm's average cost is $AC = \alpha q^{\beta}$, where $\alpha > 0$. How can you interpret α? (*Hint*: Suppose $q = 1$.) What sign must β have if there is learning by doing? What happens to average cost as q gets large? Draw the average cost curve as a function of output for a particular set of α and β.

CHAPTER

8

Competitive Firms and Markets

The love of money is the root of all virtue. —George Bernard Shaw

One of the major questions facing firms is "How much output should we produce?" To pick a level of output that maximizes its profit, a firm must consider its cost function and how much it can sell at a given price. The amount the firm thinks it can sell depends, in turn, on the market demand of consumers and its beliefs about how other firms in the market will behave. The behavior of firms depends on the **market structure**: the number of firms in the market, the ease with which firms can enter and leave the market, and the ability of firms to differentiate their products from those of their rivals.

In this chapter, we look at a competitive market structure, one in which many firms produce identical products and firms can easily enter and exit the market. Because each firm produces a small share of the total market output and its output is identical to that of other firms, one firm cannot raise its price above the market price. If it were to try to do so, this firm would be unable to sell any of its output because consumers would buy the good at a lower price from the other firms in the market. In a competitive market, each small firm is a price taker that the firm cannot affect the market price. The market price summarizes all a firm needs to know about the demand of consumers *and* the behavior of its rivals. Thus, a competitive firm can ignore the specific behavior of individual rivals in deciding how much to produce.[1]

In this chapter, we examine five main topics:

1. Competition: A competitive firm is a price taker, and as such, it faces a horizontal demand curve.
2. Profit maximization: To maximize profit, any firm must make two decisions: how much to produce and whether to produce at all.
3. Competition in the short run: Variable costs determine a profit-maximizing, competitive firm's supply curve, the market supply curve, and with the market demand curve, the competitive equilibrium in the short run.
4. Competition in the long run: Firm supply, market supply, and competitive equilibrium are different in the long run than in the short run because firms can vary inputs that were fixed in the short run.
5. Zero profit for competitive firms in the long run: In the long-run competitive market equilibrium, profit-maximizing firms break even, so firms that do not try to maximize profits lose money and leave the market.

[1]In contrast, each oligopolistic firm must consider the behavior of each of its small number of rivals, as we discuss in Chapter 12.

8.1 COMPETITION

The first market structure that we study is competition. We start with competition because it is a common market structure and it has very desirable properties, so it is useful to compare other market structures to competition.

In this section, we describe the properties of competitive firms and markets. Next, we examine how competitive firms maximize profit to derive the short-run and long-run supply curves of competitive firms and competitive markets. Then we reexamine the competitive equilibrium.

Price Taking

When most people talk about "competitive firms," they mean firms that are rivals for the same customers. By this interpretation, any market that has more than one firm is competitive. To an economist, however, only some of these multifirm markets are competitive.

Economists say that a market is *competitive* if each firm in the market is a *competitive firm*, by which we mean that the firm is a *price taker*: a firm that cannot significantly affect the market price for its output or the prices at which it buys its inputs. If any one of the more than 40,000 apple farms in the United States were to stop producing apples or to double its production, the market price of apples would not change appreciably. Similarly, by stopping production or doubling its production, an apple farm would have little or no effect on the price for apple seeds, fertilizer, and other inputs.

Why would a competitive firm be a price taker? The main reason is that it has no choice. The firm *has to be a price taker* if it faces a demand curve that is horizontal at the market price. If the demand curve is horizontal at the market price, the firm can sell as much as it wants at the market price, so it has no incentive to lower its price. Similarly, the firm cannot increase the price at which it sells by restricting its output because it faces an infinitely elastic demand (see Chapter 3): A small increase in price results in its demand falling to zero.

Why the Firm's Demand Curve Is Horizontal

Firms are likely to be price takers in markets that have some or all of four properties:

- Consumers believe that all firms in the market sell *identical products*.
- Firms *freely enter and exit* the market.
- *Buyers and sellers know the prices* charged by firms.
- *Transaction costs*—the expenses of finding a trading partner and making a trade for a good or service other than the price paid for that good or service—*are low*.

When the products of all firms are seen as perfect substitutes, no firm can sell its product if it charges more than others because no consumer is willing to pay a premium for that product. Consumers don't ask which farm grew an apple because they view apples as *homogeneous* or *undifferentiated* products. In contrast, consumers who know that the characteristics of a Jaguar and an Escort differ substantially view automobiles as *heterogeneous* or *differentiated* products. If some customers prefer one firm's product to those of other firms, the firm's demand curve has a downward slope. One firm can charge more than other firms without losing all its customers.

No firm can raise its price above the market price if other firms are able and eager to undercut another firm's high price to attract more customers. Even in markets with only a few firms, if other firms can quickly and easily enter, a firm cannot raise its price without other firms entering the market and undercutting its price. Moreover, ease of entry may cause the number of firms in a market to be large. The more firms there are in a market, the less is the effect of a change in one firm's output on total market output and hence on the market price. If one of the 40,000 apple growers drops out of the market, market supply falls by only 0.0025% (assuming that the firms are of equal size), so the market price is unaffected.

If buyers know the prices other firms charge—the market price—a firm cannot raise its price without losing its customers. In contrast, if consumers do not know the prices other firms charge, a firm can charge more than other firms without losing all its customers, so its demand curve is downward sloping.

If transaction costs are low, it is easy for a customer to buy from a rival firm if the customer's usual supplier raises its price. Transaction costs are low if buyers and sellers do not have to spend time and money finding each other or hiring lawyers to write contracts in order to make a trade. The higher the transaction costs, the more likely it is that a firm's demand curve is downward sloping. For example, if finding a new, competent auto mechanic is very time consuming or involves traveling a great distance, consumers may continue to use their current auto repair shop even if that firm charges more than other firms. In some markets, buyers and sellers are brought together in a single room, so transaction costs are virtually zero. For example, transaction costs are very low at the auction in Amsterdam that the Verenigde Bloemenveilingen Aalsmeer cooperative holds daily for the 5,000 sellers who ship flowers from Zimbabwe, Colombia, Israel, Thailand, and the rest of Europe to the 2,500 buyers from around the world.[2]

We call a market in which all these conditions hold literally a *perfect competitive market*. In such a market, if a firm raised its price above the market price, the firm would be unable to make any sales. Its former customers would know that other firms sell an identical product at a lower price. These customers can easily find those other firms and buy from them without incurring extra transaction costs. If firms that are currently in the market cannot meet the demand of this firm's former customers, new firms can quickly and easily enter the market. Thus, firms in such a market must act as price takers.

The market for wheat is an example of an almost perfect competitive market. Many farmers produce identical products, and transaction costs are negligible. Wheat is sold in a formal exchange or market such as the Chicago Commodity

[2]Woodward, Richard B., "Business Is Blooming," *The New York Times Magazine*, May 9, 1993:33f.

Exchange. Using a formal exchange, buyers and sellers can easily place buy or sell orders in person, over the telephone, or electronically, so transaction costs are negligible. No time is wasted in finding someone who wants to trade, and the transactions are made virtually instantaneously without a lot of paperwork. Moreover, every buyer and seller in the market knows the market prices, quantities, and qualities of wheat available at any moment.

Even if some of these conditions are violated, firms and consumers may still be price takers. For example, even if entry of new firms is limited but the market has a very large number of firms and each can produce much more than its current output at about the same cost, firms are price takers. If one of these firms tries to raise its price, it will be unable to sell to consumers because other firms will expand their output if necessary to meet demand. Appendix 8A shows that a firm's demand curve is nearly horizontal as long as there are many firms in the market.

Why We Study Competition

Economists spend a great deal of time discussing perfect competition, which takes place in markets in which firms are price takers because products are homogeneous, firms enter and exit the market freely, buyers and sellers know the prices charged by firms, and transaction costs are low.[3] Perfect competitive markets are important for two reasons.

First, many markets can be reasonably described as competitive. Many agricultural and other commodity markets, stock exchanges, retail and wholesale markets, building construction markets, and others have many or all of the properties of a perfect competitive market. The competitive supply-and-demand model works well enough in these markets that it accurately predicts the effects of changes in taxes, costs, incomes, and other factors on market equilibrium.

Second, a perfect competitive market has many desirable properties. Economists use this model as the ideal against which real-world markets are compared. Throughout the rest of this book, we show that society as a whole is worse off if the properties of the competitive market fail to hold.

8.2 PROFIT MAXIMIZATION

Economists usually assume that all firms—not just competitive firms—want to maximize their profits. One reason is that many businesspeople say that their objective is to maximize profits. A second reason is that firms—especially competitive firms—that do not profit maximize are likely to lose money and be driven out of business.

In this section, we discuss how any type of firm—not just a competitive firm—maximizes its profit. We then examine how a competitive firm in particular profit maximizes.

---

[3]In addition, a perfect competitive market has no externalities such as pollution (see Chapter 18).

Profit

A firm's *profit*, π, is the difference between a firm's revenues, R, and its cost, C:

$$\pi = R - C.$$

If profit is negative, $\pi < 0$, the firm makes a *loss*.

Economists and businesspeople often measure profit differently. Because both economists and businesspeople measure revenue the same way—revenue is price times quantity—the difference in their profit measures is due to the way they measure costs. Some businesses use only explicit costs: a firm's out-of-pocket expenditures on inputs such as workers' wage payments, payments for materials, and payments for energy. *Economic cost* includes both explicit and implicit costs (see Chapter 7). Economic cost is the *opportunity cost*: the value of the best alternative use of any asset the firm uses.

Economic profit is revenue minus economic cost. Because explicit cost is less than economic cost, *business profit*—based on only explicit cost—is often larger than economic profit. The reason that this distinction is important is that a firm may make a costly mistake if it mismeasures profit by ignoring relevant opportunity costs.

A couple of examples illustrate the difference in the two profit measures and the importance of this distinction. First, let's return to the scenario in Chapter 7 in which you start your own firm.[4] You have to pay explicit costs such as workers' wages and the price of materials. Like many owners, you do not pay yourself a salary. Instead, you take home a business profit of \$20,000 per year.

Economists (well-known spoilsports) argue that your profit is less than \$20,000. Economic profit is business profit minus any additional opportunity cost. Suppose that you could have earned \$25,000 a year working for someone else instead of running your business. The opportunity cost of your time working in your business is \$25,000—your forgone salary. Thus, although your firm made a business profit of \$20,000, your economic loss (negative economic profit) was \$5,000. Put another way, the price of being your own boss is \$5,000.

By looking at only the business profit and ignoring opportunity cost, you conclude that running your business is profitable. If you consider economic profit, however, you realize that working for others maximizes your income.

Similarly, when a firm decides whether to invest in a new venture, it must consider its next best alternative use of its funds. A firm that is considering setting up a new branch in Tucson must consider all the alternatives—placing the branch in Santa Fe, putting the money that the branch would cost in the bank and earning interest, and so on. If the best alternative use of the money is to put it in the bank and earn \$10,000 per year in interest, the firm should build the new branch in Tucson only if it expects to make \$10,000 or more per year in business profits. That is, the firm should create a Tucson branch only if its economic profit from the new branch is zero or positive. If its economic profit is zero, then it is earning the same

[4]Michael Dell started a mail-order computer company while he was in college. Today, it is the world's third-largest personal computer company.

return on its investment as it would from putting the money in its next best alternative, the bank. From now on, when we use the term *profit*, we mean *economic profit* unless we specifically refer to business profit.

APPLICATION

Breaking Even on Christmas Trees

On the day after Thanksgiving each year, Tom Ruffino begins selling Christmas trees in Lake Grove, New York.[5] Table 8.1 summarizes his seasonal explicit costs.

Mr. Ruffino sells trees for 29 days at the market price of $25 each. To break even, he has to sell an average of 45 trees per day, so his average cost is $25. If he can sell an average of 52 trees per day (1,508 trees total), he makes an accounting profit of $5,090 for the season.

Table 8.1 Tom Ruffino's Accounting Costs of Selling Christmas Trees

Fixed Costs:	
Permit	$300
Security	$360
Guard patrol when the lot is closed to prevent theft	
Insurance	$700
Electricity	$1,000
Lot rental	$2,500
Undeveloped piece of land across from a major shopping mall	
Miscellaneous	$2,000
Fences, lot cleanup, snow removal	
Total fixed costs:	$6,860
Variable Costs:	
Labor	$5,500
Two full-time employees ($12 an hour for 50 hours a week) and some part-time workers	
Trees	$17,250
1,500 trees bought from a Canadian tree farm at $11.50 each	
Shipping	$3,000
1,500 trees at $2 each	
Total variable costs:	$25,750
Total accounting costs:	$32,610

[5] "How They Do It: Breaking Even in a Seasonal Business," *New York Times*, December 25, 1993:21.

To calculate his economic profit, he has to subtract his forgone earnings at another job and the interest he would have earned on the money he paid at the beginning of the month (on his fixed costs and the price of the trees, $27,110) if he had invested that money elsewhere, such as in a bank, for a month. Although the forgone interest is small, his alternative earnings could be a large proportion of his business profit. ■

Two Steps to Maximizing Profit

A firm's profit varies with its output level. The firm's profit function is

$$\pi(q) = R(q) - C(q).$$

A firm decides how much output to sell to maximize its profit. To maximize its profit, any firm (not just competitive, price-taking firms) must answer two questions:

- **Output decision:** If the firm produces, what output level, q^*, maximizes its profit or minimizes its loss?
- **Shut-down decision:** Is it more profitable to produce q^* or to shut down and produce no output?

The profit curve in Figure 8.1 illustrates these two basic decisions. This firm makes losses at very low and very high output levels and positive profits at moderate output levels. The profit curve first rises and then falls, reaching a maximum profit of π^* when its output is q^*. Because the firm makes a positive profit at that output, it chooses to produce q^* units of output.

Output Rules. A firm can use one of three equivalent rules to choose how much output to produce. All types of firms maximize profit using the same rules.

The most straightforward rule is:

Output Rule 1: The firm sets its output where its profit is maximized.

The profit curve in Figure 8.1 is maximized at π^* when output is q^*. If the firm knows its entire profit curve, it can immediately set its output to maximize its profit.

Even if the firm does not know the exact shape of its profit curve, it may be able to find the maximum by experimenting. The firm slightly increases its output. If profit increases, the firm increases the output more. The firm keeps increasing output until profit does not change. At that output, the firm is at the peak of the profit curve. If profit falls when the firm first increases its output, the firm tries decreasing its output. It keeps decreasing its output until it reaches the peak of the profit curve.

What the firm is doing is experimentally determining the slope of the profit curve. The slope of the profit curve is the firm's **marginal profit**: the change in the profit the firm gets from selling one more unit of output, $\Delta\pi/\Delta q$.[6] In the figure, the

[6]The marginal profit is the derivative of the profit function, $\pi(q)$, with respect to quantity, $d\pi(q)/dq$.

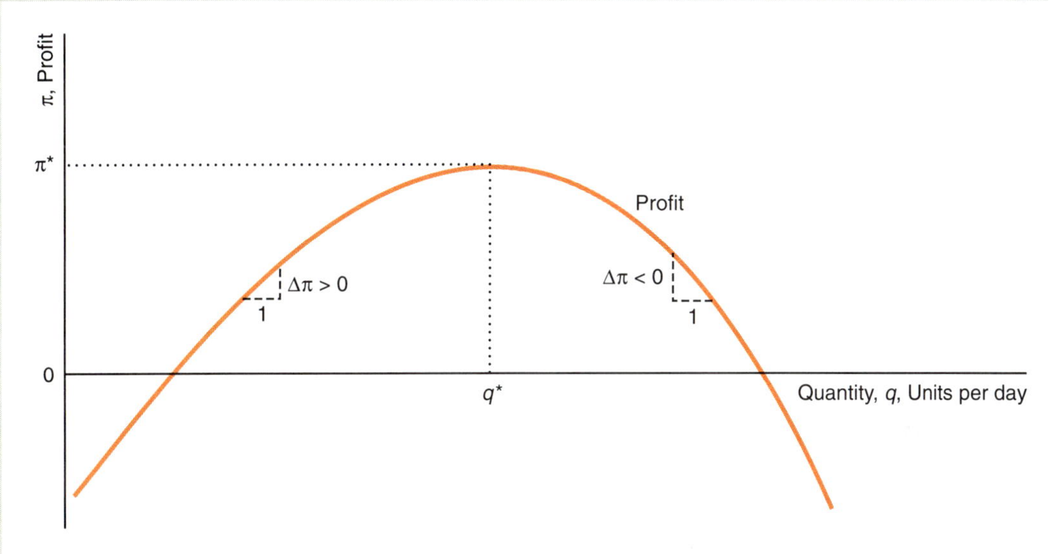

Figure 8.1 Maximizing Profit. By setting its output at q^*, the firm maximizes its profit at π^*.

marginal profit or slope is positive when output is less than q^*, zero when output is q^*, and negative when output is greater than q^*. Thus,

Output Rule 2: A firm sets its output where its marginal profit is zero.

A third way to express this profit-maximizing output rule is in terms of cost and revenue. The marginal profit depends on a firm's *marginal cost* and *marginal revenue*. A firm's *marginal cost* (MC) is the amount by which a firm's cost changes if it produces one more unit of output (Chapter 7): $MC = \Delta C/\Delta q$, where ΔC is the change in cost when output changes by Δq. Similarly, a firm's **marginal revenue**, MR, is the change in revenue it gets from selling one more unit of output: $\Delta R/\Delta q$, where ΔR is the change in revenue.[7] If a firm that was selling q units of output sells one more unit of output, the extra revenue, $MR(q)$, raises its profit, but the extra cost, $MC(q)$, lowers its profit. The change in the firm's profit is[8]

$$\text{marginal profit}(q) = MR(q) - MC(q).$$

[7]The marginal revenue is the derivative of the revenue function with respect to quantity: $MR(q) = \mathrm{d}R(q)/\mathrm{d}q$.

[8]Because profit is $\pi(q) = R(q) - C(q)$, marginal profit is the difference between marginal revenue and marginal cost:

$$\frac{\mathrm{d}\pi(q)}{\mathrm{d}q} = \frac{\mathrm{d}R(q)}{\mathrm{d}q} - \frac{\mathrm{d}C(q)}{\mathrm{d}q} = MR - MC.$$

Does it pay for a firm to produce one more unit of output? If the marginal revenue from this last unit of output exceeds its marginal cost, $MR(q) > MC(q)$, the firm's marginal profit is positive, $MR(q) - MC(q) > 0$, so it pays to increase output. The firm keeps increasing its output until its marginal profit $= MR(q) - MC(q) = 0$. There, its marginal revenue equals its marginal cost: $MR(q) = MC(q)$. If the firm produces more output where its marginal cost exceeds its marginal revenue, $MR(q) < MC(q)$, the extra output reduces the firm's profit. Thus, a third, equivalent rule is (Appendix 8B):

> *Output Rule 3:* A firm sets its output where its marginal revenue equals its marginal cost:
>
> $$MR(q) = MC(q).$$

Shut-Down Rule. The firm chooses to produce if it can make a profit. If the firm is making a loss, however, does it shut down? The answer, surprisingly, is "It depends." The general rule, which holds for all types of firms in both the short run and in the long run, is:

> *Shut-Down Rule 1:* The firm shuts down only if it can reduce its loss by doing so.

In the short run, the firm has variable and sunk fixed costs (Chapter 7). By shutting down, it can eliminate the variable cost, such as labor and materials, but usually not the fixed cost, the amount it paid for its factory and equipment. By shutting down, the firm stops receiving revenue and stops paying the avoidable costs, but it is still stuck with its fixed cost. Thus, it pays the firm to shut down only if its revenue is less than its avoidable cost.

Suppose the firm's revenue is R = \$2,000, its variable cost is VC = \$1,000, and its fixed cost is F = \$3,000, which is the price it paid for a machine that it cannot resell or use for any other purpose. This firm is making a short-run loss:

$$\pi = R - VC - F = \$2,000 - \$1,000 - \$3,000 = -\$2,000.$$

If the firm shuts down, it loses its fixed cost, –\$3,000, so it is better off operating. Its revenue more than covers its avoidable, variable cost and offsets some of the fixed cost.

On the other hand, if its revenue is only \$500, its loss is –\$3,500, which is greater than the loss from the fixed cost alone of –\$3,000. Because its revenue is less than its avoidable, variable cost, the firm reduces its loss by shutting down.

In conclusion, the firm compares its revenue to its variable cost only when deciding whether to stop operating. Because the fixed cost is *sunk*—the expense cannot be avoided by stopping operations (Chapter 7)—the firm pays this cost whether it shuts down or not. Thus, the sunk fixed cost is irrelevant to the shut-down decision.[9]

---

[9]We usually assume that fixed cost is sunk. However, if a firm can sell its capital for as much as it paid for it, its fixed cost is avoidable and should be taken into account when the firm is considering whether to shut down. A firm with a fully avoidable fixed cost always shuts down if it makes a short-run loss, when its revenue is less than its total cost. If a firm buys a specialized piece of machinery for \$1,000 that can be used only in its business but can be sold for scrap metal for \$100, then \$100 of the fixed cost is avoidable and \$900 is sunk. Here, only the avoidable portion of fixed cost is relevant for the shut-down decision.

In the long run, all costs are avoidable because the firm can eliminate them all by shutting down. Thus, in the long run where the firm can avoid all losses by not operating, it pays to shut down if the firm faces any loss at all. As a result, we can restate the shut-down rule as

> *Shut-Down Rule 2:* The firm shuts down only if its revenue is less than its avoidable cost.

This rule holds for all types of firms in both the short run and the long run.

8.3 COMPETITION IN THE SHORT RUN

Having considered how firms maximize profit in general, we now examine the profit-maximizing behavior of competitive firms, first in the short run and then in the long run. In doing so, we pay careful attention to the firm's shut-down decision.

SR Competitive Profit Maximization

A competitive firm, like other firms, first determines the output at which it maximizes its profit (or minimizes its loss). Second, it decides whether to produce or to shut down.

SR Output Decision. We've already seen that *any* firm maximizes its profit at the output where its marginal profit is zero, or, equivalently, where its marginal cost equals its marginal revenue. A competitive firm's marginal revenue is the market price. Because it faces a horizontal demand curve, a competitive firm can sell as many units of output as it wants at the market price, p. Thus, a competitive firm's revenue, $R = pq$, increases by p if it sells one more unit of output, so its marginal revenue is p.[10] For example, if the price a firm faces is \$2 per unit, its revenue is \$10 if it sells five units and \$12 if it sells six units, so its marginal revenue for the sixth unit is \$2 = \$12 – \$10, which is the market price. Because a competitive firm's marginal revenue equals the market price, *a profit-maximizing competitive firm produces the amount of output at which its marginal cost equals the market price*

$$MC = p. \tag{8.1}$$

To illustrate how a competitive firm maximizes its profit, we examine a typical Canadian lime manufacturing firm, which we assume is a price taker. Lime is a nonmetallic mineral used in mortars, plasters, cements, bleaching powders, steel, paper, glass, and other products. The lime plant's estimated cost curve, C, in panel a of Figure 8.2 rises less rapidly with output at low quantities than at higher

[10]Because $R(q) = pq$, $MR = dR(q)/dq = d(pq)/dq = p$.

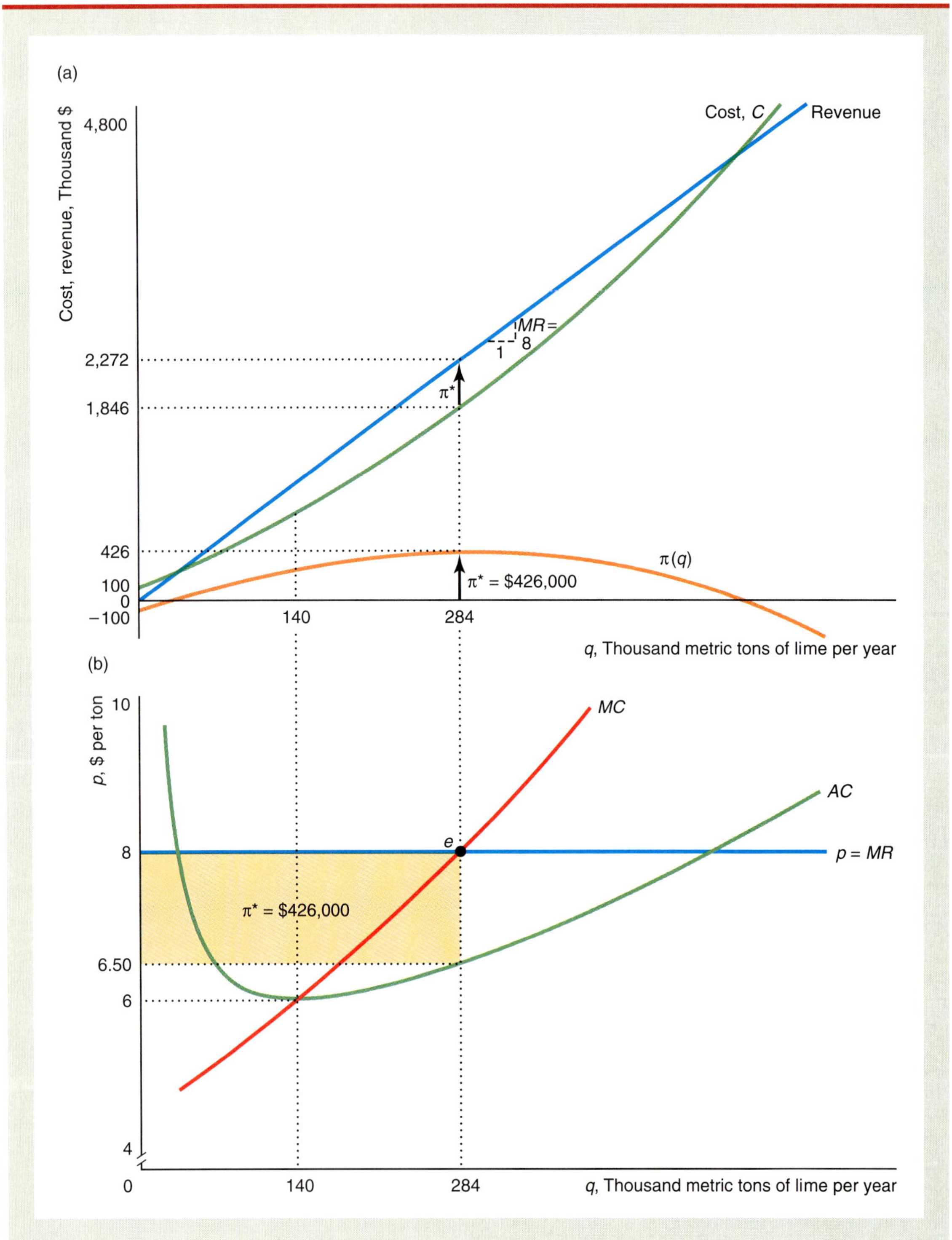

(a)
Cost, revenue, Thousand $
4,800
2,272
1,846
426
100
0
−100
Cost, C
Revenue
MR =
8
1
π*
π(q)
π* = $426,000
140
284
q, Thousand metric tons of lime per year
(b)
p, $ per ton
10
8
6.50
6
4
0
MC
AC
e
p = MR
π* = $426,000
140
284
q, Thousand metric tons of lime per year

Figure 8.2 Competitive Firm Maximizes Profit. (a) A competitive lime manufacturing firm (Robidoux and Lester 1988) produces 284 units of lime so as to maximize its profit at $\pi^* = \$426{,}000$. (b) The firm's profit is maximized where its marginal revenue, *MR*, which is the market price, $p = \$8$, equals its marginal cost, *MC*.

quantities.[11] If the market price of lime is $p = \$8$, the competitive firm faces a horizontal demand curve at \$8 (panel b), so the revenue curve, $R = pq = \$8q$, in panel a is an upward-sloping straight line with a slope of 8.

By producing 284 units (one unit being a thousand metric tons), the firm maximizes its profit at $\pi^* = \$426{,}000$, which is the height of the profit curve and the difference between the revenue and cost curves at that quantity in panel a. At the competitive firm's profit-maximizing output, its marginal cost equals the market price of \$8 (Equation 8.1) at point *e* in panel b.

Point *e* is the competitive firm's equilibrium. Were the firm to produce less than the equilibrium quantity, 284 units, the market price would be above its marginal cost. As a result, the firm could increase its profit by expanding output because the firm earns more on the next ton, $p = \$8$, than it costs to produce it, $MC < \$8$. If the firm were to produce more than 284 units, so market price was below its marginal cost, $MC > \$8$, the firm could increase its profit by reducing its output. Thus, the firm does not want to change its quantity only at output when its marginal cost equals the market price.

The firm's maximum profit, $\pi^* = \$426{,}000$, is the shaded rectangle in panel b. The length of the rectangle is the number of units sold, $q = 284$ units. The height of the rectangle is the firm's average profit, which is the difference between the market price, or average revenue, and its average cost:

$$\frac{\pi}{q} = \frac{R - C}{q} = \frac{pq}{q} - \frac{C}{q} = p - AC. \tag{8.2}$$

Here, the average profit per unit is $\$1.50 = p - AC(284) = \$8 - \$6.50$.

As panel b illustrates, the firm chooses its output level to maximize its total profit rather than its profit per ton. By producing 140 units, where its average cost is minimized at \$6, the firm could maximize its average profit at \$2. Although the firm gives up 50¢ in profit per ton when it produces 284 units instead of 140 units, it more than makes up for that by selling an extra 144 units. The firm's profit is \$146,000 higher at 284 units than at 140 units.

Using the $MC = p$ rule, a firm can decide how much to alter its output in response to a change in its cost due to a new tax. For example, one of the many lime plants in Canada is in the province of Manitoba. If that province taxes that lime firm, the

[11]Robidoux and Lester (1988) estimate the variable cost function. In the figure, we assume that the minimum of the average variable cost curve is \$5 at 50,000 metric tons of output. By using information from Statistics Canada, *Annual Census of Manufactures*, 1984, the fixed cost is set so that the average cost is \$6 at 140,000 tons.

Manitoba firm is the only one in the lime market affected by the tax, so the tax will not affect market price. Solved Problem 8.1 shows how a profit-maximizing competitive firm would react to a tax that affected only it.

SOLVED PROBLEM 8.1

If a specific tax of τ is collected from only one competitive firm, how should that firm change its output level to maximize its profit, and how does its maximum profit change?

Answer

1. *Show how the tax shifts the marginal cost and average cost curve*: The firm's before-tax marginal cost curve is MC^1 and its before-tax average cost curve is AC^1 in Figure 8.3. Because the specific tax adds τ to the per-unit cost, it shifts the after-tax marginal cost curve up to $MC^2 = MC^1 + \tau$ and the after-tax average cost curve to $AC^2 = AC^1 + \tau$ (see Chapter 7).

2. *Determine the before-tax and after-tax equilibria and the amount by which the firm adjusts its output*: Where the before-tax marginal cost curve, MC^1, hits the horizontal demand curve, p, at e_1, the profit-maximizing quantity is q_1. The after-tax marginal cost curve, MC^2, intersects the demand curve, p, at e_2 where the profit-maximizing quantity is q_2. Thus, in response to the tax, the firm produces $q_2 - q_1$ fewer units of output.

3. *Show how the profit changes after the tax*: Because the market price is constant but the firm's average cost curve shifts upward, the firm's profit at every output level falls. The firm sells fewer units (because of the increase in MC) and makes less profit per unit (because of the increase in AC). The after-tax profit is area $A = \pi_2 = [p - AC^2(q_2)]q_2$, and the before-tax profit is area $A + B = \pi_1 = [p - AC^1(q_1)]q_1$, so profit falls by area B due to the tax. ■

SR Shut-Down Decision. Does the competitive lime firm operate or shut down? At the market price of \$8 in Figure 8.2, the lime firm is making an economic profit, so it chooses to operate.

If the market price falls below \$6, which is the minimum of the average cost curve, the price does not cover average cost, so average profit is negative (using Equation 8.2), and the firm makes a loss.[12] The firm shuts down only if doing so reduces or eliminates its loss.

[12]A firm cannot "lose a little on every sale but make it up on volume."

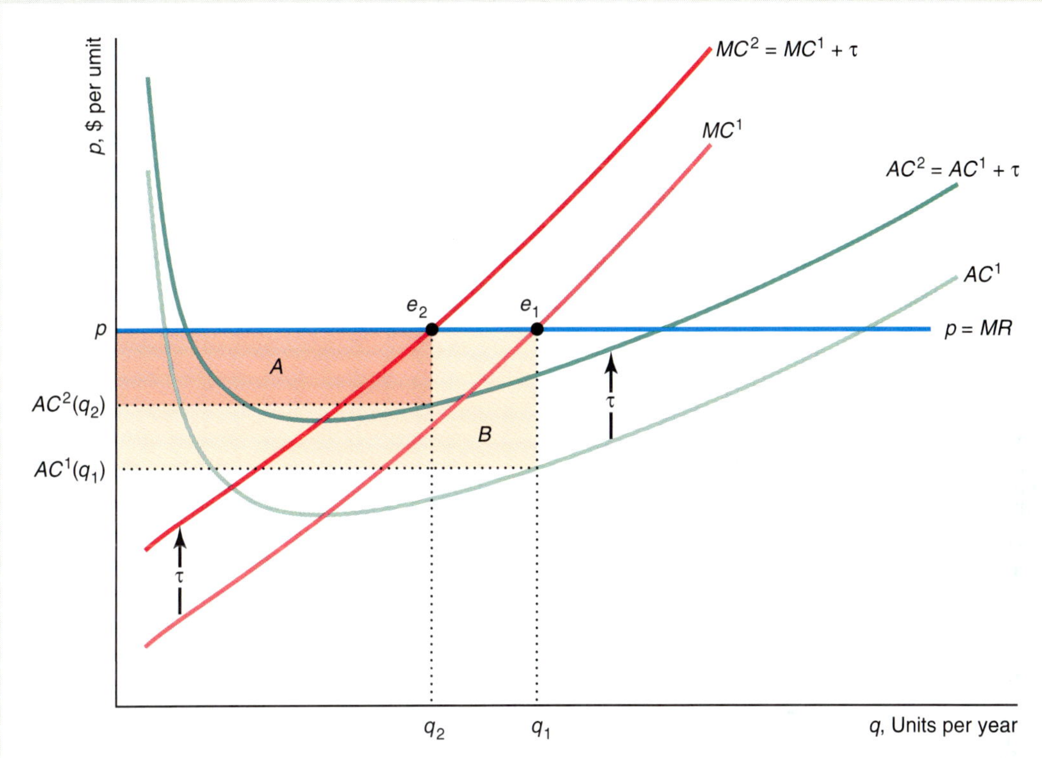

Figure 8.3 Effect of a Specific Tax. A specific tax of τ per unit is applied to only one competitive firm, so the market price remains constant at p. At every quantity, the tax shifts the marginal cost upward by τ from MC^1 to MC^2 and the average cost upward by τ from AC^1 to AC^2. As a result, the after-tax equilibrium e_2 lies to the left of the before-tax equilibrium e_1, so equilibrium quantity falls from q_1 to q_2. The after-tax profit is area A, and the before-tax profit is area $A + B$, so profit falls by B because of the tax.

The firm can gain by shutting down only if its revenue is less than its short-run variable cost:

$$pq < VC. \tag{8.3}$$

By dividing both sides of Equation 8.3 by output, we can write this condition as

$$p < AVC(q).$$

A competitive firm shuts down if the market price is less than the minimum of its short-run average variable cost curve.

We illustrate this rule in Figure 8.4 using the lime firm's cost curves. The minimum of the average variable cost, point a, is \$5 at 50 units (one unit again being a thousand metric tons). If the market price is less than \$5 per ton, the firm shuts

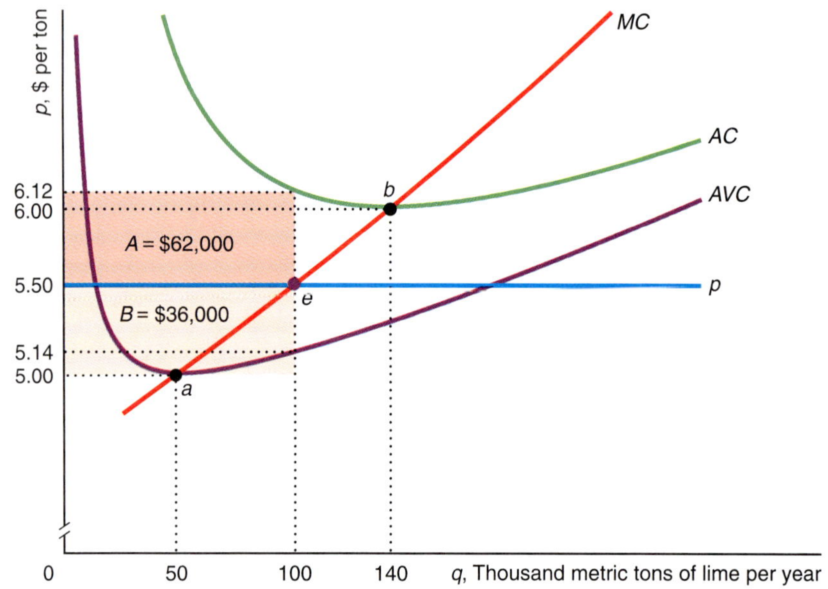

Figure 8.4 The SR Shut-Down Decisions. The competitive lime manufacturing plant operates if price is above the minimum of the average variable cost curve, point *a*, at $5. With a market price of $5.50, the firm produces 100 units because that price is above *AVC*(100) = $5.14, so the firm more than covers its out-of-pocket, variable costs. At that price, the firm makes a loss of area *A* = $62,000 because the price is less than the average cost of $6.12. If it shuts down, its loss is its fixed cost, area *A* + *B* = $98,000. Thus, the firm does not shut down.

down. The firm stops hiring labor, buying materials, and paying for energy, thereby avoiding these variable costs. If the market price rises above $5, the firm starts operating again.

In this figure, the market price is $5.50 per ton. Because the minimum of the firm's average cost, $6 (point b), is more than $5.50, the firm loses money if it produces.

If the firm produces, it sells 100 units at *e*, where its marginal cost curve intersects its demand curve, which is horizontal at $5.50. By operating, the firm loses area *A* or –$62,000. The length of *A* is 100 units, and the height is the average loss per ton or –62¢, which equals the price of $5.50 minus the average cost at 100 units of $6.12.

The firm is better off producing than shutting down. If the firm shuts down, it has no revenue or variable cost, so its loss is the fixed cost, –$98,000, which equals area *A* + *B*. The length of this box is 100 units, and its height is the lost average fixed cost of –98¢, which is the difference between the average variable cost and the average cost at 100 units.

The firm saves area B = \$36,000 by producing rather than shutting down. This amount is the money left over from the revenue after paying for the variable cost, which helps to cover part of the fixed cost.

In summary, a competitive firm uses a two-step decisionmaking process to maximize its profit. First, the competitive firm determines the output that maximizes its profit or minimizes its loss when its marginal cost equals the market price (which is its marginal revenue): $MC = p$. Second, the firm chooses to produce that quantity unless it would lose more by operating than by shutting down. The firm shuts down only if the market price is less than the minimum of its average variable cost, $p < AVC$.

SOLVED PROBLEM 8.2

A competitive firm's bookkeeper, upon reviewing the firm's books, finds that the firm spent twice as much on its plant, a fixed cost, as the firm's manager had previously thought. Should the manager change the output level because of this new information? How does this new information affect profit?

Answer

1. *Show that a change in fixed costs does not affect the firm's decisions*: How much the firm produces and whether it shuts down in the short run depend only on the firm's variable costs. (The firm picks its output level so that its marginal cost—which depends only on variable costs—equals the market price, and shuts down only if market price is less than its minimum average variable cost.) Learning that the amount spent on the plant was greater than previously believed should not change the manager's decisions about output.

2. *Show that the change in how the bookkeeper measures fixed costs does not affect economic profit*: The change in the bookkeeper's valuation of the historical amount spent on the plant may affect the firm's short-run business profit but does not affect the firm's true economic profit. The economic profit is based on opportunity costs—the amount for which the firm could rent the plant to someone else—and not on historical payments. ■

SR Firm Supply Curve

We just demonstrated how a competitive firm chooses its output for a given market price so as to maximize its profit. By repeating this analysis at different possible market prices, we learn how the amount the competitive firm supplies varies with the market price.

Tracing Out the SR Supply Curve. As the market price increases from p_1 = \$5 to p_2 = \$6 to p_3 = \$7 to p_4 = \$8, the lime firm increases its output from 50 to 140 to

215 to 285 units per year in Figure 8.5. The equilibrium at each market price, e_1 through e_4, is determined by the intersection of the relevant demand curve—market price line—and the firm's marginal cost curve. That is, as the market price increases, the equilibria trace out the marginal cost curve.

If the price falls below the firm's minimum average variable cost at \$5, the firm shuts down. Thus, *the competitive firm's short-run supply curve is its marginal cost curve above its minimum average variable cost.*

The firm's short-run supply curve, *S*, is a thick line in the figure. At prices above 5, the short-run supply curve is the same as the marginal cost curve. The supply is zero when price is less than the minimum of the *AVC* curve of 5. (From now on, we will not show the supply curve at prices below minimum *AVC*, to keep the graph as simple as possible.)

Factor Prices and the SR Firm Supply Curve. An increase in factor prices causes the production costs of a firm to rise, shifting the firm's supply curve to the left. If all factor prices double, it costs the firm twice as much as before to produce a given level of output. If only one factor price rises, costs rise less than in proportion.

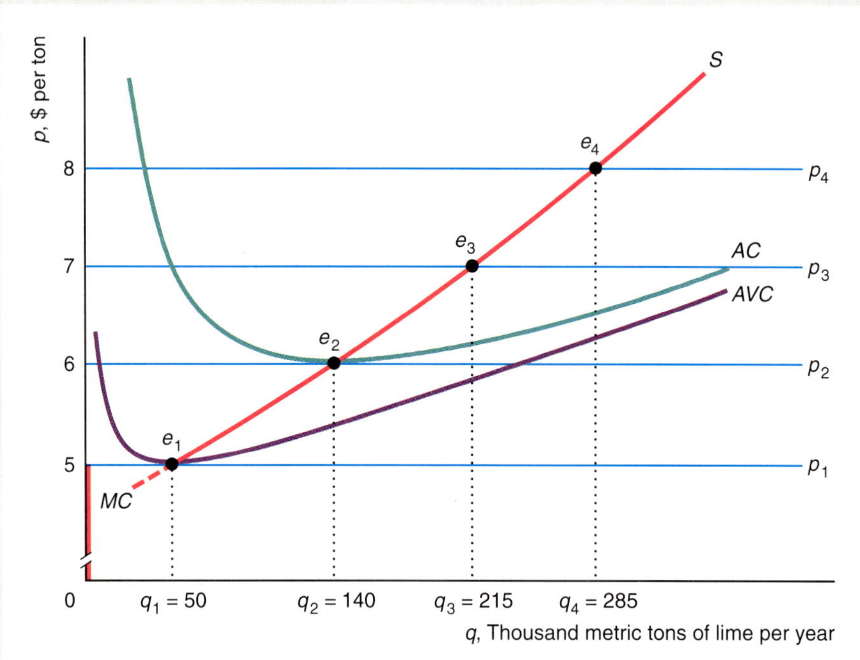

Figure 8.5 The Profit-Maximizing Quantity Varies with Price. As the market price increases, the lime manufacturing firm produces more output. The change in the price traces out the marginal cost curve of the firm.

To illustrate the effect of an increase in a single factor price on supply, we examine a vegetable oil mill. This firm uses vegetable oil seed to produce canola and soybean oils, which customers use in commercial baking and soap making, as lubricants, and for other purposes. At the initial factor prices, a Canadian oil mill's average variable cost curve, AVC^1, reaches its minimum of \$7 at 100 units (where one unit is a hundred metric tons) of vegetable oil, as in Figure 8.6 (based on the estimates of the variable cost function for vegetable oil mills by Robidoux and Lester 1988). As a result, the firm's initial short-run supply curve, S^1, is the initial marginal cost curve, MC^1, above \$7.

If the wage, the price of energy, or the price of oil seeds increases, the cost of production rises for a vegetable oil mill. The vegetable oil mill cannot substitute between oil seeds and other factors of production. The cost of oil seeds is 95% of the variable cost. Thus, if the price of raw materials increases by 25%, variable cost rises by 95% × 25% or 23.75%. This increase in the price of oil seeds causes the marginal cost curve to shift from MC^1 to MC^2 and the average variable cost curve

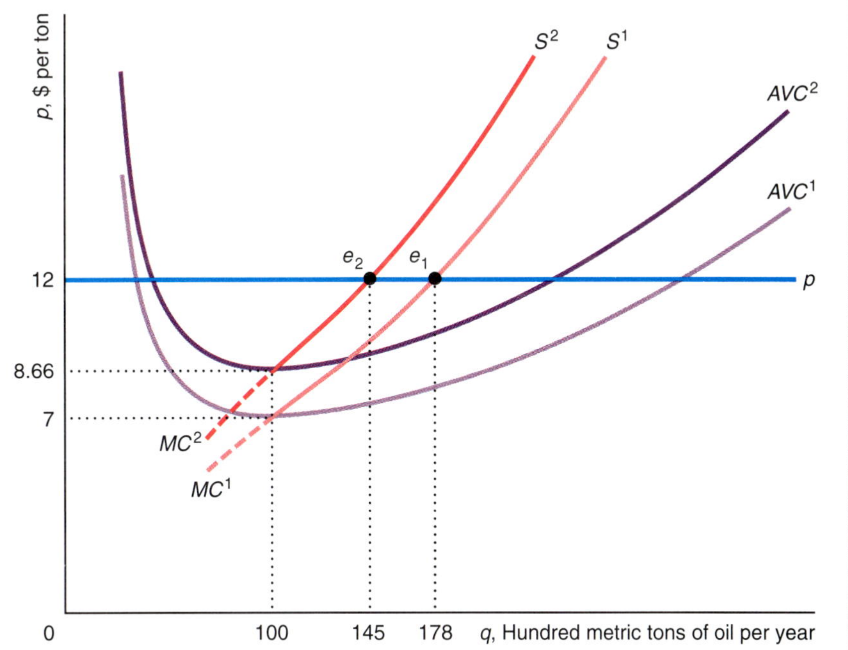

Figure 8.6 An Increase in the Cost of Materials Shifts the Supply Curve of Vegetable Oil Upward. Materials are 95% of variable costs, so when the price of materials rises by 25%, variable costs rise by 23.75% (95% of 25%). As a result, the supply curve of a vegetable oil mill shifts up from S^1 to S^2. If the market price is \$12, the quantity supplied falls from 178 to 145 units.

from AVC^1 to AVC^2 in the figure. As a result, the firm's short-run supply curve shifts upward from S^1 to S^2. The price increase causes the shut-down price to rise from \$7 per unit to \$8.66. At a market price of \$12 per unit, at the original factor prices, the firm produces 178 units. After the increase in the price of vegetable oil seeds, the firm produces only 145 units if the market price remains constant.

SR Market Supply Curve

The market supply curve is the horizontal sum of the supply curves of all the individual firms in the market (see Chapter 2). In the short run, the maximum number of firms in a market, n, is fixed because new firms need time to enter the market. If all the firms in a competitive market are identical, each firm's supply curve is identical, so the market supply at any price is n times the supply of an individual firm. Where firms have different shut-down prices, the market supply reflects a different number of firms at various prices even in the short run. We examine competitive markets first with firms that have identical costs and then with firms that have different costs.

SR Market Supply with Identical Firms. To illustrate how to construct a short-run market supply curve, we suppose that the lime manufacturing market has $n = 5$ competitive firms with identical cost curves. Panel a of Figure 8.7 plots the short-

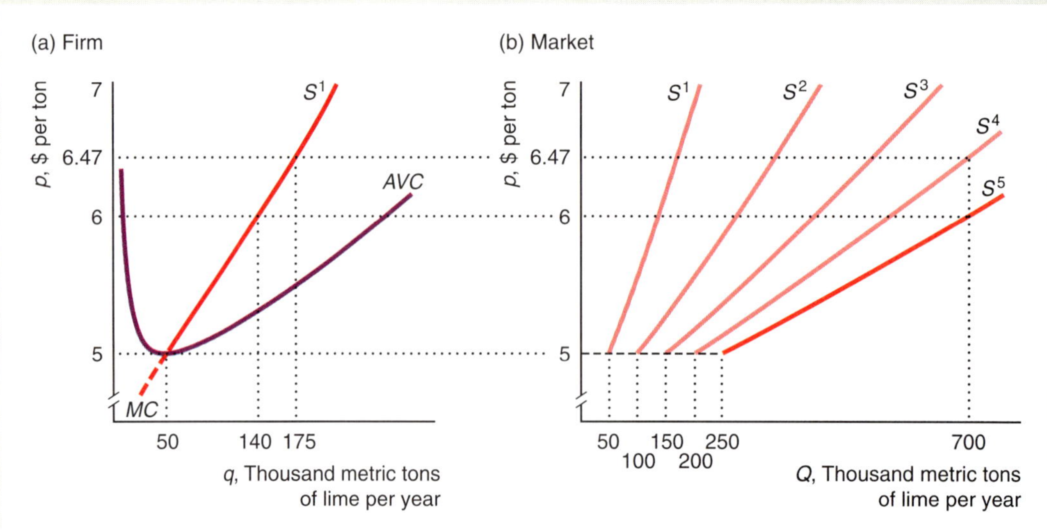

Figure 8.7 SR Market Supply with Five Identical Lime Firms. (a) The SR supply curve, S^1, of a typical lime manufacturing firm is its MC above the minimum of its AVC. (b) The market supply curve, S^5, is the horizontal sum of the supply curve of each of the five identical firms. The curve S^4 shows what the market supply curve would be if there were only four firms in the market.

run supply curve, S^1, of a typical firm—the *MC* curve above the minimum *AVC*—where the horizontal axis shows the firm's output, *q*, per year. Panel b illustrates the competitive market supply curve, the thick line S^5, where the horizontal axis is market output, *Q*, per year. The price axis is the same in the two figures.

If the market price is less than \$5 per ton, no firm supplies any output, so the market supply is zero. At \$5, each firm is willing to supply $q = 50$ units, as in panel a. Consequently, the market supply is $Q = 5q = 250$ units in panel b. At \$6 per ton, each firm supplies 140 units, so the market supply is 700 (= 5 × 140) units.

Suppose, however, that there were fewer than five firms in the short run. The dashed lines in panel b show the market supply curves for various other numbers of firms. The market supply curve is S^1 if there is one price-taking firm, S^2 with two firms, S^3 with three firms, and S^4 with four firms. The market supply curve flattens as the number of firms in the market increases because the market supply curve is the horizontal sum of more and more upward-sloping firm supply curves. As the number of firms grows very large, the market supply curve approaches a horizontal line at \$5. Thus, *the more identical firms producing at a given price, the flatter (more elastic) is the short-run market supply curve at that price.* As a result, the more firms in the market, the less the price has to increase for the short-run market supply to increase substantially. Consumers pay \$6 per ton to obtain 700 units of lime if there are five firms but must pay \$6.47 per ton to obtain that much with only four firms.

SR Market Supply with Firms That Differ. If the firms in a competitive market have different minimum average variable costs, not all firms produce at every price, a situation that affects the shape of the short-run market supply curve. Suppose that the only two firms in the lime market are our typical lime firm with a supply curve of S^1 and another firm with a higher marginal and minimum average cost with the supply curve of S^2 in Figure 8.8. The first firm produces at a market price of \$5 or above, whereas the second firm does not produce unless the price is \$6 or more. At \$5, the first firm produces 100 units, so the quantity on the market supply curve, *S*, is 100 units. Between \$5 and \$6, only the first firm produces, so the market supply, *S*, is the same as the first firm's supply, S^1. At and above \$6, both firms produce, so the market supply curve is the horizontal summation of their two individual supply curves. For example, at \$7, the first firm produces 215 units, and the second firm supplies 100 units, so the market supply is 315 units.

As with the identical firms, where both firms are producing, the market supply curve is flatter than that of either firm. Because the second firm does not produce at as low a price as the first firm, the short-run market supply curve has a steeper slope (less elastic supply) at relatively low prices than it would if the firms were identical.

Where firms differ, only the low-cost firm supplies goods at relatively low prices. As the price rises, the other, higher-cost firm starts supplying, creating a stairlike market supply curve. The more suppliers there are with differing costs, the more "steps" there are in the market supply curve. As price rises and more firms are supplying goods, the market supply curve flattens, so it takes a smaller increase in price to increase supply by a given amount. Stated the other way, the more firms differ in costs, the steeper is the market supply curve at low prices. Differences in costs are one explanation for why some market supply curves are upward sloping.

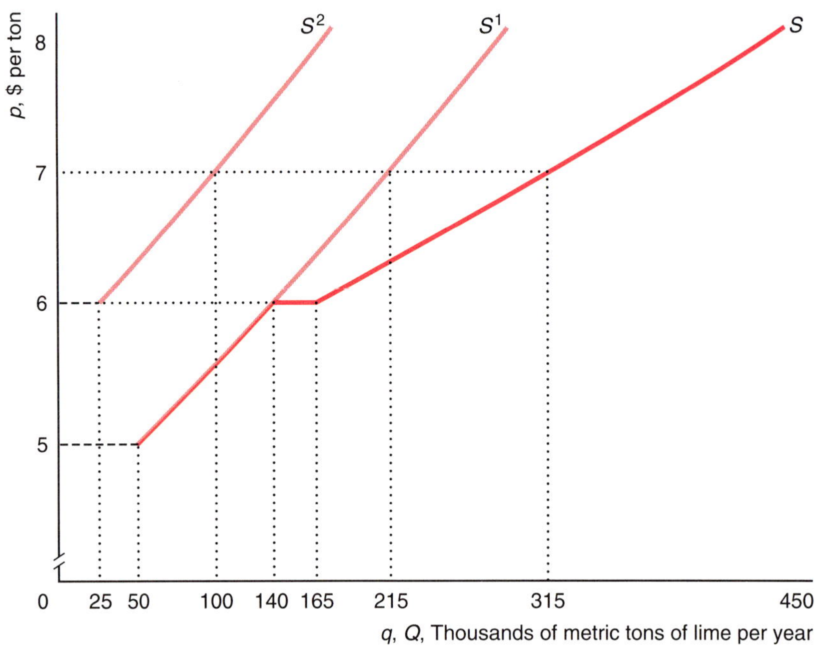

Figure 8.8 SR Market Supply with Two Different Lime Firms. The supply curve S^1 is the same as for the typical lime firm in the previous figure. A second firm has a *MC* that lies to the left of the original firm's cost curve and a higher minimum of its *AVC*. Thus, its supply curve, S^2, lies above and to the left of the original firm's supply curve, S^1. The market supply curve, *S*, is the horizontal sum of the two supply curves. When prices are high enough for both firms to produce, $6 and above, the market supply curve is flatter than the supply curve of either individual firm.

SR Competitive Equilibrium

By combining the short-run market supply curve and the market demand curve, we can determine the short-run competitive equilibrium. We first show how to determine the equilibrium in the lime market, and we then examine how the equilibrium changes when firms are taxed.

SR Equilibrium in the Lime Market. Suppose there are five identical firms in the short-run equilibrium in the lime manufacturing industry. Panel a of Figure 8.9 shows the short-run cost curves and the supply curve, S^1, for a typical firm, and panel b shows the corresponding short-run competitive market supply curve, *S*.

In panel b, the initial demand curve D^1 intersects the market supply curve at E_1, the market equilibrium. The equilibrium quantity is Q_1 = 1,075 units of lime per year, and the equilibrium market price is $7.

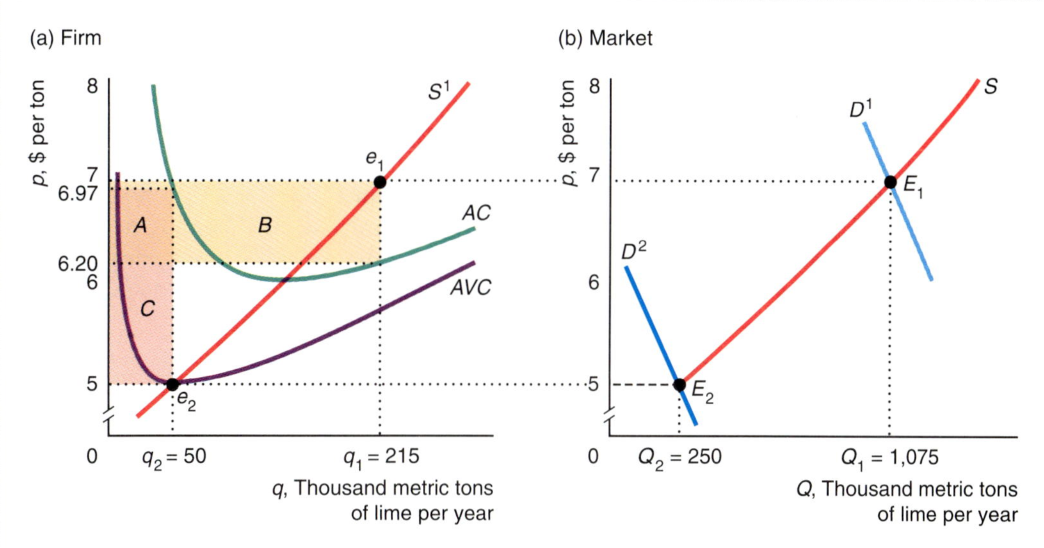

Figure 8.9 SR Competitive Equilibrium in the Lime Market. (a) The short-run supply curve is the marginal cost above minimum average variable cost of \$5. At a price of \$5, each firm makes a short-run loss of $(p - AC)q = (\$5 - \$6.97) \times 50{,}000 = -\$98{,}500$, area $A + C$. At a price of \$7, the short-run profit of a typical lime firm is $(p - AC)q = (\$7 - \$6.20) \times 215{,}000 = \$172{,}000$, area $A + B$. (b) If there are five firms in the lime market in the short run, so the market supply is S, and the market demand curve is D^1, then the short-run equilibrium is E_1, the market price is \$7, and market output is $Q_1 =$ 1,075 units. If the demand curve shifts to D^2, the market equilibrium is $p = \$5$ and $Q_2 = 250$ units.

In panel a, each competitive firm faces a horizontal demand curve at the equilibrium price of \$7. Each price-taking firm chooses its output where its marginal cost curve intersects the horizontal demand curve at e_1. Because each firm is maximizing its profit at e_1, no firm wants to change its behavior, so e_1 is the firm's equilibrium. In panel a, each firm makes a short-run profit of area $A + B = \$172{,}000$, which is the average profit per ton, $p - AC = \$7 - \$6.20 = 80¢$, times the firm's output, $q_1 =$ 215 units. The equilibrium market output, Q_1, is the number of firms, n, times the equilibrium output of each firm: $Q_1 = nq_1 = 5 \times 215$ units = 1,075 units (panel b).

Now suppose that the demand curve shifts to D^2. The new market equilibrium is E_2, where the price is only \$5. At that price, each firm produces $q = 50$ units, and market output is $Q = 250$ units. In panel a, each firm loses –\$98,500, area $A + C$, because it makes an average loss per ton of $(p - AC) = (\$5 - \$6.97) = -\$1.97$ and it sells $q_2 = 50$ units. Such a firm does not shut down, however, because price equals the firm's average variable cost so the firm is covering its out-of-pocket expenses.

Effect of a Specific Tax on SR Equilibrium. A tax that is applied to all firms in the market shifts the market supply curve, thereby altering the short-run equilibrium. In

Figure 8.10, the government collects a specific tax of τ per unit from each of the identical firms in a competitive market. The specific tax causes both the marginal and average cost curves of each firm to shift up by τ in panel a (Solved Problem 8.1), which causes the firm's supply curve to move upward by τ.

As a result, the short-run market supply curve, which is the sum of all the individual firm supply curves, also shifts upward by τ from S^1 to $S^1 + \tau$ in panel b. If the market demand curve is D, the pretax market equilibrium is E_1 and the post-tax equilibrium is E_2. The corresponding firm equilibria are e_1 and e_2 in panel a. The tax causes the equilibrium market quantity to fall from Q_1 to Q_2 in panel b and each firm's output to fall from q_1 to q_2 in panel a. Because price is above post-tax average variable cost, $AVC + \tau$, all firms continue to produce. The after-tax price, p_2, rises above the before-tax price, p_1, by less than the full amount of the tax: $p_2 < p_1 + \tau$. The reason that the incidence of the tax is shared between consumers and producers is that both the supply and the demand curve are sloped (see Chapter 3).

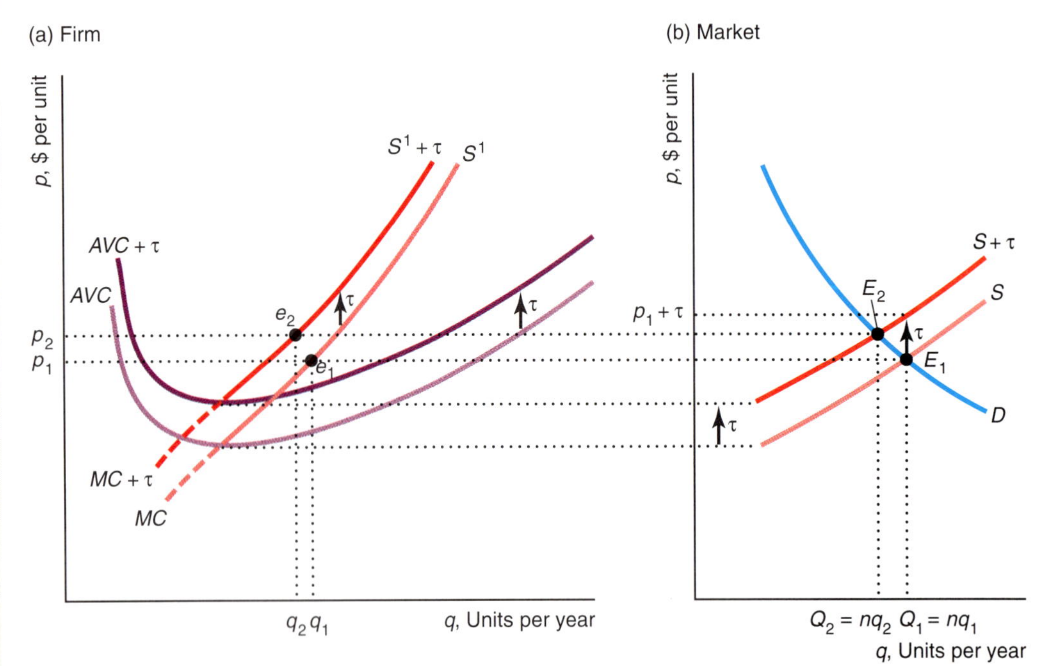

Figure 8.10 SR Effect of a Specific Tax in the Lime Market. (a) A specific tax of τ per unit causes each identical firm's *MC* and *AC* curves to shift upward by τ, so the firm's short-run supply curve shifts upward from S^1 to $S^1 + \tau$. (b) As a result, the short-run market supply curve shifts from S to $S + \tau$. If the market demand curve is D, price rises by less than τ, and both market quantity and each firm's output fall.

8.4 COMPETITION IN THE LONG RUN

I think there is a world market for about five computers.

—Thomas J. Watson, IBM chairman, 1943

In the long run, competitive firms can vary inputs that were fixed in the short run, so the long-run firm and market supply curves differ from the short-run curves. After briefly looking at how a firm determines its long-run supply curve so as to maximize its profit, we examine the relationship between short-run and long-run market supply curves and competitive equilibria.

LR Competitive Profit Maximization

The firm's two profit-maximizing decisions—how much to produce and whether to produce at all—are simpler in the long run than in the short run. In the long run, all costs are variable, so the firm does not have to consider whether fixed costs are sunk or avoidable.

LR Output Decision. The firm chooses the quantity that maximizes its profit using the same rules as in the short run. The firm picks the quantity that maximizes long-run profit, the difference between revenue and long-run cost. Equivalently, it operates where long-run marginal profit is zero and where marginal revenue equals long-run marginal cost.

LR Shut-Down Decision. After determining the output level, q^*, that maximizes its profit or minimizes its loss, the firm decides whether to produce or shut down. The firm shuts down if its revenue is less than its avoidable or variable cost. In the long run, however, all costs are variable. As a result, in the long run, the firm shuts down if it would make an economic loss by operating.

LR Firm Supply Curve

A firm's long-run supply curve is its long-run marginal cost curve above the minimum of its long-run average cost curve (because all costs are variable in the long run). The firm is free to choose its capital in the long run, so the firm's long-run supply curve may differ substantially from its short-run supply curve.

The firm chooses a plant size to maximize its long-run economic profit in light of its beliefs about the future. If its forecast is wrong, it may be stuck with a plant that is too small or too large for its level of production in the short run. The firm acts to correct this mistake in plant size in the long run.

The firm in Figure 8.11 has different short- and long-run cost curves. In the short run, the firm uses a plant that is smaller than the optimal long-run size if the price is \$35. (Of course, having a short-run plant size that is too large is also possible.) The firm produces 50 units of output per year in the short run, where its short-run marginal cost, *SRMC*, equals the price, and makes a short-run profit

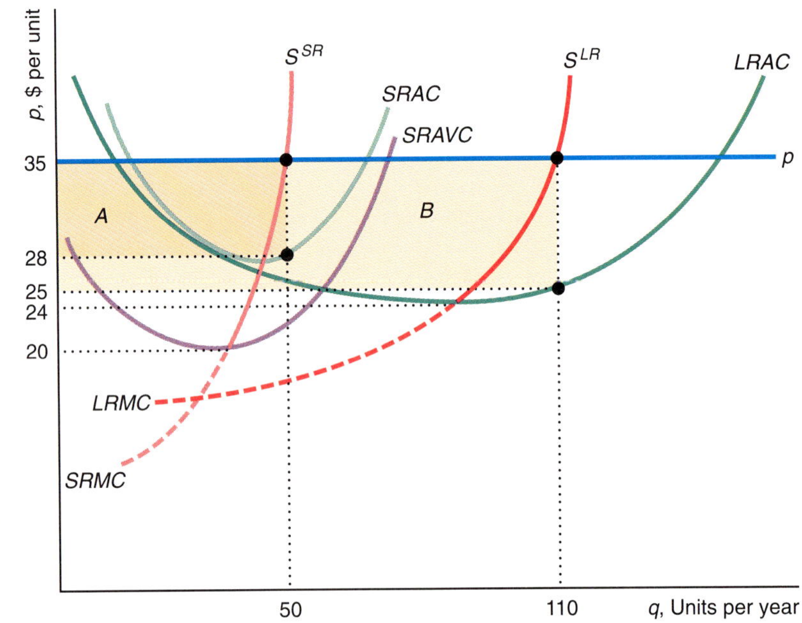

Figure 8.11 The SR and LR Supply Curves. The firm's long-run supply curve, S^{LR}, is zero below its minimum average cost of $24 and equals the long-run marginal cost, *LRMC*, at higher prices. The firm produces more in the long run than in the short run, 110 units instead of 50 units, and earns a higher profit, area *A* + *B* instead of just area *A*.

equal to area *A*. The firm's short-run supply curve, S^{SR}, is its short-run marginal cost above the minimum, $20, of its short-run average variable cost, *SRAVC*.

If the firm expects the price to remain at $35, it builds a larger plant in the long run. Using the larger plant, the firm produces 110 units per year, where its long-run marginal cost, *LRMC*, equals the market price. It expects to make a long-run profit, area *A* + *B*, which is greater than its short-run profit by area *B* because it sells 60 more units and its equilibrium long-run average cost, *LRAC* = $25, is lower than its short-run average cost in equilibrium, $28.

The firm does not operate at a loss in the long run when all inputs are variable. It shuts down if the market price falls below the firm's minimum long-run average cost of $24. Thus, the competitive firm's long-run supply curve is its long-run marginal cost curve above $24.

LR Market Supply Curve

The competitive market supply curve is the horizontal sum of the supply curves of the individual firms in both the short run and the long run. Because the maximum number of firms in the market is fixed in the short run, we add the supply curves of a known number of firms to obtain the short-run market supply curve. The only way for the market to supply more output in the short run is for existing firms to produce more.

In the long run, firms can enter or leave the market. Thus, before we can add all the relevant firm supply curves to obtain the long-run market supply curve, we need to determine how many firms are in the market at each possible market price.

To construct the long-run market supply curve properly, we also have to determine how input prices vary with output. As the market expands or contracts substantially, changes in factor prices may shift firms' cost and supply curves. If so, we need to determine how such shifts in factor prices affect firm supply curves so that we can properly construct the market supply curve. The effect of changes in input prices is greater in the long run than in the short run because market output can change more dramatically in the long run.

We now look in detail at how entry and changing factor prices affect long-run market supply. We first derive the long-run market supply curve assuming that the price of inputs remains constant as market output increases, so as to isolate the role of entry. We then examine how the market supply curve is affected if the price of inputs changes as market output rises.

Role of Entry and Exit. The number of firms in a market in the long run is determined by *entry* and *exit* of firms. In the long run, each firm decides whether to enter or exit depending on whether it can make a long-run profit.

In many markets, firms face barriers to entry or must incur significant costs to enter. Many city governments limit the number of cab drivers, creating an insurmountable barrier that prevents additional firms from entering. To enter other markets, a new firm has to hire consultants to determine the profit opportunities, pay lawyers to write contracts, and incur other expenses. Typically, such costs of entry (or exit) are fixed costs.

Even if existing firms are making positive profits, no entry occurs in the short run if entering firms need time to find a location, build a new plant, and hire workers. In the long run, firms enter the market if they can make profits by so doing. The costs of entry are often lower, and hence the profits from entering are higher, if a firm takes its time to enter. As a result, firms may enter markets long after profit opportunities first appear.

For example, McDonald's announced that it would spend about \$100 million to open 50 restaurants in Britain in 1995, bringing the number of its outlets to 630. It planned to increase the number of restaurants in Britain to 1,100 within the following four years.[13] Thus, McDonald's prepared to take up to four years to enter certain local restaurant markets that it believed it could enter profitably.

In contrast, firms can stop production quickly in most markets. Thus, firms usually react faster to losses than to potential profits. We expect firms to shut down quickly or exit the market in the short run when price is below average variable cost.

[13]"McDonald's Plans 50 New Restaurants in Britain," *New York Times*, December 29, 1994:C4.

In some markets, there are no barriers or fixed costs to entry, so firms can freely enter and exit. For example, many construction firms, which have no capital and provide only labor services, engage in *hit-and-run* entry and exit: They enter the market whenever they can make a profit and exit when they can't. These firms may enter and exit markets several times a year.

In such markets, a shift of the market demand curve to the right causes firms to enter. For example, if there were no government regulations, the market for taxicabs would have free entry and exit. Car owners could enter or exit the market virtually instantaneously. If the demand curve for cab rides shifted to the right, the market price would rise, and existing cab drivers would make unusually high profits in the short run. Seeing these profits, other car owners would enter the market, causing thc market supply curve to shift to the right and the market price to fall. Entry occurs until the last firm to enter the market—the *marginal firm*—makes zero long-run profit.

Similarly, if the demand curve shifts to the left so the market price drops, firms suffer losses. Firms with minimum average costs above the new, lower market price exit the market. Firms continue to leave the market until the next firm considering leaving, the marginal firm, is again earning a zero long-run profit.

Thus, in a market with free entry, a firm

- enters the market if it can make a long-run profit, $\pi > 0$, and
- exits the market to avoid a long-run loss, $\pi < 0$.

If firms in a market are making zero long-run profit, they are indifferent between staying in the market and exiting. We presume that if they are already in the market, they stay in the market when they are making zero long-run profit.

Most transportation markets are thought to have free entry and exit unless governments regulate them. Relatively few airline, trucking, or shipping firms may serve a particular route, but they face extensive potential entry. Other firms can and will quickly enter and serve a route if a profit opportunity appears. Entrants shift their highly mobile equipment from less profitable routes to more profitable ones.

APPLICATION

Threat of Entry in Shipping

Davies (1986) argued that in international ocean liner shipping, a market in which only a few firms serve a route, firms enter and exit frequently, so the threat of entry drives economic profits to zero. Only seven firms provide services between East Canada and Japan, China, Korea, and Pacific Russia; only eight firms serve the West Coast Canada–Continental Europe route.

Existing firms can quickly shift ships from one route to another. With the increased use of internationally standardized container ships, liners can travel any route (in the past, the type of ship differed across routes). New and used

vessels and equipment are sold on a world market that is accessible to all firms. As a result, potential entrants can easily rent equipment rather than have to raise large sums to buy liners. Similarly, exit is easy today. A firm exiting all markets can readily sell its used equipment.

As a result, firms engage in hit-and-run entry and exit to take advantage of fleeting profit opportunities. For example, for the nine principal trade routes to and from Canada, in a two-year period, the number of new services (152) on routes was 41% of the original number (373), while services terminated (109) were 29% of the original number. Thus, even though relatively few firms serve any given route, firms can enter and exit easily and do so frequently. ■

Evidence on Ease of Entry and Exit. Entry and exit are relatively difficult in many manufacturing, mining, and government-regulated industries, such as public utilities and insurance. Firms can enter and exit easily in many agriculture, construction, wholesale and retail trade, and service industries.

Dunne, Roberts, and Samuelson (1988) reported the entry rate (percentage of firms that enter in the last year relative to total firms) and exit rate in various U.S. industries, some of which Table 8.2 lists. Entry rates ranged from a low of 21% in

Table 8.2 Entry and Exit Rates in Selected U.S. Industries, 1972–1982

Industry	Entry Rate (%)	Exit Rate (%)
Food processing	24	31
Tobacco	21	22
Textiles	37	37
Apparel	40	45
Lumber	50	44
Printing	49	43
Petroleum and coal	34	30
Rubber and plastics	43	30
Leather	29	39
Primary metals	32	28
Fabricated metals	43	36
Transportation equipment	47	33
Instruments	60	47

Source: Dunne, Roberts, and Samuelson (1988), Table 5, p. 506.

tobacco (which is government regulated) to a high of 60% in instruments. Exit rates varied from a low of 22% in tobacco to a high of 47% in instruments. In general, industries with high entry rates tend to have high exit rates. That is, entry and exit barriers are likely to be related.

LR Market Supply with Identical Firms and Free Entry. The *long-run market supply curve is flat* at the minimum long-run average cost *if firms can freely enter and exit* the market, an unlimited number of *firms have identical costs*, and *input prices are constant*. This result follows from our reasoning about the short-run supply curve, in which we showed that the market supply was flatter, the more firms there were in the market. With many firms in the market in the long run, the market supply curve is effectively flat. ("Many" is ten firms in the vegetable oil market: The long-run supply curve is essentially horizontal with ten firms.)

The long-run supply curve of a typical vegetable oil mill, S^1 in panel a of Figure 8.12, is the long-run marginal cost curve above a minimum long-run average cost of \$10. Because each firm shuts down if the market price is below \$10, the long-run market supply curve is zero at a price below \$10. If the price rises above \$10, firms

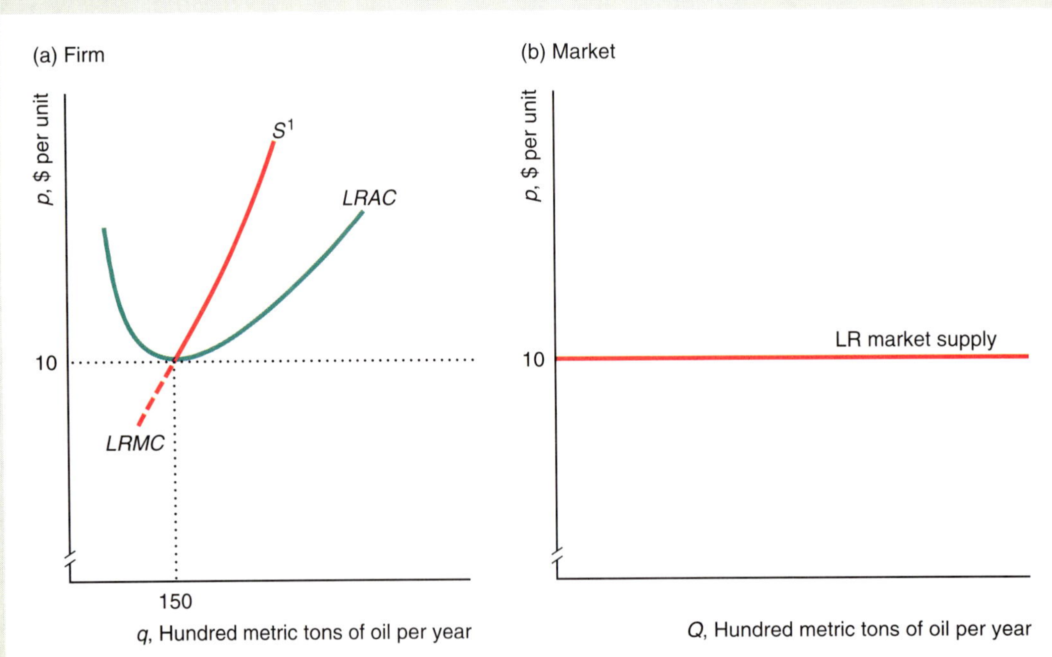

Figure 8.12 LR Firm and Market Supply with Identical Vegetable Oil Firms. (a) The long-run supply curve of a typical vegetable oil mill, S^1, is the long-run marginal cost curve above the minimum average cost of 10. (b) The long-run market supply curve is horizontal at the minimum of the long-run minimum average cost of a typical firm. Each firm produces 150 units, so market output is $150 \times n$, where n is the number of firms.

are making positive profits, so new firms enter, expanding market output until profits are driven to zero, where price is again \$10. The long-run market supply curve in panel b is a horizontal line at the minimum long-run average cost of the typical firm, \$10. At a price of \$10, each firm produces $q = 150$ units (where one unit equals a hundred metric tons). Thus, the total output produced by n firms in the market is $Q = nq = n \times 150$ units. Extra market output is obtained by new firms entering the market.

In summary, the long-run market supply curve is horizontal if the market has free entry and exit, an unlimited number of firms have identical costs, and input prices are constant. When these strong assumptions do not hold, the long-run market supply curve has a slope, as we now show.

LR Market Supply When Entry Is Limited. If the number of firms in a market is limited in the long run, the market supply curve slopes upward. The number of firms is limited if the government restricts that number, if firms need a scarce resource, or if entry is costly. An example of a scarce resource is the limited number of lots on which a luxury, beachfront hotel can be built in Miami. High entry costs restrict the number of firms in a market because firms enter only if the long-run economic profit is greater than the cost of entering.

The only way to get more output if the number of firms is limited is for existing firms to produce more. Because individual firms' supply curves slope upward, the long-run market supply curve is also upward sloping. The reasoning is the same as in the short run, as panel b of Figure 8.7 illustrates, given that no more than five firms can enter. The market supply curve is the upward-sloping S^5 curve, which is the horizontal sum of the five firms' upward-sloping marginal cost curves above minimum average cost.

LR Market Supply When Firms Differ. A second reason why some long-run market supply curves slope up is that firms differ. Firms with relatively low minimum long-run average costs are willing to enter the market at lower prices than others, resulting in an upward-sloping long-run market supply curve.

The long-run supply curve is upward sloping because of differences in costs across firms *only* if the amount that lower-cost firms can produce is limited. If there were an unlimited number of the lowest-cost firms, we would never observe any higher-cost firms producing. Effectively, then, the only firms in the market would have the same, low costs of production.

APPLICATION

Upward-Sloping LR Supply Curve of Cotton

Many countries produce cotton. Production costs differ among countries because of differences in the quality of land, rainfall, costs of irrigation, costs of labor, and other factors.

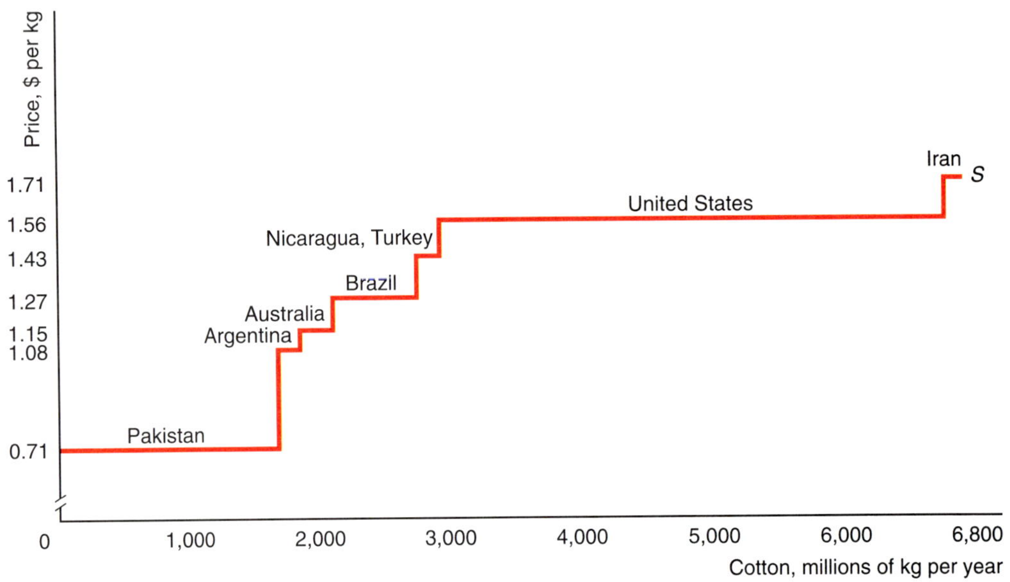

Figure 8.13 International LR Market Supply Curve for Cotton. The average cost of producing cotton and the quantity of cotton each can produce differ across countries. As a consequence, the long-run market supply curve for cotton has an upward slope.

The length of each steplike segment of the long-run supply curve of cotton in Figure 8.13 is the quantity produced by the labeled country.[14] The amount that the low-cost countries can produce must be limited, or we would not observe production by the higher-cost countries.

The height of each segment of the supply curve is the typical minimum average cost of production in that country. The average cost of production in Pakistan is less than half that in Iran. The supply curve has a steplike appearance because we are using an average of the estimate average cost in each country, which is a single number. If we knew the individual firms' supply curves in each of these countries, the market supply curve would have a smoother shape.

As the market price rises, the number of countries producing rises. At market prices below a dollar, only Pakistan produces. If the market price is below $1.50 per kilogram (kg), the United States and Iran do not produce. If the

[14]International Cotton Advisory Committee, *Survey of the Cost of Production of Raw Cotton*, September 1992, p. 5; and *Cotton: World Statistics*, April 1993, pp. 4–5. The figure shows the supply of the major producing countries for which we have cost information. The only large producers for which we lack cost data are India and China.

price increases to \$1.56, the United States supplies a large amount of cotton. In this range of the supply curve, supply is very elastic. For Iran to produce, the price has to rise to \$1.71. Price increases in that range result in only a relatively small increase in supply. Thus, the supply curve is relatively inelastic at prices above \$1.56. ■

LR Market Supply When Input Prices Vary with Output. A third reason why market supply curves may slope is nonconstant input prices. In markets in which factor prices rise or fall when output increases, the long-run supply curve slopes even if firms have identical cost and can freely enter and exit.

If the market buys a relatively small share of the total amount of a factor of production that is sold, then, as market output expands, the price of the factor is unlikely to be affected. For example, dentists do not hire enough receptionists to affect the market wage for receptionists.

In contrast, if the market buys most of the total sales of a factor, the price of that input is more likely to vary with market output. As jet plane manufacturers expand and buy more jet engines, the price of these engines rises because the jet plane manufacturers are the sole purchaser of these engines.

To produce more goods, firms must use more inputs. If the prices of some or all inputs rise when more inputs are purchased, the cost of producing the final good also rises. We call a market in which input prices rise with output an *increasing-cost market.* Few steel workers have no fear of heights and are willing to construct tall buildings, so their supply curve is steeply upward sloping. As more skyscrapers are built at one time, the demand for these workers shifts to the right, driving up their wage.

We assume that all firms in a market have the same cost curves and that input prices rise as market output expands. We use the cost curves of a representative firm in panel a of Figure 8.14 to derive the upward-sloping market supply curve in panel b.

When input prices are relatively low, each identical firm has the same long-run marginal cost curve, MC^1, and average cost curve, AC^1, in panel a. A typical firm produces at minimum average cost, e_1, and sells q_1 units of output. The market supply is Q_1 in panel b when the market price is p_1. The n_1 firms collectively sell $Q_1 = n_1q_1$ units of output, which is point E_1 on the market supply curve in panel b.

If the market demand curve shifts outward, the market price rises to p_2, new firms enter, and market output rises to Q_2, causing input prices to rise. As a result, the marginal cost curve shifts from MC^1 to MC^2, and the average cost curve rises from AC^1 to AC^2. The typical firm produces at a higher minimum average cost, e_2. At this higher price, there are n_2 firms in the market, so market output is $Q_2 = n_2q_2$ at point E_2 on the market supply curve.

Thus, in both an increasing-cost market and a constant-cost market—in which input prices remain constant as output increases—firms produce at minimum average cost in the long run. The difference is that the minimum average cost rises as market output increases in an increasing-cost market, whereas minimum average

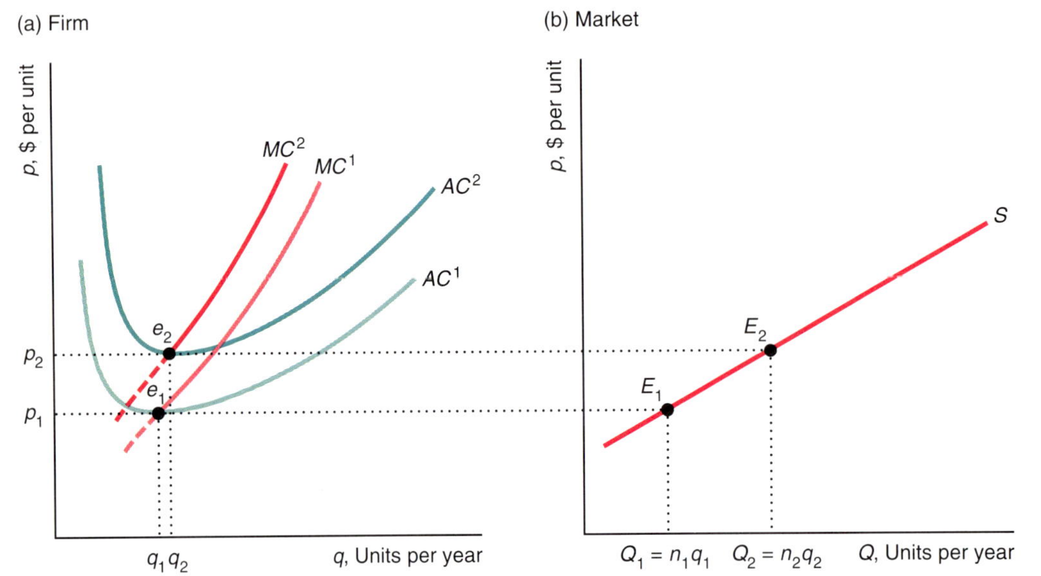

Figure 8.14 LR Market Supply in an Increasing-Cost Market. (a) At a relatively low market output Q_1, the firm's long-run marginal and average cost curves are MC^1 and AC^1. At the higher market quantity Q_2, the cost curves shift upward to MC^2 and AC^2 because of the higher input prices. Given identical firms, each firm produces at minimum average cost, such as points e_1 and e_2. (b) Long-run market supply, S, is upward sloping.

cost is constant in a constant-cost market. In conclusion, *the long-run supply curve is upward sloping in an increasing-cost market and flat in a constant-cost market.*

In decreasing-cost markets, as market output rises, at least some factor prices fall. As a result, *in a decreasing-cost market, the long-run market supply curve is downward sloping.*

Increasing returns to scale may cause factor prices to fall. For example, in the early 1980s, when the personal computer market was young, there was much less demand for floppy drives than there is today. As a result, those drives were partially assembled by hand at relatively high cost. As demand for floppy drives increased, it became practical to automate more of the production process so that floppy drives could be produced at lower per-unit cost. The decrease in the price of floppy drives lowers the cost of personal computers.

Figure 8.15 shows a decreasing-cost market. As the market output expands from Q_1 to Q_2 in panel b, the prices of inputs fall, so a typical firm's cost curves shift downward, and the minimum average cost falls from e_1 to e_2 in panel a. On the long-run market supply curve in panel b, point E_1, which corresponds to e_1, is above E_2, which corresponds to e_2. As a consequence, *a decreasing-cost market supply curve is downward sloping.*

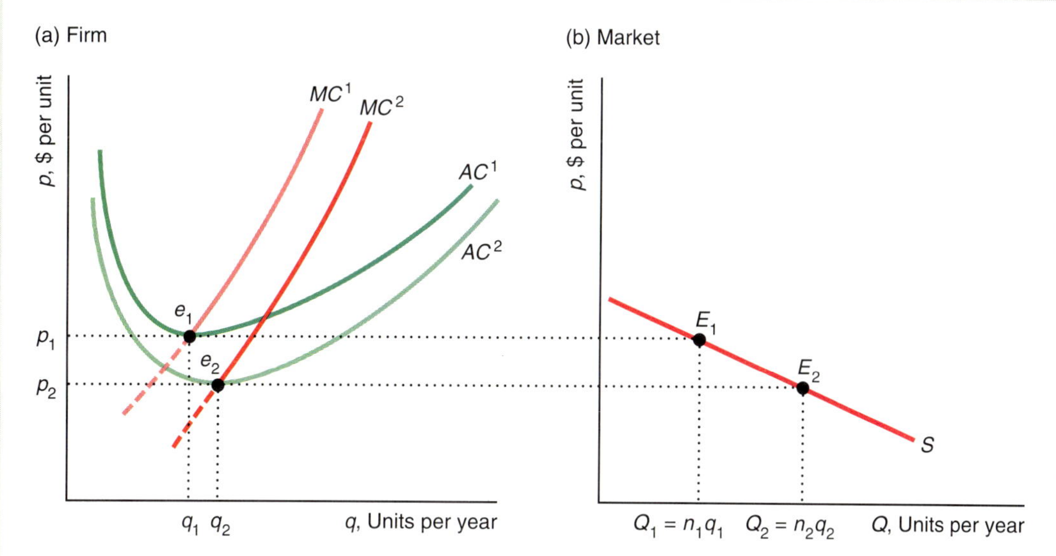

Figure 8.15 LR Market Supply in a Decreasing-Cost Market. (a) At a relatively low market output Q_1, the firm's long-run marginal and average cost curves are MC^1 and AC^1. At the higher market quantity Q_2, the cost curves shift downward to MC^2 and AC^2 because of lower input prices. Given identical firms, each firm produces at minimum average cost, such as points e_1 and e_2. (b) Long-run market supply, S, is downward sloping.

To summarize, theory tells us that competitive long-run market supply curves may be flat, upward sloping, or downward sloping. If all firms are identical in a market in which firms can freely enter and input prices are constant, the long-run market supply curve is flat. If entry is limited, firms differ in costs, or input prices rise with output, the long-run supply curve is upward sloping. Finally, if input prices fall with market output, the long-run supply curve is downward sloping.

APPLICATION

Slope of LR Market Supply Curves

Determining the slope of the supply curve in a particular market requires careful studying of that market. Shea (1993) examined the slopes of the supply curves in 26 American manufacturing industries (which are assumed to be competitive). Only three of these industries have downward-sloping long-run supply curves: prepared feeds, construction equipment, and aircraft. Of the rest, more than twice as many are upward sloping as are flat. Sixteen industries have upward-sloping long-run supply curves, including lumber; drugs; paints; tires; stone, clay, and glass; cement; and electronic components. Seven industries, among them plumbing and heating products, floor coverings, and animal and marine fats and oils, have flat supply curves.

On average across all these industries, however, the long-run supply curves have a moderate upward slope. The supply elasticity is 5.5 on average across all these manufacturing industries, so a 1% increase in price leads to a 5.5% increase in quantity. ■

LR Competitive Equilibrium

The intersection of the long-run market supply and demand curves determines the long-run competitive equilibrium. With identical firms, constant input prices, and free entry and exit, the long-run competitive market supply is horizontal at minimum long-run average cost, so the equilibrium price equals long-run average cost. A shift in the demand curve affects only the equilibrium quantity and not the equilibrium price, which remains constant at minimum long-run average cost.

The market supply curve is different in the short run than in the long run, so the long-run competitive equilibrium differs from the short-run equilibrium. The relationship between the short- and long-run equilibria depends on where the market demand curve crosses the short- and long-run market supply curves. Figure 8.16 illustrates this point using the short- and long-run supply curves for the vegetable oil mill market.

The short-run firm supply curve for a typical firm in panel a is the marginal cost above the minimum of the average variable cost, \$7. At a price of \$7, each firm produces 100 units, so the 20 firms in the market in the short run collectively supply 2,000 (= 20 × 100) units of oil in panel b. At higher prices, the short-run market supply curve slopes upward, because it is the horizontal summation of the firm's upward-sloping marginal cost curves.

We assume that the firms use the same size plant in the short and long run so that the minimum average cost is \$10 in both the short and long run. Because all firms have the same costs and can enter freely, the long-run market supply curve is flat at the minimum average cost, \$10, in panel b. At prices between \$7 and \$10, firms supply goods at a loss in the short run but not in the long run.

If the market demand curve is D^1, the short-run market equilibrium, F_1, is below and to the right of the long-run market equilibrium, E_1. This relationship is reversed if the market demand curve is D^2.[15]

In the short run, if the demand is as low as D^1, the market price in the short-run equilibrium, F_1, is \$7. At that price, each of the 20 firms produces 100 units, at f_1

[15]Using data from *Statistics Canada*, I estimate that the elasticity of demand for vegetable oil is –0.8. Both D^1 and D^2 are constant –0.8 elasticity demand curves, but the demand at any price on D^2 is 2.4 times that on D^1.

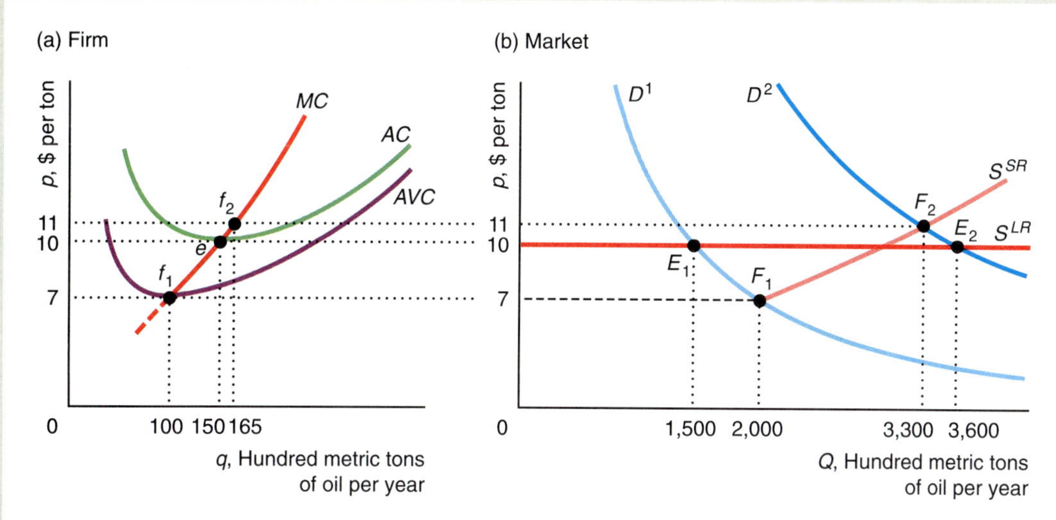

Figure 8.16 The SR and LR Vegetable Oil Equilibria. (a) A typical vegetable oil mill is willing to produce 100 units of oil at \$7, 150 units at \$10, or 165 units at \$11. (b) The short-run market supply curve, S^{SR}, is the horizontal sum of 20 individual firms' short-run marginal cost curves above minimum average variable cost, \$7. The long-run market supply curve, S^{LR}, is horizontal at the minimum average cost, \$10. If the demand curve is D^1, in the short-run equilibrium, F_1, 20 firms sell 2,000 units of oil at \$7. In the long-run equilibrium, E_1, 10 firms sell 1,500 units at \$10. If demand is D^2, the short-run equilibrium is F_2 (\$11; 3,300 units; 20 firms) and the long-run equilibrium is E_2 (\$10; 3,600 units; 24 firms).

in panel a. The firms lose money because the price of \$7 is below average cost at 100 units. These losses drive some of the firms out of the market in the long run, so market output falls and the market price rises. In the long-run equilibrium, E_1, price is \$10, and each firm produces 150 units, *e*, and breaks even. As the market demands only 1,500 units, only 10 (= 1,500/150) firms produce, so half the firms that produced in the short run exit the market.[16] Thus, with the D^1 demand curve, price rises and output falls in the long run.

If demand expands to D^2, in the short run, each of the 20 firms expands its output to 165 hundred tons, f_2, and the price rises to \$11, where the firms make profits: The price of \$11 is above the average cost at 165 hundred tons. These profits attract entry in the long run, and the price falls. In the long-run equilibrium, each firm produces 150 units, *e*, and 3,600 units are sold by the market, E_2, by 24 (= 3,600/150) firms. Thus, with the D^2 demand curve, price falls and output rises in the long run.

---

[16]How do we know which firms leave? If the firms are identical, the theory says nothing about which ones leave and which ones stay. The firms that leave make zero economic profit, and those that stay make zero economic profit, so firms are indifferent as to whether they stay or exit.

Because firms may enter and exit in the long run, taxes can have a counterintuitive effect on the competitive equilibrium. For example, as Solved Problem 8.3 shows, a lump-sum franchise tax causes the competitive equilibrium output of a firm to increase, although market output falls.

SOLVED PROBLEM 8.3

If the government starts collecting a lump-sum franchise tax of $\mathcal{L}$ each year from each identical firm in a competitive market with free entry and exit, how do the long-run market and firm equilibria change?

Answer

1. *Show that the franchise tax causes the minimum long-run average cost to rise*: Figure 8.17 shows a typical firm's cost curves in panel a and the market equilibrium in panel b. In panel a, a lump-sum, franchise tax shifts up the typical firm's average cost curve from AC^1 to $AC^2 = AC^1 + \mathcal{L}/q$ but

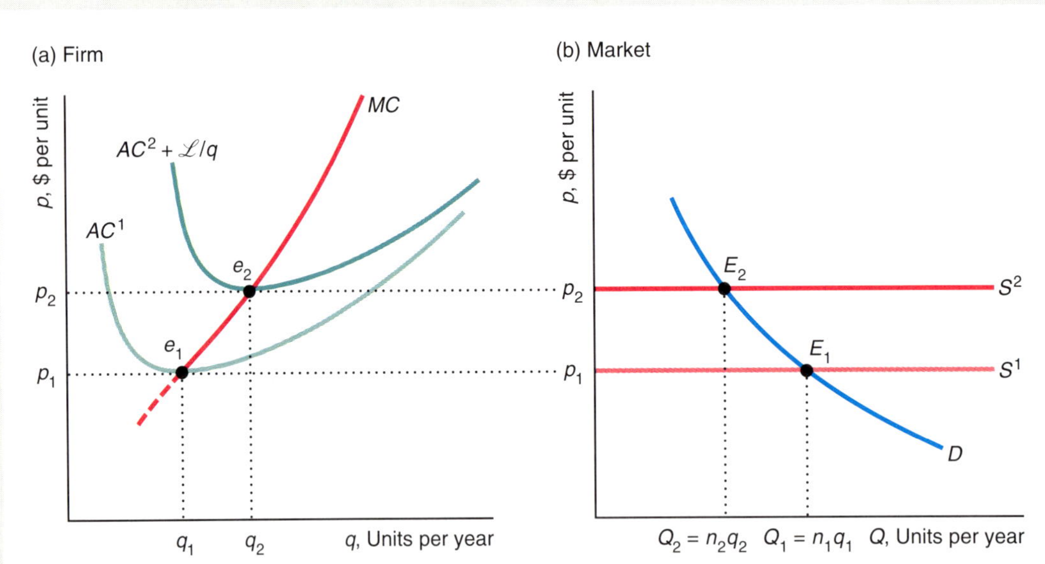

Figure 8.17 LR Effect of a Lump-Sum Franchise Tax on Competitive Equilibrium. (a) A franchise tax, $\mathcal{L}$, shifts a typical firm's average cost curve upward but does not affect the firm's marginal cost, so the minimum of the average cost shifts upward and to the right, from e_1 to e_2. (b) As a result, the long-run market supply curve shifts upward from S^1 to S^2. Because market demand curves slope downward, the equilibrium market quantity falls from Q_1 to Q_2 and equilibrium price rises from p_1 to p_2. Firms that continue to produce sell more, $q_2 > q_1$, but there are fewer firms in the market, $n_2 = Q_2/q_2 < n_1 = Q_1/q_1$.

does not affect the marginal cost (see the answer to Solved Problem 7.1). As a result, the minimum average cost rises from to e_1 to e_2.

2. *Show that the shift in the minimum average cost causes the market supply curve to shift up, equilibrium quantity to fall, and equilibrium price to rise*: The long-run market supply is horizontal at minimum average cost. Thus, the market supply curve shifts upward by the same amount as the minimum average cost increases in panel b. With a downward-sloping market demand curve, the new equilibrium, E_2, has a lower quantity, $Q_2 < Q_1$, and higher price, $p_2 > p_1$, than in the original equilibrium, E_1.
3. *Show that the increase in the equilibrium price causes output of an individual firm to rise*: Because the market price rises, the quantity that a firm produces rises from q_1 to q_2. Thus, if the firm remains in the market, it will produce more.
4. *Use the market quantity and individual firm quantity to determine how the number of firms changes*: In the initial equilibrium, the number of firms was $n_1 = Q_1/q_1$. The new equilibrium number of firms, $n_2 = Q_2/q_2$, must be smaller than n_1 because $Q_2 < Q_1$ and $q_2 > q_1$. Thus, there are fewer firms but each remaining firm produces more output in the new equilibrium. ■

8.5 ZERO PROFIT FOR COMPETITIVE FIRMS IN THE LONG RUN

Competitive firms earn zero profit in the long run whether or not entry is completely free. As a consequence, competitive firms must profit maximize.

Zero LR Profit with Free Entry

The long-run supply curve is horizontal if firms are free to enter the market, firms have identical cost, and input prices are constant. All firms in the market are operating at minimum long-run average cost. That is, they are indifferent between shutting down or not because they are earning zero profit.

One implication of the shut-down rule is that the firm is willing to operate in the long run even if it is making zero profit. This conclusion may seem strange unless you remember that we are talking about an *economic profit*, which is revenue minus opportunity costs. Because opportunity cost includes the value of the next best investment, at a zero long-run economic profit, the firm is earning the normal business profit that the firm could earn by investing elsewhere in the economy.

For example, if a firm's owner had not built the plant the firm uses to produce, the owner could have spent that money on another business or put the money in a bank. The opportunity cost of the current plant, then, is the forgone profit from what the owner could have earned by investing the money elsewhere.

The five-year median accounting return on capital across all retailing firms was 9.3%, indicating that the typical retailer earned a business profit of 9.3¢ for every dollar it invested in capital.[17] These firms were earning about what they would earn if they invested in other markets: The median return on capital for all markets was 9.4%. Thus, these retailers were earning roughly zero economic profits but positive business profit.

Because business cost does not include all opportunity costs, business profit is larger than economic profit. Thus, *a profit-maximizing firm may stay in business if it earns zero long-run economic profit but shuts down if it earns zero long-run business profit.*

Zero LR Profit When Entry Is Limited

In some markets, firms cannot enter in response to long-run profit opportunities. One reason for the limited number of firms is that the supply of an input is limited. Only so much land is suitable for mining uranium, and only a few people have the superior skills need to play professional basketball.

One might think that firms could make positive long-run economic profits in such markets; however, that's not true. The reason why firms do not earn zero economic profits is that firms bidding for the scarce input drive its price up until the firms' profits are zero.

Suppose the number of acres suitable for growing tomatoes is limited. Figure 8.18 shows a typical farm's average cost curve if the rental cost of land is zero (the average cost curve includes only the farm's costs of labor, capital, materials, and energy—not land). At the market price p^*, the firm produces q^* bushels of tomatoes and makes a profit of π^*, the shaded rectangle in the figure.

Thus, if the owner of the land does not charge rent, the farmer makes a profit. Unfortunately for the farmer, the landowner rents the land for π^*, so the farmer actually earns zero profit. Why does the landowner charge that much? The reason is that π^* is the opportunity cost of the land: The land is worth π^* to other potential farmers. These farmers will bid against each other to rent this land until the rent is driven up to π^*.

This rent is a fixed cost to the farmer because it doesn't vary with the amount of output. Thus, the rent affects the farm's average cost curve but not its marginal cost curve.

As a result, if the farm produces at all, it produces q^*, where its marginal cost equals the market price, no matter what rent is charged. The higher average cost curve in the figure includes a rent equal to π^*. The minimum point of this average cost curve is p^* at q^* bushels of tomatoes, so the farmer earns zero economic profit.

If demand falls, so the market price falls, these farmers will make short-run losses. In the long run, the rental price of the land will fall enough that, once again, each firm earns zero economic profit.

Does it make a difference whether farmers own or rent the land? Not really. The opportunity cost to a farmer who owns superior land is the amount for which that

[17]Moukheiber, Zina, "Retailing," *Forbes*, 155(1), January 1995:190–193.

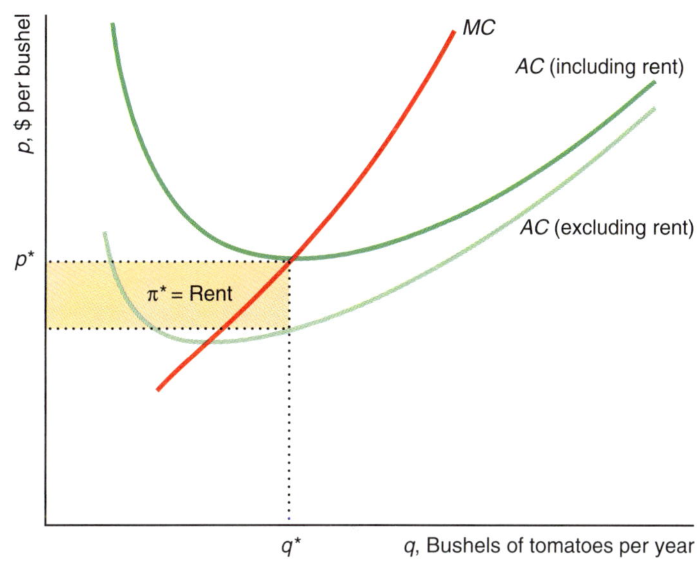

Figure 8.18 Rent. If it did not have to pay rent for its land, a farm with high-quality land would earn a positive long-run profit of π^*. Due to competitive bidding for this land, however, the rent equals π^*, so the landlord reaps all the benefits of the superior land, and the farmer earns a zero long-run economic profit.

land could be rented in a competitive land market. Thus, the economic profit of both owned and rented land is zero in the long-run equilibrium.

Good-quality land is not the only scarce resource. The price of any fixed factor will be bid up in the same way so that economic profit for the firm is zero in the long run.

Another example is an industry in which the government requires that a firm have a license to operate and then limits the number of licenses. As we discuss at length in Chapter 9, the price of the license gets bid up by potential entrants, driving profit to zero.

Economists refer to the extra, opportunity value of a scarce input as a "rent"—even if the fixed factor is a person with high ability rather than land. Indeed, to economists, a **rent** is a payment to the owner of an input beyond the minimum necessary for the factor to be supplied.

Bonnie manages a store for the salary of $30,000, which is what a typical manager is paid. Because she's a superior manager, however, the firm earns an economic profit of $50,000 a year. Other firms, seeing what a good job Bonnie is doing, offer her a higher salary. The bidding for her services drives her salary up to $80,000: her $30,000 base salary plus the $50,000 rent. After paying this rent to Bonnie, the store makes zero economic profit.

Similarly, people with unusual abilities can earn staggering rents. Though no law stops anyone from trying to become a professional entertainer, most of us do not have enough talent that others will pay to watch us perform. The Rolling Stones earned $121.2 million from their 1994 concert tour, according to *Pollstar* magazine. To put this amount in perspective, the 1993 gross national product (national income of the entire country) of Grenada, a country of a 100,000 people, was $215 million; that of Kiribati, $51.1 million; and that of Bhutan, $234 million.

In short, if some firms in a market make short-run economic profits due to a scarce input, the other firms in the market bid for that input. This bidding drives the price of the factor upward until all firms earn zero long-run profits. In such a market, the supply curve is flat because all firms have the same minimum long-run average cost.

Competitive Firms' Need to Maximize Profit

In a competitive market with identical firms and free entry, if most firms are profit-maximizing, profits are driven to zero in the long-run equilibrium. Any firm that did not profit maximize—that is, any firm that set its output so that price did not equal its marginal cost or did not use the most cost-efficient methods of production—would lose money. Thus, *a firm that survives in a competitive market must maximize its profit.*

Summary

1. **Competition:** Competitive firms are price takers that cannot influence market price. Markets are likely to be competitive if all firms in the market sell identical products, firms can enter and exit the market freely, buyers and sellers know the prices charged by firms, and transaction costs are low. A competitive firm faces a horizontal demand curve at the market price.
2. **Profit maximization:** Most firms maximize economic profit, which is revenue minus economic cost (explicit and implicit cost). Because business profit, which is revenue minus only explicit cost, does not include implicit cost, economic profit tends to be less than business profit. A firm earning zero economic profit is making as much as it could if its resources were devoted to their best alternative uses. To maximize profit, all firms (not just competitive firms) must make two decisions. First, the firm determines the quantity at which its profit is highest. Profit is maximized when marginal profit is zero, or, equivalently, marginal revenue equals marginal cost. Second, the firm decides whether to produce at all.
3. **Competition in the short run:** Because a competitive firm is a price taker, its marginal revenue equals the market price. As a result, a competitive firm maximizes its profit by setting its output so that its short-run marginal cost equals the market price. The firm shuts down if the market price is less than its minimum average variable cost. Thus, a profit-maximizing, competitive firm's short-run supply curve is its marginal cost curve above its minimum average variable cost. The short-run market supply curve, which is the sum of the supply curves of the fixed number of firms producing in the short run, is flat at low output levels and upward sloping at larger levels. The short-run competitive equilibrium is determined by the intersection of the market demand curve and the short-run market supply curve. The effect of an increase in demand depends on whether demand intersects the market supply in the flat or upward-sloping section.
4. **Competition in the long run:** In the long run, a competitive firm sets its output where the market price equals its long-run marginal cost. It shuts down if the market price is less than the minimum

of its average long-run cost because all costs are variable in the long run. Consequently, the competitive firm's supply curve is its long-run marginal cost above its minimum long-run average cost. The long-run supply curve of a firm may have a different slope than the short-run curve because it can vary its fixed factors in the long run. The long-run market supply curve is the horizontal sum of the supply curves of all the firms in the market. If all firms are identical, entry and exit are easy, and input prices are constant, the long-run market supply curve is flat at minimum average cost. If firms differ, entry is difficult or costly, or input prices vary with output, the long-run market supply curve has an upward slope. The long-run market supply curve slopes upward if input prices increase with output and slopes downward if input prices decrease with output. The long-run market equilibrium price and quantity are different than the short-run price and quantity.

5. **Zero profits for competitive firms in the long run:** Although firms may make profits or losses in the short run, they earn zero economic profits in the long run. If necessary, the prices of scarce inputs adjust to ensure that competitive firms make zero long-run profits. Because profit-maximizing firms just break even in the long run, firms that do not try to maximize profits must lose money. Thus, competitive firms must profit maximize to survive.

Problems

1. Should a competitive firm ever produce when it is losing money? Why or why not?
2. Many marginal cost curves are U-shaped. As a result, it is possible that the *MC* curve hits the demand or price line at two output levels. Which is the profit-maximizing output? Why?
3. Suppose the government imposes an ad valorem tax (Chapter 3) of α per dollar on a competitive firm. What happens to its long-run supply curve?
4. In Solved Problem 8.3, would it make a difference to the analysis whether the franchise tax were collected annually or only once when the firm starts operation? How would each of these franchise taxes affect the firm's long-run supply curve? Explain your answer.
5. Answer Solved Problem 8.3 for the short run rather than for the long run. (*Hint*: The answer depends on where the demand curve intersects the original short-run supply curve.)
6. Competitive firms in the United States and in France produce cheese. The French government gives each cheese manufacturer an annual subsidy (a negative tax) of s that is independent of the amount of cheese it produces. What happens to the long-run supply curve of cheese to the world?
7. How does the cheese subsidy discussed in Problem 6 affect the world price, the amount sold by French and American firms, and the profits of both types of firms?
8. What is the effect on firm and market equilibrium of a law requiring a firm to give its workers six months' notice before it can shut down its plant?
9. Redraw Figure 8.11 showing a situation in which the short-run plant size is too large relative to the optimal long-run plant size.
10. Is it true that the long-run supply curve of a good is horizontal only if the long-run supply curves of all factors are horizontal? Explain.
11. Navel oranges are grown in California and Arizona. If Arizona starts collecting a specific tax per orange from its firms, what happens to the long-run market supply curve? (*Hint*: You may assume that all firms initially have the same costs. Your answer may depend on whether unlimited entry occurs.)
12. Americans used 33 million real Christmas trees and 40 million artificial trees in 1994.[18] The number of tree producers fell by about a third over the previous 10 years, to about 2,000 in 1994, due to artificial tree sales. That year, trees sold for an average of \$26.50, about 50¢ more than the previous year. Retailers' average cost was \$20. Use graphs to illustrate this information.

[18]Kazakoff, Lois, "Tree Sellers Expecting More Green," *San Francisco Chronicle*, December 6, 1995:B1, B3.

Math Problems

13. If a competitive firm's cost function is $C(q) = 100 + 10q - q^2 + \frac{1}{3}q^3$, what is the firm's marginal cost function? What is the firm's profit-maximizing condition?

14. If a competitive firm's cost function is $C(q) = a + bq + cq^2 + dq^3$, where a, b, c, and d are constants, what is the firm's marginal cost function? What is the firm's profit-maximizing condition?

15. Each firm in a competitive market has a cost function of $C = 16 + q^2$. The market demand function is $Q = 24 - p$. Determine the equilibrium price, quantity per firm, market quantity, and number of firms.

16. There are 10 identical competitive firms in a market. The linear market demand curve is $Q = 100 - p$, and the linear supply curve of each firm is $q = p$. What is the residual demand (Appendix 8A) facing a typical firm?

17. There are n identical competitive firms in a market. The linear market demand curve is $Q = a - bp$, and the linear supply curve of each firm is $q = c + dp$, where a, b, c, and d are positive constants. What is the residual demand (Appendix 8A) facing a typical firm?

18. At least 40,000 U.S. farms produce apples. The market demand elasticity of apples is about -0.2. At least how great must the residual demand elasticity (Appendix 8A) facing a single farm be?

CHAPTER

9

Applying the Competitive Model

We've reached a compromise. We're going to raise the minimum wage by half a gallon of gas per hour.

In June 1995, the United States and Japan almost had a trade war in which both countries would heavily tax imported goods. How would such taxes have affected consumers and producers? In this chapter, we show how the competitive model can answer this type of question. One of the major strengths of the competitive market model is that it can predict how trade wars, changes in government policies, global warming, and major cost-saving discoveries affect consumers and producers.

This chapter introduces the measure that economists commonly use to determine whether consumers or firms gain or lose when the equilibrium of a competitive market changes. Using such a measure, we can predict whether a policy change benefits the winners more than it harms the losers. To decide whether to adopt a particular policy, policymakers can combine these predictions with their normative views (values), such as whether they are more interested in helping the group that gains or the group that loses.

To most people, the term *welfare* refers to the government's payments to poor people. No such meaning is implied when economists employ the term. Economists use *welfare* to refer to the well-being of various groups such as consumers and producers. They call an analysis of the impact of a change on various groups' well-being a study of *welfare economics*.

In this chapter, we examine six main topics:

1. Consumer welfare: How much consumers are helped or harmed by a change in the equilibrium price can be measured by using information from demand curves or utility functions.
2. Producer welfare: How much producers gain or lose from a change in the equilibrium price can be measured by using information from the marginal cost curve or by measuring the change in profits.
3. Competition maximizes welfare: Competition maximizes a measure of social welfare based on consumer and produce welfare.
4. Policies that shift supply curves: Government policies that limit the number of firms in competitive markets harm consumers and lower welfare.
5. Policies that create a wedge between supply and demand: Government policies such as taxes, price ceilings, price floors, and tariffs that create a wedge between the supply and demand curves (Chapter 3) reduce equilibrium quantity, raise the equilibrium price to consumers, and lower welfare.
6. Comparing both types of policies: imports: Policies that limit supply (such as quotas or bans on imports) or create a wedge between supply and demand (such as *tariffs*, which are taxes on imports) have different welfare effects when both polices reduce imports by equal amounts.

9.1 CONSUMER WELFARE

Economists and policymakers want to know how much consumers benefit from or are harmed by shocks that affect the equilibrium price and quantity. To what extent are consumers harmed if a local government imposes a sales tax to raise additional revenues? To answer such a question, we need some way to measure consumers' welfare. Economists use measures of welfare based on consumer theory (Chapters 4 and 5).

If we knew a consumer's utility function, we could directly answer the question of how an event affects a consumer's welfare. If the price of beef increases, the budget line facing someone who eats beef rotates inward, so the consumer is on a lower indifference curve in the new equilibrium. If we knew the levels of utility associated with the original indifference curve and the new one, we could measure the impact of the tax in terms of the change in the utility level.

This approach is not practical for a couple of reasons. First, we rarely, if ever, know individuals' utility functions. Second, even if we had utility measures for various consumers, we would have no obvious way to compare them. One person might say that he got 1,000 utils (units of utility) from the same bundle that another consumer says gives her 872 utils of pleasure. The first person is not necessarily happier—he may just be using a different scale.

As a result, *we measure consumer welfare in terms of dollars*. Instead of asking the rather silly question "How many utils would you lose if your daily commute increased by 15 minutes?" we could ask "How much would you pay to avoid having your daily commute grow a quarter of an hour longer?" or "How much would it cost you in forgone earnings if your daily commute were 15 minutes longer?" It is easier to compare dollars across people than utils.

We first present the most widely used method of measuring consumer welfare. Then we show how it can be used to measure the effect of a change in price on consumer welfare.

Measuring Consumer Welfare Using a Demand Curve

Consumer welfare from a good is the benefit a consumer gets from consuming that good minus what the consumer paid to buy the good. How much pleasure do you get from a good above and beyond its price? If you buy a good for exactly what it's worth to you, you are indifferent between making that transaction and not. Frequently, however, you buy things that are worth more to you than what they cost. Imagine that you've played tennis in the hot sun and are very thirsty. You can buy a soft drink from a vending machine for 75¢, but you'd be willing to pay much more because you are so thirsty. As a result, you're much better off making this purchase than not.

If we can measure how much more you'd be willing to pay than you did pay, we'd know how much you gained from this transaction. Luckily for us, the demand curve contains the information we need to make this measurement.

Marginal Willingness to Pay. To develop a welfare measure based on the demand curve, we need to know what information is contained in a demand curve. The demand curve reflects a consumer's *marginal willingness to pay*: the maximum amount a consumer will spend for an extra unit. The consumer's marginal willingness to pay is the *marginal value* the consumer places on the last unit of output.

David's demand curve for magazines per week, panel a of Figure 9.1, indicates his marginal willingness to buy various numbers of magazines. David places a marginal value of \$5 on the first magazine. As a result, if the price of a magazine is \$5, David buys one magazine, point *a* on the demand curve. His marginal willingness to buy a second magazine is \$4, so if the price falls to \$4, he buys two magazines, *b*. His marginal willingness to buy three magazines is \$3, so if the price of magazines is \$3, he buys three magazines, *c*.

Consumer Surplus. The monetary difference between what a consumer is willing to pay for the quantity of the good purchased and what the good actually costs is called **consumer surplus** (*CS*). Consumer surplus is a dollar-value measure of the extra pleasure the consumer receives from the transaction beyond its price.

David's consumer surplus from each additional magazine is his marginal willingness to pay minus what he pays to obtain the magazine. His marginal willingness to pay for the first magazine, \$5, is area $CS_1 + E_1$. If the price is \$3, his expenditure to obtain the magazine is area $E_1 = \$3$. Thus, his consumer surplus on the first magazine is area $CS_1 = (CS_1 + E_1) - E_1 = \$5 - \$3 = \$2$. Because his marginal willingness to pay for the second magazine is \$4, his consumer surplus for the second magazine is the smaller area $CS_2 = \$1$. His marginal willingness to pay for the third magazine is \$3, which equals what he must pay to obtain it, so his consumer surplus is zero, $CS_3 = \$0$. He is indifferent between buying and not buying the third magazine.

At a price of \$3, David buys three magazines. His total consumer surplus from the three magazines he buys is the sum of the consumer surplus he gets from each of these magazines: $CS_1 + CS_2 + CS_3 = \$2 + \$1 + \$0 = \$3$. This total consumer surplus of \$3 is the extra amount that David is willing to spend for the right to buy three magazines at \$3 each. Thus, *an individual's consumer surplus is the area under the demand curve and above the market price up to the quantity the consumer buys.*

David is unwilling to buy a fourth magazine unless the price drops to \$2 or less. If David's mother gives him a fourth magazine as a gift, the marginal value that David puts on that fourth magazine, \$2, is less than what it cost his mother, \$3.

We can determine consumer surplus for smooth demand curves in the same way as with David's unusual stairlike demand curve. Steven has a smooth demand curve for baseball trading cards, panel b of Figure 9.1. The height of this demand curve measures his willingness to pay for one more card. This willingness varies with the number of cards he buys in a year. The total value he places on obtaining q_1 cards per year is the area under the demand curve up to q_1, the areas *CS* and *E*. Area *E* is his actual expenditure on q_1 cards. Because the price is p_1, his expenditure is $p_1 q_1$. Steven's consumer surplus from consuming q_1 trading cards is the value of consuming those cards, areas *CS* and *E*, minus his actual expenditures *E* to obtain them, or *CS*. Thus, his consumer surplus, *CS*, is the area under the demand curve and above the horizontal line at the price p_1 up to the quantity he buys, q_1.

Just as we measure the consumer surplus for an individual using that individual's demand curve, we measure the consumer surplus of all consumers in a market using

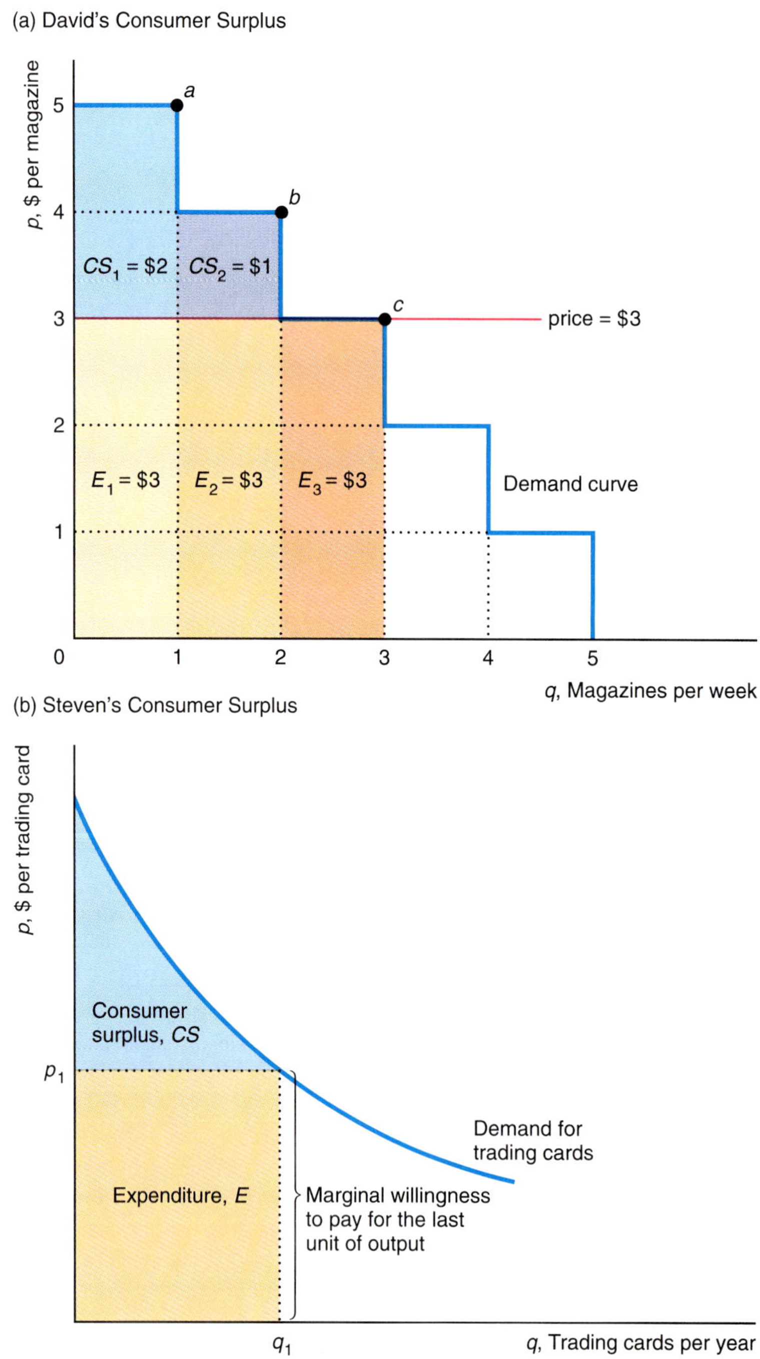
(a) David's Consumer Surplus
p, $ per magazine
5
4
3
2
1
0
a
b
c
CS1 = $2
CS2 = $1
price = $3
E1 = $3
E2 = $3
E3 = $3
Demand curve
1
2
3
4
5
q, Magazines per week
(b) Steven's Consumer Surplus
p, $ per trading card
Consumer surplus, CS
p1
Expenditure, E
Marginal willingness to pay for the last unit of output
Demand for trading cards
q1
q, Trading cards per year

Figure 9.1 Consumer Surplus. (a) David's demand curve for magazines has a steplike shape. When the price is \$3, he buys three magazines, point *c*. David's marginal value for the first magazine is \$5, areas $CS_1 + E_1$, and the price of that magazine is \$3, area E_1, so his consumer surplus from buying it is CS_1 = \$2. His consumer surplus is \$1 for the second magazine, area CS_2, and is \$0 for the third (he is indifferent between buying and not buying it). Thus, his total consumer surplus is the shaded area $CS_1 + CS_2 + CS_3 = \$3$. (b) Steven's willingness to pay is the height of his smooth demand curve. At price p_1, Steven's expenditure is E (= p_1q_1), his consumer surplus is CS, and the total value he places on consuming q_1 trading cards per year is the sum of the two shaded areas (labeled CS and E).

the market demand curve. *Market consumer surplus is the area under the market demand curve above the market price up to the quantity consumers buy.*

To summarize, consumer surplus is a practical and convenient measure of consumer welfare. There are two advantages of using consumer surplus rather than utility to discuss the welfare of consumers. First, the dollar-denominated consumer surplus of several individuals can be easily compared or combined, whereas the utility of various individuals cannot be easily compared or combined. Second, it is relatively easy to measure consumer surplus, whereas it is difficult to get a meaningful measure of utility directly. To calculate consumer surplus, all we have to do is measure the area under a demand curve.

APPLICATION

Consumer Surplus from Television

Do you get consumer surplus from television? Fewer than one in four (23%) Americans say that they would be willing to "give up watching absolutely all types of television" for the rest of their lives in exchange for \$25,000.[1] Almost half (46%) say that they'd refuse to give up TV for anything under a million dollars. One in four Americans wouldn't give it up for \$1 million. Indeed, one quarter of those who earn under \$20,000 a year wouldn't give up TV for \$1 million—more than they will earn in 50 years.

Thus, if you ask consumers how much consumer surplus they receive from television, many of them give implausibly high answers. For this reason, economists typically calculate consumer surplus by using estimated demand curves, which are based on actual observed behavior, rather than simply asking consumers. ■

[1]Delsol, Michel, "Would You Give Up TV for a Million Bucks?" *TV Guide*, 40(41[2063]), October 10, 1992:11.

Effect of a Price Change on Consumer Surplus

If the supply curve shifts upward or a government imposes a new sales tax, the equilibrium price rises, reducing consumer surplus. We first use our old friend, the processed pork example from Chapters 2 and 3, to illustrate the effect of a price increase on market consumer surplus. Then we discuss which markets are likely to have the greatest loss of consumer surplus from a price increase.

Consumer Surplus Loss from a Higher Pork Price. Suppose the price of processed pork in Canada rises from the original equilibrium price of \$3.30 per kg to \$4 per kg (perhaps due to a shift in supply or a tax), causing a shift along the demand curve (based on estimates by Moschini and Meilke 1992) in Figure 9.2.[2] The consumer

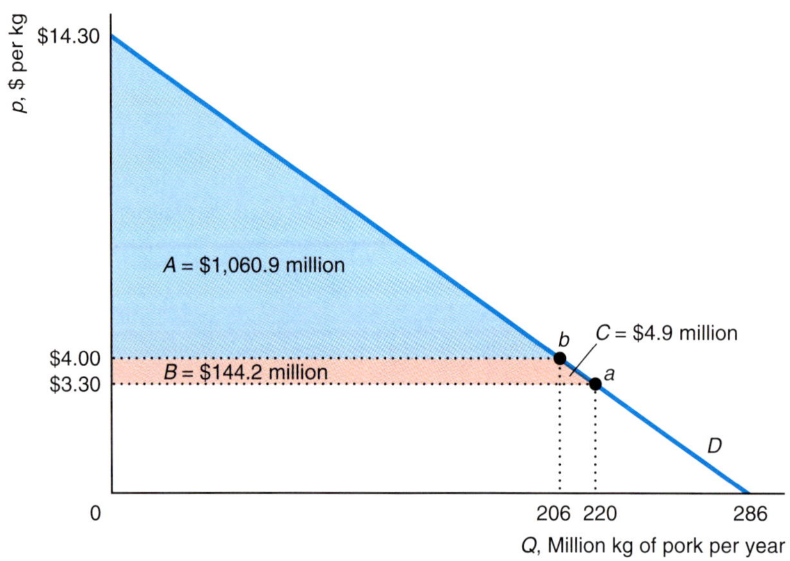

	Original Price, \$3.30	Higher Price, \$4	Change (\$ millions)
Consumer Surplus	$A + B + C$ = \$1,210	A = \$1,060.9	$-(B + C) = -149.1$

Figure 9.2 Fall in Consumer Surplus from Pork as Price Rises. As the price of pork rises 70¢ (Canadian) per kg from \$3.30 per kg, the quantity demanded falls from 220 to 206 million kg per year. The loss in consumer surplus from the higher price, areas *B* and *C*, is –\$149.1 million per year.

[2]Using the demand function from Chapter 2, $Q = 286 - 20p$, we know that the quantity demanded at \$3.30 is 220 million kg per year and the quantity demanded at \$4 is 206 million kg per year.

surplus is area $A + B + C$ = \$1,210 million per year at a price of \$3.30, and it is A = \$1,060.9 million per year at a price of \$4.[3] Thus, the loss in consumer surplus from the increase in the price is $-(B + C)$ = –\$149.1 (= 1,210 – 1060.9) million per year.

Markets in Which Consumer Surplus Losses are Large. In general, as the price increases, consumer surplus falls more (1) the greater the initial revenues spent on the good and (2) the less elastic is the demand curve.[4] More is spent on a good when its demand curve is farther to the right so that areas like A, B, and C in Figure 9.2 are larger. The larger is $B + C$, the greater is the drop in consumer surplus from a given percentage increase in price. Similarly, the less elastic is a demand curve (the closer it is to vertical), the less willing consumers are to give up the good, so consumers do not cut their consumption much as the price increases, with the result of greater consumer surplus losses.

Higher prices cause greater consumer surplus loss in some markets than in others. Consumers would benefit if policymakers, before imposing a tax, considered in which market the tax is likely to harm consumers the most.

We can use estimates of demand curves to predict for which good a price increase causes the greatest loss of consumer surplus. Table 9.1 shows the consumer surplus loss in billions of 1992 dollars from a 10% increase in the price of various goods. The table shows that the loss in consumer surplus is larger, the larger the initial revenue (price times quantity) that is spent on a good. A 10% increase in price causes a much greater loss of consumer surplus if it is imposed on food, –\$50 billion, than if it is imposed on alcohol and tobacco, –\$10.4 billion, because much more is spent on food.

At first glance, the relationship between elasticities of demand and the loss in consumer surplus in Table 9.1 looks backward: A given percent change in prices has a larger effect on consumer surplus for the relatively elastic demand curves. However, this relationship is coincidental: The large revenue goods happen to have

---

[3]The height of the $A + B + C$ triangle is \$11 = \$14.30 – \$3.30 per kg, and the base of the triangle is 220 million kg per year, so the area of the triangle is \$1,210 (= $\frac{1}{2} \times 11 \times 220$) million per year. The height of triangle A is \$10.30 (= \$14.30 – \$4) per kg, the base is 206 million kg per year, so the area is \$1,060.9 (= $\frac{1}{2} \times 10.30 \times 206$) million kg per year.

[4]If the demand curve is linear, as in Figure 9.2, the lost consumer surplus, area $B + C$, equals the sum of the area of a rectangle, $Q\Delta p$, with length Q and height Δp, plus the area of a triangle, $\frac{1}{2}\Delta Q\Delta p$, of length ΔQ and height Δp. We can approximate any demand curve with a straight line, so $\Delta CS = Q\Delta p + \frac{1}{2}\Delta Q\Delta p$ is a reasonable approximation of the true change in consumer surplus. We can rewrite this expression for ΔCS as

$$\Delta p\left[Q + \frac{1}{2}\Delta Q\right] = Q\Delta p\left[1 + \frac{1}{2}\left(\frac{\Delta Q}{Q}\frac{p}{\Delta p}\right)\frac{\Delta p}{p}\right]$$
$$= (pQ)\frac{\Delta p}{p}\left[1 + \frac{1}{2}\varepsilon\frac{\Delta p}{p}\right]$$
$$= Rx\left[1 + \frac{1}{2}\varepsilon x\right],$$

where $x = \Delta p/p$ is the percentage increase in the price, R (= pQ) is the total revenue from the sale of good Q, and ε is the elasticity of demand. (This equation is used to calculate the last column in Table 9.1.)

Table 9.1 Effect of a 10% Increase in Price on Consumer Surplus (Revenue and Consumer Surplus in Billions of 1992 Dollars)

	Revenue	Elasticity of Demand, ε	Change in Consumer Surplus, ΔCS
Food	506	–0.245	–50.0
Housing	424	–0.633	–41.1
Medical	277	–0.604	–26.9
Transportation	238	–0.461	–23.3
Clothing	231	–0.405	–22.6
Utilities	122	–0.448	–11.9
Alcohol and tobacco	105	–0.162	–10.4

Source: The elasticities and revenues are from Blanciforti (1982).

relatively elastic demand curves. The effect of a price change depends on both revenue and the demand elasticity. In this table, the relative size of the revenues is more important than the relative elasticities.

If we could hold revenue constant and vary the elasticity, we would find that consumer surplus loss from a price increase is larger as the demand curve becomes less elastic. If the demand curve for alcohol and tobacco were 10 times more elastic, –1.62, while the revenue stayed the same—the demand curve became flatter at the initial price and quantity—the consumer surplus from a 10% price increase would be only \$9.6 million instead of \$10.4 million.

SOLVED PROBLEM 9.1

Suppose two linear demand curves go through the initial equilibrium e_1. One demand curve is less elastic than the other at e_1. For which demand curve will a price increase cause the largest consumer surplus loss?

Answer

1. *Draw the two demand curves and indicate which one is less elastic at the initial equilibrium*: Two demand curves cross at e_1 in Figure 9.3. The steeper demand curve is less elastic at e_1.[5]

[5]As we discussed in Chapter 3, the price elasticity of demand, ε, = $(\Delta Q/\Delta p)(p/Q)$, is 1 over the slope of the demand curve, $\Delta p/\Delta Q$, times the ratio of the price to the quantity. At the point of intersection, where both demand curves have the same price, p_1, and quantity, Q_1, the steeper the demand curve, the lower is the elasticity of demand.

2. *Illustrate that a price increase causes a larger consumer surplus loss with the less elastic demand curve*: If the price rises from p_1 to p_2, the consumer surplus falls by only $-C$ with the relatively elastic demand curve and by $-C - D$ with the relatively inelastic demand curve. ■

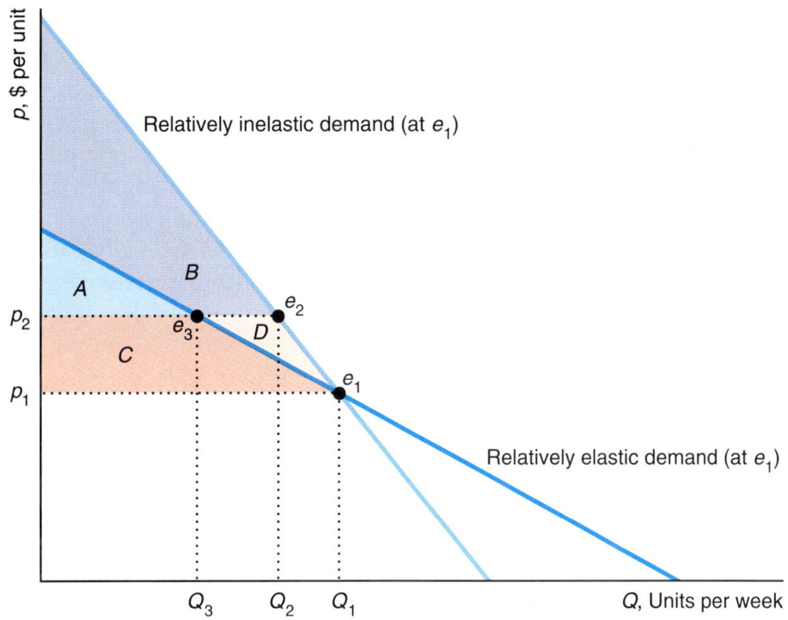

	Relatively Elastic Demand Curve	Relatively Inelastic Demand Curve
Consumer Surplus at p_1	$A + C$	$A + B + C + D$
Consumer Surplus at p_2	A	$A + B$
Consumer Surplus Loss	$-C$	$-C - D$

Figure 9.3 A Price Increase Causes a Larger Consumer Surplus Loss When Demand Is Relatively Inelastic. At the initial price, p_1, consumers buy Q_1 quantity at point e_1 on either demand curve. If the price rises to p_2, demand falls to Q_2 on the demand curve that is relatively inelastic at e_1 and to Q_3 on the other demand curve. After the price increase, consumer surplus is $A + B$ with the relatively inelastic demand curve (a loss of consumer surplus of $-C - D$) and A with the elastic demand curve (a loss of $-C$). The loss in consumer surplus is greater with the less elastic demand curve.

9.2 PRODUCER WELFARE

A supplier's gain from participating in the market is measured by its **producer surplus** (*PS*), which is the difference between the amount for which a good sells and the minimum amount necessary for the seller to be willing to produce the good. The minimum amount a seller must receive to be willing to produce is the firm's avoidable production cost (the shut-down rule in Chapter 8).

Measuring Producer Surplus Using a Supply Curve

To determine a competitive firm's producer surplus, we use its supply curve: its marginal cost curve above its minimum average variable cost (Chapter 8). The firm's supply curve in panel a of Figure 9.4 looks like a staircase. The marginal cost of producing the first unit is $MC_1 = \$1$, which is the area under the marginal cost curve between 0 and 1. The marginal cost of producing two units is $MC_2 = \$2$, and so on. The variable cost, *VC*, of producing four units is the sum of the marginal costs for the first four units: $VC = MC_1 + MC_2 + MC_3 + MC_4 = \$1 + \$2 + \$3 + \$4 = \$10$.

If the market price, p, is \$4, the firm's revenue from the sale of the first unit exceeds its cost by $PS_1 = p - MC_1 = \$4 - \$1 = \$3$, which is its producer surplus on the first unit. The firm's producer surplus is \$2 on the second unit and \$1 on the third unit. On the fourth unit, the price equals marginal cost, so the firm just breaks even. As a result, the firm's total producer surplus, *PS*, from selling four units at \$4 each is the sum of its producer surplus on these four units: $PS = PS_1 + PS_2 + PS_3 + PS_4 = \$3 + \$2 + \$1 + \$0 = \$6$. Graphically, the total producer surplus is the area above the supply curve and below the market price up to the quantity actually produced. This same reasoning holds when the firm's supply curve is smooth.

Producer Surplus and Profits. The producer surplus is closely related to profits. Producer surplus is revenue, *R*, minus variable cost, *VC*:

$$PS = R - VC.$$

In panel a of Figure 9.4, revenue is $\$4 \times 4 = \$16$ and variable cost is \$10, so producer surplus is \$6.

Profit is revenue minus total cost, *C*, which equals variable cost plus fixed cost, *F*:

$$\pi = R - C = R - (VC + F).$$

Figure 9.4 Producer Surplus. (a) The firm's producer surplus, \$6, is the area below the market price, \$4, and above the marginal cost (supply curve) up to the quantity, 4, sold. The area under the marginal cost curve up to the number of units actually produced is the variable cost of production. (b) The market producer surplus is the area above the supply curve and below the line at the market price, p^*, up to the quantity produced, Q^*. The area below the supply curve and to the left of the quantity produced by the market, Q^*, is the variable cost of producing that level of output.

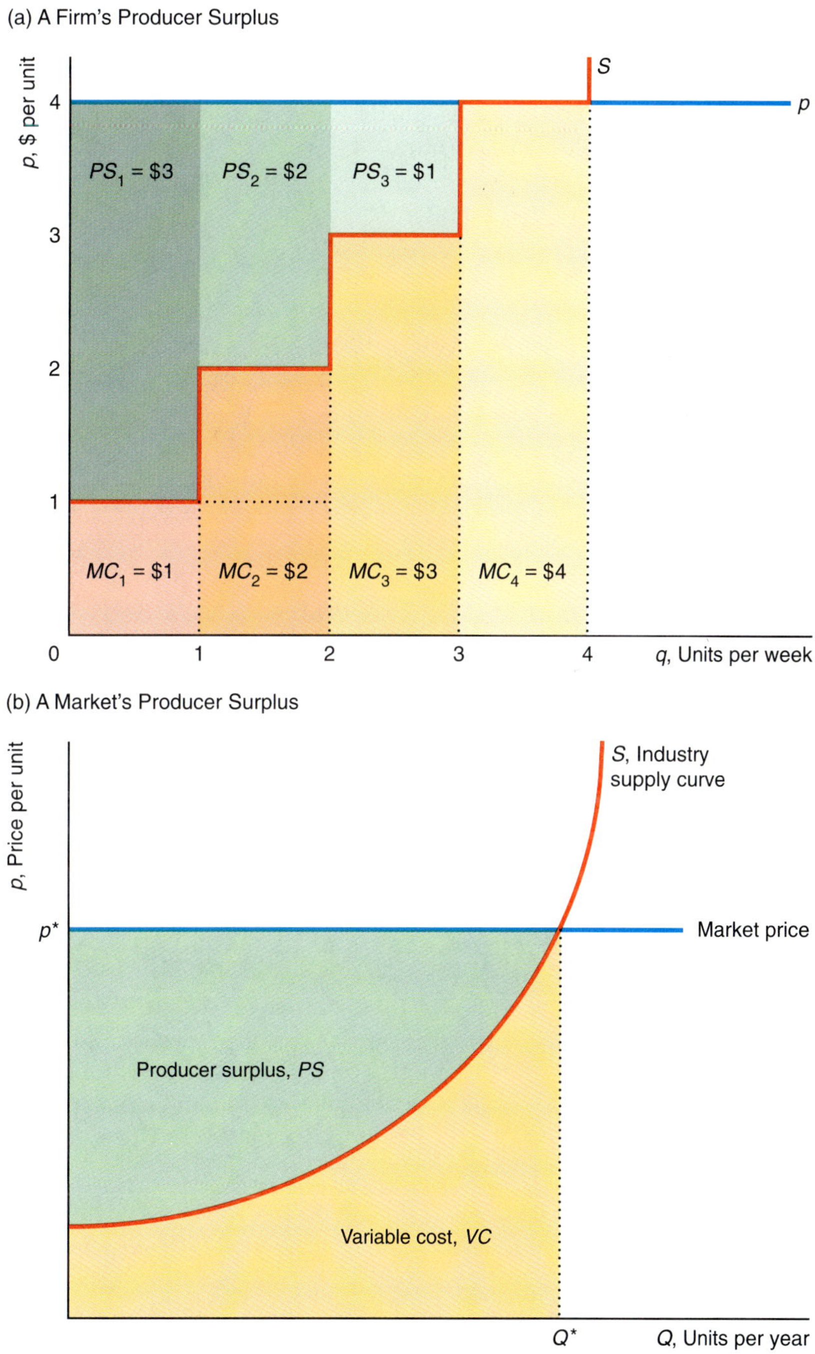
(a) A Firm's Producer Surplus
p, $ per unit
S
p
PS1 = $3
PS2 = $2
PS3 = $1
MC1 = $1
MC2 = $2
MC3 = $3
MC4 = $4
0
1
2
3
4
q, Units per week
(b) A Market's Producer Surplus
p, Price per unit
S, Industry supply curve
p*
Market price
Producer surplus, PS
Variable cost, VC
Q*
Q, Units per year

In the short run, the difference between producer surplus and profit is fixed cost, F. In the long run, in which fixed cost is zero, there is no important distinction between the two concepts.

Producer Surplus as a Gain to Trade. Another interpretation of producer surplus is as a gain to trade. In the short run, if the firm produces and sells its good—trades—it earns a profit of $R - VC - F$. If the firm shuts down—does not trade—it loses its fixed cost of $-F$. Thus, producer surplus equals the profit from trade minus the profit (loss) from not trading of

$$(R - VC - F) - (-F) = R - VC = PS.$$

Using Producer Surplus

Even in the short run, we can use producer surplus to study the effects of any shock that does not affect the fixed cost of firms, such as a change in the price of a substitute or an input. Such shocks change profit by exactly the same amount as they change producer surplus because fixed costs do not change.

A major advantage of producer surplus is that we can use it to measure the effect of a shock on *all* the firms in a market without having to measure the profit of each firm in the market separately. We can calculate market producer surplus using the market supply curve in the same way as we calculate a firm's producer surplus using its supply curve. The market producer surplus in panel b of Figure 9.4 is the area above the supply curve and below the market price, p^*, line up to the quantity sold, Q^*. The market supply curve is the horizontal sum of the marginal cost curves of each of the firms (Chapter 8). As a result, the variable cost for all the firms in the market of producing Q is the area under the supply curve between 0 and the market output, Q.

SOLVED PROBLEM 9.2

How much producer surplus is lost when the market price of pork falls from \$3.30 to \$2.95 per kg? (*Hint:* Using the supply function of pork from Chapter 2, we know that firms supply 220 million kg of processed pork per year when price is \$3.30 and 206 million kg per year when price is \$2.95.)

Answer

1. *Draw the supply curve and show the change in producer surplus from the price change*: Figure 9.5 shows the supply curve for processed pork (based on Moschini and Meilke 1992). Point a is the supply at the original price, and b is the supply at the lower price. The loss in producer surplus is the sum of rectangle D and triangle E.

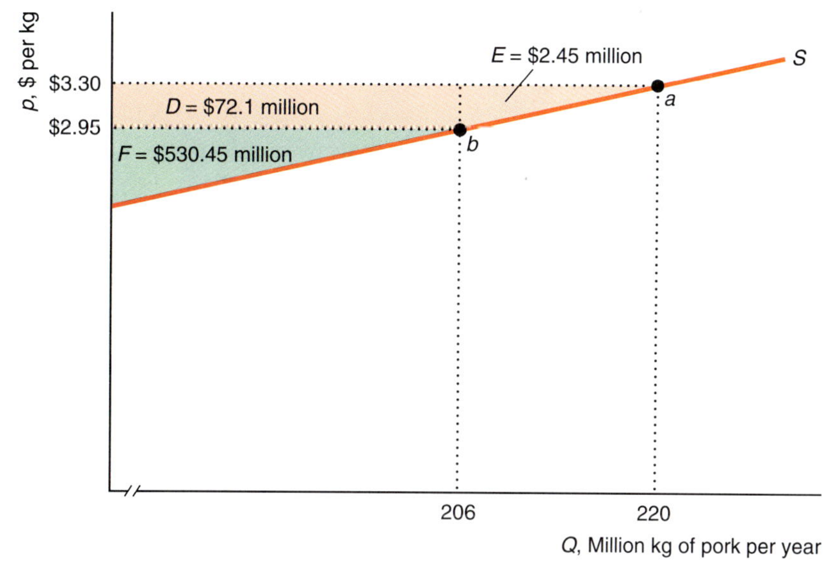

	Original Price, \$3.30	Lower Price, \$2.95	Change (\$ millions)
Producer Surplus	$D + E + F$	F	$-D - E = -74.55$

Figure 9.5 Effect of a Fall in the Price of Pork on Producer Surplus. The loss in producer surplus, \$74.55 million, from a 35¢ fall in price is the sum of the rectangle D = \$72.1 million and the triangle E = \$2.45 million.

2. *Calculate the lost producer surplus by adding areas of rectangle D and triangle E*: The height of both D and E is the difference between the original price and the new price, 35¢. The length of D is 206, and the length of E is 14 million kg per year. Area D (not all of which is shown in the figure because the quantity axis starts at 175) is (\$0.35 per kg) × (206 million kg per year) = \$72.1 million per year. Area E is $\frac{1}{2}$ × (\$0.35 per kg) × (14 million kg per year) = \$2.45 million per year. Thus, the loss in producer surplus from the drop in price is \$74.55 million per year. ■

9.3 COMPETITION MAXIMIZES WELFARE

How should we measure society's welfare? There are many reasonable answers to this question. One commonly used measure of the welfare of society, W, is the sum of consumer surplus plus producer surplus:

$$W = CS + PS.$$

This measure implicitly weights the well-being of consumers and producers equally. By using this measure, we are making a value judgment that the well-being of consumers and that of producers are equally important.

Not everyone agrees that society should try to maximize this measure of welfare. Groups of producers argue for legislation that helps them even if it hurts consumers by more than the producers gain—as though only producer surplus matters. Similarly, some consumer advocates argue that we should care only about consumers, so social welfare should include only consumer surplus.[6]

We use the consumer surplus plus producer surplus measure of welfare in this chapter (and postpone a further discussion of other welfare concepts until the next chapter). One of the most striking results in economics is that competitive markets maximize this measure of welfare. If either less or more output than the competitive level is produced, welfare falls.

Producing Less Than the Competitive Output Lowers Welfare

Producing less than the competitive output lowers welfare. At the competitive equilibrium in Figure 9.6, e_1, where output is Q_1 and price is p_1, consumer surplus equals areas $CS_1 = A + B + C$, producer surplus is $PS_1 = D + E$, and total welfare is $W_1 = A + B + C + D + E$. If output is reduced to Q_2 so price rises to p_2 at e_2, consumer surplus is $CS_2 = A$, producer surplus is $PS_2 = B + D$, and welfare is $W_2 = A + B + D$.

The change in consumer surplus is

$$\Delta CS = CS_2 - CS_1 = A - (A + B + C) = -B - C.$$

Consumers lose $-B$ because they have to pay $p_2 - p_1$ more than at the competitive price for the Q_2 units they buy. Consumers lose $-C$ because they buy only Q_2 rather than Q_1 at the higher price.

The change in producer surplus is

$$\Delta PS = PS_2 - PS_1 = (B + D) - (D + E) = B - E.$$

Producers gain B because they now sell Q_2 units at p_2 rather than p_1. They lose E because they sell $Q_2 - Q_1$ fewer units.

The change in welfare, $\Delta W = W_2 - W_1$, is[7]

$$\Delta W = \Delta CS + \Delta PS = (-B - C) + (B - E) = -C - E.$$

---

[6]Such a conclusion would not really follow from a desire to help consumers. Suppliers or producers are consumers of other goods. Changes in producers' surplus affect their incomes and hence their ability to buy other goods and the consumer surplus they receive from those goods. Moreover, the distinction between buyers and sellers is not always a clean one. Children (and these days, adults) who trade old baseball cards may act as both buyers and sellers. A law that reduced the price at which cards can be sold would benefit people when they were buyers but would harm them as sellers.

[7]The change in welfare is

$$\Delta W = W_2 - W_1 = (CS_2 + PS_2) - (CS_1 + PS_1) = (CS_2 - CS_1) + (PS_2 - PS_1) = \Delta CS + \Delta PS.$$

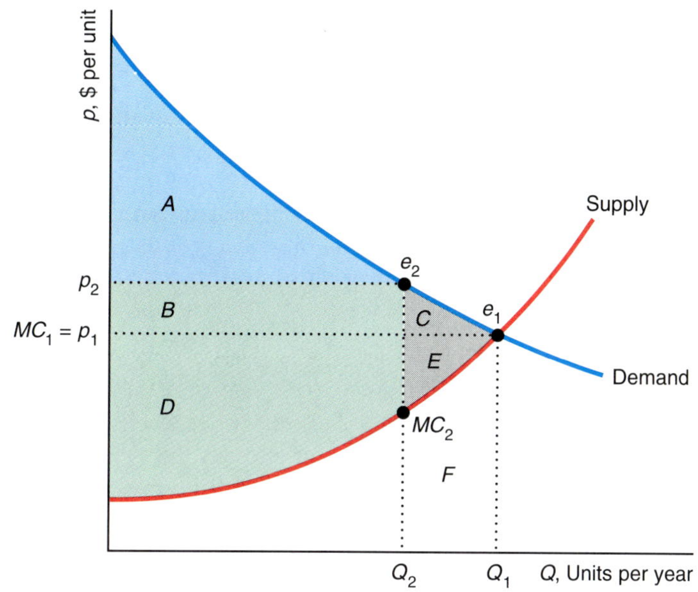

	Competitive Output, Q_1 (1)	Smaller Output, Q_2 (2)	Change (2) – (1)
Consumer Surplus, *CS*	$A + B + C$	A	$-B - C = \Delta CS$
Producer Surplus, *PS*	$D + E$	$B + D$	$B - E = \Delta PS$
Welfare, $W = CS + PS$	$A + B + C + D + E$	$A + B + D$	$-C - E = \Delta W = DWL$

Figure 9.6 Reducing Output from the Competitive Level Lowers Welfare. Reducing output from the competitive level, Q_1, to Q_2 increases price from p_1 to p_2. Consumers suffer: Consumer surplus is now A, a fall of $\Delta CS = -B - C$. Producers may gain or lose: Producer surplus is now $B + D$, a change of $\Delta PS = B - E$. Overall, welfare falls by $\Delta W = -C - E$, which is a deadweight loss (DWL) to society.

The area B is a transfer from consumers to producers—the extra amount consumers pay for the Q_2 units goes to the sellers—so it does not affect welfare. Welfare drops because the consumer loss of $-C$ and the producer loss of $-E$ benefit no one. This drop in welfare, $\Delta W = -C - E$, is a **deadweight loss** (DWL): the net reduction in welfare from losses of surplus by one group that are not offset by a gain to another group from an action that alters a market equilibrium.

The deadweight loss results because consumers value extra output by more than the marginal cost of producing it. At each output between Q_2 and Q_1, consumers' marginal willingness to pay for another unit—the height of the demand curve—is greater than the marginal cost of producing the next unit—the height of the supply curve. For example, at e_2, consumers value the next unit of output at p_2, which is much greater than the marginal cost, MC_2, of producing it. Increasing output from Q_2 to Q_1 raises firms' variable cost by area F, the area under the marginal cost (supply) curve between Q_2 and Q_1. Consumers value this extra output by the area under the demand curve between Q_2 and Q_1, area $C + E + F$. Thus, consumers value the extra output by $C + E$ more than it costs to produce it.

Society would be better off producing and consuming extra units of this good than spending this amount on other goods. In short, *the deadweight loss is the opportunity cost of giving up some of this good to buy more of another good.*

Producing More Than the Competitive Output Lowers Welfare

Increasing output beyond the competitive level also decreases welfare because the cost of producing this extra output exceeds the value consumers place on it. Figure 9.7 shows the effect of increasing output from the competitive level Q_1 to Q_2 and letting the price fall to p_2, point e_2 on the demand curve, so consumers buy the extra output.

Because price falls from p_1 to p_2, consumer surplus rises by

$$\Delta CS = C + D + E,$$

which is the area between p_2 and p_1 to the left of the demand curve. At the original price, p_1, producer surplus was $C + F$. The cost of producing the larger output is the area under the supply curve up to Q_2, $B + D + E + F + G$. The firms sell this quantity for only p_2Q_2, area $F + G + H$. Thus, the new producer surplus is $F - B - D - E$. As a result, the increase in output causes producer surplus to fall by

$$\Delta PS = -B - C - D - E.$$

Because producers lose more than consumers gain, the deadweight loss is

$$\Delta W = \Delta CS + \Delta PS = (C + D + E) + (-B - C - D - E) = -B.$$

A net loss occurs because consumers value the $Q_2 - Q_1$ extra output by only $E + H$, which is less than the extra cost, $B + E + H$, of producing it. The new price, p_2, is less than the marginal cost, MC_2, of producing Q_2. Too much is being produced.

The reason that competition maximizes welfare is that price equals marginal cost in the competitive equilibrium. In the competitive equilibrium, demand equals supply, which ensures that price equals marginal cost. When price equals marginal cost, consumers value the last unit of output by exactly the amount that it costs to produce it. If consumers value the last unit by more than the marginal cost of production, welfare rises if more is produced. Similarly, if consumers value the last unit by less than its marginal cost, welfare is higher at a lower level of production.

A **market failure** is inefficient production or consumption, often because a price exceeds marginal cost. In the next application, we show that the surplus of the recipient of a gift is less than the cost of the giver.

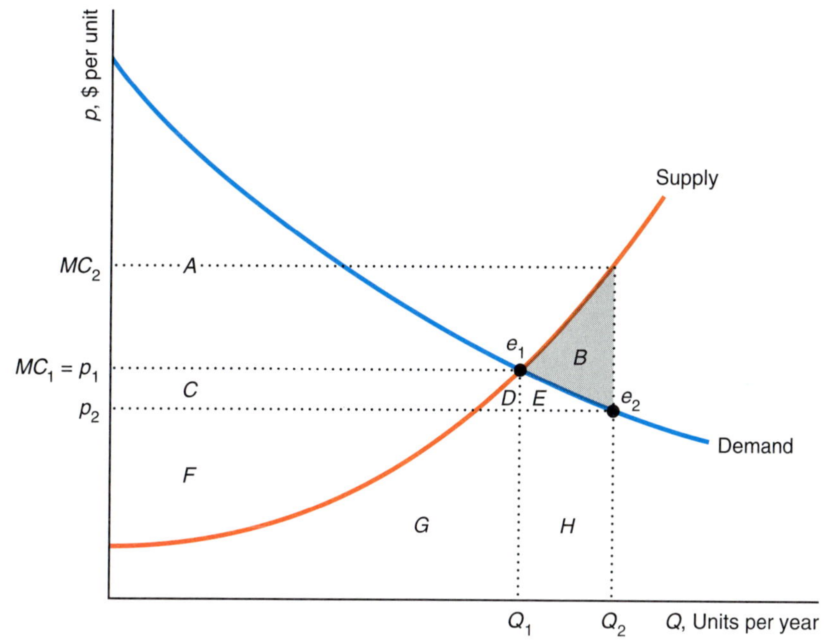

	Competitive Output, Q_1	Larger Output, Q_2	Change
Consumer Surplus, *CS*	A	$A + C + D + E$	$C + D + E = \Delta CS$
Producer Surplus, *PS*	$C + F$	$F - B - D - E$	$-B - C - D - E = \Delta PS$
Welfare, $W = CS + PS$	$A + C + F$	$A + C + E - B$	$-B = \Delta W = DWL$

Figure 9.7 **Increasing Output from the Competitive Level Lowers Welfare.** Increasing output from the competitive level, Q_1, to Q_2 lowers the price from p_1 to p_2. Consumer surplus rises by $C + D + E$, producer surplus falls by $-B - C - D - E$, and welfare falls by $-B$, which is a deadweight loss to society.

APPLICATION

Deadweight Loss of Christmas Presents

Just how much did you enjoy the expensive woolen socks with the dancing purple teddy bears on the international orange background that your Aunt Fern gave you last Christmas? Often, the cost of a gift exceeds the value that the recipient places on the gift.

A gift of cash typically gives as much or more pleasure to the recipient than a gift that costs the same but can't be exchanged for cash. (So what if giving cash is tacky?) Of course, it's possible that a gift can give more pleasure to the recipient than it costs the giver—but how often does that happen to you?

An "efficient" gift is one that the recipient values as much as the gift costs the giver. The difference between the price of the gift and its value to the recipient is a deadweight loss to society. Joel Waldfogel (1993) asked Yale undergraduates just how large this deadweight loss is. He estimates that the deadweight loss is between 10% and 33% of the value of gifts. He finds that gifts from friends and "significant others" are most efficient, while noncash gifts from members of the extended family are least efficient (one-third of the value is lost). Luckily, grandparents, aunts, and uncles are most likely to give cash.

Given holiday expenditures of about $40 billion per year in the United States, he concludes that a conservative estimate of the deadweight loss of Christmas, Hanukkah, and other holidays with gift-giving rituals is between a tenth and a third as large as estimates of the deadweight loss from inefficient income taxation.

The question remains why people don't give cash instead of presents. If the reason is that they get pleasure from picking the "perfect" gift, the deadweight loss that adjusts for the pleasure of the giver is lower than these calculations suggest. (Bah, humbug!) ■

9.4 POLICIES THAT SHIFT SUPPLY CURVES

> *I know more about the private lives of celebrities than I do about any governmental policy that will actually affect me. . . . Maybe the economy should be discussed in cheap motel rooms.* —Calvin & Hobbes

One of the main reasons that economists developed these welfare tools was to predict the impact of government policies and other events that alter a competitive equilibrium, which we consider next. We focus on government policies rather than other shocks caused by random events or other members of society because we—as part of the electorate—can influence these decisions.

Virtually all government actions affect a competitive equilibrium in one of two ways. Some government policies, such as limits on the number of firms in a market, shift the supply or demand curve. Other government actions, such as sales taxes, create a wedge between price and marginal cost so that they are not equal, as they were in the original competitive equilibrium.

These government actions move us from an unconstrained competitive equilibrium to a new, constrained competitive equilibrium. Because welfare was maximized in the initial competitive equilibrium, the following examples of government-induced changes lower welfare. In later chapters, we examine markets in which welfare was not maximized initially, so government intervention may raise welfare.

Although government policies may cause either the supply curve or the demand curve to shift, we concentrate on policies that limit supply because they are frequently used and have clear-cut effects. The two most common types of government policies that shift the supply curve are limits on the number of firms in a market and quotas or other limits on the amount of output that firms may produce. We study restrictions on entry and exit of firms in this section and examine quotas later in the chapter.

Government policies that cause a decrease in supply at each possible price (shift the supply curve to the left) lead to fewer purchases by consumers at higher prices, an outcome that lowers consumer surplus and welfare. Welfare falls when governments restrict the consumption of competitive products that we all agree are *goods*, such as food and medical services. In contrast, if most of society wants to discourage the use of certain products, such as hallucinogenic drugs and poisons, policies that restrict consumption may increase some measures of society's welfare.

Governments, other organizations, and social pressures limit the number of firms in at least three ways. The number of firms is restricted explicitly in some markets, such as the one for taxi service. In other markets, some members of society are barred from owning firms or performing certain jobs or services. In yet other markets, the number of firms is controlled indirectly by raising the cost of entry.

Restricting the Number of Firms

A limit on the number of firms causes a shift of the supply curve to the left, which raises the equilibrium price and reduces the equilibrium quantity. Consumers are harmed: They don't buy as much as they would at lower prices. Firms that are in the market when the limits are first imposed benefit from higher profits.

To illustrate these results, we examine the regulation of taxicabs. Virtually every country in the world regulates taxicabs (except Sweden, which deregulated in 1991). Many American cities limit the number of taxicabs. To operate a cab in these cities legally, you must possess a city-issued permit, which may be a piece of paper or a medallion (a coinlike metal object).

Two explanations are given for such regulation. First, using permits to limit the number of cabs raises the earnings of permit owners—usually taxi fleet owners—who lobby city officials for such restrictions. Second, some city officials contend that limiting cabs allows for better regulation of cabbies' behavior and protection of consumers. (It would seem possible, however, that cities could directly regulate behavior and not restrict the number of cabs.)

Whatever the justification for such regulation, the limit on the number of cabs raises the market prices. If the city doesn't limit entry, a virtually unlimited number of potential taxi drivers with identical costs can enter freely.

Panel a of Figure 9.8 shows a typical taxi owner's marginal cost curve, MC, and average cost curve, AC^1. An outward shift of the demand curve is met by new firms entering, so the long-run supply curve of taxi rides, S^1 in panel b, is horizontal at AC^1 (Chapter 8). For the market demand curve in the figure, the equilibrium is E_1, where the equilibrium price, p_1, equals the minimum of AC^1 of a typical cab. The total number of rides is $Q_1 = n_1 q_1$, where n_1 is the equilibrium number of cabs and q_1 is the number of rides per month provided by a typical cab.

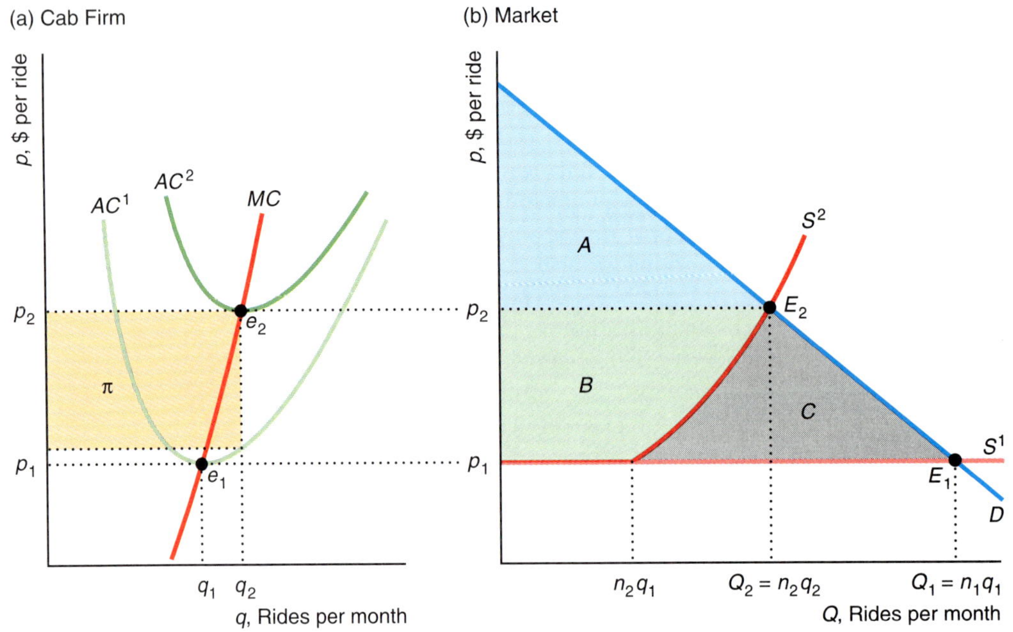

	No Restrictions	Restrictions	Change
Consumer Surplus, CS	$A + B + C$	A	$-B - C = \Delta CS$
Producer Surplus, PS	0	B	$B = \Delta PS$
Welfare, $W = CS + PS$	$A + B + C$	$A + B$	$-C = \Delta W = DWL$

Figure 9.8 Effect of a Restriction on the Number of Cabs. A restriction on the number of cabs causes the supply curve to shift from S^1 to S^2 in the short run, and the equilibrium to change from E_1 to E_2. The resulting lost surplus, $-C$, is a deadweight loss to society. In the long run, the unusual profit, π, created by the restriction becomes a rent to the owner of the license. As the license owner increases the charge for using the license, the average cost curve rises to AC^2, so the cab driver earns a zero long-run profit. That is, the producer surplus goes to the permit holder, not to the cab driver.

Consumer surplus, $A + B + C$, is the area under the market demand curve above p_1 up to Q_1. There is no producer surplus because the supply curve is horizontal at the market price, which equals marginal and average cost. Thus, welfare is the same as consumer surplus.

Legislation limits the number of permits to operate cabs to $n_2 < n_1$. The market supply curve, S^2, is the horizontal sum of the marginal cost curves above minimum average cost of the n_2 firms in the market. For the market to produce more than n_2q_1 rides, the price must rise to induce the n_2 firms to supply more.

With the same demand curve as before, the equilibrium market price rises to p_2. At this higher price, each licensed cab firm produces more than before by operating longer hours, $q_2 > q_1$, but the total number of rides, $Q_2 = n_2q_2$, falls because there are fewer cabs, n_2. Consumer surplus is A, producer surplus is B, and welfare is $A + B$.

Thus, because of the higher fares (prices) under a permit system, consumer surplus falls by

$$\Delta CS = -B - C.$$

The producer surplus of the lucky permit owners rises by

$$\Delta PS = B.$$

As a result, total welfare falls:

$$\Delta W = \Delta CS + \Delta PS = (-B - C) + B = -C,$$

which is a deadweight loss.

By preventing other potential cab firms from entering the market, limiting cab permits creates economic profit, the area labeled π in panel a, for permit owners. In many cities, these permits can be sold or rented, so the owner of the scarce resource, the permit, can capture the unusual profit, or *rent* (Chapter 8). The rent for the permit or the implicit rent paid by the owner of a permit causes the cab driver's average cost to rise to AC^2. Cab drivers earn zero economic profits because the market price, p_2, equals their average cost, the minimum of AC^2. The producer surplus, B, created by the limits on entry go to the original owners of the permits rather than to the current cab drivers. Thus, the permit owners are the *only* ones that benefit from the restrictions, and their gains are less than the losses to others.

In many cities, the rents and welfare effects that result from these laws are large. The size of the loss to consumers and the benefit to permit holders depend on how severely a city limits the number of cabs.

APPLICATION

Taxicab Medallions

Limiting the number of cabs has large effects in San Francisco, New York, and many other U.S. cities.[8] Only 856 cabs have permits to operate legally

---

[8]The following discussion is based on Fisher, Ian, "A Bumpier Ride for New York Taxis," *New York Times*, October 6, 1991:7; Marshall, Jonathan, "Cab Companies Haled into Court," *San Francisco Chronicle*, July 1, 1993:A1, A11; Fragin, Sheryl, "Taxi!" *The Atlantic Monthly*, 273(5), May 1994:30f; and Bowman, Catherine, "Why San Francisco Taxis Are Catch as Catch Can," *San Francisco Chronicle*, September 16, 1995:A1, A11.

in San Francisco, a tenth as many as in Washington, D.C., which has a smaller population but does not restrict the number of cabs. San Francisco does not allow the permits to be resold. The 3,500 active cab drivers rent medallions from permit holders for $80 per 10-hour shift. Many San Francisco permit holders lease their permits for $1,800 a month to taxi companies (which own only about a quarter of all permits). Thus, each permit is worth $21,600 a year, and the 856 permits are collectively worth approximately $18.5 million a year. This rent is the extra producer surplus of the lucky permit holders that would be eliminated if anyone could supply taxi services.

In 1937, when New York City started regulating the number of cabs, all 11,787 cab owners received permits in the form of medallions. New York City allows these medallions to be sold. Thus, a medallion holder does not actually have to operate the cab to benefit from the restriction on the number of cabs. The owner of a medallion can sell it for an amount that captures the unusually high future profits from the limit on the number of cabs. Cab drivers who lease medallions certainly don't make these unusual returns: Some earn as little as $50 a day.

Even by the late 1940s, people must have believed that the number of cabs with permits was not much different from the equilibrium number in the absence of this law because permits sold for very little money. Apparently, this limit has become more binding over time: The price of a medallion nearly tripled from 1980 to 1989 to $140,000. The price of a medallion increased another 30% from 1989 to 1993 to $182,000.

A 1984 study for the U.S. Department of Transportation estimated the annual extra cost to consumers from restrictions on the number of taxicabs throughout the United States at nearly $800 million. The total lost consumer surplus exceeds $800 million, because this amount does not include lost waiting time and other inconveniences associated with having fewer taxis. ■

Excluding Certain Groups from Owning Firms

By excluding certain groups, other groups can limit the number of firms or service providers in a market. If the favored group has so few firms that they earn economic profits, the exclusion of the other group restricts the total number of firms in the market. Such restrictions harm consumers and benefit members of the favored group who own firms.

APPLICATION

Discriminating Against Groups

Sometimes by themselves and sometimes with the help of governments, certain groups have excluded other groups from owning firms or providing certain services. Examples include unions and guilds and apartheid.

Unions and Guilds

Historically, only members of unions and guilds could run certain types of firms or perform certain services. As these groups limited membership, the number of firms was similarly limited.

Many guilds and unions were able to enforce these restrictions themselves. Some, however, relied on governments to enforce these restrictions.

During the first half of this century in New York, only members of the Bagel Bakers' Local 338 could make bagels legally.[9] As a result, there were relatively few bagel makers. Today, anyone with $100,000 to $200,000 can enter the market by buying a bagel bakery package, which includes cooking equipment and just about anything else needed to start a firm. The number of firms selling bagels has greatly increased since these restrictions ended. Eliminating this restriction raised consumer surplus because people buy more at lower prices.[10] Ending the restriction reduced producer surplus of firms that were protected from competition.

Apartheid

For years, apartheid laws denied black South Africans the right to own property, restricted where they could work, and made it difficult for them to obtain loans needed to start and run businesses. Since the repeal of the Group Areas Act in May 1991, which effectively ended apartheid, new black-owned businesses entered markets in previously white-only central business districts of South Africa.

For example, Africa Hut offers pap (a stiff corn porridge) served with malamagodu (tripe) or morogo (a leafy green vegetable), samp (a mixture of

---

[9]Burros, Marian, "Eating Well," *New York Times*, July 6, 1994:B7.

[10]According to Gary Gerdemann, spokesman for Einstein Bros. Bagels, "Bagels are the hottest thing since sliced bread. In fact, they are sliced bread." Bagel sales have shot up in the last decade: 3.5% of Americans eat bagels in the home for breakfast—triple the share of a decade ago; and 5.5% of Americans eat bagels outside the home—a 150% increase. Retail sales of bagels increased fourfold from $0.4 billion in retail sales in 1993 to $1.6 billion in 1995. The estimated sales in 1996 were $2.3 billion. Canedy, Dan, "The Shmeering of America," *New York Times*, December 26, 1996:C1.

hominy and beans) and steak, skop (sheep heads), and fat cakes (a greasy fried dough) while "township jive" blares in the background.[11] Until recently, these African foods were not available in downtown Johannesburg, where one found American-style chicken and burger shops on every corner.

Africa Hut has many customers. One reason is price: A large portion of pap with chicken stew and morogo costs about $1.60, half of the price of a two-piece chicken dinner at a KFC outlet across the street. Because it is cost-effective, this restaurant is thriving. By 1994, the black and white investors in Africa Hut already had three locations in Johannesburg, expected to open ten franchises throughout South Africa soon, and were planning to acquire a U.S. trademark. The end of apartheid resulted in entry by many black-owned firms in a variety of markets. This new entry benefits consumers, who can buy more varied food at lower prices, and harms white-owned firms that were receiving unusually high profits under apartheid.

In the United States, Canada, the United Kingdom, and many other countries, barriers to various ethnic, racial, and gender groups are created by *discrimination* rather than by overt government acts. To the degree that discrimination keeps racial minorities, women, or other groups from fully participating in the market, it reduces the degree of competition in that market. ■

Raising Entry and Exit Costs

Instead of directly restricting the number of firms that may enter a market, governments and other organizations may raise the cost of entering, thereby indirectly restricting that number. Similarly, raising the cost of exiting a market discourages some firms from entering.

Entry Barriers. If its cost will be greater than that of firms already in the market, a potential firm might not enter a market even if existing firms are making a profit. Any cost that falls only on potential entrants and not on current firms discourages entry. A long-run **barrier to entry** is an explicit restriction or a cost that applies only to potential new firms—existing firms are not subject to the restriction or do not bear the cost.

At the time they entered, incumbent firms had to pay many of the costs of entering a market that new entrants incur, such as the fixed costs of building plants and buying equipment. For example, the fixed cost to McDonald's and other fast-food chains of opening a new fast-food restaurant is about $2 million. These fixed costs are *costs of entry* but are *not* barriers to entry in our definition because they apply equally to incumbents and entrants. Costs incurred by both

[11] "It's Soul Food at Africa Hut," *San Francisco Chronicle*, June 8, 1994:C1.

incumbents and entrants do not discourage potential firms from entering a market if existing firms are making money. Potential entrants know that they will do as well as existing firms once they are in business, so they are willing to enter as long as profit opportunities exist.[12]

If barriers to entry limit the ability of firms to enter a market in response to a profit opportunity, equilibrium price and firms' profits may remain high indefinitely. When a federal court declared unconstitutional a 50-year-old statute that allowed only five wholesalers to sell milk in New York City, a new firm entered the market and the price per gallon fell 70¢, producing a savings to consumers of $80 million a year.[13]

There are many, varied government-created barriers to entry. Laws frequently require that new factories be built with extra features to prevent pollution or avoid seismic problems, while exempting older factories. Many U.S. communities imposed the bizarre rule that potential psychiatric hospitals had to incur the expense of "proving" that there was a need for more hospitals in the community.

Exit Barriers. Some markets have barriers that make it difficult (though, typically, not impossible) for a firm to exit by going out of business. In the short run, exit barriers can keep the number of firms in a market relatively high. In the long run, exit barriers may limit the number of firms in a market.

Why do exit barriers limit the number of firms in a market? Suppose you are considering starting a construction firm with no capital or other fixed factors. The firm's only input is labor. You know that there is relatively little demand for construction during business downturns and in the winter. To avoid paying workers when business is slack, you plan to shut down during those periods. If you can avoid losses by shutting down during those periods, you enter this market if your expected economic profits during good periods are zero or positive.

Now suppose that a new law requires that you give your workers six months' warning before laying them off. Because the new law prevents you from shutting down quickly, you know that you'll regularly suffer losses during business downturns because you'll have to pay your workers for up to six months during periods when you have nothing for them to do. Knowing that you'll incur these regular losses, you are less inclined to enter the market. Unless the economic profits during good periods are much higher than zero—high enough to offset your losses—you will not enter the market.

If exit barriers limit the number of firms, then the same analysis that we used to examine entry barriers applies. Thus, exit barriers may raise prices, lower consumer surplus, and reduce welfare.

---

[12]Large sunk costs can be barriers to entry under two conditions. First, if capital markets do not work well, so new firms have difficulty raising money, new firms may be unable to enter profitable markets. Second, if a firm must incur a large *sunk* cost, which makes the loss if it exits great, the firm may be reluctant to enter a market in which it is uncertain of success.

[13]Oliver, Daniel, "Competition Deserves More Than Lip Service," Center for the Study of American Business, Contemporary Issues Series 27, March 1988.

APPLICATION

Job Termination Laws

Many government-imposed exit barriers are designed to protect workers who would be laid off in the event of a plant closure. In Canada, how far in advance employers must give notice of termination varies by the size of the firm, reaching a maximum of 16 weeks for firms with more than 300 employees. In the United Kingdom, the amount of advance warning varies with length of service, ranging from 1 week to 8 weeks for workers with 15 or more years of service.

These warning periods may raise costs to firms enough to reduce the number of firms in markets in which downturns are frequent. Thus, although these warnings help workers in some markets to prepare for layoffs, these exit barriers may reduce the number of employers in an industry—and hence the number of workers employed in that industry. ■

9.5 POLICIES THAT CREATE A WEDGE BETWEEN SUPPLY AND DEMAND

The most common government policies that create a wedge between supply and demand curves are sales taxes and price controls. Such policies frequently result in prices that are greater than marginal cost. Because consumers value the good more than it costs to produce it, these polices lower consumer surplus and welfare.

Welfare Effects of a Sales Tax

A new sales tax causes the price consumers pay to rise (Chapter 3), resulting in a loss of consumer surplus, $\Delta CS < 0$, and a fall in the price firms receive, resulting in a drop in producer surplus, $\Delta PS < 0$. However, the new tax provides the government with new tax revenue, $\Delta T = T > 0$ (if tax revenue was zero before this new tax).

Assuming that the government does something useful with the tax revenue, we should include tax revenue in our definition of welfare:

$$W = CS + PS + T.$$

As a result, the change in welfare is

$$\Delta W = \Delta CS + \Delta PS + \Delta T.$$

Even when we include tax revenue in our welfare measure, a specific tax must lower welfare in a competitive market. A specific tax of τ = \$1.05 per kg on the Canadian pork market lowers welfare.

Without a tax, the competitive equilibrium is determined by the intersection of the demand curve and the supply curve at e_1, where Q_1 = 220 million kg of pork are sold at p_1 = \$3.30 per kg in Figure 9.9. Consumer surplus is $A + B + C$; producer surplus is $D + E + F$, tax revenue is zero, and there is no deadweight loss.

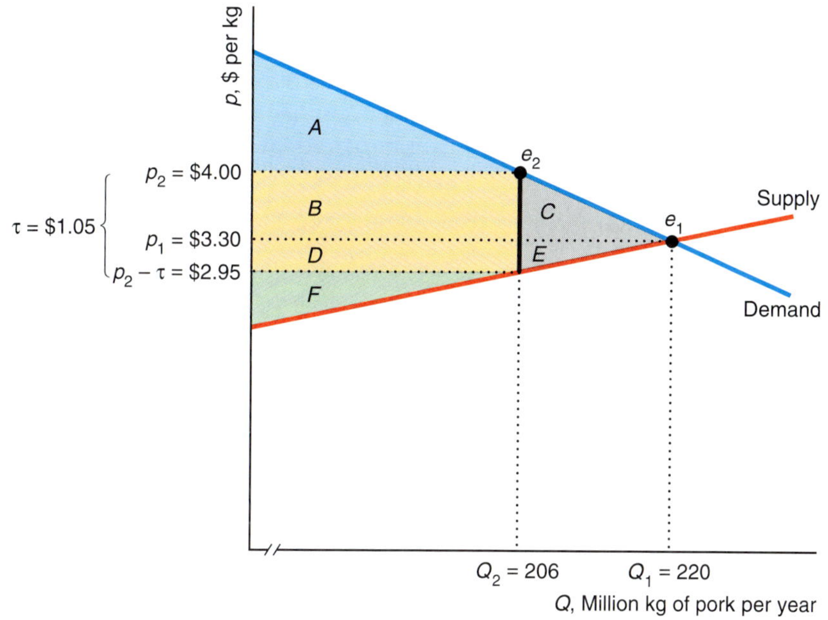

	No Tax	Specific Tax	Change ($ millions)
Consumer Surplus, *CS*	$A + B + C$	A	$-B - C = -149.1 = \Delta CS$
Producer Surplus, *PS*	$D + E + F$	F	$-D - E = -74.55 = \Delta PS$
Tax Revenue, $T = \tau Q$	0	$B + D$	$B + D = 216.3 = \Delta T$
Welfare, $W = CS + PS + T$	$A + B + C + D + E + F$	$A + B + D + F$	$-C - E = -7.35 = DWL$

Figure 9.9 Welfare Effects of a Specific Tax on Pork. The τ = \$1.05 specific tax on pork creates a \$1.05 per kg wedge between the price Canadian pork consumers pay, p_2, and the price producers receive, $p_2 - \tau$. Tax revenues are $T = \tau Q_2$ = \$216.3 million per year. The deadweight loss to society is $-C - E$ = −\$7.35 million per year.

The specific tax creates a \$1.05 wedge (Chapter 3) between the price consumers pay, p_2 = \$4, and the price producers receive, $p_2 - \tau$ = \$2.95.[14] Equilibrium output falls to Q_2 = 206 million kg of pork per year.

[14]Instead of using a wedge, we can think of the tax as shifting the demand curve downward and use it to determine the after-tax equilibrium. If we do that, however, we should use the original demand curve, which shows consumers' true willingness to pay, and the original supply curve, which shows the firms' actual marginal costs, to determine consumer surplus and producer surplus. The new "after-tax demand curve" is only a hypothetical demand curve that we use to determine the equilibrium.

The price increase to consumers of 70¢ per kg causes consumer surplus to fall by $-B - C$ = –\$149.1 million, as we showed earlier. The 35¢ reduction in the price received by firms causes them to lose producer surplus of $-D - E$ = –\$74.55 million (Solved Problem 9.2). The government gains tax revenue of $B + D = \tau Q^*$ = (\$1.05 per kg) × (206 million kg per year) = \$216.3 million per year.

The combined loss of consumer surplus and producer surplus is only partially offset by the government's gain in tax revenue, so there is a net loss to society (in millions of dollars) of

$$\Delta W = \Delta CS + \Delta PS + \Delta T = -\$149.1 - \$74.55 + \$216.3 = -\$7.35.$$

This deadweight loss is area $-C - E$.

Why does society suffer a deadweight loss? The reason is that the tax lowers output from the competitive level, Q_1, where welfare is maximized, to Q_2. An equivalent explanation for this inefficiency or loss to society is that the tax puts a wedge between price and marginal cost: At Q_2, price, p_2, is above marginal cost, which equals $p_2 - \tau$. Consumers are willing to pay \$4 for one more kg of pork, where the marginal cost to firms is only \$2.95. Shouldn't more pork be produced if consumers are willing to pay a third more than it costs to produce? That's what our welfare study indicates.

Welfare Effects of a Price Floor

In some markets, the government sets a *price floor*, or minimum price, which is the lowest price a consumer can pay legally for the good. For example, in most countries, the government creates price floors under at least some agricultural prices to guarantee producers that they will receive at least a price of $\underline{p}$ for their good. If the market price is above $\underline{p}$, the support program is irrelevant. If the market price would be below $\underline{p}$, however, the government buys as much output as necessary to drive the price up to $\underline{p}$. Since 1929 (the start of the Great Depression), the U.S. government has used price floors or similar programs to keep prices of many agricultural products above the price that competition would determine in unregulated markets.[15]

We now show the effect of a price support using estimated supply and demand curves for the soybean market (Holt 1992). The intersection of the market demand curve and the market supply curve in Figure 9.10 determines the competitive equilibrium, e, in the absence of a price support program, where the equilibrium price is p_1 = \$4.59 per bushel and the equilibrium quantity is Q_1 = 2.1 billion bushels per year.

With a price support on soybeans of $\underline{p}$ = \$5 per bushel and the government's pledge to buy as much output as farmers want to sell, quantity sold is Q_s = 2.2 billion bushels.[16] At $\underline{p}$, consumers buy less output, Q_d = 1.9 billion bushels, than the

[15] My favorite program was the wool and mohair (made from the fleece of Angora goats) subsidy. The federal government instituted wool subsidies after the Korean War to ensure "strategic supplies" for uniforms. Congress later added the mohair subsidies, though mohair has no military use. In some years, the mohair subsidy exceeded the amount consumers paid for mohair, and the subsidies on wool and mohair reached a fifth of a billion dollars. (No doubt, the end of these subsidies on December 31, 1995, has endangered national security.)

[16] In 1985, the period Holt studies, the price support was \$5.02. As of 1998, the support in any given year lies between \$4.92 and \$5.26.

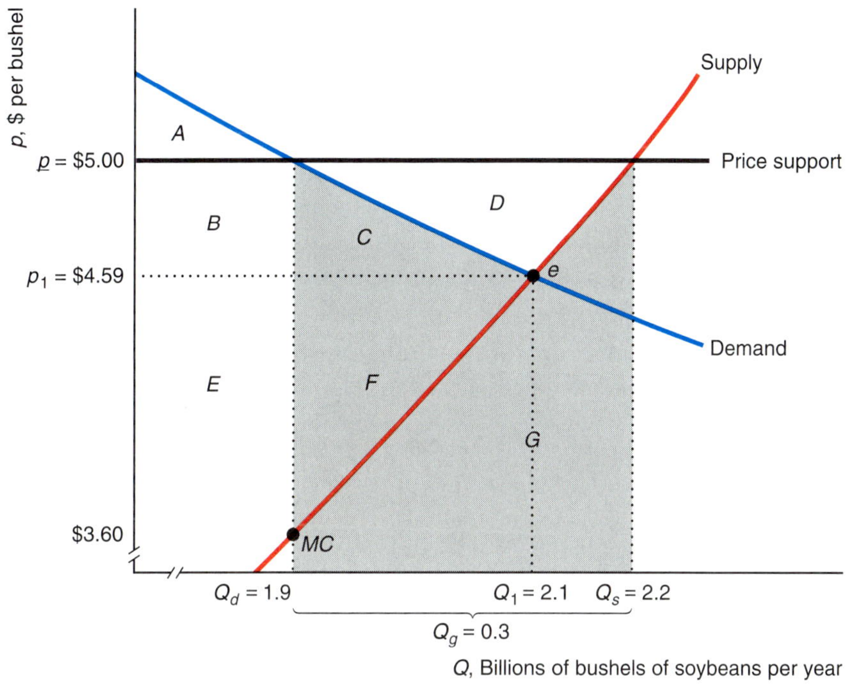

	No Price Support	Price Support	Change ($ millions)
Consumer Surplus, CS	$A + B + C$	A	$-B - C = -864 = \Delta CS$
Producer Surplus, PS	$E + F$	$B + C + D + E + F$	$B + C + D = 921 = \Delta PS$
Government Expense, $-X$	0	$-C - D - F - G$	$-C - D - F - G = -1{,}283 = \Delta X$
Welfare, $W = CS + PS - X$	$A + B + C + E + F$	$A + B + E - G$	$-C - F - G = -1{,}226 = \Delta W = DWL$

Figure 9.10 Effect of Price Supports in Soybeans. Without government price supports, the equilibrium is e, where p_1 = \$4.59 bushel and Q_1 = 2.1 billion bushels of soybeans per year (based on estimates in Holt 1992). With the price support at $\underline{p}$ = \$5.00 per bushel, output sold increases to Q_s and consumer purchases fall to Q_d, so the government must buy $Q_g = Q_s - Q_d$ at a cost of \$1.283 billion per year. The deadweight loss is $-C - F - G$ = \$1.226 billion per year, not counting storage and administrative costs.

Q_1 they would have bought at the market-determined price p_1. As a result, consumer surplus falls by $-B - C = -\$864$ million.[17] The government buys $Q_g = Q_s - Q_d \approx 0.3$ billion bushels per year, which is the excess supply, at a cost of $T = \underline{p} \times Q_g = C + D + F + G = \$1.283$ billion.

The government cannot resell the output domestically because if it tried to do so, it would succeed only in driving down the price consumers pay. The government stores the output or sends it abroad.

Although farmers gain producer surplus of $B + C + D = \$921$ million, this program is an inefficient way to transfer money to them. Assuming that the government's purchases have no alternative use, the deadweight loss is $\Delta W = \Delta CS + \Delta PS - T = -C - F - G = \$1.226$ billion per year.[18] The deadweight loss reflects two distortions in this market:

- **Excess production:** More output is produced than is consumed, so Q_g is stored, destroyed, or shipped abroad.
- **Inefficiency in consumption:** At the quantity they actually buy, Q_d, consumers are willing to pay \$5 for the last bushel of soybeans, which is more than the marginal cost, $MC = \$3.60$, of producing that bushel.

Price Floors and Quotas. Because of price supports, the government was buying and storing large quantities of food, much of which was allowed to spoil. As a consequence, the government started limiting the amount farmers could produce. Because there is uncertainty about how much a farmer will produce, the government set quotas or limits on the amount of land farmers could use, so as to restrict their output. However, a peanut or tobacco farmer whose acreage is limited could increase the amount of fertilizer and other inputs used to increase yields per acre. Thus, the quotas can lead to inefficient production in which too much of noncontrolled inputs are used relative to controlled inputs.

SOLVED PROBLEM 9.3

For simplicity, suppose that the government could put a binding quota, $\bar{Q}$, on the amount of soybeans farmers may produce (as opposed to a restriction on inputs), equal to the equilibrium quantity in the absence of a price support. What is the impact of such a quota on consumers, producers, the government purchases, and overall welfare in the soybean market, in which the price support is \$5 per bushel?

---

[17] The demand and supply curves are slightly curved, so the welfare areas cannot be calculated exactly by using triangle formulas.

[18] This measure of deadweight loss is an underestimate of the true loss. The government also pays storage and administration costs. In 1991, the U.S. Department of Agriculture, which runs the price support program, had 125,640 employees, or roughly 1 employee for every 2.4 farms that received price supports for any supported crop (though many of these employees are working on other activities).

Answer

1. *Describe the market if there is only a price support*: At a price support of \$5 per bushel, farmers sell Q_2, of which consumers buy Q_d and the government buys Q_g (= $Q_2 - Q_d$) in Figure 9.11. Consumer surplus is A, producer surplus is $B + C + D_1 + D_2 + E + F$, and the loss from government expenditures is $-C - D_1 - D_2 - F - G_1 - G_2$.

2. *Show the effect of the quota*: The quota equals the equilibrium quantity in the absence of a price support, $\bar{Q} = Q_1$, so we add a vertical line showing the quota constraint at Q_1. The government now buys Q_g^* (= $Q_1 - Q_d$). Consumer surplus is A, producer surplus is $B + C + D_1 + E + F$, and loss from government expenditures is $-C - D_1 - F - G_1$.

3. *Compare prices, quantity, and welfare with and without the quota*: The quota reduces the amount the government buys by $Q_g^* - Q_g$, causing the government expenditures to fall by $D_2 + G_2$. Farmers' producer surplus drops by $-D_2$. Because the price to consumers is still $\underline{p}$, consumers buy the same amount, Q_d, as before the quota, and their consumer surplus, A, is unchanged. The welfare is higher than it would be with price supports alone by G_2, but there's still deadweight loss. Compared to an unregulated market, welfare is lower with a price support and a quota by $-C - F - G_1$. ■

Recent Government Responses to Surpluses. In some years, the government paid to destroy some of a subsidized crop or some of the inputs. In the 1980s, the government was overwhelmed by the surpluses of butter and powdered milk due to subsidies. It sent some of these milk products to other countries by providing export subsidies. In 1986, though, the government announced that it would pay dairy farmers to kill 1.6 million cows. (As some of these slaughtered animals were sold for meat, this program lowered the price of cattle, thus hurting cattle ranchers.)

Today, the U.S. government relies primarily on a different type of price support program, in which it adds a subsidy to whatever price consumers pay on the quantity actually sold to them. As a result of this change, the government buys no output at all, and the inefficiency of the programs has largely been eliminated.

Who Benefits. Presumably, the purpose of these programs is to help poor farmers, not to hurt consumers and taxpayers. However, the lion's share of American farm subsidies goes to large agricultural corporations, not to poor farmers. More than half (58%) of U.S. farms have sales of less than \$20,000 per year, yet these farms received only 4.1% of the total direct government payments for agriculture in 1994.[19] In contrast, farms with over a million dollars in annual sales are only 0.7%

[19]Economic Research Service, U.S. Department of Agriculture, *Farm Business Economic Report, 1994*, August 1996.

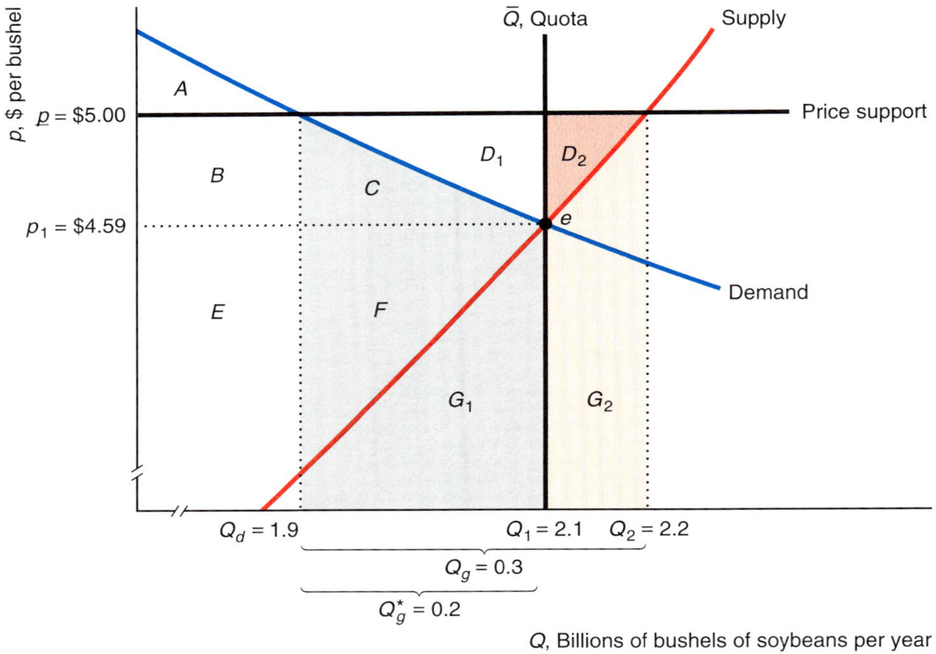

	No Price Support	Price Support	Price Support and Quota	Change: Support Alone Versus Support and Quota ($ millions)
Consumer Surplus, CS	$A + B + C$	A	A	$0 = \Delta CS$
Producer Surplus, PS	$E + F$	$B + C + D_1 + D_2 + E + F$	$B + C + D_1 + E + F$	$-D_2 = -16 = \Delta PS$
Government Expense, $-X$	0	$-C - D_1 - D_2 - F - G - G_2$	$-C - D_1 - F - G_1$	$D_2 + G_2 = 364 = \Delta T$
Welfare, $W = CS + PS - X$	$A + B + C + E + F$	$A + B + E - G_1 - G_2$	$A + B + E - G_1$	$G_2 = 348 = \Delta W$

Figure 9.11 Effect of Price Supports and a Quota on Soybeans:. The quota limits the amount of soybeans the government promises to purchase to $\overline{Q}$. Adding a quota to a price support leaves consumers unaffected, causes producer surplus to fall $-D_2 = -\$16$ million per year, saves the government $D_2 + G_2 = \$364$ per year, and reduces the deadweight loss by $G_2 = \$348$ million per year. Welfare would be higher if both the price support and quota were removed.

of all farms, yet they received 5.5% of all direct government payments. Farms with over a quarter of a million dollars in sales (top 6% of all farms) received one-third of the payments, and farms with over $100,000 in sales (top 18% of all farms) received two-thirds of the direct government payments. As a specific example, the 287 largest beekeeper firms, about 7% of the beekeepers who received the honey subsidy, got over half of the $11.2 million distributed in 1991.[20]

APPLICATION

International Cost of Agricultural Subsidies

In some countries, government farm subsidy payments exceed the amount farmers receive from consumers for the products. The Organization for Economic Co-Operation and Development (OECD) collects information about such subsidies in its member nations, which include most European and Scandinavian countries, Australia, Canada, Japan, New Zealand, and the United States.[21] Farmers in OECD countries received $180 billion in subsidies for their major crops in 1992 and $166 billion in 1996. These subsidies were 44% of the amount consumers paid in 1992 and 36% in 1996. Subsidy payments for minor crops are about half as much as for the major crops.

The European Community had the largest subsidies, $85 billion in 1996. Subsidies were $41 billion in Japan and $24 billion in the United States.

Among OECD nations, Switzerland's farm subsidies constituted the largest fraction of consumer payments. Their $5.5 billion of subsidies were 78% of the value of production: The Swiss government gives farmers nearly $4 for every $1 farmers earn from the market.

New Zealand is the only OECD country in which subsidies fell as a percentage of the value of farm production. The subsidies were 25% of total value in 1979 but only 3% from 1992 through 1996.

The cost of these supports to the average taxpayer is substantial. In 1996, a person living in the European Community paid $322 a year in subsidies to farmers. However, Swiss citizens paid $935 a year. Japanese citizens spent $617 per person, Americans paid $259 each, Canadians $161, Australians $89, and Mexicans $23. ■

---

[20]Brasher, Philip, "Sweet Deal for Biggest Beekeepers," *San Francisco Examiner*, April 18, 1993:E7.

[21]*Agricultural Policies, Markets and Trade: Monitoring and Outlook*, Organization for Economic Co-Operation and Development, 1994 through 1997.

Welfare Effects of a Price Ceiling

In some markets, the government sets a *price ceiling*: the highest price that a firm can legally charge. If the government sets the ceiling below the precontrol competitive price, consumers demand more than the precontrol equilibrium quantity and firms supply less than that quantity (Chapter 2). Producer surplus must fall because firms receive a lower price and sell fewer units.

Because of the price ceiling, consumers can buy the good at a lower price but cannot buy as much of it as they'd like. Because less is sold than in the precontrol equilibrium, there is deadweight loss: Consumers value the good more than the marginal cost of producing extra units.

In the 1970s, the U.S. government used price controls to keep gasoline prices below the market price (Chapter 2). This policy led to long lines at gas stations and large deadweight losses. Frech and Lee (1987) estimate that the loss in consumer surplus in California in 1985 dollars was \$1.2 billion during the December 1973 to March 1974 price controls and \$800 million during the May 1979 to July 1979 controls.

SOLVED PROBLEM 9.4

If the Canadian government places a price ceiling on pork at $\bar{p}$ = \$2.95 per kg—which is below the unregulated competitive equilibrium price of p_1 = \$3.30—what is the qualitative effect on the equilibrium and welfare?

Answer

1. *Show the initial, unregulated equilibrium*: The intersection of the demand curve and the supply curve determines the unregulated, competitive equilibrium e_1 in Figure 9.12, where the equilibrium quantity is Q_1.

2. *Show how the equilibrium changes with the price ceiling*: Because the price ceiling, $\bar{p}$ = \$2.95, is set below the equilibrium price of p_1 = \$3.30, the ceiling binds. At this lower price, consumer demand increases to Q_d while the quantity firms are willing to supply falls to Q_s, so only $Q_s = Q_2$ units are sold in the new equilibrium, e_2. Thus, the price control causes the equilibrium quantity and price to fall, but consumers have excess demand of $Q_d - Q_s$.

3. *Describe the welfare effects*: Because consumers are able to buy Q_s units at a lower price than before the controls, they gain area *D*. Consumers lose consumer surplus of C, however, because they can purchase only Q_s instead of Q_1 units of output. Thus, consumers gain net consumer surplus of $D - C$. Because they sell fewer units at a lower price, firms lose producer surplus $-D - E$. Part of this loss, *D*, is transferred to consumers because of lower prices, but the rest, *E*, is a loss to society. The total deadweight loss to society, $\Delta W = \Delta CS + \Delta PS = -C - E$. ■

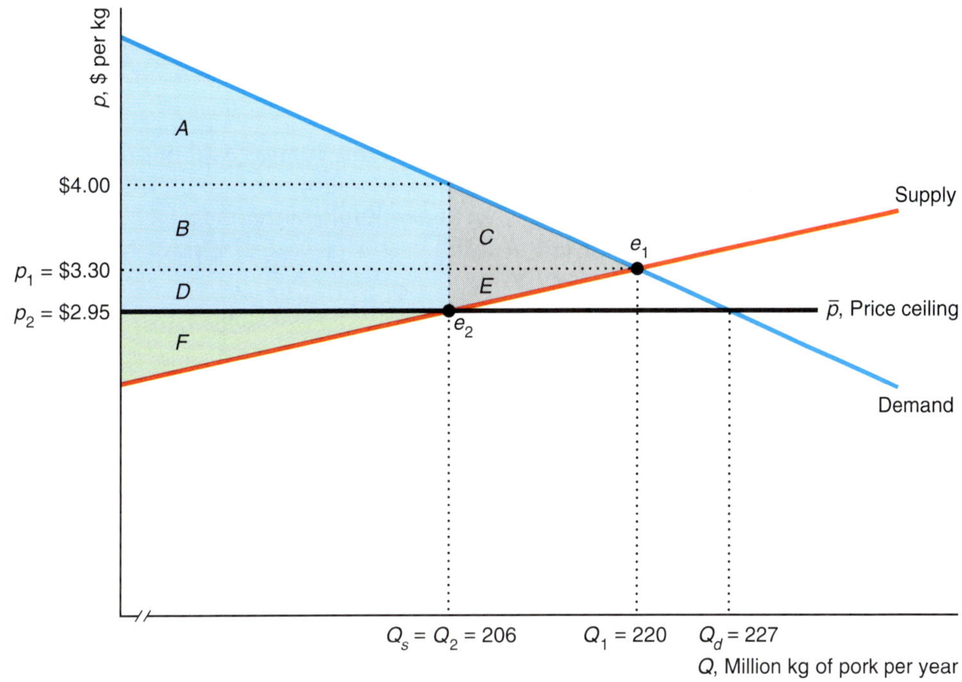

	No Ceiling	Price Ceiling	Change ($ millions)
Consumer Surplus, *CS*	$A + B + C$	$A + B + D$	$D - C = 67.2 = \Delta CS$
Producer Surplus, *PS*	$D + E + F$	F	$-D - E = -74.55 = \Delta PS$
Welfare, $W = CS + PS$	$A + B + C + D + E + F$	$A + B + D + F$	$-C - E = -7.35 = \Delta W = DWL$

Figure 9.12 Effect of a Price Ceiling on Pork. In the unregulated pork market, the equilibrium is e_1, where the price is \$3.30 per kg and Q_1 million kg of pork are sold per year. If the government sets a price ceiling of $\bar{p}$ = \$2.95 per kg, consumers would like to buy Q_d but firms want to sell only Q_s, resulting in excess demand of $Q_d - Q_s$. Welfare falls by $C - E$ = –\$7.35 million, which is a deadweight loss to society. The new consumer surplus is $A + B + D$, and the new producer surplus is only F. To increase consumer welfare by \$67.2 million costs society –\$7.35 million or about \$1 for every \$9 transferred from producers to consumers.

9.6 COMPARING BOTH TYPES OF POLICIES: IMPORTS

Traditionally, most of Australia's imports come from overseas.

—Keppel Enderbery, Former Australian Cabinet Minister

We've examined examples of government policies that shift supply or demand curves and policies that create a wedge between supply and demand. Governments use both types of policies to control international trade.

Allowing imports of foreign goods benefits the importing country. If a government reduces imports of a good, the domestic price rises; the profits of domestic firms that produce the good increase, but domestic consumers are hurt. Our analysis will show that the loss to consumers exceeds the gain to producers.

The government of the (potentially) importing country can use one of four import policies:

- **Allow free trade:** Any firm can sell in this country without restrictions.
- **Ban all imports:** The government sets a quota of zero on imports.
- **Set a positive quota:** The government limits imports to $\bar{Q}$.
- **Set a tariff:** The government imposes a tax called a **tariff** (or a *duty*) on only imported goods.

We compare welfare under free trade to welfare under bans and quotas, which change the supply curve, and to welfare under tariffs, which create a wedge between supply and demand.

To illustrate the differences in welfare under these various policies, we examine the U.S. market for crude oil.[22] We make two assumptions for the sake of simplicity. First, we assume that transportation costs are zero. Second, we assume that the supply curve of the potentially imported good is horizontal at the world price p^*. Given these two assumptions, the importing country, the United States, can buy as much of this good as it wants at p^* per unit: It is a price taker in the world market because its demand is too small to influence the world price.

Free Trade Versus a Ban on Imports

No nation was ever ruined by trade. —Benjamin Franklin

Preventing imports into the domestic market raises the price, as we illustrated in Chapter 2 for the Japan rice market. The estimated American domestic supply curve, S^a, is upward sloping, and the foreign supply curve is horizontal at the world price of \$14.70 in Figure 9.13. The total American supply curve, S^1, is the horizontal sum of the domestic supply curve and the foreign supply curve. Thus, S^1 is the same as the upward-sloping domestic supply curve for prices below \$14.70 and is horizontal at \$14.70. Under free trade, the United States imports crude oil if its domestic price in the absence of imports would exceed the world price, \$14.70 per barrel.

The free-trade equilibrium, e_1, is determined by the intersection of S^1 and the demand curve, where the U.S. price equals the world price, \$14.70, and the quantity is 13.1 million barrels per day. At the equilibrium price, domestic supply is 8.2, so imports are 4.9 (= 13.1 – 8.2). Consumer surplus is $A + B + C$, producer surplus is D, and welfare is $A + B + C + D$.

[22]We assume that the market is competitive. The following figures are based on short-run, constant-elasticity supply and demand equations for crude oil in 1988 using the short-run supply and demand elasticities reported in Anderson and Metzger (1991). These numbers differ slightly from those in Anderson and Metzger because they use different-shaped curves, examine a different period, and discuss policies that affect both the crude oil and the refined product markets.

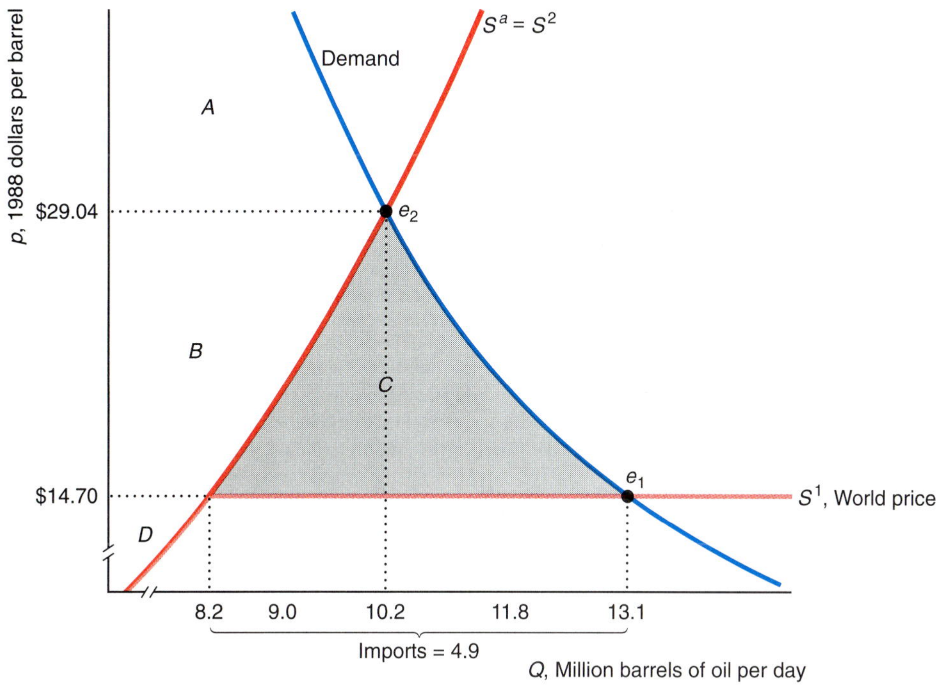

U.S.	Free Trade	U.S. Import Ban	Change ($ millions)
Consumer Surplus, *CS*	$A + B + C$	A	$-B - C = -163.7 = \Delta CS$
Producer Surplus, *PS*	D	$B + D$	$B = 132.5 = \Delta PS$
Welfare, $W = CS + PS$	$A + B + C + D$	$A + B + D$	$-C = -31.2 = \Delta W = DWL$

Figure 9.13 Loss from Eliminating Free Trade. Because the supply curve of foreigners is horizontal at the world price of $14.70, the total U.S. supply curve of crude oil is S_1 when there is free trade. The free-trade equilibrium is e_1. With a ban on imports, the equilibrium e_2 occurs where the domestic supply curve, $S^a = S^2$, intersects D. The ban increases producer surplus by $B = \$132.5$ million per day and decreases consumer surplus by $-B - C = -\$163.7$ million per day, so the deadweight loss is $-C = -\$31.2$ million per day or $-\$11.4$ billion per year.

If imports are banned, the total U.S. supply curve, S^2, is the American domestic supply curve, S^a. The equilibrium is at e_2, where S^2 intersects the demand curve. The new equilibrium price is $29.04, and the new equilibrium quantity, 10.2 million barrels per day, is produced domestically. Consumer surplus is A, producer surplus is $B + D$, and welfare is $A + B + D$.

The ban helps producers but harms consumers. Because of the higher price, domestic firms gain producer surplus of $\Delta PS = B = \$132.5$ million per day. Consumers lose $\Delta CS = -B - C = -\$163.7$ million per day.

Does the ban help the United States? The change in total welfare, ΔW, is the difference between the gain to producers and the loss to consumers, $\Delta W = \Delta PS + \Delta CS = -\$31.2$ million per day or –\$11.4 billion per year. This deadweight loss is 24% of the gain to producers. Consumers lose \$1.24 for every \$1 that producers gain from a ban.

Free Trade Versus a Tariff

There are two common types of tariffs: *specific tariffs*—τ dollars per unit—and *ad valorem tariffs*—α percent of the sales price. In recent years, tariffs have been applied throughout the world, most commonly to agricultural products.[23] American policymakers have frequently debated the optimal tariff on crude oil as a way to raise revenue or to reduce "dependence" on foreign oil.

You may be asking yourself, "Why should we study tariffs if we've already looked at taxes? Aren't tariffs just another tax?" Good point! Tariffs are just taxes. If the only goods sold were imported, the effect of a tariff in the importing country is the same as we showed for a sales tax. We study tariffs separately, however, because a tariff is applied only to imported goods, so it affects domestic and foreign producers differently.

Because tariffs are applied to only imported goods, all else the same, they do not raise as much tax revenue or affect equilibrium quantities as much as taxes placed on all goods in a market. De Melo and Tarr (1992) find that almost five times more tax revenue would be generated by a 15% additional ad valorem tax on petroleum products (\$34.6 billion) than by a 25% additional import tariff on oil and gas (\$7.3 billion).

To illustrate the effect of a tariff, suppose that the government imposes a specific tariff of $\tau = \$5$ per barrel of crude oil. Given this tariff, firms will not import oil into the United States unless the U.S. price is at least \$5 above the world price, \$14.70. The tariff creates a wedge between the world price and the American price. This tariff causes the total supply curve to shift from S^1 to S^3 in Figure 9.14. Given that the world supply curve is horizontal at \$14.70, a tariff shifts this supply curve upward so that it is horizontal at \$19.70. As a result, the total U.S. supply curve with the tariff, S^3, equals the domestic supply curve for prices below \$19.70 and is horizontal at \$19.70.

The new equilibrium, e_3, occurs where S^3 intersects the demand curve. In this equilibrium, price is \$19.70 and quantity is 11.8 million barrels of oil per day. At this higher price, domestic firms supply 9.0 so imports are 2.8 (= 11.8 – 9.0).

---

[23] After World War II, most trading nations signed the General Agreement on Tariffs and Trade (GATT), which limited their ability to subsidize exports or limit imports using quotas and tariffs. These rules prohibited most export subsidies and import quotas, except when imports threaten "market disruption" (a term that was, unfortunately, not defined). The GATT also required that any new tariff be offset by a reduction in other tariffs to compensate the exporting country. Since then, modifications of the GATT have reduced or eliminated most tariffs.

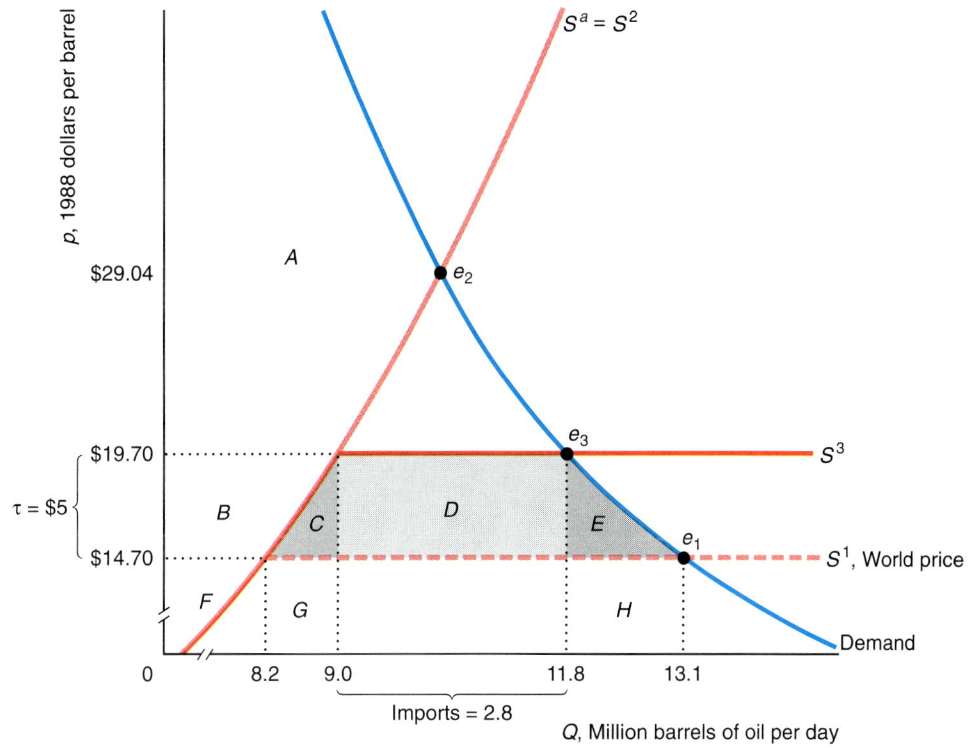

U.S.	Free Trade	U.S. Tariff or Quota	Change ($ millions)
Consumer Surplus, *CS*	$A + B + C + D + E$	A	$-B - C - D - E = -61.9$
Producer Surplus, *PS*	F	$B + F$	$B = 42.8$
Tariff Revenues, *T*	0	D (tariff)	$D = 14.0$ (tariff)
		0 (quota)	0 (quota)
Welfare from a Tariff, $W = CS + PS + T$	$A + B + C + D + E + F$	$A + B + D + F$	$-C - E = -5.1 = DWL$
Welfare from a Quota, $W = CS + PS$	$A + B + C + D + E + F$	$A + B + F$	$-C - D - E = -19.1 = DWL$

Figure 9.14 Effect of a Tariff (or Quota). A tariff of $\tau = \$5$ per barrel of oil imported or a quota of $\bar{Q} = 2.8$ drives the U.S. price of crude oil to $19.70, which is $5 more than the world price. Under the tariff, the equilibrium, e_3, is determined by the intersection of the S_3 total U.S. supply curve and the D demand curve. Under the quota, e_3 is determined by a quantity wedge of 2.8 million barrels per day between the quantity demanded, 9.0 million barrels per day, and the quantity supplied, 11.8 million barrels per day. Compared to free trade, producers gain $B = \$42.8$ million per day and consumers lose $-B - C - D - E = -\$61.9$ million per day from the tariff or quota. The deadweight loss under the quota is $-C - D - E = -\$19.1$ million per day. With a tariff, the government's tariff revenue increases by $D = \$14$ million a day, so the deadweight loss is only $-C - E = -\$5.1$ million per day.

The tariff *protects* American producers from foreign competition. The larger the tariff, the less is imported, hence the higher the price that domestic firms can charge. (With a large enough tariff, nothing is imported, and the price rises to the no-trade level, \$29.04.) With a tariff of \$5, domestic firms' producer surplus increases by area B = \$42.8 million per day.

Because of the rise in the price from \$14.70 to \$19.70, consumer surplus falls by \$61.9 million per day. The government receives tariff revenues, T, equal to area D = \$14 million per day, which is τ = \$5, times the quantity imported, 2.8.

The deadweight loss is $-C - E$ = –\$5.1 million per day, or nearly –\$1.9 billion per year.[24] This deadweight loss is almost 12% of the gain to producers. Consumers lose \$1.45 for each \$1 domestic producers gain. Because the tariff doesn't completely eliminate imports, the welfare loss is smaller than it is if all imports are banned.

We can interpret the two components of this deadweight loss. First, $-C$ is the loss from producing 9.0 million barrels per day instead of 8.2 million barrels per day. Domestic firms produce this extra output because the tariff drove up the price from \$14.70 to \$19.70. The cost of producing this extra 0.8 million barrels of oil per day domestically is $C + G$, the area under the domestic supply curve, S^a, between 8.2 and 9.0. Had Americans bought this oil at the world price, the cost would have been only G = \$11.8 million per day. Thus, $-C$ is the extra cost from producing the extra 0.8 million barrels of oil per day domestically instead of importing it.

Second, $-E$ is a *consumption distortion loss* from American consumers' buying too little oil, 11.8 instead of 13.1, because the price rose from \$14.70 to \$19.70 owing to the tariff. American consumers value this extra output as $E + H$, the area under their demand curve between 11.8 and 13.1, whereas the value in international markets is only H, the area below the line at \$14.70 between 11.8 and 13.1. Thus, $-E$ is the difference between the value at world prices and the value American consumers place on this extra 1.3 million barrels per day.

Free Trade Versus a Quota

The effect of a positive quota is similar to that of a tariff. If the government limits imports to $\bar{Q}$ = 2.8 million barrels per day, the quota is binding because 4.9 million barrels per day were imported under free trade. Given this binding quota, at the equilibrium price, the quantity demanded minus the quantity supplied by domestic producers equals 2.8 million barrels per day. In Figure 9.14, where the price is \$19.70, the gap between the quantity demanded, 11.8 million barrels per day, and the quantity supplied, 9.0 million barrels per day, is 2.8 million barrels per day. Thus, a quota on imports of 2.8 leads to the same equilibrium, e_3, as does a tariff of \$5.

The gain to domestic producers, B, and the loss to consumers, $-C - E$, are the same as those with a tariff. With the quota, however, the government does not receive any tariff revenues. Area D goes to foreign producers. As a result, the deadweight loss from the quota, \$19.1 million per day, or \$7.0 billion per year, is greater than under the tariff. This deadweight loss is nearly half (45%) of the gains to producers.

---

[24]If the foreign supply is horizontal, welfare in the importing country *must* fall. However, if the foreign supply is upward sloping, welfare in the importing country may rise.

Thus, the importing country fares better using a tariff than setting a quota that reduces imports by the same amount. Consumers and domestic firms do as well under the two policies, but the government gains tariff revenues, *D*, only when the tariff is used.

APPLICATION

Japanese Nontariff Barriers

In recent years, Japan has used both formal trade barriers, such as tariffs and quotas, and informal measures, such as government "guidance" to firms, to limit imports in agriculture and several manufacturing industries. Table 9.2 shows how much higher were the prices that Japanese consumers paid than the corresponding world prices for a number of goods in 1989. The price Japanese consumers paid for rice had over a sevenfold (737%) markup over the world price, which would have been the Japanese price in the absence of trade barriers. The markup was over six times for radios and televisions. Most of the markup is due to nontariff barriers such as quotas and informal barriers rather than tariffs. The 718.4% markup for tea and coffee represents a 11.9% markup due to tariffs and a 706.5% markup due to nontariff barriers.

One estimate of the cost of this protection to Japanese consumers is around $110 billion a year at 1989 exchange rates, or 3.8% of the Japanese national income. The net welfare loss is estimated to be 0.6% of Japanese national income.[25] ■

Rent Seeking

Given that tariffs and quotas hurt the importing country, why do the Japanese, American, and many other governments impose tariffs, quotas, or other trade barriers? The reason is that domestic producers stand to make large gains from such government actions; hence, it pays for them to organize and lobby the government to enact these trade policies. Although consumers as a whole suffer large losses, most individual consumers face a negligible loss. Moreover, consumers rarely organize to lobby the government about trade issues. Thus, in most countries, producers are often able to convince (cajole, influence, or bribe) legislators or government officials to aid them, even though consumers suffer more-than-offsetting losses.

If domestic producers can talk the government into a tariff, a quota, or other policies that reduce imports, they gain extra producer surplus (rents), such as area *B* in Figures 9.13 and 9.14. Economists call efforts and expenditures to gain a rent

[25]"Japan's Protection Racket," *The Economist*, January 7, 1995:58, based on Sazanami, Urata, and Kawai (1995). These numbers are probably upper bounds on the true losses, as they do not fully control for quality differences in Japanese and imported goods.

Table 9.2 Japanese Price Differences Due to Trade Barriers: Percentage Markup of Prices Japanese Consumers Paid over World Prices, 1989

	Markup of Japanese Consumer Price over World Price (%)	Tariff Rate (%)	Implied Nontariff Barrier Rate (%)
Milled rice	737.1	0	737.1
Soybeans	423.6	0	423.6
Tea and coffee	718.4	11.9	706.5
Wheat	477.8	0	477.8
Clothing	292.6	10.4	282.2
Cosmetics	661.6	2.0	659.6
Gasoline	229.0	5.5	223.5
Radio and televisions	607.0	0	607.0

Source: "Japan's Protection Racket," *The Economist*, January 7, 1995:58, and Sazanami, Urata, and Kawai (1995).

or a profit from government actions **rent seeking**. If this rent-seeking behavior—such as hiring lobbyists and engaging in advertising to influence legislators—uses up resources, the deadweight loss from tariffs and quotas understates the true loss to society. The domestic producers may spend up to the gain in producer surplus to influence the government.[26]

Indeed, some economists argue that the government revenues from tariffs are completely offset by administrative costs and rent-seeking behavior. If so (and if the tariffs and quotas do not affect world prices), the loss to society from tariffs and quotas is all of the change in consumer surplus, such as areas $B + C$ in Figure 9.13 and areas $B + C + D + E$ in Figure 9.14.

Lopez and Pagoulatos (1994) estimate the deadweight loss and an estimate of the maximum additional losses due to rent-seeking activities in the United States in food and tobacco products in 1987. Table 9.3 summarizes their estimates for several industries in 1997 dollars. They estimate that the deadweight loss is –\$12.3 billion, which is 2.6% of the domestic consumption of these products. The gain in producer surplus is \$44.6 billion, or 9.5% of domestic consumption. The government obtained \$1.8 billion in tariff revenues, or 0.4% of consumption. If all of producer surplus and government revenues were expended in rent-seeking behavior and other wasteful activities, the total loss is \$58.7 billion, or 12.5% of consumption, which is 4.75 times larger than the deadweight loss alone. In other words, the loss to society is somewhere between the deadweight loss of \$12.3 billion and \$58.7 billion. The largest deadweight losses were in milk products and sugar manufacturing, which primarily use import quotas to raise domestic prices.

[26]This argument is made in Tullock (1967) and Posner (1975). Fisher (1985) and Varian (1989) argue that the expenditure is typically less than the producer surplus.

Table 9.3 Welfare Cost of Trade Barriers in 1987 (Millions of 1997 Dollars)

	DWL	ΔPS	Government Revenues	ΔCS
Meat products	−26	2,145	62	−2,233
Dairy products*	−13,995	25,554	959	−37,478
Sugar confectionery*	−874	4,008	254	−5,134
Grain mill products	−9	1,043	8	−1,061
Fats and oils	−121	2,164	4	−2,290
Beverages	−8	1,000	134	−1,142
Tobacco	−187	3,492	87	−3,765
All food and tobacco	−12,329	44,612	1,809	−58,749

*Import quotas are the primary instrument of protection.

Notes: As estimated, $\Delta CS = DWL - \Delta PS$ − Government Revenues. Dollar quantities were adjusted using the Consumer Price Index.

Source: Lopez and Pagoulatos (1994).

Summary

1. **Consumer welfare:** The pleasure a consumer receives from a good in excess of its cost is called *consumer surplus*. Consumer surplus equals the area under the consumer's demand curve above the market price up to the quantity that the consumer buys. How much consumers are harmed by an increase in price is measured by the change in consumer surplus.

2. **Producer welfare:** A firm's gain from trading is measured by its producer surplus. Producer surplus is the largest amount of money that could be taken from a firm's revenue and still leave the firm willing to produce. That is, the producer surplus is the amount the firm is paid minus its variable cost of production, which is profit in the long run. It is the area below the price and above the supply curve up to the quantity that the firm sells. The effect of a change in a price on a supplier is measured by the change in producer surplus.

3. **How competition maximizes welfare:** One standard measure of welfare is the sum of consumer surplus and producer surplus. The more price is above marginal cost, the lower is this measure of welfare. In the competitive equilibrium, in which price equals marginal cost, welfare is maximized.

4. **Policies that shift supply curves:** Governments frequently limit the number of firms in a market directly, by licensing them, or indirectly, by raising the costs of entry to new firms or raising the cost of exiting. A reduction in the number of firms in a competitive market raises price, hurts consumers, helps producing firms, and lowers the standard measure of welfare. This reduction in welfare is a deadweight loss: The gain to producers is less than the loss to consumers.

5. **Policies that create a wedge between supply and demand:** Taxes, price ceilings, and price floors create a gap between the price consumers pay and the price firms receive. These policies force price above marginal cost, which raises the price to consumers and lowers the amount consumed. The wedge between price and marginal cost results in a deadweight loss: The loss of consumer surplus and producer surplus is not offset by increased taxes or by benefits to other groups.

6. **Comparing both types of policies: imports:** A government may use either a quantity restriction such as a quota, which shifts the supply curve, or a tariff, which creates a wedge, to reduce imports or achieve other goals. These policies may have different welfare implications. A tariff that reduces imports by the same amount as a quota has the same harms—a larger loss of consumer surplus than increased domestic producer surplus—but has a partially offsetting benefit—increased tariff revenues for the government. Rent-seeking activities are attempts by firms or individuals to influence a government to adopt a policy that favors them. By using resources, rent seeking exacerbates the welfare loss beyond the deadweight loss caused by the policy itself. In a perfectly competitive market, government policies frequently lower welfare. As we show in later chapters, however, in markets that are not perfectly competitive, government policies may increase welfare.

Problems

1. How would the quantitative effect of a specific tax on welfare change as demand becomes more elastic? As it becomes less elastic? (*Hint:* See Solved Problem 9.1.)
2. What were the welfare effects (who gained, who lost, what was the deadweight loss) of the gasoline price controls described in Chapter 2? Show these effects in a figure.
3. Use an indifference curve diagram (gift goods on one axis and all other goods on the other) to illustrate that one is better off receiving cash than a gift. (*Hint*: See the discussion of gifts in this chapter and the discussion of food stamps in Chapter 4.)
4. What is the welfare effect of a profit tax, ρ, assessed on each competitive firm in a market?
5. What is the welfare effect of an ad valorem sales tax, α, assessed on each competitive firm in a market?
6. What are the welfare effects of a minimum wage? Use a graphical approach to show what happens if all workers are identical. Then verbally describe what is likely to happen to workers who differ by experience, education, age, gender, and race.
7. What effect does a per unit subsidy (negative specific tax) have on equilibrium and on welfare?
8. What is the welfare effect of a lump sum tax, $\$L$, assessed on each competitive firm in a market?
9. What happens to welfare in Solved Problem 9.3 on soybeans if the government maintains a price support, p_2, but restricts output to Q_d using a quota?
10. The government wants to drive the price of soybeans above the equilibrium price p_1 to p_2. It offers growers a payment of x to reduce their output from Q_1 (the equilibrium level) to Q_2, which is the quantity demanded by consumers at p_2. How large must x be for growers to reduce output to this level? What are the effects of this program on consumers, farmers, and total welfare? Compare this approach to (a) offering a price support of p_2, (b) offering a price support and a quota set at Q_1, and (c) offering a price support and a quota set at Q_2.
11. In 1995, the U.S. Congress debated various bills that would lower the federal price supports for sugar from 18¢ to 17¢ per pound. Given that the current world wholesale price was 10–12¢, what would be the likely effect of this change?
12. By 1996, the world price for raw sugar, 11.75¢ per pound, was about half the domestic price, 22.5¢ per pound, because of quotas and tariffs on sugar imports. As a consequence, American-made corn sweetener, which costs 12¢ a pound to make, can be profitably sold. Archer-Daniels-Midland made an estimated profit of $290 million in 1994 from selling corn sweetener. The U.S. Commerce Department says that the quotas and price support reduce American welfare by about $3 billion a year. If so, each dollar of Archer-Daniels-Midland's profit costs Americans about $10.[27] Model the effects of a quota on sugar in both the sugar and corn sweetener markets.
13. A government is considering a quota and a tariff, both of which will reduce imports by the same

[27]Weiner, Tim, "It's Dwayne's World: Archer-Daniels's Influence Is Wide as Well as Deep," *New York Times*, January 16, 1996:C1, C4.

amount. Which does the government prefer, and why?

14. Given that the world supply curve is horizontal at the world price for a given good, can a subsidy on imports raise welfare in the importing country? Explain your answer.

Math Problems

15. If the inverse demand function is $p = 60 - Q$, what is the consumer surplus if price is 30?
16. If the inverse demand function is $p = a - bQ$, what is the consumer surplus if price is $a/2$?
17. If the supply function is $Q = Ap^{\eta}$, what is the producer surplus if price is p^*?
18. If the inverse demand function is $p = 60 - Q$ and the supply function is $Q = p$, what is the initial equilibrium? What is the welfare effect of a specific tax of $\tau = \$2$?
19. If the inverse demand function is $p = a - bQ$ and the supply function is $Q = c + dp$, what is the initial equilibrium? What is the welfare effect of a specific tax of $\tau = \$1$?

CHAPTER

10

General Equilibrium and Economic Welfare

More than any time in history mankind faces a crossroads. One path leads to despair and utter hopelessness, the other to total extinction. Let us pray that we have the wisdom to choose correctly.

—Woody Allen

A change in government policies, a natural disaster, or other shocks often affect equilibrium price and quantity in more than one market. To determine the effects of such a change, we must examine the interrelationships among markets. In this chapter, we extend our analysis of an equilibrium in a single market to an equilibrium in all markets.

We then examine how a society decides whether a particular equilibrium (or change in equilibrium) in all markets is desirable. To do so, society must answer two questions: "Is the equilibrium efficient?" and "Is the equilibrium equitable?"

For the equilibrium to be efficient, both consumption and production must be efficient. Production is efficient only if it is impossible to produce more output at current cost given current knowledge (Chapter 6). Consumption is efficient only if goods cannot be reallocated across people so that at least someone is better off and no one is harmed. In this chapter, we show how to determine whether consumption is efficient.

Whether the equilibrium is efficient is a scientific question. It is possible that all members of society could agree on how to answer scientific questions concerning efficiency.

To answer the equity question, society must make a value judgment as to whether each member of society has his or her "fair" or "just" share of all the goods and services. A common view in Western, individualistic cultures is that each person is the best—and possibly only legitimate—judge of his or her own welfare. Nonetheless, to make social choices about events that affect more than one person, we have to make interpersonal comparisons, through which we decide whether one person's gain is more or less important than another person's loss. For example, in Chapter 9, we argued that a price ceiling on pork lowers a measure of total welfare given the value judgment that the well-being of consumers (consumer surplus) and the well-being of the owners of firms (producer surplus) should be weighted equally. People of good will—and others—may disagree greatly about equity issues.

As a first step in studying welfare issues, many economists use a narrow value criterion, called the *Pareto principle* (after an Italian economist, Vilfredo Pareto), to rank different allocations of goods and services for which no interpersonal comparisons need to be made. According to this principle, a change that makes one person better off without harming anyone else is desirable. Any allocation such that any reallocation would harm at least one person is said to be **Pareto efficient**.

Presumably, you agree that any government policy that makes all members of society better off is desirable. Do you also agree that a policy that makes some members better off without harming others is desirable? What about a policy that helps one group more than it hurts another group? What about a policy that hurts another group more than it helps your group? It is very unlikely that all members of society will agree on how to answer these questions—much less on the answers.

The efficiency and equity questions arise even in small societies, such as your family. Suppose that your family has gathered together in November and everyone wants pumpkin pie. How much pie you get will depend on the answer to efficiency and equity questions: "How can we make the pie as large as possible with available resources?" and "How should we divide the pie?" It is probably easier to get agreement about how to make the largest possible pie than about how to divide it equitably.

So far in this book (aside from Chapter 9's welfare analysis), we've used economic theory to answer the scientific, efficiency question. We've concentrated on that question because the equity question requires a value judgment. (Strangely, most members of our society seem to believe that economists are no better at making value judgments than anyone else.) In this chapter, however, we examine various views on equity.

In this chapter, we examine five main topics:

1. **General equilibrium:** The welfare analysis in Chapter 9 (involving gains and losses in consumer and producer surplus) changes when a government policy change or other shock affects several markets at once.
2. **Trading between two people:** Where two people have goods but cannot produce more goods, both parties benefit from mutually agreed-upon trades.
3. **Competitive exchange:** The competitive equilibrium has two desirable properties: Any competitive equilibrium is Pareto efficient, and any Pareto-efficient allocation can be obtained by using competition, given an appropriate income distribution.
4. **Production and trading:** The benefits from trade continue to hold when production is introduced.
5. **Efficiency and equity:** Because there are many Pareto-efficient allocations, a society uses its views about equity to choose among them.

10.1 GENERAL EQUILIBRIUM

So far, we have used a **partial-equilibrium analysis**: an examination of equilibrium and changes in equilibrium in one market in isolation. In a partial-equilibrium analysis in which we hold the prices and quantities of other goods fixed, we implicitly ignore the possibility that events in this market affect other markets' equilibrium prices and quantities.

When stated this baldly, partial-equilibrium analysis sounds foolish. It needn't be, however. Suppose the government puts a specific tax on the price of Hula-Hoops. If the tax is sizable, it will dramatically affect the sales of Hula-Hoops. However, even a very large tax on Hula-Hoops is unlikely to affect the markets for automobiles, doctor services, or orange juice. Indeed, it is unlikely to affect the demand for other toys greatly. Thus, a partial-equilibrium analysis of the effect of such a tax should serve us well. Studying all markets simultaneously to analyze this tax would be unnecessary at best and confusing at worst.

Sometimes, however, we need to use a **general-equilibrium analysis:** the study of how equilibrium is determined in all markets simultaneously. For example, the discovery of a major oil deposit in a small country raises the income of its citizens, and the increased income affects all that country's markets. Economists sometimes model many markets in an economy and solve for the general equilibrium in all of them simultaneously, using high-speed computers.

Frequently, economists look at equilibrium in several—but not all—markets simultaneously. We'd expect a tax on comic books to affect the price of comic books, which in turn affects the price of video games because video games are substitutes for comics. However, we would not expect that this tax on comics would have a measurable effect on the demand for washing machines. It's therefore reasonable to conduct a "general-equilibrium" analysis of the effects of a tax on comics by looking at just the markets for comics, video games, and a few other closely related markets such as those for movies and trading cards.

Markets are closely related if a shift in the price in one market causes the demand or supply curve in another market to shift measurably. Suppose a tax on coffee causes the price of coffee to rise. The rise in the price of coffee causes the demand curve for tea to shift outward (more is demanded at any given price of tea) because tea and coffee are substitutes. The price increase in coffee also causes the demand curve for cream to shift in because coffee and cream are complements.

Similarly, supply curves in different markets may be related. If a farmer produces both corn and soybeans, an increase in the price of corn will affect the relative amounts of both crops the farmer chooses to produce.

Markets may also be linked if the output of one market is an input in another market. A shock that raises the price of computer chips will also raise the price of computers.

Thus, an event in one market may have a *spillover effect* on other, related markets for a number of reasons. Indeed, a single event may start a chain reaction of spillover effects that reverberates back and forth between markets.

Feedback Between Competitive Markets

To illustrate the feedback of spillover effects between markets, we examine the corn and soybean markets using demand and supply curves estimated by Holt (1992). Consumers and producers substitute between corn and soybeans, so the demand and supply curves in these two markets are related. The quantity of corn demanded and the quantity of soybeans demanded both depend on the price of corn, the price of soybeans, and other variables. Similarly, the quantities of corn and soybeans supplied depend on their relative prices.

Sequence of Events. We can demonstrate the effect of a shock in one market on both markets by tracing the sequence of events in the two markets. Whether these steps occur nearly instantaneously or take some time depends on how quickly consumers and producers react.

The initial supply and demand curves for corn, S_0^c and D_0^c, intersect at the initial equilibrium for corn, e_0^c, in panel a of Figure 10.1.[1] The price of corn is \$2.15 per bushel, and the quantity of corn is 8.44 billion bushels per year. The initial supply and demand curves for soybeans, S_0^s and D_0^s, intersect at e_0^s in panel b, where price is \$4.12 per bushel and quantity is 2.07 billion bushels per year. The first row of Table 10.1 shows the initial equilibrium prices and quantities in these two markets.

Now suppose that the foreign demand for American corn decreases, causing the export of corn to fall by 10% and the total American demand for corn to shift from D_0^c to D_1^c in panel a. The new equilibrium is at e_1^c, where D_1^c intersects S_0^c. The price of corn falls by nearly 11% to \$1.9171 per bushel, and the quantity falls 2.5% to 8.2270 billion bushels per year, as the Step 1 row of the table shows.

If we were conducting a partial-equilibrium analysis, we would stop here. In a general-equilibrium analysis, however, we next consider how this shock to the corn market affects the soybean market. Because this shock initially causes the price of corn to fall relative to the price of soybeans (which stays constant), consumers substitute toward corn and away from soybeans: The demand curve for soybeans shifts to the left from D_0^s to D_2^s in panel b.

In addition, because the price of corn falls relative to the price of soybeans, farmers produce more soybeans at any given price of soybeans: The supply curve for soybeans shifts out to S_2^s. The new soybean demand curve, D_2^s, intersects the new soybean supply curve, S_2^s, at the new equilibrium e_2^s, where price is \$3.8325 per bushel, a fall of 7%, and quantity is 2.0514 billions of bushels per year, a drop of less than 1% (Step 2 row).

Table 10.1 Adjustment in the Corn and Soybean Markets

	Corn		Soybeans	
Step	*Price*	*Quantity*	*Price*	*Quantity*
Initial (0)	2.15	8.44	4.12	2.07
1	1.9171	8.2270		
2			3.8325	2.0514
3	1.9057	8.2613		
4			3.8180	2.0505
5	1.90508	8.26308		
6			3.81728	2.05043
.	.	.	.	.
.	.	.	.	.
.	.	.	.	.
Final	1.90505	8.26318	3.81724	2.05043

[1]Until recently, the corn and soybean markets were subject to price controls (Chapter 9). However, we use the estimated demand and supply curves to ask what would happen in these markets in the absence of price controls.

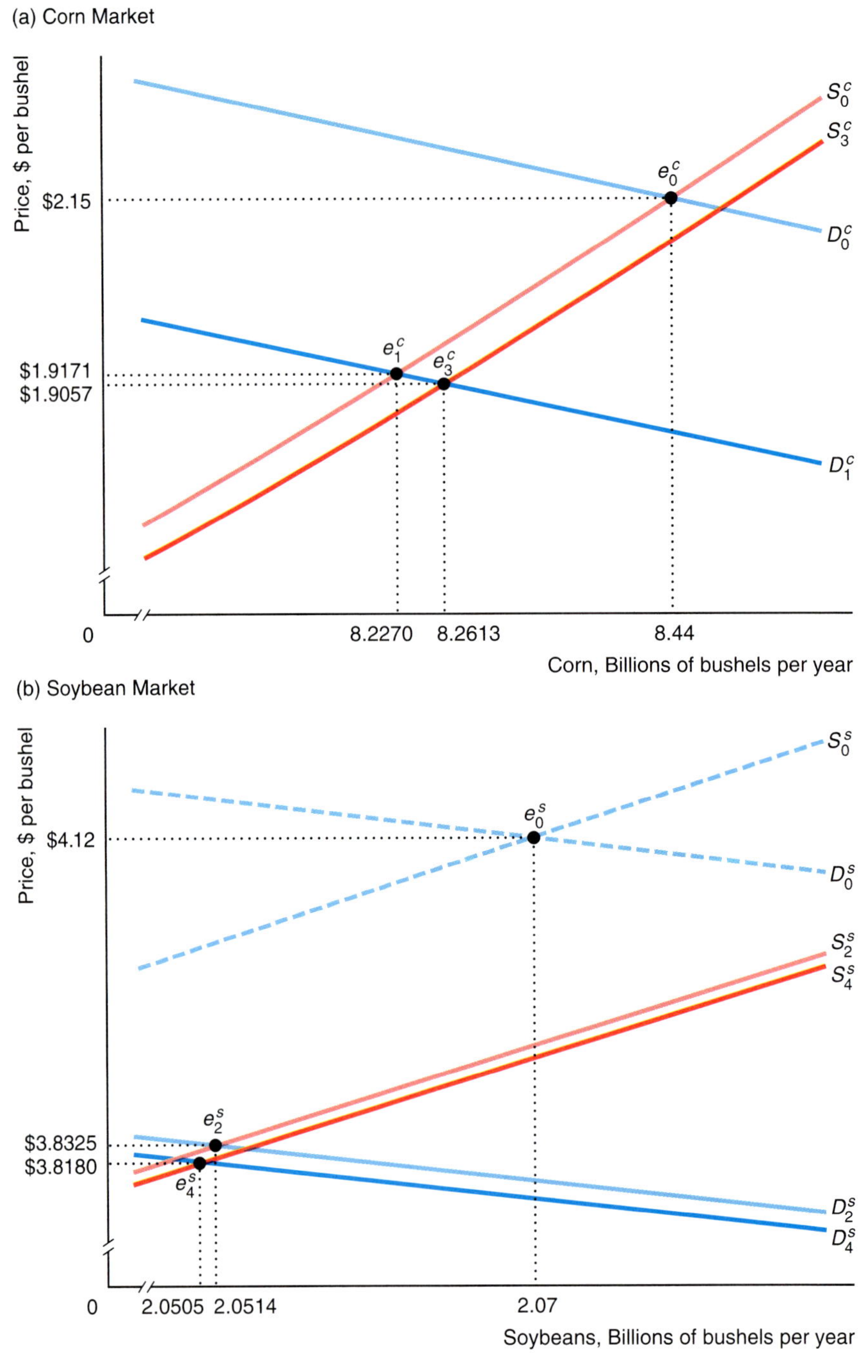
(a) Corn Market
Price, $ per bushel
$2.15
$1.9171
$1.9057
S_0^c
S_3^c
e_0^c
D_0^c
e_1^c
e_3^c
D_1^c
0
8.2270
8.2613
8.44
Corn, Billions of bushels per year
(b) Soybean Market
Price, $ per bushel
$4.12
$3.8325
$3.8180
S_0^s
e_0^s
D_0^s
S_2^s
S_4^s
e_2^s
e_4^s
D_2^s
D_4^s
0
2.0505
2.0514
2.07
Soybeans, Billions of bushels per year

Figure 10.1 The Relationship Between the Corn and Soybean Markets (based on Holt 1992).

As it turns out, this fall in the price of soybeans relative to the price of corn causes essentially no shift in the demand curve for corn (panel a shows no shift) but shifts the supply curve of corn, S_3^c, to the right. The new equilibrium is e_3^c, where S_3^c and D_1^c intersect. Price falls to \$1.9057 per bushel of corn and quantity to 8.2613 billions of bushels per year (Step 3 row).

This new fall in the relative price of corn causes the soybean demand curve, D_4^s, to shift farther to the left and the supply curve, S_4^s, to shift farther to the right in panel b. In the new equilibrium at e_4^s, where D_4^s and S_4^s intersect, the price and quantity of soybeans fall slightly to \$3.8180 per bushel and 2.0505 billions of bushels per year, respectively (Step 4 row).

These reverberations between the markets continue, with additional, smaller shifts of the supply and demand curves. Eventually, a final equilibrium is reached at which none of the supply and demand curves will shift further. The final equilibria in these two markets (last row of Table 10.1) are virtually the same as e_3^c in panel a and e_4^s in panel b.

Bias in a Partial-Equilibrium Analysis. Suppose that we were interested only in the effect of the shift in the foreign demand curve on the corn market. Could we rely on a partial-equilibrium analysis? According to the partial-equilibrium analysis, the price of corn falls 10.8% to \$1.9171. In contrast, in the general-equilibrium analysis, the price falls 11.4% to \$1.905, which is 1.2¢ less per bushel. Thus, the partial-equilibrium analysis underestimates the price effect by 0.6 percentage point. Similarly, the fall in quantity is 2.5% according to the partial-equilibrium analysis and only 2.1% according to the general-equilibrium analysis. In this market, then, the biases from using a partial-equilibrium analysis are small. The following application demonstrates that the biases from using a partial-equilibrium analysis are large in some other markets.

APPLICATION

Sin Taxes

Sin taxes—taxes on alcohol, tobacco, and other goods and services with poor reputations—are often justified on the grounds that they raise revenues for the government and discourage bad behavior. But do these taxes significantly affect other markets? After all, as consumers spend less on sinful activities, they increase their consumption of other goods. Further, resources that are freed from producing alcohol and cigarettes increase output in other sectors.

Boyd and Seldon (1991) estimated the effects of alcohol and tobacco taxes using a general-equilibrium model that considered 13 goods and services that are consumed by six groups of consumers of differing incomes. They considered a proposal whereby a $1.3 billion shortfall in drug rehabilitation programs would be paid for by higher cigarette and alcohol taxes.

These new sin taxes lowered alcohol and tobacco consumption by 2.03%. They raised prices to consumers by 2.08% and lowered prices to retailers by 0.02%, so almost all the price effect of the tax fell on consumers. As a consequence of these effects, prices of foods fell 0.03%; candy, 0.006%; clothing, 0.001%; and recreation, 0.004% (among others). Though these price changes were small, the revenue effects were sizable. After-tax revenues from alcohol and tobacco fell by $1.29 billion; revenues increased by $53 million for food, $9 million for candy, $20 million for clothing, and $19 million for recreation. Moreover, savings grew by $110 million.

Alcohol and tobacco are produced by using inputs from the food, alcohol, and tobacco processing sector and the service sector. The tax-induced drop in alcohol and tobacco sales resulted in the service sector's price and output falling by 0.003% and 0.024%, while the corresponding declines in the processing sector were 0.050% and 0.20%. The food, alcohol, and tobacco production sector lost $883 million in revenues, agriculture other than alcohol and tobacco lost $470 million, and services lost $664 million.

How important are these general-equilibrium effects in making policy? If a partial-equilibrium analysis were used that ignored spillover effects into other markets, the estimated change in the government revenues due to these taxes would be $1.29 billion. According to the general-equilibrium analysis, however, government revenues grow by only $772 million due to changes in taxes collected from other sectors. Thus, the partial-equilibrium analysis overstates the increase in tax revenues by two-thirds. ■

Minimum Wages with Incomplete Coverage

We used a partial-equilibrium analysis in Chapter 2 to examine the effects of a minimum wage law that holds throughout the entire labor market. The minimum wage causes the quantity of labor demanded to be less than the quantity of labor supplied. Workers who lose their jobs cannot find work elsewhere, so they become unemployed.

The story changes substantially, however, if the minimum wage law covers workers in only some sectors of the economy, as we show using a general-equilibrium analysis. This analysis is relevant because the U.S. minimum wage law has not covered all workers historically.

When a minimum wage is applied to a covered sector of the economy, the increase in the wage causes the quantity of labor demanded in that sector to fall. Workers who are displaced from jobs in the covered sector move to the uncovered sector, driving down the wage in that sector. When the U.S. minimum wage law was first passed in 1938, some economists joked that its purpose was to maintain family farms. The law drove workers out of manufacturing and other covered industries into agriculture, which the law did not cover.

Figure 10.2 shows the effect of a minimum wage law when coverage is incomplete. The total demand curve, D in panel c, is the horizontal sum of the demand curve for labor services in the covered sector, D^c in panel a, and the demand curve in the uncovered sector, D^u in panel b. In the absence of a minimum wage law, the wage in both sectors is w_1, which is determined by the intersection of the total demand curve, D, and the total supply curve, S. At that wage, L_c^1 annual hours of work are hired in the covered sector, L_u^1 annual hours in the uncovered sector, and $L_1 = L_c^1 + L_u^1$ total annual hours of work.

If a minimum wage of $\underline{w}$ is set in only the covered sector, employment in that sector falls to L_c^2. To determine the wage and level of employment in the uncovered sector, we first need to determine how much labor service is available to that sector.

Anyone who can't find work in the covered sector goes to the uncovered sector. The supply curve of labor to the uncovered sector in panel b is a **residual supply curve**: the market supply that is not met by demanders in other sectors at any given wage. With a binding minimum wage in the covered sector, the residual supply

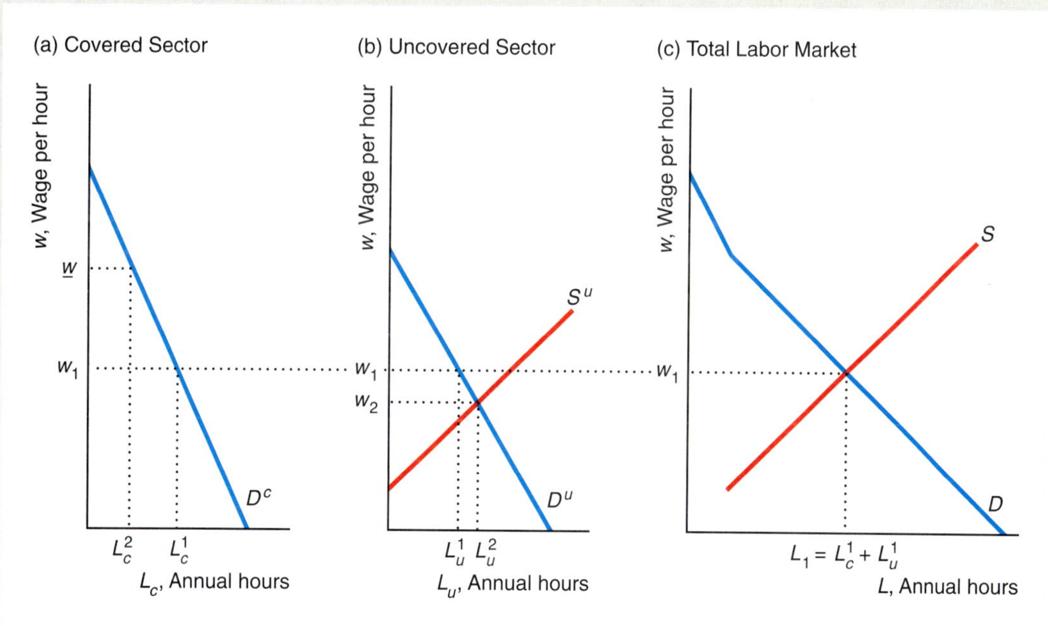

Figure 10.2 Minimum Wage with Incomplete Coverage. In the absence of a minimum wage, the equilibrium wage is w_1. Applying a minimum wage, $\underline{w}$, to only one sector causes the quantity of labor services demanded in the covered sector to fall. The extra labor moves to the uncovered sector, driving the wage there down to w_2.

function in the uncovered sector is[2]

$$S^u(w) = S(w) - D^c(\underline{w}).$$

Thus, the residual supply to the uncovered sector, $S^u(w)$, is the total supply, $S(w)$, at any given wage w minus the amount of labor used in the covered sector, $L_c^2 = D^c(\underline{w})$.

The intersection of D^u and S^u determines w_2, the new wage in the uncovered sector, and L_u^2, the new level of employment.[3] This general-equilibrium analysis shows that a minimum wage causes employment to drop in the covered sector, employment to rise (by a smaller amount) in the uncovered sector, and the wage in the uncovered sector to fall below the original competitive level. Thus, a minimum wage law with only partial coverage affects wage levels and employment levels in various sectors but need not create unemployment.

APPLICATION

U.S. Minimum Wage Laws and Teenagers

The first important American minimum wage legislation was the Fair Labor Standards Act of 1938. That law primarily covered the industrial sectors of the economy. Most agriculture, government, retail, and service workers were not subject to minimum wages. Almost half of the economy was not covered by the initial minimum wage legislation in 1938. The fraction of workers covered rose to 56% in 1947, 61% in 1962, 86% in 1978, and 88% in 1991. Today, all major industry and government sectors are covered to some extent, but coverage in agriculture and private household employment is still less than complete.

Teenagers, who earn relatively low wages, were particularly affected when the law first took effect (Welsh 1974). Table 10.2, which shows the law's effect on employment for this age group, illustrates that teenagers were driven out of the covered sector into the uncovered sector from 1930 to 1940 (though other changes, including the Great Depression, took place over this period as well). The first column lists some key industries, starting with mining—in which 99% of all workers were employed in firms subject to the minimum wage—and then presents other industries in decreasing order of coverage. The next two columns show the share of teenagers employed in each industry in 1930 and 1940. In 1930, 9.2% of all employees were teenagers. Their share

---

[2]A residual supply curve is similar to a residual demand curve (Appendix 8A). If there is no minimum wage, the residual supply curve to the uncovered sector is $S^u(w) = S(w) - D^c(w)$.

[3]This analysis is incomplete if the minimum wage causes the price of goods in the covered sector to rise relative to those in the uncovered sector, which, in turn, causes the demands for labor in those two sectors, D^c and D^u, to shift. Ignoring that possibility is reasonable if labor costs are a small fraction of total costs (hence the effect of the minimum wage is minimal on total costs) or if the demands for the final goods are relatively price insensitive.

Table 10.2 Effect of the Minimum Wage Law on Teenage Employment

	Teenagers as a Percent of All Employed Persons 14 and Over		Percentage Change in Teenage Employment from 1930 to 1940	Percentage of Workers in Covered Firms
	1930	*1940*		
Industries with Coverage Above the National Average				
Mining	5.3	2.3	−57	99
Manufacturing	9.6	4.8	−50	95
Transportation and communications	5.5	2.1	−62	88
Finance, insurance, and real estate	7.1	2.9	−59	74
U.S. Total	9.2	5.9	−36	56
Industries with Coverage Below the National Average				
Construction	3.2	2.5	−22	44
Services	7.5	6.0	−20	19
Wholesale and retail trade	8.8	6.0	−32	13
Agriculture, forestry, and fishing	14.2	10.6	−25	—
Miscellaneous	11.2	10.5	−6	—
Governments	3.2	3.4	+6	—

Source: Welsh (1974).

fell to 5.9% in 1940 due to the Depression, the minimum wage law, other labor laws, and additional factors.

The next column gives the percentage change in the share of teenage employment from 1930 to 1940. It shows that teenagers' share of employment fell everywhere except the government sector. Teenage employment dropped more in industries with minimum wage coverage that was greater than the national average and less in industries with lower levels of coverage. Thus, teenagers moved from the relatively covered sector to the relatively uncovered sector. ■

SOLVED PROBLEM 10.1

After the government starts subsidizing the cost of labor by a payment of s per hour only in a covered sector, the wage that workers in both sectors receive is w, but the wage paid by firms in the covered sector is $w - s$. What effect does the subsidy have on the wages, total employment, and employment in the covered and uncovered sectors of the economy?

Answer

1. *Determine the original equilibrium*: In Figure 10.3, the intersection of the total demand curve, D^1, and the total supply curve of labor, S, determines the original equilibrium, e_1, where the wage is w_1 and total employment is L_1. The total demand curve is the horizontal sum of the demand curves in the covered, D_1^c, and uncovered, D^u, sectors.

2. *Show the shift in the demand for labor in the covered sector and the resulting shift in the total demand curve*: The subsidy causes the demand curve for labor in the covered sector to shift upward from D_1^c to D_2^c. As a result, the total demand curve shifts out to D^2.

3. *Determine the equilibrium wage using the total demand and supply curves, then determine employment in the two sectors*: Workers shift between sectors until the new wage is equal in both sectors at w_2, which is determined by the intersection of the new total demand curve, D^2, and the total supply curve, S. Employment in the two sectors is L_2^c and L_2^u.

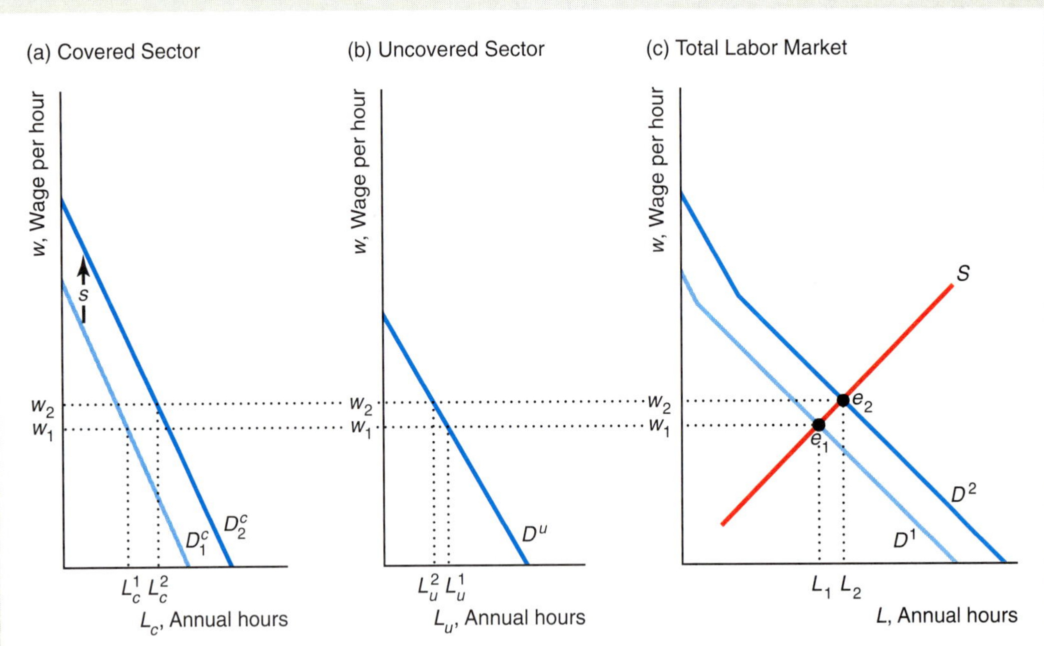

Figure 10.3 Wage Subsidy with Incomplete Coverage. Before the subsidy, the equilibrium wage, w_1, is determined by the intersection of D^1 and S. The subsidy of s per hour of labor to the covered sector shifts the demand in the covered sector to D_2^c, so the total demand curve shifts to D^2. As a result, the wage rises to w_2, total employment and employment in the covered sector rise, and employment in the uncovered sector falls.

4. *Compare the equilibria*: The subsidy causes the wage, total employment, and employment in the covered sector to rise and employment in the uncovered sector to fall. ■

10.2 TRADING BETWEEN TWO PEOPLE

In Chapter 9, we learned that tariffs, quotas, and other restrictions on trade usually harm both importing and exporting nations. The reason is that both parties to a voluntary trade benefit from that trade or else they would not have traded. Using a general-equilibrium model, we will show that free trade is Pareto efficient: After all voluntary trades have occurred, we cannot reallocate goods so as to make one person better off without harming another person. We first demonstrate that trade between two people has this Pareto property. We then show that the same property holds when many people trade using a competitive market.

Endowments

Suppose that Jane and Denise live near each other in the wilds of Massachusetts. A snowstorm strikes, isolating them from the rest of the world. They must either trade with each other or consume only what they have at hand.

Collectively, they have 50 cords of firewood and 80 bars of candy and no way of producing more of either good. Jane's **endowment**—an initial allocation of goods—is 30 cords of firewood and 20 candy bars. Denise's endowment is 20 (= 50 − 30) cords of firewood and 60 (= 80 − 20) candy bars. That is, Jane has relatively more wood, and Denise has relatively more candy.

We show these endowments in Figure 10.4. Panels a and b are typical indifference curve diagrams (Chapters 4 and 5) in which we measure cords of firewood on the vertical axis and candy bars on the horizontal axis. Jane's endowment is e_j (30 cords of firewood and 20 candy bars) in panel a, and Denise's endowment is e_d in panel b. Both panels show the indifference curve through the endowment.

If we take Denise's diagram, rotate it, and put it on Jane's diagram, we obtain the box in panel c. This type of figure, called an *Edgeworth box* (after an English economist, Francis Ysidro Edgeworth), illustrates trade between two people with fixed endowments of two goods. We use this Edgeworth box to illustrate a general-equilibrium model in which we examine simultaneous trade in firewood and trade in candy.

The height of the Edgeworth box represents 50 cords of firewood, and the length represents 80 candy bars, which are the combined endowments of Jane and Denise. The Bundle *e* shows both Jane's endowment and Denise's endowment. Measuring from Jane's origin, O_j, at the lower left of the diagram, we see that Jane has 30 cords of firewood and 20 candy bars at endowment *e*. Similarly, measuring from Denise's origin, O_d, at the upper-right corner, we see that Denise has 60 bars of candy and 20 cords of firewood at *e*.

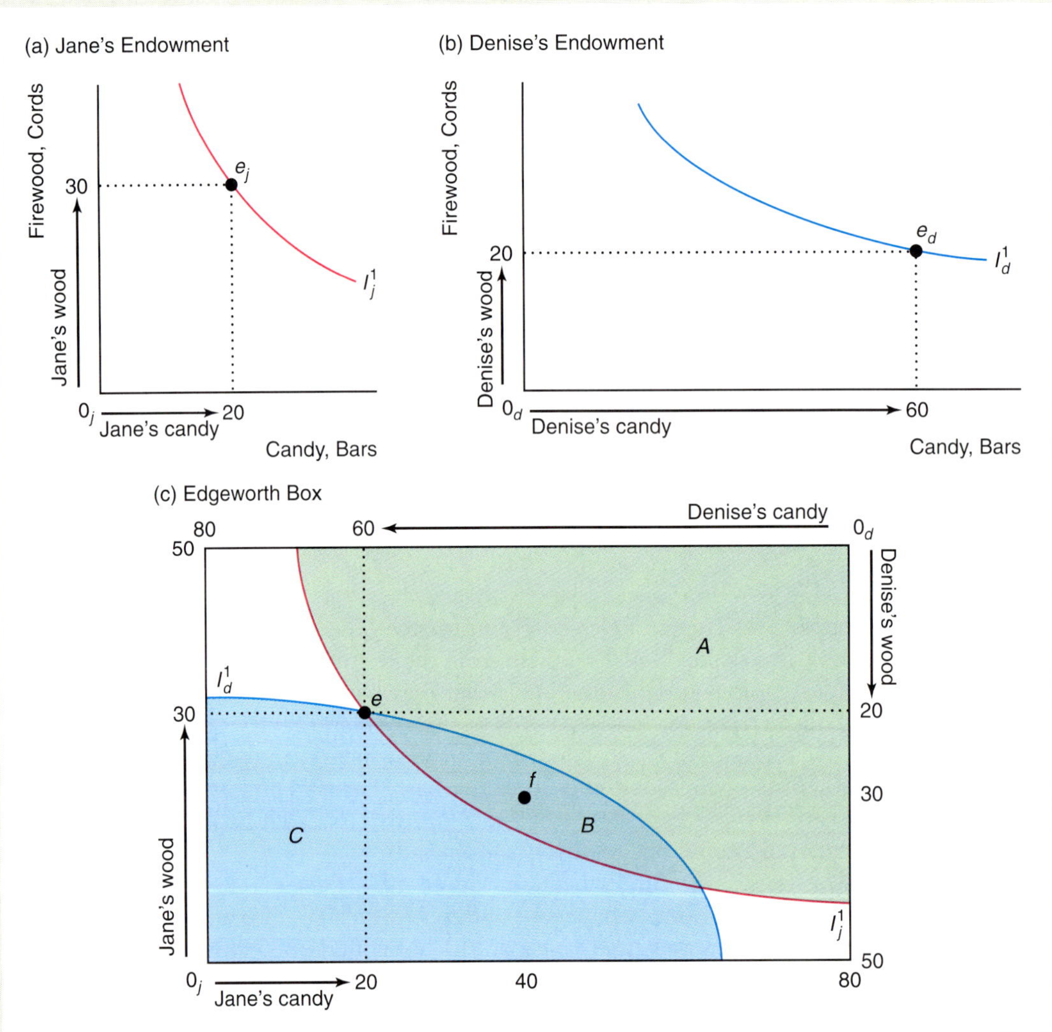

Figure 10.4 Endowments in an Edgeworth Box. (a) Jane's endowment is e_j, where she has 20 candy bars and 30 cords of firewood. She is indifferent between that bundle and the others that lie on her indifference curve I_j^1. (b) Denise is indifferent between her endowment, e_d (60 candy bars and 20 cords of wood), and the other bundles on I_d^1. (c) Their endowments are at e in the Edgeworth box formed by combining the figures in (a) and (b). Jane prefers bundles in A and B to e. Denise prefers bundles in B and C to e. Thus, both prefer any bundle in area B to e.

Mutually Beneficial Trades

Should Jane and Denise trade? The answer depends on their tastes, which are summarized by their indifference curves. We make four assumptions about their tastes and behavior:

- **Utility maximization:** Each person *maximizes* her *utility*.
- **Usual-shaped indifference curves:** Each person's indifference curves have the usual convex shape.
- **Nonsatiation:** Each person has strictly positive *marginal utility* for each good, so each person wants as much of the good as possible (neither person is ever satiated).
- **No interdependence:** Neither person's utility depends on the other's consumption (neither person gets pleasure or displeasure from the other's consumption), and neither person's consumption harms the other (one person's consumption of firewood does not cause smoke pollution that bothers the other person).

Figure 10.4 reflects these assumptions.

In panel a, Jane's indifference curve, I_j^1, through her endowment point, e_j, is convex to her origin, O_j. Jane is indifferent between e_j and any other bundle on I_j^1. She prefers bundles that lie above I_j^1 to e_j and prefers e_j to points that lie below I_j^1. Panel c also shows her indifference curve, I_j^1. The bundles that Jane prefers to her endowment are in the shaded areas *A* and *B*, which lie above her indifference curve I_j^1.

Similarly, Denise's indifference curve, I_d^1, through her endowment is convex to her origin, O_d, in the lower left of panel b. This indifference curve, I_d^1, is still convex to O_d in panel c, but O_d is in the upper right of the Edgeworth box. (It may help to turn this book around when viewing Denise's indifference curves in an Edgeworth box. Then again, possibly many points will be clearer if the book is held upside down.) The bundles Denise prefers to her endowment are in shaded areas *B* and *C*, which lie on the other side of her indifference curve I_d^1 from her origin O_d (above I_d^1 if you turn the book upside down).

At the endowment *e* in panel c, Jane and Denise can both benefit from a trade. Jane prefers bundles in *A* and *B* to *e*, and Denise prefers bundles in *B* and *C* to *e*, so *both* prefer bundles within the football-shaped area *B* to their endowment at *e*.

Suppose they trade, reallocating goods from Bundle *e* to *f*. Jane gives up 10 cords of firewood for 20 more candy bars, and Denise gives up 20 candy bars for 10 more cords of wood. As Figure 10.5 illustrates, both gain from such a trade. Jane's indifference curve I_j^2 through allocation *f* lies above her indifference curve I_j^1 through allocation *e*, so she is better off at *f* than at *e*. Similarly, Denise's indifference curve I_d^2 through *f* lies above (if you hold the book upside down) her indifference curve I_d^1 through *e*, so she also benefits from the trade.

Now that they've traded to Bundle *f*, do Jane and Denise want to make further trades? To answer this question, we can repeat our analysis. Jane prefers all bundles above I_j^2, her indifference curve through *f*. Denise prefers all bundles above (when the book is held upside down) I_d^2 to *f*. However, there are no bundles that both prefer because I_j^2 and I_d^2 are tangent at *f*. Neither Jane nor Denise wants to trade from *f* to a bundle such as *e*, which is below both of their indifference curves. Jane would love to trade from *f* to *c*, which is on her higher indifference curve I_j^3, but such a trade would make Denise worse off because this bundle is on a lower indifference curve I_d^1. Similarly, Denise prefers *b* to *f*, but Jane does not. Thus *any* move from *f* harms at least one of them.

The reason no further trade is possible at a bundle like *f* is that Jane's marginal rate of substitution (the slope of her indifference curve), MRS_j, between wood and

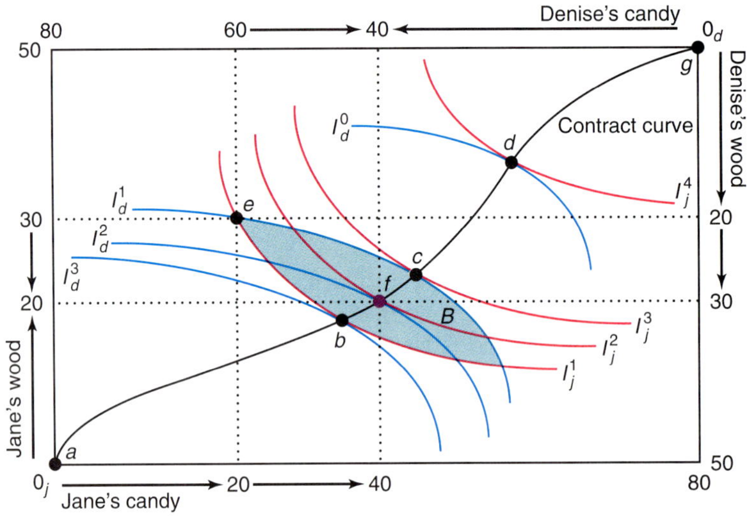

	Endowment, *e*		Trade		New Allocation, *f*	
	Wood	Candy	Wood	Candy	Wood	Candy
Jane	30	20	–10	+20	20	40
Denise	20	60	+10	–20	30	40

Figure 10.5 Contract Curve. The contract curve contains all the Pareto-efficient allocations. Any bundle for which Jane's indifference curve is tangent to Denise's indifference curve lies on the contract curve, because no further trade is possible, so we can't reallocate goods to make one of them better off without harming the other. Starting at an endowment of *e*, Jane and Denise will trade to a bundle on the contract curve in area *B*: bundles between *b* and *c*. The table above shows how they would trade to Bundle *f*.

candy equals Denise's marginal rate of substitution, MRS_d. Jane's MRS_j is $-\frac{1}{2}$: She is willing to trade one cord of wood for two candy bars. Because Denise's indifference curve is tangent to Jane's, Denise's MRS_d must also be $-\frac{1}{2}$. When they both want to trade wood for candy at the same rate, they can't agree on further trades.

In contrast, at a bundle, such as *e*, where their indifference curves are not tangent, MRS_j does not equal MRS_d. Denise's MRS_d is $-\frac{1}{3}$, and Jane's MRS_j is –2. Denise is willing to give up one cord of wood for three more candy bars or to sacrifice three candy bars for one more cord of wood. If Denise offers Jane three candy bars for one cord of wood, Jane will accept because she is willing to give up one cord of wood for two candy bars. This example illustrates that trades are possible where indifferent curves intersect because marginal rates of substitution are unequal.

To summarize, we can make four equivalent statements about allocation *f*:

1. The indifference curves of the two parties are tangent at *f*.
2. The parties' marginal rates of substitution are equal at *f*.
3. No further mutually beneficial trades are possible at *f*.
4. The allocation at *f* is Pareto efficient: One party cannot be made better off without harming the other.

Indifference curves are also tangent at bundles *b*, *c*, and *d*, so these allocations, like *f*, are Pareto efficient. By connecting all such bundles, we draw the **contract curve**: the set of all Pareto-efficient bundles. The reason for this name is that only at these points are the parties unwilling to engage in further trades or contracts: These allocations are the final contracts. A move from any bundle on the contract curve must harm at least one person.

SOLVED PROBLEM 10.2

Are allocations a and g in Figure 10.5 part of the contract curve?

Answer

By showing that no mutually beneficial trades are possible at those points, demonstrate that those bundles are Pareto efficient: The allocation at which Jane has everything, allocation *g*, is on the contract curve because no mutually beneficial trade is possible: Denise has no goods to trade with Jane. As a consequence, we cannot make Denise better off without taking goods from Jane. Similarly, when Denise has everything, *a*, we can make Jane better off only by taking wood or candy from Denise and giving it to Jane. ■

Bargaining Ability

For every allocation off the contract curve, there are allocations on the contract curve that benefit at least one person. If they start at endowment *e*, Jane and Denise should trade until they reach a point on the contract curve between bundles *b* and *c* in Figure 10.5. All the allocations within the football-shaped area *B* are beneficial. However, if they trade to any allocation in *B* that is not on the contract curve, further beneficial trades are possible because their indifference curves intersect at that allocation.

Where will they end up on the contract curve between *b* and *c*? That depends on who is better at bargaining. Suppose that Jane is better at bargaining. Jane knows that the more she gets, the worse off Denise will be and that Denise will not agree to any trade that makes her worse off than she is at *e*. Thus, the best trade Jane can make is one that leaves Denise only as well off as at *e*, which are the bundles on I_d^1. If Jane could pick any point she wanted along I_d^1, she'd choose the bundle on her highest possible indifference curve, which is Bundle *c*, where I_j^3 is just tangent to I_d^1. After this trade, Denise is no better off than before, but Jane is much happier. By similar reasoning, if Denise is better at bargaining, the final allocation will be at *b*.

10.3 COMPETITIVE EXCHANGE

Most trading throughout the world occurs without one-on-one bargaining between people. When you go to the store to buy a bottle of shampoo, you read its posted price and then decide whether to buy it or not. You've probably never tried to bargain with the store's clerk over the price of shampoo: You're a price taker in the shampoo market.

If we don't know much about how Jane and Denise bargain, all we can say is that they will trade to some allocation on the contract curve. If we know the exact trading process they use, however, we can apply that process to determine the final allocation. In particular, we can examine the competitive trading process to determine the competitive equilibrium in a pure exchange economy.

In Chapter 9, we used a partial-equilibrium approach to show that one measure of welfare, W, is maximized in a competitive market in which many voluntary trades occur. We now use a general-equilibrium model to show that a competitive market has two desirable properties:

- **The competitive equilibrium is efficient:** Competition results in a Pareto-efficient allocation—no one can be made better off without making someone worse off—in all markets.
- **Any efficient allocations can be achieved by competition:** All possible efficient allocations can be obtained by competitive exchange, given an appropriate initial allocation of goods.

Economists call these results the *First Theorem of Welfare Economics* and the *Second Theorem of Welfare Economics*, respectively. These properties hold if everyone knows the preferences of all traders, there are no transaction costs, and indifference curves have the usual shapes.

Competitive Equilibrium

When two people trade, they are unlikely to view themselves as price takers. However, if there were a large number of people with tastes and endowments like Jane's and a large number of people with tastes and endowments like Denise's, each person would be a price taker in the two goods. We can use an Edgeworth box to examine how such price takers would trade.

Because they can trade only two goods, each person needs to consider only the relative price of the two goods when deciding whether to trade. If the price of a cord of wood, p_w, is \$2, and the price of a candy bar, p_c, is \$1, then a candy bar costs half as much as a cord of wood: $p_c/p_w = \frac{1}{2}$. An individual can sell one cord of wood and use that money to buy two candy bars.

At the initial allocation, *e*, Jane has goods worth \$80 = (\$2 per cord × 30 cords of firewood) + (\$1 per candy bar × 20 candy bars). At these prices, Jane could keep her endowment or trade to an allocation with 40 cords of firewood and no candy, 80 bars of candy and no firewood, or any combination in between as the price line (budget line) in panel a of Figure 10.6 shows. The price line is all the combinations

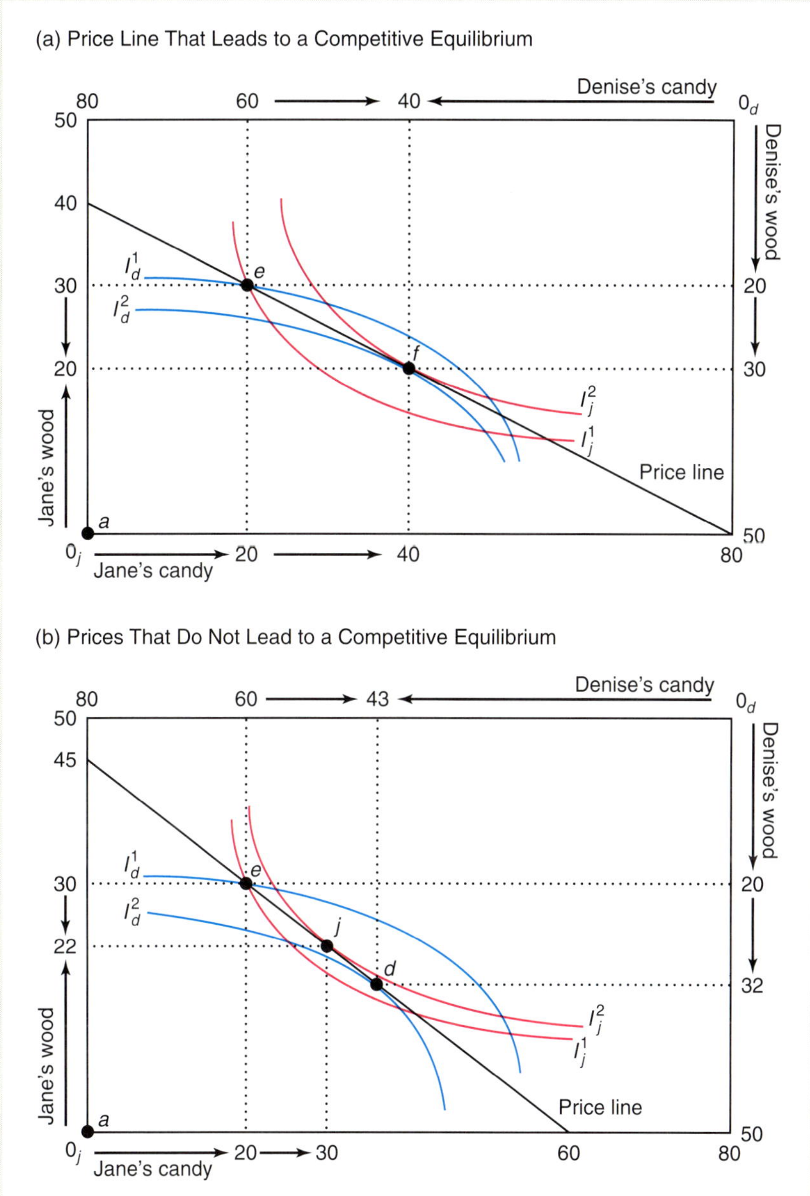

Figure 10.6 Competitive Equilibrium. The initial endowment is *e*. (a) If along the price line facing Jane and Denise p_w = \$2 and p_c = \$1, they trade to point *f*, where Jane's indifference curve, I_j^2, is tangent to the price line and to Denise's indifference curve, I_d^2. (b) No other price line results in an equilibrium. If p_w = \$1.33 and p_c = \$1, Denise wants to buy 12 (= 32 – 20) cords of firewood at these prices, but Jane wants to sell only 8 (= 30 – 22) cords. Similarly, Jane wants to buy 10 (= 30 – 20) candy bars, but Denise wants to sell 17 (= 60 – 43). Thus, these prices are not consistent with a competitive equilibrium.

of goods Jane could get by trading, given her endowment. The price line goes through point *e* and has a slope of $-p_c/p_w = -\frac{1}{2}$.

Given the price line, what bundle of goods will Jane choose? She wants to maximize her utility by picking the bundle where one of her indifference curves, I_j^2, is tangent to her budget or price line. Denise wants to maximize her utility by choosing a bundle in the same way.

In a competitive market, prices adjust until the quantity supplied equals the quantity demanded. An auctioneer could help to determine the equilibrium. The auctioneer could call out relative prices and ask how much is demanded and how much is offered for sale at those prices. If demand does not equal supply, the auctioneer calls out another relative price. When demand equals supply, the transactions actually occur and the auction stops. At some ports, fishing boats sell their catch to fish wholesalers at a daily auction run in this manner.

Panel a shows that, when candy costs half as much as wood, the quantity demanded of each good equals the quantity supplied. Jane (and every person like her) wants to sell 10 cords of firewood and use that money to buy 20 additional candy bars. Similarly, Denise (and everyone like her) wants to sell 20 candy bars and buy 10 cords of wood. Thus, the quantity of wood sold equals the quantity bought, and the quantity of candy demanded equals that supplied. We can see in the figure that the quantities demanded equal the quantities supplied because the optimal bundle for both types of consumers is the same Bundle, *f*.

At any other price ratio, the quantity demanded of each good would not equal the quantity supplied. For example, if the price of candy remained constant at $p_c =$ \$1 per bar but the price of wood fell to $p_w =$ \$1.33 per cord, the price line would be steeper, with a slope of $-p_c/p_w = -1/1.33 = -0.75$ in panel b. At these prices, Jane wants to trade to Bundle *j* and Denise wants to trade to Bundle *d*. Because Jane wants to buy 10 extra candy bars but Denise wants to sell 17 extra candy bars, the quantity supplied does not equal the quantity demanded, so this price ratio does not result in a competitive equilibrium when the endowment is *e*.

Competition Is Efficient

In a competitive equilibrium, the indifference curves of both types of consumers are tangent at the same bundle on the price line. As a result, the slope (*MRS*) of each person's indifference curve equals the slope of the price line, so the slopes of the indifference curves are equal:

$$MRS_j = -\frac{p_c}{p_w} = MRS_d. \tag{10.1}$$

The marginal rates of substitution are equal across consumers in the competitive equilibrium, so the competitive equilibrium must lie on the contract curve. Thus, we have demonstrated the First Theorem of Welfare Economics:

Any competitive equilibrium is Pareto efficient.

The intuition for this result is that people (who face the same prices) make all the voluntary trades they want in a competitive market. Because no additional voluntary trades can occur, there is no way to make someone better off without making someone worse off in a competitive equilibrium. (If an involuntary trade occurs, at least one person is made worse off. A person who steals goods from another person—an involuntary exchange—gains at the expense of the victim.)

Any Efficient Allocation Is Obtainable by Using Competition

Of the many possible Pareto-efficient allocations, the government may want to choose one. Can it achieve that allocation using the competitive market mechanism?

Our previous example illustrates that the competitive equilibrium depends on the endowment: the initial distribution of wealth. For example, if the initial endowment were *a* in panel a of Figure 10.6—where Denise has everything and Jane has nothing—the competitive equilibrium would be *a* because no trades would be possible.

Thus, for competition to lead to a particular allocation, say *f*, the trading must start at an appropriate endowment. If the consumers' endowment is *f*, a Pareto-efficient point, their indifference curves are tangent at *f*, so no further trades occur. That is, *f* is a competitive equilibrium.

Many other endowments also will result in a competitive equilibrium at *f*. Panel a shows that the resulting competitive equilibrium is *f* if the endowment is *e*. In that figure, a price line goes through both *e* and *f*. If the endowment is any bundle along this price line—not just *e* or *f*—the competitive equilibrium is *f*, because only at *f* are the indifference curves tangent.

To summarize, any Pareto-efficient bundle *x* can be obtained as a competitive equilibrium if the initial endowment is *x*. That allocation can also be obtained as a competitive equilibrium if the endowment lies on a price line through *x*, where the slope of the price line equals the marginal rate of substitution of the indifference curves that are tangent at *x*. Thus, we've demonstrated the Second Theorem of Welfare Economics:

> *Any Pareto-efficient equilibrium can be obtained by competition, given an appropriate endowment.*

The first welfare theorem tells us that society can achieve efficiency by allowing competition. The second welfare theorem adds that society can obtain the particular efficient allocation it prefers based on its value judgments about equity by appropriately redistributing endowments (income).

10.4 PRODUCTION AND TRADING

So far, our discussion has been based on a pure exchange economy with no production. We now examine an economy in which a fixed amount of a single input can be used to produce two different goods.

Comparative Advantage

Jane and Denise can produce candy or chop firewood using their own labor. They differ, however, in how much of each good they produce from a day's work.

Production Possibility Frontier. Jane can produce either three candy bars or six cords of firewood in a day. By splitting her time between the two activities, she can produce various combinations of the two goods. If α is the fraction of a day she spends making candy and $1 - \alpha$ is the fraction cutting wood, she produces 3α candy bars and $6(1 - \alpha)$ cords of wood.

By varying α between 0 and 1, we trace out the line in panel a of Figure 10.7. This line is Jane's *production possibility frontier* (PPF^j, Chapter 7), which shows the maximum combinations of wood and candy that she can produce from a given amount of input. If Jane works all day using the best available technology (such as a sharp axe), she achieves *efficiency in production* and produces combinations of goods on PPF^j. If she sits around part of the day or does not use the best possible technologies, she produces an inefficient combination of wood and candy inside PPF^j.

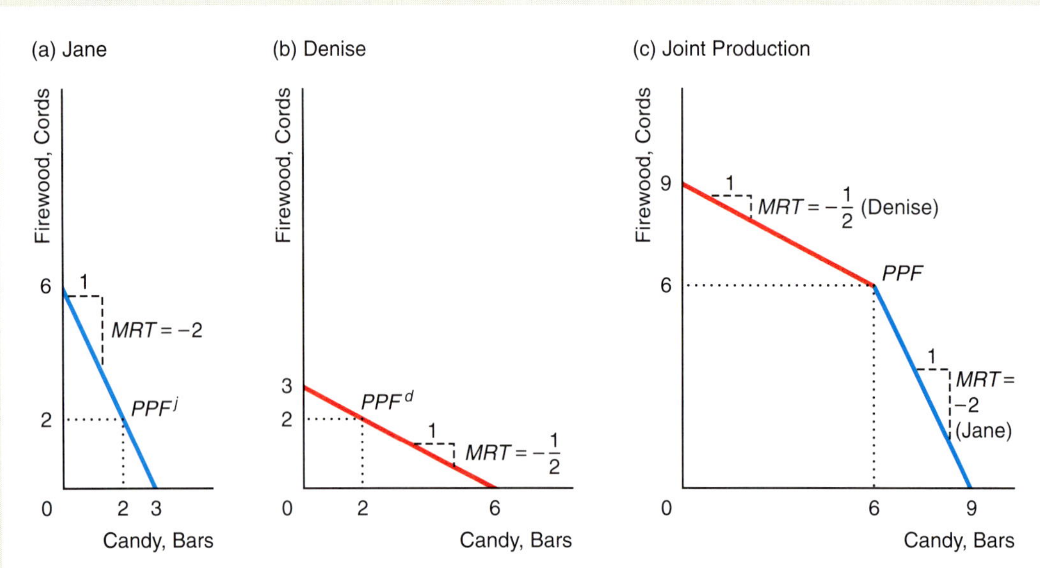

Figure 10.7 Comparative Advantage and Production Possibility Frontiers. (a) Jane's production possibility frontier, PPF^j, shows that, in a day, she can produce six cords of firewood or three candy bars or any combination of the two. Her marginal rate of transformation (*MRT*) is –2. (b) Denise's production possibility frontier, PPF^d, has an *MRT* of $-\frac{1}{2}$. (c) Their joint production possibility frontier, *PPF*, has a kink at six cords of firewood (produced by Jane) and six candy bars (produced by Denise) and is concave to the origin.

Marginal Rate of Transformation. The slope of the production possibility frontier is the *marginal rate of transformation* (*MRT*).[4] The marginal rate of transformation tells us how much more wood can be produced if the production of candy is reduced by one bar. Because Jane's PPF^j is a straight line with a slope of –2, her *MRT* is –2 at every allocation.

Denise can produce up to three cords of wood or six candy bars in a day. Panel b shows her production possibility function, PPF^d, with an $MRT = -\frac{1}{2}$. Thus, with a day's work, Denise can produce relatively more candy, and Jane can produce relatively more wood, as reflected by their differing marginal rates of transformation.

The marginal rate of transformation shows how much it costs to produce one good in terms of the forgone production of the other good. A person who, when producing one good, gives up producing less of a second good compared to another person is said to have a **comparative advantage** in producing the first good. Denise has a comparative advantage in producing candy, and Jane has a comparative advantage in producing wood.

By combining their outputs, they have the joint production possibility frontier *PPF* in panel c. If Denise and Jane spend all their time producing wood, Denise produces three cords and Jane produces six cords for a total of nine, which is where the joint *PPF* hits the wood axis. Similarly, if they both produce candy, they can jointly produce nine bars. If Denise specializes in making candy and Jane specializes in cutting wood, they produce six candy bars and six cords of wood, a combination that appears at the kink in the *PPF*.

If they choose to produce a relatively large quantity of candy and a relatively small amount of wood, Denise produces only candy and Jane produces some candy and some wood. Jane chops the wood because that's her comparative advantage. The marginal rate of transformation in the lower portion of the *PPF* is Jane's, –2, because only she produces both candy and wood.

Similarly, if they produce little candy, Jane produces only wood and Denise produces some wood and some candy, so the marginal rate of transformation in the higher portion of the *PPF* is Denise's, $-\frac{1}{2}$. In short, the *PPF* has a kink at six cords of wood and six candy bars and is concave (bowed away from the origin).[5]

Benefits of Trade. Because of the difference in their marginal rates of transformation, Jane and Denise can benefit from a trade. Suppose Jane and Denise like to consume wood and candy in equal proportions. If they do not trade, each produces two candy bars and two cords of wood in a day. If they agree to trade, Denise, who excels at making candy, spends all day producing six candy bars. Similarly, Jane, who has a comparative advantage at chopping, produces six cords of wood. If they split this production equally, they can each have three cords of wood and three candy bars—or 50% more than if they don't trade.

[4]In Chapter 4, we called the slope of a consumer's budget line the marginal rate of transformation. For a price-taking consumer who obtains goods by buying them, the budget line plays the same role as the production possibility frontier for someone who produces the two goods.

[5]Problem 9 at the end of this chapter asks you to prove that the joint production possibility frontier is concave, not convex (bowed toward the origin).

They do better if they trade because each person uses her comparative advantage. Without trade, if Denise wants an extra cord of wood, she must give up two candy bars. Producing an extra cord of wood costs Jane only half a candy bar in forgone production. Denise is willing to trade up to two candy bars for a cord of wood, and Jane is willing to trade the wood as long as she gets at least half a candy bar. Thus, there is room for a mutually beneficial trade.

SOLVED PROBLEM 10.3

How does the joint production possibility frontier in panel c of Figure 10.7 change if Jane and Denise can also trade with Harvey, who can produce five cords of wood, five candy bars, or any linear combination of wood and candy in a day?

Answer

1. *Describe each person's individual production possibility frontier*: Panels a and b of Figure 10.7 show the production possibility frontiers of Jane and Denise. Harvey's production possibility frontier is a straight line that hits the firewood axis at five cords and the candy axis at five candy bars.
2. *Draw the joint PPF, by starting at the quantity on the horizontal axis that is produced if everyone specializes in candy and then connecting the individual production possibility frontiers in order of comparative advantage in chopping wood*: If everyone produces candy, they make 14 candy bars (on the horizontal axis of Figure 10.8). Jane has a comparative advantage at chopping wood over Harvey and Denise, and Harvey has a comparative advantage over Denise. Thus, Jane's production possibility frontier is the first one (starting at the lower right), then comes Harvey's, and then Denise's. The resulting *PPF* is concave to the origin. (If we change the order of the individual frontiers, the resulting kinked line lies inside the *PPF* in Figure 10.8. Thus, the new line cannot be the joint production possibility frontier, which shows the maximum possible production from the available labor inputs.) ■

The Number of Producers. When there are only two ways of producing wood and candy—Denise's and Jane's methods with different marginal rates of transformation—the joint production possibility frontier has a single kink (panel c of Figure 10.7). If another method of production with a different marginal rate of transformation—Harvey's—is added, the joint production possibility frontier has two kinks (Figure 10.8).

If many firms can produce candy and firewood with different marginal rates of transformation, the joint production possibility frontier has even more kinks. As the

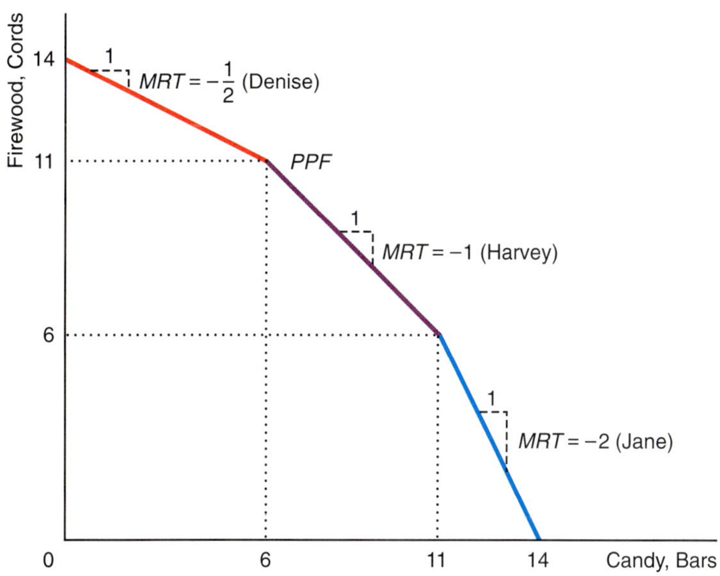

Figure 10.8 Joint Production Possibility Frontier with Three Producers. The joint *PPF* with three producers with different marginal rates of transformation (Jane's *MRT* is –2, Harvey's is –1, and Denise's is $-\frac{1}{2}$) has two kinks and is concave to the origin.

number of firms becomes very large, the PPF becomes a smooth curve that is concave to the origin, as in Figure 10.9.

Because the *PPF* is concave, the marginal rate of transformation decreases (in absolute value) as we move up the *PPF*. The *PPF* has a flatter slope at *a*, where the $MRT = -\frac{1}{2}$, than at *b*, where the $MRT = -1$. At *a*, giving up a candy bar leads to half a cord more wood production. In contrast, at *b*, where relatively more candy is produced, giving up producing a candy bar frees enough resources that an additional cord of wood can be produced.

The marginal rate of transformation along this smooth *PPF* tells us about the marginal cost of producing one good relative to the marginal cost of producing the other good. The marginal rate of transformation equals the negative of the ratio of the marginal cost of producing candy, MC_c, and wood, MC_w:

$$MRT = -\frac{MC_c}{MC_w}. \tag{10.2}$$

Suppose that at point *a* in Figure 10.9, a firm's marginal cost of producing an extra candy bar is \$1 and its marginal cost of producing an additional cord of firewood is \$2. As a result, the firm can produce one extra candy bar or half a cord of

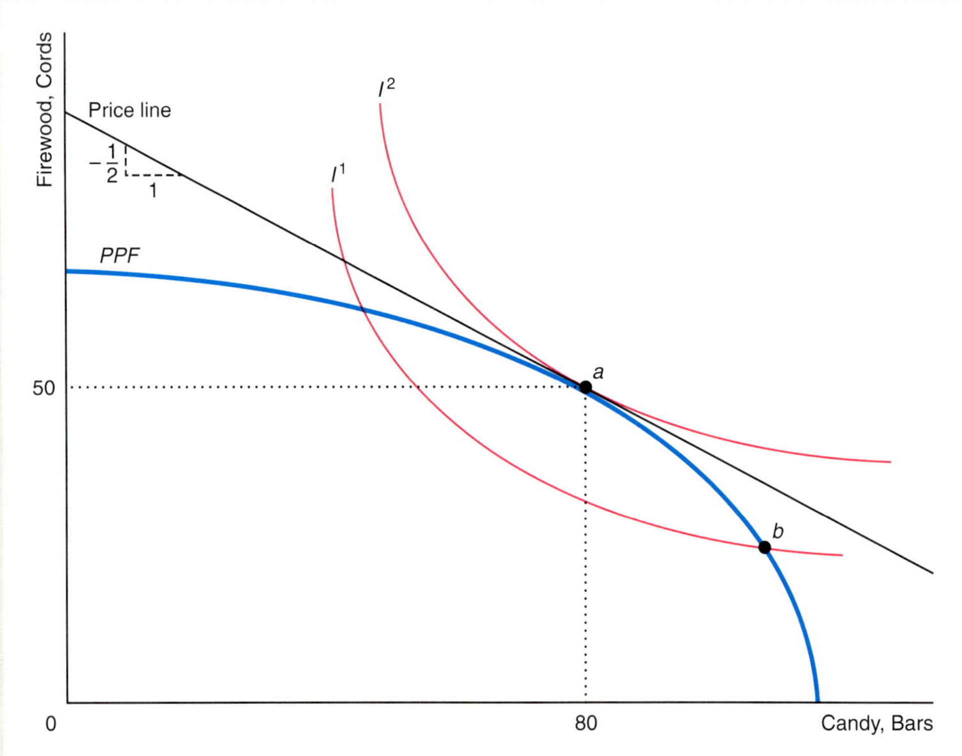

Figure 10.9 Optimal Product Mix. The optimal product mix, *a*, could be determined by maximizing an individual's utility by picking the allocation for which an indifference curve is tangent to the production possibility frontier. It could also be determined by picking the allocation where the relative competitive price, p_c/p_f, equals the slope of the *PPF*.

wood at a cost of $1. The marginal rate of transformation is the negative of the ratio of the marginal costs, $-(\$1/\$2) = -\frac{1}{2}$. To produce one more candy bar, the firm must give up producing half a cord of wood.

Efficient Product Mix

Which combination of products along the *PPF* does society choose? If a single person were to decide on the product mix, that person would pick the allocation of wood and candy along the *PPF* that maximized his or her utility. A person with the indifference curves in Figure 10.9 would pick Allocation *a*, which is the point where the *PPF* touches indifference curve I^2.

Because I^2 is tangent to the *PPF* at *a*, that person's marginal rate of substitution (the slope of indifference curve I^2) equals the marginal rate of transformation (the slope of the *PPF*). The marginal rate of substitution, *MRS*, tells us how much a consumer is willing to give up of one good to get another. The marginal rate of transformation, *MRT*, tells us how much of one good we need to give up to produce more of another good.

If the *MRS* doesn't equal the *MRT*, the consumer will be happier with a different product mix. At Allocation *b*, the indifference curve I^1 intersects the *PPF*, so the *MRS* does not equal the *MRT*. At *b*, the consumer is willing to give up one candy bar to get a third of a cord of wood ($MRS = -\frac{1}{3}$), but firms can produce one cord of wood for every candy bar not produced ($MRT = -1$). Thus, at *b*, too little wood is being produced. If the firms increase wood production, the *MRS* will fall and the *MRT* will rise until they are equal at *a*, where $MRS = MRT = -\frac{1}{2}$.

We can extend this reasoning to look at the product mix choice of all consumers simultaneously. Each consumer's marginal rate of substitution must equal the economy's marginal rate of transformation, $MRS = MRT$, if the economy is to produce the optimal mix of goods for each consumer. How can we ensure that this condition holds for all consumers? One way is to use the competitive market.

Competition

Each price-taking consumer picks a bundle of goods so that the consumer's marginal rate of substitution equals the slope of the consumer's price line (the negative of the relative prices):

$$MRS = -\frac{p_c}{p_w}. \tag{10.3}$$

Thus, if all consumers face the same relative prices, in the competitive equilibrium, all consumers will buy a bundle where their marginal rates of substitution are equal (Equation 10.1). Because all consumers have the same marginal rates of substitution, no further trades can occur. Thus, the competitive equilibrium achieves *consumption efficiency*: We can't redistribute goods among consumers to make one consumer better off without harming another one. That is, the competitive equilibrium lies on the contract curve.

If candy and wood are sold by competitive firms, each firm sells a quantity of a candy for which its price equals its marginal cost,

$$p_c = MC_c, \tag{10.4}$$

and a quantity of wood for which its price and marginal cost are equal,

$$p_w = MC_w. \tag{10.5}$$

Taking the ratio of Equations 10.4 and 10.5, we find that in competition, $p_c/p_w = MC_c/MC_w$. From Equation 10.2, we know that the marginal rate of transformation equals $-MC_c/MC_w$, so

$$MRT = -\frac{p_c}{p_w}. \tag{10.6}$$

We can illustrate why firms want to produce where Equation 10.6 holds. Suppose that a firm were producing at b in Figure 10.9, where its MRT is –1, and that p_c = \$1 and p_w = \$2, so $-p_c/p_w = -\frac{1}{2}$. If the firm reduces its output by one candy bar, it loses \$1 in candy sales but makes \$2 more from selling the extra cord of wood, for a net gain of \$1. Thus, at b, where the $MRT < -p_c/p_w$, the firm should reduce its output of candy and increase its output of wood. In contrast, if the firm is producing at a, where the $MRT = -p_c/p_w = -\frac{1}{2}$, it has no incentive to change its behavior: The gain from producing a little more wood exactly offsets the loss from producing a little less candy.

Combining Equations 10.3 and 10.6, we find that in the competitive equilibrium, the MRS equals the relative prices, which equals the MRT:

$$MRS = -\frac{p_c}{p_w} = MRT.$$

Because competition ensures that the MRS equals the MRT, a competitive equilibrium achieves an *efficient product mix*: The rate at which firms can transform one good into another equals the rate at which consumers are willing to substitute between the goods, as reflected by their willingness to pay for the two goods.

By combining the production possibility frontier and an Edgeworth box, we can show the competitive equilibrium in both production and consumption. Suppose that firms produce 50 cords of firewood and 80 candy bars at a in Figure 10.10. The size of the Edgeworth box—the maximum amount of wood and candy available to consumers—is determined by point a on the PPF.

The prices consumers pay must equal the prices producers receive, so the price lines facing consumers and producers must have the same slope of $-p_c/p_w$. In equilibrium, the price lines are tangent to each consumer's indifference curve at f and to the PPF at a.

In this competitive equilibrium, supply equals demand in all markets. The consumers buy the mix of goods at f. Consumers like Jane, whose origin, O_j, is at the lower left, consume 20 cords of firewood and 40 candy bars. Consumers like Denise, whose origin is a at the upper right of the Edgeworth box, consume 30 (= 50 – 20) cords of firewood and 40 (= 80 – 40) candy bars.

The two key results concerning competition still hold in an economy with production. First, a competitive equilibrium is Pareto efficient, achieving efficiency in consumption and in output mix.[6] Second, any particular Pareto-efficient allocation between consumers can be obtained through competition, given that the government chooses an appropriate endowment.

[6]Although we have not shown it here, competitive firms choose factor combinations so that their marginal rates of technical substitution between inputs equal the ratios of the relative factor prices (see Chapter 7). That is, competition also results in *efficiency in production*: We could not produce more of one good without producing less of another good.

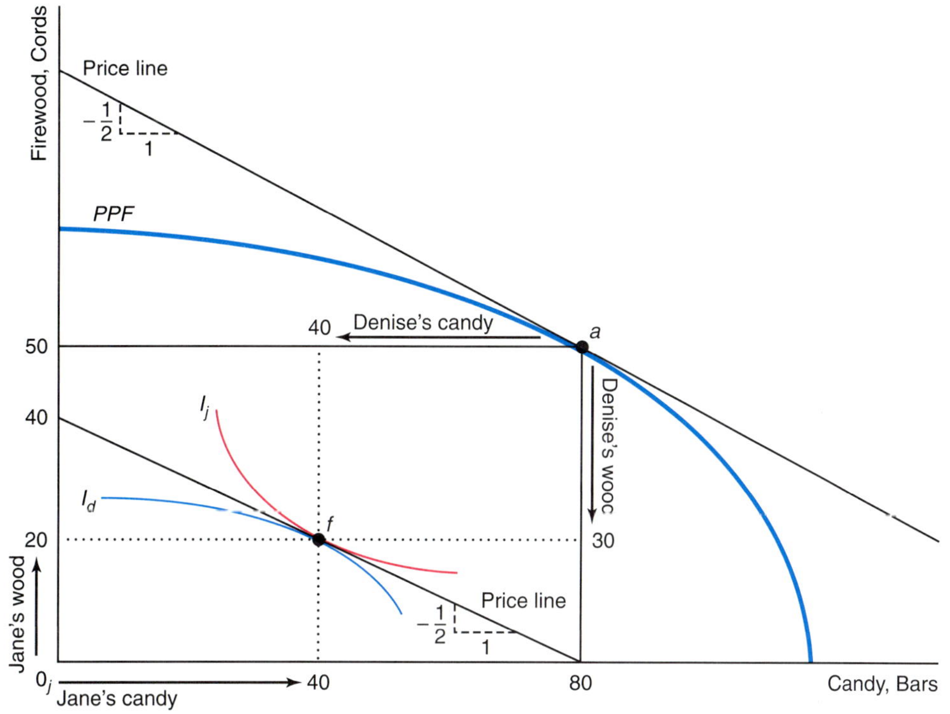

Figure 10.10 Competitive Equilibrium. At the competitive equilibrium, the relative prices facing firms and consumers are the same (the price lines are parallel), so the $MRS = -p_c/p_w = MRT$.

APPLICATION

Auto Trade Barriers

Traditionally, customers in one European nation have not be able to buy cars easily from dealers in other countries. If they could, competition would equalize prices across countries. Without this competition, prices are much higher in some European nations than in others. In 1996, cars often sold for more in the country in which they were manufactured than in other European countries: A Mercedes-Benz S320 cost \$72,614 in Germany and \$66,920 in Italy; a Renault Twingo went for \$13,265 in France and \$11,120 in Spain; a Peugeot

106 cost $12,129 in France and $11,532 in Spain; and a Volkswagen Polo priced at $8,562 in Italy sells for $1,250 more in Germany or Austria.[7]

The European Commission was supposed to create a single European market for automobiles in the last quarter of 1994. With a single market, consumers could shop where they wanted, including across national borders. Allowing firms in various countries to compete would decrease price differentials across countries. However, rules on the exchange of funds across countries that allow banks to charge extremely high fees limit the extent to which consumers buy cars in other countries. Nonetheless, some commercial reimporting of cars is taking place, which reduces price differentials.

Policies that create price differentials across countries lower efficiencies (and hence lower welfare). At least in high-price countries, price is above marginal cost. Because consumers are willing to pay more for cars than they cost to produce, welfare is lower than if price equaled marginal cost. Moreover, because these price distortions are unequal across types of cars, the product mix is inefficient. ■

10.5 EFFICIENCY AND EQUITY

How well various members of society live depends on how society deals with efficiency (the size of the pie) and equity (how the pie is divided). The actual outcome depends on choices by individuals and on government actions.

Role of the Government

By altering the efficiency with which goods are produced and distributed and the endowment of resources, governments help to determine how much is produced and how goods are allocated. By redistributing endowments or by refusing to redistribute endowments, governments, at least implicitly, are making value judgments about which members of society should get relatively more of society's goodies.

Virtually every government program, tax, or action redistributes wealth. A British lottery, played mostly by lower-income people, supports the "rich toffs" who attend the Royal Opera House at Covent Garden.[8] Agricultural price support programs (Chapter 9) redistribute wealth to farmers from other taxpayers. Income taxes (Chapter 5) and food stamp programs (Chapter 3) redistribute income from the rich to the poor.

---

[7]"Caveat Emptor," *The Economist*, 332(7878), August 27, 1994:43; "A Car Buyer's Heaven in a Borderless Europe," *New York Times*, January 17, 1996:C1, C4.

[8]Riding, Alan, "Lottery's Art Grants Stir Furor in Britain," *New York Times*, August 7, 1995:B1.

APPLICATION

Distribution of Wealth in the United States

Over the last 200 years, changes in the U.S. economy have altered the share of the nation's wealth concentrated in the hands of the richest 1% of Americans, as Figure 10.11 illustrates. A variety of social changes—sometimes occurring during or after wars and often codified into new laws—has led to new equilibria and new distributions of wealth. For example, the emancipation of slaves transferred vast "wealth"—the labor of the former slaves—from rich Southern landowners to the poor freed slaves. Anti-immigration laws have helped the domestic poor, because immigrant labor is typically a substitute for low-skilled domestic labor, and have hurt the middle and upper classes because low-skilled immigrant labor is a complement to capital and high-skilled labor.

From the founding of the country to the Great Depression, the share of wealth held by the richest 1% generally increased. Their share generally declined from then through the mid-1970s. The trend then reversed with a vengeance. One reason for this increase in the concentration of wealth was that the top income tax rate fell from 70% to less than 30% at the beginning of the Reagan administration, shifting more of the tax burden to the middle class. ■

Efficiency

Many economists and political leaders make the value judgment that governments *should* use the Pareto principle and prefer allocations by which someone is made better off if no one else is harmed. That is, governments should allow voluntary trades, encourage competition, and otherwise try to prevent problems that reduce efficiency.

We can use the Pareto principle to rank allocations or government policies that alter allocations. The Pareto criterion ranks Allocation x over Allocation y if some people are better off at x and no one else is harmed. If that condition is met, we say that x is *Pareto superior* to y.

The Pareto principle cannot always be used to compare allocations. Because there are many possible Pareto-efficient allocations, however, a value judgment based on interpersonal comparisons must be made to choose between them. Issues of interpersonal comparisons often arise when we evaluate various government policies. If both Allocation x and Allocation y are Pareto efficient, we cannot use this criterion to rank them. For example, if Denise has all the goods in x and Jane has all of them in y, we cannot rank these allocations using the Pareto rule.

Suppose that, when a country ends a ban on imports and allows free trade, domestic consumers benefit by many times more than domestic producers suffer. Nonetheless, this policy change does not meet the Pareto-efficiency criterion that someone be made better off without anyone's suffering. However, the government

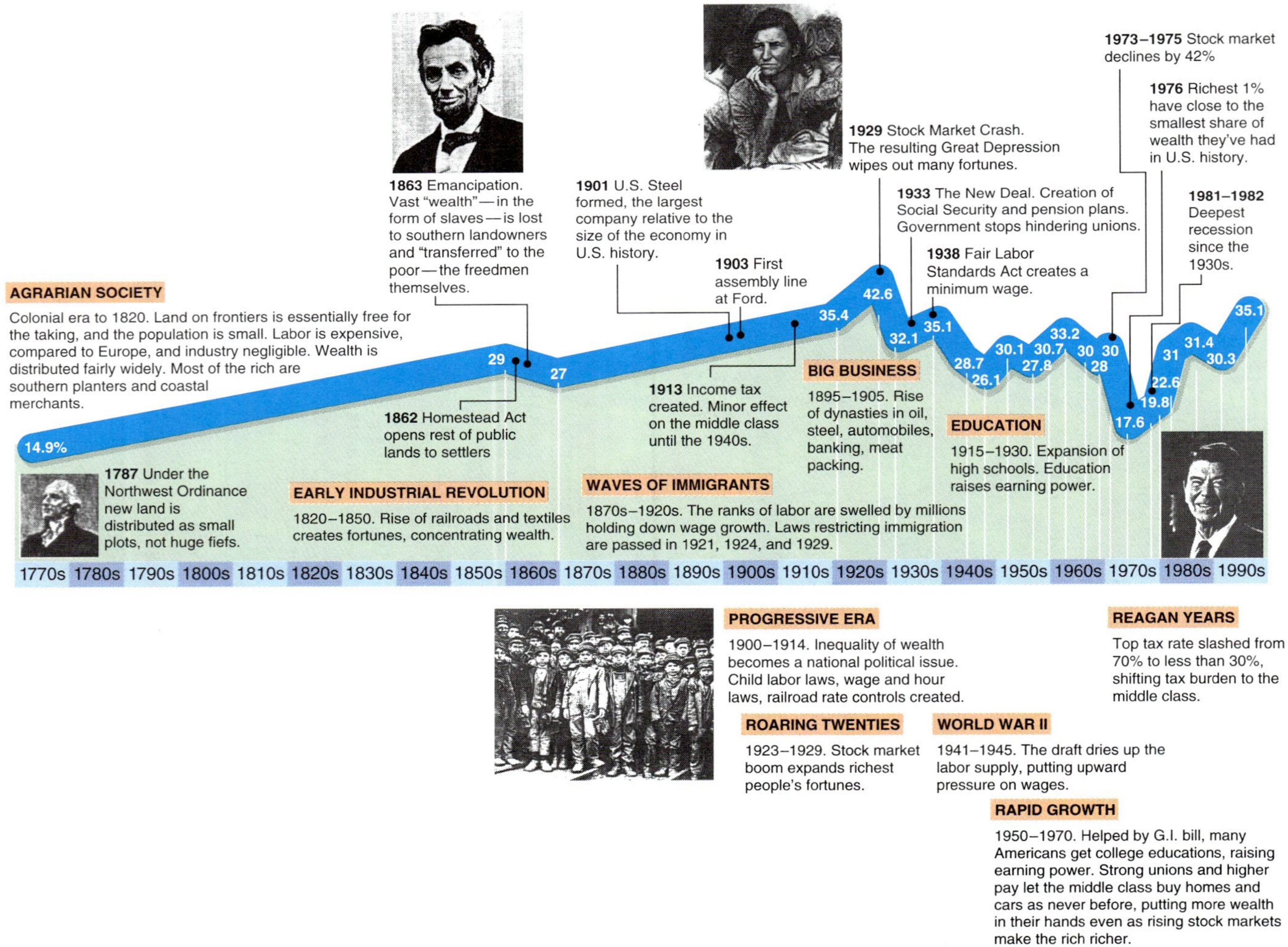
AGRARIAN SOCIETY
Colonial era to 1820. Land on frontiers is essentially free for the taking, and the population is small. Labor is expensive, compared to Europe, and industry negligible. Wealth is distributed fairly widely. Most of the rich are southern planters and coastal merchants.
1787 Under the Northwest Ordinance new land is distributed as small plots, not huge fiefs.
EARLY INDUSTRIAL REVOLUTION
1820–1850. Rise of railroads and textiles creates fortunes, concentrating wealth.
1863 Emancipation. Vast "wealth"—in the form of slaves—is lost to southern landowners and "transferred" to the poor—the freedmen themselves.
1862 Homestead Act opens rest of public lands to settlers
1901 U.S. Steel formed, the largest company relative to the size of the economy in U.S. history.
1903 First assembly line at Ford.
1913 Income tax created. Minor effect on the middle class until the 1940s.
WAVES OF IMMIGRANTS
1870s–1920s. The ranks of labor are swelled by millions holding down wage growth. Laws restricting immigration are passed in 1921, 1924, and 1929.
BIG BUSINESS
1895–1905. Rise of dynasties in oil, steel, automobiles, banking, meat packing.
1929 Stock Market Crash. The resulting Great Depression wipes out many fortunes.
1933 The New Deal. Creation of Social Security and pension plans. Government stops hindering unions.
1938 Fair Labor Standards Act creates a minimum wage.
EDUCATION
1915–1930. Expansion of high schools. Education raises earning power.
1973–1975 Stock market declines by 42%
1976 Richest 1% have close to the smallest share of wealth they've had in U.S. history.
1981–1982 Deepest recession since the 1930s.
14.9%
29
27
35.4
42.6
32.1
35.1
28.7
26.1
30.1
27.8
30.7
33.2
30
28
30
17.6
19.8
22.6
31
31.4
30.3
35.1
1770s 1780s 1790s 1800s 1810s 1820s 1830s 1840s 1850s 1860s 1870s 1880s 1890s 1900s 1910s 1920s 1930s 1940s 1950s 1960s 1970s 1980s 1990s
PROGRESSIVE ERA
1900–1914. Inequality of wealth becomes a national political issue. Child labor laws, wage and hour laws, railroad rate controls created.
ROARING TWENTIES
1923–1929. Stock market boom expands richest people's fortunes.
WORLD WAR II
1941–1945. The draft dries up the labor supply, putting upward pressure on wages.
REAGAN YEARS
Top tax rate slashed from 70% to less than 30%, shifting tax burden to the middle class.
RAPID GROWTH
1950–1970. Helped by G.I. bill, many Americans get college educations, raising earning power. Strong unions and higher pay let the middle class buy homes and cars as never before, putting more wealth in their hands even as rising stock markets make the rich richer.

Figure 10.11 Wealth Held by the Richest 1% of Americans. *Source:* Nasar, Sylvia, "The Rich Get Richer, but Never the Same Way Twice," *New York Times*, August 16, 1992:3, based on the work of Claudia Goldin, Bradford DeLong, and Edward Wolff. Updates based on Kennickell and Woodburn (1997).

could adopt a more complex policy that meets the Pareto criterion. Because consumers benefit by more than producers suffer, the government could take enough of the gains from free trade from consumers to compensate the producers so that no one is harmed and some people benefit.

The government rarely uses policies by which winners subsidize losers, however. If such subsidization does not occur, then additional value judgments involving interpersonal comparisons must be made before deciding whether to adopt the policy.

We've been using a welfare measure, W = consumer surplus + producer surplus, that weights benefits and losses to consumers and producers equally. On the basis of that particular interpersonal comparison criterion, if the gains to consumers outweigh the loss to producers, then the policy change should be made.

Thus, calling for policy changes that lead to Pareto-superior allocations is a weaker rule than calling for all policy changes that increase the welfare measure W. Any policy change that leads to a Pareto-superior allocation must increase W; however, some policy changes that increase W are not Pareto superior: There are both winners and losers.

Equity

All animals are equal, but some animals are more equal than others.

—George Orwell, *Animal Farm* (1945)

If we are unwilling to use the Pareto principle or if that criterion does not allow us to rank the relevant allocations, we must make additional value judgments to rank these allocations. A way to summarize these value judgments is to use a *social welfare function* that combines various consumers' utilities to provide a collective ranking of allocations. Loosely speaking, a social welfare function is a utility function for society.

We illustrate the use of a social welfare function using the pure exchange economy in which Jane and Denise trade wood and candy. There are many possible Pareto-efficient allocations along the contract curve in Figure 10.5. Jane and Denise's utility levels vary along the contract curve. Figure 10.12 shows the *utility possibility frontier* (*UPF*): the set of utility levels corresponding to the Pareto-efficient allocations along the contract curve. Point *a* in panel a corresponds to the end of the contract curve at which Denise has all the goods, and *c* corresponds to the allocation at which Jane has all the goods.

The curves labeled W^1, W^2, and W^3 in panel a are *isowelfare curves* based on the social welfare function. These curves are similar to indifference curves for

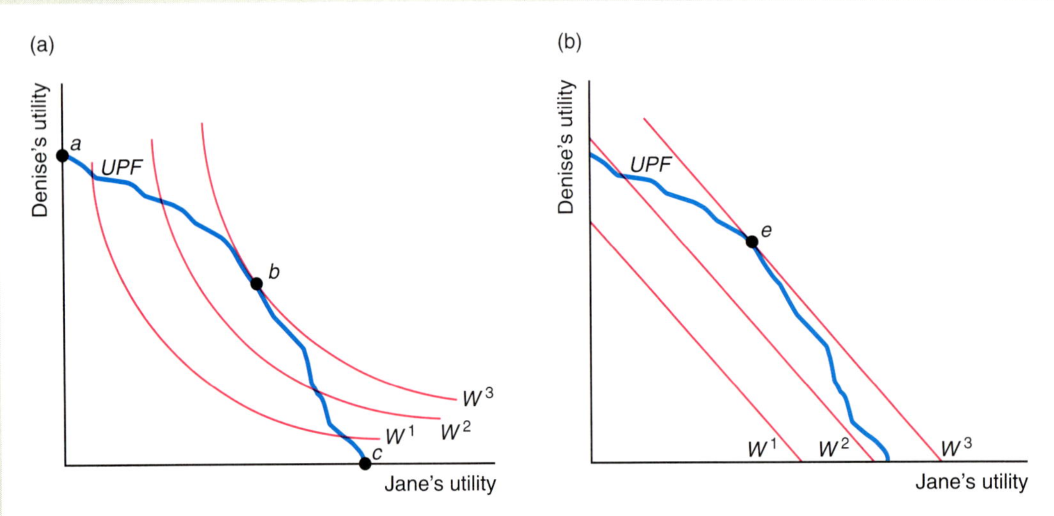

Figure 10.12 Welfare Maximization. Society maximizes welfare by choosing the allocation for which the highest possible isowelfare curve touches the utility possibility frontier, *UPF*. (a) The isowelfare curves have the shape of a typical indifference curve. (b) The isowelfare lines have a slope of –1, indicating that the utilities of both people are treated equally at the margin.

individuals. They summarize all the allocations with identical levels of welfare. Society maximizes its welfare at point *b*.

Who decides on the welfare function? In most countries, government leaders make decisions about which allocations are most desirable. These officials may believe that transferring money from wealthy people to poor people raises welfare, or vice versa. When government officials choose a particular allocation, they are implicitly or explicitly judging which consumers are relatively deserving and hence should receive more goods than others.

Voting. In a democracy, important government policies that determine the allocation of goods are made by voting. Such democratic decisionmaking is often difficult because people fundamentally disagree on how issues should be resolved and which groups of people should be favored.

In Chapter 4, we assumed that consumers could order all bundles of goods in terms of their preferences (completeness) and that their rank over goods was transitive.[9] Suppose now that consumers have preferences over allocations of goods across consumers. One possibility, as we assumed above, is that individuals care only about how many goods they receive—they don't care about how much others

[9]The transitivity (or *rationality*) assumption is that a consumer's preference over bundles is consistent in the sense that if the consumer weakly prefers Bundle *a* to Bundle *b* and weakly prefers Bundle *b* to Bundle *c*, then the consumer weakly prefers Bundle *a* to Bundle *c*.

have. Another possibility is that, because of envy, charity, pity, love, or other interpersonal feelings, individuals do care about how much everyone has.[10]

Let *a* be a particular allocation of goods that describes how much of each good an individual has. Each person can rank this allocation relative to Allocation *b*. For instance, individuals know whether they prefer an allocation by which everyone has equal amounts of all goods to another allocation by which people who work hard—or those of a particular skin color or religion—have relatively more goods than others.

Through voting, individuals express their rankings. One possible voting system requires that before the vote is taken, everyone agrees to be bound by the outcome in the sense that if a majority of people prefer Allocation *a* to Allocation *b*, then *a* is *socially preferred* to *b*.

Using majority voting to determine which allocations are preferred by society sounds reasonable, doesn't it? Such a system might work well. For example, if all individuals have the same transitive preferences, the social ordering has the same transitive ranking as that of each individual.

Unfortunately, sometimes voting does not work well, and the resulting social ordering of allocations is not transitive. To illustrate this possibility, suppose that three people have the transitive preferences in Table 10.3. Individual 1 prefers Allocation *a* to Allocation *b* to Allocation *c*. The other two individuals have different preferred orderings. Two out of three of these individuals prefer *a* to *b*; two out of three prefer *b* to *c*; and two out of three prefer *c* to *a*. Thus, voting leads to nontransitive preferences, even though the preferences of each individual are transitive. As a result, there is no clearly defined socially preferred outcome. A majority of people prefers some other allocation to any particular allocation. Compared to Allocation *a*, a majority prefers *c*. Similarly, a majority prefers *b* over *c*, and a majority prefers *a* over *b*.

If people have this type of ranking of allocations, the chosen allocation will depend crucially on the order in which the vote is taken. Suppose that these three people first vote on whether they prefer *a* or *b* and then compare the winner to *c*. Because a majority prefers *a* to *b* in the first vote, they will compare *a* to *c* in the second vote, and *c* will be chosen. If, instead, they first compared *c* to *a* and the winner to *b*, then *b* will be chosen. Thus, the outcome depends on the political skill of various factions in determining the order of voting.

Table 10.3 Preferences over Allocations of Three People

	Individual 1	Individual 2	Individual 3
First choice	*a*	*b*	*c*
Second choice	*b*	*c*	*a*
Third choice	*c*	*a*	*b*

[10]To an economist, love is nothing more than interdependent utility functions. Thus, it's a mystery how each successive generation of economists is produced.

Similar problems arise with other types of voting schemes. Kenneth Arrow (1951), who received a Nobel Prize in Economics in part for his work on social decisionmaking, proved a startling and depressing result about democratic voting. This result is often referred to as Arrow's Impossibility Theorem. Arrow suggested that a socially desirable decisionmaking system, or social welfare function, should satisfy the following criteria:

- Social preferences should be complete (Chapter 4) and transitive, as are individual preferences.
- If everyone prefers Allocation *a* to Allocation *b*, then *a* should be socially preferred to *b*.
- Society's ranking of *a* and *b* should depend only on individuals' ordering of these two allocations, not on how they rank other alternatives.
- Dictatorship is not allowed: Social preferences must not reflect the preferences of only a single individual.

Although each of these criteria seems reasonable—indeed, innocuous—Arrow proved that it is impossible to find a social decisionmaking rule that *always* satisfies all of these criteria. His result indicates that democratic decisionmaking *may* fail—not that democracy must fail. After all, if everyone agrees on a ranking, these four criteria are satisfied.

If society is willing to give up one of these criteria, a democratic decisionmaking rule can guarantee that the other three criteria are met. For example, if we give up the third criterion, often referred to as the *independence of irrelevant alternatives*, certain complicated voting schemes in which individuals rank their preferences can meet the other criteria.

Social Welfare Functions. How would you rank various allocations if you were asked to vote? Philosophers, economists, newspaper columnists, politicians, radio talk show hosts, and other deep thinkers have suggested various rules that society might use to decide which allocations are better than others. Basically, all these systems answer the question of which individuals' preferences should be given more weight in society's decisionmaking. Determining how much weight to give to the preferences of various members of society is usually the key step in determining a social welfare function.

Probably the simplest and most egalitarian rule is that every member of society is given exactly the same bundle of goods. If no further trading is allowed, this rule results in complete equality in the allocation of goods.

Jeremy Bentham (1748–1832) and his followers (including John Stuart Mill), the utilitarian philosophers, suggested that society should maximize the sum of the utilities of all members of society. Their social welfare function is the sum of the utilities of every member of society. The utilities of all people in society are given equal weight.[11] If U_i is the utility of Individual *i* and there are *n* people, the utilitarian

[11]It is difficult to compare utilities across individuals because the scaling of utilities across individuals is arbitrary (Chapters 4 and 9). A similar rule that avoids this utility comparison is to maximize a welfare measure that equally weights consumer surplus and producer surplus, which are denominated in dollars.

welfare function is

$$W = U_1 + U_2 + \ldots + U_n.$$

This social welfare function may not lead to an egalitarian distribution of goods. Indeed, under this system, an allocation is judged superior, all else the same, if people who get the most pleasure from consuming certain goods are given more of those goods.

Panel b of Figure 10.12 shows some isowelfare lines corresponding to the utilitarian welfare function. These lines have a slope of –1 because the utilities of both parties are weighted equally. In the figure, welfare is maximized at *e*.

A generalization of the utilitarian approach assigns different weights to various individuals' utilities. If the weight assigned to Individual i is α_i, this generalized utilitarian welfare function is

$$W = \alpha_1 U_1 + \alpha_2 U_2 + \ldots + \alpha_n U_n.$$

Society could give greater weight to adults, hardworking people, or those who meet other criteria. Under South Africa's former apartheid system, the utilities of people with white skins were given more weight than those of people with other skin colors.

John Rawls (1971), a philosopher at Harvard, believes that society should maximize the well-being of the worst-off member of society, who is the person with the lowest level of utility. In the social welfare function, all the weight should be placed on the utility of the person with the lowest utility level. The Rawlsian welfare function is

$$W = \min \{U_1, U_2, \ldots, U_n\}.$$

Rawls argues that his rule leads to a relatively egalitarian distribution of goods.

One final rule, which is frequently espoused by various members of Congress and by wealthy landowners in less developed countries, is to maintain the status quo. Exponents of this rule believe that the current allocation is the best possible allocation. They argue against any reallocation of resources from one individual to another. Under this rule, the final allocation is likely to be very unequal. Why else would the wealthy want it?

All of these rules or social welfare functions reflect value judgments in which interpersonal comparisons are made. Because each reflects value judgments, we cannot compare them on scientific grounds.

Efficiency Versus Equity

Given a particular social welfare function, *society might prefer an inefficient allocation to an efficient one*. We can show this result by comparing two allocations. In Allocation *a*, you have everything and everyone else has nothing. This allocation is Pareto efficient: We can't make others better off without harming you. In Allocation *b*, everyone has an equal amount of all goods. Allocation *b* is not Pareto efficient: I would be willing to trade all my zucchini for just about anything else. Despite Allocation *b*'s inefficiency, most people probably prefer *b* to *a*.

Although society might prefer an inefficient Allocation *b* to efficient Allocation *a*, according to most social welfare functions, society would prefer some efficient allocation to *b*. Suppose that Allocation *c* is the competitive equilibrium that would be obtained if people were allowed to trade starting from Endowment *b*, in which everyone has an equal share of all goods. By the utilitarian social welfare functions, Allocation *b* might be socially preferred to Allocation *a*, but Allocation *c* is certainly socially preferred to *b*. After all, if everyone is as well off or better off in Allocation *c* than in *b*, *c* must be better than *b* regardless of weights on individuals' utilities. According to the egalitarian rule, however, *b* is preferred to *c* because only strict equality matters. Thus, by most of the well-known social welfare functions, but not all, *there is an efficient allocation that is socially preferred to an inefficient allocation.*

Competitive equilibrium may not be very equitable even though it is Pareto efficient. Consequently, societies that believe in equity may tax the rich to give to the poor. If the money taken from the rich is given directly to the poor, society moves from one Pareto-efficient allocation to another.

Sometimes, however, in an attempt to achieve greater equity, efficiency is reduced. For example, advocates for the poor argue that providing public housing to the destitute leads to an allocation that is superior to the original competitive equilibrium. This reallocation isn't efficient: The poor view themselves as better off receiving an amount of money equal to what the government spends on public housing. They could spend the money on the type of housing they like—rather than the type the government provides—or they could spend some of the money on food or other goods.[12]

Unfortunately, there is frequently a conflict between a society's goal of efficiency and the goal of achieving an equitable allocation. Even when the government redistributes money from one group to another, there are significant costs to this redistribution. If tax collectors and other government bureaucrats could be put to work producing rather than redistributing, total output would increase. Similarly, income taxes discourage people from working as hard as they otherwise would (Chapter 5). Nonetheless, probably few people believe that the status quo is optimal and that the government should engage in no redistribution at all (though some members of Congress seem to believe that we should redistribute from the poor to the rich).

Summary

1. **General equilibrium:** A shock that affects one market may have a spillover effect in another market. A general-equilibrium analysis takes account of the direct effects of a shock in a market and the spillover effects in other markets. In contrast, a partial-equilibrium analysis (such as we used in earlier chapters) looks only at one market and ignores the spillover effects in other markets. The partial-equilibrium and general-equilibrium effects can differ.
2. **Trading between two people:** If people make all the trades they want, the resulting equilibrium will be Pareto efficient: By moving from this equilibrium, we cannot make one person better off without harming another person. At a Pareto-efficient equilibrium, the marginal rates of substitution

[12]Letting the poor decide how to spend their income is efficient by our definition, even if they spend it on "sin goods" such as cigarettes, liquor, or illicit drugs. A similar argument was made about food stamps in Chapter 4.

between people are equal because their indifference curves are tangent.

3. **Competitive exchange:** Competition, in which all traders are price takers, leads to an allocation in which the ratio of relative prices equals the marginal rates of substitution of each person. Thus, *every competitive equilibrium is a Pareto-efficient equilibrium.* Moreover, *any Pareto-efficient equilibrium can be obtained by competition, given an appropriate endowment.*

4. **Production and trading:** Where one person can produce more of one good and another person can produce more of another good using the same inputs, trading can result in greater combined production.

5. **Efficiency and equity:** The Pareto-efficiency criterion reflects a value judgment that a change from one allocation to another is desirable if it makes someone better off without harming anyone else. This criterion does not allow all allocations to be ranked, because some people may be better off in one allocation and others may be better off at another. Majority voting may not allow society to produce a consensus, transitive ordering of allocations either. Economists, philosophers, and others have proposed many criteria for ranking allocations, as summarized in welfare functions. Society may use such a welfare function to choose among Pareto-efficient (or other) allocations.

Problems

1. What is the effect of a tax of t per hour on labor in one sector of the economy on the equilibrium wage, total employment, and employment in the covered and uncovered sectors?

2. Suppose that the government gives a fixed subsidy of T per firm in one sector of the economy to encourage firms to hire more workers. What is the effect on the equilibrium wage, total employment, and employment in the covered and uncovered sectors?

3. A central city imposes a rent control law that places a binding ceiling on the rent that can be charged for an apartment. The suburbs of this city do not have a rent control law. What happens to the rental prices in the suburbs and to the equilibrium number of apartments in the total metropolitan area, in the city, and in the suburbs? (For simplicity, you may assume that people are indifferent as to whether they live in the city or suburbs.)

4. Initially, Michael has 10 candy bars and 5 cookies, and Tony has 5 candy bars and 10 cookies. After trading, Michael has 12 candy bars and 3 cookies. In an Edgeworth box, label the initial Allocation A and the new Allocation B. Draw some indifference curves that are consistent with this trade being optimal for both Michael and Tony.

5. The two people in a pure exchange economy have identical utility functions. Will they ever want to trade?

6. Two people trade two goods that they cannot produce. Suppose that one consumer's indifference curves are bowed away from the origin—the usual type of curves—but the other's are concave to the origin. In an Edgeworth box, show that a point of tangency between the two consumers' indifference curves is not a Pareto-efficient bundle. (Identify another allocation that Pareto dominates.)

7. If Jane and Denise have identical, linear production possibility frontiers, are there gains to trade?

8. Suppose Britain can produce 10 units of cloth or 5 units of food per day (or any linear combination) with available resources and Greece can produce 2 units of food per day or 1 unit of cloth (or any combination). Britain has an *absolute advantage* over Greece in producing both goods. Does it still make sense for these countries to trade?

9. In panel c of Figure 10.7, the joint production possibility frontier is concave to the origin. When the two individual production possibility frontiers are combined, however, the resulting *PPF* could have been drawn so that it was convex to the origin. How do we know which of these two ways of drawing the *PPF* to use?

10. Give an example of a social welfare function that leads to the egalitarian allocation that everyone should be given exactly the same bundle of goods.

11. Suppose that society used the "opposite" of a Rawlsian welfare function: It tried to maximize the well-being of the best-off member of society. Write this welfare function. What allocation maximizes welfare in this society?

Math Problems

12. The demand curve in Sector 1 of the labor market is $L_1 = a - bw$. The demand curve in Sector 2 is $L_2 = c - dw$. The supply curve of labor to the entire market is $L = e + fw$. In equilibrium, $L_1 + L_2 = L$.
    A. Solve for the equilibrium with no minimum wage.
    B. Solve for the equilibrium at which the minimum wage is $\underline{w}$ in Sector 1 ("the covered sector") only.
    C. Solve for the equilibrium at which the minimum wage $\underline{w}$ applies to the entire labor market.
13. The demand functions for Q_1 and Q_2 are

$$Q_1 = 10 - 2p_1 + p_2$$

$$Q_2 = 10 - 2p_2 + p_1$$

and there are five units of each good. What is the general equilibrium?

14. The demands for two goods depend on the prices of Good 1 and Good 2, p_1 and p_2,

$$Q_1 = 15 - 3p_1 + p_2,$$

$$Q_2 = 6 - 2p_2 + p_1,$$

but each supply curve depends on only its own price:

$$Q_1 = 2 + p_1,$$

$$Q_2 = 1 + p_2.$$

Solve for the equilibrium: p_1, p_2, Q_1, and Q_2.

15. In a pure exchange economy with two goods, G and H, the two traders have Cobb-Douglas utility functions. Amos's utility is

$$U_a = (G_a)^{\alpha}(H_a)^{1-\alpha}, \quad (10.8)$$

and Elise's is

$$U_e = (G_e)^{\beta}(H_e)^{1-\beta}, \quad (10.9)$$

What are their marginal rates of substitution?

★16. Continuing with Problem 15: Between them, Amos and Elise own 100 units of G and 50 units of H. Thus, if Amos has G_a and H_a, Elise has $G_e = 100 - G_a$ and $H_e = 50 - H_a$. Solve for their contract curve.

CHAPTER 11

Monopoly

Monopoly: One parrot.

Tagamet was the first drug that effectively blocked the formation of acid in the stomach for the treatment of ulcers. Existing anti-ulcer drugs were less effective because they reduced the amount of acid only after it was formed. For several years in the early 1980s, before the introduction of other, similar drugs, SmithKline Beckman, Tagamet's producer, was the only supplier of an anti-ulcer drug that blocked acid formation. Ulcer sufferers were willing to pay enormous amounts for this drug. SmithKline could definitely set its price—it was not a price taker like a competitive firm.

In this chapter, we examine the behavior of a **monopoly**: the only supplier of a good for which there is no close substitute. A monopoly's output is the market output, and the demand curve facing a monopoly is the market demand curve. Because the market demand curve is downward sloping, the monopoly (unlike a competitive firm) doesn't lose all its sales if it raises its price. As a consequence, the monopoly sets its price above marginal cost to maximize its profit. Consumers buy less at this high monopoly price than they would at the competitive price, which equals marginal cost.

In this chapter, we examine seven main topics:

1. **Monopoly profit maximization:** Like all firms, a monopoly maximizes its profit by setting its price or output so that its marginal revenue equals its marginal cost.
2. **Market power:** How much the monopoly's price is above its marginal cost depends on the shape of the demand curve it faces.
3. **Effects of a shift of the demand curve:** A shift of the demand curve may have a wider range of effects on a monopoly than on a competitive market.
4. **Welfare effects of monopoly:** By setting its price above marginal cost, a monopoly creates a deadweight loss.
5. **Cost advantages that create monopolies:** A firm can use a cost advantage over other firms (due, say, to control of a key input or economies of scale) to become a monopoly.
6. **Government actions that create monopolies:** Governments create monopolies by establishing government monopoly firms, limiting entry of other firms to create a private monopoly, and issuing patents, which are temporary monopoly rights.
7. **Government actions that reduce market power:** The welfare loss of a monopoly can be reduced or eliminated if the government regulates the price the monopoly charges or allows other firms to enter the market.

11.1 MONOPOLY PROFIT MAXIMIZATION

All firms, including competitive firms and monopolies, maximize their profits by setting *marginal revenue equal to marginal cost* (Chapter 8). We already know how to derive the marginal cost curve of a monopoly from its cost curve (Chapter 7). We now derive the monopoly's marginal revenue curve and then use the marginal revenue and marginal cost curves to examine the monopoly's profit-maximizing behavior.

Marginal Revenue

A firm's marginal revenue curve depends on its demand curve. We will show that a monopoly's marginal revenue curve lies below its demand curve at any positive quantity because its demand curve is downward sloping.

Marginal Revenue and Price. A firm's demand curve shows the price, p, it receives for selling a given quantity, q. The price is the *average revenue* the firm receives, so a firm's revenue is $R = pq$.

A firm's *marginal revenue*, MR, is the change in its revenue from selling one more unit. A firm that earns ΔR more revenue when it sells Δq extra units of output has a marginal revenue (Chapter 8) of

$$MR = \Delta R/\Delta q.$$

If the firm sells exactly one more unit, $\Delta q = 1$, its marginal revenue is $MR = \Delta R$.

The marginal revenue of a monopoly differs from that of a competitive firm because the monopoly faces a downward-sloping demand curve and the competitive firm does not. The competitive firm in panel a of Figure 11.1 faces a horizontal demand curve at the market price, p_1. Because its demand curve is horizontal, the competitive firm can sell another unit of output without dropping its price. As a result, the marginal revenue it receives from selling the last unit of output is the market price, as panel a illustrates.

Initially, the competitive firm sells q units of output at the market price of p_1, so its revenue, R_1, is area A, which is a rectangle that is $p_1 \times q$. If the firm sells one more unit, its revenue is $R_2 = A + B$, where area B is $p_1 \times 1 = p_1$. The competitive firm's marginal revenue equals the market price:

$$\Delta R = R_2 - R_1 = (A + B) - A = B = p_1.$$

A monopoly faces a downward-sloping market demand curve, as in panel b of Figure 11.1. (Until now, we called the number of units of output a firm sells q and the output of all the firms in a market, or market output, Q. Because a monopoly is the only firm in the market, there is no distinction between q and Q, so we use Q to describe both the firm's and the market's output.) The monopoly, which is initially selling Q units at p_1, can sell one extra unit only if the price falls to p_2.

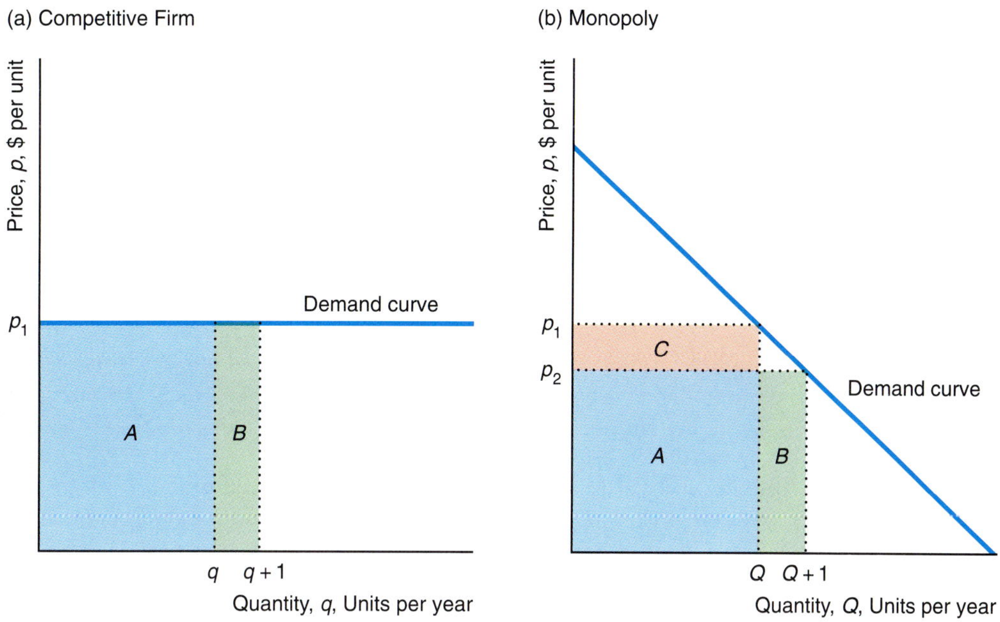

	Initial Revenue, R_1	Revenue with One More Unit, R_2	Marginal Revenue, $R_2 - R_1$
Competition	A	$A + B$	$B = p_1$
Monopoly	$A + C$	$A + B$	$B - C = p_2 - C$

Figure 11.1 Average and Marginal Revenue. The demand curve shows the average revenue or price per unit of output sold. (a) The competitive firm's marginal revenue, area B, equals the market price, p_1. (b) The monopoly's marginal revenue is less than the price p_2 by area C (the revenue lost due to a lower price on the Q units originally sold).

The monopoly's initial revenue, $p_1 \times Q$, is $R_1 = A + C$. When it sells the extra unit, its revenue, $p_2 \times (Q + 1)$, is $R_2 = A + B$. Thus, its marginal revenue is

$$\Delta R = R_2 - R_1 = (A + B) - (A + C) = B - C.$$

The monopoly sells the extra unit of output at the new price, p_2, so its extra revenue is $B = p_2 \times 1 = p_2$. The monopoly loses the difference between the new price and the original price, $\Delta p = (p_2 - p_1)$, on the Q units it originally sold: $C = \Delta p \times Q$.

Thus, the monopoly's marginal revenue, $B - C = p_2 - C$, is less than the price it charges by an amount equal to area C.

The competitive firm in panel a does not lose an area C from selling an extra unit because its demand curve is horizontal. It is the downward slope of the monopoly's demand curve that causes its marginal revenue to be less than its price.

Marginal Revenue Curve. Thus, *the monopoly's marginal revenue curve lies below the demand curve* at every positive quantity. In general, the relationship between the marginal revenue curve and demand curve depends on the shape of the demand curve.

For all *linear* demand curves, the relationship between the marginal revenue curve and demand curve is the same. The marginal revenue curve is a straight line that starts at the same point on the vertical (price) axis as the demand curve but has twice the slope of the demand curve, so the marginal revenue curve hits the horizontal (quantity) axis at half the quantity as the demand curve.[1] In Figure 11.2, the demand curve has a slope of –1 and hits the horizontal axis at 24 units, while the marginal revenue curve has a slope of –2 and hits the horizontal axis at 12 units.

★ **Deriving the Marginal Revenue Curve.** To derive the monopoly's marginal revenue curve, we write an equation summarizing the relationship between price and marginal revenue that panel b of Figure 11.1 illustrates. (Because we want this equation to hold at all prices, we drop the subscripts from the prices.) For a monopoly to increase its output by ΔQ, the monopoly lowers its price per unit by $\Delta p/\Delta Q$, which is the slope of the demand curve. By lowering its price, the monopoly loses $(\Delta p/\Delta Q) \times Q$ on the units it originally sold at the higher price (area C), but it earns an additional p on the extra output it now sells (area B). Thus, the monopoly's marginal revenue is[2]

$$MR = p + \frac{\Delta p}{\Delta Q} Q. \tag{11.1}$$

Because the slope of the monopoly's demand curve, $\Delta p/\Delta Q$, is negative, the last term in Equation 11.1, $(\Delta p/\Delta Q)Q$, is negative. Equation 11.1 confirms that the price is greater than the marginal revenue, which equals p plus a negative term.

---

[1]A linear demand curve can be written generally as

$$p = a - bQ.$$

The monopoly's revenues are quadratic, $R = pQ = aQ - bQ^2$. Differentiating revenue with respect to quantity, we find that the marginal revenue, $\mathrm{d}R(Q)/\mathrm{d}Q$, is linear,

$$MR = a - 2bQ.$$

The demand and MR curves hit the price axis at a. The slope of the demand curve, $\mathrm{d}p/\mathrm{d}Q = -b$, is half (in absolute value) the slope of the marginal revenue curve, $\mathrm{d}MR/\mathrm{d}Q = -2b$. The MR curve hits the quantity axis at half the distance, $a/(2b)$, as does the demand curve, a/b.

[2]Revenue is $R(Q) = p(Q)Q$, where $p(Q)$, the inverse demand function, shows how price changes as quantity increases along the demand curve. Differentiating, we find that the marginal revenue is

$$MR = \mathrm{d}R(Q)/\mathrm{d}Q = p(Q) + [\mathrm{d}p(Q)/\mathrm{d}Q]Q.$$

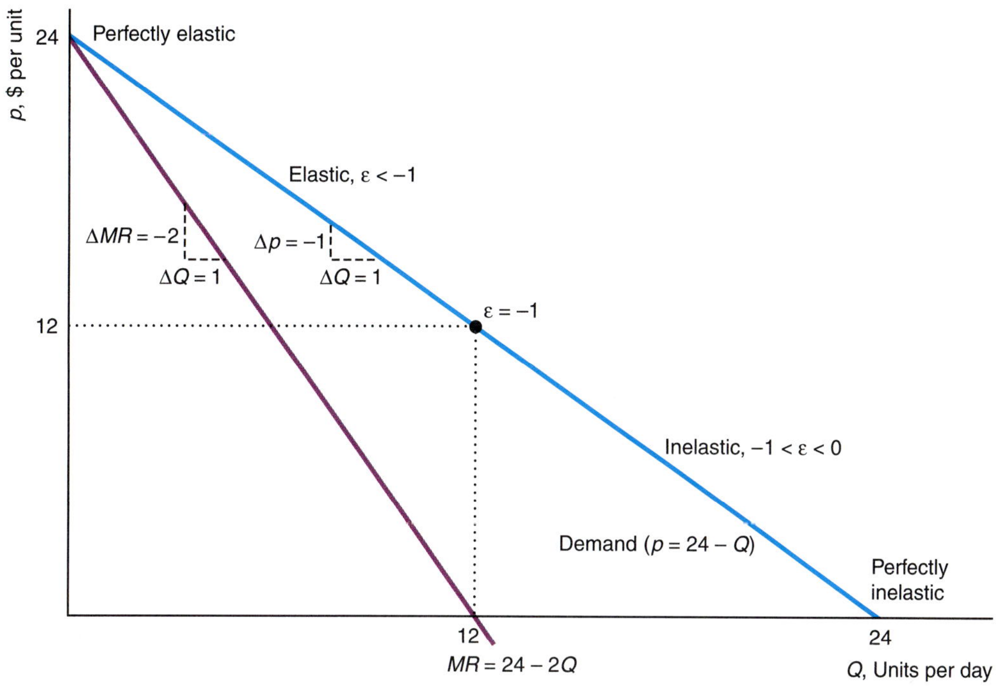

Figure 11.2 Elasticity of Demand and Total, Average, and Marginal Revenue. The demand curve (or average revenue curve), $p = 24 - Q$, lies above the marginal revenue curve, $MR = 24 - 2Q$. Where the marginal revenue equals zero, $Q = 12$, the elasticity of demand is $\varepsilon = -1$.

We now use Equation 11.1 to derive the marginal revenue curve when the monopoly faces the linear, inverse demand function,

$$p = 24 - Q, \tag{11.2}$$

in Figure 11.2. Equation 11.2 shows that the price consumers are willing to pay falls one dollar if quantity increases by one unit. More generally, if quantity increases by ΔQ, price falls by $\Delta p = -\Delta Q$. Thus, the slope of the demand curve is $\Delta p/\Delta Q = -1$.

We obtain the marginal revenue function for this monopoly by substituting into Equation 11.1 the actual slope of the demand function, $\Delta p/\Delta Q = -1$, and replacing p with $24 - Q$ (using Equation 11.2):

$$\begin{aligned} MR &= p + \frac{\Delta p}{\Delta Q} Q \\ &= (24 - Q) + (-1)Q \\ &= 24 - 2Q. \end{aligned} \tag{11.3}$$

Figure 11.2 plots Equation 11.3. The slope of this marginal revenue curve is $\Delta MR/\Delta Q = -2$, so the marginal revenue curve is twice as steeply sloped as is the demand curve.

Marginal Revenue and Price Elasticity of Demand. The marginal revenue at any given quantity depends on the demand curve's height (the price) and shape. The shape of the demand curve at a particular quantity is described by the price elasticity of demand (Chapter 3), $\varepsilon = (\Delta Q/Q)/(\Delta p/p)$, which tells us the percentage by which quantity demanded falls as the price increases by 1%.

At a given quantity, the marginal revenue equals the price times a term involving the elasticity of demand:[3]

$$MR = p\left(1 + \frac{1}{\varepsilon}\right). \tag{11.4}$$

According to Equation 11.4, marginal revenue is closer to price as demand becomes more elastic. Where the demand curve hits the price axis ($Q = 0$), the demand curve is perfectly elastic, so the marginal revenue equals price: $MR = p$.[4] Where the demand elasticity is unitary, $\varepsilon = -1$, marginal revenue is zero: $MR = p[1 + 1/(-1)] = 0$. Marginal revenue is negative where the demand curve is inelastic, $-1 < \varepsilon \leq 0$.

With the demand function in Equation 11.2, $\Delta Q/\Delta p = -1$, so the elasticity of demand is $\varepsilon = (\Delta Q/\Delta p)(p/Q) = -p/Q$. Table 11.1 shows the relationship among quantity, price, marginal revenue, and elasticity of demand for this linear example. As Q approaches 24, ε approaches 0, and marginal revenue is negative. As Q approaches zero, the demand becomes increasingly elastic, and marginal revenue approaches the price.

A Monopoly Chooses Price or Quantity

Any firm maximizes its profit by operating where its marginal revenue equals its marginal cost. Unlike a competitive firm, a monopoly can adjust its price, so it has a choice of setting its price *or* its quantity to maximize its profit. (A competitive firm sets its quantity to maximize profit because it cannot affect market price.)

---

[3]By multiplying and dividing the last term in Equation 11.1 by p and using algebra, we can rewrite the expression as

$$MR = p + p\frac{\Delta p}{\Delta Q}\frac{Q}{p} = p\left(1 + \frac{1}{\dfrac{\Delta Q}{\Delta p}\dfrac{p}{Q}}\right).$$

The last term in this expression is $1/\varepsilon$, because $\varepsilon = (\Delta Q/\Delta p)(p/Q)$.

[4]As ε approaches $-\infty$ (perfectly elastic demand), the $1/\varepsilon$ term approaches zero, so $MR = p(1 + 1/\varepsilon)$ approaches p.

Table 11.1 Quantity, Price, Marginal Revenue, and Elasticity for the Linear Demand Curve $p = 24 - Q$

Quantity, Q	Price, p	Marginal Revenue, MR	Elasticity of Demand, $\varepsilon = -p/Q$	
0	24	24	$-\infty$	↑ more elastic
1	23	22	−23	
2	22	20	−11	
3	21	18	−7	
4	20	16	−5	
5	19	14	−3.8	
6	18	12	−3	
7	17	10	−2.43	
8	16	8	−2	
9	15	6	−1.67	
10	14	4	−1.4	
11	13	2	−1.18	
12	**12**	**0**	**−1**	
13	11	−2	−0.85	
14	10	−4	−0.71	
⋮	⋮	⋮	⋮	
23	1	−22	−0.043	
24	0	−24	0	less elastic ↓

The monopoly is constrained by the market demand curve. Because the demand curve slopes downward, the monopoly faces a trade-off between a higher price and a lower quantity or a lower price and a higher quantity. The monopoly chooses the point on the demand curve that maximizes its profit. Unfortunately for the monopoly, it cannot set both its quantity and its price—thereby picking a point that is above the demand curve. If it could do so, the monopoly would choose an extremely high price and an extremely high output level and would become exceedingly wealthy.

If the monopoly sets its price, the demand curve determines how much output it sells. If the monopoly picks an output level, the demand curve determines the price. Because the monopoly wants to operate at the price and output at which its profit is maximized, it chooses the same, profit-maximizing solution whether it sets the price or output. In the following, we assume that the monopoly sets quantity.

Graphical Approach

All firms, including monopolies, use a two-step analysis to determine the output level that maximizes its profit (Chapter 8). First, the firm determines the output, Q^*, at which it makes the highest possible profit—the output at which its marginal revenue equals its marginal cost. Second, the firm decides whether to produce Q^* or shut down.

Profit-Maximizing Output. To illustrate how a monopoly chooses its output to maximize its profit, we continue to use the same linear demand and marginal revenue curves but add a linear marginal cost curve in panel a of Figure 11.3. Panel b shows the corresponding profit curve. The profit curve reaches its maximum at six units of output, where marginal profit—the slope of the profit curve—is zero. Because marginal profit is marginal revenue minus marginal cost (Chapter 8), marginal profit is zero where marginal revenue equals marginal cost. Panel a shows that marginal revenue equals marginal cost at six units. The price on the demand curve at that quantity is \$18. Thus, the monopoly maximizes its profit at point *e*, where it sells six units per day for \$18 each.

Why does the monopoly maximize its profit by producing six units where its marginal revenue equals its marginal cost? At smaller quantities, the monopoly's marginal revenue is greater than its marginal cost, so its marginal profit is positive (the profit curve is upward sloping). By increasing its output, it raises its profit. Similarly, at quantities greater than six units, the monopoly's marginal cost is greater than its marginal revenue, so it can increase its profit by reducing its output.

The profit-maximizing quantity is smaller than the revenue-maximizing quantity. The revenue curve reaches its maximum at $Q = 12$, where the slope of the revenue curve, the marginal revenue, is zero (panel a). In contrast, the profit curve reaches its maximum at $Q = 6$, where marginal revenue equals marginal cost. Because marginal cost is positive, marginal revenue must be positive where profit is maximized. Because the marginal revenue curve has a negative slope, marginal revenue is positive at a smaller quantity than where it equals zero. Thus, the profit curve must reach a maximum at a smaller quantity, 6, than does the revenue curve, 12.

As we already know, marginal revenue equals zero at the quantity where the demand curve has a unitary elasticity. Because a linear demand curve is more elastic at smaller quantities, *monopoly profit is maximized in the elastic portion of the demand curve.* (Here, profit is maximized at $Q = 6$ where the elasticity of demand is -3.) Equivalently, *a monopoly never operates in the inelastic portion of its demand curve.*

Shut-Down Decision. A monopoly shuts down to avoid making a loss in the long run, if the monopoly-optimal price is below its average cost. In the short run, the monopoly shuts down if the monopoly-optimal price is less than its average variable cost. In our short-run example in Figure 11.3, the average variable cost, $AVC = \$6$, is less than the price, $p = \$18$, at the profit-maximizing output, $Q = 6$, so the firm chooses to produce.

Price is also above average cost at $Q = 6$, so the monopoly makes a positive profit.[5] At the profit-maximizing quantity of six units, the price is $p(6) = \$18$ and the average cost is $AC(6) = \$8$. As a result, the profit, $\pi = \$60$, is the shaded rectangle with a height equal to the average profit per unit, $p(6) - AC(6) = \$18 - \$8 = \$10$, and a width of six units.

[5]Because profit is $\pi = p(Q)Q - C(Q)$, average profit is $\pi/Q = p(Q) - C(Q)/Q = p(Q) - AC$. Thus, average profit (and hence profit) is positive only if price is above average cost.

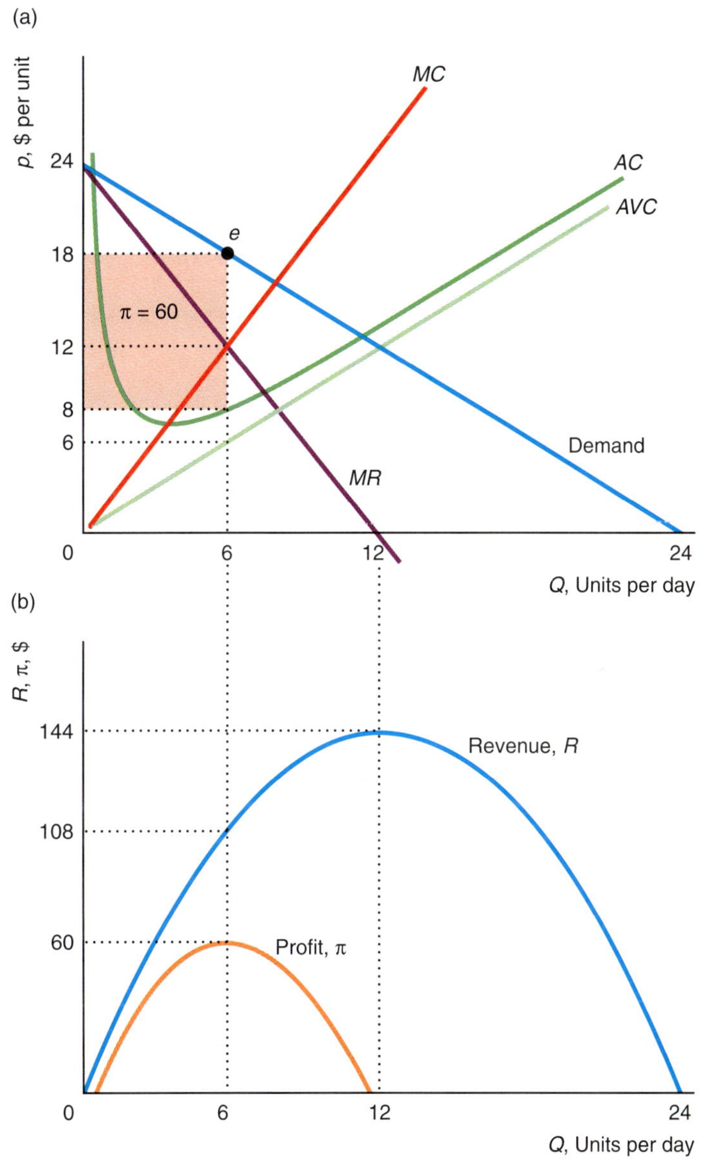

Figure 11.3 Maximizing Profit. (a) At $Q = 6$, where marginal revenue, MR, equals marginal cost, MC, profit is maximized. The rectangle showing the maximum profit \$60 is average profit per unit, $p - AC = \$18 - \$8 = \$10$, times the number of units, 6. (b) Profit is maximized at a smaller quantity, $Q = 6$ (where marginal revenue equals marginal cost), than is revenue, $Q = 12$ (where marginal revenue is zero).

Mathematical Approach

We also can solve for the profit-maximizing quantity mathematically. We already know the demand and marginal revenue functions for this monopoly. We need to determine its marginal cost curve. The monopoly's cost is a function of its output, $C(Q)$. In Figure 11.3, we assume that the monopoly faces a short-run cost function of

$$C(Q) = Q^2 + 12, \tag{11.5}$$

where Q^2 is the monopoly's variable cost as a function of output and \$12 is its fixed cost (Chapter 7). Given this cost function, the monopoly's marginal cost function is[6]

$$MC = 2Q. \tag{11.6}$$

This marginal cost curve is a straight line through the origin with a slope of 2 in panel a. The average variable cost is $AVC = Q^2/Q = Q$, so it is a straight line through the origin with a slope of 1. The average cost is $AC = C/Q = (Q^2 + 12)/Q = Q + 12/Q$, which is U-shaped.

We determine the profit-maximizing output by equating the marginal revenue (Equation 11.3) and marginal cost (Equation 11.6) functions:

$$\begin{aligned} MR = 24 - 2Q &= 2Q = MC, \\ 24Q &= 4Q, \\ Q &= 6. \end{aligned}$$

Substituting $Q = 6$ into the inverse demand function (Equation 11.2), we find that the profit-maximizing price is

$$p = 24 - Q = 24 - 6 = \$18.$$

At that quantity, the average variable cost is $AVC = \$6$, which is less than the price, so the firm does not shut down. The average cost is $AC = \$(6 + 12/6) = \$8$, which is less than the price, so the firm makes a profit.

APPLICATION

Toying with Profits and Losses

A toy manufacturer must accurately estimate its cost and the demand for its products if it is to maximize its profit. If the demand for a product is such that the profit-maximizing quantity is large and the product's average cost is relatively low, the firm makes a profit. Otherwise, it suffers a loss.

---

[6]By differentiating Equation 11.5 with respect to output, we find that the marginal cost is $MC = dC(Q)/dQ = 2Q$.

One segment of the toy industry provides dolls, such as Barbie, and other toys for young girls. In 1995, Galoob, an American toy manufacturer, introduced Sky Dancer, a flying doll complete with a launching device.[7]

To produce and sell this doll, the company incurred fixed costs of over $5 million. Of these costs, $400,000 was spent on research and development (designing Sky Dancer's shape, picking appropriate fabric for its tutu, choosing the best flying wing design), and another $400,000 was spent on "cutting steel"—industry slang for creating the expensive molds used to churn out the dolls. In addition, the firm made some early samples, which cost up to $20,000 each, to show prospective buyers. The largest fixed cost was $4 million in television commercials in 1995.

The marginal and average variable cost of the doll and its launcher is about $3.30 and is relatively constant. Thus, given the large fixed cost, the average cost curve is strictly downward sloping. Its average cost per doll is $8.30 if the firm sells one million dolls but only $5.80 if it sells two million dolls.

The firm sells the doll at $7.49 wholesale. Thus, after covering its average variable cost of $3.30, it makes an additional $4.19 per doll. To cover its fixed cost of about $5 million, it had to sell about 1.2 million (≈ $5 million/$4.19) Sky Dancers. As one executive at the firm admitted, "If we only sell a half-million of these, it's going to be very bad news." The firm hoped to sell at least 1.5 million Sky Dancers in its first year. Some executives predicted that they'd sell over 3 million.

The doll's success depended on its appeal to young girls and on the number and quality of competing toys that hit the market at the same time. Sky Dancer was a major success, selling over 10 million in its first year. It was the third-best-selling toy in Britain (after Power Rangers and Barbie). Today, you can buy many variations of the original doll, including mini–Sky Dancers and New Pretty Lights Sky Dancers that light up, or watch a Sky Dancer cartoon show. ■

[7]Sella, Marshall, "Will a Flying Doll . . . Fly?" *The New York Times Magazine*, December 25, 1994:20f; "The Real Toy Story; Is 1996 a Good Year for Toys? Check Them Out," *Time for Kids*, March 1, 1996:6; Clarke, Chris, "Go Go Power Rangers in the Year of the Doll," *Daily Mail*, December 16, 1995:14. Galoob is the only firm that may produce Sky Dancer dolls. When the toy was first produced, there were few close substitutes. Now, other toy manufacturers produce substitutes for this flying doll.

11.2 MARKET POWER

A monopoly has **market power**: the ability of a firm to charge a price above marginal cost and earn a positive profit. We now examine the factors that determine how much above its marginal cost a monopoly sets its price.

Market Power and the Shape of the Demand Curve

The degree to which the monopoly raises its price above its marginal cost depends on the shape of the demand curve at the profit-maximizing quantity. If the monopoly faces a highly elastic—nearly flat—demand curve at the profit-maximizing quantity, it would lose substantial sales if it raised its price by even a small amount. On the other hand, if the demand curve is not very elastic (relatively steep) at that quantity, the monopoly would lose fewer sales from raising its price by the same amount.

We can derive the relationship between market power and the elasticity of demand at the profit-maximizing quantity using the expression for marginal revenue in Equation 11.4 and the firm's profit-maximizing condition that marginal revenue equals marginal cost:

$$MR = p\left(1 + \frac{1}{\varepsilon}\right) = MC. \tag{11.7}$$

By rearranging terms, we can rewrite Equation 11.7 as

$$\frac{p}{MC} = \frac{1}{1 + \frac{1}{\varepsilon}}. \tag{11.8}$$

Equation 11.8 says that the ratio of the price to marginal cost depends *only* on elasticity of demand at the profit-maximizing quantity.

In our linear demand example in panel a of Figure 11.3, the elasticity of demand is $\varepsilon = -3$ at the monopoly optimum where $Q = 6$. As a result, the ratio of price to marginal cost is $p/MC = 1/[1 + 1/(-3)] = 1.5$, or $p = 1.5MC$. The profit-maximizing price, \$18, in panel a is 1.5 times the marginal cost of \$12.

Table 11.2 illustrates how the ratio of price to marginal cost varies with the elasticity of demand. When the elasticity is −1.01, only slightly elastic, the monopoly's profit-maximizing price is 101 times larger than its marginal cost: $p/MC = 1/[1 + 1/(-1.01)] \approx 101$. As the elasticity of demand approaches negative infinity (becomes perfectly elastic), the ratio of price to marginal cost shrinks to $p/MC = 1$.[8]

This table illustrates that not all monopolies can set high prices. A monopoly that faces a horizontal, perfectly elastic demand curve, where the elasticity is $-\infty$, sets its price equal to its marginal cost—as does a price-taking, competitive firm. If this

[8]As the elasticity approaches negative infinity, $1/\varepsilon$ approaches zero, so $1/(1 + 1/\varepsilon)$ approaches $1/1 = 1$.

Table 11.2 Elasticity of Demand, Price, and Marginal Cost

←more elastic less elastic→

Elasticity of Demand, ε	Price/Marginal Cost Ratio, $p/MC = 1/[1 + (1/\varepsilon)]$	Lerner Index, $(p - MC)/p = -1/\varepsilon$
−1.01	101	0.99
−1.1	11	0.91
−2	2	0.5
−3	1.5	0.33
−5	1.25	0.2
−10	1.11	0.1
−100	1.01	0.01
−∞	1	0

monopoly were to raise its price, it would lose all its sales, so it maximizes its profit by setting its price equal to its marginal cost.

The more elastic the demand curve, the less a monopoly can raise its price without losing many sales. All else the same, the more close substitutes for the monopoly's good there are, the more elastic is the demand facing a monopoly. For example, Addison-Wesley Publishing Company has the monopoly right to sell this textbook. Many other publishers, however, have the rights to sell similar microeconomics textbooks (though you wouldn't like them as much). The demand facing Addison-Wesley is much more elastic than it would be if no substitutes were available. If you think this textbook is expensive, imagine what it would cost if no substitutes were published!

Lerner Index

Another way to show how the elasticity of demand affects a monopoly's price relative to its marginal cost is to look at the firm's **Lerner Index** (or *price markup*): the ratio of the difference between price and marginal cost to the price: $(p - MC)/p$.[9] This measure is zero for a competitive firm because a competitive firm cannot raise its price above its marginal cost. The greater is the difference between price and marginal cost, the greater is the Lerner Index and the greater is the monopoly's ability to set price above marginal cost.

We can express the Lerner Index in terms of the elasticity of demand by rearranging Equation 11.8:

$$\frac{p - MC}{p} = -\frac{1}{\varepsilon}. \qquad (11.9)$$

[9]This index is named after Abba Lerner, the economist who invented it.

Because $MC \geq 0$ and $p \geq MC$, $0 \leq p - MC \leq p$, so the Lerner Index ranges from 0 to 1 for a profit-maximizing firm.[10] Equation 11.9 confirms that a competitive firm has a Lerner Index of zero because its demand curve is perfectly elastic.[11] As Table 11.2 illustrates, the Lerner Index for a monopoly increases as the demand becomes less elastic. If $\varepsilon = -5$, the monopoly's markup (Lerner Index) is $1/5 = 0.2$; if $\varepsilon = -2$, the markup is $1/2 = 0.5$; and if $\varepsilon = -1.01$, the markup is 0.99. Monopolies that face demand curves that are only slightly elastic set prices that are multiples of their marginal cost and have Lerner Indexes close to 1.

APPLICATION

Humana Hospitals

As Table 11.3 shows, Humana hospitals in 1991 had very large price/marginal cost ratios and Lerner Indexes close to 1 on many supplies they sell to patients, apparently because they faced elasticities of demand close to −1.[12] For example, Humana's Suburban Hospital in Louisville charges patients $44.90 for a container of saline solution (salt water) that costs the hospital 81¢, so its price is over 55 times higher than its marginal cost, implying a price elasticity of −1.02 and a Lerner Index of 0.98, which is close to the theoretical maximum. Although the table highlights some of the more extreme cases—the price/marginal cost ratio for supplies averages "only" 227%—at least it doesn't show the markups at some of their hospitals on $9 Tylenol tablets and $455 nursing bras. ■

Causes of Market Power

When will a monopoly face a relatively elastic demand curve and hence have little market power? Ultimately, the elasticity of demand of the market demand curve depends on consumers' tastes and options. The more consumers want a good—the more willing they are to pay "virtually anything" for it—the less elastic is the demand curve.

---

[10]For the Lerner Index to be above 1, ε would have to be a negative fraction, indicating that the demand curve was inelastic at the monopoly optimum. A profit-maximizing monopoly, however, never operates in the inelastic portion of its demand curve.

[11]As the elasticity of demand approaches $-\infty$, the Lerner Index, which equals $1/\varepsilon$, approaches zero.

[12]Frantz, Douglas, "Congress Probes Hospital Costs—$9 Tylenols, $118 Heat Pads," *San Francisco Chronicle*, October 18, 1991:A2. The elasticities in Table 11.3 were calculated by assuming that Humana sets the price of each good independently and operates where its marginal revenue equals its marginal cost: $MR = p(1 + 1/\varepsilon) = MC$. Rearranging this expression, we find that $\varepsilon = p/[MC - p]$. (If the hospital sets prices of several goods and services simultaneously, we should use a more complex formula.)

Table 11.3 Humana Hospitals' Pricing of Selected Supplies

	Price Charged Patients, p	Hospitals' Marginal Cost, MC	p/MC	Implicit Demand Elasticity, ε	Lerner Index
Saline solution	$44.90	$0.81	55.4	–1.02	0.98
Rubber arm pads for crutches	$23.75	$0.90	26.4	–1.04	0.96
Rubber tips for crutches	$15.95	$0.71	22.5	–1.05	0.96
Heating pad	$118.00	$5.74	20.6	–1.05	0.95
Pair of crutches	$103.65	$8.35	12.4	–1.09	0.92
Esophagus tube	$1,205.50	$151.98	7.9	–1.14	0.87
Average, all supplies			2.3	–1.77	0.57

Source: Frantz, Douglas, "Congress Probes Hospital Costs—$9 Tylenols, $118 Heat Pads," *San Francisco Chronicle*, October 18, 1991:A2.

All else the same, the demand curve facing a firm (not necessarily a monopoly) becomes more elastic as

- better substitutes for the firm's product are introduced,
- more firms enter the market selling the same product, or
- firms that provide the same service locate closer to this firm.

The demand curves facing Xerox, the U.S. Postal Service, and McDonald's have become more elastic in recent years for these three reasons.

When Xerox started selling its plain-paper copier, no other firm sold a close substitute. Other companies' machines produced copies on special slimy paper that yellowed quickly. As other firms developed plain-paper copiers, the demand curve that Xerox faced became more elastic.

The U.S. Postal Service (USPS) has a monopoly in first-class mail service. Today, phone calls, faxes, and E-mail are excellent substitutes for many types of first-class mail. The USPS had a monopoly in overnight delivery services until 1979. Now, Federal Express, United Parcel Service, and many other firms compete with the USPS in providing overnight deliveries. Because of this new competition, the USPS's share of business and personal correspondence fell from 77% in 1988 to 59% in 1996, and its overnight-mail market fell to 4%.[13] Thus, over time, the demand curves facing the USPS for first-class mail and overnight service have shifted down and become more elastic.

As you drive down a highway, you may notice that McDonald's restaurants are spaced miles apart. The purpose of this spacing is to reduce the likelihood that two McDonald's outlets will compete for the same customer. While McDonald's can prevent its own restaurants from competing with each other, it cannot prevent Wendy's or Burger King restaurants from locating near its restaurants. As other fast-food restaurants open near a McDonald's, that restaurant faces a more elastic demand.

[13]Passell, Peter, "Battered by Its Rivals," *New York Times*, May 15, 1997:C1.

What happens as a profit-maximizing monopoly faces more elastic demand? It has to lower its price. The next application illustrates how a monopoly adjusts its price as it changes its beliefs about the elasticity of demand it faces.

APPLICATION

Airport Monopolies

Most airports grant a single firm monopoly rights to sell food and other goods, a practice that evokes the oft-expressed sentiment that "the best way to avoid being robbed in an airport is to bring your own food." Host Marriott Corporation has had a monopoly on concessions at the San Francisco International Airport for 40 years. In 1995, however, it reduced its prices on hundreds of items.[14] One interpretation of this cut is that Marriott lowered its estimate of the elasticity of demand, ε, it faces for each of these goods.

We know Marriott's price and the corresponding prices at a 7-Eleven. Convenience stores like 7-Eleven typically charge more than grocery and other stores for the items they sell. Thus, the 7-Eleven prices are probably above Marriott's marginal cost, MC. Nonetheless, we use the 7-Eleven prices as a conservative estimate of the true MC to calculate ε. (As a consequence, our estimates of the elasticities of demand in Table 11.4 are too high in absolute value—Marriott has more market power than our estimates indicate.) Table 11.4 shows estimates of the original elasticity, ε_o, and the new elasticity, ε_n, of demand for several goods. Apparently Marriott decided that the demand curves for most of these goods were substantially more elastic than it previously believed.

Table 11.4 Changing Airport Prices and Elasticities of Demand

	7-Eleven Price	Original Airport Price	ε_o	New Airport Price	ε_n
Bottled water	0.49	1.69	−1.4	1.49	−1.5
Kodak FunSaver Camera (24)	9.99	14.95	−3.0	10.99	−11.0
Life Savers	0.59	0.85	−3.3	0.69	−6.9
Snapple	0.99	2.25	−1.8	1.59	−2.7

Source of price data: Host Marriott, Chronicle Research, as reported in Sinton, Peter, "Airport Shops Cut Prices: A Move to Subdue Fear of Gorging," *San Francisco Chronicle*, February 15, 1995:C1.

[14] Sinton, Peter, "Airport Shops Cut Prices: A Move to Subdue Fear of Gouging," *San Francisco Chronicle*, February 15, 1995:C1.

Why does the airport grant a monopoly to a single firm? The airport authority captures these monopoly profits for itself by charging high rents. Marriott pays $48 per square foot per month for its space, while retail space in surrounding areas rents for as low as $1 to $3 per square foot. Though Marriott charges high prices, it may not make positive economic profits if the airport charges a high enough rent. ■

11.3 EFFECTS OF A SHIFT OF THE DEMAND CURVE

Shifts in the demand curve or marginal cost curve affect the monopoly optimum and can have a wider variety of effects in a monopolized market than in a competitive market.[15] In a competitive market, the effect of a shift in demand on a competitive firm's output depends only on the shape of the marginal cost curve (Chapter 8). In contrast, the effect of a shift in demand on a monopoly's output depends on the shapes of both the marginal cost curve and the demand curve.

As we saw in Chapter 8, a competitive firm's marginal cost curve tells us everything we need to know about the amount that firm will supply at any given market price. The competitive firm's supply curve is its upward-sloping marginal cost curve (above its minimum average variable cost). A competitive firm's supply behavior does not depend on the shape of the market demand curve, because it always faces a horizontal demand curve at the market price. Thus, if you know a competitive firm's marginal cost curve, you can predict how much that firm will produce at any given market price.

In contrast, a monopoly's output decision depends on the shapes of its marginal cost curve and its demand curve. Unlike a competitive firm, *a monopoly does not have a supply curve*. Knowing the monopoly's marginal cost curve is not enough for us to predict how much a monopoly will sell at any given price.

Figure 11.4 illustrates that the relationship between price and quantity is unique in a competitive market but not in a monopoly market. If the market is competitive, the initial equilibrium is e_1 in panel a, where the original demand curve D^1 intersects the supply curve, MC, which is the sum of the marginal cost curves of a large number of competitive firms. When the demand curve shifts to D^2, the new competitive equilibrium, e_2, has a higher price and quantity. A shift of the demand curve maps out competitive equilibria along the marginal cost curve, so for every equilibrium quantity, there is a single corresponding equilibrium price.

Now suppose there is a monopoly. As demand shifts from D^1 to D^2 the monopoly optimum shifts from E_1 to E_2 in panel b, so the price rises but the quantity stays constant, $Q_1 = Q_2$. Thus, *a given quantity can correspond to more than one monopoly-optimal price*. A shift in the demand curve may cause the monopoly-optimal price to stay constant and the quantity to change or both price and quantity to change.

[15]We examine the effect of a shift of the demand curve on the monopoly optimum here and the effects of a shift in marginal cost in Solved Problem 11.1.

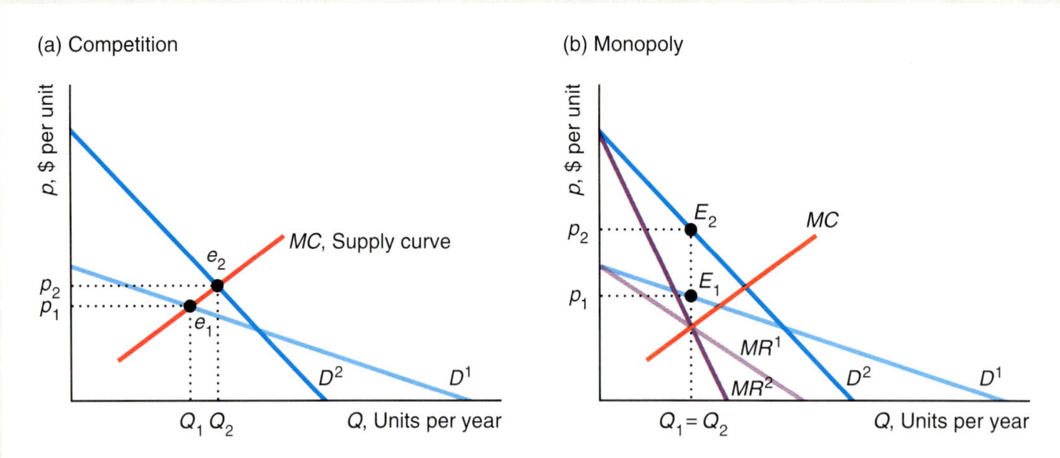

Figure 11.4 Effects of a Shift of the Demand Curve. (a) A shift of the demand curve from D^1 to D^2 causes the competitive equilibrium to move from e_1 to e_2 along the supply curve (the horizontal sum of the marginal cost curves of all the competitive firms). Because the competitive equilibrium lies on the supply curve, each quantity corresponds to only one possible equilibrium price. (b) With a monopoly, this same shift of demand causes the monopoly optimum to change from E_1 to E_2. The monopoly quantity stays the same, but the monopoly price rises. Thus, a shift in demand does not map out a unique relationship between price and quantity in a monopolized market: The same quantity, $Q_1 = Q_2$, is associated with two different prices, p_1 and p_2.

11.4 WELFARE EFFECTS OF MONOPOLY

Welfare, W (here defined as the sum of consumer surplus, CS, and producer surplus, PS), is lower under monopoly than under competition. Chapter 9 showed that competition maximizes welfare because price equals marginal cost. By setting its price above its marginal cost, a monopoly causes consumers to buy less than the competitive level of the good, so a deadweight loss to society occurs.

Graphing the Welfare Loss

We illustrate this loss using our continuing example. If the monopoly were to act like a competitive market and operate where its inverse demand curve, Equation 11.2, intersects its marginal cost (supply) curve, Equation 11.6,

$$p = 24 - Q = 2Q = MC,$$

it would sell $Q_c = 8$ units of output at a price of \$16, as in Figure 11.5. At this competitive price, consumer surplus is area $A + B + C$ and producer surplus is $D + E$.

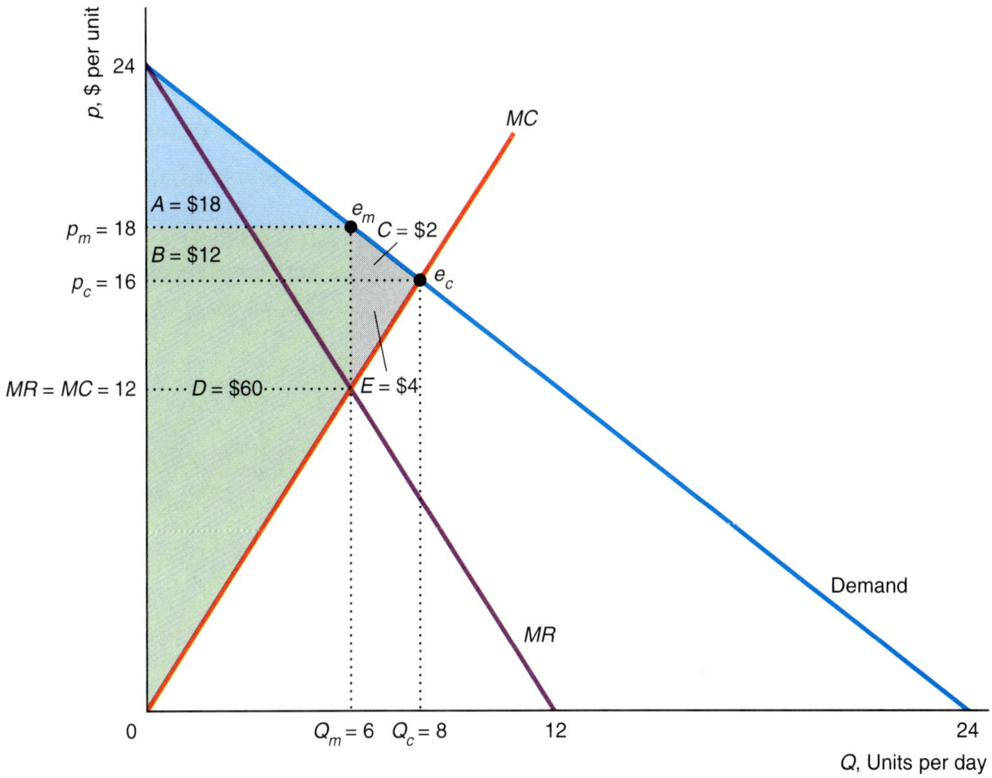

	Competition	Monopoly	Change
Consumer Surplus, *CS*	$A + B + C$	A	$-B - C = \Delta CS$
Producer Surplus, *PS*	$D + E$	$B + D$	$B - E = \Delta PS$
Welfare, $W = CS + PS$	$A + B + C + D + E$	$A + B + D$	$-C - E = \Delta W = DWL$

Figure 11.5 Deadweight Loss of Monopoly. A competitive market would produce $Q_c = 8$ at $p_c = \$16$, where the demand curve intersects the marginal cost (supply) curve. A monopoly produces only $Q_m = 6$ at $p_m = \$18$, where the marginal revenue curve intersects the marginal cost curve. Under monopoly, consumer surplus is *A*, producer surplus is $B + D$, and the lost welfare or deadweight loss of monopoly is $-C - E$.

If the firm acts like a monopoly and operates where its marginal revenue equals marginal cost, only six units are sold at the monopoly price of $18, and consumer surplus is only *A*. Part of the lost consumer surplus, *B*, goes to the monopoly; but the rest, *C*, is lost.

By charging the monopoly price of \$18 instead of the competitive price of \$16, the monopoly receives \$2 more per unit and earns an extra profit of area B = \$12 on the $Q_m = 6$ units it sells. The monopoly loses area E, however, because it sells less than the competitive output. Consequently, the monopoly's producer surplus increases by $B - E$ over the competitive level. (We know that its producer surplus increases, $B - E > 0$, because the monopoly had the option of producing at the competitive level and chose not to do so.)

Monopoly welfare is lower than competitive welfare. The deadweight loss of monopoly is $-C - E$, which represents the consumer surplus and producer surplus lost because less than the competitive output is produced. As in the analysis of a tax in Chapter 9, the deadweight loss is due to the gap between price and marginal cost at the monopoly output. At $Q_m = 6$, the price, \$18, is above the marginal cost, \$12, so consumers are willing to pay more for the last unit of output than it costs to produce it.

APPLICATION

Deadweight Loss of the U.S. Postal Service

Lenard (1994) calculated the welfare losses from the monopoly of the USPS in delivering third-class mail, which includes advertising circulars and mail-order catalogs. The welfare cost of the postal service monopoly depends on how much higher the price is above the USPS's marginal cost and whether the USPS produces inefficiently. If the USPS produces efficiently, the deadweight loss is the reduction in consumer surplus not offset by a gain to the USPS or others. If the USPS is inefficient, the deadweight loss is even greater.

Private mail carriers may deliver fliers and other pieces of mail that do not have an individual's name in the address (but they may not deliver addressed mail such as third-class letters). On the basis of a survey of private mail carriers, Lenard calculated that the private companies could deliver third-class mail at a constant price of p_c = 12.3¢ per piece in 1992. Assuming that the private mail carriers are price takers, that price equals the marginal cost. This marginal cost was only about three-quarters of the USPS monopoly price for third-class mail, p_m = 16.7¢.

The USPS delivered Q_m = 49.8 billion pieces of mail. On the basis of the USPS estimate of the elasticity of demand for third-class mail of –0.625, Q_c = 60.4 billion pieces would have been delivered at the competitive price.[16]

On the basis of these numbers, customers lose consumer surplus of \$2.46 billion dollars, which is 30% of the \$8.3 billion they spend on third-class bulk mail. Of this lost consumer surplus, \$237 million (the loss of area B in Figure 11.6),

[16]Because the USPS is operating where demand is inelastic, $\varepsilon = -0.625$, its price is less than the profit-maximizing level.

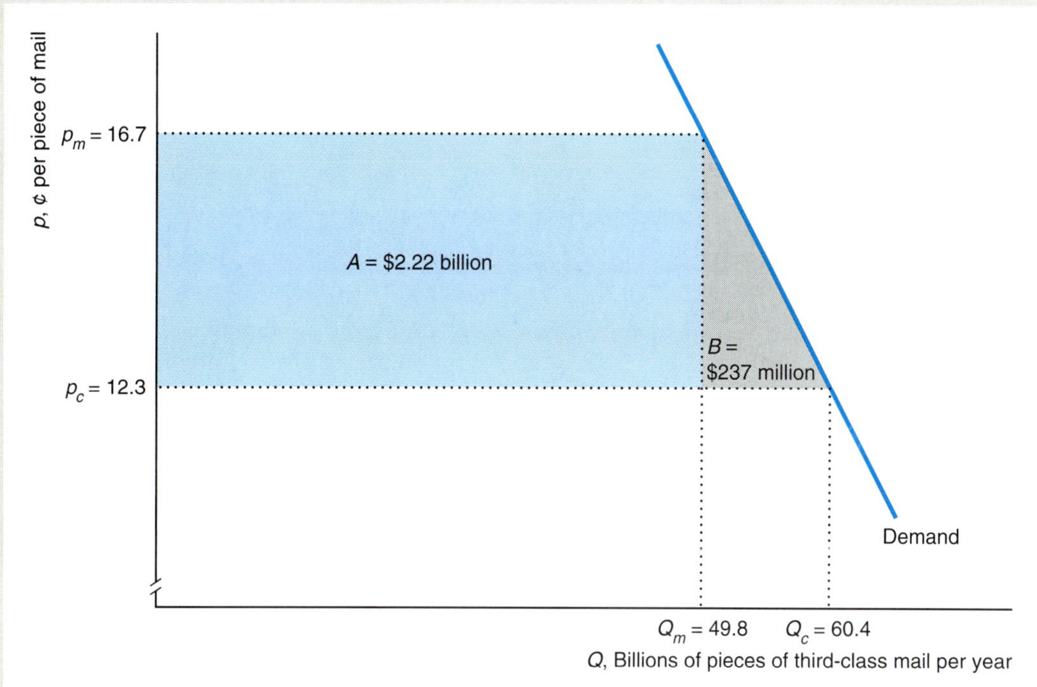

Figure 11.6 Deadweight Loss of the USPS Monopoly on Third-Class Mail. Lenard (1994) found that the USPS monopoly price for third-class mail was p_m = 16.7¢ per piece in 1992, which was more than one-third higher than the competitive price of p_c = 12.3¢. Lost consumer surplus is \$2.46 billion dollars, of which \$237 million, *B*, is a deadweight loss and \$2.22 billion, *A*, is the excess payment to the USPS from charging the monopoly price instead of the competitive price.

is a deadweight loss—a loss to customers that is not gained by the USPS—and the remaining \$2.22 billion, area *A*, is the excess payment, $(p_m - p_c)Q_m$, the USPS gets by charging the monopoly price instead of the competitive price.

The USPS is obligated by statute to break even. Thus, the \$2.22 billion transferred from customers to the USPS due to the high price of mail is either wasted on inefficient production, used to subsidize other types of mail, or transferred to postal workers through high wages. Knowing that postal workers earn 21% more than comparable private-sector employees, Lenard calculated that postal workers get up to \$1.51 billion of the third-class mail "profit." He inferred that \$0.95 billion (= \$2.46 – \$1.51 billion) is wasted through inefficient production. Much of this inefficiency is due to the existence of post offices—especially in rural areas—that are too small to use optical character readers and barcode sorters, so workers must sort by hand.

If the USPS produced efficiently, the deadweight loss would be B = \$237 million, the amount customers lose that is not transferred to the USPS. Because the USPS produces inefficiently, however, the true deadweight loss to society is \$1.19 billion: the sum of B and the \$0.95 billion lost from production inefficiency. ■

SOLVED PROBLEM 11.1

In our linear example, how does charging the monopoly a specific tax of τ = \$8 per unit affect the monopoly optimum and the welfare of consumers, the monopoly, and society (where society's welfare includes the tax revenue)? What is the incidence of the tax on consumers?

Answer

1. *Determine how imposing the tax affects the monopoly optimum*: In Figure 11.7, the intersection of the marginal revenue curve, MR, and the before-tax marginal cost curve, MC^1, determines the monopoly optimum quantity $Q_1 = 6$. At the before-tax optimum, e_1, the price is p_1 = \$18. The specific tax causes the monopoly's before-tax marginal cost curve, $MC^1 = 2Q$, to shift up by \$8 to $MC^2 = MC^1 + 8 = 2Q + 8$. After the tax is applied, the monopoly operates where $MR = 24 - 2Q = 2Q + 8 = MC^2$. In the after-tax monopoly optimum, e_2, the quantity is $Q_2 = 4$ and the price is p_2 = \$20. Thus, output falls by $\Delta Q = 2$ units and the price increases by Δp = \$2.

2. *Calculate the incidence of the tax*: Because the tax goes from \$0 to \$8, the change in the tax is $\Delta\tau$ = \$8. The incidence of the tax (Chapter 3) on consumers is $\Delta p/\Delta\tau$ = \$2/\$8 = $\frac{1}{4}$. (The monopoly absorbs \$6 of the tax and passes on only \$2.)

3. *Calculate the change in the various welfare measures*: Figure 11.7 shows how the welfare measures change. Area G is the tax revenue collected by the government, τQ = \$32, because its height is the distance between the two marginal cost curves, τ = \$8, and its width is the output the monopoly produces after the tax is imposed, $Q = 4$. The tax reduces consumer and producer surplus and increases the deadweight loss. We know that producer surplus falls because (a) the monopoly could have produced this reduced output level in the absence of the tax but did not because it was not the profit-maximizing output, so its before-tax profit falls, and (b) the monopoly must now pay taxes. The before-tax deadweight loss from monopoly is $-F$. The after-tax deadweight loss is $-C - E - F$, so the increase in deadweight loss due to the tax is $-C - E$. The table accompanying the figure shows that consumer surplus changes by $-B - C$ and producer surplus by $B - E - G$. ■

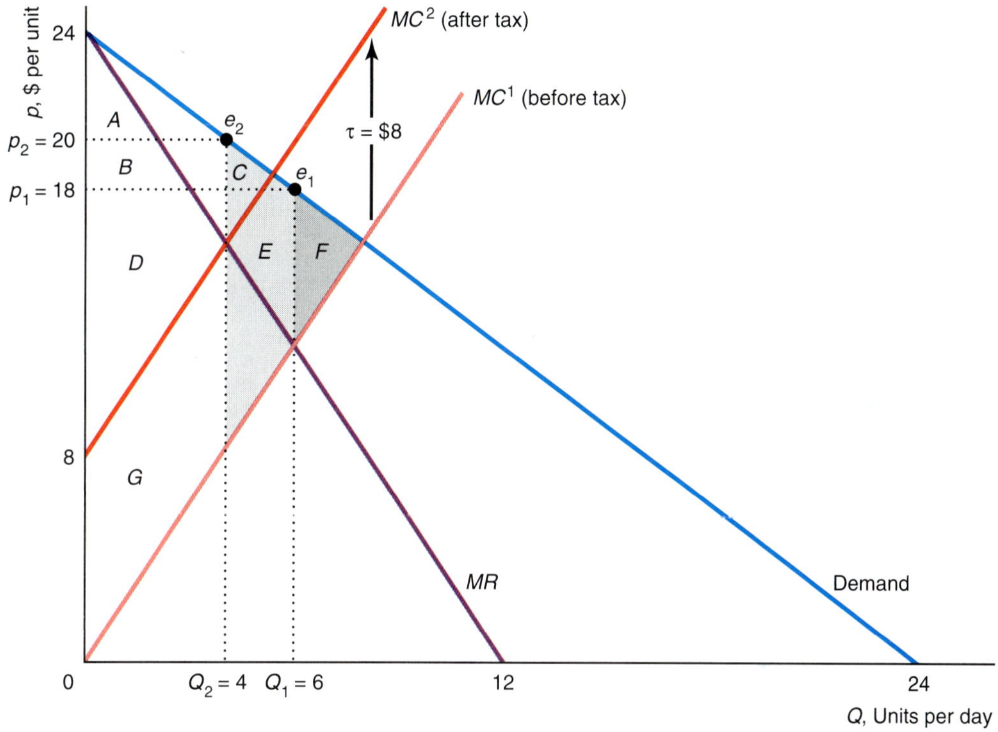

	Monopoly Before Tax	Monopoly After Tax	Change
Consumer Surplus, *CS*	$A + B + C$	A	$-B - C = \Delta CS$
Producer Surplus, *PS*	$D + E + G$	$B + D$	$B - E - G = \Delta PS$
Tax Revenues, $T = \tau Q$	0	G	$G = \Delta T$
Welfare, $W = CS + PS + T$	$A + B + C + D + E + G$	$A + B + D + G$	$-C - E = \Delta W$
Deadweight Loss, *DWL*	$-F$	$-C - E - F$	$-C - E = \Delta DWL$

Figure 11.7 Welfare Effects of a Tax on a Monopoly. A specific tax of τ = \$8 shifts the monopoly's marginal cost curve from MC^1 to MC^2, raises the monopoly price from p_1 = \$18 to p_2 = \$20, and reduces the monopoly quantity from $Q_1 = 6$ to $Q_2 = 4$. The deadweight loss from monopoly, $-F$, is less than the deadweight loss when a tax is placed on a monopoly of $-C - E - F$.

Welfare Effects of Ad Valorem Versus Specific Taxes

Solved Problem 11.1 illustrates that a specific sales tax (the monopoly pays the government τ dollars per unit sold) provides tax revenue but reduces welfare below even the monopoly level. Governments use ad valorem taxes more often than specific taxes. Is there an advantage to using an ad valorem sales tax (the monopoly pays αp per unit of output, where α is a fraction and p is the price charged) instead? The answer is that a government raises more tax revenue with an ad valorem tax applied to a monopoly than with a specific tax when α and τ are set so that the after-tax output is the same with either tax, as we now show.[17]

In Figure 11.8, the before-tax market demand curve is D, and the corresponding marginal revenue is MR. The before-tax monopoly optimum is e_1. The MR curve intersects the MC curve at Q_1 units, which sell at a price of p_1.

If the government imposes a specific tax τ, the monopoly's after-tax demand curve is D^s, which is the market demand curve D shifted down by τ dollars.[18] The

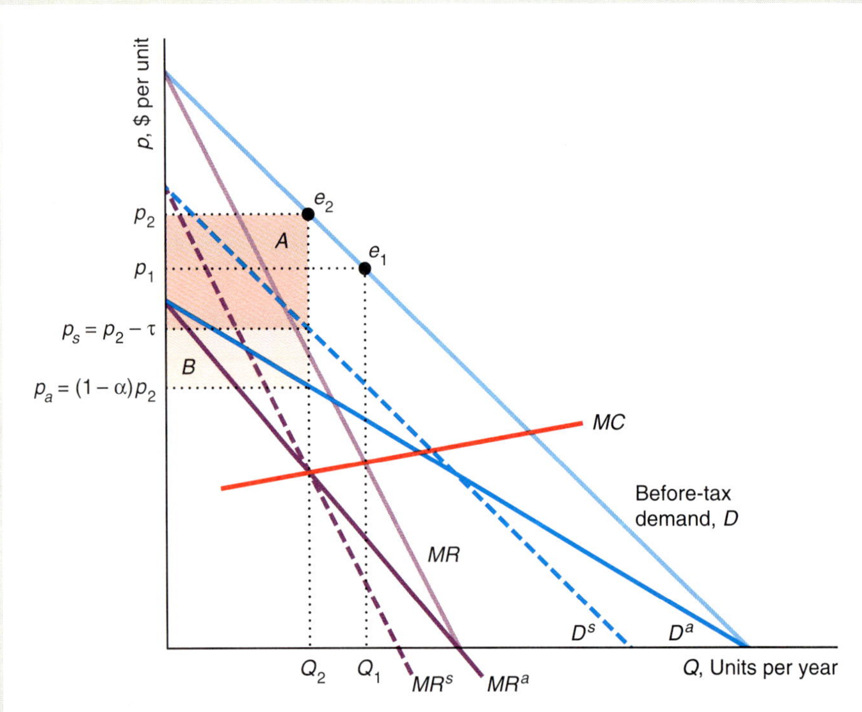

Figure 11.8 Ad Valorem Versus Specific Tax. A specific tax (τ) and an ad valorem tax (α) that reduce the monopoly output by the same amount (from Q_1 to Q_2) raise different amounts of tax revenues for the government. The tax revenue from the specific tax is area $A = \tau Q_2$. The tax revenue from the ad valorem tax is $A + B = \alpha p_2 Q_2$.

---

[17]Chapter 3 shows that both taxes raise the same tax revenue in a competitive market. As with a monopoly, the taxes raise different amounts when applied to oligopolies or other noncompetitive firms.

[18]Instead, we could capture the effect of a specific tax by shifting upward the marginal cost curve by τ, as in our answer to Solved Problem 11.1.

corresponding marginal revenue curve, MR^s, intersects the marginal cost curve at Q_2. In this after-tax equilibrium, e_2, consumers pay p_2 and the monopoly receives $p_s = p_2 - \tau$ per unit. The government's revenue from the specific tax is area $A = \tau Q_2$.

If the government imposes an ad valorem tax α, the demand curve facing the monopoly is D^a. The gap between D^a and D, which is the tax per unit, αp, is greater at higher prices. By setting α appropriately, the corresponding marginal revenue curve, MR_a, intersects the marginal cost curve at Q_2, where consumers again pay p_2. Although the ad valorem tax reduces output by the same amount as does the specific tax, the ad valorem tax raises more revenue, areas $A + B = \alpha p_2 Q_2$.

Both sales taxes harm consumers by the same amount because they raise the price consumers pay from p_1 to p_2 and reduce the quantity purchased from Q_1 to Q_2. The ad valorem tax transfers more revenue from the monopoly to the government, so the government prefers the ad valorem tax and the monopoly prefers the specific tax. (Equivalently, if the government set τ and α so that they raised the same amount of tax revenue, the ad valorem tax would reduce output and consumer surplus less than the specific tax.)

Isn't that amazing! It makes sense for governments to employ an ad valorem tax rather than a specific tax, and they usually apply the ad valorem tax.

11.5 COST ADVANTAGES THAT CREATE MONOPOLIES

Why are some markets monopolized? Two key reasons are that a firm has a cost advantage over other firms or that a government created the monopoly.[19] If a low-cost firm profitably sells at a price so low that other potential competitors with higher costs would make losses, no other firm enters the market.

Sources of Cost Advantages

A firm can have a cost advantage over potential rivals for a number of reasons. One reason is that the firm controls a key input.[20] For example, a firm that owns the only rock quarry in a region is the only firm that can profitably sell gravel to local construction firms.

A second important reason why a firm may have lower costs is that the firm knows of a superior technology or has a better way of organizing production. Henry

[19] In later chapters, we discuss three other means by which monopolies are created. One method is merger of several firms into a single firm (Chapter 12). This method creates a monopoly, however, only if new firms fail to enter the market. A second method is for firms to coordinate their activities and set their prices as a monopoly would (Chapter 12). Firms that act collectively in this way are called a *cartel*. A third method is for a monopoly to use strategies that discourage other firms from entering the market (Chapter 14).

[20] Chapter 14 discusses in greater detail how one firm may control an *essential facility*: a scarce resource that a rival needs to use to survive.

Ford's new methods of organizing production using assembly lines and standardization allowed him to produce cars at lower cost than rival firms until they copied his organizational techniques.

When a firm develops a better production method that provides an advantage—possibly enough of an advantage for the firm to be a monopoly—the firm must either keep the information secret or obtain a patent, which provides government protection from imitation. According to a survey of 650 research and development managers of U.S. firms (Levin et al. 1987), secrecy is more commonly used than patents to prevent duplication of new or improved processes by other firms but less commonly used to protect new products.

Natural Monopoly

A market has a **natural monopoly** if one firm can produce the total output of the market at lower cost than several firms could.[21] With a natural monopoly, it is more efficient to have only one firm produce than more firms. Believing that they are natural monopolies, governments frequently grant monopoly rights to *public utilities* to provide an essential good or service such as water, gas, electric power, or mail delivery.

If a firm has economies of scale (Chapter 7) at all levels of output, its average cost curve falls as output increases for any observed level of output. If all potential firms have the same strictly declining average cost curve, this market has a natural monopoly, as we now illustrate.[22]

A company that supplies water to homes incurs a high fixed cost, F, to build a plant and connect houses to the plant. The firm's marginal cost, m, of supplying water is constant, so its marginal cost curve is horizontal and its average cost, $AC = m + F/Q$, declines as output rises.

Panel a of Figure 11.9 shows such marginal and average cost curves where $m =$ \$10 and $F =$ \$60. If the market output is 12 units per day, one firm produces that output at an average cost of \$15, or a total cost of \$180 (= \$15 × 12). If two firms each produce 6 units, the average cost is \$20 and the cost of producing the market output is \$240 (= \$20 × 12), which is greater than the cost with a single firm.

If the two firms divided total production in any other way, their cost of production would still exceed the cost of a single firm (as the following question asks you to prove). The reason is that the marginal cost per unit is the same no matter how many firms produce, but each additional firm adds a fixed cost, which raises the cost of producing a given quantity. If only one firm provides water, the cost of building a second plant and a second set of pipes is avoided.

---

[21]If the cost for Firm i to produce q_i is $C(q_i)$, the condition for a natural monopoly is

$$C(Q) < C(q_1) + C(q_2) + \ldots + C(q_n),$$

where $Q = q_1 + q_2 + \ldots + q_n$ is the sum of the output of any $n \geq 2$ firms.

[22]A firm may be a natural monopoly even if its cost curve does not fall at all levels of output. If a U-shaped average cost curve reaches its minimum at 100 units of output, it may be less costly for only one firm to produce an output of 101 units even though average cost is rising at that output. Thus, a cost function with economies of scale everywhere is a sufficient but not a necessary condition for natural monopoly.

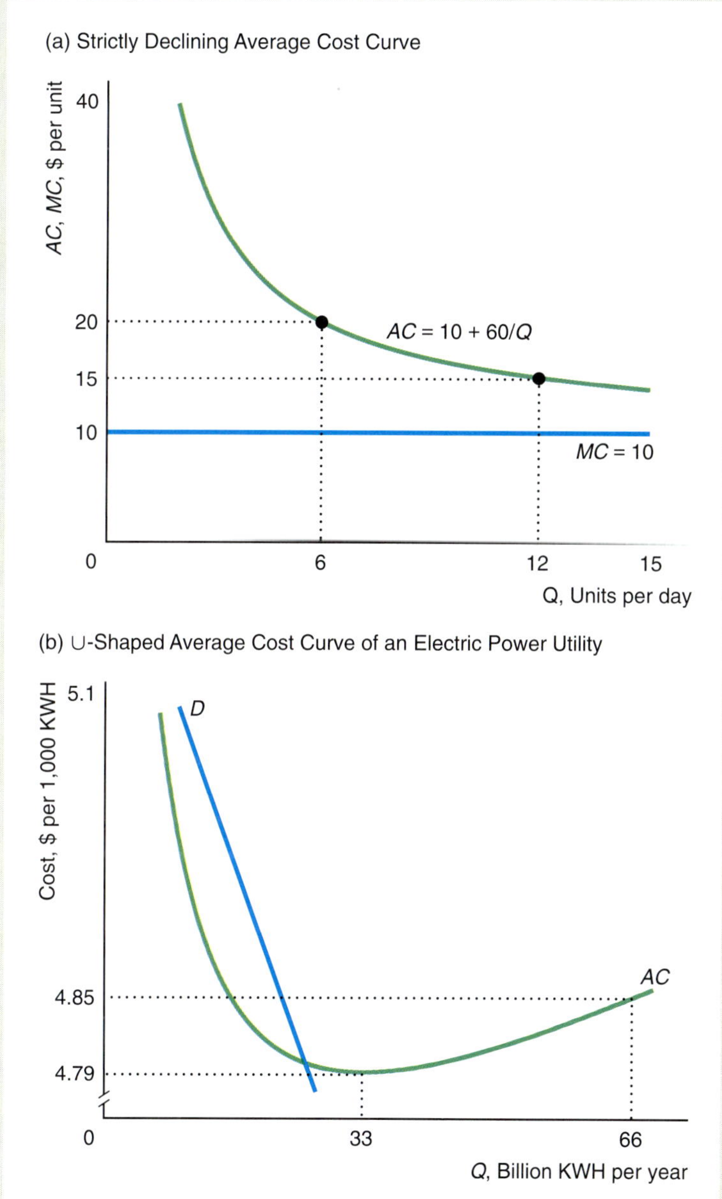

Figure 11.9 Natural Monopoly. (a) This natural monopoly has a strictly declining average cost. (b) A natural monopoly may have a U-shaped average cost curve if the quantity demanded by the market is small enough. According to Christensen and Greene's (1976) estimates, the average cost curve for U.S. electric-power-producing firms in 1970 reached its minimum at 33 billion kilowatt hours (KWH) per year. With demand curve D, one firm can produce any plausible quantity demanded at lower cost than two or more firms can because the average cost curve is strictly falling in that range.

SOLVED PROBLEM 11.2

A firm that delivers Q units of water to households has a total cost of $C(Q) = mQ + F$. If any entrant would have the same cost, does this market have a natural monopoly?

Answer

Determine whether costs rise if two firms produce a given quantity: Let q_1 be the output of Firm 1 and q_2 be the output of Firm 2. The combined cost of these two firms producing $Q = q_1 + q_2$ is

$$\begin{aligned} C(q_1) + C(q_2) &= (mq_1 + F) + (mq_2 + F) \\ &= m(q_1 + q_2) + 2F \\ &= mQ + 2F. \end{aligned}$$

If a single firm produces Q, its cost is $C(Q) = mQ + F$. Thus, the cost of producing any given Q is greater with two firms than with one firm, so this market has a natural monopoly. ■

APPLICATION

Electric Power Utilities

According to the estimates of Christensen and Greene (1976), the average cost curve for U.S. electric-power-producing firms (panel b of Figure 11.9) in 1970 was U-shaped, reaching its minimum at 33 billion kilowatt-hours (KWH) per year. Thus, whether an electric power utility was a natural monopoly depended on the demand it faced.

For example, if the demand curve facing an electric utility was D in panel b, the market demand was less than 33 billion KWH per year, so the electric utility operated in the strictly declining section of its average cost curve and was a natural monopoly. In 1970, most electric companies were operating in regions of substantial economies of scale. Newport Electric produced only 0.5 billion KWH per year, and Iowa Southern Utilities produced 1.3 billion KWH per year.

A few of these firms operated in the upward-sloping section of the average cost curve and were not natural monopolies, however. The largest electric utility in 1970, Southern, produced 54 KWH per year. It was not a natural monopoly because two firms could produce that quantity at 3¢ less per thousand KWH than a single firm could. ■

11.6 GOVERNMENT ACTIONS THAT CREATE MONOPOLIES

Governments create many monopolies. Sometimes, governments own and manage monopolies. In the United States, as in most countries, the postal service is a government monopoly. Indeed, the U.S. Constitution explicitly grants the government the right to establish a postal service. The European Commission's 1995 draft directive to liberalize European postal services allows countries to "reserve" letters lighter than 350 grams (12 ounces) for delivery by national post offices until at least the year 2000. Many local governments own and operate public utility monopolies that provide garbage collection, electricity, water, gas, phone services, and other utilities.

Frequently, however, governments create monopolies by preventing competing firms from entering a market. For example, when a government uses a patent to limit entry, it allows a firm to earn a monopoly profit from an invention—a reward to the firm for developing the new product.

Barriers to Entry

By preventing other firms from entering a market, governments create monopolies. Typically, governments create monopolies in one of three ways: by making it difficult for new firms to obtain a license to operate, by granting a firm the rights to be a monopoly, or by auctioning the rights to be a monopoly.

Frequently, firms need government licenses to operate. If governments make it difficult for new firms to obtain licenses, the first firm may maintain its monopoly. Until recently, many U.S. cities required that new hospitals or other inpatient facilities demonstrate the need for a new facility to obtain a certificate of need, which allowed them to enter the market.

Government grants of monopoly rights have been common for public utilities. Instead of running a public utility itself, a government gives a private company the monopoly rights to operate the utility. Often, there are strings attached to such grants of monopoly rights. One possibility is that the government captures some of the monopoly profits. The State of Louisiana granted Harrah's Jazz Company a 30-year pact in 1994, guaranteeing the firm a monopoly on land-based gambling. Under state law, if other firms enter, the casino can refuse to pay the state its share of the proceeds, which were (optimistically) estimated at the time of passage to be at least $100 million a year.[23] Similarly, as discussed in the application on airport monopoly concessions, a government may capture some of the monopoly profits by charging a high rent to the monopoly. Alternatively, government officials may capture the rents for monopoly rights by means of bribes.

Governments around the world have privatized many state-owned monopolies in the last several decades. By selling its monopolies to private firms, a government can capture the value of future monopoly earnings today. However, for political or other reasons, governments frequently sell at a lower price that does not capture all future profits.

---

[23]Sayre, Alan, "Louisiana's Gambling Industry Is Faltering," *San Francisco Chronicle*, September 6, 1994:B1.

In 1984, the British government sold \$4.9 billion worth of shares in British Telecom, the nation's telephone company. In 1995, France sold all but 10% of its tobacco monopoly, Seita, which makes Gauloise and Gitane cigarettes. The Clinton administration auctioned off large parts of U.S. airwaves for new wireless phone services and other uses. Recently, Mexico and Britain auctioned television stations.

Some governments auction the franchise rights to a monopoly to the highest bidder—or to the firm that promises to charge consumers the lowest price. San Francisco auctioned the monopoly rights to store cars towed for illegal parking. The monopoly, City Tow, collects \$40 per car, of which \$15.03 goes to the city (the losing company's bid would have given the city only \$7.50).[24] Many local cable television monopolies are awarded by using bidding. The United States granted a billionaire investor a 30-year monopoly on the cruise business to Hawaii in exchange for a commitment to buy two American-built cruise ships for about \$400 million each.[25]

Some governments offer monopolies in exchange for high-quality service to customers. In 1996, South Africa's Parliament granted its phone monopoly Telkom five more years of monopoly on the condition that it install 2.8 million new lines and greatly improve service. If Telkom reaches these goals, it gets a sixth year of monopoly as a reward.[26]

Patents

If a firm cannot prevent imitation by keeping its discovery secret, it may obtain government protection to prevent other firms from duplicating its discovery and entering the market. Virtually all countries provide such protection through a **patent:** an exclusive right granted to the inventor to sell a new and useful product, process, substance, or design for a fixed period of time. A patent grants an inventor the right to be the monopoly provider of the good for a number of years.

Patent Length. The length of a patent varies across countries. The U.S. Constitution explicitly gives the government the right to grant authors and inventors exclusive rights to their writings (copyrights) and to their discoveries (patents) for limited periods of time. Traditionally, U.S. patents lasted *17 years* from the date they were *granted*. The United States agreed to change its patent law as part of the most recent General Agreement on Tariffs and Trade (GATT). Starting June 7, 1995, U.S. patents last for *20 years* after the date an inventor *files* for patent protection. Under these new rules, the length of the protection is likely to be shorter, as it frequently takes years after filing for final approval of a patent.

---

[24]Matier, Phillip and Andrew Ross, "City Tow Kowtows to S.F. and Coughs Up More Cash," *San Francisco Chronicle*, February 18, 1994:A17.

[25]Bryant, Adam, "In a Bill's Shipbuilding Provision, Some See a Floating Pork Barrel," *New York Times*, October 11, 1997:A1, B2.

[26]McNeil, Donald G., "Crossed Wires in South Africa," *New York Times*, December 17, 1997:C1, C8.

Many European countries granted patent protection for very short periods of time, but these patents could be renewed upon the payment of a fee. The renewal fee was due in two years in France, three in Germany, and five in the United Kingdom. A patent could be renewed until it was 16 years old in Britain, 18 in Germany, and 20 in France.

Patents Stimulate Research. A firm with a patent monopoly sets a high price that results in deadweight loss. Why then do governments grant patent monopolies? The main reason is that inventive activity would fall if there were no patent monopolies or other incentives to inventors. The costs of developing a new drug or new computer chip are often hundreds of millions or even billions of dollars. If anyone could copy a new drug or chip and compete with the inventor, few individuals or firms would undertake costly research. Thus, the government is explicitly trading off the long-run benefits of additional inventions against the shorter-term harms of monopoly pricing during the period of patent protection.

APPLICATION

A Drug Patent

In 1977, SmithKline Beckman received a patent for its revolutionary anti-ulcer drug, Tagamet, which gave it the monopoly right to sell Tagamet in the United States.[27] It was sold as a prescription drug.

Tagamet blocks the histamine-2 (H_2) receptor on the cells of the stomach that produce gastric acid and thus reduces the amount of acid produced. This drug is much more effective than previous anti-ulcer drugs, which neutralize acids after they are produced. Three other H_2 drugs entered the market from 1983 to 1988: Zantac in June 1983, Pepcid in October 1986, and Axid in April 1988. After 1994, when Tagamet's patent expired, other firms started selling generic forms of Tagamet.

Thus, from 1977 to late 1983, Tagamet was the only H_2 drug on the market and had no close substitute. From late 1983 to 1994, the market for H_2 drugs was oligopolistic. Today, there is a more complex market structure in which both branded goods (Tagamet, Zantac, Pepcid, and Axid) and unbranded, generic Tagamet copies are sold. In addition, Tagamet, Zantac, Pepcid, and Axid are now available without a prescription.

---

[27]The following discussion is based on Berndt et al. (1994, 1995); Suslow (1996); "Ulcer Drug's Price About to Drop," *San Francisco Chronicle*, May 11, 1994:D1; Freudenheim, "New Drug Era Begins as Tagamet Patent Ends," *New York Times*, May 17, 1994:C4; "Having an Ulcer Is Getting a Lot Cheaper," *Business Week*, No. 3370, May 9, 1994:30; and Day, Kathleen, "Putting a Price on a Pill," *Washington Post*, March 21, 1993. When the firm had a monopoly, its name was SmithKline Beckman. Its current name is SmithKline Beecham.

Using a few assumptions, we can calculate the pricing and welfare implications of SmithKline's monopoly in early 1983, just before Tagamet lost its monopoly. Before Zantac entered the market, about 1.3 million daily doses of oral Tagamet were sold at pharmacies at a price of about 75¢ per daily dose in 1983 dollars. Though the firm's cost data are not publicly available, some unofficial industry estimates put the marginal cost (and average variable cost) of an H_2 drug at about 10% of the price, or $MC = AVC = 7.5$¢. If we rearrange Equation 11.9, we can use this relationship between marginal cost and price to calculate the elasticity of demand that SmithKline faced if it were maximizing its short-run profits:

$$\varepsilon = -\frac{p}{p - MC} = -\frac{0.75}{0.75 - 0.075} \approx -1.11.$$

The demand it faced was only slightly elastic: A 1% increase in price caused quantity to fall by only a little more than 1%.

If we assume that the demand curve is linear, and that the elasticity of demand is −1.11 at the monopoly optimum (1.3 million daily doses sold at 75¢ a dose), then the demand function is[28]

$$p = 1.43 - 0.52Q.$$

This demand curve, in Figure 11.10, has a slope of −0.52, hits the price axis at \$1.43, and hits the quantity axis at 2.75 million daily doses. The corresponding marginal revenue curve,

$$MR = 1.43 - 1.04Q,$$

strikes the price axis at \$1.43 and has twice the slope, −1.04, as the demand curve.

The marginal revenue and marginal cost (expressed in dollars) curves intersect,

$$MR = 1.43 - 1.04Q = 0.075 = MC,$$

at the profit-maximizing quantity of about 1.3 million daily doses. The corresponding price is 75¢.

Had Tagamet been sold at a price equal to its marginal cost, 7.5¢, consumer surplus would have equaled areas $A + B + C$ in the figure, which, given our linearity and other assumptions, was about \$1.77 million per day.[29] At the

[28]A linear demand, $p = a - bQ$, has an elasticity of $\varepsilon = -(1/b)(p/Q)$. If the elasticity of demand is $-1.11 = -(1/b)(0.75/1.3)$, where $p = 0.75$ and $Q = 1.3$, then $b = 0.52$. Solving $p = 0.75 = a - 0.52 \times 1.3$, we find that $a = 1.43$.

[29]The height of the triangle $A + B + C$ is \$1.355 = \$1.43 − \$0.075, and its length is approximately 2.61 million daily doses, so its area is $\frac{1}{2}(\$1.355 \times 2.61) \approx$ \$1.77 million per day.

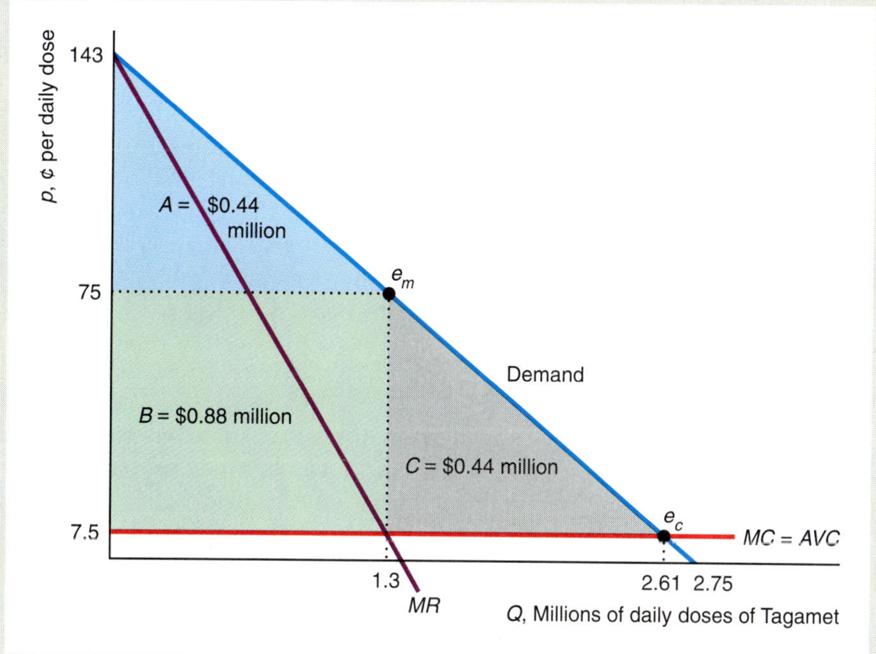

Figure 11.10 Tagamet. Tagamet had a monopoly in 1983. If we assume that the demand curve is linear, marginal cost is constant, and SmithKline set the price of Tagamet to maximize its profits, the deadweight loss from monopoly was *C* and consumer surplus was *A*. The firm's profit was *B* minus its fixed costs.

higher monopoly price of 75¢, consumer surplus was only $A \approx$ \$0.44 million per day, so consumers lost consumer surplus of $B + C$, or \$1.33 million per day. Part of this loss to consumers, B = (\$0.75 – \$0.075) × 1.3 million daily doses ≈ \$0.88 million per day, is a transfer from consumers to the firm, but the rest, $C \approx$ \$0.44 million per day or \$161 million per year, is the deadweight loss from monopoly pricing. SmithKline's profit is its producer surplus, *B*, minus its fixed cost.

SmithKline reports selling \$14 billion of Tagamet during the 17 years its patent was in force.[30] The gigantic rewards to be had from a successful drug provide a major incentive to firms to invest in developing new pharmaceuticals.

Were it not for patent protection, other companies could duplicate a new drug—as illustrated by the entry of generic copies of Tagamet when its patent expired—and competition would drive economic profits toward zero,

[30]To put that number in perspective, Mattel has sold \$1.4 billion worth of Barbie dolls over 37 years. Collins, Glenn, "Growing Pains for a Doll Maker," *New York Times*, September 17, 1996:C19.

reducing the financial incentive to engage in research. To forestall that, several drug companies proposed in 1997 to pay the government to extend their patent monopolies. The funds would be used for research on cancer, heart disease, AIDS, and other diseases.[31]

It is extremely expensive to bring a new drug to market. Firms must pay for conducting research, winning patent approval, engaging in development, performing clinical trials, and obtaining final approval from the Food and Drug Administration (FDA) to sell the drug based on a demonstration of efficacy and safety. According to one U.S. government agency's estimate, the before-tax cost of developing a new pharmaceutical averages \$359 million per drug (the after-tax cost is \$194 million).[32] Moreover, there's no guarantee that a drug will be successful. Tagamet was one of the most profitable drugs of all time; however, many other drugs, though costly to develop, produce few returns.

Thus, the justification for letting patents create monopolies is that the monopoly profits spur new research. Many people benefit greatly from a drug like Tagamet. The monetary value of the relief from ulcers they received in the short run, when they bought Tagamet at the monopoly price, is Area A; the value in the long run after the patent expired, when they buy the same drug at marginal cost, is area $A + B + C$.[33] ■

Alternatives to Patents. Instead of using patents to spur research, the government could give research grants or offer prizes. Rather than trying these alternative approaches, Congress has modified the patent system. In the 1960s and 1970s, the effective life of a patent on a drug shrank because of the additional time it took to get FDA approval to sell the drug. By 1978, the average drug had patent protection for fewer than 10 years. The Drug Price Competition and Patent Term Restoration Act of 1984 restored up to three years of the part of the patent life that was lost while the firm demonstrated efficacy and safety to the FDA. At the same time, the act made it easier for generic products to enter at the end of the patent period. Thus, the act aimed both to encourage the development of new drugs by increasing the reward—the monopoly period—and to stimulate price competition at the end of the period.

---

[31] "Drug Companies Seek Deal to Stall Generic Competitors," *Los Angeles Times*, October 22, 1997:A27.

[32] The after-tax cost is lower than the before-tax amount because the firm may subtract its research cost from its taxable income, lowering its tax burden by \$165 (= \$359 – \$194) million.

[33] According to some estimates, the rate of surgical operations for ulcers dropped from 155,000 in 1977, when Tagamet was introduced, to around 16,000 per year by 1991. Given that ulcer surgery costs \$25,000 compared to H_2 drugs' cost of about \$1,000, patients' net savings in out-of-pocket costs is over \$3 billion per year.

11.7 GOVERNMENT ACTIONS THAT REDUCE MARKET POWER

Some governments act to reduce or eliminate monopolies' market power. Most Western countries have laws forbidding a firm from driving other firms out of the market so as to monopolize it. Many governments either regulate monopolies—especially those that the government created—or destroy monopolies by breaking them up into smaller, independent firms or encouraging other firms to enter the market.

Regulating Monopolies

Governments limit monopolies' market power in a number of ways. Most utilities, for example, are subject to direct regulation. One method governments use to limit the harms of monopoly is to place a ceiling on the price that a monopoly charges.

Optimal Price Regulation. In some markets, the government can eliminate the deadweight loss of monopoly by requiring that a monopoly charge no more than the competitive price. We use our earlier linear example to illustrate this type of regulation in Figure 11.11.

If the government doesn't regulate the profit-maximizing monopoly, the monopoly optimum is e_m, at which six units are sold at the monopoly price of \$18. Suppose the government sets a ceiling price of \$16, the price at which the marginal cost curve intersects the market demand curve. Because the monopoly cannot charge more than \$16 per unit, the monopoly's regulated demand curve is horizontal at \$16 (up to eight units) and is the same as the market demand curve at lower prices. The marginal revenue, MR_r, corresponding to the regulated demand curve is horizontal where the regulated demand curve is horizontal (up to eight units) and equals the marginal revenue curve, MR, corresponding to the market demand curve at larger quantities.

The regulated monopoly sets its output at eight units, where MR_r equals its marginal cost, MC, and charges the maximum permitted price of \$16. The regulated firm still makes a profit, because its average cost is less than \$16 at eight units. The optimally regulated monopoly optimum, e_o, is the same as the competitive equilibrium, where marginal cost (supply) equals the market demand curve.[34] Thus, setting a price ceiling where the MC curve and market demand curve intersect eliminates the deadweight loss of monopoly.

How do we know that this regulation is optimal? The answer is that this regulated outcome is the same as would occur if this market were competitive, where welfare is maximized (Chapter 9). As the table accompanying Figure 11.11 shows, the deadweight loss of monopoly, $-C - E$, is eliminated by this optimal regulation.

Nonoptimal Price Regulation. Welfare is reduced if the government does not set the price optimally. Suppose that the government sets the regulated price below the

---

[34]The monopoly produces at e_o only if the regulated price is greater than its average variable cost. Here, the regulated price, \$16, exceeds the average variable cost at eight units of \$8. Indeed, the firm makes a profit because the average cost at eight units is \$9.50.

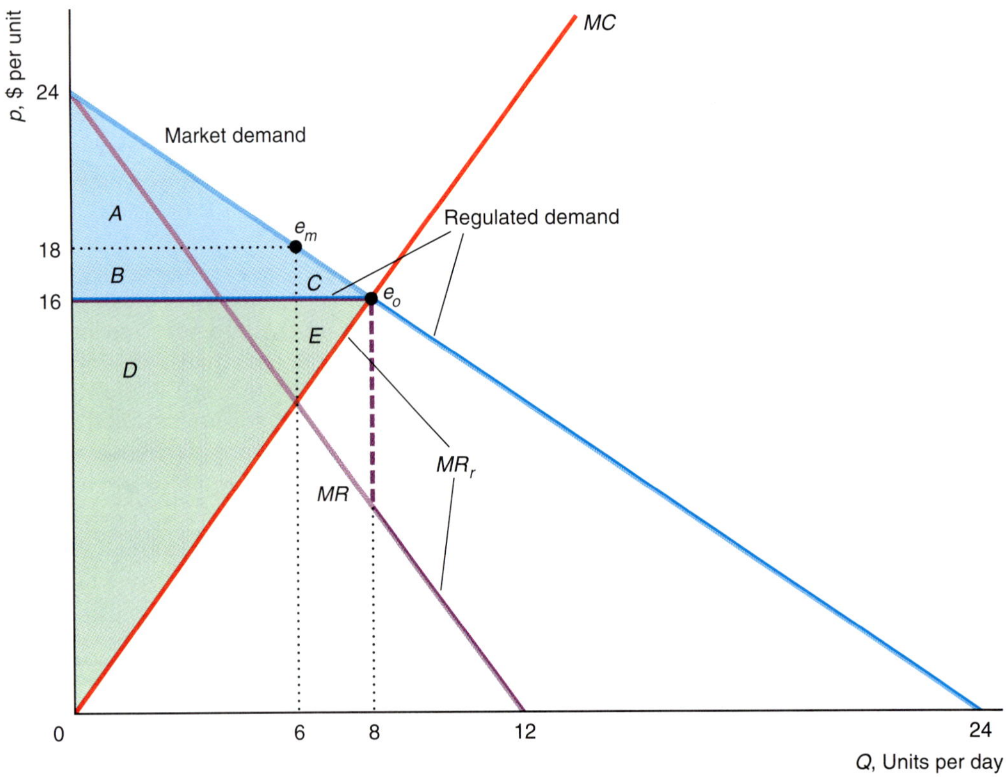

	Monopoly without Regulation	Monopoly with Optimal Regulation	Change
Consumer Surplus, *CS*	A	$A + B + C$	$B + C = \Delta CS$
Producer Surplus, *PS*	$B + D$	$D + E$	$E - B = \Delta PS$
Welfare, $W = CS + PS$	$A + B + D$	$A + B + C + D + E$	$C + E = \Delta W$
Deadweight Loss, *DWL*	$-C - E$	0	$C + E = \Delta DWL$

Figure 11.11 Optimal Price Regulation. If the government sets a price ceiling at \$16, where the monopoly's marginal cost curve hits the demand curve, the new demand curve facing the monopoly has a kink at eight units and the corresponding marginal revenue curve, MR_r, "jumps" at that quantity. The regulated monopoly sets its output where $MR_r = MC$, selling the same quantity, eight units, at the same price, \$16, as would a competitive industry. The regulation eliminates the monopoly deadweight loss, $-C - E$. Consumer surplus, $A + B + C$, and producer surplus, $D + E$, are the same as under competition.

optimal level, which is \$16 in our example. If it sets the price below the firm's minimum average cost, the firm shuts down. If that happens, the deadweight loss equals the sum of the consumer plus producer surplus under optimal regulation, $A + B + C + D + E$ in Figure 11.11.

If the government sets the price ceiling below the optimally regulated price but high enough that the firm does not shut down, consumers who are lucky enough to buy the good are better off because they can buy goods at a lower price than with optimal regulation. Some customers, however, are frustrated because the monopoly will not sell them the good, as we show next. There is a deadweight loss because less output is sold than with optimal regulation. (Problem 10 at the end of the chapter asks you to determine the effects of a regulated price that is above the optimal level.)

SOLVED PROBLEM 11.3

Suppose the government sets a price p_2 that is below the monopoly-optimal level, p_1, but above the monopoly's minimum average cost. How do the price, the quantity sold, the quantity demanded, and welfare under this regulation compare to those under optimal regulation?

Answer

1. *Describe the optimally regulated outcome*: With optimal regulation, e_1, the price is set at p_1, where the market demand curve intersects the monopoly's marginal cost curve in Figure 11.12. The optimally regulated monopoly sells Q_1 units.
2. *Describe the outcome when the government regulates the price at p_2*: Where the market demand is above p_2, the regulated demand curve facing the monopoly is horizontal at p_2 (up to Q_d). The corresponding marginal revenue curve, MR_r, is horizontal where the regulated demand curve is horizontal and equals the marginal revenue curve corresponding to the market demand curve, MR, where the regulated demand curve is downward sloping. The monopoly maximizes its profit by selling Q_2 units at p_2. The new regulated monopoly optimum is e_2, where MR_r intersects MC. The firm does not shut down when regulated as long as its average variable cost at Q_2 is less than p_2.
3. *Compare the outcomes*: The quantity that the monopoly sells falls from Q_1 to Q_2 when the government lowers its price ceiling from p_1 to p_2. At that low price, consumers want to buy Q_d, so there is excess demand equal to $Q_d - Q_2$. Compared to optimal regulation, welfare is lower by at least $-B - D$.[35] ■

[35] The welfare loss is greater if unlucky consumers waste time trying to buy the good unsuccessfully or if goods are not allocated optimally among consumers. A consumer who values the good at only p_2 may be lucky enough to buy it, while a consumer who values the good at p_1 or more may not be able to obtain it.

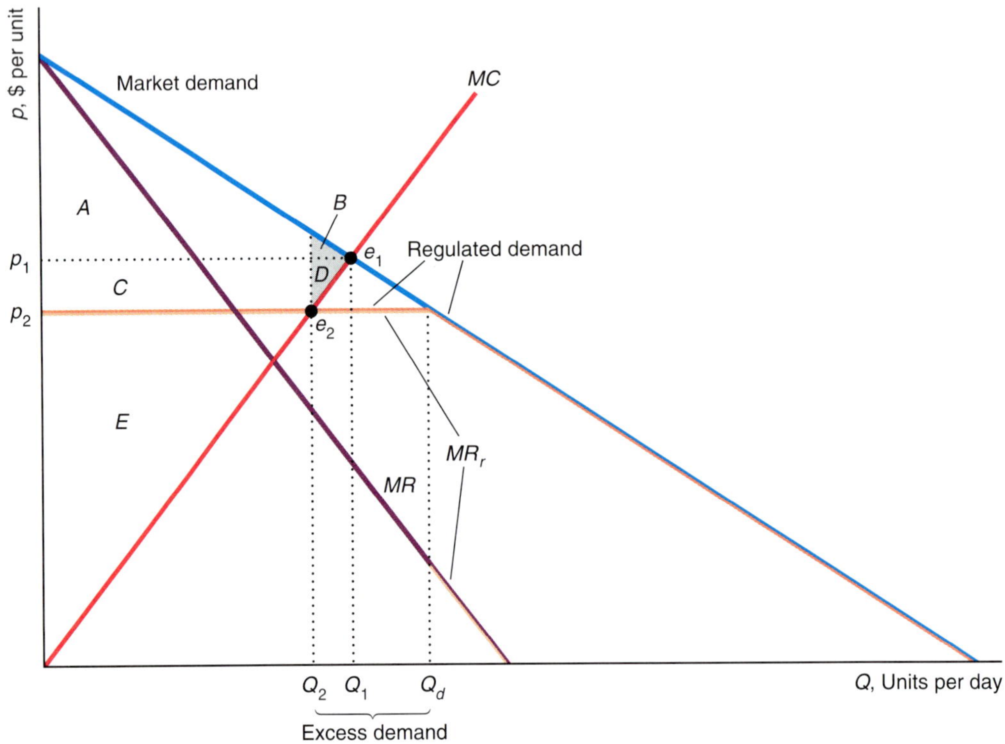

	Monopoly with Optimal Regulation	Monopoly with a Low Regulated Price	Change
Consumer Surplus, *CS*	$A + B$	$A + C$	$C - B = \Delta CS$
Producer Surplus, *PS*	$C + D + E$	E	$-C - D = \Delta PS$
Welfare, $W = CS + PS$	$A + B + C + D + E$	$A + C + E$	$-B - D = \Delta W = DWL$

Figure 11.12 Welfare Effects of a Low Regulated Price. If the government sets a maximum price of p_2, the monopoly's residual demand and the corresponding marginal revenue curve, MR_r, are horizontal at that price. The monopoly sells Q_2, where MR_r intersects the marginal cost curve, *MC*. At that price, consumers would like to buy Q_d, so there is excess demand equal to $Q_d - Q_2$. The deadweight loss is $-B - D$, which is less than without any regulation but more than with optimal regulation.

Problems in Regulating. Governments face several problems in regulating monopolies. First, because they do not know the actual demand and marginal cost curves, governments may set the price at the wrong level. Second, many governments use regulations that are less efficient than price regulation. Third, regulated firms may bribe or otherwise influence government regulators to help the firms rather than society as a whole.

Because of limited information about the demand and marginal cost curves, governments may set a price ceiling above or below the competitive level. Moreover, a regulatory agency may have to set the price higher than is optimal because it cannot offer a subsidy.

If the regulatory agency were to set the price equal to a natural monopoly's marginal cost, the price would be below the firm's average cost. The monopoly would threaten to shut down unless the regulatory agency were to subsidize it or raise the price.

To illustrate this problem, we calculate how setting the price too low would affect the electric power monopoly in Kyushu, Japan.[36] In the absence of regulation and in light of the curves in Figure 11.13, this firm maximizes its profit by operating where its marginal cost equals its marginal revenue, where it sells 23 billion KWH at ¥30.3 per hundred KWH and makes a profit equal to area *A*.

This firm would lose money if it faced a price ceiling of ¥19.5, where the demand curve intersects the marginal cost curve at 34 billion KWH. At that quantity, its average cost of ¥21.9 is greater than the price ceiling, and the firm loses an amount equal to area *B*. Thus, if the government wants the firm to charge a price equal to marginal cost, it would have to subsidize the firm by at least *B* to keep it from shutting down.

Typically, it is politically infeasible for a government regulatory agency to subsidize a firm. Instead, the agency might set the price at ¥22.3, at which the demand curve intersects the average cost curve and the monopoly breaks even. There is still a deadweight loss because that price is above marginal cost, but the deadweight loss is smaller than if the monopoly were unregulated.

The Kyushu electric utility is subject not to price regulation but to *rate-of-return regulation*, in which the government limits the firm's profit to a percentage of what it spent to buy its capital (the plant and equipment). For example, if the government limits a firm's annual rate of return to 10%, a firm that spent $100 on its capital could earn a profit no higher than $10 per year. Rate-of-return regulation has been widely used in Japan, the United States, and other countries.

Many economists argue that rate-of-return regulation is less efficient than direct price regulation and creates distortions. They contend that this type of regulation causes firms to overinvest in capital so that they can keep their rates of return low. If a firm facing a rate-of-return regulation of 10% had $200 of capital instead of $100, it would be allowed annual profits up to $20 instead of $10 per year. In part because governments now accept this reasoning, rate-of-return regulation is becoming much less common and direct price regulation is used increasingly in the United States.

---

[36]The cost curves in this example are based on the estimated short-run average cost curve in Nemoto, Nakanishi, and Madono (1993). To create an example of a possible demand curve, we assume that the demand is linear and that the electricity demand of Japanese consumers at the observed output is the same as that of American consumers (Maddock, Castano, and Vella, 1992).

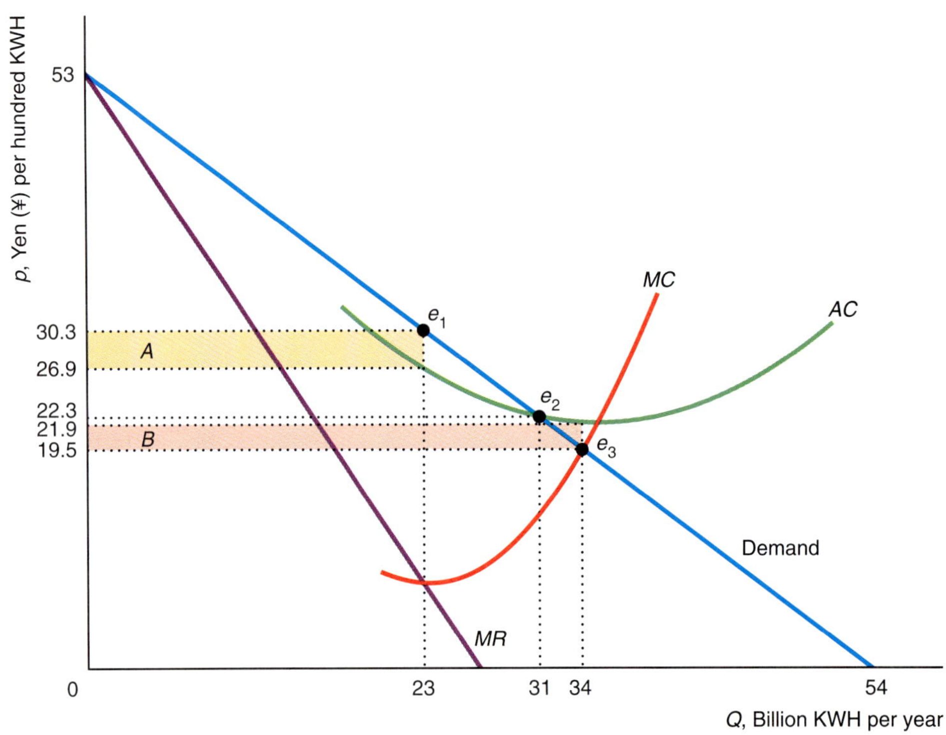

Figure 11.13 Regulating an Electric Utility. If the electric utility is an unregulated, profit-maximizing monopoly, e_1, it sets its output at 23 billion KWH and charges ¥30.3 per hundred KWH and makes a profit of area *A*. The government may regulate price so that the utility breaks even, e_2. Alternatively, the government may regulate the utility to behave like a price taker, e_3. If so, the government must subsidize the utility by area *B* to keep it from shutting down.

Unfortunately, regulation is often not effective when regulators are *captured*: influenced by the firms they regulate. Typically, this influence is more subtle than an outright bribe. Many American regulators have worked in the industry before they became regulators and hence are sympathetic to those firms.[37] Many regulators hope to obtain good jobs in the industry eventually, so they don't want to offend potential

[37]For example, before his resignation in 1995, a California Public Utilities Commissioner (PUC) enjoyed friendly games of racquetball with a lobbyist for Southern California Edison Co., a utility that is regulated by the PUC. Another commissioner played golf with an Edison lobbyist as the pair toured England with top energy lobbyists on a trip paid for by a foundation with close ties to the California energy industry. California electricity rates were 50% above the national average at the time. Sandoval, Ricardo, "PUC, Utilities: Too Close for Comfort?" *San Francisco Examiner*, March 26, 1995:B1.

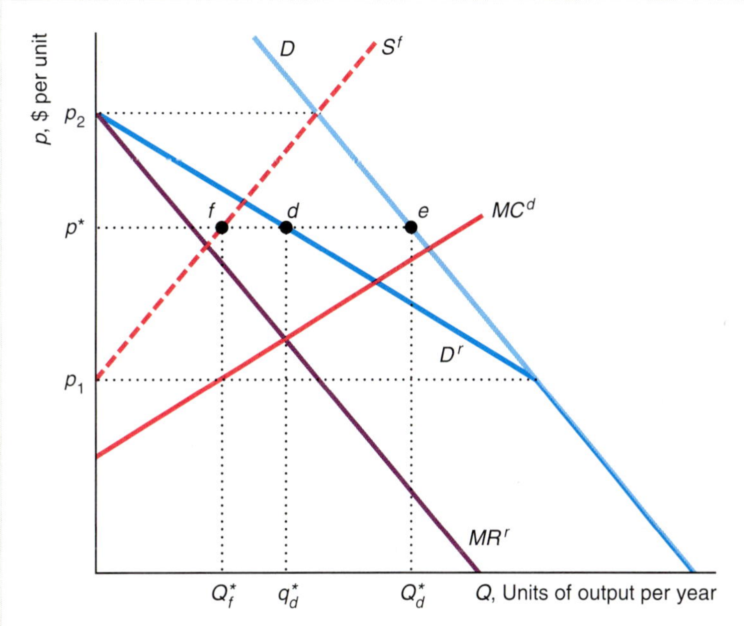

Figure 11.14 Dominant Firm–Competitive Fringe Equilibrium. The residual demand facing the dominant firm, D^r, is the horizontal difference between the market demand curve, D, and the supply curve of the fringe firms, S^f. The dominant firm maximizes its profit at d by setting a price of p^* and selling q_d units where its residual demand curve, MR^r, intersects its marginal cost curve, MC^d. The fringe operates at point f, and the market equilibrium is point e.

demand. At p^*, the residual demand is q_d^*, which equals the market demand, Q^*, minus the fringe supply, Q_f^*. At p_2, the fringe supplies as much as the market demands (S^f intersects D at p_2), so the residual demand is zero.

The dominant firm's marginal revenue curve is MR^r, which corresponds to the residual demand curve, D^r. The dominant firm maximizes its profit at point d by setting a price of p^*, where it sells q_d^* units—the quantity where MR^r intersects its marginal cost curve, MC^d. The fringe sells Q_f^* for p^*, at point f. In the market equilibrium, point e, the total amount that the dominant firm and the fringe sell, $q_d^* + Q_p^*$, equals the quantity the market demands at that price, Q^*, so neither consumers nor producers want to change their behavior.

Because of the upward-sloping supply curve of the fringe, the dominant firm's residual demand curve, D^r, lies below and is flatter than the market demand curve, D, that the monopoly faced. As a result, the dominant firm faces a more elastic demand than did the monopoly, which causes the dominant firm to set a lower price. At this lower price, consumers demand more, and the dominant firm and the fringe produce more collectively than did the monopoly alone. Thus, the fringe erodes but does not eliminate the dominant firm's market power. Consumers benefit from the entry of the fringe, and some, but not all, of the deadweight loss under monopoly is eliminated.

Summary

1. **Monopoly profit maximization:** Like any firm, a monopoly—a single seller—maximizes its profit by setting its output so that its marginal revenue equals its marginal cost. The monopoly makes a positive profit if its average cost is less than the price at the profit-maximizing output.
2. **Market power:** Market power is the ability of a firm to charge a price above marginal cost and earn a positive profit. The more elastic is the demand facing the monopoly at the quantity at which it maximizes its profit, the closer is its price to its marginal cost and the closer is the Lerner Index or price markup, $(p - MC)/p$, to zero, the competitive level.
3. **Effects of a shift of the demand curve:** Because a monopoly does not have a supply curve, the effect of a shift in demand on a monopoly's output depends on the shapes of both its marginal cost curve and its demand curve. As a monopoly's demand curve shifts, price and output may change in the same or different directions.
4. **Welfare effects of monopoly:** Because a monopoly's price is above its marginal cost, too little output is produced, and society suffers a deadweight loss. The monopoly makes higher profit than it would if it acted as a price taker. Consumers are worse off, buying less output at a higher price.
5. **Cost advantages that create monopolies:** A firm may be a monopoly if it controls a key input, has superior knowledge about producing or distributing a good, or has substantial economies of scale. In markets with substantial economies of scale, the single seller is called a natural monopoly because total production costs would rise if more than one firm produced.
6. **Government actions that create monopolies:** Governments may establish government-owned and operated monopolies, such as garbage collection firms. They may also create private monopolies by establishing barriers to entry that prevent other firms from competing. Nations grant patents, which give inventors monopoly rights for a limited period of time.
7. **Government actions that reduce market power:** A government can eliminate the welfare harm of a monopoly by forcing the firm to set its price at the competitive level. If the government sets the price at a different level or otherwise regulates nonoptimally, welfare at the regulated monopoly optimum is lower welfare than in the competitive equilibrium. A government can eliminate or reduce the harms of monopoly by allowing or facilitating entry.

Problems

1. Show that, after a shift in the demand curve, a monopoly's price may remain constant but its output may rise.
2. In Solved Problem 11.1, you are asked to show the effect of a specific tax of \$8 on a monopoly. If this market were competitive (the marginal cost curve is the market supply curve), what would be the effect of the same tax? Compare the effects of a tax on a competitive market versus a monopoly in terms of tax incidence on consumers and the size of the deadweight loss.
3. What is the effect of a profit tax on a monopoly? Assume the government takes γ fraction of the before-tax economic profit, π, and the monopoly maximizes the after-tax profit, $(1 - \gamma)\pi$.
4. Southwest Airlines' cost-per-available-seat mile is well below that of most of its large rivals. Southwest's cost is 35% lower than that of the

worst performer, USAir.[40] Assuming that Southwest and USAir compete on a route, use a graph to show how their equilibrium quantities differ.

5. A monopoly has a constant marginal cost of production of \$1 per unit and a fixed cost of \$10. Draw the firm's *MC*, *AVC*, and *AC* curves. Add a downward-sloping demand curve, and show the profit-maximizing quantity and price. Indicate the profit as an area on your diagram. Show the deadweight loss.

6. Can a firm be a natural monopoly if it has a U-shaped average cost curve? Why or why not?

7. Can a firm operating in the upward portion of its average cost curve be a natural monopoly? Explain.

8. Show why a monopoly may operate in the upward- or downward-sloping section of its long-run average cost but a competitive firm will operate only in the upward-sloping section.

9. When will a monopoly set its price equal to its marginal cost? (*Hint*: For one answer, refer to the discussion of free entry in Chapter 8.)

10. Describe the effects on output and welfare if the government regulates a monopoly so that it may not charge a price above $\bar{p}$, which lies between the unregulated monopoly price and the optimally regulated price (determined by the intersection of the firm's marginal cost and the market demand curve).

★11. Suppose that many similar price-taking consumers (like Denise in Chapter 10) have a single good (candy bars) and that Jane has a monopoly in wood. Thus, Jane can set prices. Assume that no production is possible. Using an Edgeworth box, illustrate the monopoly optimum and show that it does not lie on the contract curve (isn't Pareto efficient).

12. Suppose that a monopoly faces a linear demand curve, constant marginal cost, and no fixed costs. If the market were competitive, the price would be in the elastic portion of the demand curve. The government provides the monopoly with a per unit subsidy that induces the monopoly to set its price at the competitive level. Using a graph, show what happens to consumer surplus, producer surplus, and deadweight loss before and after the subsidy.

13. Suppose that the competitive fringe's supply curve is horizontal in the long run. Show and describe the resulting dominant firm-competitive fringe equilibrium.

14. Show that the deadweight loss is higher in a monopoly optimum than in a dominant firm-competitive fringe equilibrium.

Math Problems

★15. Show mathematically that a monopoly may raise the price to consumers by more than the specific tax imposed on it. (*Hint*: One approach is to consider a monopoly facing a constant-elasticity demand curve and a constant marginal cost, *m*.)

16. The demand curve facing a monopoly is

$$p = 100 - Q.$$

The firm's cost curve is $C(Q) = 10 + 5Q$. What is the profit-maximizing solution?

17. How does your answer to the previous math problem change if $C(Q) = 100 + 5Q$?

18. The demand curve facing a monopoly is

$$p = 10Q^{-1/2}.$$

The firm's cost curve is $C(Q) = 5Q$. What is the profit-maximizing solution?

★19. A monopoly's production function is Cobb-Douglas: $Q = L^{1/2}K^{1/2}$, where L is labor and K is capital. As a result, the marginal product functions are $MP_L = \frac{1}{2}K^{1/2}/L^{1/2}$ and $MP_K = \frac{1}{2}L^{1/2}/K^{1/2}$. The demand function is $p = 100 - Q$. The wage, w, is \$1 per hour, and the rental cost of capital, r, is \$4.
   A. What is the equation of the (long-run) expansion path? Illustrate in a graph.
   B Derive the long-run total cost curve equation as a function of q.
   C What quantity maximizes this firm's profit?
   D Find the optimal input combination that produces the profit-maximizing quantity. Illustrate with a graph.

[40]"Come Fly the Unfriendly Skies," *The Economist*, 333(7888), November 5, 1994:61–2.

CHAPTER 12

Oligopoly and Monopolistic Competition

Anyone can win unless there happens to be a second entry.
—George Ade

When deciding how many Taurus sedans to produce, Ford considers how many Camry and Accord cars Toyota and Honda are likely to sell. Each of these firms closely monitors its rivals' past behavior—the number of cars sold, their pricing, and the cars' features—to better predict their rivals' future behavior. Indeed, a firm may pay large sums to hire executives and engineers from a rival firm to gain insight into its competitor's decisionmaking and planning.

Firms pay attention to each other's behavior in an **oligopoly**: a small group of firms in a market with substantial barriers to entry. Because relatively few firms compete in such a market, each can influence the price, and hence each affects rival firms. The need to consider the behavior of rival firms makes an oligopoly firm's profit-maximization decision more difficult than that of a monopoly or a competitive firm. A monopoly has no rivals, and a competitive firm ignores the behavior of individual rivals—it considers only the market price and its own costs in choosing its profit-maximizing output.

An oligopoly firm that ignores or inaccurately predicts its rivals' behavior is likely to suffer a loss of profit. As its rivals produce more cars, the price Ford can get for its cars falls. If Ford underestimates how many cars its rivals will produce, Ford may produce too many automobiles and lose money.

Oligopolistic firms may act independently or coordinate their actions. A group of firms that explicitly agree to coordinate their activities is called a **cartel**. These firms may agree on how much each firm will sell or on a common price. By cooperating and behaving like a monopoly, the members of a cartel collectively earn the monopoly profit—the maximum possible profit.

If oligopolistic firms do not collude, they earn lower profits. Nonetheless, because there are relatively few firms in the market, oligopolistic firms that act independently may earn positive economic profits in the long run, unlike competitive firms.

A barrier to entry keeps the number of firms small in an oligopolistic market. If a market has no barriers to entry, firms enter the market until profits are driven to zero. In a perfectly competitive market, free entry results in firms' earning zero profits and acting like price takers. In some markets, however, even after entry has driven profits to zero, each firm faces a downward-sloping demand curve. Because of this slope, the firm can charge a price above its marginal cost, creating a *market failure*: inefficient (too little) consumption (Chapter 9). **Monopolistic competition** is a market structure in which firms have market power (the ability to raise price profitably above marginal cost) but no additional firm can enter and earn positive profits.

In this chapter, we examine cartel, oligopoly, and monopolistically competitive markets in which firms set quantities rather than prices. As discussed in Chapter 11, the monopoly equilibrium is the same whether a monopoly sets price or quantity. Similarly, if colluding oligopolies sell identical products, the cartel equilibrium is the same whether they set quantity or price. The oligopolistic and monopolistically competitive equilibria differ, however, if firms set prices instead of quantities. In the next chapter, we show how to determine these equilibria when firms choose prices.

In this chapter, we examine seven main topics:

1. **Market structures:** The number of firms, price, profits, and other properties of markets vary depending on whether the market is monopolistic, oligopolistic, monopolistically competitive, or competitive.
2. **Game theory:** When there are relatively few firms in a market, firms take into account how their actions affect other firms and how other firms' actions affect them. Economists use a set of tools called *game theory* to analyze conflicts and cooperation between such firms.
3. **Cooperative oligopoly models:** If firms successfully coordinate their actions, they can collectively behave like a monopoly.
4. **Cournot model of noncooperative oligopoly:** In a Cournot model, in which firms choose their output levels without colluding, the market output and firms' profits lie between the competitive and monopoly levels.
5. **Stackelberg model of noncooperative behavior:** In a Stackelberg model, in which a *leader* firm chooses its output level before its identical-cost rivals, market output is greater than if all firms chose their output simultaneously, and the leader makes a higher profit than the other firms.
6. **Comparison of collusive, Cournot, Stackelberg, and competitive equilibria:** Total market output declines from the competitive level to the Stackelberg level to the Cournot level and reaches a minimum with monopoly or collusion.
7. **Monopolistic competition:** When firms can freely enter the market but, in equilibrium, face downward-sloping demand curves, firms charge prices above marginal cost but make no profit.

12.1 MARKET STRUCTURES

Markets differ according to the number of firms in the market, the ease with which firms may enter and leave the market, and the ability of firms in a market to differentiate their products from those of their rivals. Table 12.1 lists characteristics and properties of competition, monopoly, oligopoly, and monopolistic competition. For each of these market structures, we assume that the firms face many price-taking buyers.

Regardless of market structures, a firm maximizes its profit by setting quantity so that marginal revenue equals marginal cost (row 1 of Table 12.1). The four market structures differ in terms of the market power of firms (ability to set price above marginal cost), ease of entry of new firms, and strategic behavior on the part of firms (taking account of rivals' actions). Monopolies, oligopolies, and

Table 12.1 Properties of Monopoly, Oligopoly, Monopolistic Competition, and Competition

	Monopoly	Oligopoly	Monopolistic Competition	Competition
1. Profit-maximization condition	$MR = MC$	$MR = MC$	$MR = MC$	$p = MR = MC$
2. Ability to set price	Price setter	Price setter	Price setter	Price taker
3. Market power	$p > MC$	$p > MC$	$p > MC$	$p = MC$
4. Entry conditions	No entry	Limited entry	Free entry	Free entry
5. Number of firms	1	Few	Few or many	Many
6. Economic profit in the long run	≥0	≥0	0	0
7. Whether firm's strategy depends on individual rival firm's behavior	No (has no rivals)	Yes	Yes	No (cares about market price only)
8. Products	Single product	May be differentiated	May be differentiated	Undifferentiated
9. Example	Local natural gas utility	Automobile manufacturers	Plumbers in a small town	Wheat farmers

monopolistically competitive firms are price setters rather than price takers (row 2) because they face downward-sloping demand curves. As a consequence, market failures occur in each of these market structures because price is above marginal revenue and hence above marginal cost (row 3). In contrast, a competitive firm faces a horizontal demand curve, so its price equals its marginal cost.

A monopoly or an oligopoly does not fear entry (row 4) because of insurmountable barriers to entry such as government licenses or patents. These barriers to entry restrict the number of firms so that there is only one firm ("mono") in a monopoly and—usually—a few ("oligo") in an oligopoly (row 5). The key difference between oligopolistic and monopolistically competitive markets is that firms are free to enter only in a monopolistically competitive market.

In both competitive and monopolistically competitive markets, entry occurs until no new firm can profitably enter (so the marginal firm earns zero profit, row 6). Monopolistically competitive markets have fewer firms than do perfectly competitive markets. Because they have relatively few rivals and hence are large relative to the market, each monopolistically competitive firm faces a downward-sloping demand curve.

Oligopolistic and monopolistically competitive firms pay attention to rival firms' behavior, in contrast to monopolistic or competitive firms (row 7). A monopoly has no rivals. A competitive firm ignores the behavior of individual rivals in choosing its output because the market price tells the firm everything it needs to know about its competitors.

Oligopolistic and monopolistically competitive firms may produce differentiated products (row 8). For example, Camry and Taurus automobiles differ in size, weight, and various other dimensions. In contrast, competitive wheat farmers sell undifferentiated (homogeneous) products.

For simplicity in the rest of this chapter, we concentrate on oligopolistic and monopolistically competitive markets in which undifferentiated goods are sold. In Chapter 13, we examine how product differentiation affects markets.

12.2 GAME THEORY

Business is a good game—lots of competition and a minimum of rules. You keep score with money.

—Nolan Bushnell (founder of Atari, a pioneering electronic game company)

Unlike a monopoly or a competitive firm, an oligopolistic or monopolistically competitive firm considers how its actions affect its rivals and how rivals' actions will affect it. Each firm forms a **strategy**, which is a battle plan of the actions (such as setting a price or quantity) that it will take to compete with other firms. A fairly simple strategy is to produce 100 units of output regardless of what anyone else does. A more complex strategy is for a firm to produce a small quantity as long as its rival produces a small amount and a large quantity otherwise.

We can think of oligopolies as engaging in a **game**, which is any competition between players (such as firms) in which strategic behavior plays a major role. **Game theory** is a set of tools that economists, political scientists, military analysts, and others use to analyze decisionmaking by players (such as firms) who use strategies. These same analytic tools can be used to analyze oligopolistic games, poker, coin-matching games, tic-tac-toe, elections, and wars.

Although we call the conflict between oligopolists a game, firms do not view this competition as frivolous. These games are serious business. Each firm is interested in achieving the largest possible profit (or payoff) at the end of the game. Typically, one firm's gain comes at the expense of the other firm. Each firm's profit depends on the actions taken by all the firms. For example, if one oligopolistic firm increases its output, the price falls for all firms, affecting the profits of all firms.

When is an oligopolistic market in equilibrium? In describing competitive and monopolistic markets, we said that the market is in equilibrium if no firm has a desire to change its output level given what everyone else is doing. John Nash (1951), a Nobel Prize–winning economist and mathematician, defined an oligopolistic equilibrium similarly: No firm wants to change its strategy given what everyone else is doing. Formally, a set of strategies is a **Nash equilibrium** if, holding the strategies of all other players (firms) constant, no player (firm) can obtain a higher payoff (profit) by choosing a different strategy. In a Nash equilibrium, no firm wants to change its strategy because each firm is using its **best response**—the strategy that maximizes its profit, given its beliefs about its rivals' strategies.

A Single-Period, Two-Firm, Quantity-Setting Game

We illustrate game theory and determine the Nash equilibrium for a **duopoly**: an oligopoly with two ("duo") firms. We examine how American Airlines and United

Airlines actually compete for customers on flights between Chicago and Los Angeles.[1]

The total number of passengers flown by these two firms, Q, is the sum of the number of passengers flown on American Airlines, q_A, and those flown on United Airlines, q_U. These airlines have a great deal of latitude in setting the number of flights and the number of seats per flight. For simplicity in this section, however, we assume that the airlines can pick only a relatively large quantity, 64 units (one unit being a thousand passengers) per quarter, or a relatively small quantity, 48 units per quarter. (Later, we examine the more complex game in which these firms may choose any quantity.)

A *profit matrix* (or *payoff matrix*), such as in Table 12.2, shows the strategies the firms may choose and the resulting profits. If American chooses a large quantity, $q_A = 64$ units per quarter, and United chooses a small quantity, $q_U = 48$ units per quarter, the firms' profits are in the cell in the lower-left-hand corner of the matrix. In that cell, American's profit (upper-right number) is \$5.1 million per quarter, and United's profit (bottom-left number) is \$3.8 million per quarter.

Because the firms choose their strategies simultaneously, each firm selects a strategy that maximizes its profit given what it *believes* the other firm will do. Thus, the firms are playing a *noncooperative game of imperfect information*, in which each firm must choose an action before observing the simultaneous action by its rival.

How can a firm decide its best response to the other firm's strategy if it doesn't know what the other firm will do? The firm can start by rejecting any strategy that is strictly dominated by another strategy. Strategy 1 *strictly dominates* Strategy 2 if Strategy 1 produces a profit as high as or higher than does Strategy 2 *regardless of the action chosen by the rival firm.* If one strategy strictly dominates *all* other

Table 12.2 Profit Matrix for a Quantity-Setting Game

		American Airlines	
		$q_A = 64$	$q_A = 48$
United Airlines	$q_U = 64$	American: \$4.1; United: \$4.1	American: \$3.8; United: \$5.1
	$q_U = 48$	American: \$5.1; United: \$3.8	American: \$4.6; United: \$4.6

Note: Quantities are in thousands of passengers per quarter; profits are in millions of dollars per quarter.

[1]This example is based on Brander and Zhang (1990). They reported data for economy and discount passengers taking direct flights between the two cities in the third quarter of 1985. Brander and Zhang ignored the other airlines that flew between these two cities because they had relatively few passengers. In calculating the profits reported here, we assume that Brander and Zhang's estimate of the firms' constant marginal cost is the same as the firms' relevant long-run average cost.

strategies, regardless of the actions chosen by rival firms, the firm should choose this **dominant strategy**. Where a firm has a dominant strategy, its belief about its rival's behavior is irrelevant.

Although firms do not always have dominant strategies, they do have them in this game. To determine American's dominant strategy, American's managers can use the following reasoning:

- *If United chooses the high-output strategy* (q_U = 64), *American's high-output strategy maximizes its profit*: Given United's strategy, American's profit is $4.1 million (top-right number in the upper-left cell) with its high-output strategy (q_A = 64) and only $3.8 million (top-right number in the upper-right cell) with its low-output strategy (q_A = 48). Thus, American is better off using a high-output strategy if United chooses its high-output strategy.
- *If United chooses the low-output strategy* (q_U = 48), *American's high-output strategy maximizes its profit*: Given United's strategy, American's profit is $5.1 million with its high-output strategy and only $4.6 million with its low-output strategy.
- *Thus, the high-output strategy is American's dominant strategy*: Whichever strategy United uses, American's profit is higher if it uses its high-output strategy.

By the same type of reasoning, United's high-output strategy is also a dominant strategy.

Because the high-output strategy is a dominant strategy for both firms, the pair of high-output strategies, $q_A = q_U = 64$, is a Nash equilibrium. We can use the profit matrix to confirm that this pair of strategies is a Nash equilibrium by showing that neither firm wants to change its strategy if it is certain that the other firm will use its high-output strategy. If American knew that United would use its high-output strategy, it still would not switch to its low-output strategy because its profit would fall from $4.1 million to $3.8 million. Similarly, United wouldn't switch if it knew American would use its high-output strategy. Because neither firm wants to change its strategy given that the other firm is playing its Nash equilibrium strategy, this pair of strategies ($q_A = q_U = 64$) is a Nash equilibrium.

Why Firms Do Not Cooperate in a Single-Period Game

In this Nash equilibrium, each firm earns $4.1 million, which is less than the $4.6 million it would make if firms restricted their outputs to $q_A = q_U = 48$. Thus, *the sum of the firms' profits is not maximized in this simultaneous-choice, one-period game.*

Many people are surprised the first time they hear this result. Why don't the firms cooperate and use the individually and jointly more profitable low-output strategies, by which each earns a profit of $4.6 million, instead of the $4.1 million in the Nash equilibrium? They don't cooperate due to a lack of trust: Each firm can profitably use the low-out strategy *only if it trusts the other firm.*

Suppose the two firms meet in advance and agree to restrict their outputs to the lower quantity. If the firms are going to engage in this game only once, each has an incentive to cheat on their agreement. If American believes that United will stick to the agreement and produce q_U = 48, American can increase its profit from $4.6

million to \$5.1 million by cheating on the agreement and producing $q_A = 64$. Moreover, if American thinks that United will also cheat on the agreement by producing $q_U = 64$, American wants to produce the high output (so that it will earn \$4.1 million rather than \$3.8 million). By this reasoning, each firm has a substantial profit incentive to cheat on the agreement. In this type of game—called a **prisoners' dilemma** game—all players have dominant strategies that lead to a profit (or other payoff) that is inferior to what they could achieve if they cooperated and played alternative strategies.[2]

Collusion in Repeated Games

We've just seen that in a single-period prisoners' dilemma game, the two firms produce more than they would if they colluded. However, cartels are frequently observed. What's wrong with this theory, which shows that cartels won't occur? One explanation is that firms frequently engage in multiperiod games, in which collusion is more likely than it is in a single-period game.

In a single-period game, one firm cannot punish the other firm for cheating on a cartel agreement. But if the firms meet period after period, a wayward firm can be punished by the other.

Suppose that the single-period prisoners' dilemma game is repeated period after period. In the single-period game, each firm takes its rival's strategy as given and assumes that it cannot affect its rival's strategy. If the same game is played repeatedly, however, firms engage in a **supergame** in which players may devise strategies for this period that depend on rivals' actions in previous periods. For example, a firm may set a low-output level this period only if its rival set a low-output level in the previous period.

In a repeated game, a firm can influence its rival's behavior by *signaling* and *threatening to punish*. One airline could use a low-quantity strategy for a couple of periods to signal to the other firm its desire that the two firms cooperate and produce that low quantity in the future. If the other firm does not respond by lowering its output in future periods, the first firm suffers lower profits for only a couple of periods. However, if the other firm responds to this signal and lowers its quantity, both firms can profitably produce at the low quantity thereafter.

In addition to or instead of signaling, a firm can punish a rival for not restricting output. We can illustrate how firms punish rivals to ensure collusion by using the profit matrix in Table 12.2. Suppose that American announces or somehow indicates to United that it will use the following two-part strategy:

---

[2]The prisoners' dilemma game occurs in virtually every cops-and-robbers show you've ever seen. The cops arrest Larry and Duncan and put them in separate rooms so that they cannot communicate with each other. An assistant district attorney tells Larry, "We have enough evidence to convict you both of a relatively minor crime for which you'll serve a year in prison. If you'll squeal on your partner and he stays silent, we can convict him of a major crime, for which he'll serve five years and you'll go free. If you both confess, you'll each get two years." Meanwhile another assistant district attorney is making this same offer to Duncan. By the same reasoning as in the airlines example, both Larry and Duncan confess, even though they are better off if they both keep quiet.

- American produces the smaller quantity each period as long as United does the same.
- If United produces the larger quantity in period t, then American will produce the larger quantity in period $t + 1$ and all subsequent periods.

If United believes that American will follow this strategy, United knows that it will make \$4.6 million each period if it produces the lower quantity. Although United can make a higher profit, \$5.1 million, in period t by producing the larger quantity, by doing so it lowers its potential profit to \$4.1 million in each following period. Thus, United's best policy is to produce the lower quantity in each period unless it cares greatly about current profit and little about future profits. If United values future profits nearly as much as current ones, the one-period gain from deviating from the collusive output level does not compensate for the losses from reduced profits in future periods, which is the punishment American will impose. United may take this threat by American seriously because American's best response is to produce the larger quantity if it believes it can't trust United to produce the smaller quantity.[3] Thus, if firms play the same game *indefinitely*, they should find it easier to collude.

Playing the same game many times, however, doesn't necessarily help the firms collude. Suppose, for example, that the firms know that they are going to play the game for T periods. In the last period, they know that they're not going to play again, so they know they can cheat—produce a lot of output—without fear of punishment. As a result, the last period is like a single-period game, and all firms cheat. That makes the $T - 1$ period the last interesting period. By the same reasoning, they'll cheat in $T - 1$. Thus, continuing this type of argument, we conclude that maintaining a cartel will be difficult if the game has a known stopping point. If the players know that the game will end but aren't sure when, this cheating is less likely to occur. Collusion is therefore more likely in a game that will continue forever or that will end at an uncertain time.

APPLICATION

Oligopoly Competition among Governments

To increase local employment and for other reasons, state governments offer subsidies and tax breaks to attract new businesses.[4] Utah gave Micron Technology \$200 million, Illinois showered Sears, Roebuck with \$240 million, and New Mexico, using a \$1 billion industrial revenue bond issue, won a

---

[3]American does not have to punish United forever to induce it to cooperate. All it has to do is punish it for a long enough period that it does not pay for United to deviate from the low-quantity strategy in any period.

[4]Clark, Don, "New Mexico Gets Huge Intel Plant," *San Francisco Chronicle*, April 1, 1993:C1; Holmes (1995); and Myerson, Allen R., "O Governor, Won't You Buy Me a Mercedes Plant?" *New York Times*, September 1, 1996:Sec. 3:1, 10.

bidding war with half a dozen other states for an Intel Corporation expansion of its semiconductor plant.

These state governments may be acting in the best interests of their citizens, but Americans would collectively benefit if state governments were prevented from competing in this way. If only one state government offers a tax break, it can attract a major business at relatively low cost: Any tax break dominates the zero tax break offered elsewhere. Once many governments start bidding against each other for businesses, however, the size of the tax breaks that are needed to attract firms rises. States that were not offering tax breaks originally now have to offer them to prevent a mass exodus of firms.

In 1993, Alabama gave Mercedes about $300 million in tax breaks and other subsidies, which amounted to about $200,000 for each job created. This price per job is 18 times higher than that for the Nissan plant in Tennessee in 1980, 7 times that for the General Motors Saturn plant in Tennessee in 1985, and 3 times that for the BMW plant in South Carolina in 1992.

In the terminology of game theory, the players or states compete in a game in which the strategies are handouts to firms. In the noncooperative Nash equilibrium, all states offer handouts. Collectively, the state governments would benefit by agreeing not to offer handouts. Unfortunately, so far, the state governments have not agreed to collude. ■

12.3 COOPERATIVE OLIGOPOLY MODELS

The last section argues that firms have an incentive to form a cartel in which each firm reduces its output so that firms' individual and collective profits rise. As Adam Smith observed over two centuries ago, "People of the same trade seldom meet together, even for merriment and diversion, but the conversation ends in a conspiracy against the public, or some contrivance to raise prices." Luckily for consumers, cartels often fail because a government forbids them and because each firm in a cartel has an incentive to cheat on the cartel agreement by producing extra output.

Laws Against Cartels

In the late nineteenth century, cartels (or, as they were called then, *trusts*) were legal and common in the United States. Oil, railroad, sugar, and tobacco trusts raised prices substantially above the noncartel levels.

In response to the trusts' high prices, the U.S. Congress passed the Sherman Act in 1890 and the Federal Trade Commission Act of 1914, which prohibit firms from *explicitly* agreeing to take actions that reduce competition. In particular, cartels that are formed for the purpose of jointly setting price are strictly prohibited. These laws reduce the probability that cartels form by imposing penalties on firms caught colluding. Virtually all industrialized nations have *antitrust laws*—or, as they are called in other countries, *competition policies*—that limit or forbid some or all cartels.

Some cartels persist despite these laws for three reasons. First, international cartels and cartels within certain countries operate legally. Second, some illegal cartels operate believing that they can avoid detection or that the punishment will be small. Third, some firms are able to coordinate their activity without explicitly colluding and thereby running afoul of competition laws.

Some international cartels organized by countries rather than firms are legal. The Organization of Petroleum Exporting Countries (OPEC) is an international cartel that was formed in 1960 by five major oil-exporting countries: Iran, Iraq, Kuwait, Saudi Arabia, and Venezuela. In 1971, OPEC members agreed to take an active role in setting oil prices.

Many illegal cartels flout the competition laws in major industrial countries. These firms apparently believe that they are unlikely to get caught or that the punishments they face are so low that it pays to collude anyway. For example, General Electric (GE) and Westinghouse were charged and punished repeatedly in the first 50 years after the Sherman Act went into effect. The U.S. Department of Justice brought 13 antitrust cases and the Federal Trade Commission filed 3 more against GE and Westinghouse between 1911 and 1952. The government "won" all of the cases by obtaining either a conviction, a *nolo contendere* ("no contest") plea (without admitting guilt, the firms agreed to be punished), or a consent decree by which the firms agreed to stop behaving in certain ways (Walton and Cleveland 1964).

Small fines fail to discourage cartel behavior. In a recent cartel case involving the \$9 billion American carpet industry, a firm with \$150 million annual sales agreed with the U.S. Justice Department to plead guilty and pay a fine of \$150,000.[5] It is hard to imagine that a fine of one-tenth of 1% of annual sales significantly deters cartel behavior.

American antitrust laws use evidence of conspiracy (such as explicit agreements) rather than the economic effect of monopoly to determine guilt. Charging monopoly-level prices is not necessarily illegal—only the "bad behavior" of explicitly agreeing to raise prices is illegal. As a result, some groups of firms charge monopoly-level prices without violating the competition laws. These firms may *tacitly collude* without meeting by signaling to each other through their actions (as the next application illustrates). Although the actions of this group of firms may not be illegal, they behave in much the same way as cartels.

APPLICATION

Tacit Collusion in Long-Distance Service

In 1984, with the breakup of AT&T, the former monopoly in both local and long-distance services, many people expected MCI, Sprint, and other long-distance companies to compete effectively with AT&T in long-distance service, driving prices to competitive levels. Indeed, for the rest of the 1980s, these companies under-

[5]Drummond, Bob, "Carpet Maker Pleads Guilty," *San Francisco Chronicle*, June 8, 1995:B2.

cut AT&T's prices and grabbed market share. From 1984 to 1989, AT&T's share of revenue from long-distance calls fell from 90% to 70% while the shares of MCI rose from 5% to 13% and those of Sprint increased from 3% to 9%.

In the early 1990s, however, MCI and Sprint stopped undercutting AT&T. From 1990 to 1993, these firms' market shares were relatively stable, with AT&T losing only 3 percentage points to MCI and none to Sprint. By the end of 1993, AT&T had 65% of the market, and MCI and Sprint combined had 29%.

MacAvoy (1995) concludes that the long-distance telephone services tacitly colluded. He argues that, if the three companies were acting independently, no firm would increase its price unilaterally unless its costs had increased, for fear of losing many customers. The marginal costs of the firms fell steadily from 1985 through 1993. Nonetheless, from 1991 to 1993, AT&T raised its price six times, and each time, MCI and Sprint quickly matched AT&T's price. As a result, each firm's Lerner Index (Chapter 11), $(p - MC)/p$, rose. The Lerner Indexes for the various long-distance services exceeded 60%, which is far from competitive behavior. ■

Why Cartels Form

We now consider why cartels form, why cartel members have an incentive to deviate from the cartel agreement, and why some cartels succeed where others fail. A cartel forms if members of the cartel believe that they can raise their profits by coordinating their actions. Although cartels usually involve oligopolies, cartels may form in a market that would otherwise be competitive.

If a competitive firm is maximizing its profit, why should joining a cartel increase its profit? The answer involves a subtle argument. When a competitive firm chooses its profit-maximizing output level, it considers how varying its output affects its own profit only. The firm ignores the effect that changing its output level has on other firms' profits. A cartel, on the other hand, takes into account how changes in any one firm's output affect the profits of all members of the cartel.

If a competitive firm lowers its output, it raises the market price very slightly—so slightly that the firm ignores the effect not only on other firms's profits but on its own. If all the identical competitive firms in an industry lower their output by this same amount, however, the market price will change noticeably. Recognizing this effect of collective action, a cartel chooses to produce a smaller market output than is produced by a competitive market.

Figure 12.1 illustrates this difference between a competitive market and a cartel. There are n firms in this market, and no further entry is possible. Panel a shows the marginal and average cost curves of a typical firm. If all firms are price takers, the market supply curve, S, is the horizontal sum of the individual marginal cost curves above minimum average cost, as shown in panel b. At the competitive price, p_c, each price-taking firm produces q_c units of output (where MC intersects the line at p_c in panel a). The market output is $Q_c = nq_c$ (where S intersects the market demand curve in panel b).

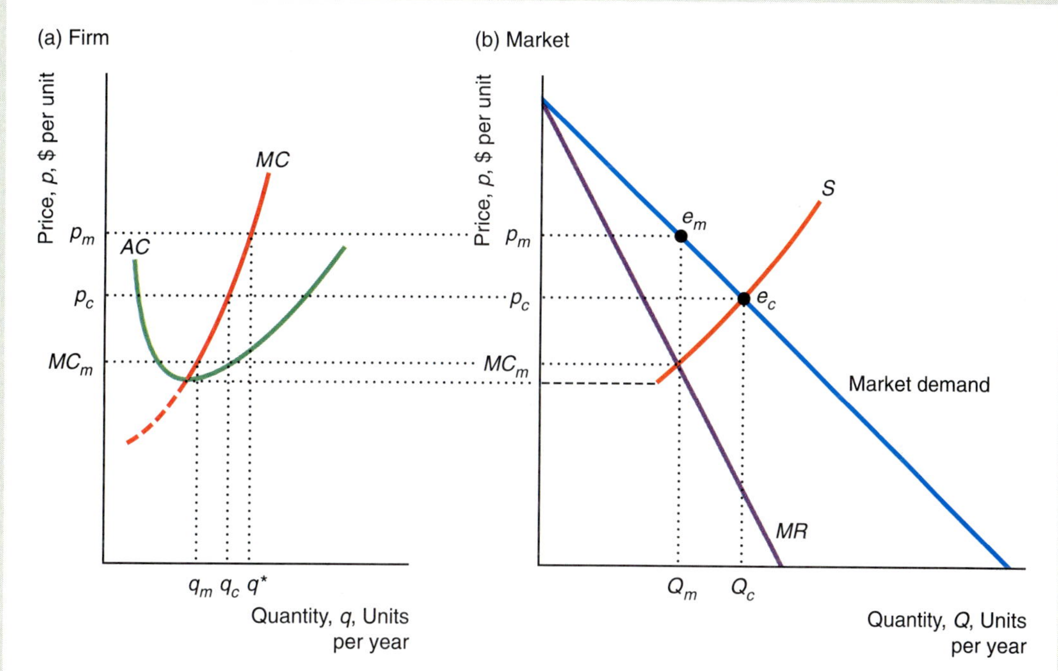

Figure 12.1 Competition Versus Cartel. (a) The marginal cost and average cost of one of the n firms in the market are shown. A competitive firm produces q_c units of output, whereas a cartel member produces $q_m < q_c$. At the cartel price, p_m, however, each cartel member has an incentive to increase its output from q_m to q^* (where p_m equals its marginal cost). (b) The competitive equilibrium, e_c, has more output and a lower price than does the cartel equilibrium, e_m.

Now suppose that the firms form a cartel. Should they reduce their output? At the competitive output, the cartel's marginal cost (which is the competitive industry supply curve, S in panel b) is greater than its marginal revenue, so the cartel's profit rises if it reduces output. The cartel's collective profit rises until output is reduced by enough that its marginal revenue equals its marginal cost at Q_m, the monopoly output. If the profit of the cartel increases, the profit of each of the n members of the cartel also increases. To achieve the cartel output level, each firm must reduce its output to $q_m = Q_m/n$, as panel a shows.

Why must the firms form a cartel to achieve these higher profits? A competitive firm produces q_c, where its marginal cost equals the market price. If only one firm reduces its output, it loses profit because it sells fewer units at essentially the same price. By getting all the firms to lower their output together, the cartel raises the market price and hence individual firms' profits. The less elastic is the market demand facing the potential cartel, all else the same, the higher is the price the cartel sets (Chapter 11) and the greater is the benefit from cartelizing. If the penalty for forming an illegal cartel is relatively low, some unscrupulous businesspeople may succumb to the lure of extra profits and join.

Why Cartels Fail

A thing worth having is a thing worth cheating for. —W. C. Fields

Cartels fail if noncartel members can supply consumers with large quantities of goods. For example, copper producers formed an international cartel that controlled only about a third of the noncommunist world's copper production and faced additional competition from firms that recycle copper from scrap materials. Because of this competition from noncartel members, the cartel was not successful in raising and keeping copper prices high.

In addition, *each member of a cartel has an incentive to cheat on the cartel agreement.* The owner of a firm may reason, "I joined the cartel to encourage others to reduce their output and increase profits for everyone. I can make more, however, if I cheat on the cartel agreement by producing extra output. I can get away with cheating if the other firms can't tell who's producing the extra output because I'm just one of many firms and because I'll hardly affect the market price." By this reasoning, it is in each firm's best interest for all *other* firms to honor the cartel agreement—thus driving up the market price—while it ignores the agreement and makes extra, profitable sales at the high price.

Figure 12.1 illustrates why firms want to cheat. At the cartel output, q_m in panel a, each cartel member's marginal cost is MC_m. The marginal revenue of a firm that violates the agreement is p_m because it is acting like a price taker with respect to the market price. Because the firm's marginal revenue (price) is above its marginal cost, the firm wants to increase its output. If the firm decides to violate the cartel agreement, it maximizes its profit by increasing its output to q^*, where its marginal cost equals p_m.

As more and more firms leave the cartel, the cartel price falls. The colluding firms act like a dominant firm facing a competitive fringe (Chapter 11). Eventually, if enough firms quit, the cartel collapses.

Maintaining Cartels

To keep firms from violating the cartel agreement, the cartel must be able to detect cheating and punish violators. Further, the members of the cartel must keep their illegal behavior hidden from customers and government agencies.

Detection. Cartels use many techniques to detect cheating. Some cartels, for example, give members the right to inspect each other's books. Similarly, governments often help cartels by reporting bids on government contracts, so other firms learn if a cartel member bids below the agreed-upon cartel price.

Cartels may divide the market by region or by customers, so a firm that tries to steal another firm's customer is more likely to be detected. The two-country mercury cartel (1928–1972) allocated America to Spain and Europe to Italy.

Other cartels use industry organizations to detect cheating. These organizations collect data on market share by firm and circulate their results. If a firm cheats on a cartel, its share would rise and other firms would know that it cheated.

You may have seen "low price" ads in which local retail stores guarantee to meet or beat the prices of any competitors. You may have thought that such a guarantee assured you of a low price. However, it may be a way for the firm to induce its customers to report cheating on a cartel agreement by other firms (Salop 1986).

Enforcement. Many methods are used to enforce cartel agreements. For example, GE and Westinghouse, the two major sellers of large steam-turbine generators, included "most-favored-nation clauses" in their contracts. These contracts stated that the seller would not offer a lower price to any other current or future buyer without offering the same price decrease to that buyer. This type of rebate clause creates a penalty for cheating on the cartel: If either company cheats by cutting prices, it has to lower prices to all previous buyers as well. Another means of enforcing a cartel agreement is through threats of violence, as the next application illustrates.

APPLICATION

Bad Bakers

For years, New York City law enforcement officials received complaints that a group of unscrupulous bakers were enforcing a cartel agreement by using threats of violence for firms that did not cooperate.[6] The cartel was said to control the distribution of fresh Italian bread to small grocery stores, in the process raising prices and eliminating competition.

Being well bred, the police did not loaf around. Finding bakers and store owners reluctant to cooperate with their investigation, the police concluded that the only way to uncover the truth was to go undercover and open a bakery themselves. For five months in 1993, six white-apron-clad New York City policemen pretended to bake bread and sold bread at a store they called Louis Basile's at 327 West Eleventh Street in Greenwich Village.

The six officers took turns getting up at 3:00 A.M. to drive to New Jersey to buy the real stuff. These loaves were wrapped in the customized white paper sleeves that signal that the loaves were authentic, fresh Italian bread. The pseudo-bakers tried to sell the bread to neighborhood grocery stores in Manhattan and Brooklyn. Though officials claim that the bread was cheaper and tasted better than that of rivals, stores routinely refused to buy from them.

Then the undercover cops heard from the Association of Independent Bakers and Distributors of Italian Bread (AIBDIB). Two members of the association told one of the detective-bakers that violence could come to Basile's and its employees if they did not play by association rules.

In response, the police arrested four AIBDIB officials and charged them with attempting to corner the Italian bread market and raise prices (maximum

[6]Faison, Seth, "Detectives Posing as Bakers Charge 4 with Price-Fixing," *New York Times*, July 14, 1994:A14; "The Bread Beat," *New Yorker*, August 8, 1994:24–25.

penalty: four years in prison and fines of $100,000 if convicted). Two were also charged with coercion, and one with tax evasion.

The cartel had divided customers among sellers to help detect cheating. According to the Manhattan district attorney, a store could buy from only a single baker under the association's rules. If a store wanted to switch to another baker, the association had to be consulted, and the former baker was given a cash payment.

The association members included 50 bakeries and 1,000 small grocery stores and delicatessens. Large supermarkets were not involved, but the conspiracy allegedly covered virtually all of Staten Island and most neighborhoods in Brooklyn and was expanding into Manhattan, Queens, and Westchester and Nassau counties. According to the district attorney, "We spent over $100,000 setting up this bakery, but over a period of time we'll save consumers a lot more than that." ■

Government Support. Sometimes governments help to create and enforce cartels. For example, U.S., European, and other governments signed an agreement in 1944 to establish a cartel that fixes prices for international airline flights and prevents competition.

Professional baseball teams have been exempted from some U.S. antitrust laws since 1922.[7] As a result, they can use the courts to help enforce certain aspects of their cartel agreement. Major league clubs are able to avoid competing for young athletes by means of a draft and contracts, limit geographic competition between teams, jointly negotiate for television and other rights, and in many other ways act collectively.

APPLICATION

A Government-Created Cartel

In recent years, a number of governments have created foreign cartels through their trade policies. In 1981, the Reagan administration negotiated voluntary export restraint (VER) agreements whereby Japanese automobile manufacturers would reduce their exports to the United States. The Japanese manufacturers also signed VER agreements with West Germany and Belgium at about the same time.

Why would the Japanese manufacturers "voluntarily" reduce their exports? One explanation is that they were under pressure from both the U.S. and

---

[7]Bud Selig, Milwaukee Brewers president and baseball's acting commissioner, claims that "[the baseball] antitrust exemption is protection for the fans."

Japanese governments and feared that quotas would be applied. A more likely explanation is that agreeing to the VERs was in their best interests.

Under these agreements, the Japanese manufacturers were to reduce their exports to the United States, thereby forcing American consumers to pay more for domestic and Japanese cars. The VER agreements achieved this goal: Domestic and foreign manufacturers benefitted at the expense of American consumers.

If the Japanese car manufacturers were operating independently before 1981, they could increase their collective profit by reducing the number of cars each exported to the United States. They would face the usual problems in trying to agree between themselves to restrict exports. The VERs, then, provided a mechanism for the firms to reduce exports collectively and profitably. By this argument, the Japanese manufacturers wanted firm-specific quotas (if not set too low), which would ensure that no manufacturer cheated on the agreement. Indeed, when the United States allowed the VER agreements to lapse in 1985, the Japanese government—presumably reflecting the sentiments of the car manufacturers—said that it wanted to continue to restrict exports.

Ries (1993) reported that the stock market value of firms in the Japanese automobile industry increased during the VER period by \$6.6 billion, of which \$2.2 billion was due to the American VER announcement. Scott (1994) estimated that the VERs raised the price of American cars by 5.4% between 1981 and 1983. Using a general-equilibrium trade model, Tarr (1989) concluded that American consumers lost \$6.9 billion (in 1984 dollars) because of these export restrictions.

The U.S. government's use of quantity restrictions is bizarre. Foreign and domestic auto manufacturers capture the extra "cartel" profits from the higher prices caused by the VER. Had the U.S. government used tariffs instead, the domestic price would have risen, helping domestic firms, but the extra profits from the increase in price would have gone to the U.S. government through tariff revenues instead of to foreign manufacturers (Chapter 9). ■

Entry and Cartel Success

Barriers to entry that limit the number of firms help the cartel to detect and punish cheating. The fewer the firms in a market, the more likely it is other firms will know if a given firm cheats and the easier it is to impose costs on that firm. Cartels with a large number of firms are relatively rare, except those involving professional associations. Hay and Kelley (1974) examined Department of Justice price-fixing cases from 1963 to 1972 and found that only 6.5% involved 50 or more conspirators, the average number of firms was 7.25, and nearly half the cases (48%) involved 6 or fewer firms.

When new firms enter their market, cartels frequently fail. For example, when only Italy and Spain sold mercury, they were able to establish and maintain a stable cartel. When a larger group of countries joined them, their attempts to cartelize the world mercury market repeatedly failed (MacKie-Mason and Pindyck 1986).

APPLICATION

Bail Bonds

The state of Connecticut sets a maximum fee that bail-bond businesses can charge for posting a given size bond (Ayres and Waldfogel, 1994). The bail-bond fee is set at virtually the maximum amount allowed by law in cities with only one active firm (Plainville, 99% of the maximum; Stamford, 99%; and Wallingford, 99%). The price is as high in cities with a duopoly (Ansonia, 99.6%; Meriden, 98%; and New London, 98%). In cities with three or more firms, however, the price falls well below the maximum permitted price, possibly because the difficulty of maintaining a cartel or tacit collusion rises with the number of firms. The fees are only 54% of the maximum in Norwalk with 3 firms, 64% in New Haven with 8 firms, and 78% in Bridgeport with 10 firms. ■

Mergers

If antitrust or competition laws prevent firms from colluding, they may try to merge instead. Recognizing this potential problem, U.S. laws restrict the ability of firms to merge if the effect would be anticompetitive. Whether the Department of Justice or the Federal Trade Commission (FTC) challenges a proposed merger turns on a large number of issues. One reason why the government limits mergers is that all the firms in a market could combine and form a monopoly.

On the other hand, it would not be a good idea to ban all mergers, because some mergers result in more efficient production. Formerly separate firms may become more efficient because of greater scale, sharing trade secrets, or closing duplicative retail outlets. For example, when Chase and Chemical banks merged in 1995, they closed or combined seven branches in Manhattan that were located within two blocks of other branches.[8]

APPLICATION

Airline Mergers

Kim and Singal (1993) studied price changes from airline mergers during the period 1985–1988 when the government did not contest most airline mergers. Prices increased on routes served by firms that merged relative to those on routes without mergers. Thus, the authors concluded that the efficiency gains from the mergers were more than offset by the exercise of increased market power in this market. ■

---

[8]Van Gelder, Lawrence, "After Merger, Chase to Shut 7 New York City Branches," *New York Times*, September 22, 1995:C17.

12.4 COURNOT MODEL OF NONCOOPERATIVE OLIGOPOLY

We just used our monopoly and dominant-firm models to analyze markets where oligopoly firms collude. We need new models, however, to explain how oligopolies behave if they act independently.

Although there is only one model of competition and one model of monopoly, there are many models of noncooperative oligopoly behavior. Because strategies matter for oligopolies, many market outcomes are possible. Here, we examine two oligopoly models in which firms choose quantities: the Cournot and Stackelberg models.

Which model is appropriate to use as a guide to understanding a market depends on the institutional features of that market. If firms set output simultaneously and let the market determine the price, a Cournot model works well. If one firm can set output before other firms, a Stackelberg model is appropriate. Similarly, if oligopolies set price instead of quantity, a price-setting oligopoly model (Chapter 13) is relevant. Where the institutional features of a market are not well understood, an economist may try each model to see which best predicts actual behavior in that market.

Augustin Cournot introduced the first formal model of oligopoly in 1838. Cournot asked how oligopoly firms behave if they choose how much to produce at the same time. As in our earlier prisoners' dilemma game, the firms are playing a noncooperative game of imperfect information; each firm must choose its output level before knowing what the other firm will choose. Now, however, the firms may choose any output level they want.

To simplify our analysis of the Cournot oligopoly model, we examine a market in which

- There are two firms, and no other firms can enter,
- The firms sell identical (undifferentiated, homogeneous) products, and
- The firms compete in a market that lasts for only one period, and the product or service that they sell cannot be stored and sold later.

How much one firm produces directly affects the profit of the other firms, because market price depends on total output. Thus, in choosing its strategy to maximize its profit, each firm takes into account its beliefs about the output other firms will sell.

A Cournot Model of an Airline Market

We again examine the duopoly market in which United Airlines and American Airlines fly passengers between Chicago and Los Angeles. We assume that no other companies can enter, perhaps because they cannot obtain landing rights at both airports.[9]

[9]With the end of deregulation, existing firms were given the right to buy, sell, or rent landing slots. By controlling landing slots, existing firms can make entry difficult. At least in Chicago, these slots are scarce. In 1992, a landing slot at Chicago's O'Hare Airport rented for $66,000 per month ("United Wins TWA Lease," *New York Times*, March 20, 1992).

How many passengers does each airline choose to carry? To answer this question, we determine the Nash equilibrium for this model. This Nash equilibrium, in which firms choose quantities, is also called a **Cournot equilibrium**: a set of quantities sold by firms such that, holding the quantities of all other firms constant, no firm can obtain a higher profit by choosing a different quantity.

To determine the Cournot equilibrium, we need to establish how each firm chooses its strategy: the quantity it produces. We start by using the total demand curve for the Chicago–Los Angeles route and a firm's belief about how much its rival will sell to determine the residual demand curve this firm faces. Next, we examine how a firm uses its residual demand curve to determine its best response: the output level that maximizes its profit, given its belief about how much its rival will produce. Finally, we apply this information about both firms' best responses to determine the Cournot equilibrium.

Graphic Approach. The strategy that each firm uses depends on the demand curve it faces and its marginal cost. American Airline's profit-maximizing output depends on how many passengers it believes United will fly. Figure 12.2 illustrates two possibilities.

If American were a monopoly, it wouldn't have to worry about United's strategy. American's demand would be the market demand curve, *D* in panel a. To maximize

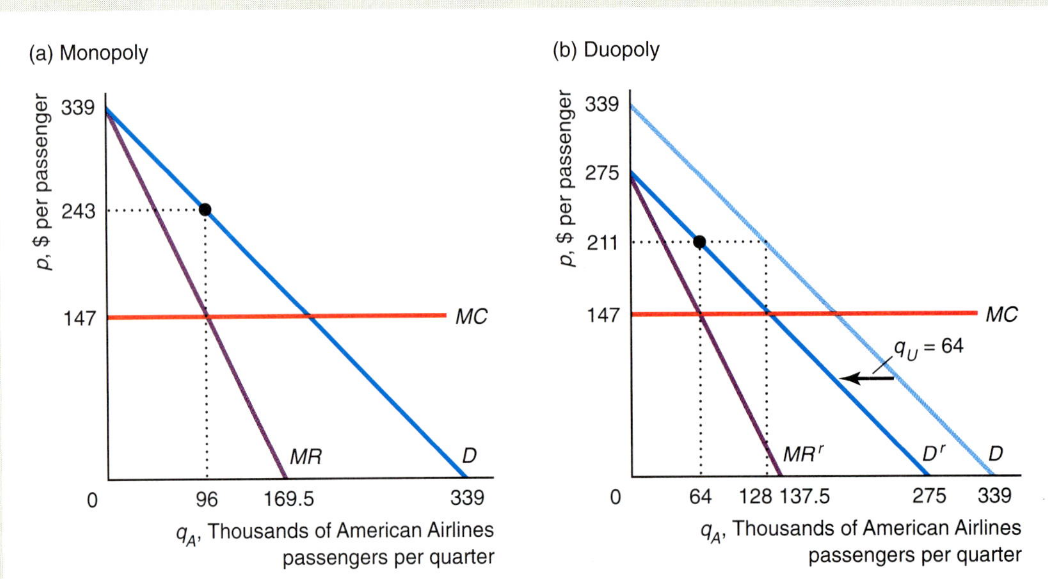

Figure 12.2 American Airline's Profit-Maximizing Output. (a) If American is a monopoly, it picks its profit-maximizing output, $q_A = 96$ units (thousand passengers) per quarter, so that its marginal revenue, *MR*, equals its marginal cost, *MC*. (b) If American believes that United Airlines will fly $q_U = 64$ units per quarter, its residual demand curve, D^r, is the market demand curve, *D*, minus q_U. American maximizes its profit at $q_A = 64$, where its marginal revenue, MR^r, equals *MC*.

its profit, American would set its output so that its marginal revenue curve, *MR*, intersected its marginal cost curve, *MC*, which is constant at \$147 per passenger (on a one-way flight). Panel a shows that the monopoly output is 96 units (thousand passengers) per quarter and the monopoly price is \$243 per passenger (one way).

Because American competes with United, American must take account of United's behavior when choosing its profit-maximizing output. American's demand is not the entire market demand. If United flies q_U passengers, then American transports only the residual demand: the total market demand, Q, minus the q_U passengers: $q_A = Q - q_U$.

Suppose that American believes that United will fly $q_U = 64$. Panel b shows that American's residual demand curve, D^r, is the market demand curve, D, moved to the left by $q_U = 64$. For example, if the price is \$211, the total number of passengers who want to fly is $Q = 128$. If United transports $q_U = 64$, American flies $Q - q_U = 128 - 64 = 64 = q_A$.

What is American's best-response, profit-maximizing output if its managers believe that United will fly q_U passengers? American can think of itself as having a monopoly with respect to the people who don't fly on United, which its residual demand curve, D^r, shows. To maximize its profit, American sets its output so that its marginal revenue corresponding to this residual demand, MR^r, equals its marginal cost. Panel b shows that if $q_U = 64$, American's best response is $q_A = 64$.

By shifting its residual demand curve appropriately, American can calculate its best response to any given q_U using this type of analysis. Figure 12.3 plots American Airline's best-response curve, which shows how many tickets American sells for each possible q_U.[10] As this curve shows, American will sell the monopoly number of tickets, 96, if American thinks United will fly no passengers, $q_U = 0$. The negative slope of the best-response curve shows that American sells fewer tickets, the more people American thinks that United will fly. American sells $q_A = 64$ if it thinks q_U will be 64. American shuts down, $q_A = 0$, if it thinks q_U will be 192 or more, because operating wouldn't be profitable.

Similarly, United's best-response curve shows how many tickets United sells if it thinks American will sell q_A. For example, United sells $q_U = 0$ if it thinks American will sell $q_A = 192$, $q_U = 48$ if $q_A = 96$, $q_U = 64$ if $q_A = 64$, and $q_U = 96$ if $q_A = 0$.

A firm wants to change its behavior if it is selling a quantity that is not on its best-response curve. In a Cournot equilibrium, neither firm wants to change its behavior. Thus, in a Cournot equilibrium, each firm is on its best-response curve: Each firm is maximizing its profit, given its correct belief about its rival's output.

These firms' best-response curves intersect at $q_A = q_U = 64$. If American expects United to sell $q_U = 64$, American wants to sell $q_A = 64$. Because this point is on its best-response curve, American doesn't want to change its output from 64. Similarly, if United expects American to sell $q_A = 64$, United doesn't want to change q_U from 64. Thus, this pair of outputs is a Cournot (Nash) equilibrium: Given its correct belief about its rival's output, each firm is maximizing its profit, and neither firm wants to change its output.

---

[10]Jargon alert: Some economists refer to the *best-response curve* as the *reaction curve*.

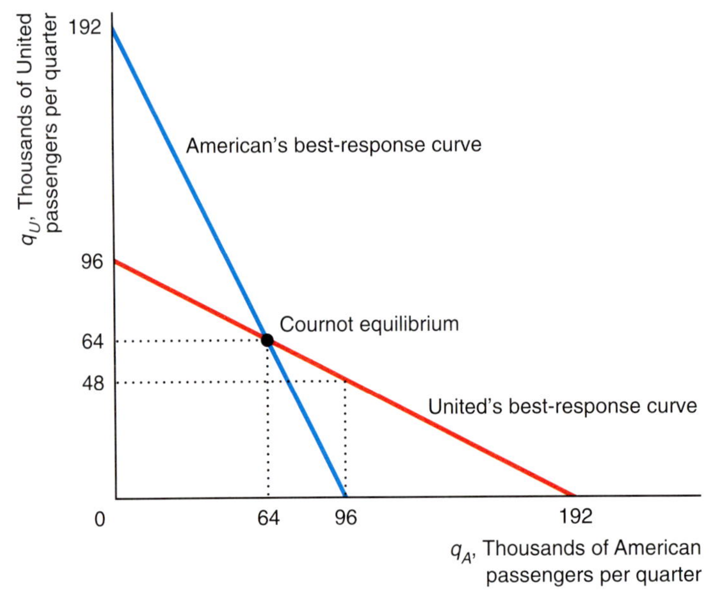

Figure 12.3 American and United's Best-Response Curves. The best-response curves show the output each firm picks to maximize its profit, given its belief about its rival's output. The Cournot equilibrium occurs at the intersection of the best-response curves.

Any pair of outputs other than the pair at an intersection of the best-response functions is *not* a Cournot equilibrium. If either firm is not on its best-response curve, it changes its output to increase its profit. For example, the output pair $q_A = 96$ and $q_U = 0$ is not a Cournot equilibrium. American is perfectly happy producing the monopoly output if United doesn't operate at all: American is on its best-response curve. United, however, would not be happy with this outcome because it is not on United's best-response curve. As its best-response curve shows, if it knows that American will sell $q_A = 96$, United wants to sell $q_U = 48$. Only at $q_A = q_U = 64$ does neither firm want to change its behavior.

Algebraic Approach. We can also use algebra to solve for the Cournot equilibrium for American and United Airlines. We use estimates of the market demand and firms' marginal costs to determine the equilibrium.

Our estimate of the market demand function is

$$Q = 339 - p, \tag{12.1}$$

where price, p, is the dollar cost of a one-way flight, and total quantity of the two airlines combined, Q, is measured in thousands of passengers flying one way per quarter. Panels a and b of Figure 12.2 show that this market demand curve, D, is a straight line that hits the price axis at \$339 and the quantity axis at 339 units (thousand passengers) per quarter. Each airline has a constant marginal cost, MC, and average cost, AC, of \$147 per passenger per flight. Using only this information and our economic model, we can find the Cournot equilibrium for the two airlines.

If American believes that United will fly q_U passengers, American expects to fly only the total market demand minus q_U passengers. At a price of p, the total number of passengers, $Q(p)$, is given by the market demand function, Equation 12.1. Thus, the residual demand facing American is

$$q_A = Q(p) - q_U = (339 - p) - q_U.$$

Using algebra, we can rewrite this residual demand function as

$$p = 339 - q_A - q_U. \tag{12.2}$$

In panel b, the linear residual demand, D^r, is parallel to the market demand, D, and lies to the left of D by $q_U = 64$.

If a demand curve is linear, the corresponding marginal revenue curve is twice as steep (Chapter 11). The slope of the residual demand curve, Equation 12.2, is $\Delta p/\Delta q_A = -1$, so the slope of the corresponding marginal revenue curve, MR^r in panel b, is –2. Thus, the marginal revenue function is[11]

$$MR^r = 339 - 2q_A - q_U. \tag{12.3}$$

American Airline's best response—its profit-maximizing output, given q_U—is the output that equates its marginal revenue, Equation 12.3, and its marginal cost:

$$MR^r = 339 - 2q_A - q_U = 147 = MC. \tag{12.4}$$

By rearranging Equation 12.4, we can write American's best-response output, q_A, as a function of q_U:

$$q_A = 96 - \tfrac{1}{2}q_U. \tag{12.5}$$

Figure 12.3 shows American's best-response function, Equation 12.5. According to this best-response function, $q_A = 96$ if $q_U = 0$, and $q_A = 64$ if $q_U = 64$. By the same reasoning, United's best-response function is

$$q_U = 96 - \tfrac{1}{2}q_A. \tag{12.6}$$

A Cournot equilibrium is a pair of quantities, q_A and q_U, such that Equations 12.5 and 12.6 both hold: Each firm is on its best-response curve. This statement is equivalent to saying that the Cournot equilibrium is a point at which the best-response curves cross.

---

[11] American's revenue is $R = pq_A = (339 - q_A - q_U)q_A$. If American treats q_U as a constant and differentiates R with respect to its output, it finds that its marginal revenue is $MR = \partial R/\partial q_A = 339 - 2q_A - q_U$.

One way to determine the Cournot equilibrium is to substitute Equation 12.6 into Equation 12.5,

$$q_A = 96 - \tfrac{1}{2}(96 - \tfrac{1}{2}q_A),$$

and solve for q_A. Doing so, we find that $q_A = 64$ is the Cournot equilibrium quantity for American. Substituting $q_A = 64$ into Equation 12.6, we find that $q_U = 64$ is the Cournot equilibrium quantity for United. As a result, the total output in the Cournot equilibrium is $Q = q_A + q_U = 128$. Setting $Q = 128$ in the market demand Equation 12.1, we learn that the Cournot equilibrium price is \$211.

Comparing the Cournot and Cartel Models

The Cournot equilibrium is the only plausible Nash outcome if oligopoly firms set quantities independently in a one-period game. It is possible, however, that the firms could collude—especially if the game is repeated over many periods.

How would American and United behave if they colluded? They would maximize joint profits by producing the monopoly output, 96 units, at the monopoly price, \$243 per passenger (panel a of Figure 12.2).

If the airlines collude, they could split the monopoly quantity in many ways. American Airlines could act as a monopoly and serve all the passengers, $q_A = 96$ and $q_U = 0$, and possibly give United some of the profits. Or they could reverse roles so that United served everyone: $q_A = 0$ and $q_U = 96$. Or the two airlines could share the passengers in any combination such that the sum of the airlines' passengers equals the monopoly number:

$$q_A + q_U = 96. \qquad (12.7)$$

Panel a of Figure 12.4 shows the possible collusive output combinations in Equation 12.7 as a line labeled the *contract curve*. Collusive firms could agree (contract) to produce at any of the points along this curve. In the figure, we assume that the collusive firms split the market equally so that $q_A = q_U = 48$.

If the firms were to act as price takers, they would each produce where their residual demand curve intersects their marginal cost curve, so price equals marginal cost of \$147. The price-taking equilibrium is $q_A = q_U = 96$. (The Stackelberg equilibrium in the figure is discussed later in this chapter.)

The cartel profits are the highest-possible level of profits the firms can earn. The contract curve shows how the firms split the total monopoly-level profit. Panel b of

Figure 12.4 Duopoly Equilibria. (a) The intersection of the best-response curves determines the Cournot equilibrium. The possible cartel equilibria lie on the contract curve. If the firms act as price takers, each firm produces where its residual demand equals its marginal cost. (b) The highest possible profit for the two firms combined is given by the profit-possibility frontier. It reflects all the possible collusive equilibria, including the one indicated where the firms split the market equally. All equilibria except collusive ones lie within the profit-possibility frontier.

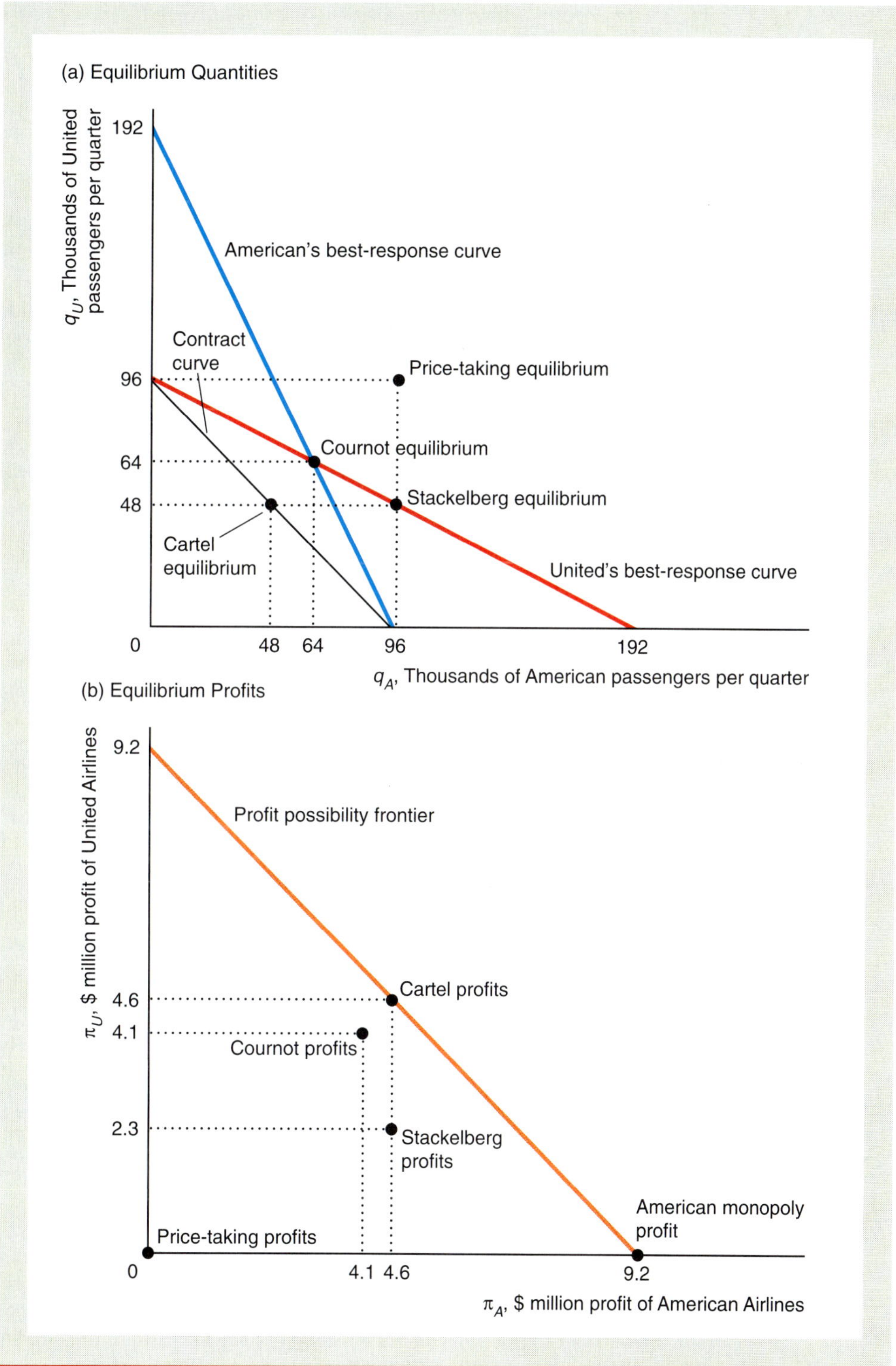
(a) Equilibrium Quantities
q_U, Thousands of United passengers per quarter
192
96
64
48
0
American's best-response curve
Contract curve
Price-taking equilibrium
Cournot equilibrium
Stackelberg equilibrium
Cartel equilibrium
United's best-response curve
48
64
96
192
q_A, Thousands of American passengers per quarter
(b) Equilibrium Profits
π_U, \$ million profit of United Airlines
9.2
4.6
4.1
2.3
0
Profit possibility frontier
Cartel profits
Cournot profits
Stackelberg profits
American monopoly profit
Price-taking profits
4.1
4.6
9.2
π_A, \$ million profit of American Airlines

Figure 12.4 shows the profit-possibility frontier, which corresponds to the contract curve. At the upper left of the profit-possibility frontier, United is a monopoly and earns the entire monopoly profit of approximately \$9.2 million per quarter.[12] At the lower right, American earns the entire monopoly profit. At points in between, they split the profit. Where they split the profit equally, each earns approximately \$4.6 million.

In contrast, if the firms act independently, each earns the Cournot profit of approximately \$4.1 million.[13] Because the Cournot price, \$211, is lower than the cartel price, \$243, consumers are better off if the firms act independently than if they collude.

The Cournot equilibrium market quantity predicted by this model, 128, is closer to the actual observed output, 128.6, than is the predicted cartel quantity, 96. Brander and Zhang (1990) reported that they could not reject the hypothesis that American and United are engaged in a Cournot game based on statistical tests.[14]

The Cournot Equilibrium Varies with the Number of Firms

We've just seen that the price to consumers is lower if two firms set output independently than if they collude. The price to consumers is even lower if there are more than two firms acting independently in the market. We now show how the Cournot equilibrium varies with the number of firms.

Each Cournot firm maximizes its profit by operating where its marginal revenue equals its marginal cost. Chapter 11 shows that a firm's marginal revenue depends on the price and the elasticity of demand it faces where it maximizes its profit. The marginal revenue for a typical Cournot firm is $MR = p(1 + 1/\varepsilon_r)$, where ε_r is the elasticity of the residual demand curve facing the firm. Appendix 12A shows that $\varepsilon_r = n\varepsilon$, where ε is the market elasticity of demand and n is the number of firms with identical costs. Thus, we can write a typical Cournot firm's profit-maximizing condition as

$$MR = p\left(1 + \frac{1}{n\varepsilon}\right) = MC. \tag{12.8}$$

[12]Each firm's profit per passenger is price minus average cost, $p - AC$, so the firm's profit is $\pi = (p - AC)q$, where q is the number of passengers the firm flies. The monopoly price is \$243 and the average cost is \$147, so the monopoly profit is $\pi = (243 - 147) \times 96$ units per quarter = \$9.216 million per quarter.

[13]The Cournot firm's profit is $(p - AC)q$ = (\$211 – \$147)64 units per quarter = \$4.096 million per quarter.

[14]Because the model described here is a simplified version of the Brander and Zhang (1990) model, the predicted output levels, $q_A = q_U = 64$, differ slightly from theirs. Nonetheless, our predictions are very close to the actual observed outcome, $q_A = 65.9$ and $q_U = 62.7$. Chance may explain the small difference in output levels between the predicted and actual levels because firms cannot perfectly control how many tickets are sold. Another possible explanation is that our assumption that the firms are identical is false. Small variations in marginal costs or other small differences between the companies (such as differences in frequent flier rules) may explain these small observed differences in output levels.

If $n = 1$, the Cournot firm is a monopoly, and Equation 12.8 is the same as the profit-maximizing monopoly condition, Equation 11.7. The more firms there are, the larger is the residual demand elasticity, $n\varepsilon$, facing a single firm. As n grows very large, the residual demand elasticity approaches $-\infty$, and Equation 12.8 becomes $p = MC$, which is the profit-maximizing condition of a price-taking competitive firm.

The Lerner Index, $(p - MC)/p$, is a measure of market power: the firm's ability to raise price above marginal cost. By rearranging the terms in Equation 12.8, we find that a Cournot firm's Lerner Index depends on the elasticity facing the firm:

$$\frac{p - MC}{p} = -\frac{1}{n\varepsilon}. \tag{12.9}$$

Thus, a Cournot firm's Lerner Index equals the monopoly level, $-1/\varepsilon$, if there is only one firm: Setting $n = 1$ in Equation 12.9, we obtain the monopoly expression (Equation 11.9). Again, as the number of firms grows large, the residual demand elasticity facing a firm approaches $-\infty$, so the Lerner Index approaches zero, which is the same as with price-taking, competitive firms.

We can illustrate these results using our airlines example. Suppose that other airlines with identical marginal cost, $MC = \$147$, were to fly between Chicago and Los Angeles. Table 12.3 shows how the Cournot equilibrium price and the Lerner Index vary with the number of firms.[15]

Table 12.3 The Cournot Equilibrium Varies with the Number of Firms

Number of Firms, n	Firm Output, q	Market Output, Q	Price, p	Market Elasticity, ε	Residual Demand Elasticity, $n\varepsilon$	Lerner Index, $(p - m)/p = -1/(n\varepsilon)$
1	96	96	\$243	–2.53	–2.53	0.40
2	64	128	211	–1.65	–3.30	0.30
3	48	144	195	–1.35	–4.06	0.25
4	38.4	154	185.40	–1.21	–4.83	0.21
5	32	160	179	–1.12	–5.59	0.18
6	27.4	165	174.43	–1.06	–6.36	0.16
7	24	168	171	–1.02	–7.13	0.14
8	21.3	171	168.33	–0.99	–7.89	0.13
9	19.2	173	166.20	–0.96	–8.66	0.12
10	17.5	175	164.45	–0.94	–9.42	0.11
50	3.8	188	150.76	–0.80	–40.05	0.02
100	1.9	190	148.90	–0.78	–78.33	0.01
200	1.0	191	147.96	–0.77	–154.89	0.01
∞	~0	192	147	–0.77	–∞	0

[15]In Appendix 12A, we derive the Cournot equilibrium quantity and price for a general linear demand. Given our particular demand curve, Equation 12.1, and marginal cost, \$147, each firm's Cournot equilibrium output is $q = (339 - 147)/(n + 1) = 192/(n + 1)$ and the Cournot market price is $p = (339 + 147n)/(n + 1)$.

As we already know, if there were only one "Cournot" firm, it would produce the monopoly quantity, 96, at the monopoly price, \$243. We also know that each duopoly firm's output is 64, so market output is 128, and price is \$211. The duopoly market elasticity is $\varepsilon = 1.65$, so the residual demand elasticity facing each duopolist is twice as large as the market elasticity, $2\varepsilon = -3.3$.

As the number of firms increases, each firm's output falls toward zero, but total output approaches 192, the quantity on the market demand curve when price equals marginal cost of \$147. Although the market elasticity of demand falls as the number of firms grows, the residual demand curve facing each firm becomes increasingly horizontal (perfectly elastic). As a result, the price approaches the marginal cost, \$147. Similarly, as the number of firms increases, the Lerner Index approaches the price-taking level of zero.

The table shows that having extra firms in the market benefits consumers. When the number of firms rises from 1 to 4, the price falls by a quarter and the Lerner Index is cut nearly in half. At 10 firms, the price is one-third less than the monopoly level, and the Lerner Index is a quarter of the monopoly level.

APPLICATION

Appliances

The European market for washing machines, refrigerators, and other appliances has many more firms than the U.S. market. The 5 largest manufacturers—Whirlpool, General Electric, Electrolux (Frigidaire), Maytag, and Raytheon—make 98% of U.S. appliance sales, whereas the top 10 firms in Europe—led by Electrolux, Bosch-Siemens, and Whirlpool—control only 72% of that market. This difference may explain why Whirlpool's American operation has a profit margin (an approximation of the Lerner Index) of 8%, while its European division earns only 4%.[16] ■

12.5 STACKELBERG MODEL OF NONCOOPERATIVE BEHAVIOR

In the Cournot model, both firms make their output decisions at the same time. Suppose, however, that one of the firms, called the *leader*, can set its output before its rival, the *follower*, sets its output. This type of game, in which the players make decisions sequentially, arises naturally if one firm enters a market before another.

Would the firm that got to act first have an advantage? Heinrich von Stackelberg showed how to modify the Cournot model to answer this question.

How does the leader decide to set its output? The leader realizes that once it sets its output, the rival firm will use its Cournot best-response curve to pick a

[16]Rehfeld, Barry, "Where Whirlpool Flies, and Maytag Sputters," *New York Times*, January 3, 1993:5.

best-response output. Thus, the leader predicts what the follower will do before the follower acts. Using this knowledge, the leader manipulates the follower, thereby benefiting at the follower's expense.

We illustrate this model using our airlines market example (Appendix 12B analyzes the model mathematically). Although it is difficult to imagine that either American Airlines or United Airlines actually has an advantage that would allow it to act before its rival, we assume (arbitrarily) that American Airlines can act before United Airlines. We first examine how the airlines would behave if they could pick one of only a few quantities. Then we examine the more general problem, in which they can choose any quantity they want.

Stackelberg Game Tree

We illustrate the importance of moving first by using a *game tree*, Figure 12.5. The game tree shows the order of the firms' moves, each firm's possible strategies at the time of its move, and the resulting profits. For simplicity, we assume that each airline can choose one of only three quantities, 48, 64, and 96.

Each line in the decision tree represents an action, and each box is a point of decision by one of the firms. American—the leader—starts by picking one of the three output levels (left side of the figure); then United—the follower—chooses one of the three quantities (middle of the figure), which determines the profits that American

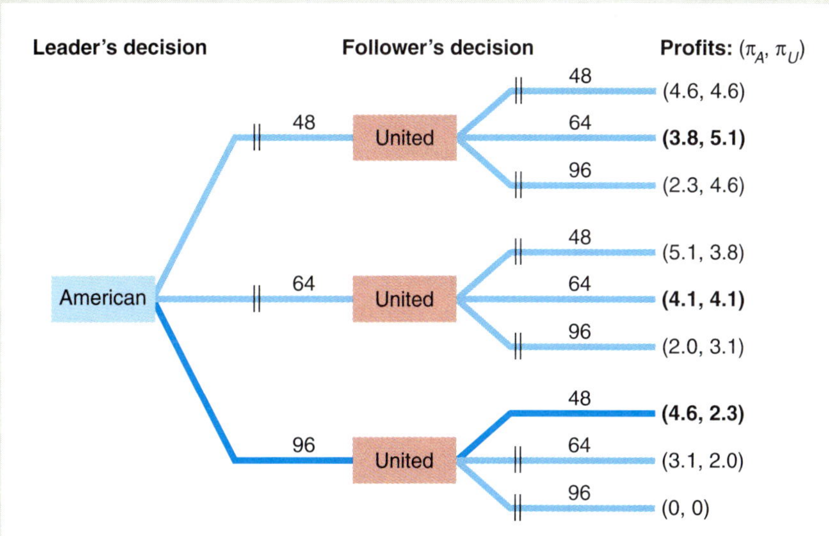

Figure 12.5 Stackelberg Game Tree. American, the leader firm, chooses its output level first. Given American's choice, United, the follower, picks an output level. The profit of the two firms that result from these decisions are shown on the right-hand side of the figure. Two lines through an action line show that the firm rejects that action.

and United earn (right side of the figure). For instance, if American picks 64 and then United picks 96, American earns $2.0 million profit per quarter and United earns $3.1 million.

How should American, the leader, pick its output? For each possible quantity it can produce, American predicts what United will do and picks the output level that maximizes its profit.

To determine the strategies the firms use, we work backward from the follower's decision to the leader's. We first ask what United, the follower, would do, given each possible output choice of American, the leader. Then, using this information about United's reasoning, we determine which strategy American chooses.

United, the follower, does not have a dominant strategy. How much output it produces depends on the quantity that American chose. If American chooses 96, United's profit is $2.3 million if its output is 48, $2 million if it produces 64, and $0 if it picks a quantity of 96. Thus, if American chose 96, United's best response is 48. The double lines through the other two action lines show that United will not use those actions.

Using the same reasoning, American determines how United will respond to each of American's possible actions, as the right-hand side of the figure illustrates. Using its predictions of United's responses, American knows that

- If American chooses 48, United will sell 64, so American's profit will be $3.8 million.
- If American chooses 64, United will sell 64, so American's profit will be $4.1 million.
- If American chooses 96, United will sell 48, so American's profit will be $4.6 million.

Thus, to maximize its profit, American chooses 96. United responds by selling 48.

This outcome is a Stackelberg (Nash) equilibrium. Given that American Airlines sets its output at 96, United is using a strategy that maximizes its profit, $q_U = 48$, so it doesn't want to change. Similarly, given how United will respond to each possible American output level, American can't make more profit than selling 96.

American, the Stackelberg leader, sells 50% more than the Cournot quantity, 64, and earns $4.6 million, which is 15% more than the Cournot level of profit, $4.1 million. United, the Stackelberg follower, sells a quantity, 48, and earns a profit, $2.3 million, both of which are less than the Cournot levels.

The value to American of being the leader is $0.5 (= $4.6 – $4.1) million, the amount its profit rises over the Cournot level. However, it is worth $1.8 (= $4.1 – $2.3) million to United Airlines not to be the follower.

Given the option to act first, American chooses a large output level to make it in United's best interest to pick a relatively small output level, 48. In this example, if the firms colluded and both produced 48, both would earn $4.6 million, which is what American earns as the leader. Why doesn't American pick the collusive output level, 48, so that both firms can earn the collusive profit? If American did so, it would be in United's best interest to sell 64 and earn $5.1 million, which would reduce American's profit to $3.8 million. Thus, American produces a large output to keep United's output low.

Stackelberg Graphical Model

Now suppose that the airlines can choose any output level they want and that American Airlines chooses its output first. How does American decide on its optimal policy now?

American uses its residual demand curve to determine its profit-maximizing output. American knows that when it sets q_A, United will use its Cournot best-response function to pick its best-response q_U. Thus, American's residual demand curve, D^r (panel a of Figure 12.6), is the market demand curve, D (panel a) minus the output United will produce as summarized by United's best-response curve (panel b). For example, if American sets $q_A = 192$, United's best response is $q_U = 0$ (as shown by United's best-response curve in panel b). As a result, the residual demand curve and the market demand curve are identical at $q_A = 192$ (panel a).

Similarly, if American set $q_A = 0$, United would choose $q_U = 96$, so the residual demand at $q_A = 0$ is 96 less than demand. The residual demand curve hits the vertical axis, where $q_A = 0$, at $p = \$243$, which is 96 units to the left of demand at that price. When $q_A = 96$, $q_U = 48$, so the residual demand at $q_A = 96$ is 48 units to the left of the demand.

American chooses its profit-maximizing output, $q_A = 96$, where its marginal revenue curve that corresponds to the residual demand curve, MR^r, equals its marginal cost, \$147. At $q_A = 96$, the price, which is the height of the residual demand curve, is \$195. Total demand at \$195 is $Q = 144$. At that price, United produces $q_U = Q - q_A = 48$, its best response to American's output of $q_A = 96$.

Thus, in this Stackelberg equilibrium, the leader produces twice as much as the follower, as Figure 12.6 and panel a of Figure 12.4 show.[17] The total Stackelberg output, 144, is greater than the total Cournot, 128, and collusive, 96, outputs. As a result, the Stackelberg price, \$195, is less than the Cournot, \$211, and collusive, \$243, prices. Thus, consumers prefer the Stackelberg equilibrium to the Cournot equilibrium and the Cournot equilibrium to the collusive equilibrium here (and in any market where all firms have identical cost functions).

The combined Stackelberg profit, \$6.9 million, is less than the combined Cournot, \$8 million, and collusive, \$9.2 million, profits, as panel b of Figure 12.4 shows. The Stackelberg leader, though, earns \$4.6 million, which is more than it could earn in a Cournot game, \$4.1 million. Total Stackelberg profit is less than total Cournot profit because the Stackelberg follower, earning \$2.3 million, is much worse off than in the Cournot equilibrium.

Why Moving Sequentially Is Essential

Why don't we get the Stackelberg equilibrium when both firms move simultaneously? Why doesn't one firm—say, American—announce that it will produce the Stackelberg leader output to induce United to produce the Stackelberg follower output level? The answer is that, when the firms move simultaneously, United doesn't view American's warning that it will produce a large quantity as a *credible threat*.

[17]Here, the leader produces the same quantity as would a monopoly, and the follower produces the same quantity as it would in the cartel equilibrium. These relations are due to the linear demand curve and the constant marginal cost—they do not hold more generally.

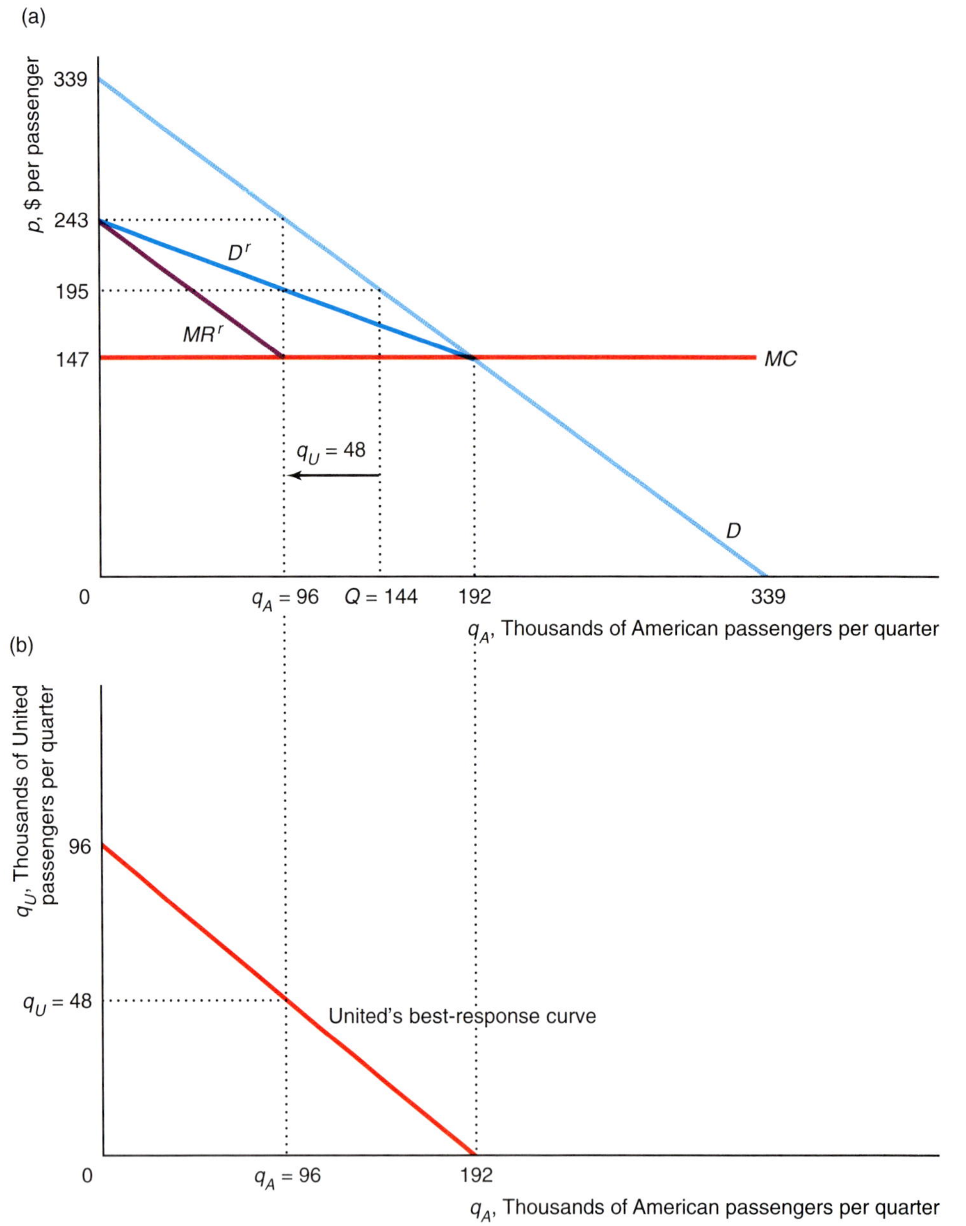

Figure 12.6 Stackelberg Equilibrium. (a) The residual demand facing the Stackelberg leader is the market demand minus the quantity produced by the follower, q_U, given the leader's quantity, q_A. The leader chooses $q_A = 96$ so that its marginal revenue, MR^r, equals its marginal cost. The total output, $Q = 144$, is the sum of the output of the two firms. (b) The quantity the follower produces is its best-response to the leader's output, as given by its Cournot best-response curve.

If United believed that threat, it would indeed produce the Stackelberg follower output level. But United doesn't believe the threat because it is not in American's best interest to produce that large a quantity of output. If American were to produce the leader level of output and United produced the Cournot level, American's profit would be lower than if it too produced the Cournot level. Because American cannot be sure that United will believe its threat and reduce its output, American will actually produce the Cournot output level.

Indeed, each firm may make the same threat and announce that it wants to be the leader. Because neither firm can be sure that the other will be intimidated and produce the smaller quantity, both produce the Cournot output level. In contrast, when one firm moves first, its threat to produce a large quantity is credible because it has already *committed* to producing the larger quantity, thereby carrying out its threat.

★ Strategic Trade Policy

> *[E]ach interference by the government in the economic system calls forth others: each industry in turn wishes to be protected and argues that is injured by the protection which other industries have received.* —Antoine-Augustin Cournot, 1877

Suppose that two identical firms in two different countries compete in a world market. Both firms act simultaneously, so neither firm can make itself the Stackelberg leader. A government may be tempted to intervene to make its firm a Stackelberg leader. The Japanese and French governments often help their domestic firms to compete with international rivals, as do the American, British, Canadian, and many other governments. If only one government intervenes, it can make its domestic firm's threat to produce a large quantity of output credible, so foreign rivals will produce the Stackelberg follower level of output (Spencer and Brander 1983).

Subsidizing an Airline. We'll modify our airline example to illustrate how one country's government can aid its firm. Suppose that United Airlines were based in one country and American Airlines in another. Initially, United Airlines and American Airlines are in a Cournot equilibrium. Each firm has a marginal cost of \$147 and flies 64 thousand passengers (64 units) per quarter at a price of \$211.

Now suppose that United Airlines's government gives United a \$48 per passenger subsidy, but the other government doesn't help American Airlines. As a result, American's marginal cost remains at \$147, but United's marginal cost after the subsidy is only \$99.

The firms continue to play Cournot, but the playing field is no longer level.[18] How does the Cournot equilibrium change? Your intuition probably tells you that United's output increases relative to that of American, as we now show.

United still acts at the same time as American, so United acts like any Cournot firm and determines its best-response curve. United's best-response to any given American output is the output at which its marginal revenue corresponding to its residual demand, MR^r, equals its marginal cost. The subsidy does not affect United's

[18] Don't you think that anyone who uses the phrase "level playing field" should have to pay a fine?

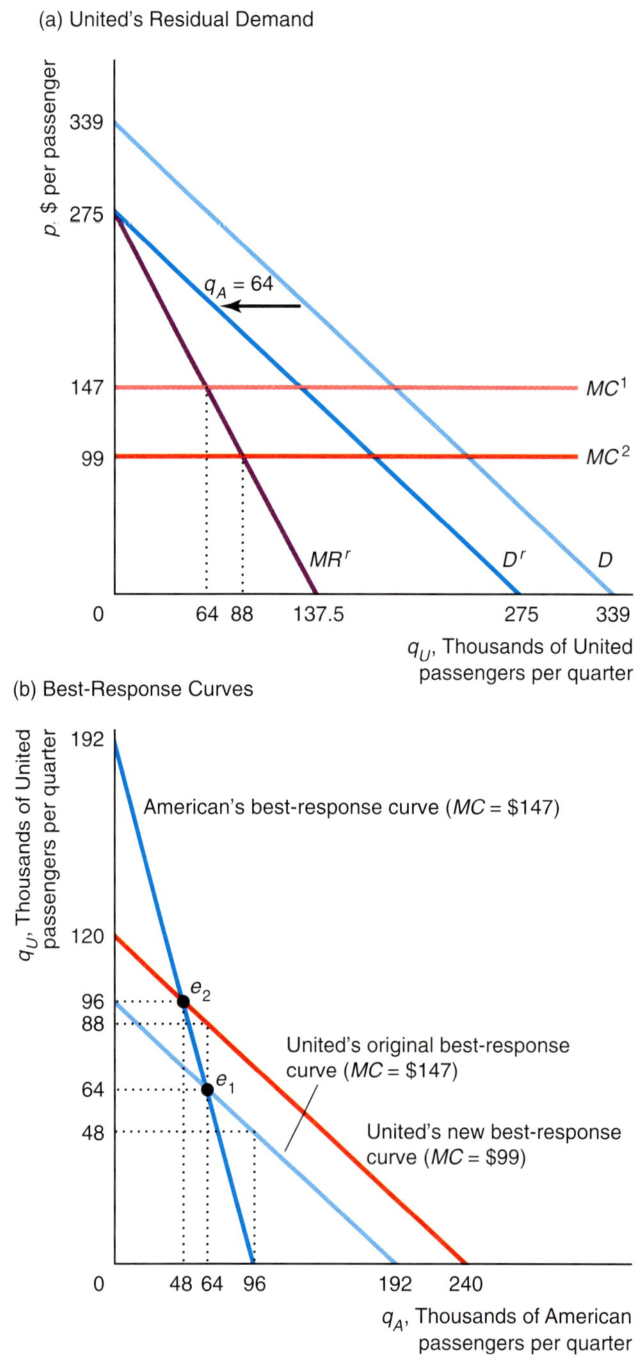
(a) United's Residual Demand
p, $ per passenger
339
275
q_A = 64
147
99
MC^1
MC^2
MR^r
D^r
D
0
64 88
137.5
275
339
q_U, Thousands of United passengers per quarter
(b) Best-Response Curves
q_U, Thousands of United passengers per quarter
192
American's best-response curve (MC = $147)
120
e_2
96
88
United's original best-response curve (MC = $147)
64
e_1
48
United's new best-response curve (MC = $99)
0
48 64 96
192
240
q_A, Thousands of American passengers per quarter

Figure 12.7 Effect of a Government Subsidy on a Cournot Equilibrium. (a) A government subsidy that lowers United's marginal cost from MC^1 = \$147 to MC^2 = \$99 causes United's best-response output to American's $q_A = 64$ to rise from $q_U = 64$ to 88. (b) If both airlines' marginal costs are \$147, the Cournot equilibrium is e_1. If United's marginal cost falls to \$99, its best-response function shifts outward. It now sells more tickets in response to any given American output than previously. In the new Cournot equilibrium, e_2, United sells $q_U = 96$ whereas American sells only $q_A = 48$.

MR^r curve, but it lowers its MC curve, so United produces more output for any given American output after the cost falls.

Panel a of Figure 12.7 illustrates this reasoning. United's residual demand, D^r, lies 64 units to the right of the market demand, D, if American produces 64. The MR^r curve intersects the original marginal cost, MC^1 = \$147, at 64 and the new marginal cost, MC^2 = \$99, at 88. Thus, if we hold American's output constant at 64, United produces more as its marginal cost falls.

Because this reasoning applies for any level of output American picks, United's best-response function in panel b shifts outward as its marginal cost falls.[19] United's best response to any given quantity that American sells is to sell more than at its previous, higher cost. As a result, the Cournot equilibrium shifts from the original e_1, at which both firms sold 64, to e_2, at which United sells 96 and American sells 48. Thus, the \$48 subsidy to United causes it to sell the Stackelberg leader quantity and American to sell the Stackelberg follower quantity. The subsidy works by convincing American that United will produce large quantities of output.

Using the market demand curve, Equation 12.1, we find that the market price falls from \$211 to \$195, benefiting consumers. United's profit increases from \$4.1 million to \$9.2 million, while American's profit falls to \$2.3 million. Thus, United and consumers gain and American loses from the fall in United's marginal cost.

This example illustrates that a government subsidy to one firm *can* lead to the same outcome as in a Stackelberg equilibrium. Would a government *want* to give the subsidy that leads to the Stackelberg outcome?

The answer depends on the government's objective. Suppose that the government is interested in maximizing its domestic firm's profit net of (not including) the government's subsidy. The subsidy is a transfer from some citizens (taxpayers) to others (the owners of United). We assume that the government doesn't care about consumers—which is certainly true if they live in another country.

Table 12.4 shows the effects of various subsidies and a tax (a negative subsidy). If the subsidy is zero, we have the usual Cournot equilibrium. A \$48-per-passenger

[19]United sets the marginal revenue that corresponds to its residual demand curve, MR^r, equal to its new marginal cost, MC:

$$\text{MR}^r = 339 - 2q_U - q_A = 99 = MC.$$

Using algebra to rearrange this expression, we find that United's best-response function is

$$q_U = 120 - \tfrac{1}{2}q_A.$$

Table 12.4 Effects of Subsidy on United Airlines

Subsidy, s	United			American	
	q_U	π_U	*Welfare*, $\pi_U - sq_U$	q_A	π_A
60	104	\$10.8	\$4.58	44	\$1.9
48	**96**	**\$9.2**	**\$4.61**	**48**	**\$2.3**
30	84	\$7.1	\$4.5	54	\$2.9
0	64	\$4.1	\$4.1	64	\$4.1
–30	44	\$1.9	\$3.3	74	\$5.5

Notes:
The subsidy is in dollars per passenger (and is a tax if negative).
Output units are in thousands of passengers per quarter.
Profits and welfare (defined as United's profits minus the subsidy) are in millions of dollars per quarter.

subsidy leads to the same outcome as in the Stackelberg equilibrium and maximizes the government's welfare measure. At a larger subsidy, such as \$60, United's profit rises, but by less than the cost of the subsidy to the government. Similarly, at smaller subsidies or taxes, welfare is also lower.

Problems with Intervention. Thus, in theory, a government may want to subsidize its domestic firm to make it produce the same output as it would if it were a Stackelberg leader. If such subsidies are to work as desired, however, five conditions must hold.

First, the government must be able to set its subsidy before the firms choose their output levels. The idea behind this intervention is that one firm cannot act before the other, but its government can act first.

Second, the other government must not retaliate. If both governments intervene, instead of having a game of strategies between firms, we have a game of strategies between governments, in which both countries may lose.

Third, the government's actions must be credible. If the foreign firm country doesn't believe that the government actually will subsidize its domestic firm, the foreign firm produces the Cournot level. Countries have difficulty in committing to long-term policies. For example, during the 1996 Republican presidential primaries, many candidates said that they would reverse President Clinton's trade policies if they were elected.

Fourth, the government must know enough about how firms behave to intervene appropriately. The government sets its subsidy at the wrong level if it doesn't know the demand function and the costs of all firms.

Fifth, the government must know which game firms are playing. If firms were not engaged in a Cournot game, the government would have to intervene in a different way (see Problem 6 at the end of the chapter).

Many economists who analyze strategic trade policies strongly oppose them because they are difficult if not impossible to implement and are mean-spirited, "beggar thy neighbor" policies. If only one government intervenes, another country's firm is harmed. If both governments intervene, both countries may suffer. For these reasons, the latest General Agreement on Tariffs and Trade (GATT) forbids the use of virtually all explicit export subsidies.

APPLICATION

Airbus and Boeing

France, Germany, Spain, and the United Kingdom own Airbus, which competes in the widebody aircraft market with Boeing, an American firm.[20] Because of the large sunk costs of starting such a firm, major economies of scale, long product lives of planes, and substantial learning by doing, there is probably room for only two firms at most in this market.[21]

Boeing vehemently complains that the governments that own Airbus provide it with large subsidies that make it difficult for Boeing to compete. Airbus responds that the military contracts Boeing receives from the U.S. government are nothing less than implicit subsidies.

Using a Cournot model similar to the one we just used to examine subsidies to an airline company, Baldwin and Krugman (1988) examined how a subsidy to Airbus would affect this market under various scenarios. They illustrated that the subsidies benefited consumers worldwide because the Stackelberg price is below the (unsubsidized) Cournot price. Their simulations, however, indicated that American firms were net losers from the subsidy: The fall in Boeing's profits was greater than the increase in the consumer surplus of U.S. airline firms that buy planes. Even more striking, they found that the European countries also lost after paying the subsidy: The subsidy was not set optimally even from the standpoint of the European governments. ■

[20]In the first quarter of 1996, Airbus had 40.2% of orders for new planes, Boeing had 56.4%, and McDonnell Douglas Corporation had 3.4%. Tagliabue, John, "Airbus Tries to Fly in a New Formation," *New York Times*, May 2, 1996:C1.

[21]Indeed, Boeing announced in 1997 that it wanted to acquire the McDonnell Douglas Corporation, the unprofitable third manufacturer. The U.S. government approved the merger, but the European Community initially objected on the grounds the merger would benefit Boeing at the expense of Airbus.

SOLVED PROBLEM 12.1

If the government charges identical Cournot duopolies a specific tax of τ per unit of output, what is the qualitative effect (direction of change) on the equilibrium quantities and price? You may assume that the before-tax best-response functions are linear.

Answer

1. *Show the initial, before-tax Cournot equilibrium*: We're told that the Cournot firms, labeled Firm A and Firm B in Figure 12.8, are identical. As a result, their best-response curves are mirror images of each other, and both firms produce the same quantity, q_1, at the Cournot equilibrium, e_1, where their best-response functions cross.

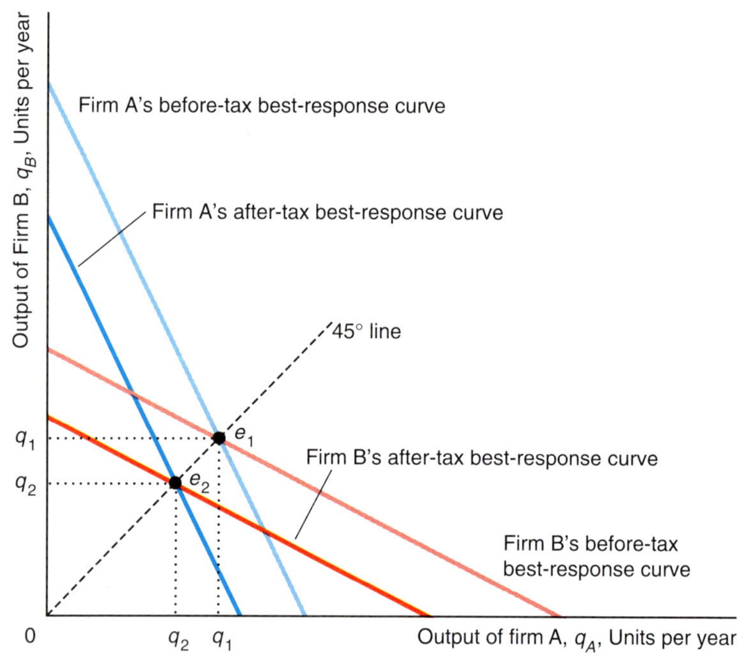

Figure 12.8 Effect of a Specific Tax on a Cournot Equilibrium. Because the two firms are identical, their best-response functions are mirror images of each other and cross at points where the firm's outputs are equal. Without a tax, the Cournot equilibrium is e_1 and each firm produces q_1. The specific tax τ causes both best-response functions to shift in by equal amounts. Thus, in the new Cournot equilibrium, e_2, the firm's outputs are equal at q_2, which is smaller than q_1.

2. *Show how the best-response curves shift in response to the tax*: We've just seen that a subsidy lowers a firm's marginal cost, causing its best-response curve to shift away from the origin. Thus, a tax (which is a negative subsidy) raises a firm's marginal cost, causing its best-response curve to shift in toward the origin. Here, because both firms face the same specific tax, marginal costs of both firms rise by the same amount. As a result, both after-tax best-response curves shift in toward the origin by the same amount and remain mirror images of each other.

3. *Compare the two Cournot equilibria*: Each firm produces a smaller quantity, q_2, at the new Cournot equilibrium, e_2, than in the original Cournot equilibrium. As a result, total equilibrium quantity falls and the equilibrium price rises. ■

12.6 COMPARISON OF COLLUSIVE, COURNOT, STACKELBERG, AND COMPETITIVE EQUILIBRIA

The welfare of consumers and firms depends on the market structure, as Table 12.5 shows for our airline example. In this table, the welfare measure is the sum of consumer surplus and the profits of the two firms.

At one extreme, if one firm has a monopoly or if the two firms form a cartel and split the market equally, total output is relatively low, price is high, consumer

Table 12.5 Comparison of Airline Market Structures

	Monopoly	Cartel	Cournot	Stackelberg	Price Taking
q_A	96	48	64	96	96
q_U	0	48	64	48	96
$Q = q_A + q_U$	96	96	128	144	192
p	\$243	\$243	\$211	\$195	\$147
π_A	\$9.2	\$4.6	\$4.1	\$4.6	\$0
π_U	\$0	\$4.6	\$4.1	\$2.3	\$0
$\Pi = \pi_A + \pi_U$	\$9.2	\$9.2	\$8.2	\$6.9	\$0
Consumer surplus, CS	\$4.6	\$4.6	\$8.2	\$10.4	\$18.4
Welfare, $W = CS + \Pi$	\$13.8	\$13.8	\$16.4	\$17.3	\$18.4
Deadweight loss, DWL	\$4.6	\$4.6	\$2.0	\$1.2	\$0

Notes:
Passengers are in thousands per quarter.
Price is in dollars per passengers.
Profits, consumer surplus, welfare, and deadweight loss are in millions of dollars per quarter.

surplus and welfare are low, and deadweight loss is high. At the other extreme, if American and United act as price takers, output is relatively high, price is low, consumer surplus and welfare are high, and society does not suffer a deadweight loss.

The duopoly Cournot and Stackelberg equilibria (in the table, American is the leader) lie between the extreme cases of monopoly or cartel and price taking. The Stackelberg equilibrium is closer to the price-taking equilibrium than is the Cournot equilibrium in terms of total output, price, consumer surplus, welfare, and deadweight loss.

We already know that the Cournot equilibrium approaches the price-taking equilibrium as the number of firms grows large. Similarly, we can show that the Stackelberg equilibrium approaches the price-taking equilibrium as the number of Stackelberg followers grows. As a result, the differences between the Cournot, Stackelberg, and price-taking market structures shrink as the number of firms grows large.

12.7 MONOPOLISTIC COMPETITION

We've assumed that the number of oligopoly firms is fixed because of barriers to entry. As a result, the oligopoly firms (such as the airlines) may earn economic profits. In contrast, monopolistically competitive markets do not have barriers to entry, so firms enter the market until no new firm can enter profitably.

If both competitive and monopolistically competitive firms make zero profits, what distinguishes these two market structures? In contrast to competitive firms (which face horizontal residual demand curves and charge prices equal to marginal cost), monopolistically competitive firms face downward-sloping residual demand curves, so they charge prices above marginal cost. Monopolistically competitive firms face downward-sloping residual demand because they have relatively few rivals or because they sell differentiated products.

The fewer monopolistically competitive firms, the less elastic is the residual demand curve each firm faces. As we saw above, the elasticity of demand facing an individual Cournot firm is $n\varepsilon$, where n is the number of firms and ε is the market elasticity. Thus, the fewer the firms in a market, the less elastic is the residual demand curve.

When monopolistically competitive firms benefit from economies of scale at high levels of output (the average cost curve is downward sloping), so each firm is relatively large in comparison to market demand, there is room in the market for only a few firms. In the short run, if fixed costs are large and marginal costs are constant or diminishing, firms have economies of scale (Chapter 7) at all output levels, so there are relatively few firms in the market. In an extreme case with substantial enough economies of scale, the market may have room for only one firm: a natural monopoly (Chapter 11). The number of firms in equilibrium is smaller, the greater are the economies of scale and the farther to the left is the market demand curve.

Monopolistically competitive firms also face downward-sloping residual demand curves if each firm sells a differentiated product. If some consumers believe that Tide laundry detergent is better than Cheer and other brands, Tide won't lose all its sales even if Tide has a slightly higher price than Cheer. Thus, Tide faces a downward-sloping demand curve—not a horizontal one.

Monopolistically Competitive Equilibrium

In a monopolistically competitive market, each firm tries to maximize its profit; however, each makes zero economic profit due to entry. Two conditions hold in a monopolistically competitive equilibrium: *Marginal revenue equals marginal cost* (because firms set output to maximize profit) and *price equals average cost* (because firms enter until no further profitable entry is possible).

Figure 12.9 shows a monopolistically competitive market equilibrium. A typical monopolistically competitive firm faces a residual demand curve D^r. To maximize its profit, the firm sets its output, q, where its marginal revenue curve corresponding to the residual demand curve intersects its marginal cost curve: $MR^r = MC$. At that quantity, the firm's average cost curve, AC, is tangent to its residual demand curve. Because the height of the residual demand curve is the price, at the point of tangency, price equals average cost, $p = AC$, and the firm makes zero profit.

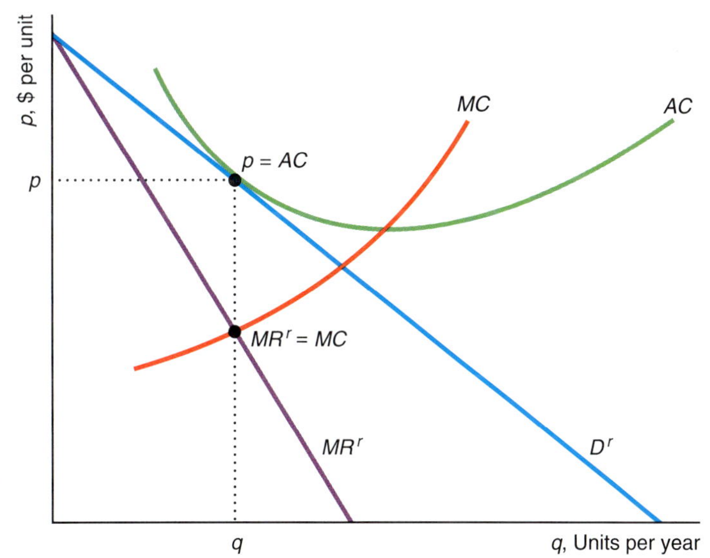

Figure 12.9 Monopolistically Competitive Equilibrium. A monopolistically competitive firm, facing residual demand curve, D^r, sets its output where its marginal revenue equals its marginal cost: $MR^r = MC$. Because firms can enter this market, the profit of the firm is driven to zero, so price equals the firm's average cost: $p = AC$.

If the average cost were less than price at that quantity, firms would make positive profits and entrants would be attracted. If average cost were above price, firms would lose money, so firms would exit until the marginal firm was breaking even.

The smallest quantity at which the average cost curve reaches its minimum is referred to as *full capacity* or **minimum efficient scale.** The firm's full capacity or minimum efficient scale is the quantity at which the firm no longer benefits from economies of scale. Because a monopolistically competitive equilibrium occurs in the downward-sloping section of the average cost curve (where the average cost curve is tangent to the downward-sloping demand curve), a monopolistically competitive firm operates at less than full capacity in the long run.

Fixed Costs and the Number of Firms

The number of firms in a monopolistically competitive equilibrium depends on firms' costs. The larger is each firm's fixed cost, the smaller is the number of monopolistically competitive firms in the market equilibrium.

Although entry is free, if the fixed costs are high, few firms may enter. In the automobile industry, just to develop a new fender costs \$8 to \$10 million.[22] Developing a new pharmaceutical drug may cost \$350 million or more.

We can illustrate this relationship using the airlines example, in which we modify our assumptions about entry and fixed costs. American and United are the only airlines providing service on the Chicago–Los Angeles route. Until now, we have assumed that a barrier to entry—such as an inability to obtain landing rights at both airports—prevented entry and that the firms had no fixed costs. If fixed cost is zero and marginal cost is constant at \$147 per passenger, average cost is also constant at \$147 per passenger. As we showed earlier, each firm in this oligopolistic market flies $q = 64$ per quarter at a price of $p = \$211$ and makes a profit of \$4.1 million per quarter.

Now suppose that there are no barriers to entry, but each airline incurs a fixed cost, F, due to airport fees, capital expenditure, or other factors. Each firm's marginal cost remains \$147 per passenger, but its average cost,

$$AC = 147 + \frac{F}{q},$$

falls as the number of passengers rises, as panels a and b of Figure 12.10 illustrate for $F = \$2.3$ million.

If there are only two firms in a monopolistically competitive market, what must the fixed costs be so that the two firms earn zero profit? We know that these firms receive a profit of \$4.1 million per firm in the absence of fixed costs. As a result, the fixed cost must be \$4.1 million per firm for the firms to earn zero profit. With this

[22]Treece, James B., "Sometimes, You Gotta Have Size," *Business Week*, Enterprise 1993:200–1. That article also illustrates the role of fixed costs on entry in the following anecdote: "In 1946, steel magnate Henry J. Kaiser boasted to a Detroit dinner gathering that two recent stock offerings had raised a huge \$50 million to invest in his budding car company. Suddenly, a voice from the back of the room shot out: 'Give that man one white chip.' "

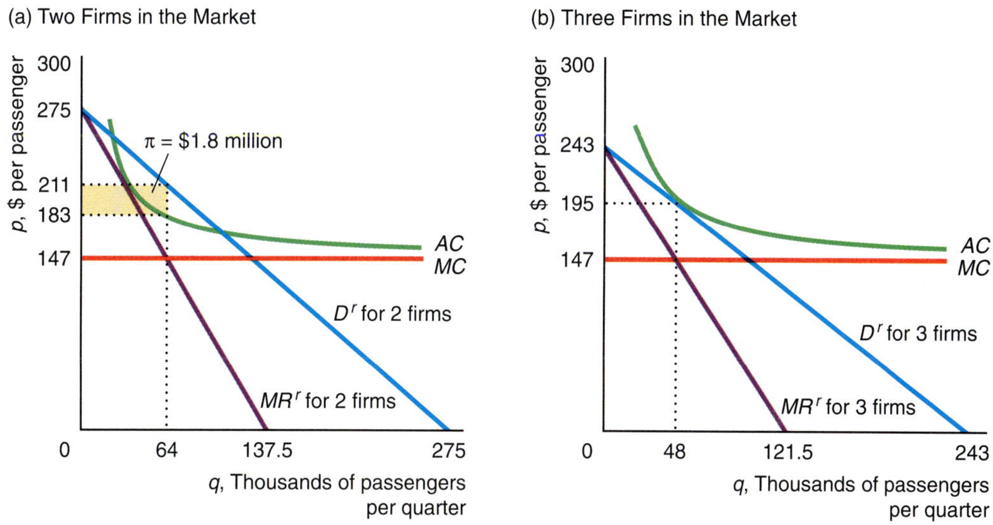

Figure 12.10 Monopolistic Competition among Airlines. (a) If each identical airline has a fixed cost of \$2.3 million and there are two firms in the market, each firm flies $q = 64$ units (thousand passengers) per quarter at a price of $p = \$211$ per passenger and makes a profit of \$1.8 million. This profit attracts entry. (b) After a third firm enters, the residual demand curve shifts, so each firm flies $q = 48$ units (thousand passengers) at $p = \$195$ and makes zero profit, which is the monopolistically competitive equilibrium.

fixed cost, the monopolistically competitive price and quantity are the same as in the oligopolistic equilibrium, $q = 64$ and $p = \$211$, and the number of firms is the same, but now each firm's profit is zero.

If the fixed cost is only \$2.3 million and there are only two firms in the market, each firm makes a profit, as panel a shows. Each duopoly firm faces a residual demand curve (labeled "D^r for 2 firms"), which is the market demand minus its rival's Cournot equilibrium quantity, $q = 64$. Given this residual demand, each firm produces $q = 64$, which equates its marginal revenue, MR^r, and its marginal cost, MC. At $q = 64$, the firm's average cost is $AC = \$147 + (\$2.3 \text{ million})/(64 \text{ units}) \approx \$183$, so each firm makes a profit of $\pi = (p - AC)q \approx (\$211 - \$183) \times 64$ units per quarter $\approx \$1.8$ million per quarter.

This substantial economic profit attracts an entrant. The entry of a third firm causes the residual demand facing any one firm to shift to the left in panel b. In the new equilibrium, each firm sets $q = 48$ and charges $p = \$195$. At this quantity, each firm's average cost is \$195, so the firms break even. No other firms enter because, if one did, the residual demand curve would shift even farther to the left and all the firms would lose money. Thus, if fixed cost is \$2.3 million, there are three firms in the monopolistically competitive equilibrium. This example illustrates a general result: *The lower the fixed costs, the more firms there are in the monopolistically competitive equilibrium.*[23]

SOLVED PROBLEM 12.2

What is the monopolistically competitive airline equilibrium if each firm has a fixed cost of \$3 million?

Answer

1. *Determine the number of firms*: We already know that the monopolistically competitive equilibrium has two firms if the fixed cost is \$4.1 million, and three firms if the fixed cost is \$2.3 million. With a fixed cost of \$3 million, if there are only two firms in the market, each makes a profit of \$1.1 (= \$4.1 – 3) million. If another firm enters, though, each firm's loss equals –\$0.7 (= 2.3 – 3) million. Thus, the monopolistically competitive equilibrium has two firms, each of which earns a positive profit that is too small to attract another firm. This outcome is a monopolistically competitive equilibrium because no other firm wants to enter.
2. *Determine the equilibrium quantities and prices*: We already know that each duopoly firm produces $q = 64$, so $Q = 128$, and $p = \$211$. ■

APPLICATION

Entry and Airline Prices

Entry lowers the oligopoly price. When People Express Airlines expanded its operations into 24 new domestic nonstop markets in 1984 and 1985, the incumbent airlines on routes entered by People Express suffered \$6.8 million to \$12.0 million in pretax losses (Whinston and Collins 1992). This loss is equivalent to what would occur if incumbents were forced to fly their planes empty for three to five months.

All else the same, prices are higher in oligopolies, in which entry is difficult, than in monopolistically competitive markets, in which entry is relatively easy.

---

[23]When Airbus Industrie announced that it planned to spend at least \$10 billion to build a large plane to compete with Boeing's 747, Boeing argued that there was not enough demand to justify the investment. Zuckerman, Laurence, "Super-Jumbo or Super-Dumbo?" *New York Times*, January 6, 1998:C1.

The effect of entry on price is illustrated by comparing airline shuttle flights on the East and West Coasts. During much of 1995, shuttle flights between Burbank or Los Angeles in southern California and Oakland or San Francisco in northern California cost $69 (and dipped as low as $39) for the roughly 330-mile trip. At the same time, flying the approximately 230-mile trip between New York and Washington, D.C., or the 190-mile trip between New York and Boston cost $147 on Delta or USAir.

Though there are many differences between these two markets that might account for the higher price on the East Coast, one explanation concerns the number of actual and potential competitors. At least five airlines fly between northern and southern California, and there is always the threat of additional entry, which helps to keep the price down in the West. In contrast, at both LaGuardia Airport in New York and National Airport in Washington, the number of landing slots is controlled, effectively guaranteeing that Delta and USAir have a duopoly on that route. As one industry expert observed when asked why Delta and USAir keep their fares higher, "So why should they get in a cat fight when they're both doing well? It isn't like the West Coast shuttle, where anybody can go into that market."[24]

Similarly, European airlines charge much more per mile for domestic flights than do U.S. domestic airlines. Most European countries strictly limit the number of airline companies, whereas entry is relatively easy for many routes in the United States. ■

Summary

1. **Market structures:** Prices, profits, and quantities in a market equilibrium depend on the market's structure. Because profit-maximizing firms set marginal revenue equal to marginal cost, price is above marginal revenue—and hence marginal cost—only if firms face downward-sloping demand curves. In monopoly, oligopoly, and monopolistically competitive markets, firms face downward-sloping demand curves, in contrast to firms in a competitive market. When entry is blocked, as with a monopoly or oligopoly, firms may earn positive profits; however, when entry is free, as in competition or monopolistic competition, profits are driven toward zero. Noncooperative oligopoly and monopolistically competitive firms, in contrast to competitive and monopoly firms, must pay attention to their rivals.

2. **Game theory:** The set of tools that economists use to analyze conflict and cooperation between firms is called game theory. Each oligopolistic or monopolistically competitive firm forms a strategy or battle plan of the actions to compete with other firms. The firms' set of strategies is a Nash equilibrium if, holding the strategies of all other firms constant, no firm can obtain a higher profit by choosing a different strategy.

3. **Cooperative oligopoly models:** If firms successfully collude, they produce the monopoly output and collectively earn the monopoly level of profit. Although their collective profits rise if all firms collude, each individual firm has an incentive to cheat on a cartel arrangement so as to raise its own profit even higher. For cartel prices to remain high, cartel

[24]Cited in McDowell, Edwin, "Shuttles in the Northeast Keep Fares Up," *New York Times*, May 8, 1995:C4.

members must be able to detect and prevent cheating, and noncartel firms must not be able to supply very much output. When antitrust laws or competition policies prevent firms from colluding, firms may try to merge if permitted by law.

4. **Cournot model of noncooperative oligopoly:** If oligopoly firms act independently, the market output and firms' profits lie between the competitive and monopoly levels. In a Cournot model, each oligopoly firm sets its output at the same time. In the Cournot (Nash) equilibrium, each firm produces its best-response output—the output that maximizes its profit—given the output its rival produces. As the number of Cournot firms increases, the Cournot equilibrium price, quantity, and profits approach the price-taking levels.

5. **Stackelberg model of noncooperative behavior:** If one firm, the Stackelberg leader, chooses its output before its rivals, the Stackelberg followers, the leader produces more and earns a higher profit than each identical-cost follower firm. A government may subsidize a domestic oligopoly firm so that it produces the Stackelberg leader quantity, which it sells in an international market.

6. **Comparison of collusive, Cournot, Stackelberg, and competitive equilibria:** Total market output is maximized and price is minimized under competition. For a given number of firms, the Stackelberg equilibrium output exceeds that of the Cournot equilibrium, which exceeds that of the collusive equilibrium (which is the same as a monopoly produces). Correspondingly, the Stackelberg price is less than the Cournot price, which is less than the collusive or monopoly price.

7. **Monopolistic competition:** In monopolistically competitive markets, after all profitable entry occurs, there are few enough firms in the market that each firm faces a downward-sloping demand curve. Consequently, the firms charge prices above marginal cost. These markets are not perfectly competitive because there are relatively few firms—possibly because of high fixed costs or economies of scale that are large relative to market demand—or because the firms sell differentiated products.

Problems

1. Show the payoff matrix and explain the reasoning in the prisoners' dilemma example involving criminals given in footnote 2 in this chapter. (*Note:* The payoffs are negative because they represent years in jail, which is a bad.)

2. Using a graph and words, explain why an individual firm has an incentive to cheat on a cartel.

3. Two firms are planning to sell 10 or 20 units of their goods and face the following payoff matrix:

   A. What is the Nash equilibrium if both firms make their decisions simultaneously? Why? (What strategy does each firm use?)

   B. Suppose that Firm 1 can decide first. What is the outcome? Why?

   C. Suppose that Firm 2 can decide first. What is the outcome? Why?

4. Southwest Airlines' cost-per-available-seat mile is well below that of most of its big rivals and 35% lower than that of the worst performer, USAir.[25]

		Firm 2: 10	Firm 2: 20
Firm 1	10	30 (Firm 1), 30 (Firm 2)	50 (Firm 1), 35 (Firm 2)
Firm 1	20	40 (Firm 1), 60 (Firm 2)	20 (Firm 1), 20 (Firm 2)

[25]"Come Fly the Unfriendly Skies," *The Economist*, 333(7888), November 5, 1994:61–62.

Assuming that Southwest and USAir compete on a route, use a graph to show that their equilibrium quantities differ.

5. Your college is considering renting space in the student union to one or two commercial textbook stores. The rent the college can charge per square foot of space depends on the profit (before rent) of the firms and hence depends on whether there is a monopoly or a duopoly. Which number of stores is best for the college in terms of rent? Which is best for students? Why?

★6. Suppose that competitive firms in two countries sell in a third country. Each country's supply curve is upward sloping. The government in Country 1 is thinking of taxing or subsidizing its firms to increase national profits (not including the subsidy). The government does not expect the government of Country 2 to retaliate. Using a graph, show that the optimal policy is a tax.

★7. Suppose that two Cournot firms, each located in a different country, sell only in a third country's market. Both governments act to help their domestic firm. Who gains and who loses?

8. In the initial Cournot duopoly equilibrium, both firms have constant marginal costs, m, and no fixed costs, and there is a barrier to entry. Show what happens to the best-response function of firms if both firms now face a fixed cost of F.

9. In the monopolistically competitive airline model, what is the equilibrium if firms face no fixed costs?

10. In a monopolistically competitive market, the government applies a specific tax of \$1 per unit of output. What happens to the profit of a typical firm in this market? Does the number of firms in the market change? Why?

11. Does an oligopoly or monopolistically competitive firm have a supply curve? Why or why not? (*Hint*: See the discussion in Chapter 11 of whether a monopoly has a supply curve.)

Math Problems

12. A duopoly faces a market demand of $p = 120 - Q$. Firm 1 has a constant marginal cost of $MC^1 = 20$. Firm 2's constant marginal cost is $MC^2 = 40$. Calculate the output of each firm, market output, and price if there is (a) a collusive equilibrium or (b) a Cournot equilibrium.

13. What is the duopoly Cournot equilibrium if the market demand function is

$$Q = 1{,}000 - 1{,}000p,$$

and each firm's marginal cost is \$0.28 per unit?

14. How would the Cournot equilibrium change in the airline example if United's marginal cost were \$100 and American's were \$200?

15. In the American–United Airlines Cournot equilibrium in the chapter, how would the equilibrium outputs change if American's constant marginal cost, m_A, does not equal United's constant marginal cost, m_U. (*Hint*: Modify Equations 12.5 and 12.6 appropriately. Your equilibrium quantities will be functions of m_A and m_U rather than numbers.)

16. What is the equilibrium in the airline example in the chapter if both American and United Airlines receive a subsidy of \$48 per passenger?

17. The demand facing the duopoly quantity-setting firms is

$$p = 90 - 2q_1 - 2q_2.$$

Firm 1 has no marginal cost of production, but Firm 2 has a marginal cost of \$30. How much does each firm produce if they move simultaneously? What is the equilibrium price?

18. Using calculus, show how the Cournot equilibrium for n firms given in Appendix 12A changes if each firm faces a fixed cost of F as well as a constant marginal cost per unit.

19. Using calculus, determine the Cournot equilibrium for n firms when the market demand function is $p = D(Q)$, which need not be linear, and each firm faces a constant marginal cost, m, and no fixed cost. (*Hint*: Appendix 12A derives the Cournot equilibrium with a linear demand.)

20. Using calculus, determine the Stackelberg equilibrium with one leader firm and two follower firms if the market demand curve is linear and each firm faces a constant marginal cost, m, and no fixed cost. (*Hint*: See Appendix 12B for the Stackelberg model with one follower.)

CHAPTER 13

Pricing

Everything is worth what its purchaser will pay for it.
—Publilius Syrus (1st Century B.C.)

If Coke raises its price, should Pepsi match this price increase? Why does Disneyland charge local residents $22 but out-of-towners $31 for admission? To answer these questions, we need to examine how noncompetitive firms set prices.

In setting prices to maximize profit, firms with market power must take into account the strategies of rivals and the shapes of individual consumers' demand curves. In contrast, a competitive firm, which passively accepts the market price, can ignore other firms' actions and the demand curves of individuals.

We start by examining the price-setting strategies of oligopolistic or monopolistically competitive firms. We find that the noncompetitive equilibrium where firms set prices differs from that where firms set quantities (Chapter 12). The degree of similarity between a firm's product and those of its rivals affects how high these firms set their prices.

Next, we demonstrate that noncompetitive firms can use information about individual consumers' demand curves to increase their profits. Instead of setting a single price, such firms use **nonuniform pricing**: charging consumers different prices for the same product or charging a single customer a price that depends on the number of units the customer buys. By replacing a single price with nonuniform pricing, a noncompetitive firm converts some or all of its customers' consumer surplus into additional profit. Moreover, this firm may sell to more customers, possibly causing welfare (consumer surplus plus producer surplus) to rise.

We examine several types of nonuniform pricing including price discrimination, two-part tariffs, and tie-in sales. The most common form of nonuniform pricing is **price discrimination**, whereby a firm charges consumers different prices for the same good. Many magazines price discriminate by charging college students less for subscriptions than they charge older adults. If a magazine were to start setting a high price for everyone, many college student subscribers—who are sensitive to price increases (have relatively elastic demands)—would cancel their subscriptions. If the magazine were to let everyone buy at the college student price, it would gain few additional subscriptions because most potential older adult subscribers are relatively insensitive to the price, and it would earn less from those older adults who are willing to pay the higher price. Thus, the magazine makes more profit by price discriminating.

Some noncompetitive firms that cannot practically price discriminate use other forms of nonuniform pricing to increase profits. One method is for a firm to charge a *two-part tariff*, whereby a customer pays one fee for the right to buy the good and another price for each unit purchased. Health club members pay an annual fee to join the club and then shell out an additional amount each time they use the facilities.

Another type of nonlinear pricing is a *tie-in sale*, whereby a customer may buy one good only if he or she also agrees to buy another good or service. Vacation package deals may include airfare and a hotel room for a single price. Some restaurants provide only full-course dinners: a single price buys an appetizer, a main dish, and dessert. A firm may sell copiers under the condition that customers agree to buy all future copier service and supplies from it.

In this chapter, we examine seven main topics:

1. **Price setting:** The oligopoly equilibrium in which firms set prices differs from the equilibrium in which firms set quantities and depends on the degree of product differentiation.
2. **Why and how firms price discriminate:** A firm can increase its profit by price discriminating if it has market power, can identify which customers are more price sensitive than others, and can prevent customers who pay low prices from reselling to those who pay high prices.
3. **Perfect price discrimination:** If a monopoly can charge the maximum each customer is willing to pay for each unit of output, the monopoly captures all potential consumer surplus, and the efficient (competitive) level of output is sold.
4. **Quantity discrimination:** Some firms profit by charging different prices for large purchases than for small ones, which is a form of price discrimination.
5. **Multimarket price discrimination:** Firms that cannot perfectly price discriminate may charge a group of consumers with relatively elastic demands a lower price than other groups of consumers.
6. **Two-part tariffs:** By charging consumers a fee for the right to buy any number of units and a price per unit, firms earn higher profits than they do by charging a single price per unit.
7. **Tie-in sales:** By requiring a customer to buy a second good or service in order to buy a good, firms make higher profits than they do by selling the goods separately.

13.1 PRICE SETTING

In Chapter 12, we examined how oligopolistic and monopolistically competitive firms set quantities to try to maximize their profits. However, many such firms set prices instead of quantities and allow consumers to decide how much to buy. The market equilibrium is different if firms set prices rather than quantities.

In monopolistic and competitive markets, the issue of whether firms set quantities or prices does not arise. Competitive firms have no choice: They cannot affect price and hence can choose only quantity (Chapter 8). The monopoly equilibrium is the same whether the monopoly sets price or quantity (Chapter 11).

Cournot's original model of oligopoly describes only quantity-setting behavior. To study price-setting behavior, we must use a different model. For years after Cournot presented his model of oligopoly in 1838, there was no alternative oligopoly model. To say that Cournot's model was ahead of its time is to put it mildly. Apparently, no one paid any attention to it for nearly half a century. Finally, in 1883, Joseph Bertrand published a critique of Cournot's work. Bertrand argued that oligopolies set prices, and then consumers decide how many units to buy. The resulting Nash equilibrium is called a **Bertrand equilibrium**: a set of prices such that no firm can obtain a higher profit by choosing a different price if the other firms continue to charge these prices.

We now show that the price and quantity in a Bertrand equilibrium are different from those in a Cournot equilibrium. We also show that a Bertrand equilibrium depends on whether firms are producing identical or differentiated products.

Bertrand Equilibrium with Identical Products

We start by examining a price-setting oligopoly in which firms have identical costs and produce identical goods. The resulting Bertrand equilibrium price equals the marginal cost, as in the price taking equilibrium. To show this result, we use best-response curves to determine the Bertrand equilibrium, as we did in the Cournot model.

Best-Response Curves. Suppose that each of the two price-setting oligopoly firms in a market produce identical products and face a constant marginal and average cost of \$5 per unit. What is Firm 1's best response—what price should it set—if Firm 2 sets a price of p_2 = \$10? If Firm 1 charges more than \$10, it makes no sales because consumers will buy from Firm 2. Firm 1 makes a profit of \$5 on each unit it sells if it also charges \$10 per unit. If the market demand is 200 units and both firms charge the same price, we'd expect Firm 1 to make half the sales, so its profit is \$500.

Suppose, however, that Firm 1 slightly undercuts its rival's price by charging \$9.99. Because the products are identical, Firm 1 captures the entire market. Firm 1 makes a profit of \$4.99 per unit and a total profit of \$998. Thus, Firm 1's profit is higher if it slightly undercuts its rival's price. By similar reasoning, if Firm 2 charges \$8, Firm 1 also charges slightly less than Firm 2.

Now suppose that Firm 2 charges p_2 = \$5. If Firm 1 charges more than \$5, it makes no sales. The firms split the market and make zero profit if Firm 1 charges \$5. If Firm 1 undercuts its rival, it captures the entire market, but it makes a loss on each unit. Thus, Firm 1 will undercut only if its rival's price is higher than Firm 1's marginal and average cost of \$5. By similar reasoning, if Firm 2 charges less than \$5, Firm 1 chooses not to produce.

Figure 13.1 shows that Firm 1's best response is to produce nothing if Firm 2 charges less than \$5. Firm 1's best response is \$5 if Firm 2 charges \$5. If Firm 2 charges prices above \$5, Firm 1's best response is to undercut Firm 2's price slightly. Above \$5, Firm 1's best-response curve is above the 45° line by the smallest amount possible. (The distance of the best-response curve from the 45° line is exaggerated in the figure for clarity.) By the same reasoning, Firm 2's best-response curve starts at \$5 and lies slightly below the 45° line.

The two best-response functions intersect only at *e*, where each firm charges \$5. It does not pay for either firm to change its price as long as the other charges \$5, so *e* is a Nash or Bertrand equilibrium. In this equilibrium, each firm makes zero profit. Thus, *the Bertrand equilibrium when firms produce identical products is the same as the price-taking, competitive equilibrium.*

Bertrand Versus Cournot. The Bertrand equilibrium differs substantially from the Cournot equilibrium. We can calculate the Cournot equilibrium price for firms with

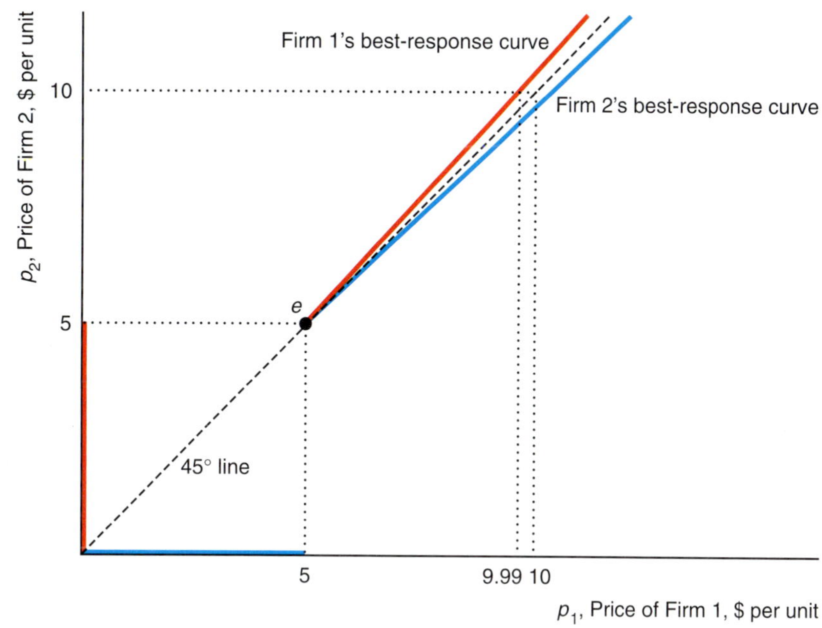

Figure 13.1 Bertrand Equilibrium with Identical Products. With identical products and constant marginal and average costs of \$5, Firm 1's best-response curve starts at \$5 and then lies slightly above the 45° line. That is, Firm 1 undercuts its rival's price as long as its price remains above \$5. The best-response curves intersect at *e*, the Bertrand or Nash equilibrium, where both firms charge \$5.

constant marginal costs of \$5 per unit by rearranging Equation 12.8:

$$p = \frac{MC}{1 + \frac{1}{n\varepsilon}} = \frac{\$5}{1 + \frac{1}{n\varepsilon}}, \qquad (13.1)$$

where n is the number of firms and ε is the market demand elasticity. If the market demand elasticity is $\varepsilon = -1$ and $n = 2$, the Cournot equilibrium price is $\$5/(1 - \frac{1}{2}) = \$10$, which is double the Bertrand equilibrium price.

When firms produce identical products and have a constant marginal cost, the Cournot model is more plausible than the Bertrand. The Bertrand model—unlike the Cournot model—appears inconsistent with real oligopoly markets in at least two ways.

First, the Bertrand model's "competitive" equilibrium price is implausible. If there is only a small number of firms, why would they compete so vigorously that they would make no profit? In contrast, the Cournot equilibrium price with a small number of firms lies between the competitive price and the monopoly price. Because oligopolies typically charge a higher price than competitive firms, the Cournot equilibrium is more plausible.

Second, the Bertrand equilibrium price, which depends only on cost, is insensitive to demand conditions and the number of firms. In contrast, the Cournot equilibrium price, Equation 13.1, depends on the number of firms and demand and cost conditions. In the example above, if the number of firms rises from two to three, the Cournot price falls from \$10 to $\$5/(1 - \frac{1}{3}) = \$7.50$, but the Bertrand equilibrium price remains \$5. Again, the Cournot model is more plausible because we usually observe market price changing with the number of firms and demand conditions—not just with changes in costs.

As a result, it seems more likely that, when firms' products are identical, firms set quantities rather than prices. For these reasons, economists are much more likely to use the Cournot model than the Bertrand model to study markets in which firms produce identical goods.

Bertrand Equilibrium with Differentiated Products

If most markets were characterized by firms producing homogeneous goods, the Bertrand model probably would have been forgotten. Markets with differentiated goods—automobiles, stereos, computers, toothpastes, and spaghetti sauces—however, are extremely common, as is price setting by firms. In such markets, the Bertrand equilibrium is plausible, and the two "problems" of the homogeneous-goods model disappear: Firms set prices above marginal cost, and prices are sensitive to demand conditions.

Indeed, many economists believe that price-setting models are more plausible than quantity-setting models when goods are differentiated. If products are differentiated and firms set prices, then consumers determine quantities. In contrast, if firms set quantities, it is not clear how the prices of the differentiated goods are determined in the market.

We illustrate a Bertrand equilibrium with the differentiated products in the cola market. We first use best-response curves in a figure to solve for the equilibrium. We then use math to illustrate the properties of the equilibrium.

Graphical Solution. Coke and Pepsi produce similar but not identical products; many consumers prefer one of these products to the other. If the price of Pepsi were to fall slightly relative to that of Coke, some consumers who prefer Coke to Pepsi would not switch. Thus, neither firm has to match exactly a price cut by its rival. As a result, neither firm's best-response curve in Figure 13.2 lies along a 45° line through the origin.[1]

The Bertrand best-response curves have different slopes than the Cournot best-response curves in Figure 12.3. The Cournot curves—which plot relationships

[1]The figure is based on estimates from Gasmi, Laffont, and Vuong (1992) under the assumption that the firms are engaged in a Bertrand price-setting game. Their estimated model allows the firms to set both prices and advertising. In the following analysis, we assume that the firms' advertising is held constant. The Coke equations are the authors' estimates (with slight rounding to get whole numbers). The Pepsi equations are rescaled so that the equilibrium prices of Coke and Pepsi are equal. Quantities are in tens of millions of cases (a case consists of 24 twelve-ounce cans) per quarter, and prices (to retailers) and costs are in real 1982 dollars per 10 cases.

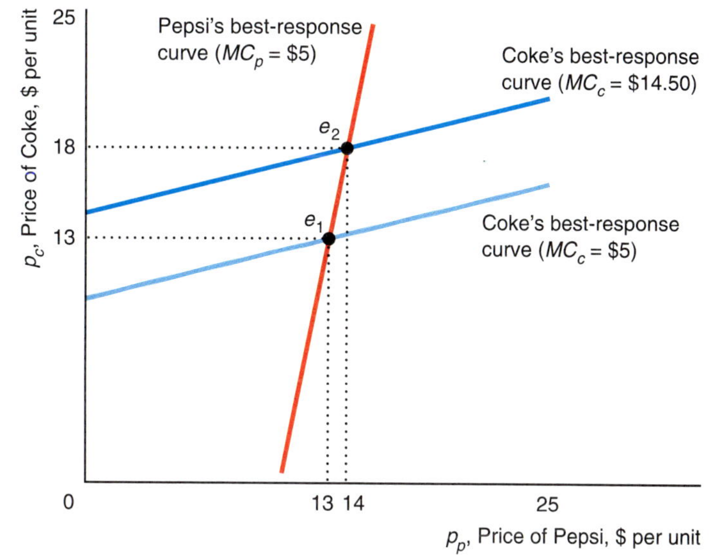

Figure 13.2 Bertrand Equilibrium with Differentiated Products. If both firms have a constant marginal cost of \$5, the best-response curves of Coke and Pepsi intersect at e_1, where each sets a price of \$13 per unit. If Coke's marginal cost rises to \$14.50, its best-response function shifts upward. In the new equilibrium, e_2, Coke charges a higher price, \$18, than does Pepsi, \$14.

between quantities—slope downward, showing that a firm produces less, the more its rival produces. In Figure 13.2, the Bertrand best-response curves—which plot relationships between prices—slope upward, indicating that a firm charges a higher price, the higher the price its rival charges.

If both Pepsi and Coke have a constant marginal cost of $MC_p = MC_c = \$5$, the Bertrand equilibrium, e_1 in Figure 13.2, occurs where the price of each firm is \$13 per unit (10 cases). In this Nash equilibrium, each firm sets its best-response price *given the price the other firm is charging*. Neither firm wants to change its price because neither firm can increase its profit by so doing.

Mathematical Solution. We can use math to determine this cola market equilibrium. First we determine the best-response functions facing each firm. Then we equate the best-response functions to determine the equilibrium prices for the two firms.

Coke's best-response function tells us what price Coke charges—the price that maximizes its profit—as a function of the price Pepsi charges. We use the demand curve facing Coke to derive the best-response function.

The reason Coke's price depends on Pepsi's price is that the quantity of Coke demanded, q_c, depends on the price of Coke, p_c, and the price of Pepsi, p_p. Coke's demand curve is

$$q_c = 58 - 4p_c + 2p_p. \tag{13.2}$$

Equation 13.2 shows that, if Coke raises its price by Δp_c while the price of Pepsi remains constant, the quantity Coke sells falls by $\Delta q_c = -4\Delta p_c$. Thus, the change in quantity for every dollar change in price is $\Delta q_c/\Delta p_c = -4$, so a \$1 per unit increase in the price of Coke causes the quantity of Coke demanded to fall by four units. Similarly, the demand for Coke rises by two units if the price of Pepsi rises by a dollar, while the price of Coke remains constant: $\Delta q_c/\Delta p_p = 2$.

If Coke faces a constant marginal and average cost of m per unit, its profit is

$$\pi_c = p_c q_c - m q_c = (p_c - m)q_c, \tag{13.3}$$

where $p_c q_c$ is Coke's revenue, mq_c is its cost, and $p_c - m$ is its profit per unit.

What happens to its profit if Coke raises its price by Δp_c? If Coke could sell as many units as it did at the original price, Coke's revenue would increase by $\Delta p \times q_c$. Unfortunately for Coke, as it raises its price, the demand for its product falls by $\Delta q_c = -4\Delta p_c$. Because its profit per unit was $p_c - m$, Coke loses $(p_c - m)\Delta q_c$ by selling Δq_c fewer units. As a result, the change in its profit as the price rises is

$$\Delta \pi_c = (\Delta p_c \times q_c) + (p_c - m)\Delta q_c. \tag{13.4}$$

Dividing both sides of Equation 13.4 by Δp_c, we find that the change in Coke's profit for every dollar it raises its price is

$$\frac{\Delta \pi_c}{\Delta p_c} = q_c + (p_c - m)\frac{\Delta q_c}{\Delta p_c},$$

where $\Delta q_c/\Delta p_c$ tells us how the quantity demanded changes as the price of Coke rises.[2] From our analysis of Coke's demand curve, we know that $\Delta q_c/\Delta p_c = -4$, so

$$\frac{\Delta \pi_c}{\Delta p_c} = q_c - 4(p_c - m).$$

What price maximizes Coke's profit? Coke should raise its price if doing so raises its profit ($\Delta \pi_c/\Delta p_c > 0$). Similarly, Coke should lower its price if doing so raises its profit ($\Delta \pi_c/\Delta p_c < 0$). Thus, Coke's profit is maximized at the price where a small change in its price does not affect its profit:

$$\frac{\Delta \pi_c}{\Delta p_c} = q_c - 4(p_c - m) = 0. \tag{13.5}$$

---

[2]We can derive a similar expression by using calculus. The profit function in Equation 13.3 is

$$\pi_c = (p_c - m)q_c(p_c, p_m),$$

where $q_c(p_c, p_p)$ shows that the quantity of Coke demanded is a function of the price of Coke and Pepsi. Differentiating the profit function, Equation 13.2, with respect to the price of Coke, holding the price of Pepsi constant, we find that

$$\partial \pi_c/\partial p_c = q_c + (p_c - m)\partial q_c/\partial p_c.$$

Replacing q_c in Equation 13.5 with the demand function from Equation 13.2 and rearranging terms, we find that the price that maximizes Coke's profit is

$$p_c = 7.25 + 0.25p_p + 0.5m. \tag{13.6}$$

Coke's best-response curve in Figure 13.2 is a plot of its best-response function in Equation 13.6. According to Equation 13.6, Coke's best-response price is 25¢ higher for every extra dollar that Pepsi charges and 50¢ higher for every extra dollar of its marginal cost.

Coke's average and marginal cost of production is \$5 per unit. Thus, Coke's best-response function is

$$p_c = 9.75 + 0.25p_p. \tag{13.7}$$

If p_p = \$13, then Coke's best response is to set p_c = \$13. Similarly, if p_p = \$9, then p_c = \$12 maximizes Coke's profit. Coke's lower best-response curve in Figure 13.2 is a plot of Equation 13.7. Using the same approach, we find that Pepsi's best-response function is

$$p_p = 10.4 + 0.2p_c. \tag{13.8}$$

The intersection of these best-response functions determines the Nash equilibrium in the figure. If we substitute Pepsi's best-response function, Equation 13.8, for p_p in Coke's best-response function, Equation 13.7, we find that

$$p_c = 9.75 + 0.25(10.4 + 0.2p_c).$$

Solving this equation for p_c, we learn that the equilibrium price of Coke is \$13. Substituting p_c = \$13 into Equation 13.8, we discover that the equilibrium price of Pepsi is also \$13.

SOLVED PROBLEM 13.1

What happens to the equilibrium prices if Coke's marginal cost rises from MC_c = \$5 per unit to \$14.50 per unit and Pepsi's marginal cost remains constant at \$5?

Answer

1. *Describe what happens to the best-response functions.* Pepsi's best-response function, Equation 13.8, is unaffected by a change in Coke's marginal cost. Using Equation 13.6, we see that Coke's new best-response function is

$$p_c = 7.25 + 0.25p_p + 0.5m = 14.5 + 0.25p_p. \tag{13.9}$$

The new best-response function lies above the original one in Figure 13.2. This upward shift in the best-response curve shows that at any given price charged by Pepsi, Coke charges a higher price because its marginal cost has risen.

2. *Show how the equilibrium shifts*: The original equilibrium is e_1, where $p_c = p_p$ = \$13. We solve for the new equilibrium by substituting Pepsi's best-response function, Equation 13.8, for p_p in Coke's best-response function, Equation 13.9:

$$p_c = 14.5 + 0.25(10.4 + 0.2p_c).$$

Solving this equation for p_c, we find that the new equilibrium price of Coke is \$18. Setting p_c = \$18 in Pepsi's best-response function, Equation 13.8, we learn that the new equilibrium price of Pepsi is \$14. Thus, the increase in Coke's marginal cost causes not only its own equilibrium price but also that of Pepsi to rise. The new equilibrium e_2 lies substantially above and slightly to the right of the original equilibrium: The price of Coke rises by more than the price of Pepsi. ■

Differentiating Products

I couldn't believe no one had addressed the mule market.

—Sharon Doherty, president of Vellus Products, on discovering a market niche for mule shampoo and conditioners

The Bertrand model demonstrates that firms can profit from selling differentiated products. If products are homogeneous, Bertrand firms cannot charge above marginal cost. With differentiated products, they can charge prices above marginal cost and make larger profits. Firms aggressively differentiate their products to raise profits. By such differentiation, they affect the average price in a market and welfare.

Economists view products as differentiated if consumers *believe* that they differ. Although few consumers can reliably distinguish Coke from Pepsi in blind taste tests, many consumers strongly prefer buying one product over the other. Conversely, if consumers view products that differ chemically or physically to be identical, the products are homogeneous for the purposes of economic analysis. A firm can differentiate its product from its rivals' by changing a product characteristic consumers view as important (taste or appearance), or the firm can convince consumers that its product differs through advertising and other means, even if the products do not differ physically.

APPLICATION

Toothbrushes

Firms constantly add features to their products to differentiate them. Oral-B toothbrushes now have blue bristles that fade to white when it's time to replace the toothbrush, as well as ribbed thumb grips to prevent the brushes from slipping when wet. Johnson & Johnson's pink Good & Plenty Color Youth Glow model has a luminescent grip; Aquafresh Flex features a built-in shock absorber and special handle for "brushing control"; and the Radius toothbrush offers a left-hand grip. For toddlers, some toothbrushes sing, others rattle, and some smell like bananas. To accommodate this proliferation of toothbrushes, the average retail store's toothbrush section is now four feet wide, up 20% from three years ago.[3] ■

Product Differentiation and Price. Whether the difference is a nonslip handle or a sneaker pump, if a firm can convince some customers that its brand is superior in some fashion, it can charge a higher price than it could if it sold plain or generic products. Clorox and Bayer are just two examples of firms that charge higher prices for products (bleach and aspirin, respectively) that have an active ingredient that is chemically identical to that of generic brands.

The reason differentiation allows a firm to charge a higher price is that the residual demand curve facing the firm (the market demand minus the quantity supplied by rivals at each price) becomes less elastic. That is, a given decrease in the price charged by a rival lowers the demand for this firm's product by *less*, the less substitutable are the two goods. If consumers view the goods as perfect substitutes, a small drop in the rival's price causes this firm to lose all its sales. If some consumers become convinced that this firm's product is superior in some way, they do not switch to the rival if the rival lowers its price slightly.

APPLICATION

Designer Glasses

Plain drinking glasses are manufactured by many firms and sell for about the same price, which is not substantially above marginal cost. Ritenzhoff, a big German industrial glassmaker, commissioned fashionable designers to decorate milk glasses. These designer glasses are distributed in 20 countries and retail at DM35 ($25) a pair—10 times more than plain glasses—although they cost only pennies more to make. They sell for a premium because some customers strongly prefer them and will pay extra for decorations.[4] ■

---

[3]Carton, Barbara, "Dental Persuasion: Fear of Droopy Gums Starts a Brush Rush," *Wall Street Journal*, April 12, 1996:A1, A10. I'm grateful to one of my students who showed me this article. She said she felt so gullible after reading it that she immediately replaced her name-brand toothbrush with the cheapest generic brush she could find.

[4]"The White Stuff," *The Economist*, 337(7943), December 2, 1995:71.

Product Differentiation and Welfare. Thus, prices are likely to be higher when products are differentiated than when they're identical, all else the same. We also know that welfare falls as the gap between price and marginal cost rises. Does it follow that differentiating products lowers welfare? Not necessarily. Although differentiation leads to higher prices, which harm consumers, differentiation is desirable in its own right. Consumers value having a choice, and some may greatly prefer a new brand to existing ones.

One way to illustrate the importance of this second effect is to consider what the value is of introducing a new, differentiated product. This value reflects how much extra income consumers would require to be as well off without the good as with it.

APPLICATION

Welfare Gain from New Cereals

Jerry Hausman (1994) calculated the consumer surplus from General Mills' introducing Apple-Cinnamon Cheerios at $67 million per year, or 26.8¢ per person. Offsetting this gain is the increase in the prices of other cereals that General Mills was already selling, including regular Cheerios and Honey-Nut Cheerios. By introducing the new product, General Mills found it profitable to raise the price of the existing brands slightly because some of their lost sales would go to Apple-Cinnamon Cheerios. Hausman calculated that the profit-maximizing increase in the price of Honey-Nut Cheerios was 8¢ a box and that of Cheerios was 1¢. (Honey-Nut Cheerios is a closer substitute to Apple-Cinnamon Cheerios than regular Cheerios is.) Overall, however, welfare increased because the consumer surplus gains from the new brand outweighs the loss from higher prices.[5] ■

13.2 WHY AND HOW FIRMS PRICE DISCRIMINATE

Until now, we've examined how a firm sets its price if it charges all its customers the same price. Many oligopolies, monopolistically competitive firms, and monopolies, however, increase their profits by charging *nonuniform prices*, which vary across customers. We start by studying the most common form of nonuniform pricing: price discrimination.

Why Price Discrimination Pays

For almost any good or service, some consumers are willing to pay more than others. A firm that sets a single price faces a trade-off between charging consumers who

[5]Hausman also concluded that the CPI for cereal overstates inflation by about 20% because the Consumer Price Index (Chapter 5) fails to take the benefit of new brands into account.

really want the good as much as they are willing to pay and charging a low enough price that the firm doesn't lose sales to less enthusiastic customers. As a result, the firm usually sets an intermediate price. A price-discriminating firm that varies its prices across customers avoids this trade-off.

A firm earns a higher profit from price discrimination than from uniform pricing for two reasons. First, a price-discriminating firm charges a higher price to customers who are willing to pay more than the uniform price, capturing some or all of their consumer surplus—the difference between what a good is worth to a consumer and what the consumer paid—under uniform pricing. Second, a price-discriminating firm sells to some people who were not willing to pay as much as the uniform price.

We use a pair of extreme examples to illustrate the two benefits of price discrimination to firms—capturing more of the consumer surplus and selling to more customers. These examples are extreme in the sense that the firm sets a uniform price at the price the most enthusiastic consumers are willing to pay or at the price the least enthusiastic consumers are willing to pay, rather than at an intermediate level.

Suppose that the only movie theater in town has two types of patrons: college students and senior citizens. The college student will see the Saturday night movie if the price is $10 or less, and the senior citizens will attend if the price is $5 or less. For simplicity, we assume that there is no cost in showing the movie, so profit is the same as revenue. In particular, the theater is large enough to hold all potential customers, so the marginal cost of admitting one more customer is zero. Table 13.1 shows how pricing affects the theater's profit.

Table 13.1 A Theater's Profit Based on the Pricing Method Used

a) No Extra Customers from Price Discrimination

Pricing	Profit from 10 College Students	Profit from 20 Senior Citizens	Total Profit
Uniform, $5	$50	$100	$150
Uniform, $10	$100	$0	$100
Price discrimination*	$100	$100	$200

b) Extra Customers from Price Discrimination

Pricing	Profit from 10 College Students	Profit from 5 Senior Citizens	Total Profit
Uniform, $5	$50	$25	$75
Uniform, $10	$100	$0	$100
Price discrimination*	$100	$25	$125

*The theater price discriminates by charging college students $10 and senior citizens $5.
Notes: The college students go to the theater if they are charged no more than $10. The senior citizens are willing to pay up to $5. The theater's marginal cost for an extra customer is zero.

In panel a, there are 10 college students and 20 senior citizens. If the theater charges everyone \$5, its profit is \$150 = \$5 × (10 college students + 20 senior citizens). If it charges \$10, the senior citizens do not go to the movie, so the theater makes only \$100. Thus, if the theater is going to charge everyone the same price, it maximizes its profit by setting the price at \$5. Charging less than \$5 makes no sense because the same number of people go to the movie as go when \$5 is charged. Charging between \$5 and \$10 is less profitable than charging \$10 because no extra seniors go and the college students are willing to pay \$10. Charging more than \$10 results in no customers.

At a price of \$5, the seniors have no consumer surplus: They pay exactly what seeing the movie is worth to them. Seeing the movie is worth \$10 to the college students, but they have to pay only \$5, so each has a consumer surplus of \$5, and their total consumer surplus is \$50.

If the theater can price discriminate by charging senior citizens \$5 and college students \$10, its profit increases to \$200. Its profit rises because the theater makes as much from the seniors as before but gets an extra \$50 from the college students. By price discriminating, the theater sells the same number of seats but makes more money from the college students, capturing all the consumer surplus they had under uniform pricing. Neither group of customers has any consumer surplus if the theater price discriminates.

In panel b, there are 10 college students and 5 senior citizens. If the theater must charge a single price, it charges \$10. Only college students see the movie, so the theater's profit is \$100. (If it charges \$5, both students and seniors go to the theater, but its profit is only \$75.) If the theater can price discriminate and charge seniors \$5 and college students \$10, its profit increases to \$125. Here the gain from price discrimination comes from selling extra tickets to seniors (not from making more money on the same number of tickets, as in panel a). The theater earns as much from the students as before and makes more from the seniors, and neither group enjoys consumer surplus. These examples illustrate that firms can make a higher profit by price discriminating either by charging some existing customers more or by selling extra units.

APPLICATION

Disneyland Prices

Disneyland, in southern California, is a well-run operation that rarely misses a trick when it comes to increasing profits. (Indeed, Disneyland mints money: When you enter the park, you can exchange U.S. currency for Disney dollars, which can be spent only in the park.)[6]

[6]Studies show that it costs an average of \$350,000 to raise a child from cradle through college. Parents can cut that total in half, however: They don't *have* to take their kids to Disneyland.

In 1994, Disneyland charged most adults \$31 to enter the park but charged southern Californians only \$22.[7] This policy makes sense if visitors from afar are willing to pay more than locals and if Disneyland can prevent locals from selling discount tickets to nonlocals. Imagine a Midwesterner who's never been to Disneyland before and wants to visit. Travel accounts for most of the cost of the trip, so an extra \$9 for entrance to Disneyland makes little percentage difference in the total cost of a visit and hence doesn't greatly affect that person's decision whether or not to go. In contrast, for a local who has gone to Disneyland many times and for whom the entrance price is a larger share of the cost of the visit, a slightly higher price might prevent a visit.

Charging both groups the same price is not in Disney's best interest. If Disney were to charge the higher price to everyone, many locals would stay away. If Disney were to use the lower price for everyone, it would be charging nonresidents much less than they are willing to pay.

By setting different prices for the two groups, Disney increases its profit if it can prevent the locals from selling discount tickets to others. Disney prevents resales by checking a purchaser's driver's license and requiring that the ticket be used for same-day entrance. ■

Who Can Price Discriminate

Not all firms can price discriminate. For a firm to price discriminate successfully, three conditions must be met.

First, a firm must have *market power*; otherwise, it cannot charge any consumer more than the competitive price. A monopoly, an oligopoly firm, a monopolistically competitive firm, or a cartel may be able to price discriminate. A competitive firm cannot price discriminate.

Second, consumers must *differ* in their sensitivity to price (demand elasticities), and a firm must be able to *identify* how consumers differ in this sensitivity. The

---

[7]Similarly, Fordham University in New York charges commuting first-year students a \$4,000 lower tuition than those from out of the metropolitan area. Arenson, Karen W., "Fordham University to Give Tuition Discounts to Freshmen Who Commute," *New York Times*, October 22, 1997:A18.

movie theater knows that college students and senior citizens differ in their willingness to pay for a ticket, and Disneyland knows that tourists and natives differ in their willingness to pay for admission. In both cases, the firms can identify members of these two groups by using drivers licenses or other forms of identification. Similarly, if a firm knows that each individual's demand curve slopes downward, it may charge each customer a higher price for the first unit of a good than for subsequent units.

Third, a firm must be able to *prevent or limit resales* to higher-price-paying customers by customers whom the firm charges relatively low prices. Price discrimination doesn't work if resales are easy because the firm would be able to make only low-price sales. A movie theater can charge different prices because senior citizens—who enter the theater as soon as they buy the ticket—do not have time to resell the ticket.

Except for competitive firms, the first two conditions—market power and ability to identify groups with different price sensitivities—frequently hold. Usually, the biggest obstacle to price discrimination is a firm's inability to prevent resales. In some markets, however, resales are inherently difficult or impossible, firms can take actions that prevent resales, or government actions or laws prevent resales.

Preventing Resales

Resales are difficult or impossible for most *services* and when *transaction costs are high*. If a plumber charges you less than your neighbor for clearing a pipe, you cannot make a deal with your neighbor to resell this service. The higher the transaction costs a consumer must incur to resell a good, the less likely that resales will occur. Suppose that you are able to buy a jar of pickles for $1 less than the usual price. Could you practically find and sell this jar to someone else, or would the transaction costs be prohibitive? The more valuable a product or the more widely consumed it is, the more likely it is that transaction costs are low enough that resales occur.

Some firms act to raise transaction costs or otherwise make resales difficult. If your college requires that someone with a student ticket must show a student identification card with a picture on it before being admitted to a sporting event, you'll find it difficult to resell your low-price tickets to nonstudents, who must pay higher prices. When students at some universities buy Apple or IBM computers at lower-than-usual prices, they must sign a *contract* that forbids them to resell the computer.

Similarly, a firm can prevent resales by *vertically integrating*: participating in more than one successive stage of the production and distribution chain for a good or service. Alcoa, the former aluminum monopoly, wanted to sell aluminum ingots to producers of aluminum wire at a lower price than was set for producers of aluminum aircraft parts. If Alcoa did so, however, the wire producers could easily resell their ingots. By starting its own wire production firm, Alcoa prevented such resales and was able to charge high prices to firms that manufactured aircraft parts (Perry 1980).

Governments frequently aid price discrimination by preventing resales. State and federal governments require that milk producers—under penalty of law—price discriminate by selling milk at a higher price for fresh use than for processing (cheese, ice cream) and forbid resales. Government *tariffs* (taxes on imports) limit resales by making it expensive to buy goods in a low-price country and resell them in a high-price country. In some cases, laws prevent such reselling explicitly. Under U.S. trade laws, certain brand-name perfumes may not be sold in the United States except by their manufacturers.

Not All Price Differences Are Price Discrimination

Not every seller who charges consumers different prices is price discriminating. Hotels charge newlyweds more for bridal suites. Is that price discrimination? Some hotel managers say no. They contend that honeymooners, unlike other customers, always steal mementos, so the price differential reflects an actual cost differential.

The price for all issues of *Time* magazine for a year is \$153.40 if you buy it at the newsstand, \$59.80 for a standard subscription, and \$29.97 for a college student subscription. The difference between the newsstand cost and the standard subscription cost reflects, at least in part, the higher cost of selling at a newsstand rather than mailing the magazine directly to customers, so this price difference doesn't reflect pure price discrimination. The price difference between the standard subscription rate and the college student rate reflects pure price discrimination because the two subscriptions are identical other than in price.

Types of Price Discrimination

There are three main types of price discrimination. With **perfect price discrimination**—also called *first-degree price discrimination*—the firm sells each unit at the maximum amount any customer is willing to pay for it, so prices differ across customers and a given customer may pay more for some units than for others.

With **quantity discrimination**—a form of *second-degree price discrimination*—the firm charges a different price for large quantities than for small quantities but all customers who buy a given quantity pay the same price. With **multimarket price discrimination** (*third-degree price discrimination*), the firm charges different groups of customers different prices, but it charges a given customer the same price for every unit of output sold. Typically, not all customers pay different prices—the firm sets different prices only for a few groups of customers. Because this last type of discrimination is the most common, the phrase *price discrimination* is often used to mean *multimarket price discrimination*.

In addition to price discriminating, many firm use other, more complicated types of nonuniform pricing. Later in this chapter, we examine two other frequently used nonuniform pricing methods—two-part tariffs and tie-in sales—that are similar to quantity discrimination.

13.3 PERFECT PRICE DISCRIMINATION

If a firm with market power knows exactly how much each customer is willing to pay for each unit of its good and it can prevent resales, the firm charges each person his or her **reservation price**: the maximum amount a person would be willing to pay for a unit of output. Such an all-knowing firm *perfectly price discriminates*. By selling each unit of its output to the customer who values it the most at the maximum price that person is willing to pay, the perfectly price-discriminating monopoly captures all possible consumer surplus. For example, the managers of the Suez Canal set tolls on an individual basis, taking into account many factors such as weather and each ship's alternative routes.[8]

We first show how a firm uses its information about consumers to perfectly price discriminate. We then compare the perfectly price-discriminating monopoly to competition and single-price monopoly. By showing that the same quantity is produced as would be produced by a competitive market and that the last unit of output sells for the marginal cost, we demonstrate that perfect price discrimination is efficient. We then illustrate how the perfect-price-discrimination equilibrium differs from single-price monopoly by using the Tagamet application from Chapter 12. Finally, we discuss how firms obtain the information they need to perfectly price discriminate.

How a Firm Perfectly Price Discriminates

Suppose a monopoly has market power, can prevent resales, and has enough information to perfectly price discriminate. The monopoly sells each unit at its reservation price, which is the height of the demand curve: the maximum price consumers will pay for a given amount of output.

Figure 13.3 illustrates how this perfectly price-discriminating firm maximizes its profit (see Appendix 13A for a mathematical treatment). The figure shows that the first customer is willing to pay \$6 for a unit, the next is willing to pay \$5, and so forth. This perfectly price-discriminating firm sells its first unit of output for \$6. Having sold the first unit, the firm can get at most \$5 for its second unit. The firm must drop its price by \$1 for each successive unit it sells.

A perfectly price-discriminating monopoly's marginal revenue is the same as its price. As the figure shows, the firm's marginal revenue is MR_1 = \$6 on the first unit, MR_2 = \$5 on the second unit, and MR_3 = \$4 on the third unit. As a result, *the firm's marginal revenue curve is its demand curve.*

This firm has a constant marginal cost of \$4 per unit. It pays for the firm to produce the first unit because the firm sells that unit for \$6, so its marginal revenue exceeds its marginal cost by \$2. Similarly, the firm certainly wants to sell the second unit for \$5, which also exceeds its marginal cost. The firm breaks even when it sells the third unit for \$4. The firm is unwilling to sell more than three units because its marginal cost would exceed its marginal revenue on all successive units. Thus, like any profit-maximizing firm, a perfectly price-discriminating firm produces at point *e*, where its marginal revenue curve intersects its marginal cost curve.

This perfectly price-discriminating firm earns revenues of $MR_1 + MR_2 + MR_3$ = \$6 + \$5 + \$4 = \$15, which is the area under its marginal revenue curve up to the number of units, 3, it sells. If the firm has no fixed cost, its cost of producing three units is \$12 = \$4 × 3, so its profit is \$3.

---

[8]Jehl, Douglas, "Trying to Revive a Canal That Is Out of the Loop," *New York Times*, April 30, 1997:A4.

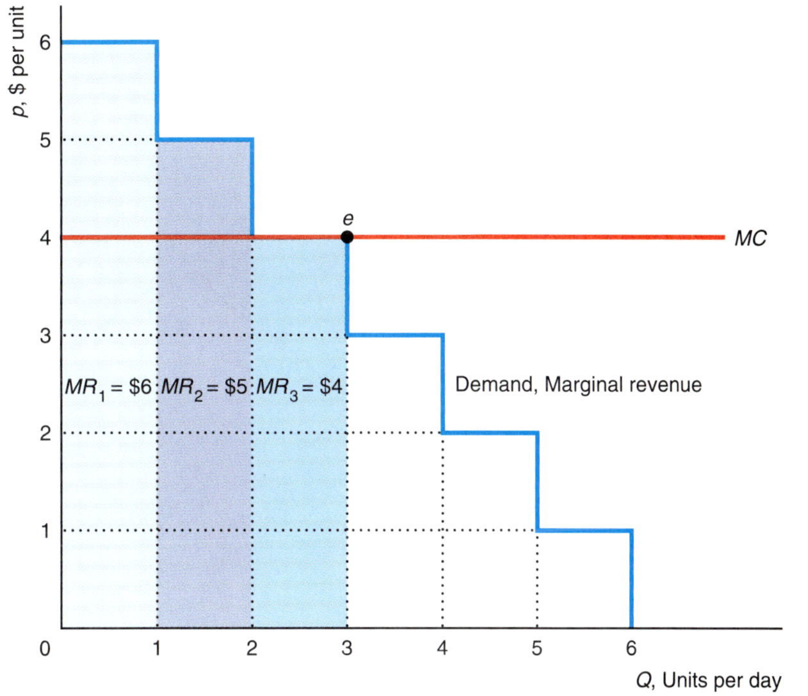

Figure 13.3 Perfect Price Discrimination. The monopoly can charge \$6 for the first unit, \$5 for the second, and \$4 for the third, as the demand curve shows. Its marginal revenue is MR_1 = \$6 for the first unit, MR_2 = \$5 for the second unit, and MR_3 = \$4 for the third unit. Thus, the demand curve is also the marginal revenue curve. Because the firm's marginal and average cost is \$4 per unit, it is unwilling to sell at a price below \$4, so it sells three units, point *e*, and breaks even on the last unit.

Perfect Price Discrimination Is Efficient but Hurts Consumers

A perfect-price-discrimination equilibrium is efficient and maximizes total welfare, where welfare is defined as the sum of consumer surplus and producer surplus. As such, this equilibrium has more in common with a competitive equilibrium than with a single-price-monopoly equilibrium.

If the market in Figure 13.4 is competitive, the intersection of the demand curve and the marginal cost curve, *MC*, determines the competitive equilibrium at e_c, where price is p_c and quantity is Q_c. Consumer surplus is $A + B + C$, producer surplus is $D + E$, and there is no deadweight loss. The market is efficient because the price, p_c, equals the marginal cost, MC_c.

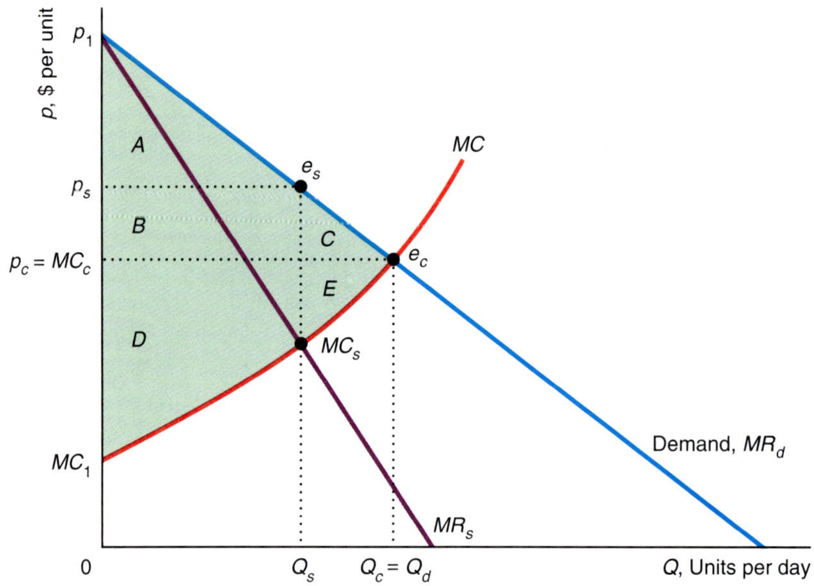

	Competition	Monopoly: Single Price	Monopoly: Perfect Price Discrimination
Consumer surplus, CS	$A + B + C$	A	0
Producer surplus, PS	$D + E$	$B + D$	$A + B + C + D + E$
Welfare, $W = CS + PS$	$A + B + C + D + E$	$A + B + D$	$A + B + C + D + E$
Deadweight loss	0	$C + E$	0

Figure 13.4 Competitive, Single-Price, and Perfect Discrimination Equilibria. In the competitive market equilibrium, e_c, price is p_c, quantity is Q_c, consumer surplus is $A + B + C$, producer surplus is $D + E$, and there is no deadweight loss. In the single-price monopoly equilibrium, e_s, price is p_s, quantity is Q_s, consumer surplus falls to A, producer surplus is $B + D$, and deadweight loss is $C + E$. In the perfect discrimination equilibrium, the monopoly sells each unit at the customer's reservation price on the demand curve. It sells Q_d (= Q_c) units, where the last unit is sold at its marginal cost. Customers have no consumer surplus, but there is no deadweight loss.

With a single-price monopoly (which charges all its customers the same price because it cannot distinguish among them), the intersection of the MC curve and the single-price-monopoly marginal revenue curve, MC_s, determines the output,

Q_s. The monopoly operates at e_s, where it charges p_s. The deadweight loss from monopoly is $C + E$. This efficiency loss is due to the monopoly's charging a price, p_s, that's above its marginal cost, MC_s, so less is sold than in a competitive market.

A perfectly price-discriminating monopoly sells each unit at its reservation price, which is the height of the demand curve. As a result, the firm's marginal revenue curve, MR_d, is the same as its demand curve. The firm sells the first unit for p_1 to the consumer who will pay the most for the good. The firm's marginal cost for that unit is MC_1, so it makes $p_1 - MC_1$ on that unit. The firm receives a lower price and has a higher marginal cost for each successive unit. It sells the Q_d unit for p_c, where its marginal revenue curve, MR_d, intersects the marginal cost curve, MC, so it just covers its marginal cost on the last unit. The firm is unwilling to sell additional units because its marginal revenue would be less than the marginal cost of producing them.

The perfectly price-discriminating monopoly's total producer surplus on the Q_d units it sells is the area below its demand curve and above its marginal cost curve, $A + B + C + D + E$. Its profit is the producer surplus minus its fixed cost, if any. Consumers receive no consumer surplus because each consumer pays his or her reservation price. The perfectly price-discriminating-monopoly equilibrium has *no deadweight loss* because the last unit is sold at a price, p_c, which equals the marginal cost, MC_c, as in a competitive market. Thus, both a perfect-price-discrimination equilibrium and a competitive equilibrium are efficient.

The perfect-price-discrimination equilibrium differs from the competitive equilibrium in two ways. First, in the competitive equilibrium, everyone is charged a price equal to the equilibrium marginal cost, $p_c = MC_c$; however, in the perfect-price-discrimination equilibrium, only the last unit is sold at that price. The other units are sold at customers' reservation prices, which are greater than p_c. Second, consumers receive some welfare (consumer surplus, $A + B + C$) in a competitive market, whereas a perfectly price-discriminating monopoly captures all the welfare. Thus, perfect price discrimination doesn't reduce efficiency—the output and total welfare are the same as under competition—but it does redistribute income away from consumers—consumers are much better off under competition.

Is a single-price or perfect-price-discriminating monopoly better for consumers? The perfect-price-discrimination equilibrium is more efficient than the single-price monopoly equilibrium because more output is produced. A single-price monopoly, however, takes less consumer surplus from consumers than a perfectly price-discriminating monopoly. Consumers who put a very high value on the good are better off under single-price monopoly, where they have consumer surplus, than with perfect price discrimination, where they have none. Consumers with lower reservation prices who purchase from the perfectly price-discriminating monopoly but not from the single-price monopoly have no consumer surplus in either case. All the social gain from the extra output goes to the perfectly price-discriminating firm. Consumer surplus is greatest with competition, lower with single-price monopoly, and eliminated by perfect price discrimination.

APPLICATION

Tagamet Revisited

We illustrate how perfect price discrimination differs from competition and single-price monopoly using the example from Chapter 11 of SmithKline's anti-ulcer drug, Tagamet. Figure 13.5 shows a linear demand curve for Tagamet and a constant marginal cost (and average cost) of 7.5¢ per dose.[9] If the market had been competitive (price equal to marginal cost at e_c), consumer surplus would have been $A + B + C \approx \$1.77$ million, and there would have been no producer surplus or deadweight loss.[10]

In the single-price-monopoly equilibrium, e_s, pharmacy customers paid 75¢ per daily dose, and 1.3 million daily doses of oral Tagamet were sold. The corresponding consumer surplus was $A \approx \$0.44$ million per day, producer surplus was $B \approx \$0.88$ million per day, and the deadweight loss was $C \approx \$0.44$ million per day.

Had SmithKline been able to perfectly price discriminate, its producer surplus would have nearly doubled to $A + B + C \approx \$1.77$ million per day, and consumers would have obtained no consumer surplus. The marginal consumer would have paid the marginal cost of 7.5¢, the same as in a competitive market.

SmithKline's inability to perfectly price discriminate costs the company and society dearly. The profit of the single-price monopoly, $B \approx \$0.88$ million per day, is lower than that of a perfectly price-discriminating monopoly by about $A + C = \$0.88$ million per day, or \$321 million per year. Similarly, society's welfare under single-price monopoly is lower than from perfect price discrimination by the deadweight loss of \$0.44 million per day, or \$161 million per year. ■

SOLVED PROBLEM 13.2

How does welfare change if the movie theater described in Table 13.1 goes from charging a single price to perfectly price discriminating?

---

[9]See Chapter 11 for the sources and the assumptions used in this analysis for 1983, the last year Tagamet had a monopoly on this type of anti-ulcer drug. In these calculations, we assume that there is no fixed cost so that average cost equals marginal cost equals 7.5¢ per dose. The estimated welfare numbers reported here are sensitive to the assumed shape of the estimated demand curve. Most drug companies charge hospitals and other organizations lower prices than pharmacies, so they do not behave as single-price monopolies. For simplicity, however, our analysis compares single-price monopoly to perfect price discrimination among pharmacy customers.

[10]The area of the triangle $A + B + C$ in the figure is $\frac{1}{2} \times (\$1.43 - \$0.075) \times 2.61$ million $=$ \$1.768275 million.

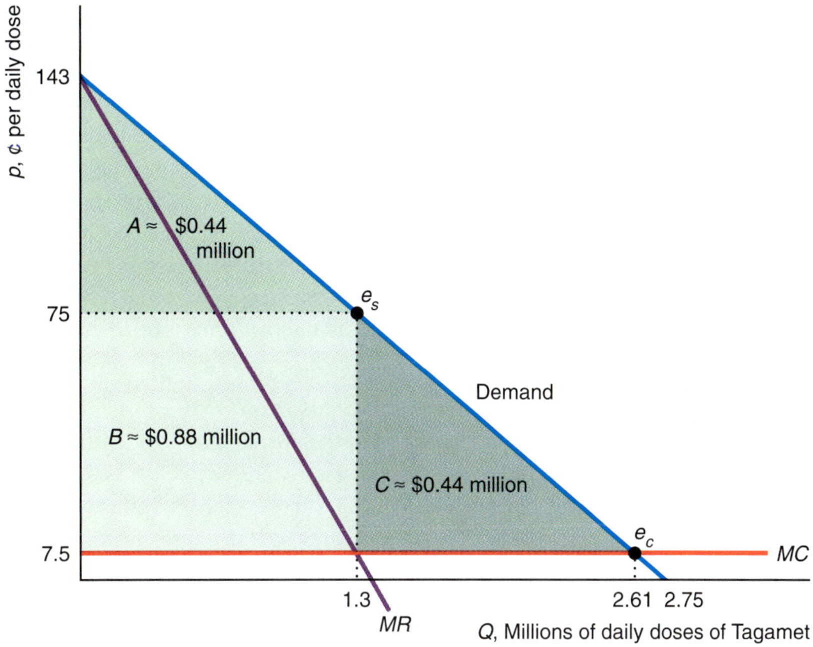

	Competition	Monopoly: Single Price	Monopoly: Perfect Price Discrimination
Consumer surplus, *CS*	*A* + *B* + *C*	*A*	0
Producer surplus, *PS*	0	*B*	*A* + *B* + *C*
Welfare, *W* = *CS* + *PS*	*A* + *B* + *C*	*A* + *B*	*A* + *B* + *C*
Deadweight loss	0	*C*	0

Figure 13.5 Welfare from Tagamet Under Three Market Structures. If Tagamet were sold competitively, the equilibrium price would be 7.5¢ per daily dose, consumers would have gained all the welfare, and there would be no deadweight loss. In the single-price-monopoly equilibrium, e_s, customers pay 75¢ and buy 1.3 million daily doses, and there is deadweight loss. If the manufacturer could have perfectly price discriminated, it would have charged the reservation price for each unit, as long as that price was at least as great as its marginal cost. By price discriminating, the monopoly would increase its producer surplus *A* + *B* + *C*, and there would be no deadweight loss.

Answer

1. *Calculate welfare for panel a (i) if the theater sets a single price and (ii) if it perfectly price discriminates, and (iii) compare them*: (i) If the theater sets the profit-maximizing single price of $5, it sells 30 tickets and makes a profit of $150. The 20 senior citizen customers are paying their reservation price, so they have no consumer surplus. The 10 college students have reservation prices of $10, so their consumer surplus is $50. Thus welfare is $200: the sum of the profit, $150, and the consumer surplus, $50. (ii) If the firm perfectly price discriminates, it charges seniors $5 and college students $10. Because the theater is charging all customers their reservation prices, there is no consumer surplus. The firm's profit rises to $200. (iii) Thus, *welfare is the same under both pricing systems where output stays the same.*

2. *Calculate welfare for panel b (i) if the theater sets a single price and (ii) if it perfectly price discriminates, and (iii) compare them*: (i) If the theater sets the profit-maximizing single price of $10, only college students attend and have no consumer surplus. The theater's profit is $100, so total welfare is $100. (ii) With perfect price discrimination, there is no consumer surplus, but profit increases to $125, so welfare rises to $125. (iii) Thus, *welfare is greater with perfect price discrimination where output increases.*[11] ■

Transaction Costs and Perfect Price Discrimination

Although some firms come close to perfect price discrimination, many more firms set a single price or use another nonlinear pricing method. Transaction costs are a major reason why these firms do not perfectly price discriminate: It is too difficult or costly to gather information about each customer's price sensitivity. Recent advances in computer technologies, however, have lowered these costs, causing hotels, car and truck rental companies, cruise lines, and airlines to price discriminate more often.[12]

Many auto dealerships try to increase their profit by perfectly price discriminating, charging each customer the most that customer is willing to pay. These firms hire salespeople to ascertain potential customers' willingness to pay for a car and to bargain with them. Not all car companies believe that it pays to price discriminate in this way, however. As we saw in Chapter 1, Saturn charges all customers the same price, believing that the transaction costs (including wages of salespeople) of such information gathering and bargaining exceeds the benefits of charging customers differential prices.

---

[11]These results—that welfare increases if and only if output increases—hold generally.

[12]Bryant, Adam, "Travelers' Growing Irritation: Many Prices for One Product," *New York Times*, January 24, 1994:A1, C2.

Many other firms believe that, taking the transaction costs into account, it pays to use quantity discrimination, multimarket price discrimination, or other nonlinear pricing methods rather than try to perfectly price discriminate. We now turn to these alternative approaches.

13.4 QUANTITY DISCRIMINATION

Many firms are unable to determine which customers have the highest reservation prices. Such firms may know, however, that most customers are willing to pay more for the first unit than for successive units: The typical customer's demand curve is downward sloping. Such a firm can price discriminate by letting the price each customer pays vary with the number of units the customer buys. Here, the price varies only with quantity: All customers pay the same price for a given quantity.

Not all quantity discounts are a form of price discrimination. Some reflect the reduction in a firm's cost with large quantity sales. For example, the cost per ounce of selling a soft drink in a large cup is less than that of selling it in a smaller cup; the cost of cups varies little with size, and the cost of pouring and serving is the same. A restaurant offering quantity discounts on drinks may be passing on actual cost savings to larger purchasers rather than price discriminating. However, if the quantity discount is not due to cost differences, the firm is engaging in quantity discrimination. Moreover, a firm may quantity discriminate by charging customers who make large purchases more per unit than those who make small purchases.

Many utilities use *block-pricing* schedules, by which they charge one price for the first few units (a *block*) of usage and a different price for subsequent blocks. Both declining-block and increasing-block pricing are common.

The utility monopoly in Figure 13.6 faces a linear demand curve for each customer. The demand curve hits the vertical axis at \$90 and the horizontal axis at 90 units. The monopoly has a constant marginal and average cost of m = \$30. Panel a shows how this monopoly maximizes its profit if it can quantity discriminate by setting two prices. The firm uses declining-block prices to maximize its profit. It sells 40 units, charging \$70 on the first 20 units (the first block) and \$50 per unit for additional units.[13]

[13]The inverse demand curve is $p = \$90 - Q$, and the marginal and average cost is $m = \$30$, so the quantity-discounting utility's profit is

$$\begin{aligned}\pi &= p(Q_1)Q_1 + p(Q_2)(Q_2 - Q_1) - mQ_2\\ &= (90 - Q_1)Q_1 + (90 - Q_2)(Q_2 - Q_1) - 30Q_2,\end{aligned}$$

where Q_1 is the largest quantity for which the first-block rate, $p_1 = \$90 - Q_1$, is charged and Q_2 is the total quantity a consumer purchases. The utility chooses Q_1 and Q_2 to maximize its profit. It sets the derivative of profit with respect to Q_1 equal to zero, $Q_2 - 2Q_1 = 0$, and the derivative of profit with respect to Q_2 equal to zero, $Q_1 - 2Q_2 + 60 = 0$. Solving these two equations, the utility determines its profit-maximizing quantities, $Q_1 = 20$ and $Q_2 = 40$. The corresponding block prices are $p_1 = \$90 - 20 = \$70$ and $p_2 = \$50$.

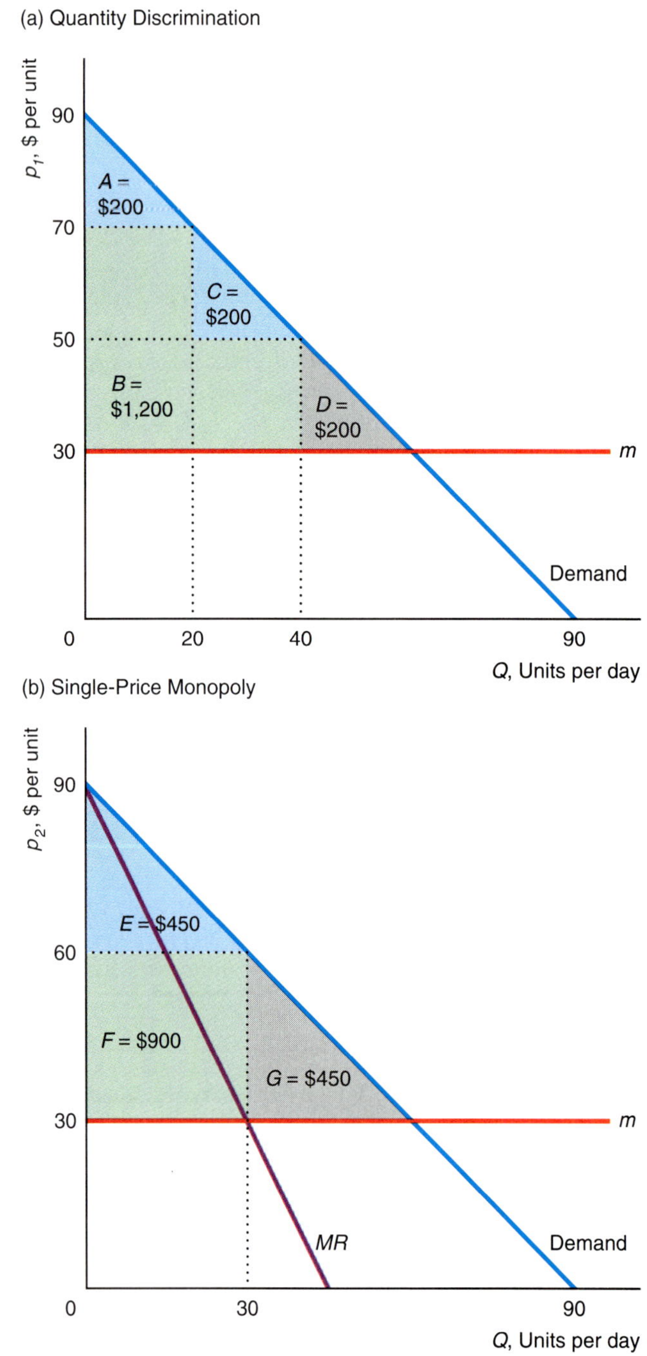
(a) Quantity Discrimination
p_1, $ per unit
90
70
50
30
A =
$200
C =
$200
B =
$1,200
D =
$200
m
Demand
0
20
40
90
Q, Units per day
(b) Single-Price Monopoly
p_2, $ per unit
90
60
30
E = $450
F = $900
G = $450
m
MR
Demand
0
30
90
Q, Units per day

	Quantity Discrimination	Single Price
Consumer surplus, *CS*	$A + C = \$400$	$E = \$450$
Producer surplus or profit, $PS = \pi$	$B = \$1,200$	$F = \$900$
Welfare, $W = CS + PS$	$A + B + C = \$1,600$	$E + F = \$1,350$
Deadweight loss, *DWL*	$D = \$200$	$G = \$450$

Figure 13.6 Quantity Discrimination. If this monopoly engages in quantity discounting, it makes a larger profit (producer surplus) than it does if it sets a single price and welfare is greater. (a) With quantity discounting, profit is $B = \$1,200$ and welfare is $A + B + C = \$1,600$. (b) If it sets a single price (so that its marginal revenue equals its marginal cost), the monopoly's profit is $F = \$900$ and welfare is $E + F = \$1,350$.

If the monopoly can set only a single price (panel b), it produces where its marginal revenue equals its marginal cost, selling 30 units at \$60 per unit. Thus, by quantity discriminating instead of using a single price, the utility sells more units, 40 instead of 30, and makes a higher profit, $B = \$1,200$ instead of $F = \$900$. With quantity discounting, consumer surplus is lower, $A + C = \$400$ instead of $E = \$450$, welfare (consumer surplus plus producer surplus) is higher, $A + B + C = \$1,600$ instead of $E + F = \$1,350$, and deadweight loss is lower, $D = \$200$ instead of $G =$ \$450. Thus, in this example, the firm and society are better off with quantity discounting, but consumers as a group suffer.

The more block prices that the monopoly can set, the closer the monopoly can get to perfect price discrimination. The deadweight loss results from the monopoly setting a price above marginal cost so that too few units are sold. The more prices the monopoly sets, the lower is the last price and hence the closer it is to marginal cost.[14]

APPLICATION

Block Pricing by Water Utilities

Many water utilities use block pricing. As they expected, Hewitt and Hanemann (1995) found that a household's demand for water increases with the size of the household's lawn, the number of family members, the size of the house, the number of bathrooms, and the average temperature. The demand for indoor use (drinking, taking baths) of water is less elastic than the demand

[14]Math Problem 19 at the end of the chapter examines what happens if the monopoly uses three block prices. In this example, the three prices are \$75, \$60, and \$45.

for outdoor use (watering lawns, washing cars). The combined demand for water is relatively sensitive to price, with an elasticity of –1.6. Given Hewitt and Hanemann's findings, an unregulated, profit-maximizing utility can increase its profit by switching from a single price to declining-block pricing, charging households that use little water (apartment dwellers with no lawns) higher prices than households with larger but more elastic demands. ■

13.5 MULTIMARKET PRICE DISCRIMINATION

Typically, a firm does not know the reservation price for each of its customers. But the firm may know which groups of customers are likely to have higher reservation prices than others. The most common method of multimarket price discrimination is to divide potential customers into two or more groups and set a different price for each group. All units of the good sold to customers within a group are sold at a single price. As with perfect price discrimination, to engage in multimarket price discrimination, a firm must have market power, be able to identify groups with different demands, and prevent resales.

For example, first-run movie theaters with market power charge senior citizens a lower price than they charge younger adults because senior citizens are not willing to pay as much as others to see a movie. By admitting people as soon as they demonstrate their age and buy tickets, the theater prevents resales.

Multimarket Price Discrimination with Two Groups

Suppose that a monopoly has a constant marginal and average cost of production, can prevent customers from reselling its product, and can divide its customers into two groups with different demands. Figure 13.7 illustrates how this monopoly maximizes its profit given that it uses multimarket price discrimination. The figure shows that the two groups of customers have different demand curves, D_1 and D_2, with corresponding marginal revenue curves, MR_1 and MR_2. The monopoly's marginal and average cost curves of selling to the two groups of customers are identical and horizontal: $MC_1 = AC_1 = m = MC_2 = AC_2$.

If the monopoly charges Group 1 members p_1 for Q_1 units, its revenue from sales to this group is p_1Q_1. The profit the monopoly makes selling to this group is $\pi_1 = p_1Q_1 - mQ_1$, where mQ_1 is its cost of producing Q_1 units. The monopoly wants to maximize its combined profit, π, which is the sum of its profits, π_1 and π_2, from selling to the two groups:

$$\pi = \pi_1 + \pi_2 = [p_1Q_1 - mQ_1] + [p_2Q_2 - mQ_2].$$

How should the monopoly set its prices p_1 and p_2—or equivalently, its quantities Q_1 and Q_2—so that its combined profit, π, is maximized? Appendix 13B gives a mathematical answer. Here we use Figure 13.7 and our understanding of a single-price monopoly's behavior to answer this question.

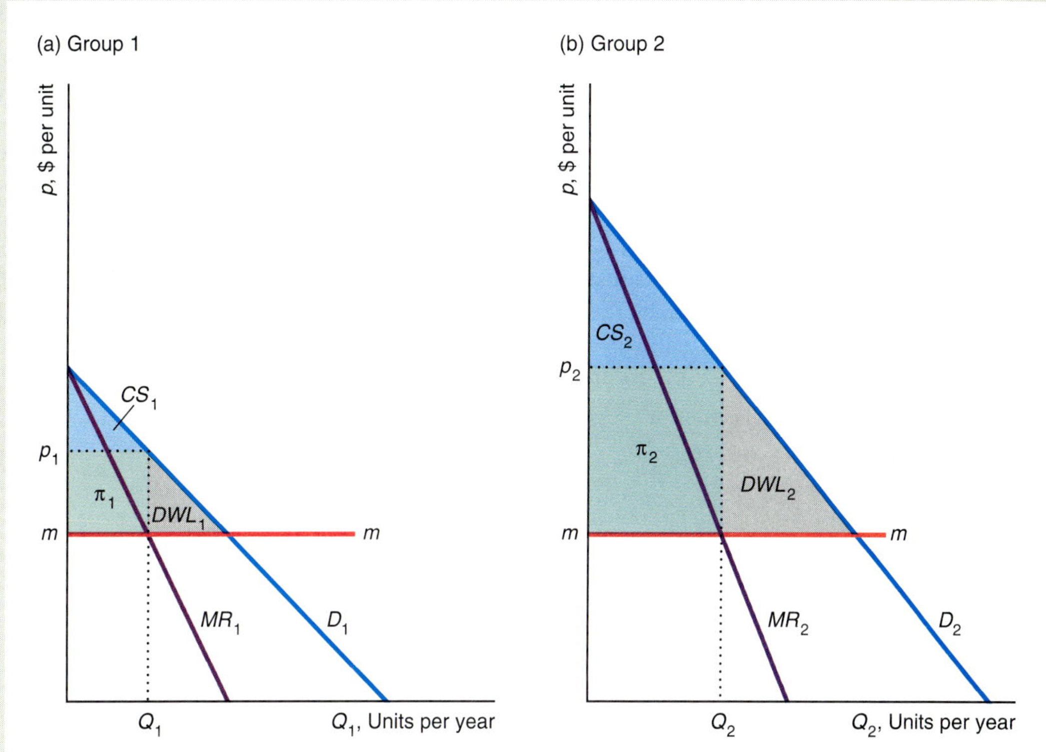

Figure 13.7 Multimarket Price Discrimination. A monopoly that can prevent resales divides its customers into two groups. Because the demand curves of these two groups differ, the monopoly finds it profitable to charge the two groups different prices. It sets each price so that the marginal revenue for that group equals the firm's constant marginal cost, m. As a result, in equilibrium, the marginal revenues are also equal: $MR_1 = MR_2 = m$.

Because it has a constant marginal cost, this multimarket-price-discriminating monopoly maximizes its total profit by maximizing its profit to each group individually. The monopoly does so by setting its quantities so that the marginal revenue for each group equals the common marginal cost, m. Panel a shows that $MR_1 = m$ at Q_1 and the resulting price is p_1. Similarly, panel b shows that $MR_2 = m$ at Q_2 and the price is p_2, which is greater than p_1.

This rule for setting prices is optimal for the monopoly if the monopoly doesn't want to change its price to either group. Would the monopoly like to lower its price and sell more output to the first group? If it did so, its marginal revenue would be below its marginal cost, $MR_1 < m$, so it would lose money from selling this extra output. Similarly, if the monopoly sold less to this group, its marginal revenue would be above its marginal cost. The same arguments can be made about the second group. Thus, the price-discriminating monopoly maximizes its profit by operating where its marginal revenue for each group equals the firm's marginal cost.

Because the monopoly equates the marginal revenue for each group to its common marginal cost, $MC = m$, the marginal revenues for the two groups are equal:

$$MR_1 = m = MR_2. \tag{13.10}$$

If the marginal revenue from selling to one group were higher than that from selling to the other group, the monopoly could increase its profit by switching sales to the high-marginal-revenue group from the other group.

We can use Equation 13.10 to determine how the prices to the two groups vary with the price elasticities of demand, which reflect the shape of the demand curves. We can write the marginal revenue in terms of the price and the price elasticity of demand. For example, the monopoly's marginal revenue to the first group is $MR_1 = p_1(1 + 1/\varepsilon_1)$, where p_1 is the price to the first group and ε_1 is the price elasticity of demand for the first group. Substituting these relationships into Equation 13.10, we find that

$$MR_1 = p_1\left(1 + \frac{1}{\varepsilon_1}\right) = m = p_2\left(1 + \frac{1}{\varepsilon_2}\right) = MR_2. \tag{13.11}$$

By rearranging Equation 13.11, we learn that

$$\frac{p_1}{p_2} = \frac{(1 + 1/\varepsilon_2)}{(1 + 1/\varepsilon_1)}. \tag{13.12}$$

Equation 13.12 shows that the price ratio to the two groups, p_1/p_2, depends on the price elasticities of demand of the two groups. For example, if $\varepsilon_1 = -3$ and $\varepsilon_2 = -2$, then $p_1/p_2 = (1 - \frac{1}{2})/(1 - \frac{1}{3}) = \frac{3}{4}$. To maximize its joint profit, this monopoly should set p_1 so that it is three-quarters as large as p_2. Thus, the monopoly charges the Group 2 consumers, who have the relatively less elastic demand, a higher price than the Group 1 consumers.

SOLVED PROBLEM 13.3

A monopoly sells its good in the U.S. and Japanese markets. The American inverse demand function is $p_a = 100 - Q_a$, and the Japanese inverse demand function is $p_j = 80 - 2Q_j$, where both prices, p_a and p_j, are measured in dollars. The firm's marginal cost of production is $m = 20$ in both countries. If the firm can prevent resale, what price will it charge in both markets? [*Hint:* The monopoly determines its optimal (monopoly) price in each country separately because customers cannot resell the good.]

Answer

1. *Determine the marginal revenue curve for each country*: The marginal revenue function corresponding to a linear inverse demand function has the

same intercept and twice as steep a slope (Chapter 11). Thus, the American marginal revenue function is $MR_a = 100 - 2Q_a$, and the Japanese one is $MR_j = 80 - 4Q_j$.

2. *Determine how many units are sold in each country*: To determine how many units to sell in the United States, the monopoly sets its American marginal revenue equal to its marginal cost, $MR_a = 100 - 2Q_a = 20$, and solves for the optimal quantity, $Q_a = 40$ units. Similarly, because $MR_j = 80 - 4Q_j = 20$, the optimal quantity is $Q_j = 15$ units in Japan.
3. *Substitute the quantities into the demand functions to determine the prices*: Substituting $Q_a = 40$ into the American demand function, we find that $p_a = 100 - 40 = \$60$. Similarly, substituting $Q_j = 15$ units into the Japanese demand function, we learn that $p_j = 80 - (2 \times 15) = \$50$. Thus, the price-discriminating monopoly charges 20% more in the United States than in Japan.[15] ■

APPLICATION

Generics and Brand-Name Loyalty

We can apply what we've learned about how rival firms set prices and how firms with market power price discriminate to explain a phenomenon that otherwise is mysterious: *The prices of some brand-name pharmaceutical drugs rise when equivalent, generic brands enter the market.*[16] When a patent for a highly profitable drug expires, many firms produce generic versions. The government allows a firm to sell a generic product after a brand-name drug's patent protection expires only if the generic-drug firm can prove that its product delivers the same amount of active ingredient or drug to the body in the same way as the *brand-name* product.[17] Sometimes the same firm manufactures both a brand-name drug and an identical generic drug, so the two have identical

---

[15]Using Equation 3.3, we know that the elasticity of demand in America is $\varepsilon_a = -p_a/Q_a$ and that in Japan it is $\varepsilon_j = -\tfrac{1}{2}p_j/Q_j$. In the equilibrium, $\varepsilon_a = -60/40 = -\tfrac{3}{2}$ and $\varepsilon_j = -50/(2 \times 15) = -\tfrac{5}{3}$. As Equation 13.12 shows, the ratio of the prices depends on the relative elasticities of demand:

$$p_a/p_j = 60/50 = (1 + 1/\varepsilon_j)/(1 + 1/\varepsilon_a) = (1 - \tfrac{3}{5})/(1 - \tfrac{2}{3}) = \tfrac{6}{5}.$$

[16]The following discussion relies on "Generics, the Impact at the Grass Roots," *Drug Topics Supplement*, 1994; Caves, Whinston, and Hurwitz (1991); Frank and Salkever (1992); Grabowski and Vernon (1992); Freudenheim, Milt, "Cleaning Out the Medicine Cabinet," *New York Times*, September 11, 1997:C1.

[17]Generic drugs are a large and growing part of the pharmaceutical market. Forty percent of U.S. pharmaceutical sales by volume are for generic drugs, and total generic sales were $4.6 billion in 1996. By 1997, brand-name drugs with sales of about $20 billion had gone off patent.

ingredients. Generics produced by other firms usually differ in appearance and name from the original product and may have different nonactive ingredients.

Most states have laws that allow (and 13 states require) a pharmacist to switch a prescription from a more expensive brand-name product to a less expensive generic equivalent unless the doctor or patient explicitly prohibits such a substitution. Many consumers, health maintenance organizations, and hospitals switch to the generics if they cost less than the brand-name drug.

What would you expect to happen when a generic enters the market? If consumers view the generic product and the brand-name product as perfect substitutes, entry by many firms will drive down the price—which is the same for both the name-brand drug and the generic drug—to the competitive level (see Chapter 8). Even if consumers view the goods as imperfect substitutes, you'd probably expect the price of the brand-name drug to fall.

Grabowski and Vernon (1992), however, find that entry by generics usually causes brand-name drug prices to rise. They examined 18 major orally administered drug products that faced generic competition between 1983 and 1987. They reported that, on average for each drug, 17 generic brands entered and captured 35% of total sales in the first year. During this period, the brand-name drug price *increased* by an average of 7% (but the average market price fell over 10% because the generic price was only 46% of the price of the brand-name drug).

One explanation for the rise in brand-name prices turns on the different elasticities of two groups of customers. Although some customers are price sensitive and willingly switch to less expensive generic drugs, others do not want to change brands. They prefer the brand-name drug because they are more comfortable with a familiar product, worried that new products may be substandard, or concerned that differences in the inactive ingredients might affect them. Elderly patients in particular are less likely to switch brands. A survey of the American Association of Retired Persons found that people aged 65 and older are 15% less likely than people aged 45 to 64 to request generic versions of a drug from their doctor or pharmacist.

Thus, the introduction of generics makes the demand facing the brand-name drug *less elastic*, rather than more elastic as usually happens when entry occurs. Before the generics enter, the brand-name drug is sold to both groups of consumers. When the generics become available, price-sensitive consumers stop buying the brand-name drug and switch to whichever generic drug is cheapest. The other consumers with less elastic demand do not switch. After the price-sensitive people switch to the generics, the demand facing the brand-name drug is less elastic than before. As a result, the brand-name drug company raises its price after entry.

Thus, differences in demands of these two groups explain both why brand-name drugs can charge higher prices than generics and why the price of the brand-name drug may increase after entry. They also explain why some firms sell both a brand-name drug at a relatively high price and an identical generic drug at a lower price so as to price discriminate. ■

Table 13.2 The Percentage by Which Europeans Pay More Than Americans for Computer Software

	Britain	Germany	France
Lotus 1-2-3	52%	66%	103%
Microsoft Windows	26%	84%	101%
WordPerfect	53%	93%	91%

Source: Levine, Jonathan B., "The Knives Come Out in Europe's Software Market," *Business Week*, 3304, February 8, 1993:37.

Identifying Groups

Firms use two approaches to divide customers into groups. One method is to divide buyers into groups based on those *observable characteristics* of consumers that the firm believes are associated with unusually high or low price elasticities. For example, movie theaters price discriminate using the age of customers. Similarly, some firms charge customers in one country higher prices than those in another country.[18] American computer software firms sell their products for more in Europe than in the United States, as Table 13.2 illustrates. These differences are much greater than can be explained by shipping costs and reflect multimarket price discrimination.

Another approach is to identify and divide consumers on the basis of their *actions*: The firm allows consumers to self-select the group to which they belong. For example, customers may be identified by their willingness to spend time to buy a good at a lower price or to order goods and services in advance of delivery.

Firms use differences in the value customers place on their time to discriminate by using queues (making people wait in line) and other time-intensive methods of selling goods. Store managers who believe that high-wage people are unwilling to "waste their time shopping" may run sales by which consumers who visit the store and pick up the good themselves get a low price while consumers who order over the phone or by mail pay a higher price. This type of price discrimination increases profit if people who put a high value on their time also have less elastic demands for the good.

APPLICATION

Getting Consumers to Identify Themselves

Firms draw on a variety of methods to induce consumers to indicate whether they have relatively high or low elasticities of demand. We examine three such approaches.

[18]A firm can charge a higher price for customers in one country than in another if the price differential is too small for many resales between the two countries to occur or if governments enforce import or export restrictions to prevent resales between countries.

Coupons

Many firms use discount coupons to multimarket price discriminate. By doing so, they divide customers into two groups, charging those who are willing to use coupons less than those who won't clip coupons. Providing coupons makes sense if people who don't use coupons are less price sensitive on average than those who clip.[19] People who are willing to spend their time clipping coupons buy cereals and other goods at lower prices than those who value their time more. Coupon-using consumers paid $24 billion less than other consumers in the first half of the 1990s.

Airline Tickets

By choosing between two different types of tickets, airline customers indicate whether they are likely to be business travelers or vacationers. Airlines give customers a choice between high-price tickets with no strings attached and low-price fares that must be purchased long in advance and require the traveler to stay over a Saturday night.

Airlines know that many business travelers have little advance warning before they book a flight and are usually unwilling to stay away over a Saturday night. These business travelers have relatively inelastic demand curves: They want to travel at a specific time even if the price is relatively high. In contrast, vacation travelers can usually plan in advance and stay over a Saturday night. Because vacation travelers can drive, take trains or buses, or postpone trips, they have relatively high elasticities of demand for air travel. The choice that airlines give customers ensures that vacationers with relatively elastic demands obtain cheap seats while most business travelers with relatively inelastic demands buy high-price tickets (often more than four times higher than the plan-ahead rate). Recently, Sheraton and other hotel chains have started offering discounts for rooms booked 14 days in advance for the same reason.

Hotel Room Prices

Harris Rosen owns six hotels in Orlando, Florida.[20] Believing that he maximizes his profit by keeping his hotel rooms filled, he cuts the price of a room over the day as necessary. Early in the day, the electronic message board outside his two lowest-price hotels shows that a room rents at between $39 and $59. If there are vacancies late in the day, the sign changes to post a rate as low as $29.95.

---

[19]As the Internet lowers transaction costs, some coupon clippers trade or sell their coupons to others, using sites such as *http://www.couponnet.com*.

[20]McDowell, Edwin, "His Goal: No Room at the Inns," *New York Times*, November 23, 1995:C1.

Customers who are willing to wait until late in the day to book rooms get a lower rate. However, they risk not finding a vacancy at his inexpensive hotels. His hotels average a much higher occupancy rate—96% versus 79%—than those of his competitors, who are less likely to vary their prices over the day.[21] ■

Welfare Effects of Multimarket Price Discrimination

Multimarket price discrimination results in inefficient production and consumption. As a result, welfare under multimarket price discrimination is lower than that under competition or perfect price discrimination. Welfare may be lower or higher with multimarket price discrimination than with a single-price monopoly, however.

Multimarket Price Discrimination Versus Competition. Consumer surplus is greater and more output is produced with competition (or perfect price discrimination) than with multimarket price discrimination. In Figure 13.7, consumer surplus with multimarket price discrimination is CS_1 (for Group 1 in panel a) and CS_2 (for Group 2 in panel b). Under competition, consumer surplus is the area below the demand curve and above the marginal cost curve: $CS_1 + \pi_1 + DWL_1$ in panel a and $CS_2 + \pi_2 + DWL_2$ in panel b.

Thus, multimarket price discrimination transfers some of the competitive consumer surplus, π_1 and π_2, to the monopoly as additional profit and causes the deadweight loss, DWL_1 and DWL_2, of some of the rest of the competitive consumer surplus. The deadweight loss is due to the multimarket-price-discriminating monopoly's charging prices above marginal cost, which results in reduced production from the optimal competitive level.

Multimarket Price Discrimination Versus Single-Price Monopoly. From theory alone, we can't tell whether welfare is higher if the monopoly uses multimarket price discrimination or if it sets a single price. Both types of monopolies set price above marginal cost, so too little is produced relative to competition. Output may rise as the firm starts discriminating if groups that did not buy when the firm charged a single price start buying. In the movie theater example in panel b of Table 13.1, welfare is higher with discrimination than with single-price monopoly because more tickets are sold when the monopoly discriminates (see Solved Problem 13.2).

The closer the multimarket-price-discriminating monopoly comes to perfectly price discriminating (say, by dividing its customers into many groups rather than just two), the more output it produces, so the less the production inefficiency there is. However, unless a multimarket-price-discriminating monopoly sells significantly more output than it would if it had to set a single price, welfare is likely to be lower with discrimination because of consumption inefficiency and time wasted shopping.

---

[21]Presumably, his competitors believe that it is impractical to change prices over the day because the transaction costs are too high, or they think that they can make more money by charging a relatively high price and having higher average levels of vacancies.

These two inefficiencies don't occur with a monopoly that charges all consumers the same price. As a result, consumers place the same marginal value (the single sales price) on the good, so they have no incentive to trade with each other. Similarly, if everyone pays the same price, consumers have no incentive to search for low prices.

APPLICATION

Taking Women to the Cleaners

Under a 1995 law, California dry cleaners, hair salons, and other firms can no longer charge women a higher price than they charge men for the same services.[22] Before passage of this law, prices frequently differed. At one San Francisco firm, cleaning a man's shirt cost $1.85, but cleaning a woman's blouse cost $7.70. One department store offered complimentary hemming for men's slacks and charged $8 to alter men's jackets, while charging $15 to hem a skirt and $12 to take in a woman's jacket.

Many firms argued that their price differences were due solely to cost differences. The 1995 law allows firms to charge higher prices for services if they are more costly, difficult, or time-consuming, such as cutting longer hair or laundering lace blouses.

For price differences to be due to price discrimination rather than disparities in costs, firms must have market power. A survey by the California state legislature before the law went into effect found that haircutting establishments that charged lower prices were more likely to charge men and women the same price. One possible explanation for why inexpensive firms charge men and women the same price is that these firms have no market power: They provide simple, nearly identical haircuts and act as price takers. In contrast, fancy establishments, whose services are viewed as differing from those of other firms, have market power and can price discriminate. ■

13.6 TWO-PART TARIFFS

We now turn to two other forms of nonlinear pricing: *two-part tariffs* in this section and *tie-in sales* in the next one. Both are similar to the type of second-degree price discrimination we examined earlier because the average price per unit varies with the number of units consumers buy.

[22]Burdman, Pamela, "New Law Not Likely to Cut Women's Costs," *San Francisco Chronicle*, October 21, 1995:A1; letter, March 17, 1993, from the Assembly, California Legislature, Assembly Office of Research to Assembly Member Jackie Speier.

With a **two-part tariff**, the firm charges a consumer a lump-sum fee (the first tariff) for the right to buy as many units of the good as the consumer wants at a specified price (the second tariff). Because of the lump-sum fee, consumers pay more per unit if they buy a small number of goods than if they buy a larger number (see Math Problem 23 at the end of this chapter).

To get telephone service, you may pay a monthly connection fee and a price per minute of use. Some car rental firms charge a per-day fee and a price per mile driven. To buy season tickets to Raiders football games, a fan pays a fee of \$250 to \$4,000 for a "personal seat license," which gives the fan the right to buy season tickets for the next eleven years at a ticket price per game ranging between \$40 and \$60. The St. Louis Rams, Carolina Panthers, Jacksonville Jaguars, and other teams use similar two-part tariffs.

To profit from two-part tariffs, a firm must have market power, know how demand differs over customers or with the quantity that a single customer buys, and successfully prevent resales. We now examine two results. First, we consider how a firm uses a two-part tariff to extract consumer surplus (as in our previous price discrimination examples). Second, we see how, if the firm cannot vary its two-part tariff across its customers, its profit is greater, the more similar the demand curves of its customers are.

We illustrate these two points for a monopoly that knows its customers' demand curves. We start by examining the monopoly's two-part tariff where all its customers have identical demand curves and then look at one where its customers' demand curves differ.

A Two-Part Tariff with Identical Consumers

If all the monopoly's customers are identical, a monopoly that knows its customers' demand curve can set a two-part tariff that has the same two properties as the perfect-price-discrimination equilibrium. First, the efficient quantity, Q_1, is sold because the price of the last unit equals marginal cost. Second, all consumer surplus is transferred from consumers to the firm.

Suppose the monopoly has a constant marginal and average cost of m = \$10 (no fixed cost), and every consumer has the demand curve D^1 in panel a of Figure 13.8. To maximize its profit, the monopoly charges a price of p equal to the constant marginal and average cost, m = \$10, and just breaks even on each unit sold. By setting price equal to marginal cost, it maximizes the *potential consumer surplus*: the consumer surplus if no lump-sum fee is charged. It charges the largest possible lump-sum fee, $\mathcal{L}$, which is the potential consumer surplus $A_1 + B_1 + C_1$ = \$2,450. Thus, its profit is \$2,450 times the number of customers.

Had the firm charged a higher per-unit price, it would sell fewer units and hence make a smaller profit. For example, if the monopoly charges p = \$20, it sells 60 units, making a profit from its unit sales of B_1 = (\$20 − \$10)60 = \$600. It must lower its fee to equal the new potential consumer surplus of A_1 = \$1,800, so its total profit per customer is only \$2,400. It loses area C_1 = \$50 by charging the higher price. Similarly, had the monopoly charged a lower per-unit price, its profit would be lower: It would sell too many units and make a loss on each unit because its price would be below its marginal cost.

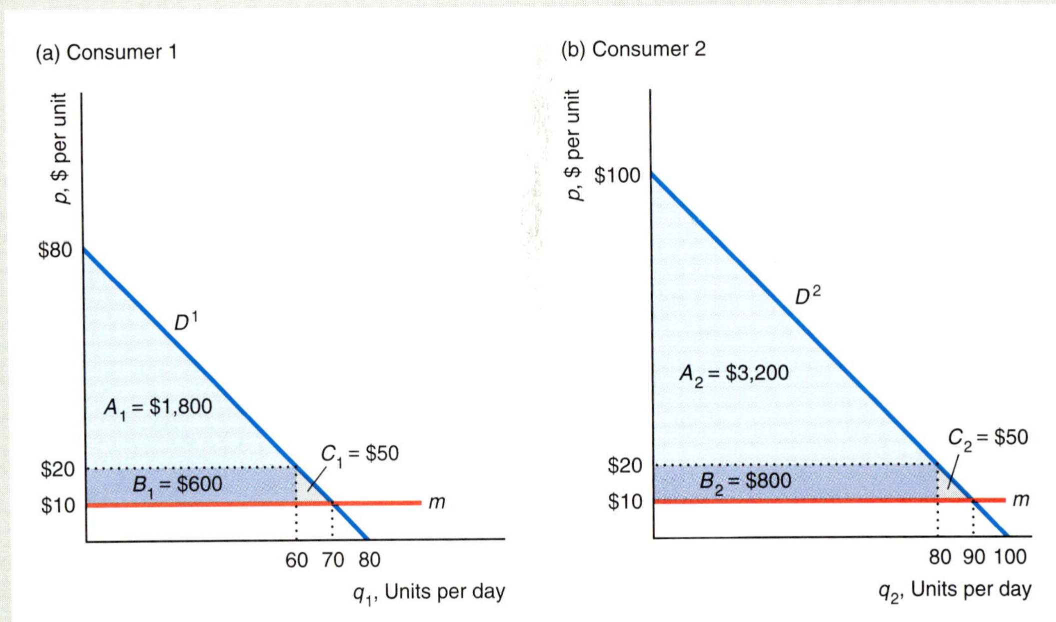

Figure 13.8 Two-Part Tariff. If all consumers have the demand curve in panel a, a monopoly can capture all the consumer surplus with a two-part tariff by which it charges a price, p, equal to the marginal cost, m = \$10, for each item and a lump-sum membership fee of $\mathcal{L} = A_1 + B_1 + C_1$ = \$2,450. Now suppose the monopoly has two customers, Consumer 1 in panel a and Consumer 2 in panel b. If the monopoly can treat its customers differently, it maximizes its profit by setting $p = m$ = \$10 and charging Consumer 1 a fee equal to its potential consumer surplus, $A_1 + B_1 + C_1$ = \$2,450, and Consumer 2 a fee of $A_2 + B_2 + C_2$ = \$4,050, for a total profit of \$6,500. If the monopoly must charge all customers the same price, it maximizes its profit at \$5,000 by setting p = \$20 and charging both customers a lump-sum fee equal to the potential consumer surplus of Consumer 1, $\mathcal{L} = A_1$ = \$1,800.

Because the monopoly knows the demand curve, it could, instead, perfectly price discriminate by charging each customer a different price for each unit purchased: the price along the demand curve. Thus, this knowledgeable monopoly can capture all potential consumer surplus either by perfectly price discriminating or by setting its optimal two-part tariff.

If the monopoly does not know its customers' demand curve, it must guess how high a lump-sum fee to set. This fee will almost certainly be less than the potential consumer surplus. If the firm sets its fee above the potential consumer surplus, it loses all its customers.

A Two-Part Tariff with Nonidentical Consumers

Now suppose there are two customers, Consumer 1 and Consumer 2, with demand curves, D_1 and D_2, in panels a and b of Figure 13.8. If the monopoly knows each customer's demand curve and can prevent resales, it can capture all the consumer surplus by varying its two-part tariffs across customers. However, if the monopoly is unable to distinguish between the types of customers or cannot charge consumers different prices, efficiency and profitability fall.

Suppose that the monopoly knows its customers' demand curves. By charging each customer $p = m = \$10$ per unit, the monopoly makes no profit per unit but sells the number of units that maximizes the potential consumer surplus. The monopoly then captures all this potential consumer surplus by charging Consumer 1 a lump-sum fee of $\mathcal{L}_1 = A_1 + B_1 + C_1 = \$2{,}450$ and Consumer 2 a fee of $\mathcal{L}_2 = A_2 + B_2 + C_2 = \$4{,}050$. The monopoly's total profit is $\mathcal{L}_1 + \mathcal{L}_2 = \$6{,}500$. By doing so, the monopoly maximizes its total profit by capturing the maximum potential consumer surplus from both customers.

Now suppose that the monopoly has to charge each consumer the same lump-sum fee, $\mathcal{L}$, and the same per-unit price, p. For example, because of legal restrictions, a telephone company charges all residential customers the same monthly fee and the same fee per call, even though the company knows that consumers' demands vary. As with multimarket price discrimination, the monopoly does not capture all the consumer surplus.

The monopoly charges a lump-sum fee, $\mathcal{L}$, equal to either the potential consumer surplus of Consumer 1, CS_1, or of Consumer 2, CS_2. Because CS_2 is greater than CS_1, both customers buy if the monopoly charges $\mathcal{L} = CS_1$, whereas only Consumer 2 buys if the monopoly charges $\mathcal{L} = CS_2$. The monopoly sets either the low lump-sum fee or the higher one depending on which produces the greater profit.

Any other lump-sum fee would lower its profit. The monopoly has no customers if it charges more than $\mathcal{L} = CS_2$. If it charges between CS_1 and CS_2, it loses money on Consumer 2 compared to what it could earn by charging CS_2, and it still does not sell to Consumer 1. By charging less than $\mathcal{L} = CS_1$, it earns less per customer and does not gain any additional customers.

In our example, the monopoly maximizes its profit by setting the lower lump-sum fee and charging a price $p = \$20$, which is above marginal cost.[23] Consumer 1 buys 60 units, and Consumer 2 buys 80 units. The monopoly makes $(p - m) = (\$20 - \$10) = \$10$ on each unit, so it earns $B_1 + B_2 = \$600 + \$800 = \$1{,}400$ from the units it sells. In addition, it gets a fee from both consumers equal to the consumer surplus of

---

[23]The demand curves for Consumers 1 and 2 are $q_1 = 80 - p$ and $q_2 = 100 - p$. The consumer surplus for Consumer 1 is $CS_1 = \frac{1}{2}(80 - p)q_1 = \frac{1}{2}(80 - p)^2$. Similarly, $CS_2 = \frac{1}{2}(100 - p)^2$. If the monopoly charges the lower fee, $\mathcal{L} = CS_1$, it sells to both consumers, and its profit is

$$\pi = 2\mathcal{L} + (p - m)(q_1 + q_2) = (80 - p)^2 + (p - 10)(180 - 2p).$$

Setting the derivative of π with respect to p equal to zero, we find that the profit-maximizing price is $p = 20$. The monopoly charges a fee of $\mathcal{L} = CS_1 = \$1{,}800$ and makes a profit of \$5,000. If the monopoly charges the higher fee, $\mathcal{L} = CS_2$, it sells only to Consumer 2, and its profit is

$$\pi = \mathcal{L} + (p - m)q_2 = \tfrac{1}{2}(100 - p)^2 + (p - 10)(100 - p).$$

The profit-maximizing price is $p = 10$, and its profit is $\mathcal{L} = CS_2 = \$4{,}050$. Thus, the monopoly makes more by setting $\mathcal{L} = CS_1$ and selling to both customers.

Consumer 1, A_1 = \$1,800. Thus, its total profit is $2 \times \$1,800 + \$1,400 = \$5,000$, which is \$1,500 less than if it could set different lump-sum fees for each customer. Consumer 1 has no consumer surplus, but Consumer 2 enjoys a consumer surplus of \$1,400 (= \$3,200 – \$1,800).

Why does the monopoly charge a price above marginal cost when using a two-part tariff? By raising its price, the monopoly earns more per unit from both types of customers but lowers its customers' potential consumer surplus. Thus, if the monopoly can capture each customer's potential surplus by charging different lump sum fees, it sets its price equal to marginal cost. However, if the monopoly cannot capture all the potential consumer surplus because it must charge everyone the same lump-sum fee, the increase in profit from Customer 2 from the higher price more than offsets the reduction in the lump-sum fee (the potential consumer surplus of Customer 1).[24]

APPLICATION

Warehouse Stores

Warehouse clubs, such as Sam's Club, Price-Costco, and BJ's Wholesale Club, use two-part tariffs for their 24 million customers. They set a membership fee to shop at the store and then charge a low price for each item.[25] For example, a Mr. Coffee 12-cup coffeemaker costs \$50 at typical discount or department stores but \$35 at a warehouse club; Scotch videotape that sells for \$2.50 elsewhere is \$1.75.

Such two-part tariffs are profitable only if the firm can prevent resales. If customers of such stores could easily resell such goods to their friends, one customer could pay the fixed membership fee, purchase a large number of goods, and then resell them to others so that the store collects only one membership fee. Particularly for relatively inexpensive items such as groceries and underwear, such resales are unlikely to be a practical problem. Apparently, even on larger items such as refrigerators, resales have not been a major problem, as these warehouses continue to sell them. ■

---

[24]If the monopoly lowers its price from \$20 to the marginal cost of \$10, it loses B_1 from Customer 1, but it can raise its lump-sum fee from A_1 to $A_1 + B_1 + C_1$, so its total profit from Customer 1 increases by C_1 = \$50. The lump-sum fee it collects from Customer 2 also rises by $B_1 + C_1$ = \$650, but its profit from unit sales falls by B_2 = \$800, so its total profit decreases by –\$150. The loss from Customer 2, –\$150, more than offsets the gain from Customer 1, \$50. Thus, the monopoly makes \$100 more by charging a price of \$20 rather than \$10.

[25]"Should You Join a Warehouse Club?" *Consumer Reports*, 60(5), May 1995:330–333.

13.7 TIE-IN SALES

Another type of nonlinear pricing is a **tie-in sale**, in which customers can buy one product only if they agree to purchase another product as well. There are two forms of tie-in sales.

The first type is a **requirements tie-in sale**, in which customers who buy one product from a firm are required to make all their purchases of another product from that firm. Some firms sell durable machines such as copiers under the condition that customers buy copier services and supplies from them in the future. Because the amount of services and supplies each customer buys differs, the per-unit price of copiers varies across customers.

The second type of tie-in sale is **bundling** (or a *package tie-in sale*), in which two goods are combined so that customers cannot buy either good separately. You can't buy new automobiles without tires or laced shoes without shoelaces.

Most tie-in sales increase efficiency by lowering transaction costs. Indeed, tie-ins for efficiency purposes are so common that we hardly think about them. Presumably, no one would want to buy a shirt without buttons, so selling shirts with buttons attached lowers transaction costs. Because virtually everyone wants certain basic software, most companies sell computers with this software already installed. Firms also often use tie-in sales to increase profits, as we now illustrate.

Requirement Tie-in Sales

Frequently, a firm cannot tell which customers are going to use its product the most and hence are willing to pay the most for the good. These firms may be able to use a requirement tie-in sale to identify heavy users of the product and charge them more.

APPLICATION

IBM

In the 1930s, IBM increased its profit by using a requirement tie. IBM produced card punch machines, sorters, and tabulating machines (precursors of modern computers) that computed by using punched cards. Rather than selling its card punch machines, IBM leased them under the condition that the lease would terminate if any card not manufactured by IBM were used. (By leasing the equipment, IBM avoided resale problems and forced customers to buy cards from it.) IBM charged customers more per card than other firms would have charged. If we think of this extra payment per card as part of the cost of using the machine, this requirement tie resulted in customers who used the machines heavily paying more for the machines than others. Such a tie-in was profitable because heavier users were willing to pay more for a machine than others were.[26] ■

Bundling

Firms that sell two or more goods may use bundling to raise profits. Bundling allows firms that can't directly price discriminate to charge customers different prices. Whether bundling is profitable depends on customers' tastes and the ability to prevent resales.

Imagine that you are in charge of selling season tickets for the local football team. Your stadium can hold all your potential customers, so the marginal cost of selling one more ticket is zero.

Should you bundle together tickets for preseason (exhibition) and regular-season games, or should you sell books of tickets for the preseason and the regular season separately?[27] To answer this question, you have to determine how the fans differ in their desires to see preseason and regular-season games.

For simplicity, suppose that there are two customers (or types of customers). These football fans are so fanatical that they are willing to pay to see preseason exhibition games: There's no accounting for tastes!

Whether you should bundle depends on your customers' tastes. It does not pay to bundle in panel a of Table 13.3, in which Fan 1 is willing to pay more for both regular and preseason tickets than Fan 2. Bundling does pay in panel b, in which Fan 1 is willing to pay more for regular-season but less for exhibition-season tickets than Fan 2.

To determine whether it pays to bundle, we have to calculate the profit-maximizing unbundled and bundled prices. We start by calculating the profit-maximizing unbundled prices in panel a. If you charge \$2,000 for the regular-season tickets, you earn only \$2,000 because Fan 2 won't buy tickets. It is more profitable to charge \$1,400, sell tickets to both customers, and earn \$2,800 for the regular season. By similar reasoning, the profit-maximizing price for the exhibition tickets is \$500, at which you sell to only Fan 1 and earn \$500. As a result, you earn \$3,300 (= \$2,800 + \$500) if you do not bundle.

---

[26]In *IBM* v. *United States*, 298 U.S. 131 (1936), the Supreme Court said that IBM's actions violated the antitrust laws because they lessened competition in the (potential) market for tabulating cards. IBM's defense was that its requirement was designed to protect its reputation. IBM claimed that badly made tabulating cards might cause its machines to malfunction and that consumers would falsely blame IBM's equipment. The Court did not accept IBM's argument. The Court apparently did not understand—or at least care about—the price discrimination aspect of IBM's actions.

[27]We assume that you don't want to sell tickets to each game separately. One reason for selling only season tickets is to reduce transaction costs. A second explanation is the same type of bundling argument that we discuss in this section.

Table 13.3 Bundling of Tickets to Football Games

a) Unprofitable Bundle

	Regular Season	Preseason	Bundle
Fan 1	$2,000	$500	$2,500
Fan 2	$1,400	$100	$1,500
Profit-maximizing price	$1,400	$500	$1,500

b) Profitable Bundle

	Regular Season	Preseason	Bundle
Fan 1	$1,700	$300	$2,000
Fan 2	$1,500	$500	$2,000
Profit-maximizing price	$1,500	$300	$2,000

If you bundle and charge $2,500, you sell only to Fan 1. Your better option if you bundle is to set a bundle price of $1,500 and sell to both fans, earning $3,000. Nonetheless, you earn $300 more if you sell the tickets separately than if you bundle.

In this first example, in which it doesn't pay to bundle, the same customer who values the regular-season tickets the most also values the preseason tickets the most. In contrast, in panel b, the fan who values the regular-season tickets more values the exhibition season tickets less than does the other fan. Here, your profit is higher if you bundle. If you sell the tickets separately, you charge $1,500 for regular-season tickets, earning $3,000 from the two customers, and $300 for preseason tickets, earning $600, for a total of $3,600. By selling a bundle of tickets for all games at $2,000 each, you'd earn $4,000. Thus, you earn $400 more by bundling than by selling the tickets separately.

By bundling, you can charge the fans different prices for the two components of the bundle. Fan 1 is paying $1,700 for regular-season tickets and $300 for exhibition tickets, while Fan 2 is paying $1,500 and $500 respectively.[28] If you could perfectly price discriminate, you'd charge each consumer his or her reservation price for the preseason and regular-season tickets and would make the same amount as you do by bundling.

These examples illustrate that bundling a pair of goods pays only if their demands are *negatively correlated*: customers who are willing to pay relatively more for regular-season tickets are not willing to pay as much as others for preseason tickets, and vice versa. When a good or service is sold to different people, the price

---

[28]As with price discrimination, you have to prevent resales for bundling to increase your profit. Someone could make a $198 profit by purchasing the bundle for $2,000, selling Fan 1 the regular-season tickets for $1,699, and selling Fan 2 the preseason tickets for $499. Each fan would prefer attending only one type of game at those prices to paying $2,000 for the bundle.

is determined by the purchaser with the *lowest* reservation price. If reservation prices differ substantially across consumers, a monopoly has to charge a relatively low price to make many sales. By bundling when demands are negatively correlated, the monopoly reduces the dispersion in reservation prices, so it can charge more and still sell to a large number of customers.

Summary

1. **Price setting:** In many oligopolistic or monopolistically competitive markets, firms set prices instead of quantities. If the product is homogeneous and firms set prices, the Bertrand equilibrium price equals marginal cost (which is lower than the Cournot equilibrium price, in which firms set quantities). If the products are differentiated, the Bertrand equilibrium price is above marginal cost. Typically, the markup of price over marginal cost is greater, the more the goods are differentiated.
2. **Why and how firms price discriminate:** A firm can price discriminate if it has market power, knows which customers will pay more for each unit of output, and can prevent customers who pay low prices from reselling to those who pay high prices. A firm earns a higher profit from price discrimination than from uniform pricing because (a) the firm captures some or all of the consumer surplus of customers who are willing to pay more than the uniform price, and (b) the firm sells to some people who would not buy at the uniform price.
3. **Perfect price discrimination:** To perfectly price discriminate, a firm must know the maximum amount each customer is willing to pay for each unit of output. If a firm charges each customer the maximum he or she is willing to pay for each unit of output, the monopoly captures all potential consumer surplus and sells the efficient (competitive) level of output. Compared to competition, total welfare is the same, consumers are worse off, and firms are better off under perfect price discrimination.
4. **Quantity discrimination:** Some firms charge customers different prices depending on how many units they purchase. If consumers who want more water have less elastic demands, a water utility can increase its profit by using declining-block pricing, in which the price for the first few gallons of water is higher than that for additional gallons.
5. **Multimarket price discrimination:** A firm that does not have enough information to perfectly price discriminate may know the relative elasticities of demand of groups of its customers. Such a profit-maximizing firm charges groups of consumers prices in proportion to their elasticities of demand, the group of consumers with the least elastic demand paying the highest price. Welfare is less under multimarket price discrimination than under competition or perfect price discrimination but may be greater or less than that under single-price monopoly.
6. **Two-part tariffs:** By charging consumers one fee for the right to buy, and a separate price per unit, firms may earn higher profits than from charging only for each unit sold. If a firm knows its customers' demand curves, it can use two-part tariffs (instead of perfectly price discriminating) to capture all the consumer surplus. Even if the firm does not know each customer's demand curve or cannot vary the two-part tariffs across customers, it can use a two-part tariff to make a larger profit than it can get if it set a single price.
7. **Tie-in sales:** A firm may increase its profit by using a tie-in sale that allows customers to buy one product only if they also purchase another one. In a requirement tie-in sale, customers who buy one good must make all of their purchases of another good or service from that firm. With bundling (a package tie-in sale), a firm sells only a bundle of two goods together. Prices differ across customers under both types of tie-in sales.

Problems

1. Will price be lower if duopoly firms set price or if they set quantity? Under what conditions can you give a definitive answer to this question?
2. Why does differentiating its product allow an oligopolist to charge a higher price?
3. Suppose that two firms with differentiated products are in a Bertrand equilibrium in which both charge the same price. Now suppose that one firm finds that, by advertising, it can increase the quantity of its product demanded (when its price and the other firm's price are held constant). If the other firm cannot advertise, what happens to the equilibrium prices?
4. In the Coke and Pepsi example, what is the effect on the equilibrium prices of a specific tax, $\tau = \$1$, applied only to Coke? First answer this question qualitatively, using a graph. Then determine the exact equilibrium price, using math. (*Hint*: What does the tax do to the firm's marginal cost?)
5. In the examples in Table 13.1, if the movie theater does not price discriminate, it charges either the highest price the college students are willing to pay or the one that the senior citizens are willing to pay. Why doesn't it charge an intermediate price? (*Hint*: Discuss how the demand curves of these two groups are unusual.)
6. A firm is a natural monopoly (Chapter 11). Its marginal cost curve is flat, and its average cost curve is downward sloping (because it has a fixed cost). The firm can perfectly price discriminate.
   A. In a graph, show how much the monopoly produces, Q^*. Will it produce to where price equals its marginal cost?
   B. Show graphically (and explain) what its profits are.
7. Are all the customers of the quantity-discriminating monopoly in panel a of Figure 13.6 worse off than they would be if the firm set a single price (panel b)?
8. A monopoly has a marginal cost of zero and faces two groups of consumers. Originally, the monopoly cannot prevent resales, so it maximizes its profit by charging everyone the same price, $p = \$5$. No one from the first group chooses to purchase. Now the monopoly can prevent resales, so it decides to price discriminate. Will total output expand? Why or why not? What happens to profit and consumer surplus?
9. Use graphs to show why the price of a brand-name pharmaceutical may increase after generics enter the market.
10. In harmonizing its patent laws, the European Economic Community outlawed exportation of bulk/fine chemicals, which are used in 85% of U.S. generic drugs. This prohibition may delay the entry of generics onto the U.S. market by two to three years, a circumstance favoring U.S. patent holders, who already have enough chemicals to produce their own generics. What is the likely effect of this law on drug prices in the United States?
11. Each week, a department store places a different item of clothing on sale. Give an explanation based on price discrimination for why the store may conduct such regular sales.
12. Does a monopoly's ability to price discriminate between two groups of consumers depend on its marginal cost curve? Why or why not? (Consider two cases: (a) the marginal cost is so high that the monopoly is uninterested in selling to one group; (b) the marginal cost is low enough that the monopoly wants to sell to both groups.)
13. The chapter shows that a multimarket-price-discriminating monopoly with a constant marginal cost maximizes its total profit by maximizing its profit to each group individually. How would the analysis change if the monopoly has an upward-sloping marginal cost curve?
14. A monopoly sells two products, of which consumers want only one. Assuming that it can prevent resales, can the monopoly increase its profit by bundling them together, thus forcing consumers to buy both goods?

Math Problems

15. Suppose identical duopoly firms have constant marginal costs of \$10 per unit. Firm 1 faces a demand function of

$$q_1 = 100 - 2p_1 + p_2,$$

where q_1 is Firm 1's output, p_1 is the price of Firm 1, and p_2 is the price of Firm 2. Similarly, the demand facing Firm 2 is

$$q_2 = 100 - 2p_2 + p_1.$$

Solve for the Bertrand equilibrium.

16. Solve for the Bertrand equilibrium for the firms described in Problem 15 if both firms have a marginal cost of \$0 per unit.

17. Solve for the Bertrand equilibrium for the firms described in Problem 15 if Firm 1's marginal cost is \$30 per unit and Firm 2's marginal cost is \$10 per unit.

18. In panel b of Figure 13.6, the single-price monopoly faces a demand curve of $p = 90 - Q$ and a constant marginal (and average) cost of $m = \$30$. Find the profit-maximizing quantity (or price) using math (Chapter 11). Determine the profit, consumer surplus, welfare, and deadweight loss.

19. The quantity-discriminating monopoly in panel a of Figure 13.6 can set three prices depending on the quantity a consumer purchases. The firm's profit is

$$\pi = p_1Q_1 + p_2(Q_2 - Q_1) + p_3(Q_3 - Q_2) - mQ_3,$$

where p_1 is the high price charged on the first Q_1 units (first block), p_2 is a lower price charged on the next $Q_2 - Q_1$ units, and p_3 is the lowest price charged on the $Q_3 - Q_2$ remaining units, Q_3 is the total number of units actually purchased, and $m = \$30$ is the firm's constant marginal and average cost. Use calculus to determine the profit-maximizing p_1, p_2, and p_3.

20. A monopoly sells its good in the United States, where the elasticity of demand is –2, and in Japan, where the elasticity of demand is –5. Its marginal cost is \$10. At what price does the monopoly sell its good in each country if resales are impossible?

21. What happens to the prices that the monopoly in Problem 20 charges in the two countries if retailers can buy the good in Japan and ship it to the United States at a cost of (a) \$10 or (b) \$0 per unit?

22. A monopoly sells in two countries, and resales between the countries are impossible. The demand curves in the two countries are

$$p_1 = 100 - Q_1,$$

$$p_2 = 120 - 2Q_2.$$

The monopoly's marginal cost is $m = 30$. Solve for the equilibrium price in each country.

23. Using math, show why a two-part tariff causes customers who purchase few units to pay more per unit than do customers who buy more units.

CHAPTER 14

Strategy

A camper awakens to the growl of a hungry bear and sees his friend putting on a pair of running shoes. "You can't outrun a bear," scoffs the camper. His friend coolly replies, "I don't have to. I only have to outrun you!"

Since its inception in the early 1980s, Virgin Atlantic Airways (VAA) waged a service war with British Airways (BA), taking customers away from BA through an innovative service program. This program—which included massages on flights and free limo service—gave VAA one of the highest customer-loyalty ratings in the airlines market. In retaliation, BA tried to sabotage its smaller rival.[1] According to VAA, BA employees spread rumors in both the United States and Britain that VAA was in financial trouble so that travel agents would warn potential passengers not to fly VAA. Other dirty tricks perpetrated by BA's staff included tapping into VAA's computers to obtain the names and numbers of passengers, then phoning or meeting VAA passengers and falsely claiming that their flights were delayed or overbooked and offering inducements to fly with BA; breaking into the homes and cars of VAA staff; hiring a consultant to dig up dirt on VAA's owner and plant negative news stories; and withdrawing cooperation between the airlines in plane maintenance and staff training. As a result of British hearings, BA paid VAA £610,000 plus large court costs and admitted to "regrettable incidents." No wonder Richard Branson, chairman of VAA, observed that dealing with BA was "like getting into a bleeding competition with a blood bank."[2]

Fortunately, firms in most markets do not employ such colorful strategies on a regular basis. Nonetheless, they use a wide variety of strategic behaviors. **Strategic behavior** is a set of actions a firm takes to increase its profit, taking into account the possible actions of other firms. A firm may act to alter the beliefs of consumers and other firms, the number of actual and potential firms, the technology the other firms use, and the cost and speed with which a rival can enter the market.

In this chapter, we focus on **noncooperative strategic behavior**: the set of actions taken by a profit-maximizing firm acting independently of other firms.[3] Conflicts

---

[1]Nelms, Douglas W., "Defending its Virtue: A Reluctant Virgin Atlantic Is in Court, Trying to Force British Airways to Do the Honorable Thing," *Air Transport World*, 29(6), July 1992:36; Dwyer, Paula, "British Air: Not Cricket," *Business Week*, January 25, 1993:50–51; "Tactics and Dirty Tricks," *The Economist*, 326, January 16, 1993:21–22; "U.S. Court to Consider Antitrust Case Against British Air," *Reuter European Business Report*, January 3, 1995.

[2]London *Times*, September 20, 1984.

[3]In contrast, *cooperative strategic behavior* is the set of actions taken by firms to increase their profits through coordinating actions and limiting their competitive responses. Cartels (Chapter 12) are examples of cooperative behavior. The distinction between noncooperative and cooperative strategic behavior is not clear cut (see the discussion of tacit collusion in Chapter 12).

between firms frequently arise because the actions of each profit-maximizing firm affect the profits of other firms.

So far, we've concentrated on one-period games in which firms simultaneously set quantity (Cournot model) or price (Bertrand model). In this chapter, we consider multiperiod or multistage games, in which firms act sequentially. The one multistage game we examined in Chapter 12 is the Stackelberg model, in which the leader firm benefits by choosing its output before the follower firm does. In this chapter, we focus on firms' efforts to limit the number of rivals by deterring rivals from entering a market, though firms may have many other motives for their strategic actions.

In Chapter 13, we noted that, in addition to choosing quantities or setting prices, many firms compete by varying quality or differentiating their products. For example, McDonald's and Burger King adjust quality and differentiate their products for competitive reasons.[4] In response to Burger King ads touting its larger burgers, McDonald's had to decide whether to increase the size of its hamburgers from 1.6 ounces to 2 "full" ounces. Similarly, in response to McDonald's Big Mac success, Burger King introduced the Big King. In this chapter, we see that firms may also compete through advertising campaigns.

In this chapter, we examine four main topics:

1. **Preventing entry: simultaneous decisions:** When firms make entry decisions simultaneously, firms cannot act strategically to prevent rivals from entering the market.
2. **Preventing entry: sequential decisions:** If an incumbent firm can commit to producing large quantities before another firm decides whether to enter the market, the incumbent may deter entry.
3. **Creating and using cost advantages:** By raising costs to rivals, a firm may be able to deter entry or gain other advantages.
4. **Advertising:** Firms use advertising to increase the demand for their product, possibly at the expense of rival firms.

14.1 PREVENTING ENTRY: SIMULTANEOUS DECISIONS

When new firms enter an oligopolistic market, the profits of existing firms fall, as in the Cournot model in Chapter 12. Using a market that has either one or two firms, we now examine when and how firms behave strategically to prevent entry.

In this section we show that neither firm has an advantage that helps it to prevent the other firm from entering if both firms *simultaneously* decide whether to enter. In contrast, in the next section, we examine a market in which one firm, the incumbent, is already in the market and the other firm decides whether to enter. In that market, decisions are *sequential*: The incumbent acts before the potential entrant.

Two firms are considering opening gas stations at a highway rest stop that has no gas stations. There's enough physical space for only two gas stations. The profit or

[4] Greenberg, Herb, "McDonald's Thinks the Unthinkable: Making Bigger Burgers," *San Francisco Chronicle*, April 18, 1996:D1; and Collins, Glenn, "As Business Gets Lean, a Big King Dares Big Mac, *New York Times*, August 28, 1997:C1, C8.

payoff matrix in panel a of Table 14.1 shows that there is enough demand for two stations to operate profitably. In the profit matrix in panel b, there's enough demand for only one station to operate profitably.

Room for Two Firms

According to the payoff matrix in panel a (in which profits are in hundreds of thousands of dollars), both firms can make a profit. The cell in the upper-right corner of the matrix shows the payoffs to the two firms if only Firm 1 enters. Firm 1 earns $3 (upper-right corner of that cell) and the nonentrant, Firm 2, earns $0 (lower left of that cell). Similarly, Firm 2 earns $3 if it is a monopoly (lower-left cell). If both firms enter (lower-right cell), both earn $1. If neither enters (upper-left cell), both earn $0.

Entering the market is a *dominant strategy* (see Chapter 12) for both firms. Firm 1 reasons that

- If Firm 2 does not enter, Firm 1 makes $3 by entering and $0 if its does not enter, so entering is Firm 1's best strategy.
- If Firm 2 enters, Firm 1 makes $1 by entering and $0 if it does not enter, so entering is Firm 1's best strategy.

Because Firm 1 wants to enter regardless of what Firm 2 does, Firm 1 enters. Using the same reasoning, Firm 2 also enters because that's a dominant strategy. The

Table 14.1 Simultaneous Entry Game

a) The market can support two firms.

		Firm 1: *Do Not Enter*	Firm 1: *Enter*
Firm 2	*Do Not Enter*	$0 / $0	$3 / $0
	Enter	$0 / $3	**$1** / **$1**

b) The market can support only one firm.

		Firm 1: *Do Not Enter*	Firm 1: *Enter*
Firm 2	*Do Not Enter*	$0 / $0	**$1** / $0
	Enter	$0 / **$1**	–$1 / –$1

strategies by which both firms enter constitute a Nash equilibrium: Neither firm wants to change its behavior, given that the other firm enters.

Room for Only One Firm

The firms' strategies change in panel b, where there is enough demand for only one firm to operate profitably.[5] Now if both firms enter, each loses $1. Neither firm has a dominant strategy. What each firm wants to do depends on the other firm's strategy.

Until now, we have examined only games in which firms use a *pure strategy*—each firm chooses an action with certainty—and there is only one Nash equilibrium. Our analysis of the game in panel b differs from these previous games in two ways. First, this game has more than one Nash equilibrium in pure strategies. Second, in addition to using a pure strategy, a firm may employ a *mixed strategy*, in which it chooses between its possible actions with given probabilities.

Pure Strategies. This game has two Nash equilibria in pure strategies: Firm 1 enters and Firm 2 does not, or Firm 2 enters and Firm 1 does not. The equilibrium at which only Firm 1 enters is Nash because neither firm wants to change its behavior. Given that Firm 2 does not enter, Firm 1 does not want to change from entering to staying out of the market. If it changed its behavior, it would go from earning $1 to earning nothing. Similarly, given that Firm 1 enters, Firm 2 does not want to switch its behavior and enter because it would lose $1 instead of making $0. Where only Firm 2 enters is a Nash equilibrium by the same type of reasoning.

How do the players know which (if any) Nash equilibrium will result? They don't. It is difficult to see how the firms choose strategies unless they collude. For example, the firm that enters could pay the other firm to stay out of the market. Without collusion, even discussions between the firms before decisions are made are unlikely to help.

★**Mixed Strategies.** These pure Nash equilibria are unappealing because they call for identical firms to use different strategies. The firms may use the same strategies if their strategies are mixed. When both firms enter with a probability of one-half—say, if a flipped coin comes up heads—there is a Nash equilibrium in mixed strategies.[6] If both firms use this mixed strategy, each of the four outcomes in the payoff matrix in panel b is equally likely. Firm 1 has a one-fourth chance of earning $1 (upper-right cell), a one-fourth chance of losing $1 (lower-right cell), and a one-half chance of earning $0 (upper-left and lower-left cells). Thus, Firm 1's expected profit is $(\$1 \times \frac{1}{4}) + (-\$1 \times \frac{1}{4}) + (\$0 \times \frac{1}{2}) = \$0$.

---

[5]This game is similar to the game of *chicken*. Two foolish people drive toward each other in the middle of a road. As they approach the impact point, each has the option of continuing to drive down the middle of the road or to swerve. Both believe that, if only one driver swerves, that driver loses face (payoff = 0) and the other gains in self-esteem (payoff = 2). If neither swerves, they die or are maimed (payoff = –1). If both swerve, no harm is done to either (payoff = 1). In Problem 1 at the end of the chapter, you are asked to analyze this game formally.

[6]Probabilities and expected values are discussed in detail in Chapter 17.

Given that Firm 1 uses this mixed strategy, Firm 2 cannot do better by using a pure strategy. If Firm 2 enters with certainty, it earns \$1 half the time and loses \$1 the other half, so its expected profit is \$0. If it stays out with certainty, Firm 2 earns \$0 with certainty.[7] Thus, both firms playing the mixed strategy or one firm playing one pure strategy of entering and the other firm playing the pure strategy of not entering are Nash equilibria.

One important reason for introducing the concept of a mixed strategy is that some games have no pure-strategy Nash equilibria. Every game with a finite number of firms and a finite number of actions, however, has at least one Nash equilibrium, which may involve mixed strategies (Nash 1950).

Nonetheless, some game theorists argue that mixed strategies are implausible because firms do not flip coins to choose strategies. One response is that firms may only appear to be unpredictable in this way. In this game with no dominant strategies, neither firm has a strong reason to believe that the other will choose a pure strategy. It may think about its rival's behavior as random. In actual games, however, a firm may use some information or reasoning that its rival does not observe in choosing a pure strategy.

Summary of the Simultaneous Decision Entry Game

In conclusion, if firms make simultaneous entry decisions, their actions depend on the size of the market. If the market is large enough for both firms to make a profit, both firms enter. If the market can support only one firm, there are many possible Nash equilibria, and it is difficult to predict the outcome. *Neither firm can do anything to discourage the other firm from entering because the firms make their decisions simultaneously.*

SOLVED PROBLEM 14.1

Suppose that Ford and GM are considering entering a new market for electric automobiles and that their profits (in millions of dollars) from entering or staying out of the market are

---

[7]Why would a firm pick a mixed strategy where its probability of entering is one-half? Because the payoff matrix is symmetric, we can look for an equilibrium in which each firm has the same probability of entering. If Firm 1 uses a mixed strategy, it must be willing to use either of the pure strategies, so it must be indifferent between staying out or entering. Thus, the probability that Firm 2 enters, α, must be such that Firm 1's expected profit from staying out, $E\pi_n^1$, equals its expected profit from entering, $E\pi_e^1$:

$$E\pi_n^1 = 0 \times (1 - \alpha) + 0 \times \alpha = 1 \times (1 - \alpha) + (-1) \times \alpha = E\pi_e^1.$$

For the expected profits to be equal, it must be true that $E\pi_e^1 = 1(1 - \alpha) + (-1)\alpha = 0$, so $\alpha = \frac{1}{2}$. Similarly, Firm 2 uses a mixed strategy if it thinks the probability that Firm 1 enters is $\frac{1}{2}$. (In general, firms' mixed strategies can differ, and the probability that a firm chooses a strategy need not equal one-half.)

		GM	
		Enter	*Do Not Enter*
Ford	*Enter*	Ford: 10, GM: –40	Ford: 250, GM: 0
	Do Not Enter	Ford: 0, GM: 200	Ford: 0, GM: 0

If the firms make their decisions simultaneously, which firms enter? How would your answer change if the government committed to paying GM a lump-sum subsidy of $50 million on the condition that it produce this new type of car?

Answer

1. *Check for dominant strategies and determine the Nash equilibrium*: Given the payoff matrix, Ford always does as well or better by entering the market. If GM enters, Ford earns 10 by entering and 0 by staying out of the market. If GM does not enter, Ford earns 250 if it enters and 0 otherwise. Thus, entering is Ford's dominant strategy. GM does not have a dominant strategy. It wants to enter if Ford does not enter (earning 200 rather than 0), and it wants to stay out if Ford enters (earning 0 rather than –40). Because GM knows that Ford will enter (entering is Ford's dominant strategy), GM stays out of the market. Ford's entering and GM's not entering is a Nash equilibrium. Given the other firm's strategy, neither firm wants to change its strategy.

2. *See how the subsidy affects the payoff matrix and dominant strategies*: The subsidy does not affect Ford's payoff, so Ford still has a dominant strategy: It enters the market. With the subsidy, GM's payoffs if it enters increase by 50: GM earns 10 if both enter and 250 if it enters and Ford does not. With the subsidy, entering is a dominant strategy for GM. Thus, both firms' entering is a Nash equilibrium. ■

14.2 PREVENTING ENTRY: SEQUENTIAL DECISIONS

Additional strategic considerations arise if firms act sequentially. Suppose that an *incumbent* monopoly firm knows that a *potential entrant* is considering entering. These firms make sequential decisions about what actions to take. In the first stage, the incumbent chooses whether to take an action that will prevent the potential entrant from actually entering the market. In the second stage, the potential entrant decides whether to enter, and the firms choose output levels. The incumbent earns the monopoly profit if entry does not occur. If entry occurs, each firm sets its output to maximize its profit—taking account of the possible actions of its rival—and earns a duopoly profit. We assume that the potential entrant will not bother entering if it just breaks even—it enters only if it can make a positive profit.

Whether the incumbent acts to prevent entry depends on the answer to three questions:

- Does it pay for an incumbent to act to prevent entry?
- When can an incumbent prevent entry?
- What strategic acts and threats of future actions can an incumbent use to prevent entry?

We consider these questions in order. First, we examine whether a firm would pay a fee to prevent a rival from entering. Second, we show how the size of the fee depends on the potential rival's fixed cost of entering and the quantity demanded in this market. Third, we demonstrate that a threat of actions by the incumbent deters entry only if the potential rival believes the threat.

To Act or Not to Act?

Whether the incumbent acts to prevent entry depends on whether it *can take actions* that will prevent entry and whether it *pays to take those actions*. We start by assuming that the incumbent can take a strategic action that will prevent the other firm from entering and by asking whether it pays for it to take this action. There are three possibilities:

- **Blockaded entry:** Market conditions are such that no additional firm can profitably enter the market, even if the incumbent produces the monopoly output—so it is *unnecessary* for the incumbent to act strategically to prevent entry.
- **Deterred entry:** The incumbent acts to prevent an additional firm from entering because it *pays* to do so.
- **Accommodated entry:** Because it *doesn't pay* for the incumbent to prevent entry through strategic action, it does nothing to prevent entry but reduces its output (or price) from the monopoly to duopoly level to maximize its post-entry profit.

Paying to Prevent Entry. We use the gas station example to illustrate these three possibilities. One gas station, the incumbent, is already operating at the rest stop. The incumbent engages in a two-stage game with a potential entrant. In the first stage, the incumbent decides whether to pay the landlord of the rest stop b dollars for the *exclusive right* to be the only gas station at the rest stop. If this amount is paid, the landlord will rent the remaining land only to a restaurant or some other business that does not sell gasoline. If the incumbent doesn't take this strategic action to prevent entry, the potential entrant decides whether or not to enter in the second stage.[8]

---

[8]Recently, Coca-Cola wanted McDonald's restaurant owners to carry its drinks exclusively and offered each franchise a payment of enough soda syrup to make from 30,000 to 90,000 drinks. Dr Pepper made a comparable counteroffer. Collins, Glenn, "Top Soft-Drink Makers Raise Stakes in Brand War," *New York Times*, June 3, 1997:C2.

Figure 14.1 shows the game tree. In the first stage (left side of the diagram), the incumbent decides whether to pay for exclusive rights (bottom line) or not (top line). In the second stage (middle of the diagram), the potential entrant decides whether or not to enter if entry is possible. The right side of the diagram shows the profit of the incumbent, π_i, and then the profit of the potential entrant, π_e.

The top part of the tree shows what happens if the incumbent doesn't pay b to the landlord. If the other firm does not enter, the incumbent earns the monopoly profit, π_m, and the other firm earns zero. If the other firm enters, both the incumbent and the new firm earn the duopoly profit, π_d.

The bottom part of the tree shows what happens if the incumbent pays b for the exclusive rights. The incumbent earns $\pi_m - b$, and the other firm earns zero. (The landlord may set b so as to capture virtually all the extra profit.)

Entry is *blockaded* if the duopoly profit is negative, $\pi_d < 0$, so entry doesn't pay. The incumbent firm earns the monopoly profit, π_m, without having to pay b for exclusive rights.

If the duopoly profit, π_d, is positive, entry occurs unless the incumbent engages in strategic action to stop it. The incumbent can prevent entry by paying b, but it might not pay for the incumbent to do so. It pays if the incumbent's profit with *deterred* entry, $\pi_m - b$, is greater than the duopoly profit, π_d. However, if the duopoly profit is greater than the profit when the incumbent deters entry, $\pi_d > \pi_m - b$, it is better off with *accommodated* entry.

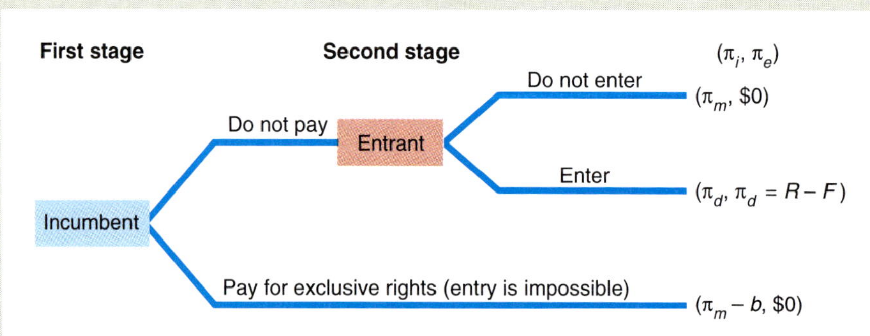

Figure 14.1 Whether an Incumbent Pays to Prevent Entry. If the potential entrant stays out of the market, it makes no profit, $\pi_e = 0$, and the incumbent firm makes the monopoly profit, $\pi_i = \pi_m$. If the potential entrant enters the market, both firms make the duopoly profit, π_d. Entry occurs if the duopoly profit is positive, $\pi_d > 0$. Entry is *blockaded* (does not occur regardless of actions by the incumbent) if the duopoly profit is negative because of low demand or high fixed costs of entering, both of which lower profit. If entry is not blockaded, the incumbent acts to *deter* entry by paying for exclusive rights to be the only firm at the rest stop only if $\pi_m - b > \pi_d$. Otherwise (if $\pi_m - b < \pi_d$), the incumbent *accommodates* entry.

Fixed Costs, Demand, and Blockaded Entry. A second firm can profitably enter this market only if π_d is positive in Figure 14.1. Whether π_d is positive depends on the fixed cost of entering and demand.

Suppose that the firms have no variable cost of production but incur a fixed cost F to enter the market. With two firms in the market, each firm has revenue R and duopoly profit of $\pi_d = R - F$. If revenue is less than the fixed cost of entering, $R < F$, the duopoly profit is negative, $\pi_d < 0$, and the second firm doesn't enter. Even though there is not enough demand, given the fixed cost of entry to support two firms, the incumbent may earn a positive, monopoly profit: $\pi_m > 0$.

Entry is blockaded only if a firm must incur a fixed cost to enter. If $F = 0$, then $R > F$, so an entrant can make a profit even if demand is low: $\pi_d > 0$. With fixed entry costs and demand so low that there's room for only one firm in the market, that firm is a *natural monopoly* (Chapter 11). If demand grows, additional firms can enter profitably. Chapter 12 shows that the number of monopolistically competitive firms in a market depends on how high fixed costs are relative to demand.

Because the incumbent is already in the market, its fixed entry cost is sunk. The incumbent firm ignores its sunk cost in deciding whether to operate. In contrast, the fixed cost of entry is an avoidable cost to the potential entrant, which incurs the cost only if entry takes place.

Whether an incumbent takes strategic action depends on the size of fixed costs and demand conditions, which determine π_m and π_d, and the cost of taking the strategic action, b. If entry is blockaded, there is no need for an incumbent firm to take strategic action. In the rest of this chapter, we concentrate on markets in which entry is not blockaded, so firms consider strategic actions.

APPLICATION

Government Deterrence

Existing firms often lobby legislatures and regulatory bodies to block entry by potential rivals. Some laws (for example, those regulating taxis and beer distributorships) limit the number of firms in a market, while others (including those pertaining to psychiatric hospitals, lawyers, doctors, and electricians) set up substantial barriers to entry.

Zoning laws are often used to block entry. When Home Depot tried to open a warehouse store in a New Jersey suburb, Pequannock, in 1993–1994, it encountered fierce opposition.[9] A group called Concerned Citizens for Community Preservation posted fliers and signs alleging that Home Depot had a "legacy" of crime and traffic safety violations. One flier ominously warned,

[9]De Lisser, Eleena, and Anita Sharpe, "Stealth Warfare," *Wall Street Journal*, August 18, 1995:A1, A5; Cory, James M., "Rickel Woes Are Self-Made," *Home Improvement Market*, 233(2)February 1996:13.

"Our kids will be crossing through this deathtrap!" The group's leader, a local attorney, got five experts to write reports and testify at a township planning board meeting to oppose Home Depot's zoning application. Their opposition effort worked: The zoning application was denied.

Then Home Depot tried to open a store in another New Jersey suburb, Bloomfield. Again the firm ran into a citizen's group, headed by the same lawyer. One of its fliers claimed that "over the past three years, 15% of the crime in Clifton has occurred at the Home Depot. 30% of Clifton's car thefts have occurred at Home Depot." But, according to the Clifton, N.J. Police Department, this lawyer had obtained a copy of their report that said that less than 2% of crime and fewer than 4% of car thefts had occurred at Home Depot in the past three years.

Who was paying for the lawyer and these groups? When Pequannock township officials asked involved residents, they got no answer. In 1995, Home Depot brought a lawsuit charging that Rickel Home Centers, a competitor based in South Plainfield, N.J., had used smear tactics to keep Home Depot from opening the stores in Pequannock and Bloomfield. In a motion that it filed to dismiss Home Depot's suit, Rickel acknowledged its involvement with the formation of the Bloomfield citizens' group.

Rickel had reason to be concerned about Home Depot. With 92 stores in 5 states, Rickel had sales in excess of $680 million a year. It saw Home Depot go from no stores in 1989 to sales of $500 million annually in New Jersey (and national sales of $12.5 billion). It seems likely that a firm would consider it prudent to spend money to try to prevent entry of a potentially effective rival. Following bad publicity from newspaper articles about its strategic actions and the success of Home Depot, Rickel declared bankruptcy in January 1996. ■

Commitment and Entry Prevention

Imagine that you run the incumbent firm. You may not be able to prevent entry. You can't expect to deter entry merely by telling a potential entrant, "Don't enter! This market ain't big enough for the two of us." The potential entrant will laugh and suggest that your firm exit if it doesn't want to share the market.

If the potential entrant won't agree to stay out of the market just because you've politely asked it to do so, you may be tempted to threaten it. (Actually, you surely wouldn't *threaten*, which is something only a thug would do. You might merely *suggest* that the potential entrant will suffer "adverse consequences" if it enters.) You might announce that your firm will produce such a large quantity if your rival enters that it will lose $100, as the game tree in Figure 14.2 shows.

Unfortunately for you, the potential entrant is almost certain to doubt the veracity of your statement: "Yeah! Right! You'll produce so much output that we'll both lose money. I don't think so." Your rival realizes that, once it enters, you are better off producing a smaller, Cournot output so that you'll make a $300 profit instead of suffering a $100 loss.

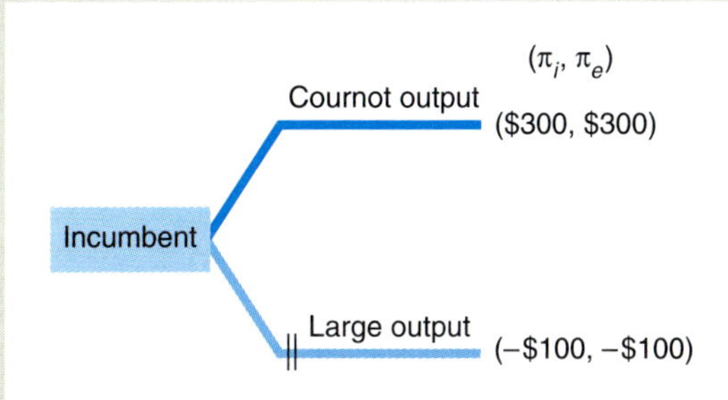

Figure 14.2 Noncredible Threat. The incumbent announces that it will produce such a large amount of output (lower path) if entry occurs that the entrant will lose money. The potential entrant doesn't believe this threat because it is not credible: The incumbent would make a higher profit by accommodating the entrant and the smaller, Cournot level of output.

For a firm's announced strategy to be a **credible threat**, rivals must believe that the firm's strategy is rational in the sense that it is in the firm's best interest to use it.[10] It wouldn't make sense for you to produce large quantities of output and lose money just to punish the other firm after it enters. Once entry occurs, it's too late for you to try to deter your rival. You might as well make the best of the situation and produce only the Cournot amount of output.

We now show that the situation changes if an incumbent can *commit* to producing a large quantity before the potential rival decides to enter. One way a firm can make such a commitment is to sign contracts to sell that amount of output to customers at a future date. By committing to produce a large quantity *whether or not entry occurs*, the incumbent discourages entry. Other firms know they will lose money if they enter because the incumbent is committed to selling a large quantity. Because entry does not occur, the incumbent makes a profit even though it produces a large enough quantity that it would make a loss if entry occurred.

Commitment as a Credible Threat. The intuition for why commitment makes a threat credible is that of "burning bridges." If the general burns the bridge behind the army so that it can only advance and not retreat, the army becomes a more fear-

[10]No doubt you've been in a restaurant and listened to an exasperated father trying to control his brat with an extreme threat such as, "If you don't behave, you'll have to sit in the car while we eat dinner" or "If you don't behave, you'll never see television again." The kid, of course, does not view such threats as credible and continues to terrorize the restaurant—proving that the kid is a better game theorist than the father.

some foe (like a cornered animal). Similarly, by limiting its future options, a firm makes itself stronger.[11]

Not all firms can make credible threats, however, because not all firms can make commitments. Typically, for a threat to succeed, a firm must have an advantage that allows it to harm the other firm before that firm can retaliate. Identical firms that act simultaneously cannot credibly threaten each other. A firm may be able to make its threatened behavior believable if firms differ. An important difference is the ability of one firm to act before the other—as could an incumbent firm that got a law passed preventing further entry.

The Cournot and Stackelberg models illustrate these points, as we saw in Chapter 12. In the Stackelberg model, the leader firm chooses its output level before the follower firm and thus has a *first-mover advantage*. Moving first allows the leader to *commit* to producing a relatively large quantity, q_s. Knowing that the leader will definitely produce that large quantity, the follower chooses a relatively small quantity, $q_f < q_s$, as in Figure 12.6.

In contrast, in the Cournot model, in which the two firms choose their output levels simultaneously, neither firm has an advantage over the other: Neither can commit credibly to producing a large quantity. If one firm announced in advance that it was going to produce a large quantity, the other firm would not view that claim as a credible threat (see the section "Why Moving Sequentially Is Essential" in Chapter 12).

Commitment Options. Suppose that an incumbent can commit to producing a large quantity of output before the potential entrant decides whether to enter. If the incumbent does not make a commitment before its rival enters, entry occurs and the incumbent earns a Cournot duopoly profit. By committing to produce the larger, Stackelberg leader quantity before entry occurs, the incumbent makes a larger profit. However, the incumbent may have a better option. Instead of accommodating entry, it may be able to commit to produce such a large quantity (larger than the Stackelberg leader quantity) that the potential entrant decides not to enter because it cannot make a positive profit.

Does the incumbent commit to producing the Stackelberg leader quantity or the larger, entry-deterring quantity? The incumbent uses the strategy that maximizes its profit, as the two game trees in Figure 14.3 illustrate. In each of these, the incumbent can accommodate entry by committing to produce the Stackelberg quantity (upper action), or it can deter entry by producing a larger quantity (which is the smallest quantity such that the potential entrant cannot make a profit).

The incumbent determines its optimal strategy by working backward (Chapter 12). First the incumbent determines what its rival will do, given that the incumbent

[11]Some psychologists use the idea of commitment to treat behavioral problems. A psychologist may advise an author with writer's block to set up an irreversible procedure whereby, if the author's book is not finished by a certain date, the author's check for $10,000 will be sent to the group the author hates most in the world—be it the Nazi Party, the Ku Klux Klan, or the National Save the Skeets Foundation. Such an irreversible commitment helps the author to get the project done by raising the cost of failure. (We can imagine the author as playing a game against the author's own better self.)

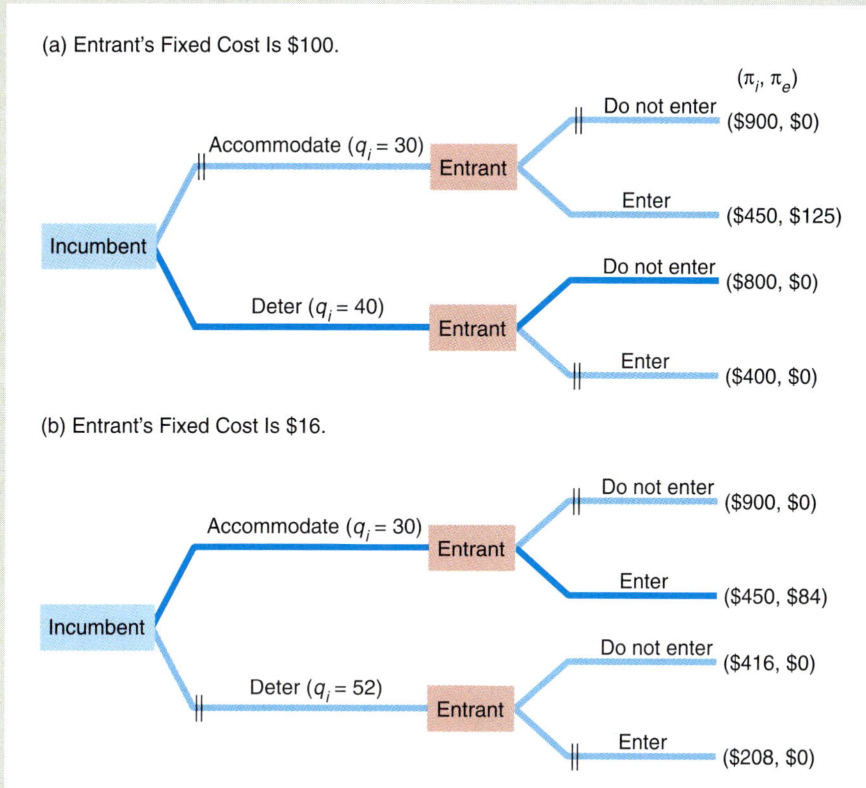

Figure 14.3 Game Trees for the Deterred Entry and Stackelberg Equilibria. (a) When the fixed cost of entry is $100, the incumbent earns more ($800) by deterring entry than accommodating it ($450). (b) When the fixed cost is only $16, the incumbent's profit is higher ($450) if it accommodates entry than if it deters it ($416).

takes each of its possible actions believing that its rival will behave rationally. Then the incumbent picks the action that maximizes its profit.

The two panels in Figure 14.3 differ as to the entrant's fixed cost of entering the market. Its fixed cost of entry is $100 in panel a and only $16 in panel b.

In panel a, the incumbent chooses to deter entry. If the incumbent commits to the Stackelberg leader quantity, q_i = 30, its rival makes $125 if it enters and $0 otherwise. Thus, the rival chooses to enter if the incumbent commits to 30 units (the double line shows that it rejects the no-entry path). If the incumbent commits to producing at least q_i = 40, the best the entrant can do if it enters is earn $0, the same amount it would earn if it didn't enter. The rival does not enter.[12]

[12]If the incumbent commits to producing more than 40 units, its rival will definitely lose money if it enters, but the incumbent's profit would be lower than if it produced only 40 units.

Thus, if the incumbent commits to the Stackelberg quantity, its rival enters and the incumbent earns \$450. If the incumbent commits to the larger quantity, its rival does not enter and the incumbent earns \$800. Clearly, the incumbent should commit to the larger quantity because it earns a larger profit. However, where the fixed cost of entry is lower, as in panel b, the incumbent's decision is reversed.

SOLVED PROBLEM 14.2

In panel b of Figure 14.3, does the incumbent firm make more profit by deterring entry?

Answer

1. *Determine the best responses of the potential entrant for each possible action by the incumbent firm*: The incumbent firm must first determine how its rival will react to each possible action. If the incumbent produces the smaller output, $q_i = 30$, the potential entrant makes more by entering, \$84, than staying out, \$0, so it enters. If the incumbent produces the larger output, $q_i = 52$, the best its rival can do is break even, so it does not enter.
2. *Given the best responses of the potential entrant, determine the strategy that maximizes the incumbent's profit*: If the incumbent firm produces the smaller output, its rival enters and the incumbent earns \$450. With the larger output, its rival doesn't enter and the incumbent earns \$416. Because it prefers \$450 to \$416, the incumbent commits to the smaller output. By doing so, it accommodates its rival's entry and acts as a Stackelberg leader. ■

★ Commitment and Fixed Costs

What causes these two examples to differ? A key factor is the fixed cost of entry. We illustrate the role that fixed cost plays in the incumbent's decision by looking at the demand and cost structure that underlie the game trees in Figure 14.3.

How well the incumbent firm does when faced with a potential entrant depends on whether it can commit and how large a fixed entry cost its rival must incur. There are three possibilities if the fixed cost is below the level where entry is blockaded:

- **Cournot equilibrium**: If the incumbent can't commit—so both firms are on an equal footing—the incumbent produces the Cournot equilibrium quantity.
- **Stackelberg (accommodated-entry) equilibrium**: If the incumbent can commit and the fixed cost of entry is relatively low, the incumbent commits to the Stackelberg leader quantity (larger than the Cournot quantity).
- **Deterred-entry equilibrium**: If the incumbent can commit and the fixed cost of entry is relatively high, it commits to a large enough quantity (larger than the Stackelberg quantity) to deter entry.

Table 14.2 Entrant's Best-Response and Profit

Incumbent's Output, q_i	Entrant's Best Response if $F = 0$, q_e	Entrant's Profit, $R - F$			Incumbent's Profit	
		$F = 0$	$F = \$16$	$F = \$100$	Entry π_s	No Entry π_m
60	0	0	−16*	−100*	0	0
52	4	16	0	−84*	208	416
50	5	25	9	−75*	250	500
40	10	100	84	0	400	800
30	15	225	209	125	450	900
20	20	400	384	300	400	800
10	25	625	609	525	250	500
0	30	900	884	800	0	0

*The entrant's profit if it produces the loss-minimizing output level. Profit is maximized at zero by not entering.

To illustrate these three possibilities, we suppose that the market demand is

$$p = 60 - Q, \tag{14.1}$$

where p is the market price and $Q = q_i + q_e$, the market quantity, is the sum of the incumbent's quantity, q_i, and the entrant's quantity, q_e. The marginal cost of production is zero (for simplicity), but a firm incurs a fixed cost of F to enter the market.

No Fixed Cost. Suppose that the fixed cost of entry is zero. Initially, we also assume that the incumbent firm cannot commit to an output level, so both firms must set their quantities at the same time. The incumbent's best-response function is[13]

$$q_i = 30 - \frac{q_e}{2}, \tag{14.2}$$

and the best-response function of its rival, the potential entrant, is

$$q_e = 30 - \frac{q_i}{2}. \tag{14.3}$$

The second column of Table 14.2 shows the rival's best responses to several of the incumbent's possible output levels.

[13]The demand intercept in Equation 14.1 is $a = \$60$, the absolute value of the slope of the demand curve is $b = 1$, the marginal cost is $m = \$0$, and there are two firms, $n = 2$. Substituting these values into Equation 12A.7 in Appendix 12A, the incumbent's best-response function is

$$q_i = (a - m)/(2b) - (n - 1)q_e/2 = 30 - q_e/2.$$

Solving Equations 14.2 and 14.3, we find that the Cournot equilibrium quantity is $q_i = q_e = 20$.[14] The intersection of the two best-response curves in panel a of Figure 14.4 determines the Cournot equilibrium, e_c.

Now suppose that the incumbent firm can commit to an output level before its rival makes its entry decision. Once the incumbent picks a level of output q_i, the rival uses its best-response curve in panel a of the figure (or column 2 of Table 14.2) to decide how much to produce. Thus, by setting its own output, the incumbent determines its rival's output level and hence the total market output. As a result, the incumbent's output level determines its profit, π_s, as panel b of the figure and the next to last (π_s with entry) column in Table 14.2 show.

The incumbent maximizes its profit at \$450 by committing to producing the Stackelberg leader output of 30 units, as panel b of Figure 14.4 shows. Its rival's best response is to produce the Stackelberg follower quantity, 15 units. By committing to the relatively large Stackelberg leader output, the incumbent increases its profit by \$50 over the Cournot level. This additional profit is the result of its commitment, which eliminates its flexibility in the amount of output it can produce.

Fixed Cost. Now suppose that the rival incurs a fixed cost to enter. If the incumbent firm can commit, it should produce at least the Stackelberg output because that raises its profit above the Cournot level.

Should the incumbent produce even more output and deter the potential entrant from producing at all? The answer depends on the size of the fixed cost. We look first at a relatively large fixed cost, F = \$100, and then at a smaller fixed cost, F = \$16.

The potential entrant's profit is its revenue minus its fixed cost (because it has no variable cost of production) if it enters and zero if it does not enter.[15] The rival enters only if it makes a profit from entering. Given that the fixed cost of entry is F = \$100, the rival enters only if its revenue is at least \$100. Table 14.2 shows how the potential entrant's profit varies with the incumbent's output. This table illustrates that the rival shouldn't enter the market if the incumbent produces 40 or more units of output. Similarly, the entrant's best-response curve in panel a of Figure 14.5 is zero when the incumbent's output is 40 or more units.

If the incumbent produces less than 40 units, entry occurs and the incumbent's profit is the solid portion of the π_s curve in panel b. For example, if it produces the Stackelberg leader output of 30 units, it earns \$450.

However, if the incumbent increases its output to 40 or more units, it deters entry and is a monopoly. The incumbent's profit is the solid portion of the π_m curve. As panel b shows, the incumbent maximizes its profit at \$800 by producing 40 units.

If the incumbent didn't have to worry about entry, it would produce 30 units and earn a profit of \$900. Because it fears entry, the incumbent commits to producing more than the monopoly equilibrium quantity to deter entry.

---

[14]Because both firms are identical, we can set both q_e and q_i equal to q in Equation 14.2 or 14.3 and solve for q. Alternatively, we can substitute the expression for q_e from Equation 14.3 into 14.2, solve for q_i, and then substitute the resulting expression for q_i into Equation 14.3 to obtain q_e.

[15]The analysis would be similar with a positive variable cost. Indeed, if demand were $p = 100 - Q$ and the marginal cost were constant at \$40, the analysis would be identical.

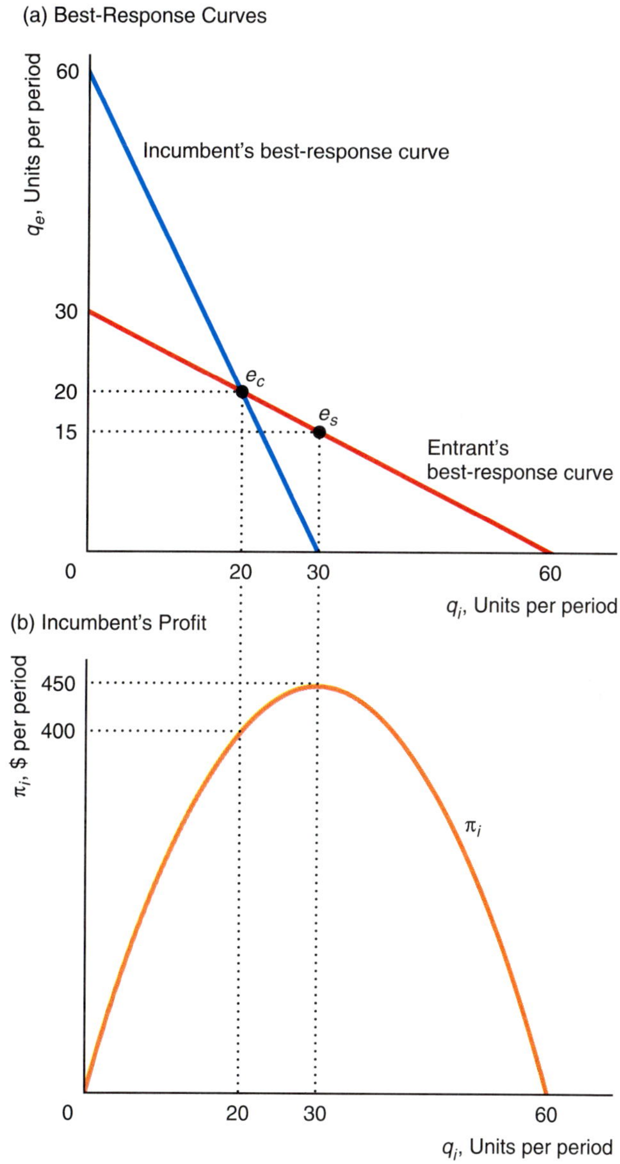

Figure 14.4 Cournot and Stackelberg Equilibria. (a) The Cournot equilibrium, e_c, is determined by the intersection of the best-response curves (where $F = 0$). If the incumbent can commit to a larger quantity, it produces the Stackelberg leader output, 30. (b) The incumbent's profit is maximized at the Stackelberg equilibrium, e_s.

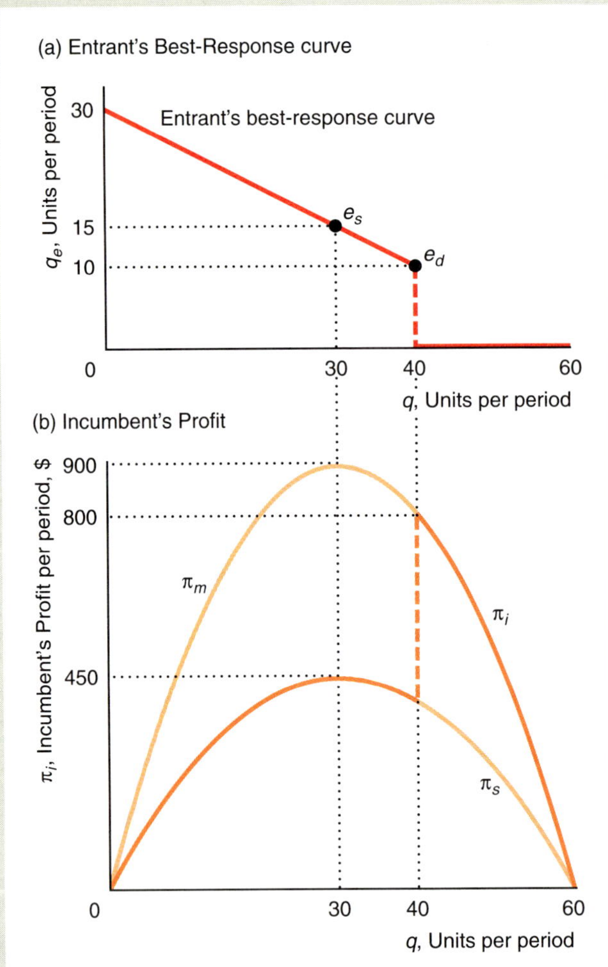

Figure 14.5 Incumbent Commits to a Large Quantity to Deter Entry. (a) Because it must pay a fixed cost of F = \$100 to enter, the potential entrant does not enter, and its best-response function is zero if $q_i \geq 40$. (b) The incumbent's profit, π_i (the solid portions of the π_s and π_m curves), is higher at $q_i = 40$, where it deters entry and is a monopoly (π_m = \$900), than at $q_i = 30$, where it is a Stackelberg leader (π_s = \$450).

Thus, if the potential entrant incurs a sizable fixed cost to enter and the incumbent can commit to a large quantity, it pays for the incumbent to produce more than the Stackelberg leader quantity and deter entry. Does it follow that the incumbent always deters entry as long as there is a fixed cost of entry? No, the incumbent doesn't deter entry if the fixed cost of entry is relatively small.

Suppose that the fixed cost of entry is only F = \$16. As Table 14.2 and panel a of Figure 14.6 show, the rival does not enter if the incumbent commits to produc-

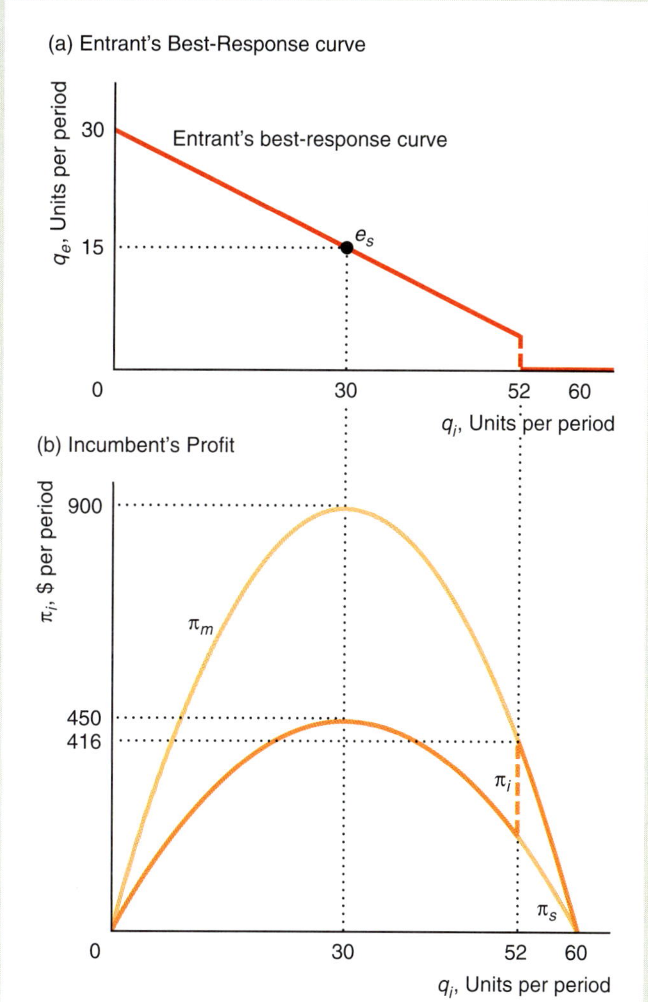

Figure 14.6 The Incumbent Loses if It Deters Entry. (a) If the fixed cost of entry is F = \$16, the potential entrant does not enter, and its best-response function is zero if $q_i \geq 52$. (b) The incumbent's profit, π_i, is higher at $q_i = 30$ ($\pi_i = \pi_s$ = \$450), where it doesn't deter entry, than at $q_i = 30$ ($\pi_i = \pi_d$ = \$416), where it deters entry.

ing 52 or more units of q_i. If the incumbent commits to selling 52 units to deter entry, its profit is \$416. That's less than the \$450 it earns if it commits to the Stackelberg quantity, $q_i = 30$, and accommodates entry. *Thus, if the fixed cost is relatively low or zero, the incumbent commits to the Stackelberg leader quantity. If the fixed cost is relatively high, the incumbent commits to a larger output to deter entry.*

SOLVED PROBLEM 14.3

Netscape and Microsoft both produce browsers for the Internet.[16] Each firm apparently believes that its software will be successful only if it performs the same tasks as the other firm's software does. Netscape would like to set the standard (determine the tasks the browser can perform), which we call *N*, while Microsoft would like to set its standard, *M*. Suppose that the payoffs to the firms are:[17]

		Microsoft	
		N Standard	*M Standard*
Netscape	*N Standard*	3 / 1	−1 / −1
	M Standard	−1 / −1	1 / 3

What are the pure-strategy Nash equilibria if the firms must pick their standards simultaneously? If Netscape can commit to a standard before Microsoft chooses, what is the Nash equilibrium?

Answer

1. *Determine the pure-strategy Nash equilibria if the firms must decide simultaneously*: There are two Nash equilibria in which both firms choose the same standard. If both choose the *N* standard, neither firm would change its strategy if it knew that the other was using the *N* standard. Netscape's profit falls from 3 to −1 if it changes its strategy from *N* to *M*, whereas Microsoft's profit falls from 1 to −1 if it makes that change.

[16] "The Internet is a great way to get on the net" (Bob Dole, former senator and Republican presidential candidate).

[17] This game is of the same form as the one that game theorists call *the battle of the sexes*. In that game, the husband likes to go to the mountains on vacation, and the wife prefers the ocean, but they both prefer to take their vacations together.

Similarly, neither firm would change its strategy from the *M* standard if it believed that the other firm would use the *M* standard.[18]

2. *Determine the Nash equilibrium if Netscape can commit to a strategy first*: If it can commit first, Netscape chooses the *N* standard. Netscape knows that, because Microsoft realizes that Netscape is using the *N* standard, Microsoft chooses the *N* standard because it makes more (1) than if it chooses the *M* standard (–1). Thus, with a first-mover advantage, Netscape chooses its own standard, which its rival accepts.[19] ■

14.3 CREATING AND USING COST ADVANTAGES

So far, we have examined how an incumbent firm obtains a complete barrier to entry (buys exclusive rights or gets the government to intervene) or commits to producing such large quantities that entry doesn't pay. We now examine the types of commitments an incumbent makes in an initial period to lower its marginal cost (relative to that of rivals) in later periods so as to deter entry.

A firm with a lower marginal cost has a larger market share and a higher profit than its higher-cost rival (Chapter 12). If its cost is very low relative to that of potential rivals, a firm can set a price low enough to prevent rivals from entering (Chapter 11). Thus, a firm benefits if it can lower its cost relative to that of its rivals or if it can raise its rivals' costs. We look at three techniques an incumbent may use: investing in new equipment, learning by doing, and raising rivals' costs.

Lowering Marginal Cost but Raising Total Cost

Should a monopoly buy a new piece of equipment that lowers its marginal cost but raises its total cost? The answer depends on whether buying the equipment will prevent potential rivals from entering.

---

[18]Each firm may also use a mixed strategy in which it is equally likely to choose either standard. If Microsoft chooses the *N* standard with a probability of $\frac{1}{3}$, then Netscape's expected profit is $(3 \times \frac{1}{3}) + (-1 \times \frac{2}{3}) = \frac{1}{3}$ if it chooses the *N* standard and $(-1 \times \frac{1}{3}) + (1 \times \frac{2}{3}) = \frac{1}{3}$ if it chooses the *M* standard. Thus, Netscape is indifferent as to which strategy it uses if it expects Microsoft to use this mixed strategy. Similarly, if Netscape uses that mixed strategy where it chooses *N* with a probability of $\frac{2}{3}$ and *M* with a probability of $\frac{1}{3}$, Microsoft is indifferent.

[19]Netscape was the first mover and had a tremendous advantage over Microsoft with its initial browsers. As the browsers were revised repeatedly, however, the issue of which firm moves first became moot. In 1997, the Department of Justice sued Microsoft, claiming that the firm was tying in its browser with its Windows operating system in an attempt to eliminate competitors from the browser market. Thus, the Department of Justice claimed that the firms' strategies are more complex and involve more products than in this simple example.

A monopoly manufacturing plant currently uses many workers to pack its product into boxes. It can replace these workers with an expensive set of robotic arms. Although the robotic arms raise the monopoly's fixed cost substantially, they lower its marginal cost because it no longer has to hire as many workers.

The monopoly would be enthusiastic about buying this equipment if the labor savings were large enough that its total cost of production would fall. Unfortunately for the monopoly, buying the robotic arms raises its total cost: The monopoly can't sell enough boxes to make the machine pay for itself, given the market demand curve.

Should the monopoly buy the machine anyway? Your response may be, "Is this a trick question? Why should the firm buy a machine that'll cause it to lose money?" Clearly, the firm shouldn't buy the machine if it is sure that it's going to remain a monopoly. However, if the incumbent fears that another firm will enter the market, it may make sense for the incumbent to buy the machine.

Purchasing the robotic equipment is a credible commitment. A potential entrant knows that, the lower is the incumbent's marginal cost, the more output the incumbent will produce. The incumbent can deter entry by buying the robotic arms if the incumbent produces so much output that its rival will lose money if it enters.

The game tree in Figure 14.7 illustrates why the incumbent may install the robotic arms to discourage entry even though its total cost rises. Problem 16 at the end of the chapter asks you to use best-response functions to derive the values in this game tree.) The robotic arms cost $1,804, but they lower the marginal cost of manufacturing from $40 to $4.

If the incumbent does not fear entry, it does not buy the machine. Its profit is $900 without the investment and only $500 with it.

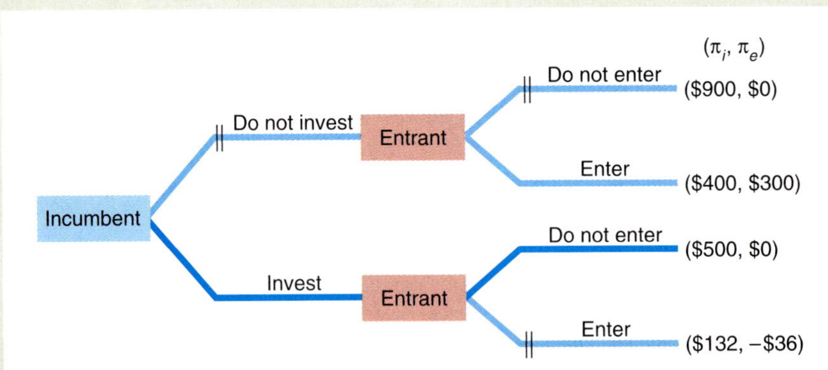

Figure 14.7 Investment Game Tree. The incumbent can invest in equipment that lowers its marginal cost. With the lowered marginal cost, it is credible that the incumbent will produce larger quantities of output, which discourages entry. The incumbent's monopoly (no entry) profit drops from $900 to $500 if it makes the investment, because the investment raises its total cost.

If the incumbent fears that a rival is poised to enter, it invests to discourage entry. If the incumbent doesn't buy the robotic arms, the rival enters because it makes $300 by entering and nothing if it stays out of the market. With entry, the incumbent's profit is $400. With the investment, the rival loses $36 if it enters, so it stays out of the market, losing nothing. Because of the investment, the incumbent earns $500. Nonetheless, earning $500 is better than earning only $400, so the incumbent invests.

Learning by Doing

A firm can often lower its marginal cost of production through *learning by doing*, by which workers and managers become more skilled at their jobs and discover better ways to produce as they gain experience (Chapter 7). Such a firm may want to increase its workers' experience by producing more in the first period so that it can produce at a lower marginal cost than its potential rivals in the second period. The firm produces more output in Period 1 than the quantity that maximizes its profit in that period, ignoring the future. Due to the resulting learning by doing, the incumbent's marginal cost is so low in Period 2 that the potential rival does not enter. (Problem 9 at the end of this chapter asks you to illustrate this result by using a game tree.)

An incumbent's gain from learning by doing depends on the amount by which a firm can lower its cost relative to its rival's and the length of time it takes to learn. The advantage of being in the market first is diminished if learning is extremely rapid *or* extremely slow. If learning is rapid, a late entrant can catch up quickly. When learning is slow, the first firm cannot lower its cost much by accelerating production. Thus, learning by doing is most likely to provide a strategic advantage for intermediate rates of learning (Spence 1981). If the cost advantage from learning by doing is substantial enough, the incumbent may successfully discourage the second firm from entering.

Raising Rivals' Costs

By raising its rivals' variable costs relative to its own, a firm may be able to increase its own profit (Krattenmaker and Salop 1986; Salop and Sheffman 1987). A firm can raise rivals' variable costs either directly or indirectly.

Direct Methods. By interfering with its rivals' production or selling methods, a firm can drive up its rivals' costs. The anecdote at the beginning of this chapter about British Airways' alleged treatment of Virgin Atlantic Airways illustrates this approach. Another (particularly sneaky) technique is to buy up all of a rival's product during periods of heavy advertising and return it later, depriving the rival of its extra advertising-induced sales.

By making it difficult for rivals to collect marketing information, a firm may raise their costs. For example, firms sometimes conduct marketing experiments by introducing a new brand or adjusting a price at only a single location. Rival firms can disrupt such an experiment by offering large discounts, engaging in a massive advertising campaign, or otherwise "jamming the signal" (Fudenberg and Tirole 1986).

In May 1995, the U.S. Customs Service raided a warehouse and confiscated 74.5 million large-caliber bullets—enough to fill at least 10 railroad cars—in one of the biggest seizures of ammunition in U.S. history. The accompanying import documents stated that the ammunition came from Russia at a time when the importing firm had a federal permit to import Russian ammunition, but federal investigators claimed that the ammunition was illegally smuggled in from a manufacturer in China. Shooting down the charge as ridiculous, the firm's president said, "We know who caused this problem. It was a competitor." Apparently, he believed that a competitor had called the feds. A month later, the government sheepishly returned the bullets, lending credence to the firm's claims.[20]

APPLICATION

Buttering Up Legislatures

Margarine was introduced in the United States in 1874.[21] Claiming that they wanted to protect customers from being misled by margarine manufacturers, butter producers lobbied for legislative controls on margarine. Allegedly, these laws were designed to protect consumers from having margarine passed off as butter. Actually, butter producers effectively got friendly legislatures to handicap their new rivals.

In 1877, New York and Maryland introduced labeling laws. Other states followed. Later, more stringent restrictions were passed. In 1886, New York imposed a special tax of two cents per pound on margarine and required annual license fees ($600 a year for manufacturers, $480 for wholesalers, and $48 for retailers). These higher costs lowered the profits of margarine producers and drove them from the market. In early 1887, there were six margarine manufacturers in New York City; a year later, there was only one; and by 1889, there was none.

In 1884 and 1885, several states passed laws forbidding the manufacture or sale of artificial butter

[20]Burdman, Pamela, and Charles Burress, "75 Million Rounds Seized in Santa Clara Ammo Raid," *San Francisco Chronicle*, May 4, 1995:A1, A13; Wallace, Bill, "Feds Return All Ammo from Raid; Santa Clara Firm Won't Sue over Botched Bust," *San Francisco Chronicle*, June 14, 1995:A19.

[21]Bergoffen, Celia, "Margarine Wars," *Audacity*, 3(4), Summer 1995:52–61.

within their borders, though the courts threw out some of these. Most states, except Massachusetts, repealed these bans. In 1894, the U.S. Supreme Court ruled that Massachusetts could prohibit the import of artificially colored margarine but not of uncolored margarine. The Court reasoned that consumers were protected against fraud because uncolored margarine could be distinguished easily from butter. By 1895, nineteen states had adopted their own anticolor laws. Five states required that margarine be dyed an unappetizing pink. Others required red or black colors. The Federal Margarine Act placed a 10¢ tax on colored margarine in 1902. Margarine manufacturers' profits fell because of the tax, the extra costs of coloring, and the reduced consumer demand for the weird-tinted margarine.

The color restrictions of the Federal Margarine Act were repealed in 1950. By 1955, every state except Minnesota and Wisconsin had repealed its anticolor laws. Minnesota held out until 1963, and Wisconsin, the Dairy State, did not concede until 1967. Only then were margarine producers able to compete with butter manufacturers on an even footing. ■

Indirect Methods. Firms may also use a variety of indirect methods to raise rivals' costs. Incumbent firms may lobby for a government regulation that disproportionately affects new firms. Many such regulations *grandfather* older firms—that is, exempt them from the law. Some environmental regulations, for example, require new plants to install pollution-control devices but exempt existing factories, thereby raising the relative costs of new firms.

Where one firm produces two products that must be used together and an entrant produces only one of these products, the firm that produces both can impose costs on the other firm. Apple Computer sells computers, operating systems, and peripheral equipment such as hard drives and printers. Some other firms produce only peripheral equipment. If it wants to do so, Apple can repeatedly change its hardware and operating systems for its computers, imposing extra costs on the peripheral manufacturers.

Many antitrust suits charge that incumbent firms buy up market supplies of scarce resources to prevent rivals from using them. For example, it was alleged (in *U.S.* v. *Aluminum Co. of America,* 148 F.2d 416 (1945)) that, by certain provisions in its contracts with power companies, Alcoa prevented those companies from supplying power to any other firm for the purpose of making aluminum.

In extreme cases, a resource may be an **essential facility**: a scarce resource that a rival must use to survive. Because all the railroad bridges in St. Louis were owned by a group of railroads, the railroads could have prevented entry by rivals by refusing them access to their essential facilities, the bridges. However, the U.S. Supreme Court ruled [in *United States* v. *Terminal Railroad Association of St. Louis*, 224 U.S. 383 (1912)] that the owning group had to provide access to rival railroads on reasonable terms. U.S. courts apparently are more likely to require that access to such facilities be provided if the owners have a monopoly.

APPLICATION

Preventing Customers from Switching

If an incumbent firm can make it difficult for its customers to switch to an entrant's brand in the future, it can discourage entry. A case in point involves the customers of Pacific Gas and Electric Company (PG&E), who were told that they'd have to pay a fee to stop buying from PG&E.[22]

When the federal Energy Regulatory Commission ordered electrical utilities to open up their transmission lines to competitors, it left a loophole for utilities that were stuck with high-cost nuclear power plants. If such a utility can show that it will lose revenue from the defection of some wholesale customers to cheaper energy suppliers, the utility can charge the departing customer a fee to help recover the lost revenues.

In 1996, California state regulators acted to block customers from bypassing PG&E—the former monopoly—and buying electricity from less expensive suppliers. Responding to a motion filed by PG&E, the regulators ruled that customers who stopped buying power from PG&E must pay it an exit fee as compensation for lost revenues.

PG&E asked for this help because other suppliers were on the verge of taking away billions of dollars a year of its business. PG&E was vulnerable to this competition because its costs were 40% above the national average (in part because of unusually high costs at the utility's Diablo Canyon nuclear plant). Competitors at the California-Oregon border could buy power from other Western utility companies at about 1¢ per kilowatt hour, which is about one-tenth of PG&E's average retail price.

This ruling clearly helped PG&E by making it difficult for other firms to enter the market and attract customers. You can probably sympathize with PG&E customers. Imagine how you'd feel if someone told you you'd have to pay money to walk out of your economics class early. ■

Raising All Firms' Costs

In some markets, an incumbent raises the costs of all firms, including its own. An incumbent wants higher costs if its cost is sunk, while its potential rivals' entry costs are still avoidable. Because its costs are sunk, the incumbent is more likely to remain in the market if costs rise than potential entrants are to enter. The incumbent derives a strategic advantage from its sunk-cost commitment: An incumbent is willing to spend more money to keep other firms out of the market than they are willing to spend to get into it (Salop 1979, Gilbert 1989), as we now illustrate in Figure 14.8.

[22]Salpukas, Agis, "Electric Utilities Ordered to Open Distribution Systems to Rivals," *San Francisco Chronicle*, April 25, 1996:A3; Marshall, Jonathan, "Regulators Give PG&E a Big Win," *San Francisco Chronicle*, April 11, 1996:D1.

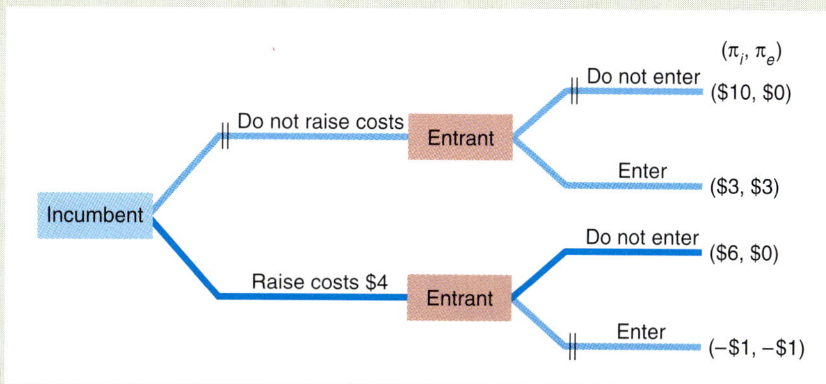

Figure 14.8 Raising Costs Game Tree. The incumbent induces the government to raise costs to all firms in the market by $4 so as to prevent entry.

Before entry, the incumbent earns a monopoly profit of π_m = $10 (million). If entry occurs, the incumbent and entrant together split the total duopoly profits of π_d = $6. If the incumbent and entrant share the duopoly profits equally, the entrant would pay up to $\pi_d/2$ = $3 to enter, whereas the incumbent would pay up to $\pi_m - \pi_d/2$ = $7 to exclude the potential entrant. Because π_m always exceeds π_d, $\pi_m - \pi_d/2 > \pi_d/2$, so it is always worth more to the monopoly to keep the entrant out than it is worth to the entrant to enter.

Suppose that the incumbent can induce the government to insist on pollution-control devices or other investments that raise the costs of all firms in the market. If the incumbent can raise an entrant's cost as well as its own by $4, the incumbent's profit is $6 if entry does not occur and it loses $1 if entry occurs. Because the new firm would lose $1 if it were to enter, it does not enter. Thus, the incumbent has an incentive to raise costs by $4 to both firms. The incumbent's profit is $6 if it raises costs rather than $3 if it does not.

Advantages and Disadvantages to Moving First

We've seen how a firm that enters the market first gains an advantage over potential rivals by moving first. The first-mover firm may prevent entry by building a reputation, committing to a large plant, raising costs to potential entrants, or getting an early start on learning by doing.

The downside of entering early is that the cost of entering quickly is higher, the odds of miscalculating demand are greater, and later entrants may build on the pioneer's research to produce a superior product. As the first of a new class of anti-ulcer drugs, Tagamet was extremely successful when it was introduced. However, the second entrant, Zantac, rapidly took the lion's share of the market. Zantac works similarly to Tagamet but has fewer side effects, could be taken less frequently when it was first introduced, and has been more effectively promoted.

Such examples of domination by second entrants are unusual. Urban, Carter, and Gaskin (1986) examined 129 successful consumer products and found that the second entrant gained, on average, only three-quarters of the market share of the pioneer and that later entrants captured even smaller shares.

Summary on Preventing Entry

An incumbent firm prefers that no other firm enter its market. If it is lucky, entry is blockaded: Even if this firm acts like a profit-maximizing monopoly, no other firm finds it profitable to enter. Other firms may find entry unprofitable because there is relatively little demand in this market or because entry costs are high.

If there is enough demand to support more than one firm and the incumbent moves first, the incumbent firm may take strategic actions to prevent entry. We examined how an incumbent may buy exclusive rights, lobby governments for laws limiting new entry, make commitments that reduce the incumbent's flexibility in production, and raise costs of all firms or just its rivals. There are many other strategies that firms can use. The next application shows that many firms admit that entry-preventing strategies are ubiquitous.[23]

APPLICATION

Evidence on Strategic Entry Deterrence

In theory, firms can prevent entry by manipulating price, product variety, reputation, information, scale or capacity, or in other ways. How commonly do they act to restrict entry?

Smiley (1988) surveyed firm managers in most industries about whether they attempted to limit entry by rivals. One might expect that firms that try to prevent entry in ways of questionable legality would be more likely to deny such behavior or refuse to respond to the survey at all. Thus, the following responses should probably be viewed as conservative estimates of the frequency with which entry-deterring strategies are used.

Firms were asked whether they employed the following techniques to deter entry:

- **Excess capacity**: Did the firm build a production plant large enough that the firm would be able to meet all expected demand for the new product so as to reduce the attractiveness of entry?

[23]*Ubiquitous* means "all over." This discussion of entry-preventing strategies is all over.

- **Advertising:** Did the firm advertise and promote the new product intensively so as to create sufficient product loyalty that potential rivals would find entry unattractive?
- **R&D-Patent:** Did the firm acquire patents for all similar products for a new product so as to prevent entry of similar products?
- **Reputation:** Did the firm signal (using the media or other means) that it would compete especially vigorously against new rivals so as to discourage entry?
- **Limit pricing:** Did the firm set a price lower than would otherwise be profitable so that a potential competitor would not imitate its new product or would slow its rate of entry?
- **Learning curve:** Did the firm market products aggressively in early stages to obtain low future costs and discourage entry?
- **Filling all niches:** Did the firm market so many (similar) products that a new entrant could not find sufficient demand to justify entering?
- **Hiding profit:** Did the firm move profits to other divisions within the firm to make the attractiveness of entry less apparent?

Table 14.3 shows the percentage of responding firms that reported using these techniques, depending on whether their product was new or had been in existence for a while. More than half of the respondents thought that entry considerations were at least as important as other strategic marketing and production decisions. Only 13% felt that entry considerations were unimportant. ■

Table 14.3 Strategies to Prevent Entry

	New Products			Existing Products		
Strategy	*Frequently*	*Sometimes*	*Never*	*Frequently*	*Sometimes*	*Never*
Excess capacity	6	58	36	7	63	30
Advertising	32	63	5	24	68	7
R&D-Patents	31	52	17	11	67	23
Reputation	10	68	23	8	72	21
Limit pricing (to prevent entry)	2	55	44	7	68	25
Limit pricing (to slow entry)	3	62	35	6	67	27
Learning curve	9	73	18			
Filling all niches				26	67	6
Hiding profits				31	58	12

14.4 ADVERTISING

> *Thirty-five percent of Americans say that they would be in favor of printing ads on dollar bills if it would result in lower taxes.*[24]

In addition to setting prices or quantities, choosing investments, and lobbying governments, firms engage in many other strategic actions to boost their profits. One of the most important is advertising.

Consumers are constantly exposed to advertising. When MCA/Universal Home Video released its *Jurassic Park* videotape at the end of 1994, it blitzed the market with ads designed to reach 98% of the adult population in the United States 25.2 times each.[25]

Promotional Activities

Advertising is only one way to promote a product. Other promotional activities include providing free samples and using sales agents. Some promotional tactics are subtle. For example, grocery stores place sugary breakfast cereals on lower shelves so that they are at children's eye level. According to a survey of 27 supermarkets nationwide by the Center for Science in the Public Interest, the average position of 10 child-appealing brands was on the next-to-bottom shelf, while the average position of 10 adult brands was on the next-to-top shelf.[26]

Before 1991, media advertising (television, radio, newspaper, and magazine ads) absorbed the major share of marketing budgets. Since 1991, consumer promotions—giveaways, tie-ins, coupons, contests, and the like—have taken the larger share. For example, in the summer of 1994, Frito-Lay put all its marketing dollars into sponsoring country singer Reba McEntire's concert tour.[27]

We begin this discussion by examining advertising (or other promotional activities) by a monopoly, which has no rivals. Then we consider strategic advertising in a duopoly, in which a firm advertises to attract customers from its rival.

Monopoly Advertising

A monopoly advertises to raise its profit. A successful advertising campaign shifts the market demand curve by changing consumers' tastes or informing them about new products. The monopoly may be able to change the tastes of some consumers

---

[24]Garchik, Leah, "Personal," *San Francisco Chronicle*, November 6, 1995:D10 (citing a poll reported in the *New Republic*).

[25]"*Jurassic Park* Video Due in Stores in October," *San Francisco Chronicle*, May 27, 1994:C14.

[26]Adult cereals contain an average of 10% sugar, while the kids' products average 44% sugar. *The Washington Post*, "Sugary Cereals Tempt the Tots," *San Francisco Chronicle*, April 11, 1990:Food 3.

[27]"Wilma! What Happened to the Plain Old Ad?" *Business Week*, 3375, June 6, 1994:54.

by telling them that a famous athlete or performer uses the product. Children and teenagers are frequently the targets of such advertising. If the advertising convinces some consumers that they can't live without the product, the monopoly's demand curve may shift outward and become less elastic at the new equilibrium, at which the firm charges a higher price for its product (see Chapter 11). If the firm informs potential consumers about a new use for the product—for example, "Vaseline petroleum jelly protects lips from chapping"—demand at each price increases.

APPLICATION

Smoking Gun Evidence?

Many advertising campaigns are designed to shift the tastes of children or teenagers. Presumably, ads claiming that a famous athlete or rock musician uses a firm's product are more likely to influence the demands of young people than of adults.

The Centers for Disease Control and Prevention (CDC) found that the three brands of cigarettes most often purchased by teenagers—Marlboro, Camel, and Newport—had the largest advertising budgets.[28] In 1994, the CDC asserted that cigarette manufacturers' promotional activities (including sponsoring rock concerts and sporting events and distributing jackets, T-shirts, and other products with brand logos) were increasingly designed to appeal to young people.

The CDC reports that teenagers' buying patterns for Marlboro and Camel over a four-year period corresponded to changes in brand-specific promotional spending and not to fluctuations in the brands' overall market shares. From 1989 to 1993, Marlboro's market share among youngsters fell, while Camel's increased. During that same period, Marlboro's advertising expenditures dropped from $102 million to $75 million, while Camel's rose from $27 million to $43 million. (Newport's market share grew, however, even though its advertising budget fell from $49 million to $35 million.) The CDC did not find a close connection with advertising and adult buying behavior.

In 1997, facing the threat of lawsuits and new laws, Camel's manufacturer agreed to remove the cartoon character Joe Camel from its advertising campaigns. One memo from Camel's manufacturer notes that the use of Joe Camel was an attempt to "'youthen' the brand: the entire advertising and promotional campaign used at the time was geared to this end, with the 'funny' Camel playing a key role in the advertising."[29] ■

---

[28]Reuters, "Cigaret Ads Linked to Teenage Smoking," *San Francisco Chronicle*, August 19, 1994:A5.

[29]Lockhead, Carolyn, "Joe Camel Designed to Lure Teens," *San Francisco Chronicle*, January 15, 1998:A1, A15.

The Decision Whether to Advertise. Even if advertising succeeds in shifting demand, it may not pay for the firm to advertise. If advertising shifts demand out or makes it less elastic, the firm's *gross profit*, which ignores the cost of advertising, must rise. The firm undertakes this advertising campaign, however, only if it expects its *net profit* (= gross profit – the cost of advertising) to increase.

To illustrate a monopoly's decisionmaking, Figure 14.9, we return to the Coke and Pepsi example from the last chapter. Initially, suppose that Coke is a monopoly in the United States. If it does not advertise, it faces the demand curve, D^1 (based on the estimates of Gasmi, Laffont, and Vuong, 1992). If Coke advertises at its current level, its demand curve shifts from D^1 to D^2.

Coke's marginal cost, MC, is constant and equals its average cost, AC, at \$5 per unit (10 cases). Before advertising, Coke chooses its output, Q_1 = 24 million units, where its marginal cost equals its marginal revenue, MR^1, based on its demand curve D^1. The profit-maximizing equilibrium is e_1, and the monopoly charges a price of p_1 = \$11. The monopoly's profit, π_1, is a box whose height is the difference

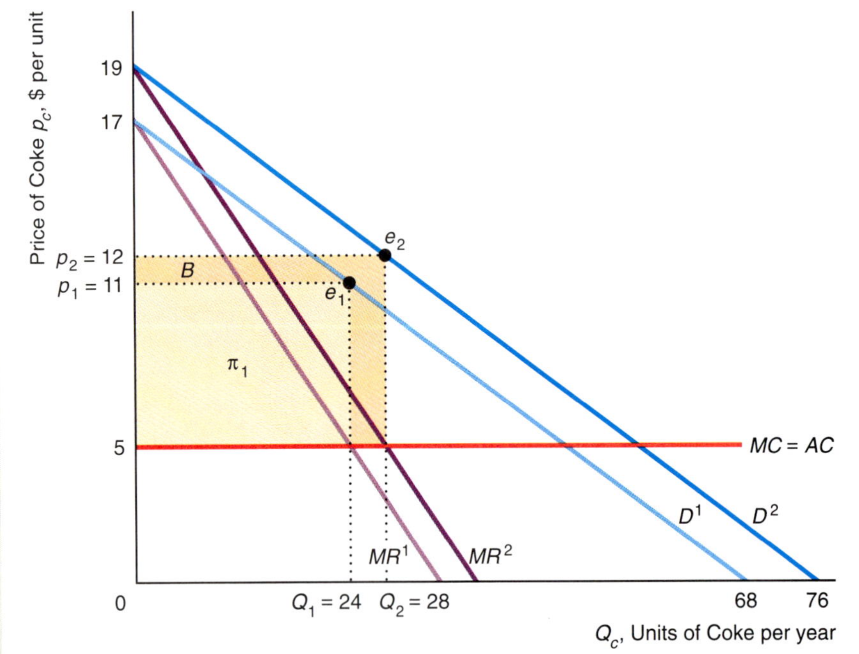

Figure 14.9 Advertising. Suppose Coke were a monopoly. If it does not advertise, its demand curve is D^1. At its actual level of advertising, its demand curve is D^2. Advertising increases Coke's gross profit (ignoring the cost of advertising) from π_1 to $\pi_2 = \pi_1 + B$. Thus, if the cost of advertising is less than the benefits from advertising, B, Coke's net profit (= gross profit – the cost of advertising) rises.

between the price and the average cost, \$6 (= \$11 – \$5) per unit, and whose length is the quantity, 24 units (tens of millions of cases of twelve-ounce cans).

After its advertising campaign (involving dancing polar bears or whatever) shifts its demand curve to D^2, Coke chooses a higher quantity, $Q_2 = 28$, where the MR^2 and MC curves intersect. In this new equilibrium, e_2, Coke charges $p_2 = \$12$. Despite this higher price, Coke sells more Coke after advertising because of the outward shift of its demand curve.

As a consequence, Coke's gross profit rises over 36%. Coke's new gross profit is the rectangle $\pi_1 + B$, where the height of the rectangle is the new price minus the average cost, \$7, and the length is the quantity, 28. Thus, the benefit, B, to Coke from advertising at this level is the increase in its gross profit. If its cost of advertising is less than B, its net profit rises and it pays for Coke to advertise at this level rather than not to advertise at all.

How Much to Advertise. In general, how much should a monopoly advertise to maximize its net profit? To answer this question we consider what happens if the monopoly raises or lowers its advertising expenditures by a dollar, which is its marginal cost of an additional unit of advertising. If a monopoly spends one more dollar on advertising and its gross profit rises by more than a dollar, its net profit rises, so the extra advertising pays. In contrast, the monopoly should reduce its advertising if the last dollar of advertising raises its gross profit by less than a dollar, so its net profit falls. Thus, the monopoly's level of advertising maximizes its net profit if the last dollar of advertising increases its gross profit by a dollar (see Appendix 14A for an alternative analysis). In short, the rule for setting the profit-maximizing amount of advertising is the same as that for setting the profit-maximizing amount of output: Set advertising or quantity where the marginal benefit (the extra gross profit from one more unit of advertising or the marginal revenue from one more unit of output) equals its marginal cost.

We can illustrate how firms use such marginal analysis to determine how much time to purchase from television stations for infomercials, those interminably long television advertisements sometimes featuring unique (and typically bizarre) plastic products: "Isn't that amazing?! It slices! It dices! It minces! ... But wait! That's not all!" As Figure 14.10 shows, the marginal cost per minute of broadcast time, MC, on small television stations is constant. The firm buys A_1 minutes of advertising time, where its marginal benefit, MB^1, equals its marginal cost.

APPLICATION

O. J. Trial Effect

Often, a major event such as the Super Bowl affects TV watchers' viewing behavior and the benefits from advertising. A particularly dramatic event was O. J. Simpson's 1995 trial for murder, which many television and radio stations broadcast. The *O. J. Factor* cut the take from infomercials on other television stations.[30] Sales sagged as viewers skipped program-length product pitches to watch trial coverage on weekday mornings.

The reason for the sales slump was that the marginal benefit curve for infomercials shifted. Where every \$1,000 spent on commercial time at 12:30 P.M. brought in an average of \$2,190 in sales in Charlotte, North Carolina, before the trial, it produced only \$1,790 (a drop of 18.3%) during the trial. The comparable figures for San Francisco at 9:30 A.M. were \$1,740 and \$790, a fall of 54.6%. Thus, for a given quantity (\$1,000 worth of advertising time), the marginal benefit for San Francisco shifted down by 54.6% from MB^1 to MB^2.

Because the marginal benefit curve shifted, a typical firm reduced the amount of advertising time it purchased to A_2, where MB^2 intersects MC. Estimates of average infomercial sales declines due to the Simpson trial ranged from 10% to 60% across cities. ■

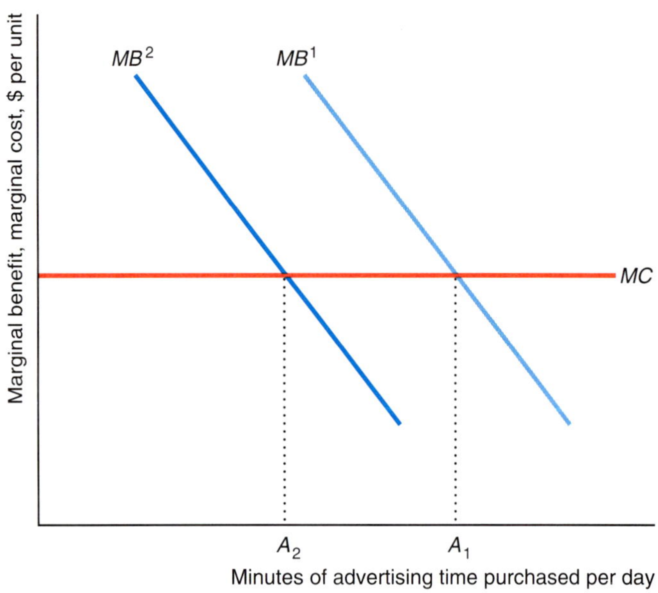

Figure 14.10 Shifts in the Marginal Benefit of Advertising. Before the Simpson trial, the marginal benefit of advertising is MB^1. The firm purchases A_1 minutes of advertising time, where MB^1 intersects its marginal cost per minute of broadcast time, MC, curve. During the trial, the marginal benefit curve shifts to the left to MB^2. As a result, the firm reduces its purchase of advertising time to A_2.

[30]Elliott, Stuart, "Advertising: The 'O. J. Factor' Takes a Toll on Producers of Infomercials," *New York Times*, March 24, 1995:C4.

Strategic Advertising

If there are several firms in a market, each chooses its optimal level of advertising by taking into account the advertising, pricing, and other strategies of its rivals. Advertising by one firm may help or hurt other firms.

Advertising That Helps Rivals. One firm may inform consumers about a new use for its product. By doing so, its advertising may cause demand for its own *and* rival brands to rise. A number of industry groups advertise collectively to increase demand for their product. In recent years, raisin growers (dancing raisins) and milk producers (milk mustache) have joined forces to run successful campaigns.

APPLICATION

Pink Toothbrush

Before World War I, only 26% of Americans brushed their teeth. By 1926, in part because of ads like those in Ipana's "pink toothbrush" campaign, which detailed the perils of bleeding gums, the share that brushed rose to 40%. Ipana's advertising helped all manufacturers of toothbrushes and toothpaste.[31] ■

Advertising That Hurts Rivals. Alternatively, a firm's advertising may increase demand for its product by taking customers from other firms. A firm may use advertising to differentiate its products from those of rivals. The advertising may describe actual physical differences in the products or try to convince customers that essentially identical products differ. If a firm succeeds with this latter type of advertising, the products are sometimes described as *spuriously* differentiated.

APPLICATION

Secret Ingredients

A firm can raise its profit if it can convince consumers that its product is superior to other brands. From the 1930s through the early 1970s, *secret ingredients* were a mainstay of consumer advertising.[32] These ingredients

---

[31]"50 Years Ago ...," *Consumer Reports*, January 1986.

[32]Elliott, Stuart, "Advertising," *New York Times*, April 28, 1994:C7.

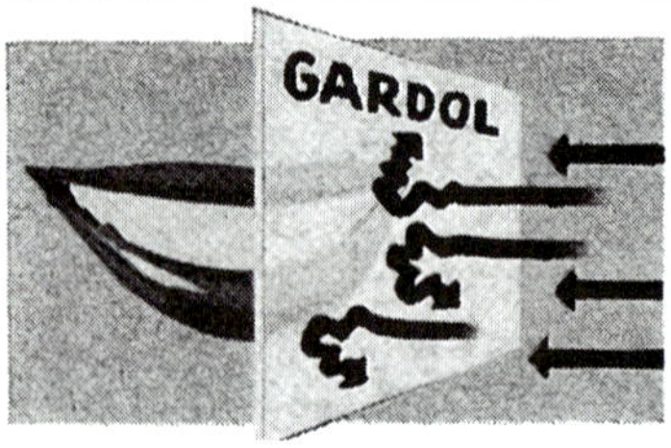

Gardol, Colgate's patented new decay-fighter, forms an invisible shield around your teeth. You can't feel it, taste it, or see it — but Gardol's protection won't rinse off or wear off all day. That's why Colgate's — the only leading toothpaste to contain Gardol — gives the *surest* protection ever offered by any toothpaste!

were given names combining letters and numbers to suggest that they were cooked up in laboratories rather than by Madison Avenue. Dial soap boasted that it contained AT-7. Rinso detergent had solium; Comet included chlorinol; and Bufferin had di-alminate. Among the toothpastes, Colgate had Gardol, Gleem had GL-70, Crest had fluoristan, and Ipana had hexachlorophene and Durenamel ("Bristol-Myer's brand of solium fluoride and soluble orthophosphate.")

About 20 years ago, secret-ingredient claims fell out of favor, and manufacturers asserted that their brands contained *natural* ingredients such as baking soda. In the last couple of years, however, the secret ingredient approach has been reintroduced to differentiate brand names from cheaper competitors. Recent ads remind us that Clorets breath-freshening gum and mints contain Actizol. Cheer detergent now touts an enzyme called Color Guard; Shade UVA Guard sunscreen lotion has Parasol 1789 and oxybenzone sunblock agents; and Pond's Dramatic Results Skin Smoothing Capsules have Nutrium, "a miraculous oil-free complex." ■

Empirical Evidence. We do not know from theory alone whether advertising by a firm will help or hurt other firms. At one extreme is cigarette advertising. Roberts and Samuelson (1988) found that cigarette advertising is cooperative: It increases the size of the market but doesn't change market shares substantially.[33] At the other extreme is cola advertising. Gasmi, Laffont, and Vuong (1992) reported that each firm's gain from advertising comes at the expense of its rival. Cola advertising has almost no effect on total market demand. Slade (1995) found results for saltine crackers that lie between these extremes.

Strategic Advertising Equilibria. Whether advertising hurts or helps rivals may affect the advertising strategies that firms use and the outcome. Table 14.4 shows two possible duopoly games in which firms decide whether to advertise or not.

Advertising only takes customers from rivals in panel a. If only one firm advertises, its advertising lures customers from the other firm. The advertising firm's profit does not rise by as much (from \$2 to \$3) as the other firm's profit falls (from \$2 to \$0) because of the cost of advertising. Both firms have a dominant strategy: Advertise. The Nash equilibrium is for both firms to advertise. This game is an example of the prisoners' dilemma. Both firms would be better off if they colluded and agreed not to advertise.

---

[33]Note, however, that the CDC's evidence suggests that advertising may shift the brand loyalty of youths.

Table 14.4 Advertising Game

a) Advertising Only Takes Customers from Rivals.

		Firm 1	
		Do Not Advertise	*Advertise*
Firm 2	*Do Not Advertise*	$2 $2	$3 $0
	Advertise	$0 $3	**$1** **$1**

b) Advertising Attracts New Customers to the Market.

		Firm 1	
		Do Not Advertise	*Advertise*
Firm 2	*Do Not Advertise*	$2 $2	$4 $3
	Advertise	$3 $4	**$5** $5

Advertising attracts new customers to both firms in panel b. If only one firm advertises, its profit rises by more ($2 to $4) than does that of the other firm ($2 to $3). If both advertise, however, they are better off than if only one advertises or neither advertises. Again, advertising is a dominant strategy for both firms.

In each of these games, both firms advertise. The distinction is that the Nash equilibrium in advertising is the same as the collusive equilibrium when advertising increases the market size (panel b, or the cigarette market). When advertising cannibalizes the sales of other firms in the market (panel a or the cola market), firms are worse off in an equilibrium in which they advertise. Consequently, cola firms would be delighted to have their advertising banned, but cigarette firms oppose an advertising ban.[34] In a more general model in which firms set the amount of advertising (rather than just decide to advertise or not), the amount of advertising depends critically on whether advertising increases the market size or only steals customers from rivals.

[34]In 1997 and 1998 under substantial legal and government pressure, the cigarette companies negotiated various restrictions on their advertising in the United States. However, they tried to avoid any restrictions on other types of promotional activities, which presumably they planned to use when they could no longer advertise.

Summary

1. **Preventing entry: simultaneous decisions:** If firms make simultaneous decisions about entering a market, the strategies that they choose depend on the size of the market and possibly on chance. If the market is large enough that two firms can make a profit, both enter. If only one firm can profitably produce, there are many possible Nash equilibria.

2. **Preventing entry: sequential decisions:** If an incumbent firm can commit to producing large quantities before another firm decides whether to enter the market, the incumbent may deter entry. The incumbent has a *first-mover advantage*.

   An incumbent acts to prevent entry only if it pays to do so. In a *blockaded* market, no potential entrant can make a profit even if the incumbent continues to act as a monopoly, so the incumbent ignores the threat of entry. When there is room for another firm to enter, the incumbent acts to *deter* entry if it is profitable to do so. Otherwise, the incumbent *accommodates* the entrant by doing nothing to prevent entry and reducing its output or price from the monopoly to duopoly level to maximize its postentry profit. Which outcome occurs depends on the cost of entry.

   An incumbent with first-mover advantage prevents entry by making a *credible threat*: It *commits* to taking an action (whether or not entry occurs) that lowers a potential entrant's profit. For example, the incumbent may commit to producing so much output that it will not be profitable for a rival to enter the market, a course the incumbent follows if the fixed costs of entering are relatively high. Otherwise, if entry costs are low, the incumbent produces a smaller amount that makes it a Stackelberg leader after entry occurs.

3. **Creating and using cost advantages:** A firm with a lower marginal cost has a larger market share and a higher profit than a higher-cost rival. A firm with substantially lower costs may prevent entry by a higher-cost rival. Thus, firms benefit from lowering their marginal costs relative to those of rivals. It may pay for a firm to invest in a new technology that raises its total cost of production if such an investment lowers its marginal cost substantially. By lowering its marginal cost, the firm credibly commits to producing relatively large levels of output and thereby discourages entry. Firms may also use learning by doing or various direct and indirect methods so that their costs fall relative to those of their rivals (or so that their rivals' costs rise relatively).

4. **Advertising:** Firms advertise to shift their demand curve outward or to reduce the elasticity of demand they face in equilibrium. Advertising may differentiate a firm's product or inform consumers about new products or new uses for a product. The strategies that firms use in deciding how much to advertise depend on the effect of advertising on rivals' customers. If a firm's advertising increases total market demand, all firms may benefit. Alternatively, if a firm's advertising takes customers from a rival, one firm's gain comes at the expense of the other firm.

Problems

1. Show the payoff matrix for two drivers engaged in the game of chicken (described in footnote 5). Describe the possible Nash equilibria for this game.
2. Modify the payoff matrix in the game of chicken in Problem 1 so that, if neither driver swerves, the payoff is –2. How does that change the equilibria?
3. Suppose that Solved Problem 14.1 were modified so that GM has no subsidy but does have a head start over Ford and can move first. What is the Nash equilibrium? Explain.
4. Suppose that Panasonic and Zenith are the only two firms that can produce a new type of high-definition television. The payoffs (in millions of dollars) from entering this product market are shown in the following payoff table.
   A. If both firms move simultaneously, does either firm have a dominant strategy? Explain.
   B. What are the Nash equilibria, given that both firms move simultaneously?

C. If the U.S. government commits to paying Zenith a lump-sum subsidy of \$50 million if it enters this market, what is the Nash equilibrium?

D. If Zenith does not receive a subsidy but has a head start over Panasonic, what is the Nash equilibrium?

		Panasonic	
		Enter	*Do Not Enter*
Zenith	*Enter*	Zenith: –40; Panasonic: –40	Zenith: 250; Panasonic: 0
	Do Not Enter	Zenith: 0; Panasonic: 250	Zenith: 0; Panasonic: 0

5. Suppose that the payoffs facing two firms are as shown in the following payoff table.
   Given these payoffs, Firm 2 wants to match Firm 1's price, but Firm 1 does not want to match Firm 2's price. What—if any—are the pure-strategy Nash equilibria of this game?

		Firm 1	
		Low Price	*High Price*
Firm 2	*Low Price*	Firm 2: \$2; Firm 1: \$0	Firm 2: \$1; Firm 1: \$2
	High Price	Firm 2: \$0; Firm 1: \$7	Firm 2: \$6; Firm 1: \$6

★6. What is the mixed-strategy Nash equilibrium for the game in Problem 5?

7. Currently, there is an incumbent monopoly in the market. Next year, a potential entrant may enter. If the incumbent spends *b* dollars lobbying, it can get the legislature to pass a law that places a lump-sum tax of *T* on the potential entrant if it enters. If the potential entrant stays out of the market, it makes no profit, $\pi_e = 0$, and the incumbent firm makes the monopoly profit, $\pi_m > 0$, minus the expenditure on lobbying if any (*b* or 0). If the potential entrant enters the market, it gets the duopoly profit, $\pi_d > 0$, minus the tax, if any, and the incumbent earns the duopoly profit minus the lobbying costs, if any. Draw the game tree. If the incumbent lobbies, under what conditions (in terms of π_m, π_d, *b*, or *T*) will the potential entrant NOT enter? If the potential entrant will not enter when the incumbent lobbies, under what conditions (in terms of π_m, π_d, *b*, and/or *T*) will the incumbent act to deter entry by lobbying?

8. Suppose that you and a friend play a "matching pennies" game, in which each of you uncovers a penny. If both pennies show heads or both show tails, you keep both. If one shows heads and the other shows tails, your friend keeps them. Show the payoff matrix. What—if any—is the pure strategy Nash equilibrium to this game?

9. The more an incumbent firm produces in the first period, the lower is its marginal cost in the second period. If a potential entrant expects the incumbent to produce a large quantity in the second period, it does not enter. Draw a game tree to illustrate why an incumbent would produce more in the first period than the single-period profit-maximizing level. Now change the payoffs in the tree to show a situation in which the firm does not increase production in the first period.

10. According to a newspaper article cited in the chapter, if a firm spent \$1,000 on commercial television time at 12:30 P.M. in Charlotte, North Carolina, its sales rose by \$2,190 before the O. J. Simpson trial. If a firm bought \$1,000 of advertising time, was it advertising optimally? If not, should it have increased or decreased the amount it advertised?

11. If using the Internet allows a monopoly to reduce its cost of advertising, how will the total amount that the firm spends on advertising change?

Math Problems

12. Duopoly quantity-setting firms face a market demand

$$p = 150 - q_1 - q_2.$$

Each firm has a marginal cost of \$60 per unit. What is the Cournot equilibrium?

13. In Problem 12, what is the Stackelberg equilibrium where Firm 1 moves first?

14. Given the information in Problems 12 and 13, derive (and draw) the best-response curve of Firm 2 if it has a fixed cost of entry of \$100.

15. Given the information in Problems 12–14, what is the optimal strategy for Firm 1, the first mover, to use? What is the equilibrium? Draw the game tree.

16. Using best-response functions, show that the numbers in Figure 14.7 are correct. The market demand is $p = 100 - Q$, where $Q = q_i + q_e$. The potential entrant incurs a fixed cost of \$100 to enter, and its constant marginal cost is \$40. The incumbent's marginal cost is \$40 without investment and \$4 if it buys the robotic arms at a cost of \$1,804. (*Hint*: Use Equation 12A.7 in Appendix 12A to derive the best-response functions.)

17. The demand facing a monopoly is

$$p = 100 - Q + A^{1/2},$$

where Q is its quantity, p is its price, and A is the advertising. Its marginal cost of production is 10, and its cost of a unit of advertising is 1. What is the firm's profit equation? Solve for the firm's profit-maximizing price, quantity, and level of advertising. (*Hint*: See Appendix 14A.)

18. What is the monopoly's profit-maximizing output, Q, and level of advertising, A, if it faces a demand curve of $p = a - bQ + cA^{\alpha}$, its constant marginal cost of producing output is m, and the cost of a unit of advertising is \$1?

★19. Determine the Nash equilibrium where the duopoly firms set price and advertising. The firms face demand curves

$$q_1 = \alpha_1 - \beta_{11}p_1 + \beta_{12}p_2 + \gamma_{11}(A_1)^{1/2} - \gamma_{12}(A_2)^{1/2},$$

$$q_2 = \alpha_2 + \beta_{21}p_1 - \beta_{22}p_2 - \gamma_{21}(A_1)^{1/2} + \gamma_{22}(A_2)^{1/2},$$

where the Greek letter coefficients are positive numbers, p_i is the price, q_i is the quantity, and A_i is the level of advertising of Firm i. Each firm has a constant marginal cost, m, of production, and the marginal cost of advertising is \$1.

CHAPTER 15

Factor Markets and Vertical Integration

Work is of two kinds: first, altering the position of matter at or near the earth's surface relative to other matter; second, telling other people to do so. —Bertrand Russell

To broadcast a television show, a local television station uses a variety of inputs. It builds or leases a studio, purchases or rents transmission equipment, hires labor, and buys or produces its own shows.[1] The firm that owns the station may buy all these inputs from a market or produce some of them itself.

In the last few years, many media and communications companies have merged so that each could provide most of the services needed to bring entertainment into your home. Disney, Time Warner, and other major media firms are **vertically integrated**: firms that participate in more than one successive stage of the production or distribution of goods or services.

Rupert Murdoch's News Corporation is one of the most integrated firms.[2] Its Fox Film Entertainment Group makes movies (*Speed*), TV shows (*Married. . . With Children*), and animated features (*The Simpsons*). The Fox network provides Fox-made shows to Fox-owned TV stations and affiliated stations in the United States and Australia. Twelve Fox TV stations broadcast the network's shows to major local markets, including New York City, Los Angeles, and Chicago. Fox also delivers its shows directly via cable stations and satellite dishes around the world through companies that it partially or totally owns, such as fx, fxM, Fox Sports Net, Fox Sports International, ASkyB, and SkyMCI in the United States; BSkyB in the United Kingdom; Star TV, Zee TV, and JSkyB in Asia; Vox in Germany; Foxtel in Australia; and Sky Entertainment Latin American and Canal Fox in Latin America and the Caribbean. The parent company even owns *TV Guide*.

When does a firm buy factors from a market, and when does it produce those factors itself? The answer is that firms vertically integrate if the benefits outweigh the costs. Before we can examine the trade-off between these costs and benefits, we need to analyze how factor markets work.

We show that the factor-market equilibrium price depends on the structure of factor markets and the output market. We first look at competitive factor and output markets. We then examine the effect of a monopoly in either or both markets.

---

[1]In this chapter, we consider only nondurable inputs such as labor services, capital services, materials, and energy. We examine the factor markets for durable goods such as capital in the next chapter. A firm may buy durable capital (say, a truck) that lasts for several periods but rent capital services as needed (for example, by the week or month).

[2]Fabrikant, Geraldine, "Murdoch Bets Heavily on a Global Vision," *New York Times*, July 29, 1996:C1, C6, C7.

We next consider markets in which there is a **monopsony**: the only buyer of a good in a market. A monopsony is the mirror image of a monopoly. Whereas a monopoly sells at a price higher than a competitive industry would charge, a monopsony buys at a lower price than does a competitive industry. Finally, we investigate when a firm vertically integrates to produce inputs itself and when it buys the inputs from a factor market.

In this chapter, we examine four main topics:

1. **Competitive factor market:** The intersection of the factor supply curve and factor demand curve (which depends on firms' production functions and the market price for output) determines the equilibrium in a competitive factor market.
2. **Effect of monopolies on factor markets:** If firms exercise market power in either factor or output markets, the quantities of inputs and outputs sold fall.
3. **Monopsony:** A monopsony maximizes its profit by paying a price below the competitive level, which creates a deadweight loss for society.
4. **Vertical integration:** A firm engages in many sequential stages of production itself, performs in only a few stages and relies on markets for others, or uses contracts or other means to coordinate its activities with those of other firms, depending on which approach is the most profitable.

15.1 COMPETITIVE FACTOR MARKET

Virtually all firms rely on factor markets for at least some inputs. The firms that buy factors may be competitive price takers or noncompetitive price setters, such as a monopsony. Competitive, monopolistically competitive, oligopolistic, or monopolistic firms sell factors. Here we examine factor markets in which buying and selling firms are competitive price takers. In the next section, we consider noncompetitive factor markets.

Factor markets are competitive when there are many small buyers and sellers. The flower auction in Amsterdam that the Verenigde Bloemenveilingen Aalsmeer cooperative holds daily (Chapter 8) typifies such a competitive market with many sellers and buyers. The sellers supply inputs (flowers in bulk) to buyers, which sell outputs (a few trimmed flowers in vases, or bouquets wrapped in paper) at retail to final customers.

Our earlier analysis of the competitive supply curve applies to factor markets. Chapter 5 derives the supply curve of labor by examining how individuals' choices between labor and leisure depend on tastes and the wage rate. Chapter 8 determines the competitive supply curves of firms in general, including those that produce factors for other firms. Given that we know the supply curve, all we need to do to analyze a competitive factor market is to determine the factor's demand curve.

Short-Run Factor Demand of a Firm

A profit-maximizing firm's demand for a factor of production is downward sloping: The higher the price of an input, the less the firm wants to buy. To understand what is behind a firm's factor demand, we examine a firm that uses capital and labor to produce output from factors. Using the theory of the firm (Chapters 6 and 7), we show how the amount of an input the firm demands depends on the prices of the factors and the price of the final output.

We start by considering the short-run factor demand for labor of a firm that can vary labor but not capital. Then we examine long-run factor demands when both inputs are variable.

In the short run, a firm has a fixed amount of capital, $\bar{K}$, and can vary the number of workers, L, it employs. Will the firm's profit rise if it hires one more worker? The answer depends on whether its revenue or labor costs rise more when output expands.

An extra worker per hour raises the firm's output per hour, q, by the marginal product of labor, $MP_L = \Delta q/\Delta L$ (Chapter 6). How much is that extra output worth to the firm? The extra revenue, R, from the last unit of output is the firm's marginal revenue, $MR = \Delta R/\Delta q$. As a result, the **marginal revenue product of labor** (MRP_L), the extra revenue from hiring one more worker, is[3]

$$MRP_L = MR \times MP_L.$$

For a firm that is a competitive employer of labor, the marginal cost of hiring one more worker per hour is the wage, w. Hiring an extra worker raises the firm's profit if the marginal benefit—the marginal revenue product of labor—is greater than the marginal cost—the wage—from one more worker: $MRP_L > w$. If the marginal revenue product of labor is less than the wage, $MRP_L < w$, the firm can raise its profit by reducing the number of workers it employs. Thus, the *firm maximizes its profit by hiring workers until the marginal revenue product of the last worker exactly equals the marginal cost of employing that worker, which is the wage*:

$$MRP_L = w.$$

For now, we restrict our attention to competitive firms. A competitive firm faces an infinitely elastic demand for its output at the market price, p, so its marginal revenue is p (Chapter 8), and its marginal revenue product of labor is

$$MRP_L = p \times MP_L.$$

The marginal revenue product for a competitive firm is also called the *value of the marginal product* because it equals the market price times the marginal product of labor: the market value of the extra output. The competitive firm hires labor to the point at which its marginal revenue product of labor equals the wage:

$$MRP_L = p \times MP_L = w. \quad (15.1)$$

---

[3]In the short run, output is a function of only labor, $q(L)$. The price the firm receives from selling q units of output is given by its demand function, $p(q)$. Thus, the revenue that the firm receives is $R(L) = p(q(L))q(L)$. The extra revenue that the firm obtains from using an extra amount of labor services is derived using the chain rule of differentiation:

$$MRP_L \equiv \frac{dR}{dL} = \frac{dR}{dq} \times \frac{dq}{dL} \equiv MR \times MP_L.$$

Table 15.1 illustrates the relationship in Equation 15.1. If the firm hires $L = 3$ workers per hour, the marginal product from the third worker is 5 units of output per hour. Because the firm can sell the output at the market price $p = \$3$ per unit, the extra revenue from hiring the third worker is $MRP_L = p \times MP_L = \$3 \times 5 = \$15$. By hiring this worker, the firm increases its profit because the wage of this worker is only $w = \$12$. If the firm hires a fourth worker, the marginal product of labor from this last worker falls to 4, and the marginal revenue product of labor falls to \$12. Thus, the extra revenue from the last worker exactly equals that worker's wage, so the firm's profit is unchanged. Were the firm to hire a fifth worker, the $MRP_L = \$9$ is less than the wage of \$12, so its profit would fall.

Panel a of Figure 15.1 shows the same relationship. The wage line, $w = \$12$, intersects the MRP_L curve at $L = 4$ workers per hour. *The wage line is the supply of labor facing the firm.* As a competitive buyer of labor services, the firm can hire as many workers as it wants at a constant wage of \$12. *The marginal revenue product of labor curve, MRP_L, is the firm's demand curve for labor* when other inputs are fixed. It shows the maximum wage a firm is willing to pay to hire a given number of workers. Thus, the intersection of the supply curve of labor facing the firm and the firm's demand curve for labor, Equation 15.1, determines the profit-maximizing number of workers.

A firm's labor demand curve is usually downward sloping because of the law of diminishing marginal returns (Chapter 6). The marginal product from extra workers, MP_L, of a firm with fixed capital eventually falls as the firm increases the amount of labor it uses. Table 15.1 illustrates that the marginal product of labor falls from 6 for the second worker to 2 for the sixth worker. Because the marginal product of labor declines as more workers are hired, the marginal revenue product of labor (which equals a constant price times the marginal product of labor) or demand curve must slope downward as well.

Profit Maximization Using Labor or Output. Chapter 8 presents another profit-maximization condition: A competitive firm maximizes its profit by operating where the market price, p, equals the marginal cost of an extra unit of output, MC (Equation

Table 15.1 Marginal Product of Labor, Marginal Revenue Product of Labor, and Marginal Cost

Labor, L	Marginal Product of Labor, MP_L	Marginal Revenue Product of Labor, $MRP_L = 3MP_L$	Output, q	Marginal Cost, $MC = 12/MP_L$
2	6	\$18	13	\$2
3	5	\$15	18	\$2.4
4	4	\$12	22	\$3
5	3	\$9	25	\$4
6	2	\$6	27	\$6

Note: Wage, w, is \$12 per hour of work. Price, p, is \$3 per unit of output. Labor is variable and capital is fixed.

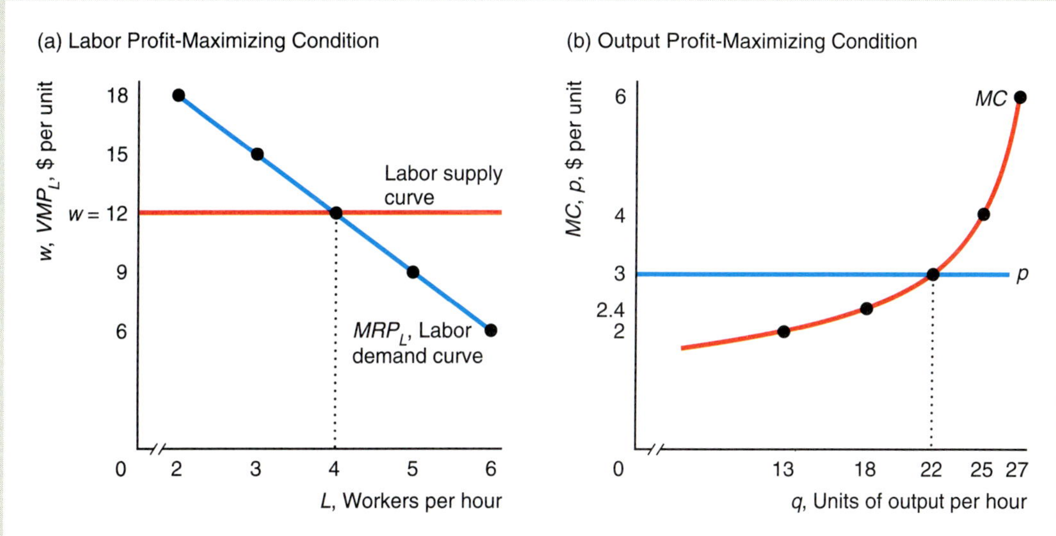

Figure 15.1 Labor Market and Output Market Equilibria Are Related. (a) The firm's profit is maximized at L = 4 workers per hour where the wage line, w = \$12, crosses the marginal revenue product of labor, MRP_L, curve, which is also the demand curve for labor. (b) The firm's profit is maximized at 22 units of output (produced by 4 workers), for which its marginal cost, $MC = w/MP_L$, curve equals the market price, p = \$3.

8.1). This output profit-maximizing condition is equivalent to the labor profit-maximizing condition in Equation 15.1. Dividing Equation 15.1 by MP_L, we find that

$$p = \frac{w}{MP_L} = MC.$$

As Chapter 7 shows, the marginal cost equals the wage, w, times one over the marginal product of labor, which is the extra labor, $\Delta L/\Delta q$, necessary to produce one more unit of output. The marginal cost is the cost of the extra labor, $w\Delta L$, needed to produce the extra output, Δq.

Table 15.1 illustrates this relationship. The fourth column shows how the amount of output produced varies with the number of workers. Because 3 workers produce 18 units of output and 4 workers produce 22 units of output, the marginal product of the fourth worker is 4 units of output. With a wage of \$12, the marginal cost for the last unit of output is $MC = w/MP_L$ = \$12/4 = \$3. The market price is also \$3, so the firm maximizes its profit by producing 22 units of output, as panel b of Figure 15.1 illustrates.

In summary, the two profit-maximizing equilibria in Figure 15.1 give the same answer: The firm maximizes its profit by hiring 4 workers to produce 22 units of output. Panel a shows that the firm maximizes its profit by hiring 4 workers, for which the marginal benefit or marginal revenue product from the last worker,

MRP_L, equals the marginal cost of that worker, w. Panel b shows that the firm maximizes its profit by producing 22 units of output, for which the marginal benefit or marginal revenue from the last unit of output, p = \$3, equals the marginal cost of the last unit of output, MC.

How Changes in Wages and Prices Affect Factor Demand. The number of workers a firm hires depends on the wage and the price of the final good, as Equation 15.1 shows. Suppose that the supply of labor shifts so that the wage falls from w_1 = \$12 to w_2 = \$6 while the market price remains constant at \$3. The firm hires more workers because the cost of more labor falls while the incremental revenue from additional output is unchanged. Figure 15.2 shows that a fall in the wage due

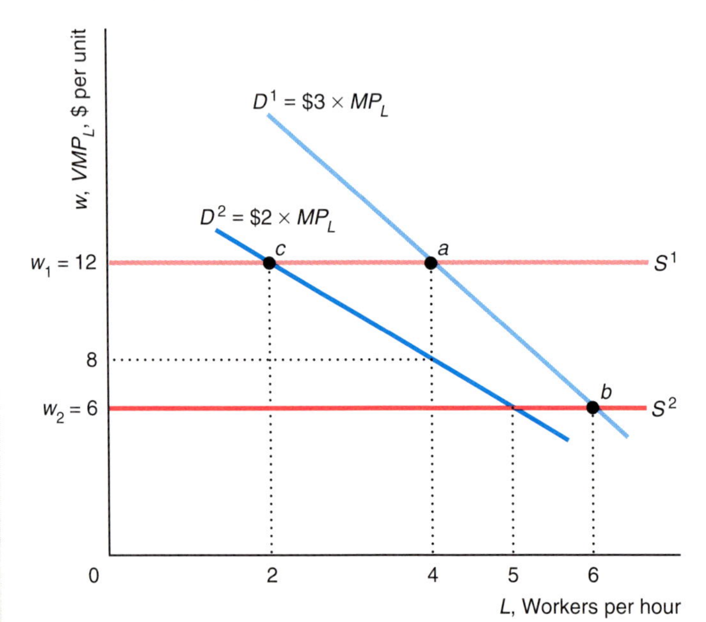

Figure 15.2 Shift of and Movement Along the Labor Demand Curve. If the market price is \$3, the firm's labor demand curve is D^1. A fall in the wage causes a *shift of the supply curve* from S^1 to S^2 and a *shift along the demand curve for labor*. If the wage is w_1 = \$12, the firm hires 4 workers per hour, equilibrium point *a*. If the wage falls to w_2 = \$6, the firm hires 6 workers, point *b*. A fall in the market price causes a *shift of the demand curve for labor*. A fall in the market price to \$2 causes a *shift of the firm's demand curve for labor* from D^1 to D^2. If the wage stays constant at w_1 = \$12, the fall in the market price causes a *movement along the supply curve* S^1: The number of workers the firm hires falls from 4, point *a* on D^1 and S^1, to 2, point *c* on D^2 and S^1.

to a downward shift of the labor supply curve from S^1 to S^2 causes a shift along the labor demand curve D^1 from point *a*, where the firm hires 4 workers, to point *b*, where the firm hires 6 workers per hour.

If the market price falls from \$3 to \$2, the demand curve for labor shifts down from D^1 to D^2. Demand D^2 is only $\frac{2}{3} = (2MP_L)/(3MP_L)$ as high as D^1 at any given quantity of labor. If the wage stays constant at w_1 = \$12, the firm reduces its demand for workers from 4, point *a*, to 2, point *c*.

Thus, a shift in either the market wage or the market price affects the amount of labor that a firm employs. A study of German manufacturing firms in 1980 (Ross and Zimmerman 1993) finds that changes in the price of the final good—output demand—were more important than changes in relative wages in determining shifts in labor demand.

SOLVED PROBLEM 15.1

How does a competitive firm adjust its demand for labor when the government imposes a specific tax of τ on each unit of output?

Answer

1. *Intuition*: The specific tax lowers the price per unit the firm receives, so we can apply the same type of analysis we just used for a fall in the market price.

2. *Show how the tax affects the marginal revenue product of labor*: The marginal revenue product of labor for a competitive firm is the price the firm receives for the good times the marginal product of labor. The tax reduces the price the firm receives. The tax does not affect the relative prices of labor and capital, so it does not affect the marginal product of labor for a given amount of labor, $MP_L(L)$. For a given amount of labor, the marginal revenue product of labor falls from $p \times MP_L(L)$ to $(p - \tau) \times MP_L(L)$. The marginal revenue product of labor curve—the labor demand curve—shifts downward until it is only $(p - \tau)/p$ as high as the original labor demand curve at any quantity of labor. ■

APPLICATION

Thread Mill

By calculating the marginal revenue product of labor, we can derive the labor demand curve for a Canadian thread mill. The firm has a Cobb-Douglas production function:[4]

$$q = L^{0.6}K^{0.2}. \quad (15.2)$$

Suppose that, in the short run, the mill's capital, K, is fixed at 32 units, so it can increase its output, q, only by increasing the amount of labor, L it uses. To determine the firm's short-run production function, we set $K = 32$ in Equation 15.2:

$$q = L^{0.6}32^{0.2} = 2L^{0.6}.$$

The extra output or marginal product of labor from the last worker can be determined by using a calculator. We find that the extra output from the last worker when the firm goes from 31 to 32 workers is

$$\Delta q = [2 \times 32^{0.6}] - [2 \times 31^{0.6}] \approx 0.3.$$

The firm can sell its output at \$50 per unit. The firm's marginal revenue product of labor at $L = 32$ is

$$MRP_L = p \times MP_L = \$50 \times 0.3 = \$15.$$

Thus, when the price is \$50 and the wage is \$15, the firm hires 32 workers.
More generally, the marginal product of labor function, when we hold capital fixed at $K = 32$, is[5]

$$MP_L = 1.2L^{-0.4}.$$

Thus, if a competitive thread mill faces a market price of \$50, its labor demand curve is

$$MRP_L \equiv p \times MP_L = \$50 \times 1.2L^{-0.4} = \$60L^{-0.4}.$$

Figure 15.3 shows this MRP_L curve or short-run labor demand curve for the firm when capital is fixed at $K = 32$. ■

---

[4]This production function is from the estimates of Baldwin and Gorecki (1986). The units of output are chosen appropriately so that the constant multiplier A in the general Cobb-Douglas, $q = AL^{\alpha}K^{\beta}$, equals 1. Chapter 6 reports two significant digits for α and β. We round those numbers to one digit here to simplify the calculations.

[5]We determine the marginal product of labor function holding capital fixed at $K = 32$ by differentiating the short-run production function, $q = 2L^{0.6}$, with respect to labor:

$$MP_L \equiv dq/dL = 0.6 \times 2 \times L^{0.6-1} = 1.2L^{-0.4}.$$

The calculator method, which compares a discrete change from 31 to 32 workers, gives approximately the correct MP_L. Using this exact formula, which is based on an infinitesimal change in labor, we find that the MP_L at $L = 32$ is exactly $0.3 = 1.2(32)^{-0.4}$.

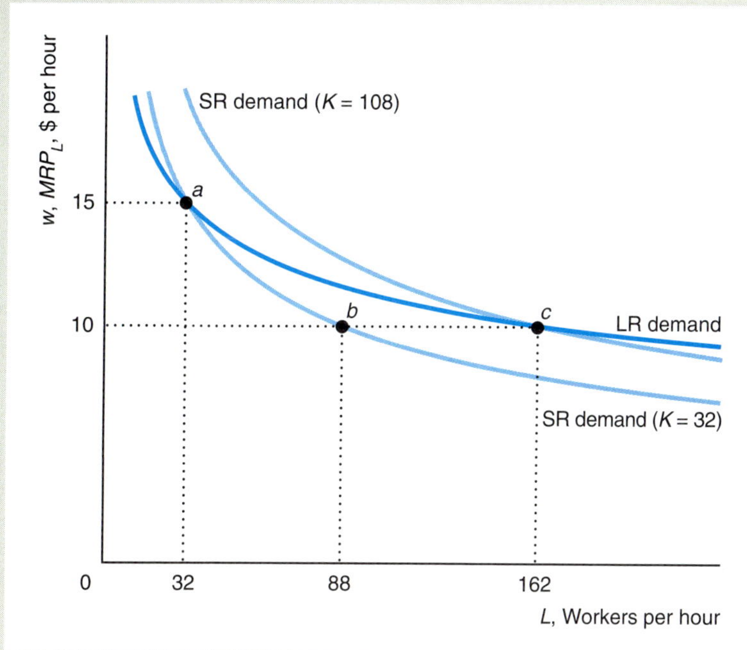

Figure 15.3 Labor Demand of a Thread Mill. In the long run, if the market price is \$50 per unit, the rental rate of capital services is r = \$5, and the wage is w = \$15 per hour, a Canadian thread mill hires 32 workers (and uses 32 units of capital) at point *a* on its LR labor demand curve. In the short run, if capital is fixed at 32 workers, the firm still hires 32 workers per hour at point *a* on its SR labor demand curve. If the wage drops to \$10 and capital were fixed at $K = 32$, the firm would hire 88 workers, point *b* on the SR labor demand curve. In the long run, however, it would increase its capital to $K = 108$ and hire 162 workers, point *c* on the LR labor demand curve and on the SR labor demand curve with $K = 108$.

Long-Run Factor Demand

In the long run, the firm may vary all of its inputs. Now if the wage of labor rises, the firm adjusts both labor and capital. As a result, the short-run marginal revenue product of labor curve that holds capital fixed is not the firm's long-run labor demand curve. The long-run labor demand curve takes account of changes in the firm's use of capital as the wage rises.

In both the short run and the long run, the labor demand curve is the marginal revenue product curve of labor. In the short run (SR), the firm cannot vary capital, so the SR MP_L curve and hence the SR MRP_L curve are relatively steep. In the long run (LR), when the firm can vary all inputs, its LR MP_L curve and MRP_L curves are flatter.

Figure 15.3 shows the relationship between the LR and SR labor demand curves for the thread mill.[6] In the short run, capital is fixed at $K = 32$, the wage is $w = \$15$, and the rental rate of capital is $r = \$5$. The firm hires 32 workers per hour, point *a* on its SR labor demand curve, where $K = 32$. Using 32 workers and 32 units of capital is profit maximizing in the long run, so point *a* is also on the firm's LR labor demand curve.

In the short run, if the wage fell to \$10, the firm could not increase its capital, so it would hire 88 workers, point *b* on the SR labor demand curve, where $K = 32$. In the long run, however, the firm would employ more capital and even more labor (because it can sell as much output as it wants at the market price). It would hire 162 workers and use 108 units of capital, which is point *c* on both the LR labor demand curve and the SR labor demand curve for $K = 108$.

Factor-Market Demand

A factor-market demand curve is the sum of the factor demand curves of the various firms that use the input. Determining a factor-market demand curve is more difficult than deriving consumers' market demand for a final good. When horizontally summing the demand curves for individual consumers in Chapter 2, we were concerned with only a single market.

Inputs such as labor and capital are used in many output markets, however. Thus, to derive the labor market demand curve, we first determine the labor demand curve for each output market and then sum across output markets to obtain the factor-market demand curve.

The Marginal Revenue Product Approach. Earlier, we derived the factor demand of a competitive firm that took the output market price as given. The problem we face is that the output market price depends on the factor's price. As the factor's price falls, each firm, taking the original market price as given, uses more of the factor to produce more output. This extra production by all the firms in the market causes the market price to fall. As the market price falls, each firm reduces its output and hence its demand for the input. Thus, a fall in an input price causes less of an increase in factor demand than would occur if the market price remained constant, as Figure 15.4 illustrates.

At the initial output market price of \$9 per unit, the competitive firm's labor demand curve (panel a) is $MRP_L(p = \$9) = \$9 \times MP_L$. When the wage is \$25 per hour, the firm hires 50 workers: point *a*. The 10 firms in the market (panel b) demand 500 hours of work: point *A* on the demand curve $D(p = \$9) = 100 \times \$9 \times MP_L$. If the wage falls to \$10 while the market price remains fixed at \$9, each firm

---

[6]Appendix 15A formally shows that the LR labor demand and capital demand functions for a Cobb-Douglas production function are functions of the market price, p, the wage rate, w, and the rental rate of capital, r. Substituting the parameters for the Canadian thread mill, $\alpha = 0.6$, $\beta = 0.2$, and $A = 1$, into Equation 15A.8, we find that the firm's LR labor demand curve is

$$L = (0.6/w)^4(0.2/r)p^5.$$

Its LR capital demand curve, Equation 15A.9, is

$$K = (0.6/w)^3(0.2/r)^2p^5.$$

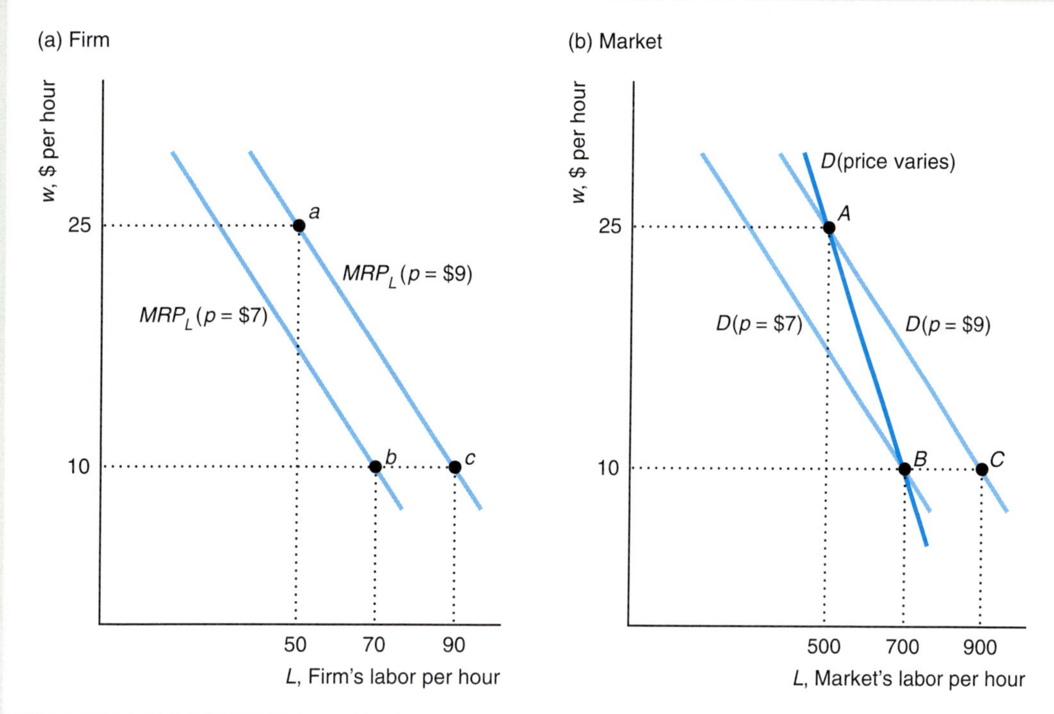

Figure 15.4 Output Market's Demand for Labor. When the output price is p = \$9, the individual competitive firm's labor demand curve is $MRP_L(p = \$9)$. If w = \$25 per hour, the firm hires 50 workers, point a in panel a, and the 10 firms in the market demand 500 workers, point A on the labor demand curve $D(p = \$9)$ in panel b. If the wage falls to \$10, each firm would hire 90 workers, point c, if the market price stayed fixed at \$9. The extra output, however, drives the price down to \$7, so each firm hires 70 workers, point b. The output market's demand for labor that takes price adjustments into account, D(price varies), goes through points A and B.

hires 90 workers, point c, and all the firms in the market would hire 900 workers, point C. However, the extra output drives the price down to \$7, so each firm hires 70 workers, point b, and the firms collectively demand 700 workers, point B. The market labor demand curve for this output market that takes price adjustments into account, D(price varies), goes through points A and B. Thus, the output market's demand for labor is steeper than it would be if output prices were fixed.

To derive the labor market demand curve, we need to combine all the demand curves for the various output markets that use labor. We apply the same method as in Chapter 2: We horizontally sum the individual labor demand curves for all the output markets.

An Alternative Approach. For certain types of production functions, it is easier to determine the market demand curve by using the output profit-maximizing equation

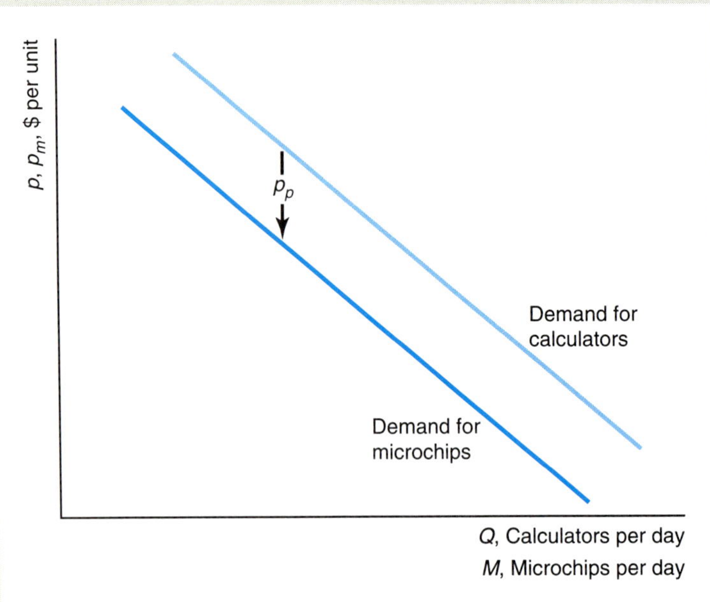

Figure 15.5 The Demand for Microchips in Calculators. It takes one microchip, which costs p_m, and one plastic case, which costs p_p, to produce a calculator, so the marginal cost of a calculator is $MC = p_m + p_p$. Competitive firms operate where the price of a calculator is $p = p_m + p_p$. Thus, the demand curve for a microchip lies p_p below that of a calculator.

rather than the marginal revenue product approach. Suppose calculator manufacturers are competitive and use a fixed-proportions production function, producing each calculator using one microchip and one plastic case. Each plastic case costs p_p, and each microchip costs p_m. What is the calculator market's demand for microchips?

Figure 15.5 shows the demand both for calculators, Q, and microchips, M. Because the numbers of chips and calculators are equal, $Q = M$, the horizontal axes for chips and calculators are the same.

Because each calculator requires one chip and one case, the marginal cost of producing a calculator is $MC = p_p + p_m$. Each competitive firm operates where the market price equals the marginal cost: $p = p_p + p_m = MC$. As a result, the most that any firm would pay for a silicon chip is $p_m = p - p_p$, the amount left over from selling a calculator after paying for the plastic case. Thus, the calculator market's demand curve for microchips lies p_p below the demand curve for calculators, as the figure shows.[7]

[7]The inverse demand function for calculators is a decreasing function of quantity, $p(Q)$. Similarly, the inverse demand function for microchips is $p_m(M)$. Because $Q = M$, we can write the profit-maximization condition as $p(Q) = p_m(M) + p_p$. Thus, the demand for chips lies p_p below the demand for calculators: $p_m(M) = p(Q) - p_p$.

Competitive Factor-Market Equilibrium

The intersection of the factor-market demand curve and the factor-market supply curve determines the competitive factor-market equilibrium. We've just derived the factor-market demand. There's nothing unusual about the factor supply curve. The long-run factor supply curve for each firm is its marginal cost curve above the minimum of its average cost curve, and the factor-market supply curve is the horizontal sum of the firm supply curves (Chapter 8). As we've already analyzed competitive market equilibria for markets in general in Chapters 2, 3, 8, and 9, there's no point in repeating the analysis. (Been there. Done that.)

Chapter 10 shows that factor prices are equalized across markets. For example, if wages were higher in one industry than in another, workers would shift from the low-wage industry to the high-wage industry until the wages were equalized.

15.2 EFFECT OF MONOPOLIES ON FACTOR MARKETS

Having examined the factor-market equilibrium where competitive firms sell a factor to a competitive output market, we now survey the effects of market power on factor-market equilibrium. If firms in the output market *or* the factor market exercise market power by setting price above marginal cost, less of a factor is sold than would be sold if all firms were competitive.

Market Structure and Factor Demands

Factor demand curves vary with market power. As we saw in Chapters 11 and 12, the marginal revenue of a profit-maximizing firm, $MR = p(1 + 1/\varepsilon)$, is a function of the elasticity, ε, of its output demand curve and the market price, p. Thus, the firm's marginal revenue product of labor function is

$$MRP_L = p\left(1 + \frac{1}{\varepsilon}\right)MP_L.$$

The labor demand curve is $p \times MP_L$ for a competitive firm because it faces an infinitely elastic demand at the market price, so its marginal revenue equals the market price.

The marginal revenue product of labor or labor demand curve for a competitive market is above that of a monopoly or oligopoly firm. Figure 15.6 shows the market factor demand for a thread mill if it is a competitive firm; one of two identical Cournot, quantity-setting firms; or a monopoly.[8]

[8]In the short run, the thread mill's marginal product function is $MP_L = 1.2L^{-0.4}$. The labor demand is $p \times 1.2L^{-0.4}$ for a competitive firm, $p(1 + 1/[2\varepsilon]) \times 1.2L^{-0.4}$ for one of two identical Cournot duopoly firms, and $p(1 + 1/\varepsilon) \times 1.2L^{-0.4}$ for a monopoly. In the figure, the market demand curve is linear so the elasticity of demand varies along the demand curve.

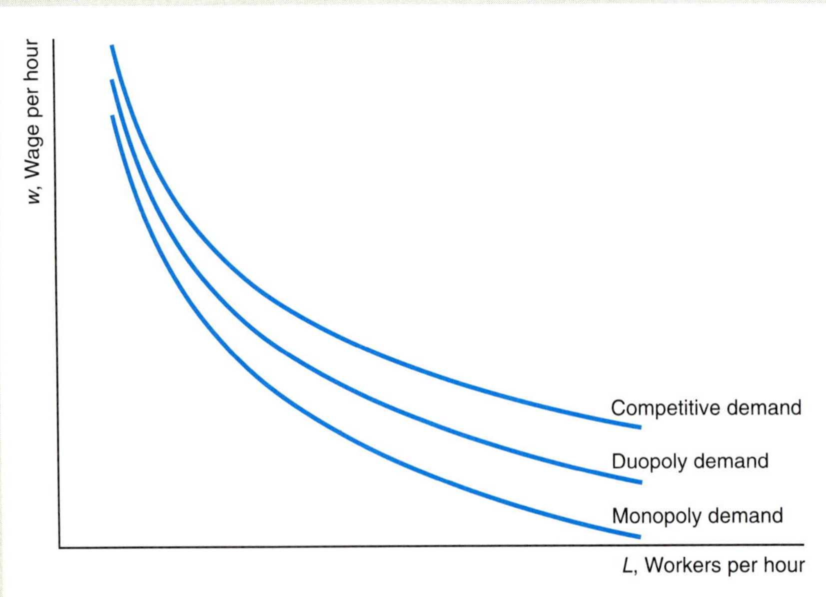

Figure 15.6 Labor Demand Varies with Market Structure. For all profit-maximizing firms, the labor demand curve is the marginal revenue product of labor: $MRP_L = MR \times MP_L$. Because the marginal revenue differs with market structure, so does the MRP_L. At a given wage, a competitive thread firm demands more workers than does a Cournot duopoly firm, which demands more workers than does a monopoly.

A monopoly operates in the elastic section of its downward-sloping demand curve (Chapter 11), so its demand elasticity is less than −1 and finite: $-\infty < \varepsilon \leq -1$. As a result, at any given price, the monopoly's labor demand, $p(1 + 1/\varepsilon)MP_L$, lies below the labor demand curve, pMP_L, of a competitive firm with an identical marginal product of labor curve.

The elasticity of demand facing a Cournot firm is $n\varepsilon$, where n is the number of identical firms and ε is the market elasticity of demand (Chapter 12). Given that they have the same market demand curve, a duopoly Cournot firm faces twice as elastic a demand curve as a monopoly faces. Consequently, a Cournot duopoly firm's labor demand curve, $p(1 + 1/[2\varepsilon])MP_L$, lies above that of a monopoly but below that of a competitive firm. From now on, we concentrate on the competitive and monopoly equilibria because the oligopoly and monopolistically competitive equilibria lie between these polar cases.

A Model of Market Power in Input and Output Markets

When a firm with market power in either the factor or the output market raises its price, the price to final consumers rises. As a result, consumers buy fewer units, so fewer units of the input are demanded. We use a linear example to illustrate how monopolies affect factor-market equilibrium. The inverse demand, $p(Q)$, for the final good is

$$p = 80 - Q. \tag{15.3}$$

Figure 15.7 plots this demand curve. An unlimited number of workers can be hired at \$20 an hour. Each unit of output, Q, requires one unit of labor, L, and no other factor, so the marginal product of labor is one.[9]

As a benchmark, we start our analysis with competitive factor and output markets. Then we ask how the factor-market equilibrium changes if the output market is monopolized. Next we examine a monopolized factor market and a competitive output market. Finally, we investigate the effect of market power in both markets.

Competitive Factor and Output Markets. The intersection of the relevant supply and demand curves determines the competitive equilibria in both input and output markets in Figure 15.7. Because $Q = L$, the figure measures both output and labor on the same horizontal axis.

The marginal product of labor is 1 because one extra worker produces one more unit of output. Thus, the competitive market's demand for labor, $MRP_L = p \times MP_L = p$, is identical to the output demand curve. The labor demand function is the same as the output demand function, where we replace p with w and Q with L:

$$w = 80 - L. \tag{15.4}$$

The competitive supply of labor is a horizontal line at \$20. Given a competitive output market, the intersection of this supply curve of labor and the competitive demand for labor (Equation 15.4) determines the labor market equilibrium, e_1, where

$$20 = 80 - L.$$

Thus, the competitive equilibrium amount of labor services is $L_1 = 60$, and the equilibrium wage is $w_1 = \$20$.

The cost of producing a unit of output equals the wage, so the supply curve of output is also horizontal at \$20. The intersection of this output supply curve and the output demand curve, Equation 15.3, occurs at $Q_1 = 60$ and $p_1 = \$20$. A competitive firm's average cost, w_1, exactly equals the price at which it sells its good, p_1, so the competitive firm breaks even.

Competitive Factor Market and Monopolized Output Market. Because a monopoly in the output market charges a higher price than a competitive market would, it sells fewer units of output and hires fewer workers. The monopoly faces a competitive labor supply curve that is horizontal at the wage $w_2 = \$20$. Thus, the output monopoly's marginal cost is \$20 per unit.

[9]This production function is a special case of the fixed-proportions production function above, for which output involves both labor and capital. Here production requires only labor, but the amount of labor per unit of output is still fixed.

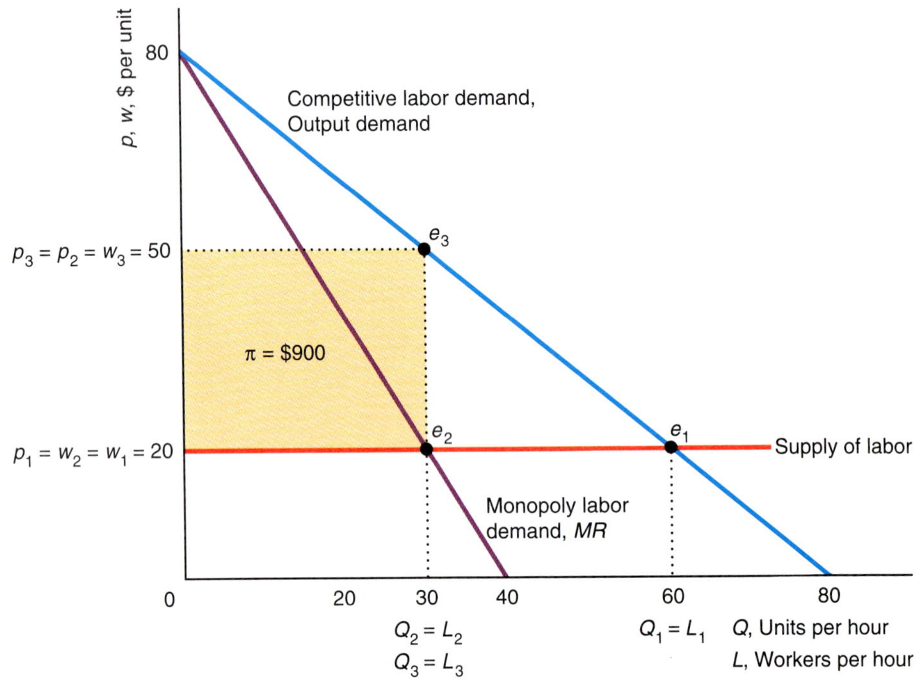

Figure 15.7 Labor Market Equilibrium Depends on the Market Structure in the Output Market. Because one unit of output is produced with one unit of labor, the marginal product of labor is 1, so the competitive labor demand curve is the same as the output demand curve. If both markets are competitive, the labor market equilibrium is e_1. A monopoly's labor demand curve is identical to its marginal revenue curve. An output monopoly charges final consumers a higher price, so it buys less labor. The new labor equilibrium is e_2. With a labor monopoly (union), the equilibrium is e_3.

The monopoly's marginal revenue curve is twice as steep as the linear output demand curve it faces (Chapter 11):

$$MR_Q = 80 - 2Q.$$

The monopoly maximizes its profit where its marginal revenue equals its marginal cost:

$$MR_Q = 80 - 2Q = 20 = MC.$$

Thus, the equilibrium quantity is $Q_2 = 30$. Substituting this quantity into the output demand, Equation 15.3, we find that the equilibrium price is \$50. The monopoly makes $p_2 - w_2 = \$50 - \$20 = \$30$ per unit. Its profit is $\pi = \$900$, as the shaded rectangle in Figure 15.7 shows.

Because the monopoly's marginal product of labor is 1, its demand curve for labor equals its marginal revenue curve:

$$MRP_L = MR_Q \times MP_L = MR_Q.$$

We obtain its labor demand function by replacing Q with L and MR_Q with w in its marginal revenue function:

$$w = 80 - 2L.$$

The intersection of the competitive labor supply curve, w_2 = \$20, and the monopoly's demand for labor curve determines the labor market equilibrium, e_2, where

$$80 - 2L = 20.$$

Thus, the equilibrium amount of labor is $L_2 = 30$.

This example illustrates that a monopoly hurts final consumers and drives some sellers of the factor (workers) out of this market. Final consumers pay \$30 more per unit than they would pay if the market were competitive. Because of the higher price, consumers buy less output, $Q_2 = 30 < 60 = Q_1$. As a consequence, the monopoly demands less labor than does a competitive market: $L_2 = 30 < 60 = L_1$. If the supply curve of labor were upward sloping, this reduction in demand would also reduce workers' wages.

APPLICATION

Record Prices

The exercise of downstream market power substantially raises the price of a CD. Table 15.2 shows the elements that determined the price of Rod Stewart's *Spanner in the Works* CD.[10] The plastic and various other inputs needed to produce the CD cost Warner Brothers Records, the manufacturer, about half a dollar per disk. Mr. Stewart was paid royalties of about \$2.50 per disk. Warner Brothers set its wholesale price at \$10.72 to \$11.20, which reflects a markup of more than 2,000% above the cost of the physical inputs and 350% above the marginal costs, including Mr. Stewart's royalty. (However, Time Warner incurs various fixed costs, including more than \$1 million to record *A Spanner in the Works*.) The CDs were shipped to record chains and independent distributors with a suggested retail price of \$16.98. The number of CDs sold would have been substantially higher had the retail price been set closer to \$5. Because it sold fewer units at the higher price, Time Warner's demand for Lexan, benzene, oil, and other inputs was reduced. ■

[10]Strauss, Neil, "Pennies That Add Up to \$16.98: Why CDs Cost So Much," *New York Times*, July 5, 1995:B1, B6.

Table 15.2 Why CDs Are Expensive

Steps Involved in Producing Rod Stewart's *Spanner in the Works* CD (Warner Brothers)	Cost, Price, or Markup per CD
1. *Oil is pumped* in Saudia Arabia.	Cost: Fraction of a cent
2. *Benzene is removed* from the oil by a refinery in Pascagoula, Mississippi.	Cost: Fraction of a cent
3. *Benzene is pressed into pellets* of a high-grade, super-clear plastic polycarbonate called Lexan at a plastics factory in Pittsfield, Massachusetts.	Cost: About a cent
4. *Lexan is pressed into a disk*, and Mr. Stewart's songs are encoded on the CD, which is then coated with aluminum and covered with ultraviolet lacquer by a manufacturer in Oliphant, Pennsylvania.	Cost: 10¢ to 15¢
5. *A plastic case and cover are made* by a printing plant in Louisville, Kentucky.	Cost: 30¢ to 35¢
6. *Mr. Stewart is paid* royalties.	Cost: About \$2.50
7. *CDs are assembled and shipped* by Warner Brothers from warehouses in Atlanta, Los Angeles, Chicago, and Philadelphia.	Wholesale price: \$10.72 to \$11.20 Markup: More than 350%

Source: Strauss, Neil, "Pennies That Add Up to \$16.98: Why CDs Cost So Much," *New York Times*, July 5, 1995:B1.

Monopolized Factor Market and Competitive Output Market. Now suppose that the output market is competitive and that there is a labor monopoly. One possibility is that the workers form a union that acts as a monopoly. Instead, for simplicity, we'll assume that the labor monopoly is the only firm that can supply the workers employed in the output market.[11]

The labor monopoly sets its marginal revenue equal to its marginal cost, which is \$20. Because the competitive output market's labor demand curve is the same as the output demand curve, the marginal revenue curve facing this labor monopoly is the same as the marginal revenue curve of an output monopoly, where we replace Q with L:

$$MR_L = 80 - 2L.$$

The labor monopoly operates at e_3 in Figure 15.7 where its marginal revenue equals its marginal cost of \$20:

$$80 - 2L = 20.$$

[11]Many markets have firms that only supply labor to other firms. Manpower, Kelly Services, and Accountemps provide temporary office workers and other employees. Many construction firms supply only skilled craftspeople. Still other firms specialize in computer programmers.

The labor monopoly sells $L_3 = 30$ hours of labor services. Substituting this quantity into the labor demand curve, Equation 15.4, we find that the monopoly wage is $w_3 = \$50$. Because the labor monopoly makes $w_3 - \$20 = \$30$ per hour of labor services and it sells 30 hours, its profit is $\pi = \$900$.

The competitive supply to the output market is horizontal at $w_3 = \$50$. The output equilibrium occurs where this supply curve hits the output demand curve, Equation 15.3: $50 = 80 - Q$. Thus, the equilibrium quantity is $Q_3 = 30$. The equilibrium price is the same as the wage, $p_3 = w_3 = \$50$. As a result, the output firms break even.

In our example, in which one unit of labor produces one unit of output, consumers fare the same whether the labor market or the output market is monopolized. Consumers pay $p_2 = p_3 = \$50$ and buy $Q_2 = Q_3 = 30$ units of output. The labor market equilibria are different: The wage is higher if the monopoly is in the labor market rather than the output market. The profit goes to the monopoly regardless of which market is monopolized.

APPLICATION

Union Monopoly Power

Workers acting collectively within a union can raise their wage much in the same manner as any other monopoly. A union's success in raising the wage depends on the elasticity of demand it faces, members' ability to act collectively, laws, and the share of the labor market that is unionized. Just as the entry of competitive firms reduces the power of a monopoly (Chapter 11), we expect that the markup of the union wage over the nonunion wage is smaller, the smaller is the fraction of the labor market controlled by unions.

The union markup in Britain has fallen over time. Table 15.3 shows estimates of how much higher British union wages were than nonunion wages in various years for three labor-skill groups.

Table 15.3 U.K. Union Markup over Nonunion Wages

	1889–1890[a]	1984[b]	1990[b]
Unskilled	25.2%	10.2%	7.2%
Semiskilled	17.4%	10.0%	6.3%
Skilled	19.3%	3.4%	1.5%

[a]Hatton, Boyer, and Bailey's (1994) estimates for 1889–1890 are based on data for individual workers, controlling statistically for age, skill level, industry, and other worker characteristics.

[b]Stewart's (1995) estimates for 1984 and 1990 reflect a comparison between union and nonunion firms that controls for firm attributes.

In the late nineteenth century, unions were thriving. Union membership more than doubled from 1888 to 1892, rising from 6.2% of the work force to 13.0%. Most of the workers in the 1889–1890 survey reported in the table were employed in industries in which unions' share of the market was substantially higher (reaching up to 90% in some occupations and industries). Unions engaged in many strikes to demonstrate their market power aggressively.

In the last couple of decades, the union wage markup has fallen. Factors contributing to this decline include legislation that reduced the bargaining strength of trade unions, a drop in the share of union workers from 54% in 1980 to 38% in 1990, and changes in the mix of occupations with strong union representation. ■

Monopoly in Successive Markets. If the labor and output markets are both monopolized, consumers get hit with a double monopoly markup. The labor monopoly raises the wage, in turn raising the cost of producing the final output. The output monopoly then increases the final price even further.[12]

Figure 15.8 illustrates this double markup. The output monopoly's marginal revenue curve, $MR_Q = 80 - 2Q$, is the same as its labor demand curve, $w = 80 - 2L$. Because the labor demand curve is linear, the labor monopoly's marginal revenue curve is twice as steeply sloped:

$$MR_L = 80 - 4L.$$

The labor monopoly maximizes its profit by setting its marginal revenue equal to its marginal cost: $80 - 4L = 20$. Thus, in the labor market equilibrium, e_4, the labor monopoly provides $L_4 = 15$ workers. Substituting this quantity into the labor demand curve, $w = 80 - 2L$, we find that the labor monopoly's equilibrium wage is $w_4 = \$50$. Thus, the labor monopoly marks up its wage \$30 above its marginal cost. Its profit is area $B = \$30 \times 15 = \$450$ in the figure.

To maximize its profit, the output monopoly sets its marginal revenue, $MR_Q = 80 - 2Q$, equal to its marginal cost, $w_4 = \$50$. It sells $Q_4 = 15$ units of output. Substituting this quantity into the output demand curve, we learn that the output monopoly's equilibrium price is $p_4 = \$65$. The output monopoly's markup is \$15 above its marginal cost. Its profit is area $A = \$225$.

This double markup harms consumers. They pay a higher price—\$65 rather than \$50—than they would pay if there were a monopoly in just one or the other market.

---

[12]In our example, the labor monopoly has a constant marginal cost of $m = \$20$. It operates where its marginal cost equals its marginal revenue, $w(1 + 1/\varepsilon_L)$, where ε_L is the elasticity of labor demand. As a result, the wage is greater than marginal cost: $w = m\mu_L$, where $\mu_L = 1/(1 + 1/\varepsilon_L) > 1$ is the multiplicative labor monopoly markup. The wage is the output monopoly's marginal cost. The output monopoly further marks up the price: $p = w\mu_Q = m\mu_L\mu_Q$, where $\mu_Q = 1/(1 + 1/\varepsilon_Q) > 1$ is the multiplicative output monopoly markup and ε_Q is the output demand elasticity.

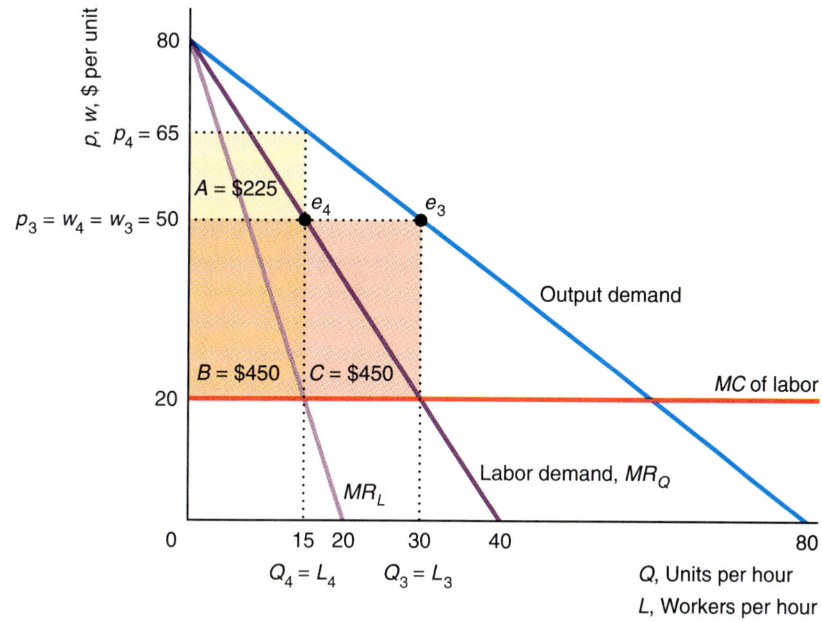

Figure 15.8 Double Monopoly Markup. If there are two successive monopolies, consumers are hit with a double monopoly markup. The labor market equilibrium is e_4, where the wage, w_4, is \$30 above the labor market's marginal and average cost of \$20. The product market monopoly's price, p_4, is \$15 above its marginal cost, w_4. If the labor monopoly vertically integrates, consumers gain ($p_3 < p_4$) and total profit increases from $A + B$ to $B + C$.

SOLVED PROBLEM 15.2

How are consumers affected and how do profits change in the preceding example if the labor monopoly buys the monopoly producer (vertically integrates)?

Answer

1. *Solve for the postmerger equilibrium*: The new, merged monopoly's output demand is the market demand, and its marginal revenue from extra output is $MR_Q = 80 - 2Q$, as Figure 15.8 shows. Now that the firms are one, the former labor monopoly no longer marks up the labor to its production unit. Its marginal cost of an extra unit of output is \$20. The

monopoly maximizes its profit by setting its marginal cost equal to MR_Q. The resulting output equilibrium is the same as it is when there was a single labor monopoly. Equilibrium output is $Q_3 = 30$ and $p_3 = \$50$. The integrated monopoly's profit is $\$30 \times 30 = \$900$, area $B + C$.

2. *Compare the premerger and postmerger equilibria*: Consumers benefit from this merger. Because the price they pay falls from $p_4 = \$65$ to $p_3 = \$50$, they buy 15 extra units of output. The firms also benefit. The combined profit with two monopolies is areas $A + B = \$675$, which is less than the profit of the integrated firm, areas $B + C = \$900$. The labor monopoly can offer the output monopoly more than it earns as a separate firm and still increase its own profit: The firms can split the extra \$225. Thus, everyone may gain from a vertical merger that eliminates one of the two monopoly markups. ■

15.3 MONOPSONY

In Chapter 11, we saw that a *monopoly*, a single *seller*, picks a point—a price and a quantity combination—on the market *demand* curve that maximizes its profit. A *monopsony*, a single *buyer* in a market, chooses a price-quantity combination from the industry *supply* curve that maximizes its profit. A monopsony is the mirror image of monopoly, and it exercises its market power by buying at a price *below* the price that competitive buyers would pay.

An American manufacturer of state-of-the-arts weapons systems can legally sell only to the federal government. U.S. professional football teams, which act collectively, are the only firms that hire professional football players.[13] In many fisheries, there is only one buyer of fish (or at most a small number of buyers, an *oligopsony*).

Monopsony Profit Maximization

Suppose that a firm is the sole employer in town: a monopsony in the local labor market. The firm uses only one factor, labor (L), to produce a final good. The value the firm places on the last worker it hires is the marginal revenue product of that worker—the value of the extra output the worker produces—which is the height of the firm's labor demand curve for the number of workers the firm employs.

The firm has a downward-sloping demand curve in panel a of Figure 15.9. The firm faces an upward-sloping supply curve of labor: The higher is its daily wage, w, the more people want to work for the firm. The firm's *marginal expenditure*—the additional cost of hiring one more worker—depends on the shape of the supply curve.

[13]Football players belong to a union that acts collectively, like a monopoly, in an attempt to offset the monopsony market power of the football teams.

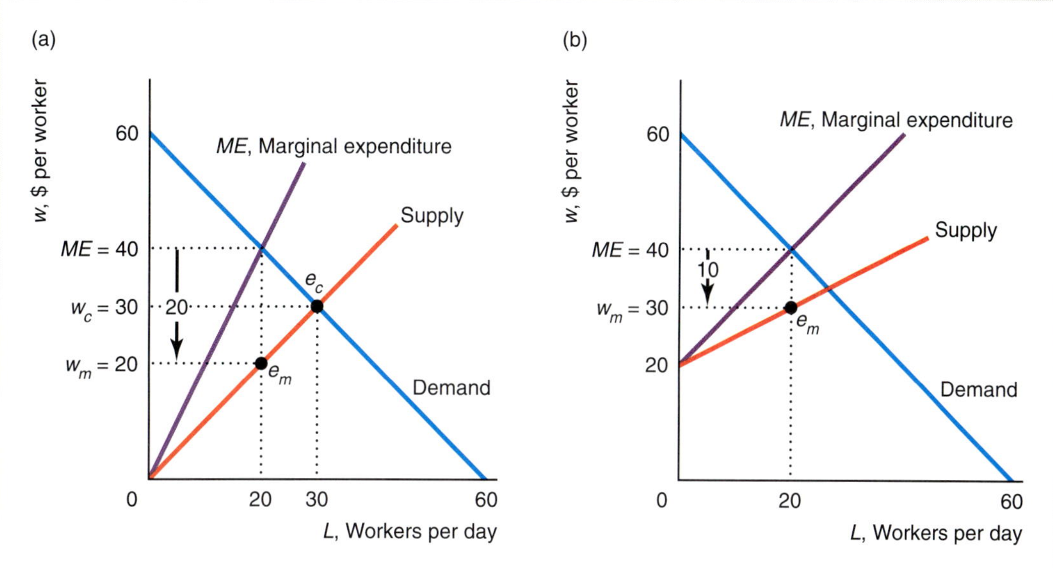

Figure 15.9 Monopsony. (a) The marginal expenditure curve—the monopsony's marginal cost of buying one more unit—lies above the upward-sloping market supply curve. The monopsony equilibrium, e_m, occurs where the marginal expenditure curve intersects the monopsony's demand curve. The monopsony buys fewer units at a lower price, $w_m = \$20$, than would a competitive market, $w_c = \$30$. (b) The supply curve is more elastic at the optimum than in (a), so the value that the monopsony places on the last unit (which equals the marginal expenditure of $40) exceeds the price the monopsony pays, $w_m = \$30$, by less than in (a).

The supply curve shows the average expenditure, or wage, the monopsony pays to hire a certain number of workers. For example, the monopsony's average expenditure or wage is $20 if it hires $L = 20$ workers per day. If the monopsony wants to obtain one more worker, it must raise its wage because the supply curve is upward sloping. Because it pays all workers the same wage, the monopsony must also pay more to each worker it was already employing. Thus, the monopsony's marginal expenditure on the last worker is greater than that worker's wage.[14] The marginal expenditure curve in the figure has twice as steep a slope as the linear supply curve.[15]

[14]The monopsony's total expenditure is $E = w(L)L$, where $w(L)$ is the wage given by the supply curve. Its marginal expenditure is $ME = \mathrm{d}E/\mathrm{d}L = w(L) + L[\mathrm{d}w(L)/\mathrm{d}L]$, where $w(L)$ is the wage paid the last worker and $L[\mathrm{d}w(L)/\mathrm{d}L]$ is the extra amount the monopsony pays the workers it was already employing. Because the supply curve is upward sloping, $\mathrm{d}w(L)/\mathrm{d}L > 0$, the marginal expenditure, ME, is greater than the average expenditure, $w(L)$.

[15]Appendix 15B shows that the ME curve is twice as steep as the labor supply curve for any linear labor supply curve.

In contrast, if the firm were a competitive price taker in the labor market, it would face a supply curve that was horizontal at the market wage. Consequently, such a competitive firm's marginal expenditure to hire one more worker would be the market wage.

Any buyer—including a monopsony or a competitive firm—buys labor services up to the point at which the marginal value of the last unit of a factor equals the firm's marginal expenditure (Appendix 15B). If the last unit is worth more to the buyer than its marginal expenditure, the buyer purchases another unit. Similarly, if the last unit is less valuable than its marginal expenditure, the buyer purchases one less unit.

The monopsony buys 20 units of the factor. The intersection of its marginal expenditure curve and the demand curve determines the monopsony equilibrium e_m. The monopsony values the labor services of the last worker at $40 (height of its demand curve), and its marginal expenditure on that unit (height of its marginal expenditure curve) is $40. It pays only $20 (height of the supply curve). In other words, the monopsony values the last unit at $20 more than it actually has to pay.

If the market in Figure 15.9 were competitive, the intersection of the demand curve and the supply curve would determine the competitive equilibrium at e_c, where buyers purchase 30 units at p_c = $30 per unit. Thus, the monopsony hires fewer workers, 20 versus 30, than a competitive market would hire and pays a lower wage, $20 versus $30.

Monopsony power is the ability of a single buyer to pay less than the competitive price profitably. The size of the gap between the value the monopsony places on the last worker (the height of its demand curve) and the wage it pays (the height of the supply curve) depends on the elasticity of supply at the monopsony optimum. The markup of the marginal expenditure (which equals the value to the monopsony) over the wage is inversely proportional to the elasticity of supply at the optimum (Appendix 15B):

$$\frac{ME - w}{w} = \frac{1}{\eta}.$$

By comparing panels a and b in Figure 15.9, we see that the less elastic the supply curve is at the optimum, greater is the gap between marginal expenditure and the wage. At the monopsony optimum, the supply curve in panel b of Figure 15.9 is more elastic than the supply curve in panel a.[16] The gap between the marginal expenditure and wage is greater in panel a, $ME - w$ = $20, than in panel b, $ME - w$ = $10. Similarly, the markup in panel a, $(ME - w)/w = 20/20 = 1$, is much greater than that in panel b, $(ME - w)/w = 10/30 = \frac{1}{3}$.

[16]The supply curve in panel a is $w = L$, while that in panel b is $w = 20 + \frac{1}{2}L$. The elasticity of supply, $\eta = (dL/dw)(w/L)$, at the optimum is $w/L = 20/20 = 1$ in panel a and $2w/L = 2 \times 30/20 = 3$ in panel b. Consequently, the supply curve is three times as elastic in panel b as in panel a at the optimum.

APPLICATION

Monopsony Wage Setting

The following two examples of monopsony wage setting illustrate the degree to which a firm can alter prices through the exercise of monopsony power.

Hospitals

In small communities with a single hospital, we expect hospitals to have substantial monopsony power over the nurses they hire. Sullivan (1989) found that the value of a nurse's service to the hospital (the height of the demand or marginal expenditure curve) is 1.79 times what the hospital pays a nurse in the short run (the height of the labor supply curve). However, he estimated that the value of the nurse's service to the wage payment is only 1.26 over a three-year period. Thus, hospitals have more monopsony power in the short run than in the long run.

College Sports Scholarships

The National Collegiate Athletic Association (NCAA) controls college athletics. The NCAA effectively limits payments (the value of a scholarship, room and board, and book allowances) to college football players for their athletic services to between \$5,000 and \$20,000. Thus, the NCAA turns colleges into monopsony employers. Brown (1993) estimated that the value of a premium player—one who is good enough to be drafted by the pros—to a college is over half a million dollars due to increased ticket sales and television revenues. In short, the value of the services of a star athlete is at least 25 times greater than what the college provides in direct payments. ■

Welfare Effects of Monopsony

By creating a wedge between the value to the monopsony and the value to the suppliers, the monopsony causes a welfare loss in comparison to a competitive market. In Figure 15.10, sellers lose producer surplus, $-D - E$, because the monopsony price, p_m, for a good is below the competitive price, p_c. Area D is a transfer from the sellers to the monopsony and represents the savings of $(p_c - p_m)$ on the Q_m units the monopsony buys. The monopsony loses $-C$ because suppliers sell it less output, Q_m instead of Q_c, at the low price. Thus, the deadweight loss of monopsony is $-C - E$. This loss is due to the wedge between the value the monopsony places on the Q_m units, the monopoly expenditure ME in the figure, and the price it pays, p_m. The greater the difference between Q_c and Q_m and the larger the gap between ME and p_m, the greater is the deadweight loss.

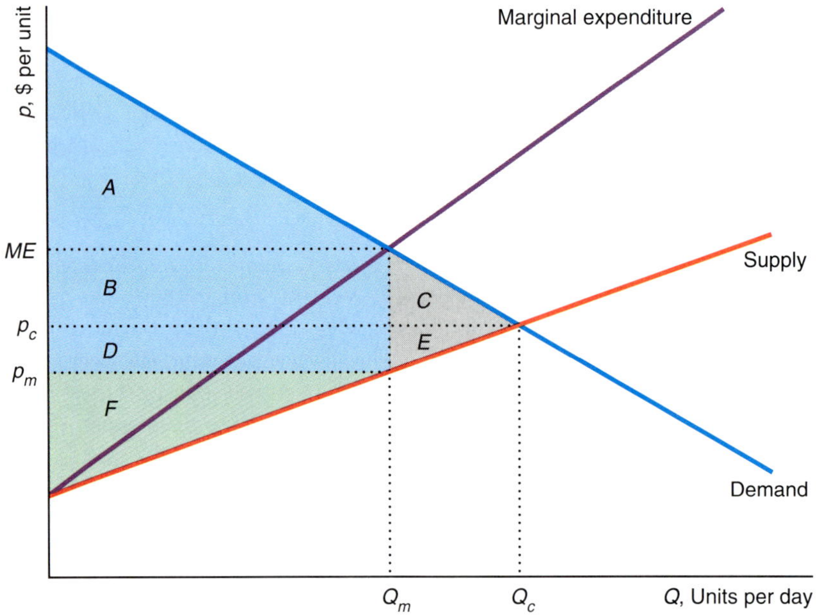

	Competition	Monopsony	Change
Consumer Surplus, *CS*	$A + B + C$	$A + B + D$	$D - C = \Delta CS$
Producer Surplus, *PS*	$D + E + F$	F	$-D - E = \Delta PS$
Welfare, $W = CS + PS$	$A + B + C + D + E + F$	$A + B + D + F$	$-C - E = \Delta W = DWL$

Figure 15.10 Welfare Effects of Monopsony. By setting a price below the competitive level, a monopsony causes too little to be sold by the supplying market, thereby reducing welfare.

SOLVED PROBLEM 15.3

How does the equilibrium in a labor market with a monopsony employer change if a minimum wage is set at the competitive level?

Answer

1. *Determine the original monopsony equilibrium*: Given the supply curve in Figure 15.11, the marginal expenditure curve is ME^1. The intersection of ME^1 and the demand curve determines the monopsony equilibrium, e_1. The monopsony hires L_1 workers at a wage of w_1.

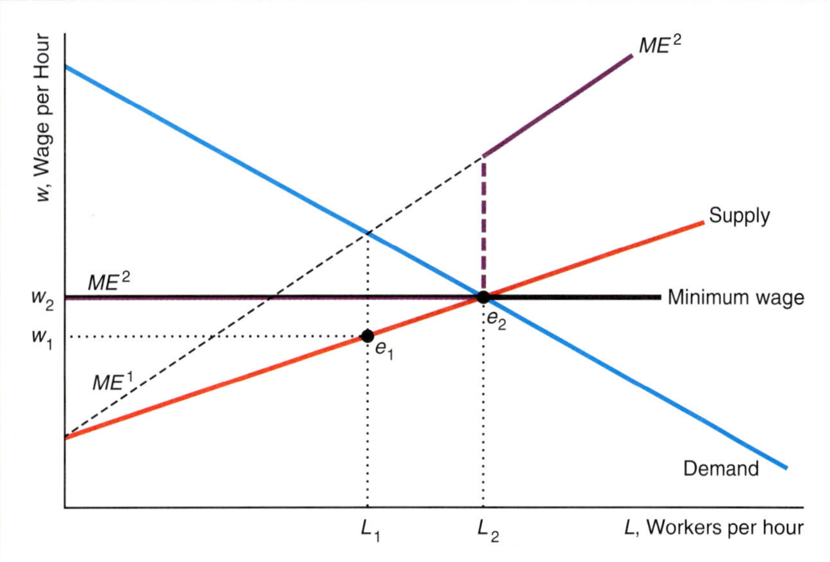

Figure 15.11 Effect of a Minimum Wage on a Monopsony. The marginal expenditure curve is flat where the minimum wage is above the supply curve and follows the original marginal expenditure curve where the supply curve is above the minimum wage. As a result, the wage rises from the original monopsony wage of w_1 to the minimum wage, w_2. The number of workers employed increases from L_1 to L_2.

2. *Determine the effect of the minimum wage on the marginal expenditure curve*: The minimum wage makes the supply curve, as viewed by the monopsony, flat in the range where the minimum wage is above the original supply curve (fewer than L_2 workers). The new marginal expenditure curve, ME^2, is flat where the supply curve is flat. Where the supply curve is upward sloping, ME^2 is the same as ME^1.

3. *Determine the post-minimum-wage equilibrium*: The monopsony operates where its new marginal expenditure curve, ME^2, intersects the demand curve. With the minimum wage, the demand curve crosses the ME^2 curve at the end of the flat section. Thus, in the new equilibrium, e_2, the monopsony pays the minimum wage, w_2, and employs L_2 workers.

4. *Compare the equilibria*: The post-minimum-wage equilibrium is the same as the competitive equilibrium determined by the intersection of the demand and supply curves. Workers receive a higher wage, and more are employed than in the monopsony equilibrium. The minimum wage helps workers and hurts the monopsony. ■

Table 15.4 HMOs Pay Less for an Organ Transplant

Transplant	Average Billed Price	Discounted Contract Price
Kidney	$92,700	$50,000–$60,000 (Cleveland Clinic)
Bone marrow	$172,900	$65,000 (Duke University)
Liver	$280,200	$150,000–200,000 (Johns Hopkins)
Heart	$222,700	$110,000 (Cleveland Clinic)
Lung	$265,100	$130,000 (Cleveland Clinic)

Source: Anders, George, "On Sale Now at Your HMO: Organ Transplants," *Wall Street Journal*, 225(11), January 17, 1995:B1, B5.

Monopsony Price Discrimination

If some consumers have monopsony power while others do not, sellers offer those with monopsony power lower prices. The prices of organ transplants at the Cleveland Clinic, Duke University, and Johns Hopkins hospitals are 29–62% lower to health maintenance organizations (HMOs) than to fee-for-service patients, as Table 15.4 shows. One explanation is that the HMOs threaten to take the business of their millions of members to other hospitals unless a hospital offers them a low, fixed-price contract. By getting bids from several hospitals, the HMOs convince each individual hospital that they have a higher elasticity of demand than do other patients.

A monopsony may directly price discriminate in much the same way as a monopoly or oligopoly. For example, suppose that a monopsony employer can hire either of two types of workers. One type is willing to move to any other firm that pays more. The second type is unwilling to move. The employer may pay those who are willing to move more than it pays other workers, all else the same, as the next application illustrates.

APPLICATION

Monopsony Price Discrimination

Ransom (1993) found that university professors are an exception to the rule in other labor markets that earnings rise with experience. According to statistics from all labor markets, young workers earn 3% more with each year of seniority, and workers with average seniority (about 10 years) earn 2% more for each additional year. A worker with 10 years' experience earns 30% more than a worker of the same age with no experience. In contrast, more than half of doctorate-granting institutions responded in a recent survey that they had hired "new, junior faculty members at a salary above that of some senior faculty members in the same department." Controlling for degree, field, and other factors, faculty with 10–14 years of seniority earn about 7% less and those with 30 years of seniority earn 15% less than individuals with less than 2 years of seniority. Salaries decline by about 0.5% per year of seniority.

In most labor markets, earnings rise with experience because workers become more productive as they gain experience or because firms use higher wages for seniority as an incentive that makes employees work hard for years (see Chapter 20). Apparently, only professors who move to a different institution prevent their salaries from falling with seniority. A professor of average seniority gains a 5–10% higher salary by moving. Why is academia different?

One possible explanation for the negative effect of seniority is that the faculty members who do not move are less productive. According to this argument, the best professors change colleges and gain higher salaries, leaving the less able where they are. This explanation appears to be false, however. Even after Ransom controlled for how many articles faculty members publish (one measure of productivity at research-oriented universities), he found a pronounced negative effect to seniority.

A more plausible explanation is monopsonistic discrimination by universities. A university professor is more likely to have to move between cities to find a higher-salary job than is a worker in other labor markets. A faculty member must take moving costs into account in deciding whether it pays to move to another city for a slightly higher salary. Moving costs are a more important factor for senior faculty members than for junior faculty members, because senior faculty members are more likely to be home owners with children in school and to have other roots in the community.

Universities hire junior faculty members—who almost certainly have to move regardless of which job they take—at the market wage. Universities pay senior faculty members relatively low wages because they know that few will incur sizable moving costs by leaving. In short, universities exploit senior faculty members. (Try to control your tears.)

15.4 VERTICAL INTEGRATION

To sell a good or service to consumers involves many sequential stages of production and sales activities. Profitability determines how many stages a firm performs itself.

Stages of Production

The turkey sandwiches you purchase at your local food stand are produced and delivered through the actions of many firms and individuals. Farmers grow wheat and raise turkeys using inputs they purchase from other firms; processors convert these raw inputs into bread and turkey slices; wholesalers transfer these products from the food processors to the food stand; and finally, employees at the food stand combine various foods to make a sandwich, wrap it, and sell it to you.

Figure 15.12 illustrates the sequential or *vertical* stages of production. First, firms use raw inputs (such as wheat) to produce semiprocessed materials (such as flour).

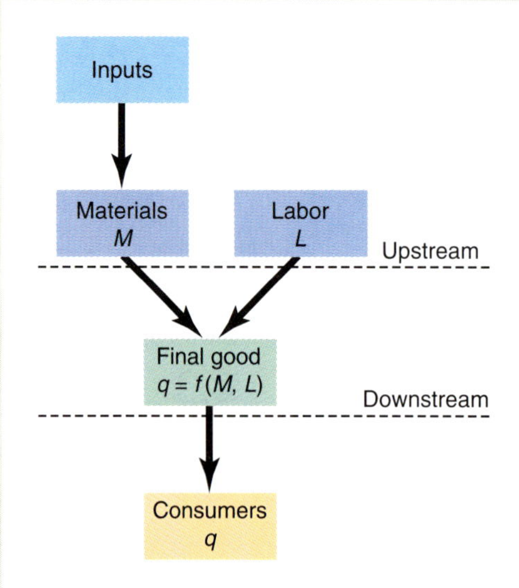

Figure 15.12 Vertical Organization. Raw inputs produced upstream are combined using a production process, $Q = f(M, L)$, downstream to produce a final good, which is sold to consumers.

Then, the same or other firms use the semiprocessed materials and labor to produce the final good (such as bread). In the last stage, the final consumers buy the product.

Before this century, production often took place along a river. Early stages of production occurred upstream, and then the partially finished goods were shipped by barge downstream—going with the flow of the river—to other firms that finished the product. We still use anachronistic river terms to indicate the order of production: *Upstream* refers to factors of production, and *downstream* refers to final goods.

Degree of Vertical Integration

The number of separate firms involved in producing your turkey sandwich depends on how many steps of the process each handles. One possibility is the food stand carries out many steps itself: making the sandwich, wrapping it, and selling it to you. Alternatively, one firm makes and wraps the sandwich and delivers it to another firm that sells it to you.

A firm that participates in more than one successive stage of the production or distribution of goods or services is **vertically integrated.** A firm may vertically integrate backward and produce its own inputs. After years of buying its unique auto bodies from Fisher Body, General Motors purchased Fisher. Or a firm may vertically integrate forward and buy its former customer. In 1926, General Motors (GM), a former supplier, purchased Hertz (the first car-rental company, founded in 1918). In

1954, Hertz went public. It was sold to a Ford Motor subsidiary in 1987 and became a fully owned Ford subsidiary in 1994.[17]

All firms are vertically integrated to some degree, but they differ substantially as to how many successive stages of production they perform internally. Although you can't be a little bit dead, a firm *can* be partially vertically integrated. It may produce a good but rely on others to market it. Or it may produce some inputs itself and buy others from the market.

Some firms buy from a small number of suppliers or sell through a small number of distributors. These firms often control the actions of the firms with whom they deal by writing contracts that restrict the actions of those other firms. Such contractual *vertical restraints* approximate the outcome from vertically merging. Such tight relationships between firms are referred to as *quasi-vertical integration*.

For example, a franchisor and a franchisee have a close relationship that is governed by a contract. Some franchisors (such as McDonald's) sell a proven method of doing business to individual franchisees (owners of McDonald's outlets). A fast-food franchisor may dictate the types of raw products its franchisees buy, the franchisees' cooking methods, the restaurants' appearance, and the franchisees' advertising.

APPLICATION

Outsourcing

During the 1990s, many firms, government agencies, and others switched to *outsourcing*: purchasing products and services from other firms rather than producing these products and services internally. A firm that uses subcontractors can produce the same output with fewer employees and less capital than a firm that carries out all activities itself.

TopsyTail, a Texan company that sold $100 million of hair-styling gadgets between 1991 and 1995, is an extreme case of an outsourcing firm.[18] It has virtually no permanent employees of its own. Subcontractors handle virtually all its activities: design, manufacturing, marketing, distribution, and packing.

In the 1990s, management gurus advised companies of all sizes to shrink and reorganize themselves in order to focus on their "core competencies." Outsourcing proponents tell firms not to integrate vertically but to rely on others. Some large firms even use subcontractors to supply labor: janitors, guards, machine operators, sales representatives, and other specialized workers.

Electronic Data Systems (EDS) has a $3.2 billion contract to provide information technology outsourcing services to Xerox. EDS runs Xerox's computer and telecommunications network. The deal involved transferring 1,700 Xerox employees to EDS.

---

[17]Jacobson, Gianna, "Enterprise's Unconventional Path," *New York Times*, January 23, 1997:C4, C6.

[18]"The Outing of Outsourcing," *The Economist*, 337(7942), November 25, 1995:57–58.

Many outsourcers and subcontractors in turn subcontract with one another. Octel Network Services, which operates more than a million electronic voice mailboxes, has EDS as a client. EDS's client, Xerox, provides invoicing and billing services for Motorola. Motorola designs and makes parts for Octel's voice-messaging systems.

By specializing, firms that provide outsourcing services take advantage of economies of scale and efficiency-creating divisions of labor (such as the gigantic gains to specialization in producing pins discussed in Chapter 6). According to the executive director of the Outsourcing Institute in New York, American firms spent about $100 billion on outsourcing and cut their costs by 10–15%. In Japan, where outsourcing represents one-third of companies' total manufacturing costs, the practice reportedly has reduced these firms' costs by over 20%.

In addition to lowering their costs, firms that outsource can reduce the amount of capital they need to invest, may be able to decrease risk, and can cut back the number of activities they must directly manage. The disadvantages are that quality may be more difficult to monitor and that aggressive outsourcing may spark labor tensions with current workers. ■

Produce or Buy

Whether a firm vertically integrates, quasi-vertically integrates, or relies on markets depends on which approach is the most profitable.[19] If a firm can perform most of the necessary stages of production at lower cost than it would incur buying from other firms, it vertically integrates.

When deciding whether to integrate vertically, the firm must take into account not only the direct costs of integrating, such as legal fees, but also the higher cost of managing a larger, more complex company. Five possible benefits from vertical integration are lowering transaction costs, ensuring a steady supply, avoiding government intervention, extending market power to another market, and eliminating market power.

APPLICATION

Vertical Integration of Auto Manufacturers

Some firms in a market may vertically integrate while others do not. As Table 15.5 shows, the major American auto manufacturers differ substantially in the degree to which they produce parts themselves. According to "common wisdom in Detroit," General Motors produces 70% of its own parts, Ford 50%, and Chrysler 30%.[20]

---

[19]For a more detailed analysis of the pros and cons of vertical integration, see Perry (1989) and Carlton and Perloff (1994). The classic articles on vertical integration are Coase (1937) and Williamson (1975).

[20]Bradsher, Keith, "G.M.'s Labor Costs on Parts Said to Be Higher Than Rivals'," *New York Times*, June 25, 1996:C2.

Table 15.5 Percentage of Parts Produced in House by Auto Manufacturers

Component	Chrysler	Ford	General Motors
Automatic transmissions	100%	65%	100%
Axles for rear-wheel-drive	50	70	30
Axles for front-wheel-drive	0	50	100
Body panel stampings and assemblies	73[a]	66[a]	90[a]
Brakes (excluding antilock type)	0	0	100
Cylinder blocks and foundry products	50[b]	100	100
Engines	82	80	98
Fuel-injection systems	0	50	100
Glass	65	100	0
Heating/cooling systems	70[a]	100	100
Lighting systems	0	0	100
Seat tracks and fasteners	0	0	100
Steering gears	0	100	100
Suspensions	50	100	100

[a] Minimum estimate.
[b] Maximum estimate.

Source: Bradsher, Keith, "G.M.'s Labor Costs on Parts Said to Be Higher Than Rivals'," *New York Times*, June 25, 1996:C2, based on figures from Harbour & Associates.

Although these firms differ greatly in degree of integration, it does not follow that any of them is making a mistake, because the firms face different costs and benefits. For example, GM may itself produce certain inputs that Chrysler buys in the market because GM is much larger and can benefit from economies of scale that are not available to Chrysler. ■

Lowering Transaction Costs. Probably the most important reason to integrate is to avoid *transaction costs*: the costs of trading with others besides the price, including the costs of writing and enforcing contracts. A firm that vertically integrates avoids many transaction costs, but its managerial costs rise as the firm becomes larger and more complex.

An important source of transaction costs is **opportunistic behavior**: taking advantage of someone when circumstances permit. When firms agree to a future transaction, each firm may try to interpret the terms of a contract to its advantage, especially when terms are vague or even missing.

Opportunistic behavior is particularly likely when a firm deals with only one other firm. If an electronic-game manufacturer can buy computer chips from only one firm, it is at the mercy of the chip supplier, a situation that could increase its price substantially just before the Christmas buying season.

Some firms vertically integrate to avoid the transaction costs imposed by opportunistic behavior. By manufacturing the chip itself, the electronic-game company can avoid such opportunistic behavior.

Similarly, when one firm has more information than another—where there is asymmetric information—the knowledgeable firm may take advantage of the relatively ignorant firm. For example, a buyer may incur substantial transaction costs in monitoring the quality of the seller's product. If the buyer vertically integrates to ensure that critical components are built to a high standard, its quality-control problem changes from monitoring another firm to monitoring its own employees in ways that are not possible when firms are completely independent.[21]

Ensuring a Steady Supply. Like the electronic-game manufacturer, many firms are at the mercy of their suppliers. A supplier that delivers a crucial part late imposes substantial costs on these manufacturers. One possibility is for a manufacturer to replace unreliable suppliers in the long run.

Another possibility is quasi-vertical integration, in which the buyer signs a contract that rewards the supplier for prompt delivery and penalizes delays. Toyota and other Japanese manufacturers pioneered the *just-in-time* system of having suppliers deliver inputs at the time needed to process them, thus minimizing inventory costs and avoiding bottlenecks. If replacing unreliable suppliers or using quasi-vertical integration fails, a firm can ensure a steady supply and avoid costs from delays by vertically integrating.

APPLICATION

Aluminum

Opportunistic behavior and the need to ensure a steady supply explains why upstream vertical integration is common in aluminum, according to Hennart (1988). Aluminum production has four main stages: mining, refining, smelting, and fabricating. After mining bauxite, a firm mixes it with caustic soda to refine it into alumina. Next, the firm uses electrolysis to produce primary aluminum metal from alumina. Finally, other firms fabricate the metal into foil, wire, cookware, airplane parts, and many other products.

The upstream activities of mining and refining bauxite are both oligopolistic. Bauxite mines and refineries require large capital investments, have large minimum efficient scales (Chapter 12), and face substantial barriers to entry. There were only about 80 alumina refineries worldwide in 1980. Moreover, bauxite is expensive to ship, so the market for bauxite is regional (77% of bauxite imported by the United States in 1976 came from the Caribbean region, while Japan imported close to 90% of its bauxite from Australia and Indonesia). Thus, a mine or a refiner has few if any other firms with which it can deal.

To guarantee a steady supply, some refineries sign 20- to 25-year contracts with mines. Because these firms cannot foresee all possible contingencies during such long periods, however, one trading party can inflict substantial costs

[21]Chapters 19 and 20 examine problems arising from *asymmetric information* in detail.

on the other by refusing to deal with it (say, when prices are unusually high or low). These firms have no alternative uses for bauxite and the plants that mine and refine it.

To avoid the potential for such opportunistic behavior, many firms vertically integrate. Vertically integrated firms mine and refine most of the world's bauxite (91% in 1976). ■

Avoiding Government Intervention. Firms may also vertically integrate to avoid government price controls, taxes, and regulations. A vertically integrated firm avoids *price controls* by selling to itself. The federal government has set a maximum price that could be charged for steel products on several occasions since World War II. Under such price controls, steel producers did not want to sell as much steel as before the controls took effect. Consequently, they rationed steel, selling their long-time customers only a fraction of what they sold before the controls went into effect.

Because transactions within a company were unaffected by price controls, a buyer who really desired more steel could purchase a steel company and obtain all the steel it wanted (and at least one firm did so). Thus, purchasing a steel company allowed firms to avoid price controls. Were it not for the high transaction costs, firms could completely avoid price controls by vertically integrating.

Firms also integrate to lower their *taxes*. Tax rates vary by country, state, or type of product. A vertically integrated firm can shift profits from one of its operations to another simply by changing the *transfer price* at which it sells its internally produced materials from one division to another. By shifting profits from a high-tax jurisdiction to a low-tax jurisdiction, a firm can increase its after-tax profits. The Internal Revenue Service tries to restrict such behavior by requiring that firms use market prices for internal transfers where possible.

Government *regulations* create additional incentives for a firm to integrate vertically (or horizontally) when the profits of only one division of a firm are regulated. When the government restricts the profits that a local telephone company earns on local services, but not its profits on other services, such as selling telephones in competition with other suppliers, the telephone company tries to shift profits from its regulated division to its unregulated division.

Extending Market Power. By vertically integrating, a firm may be able to increase its monopoly profits by price discriminating or by monopolizing. The Alcoa example in Chapter 13 shows how a monopoly supplier vertically integrates to prevent resales so that it can price discriminate.

An upstream monopoly supplier of a key input in a production process for a downstream, competitive market may be able to boost its profit by vertically integrating forward to monopolize the production industry.[22] Similarly, a vertically integrated firm that supplies itself and others with inputs may be able to restrict essential inputs to potential competitors (Chapter 14).

APPLICATION

Cutting Off Oxygen

Under federal antitrust law, the Federal Trade Commission (FTC) challenged two firms that supplied oxygen and oxygen equipment.[23] The firms were formed by doctors who then referred their patients with heart and lung diseases there. In 1993, the companies and the 28 doctors involved agreed to settlements that were to reduce the doctors' financial interest in the businesses.

The doctor-owners comprised 60% of the lung specialists in two California counties. The FTC contended that the doctors had obtained illegal dominance of a market by combining their power to refer patients to a company they jointly owned. Moreover, several of the doctors ran respiratory therapy centers at major hospitals and were able to influence referrals by hospitals and other doctors. Although such referrals are not necessarily illegal, they could be used to build up market power and to exclude competitors from the market, in violation of the law according to the FTC. Without referrals, another firm could not compete, no matter how good its product or how low its price. Under the settlement, no more than 25% of the lung specialists in the relevant market area could be affiliated with the companies.

A 1993 California law makes such self-referrals a misdemeanor subject to a $5,000 civil penalty. New federal laws also limit such referrals. ■

---

[22]If the downstream firms use a fixed-proportions production function (as in our earlier examples), a monopoly supplier does not gain additional market power by vertically integrating. See Carlton and Perloff (1994) for the relevant theory and a discussion of the empirical evidence.

[23]Pear, Robert, "U.S. Uses Antitrust Law over Doctors' Ventures," *New York Times*, November 3, 1993:A16; Barnum, Alex, "East Bay Doctors Settle with FTC," *San Francisco Chronicle*, November 4, 1993:B1–B2.

Eliminating Market Power. A firm that faces a monopsony buyer or monopoly seller may try to eliminate that market power by vertically integrating. During the Great Depression, farms in a given area could sell their milk to only a single processor that paid them a low monopsony price. Many farmers banded together to create cooperatives that processed their own milk. As we've seen, everyone may benefit from vertical integration if both the buyer and seller have monopoly power.

Summary

1. **Competitive factor market:** Any firm maximizes its profit by choosing the quantity of a factor such that the marginal revenue product (*MRP*) of that factor—the marginal revenue times the marginal product of the factor—equals the factor price. The *MRP* is the firm's factor demand. A competitive firm's marginal revenue is the market price, so its *MRP* is the market price·times the marginal product. The firm's long-run factor demand is usually flatter than its short-run demand because it can adjust more factors, thus giving it more flexibility. The market demand for a factor reflects how changes in factor prices affect output prices and hence output levels in product markets.
2. **Effect of monopolies on factor markets:** If firms exercise market power to raise price above marginal cost in an output market or factor market, the quantity demanded by consumers falls. Because the quantity of output and the quantity of inputs are closely related, a reduction in the quantity of an input reduces output, and a reduction in output reduces the demand for inputs.
3. **Monopsony:** A profit-maximizing monopsony—a single buyer—sets its price so that the marginal value to the monopsony equals its marginal expenditure. Because the monopsony pays a price below the competitive level, fewer units are sold than in a competitive market, producers of factors are worse off, the monopsony earns higher profits than it would if it were a price taker, and society suffers a deadweight loss. A monopsony may also price discriminate.
4. **Vertical integration:** A firm may vertically integrate (participate in more than one successive stage of the production or distribution of goods or services), quasi-vertically integrate (use contracts or other means to control firms with which it has vertical relations), or buy from a factor market. Depending on which is more profitable, a firm vertically integrates and produces an input itself or buys the input from others. Because vertical integration is costly, firms integrate only if there are significant benefits. Five possible benefits from vertically integrating are lowering transaction costs, ensuring a steady supply, avoiding government restrictions, extending market power to another market, and eliminating market power.

Problems

1. What does a competitive firm's labor demand curve look like at quantities of labor such that the marginal product of labor curve is upward sloping or is negative? Why?
2. What effect does an ad valorem tax of α on the revenue of a competitive firm have on that firm's demand for labor?
3. Is a firm more likely to be the victim of opportunistic behavior if it buys parts from (A) a single firm that it will not deal with again next year, (B) a single firm with which it has a long-term relationship, or (C) a market?
4. How does a fall in the rental price of capital affect a firm's demand for labor in the long run?
5. How does a monopoly's demand for labor shift if a competitive fringe (Chapter 11) enters its output market?
6. Does a shift in the supply curve of labor have a greater effect on wages if the output market is competitive or if it is monopolistic?

7. What is a monopoly's demand for labor if it uses a fixed-proportions production function in which each unit of output takes one unit of labor and one of capital?
8. A firm is a monopoly in the output market and a monopsony in the input market. Its only input is the finished good, which it buys from a competitive market with an upward-sloping supply curve. The firm sells the same good to competitive buyers in the output market. Determine its profit-maximizing output. What price does it charge in the output market? What price does it pay to its suppliers?
9. Compare the equilibrium in a market in which a firm is both a monopoly and a monopsony (previous problem) to the competitive equilibrium.
10. Compare the equilibrium quantity and price in two markets: one in which a firm is both a monopsony and a monopoly (Problem 8) and one in which the firm buys inputs competitively but has a monopoly in the output market.
11. Compare welfare in a market where a firm that is both a monopsony and monopoly to welfare in markets in which the firm has a monopsony in the input market but acts as a price taker in the output market.
12. Suppose that the original labor supply curve, S^1, facing a monopsony shifts to the right to S^2 if it spends \$1,000 in advertising. Under what condition should the monopsony engage in this advertising? (*Hint*: See the monopoly analysis in Chapter 13.)
13. What happens to the monopsony equilibrium if the minimum wage is set slightly above or below the competitive wage?
14. Can a monopsony exercise monopsony power—profitably setting its price below the competitive level—if the supply curve that it faces is horizontal?
15. Some health reform proposals call for taxing firms to pay for workers' medical care. How is the incidence of a specific tax per worker shared between competitive firms and workers? How does your answer change if the firm is a monopsony?
16. In 1998, four television networks (including ESPN) agreed to pay \$17.6 billion for eight years of National Football League broadcast rights. In three of the deals, the price was more than double that of the previous contracts. What effect will this deal have on advertising rates and the number of commercials, and why?

Math Problems

17. A competitive firm's production function is $q = L + 2LK + K$. What is its marginal revenue product of labor?
18. Suppose that a firm's production function is $q = L + K$. Can it be a competitive firm? Explain.
19. A firm's production function is Cobb-Douglas: $Q = AL^{\alpha}K^{\beta}$. What is the firm's marginal revenue product of labor?
20. If the firm in the previous question is a monopoly that faces a constant elasticity demand curve, what is its marginal revenue product of labor?
21. A monopsony faces a supply curve:

$$p = 10 + Q.$$

What is its marginal expenditure curve?

22. If the monopsony in the previous problem has a demand curve of

$$p = 50 - Q,$$

what are the equilibrium quantity and price? How does this equilibrium differ from the competitive equilibrium?

CHAPTER 16

Interest Rates, Investments, and Capital Markets

I'd gladly pay you Tuesday for a hamburger today. —Wimpy

This chapter examines *capital* and other *durable goods*: products that are usable for years. Firms use durable goods—such as manufacturing plants, machines, and trucks—to produce and distribute goods and services. Consumers spend one in every eight of their dollars on durable goods such as houses, cars, and refrigerators.

Until now, we have examined the choices between *nondurable* goods and services, which are consumed when they are purchased or soon thereafter. You eat an ice cream cone or see a movie just after paying.

If a firm rents a durable good by the week, it faces a similar decision to that of buying a nondurable good or service. A firm demands workers' services (or other nondurable input) up to the point at which its *current* marginal cost (the wage) equals its *current* marginal benefit (the marginal revenue product of the workers' services). A firm that rents a durable good, such as a truck, by the month can use the same rule to decide how many trucks to employ per month. The firm rents trucks up to the point at which the *current* marginal rental cost equals its *current* marginal benefit—the marginal revenue product of the trucks.

If the capital good must be bought or built rather than rented, the firm cannot apply this rule on the basis of current costs and benefits alone. (There are many types of capital, such as factories or specialized pieces of equipment, that a firm *cannot* rent.) In deciding whether to build a long-lived factory, a firm must compare the *current* cost of the capital to the *future* higher profits it will make from using the plant.

Often such comparisons involve *stocks* and *flows*. A **stock** is a quantity or value that is measured independently of time. Because a durable good lasts for many periods, its stock is discussed without reference to its use within a particular time period. We say that a firm owns "an apartment building *this* year" (not "an apartment building *per* year"). If a firm buys the apartment house for \$500,000, we say that it has a capital stock worth \$500,000.

A **flow** is a quantity or value that is measured per unit of time. The consumption of nondurable goods, such as the number of ice cream cones you eat per week, is a flow. Similarly, the stock of a durable good provides a flow of services. A firm's apartment house—its capital stock—provides a flow of housing services (apartments rented per month or year) to tenants. In exchange for these housing services, the firm receives a flow of rental payments from the tenants.

Does it pay for the firm to buy the apartment house? To answer this question, we need to extend our analysis in two ways. First, we must develop a method of comparing a flow of dollars in the future to a dollar today, as we do in this chapter.

Second, we need to consider the role of uncertainty about the future (can the firm rent all the apartments each month?), a subject that we discuss in Chapter 17.

In this chapter, we examine four main topics:

1. **Comparing money today to money in the future:** Interest rates tell us how much more money is worth today than in the future.
2. **Choices over time:** Investing money in a project pays if the return from that investment is greater than that on the best alternative when both returns are expressed on a comparable basis.
3. **Exhaustible resources:** Scarcity, rising costs of extraction, and positive interest rates may cause the price of exhaustible resources like coal and gold to rise exponentially over time.
4. **Capital markets, interest rates, and investments:** Supply and demand in capital markets determine the market rate of interest, which affects how much people invest.

16.1 COMPARING MONEY TODAY TO MONEY IN THE FUTURE

Even if there were no inflation—so a bundle of goods would sell for the same price today, next year, and a hundred years from now—most people would still value receiving a dollar today more than a dollar to be received tomorrow. Wouldn't you rather eat a dollar's worth of chocolate today than wait 10 years to eat that same amount of chocolate?

Interest Rates

Because virtually everyone values having a dollar today more than having a dollar in the future, getting someone to loan you a dollar today requires agreeing to pay back more than a dollar in the future. You may have borrowed money to pay for your college education in exchange for a credible promise to repay a greater amount after you graduate. How much more you must pay in the future is specified by an **interest rate:** the percentage more that must be repaid to borrow money for a fixed period of time.[1]

If you put money in a savings account, you are in effect lending the bank your money, which it may in turn loan to someone who wants to buy a car or a house. For the use of your deposited funds for one year, the bank agrees to pay you an interest rate, i, of, say, 4%. That is, the bank promises to return to you \$1.04 (= $1 + i$) one year from now for every dollar you loan it. If you put \$100 in your savings account, you will have your \$100 plus interest of \$100 × 0.04 = \$4 for a total of \$104 at the end of the year.

[1] For simplicity, we refer to *the* interest rate throughout this chapter, but there are many interest rates in most economies. For example, a bank charges a higher interest rate to loan you money than it pays you to borrow your money.

APPLICATION

Usury

Today, interest payments are not only widely accepted but required by virtually all lenders. Some cultures, however, frown upon interest.

The ancient Greek philosopher Aristotle, lawmakers, and at least three of the world's major religions condemned *usury*, which traditionally meant nothing more than lending money for interest.[2] Two common arguments against charging interest are that lenders are getting something for nothing and that one should help one's neighbor without hope of gain.

Islamic societies honor specific injunctions against *riba* (interest). However, a broader Islamic principle—that risk should be shared between borrower and lender—has allowed Muslim lenders to share in any profits from a venture they helped to finance.

In the fifth century, Pope Leo the Great forbade Christian clerics from acting as usurers and warned that laypeople who did so would be guilty of *turpe lucrum*: shameful gain. By 850, Christian clergy called for the excommunication of usurers. By 1179, usurers were to be denied a Christian burial.

Jews, drawing on biblical tradition and Talmudic writings, also condemned usury. Deuteronomy, Chapter 23, holds that "unto foreigners thou mayst lend upon interest but unto thy brother thou shalt not lend." Medieval Christians saw this passage as an excuse to exempt Jews—whom they chose to view as "foreigners"—from their prohibition against usury.

Given the importance of lending to the functioning of an economy, both Jews and Christians loaned money during the Middle Ages. Even royalty borrowed (though when their debts grew large, they tended to expel all the usurers from the land). Reluctantly, the Catholic church relaxed its ban on lending over time as the European economy expanded and the demand for credit rose. According to Jacques Le Goff, a French historian, the thirteenth-century invention of Purgatory helped the development of modern banking. Because usurers no longer expected to go straight to Hell but to linger in Purgatory, moneylenders could hope for redemption—and gained some respectability.

Gradually, a distinction was made between low interest rates, which were viewed as socially acceptable, and high ones. In 1545, England removed the general prohibition on interest charges and set a maximum rate that a lender could legally charge. Charging more than that rate was *usurious*. Other European countries followed suit. Merchant bankers gained social status

[2] This application is based on "Usury: The Lender's Long Lament," *The Economist*, 329(7843), December 24, 1993–January 7, 1994:103–105; *New Columbia Encyclopedia*, New York: Columbia University Press, 1975; and the *Encyclopedia Britannica*, 1997 CD.

doing much the same as traditional moneylenders. Governments set up central banks. However, European countries regularly debated moneylending. In this century, many countries have usury laws that limit the interest rate that can be charged (many of the states in the United States set such laws) or allow courts to limit the rates (Great Britain). ■

Discount Rate. You may value future consumption more or less than other members of society. If you knew you had a fatal disease that would kill you within two years, you would place less value on payments three or more years in the future than most other people do. We call an individual's personal "interest" rate that person's **discount rate:** a rate reflecting the relative value an individual places on future consumption compared to current consumption.

A person's willingness to borrow or lend depends on whether his or her discount rate is greater or less than the market interest rate. If your discount rate is nearly zero—you view current and future consumption as equally desirable—you would gladly loan money in exchange for a positive interest rate. Similarly, if your discount rate is high—current consumption is much more valuable to you than future consumption—you would be willing to borrow at a lower interest rate. In the following discussion, we assume for simplicity that an individual's discount rate is the same as the market interest rate unless we explicitly state otherwise.

Compounding. If you place \$100 in a bank account that pays 4%, at the end of a year, you can take out the interest payment of \$4 and leave your \$100 in the bank to earn more interest in the future. If you leave your \$100 in the bank indefinitely and the interest rate remains constant over time, you will receive a payment of \$4 each year. In this way, you can convert your \$100 stock into a flow of \$4-a-year payments forever.

In contrast, if you leave both your \$100 and your \$4 interest in the bank, the bank must pay you interest on \$104 at end of the second year. The bank owes you interest of \$4 on your original deposit of \$100 and interest of $\$4 \times 0.04 = \$0.16$ on your interest from the first year, for a total of \$4.16.

Thus, at the end of Year 1, your account contains

$$\$104.00 = \$100 \times 1.04 = \$100 \times 1.04^1.$$

By the end of the Year 2, you have

$$\$108.16 = \$104 \times 1.04 = \$100 \times 1.04^2.$$

At the end of Year 3, your account has

$$\$112.49 \approx \$108.16 \times 1.04 = \$100 \times 1.04^3.$$

If we extend this reasoning, by the end of Year t, you have

$$\$100 \times 1.04^t.$$

We can state this relationship more generally. If you let your interest accumulate in your account, for every dollar you loan the bank, it owes you $1 + i$ dollars after 1 year, $(1 + i) \times (1 + i) = (1 + i)^2$ dollars after 2 years, $(1 + i) \times (1 + i) \times (1 + i) = (1 + i)^3$ after three years, and $(1 + i)^t$ dollars at the end of t years. This accumulation of interest on interest is called *compounding*.

Frequency of Compounding. To get the highest return on your savings account, you need to check both the interest rate and the frequency with which each bank compounds the interest. So far, we've assumed that interest is paid only at the end of the year. Many banks, however, pay interest more frequently than once a year. If you leave your interest in the bank for the entire year, you receive compounded interest—interest on the interest—at the end of the year.

If a bank's annual interest rate is $i = 4\%$, but it pays interest two times a year, the bank pays you half a year's interest, $i/2 = 2\%$, after six months. For every dollar in your account, the bank pays you $(1 + i/2) = 1.02$ dollars after six months. If you leave the interest in the bank, at the end of the year, the bank must pay you interest on your original dollar and on the interest you received at the end of the first six months. At the end of the year, the bank owes you $(1 + i/2) \times (1 + i/2) = (1 + i/2)^2 = (1.02)^2 = \$1.0404$, which is your original \$1 plus 4.04¢ in interest.

If the bank were to compound your money more frequently, you would earn even more interest. Some banks offer continuous compounding, in which interest is paid at every instant. Such compounding is only slightly better for you than daily compounding. Table 16.1 shows you that the amount you would earn after one year of investing \$10,000 at a 4% or at an 18% annual rate of interest depends on the frequency of compounding.

Because most people cannot easily perform such calculations, the U.S. Truth-in-Lending Act requires lenders to tell borrowers the equivalent noncompounded annual percentage rate (APR) of interest. As the table shows, twice-a-year compounding at 4% has an APR of 4.04%. That is, over a year, an account with a noncompounded interest rate of 4.04% pays you the same interest as a 4% account that was compounded twice during the year.

Thus, when considering various loans or interest rates, you should compare the APRs; comparing rates that are compounded at different frequencies can be

Table 16.1 Interest Payments Depend on the Frequency of Compounding

	Interest Payments on a \$10,000 Investment at the End of 1 Year	
Frequency of Compounding	4%	18%
Once a year	\$400.00	\$1,800.00
Twice a year	\$404.00	\$1,881.00
Four times a year	\$406.04	\$1,925.19
Daily	\$408.08	\$1,971.64
Continuous	\$408.11	\$1,972.17

misleading. If you use credit cards to borrow money, it's particularly important that you compare APRs across accounts because credit card interest rates are usually high. If the interest rate on your card is 18%, a continuously compounded rate has an APR of over 19.7%. If you borrow \$10,000 for a year, you'll owe \$1,972.17 with continuous compounding, which is 9.6% more than the \$1,800 you'd owe with annual compounding. From now on, we assume that compounding takes place annually.

Interest Rates Connect the Present and Future

Interest rates connect the value of the money you put in the bank today, the *present value* (*PV*), and the *future value* (*FV*) that you are later repaid, which is the present value plus interest. Understanding this relationship allows us to evaluate the attractiveness of investments involving payments today for profits in the future and of purchases made today but paid for later. Knowing the interest rate and the present value allows us to calculate the future value. Similarly, we can determine the present value if we know the future value and the interest rate.

Future Value. If you deposit PV dollars in the bank today and allow the interest to compound for t years, how much money will you have at the end? The future value, FV, is the present value times a term that reflects the compounding of the interest payments:

$$FV = PV \times (1 + i)^t. \tag{16.1}$$

Table 16.2 shows how much \$1 put in the bank today will be worth in the future at various annually compounded interest rates. For example, \$1 left in the bank for 50 years will be worth only \$1.64 at a 1% interest rate. However, that same investment is worth \$7.11 at a 4% interest rate, \$11.47 at a 5% rate, \$117.39 at a 10% rate, and \$9,100.44 at a 20% rate.

Table 16.2 Future Value, *FV*, to Which \$1 Grows by the End of Year *t* at Various Interest Rates, *i*, Compounded Annually

Year *t*	1%	4%	5%	10%	20%
1	1.01	1.04	1.05	1.10	1.20
5	1.05	1.22	1.28	1.61	2.49
10	1.10	1.48	1.63	2.59	6.19
25	1.28	2.67	3.39	10.83	95.40
50	1.64	7.11	11.47	117.39	9100.44

Note: $FV = (1 + i)^t$, where FV is the future value of \$1 invested for t years at an annual interest rate of i.

APPLICATION

Power of Compounding

> *One thousand dollars left to earn interest at 8% a year will grow to $43 quadrillion in 400 years, but the first 100 years are the hardest.*
>
> —Sidney Homer, Salomon Brothers analyst

No doubt you've read that the Dutch got a good deal buying Manhattan from the original inhabitants in 1626 for about $24 worth of beads and trinkets. That conclusion may be wrong.[3] If these native Americans had had the opportunity to sell the beads and invest in tax-free bonds with an APR of 7%, the bond would now be worth over $2.0 trillion, which is much more than the assessed value of Manhattan Island. On the other hand, if the United States had taken the $7.2 million it paid for the purchase of Alaska from Russia in 1867 and invested in the same type of bonds, that money would now be worth only $50.9 billion, which is much less than Alaska's current value. ■

Present Value. Instead of asking how much a dollar today is worth in the future, we can ask how much a dollar in the future is worth today given the market interest rate. For example, we may want to know how much money, PV, we have to put in the bank today at an interest rate i to get a specific amount of money, FV, in the future. If we want to have FV = $100 at the end of a year and the interest rate is i = 4%, then, from Equation 16.1, we know that $PV \times 1.04$ = $100. Dividing both sides of this expression by 1.04, we learn that we need to put PV = $100/1.04 = $96.15 in the bank today to have $100 next year.

A more general formula relating money t periods in the future to money today is obtained by dividing both sides of Equation 16.1 by $(1 + i)^t$ to obtain

$$PV = \frac{FV}{(1 + i)^t}. \qquad (16.2)$$

[3] Huntley, Helen, Kim Norris, and Robert Trigaux, "An Early Lesson in Investing for the Long Term," *St. Petersburg Times*, March 14, 1994: Business Section 3.

This equation tells us what FV dollars in year t are worth today at an interest i compounded annually. Table 16.3 and Figure 16.1 show what \$1 in the future is worth today for various interest rates. At high interest rates, money in the future is virtually worthless today: A dollar paid to you in 25 years is worth only 1¢ today at a 20% interest rate.

Stream of Payments

Sometimes, we need to deal with payments per period, which are flow measures, rather than a present value or future value, which are stock measures. Often, a firm pays for a new factory or an individual pays for a house by making monthly mortgage payments. In deciding whether to purchase the factory or house, the decisionmaker compares the value of the stock (factory or home) to a flow of payments over time.

Present Value of Payments over Time. One way to make such an evaluation is to use our knowledge of the relationship between present and future values to determine the present value of the stream of payments. To do so, we calculate the present value of each future payment and add.

Payments for a Finite Number of Years. To motivate the general case, we start with a specific example. Suppose you agree to pay \$10 at the end of each year for three years to repay a debt. If the interest rate is 10%, the present value of this series of payments is

$$PV = \$10/1.1 + \$10/1.1^2 + \$10/1.1^3 \approx \$24.87.$$

More generally, if you make a *future payment* of f per year for t years at an interest rate of i, the present value (stock) of this flow of payments is

$$PV = f\left[\frac{1}{(1+i)^1} + \frac{1}{(1+i)^2} + \ldots + \frac{1}{(1+i)^t}\right]. \tag{16.3}$$

Table 16.4 shows that the present value of a payment of f = \$10 a year for 5 years is \$43 at 5%, \$38 at 10%, and \$30 at 20% annual interest.

Table 16.3 Present Value, *PV*, of a Payment of \$1 at the End of Year *t* at Various Interest Rates, *i*, Compounded Annually

Year t	1%	4%	5%	10%	20%
1	0.99	0.96	0.95	0.91	0.83
5	0.95	0.82	0.78	0.62	0.40
10	0.91	0.68	0.61	0.39	0.16
25	0.78	0.38	0.30	0.09	0.01
50	0.61	0.14	0.09	0.009	0.00011

Note: $PV = 1/(1+i)^t$, where PV is the present value of \$1 at the end of year t at an annual interest rate of i.

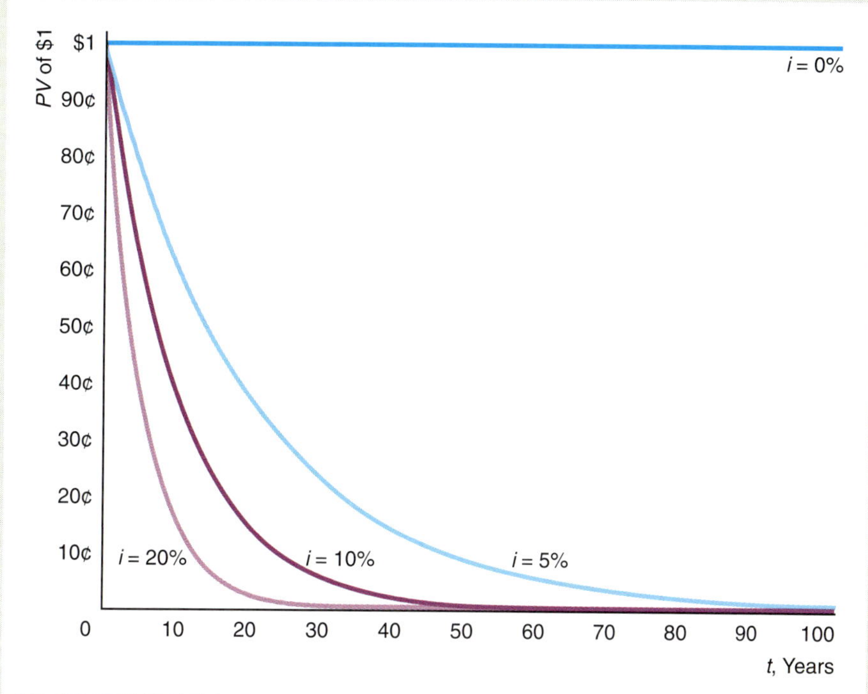

Figure 16.1 Present Value of a Dollar in the Future. The present value of a dollar is lower the farther in the future it is paid. At a given time in the future, the present value is lower when the interest rate is higher.

Table 16.4 Present Value, *PV* of a Flow of $10 a Year for *t* Years at Various Interest Rates, *i*, Compounded Annually

t Years	5%	10%	20%
5	$43	$38	$30
10	77	61	42
50	183	99	50*
100	198	100*	50*
∞	200	100	50

*The actual numbers are a fraction of a cent below the rounded numbers in the table. For example, the *PV* at 10% for 100 years is $99.9927.

Note: The payments are made at the end of the year.

Payments Forever. If these payments must be made at the end of each year forever, the present value formula is easier to calculate than is Equation 16.3. If you put PV dollars into a bank account earning an interest rate of i, you can get an interest or future payment of $f = i \times PV$ at the end of year. Dividing both sides of this expression by i, we find that, to get a payment of f each year forever, you'd have to put

$$PV = \frac{f}{i} \tag{16.4}$$

in the bank. Thus, you'd have to deposit $10/$i$ in the bank to ensure a future payment of f = $10 forever. Using this formula, we determine that the present value of $10 a year forever is $200 at 5%, $100 at 10%, and $50 at 20%.[4]

SOLVED PROBLEM 16.1

Melody Toyota advertises that it will sell you a 1997 Corolla for $14,000 or lease it to you. To lease it, you must make a down payment of $1,650 and agree to pay $1,800 at the end of each of the next two years. After the last lease payment, you may buy the car for $12,000. If you plan to keep the car until it falls apart (at least a decade) and the interest rate is 10%, which approach has a lower present value of costs?

Answer

1. *Calculate the present value of leasing*: The present value of leasing the car and then buying it is the sum of the down payment of $1,650, the present value of paying f = $1,800 at the end of each year for $t = 2$ years, and the present value of purchasing the car for FV = $12,000 in $t = 2$ years. Equation 16.3 shows the present value of the lease payments to be

$$\$1,800\left(\frac{1}{1.1^1} + \frac{1}{1.1^2}\right) \approx \$3,124.$$

Using Equation 16.2, we find that the present value of buying the car at the end of the lease period is

$$\$12,000/1.1^2 \approx \$9,917.$$

[4] This payment in perpetuity formula, Equation 16.4, provides a good approximation of a payment for a large but finite number of years. As Table 16.4 shows, at a 5% interest rate, the present value of a payment of $10 a year for 100 years, $198, is close to the present value of a permanent stream of payments, $200. At higher interest rates, this approximation is nearly perfect. At 10%, the present value of payments for 100 years is $99.9927 compared to $100 for perpetual payments. The reason this approximation works better at high rates is that a dollar paid more than 50 or 100 years from now is essentially worthless today, as Table 16.3 shows.

Thus, the present value of leasing the car and then buying it is approximately

$$\$1,650 + \$3,124 + \$9,917 = \$14,691.$$

2. *Compare leasing to buying the car*: The present value of buying the car is $14,000, which is $691 less than the present value of leasing it. ■

Future Value of Payments over Time. We just calculated the present value of a stream of payments. This type of computation can help you to decide whether to buy something today that you'll pay for over time. Sometimes, however, we want to know about the future value of a stream of payments.

For example, suppose you want to know how much you'll have in your savings account, FV, at some future time if you save f each year. The first year, you place f dollars in your account. The second year, you add another f and you have the first year's payment plus its accumulated interest, $f(1 + i)^1$. Thus, at the end of the second year, your account has $f[1 + (1 + i)^1]$. In the third year, you have the third year's payment, f, plus the current value of the second year's payment, $f(1 + i)$, plus the current value of the first year's payment, $f(1 + i)^2$, for a total of $f[1 + (1 + i) + (1 + i)^2]$. Continuing in this way, we see that, at the end of t years, the account has[5]

$$FV = f[1 + (1 + i)^1 + (1 + i)^2 + \ldots + (1 + i)^t]. \qquad (16.5)$$

APPLICATION

Saving for Retirement

If all goes well, you'll live long enough to retire. Will you live like royalty off your savings, or will you depend on Social Security to provide enough income that you can avoid having to eat dog food to stay alive?

You almost certainly don't want to hear this, but it isn't too early to think about saving for retirement. Thanks to the power of compounding, if you start saving when you're young, you don't have to save as much per year as you would if you start saving when you're middle aged.

Suppose that you plan to work full-time from age 22 until you retire at 70 and that you can earn 7% on your retirement savings account. Let's consider two approaches to savings:

- **Early bird:** You save $3,000 a year for the first 15 years of your working life and then let your savings accumulate interest until you retire.

[5]This equation can also be written as

$$FV = f[(1 + i)^0 + (1 + i)^1 + (1 + i)^2 + \ldots + (1 + i)^t].$$

because $(1 + i)^0 = 1$.

- **Late bloomer:** After not saving for the first 15 years, you save \$3,000 a year for the next 33 years until retirement.

Which scenario leads to a bigger retirement nest egg? To answer this question, we calculate the future value at retirement of each of these streams of investments.

The early bird adds \$3,000 each year for 15 years into a retirement account. Using Equation 16.5, we calculate that the account has

$$\$3{,}000[1 + 1.07^1 + 1.07^2 + \ldots + 1.07^{14}] = \$75{,}387$$

at the end of 15 years. This amount then grows as the interest compounds for the next 33 years. Using Equation 16.1, we determine that the fund grows about 9.3 times to

$$\$75{,}387.07 \times 1.07^{33} = \$703{,}010$$

by retirement.

The late bloomer makes no investments for 15 years and then invests \$3,000 a year until retirement. Again using Equation 16.5, we calculate that the funds at retirement are

$$\$3{,}000[1 + 1.07 + 1.07^2 + \ldots + 1.07^{32}] = \$356{,}800.$$

Thus, even though the late bloomer contributes to the account for more than twice as long as the early bird, the late bloomer has saved only about half as much at retirement. Indeed, to have roughly the same amount at retirement as the early bird, the late bloomer would have to save nearly \$6,000 a year for the 33 years. (By the way, someone who saved \$3,000 each year for all 48 years would have \$703,010 + \$356,800 = \$1,059,810 salted away by retirement.) ■

Inflation and Discounting

So far, we've ignored inflation (implicitly assumed an inflation rate of zero). Now, we suppose that general inflation occurs so that *nominal prices*—actual prices that are not adjusted for inflation—rise at a constant rate over time. By adjusting for this rate of inflation (Chapter 5), we can convert nominal prices to *real prices*, which are constant prices that are independent of inflation. To calculate the real present value of future payments, we adjust for inflation and use interest rates to discount future real payments.

To illustrate this process, we calculate the real present value of a payment made next year. First, we adjust for inflation so as to convert next year's nominal payment to a real amount. Then we determine the real interest rate. Finally, we use the real interest rate to convert the real future payment to a real present value.

Adjusting for Inflation. Suppose that the rate of inflation is γ ("gamma") and the nominal amount you pay next year is $\tilde{f}$. This future debt in today's dollars—the real amount you owe—is $f = \tilde{f}/(1 + \gamma)$. If the rate of inflation is $\gamma = 10\%$, a nominal payment of $\tilde{f}$ next year is $\tilde{f}/1.1 \approx 0.909\tilde{f}$ in today's dollars.

Nominal and Real Rates of Interest. To calculate the present value of this future real payment, we discount using an interest rate. Just as we converted the future payments into real values by adjusting for inflation, we convert a nominal interest rate into a real interest rate by adjusting for inflation.

Without inflation, a dollar today is worth $1 + i$ next year, where i is the real interest rate. With an inflation rate of γ, a dollar today is worth $(1 + i)(1 + \gamma)$ nominal dollars tomorrow. If $i = 5\%$ and $\gamma = 10\%$, a dollar today is worth $1.05 \times 1.1 = 1.155$ nominal dollars next year.

Banks pay a nominal interest rate, $\tilde{i}$, rather than a real one. If they're going to get people whose real discount rate is i to save, banks' nominal interest rate must be such that a dollar pays $(1 + i)(1 + \gamma)$ dollars next year. For that to be true, $1 + \tilde{i} = (1 + i)(1 + \gamma) = 1 + i + i\gamma + \gamma$, so the nominal rate is

$$\tilde{i} = i + i\gamma + \gamma.$$

By rearranging this equation, we see that the real rate of interest depends on the nominal rate of interest and the rate of inflation:

$$i = \frac{\tilde{i} - \gamma}{1 + \gamma}. \tag{16.6}$$

Equation 16.6 shows that the real rate of interest is less than the nominal rate in the presence of inflation.

If the inflation rate is small, the denominator of Equation 16.6, $1 + \gamma$, is close to 1. As a result, many people approximate the real rate of interest as the nominal rate of interest minus the rate of inflation:

$$\tilde{i} - \gamma.$$

If the nominal rate of interest is 15.5% and the rate of inflation is 10%, the real rate of interest is $(15.5\% - 10\%)/1.1 = 5\%$. The approximation to the real rate, $15.5\% - 10\% = 5.5\%$, is above the true rate by half a percentage point. The lower the rate of inflation, the closer the approximation is to the real rate of interest. If the inflation rate falls to $\gamma = 2\%$ while the nominal rate remains 15.5%, the approximation to the real rate, 13.5%, is above the real rate, 13.24%, by only slightly more than a quarter of a percentage point.

Real Present Value. To obtain a real present value of a payment one year from now, we discount the future real payment of $f = \tilde{f}/(1 + \gamma)$ using the real interest rate:

$$PV = \frac{f}{1 + i} = \frac{\tilde{f}}{(1 + \gamma)(1 + i)}.$$

Thus, the real present value is obtained by adjusting for inflation and by discounting using the real interest rate.

Suppose that you sign a contract with a store to pay \$100 next year for a tape recorder you get today. The rate of inflation is $\gamma = 10\%$, and the real rate of interest is $i = 5\%$. We calculate the real present value by converting the future payment into real dollars and by using the real interest rate to discount. Next year's nominal payment of \$100 is only \$100/1.1 ≈ \$90.91 in real dollars. Discounting by the real rate of interest, we find that the real present value of that payment is \$90.91/1.05 ≈ \$86.58.

If everyone anticipates a particular inflation rate, γ, the nominal interest is roughly $i + \gamma$. Suppose, however, that the inflation rate turns out to be higher than the anticipated rate of γ. Such unanticipated inflation helps debtors because it lowers the real cost of future payments that are set in nominal rather than real terms.

Suppose that when you buy the tape recorder, no one expects inflation ($\gamma = 0$), so both you and the store's owner believe that the present value of your future payment is \$100/1.05 ≈ \$95.24. Immediately after you make the deal, the inflation rate suddenly increases to $\gamma = 10\%$, so the actual present value is only \$86.58. Thus, because of the unexpected inflation, the present value of what you owe is less than either you or the store owner initially expected.

APPLICATION

Winning the Lottery

Lottery: A tax on people who are bad at math.

Several states boast that their lottery pays a winner one million dollars. This claim is, at best, misleading (translation: they lie through their teeth). Typically, a lottery winner gets \$50,000 a year for 20 years, which means that the winner receives 20 × \$50,000 = 1 million nominal dollars over time. After adjustment for inflation and discounting, however, the real present value of these prize payments over time is much less than a million dollars.

What is a payment of \$50,000 for 20 years worth today? If the first payment is made today, its real present value is \$50,000, regardless of the inflation and interest rates. The later payments, however, need to be adjusted for inflation and discounted to the present to be comparable to this year's payment.

If the rate of inflation is 5% and the real rate of interest is 4%, a \$50,000 payment next year is worth only \$45,788 ≈ \$50,000/(1.05 × 1.04) this year. Generalizing, we determine that the real present value of a dollar t years from now is

$$\frac{1}{(1.05)^t(1.04)^t}$$

The $(1.05)^t$ term in the denominator adjusts for inflation between now and the year t: It expresses the payment in the future in terms of today's dollars. The $(1.04)^t$ term in the denominator converts the payment in year t to a present value.

At these rates, the real present value of the 20 payments is less than half a million dollars: \$491,396. If there were no inflation ($\gamma = 0$), the real present value would be \$706,697. With 5% inflation and a real interest rate of 10%, the present value of the prize is only \$351,708.[6] ■

16.2 CHOICES OVER TIME

Earlier chapters discuss how consumers and firms make choices that do not involve time. Often, however, such decisions involve comparisons over time. Individuals and firms must choose between two or more options—such as investments and contracts—that have different present and future values. A land speculator decides whether to sell a plot of land today for \$100,000 or next year for \$200,000. Margi decides among putting \$1,000 into a bank account, buying \$1,000 worth of stocks, paying \$1,000 for a course in computer programming, and consuming the \$1,000 now. Metro-Goldwyn-Mayer (MGM), a conglomerate, decides whether to produce a movie that stars a muscle-bound hero who solves the pollution problem by beating up an evil capitalist, to build a new hotel in Reno, to buy a television studio, or to put money in a long-term savings account.

One way to make a choice involving time is to *pick the option with the highest present value*. By borrowing or lending at the market interest rate, we can shift wealth from one period to another. Thus, if we choose the option that has the highest present value, we can shift our wealth between periods so that we have more money in every period than we'd have if we made the less attractive choice.

APPLICATION

Comparing Two Contracts

A professional basketball player is offered contracts by two different teams for playing this year. Both contracts are guaranteed, and payments will be made even if the athlete is injured and cannot play. One team offers him a contract that pays him \$1 million today. The other team's contract pays him \$500,000 today and \$2 million 10 years from now.

Assuming that there is no inflation and that our pro is concerned only about the money, which contract does he accept? Our hero knows that, if he takes the second contract, he will be paid a total of \$2.5 million—but most of

[6]This discussion of lottery prizes is not intended to encourage you to play the lottery. The important thing to remember about a lottery is that the probability of winning if you buy a ticket is almost exactly the same as the probability of winning if you don't buy a ticket: zero.

it won't be available for 10 years. He also knows that if he takes the $1 million today, he can spend it immediately or invest it and have more than $1 million in the future.

He prefers the contract with the higher present value. The present value of the first contract is $1 million.

To calculate the present value of the second contract, he uses the market interest rate. We consider two possible interest rates, 5% and 20%. He can use Equation 16.2 to calculate the present value of the second contract—or hire you to do it for him. For example, you can use a calculator to determine that the present value of $2 million 10 years from now is $\$2{,}000{,}000/(1.05)^{10} \approx \$1{,}227{,}827$ with a 5% interest rate and $\$2{,}000{,}000/(1.2)^{10} \approx \$323{,}011$ with a 20% interest rate. Consequently, the present value of the second contract is approximately $1,727,827 at 5% and $823,011 at 20%, as the following calculations show:

Payment	Present Value at 5%	Present Value at 20%
$500,000 today	$500,000	$500,000
$2 million in 10 years	$1,227,827	$323,011
Total	$1,727,827	$823,011

At an interest rate of 5%, he should definitely take the second contract, which is worth nearly one and three-quarter million dollars today—almost three-quarters of a million dollars more than the present value of the first contract. At an interest rate of 20%, he prefers the contract that pays him $1 million today to the second contract, which is worth only $823,011 today.[7] ■

Investing

Investment decisions may be made by comparing present values. *A firm makes an investment if the expected return from the investment is greater than the opportunity cost* (Chapter 7). The opportunity cost is the best alternative use of its money, which is what it would earn in the next best use of the money.

Thus, to decide whether to make an investment, the firm needs to compare the potential outlay of money to the firm's best alternative. One possibility is that its best alternative is to put the money that it would otherwise spend on this investment in an interest-bearing bank account. We consider two methods for making this comparison: the *net present value* approach and the *internal rate of return* approach.

[7]He prefers the second contract for any discount rate less than 14.87%, and he prefers the first contract at any discount rate greater than 14.87%.

Net Present Value Approach. A firm has to decide whether to buy a truck for \$20,000. Because the opportunity cost is \$20,000, the firm should make the investment only if the present value of expected future returns from the truck is greater than \$20,000.

More generally, *a firm should make an investment only if the present value of the expected return exceeds the present value of the costs.* If R is the present value of the expected returns to an investment and C is the present value of the costs of the investment, the firm should make the investment if $R > C$.[8]

This rule is often restated in terms of the net present value, $NPV = R - C$, which is the difference between the present value of the returns, R, and the present value of the costs, C. *A firm should make an investment only if the net present value is positive*:

$$NPV = R - C > 0.$$

Assume that the initial year is $t = 0$, the firm's revenue in year t is R_t, and its cost in year t is C_t. If the last year in which either revenue or cost is nonzero is T, the net present value rule holds that the firm should invest if

$$\begin{aligned} NPV &= R - C \\ &= \left[R_0 + \frac{R_1}{(1+i)^1} + \frac{R_2}{(1+i)^2} + \ldots + \frac{R_T}{(1+i)^T}\right] \\ &\quad - \left[C_0 + \frac{C_1}{(1+i)^1} + \frac{C_2}{(1+i)^2} + \ldots + \frac{C_T}{(1+i)^T}\right] > 0. \end{aligned}$$

Instead of comparing the present values of the returns and costs, we can examine whether the present value of the *cash flow* in each year (loosely, the annual *profit*), $\pi_t = R_t - C_t$, is positive. By rearranging the terms in the previous expression, we can rewrite the net present value rule as

$$\begin{aligned} NPV &= (R_0 - C_0) + \frac{R_1 - C_1}{(1+i)^1} + \frac{R_2 - C_2}{(1+i)^2} + \ldots + \frac{R_T - C_T}{(1+i)^T} \\ &= \pi_0 + \frac{\pi_1}{(1+i)^1} + \frac{\pi_2}{(1+i)^2} + \ldots + \frac{\pi_T}{(1+i)^T} > 0. \end{aligned} \tag{16.7}$$

This rule does not restrict the firm to making investments only where its cash flow is positive each year. For example, a firm buys a piece of equipment for \$100 and spends the first year learning how to use it, so it makes no revenues from the machine and has a negative cash flow that year: $\pi_0 = -100$. The next year, its revenue is \$350 and the machine's maintenance cost is \$50, so its second year's cash flow is $\pi_1 = \$300$. At the end of that year, the machine wears out, so the annual cash flow from this investment is zero thereafter. Setting the interest rate at 5% in Equation 16.7, we learn that the firm's net present value is

$$NPV = -100 + 300/1.05 \approx \$185.71.$$

Because this net present value is positive, the firm makes the investment.

[8]This rule holds when future costs and returns are known with certainty and investments can be reversed but cannot be delayed (Dixit and Pindyck, 1994).

SOLVED PROBLEM 16.2

A baseball team's annual profit, *f*, is \$6 million, and the purchase price of this franchise is \$107 million.[9] A firm that is interested only in making money is considering buying the team. It believes that the club will continue to earn \$6 million (after adjusting for inflation) a year forever. If it does not buy the team, the firm plans to put the \$107 million in a savings account that pays an interest rate of $i = 5\%$. Does the firm buy the ball club?

Answer

Determine the net present value of the team: The net present value is positive if the present value of the expected returns, \$6 million/0.05 = \$120 million, minus the present value of the cost, which is the purchase price of \$107 million, is positive:

$$NPV = \$120 \text{ million} - \$107 \text{ million} = \$13 \text{ million} > 0.$$

Thus, the firm buys the team. ■

Internal Rate of Return Approach. Whether the net present value of an investment is positive depends on the interest rate. In Solved Problem 16.2, the firm buys the baseball team, given an interest rate of 5%. However, if the interest rate were 10%, the net present value would be \$6 million/0.1 – \$107 = –\$47 million, so the firm would not buy the team.

At what discount rate (rate of return) is the firm indifferent between making the investment and not? The **internal rate of return** (*irr*) is the discount rate that results in a net present value of an investment of zero. Replacing the interest rate, *i*, in Equation 16.7 with *irr* and setting the *NPV* equal to zero, we implicitly determine the internal rate of return by solving

$$NPV = \pi_0 + \frac{\pi_1}{1 + irr} + \frac{\pi_2}{(1 + irr)^2} + \ldots + \frac{\pi_T}{(1 + irr)^T} = 0$$

for *irr*.

It is easier to calculate the *irr* when the investment pays a steady stream of profit, *f*, forever and the cost of the investment is *PV*. The investment's rate of return is

[9] These numbers are the averages for 1993 according to *Financial World*, as cited in Curtis, Jake, "Local Teams Want Share of Revenues," *San Francisco Chronicle*, August 16, 1994:D1. This profit figure does not include returns from licensing the team's name and merchandising. Further, some people buy baseball teams for unusual tax advantages and for nonprofit-maximizing purposes, which we ignore here.

found by rearranging Equation 16.4 and replacing i with irr:

$$irr = \frac{f}{PV}. \tag{16.8}$$

Instead of using the net present value rule, we can decide whether to invest by comparing the internal rate of return to the interest rate. If the firm is borrowing money to make the investment, *it pays for the firm to borrow to make the investment if the internal rate of return on that investment exceeds that of the next best alternative* (which we assume is the interest rate):[10]

$$irr > i.$$

SOLVED PROBLEM 16.3

A firm can buy a baseball team for PV = \$107 million. It expects an annual real flow of payments of f = \$6 million a year forever. If the interest rate is 5%, does the firm buy the team?

Answer

Determine the internal rate of return to this investment and compare it to the interest rate: Using Equation 16.8, we calculate that the internal rate of return from buying a baseball club is

$$irr = f/PV = \$6 \text{ million}/\$107 \text{ million} \approx 5.6\%.$$

Because this rate of return, 5.6%, is greater than the interest rate, 5%, the firm buys the team. ■

Rate of Return on Bonds

Instead of investing in capital or putting their money in a bank, firms or individuals may invest in a *bond*, a piece of paper issued by a government or a corporation that promises to repay the borrower with a payment stream. The amount borrowed is called the *face value* of the bond. Some bonds have a number of *coupons*. Each year, the holder of the bond clips one coupon, returns it to the issuer, and receives a payment of a fixed amount of money. At the *maturity date* shown on the bond—when no coupons remain—the borrower redeems the bond by returning the face value, the amount borrowed.

---

[10]The *NPV* approach always works. The internal rate of return method is inapplicable if the *irr* is not unique. In Solved Problem 16.3, the *irr* is unique, and using this approach gives the same answer as the *NPV* approach.

Some bonds, *perpetuities*, have no maturity date and the face value is never returned. Instead, the bond holder receives annual payments forever.

For example, last year, Jerome paid PV = \$2,000 to buy a government-issued bond that guarantees the holder a payment of f = \$100 a year forever. According to Equation 16.8, the rate of return on Jerome's bond was 5% = \$100/\$2,000. At the time, banks were paying 5% on comparable accounts and were expected to do so in the future. As a result, Jerome was indifferent between buying a bond and keeping his money in a bank account.

This year, however, because of *unanticipated* inflation, the nominal interest rate that banks paid *unexpectedly* rose to 10%, and everyone expects this new interest rate to persist. If the bonds were to continue to sell for \$2,000, the rate of return would remain 5%, so everyone would prefer to keep their money in the bank. Thus, if Jerome wants to sell his bond, he must lower the price until the rate of return on the bond reaches 10%. As a result, the present value of Jerome's bond falls to \$1,000 = \$100/0.1 this year, according to Equation 16.4. In general, a bond's selling price falls from the face value of the bond if the nominal interest rate rises over time (and the price rises if the interest rate falls).

Similarly, the real return to a bond that pays a nominal rate of return varies with the inflation rate. During the high-inflation 1970s and early 1980s, holders of U.S. bonds lost much of their wealth for this reason. Following Canada, Britain, and other countries, the United States, in 1997, started offering bonds that adjust for the inflation rate. These bonds are supposed to provide a constant, real rate of return.

Durability

Many firms must decide how durable to make the products they sell or those they produce for their own use. Should they make long-lasting products at a relatively high cost or less durable goods at a lower cost?

Suppose that the company can vary the quality of a factor (a machine) that it uses in its own production process. If it needs exactly one machine, it must replace the machine when it wears out. Thus, *the firm should pick that durability level for the machine that minimizes the present discounted cost of having a machine forever.*

APPLICATION

Durability of Phone Poles

Pacific Gas & Electric (PG&E), a western power utility, must decide how durable to make its 132 million wooden utility poles.[11] The poles are a capital stock for PG&E, which uses them to provide a flow of services: supporting

[11]Marshall, Jonathan, "PG&E Cultivates Its Forest," *San Francisco Chronicle*, May 5, 1995:D1. In the following calculations, we assume that the figures reported are real costs that do not change over time.

power and phone lines year after year. A wooden utility pole provides the same services each year for T years under normal use. After T years, the pole breaks and is replaced because it can't be repaired, but the flow of services must be maintained. Until recently, PG&E used poles with a life span of $T = 25$ years.

The constant marginal cost of manufacturing and installing the poles depends on how long they last, $m(T)$. For an additional cost, the firm can extend the life span of a pole by treating it with chemicals to prevent bug infestations and rot, reinforcing it with metal bands, varying its thickness, or using higher-quality materials. Because the marginal cost increases with the pole's expected life span, a pole that lasts 50 years costs more than one that lasts 25 years: $m(50) > m(25)$.

The replacement cost of a pole that lasts 25 years is $m(25) = \$1{,}500$. Thus, replacing all of PG&E poles today would amount to $198 billion—which is more than the cost of many of PG&E's giant power plants.

PG&E believes that it can save money by switching to a longer-lasting pole. The firm picks the duration, T, that minimizes its cost of maintaining its forest of poles. Because the utility keeps the same number of poles in place every year, after a pole wears out at T years, the firm incurs an expense of $m(T)$ to replace it. The present value of providing each pole is the cost of producing it today, $m(T)$, plus the discounted cost of producing another one in T years, $m(T)/(1 + i)^T$, plus the discounted cost of producing another one in $2T$ years, $m(T)/(1 + i)^{2T}$, and so on.

Table 16.5 shows the present value of the cost of maintaining one pole for the next 100 years, given that the utility faces an interest rate of 5%. Because the cost of producing a pole that lasts for 25 years is $m(25) = \$1{,}500$, the present value of the cost of providing a pole for the next 100 years is $2,112 (column 2). If the cost of a pole that lasts 50 years were $m(50) = \$1{,}943$ (column 4), the present value would be the same as that for the 25-year pole. If so, the

Table 16.5 Present Discounted Cost of Providing a Utility Pole for a Century (5% Interest Rate Compounded Annually)

	25-Year Pole	50-Year Pole	
Marginal Cost, m(T):	$1,500	$1,650	$1,943
Year			
0	$1,500	$1,650	$1,943
25	443	0	0
50	131	$144	169
75	39	0	0
Present value of the cost of providing a pole for 100 years	$2,112	$1,794	$2,112

Note: The second column does not add to the present value because the reported numbers are rounded.

utility would be indifferent between using poles that last 25 years and poles that last 50 years.

Thus, PG&E will not use 50-year poles if the extra cost is greater than \$443 = \$1,943 – \$1,500 but will use them if the difference in cost is less than that. The actual extra cost is less than \$150. Thus, the present value of the cost of a 50-year pole is only about \$1,794 (column 3 of the table). Because using the 50-year poles reduces the present value by \$318, or about 15% per pole, the utility wants to use the longer-lasting poles. By so doing, PG&E cuts the present value of the cost of maintaining all its poles for 100 years by about \$42 billion. Solved Problem 16.4 shows that the length of time one maintains a durable good depends on the alternatives and the rate of interest. ■

SOLVED PROBLEM 16.4

Your car is a gas guzzler that gets only 10 miles to the gallon and has no resale value, but you are sure that it will last 5 years. You know that you can always buy a used car for \$5,000 that gets 20 miles to the gallon. A gallon of gas costs \$1.50, and you drive 6,000 miles a year. If the interest rate is 5% and you are interested only in saving money, should you buy a new car now rather than wait until your current car dies? Would you make the same decision if you faced a 10% interest rate?

Answer

1. *Determine the present values of the fuel savings*: Currently, you buy 600 gallons of gas at a cost of \$900 per year. With a more fuel-efficient car, you would spend only \$450 a year, saving \$450 a year in gas payments. If we assume that these payments are made at the end of each year, the present value of this savings is \$1,935 at a 5% annual interest rate and \$1,710 at 10% (using Table 16.4).
2. *Calculate the present value of the savings from postponing the car purchase*: If you buy the car today, the present value of the cost is \$5,000. If you spend \$5,000 to buy the car in 5 years, the present value of the cost is \$3,900 at 5% and \$3,100 at 10% (using Table 16.3). Thus, the present value of the additional cost of buying now rather than later is \$1,100 at 5% and \$1,900 at 10%.
3. *Decide whether the benefits outweigh the costs*: The benefit from buying now is the present value of the reduced gas payments. The cost is the present value of the additional cost of buying the car sooner rather than later. At 5%, the benefit is \$1,935 and the cost is \$1,100, so you should buy now. At 10%, the benefit, \$1,710, is less than the cost, \$1,900, so you should buy later. ■

Human Capital

Just as a firm considers whether or not to invest in physical capital, individuals decide whether to invest in their own *human capital*. Where a firm chooses the durability of a piece of equipment, some people invest in lengthening their expected life spans by exercising or purchasing medical care. Where a firm buys machinery and other capital to produce more output and increase its future profits, individuals invest in education to raise their productivity and their future earnings.

One of the most important human capital decisions you've had to make is whether to attend college. If you opted to go to college solely for the purpose of increasing your lifetime earnings, have you made a good investment?

Let's look back to the day you graduate from high school. You have to decide whether to invest in a college education or go directly into the job market. If you venture straight into the job market, we assume that you work from age 18 until you retire at age 70.

If your motivation for attending college is to increase your lifetime earnings, you should start college upon finishing high school so that you can earn a higher salary for as long as possible. Let's assume that you graduate from college in 4 years, during which time you do not work and you spend $10,000 a year on tuition and other schooling expenses such as books and fees. When you graduate from college, you work from age 22 to 70. Thus, the opportunity cost of a college education includes the tuition payments plus the four years of forgone earnings based on a high school degree. The expected benefit is the stream of higher earnings in the future.

Figure 16.2 shows how much the typical person earns with a high school diploma and with a college degree at each age.[12] At age 22, a typical person with a college degree earns $29,000 while that person earns $18,000 with only a high school diploma. The college grad's earnings peak at 40 years of age, at $39,000. A high school grad's earnings reach a maximum at 43 years, at $34,000.

If one stream of earnings is higher than the other at every age, we would pick the higher stream. Because these streams of earnings cross at age 22, we cannot use that method. One way to decide whether investing in a college education pays is to compare the present values at age 18 of the two earnings streams. The present values depend on the interest rate used, as Table 16.6 shows.

If potential college students can borrow money at an interest rate of 0%, money in the future is worth as much as money today, so the present value equals the sum of earnings over time. According to the table, the sum of a college graduate's earnings (including the initial negative earnings) is $1.53 million, which is about 15% more than the earnings of a high school grad. Thus, it pays to go to college. The figure also illustrates that attending college pays at a 0% discount rate because the sum of the (negative) cost and (positive) benefit areas—the difference in earnings between going to college and going to high school—is positive.

---

[12]This figure is based on our statistical analysis of weekly earnings in the March 1995 U.S. *Current Population Survey* and that controls for work experience, education, and demographic characteristics (but not for innate ability). We assume that people are paid for 48 weeks per year and that wages increase at the same rate as inflation, so real earnings are constant over time. No adjustment is made for the greater likelihood of unemployment of high school graduates.

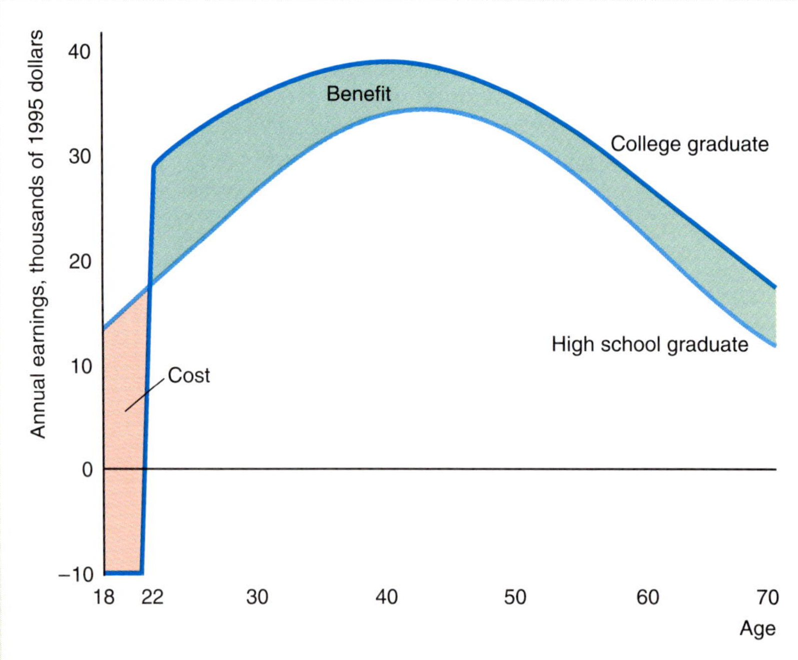

Figure 16.2 Annual Earnings of College and High School Graduates. On the basis of a statistical analysis, the earnings of high school and college graduates vary by age. The cost of getting a college education is 4 years of forgone earnings (at the rate high school graduates earn) and tuition, which is assumed to be $10,000 a year. The benefit is that the college graduate earns more each year thereafter than does a high school graduate.

Table 16.6 demonstrates that the present value of earnings for a college grad is greater than that of a high school grad for any interest rate below 6.9%. That is, the average internal rate of return to the college education is 6.9%. Thus, income-maximizing people with average characteristics go to college if the real interest rate at which they can borrow or invest is less than 6.9%.[13]

The decision whether to go to college is more complex for people for whom education has a consumption component. Somebody who loves school may go to college even if alternative investments pay more. Someone who hates going to school invests in a college education only if the financial rewards are much higher than those for alternative investments.

[13]Real interest rates at which college students can loan money to a bank and the rates at which they can borrow using government loan programs are almost always lower than 6.9%. However, the commercial rates at which they can borrow money from banks may be higher than 6.9%. Some poor people who cannot borrow to pay for college at all—effectively, they face extremely high interest rates—do not go to college, unlike wealthier people with comparable abilities.

Table 16.6 Present Value of Earnings

Discount Rate (%)	Present Value (thousands of 1995 dollars) High School	College
0	1,333	**1,531**
1	1,033	**1,170**
2	817	**911**
3	657	**720**
4	538	**578**
5	448	**471**
6	378	**388**
6.9	**329**	**329**
7	**324**	323
8	**281**	272
9	**246**	231
10	**218**	197

★ 16.3 EXHAUSTIBLE RESOURCES

The meek shall inherit the earth, but not the mineral rights. —J. Paul Getty

Discounting plays an important role in decisionmaking about how fast to consume oil, gold, copper, uranium, and other **exhaustible resources**: nonrenewable natural assets that cannot be increased, only depleted. An owner of an exhaustible resource decides when to extract and sell it so as to maximize the present value of the resource. Scarcity of the resource, mining costs, and market structure affect whether the price of such a resource rises or falls over time.

When to Sell an Exhaustible Resource

Suppose that you own a coal mine. In what year do you mine the coal and in what year do you sell it to maximize the present value of your coal? To illustrate how to answer these questions, we assume that you can sell the coal only this year or next in a competitive market, that the interest rate is i, and that the cost of mining each pound of coal, m, stays constant over time.

Given the last two of these assumptions, the present value of mining a pound of coal is m if you mine this year and $m/(1 + i)$ if you mine next year. As a result, if you're going to sell the coal next year, you're better off mining it next year because you postpone incurring the cost of mining. You mine the coal this year only if you plan to sell it this year.

Now that you have a rule that tells you when to mine the coal—at the last possible moment—your remaining problem is when to sell it. That decision depends on how the price of a pound of coal changes from one year to the next. Suppose that you know that the price of coal will increase from p_1 this year to p_2 next year.

To decide in which year to sell, you compare the present value of selling today to that of selling next year. The present value of your profit per pound of coal is $p_1 - m$ if you sell your coal this year and $(p_2 - m)/(1 + i)$ if you sell it next year. Thus, to maximize the present value from selling your coal you

- *Sell all the coal this year* if the present value of selling this year is greater than the present value of selling next year:

$$p_1 - m > (p_2 - m)/(1 + i).$$

- *Sell all the coal next year* if $p_1 - m < (p_2 - m)/(1 + i)$.
- *Sell the coal in either year* if $p_1 - m = (p_2 - m)/(1 + i)$.

The intuition behind these rules is that storing coal in the ground is like keeping money in the bank. You can sell a pound of coal today, netting $p_1 - m$, invest the money in the bank, and have $(p_1 - m)(1 + i)$ next year. Alternatively, you can keep the coal in the ground for a year and then sell it. If the amount you'll get next year, $(p_2 - m)$, is less than what you can earn from selling now and keeping the money in a bank account, you sell the coal now. On the other hand, if the price of coal is rising so rapidly that the coal will be worth more in the future than wealth left in a bank, you leave your wealth in the mine.

Price of a Scarce Exhaustible Resource

This two-period analysis generalizes to many time periods (Hotelling, 1931). We use a multiperiod analysis to show how the price of an exhaustible resource changes over time.

The resource is sold both this year, year t, and next year, $t + 1$, only if the present value of a pound sold now is the same as the present value of a pound sold next year: $p_t - m = (p_{t+1} - m)/(1 + i)$, where the price is p_t in year t and is p_{t+1} in the following year. Using algebra to rearrange this equation, we obtain an expression that tells us how price changes from one year to the next:

$$p_{t+1} = p_t + i(p_t - m). \tag{16.9}$$

If you're willing to sell the coal in both years, the price next year must exceed the price this year by $i(p_t - m)$, which is the interest payment you'd receive if you sold a pound of coal this year and put the profit in a bank that paid interest at rate i.

The gap between the price and the constant marginal cost of mining grows over time, as panel a of Figure 16.3 shows. To see why, we subtract p_t from both sides of Equation 16.9 to obtain an expression for the change in the price from one year to the next:

$$\Delta p \equiv p_{t+1} - p_t = i(p_t - m).$$

This equation shows that the gap between this year's price and next year's price widens as your cash flow this year, $p_t - m$, increases. Thus, the price rises over time and the gap between the price line and the flat marginal cost of mining line grows, as the figure illustrates.

Although we now understand how price changes over time, we need more information to determine the price in the first year and hence in each subsequent year.

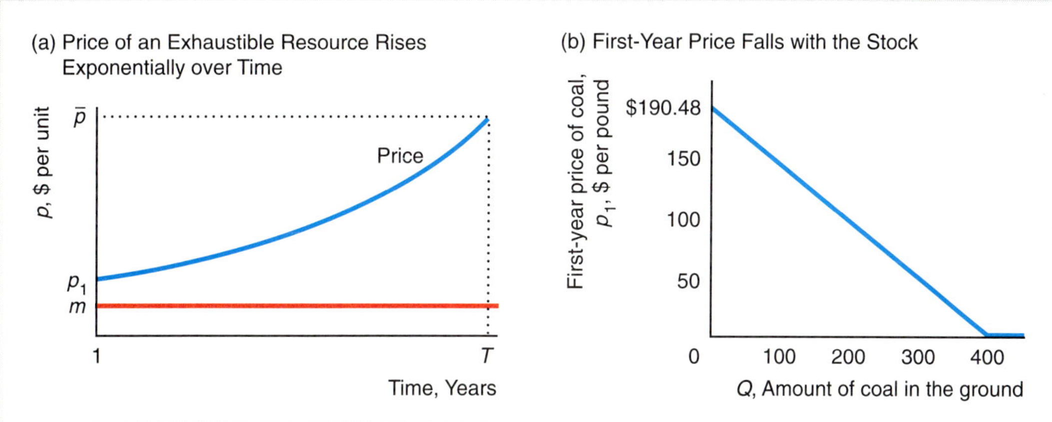

Figure 16.3 Price of an Exhaustible Resource. (a) The price of an exhaustible resource in year $t + 1$ is higher than the price in year t by the interest rate times the difference between the price in year t and the marginal cost of mining, $i(p_t - m)$. Thus, the gap between the price line and the marginal cost line, $(p_t - m)$, grows with the interest rate. (b) In a two-period model, the price of coal in the first year, p_1, falls as the amount of coal in the ground initially, Q, increases. This figure is based on an interest rate of 10%.

Suppose that coal mine owners know that the government will ban the use of coal in year T (or that a superior energy substitute will become available that year). They want to price the coal so that all of it is sold by the year T, because any resource that is unsold by then is worthless. The restriction that all the coal is used up by T and Equation 16.9 determine the price in the first year and the increase in the price thereafter.

Price in a Two-Period Example. To illustrate how the price is determined in each year, we assume that there are many identical competitive mines, that no more coal will be sold after the second year because of a government ban, and that the marginal cost of mining is zero in each period. Setting $m = 0$ in Equation 16.9, we learn that the price in the second year equals the price in the first year plus the interest rate times the first-year price:

$$p_2 = p_1 + (i \times p_1) = p_1(1 + i). \tag{16.10}$$

Thus, the price increases with the interest rate from the first year to the second year.

The mine owners face a resource constraint: They can't sell more coal than they have in their mines. The coal they sell in the first year, Q_1, plus the coal they sell in the second year, Q_2, equals the total amount of coal in the mines, Q. The mine owners want to sell all their coal within these two years because any coal they don't sell does them no good.

Suppose that the demand curve for coal is $Q_t = 200 - p_t$ in each year t. If the amount of coal in the ground is less than would be demanded at a zero price, the sum of the amount demanded in both years equals the total amount of coal in the ground:

$$Q_1 + Q_2 = [200 - p_1] + [200 - p_2] = Q.$$

Substituting the expression for p_2 from Equation 16.10 into this resource constraint to obtain $[200 - p_1] + [200 - p_1(1 + i)] = Q$ and rearranging terms, we find that

$$p_1 = (400 - Q)/(2 + i). \tag{16.11}$$

Thus, the first-year price depends on the amount of coal in the ground and the interest rate.

If the mines initially contain $Q = 169$ pounds of coal, p_1 is \$110 at a 10% interest rate and only \$105 at a 20% interest rate, as Table 16.7 shows. At the lower interest rate, the difference between the first- and second-year price is smaller (\$11 versus \$21), so relatively more of the original stock of coal is sold in the second year (47% versus 44%).

Rents. If coal is a scarce good, its competitive price is above the marginal cost of mining the coal ($m = 0$ in our example). How can we reconcile this result with our earlier finding that price equals marginal cost in a competitive market? The answer is that, when coal is scarce, it earns a *rent*: a payment to the owner of an input beyond the minimum necessary for the factor to be supplied (Chapter 8).

The owner of the coal need not be the same person who mines the coal. A miner could pay the owner for the right to take the coal out of the mine. After incurring the marginal cost of mining the coal, m, the miner earns $p_1 - m$. The owner of the mine, however, charges that amount in rent for the right to mine this scarce resource, rather than giving any of this profit to the miner. Even if the owner of the coal and the miner are the same person, the amount beyond the marginal mining cost is a rent to scarcity.

If the coal were not scarce, no rent would be paid and the price would equal the marginal cost of mining. Given the demand curve in the example, the most coal anyone would buy in a year is 200 pounds, which is the amount demanded at a

Table 16.7 Price and Quantity of Coal Depend on the Amount of Coal and the Interest Rate

	$Q = 169$		$Q = 400$
	$i = 10\%$	$i = 20\%$	any i
$p_1 = [400 - Q]/(2 + i)$	\$110	\$105	\$0
$p_2 = p_1(1 + i)$	\$121	\$126	\$0
$\Delta p \equiv p_2 - p_1 = i \times p_1$	11	21	0
$Q_1 = 200 - p_1$	90	95	200
$Q_2 = 200 - p_2$	79	74	200
Share sold in Year 2	47%	44%	50%

price of zero. If there is 400 pounds of coal in the ground initially—enough to provide 200 pounds in each year—the coal is not scarce, so the price of coal in both years is zero, as Table 16.7 illustrates.[14] As panel b of Figure 16.3 shows, the less coal is initially in the ground, Q, the higher is the initial price of coal.

Rising Prices. Thus, according to our theory, the price of an exhaustible resource rises if the resource (1) is scarce, (2) can be mined at a marginal cost that remains constant over time, and (3) is sold in a competitive market. The price of old-growth redwood trees rose as predicted by this theory.

APPLICATION

Redwood Trees

Many of the majestic old-growth redwood trees in America's western forests are 400 to several thousand years old.[15] If a mature redwood is cut, young redwoods will not grow to a comparable size within our lifetime. Thus, an old-growth redwood forest, like fossil fuels, is effectively a nonrenewable resource, even though new redwoods are being created (very slowly). In contrast, many other types of trees, such as those grown as Christmas trees, are quickly replenished and therefore are renewable resources like fish.

The exponential trend line in panel a of Figure 16.4 shows that the real price of redwoods rose from 1953 to 1983 at an average of 8% a year. By the end of this period, virtually no redwood trees were available for sale. The trees either had been harvested or were growing in protected forests. The last remaining privately owned stand was purchased by the U.S. government and the state of California from the Maxxam Corporation in 1996.

The unusually high prices observed in the late 1960s through the 1970s are in large part due to actions of the federal government, which used its power of eminent domain to buy a considerable fraction of all remaining old-growth redwoods for the Redwood National Park at the market price. The government bought 1.7 million million board feet (MBF) in 1968 and 1.4 million MBF in 1978. The latter purchase represented about two and a quarter years of cutting at previous rates. These two government purchases combined equaled 43% of private holdings in 1978 of about 7.3 million MBF. Thus, the government purchases were so large that they moved up the time of exhaustion of privately held redwoods by several years, causing the price to jump to the level it would have reached several years later. ■

[14]Equation 16.11 holds only where coal is scarce: $Q \leq 400$. According to this equation, $p_1 = 0$ when $Q = 400$. If the quantity of coal in the ground is even greater, $Q > 400$, coal is not scarce—people don't want all the coal even if the price is zero—so the price in the first year equals the marginal mining cost of zero. That is, the price is not negative, as Equation 16.11 would imply if it held for quantities greater than 400.

[15]The following discussion is based on Berck and Bentley (1997) and data supplied by Peter Berck.

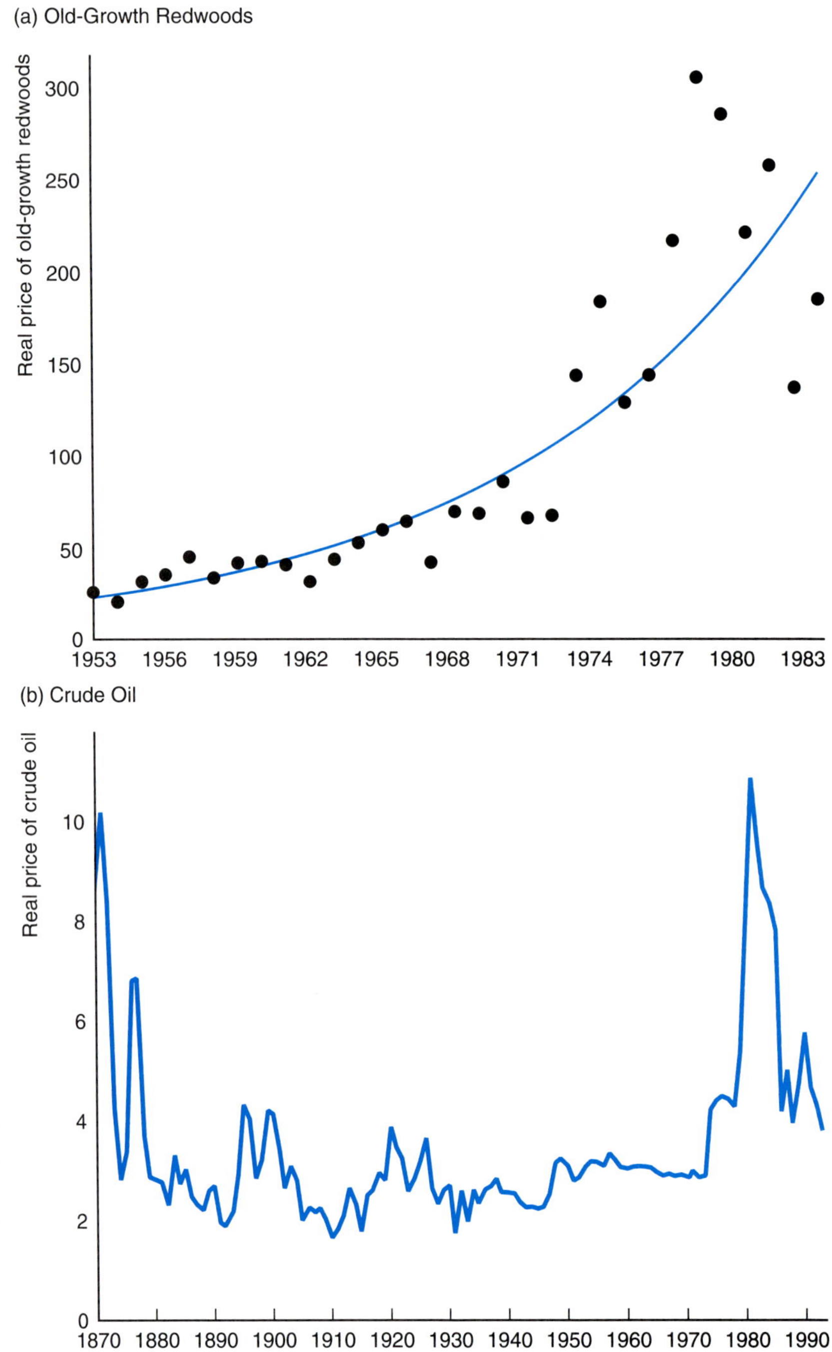
(a) Old-Growth Redwoods
Real price of old-growth redwoods
300
250
200
150
100
50
0
1953 1956 1959 1962 1965 1968 1971 1974 1977 1980 1983
(b) Crude Oil
Real price of crude oil
10
8
6
4
2
0
1870 1880 1890 1900 1910 1920 1930 1940 1950 1960 1970 1980 1990

Figure 16.4 Price of Resources over Time. (a) The real price of old-growth redwoods (price index is 100 between 1972 and 1973) rose in recent years until virtually all private holdings were sold. The dots are the actual prices, and the line is a trend line through these points that rises at 8% per year. (b) The real price index of crude oil fell at the end of the previous century, was relatively constant for many decades, increased rapidly in the late 1970s and early 1980s, then fell back to historical levels.

Why Price May Be Constant or Fall

If any one of the three conditions we've been assuming—*scarcity*, *constant marginal mining costs*, and *competition*—is not met, the price of an exhaustible resource may remain steady or fall.[16] Most exhaustible resources, such as aluminum, coal, lead, natural gas, silver, and zinc, have had decades-long periods of falling or constant real prices. Indeed, the 1993 index of the real prices of all major minerals and metals was less than half of the 1980 level.

Abundance. As we've already seen, the initial price is set at essentially the marginal cost of mining if the exhaustible resource is not scarce. The gap between the price and the marginal cost grows with the interest rate. If the good is so abundant that the initial gap is zero, the gap does not grow and the price stays constant at the marginal cost. Further, if the gap is initially very small, it has to grow for a long time before the increase becomes noticeable.

Because of abundance, the real prices for many exhaustible resources have remained relatively constant for decades. Moreover, the price falls when the discovery of a large deposit of the resource is announced.

The amount of a resource that can be profitably recovered with current methods is called a *reserve*. Known reserves of some resources are enormous, while reserves are more limited for others.[17] We have enough silicon (from sand) and magnesium to last virtually forever at the rates we use them; however, known reserves of lead, gold, silver, and zinc will last only about two decades at the 1991–1992 rates of extraction.

Known reserves of aluminum (bauxite) will last 216 years at current rates, and additional reserves are constantly being discovered. Because of this abundance, the real price of aluminum has remained virtually constant for the last 50 years.

Technical Progress. Over long periods of time, steady technical progress has reduced the marginal cost of mining many natural resources and thereby has

[16]The following discussion of why prices of exhaustible resources may not rise, and the accompanying examples, are based on Berck and Roberts (1996) and additional data supplied by these authors. Their paper also shows that pollution and other environmental controls can keep resource prices from rising.

[17]Data are from the U.S. Bureau of Mines as reported in Crowson, Phillip, *Minerals Handbook 1994–95*, New York: Stockton Press, 1994.

lowered the price of those exhaustible resources. A large enough drop in the marginal mining cost may more than offset the increase in the price due to the interest rate, so the price falls from one year to the next.[18]

The era spanning the end of the nineteenth century and the beginning of the twentieth century witnessed many advances in mining. As a result of technical progress in mining and discoveries of new supplies, the real prices of many exhaustible resources fell. For example, the real price of aluminum in 1945 was only 12% of the price 50 years earlier, in 1895. Eventually, as mines play out, prospectors have to dig ever deeper to find resources, causing marginal costs to increase and prices to rise faster than they would with constant marginal costs.

Changing Market Power. Changes in market structure can result in either a rise or a fall in the price of an exhaustible resource. The real price of oil remained virtually constant from 1880 through 1972. But when the Organization of Petroleum Exporting Countries (OPEC) started to act as a cartel in 1973, the price of oil climbed rapidly, as panel b of Figure 16.4 shows. At its peak in 1981, the real price of oil was nearly five times higher than its nearly constant level during the period 1880–1972. When Iran and Iraq went to war in 1980, the OPEC cartel began to fall apart and the real price of oil sank. Today, the real price is not substantially above its traditional level.

16.4 CAPITAL MARKETS, INTEREST RATES, AND INVESTMENTS

We've seen that an individual's decision about whether to make an investment depends on the market interest rate. As Figure 16.5 shows, the intersection of the demand and supply of loanable funds determines the equilibrium price or interest rate and the equilibrium quantity of funds in this capital market. In equilibrium, the amount borrowed (demanded) equals the amount loaned (supplied).

Funds are demanded by individuals buying homes or paying for a college education, governments borrowing money to build roads or wage wars, and firms investing in new plants or equipment. The demand curve, *D*, is downward sloping because more is borrowed as the interest rate falls.

The supply curve reflects loans made by individuals and firms. Many people, when their earnings are relatively high, save money in bank accounts and buy bonds (which they convert back to money for consumption when they retire or during lean times). Firms that have no alternative investments with higher returns may also loan

---

[18]When the marginal cost of mining is constant at m, Equation 16.9 shows that $p_{t+1} = p_t + i(p_t - m)$, so p_{t+1} must be above p_t. If we allow mining costs to vary from year to year, then

$$p_{t+1} = p_t + i(p_t - m_t) + (m_{t+1} - m_t).$$

Thus, if the drop in the mining costs, $m_{t+1} - m_t$, is greater than $i(p_t - m)$, the price in p_{t+1} is less than p_t.

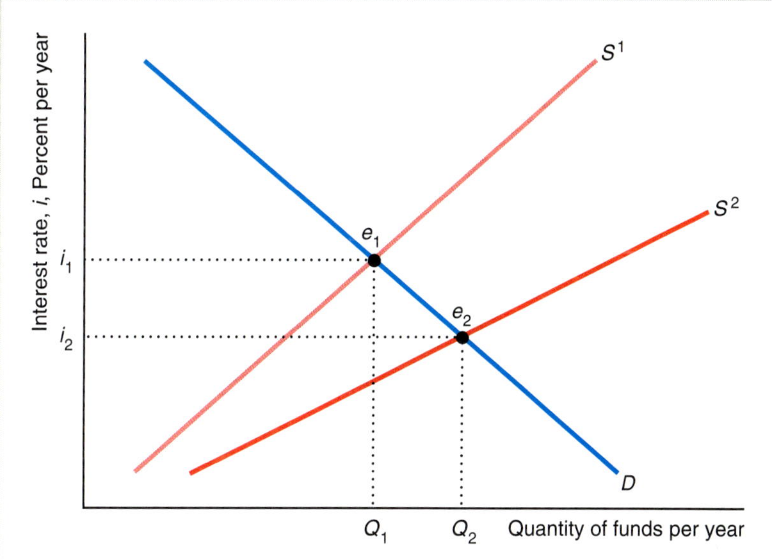

Figure 16.5 Capital Market Equilibrium. The initial equilibrium, e_1, is determined by the intersection of the demand curve for loans, D, and the initial supply curve, S^1. Changes in laws induce more people to save, shifting the supply curve to S^2. The interest rate, i_2, in the new equilibrium, e_2, is lower than the original interest rate, i_1. More funds are loaned than originally: $Q_2 > Q_1$.

money to banks or others. Higher interest rates induce greater savings by both groups, so the initial supply curve, S^1, is upward sloping.

The initial equilibrium is e_1, with an equilibrium rate of interest of i_1 and an equilibrium quantity of funds loaned and borrowed of Q_1. As usual, this equilibrium changes if any of the variables—such as tastes and government regulations—that affect demand and supply shifts.

Increased Savings Encourages More Investment

The supply curve of funds may shift to the right for many reasons. The government may remove a restriction on investment by foreigners. Or the government may make Individual Retirement Accounts (IRAs) tax exempt until retirement, a policy that induces additional savings at any given interest rate.

Such a change causes the supply curve to shift to the right to S_2 in Figure 16.5. The new equilibrium is e_2, with a lower interest rate, i_2. At the lower interest rate, firms and others undertake investment projects with lower rates of return than before the shift. They borrow more funds, so the new equilibrium is at $Q_2 > Q_1$.

Increased Government Demand Discourages Private Investment

Increased borrowing by the government raises the equilibrium interest rate, which discourages—*crowds out*—private investment. Figure 16.6 illustrates this effect. The total demand for funds, D^1 (panel c), is the horizontal sum of the demand from the private sector, D_p (panel a), and the initial demand from the public sector, D_g^1 (panel b). Given the market supply curve of funds S, the initial market equilibrium is e_1, with an equilibrium market interest rate of i_1 and quantity of Q_1.

When the government borrows money to fight a war in a distant land, its demand for funds shifts out to D_g^2. As a result, the market demand increases to D^2, which is the horizontal sum of D_p and D_g^2. In the new equilibrium, e_2, the market interest rate, i_2, is higher than the initial rate (panel c). The government borrows more than before in equilibrium: $Q_g^2 > Q_g^1$ (panel b). The higher market interest rate, however, causes private investment to fall from Q_p^1 to Q_p^2 (panel a).

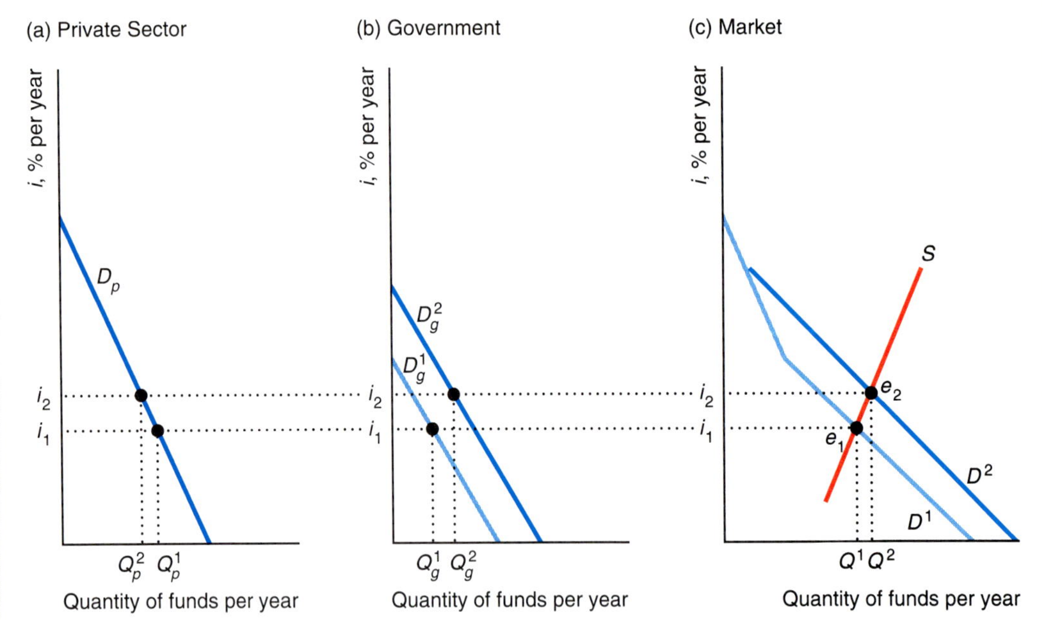

Figure 16.6 Government Borrowing Squeezes Out Private Investment. (a) Private demand for funds for investment, D_p, remains constant. (b) Government demand for loans increases from D_g^1 to D_g^2, as the government borrows to finance a war. (c) As a result, total demand shifts from D^1 to D^2, and the equilibrium shifts from e_1 to e_2. In the new equilibrium, government borrowing increases, $Q_g^2 > Q_g^1$, while private borrowing falls, $Q_p^2 < Q_p^1$.

APPLICATION

Taking from Future Generations

Blessed are the young, for they shall inherit the national debt. —Herbert Hoover

Governments are increasingly spending money today that they expect future generations (including yours) to repay. Public-sector debt in Western countries grew from an average of 16% in 1974 to 42% of gross domestic product in 1994.[19]

These figures understate the future debt because they do not include the implicit promises governments have made to future pensioners, such as Social Security. As populations age, the amount that current workers must pay to maintain such retirement systems will grow or the payments will diminish.

Many countries are transferring money to current older generations that will have to be paid for by later generations, as Table 16.8 shows. According to one set of estimates, in 1989, a retired 70-year-old American man could expect net government benefits of $46,100 over his lifetime. At the same time, a 25-year-old man could expect to make net payments of $220,100. It is difficult to believe that governments will be able to continue taking from the young to give to the old indefinitely as the tax burdens on younger generations will become extremely onerous and private investments will drop. ■

Table 16.8 Increasing Tax Burdens

	Present Value of Net Lifetime Tax Payments per Person*		
	Current Generation	Future Generation	Ratio of Future to Current
Germany	197	250	1.3
Italy	65	354	5.4
Sweden	156	204	1.3
United States	121	243	2.0

*The present value of net tax payments (in thousands of U.S. dollars) calculation assumes that productivity grows at 1.5% annually and that the discount rate is 5%.

Sources: "The Hole in Your Future," *The Economist*, 336(7931), September 9, 1995:78, which relies on data from the OECD and the work of Auerbach, Gokhale, and Kotlikoff.

[19]The numbers in this application pertain to Organization for Economic Cooperation and Development (OECD) countries: "The Hole in Your Future," *The Economist*, 336(7931), September 9, 1995:78.

Summary

1. **Comparing money today to money in the future:** Inflation aside, most people value money in the future less than money today. An interest rate reflects how much more people value a dollar today to a dollar in the future. To compare a payment made in the future to one made today, we can express the future payment in terms of current dollars by adjusting it using the interest rate. Similarly, a flow of payments over time is related to the present or future value of these payments by the interest rate.

2. **Choices over time:** An individual or firm may choose between two options with different cash flows over time by picking the one with the highest present value. Similarly, a firm invests in a project if its net present value is positive or its internal rate of return is greater than the interest rate.

3. **Exhaustible resources:** Nonrenewable resources such as coal, gold, and oil are used up over time and cannot be replenished. If these resources are scarce, the marginal cost of mining them is constant or increasing, and the market structure remains unchanged, their prices rise rapidly over time because of positive interest rates. However, if the resources are abundant, the marginal cost of mining falls over time, or the market becomes more competitive, nonrenewable resource prices may remain constant or fall over time.

4. **Capital markets, interest rates, and investments:** Supply and demand in capital markets determine the market rate of interest. A shock that shifts the supply curve to the left or the demand curve to the right raises the interest rate. As the interest rate increases, firms want to make fewer investments.

Problems

1. Some past and current civilizations, believing that interest should not be charged, passed usury laws forbidding it. What are the private and social benefits or costs of allowing interest to be charged?
2. What is the effect of a usury law on the market rate of interest if some potential lenders, hoping that the authorities do not catch them, are still willing to loan money?
3. How does an individual with a zero discount rate compare current and future consumption? How does your answer change if the discount rate is infinite?
4. If the interest rate is near zero, should an individual go to college, given the information in Figure 16.2? State a simple rule for determining whether this individual should go to college in terms of the areas labeled "benefit" and "cost" in the figure.
5. Discussing the $350 price of tickets at her live concert, Barbra Streisand said, "If you amortize the money over 28 years, it's $12.50 a year. So is it worth $12.50 a year to see me sing? To hear me sing live?"[20] Under what condition is it useful for an individual to apply Ms. Streisand's rule to decide whether to go to the concert? What do we know about the discount rate of a person who made such a purchase?

Math Problems

6. If you buy a car for $100 down and $100 a year for two more years, what is the present value of these payments at a 5% rate of interest?
7. How much money do you have to put into a bank account that pays 10% interest compounded annually to receive annual payments of $200?

[20]"In Other Words. . ." *San Francisco Chronicle*, January 1, 1995: Sunday Section, p. 3. She uses the term *amortize* in a nonstandard way. Apparently, she means to divide the $350 ticket price by 28 years to get $12.50 as the "payment" per year.

8. What is the present value of \$100 paid a year from now and another \$100 paid two years from now if the interest rate is i?

9. How much money do you have to put into a bank account that pays 10% interest compounded annually to receive perpetual annual payments of \$200 in today's dollars if the rate of inflation is 5%?

10. At a 10% interest rate, do you prefer to buy a phone for \$100 or to rent the same phone for \$10 a year? Does your answer depend on how long you think the phone will last?

11. What is the present value of a stream of payments of f per year for t years that starts T years from now if the interest rate is i?

12. In 1996, Pacific Gas and Electric sent its customers a comparison showing that a person could save \$80 per year in gas, water, and detergent expenses by replacing a traditional clothes washer with a new tumble-action washer. Suppose that the interest rate is 5%. You expect your current washer to die in 5 years. If the cost of a new tumble-action washer is \$800, should you replace your washer now or in five years?

13. You plan to buy a used refrigerator this year for \$200 and to sell it when you graduate in two years. Assuming that you can get \$100 for the refrigerator at that time, there is no inflation, and the interest rate is 5%, what is the true cost (your current outlay minus the resale value in current terms) of the refrigerator to you?

14. You want to buy a room air conditioner. The price of one machine is \$200. It costs \$20 a year to operate. The price of the other air conditioner is \$300, but it costs only \$10 a year to operate. Assuming that both machines last 10 years, which is a better deal? (Do you need to do extensive calculations to answer this question?)

15. Which is worth more to you: (a) a \$10,000 payment today or (b) a \$1,000 per year higher salary for as long as you work? At what interest rate would (a) be worth more to you than (b)? Does your answer depend on how many years you expect to work?

16. You rent an apartment for two years. You owe a payment of $\tilde{f}$ today and another equal nominal payment next year. If the inflation rate is γ and the real interest rate is i, what is the present value of these rental payments?

17. A firm's profit is π = revenue – labor costs – capital costs. Its capital cost can be stated as its rate of return on capital, rr, times the value of its capital, $p_K K$, where p_K is the price of a unit of capital and K is the number of units of capital. What is the firm's implicit rate of return on its capital?

18. A firm is considering an investment where its cash flow is π_1 = \$1 (million), $\pi_2 = -\$12$, $\pi_3 = 20$, and $\pi_t = 0$ for all other t. The interest rate is 7%. Use the net present value rule to determine whether the firm should make the investment. Can the firm use the internal rate of return rule to make this decision?

19. You have a barrel of oil that you can sell today for p dollars. Assuming no inflation and no storage cost, how high would the price have to be next year for you to sell the oil next year rather than now?

20. If all the coal in the ground, Q, is to be consumed in two years and the demand for coal is $Q_t = A(p_t)^{-\varepsilon}$ in each year t where ε is a constant demand elasticity, what is the price of coal each year?

CHAPTER 17

Uncertainty

Only slightly more than a quarter of 18- to 34-year-olds think Social Security will still exist when they retire, and only 9% believe that Social Security will have enough money to pay their retirement benefits, compared to 46% who think there are UFOs.[1]

Life's a series of gambles. Will you receive Social Security when you retire? Will you win the lottery tomorrow? Will your stock increase in value? Will you avoid disease, earthquakes, and fire? In this chapter, we extend the model of decisionmaking by individuals and firms to include uncertainty. We look at how uncertainty affects consumption decisions (Chapters 4 and 5)—such as how much insurance to buy—as well as investment decisions (Chapter 16).

When making decisions about investments and other matters, you consider the possible *outcomes* under various circumstances, or *states of nature*. When deciding about whether to carry a new type of doll, a toy store owner considers how many dolls will be sold if the doll is popular and how many if it is unpopular—two possible outcomes—and how likely these two states of nature are.

Although we cannot know with certainty what the future outcome will be, we may know that some outcomes are more likely than others. When uncertainty can be quantified, it is sometimes called **risk**: the likelihood of each possible outcome is known or can be estimated, and no single possible outcome is certain to occur. All the examples in this chapter concern quantifiable or risky situations.[2]

Consumers and firms modify their decisions about consumption and investment as the degree of risk varies. Indeed, most people are willing to spend money to reduce risk by buying insurance or taking preventative measures. Moreover, most people will choose a riskier investment over a less risky one only if they expect a higher return from the riskier investment.

In this chapter, we examine four main topics:

1. **Degree of risk:** Probabilities are used to measure the degree of risk and the likely profit from a risky undertaking.
2. **Decisionmaking under uncertainty:** Whether people choose a risky option over a nonrisky one depends on their attitudes toward risk and on the expected payoffs of each option.
3. **Avoiding risk:** People try to reduce their overall risk by not making risky choices, taking actions to lower the likelihood of a disaster, combining offsetting risks, insuring, and in other ways.

---

[1]"Young Adults Doubt Social Security Will Be There for Them," *San Francisco Chronicle*, September 27, 1994:A7.

[2]Jargon alert: Many people do not distinguish between the terms *risk* and *uncertainty*. Henceforth, we use these terms interchangeably.

4. **Investing under uncertainty:** Whether people make an investment depends on the riskiness of the payoff, the expected return, attitudes toward risk, the interest rate, and whether it is profitable to alter the likelihood of a good outcome.

17.1 DEGREE OF RISK

You are thinking about buying lunch at a new restaurant. There are two possible outcomes: The lunch will or will not taste good to you. Knowing the likelihood of each of these outcomes would help you to decide whether to try this new restaurant.

Before we can analyze decisionmaking under uncertainty, we need a way to describe and quantify risk. A particular event—such as eating lunch at a new restaurant—has a number of possible outcomes—say, an enjoyable meal or an unenjoyable meal. Because you don't know whether you will enjoy the meal, eating at this new restaurant is risky. To describe how risky this activity is, we need to quantify the likelihood that each possible outcome occurs.

We can use our estimate of how risky each outcome is to estimate the most likely outcome. We then present measures of risk that reflect how much actual outcomes deviate from the most likely outcome.

Probability

A *probability* is a number between 0 and 1 that indicates the likelihood that a particular outcome occurs. You might, for example, have a 25% probability—a 1 in 4 chance—of enjoying the meal at the restaurant. How do we estimate a probability?

Frequency. If we have a history of the outcomes for an event, we can use the frequency with which a particular outcome occurred as our estimate of the probability. Let n be the number of times one particular outcome occurred during the N total number of times an event occurred. We set our estimate of the probability, θ (theta), equal to the frequency:

$$\theta = n/N.$$

A house either burns or does not burn. If $n = 13$ similar houses burned in your neighborhood of $N = 1{,}000$ homes last year, you might estimate the probability that your house will burn this year as $\theta = 13/1{,}000 = 1.3\%$.

Subjective Probability. Often, we don't have a history that allows us to calculate the frequency. We use whatever information we have to form a *subjective probability*, which is our best estimate of the likelihood that an outcome will occur. We may use all available information—even information that is not based on a conscious, scientific estimation procedure.

How do you derive a subjective probability about the likelihood that you'll like the new restaurant? You might know that your friend liked the restaurant but your economics professor did not. If you're not sure whether either of these people likes the same food you do, you may estimate the probability that you'll like the restaurant at 50%. However, if you know that your friend usually likes the same type of food you do but you're less sure about whether your professor likes the same type of food, you might put more weight on your friend's report and estimate the probability that you'll like the restaurant as a number greater than half, perhaps 85%.[3]

Probability Distribution. A *probability distribution* relates the probability of occurrence to each possible outcome. Panel a of Figure 17.1 shows a probability distribution over five possible outcomes: zero to four days of rain per month in a

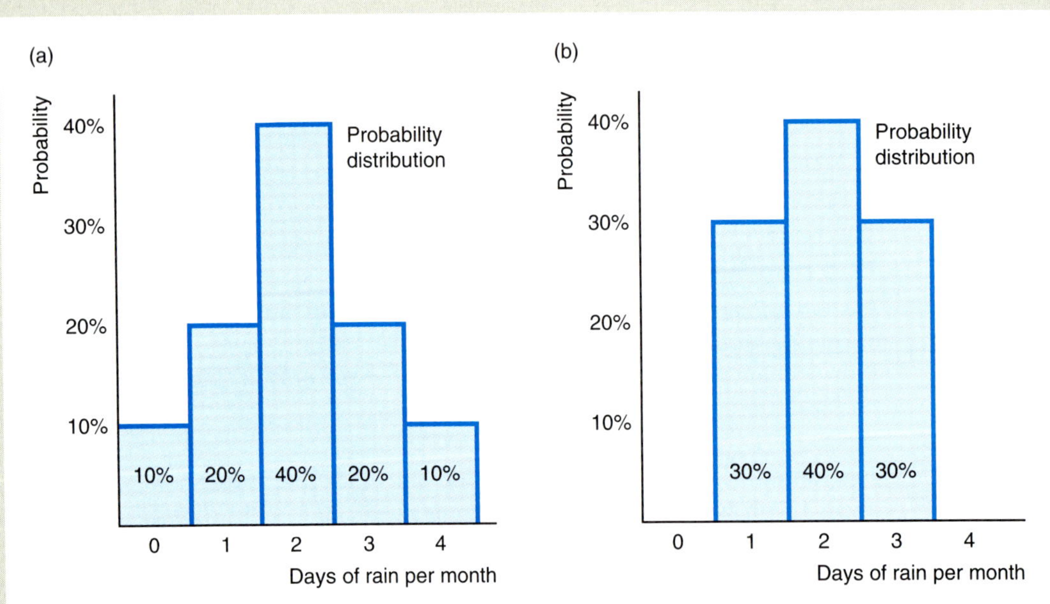

Figure 17.1 Probability Distribution. The probability distribution shows the probability each of the mutually exclusive outcomes occur. In panel a, there are five mutually exclusive outcomes that may occur. The probability that it rains exactly 2 days per month is 40%. The probability that it rains 5 or more days per month is 0%. The probability distributions in panels a and b have the same mean. The variance is smaller in panel b, where the probability distribution is more concentrated around the mean than is the distribution in panel a.

[3]When events are repeated, we can compare our subjective probabilities to observed frequencies. Your subjective probability (guess) that it rains 50% of the days in January can be compared to the frequency of rain in January during the recorded history for your city. If an event is not going to be

relatively dry city. The probability that it rains no days during the month is 10%, as is the probability of exactly four days of rain. The chance of two rainy days is 40%, and the chance of one or three rainy days is 20% each. The probability that it rains five or more days a month is 0%.

These weather outcomes are *mutually exclusive*—only one of these outcomes can occur at a given time—and *exhaustive*—no other outcomes than those listed are possible. Where outcomes are mutually exclusive and exhaustive, exactly one of these outcomes will occur with certainty, and the probabilities must add up to 100%. For simplicity, we concentrate on situations in which there are only two possible outcomes.

Expected Value

Gregg, a promoter, schedules an outdoor concert for tomorrow.[4] How much money he'll make depends on the weather. If it doesn't rain, his profit or value from the concert is V = $15. (If it will make you happier—and it will certainly make Gregg happier—you can think of the profits in this example as $15,000 instead of $15.) If it rains, he'll have to cancel the concert and he'll lose V = –$5, which he must pay the band. Although Gregg does not know what the weather will be with certainty, he knows that the weather department forecasts a 50% chance of rain.

The amount Gregg expects to earn is called his *expected value* (here, his *expected profit*). The expected value, *EV*, is the value of each possible outcome times the probability of that outcome:[5]

$$\begin{aligned} \text{EV} &= [\Pr(\text{No rain}) \times \text{Value}(\text{No rain})] + [\Pr(\text{Rain}) \times \text{Value}(\text{Rain})] \\ &= [\tfrac{1}{2} \times \$15] + [\tfrac{1}{2} \times (-\$5)] = \$5, \end{aligned}$$

where Pr is the probability of an outcome, so Pr(Rain) is the "probability that rain occurs."

The expected value is the amount Gregg would earn on average if the event were repeated many times. If he puts on such concerts many times over the years and the weather follows historical patterns, he will earn $15 at half of the concerts without rain, and he will get soaked for –$5 at the other half of the concerts, at which it rains. Thus, he'll earn an average of $5 per concert over a long period of time.

---

repeated, however, it may not be possible to check whether your subjective probability is reasonable or accurate by comparing it to a frequency. You might believe that there's a 75% chance of dry weather tomorrow. If it does rain tomorrow, that doesn't mean you were wrong. Only if you believed that the probability of rain was 0% would observing rain tomorrow prove you wrong.

[4]My brother Gregg, a successful concert promoter, wants me to inform you that the hero of the following story is some other Gregg who is a concert promoter.

[5]If there are n possible outcomes, the value of Outcome i is V_i, and the probability of that outcome is Pr_i, then the expected value is

$$EV = Pr_1 V_1 + Pr_2 V_2 + \ldots + Pr_n V_n.$$

SOLVED PROBLEM 17.1

How much more would Gregg expect to earn if he knew that he would obtain perfect information about the probability of rain far enough before the concert that he could book the band only if needed? How much does he gain from having this perfect information?

Answer

1. *Determine how much Gregg would earn if he had perfect information in each state of nature*: If Gregg knew with certainty that it would rain at the time of the concert, he would not book the band, so he would make no loss or profit. If Gregg knew that it would not rain, he would hold the concert and make \$15.

2. *Determine how much Gregg would expect to earn before he learns with certainty what the weather will be*: Gregg knows that he'll make \$15 with a 50% probability and \$0 with a 50% probability, so his expected value, given that he'll receive perfect information in time to act on it, is

$$[\tfrac{1}{2} \times \$15] + [\tfrac{1}{2} \times \$0] = \$7.50.$$

3. *His gain from perfect information is the difference between his expected earnings with perfect information and with imperfect information*: Gregg expects to earn \$2.50 = \$7.50 – \$5 more with perfect information than with imperfect information. This answer can be reached more directly. Perfect weather information is valuable to him because he can avoid hiring the band unnecessarily when it rains.[6] The *value of this information* is his expected savings from not hiring the band when it rains: $\frac{1}{2} \times \$5 = \$2.50$. ■

Variance and Standard Deviation

If Gregg would earn the same amount—the expected value—whether it rained or not, he would face no risk. We can measure the risk he faces in many different ways. One approach is to look at the degree by which actual outcomes vary from the expected value, *EV*.

The *difference* between his actual earnings and his expected earnings if it does not rain is \$10 = \$15 – \$5. The difference if it does rain is –\$10 = –\$5 – \$5. Because there are two differences—one difference for each state of nature—it is convenient to combine them in a single measure of risk.

One such measure of risk is the *variance*, which measures the spread of the probability distribution. For example, the variance in panel a of Figure 17.1, where the probability distribution ranges from zero to four days of rain per month, is greater

[6] Having information has no value if it doesn't alter behavior.

than the variance in panel b, where the probability distribution ranges from one to three days of rain per month.

Formally, the variance is the probability-weighted average of the squares of the differences between the observed outcome and the expected value.[7] The variance of the value Gregg obtains from the outdoor concert is

$$\begin{aligned}\text{Variance} &= [\Pr(\text{No rain}) \times (\text{Value}(\text{No rain}) - EV)^2] + [\Pr(\text{Rain}) \times (\text{Value}(\text{Rain}) - EV)^2] \\ &= [\tfrac{1}{2} \times (\$15 - \$5)^2] + [\tfrac{1}{2} \times (-\$5 - \$5)^2] \\ &= [\tfrac{1}{2} \times \$10^2] + [\tfrac{1}{2} \times (-\$10)^2] = \$100.\end{aligned}$$

Panel a of Table 17.1 shows how to calculate the variance of the profit from this concert step by step. The first column lists the two outcomes: rain and no rain. The next column gives the probability. The third column shows the value or profit of each outcome. The next column calculates the difference between the values in the third column and the expected value, $EV = \$5$. The following column squares these differences, and the last column multiplies these squared differences by the probabilities in the second column. The sum of these probability weighted differences, \$100, is the variance.

Table 17.1 Variance and Standard Deviation: Measures of Risk

a) Outdoor Concert

Outcome	Probability	Value	Difference = Value – \$5	Difference^2	Difference^2 × Probability
No rain	$\frac{1}{2}$	\$15	\$10	\$100	\$50
Rain	$\frac{1}{2}$	–\$5	–\$10	\$100	\$50
				Variance	\$100
				Standard Deviation	\$10

b) Indoor Concert

Outcome	Probability	Value	Difference = Value – \$5	Difference^2	Difference^2 × Probability
No rain	$\frac{1}{2}$	\$10	\$5	\$25	\$12.50
Rain	$\frac{1}{2}$	\$0	–\$5	\$25	\$12.50
				Variance	\$25
				Standard Deviation	\$5

[7]If there are n possible outcomes with an expected value of EV, the value of Outcome i is V_i, and the probability of that outcome is Pr_i, then the variance is

$$Pr_1(V_1 - EV)^2 + Pr_2(V_2 - EV)^2 + \ldots + Pr_n(V_n - EV)^2.$$

The variance puts more weight on large deviations from the expected value than on smaller ones.

Instead of describing risk using the variance, economists and businesspeople often report the *standard deviation*, which is the square root of the variance. The usual symbol for the standard deviation is σ (sigma), so the symbol for variance is σ^2. For the outdoor concert, the variance is $\sigma^2 = \$100$ and the standard deviation is $\sigma = \$10$.

Holding the expected value constant, the smaller the standard deviation (or variance), the smaller the risk. Panel b illustrates that Gregg's expected value of profit is the same if he stages the concert indoors, but the standard deviation of his profit is less. The indoor theater does not hold as many people as the outdoor venue, so the most Gregg can earn if it does not rain is \$10. Rain discourages attendance even at the indoor theater, so he just breaks even, earning \$0. The expected value of the indoor concert,

$$EV = [\tfrac{1}{2} \times \$10] + [\tfrac{1}{2} \times \$0] = \$5,$$

is the same as that for the outdoor concert. Staging the concert indoors involves less risk, however. As panel b shows, the variance of the profit at the indoor concert is \$25 and the corresponding standard deviation is \$5.

17.2 DECISIONMAKING UNDER UNCERTAINTY

Will Gregg stage an indoor or outdoor concert? To answer such a question, we need to know his attitude toward bearing risk.

Although the indoor and outdoor concerts have the same expected value, the outdoor concert involves more risk. Gregg will earn more with good weather or lose more with bad weather by holding his concert outdoors instead of indoors. He'll book an outdoor concert only if he likes to gamble.

Even if he dislikes risk, Gregg may prefer a riskier option if it has a higher expected value. Suppose that he strikes a new agreement with the band by which he pays them only if the weather is good and the concert is held. Now the band, rather than Gregg, bears the risk of bad weather. Gregg's expected value is \$7.50, the variance is \$56.25, and the standard deviation is \$7.50.[8] By holding the concert outdoors instead of inside, Gregg's expected value is higher (\$7.50 instead of \$5) and the standard deviation is higher (\$7.50 instead of \$5). He earns the same, \$0, from both types of concerts in bad weather. In good weather, he earns more from the outdoor concert. Because he always does as well with an outdoor concert as with an indoor show, Gregg clearly prefers the riskier outdoor concert with its higher expected value.

If he dislikes risk, Gregg won't necessarily stage the concert with the highest expected value. Suppose that his choice is between the indoor concert and an outdoor concert from which he earns \$100,015.50 if it doesn't rain and loses \$100,005 if it rains. His expected value is greater with the outside concert, \$5.25 instead of

---

[8]The expected value is the same as in Solved Problem 17.1: $(\tfrac{1}{2} \times \$15) + (\tfrac{1}{2} \times \$0) = \$7.50$. The variance is $\tfrac{1}{2}(\$15 - \$7.50)^2 + \tfrac{1}{2}(\$0 - \$7.50)^2 = \$56.25$, so the standard deviation is \$7.50.

\$5, but he faces much more risk. The standard deviation of the outdoor concert is \$100,010.25 compared to \$5. Gregg might reasonably opt for the indoor concert with the lower expected value if he dislikes risk. After all, he may be loath to risk losing \$100,005 with a 50% probability.

Expected Utility

We can formalize this type of reasoning by extending our model of utility maximization (Chapter 4) to show how people's taste for risk affects their choice among options (investments, career choices, consumption bundles) that differ in both value and risk. If people made choices to maximize expected value, they would always choose the option with the highest expected value regardless of the risks involved. However, most people care about risk as well as expected value. Indeed, most people are *risk averse*—they dislike risk—and will choose a bundle with higher risk only if its expected value is substantially higher than that of a less-risky bundle.

In Chapter 4, we noted that we can describe an individual's preferences over various bundles of goods by using a utility function. John von Neumann and Oskar Morgenstern (1944) suggested an extension of this standard utility-maximizing model that includes risk.[9] In their reformulation, a rational person maximizes *expected utility*. Expected utility is the probability-weighted average of the utility from each possible outcome. For example, Gregg's expected utility, EU, from the indoor concert is

$$\begin{aligned} \text{EU} &= [\Pr(\text{No rain}) \times U(\text{Value}(\text{No rain}))] + [\Pr(\text{Rain}) \times U(\text{Value}(\text{Rain}))] \\ &= [\tfrac{1}{2} \times U(\$15)] + [\tfrac{1}{2} \times U(-\$5)], \end{aligned}$$

where his utility function, U, depends upon his earnings. For example, $U(\$15)$ is the amount of utility Gregg gets from \$15.[10]

In short, the expected utility calculation is similar to the expected value calculation. Both are weighted averages in which the weights are the probability (Pr) that the state of nature will occur. The difference is that the expected value is the probability-weighted average of the monetary value, whereas the expected utility is the probability-weighted average of the utility from the monetary value.

If we know how an individual's utility increases with wealth, we can determine how that person reacts to risky propositions. We can classify people in terms of their willingness to make a **fair bet**: a wager with an expected value of zero. An example of a fair bet is one in which you pay a dollar if a flipped coin comes up heads and receive a dollar if it comes up tails. Because you expect to win half the time and lose

---

[9]This approach to handling choice under uncertainty is the most commonly used method. Schoemaker (1982) discusses the logic underlying this approach, the evidence for it, and several variants. Machina (1989) discusses a number of alternative methods. Here, we treat utility as a cardinal measure rather than an ordinal measure as we did in Chapters 4 and 5.

[10]People have preferences over the goods they consume. For simplicity, however, we'll say that a person receives utility from earnings or wealth, which can be spent on consumption goods.

half the time, the expected value of this bet is zero:

$$[\tfrac{1}{2} \times (-\$1)] + [\tfrac{1}{2} \times \$1] = 0.$$

In contrast, a bet in which you pay \$1 if you lose the coin flip and receive \$2 if you win is an unfair bet that favors you, with an expected value of

$$[\tfrac{1}{2} \times (-\$1)] + [\tfrac{1}{2} \times \$2] = 50¢.$$

Someone who does not want to make a fair bet is **risk averse**. A person who is indifferent about making a fair bet is **risk neutral**. A person who is **risk preferring** will make a fair bet.

Risk Averse

He is no wise man who will quit a certainty for an uncertainty.

—Samuel Johnson, 1760

We can use our expected utility model to examine how Irma, who is risk averse, makes a choice under uncertainty. Figure 17.2 shows Irma's utility function. The utility function is concave to the wealth axis, indicating that Irma's utility rises with wealth but at a diminishing rate.[11] She has *diminishing marginal utility of wealth*: The extra pleasure from each extra dollar of wealth is smaller than the pleasure from the previous dollar. An individual whose utility function is concave to the wealth axis is risk averse, as we now illustrate.

A person whose utility function is concave picks the less risky choice if both choices have the same expected value. Suppose that Irma has an initial wealth of \$40 and has two options. One option is for her to do nothing and keep the \$40. If she does so, her utility is $U(\$40) = 120$ (point d in Figure 17.2) with certainty.

Her other option is to buy a vase. Her wealth is \$70 if the vase is a Ming and \$10 if it is an imitation. Irma's subjective probability is 50% that it is a genuine Ming vase. Her expected value or wealth remains

$$\$40 = [\tfrac{1}{2} \times \$10] + [\tfrac{1}{2} \times \$70].$$

Thus, buying the vase is a fair bet because she has the same expected wealth whether she purchases the vase or not.

[11]Irma's utility from W wealth is $U(W)$. She has positive marginal utility from extra wealth, $dU(W)/dW > 0$; however, her utility increases with wealth at a diminishing rate, $d^2U(W)/dW^2 < 0$.

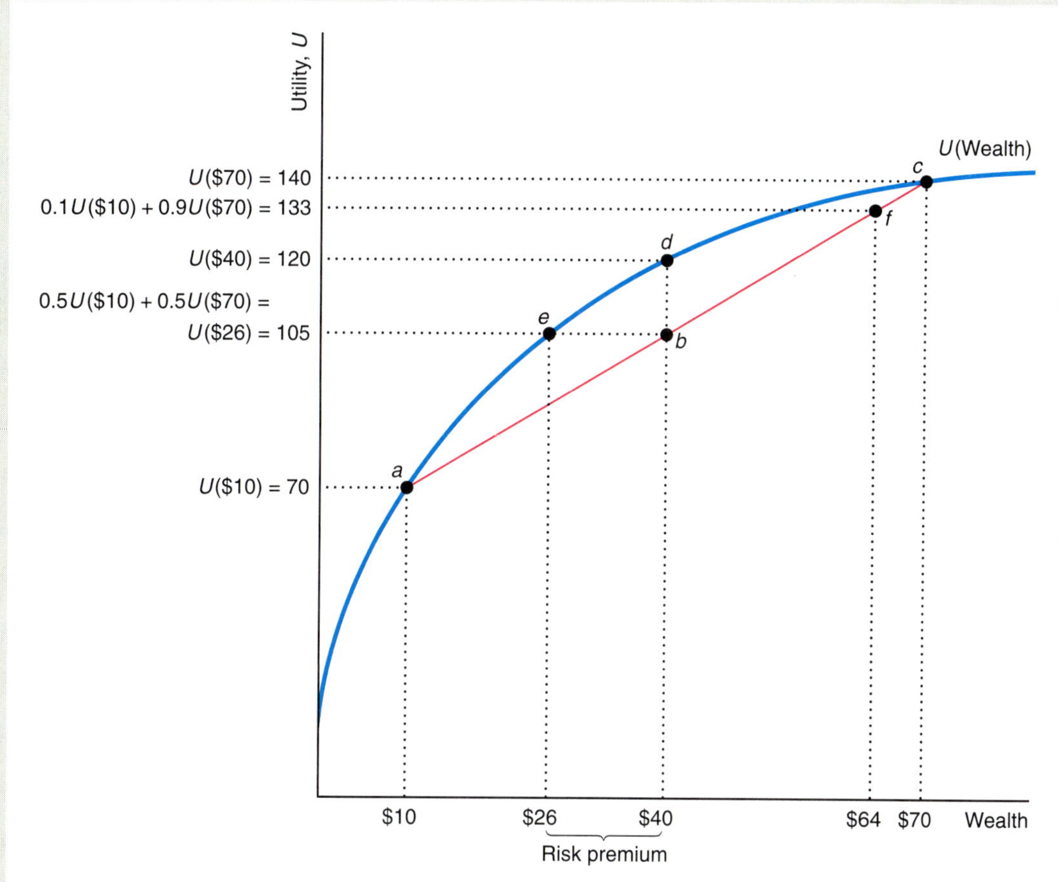

Figure 17.2 Risk Averse. Initially, Irma's wealth is \$40, so her utility is $U(\$40) = 120$, point *d*. If she buys the vase and it's a Ming, she is at point *c*, where her utility is $U(\$70) = 140$. If the purchased vase is an imitation, she is at point *a*, where $U(\$10) = 70$. If her subjective probability that the vase is a Ming is 50%, her expected utility from buying the vase, point *b*, is $\frac{1}{2}U(\$10) + \frac{1}{2}U(\$70) = 105$, which is less than her utility with a certain wealth of \$40, $U(\$40) = 120$. Thus, she does not buy the vase. If Irma's subjective probability that the vase is a Ming is 90%, her expected utility from buying the vase is $0.1U(\$10) + 0.9U(\$70) = 133$, point *f*, which is more than her utility with a certain wealth of \$40, $U(\$40) = 120$, *d*, so she buys the vase.

Irma prefers the certain wealth from not buying the vase because that option carries less risk. Her utility if the vase is a Ming is $U(\$70) = 140$, point *c*. If it's an imitation, her utility is $U(\$10) = 70$, point *a*. Thus, her expected utility is

$$[\tfrac{1}{2} \times U(\$10)] + [\tfrac{1}{2} \times U(\$70)] = [\tfrac{1}{2} \times 70] + [\tfrac{1}{2} \times 140] = 105.$$

The graph shows that her expected utility is point *b*, the midpoint of a line (called a *chord*) between *a* and *c*.[12]

Because Irma's utility function is concave, her utility from certain wealth, 120 at point *d*, is greater than her expected utility from the risky activity, 105 at point *b*. As a result, she does not buy the vase. Buying this vase, which is a fair bet, increases the risk she faces without changing her expected wealth.

The **risk premium** is the amount that a risk-averse person would pay to avoid taking a risk. The figure shows how much Irma would be willing to pay to avoid this risk. Her certain utility from having a wealth of \$26, *U*(\$26) = 105, is the same as her expected utility if she buys the vase. Thus, Irma would be indifferent between buying the vase and having \$26 with certainty. Irma would be willing to pay an amount up to \$14 = \$40 – \$26 to avoid bearing the risk from owning the vase.

A risk-averse person chooses a riskier option only if it has a sufficiently higher expected value. If Irma were much more confident that the vase were a Ming, her expected value would rise and she'd buy the Ming, as Solved Problem 17.2 shows.[13]

SOLVED PROBLEM 17.2

Suppose that Irma's subjective probability is 90% that the vase is a Ming. What is her expected wealth if she buys the vase? What is her expected utility? Does she buy the vase?

Answer

1. *Calculate Irma's expected wealth*: Her expected value or wealth is 10% times her wealth if the vase is not a Ming plus 90% times her wealth if the vase is a Ming:

$$[0.1 \times \$10] + [0.9 \times \$70] = \$64.$$

In Figure 17.2, \$64 is the distance along the wealth axis corresponding to point *f*.

[12]The line represents all the possible weighted averages of the utility at point *a* and the utility at *c*. When the probabilities of the two outcomes are equal, the expected value is the midpoint. If the probability that the vase is Ming is greater than $\frac{1}{2}$, the expected value is closer to point *c*, as Solved Problem 17.2 illustrates.

[13]My colleague Irma Adelman visited an antique store and was offered a vase for \$10. In addition to being an outstanding economist, she's an art expert. At first glance, she thought that the vase was a Ming. Turning it over, she found marks on the bottom that convinced her that it was a Ming (or a near-perfect counterfeit). Because her subjective probability that the vase was a genuine Ming was very high, she bought it, even though she is risk averse. This lovely Ming vase graced her home until her !#@\$! cat broke it.

2. *Calculate Irma's expected utility*: Her expected utility is the probability-weighted average of her utility under the two outcomes:

$$[0.1 \times U(\$10)] + [0.9 \times U(\$70)] = [0.1 \times 70] + [0.9 \times 140] = 133.$$

Her expected utility is the height on the utility axis of point *f*. Point *f* is nine-tenths of the distance along the line connecting point *a* to point *c*.

3. *Compare Irma's expected utility to her certain utility if she does not buy*: Irma's expected utility from buying the vase, 133 (point *f*), is greater than her certain utility, 120 (point *d*), if she does not. Thus, if Irma is this confident that the vase is a Ming, she buys it. Although the risk is greater from buying than from not buying, her expected wealth is enough higher ($64 instead of $40) that it's worth it to her to take the chance. ■

Risk Neutral

Someone who is risk neutral has a constant marginal utility of wealth: Each extra dollar of wealth raises utility by the same amount as the previous dollar. With constant marginal utility of wealth, the utility curve is a straight line in a utility and wealth graph.

Suppose that Irma is risk neutral and has the straight-line utility curve in panel a of Figure 17.3. She would be indifferent between buying the vase and not buying it if her subjective probability is 50% that it is a Ming. Her expected utility from buying the vase is the average of her utility at points *a* ($10) and *c* ($70):

$$[\tfrac{1}{2} \times U(\$10)] + [\tfrac{1}{2} \times U(\$70)] = [\tfrac{1}{2} \times 70] + [\tfrac{1}{2} \times 140] = 105.$$

Her expected utility exactly equals her utility with certain wealth of $40 (point *b*) because the line connecting points *a* and *c* lies on the utility function and point *b* is the midpoint of that line.

Here, Irma is indifferent between buying and not buying the vase, a fair bet, because she doesn't care how much risk she faces. Because the expected wealth from both options is $40, she is indifferent between them.

In general, *a risk-neutral person chooses the option with the highest expected value, because maximizing expected value maximizes utility*. A risk-neutral person chooses the riskier option if it has even a slightly higher expected value than the less risky option. Equivalently, the risk premium for a risk-neutral person is zero.

Risk Preferring

An individual with an increasing marginal utility of wealth is risk preferring: willing to take a fair bet. If Irma has the utility curve in panel b of Figure 17.3, she is risk preferring. Her expected utility from buying the vase, 105 at *b*, is higher then her certain utility if she does not buy the vase, 82 at *d*. Thus, she buys the vase.

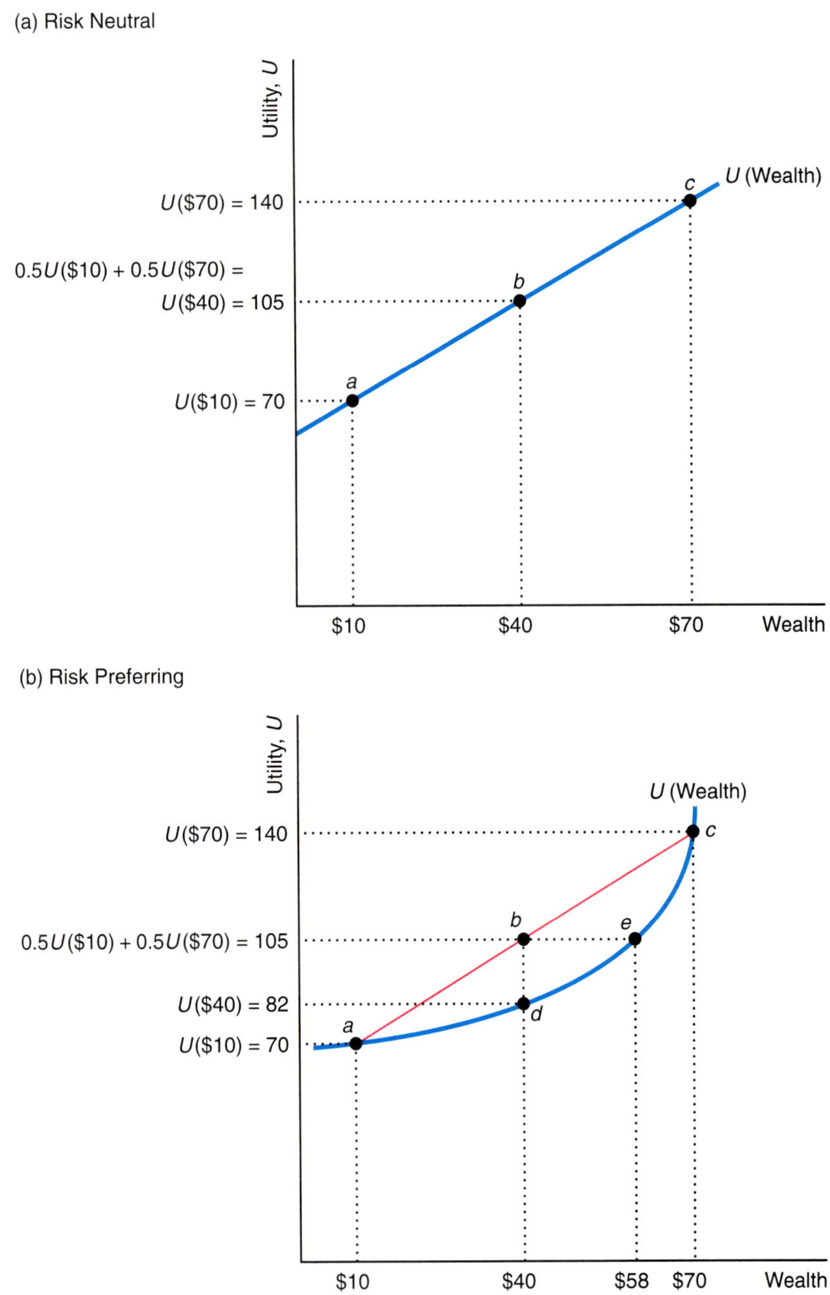
(a) Risk Neutral
Utility, U
U($70) = 140
0.5U($10) + 0.5U($70) =
U($40) = 105
U($10) = 70
a
b
c
U (Wealth)
$10
$40
$70
Wealth
(b) Risk Preferring
Utility, U
U (Wealth)
U($70) = 140
0.5U($10) + 0.5U($70) = 105
U($40) = 82
U($10) = 70
a
b
c
d
e
$10
$40
$58
$70
Wealth

Figure 17.3 Risk Neutrality and Risk Preferring. (a) If Irma's utility curve is a straight line, she is risk neutral and is indifferent as to whether or not to make a fair bet. Her expected utility from buying the vase, 105 at *b*, is the same as from a certain wealth of wealth of $40 at *d*. (b) If Irma's utility curve is convex to the horizontal axis, Irma has increasing marginal utility to wealth and is risk preferring. She buys the vase because her expected utility from buying the vase, 105 at *b*, is higher than her utility from a certain wealth of $40, 82 at *d*.

A risk-preferring person is willing to pay for the right to make a fair bet (a negative risk premium). As the figure shows, Irma's expected utility from buying the vase is the same as the utility from a certain wealth of $58. Given her initial wealth of $40, if you offer her the opportunity to buy the vase or offer to give her $18, she is indifferent. With any payment smaller than $18, she prefers to buy the vase.

APPLICATION

Gambling

If you ask them, most people say that they don't like bearing risk. Consistent with such statements, they reduce the risk they face by buying insurance. Nonetheless, many of these people engage in games of chance from time to time. Not only do they gamble, but they make unfair bets, in which the expected value of the gamble is negative. That is, if they play the game repeatedly, they are likely to lose money in the long run.

Lotteries

People have been betting (and losing) on government-run lotteries throughout history.[14] Queen Elizabeth I used lottery profits to fund the British navy. Lotteries helped the American colonists to pay for their Revolutionary War. Lotteries also paid for the British Museum.

The chance of winning a lottery is very low—even in comparison to games of chance at casinos. The odds of winning the British lottery are 1 in 13,983,813.[15] More important, lottery payoffs are usually a small percentage of the amount bet. For the bets to be fair, the lottery's payments to lucky bettors would have to equal the amount bet on average. Betting on lotteries is not

[14]This section is based, in part, on Gurdon, Meghan Cox, "British Accuse Their Lottery of Robbing the Poor to Give to the Rich," *San Francisco Chronicle*, November 25, 1995:D1.

[15]The odds of winning the New York lotto game are almost twice as bad, about 1 in 26 million, which is 7,000 times less probable than the 1 in 3,763 chance of being murdered in New York City.

fair because the expected value of a bet is negative. For example, the British lottery pays winners only 50% of the total amount bet, so collectively, bettors lose half the amount they bet week after week.

Nonetheless, most people, including the poor, bet on government lotteries. Seventy percent of British households buy a lottery ticket every week. A recent British government survey found that all socioeconomic groups spend about the same, £2($3.28) on average, each week on lottery tickets. This amount, though, is a larger share of a poor family's available income.

Theories on Why People Gamble

Why do people take unfair bets? Some people gamble because they are risk preferring or because they have a compulsion to gamble.[16] However, neither of these explanations is likely to explain noncompulsive gambling by most people who exhibit risk-averse behavior in the other aspects of their lives (such as buying insurance). Risk-averse people may make unfair bets because they enjoy the game, have a utility curve with both risk-averse and risk-preferring regions, or falsely believe that the gamble favors them.

The first explanation is that gambling provides entertainment as well as risk. Risk-averse people insure their property, such as their house, because there's nothing enjoyable about bearing the risk of theft, flooding, and fire. However, these same people may play poker or bet on horse races because they get enough pleasure from playing those games to put up with the financial risk and the expected loss.[17]

The second explanation also involves tastes. Friedman and Savage (1948) suggested that gamblers place a high value on the chance to increase their wealth greatly. Figure 17.4 shows Sylvia's utility curve, which has the shape that Friedman and Savage described. Sylvia is risk averse with respect to small gambles but risk preferring with respect to bets that allow for large potential winnings. Suppose that Sylvia is offered a choice between receiving W_2 with certainty of making a small bet with an expected value of W_2: She has an equal probability of receiving wealth W_1 or W_3. Sylvia chooses the certain wealth because her certain utility at b^* is above the expected utility at b. On the other hand, Sylvia prefers a bet with an equal chance of W_2 and W_5 to the certain

---

[16]The *British Medical Journal* says that calls to Gamblers' Anonymous have risen 17% since the current British lottery began November 14, 1995.

[17]Many British citizens exhibit their love of games by engaging in truly weird bets. For example, in 1994, Jenni Reid, a British businesswoman, told her father-in-law that it was inevitable that advances in science would permit men to give birth. He laughed so hard that she called her bookie about placing a bet. The bookie accepted a $75 bet at 500 to 1 odds of a "normal male with XY chromosomes" giving birth to a "living viable child" before 2005. The British, who have one of the highest per capita gambling rates in the world, wagered about $9 billion with bookmakers in 1993 on bets that Elvis lives and that humanoids will be found on Mars, as well as on other, more prosaic events such as the winner of a horse race. Coll, Steve, "Chances Are Brits Have Bet on It," *San Francisco Examiner*, July 10, 1994:Sunday Punch, 4.

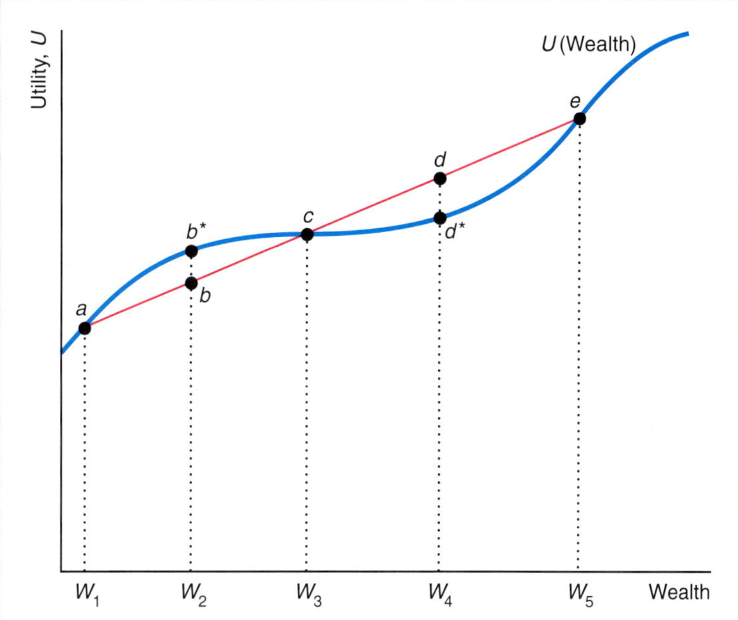

Figure 17.4 Friedman-Savage Utility. This person with Friedman-Savage utility is risk averse with respect to a small gamble (50% W_1, 50% W_3) but risk preferring with respect to a larger gamble (50% W_3, 50% W_5). The small gamble has an expected value of W_2. The expected utility, b, is less than the utility if W_2 were certain, b^*. With the larger gamble, the expected utility, d, is greater than the utility of the certain wealth W_4.

wealth of W_4, which is the expected value of the bet, because the expected utility at d from the bet is greater than the certain utility at d^*.

The third explanation is that people make mistakes. Either people do not know the true probabilities or they cannot properly calculate expected values, so they do not realize that they are participating in an unfair bet.

These three explanations are not mutually exclusive. A person could get entertainment value from gambling *and* have a Friedman-Savage utility *and* be unable to calculate odds correctly.[18]

[18]Economists, knowing how to calculate expected values and deriving most of their excitement from economic models, apparently are less likely to gamble than are real people. A number of years ago, a meeting of economists was held in Reno, Nevada. Reno hotels charge low room rates on the assumption that they'll make plenty from guests' gambling losses. However, the economists gambled so little that they were asked pointedly not to return.

Evidence on Why People Gamble

Evidence supports all three of these explanations to some degree. People definitely like games of chance. One survey found that 65% of Americans say that they engage in games of chance, even when the games involve no money or only trivial sums (Brunk 1981). That is, they play because they enjoy the games.[19]

It is difficult to test the Friedman-Savage explanation directly. Brunk (1981) indirectly examined whether the Friedman-Savage explanation (risk-preferring behavior with respect to bets with large rewards) or love of the game explains bets. He asked people whether they were dissatisfied with their current income. Presumably, their answers would indicate whether they have increasing marginal utilities of wealth, at least over certain ranges of wealth. Brunk argued that, if the Friedman-Savage explanation is correct, people who were dissatisfied with their incomes would be more likely to buy lottery tickets, after controlling for other individual differences such as education. He also argued that this factor would not be an important explanation for social gambling activities such as bingo, which people play because they enjoy the game. He found that people who were dissatisfied with their income were more likely than others to buy lottery tickets but not to engage in social gambling. Although this evidence is consistent with the Friedman-Savage explanation, it is not proof that many people have such utility functions.

A number of studies show that many people have biased estimates of probabilities and cannot calculate expected values. For example, Golec and Tamarkin (1995) concluded that football bettors tend to make low-probability bets because they are overconfident.

Golec and Tamarkin found that bettors greatly overestimate their probabilities of winning certain types of exotic football bets (an *exotic bet* depends on the outcome of more than one game). In a small survey, gamblers estimated their chance of winning a particular bet at 45% when the objective probability was 20%. Of course, these people may also place exotic bets because they enjoy them more than simple bets. ■

---

[19]When I was an undergraduate at the University of Chicago, I lived in a dorm and saw overwhelming evidence that the "love of the game" is a powerful force. As the neighborhood provided few forms of entertainment, the dorm's denizens regularly watched the man from the vending company refill the candy machine with fresh candy. He took the old, stale, unpopular bars that remained in the machine and placed them in the "mystery candy" bin. Thanks to our careful study of stocking techniques, we all knew that buying the mystery candy was not a fair bet—who would want unpopular, stale candy bars at the same price as a fresh, popular bar? Nonetheless, one of the dorm dwellers always bought the mystery candy. When asked why, he responded, "I love the excitement of not knowing what'll come out." Life was very boring indeed on the south side of Chicago.

17.3 AVOIDING RISK

> *If 75% of all accidents happen within 5 miles of home, why not move 10 miles away?* —Steven Wright

Risk-averse people want to eliminate or reduce risk whether the bet is fair or biased against them. Risk-neutral people avoid unfair bets, and even risk-preferring people avoid very unfair bets.

Individuals can avoid optional risky activities, but often they can't escape risk altogether. Property owners, for instance, always face the possibility that their property will be damaged or stolen or will burn. They may be able to reduce the probability that bad states of nature occur, however.

Just Say No

The simplest way to avoid risk is to abstain from optional risky activities. No one forces you to bet on the lottery, go into a high-risk occupation, or buy stock in a start-up biotech firm. If one brand of a product you use comes with a warranty and an otherwise comparable brand does not, you lower your risk by buying the guaranteed product. Some big chemical firms that supplied materials used to make heart valves, artificial blood vessels, and other implants told medical equipment companies that they were cutting off deliveries because of fears of lawsuits.[20]

Even when you can't avoid risk altogether, you can take precautions to reduce the probability of bad states of nature or the size of any loss that might occur. For example, you can maintain your car as the manufacturer recommends to reduce the probability that it will break down. By locking your apartment door, you lower the chance that your television will be stolen. Getting rid of your four-year-old collection of newspapers lessens the likelihood that your house will burn. Not only do these actions reduce your risk, but they also raise the expected value of your asset.

Obtain Information

Collecting accurate information before acting is one of the most important ways in which people can reduce risk and increase expected value and expected utility, as Solved Problem 17.1 illustrated. Armed with information, you may avoid a risky choice or you may be able to take actions that reduce the probability of a disaster or the size of the loss.

Before buying a car or refrigerator, many people read *Consumer Reports* to determine how frequently a particular brand is likely to need repairs. By collecting such information before buying, they can reduce the likelihood of making a costly mistake.

---

[20]Feder, Barnaby J., "Implant Industry Is Facing Cutback by Top Suppliers," *New York Times*, April 25, 1994:A1, C3. The firms believe that the probability of suits and the size of awards have changed over time. They may be getting out of this business because they dislike the increased risk or because their expected returns fell.

APPLICATION

Bond Ratings

Investors obtain information about the riskiness of bonds by checking reports on their riskiness, such as the Moody's and Standard & Poor's ratings in Table 17.2. These letter-grade ratings reflect whether a bond's issuer has made timely payments in the past, whether the issuer is in danger of becoming bankrupt, and other problems. Bonds with an *investment grade* are said to be suitable for purchase by an institutional money manager, who is legally obligated to be a *prudent investor*—one who does not take great risks. Lower-ranked bonds offer unusually high rates of return as inducements for people to buy them. Junk bonds are issued by new firms that have little or no financial history or by established firms that have had severe financial problems, so their Moody's and Standard & Poor's ratings are low. Knowledgeable investors use this information and information about the current rates of return to decide which bonds to buy. ■

Diversify

Although it may sound paradoxical, individuals and firms often reduce their overall risk by making many risky investments instead of only one. This practice is called *risk pooling* or *diversifying*. Your grandparents may have put it this way: "Don't put all your eggs in one basket."

Table 17.2 Bond Ratings

	Moody's	Standard & Poor's
Investment Grade		
Highest quality	Aaa	AAA
High quality	Aa	AA
Upper medium grade	A	A
Medium grade	Baa	BBB
High Yield or Junk Bonds		
Predominately speculative	Ba	BB
Low grade	B	B
Default likely	Caa	CCC
Very speculative	Ca	CC
Lowest quality	C	C
Default		DDD

Correlation and Diversification. The extent to which diversification reduces risk depends on the degree to which various events are correlated over states of nature. The degree of correlation ranges from negatively correlated to uncorrelated to positively correlated.[21] If you know that the first event occurs, you know that the probability that the second event occurs is lower if the events are *negatively correlated* and higher if the events are *positively correlated*. The outcomes are *independent* or *uncorrelated* if knowing whether the first event occurs tells you nothing about the probability that the second event occurs.

Diversification can eliminate risk if two events are perfectly negatively correlated. Suppose that two firms are competing for a government contract and have an equal chance of winning. Because only one firm can win, the other must lose, so the two events are *perfectly negatively correlated*. You can buy a share of stock in either firm for \$20. The stock of the firm that wins the contract will be worth \$40, while the stock of the loser will be worth \$10. If you buy two shares of the same company, your shares are going to be worth either \$80 or \$20 after the contract is awarded. Thus, their expected value is

$$\$50 = [\tfrac{1}{2} \times \$80] + [\tfrac{1}{2} \times 20]$$

with a variance of

$$\$900 = [\tfrac{1}{2} \times (\$80 - \$50)^2] + [\tfrac{1}{2} \times (\$20 - \$50)^2].$$

On the other hand, if you buy one share of each, your two shares will be worth \$50 no matter which firm wins, and the variance is zero.

Diversification reduces risk even if the two events are imperfectly negatively correlated, uncorrelated, or imperfectly positively correlated. *The more negatively correlated two events are, the more diversification reduces risk.*

Now, suppose that the values of the two stocks are uncorrelated. Each of the two firms has a 50% chance of getting a government contract, and whether one firm gets a contract does *not* affect whether the other firm wins one. Because of this independence, the chance that each firm's share is worth \$40 is $\tfrac{1}{4}$, the chance that one is worth \$40 and the other is worth \$10 is $\tfrac{1}{2}$, and the chance that each is worth \$10 is $\tfrac{1}{4}$. If you buy one share of each firm, the expected value of these two shares is

$$\$50 = [\tfrac{1}{4} \times \$80] + [\tfrac{1}{2} \times \$50] + [\tfrac{1}{4} \times \$20],$$

and the variance is

$$\$450 = [\tfrac{1}{4} \times (\$80 - \$50)^2] + [\tfrac{1}{2} \times (\$50 - \$50)^2] + [\tfrac{1}{4} \times (\$20 - \$50)^2].$$

---

[21]A measure of the correlation between two random variables x and y is

$$\rho = \mathrm{E}\left(\left[\frac{x - \bar{x}}{\sigma_x}\right]\left[\frac{y - \bar{y}}{\sigma_y}\right]\right),$$

where the E(·) means "take the expectation" of the term in parentheses, $\bar{x}$ and $\bar{y}$ are the means, and σ_x and σ_y are the standard deviations of x and y. The two events are said to be uncorrelated if $\rho = 0$.

The expected value is the same as buying two shares in one firm, but the variance is only half as large. Thus, diversification lowers risk when the values are uncorrelated but does not eliminate risk when the values are perfectly negatively correlated.

In contrast, *diversification does not reduce risk if two events are perfectly positively correlated.* If the government will award contracts either to both firms or to neither firm, the risks are perfectly positively correlated. The expected value of the stocks and the variance are the same whether you buy two shares of one firm or one share of each firm.

APPLICATION

Checking Correlations

Savvy investors pay attention to the degree of correlation of their investments. Each afternoon at 4:15 P.M., Dennis Weatherstone, chair of J. P. Morgan, a large American investment bank, receives estimates of how much money the bank stands to lose if certain events occur.[22] This calculation summarizes the 20,000 daily transactions made by the bank's 120 risk-taking units. The calculation represents the volatility of each investment and *the degree to which the returns on 300 financial instruments move together*: the correlations among them. The bank uses this information on expected returns, risks, and correlations among risky investments in its daily decisionmaking about how to modify its portfolio of investments. The firm can lower its exposure to risk by investing in pairs of assets that are very negatively correlated, all else the same. ■

Mutual Funds. Individual investors usually do not have the benefit of such detailed information about correlations. They know, however, that the value of the stock of most firms is not perfectly positively correlated with the value of other stocks, so buying stock in several companies tends to reduce risk. Many of these people effectively own shares in a number of companies at once by buying shares in a *mutual fund* of stocks. A mutual fund share is issued by a company that buys stocks in many other companies.

The *Standard & Poor's Composite Index of 500 Stocks* (S&P 500) is a value-weighted average of 500 stocks, mostly those of companies listed on the New York Stock Exchange (NYSE), though some are listed on the Amex or are over-the-counter stocks. The value of the stocks contained in this index is approximately 80% of the value of all stocks listed on the NYSE. The *New York Stock Exchange Composite Index* includes more than 1,500 common stocks traded on the NYSE. The *Amex Major Market Index* is a price-weighted average of 20 blue-chip industrial stocks. Some other mutual funds are based on bonds or a mixture of stocks, bonds, and other types of investments.

[22]"Safety in Numbers," *The Economist*, 333(7885), October 15, 1994:102.

Mutual funds allow you to reduce the risk associated with uncorrelated price movements across stocks. Suppose that two companies look very similar on the basis of everything you know about them. You have no reason to think that the stock in one firm will increase more in value or be riskier than the stock of the other firm. However, luck may cause one stock to do better than the other. You can reduce this type of random, unsystematic risk by diversifying and buying stock in both firms.

A stock mutual fund, however, has a systematic risk. The prices of all stocks tend to rise when the economy is expanding and tend to fall when the economy is contracting. By buying a diversified mutual stock fund, you are not able to avoid the systematic risks associated with shifts in the economy that affect all stocks at once.

APPLICATION

Laws Limiting Diversification

To lower risk, insurance companies and various other firms invest in many countries. Laws that limit diversification by insurance companies force these firms to bear extra risk.

In 1994, Hong Kong enacted a new law to force general (nonlife) insurers to hold assets in Hong Kong equal to at least 80% of their liabilities. Some legislators claimed that this policy would protect policyholders by keeping the assets of shareholders within Hong Kong. However, this law may have the exact opposite effect, by reducing a firm's ability to diversify and avoid bankruptcy if a major natural disaster strikes Hong Kong.[23] ■

Insure

> *I detest life-insurance agents; they always argue that I shall some day die, which is not so.* —Stephen Leacock

As we've already seen, a risk-averse person is willing to pay money—a risk premium—to avoid risk. The demand for risk reduction is met by insurance companies, which bear the risk for anyone who buys an insurance policy. Many risk-averse individuals and firms buy insurance; global insurance premiums were nearly $2 trillion in 1993.

How Much Insurance Individuals Want. The way insurance works is that a risk-averse person or firm gives money to the insurance company in the good state of nature, and the insurance company transfers money to the policyholder in the bad

---

[23]"Asian Insurance: Concentrating," *The Economist*, 321(7862), May 7, 1994:87. Moreover, by increasing investment in Hong Kong, this law might lower returns on investment in Hong Kong. In 1992, Hong Kong's 170 general insurers had liabilities of HK$7.8 billion. Had the law been in effect then, they would have had to invest an extra HK$3 billion in Hong Kong.

state of nature. This transaction allows the risk-averse person or firm to shift some or all of the risk to the insurance company.

Because Scott is risk averse, he wants to insure his house, which is worth \$80 (thousand). There is a 25% probability that his house will burn next year. If a fire occurs, the house will be worth only \$40.

With no insurance, the expected value of his house is

$$[\tfrac{1}{4} \times \$40] + [\tfrac{3}{4} \times \$80] = \$70.$$

Scott faces a good deal of risk. The variance of the value of his house is

$$[\tfrac{1}{4} \times (\$40 - \$70)^2] + [\tfrac{3}{4} \times (\$80 - \$70)^2] = \$300.$$

Now suppose that an insurance company offers a *fair bet*, or **fair insurance**: a bet between an insurer and a policyholder in which the value of the bet to the policyholder is zero. The insurance company offers to let Scott trade \$1 in the good state of nature (no fire) for \$3 in the bad state of nature (fire).[24] This insurance is fair because the expected value of this insurance to Scott is zero:

$$[\tfrac{1}{4} \times (-\$3)] + [\tfrac{3}{4} \times \$1] = \$0.$$

Because Scott is risk averse, he *fully insures* by buying enough insurance to eliminate his risk altogether. With this amount of insurance, he has the same amount of wealth in either state of nature.

Scott pays the insurance company \$10 in the good state of nature and receives \$30 in the bad state. In the good state, he has a house worth \$80 less the \$10 he pays the insurance company, for a net wealth of \$70. If the fire occurs, he has a house worth \$40 plus a payment from the insurance company of \$30, for a net wealth, again, of \$70.

Scott's expected value with fair insurance, \$70, is the same as his expected value without insurance. The variance he faces drops from \$300 without insurance to \$0 with insurance. Scott is better off with insurance because he has the same expected value and faces no risk.

SOLVED PROBLEM 17.3

The local government assesses a property tax of \$4 (thousand) on Scott's house. If the tax is collected whether or not the house burns, how much fair insurance does Scott buy? If the tax is collected only if the house does not burn, how much fair insurance does Scott buy?

---

[24] As a practical matter, the insurance company collects money up front. If the fire doesn't occur, the company keeps the money. If the fire occurs, it gives back the amount paid originally plus additional funds. Scott's insurance company charges him \$1 up front for every \$4 it will pay him in the bad state. Thus, Scott effectively pays \$1 in the good state of nature and receives a net payment of \$3 in the bad state.

Answer

1. *Determine the after-tax expected value of the house without insurance*: The expected value of the house is

$$\$66 = [\tfrac{1}{4} \times \$36] + [\tfrac{3}{4} \times \$76]$$

if the tax is always collected and

$$\$67 = [\tfrac{1}{4} \times \$40] + [\tfrac{3}{4} \times \$76]$$

if the tax is collected only in the good state of nature.

2. *Calculate the amount of fair insurance Scott buys if the tax is always collected*: Because Scott is risk averse, he wants to be fully insured so that the after-tax value of his house is the same in both states of nature. If the tax is always collected, Scott pays the insurance company \$10 in the good state of nature, so he has \$76 – \$10 = \$66, and receives \$30 in the bad state, so he has \$36 + \$30 = \$66. That is, he buys the same amount of insurance as he would without any taxes. The tax has no effect on his insurance decision because he owes that amount regardless of the state of nature.

3. *Calculate the amount of fair insurance Scott buys if the tax is collected only if there is no fire*: If the tax is collected only in the good state of nature, Scott pays the insurance company \$9 in the good state (\$76 – \$9 = \$67) and receives \$27 in the bad state (\$40 + \$27 = \$67). Thus, he has the same after-tax income in both states of nature. Effectively, Scott is partially insured by the tax system, so he purchases less insurance than he otherwise would. ■

Fairness and Insurance. When fair insurance is offered, risk-averse people fully insure. If insurance companies charge more than the fair-insurance price, individuals buy less insurance.[25]

Because insurance companies do not offer fair insurance, most people do not fully insure. An insurance company could not stay in business if it offered fair insurance. With fair insurance, the insurance company's expected payments would equal the amount the insurance company collects. Because the insurance company has operating expenses—costs of maintaining offices, printing forms, hiring sales agents, and so forth—an insurance firm providing fair insurance would lose money. Insurance companies' rates must be high enough to cover their operating expenses, so the insurance is less than fair to policyholders.

How much can insurance companies charge for insurance? A monopoly insurance company could charge an amount up to the risk premium a person is willing

[25]As Solved Problem 17.3 shows, tax laws may act to offset this problem, so some insurance is fair or more than fair after tax.

to pay to avoid risk. For example, in Figure 17.2, Irma would be willing to pay up to \$14 for an insurance policy that would compensate her if her vase were not a Ming. The more risk averse an individual is, the more that a monopoly insurance company can charge. If there are many insurance companies competing for business, the price of an insurance policy is less than the maximum that risk-averse individuals are willing to pay—but still high enough that the firms cover their operating expenses.

APPLICATION

Flight Insurance

Recently, American Express (AE) sent me a letter offering to enroll me in its automatic flight insurance program. If I agree to this plan, AE will charge me \$4 for insurance every time I take a scheduled flight. If I die on that flight, AE will pay my family \$250,000. (AE also offered much larger amounts of insurance, but I figure there's no point in making myself worth more to my family dead than alive.)

If θ is my probability of dying on a flight, my family's expected value from this bet with AE is

$$[\theta \times \$250{,}000] + [(1 - \theta) \times (-4)].$$

If the insurance is to be fair, this expected value must be zero, which is true if $\theta \approx 0.000016$, that is, if 1 out of every 62,500 flights has a fatal crash.

I'm not tempted by AE's offer because their insurance is not at all close to being fair. The chance that I'll die on a flight is much, much less than 0.000016.

How great *is* my danger of being in a fatal airline crash? According to the Air Transport Association, no passengers died in an accident involving U.S. aircraft with more than 30 seats in 1993. In 1994, 228 passengers died in 4 fatal crashes out of the more than seven million flights. The probability that one of the more than 528 million passengers in 1994 was involved in a fatal crash was only 0.000000432, or 1 in 2,317,439.

If I randomly choose a seat on a flight each day for 10 years, my probability of *not* being in an accident is 99.84%. If I fly each day for 100 years, my probability of not being in a fatal accident is 98.44%. Indeed, only by flying every day for about 4,800 years would my probability of being in a fatal crash rise as high as 50%. (The greatest risk of an airplane trip for many people is the drive to and from the airport.)

Because the chance of being in a fatal crash is 0.00000043, the fair rate to pay for \$250,000 of flight insurance is about a dime. As I see it, AE is offering to charge me 40 times more than the fair rate for this insurance.

I'd have to be incredibly risk averse to be tempted by this offer. Indeed, I wouldn't buy this insurance even if I were that risk averse. Instead, I'd buy general life insurance, which is much less expensive than flight insurance and covers me for all types of fatal accidents and diseases. ■

Insurance Only for Diversifiable Risks. Why is an insurance company willing to sell policies and take on risk? By pooling the risks of many people, the insurance company can lower its risk much below that of any individual. If the probability that one car is stolen is independent of whether other cars are stolen, the risk to an insurance company of insuring one person against theft is much greater than the average risk of insuring many people.

An insurance company sells policies only for risks that it can diversify. If the risks from disasters to its policyholders are highly positively correlated, an insurance company is not well diversified by holding many policies. A war affects all policyholders, so the outcomes that they face are perfectly correlated. Because wars are *nondiversifiable risks*, insurance companies do not offer policies insuring against wars.

APPLICATION

Natural Disasters

In recent years, some insurance companies have started viewing major natural disasters as nondiversifiable risks because such catastrophic events cause many insured people to suffer losses at the same time. As more homes have been built in parts of the country where damage from storms or earthquakes is likely, the size of the potential losses to insurers from nondiversifiable risks has grown.

In the 1990s, insurance companies suffered major losses. Insurers paid $12.5 billion for losses in the 1994 Los Angeles earthquake.[26] The estimated losses were $4.2 billion from Hurricane Hugo in 1989, $15.5 billion from Hurricane Andrew in 1992, and $2.1 billion from Hurricane Opal in 1995. Blizzards and tornadoes in 1993 caused $1.8 billion in damages.

In response to these major disasters, Allstate and State Farm, the two largest U.S. providers of home owner insurance, now limit their sales of new policies in Florida and parts of North and South Carolina out of fear of hurricanes and in California because of concerns about the high probability of earthquakes.

---

[26]Treaster, Joseph B., "Insurer Curbing Sales of Policies in Storm Areas," *New York Times*, October 10,1996:A1, C4.

In 1996, Nationwide Insurance Company, the fifth-largest insurer of U.S. homes, announced that it was sharply curtailing sales of new policies along the Gulf of Mexico and the eastern seaboard from Texas to Maine. A company official explained, "Prudence requires us to diligently manage our exposure to catastrophic losses." ■

17.4 INVESTING UNDER UNCERTAINTY

In Chapter 16, we ignored uncertainty when we analyzed how firms take account of discounting in making investment decisions. We now investigate how uncertainty affects the investment decision. In particular, we examine how attitudes toward risk affect individuals' willingness to invest, how people evaluate risky investments that last for many periods, and how investors pay to alter their probabilities of success.

In the following examples, the owner of a monopoly decides whether to open a new retail outlet. Because the firm is a monopoly, the owner's return from the investment does not depend on the actions of other firms. As a result, the owner faces no strategic considerations. The owner knows the cost of the investment but is unsure about how many people will patronize the new store; hence, the profits are uncertain.

Investing Depends on Attitudes Toward Risk

We start by considering a potential investment by the monopoly's owner that has an uncertain payoff this year. The owner must take risk into account but can ignore discounting. Whether the owner invests depends on how risk averse he or she is and on the risks involved.

Risk-Neutral Investing. Chris, the owner of the monopoly, is risk neutral. She maximizes her expected utility by making the investment only if the expected value of the return from the investment is positive.

To determine whether to invest, Chris uses the *decision tree* in panel a of Figure 17.5. The rectangle, called a *decision node*, indicates that she must make a decision about whether to invest or not. The circle, a *chance node*, denotes that a random process determines the outcome (consistent with the given probabilities). If Chris does not open the new store, she makes \$0. If she does open the new store, she expects to make \$200 with 80% probability and to lose \$100 with 20% probability. The expected value from a new store (see the circle in panel a) is

$$EV = [0.8 \times \$200] + [0.2 \times (-\$100)] = \$140.$$

Because she is risk neutral, she prefers an expected value of \$140 to a certain one of \$0, so she invests. Thus, her expected value in the rectangle is \$140.

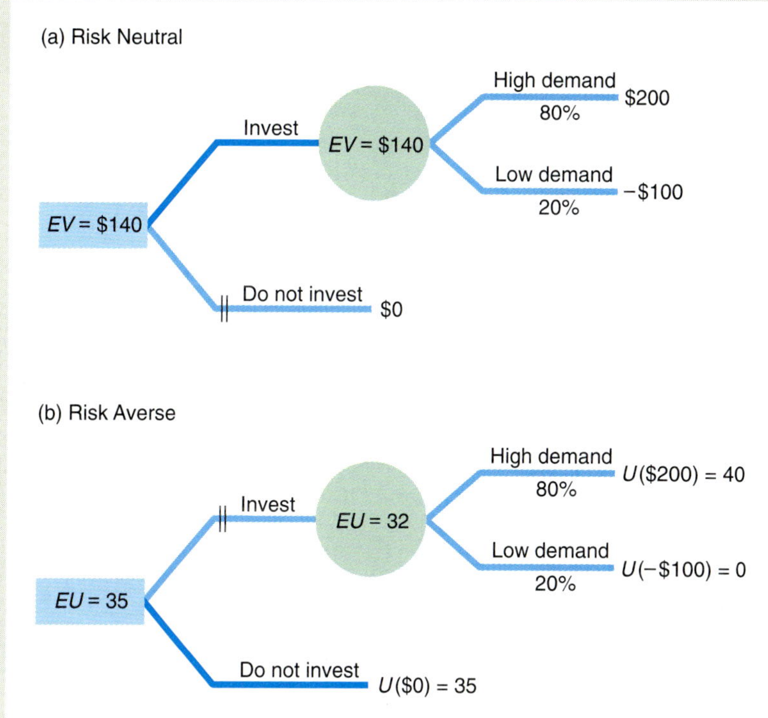

Figure 17.5 Investment Decision Tree with Risk Aversion. The owner of a monopoly must decide whether to invest in a new store. (a) The expected value is \$140, so it pays for a risk-neutral owner to invest. (b) The utility from not investing for this risk-averse owner is greater than the expected utility from investing, so the owner does not invest.

Risk-Averse Investing. Ken, who is risk averse, faces the same decision as Chris. Ken invests in the new store if his expected utility from investing is greater than his certain utility from not investing. Panel b shows the decision tree for a particular risk-averse utility function. The circle shows that Ken's expected utility from the investment is

$$EU = [0.2 \times U(-\$100)] + [0.8 \times U(\$200)]$$

$$= [0.2 \times 0] + [0.8 \times 40] = 32.$$

The certain utility from not investing is $U(\$0) = 35$. Thus, Ken does not invest. As a result, his expected utility (here, certain utility) in the rectangle is 35.

APPLICATION

Premium for a Riskier Investment

Risk-averse people will make risky investments only if these investments have an expected return that is sufficiently higher than that on a nonrisky investment such as a U.S. government bond, as Figure 17.2 illustrates.[27] Because most people are risk averse, they will make risky investments only if *the expected rate of return on a risky investment exceeds the rate of return on a nonrisky investment by a risk premium.*

Most stock funds have more nondiversifiable risks—as reflected by a higher standard deviation in returns—than bond funds, even junk bond funds. Table 17.3 shows that the historical standard deviation varies substantially across a number of diversified stock and bond funds.

Because stocks are riskier than bonds, the rates of return on stocks exceed those on bonds over long periods of time. Over the 20-year period from 1974 through 1993, stocks had higher rates of return than bonds in 13 years in Britain, 12 in France, 11 in the United States, and 14 in Japan.[28] The total

Table 17.3 Riskiness of Various Investments Funds

Investment	Standard Deviation	
Japan stock funds	8.3	riskier→
Gold funds	7.3	
Technology stock funds	5.8	
International stock funds	4.4	
Growth stock funds	4.0	
Standard & Poor's 500 stock funds	3.5	
Stock income funds	3.0	
Balanced funds	2.6	
T. Rowe Price International Bond Fund	2.4	
Junk bond funds	2.2	
World income funds	1.9	
Ginnie Mae funds	1.1	←less risky

Source: Eaton, Leslie, "Assessing a Fund's Risk Is Part Math, Part Art," *New York Times*, April 2, 1995:§3,9.

[27] The Tappet Brothers (the hosts of National Public Radio's *Car Talk*) offer a risk-free investment. Their Capital Depreciation Fund guarantees a 50% return. You send them $100 and they send you back $50.

[28] "The Cost of Looking," *The Economist*, 328(7828), September 11, 1993:74.

annual real rate of return on U.S. stocks averaged 7% between 1926 and 1990, compared to 1% on relatively risk-free U.S. Treasury bills (which are short-term bonds). The cumulative nominal rate over a 10-year period ending March 31, 1996, was 269% on a S&P 500 Index Fund, 124% for the Lehman Brothers Government/Corporate Bond Index, 87% for a (low-risk) money market account, and 81% for virtually risk-free U.S. Treasury bills.[29] In comparison, the Consumer Price Index (a measure of inflation) rose by 43% during this period. Because stocks are the riskiest of these assets, we would expect them to provide by far the highest rate of return over the long haul, as they do. ■

Investing with Uncertainty and Discounting

Now suppose that the uncertain returns or costs from an investment are spread out over time. In Chapter 16, we derived an investment rule by which we know future costs and returns with certainty. We concluded that an investment pays if its *net present value* (calculated by discounting the difference between the return and cost in each future period) is positive.

How does this rule change if the returns are uncertain? A risk-neutral person chooses to invest if the *expected net present value* is positive. We calculate the expected net present value by discounting the difference between expected return and expected cost in each future period.

Sam is risk neutral. His decision tree, Figure 17.6, shows that his cost of investing is C = $25 this year. Next year, he receives uncertain revenues from the investment of $125 with 80% probability or $50 with 20% probability. Thus, the expected value of the revenues next year is

$$EV = [0.8 \times \$125] + [0.2 \times \$50] = \$110.$$

With a real interest rate of 10%, the expected present value of the revenues is

$$EPV = \$110/1.1 = \$100.$$

Subtracting the $25 cost incurred this year, Sam determines that his expected net present value is $ENPV$ = $75. As a result, he invests.

Investing with Altered Probabilities

We have been assuming that nature dictates the probabilities of various states of nature. Sometimes, however, we can alter the probabilities, though usually at some expense.

Gautam, who is risk neutral, is considering whether to invest in a new store, as Figure 17.7 shows. After investing, he can increase the probability that demand will be high at the new store by advertising at a cost of $50.

---

[29]Source: University of California.

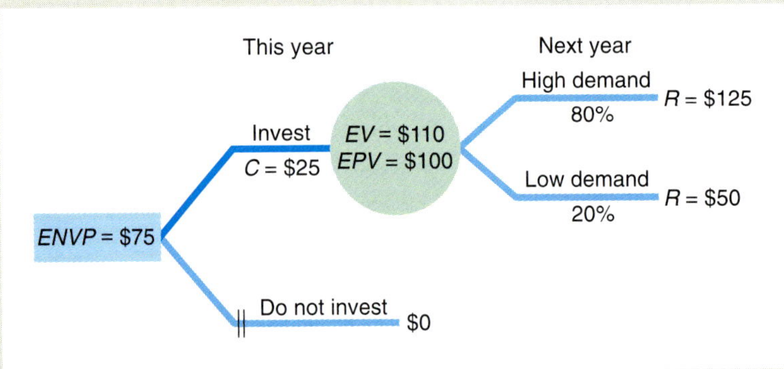

Figure 17.6 Investment Decision Tree with Uncertainty and Discounting. The risk-neutral owner invests if the expected net present value is positive. The expected value, *EV*, of the revenue from the investment next year is \$110. With an interest rate of 10%, the expected present value, *EPV*, of the revenue is \$100. The expected net present value, *ENPV*, is the *EPV* = \$100 minus the \$25 cost of the investment this year, which is \$75. Thus, the owner invests.

If he makes the investment but does not advertise, he has a 40% probability of making \$100 and a 60% probability of losing \$100. His expected value without advertising is

$$[0.4 \times \$100] + [0.6 \times (-\$100)] = -\$20.$$

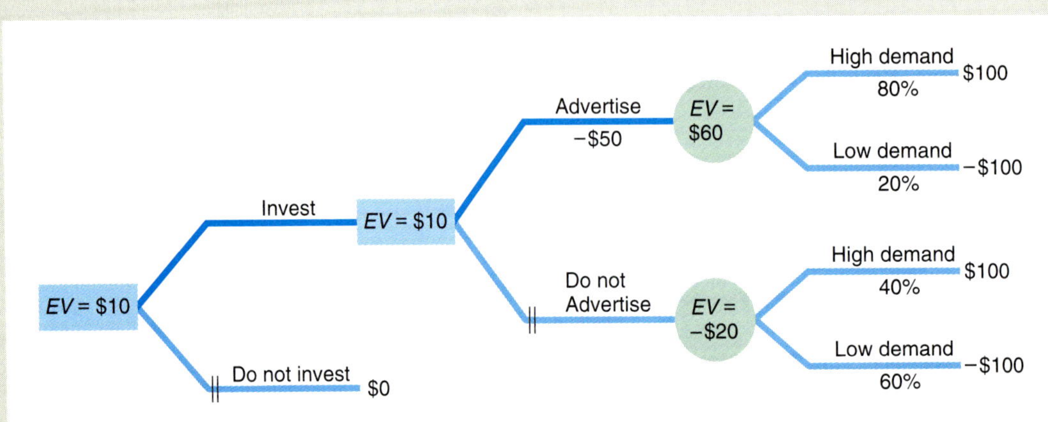

Figure 17.7 Investment Decision Tree with Advertising. By advertising, the risk-neutral owner can alter the probability of high demand. The expected value of the investment is –\$20 without advertising and \$60 with advertising. Because the cost of advertising is \$50, the expected value of investing and advertising is \$10 (= \$60 – \$50). Thus, the owner invests and advertises.

Thus, if he could not advertise, he would not make this investment.

With advertising, the probability of his making \$100 rises to 80%, so his expected value is

$$[0.8 \times \$100] + [0.2 \times (-\$100)] = \$60.$$

His expected value net of the cost of advertising is \$10 (= \$60 – \$50). Thus, he is better off investing and advertising than not investing at all or investing without advertising.

APPLICATION

Loans, Defaults, and Usury Laws

The following discussion of bank mortgage loans illustrates many of the key ideas of this chapter: measuring risk, diversifying to lower risk, insisting on higher returns for riskier investments, and altering probabilities. It also demonstrates how laws that prevent investors from receiving a risk premium reduce investments.

Banks and other firms (such as credit unions and savings and loans) invest by providing consumers with loans. These loans are risky: Banks worry that their customers will not repay the loans.

Banks know that random bad luck will cause some customers to *default*: fail to repay the money owed. The banks can reduce their risk from such random bad luck by pooling many loans, a form of diversification.

Banks are even more worried about systematic, nondiversifiable risks of default. According to research by banks, people who have had trouble repaying loans in the past are more likely to default than others. The banks could lower their risk by not loaning to these people, but such a policy would substantially reduce the number of loans they could make. Instead, to compensate for the greater risk of default, banks charge people who have weak financial histories or low and unsteady incomes higher mortgage rates.

Banks usually grade borrowers *A* through *D* for risk. Table 17.4 shows how mortgage payments varied by risk class for a typical bank in 1994. People with spotty records of repaying debts pay higher interest rates for mortgages.

Banks also take other steps to alter the odds of a default. They provide smaller loans to relatively bad-risk borrowers by requiring that these people *put more money down*—pay for a larger share of the house in cash—and pay more *points*, which are fees equal to 1% of the loan that are paid up front. By putting more money down and paying more points, a borrower has more to lose and so is less likely to default on the loan.

Thus, when banks are free to set their loan rates and other conditions for loans, people who are poor risks can get loans by paying a relatively higher rate to borrow money. A binding usury law (Chapter 16) that sets a maximum

Table 17.4 Mortgage Terms by Risk Class

Borrower's Risk Category	Adjustable Rate	Fixed Rate	Down Payment	Points
A: Clean credit	5.75%	8.65%	5–20%	0–2
B: Clean credit last 12 months but a few missed payments previously	7%	11%	20–25%	3–3.5
C: Clean credit last 12 months but previous possibly serious credit problems	7%	11%	20–30%	3–3.5
D: A serious credit problem last 2 years, such as a foreclosure or bankruptcy	—	14–18%	30–60%	3–6

Note: An adjustable-rate mortgage varies with inflation and market conditions. A fixed-rate mortgage has a nominal interest rate that remains constant for the term of the loan. The down payment is the share of the purchase price that the borrower must pay in cash at the time the house is purchased. A point is an amount of money paid at the start of the mortgage, equal to 1% of the loan.

Source: Ravo, Nick, "Mortgages: Lenders More Forgiving of Poor Credit Records," *New York Times*, September 3, 1994:27.

rate that banks can charge forces banks to set the same interest rates for many or all of their customers. In response, banks loan only to relatively low-risk borrowers. High-risk borrowers cannot get loans.

Villegas (1989) compared short-term consumer credit for households in states with usury ceilings and in those without limits. He found that the amount of credit a low-income family has in a state with a usury limit is $1,013 less than that of a comparable household in a state without such a price control. For middle-income households, the difference is $478. There is no significant difference for high-income families.

On the basis of statistical tests, Villegas did not find that households in states with usury laws were able to obtain auto loans at significantly lower interest rates than those in other states. Thus, if his results are correct, usury laws hurt poor consumers by limiting their ability to borrow and do not significantly reduce the rate at which wealthier consumers borrow. ■

Summary

1. **Degree of risk:** A probability measures the likelihood that a particular state of nature occurs. People may use historical frequencies, if available, to calculate a probability. Lacking detailed information, people form subjective estimates of the probability on the basis of available information. The expected value is the probability-weighted average of the values in each state of nature. One widely used measure of risk is the variance (or the standard deviation, which is the square root of the variance). The variance is the probability-weighted average of the squared difference of the value in each state of nature and the expected value.

2. **Decisionmaking under uncertainty:** Whether people choose a risky option over a nonrisky one depends on their attitudes toward risk and the expected payoffs of the various options. Most people are *risk averse* and will choose a riskier option only if its expected value is substantially higher

than that of a less-risky option. *Risk-neutral* people choose whichever option has the higher rate of return because they do not care about risk. *Risk-preferring* people may choose the riskier option even if it has a lower rate of return. An individual's utility function reflects that person's attitude toward risk. People choose the option that provides the highest expected utility. Expected utility is the probability-weighted average of the utility from the outcomes in the various states of nature.

3. **Avoiding risk:** People try in several ways to reduce the risk they face. They avoid some optional risks and take actions that lower the probabilities of bad events or reduce the harm from those events. By collecting information before acting, investors can make better choices. People can further reduce risk by pooling their risky investments, a strategy that is called diversification. Unless returns are perfectly positively correlated, diversification reduces risk. Insurance companies offer policies for risks that they can diversify by pooling risks across many individuals. Risk-averse people fully insure if they are offered fair insurance, from which the expected return to the policyholder is zero. They may buy some insurance even if the insurance is not fair. When buying unfair insurance, they exchange the risk of a large loss for the certainty of a smaller loss.

4. **Investing under uncertainty:** Whether a person makes an investment depends on the uncertainty of the payoff, the expected return, the individual's attitudes toward risk, the interest rate, and the cost of altering the likelihood of a good outcome. For a risk-neutral person, an investment pays if the expected net present value is positive. A risk-averse person invests only if that person's expected utility is higher after investing. Thus, risk-averse people make risky investments if those investments pay higher rates of return than safer investments pay. If an investment takes place over time, a risk-neutral investor uses a real interest rate to discount expected future values and invests if the expected net present value is positive. People pay to alter the probabilities of various outcomes from an investment if doing so raises their expected utility.

Problems

1. Suppose that an individual is risk averse and has to choose between \$100 with certainty and a risky option with two equally likely outcomes, $\$100 - x$ and $\$100 + x$. Use a graph (or math) to show that this person's risk premium is smaller, the smaller x is (the less variable the gamble is).
2. Given the information in Solved Problem 17.2, Irma prefers to buy the vase. Show graphically how high her certain income would have to be for her to choose not to buy the vase.
3. To discourage people from breaking the traffic laws, society can increase the probability that someone exceeding the speed limit will be caught and punished, or it can increase the size of the fine for speeding. Explain why either method can be used to discourage speeding. Which approach is a government likely to prefer, and why?
4. Use a decision tree to illustrate how a kidney patient would make a decision about whether to have a transplant operation. The patient currently uses a dialysis machine, which lowers her utility. If the operation is successful, her utility will return to its level before the onset of her kidney problems. However, there is a 5% probability that she will die if she has the operation. (If it will help, make up utility numbers to illustrate your answer.)
5. Use a decision tree to illustrate how a risk-neutral plaintiff in a lawsuit decides whether to settle a claim or go to trial. The defendants offer \$50,000 to settle now. If the plaintiff does not settle, the plaintiff believes that the probability of winning at trial is 60%. If the plaintiff wins, the amount awarded is X. How large can X be before the plaintiff refuses to settle? How does the plaintiff's attitudes toward risk affect this decision?
6. Would risk-neutral people ever buy insurance that was not fair (that was biased against them)?
7. After a flood, the government offers subsidies to people whose houses were destroyed. How do these subsidies affect the probability that these people buy insurance and the amount they buy? (*Hint*: Use a utility curve for a risk-averse person to illustrate your answer.)

8. Use a supply-and-demand analysis to show the effects of usury laws on consumer loans. (*Hint*: Draw supply curves and demand curves for a group of individuals who have a high probability of defaulting on their loans.)
9. Many people who live in areas where earthquakes and floods are common do not purchase insurance. One explanation is that they expect to receive aid from the government if a disaster occurs. Show how such aid affects a risk-averse individual's decision about whether to buy insurance.
10. Draw a person's utility curve and illustrate that that person is risk averse with respect to a loss but risk preferring with respect to a gain.

Math Problems

11. Asa buys a painting. There is a 20% probability that the artist will become famous and the painting will be worth \$1,000. There is a 10% probability that the painting will be destroyed by fire or some other disaster. If the painting is not destroyed and the artist does not become famous, it will be worth \$500. What is the expected value of the painting?
12. Suppose that most people will not speed if the expected fine is at least \$500. The actual fine for speeding is \$800. How high must the probability of being caught and convicted be to discourage speeding?
13. Lori, who is risk averse, has two pieces of jewelry, each worth \$1,000. She wants to send them to her sister in Thailand. She is concerned about the safety of shipping them. She believes that the probability that the jewelry won't arrive is θ. Is her expected utility higher if she sends the articles together or in two separate shipments?
14. Suppose that Mary's utility function is $U(W) = W^{0.5}$, where W is wealth. Is she risk averse? Why?
15. Suppose that Mary (see Problem 14) has an initial wealth of \$100. How much of a risk premium would she want to participate in a gamble that has a 50% probability of raising her wealth to \$120 and a 50% probability of lowering her wealth to \$80?
16. First answer the following two questions about your preferences:
    - A. You are given \$5,000 and offered a choice between receiving an extra \$2,500 with certainty or flipping a coin and getting \$5,000 if heads or \$0 if tails. Which option do you prefer?
    - B. You are given \$10,000 if you will make the following choice: Return \$2,500 or flip a coin and return \$5,000 if heads and \$0 if tails. Which option do you prefer?

    Most people choose the sure \$2,500 in the first case but flip the coin in the second. Explain why this behavior is not consistent. What do you conclude about how people make decisions concerning uncertain events?

CHAPTER 18

Externalities, Commons, and Public Goods

There's so much pollution in the air now that if it weren't for our lungs there'd be no place to put it all. —Robert Orben

In comic books, superheroes fight the smog monster or the evil entrepreneur who dumps deadly toxins in children's playgrounds. If only reducing pollution were that easy! Unfortunately, there isn't a single monster causing the problem. People and firms that do not bear the full damages from their actions pollute excessively. As Pogo remarked, "We have met the enemy and he is us."

This chapter examines why unregulated markets do not adequately control pollution and other externalities. An *externality* occurs if someone's consumption or production activities hurt or help others outside a market. For example, a manufacturing plant produces noxious fumes as a by-product of its production process. The emission of these fumes creates an externality that harms people in surrounding areas. If the government does not intervene, the firm is uninterested in the fumes—it does not sell the fumes, and it does not have to pay for the harm they cause. Because the firm has no financial incentive to reduce its level of pollution and it would be costly to do so, the firm pollutes excessively.

We start by examining externalities that arise as a by-product of production (such as water pollution from a factory) and consumption (such as air pollution from a car). We demonstrate that a competitive market produces more pollution than a market that is optimally regulated by the government and that a monopoly may not create as much of a pollution problem as a competitive market. Next we show that externalities are caused by a lack of clearly defined *property rights*, which allow owners to prevent others from using their resources.

We then turn to other issues arising from externalities. Externalities create problems for a *common property*, which is a resource available to anyone, such as a city park. Each person using the park causes an externality by crowding other people. Because no one has a property right to exclude others, such common property is overused.

When externalities benefit others, too little of the externality may be produced. A *public good*—a commodity or service whose consumption by one person does not preclude others from also consuming it—provides a positive externality if no one can be excluded from consuming it. National defense is an example of such a public good, which is called a *pure public good*. Private firms cannot profitably charge people to provide national defense because people who did not pay would also benefit from it. Supplying anyone with a pure public good makes it available to others, so pure public goods provide a positive externality. Either markets for pure public goods do not exist or such markets undersupply the good.

When an externality problem arises, government intervention may be necessary. A government may directly regulate an externality such as pollution or may provide a public good. Alternatively, a government may indirectly control an externality through taxation or laws that make polluters liable for the damage they cause.

In this chapter, we examine six main topics:

1. **Externalities:** By-products of consumption and production may benefit or harm other people.
2. **The inefficiency of competition with externalities:** A competitive market produces too much of a harmful externality, but that overproduction can be prevented through taxation or regulation.
3. **Market structure and externalities:** With a harmful externality, a noncompetitive market equilibrium may be closer to the socially optimal level than a competitive equilibrium.
4. **Allocating property rights to reduce externalities:** Clearly assigning property rights allows exchanges that reduce or eliminate externality problems.
5. **Common property:** People overexploit common property when property rights are not clearly defined.
6. **Public goods:** Private markets supply too few public goods (especially pure public goods), and governments have difficulty determining their optimal levels.

18.1 EXTERNALITIES

An **externality** occurs when a person's well-being or a firm's production capability is directly affected by the actions of other consumers or firms rather than indirectly through changes in prices. A firm whose production process lets off fumes that harm its neighbors is creating an externality for which there is no market. In contrast, the firm is not causing an externality when it harms a rival by selling extra output that lowers the market price.

Externalities may either help or harm others. An externality that harms someone is called a *negative externality*. You are harmed if your neighbors keep you awake by screaming at each other late at night. A chemical plant that dumps its waste products into a lake, spoiling the lake's beauty, harms a firm that rents boats for use on that waterway.

A *positive externality* benefits others. By installing attractive shrubs and outdoor sculpture around its plant, a firm provides a positive externality to its neighbors.

A single action may confer positive externalities on some people and negative externalities on others. The smell of pipe smoke pleases some people and annoys others. Some people think that their wind chimes please their neighbors—whereas anyone with an ounce of sense would realize that those chimes make us want to strangle them! An atmospheric scientist reports that cleaning up the air in Los Angeles over the last decade, while helping people to breathe, caused radiation levels to increase $1\frac{1}{2}$ times more rapidly than they would have risen if the air had remained dirty.[1]

[1] According to John Frederick of the University of Chicago as reported in Lundgren, Mark, "Who Said What," *San Francisco Chronicle*, March 23, 1992:C3.

APPLICATION

Michael Jordan's Positive Externalities

Michael Jordan is an employee of the Chicago Bulls, but he raises sales throughout the National Basketball Association (NBA), thus creating positive externalities. Controlling for team records, Hausman and Leonard (1997) showed that Jordan's presence increased ticket revenues at away games throughout the league by $2.5 million during the 1991–1992 regular season. (Jordan didn't affect gate receipts for playoff games because they sell out even without him.) Local television advertising revenues also rose by $2.4 million for these games. These increased ticket and local television advertising receipts reflect a positive externality because they go to the home team rather than to Jordan's employer, the Bulls.

Jordan's presence increased national television advertising by $6.6 million during the regular season and by $13.9 million during the playoffs. Jordan also boosted the earnings of NBA Properties, which licenses NBA paraphernalia such as clothing and videos, by $15.1 million. National television revenues and NBA Properties' earnings are shared equally by all teams, so most of this increase was a positive externality for other teams. All told, the value of Michael Jordan's positive externalities was $40.3 million. ■

18.2 THE INEFFICIENCY OF COMPETITION WITH EXTERNALITIES

I shot an arrow in the air and it stuck.

Competitive firms and consumers do not have to pay for the harms of their negative externalities, so they create excessive amounts. Similarly, because producers are not compensated for the benefits of a positive externality, too little of such externalities are produced.

To illustrate why externalities lead to nonoptimal production, we examine a (hypothetical) competitive market in which firms produce paper and by-products of the production process—such as air and water pollution—that harm people who live near paper mills. We'll call the pollution *gunk*. Each ton of paper that is produced increases the amount of gunk by one unit, and the only way to decrease the volume of gunk is to reduce the amount of paper manufactured. No less polluting technologies are available, and it is not possible to locate plants where the gunk bothers no one.

Paper firms do not have to pay for the harm from the pollution they cause. As a result, each firm's **private cost**—the cost of production only, not including externalities—includes its direct costs of labor, energy, and wood pulp but not the indirect costs of the harm from gunk. The true **social cost** is the private cost plus the cost of the harms from externalities.

Supply-and-Demand Analysis

A supply-and-demand diagram for the paper market, Figure 18.1, illustrates that *a competitive market produces excessive pollution because the firms' private cost is less than their social cost.*[2] In the competitive equilibrium, the firms consider only their private costs in making decisions and ignore the harms of the pollution externality they inflict on others. The market supply curve is the aggregate *private marginal cost* curve, MC^p, which is the horizontal sum of the private marginal cost curves of each of the paper manufacturing plants.

The competitive equilibrium, e_c, is determined by the intersection of the market supply curve and the market demand curve for paper. The competitive equilibrium quantity is $Q_c = 105$ tons per day, and the competitive equilibrium price is $p_c = \$240$ per ton.

The firms' *private producer surplus* is the producer surplus of the paper mills based on their *private marginal cost* curve: the area, $F + G + H$, below the market price and above MC^p up to the competitive equilibrium quantity, 105. The competitive equilibrium maximizes the sum of consumer surplus and private producer surplus (Chapter 9). If there were no externality, the sum of consumer surplus and private producer surplus would equal welfare, so competition would maximize welfare.

Because of the pollution, however, the competitive equilibrium does *not* maximize welfare. Competitive firms produce too much gunk because they do not have to pay for the harm from the gunk. This *market failure* (Chapter 9) results from competitive forces that equalize the price and *private marginal cost* rather than *social marginal cost*, which includes both the private costs of production and the externality damage.

For a given amount of paper production, the full cost of one more ton of paper to society, the *social marginal cost* (MC^s), is the cost of manufacturing one more ton of paper to the paper firms plus the additional externality damage to people in the community from producing this last ton of paper. Thus, the height of the social marginal cost curve, MC^s, at any given quantity equals the vertical sum of the height of the MC^p curve (the private marginal cost of producing another ton of paper) plus the height of the MC^g curve (the marginal externality damage) at that quantity.

[2]Appendix 18A uses algebra to analyze this model and derives the numbers in the figure.

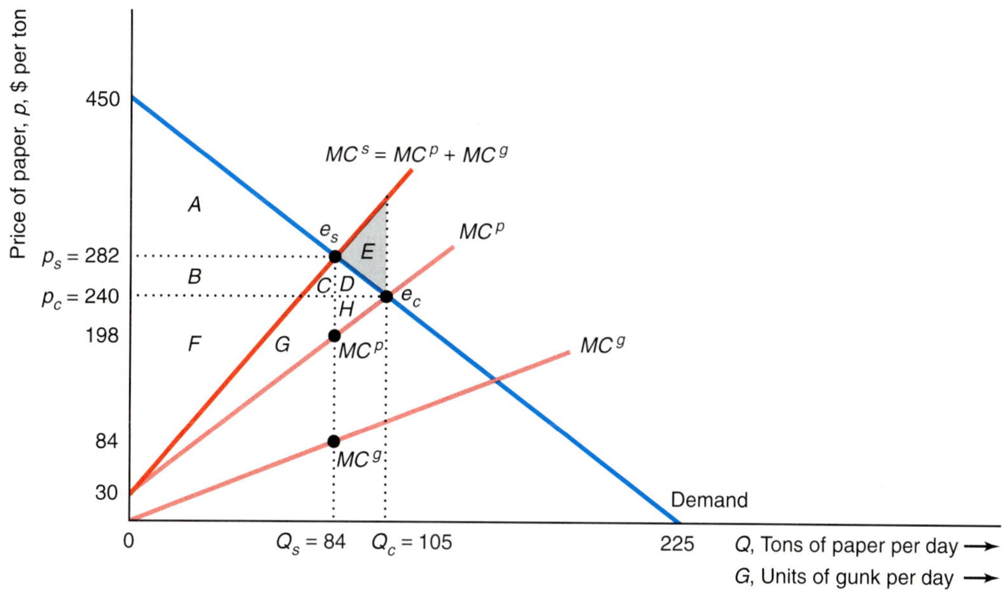

	Social Optimum	Private	Change
Consumer surplus, CS	A	$A + B + C + D$	$B + C + D$
Private producer surplus, PS_p	$B + C + F + G$	$F + G + H$	$H - B - C$
Externality cost, C_g	$C + G$	$C + D + E + G + H$	$D + E + H$
Social producer surplus, $PS_s = PS_p - C_g$	$B + F$	$F - C - D - E$	$-B - C - D - E$
Welfare, $W = CS + PS_s$	$A + B + F$	$A + B + F - E$	$-E = DWL$

Figure 18.1 Welfare Effects of Pollution in a Competitive Market. The competitive equilibrium, e_c, is determined by the intersection of the demand curve and the competitive supply or private marginal cost curve, MC^p, which ignores the cost of pollution. The social optimum, e_s, is at the intersection of the demand curve and the social marginal cost curve, $MC^s = MC^p + MC^g$, where MC^g is the marginal cost of the pollution (gunk). Private producer surplus is based on the MC^p curve, and social producer surplus is based on the MC^s curve.

The social marginal cost curve intersects the demand curve at the socially optimal quantity, $Q_s = 84$. At smaller quantities, the price—the value consumers place on the last unit of the good sold—is higher than the full social marginal cost. There, the gain to consumers of paper exceeds the cost of producing an extra unit of output (and hence an extra unit of gunk). At larger quantities, the price is below the social marginal cost, so the gain to consumers is less than the cost of producing an extra unit.

Welfare is the sum of consumer surplus and *social producer surplus*, which is based on the *social marginal cost* curve rather than the *private marginal cost* curve.

Welfare is maximized where price equals social marginal cost. At the social optimum, e_s, welfare equals $A + B + F$: the area between the demand curve and the MC^s curve up to the optimal quantity, 84 tons of paper.

Welfare at the competitive equilibrium, e_c, is lower: $A + B + F - E$, the areas between the demand curve and the MC^s curve up to 105 tons of paper. The area between these curves from 84 to 105, $-E$, is a deadweight loss because the social cost exceeds the value that consumers place on this last 21 tons of paper. *A deadweight loss results because the competitive market equates price with private marginal cost instead of with social marginal cost.*

Welfare is higher at the social optimum than at the competitive equilibrium because the gain from reducing pollution from the competitive to the socially optimal level more than offsets the loss to consumers and producers of the paper. The cost of the pollution to people who live near the factories is the area under the MC^g curve between zero and the quantity produced. By construction, this area is the same as the area between the MC^p and the MC^s curves. The total damage from the gunk is $-C - D - E - G - H$ at the competitive equilibrium, and only $-C - G$ at the social optimum. Consequently, the extra pollution damage from producing the competitive output rather than the socially optimal quantity is $-D - E - H$.

The main beneficiaries from producing the competitive output level rather than the socially optimal level are the paper buyers who pay $240 rather than $282 for a ton of paper. Their consumer surplus rises from A to $A + B + C + D$. The corresponding change in private producer surplus is $H - B - C$, which is negative in this figure.

The figure illustrates two main results concerning negative externalities. First, *a competitive market produces excessive negative externalities.* Because the price of the pollution to the firms is zero, which is less than the marginal cost that the last unit of pollution imposes on society, an unregulated competitive market produces more pollution than is socially optimal.

Second, *the optimal amount of pollution is greater than zero.* Even though pollution is harmful and we'd like to have none of it, we cannot wipe it out without eliminating virtually all production and consumption. Making paper, dishwashers, and televisions creates air and water pollution. Fertilizers used in farming pollute the water supply. Delivery people pollute the air by driving to your home.

Reducing Externalities. Because competitive markets produce too many negative externalities, government intervention may provide a social gain. Only within the last several decades, however, have any governments regulated pollution.

In developed countries, expenditures on environmental protection as a percentage of gross domestic product (national income) range between one-fifth of a percent to 1%: 0.2% in Italy, 0.4% in Portugal and the United Kingdom, 0.5% in France, 0.6% in the United States and Spain, 0.7% in Sweden, 0.8% in Germany and Switzerland, and 1.0% in Austria, Denmark, and Japan.[3] The world's poorest countries spend little, if anything, on pollution control.

---

[3]United Nations, *Statistical Yearbook*, 1994.

Consequently, emissions relative to economic output are higher in developing countries than in Western nations. China emitted 2,095 metric tons of carbon per million dollars of gross domestic product generated; the former Soviet Union, 1,517; India, 602; and Mexico, 586. In contrast, the United States emitted only 279 metric tons; Great Britain, 216; and Japan, 101.[4]

If a government has sufficient knowledge about pollution damage, the demand curve, costs, and the production technology, it can force a competitive market to produce the social optimum.[5] The government might control pollution directly by restricting the amount of pollution that firms may produce or by taxing them for pollution they create. A governmental limit on the amount of air or water pollution that may be released is called an *emissions standard.* A tax on air pollution is called an *emissions fee*, and a tax on discharges into the air or waterways is an *effluent charge.*

Frequently, however, a government controls pollution indirectly, through quantity restrictions or taxes on outputs or inputs. Whether the government restricts or taxes outputs or inputs may depend on the nature of the production process.

Emissions Standard. We use the paper mill gunk example in Figure 18.1 to illustrate how a government may use an *emissions standard* to reduce pollution. Here, the government can achieve the social optimum by forcing the paper mills to produce no more than 84 units of gunk or paper per day. (Because output and pollution move together in this example, regulating either reduces pollution in the same way.)

Unfortunately, the government usually does not know enough to regulate optimally. For example, to set quantity restrictions on output optimally, the government must know how the marginal social cost curve, the demand for paper curve, and pollution varies with output. The ease with which the government can monitor output and pollution may determine whether it sets an output restriction or a pollution standard.

Even if the government knows enough to set the optimal regulation, it must enforce this regulation to achieve the social optimum. Though the U.S. Environmental Protection Agency (EPA) sets federal smog standards, 33 metropolitan areas—including Baltimore, Boston, Chicago, Houston, Los Angeles, Milwaukee, New York, and Philadelphia—fail to meet these standards.[6]

---

[4]Whitelaw, Kevin, "All the World Is Green on the Outside," *U.S. News & World Report*, 123(14), October 13, 1997:39. Figures are for 1991.

[5]We concentrate on controlling pollution produced by firms, though pollution by consumers may be an even larger problem for the government. For example, between 30% and 70% of the human-made chemicals in the San Francisco Bay come from urban runoff rather than from firms. Petit, Charles, "Regular Folks Are Top Polluters of Waterways, Report Says," *San Francisco Chronicle*, May 22, 1995:A15, A17.

[6]To determine whether your city is on the list, see

http://www.epa.gov/oar/oaqps/greenbk/onc.html.

Emissions Fee. The government may impose costs on polluters by taxing their output or the amount of pollution produced.[7] We use our earlier paper mill example to illustrate the effect of a tax on output.

If the government knows the marginal cost of the gunk, MC^g, it can set the output tax equal to this marginal cost curve: $t(Q) = MC^g$. (We write this tax as $t(Q)$ to show that it varies with output, Q.) Figure 18.2 illustrates the manufacturers' after-tax marginal cost, $MC^s = MC^p + t(Q)$.

The output tax causes a manufacturer to **internalize the externality**: to bear the cost of the harm that one inflicts on others (or to capture the benefit that one provides to others). The after-tax private marginal cost or supply curve is the same as the social marginal cost curve. As a result, the after-tax competitive equilibrium is the social optimum.

Usually, the government sets a specific tax rather than a tax that varies with the amount of pollution, as MC^g does. As Solved Problem 18.1 shows, applying an appropriate specific tax results in the socially optimal level of production.

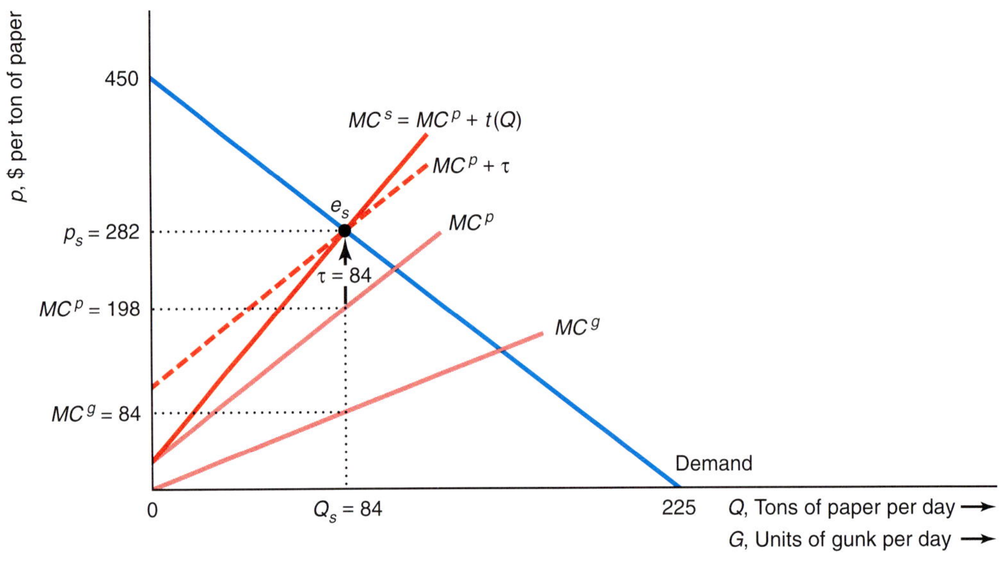

Figure 18.2 Taxes to Control Pollution. Placing a tax on the firms equal to the harm from the gunk, $t(Q) = MC^g$, causes them to internalize the externality, so their private marginal cost is the same as the social marginal cost, MC^s. As a result, the competitive after-tax equilibrium is the same as the social optimum, e_s. Alternatively, applying a specific tax of τ = $84 per unit, which is the marginal harm from the gunk at $Q_s = 84$, also results in the social optimum.

[7]Similarly, a law could make a polluter liable for damages in a court.

SOLVED PROBLEM 18.1

For the market with pollution in Figure 18.1, what constant, specific tax, τ, on output could the government set to maximize welfare?

Answer

Set the specific tax equal to the marginal harm of pollution at the socially optimal quantity: At the socially optimal quantity, $Q_s = 84$, the marginal harm from the gunk is \$84, as Figure 18.2 shows. If the specific tax is $\tau = \$84$, the after-tax private marginal cost (after-tax competitive supply curve), $MC^p + \tau$, equals the social marginal cost at the socially optimal quantity. As a consequence, the after-tax competitive supply curve intersects the demand curve at the socially optimal quantity. By paying this specific tax, the firms internalize the cost of the externality at the social optimum. All that is required for optimal production is that the tax equals the marginal cost of pollution at the optimum quantity; it need not equal the marginal cost of pollution at other quantities. ■

APPLICATION

Taxes on Fuels

Consuming fuels causes pollution. Governments may try to set taxes on fuels so that the people and firms that consume these fuels bear the full social cost, including the harms from pollution. Indeed, one of the reasons that state and federal governments tax fuels is to shift these pollution costs from victims of pollution to consumers of the fuels. (Governments also tax fuels to raise tax revenues—see Chapter 3—and to restrict imports.)

In the United States, before the ban on the use of lead in gasoline, each gallon of gasoline inflicted an estimated 1.08¢ worth of damage from lead, 8.31¢ due to particulates (grit and soot), 1.74¢ from sulfur oxides, 2.14¢ due to ozone, 0.08¢ for reduced visibility, and 2.23¢ as a result of air toxins from motor vehicles (Viscusi 1992). For many fuels, particulate emissions are the most serious problem. The harms from particulates represent 9% of the price of gasoline, 23% of the price of diesel fuel, 11% of the price of aircraft fuel, and 147% of the price of wood. Mortality losses from sulfur oxide are the major harm from heating oil, with damages that are 53% of price. Damages from coal amount to 464% of price.

Table 18.1 shows the marginal cost of pollution from one more unit of fuel as a percentage of the price of that unit and the current tax as a percent of

Table 18.1 Energy Externality Costs and Taxes

	Externality Cost as Percent of Price	Current Tax as a Percent of Price
Natural gas	1.1	6.4
Aircraft fuel	12.9	15.5
Gasoline	16.7	16.6
Diesel fuel	50.4	12.9
Heating oils	63.7	14.6
Wood	152.4	0
Coal	528.0	35.9

Note: These data are for 1986. Tax revenues that are returned as subsidies to the use of that form of energy, such as the Highway Trust Fund, are excluded in the tax calculations.

Source: Viscusi, W. Kip, and Wesley A. Magat, "Interim Draft Report on Efficient Energy Pricing," EPA Project on Economic Research for Long-Term Environmental Risks and Pollution Prevention, April 17, 1992, as reported in Viscusi (1992).

price.[8] If the tax is a lower percentage than the externality cost, too much pollution is produced. If the tax is a higher percentage, too little fuel is used. Thus, if these estimates are correct, the tax on gasoline roughly equals the marginal harm from pollution,[9] the taxes on natural gas and aircraft fuel are too high, and the taxes on other fuels—particularly coal—are far too low. Indeed, wood is not taxed at all. ■

Cost–Benefit Analysis

We've used a supply-and-demand analysis to show that *a competitive market produces too much pollution because the price of output equals the marginal private cost rather than the marginal social cost.* By using a cost–benefit analysis, we obtain another interpretation of the pollution problem in terms of the marginal cost and benefit of the pollution itself.

[8]These estimates of the harm from pollution are midpoints of estimated ranges. Estimates of the harm from gasoline vary from 3% to 31% of its price. The range of the estimates for coal is even greater, between 21% and 1,035% of price.

[9]Gasoline taxes are not the most efficient way to control auto-related air pollution. Old, ill-maintained cars, which are 10% of all automobiles, cause half the pollution from cars. Removing them from the road would be more cost effective than a gas tax that falls on both heavy and light polluters. Another option, which California is using, is to reformulate the gasoline so that it burns cleaner, at an additional cost of 5 to 15¢ a gallon. A California governmental agency claims that the new gas reduces pollution by an amount equivalent to that from taking 3.5 million of the state's 24 million cars off the road. Barnum, Alex, "Potent Smog Fighter—Cleaner Gas," *San Francisco Chronicle*, February 15, 1996:A1, A15.

In the cost–benefit diagram, panel a of Figure 18.3 (which corresponds to Figure 18.1), the quantity on the horizontal axis starts at the competitive level, 105 tons, and *decreases to the right* (in contrast to the pattern in most of our diagrams). Thus, a movement to the right indicates a reduction in paper and gunk, possibly due to a pollution-abatement policy. Again, welfare peaks at the socially optimal quantity of output or gunk of 84 tons per day.

The benefit of reducing output is the reduced damage from gunk. The height of the benefit curve at a given quantity is the difference between the pollution harm at that quantity and the harm at the competitive quantity.

The cost of reducing output is that the consumer surplus and private producer surplus fall. The height of the cost curve at a given quantity is the sum of consumer surplus and private producer surplus at that quantity minus the corresponding value at the competitive quantity.

If society reduced output to 63 tons, the quantity at which the total benefit equals the total cost, society would be no better off than it is in the competitive equilibrium. To maximize welfare, we want to set output at 84 tons, the quantity for which the gap between the total benefit and total cost is greatest. At that quantity, the slope of the benefit curve, the marginal benefit, MB, equals the slope of the cost curve, the marginal cost, MC, as panel b of the figure shows.[10] Thus, *welfare is maximized by reducing output and pollution until the marginal benefit from less pollution equals the marginal cost of less output.*

APPLICATION

Emissions Standard for Ozone

Ozone, a major pollutant, is formed in the atmosphere through a chemical reaction between reactive organic gases and nitrogen oxides in sunlight. The Clean Air Act of 1990, which sets national air-quality standards for major pollutants, mandates that atmospheric ozone levels not rise above 0.12 parts per million (ppm). The California Air Resources Board (CARB) has established an even tighter standard, 0.09 ppm.

The chief costs of reducing ozone are greater expenses of manufacturing and of driving. The main benefits are improved health and increased agricultural production.[11] The health benefits of reducing ozone are greatest in highly

---

[10]This marginal cost curve, MC, reflects the social cost of removing the last unit of paper (gunk), whereas the social marginal cost curve, MC^s, in Figure 18.1 captures the extra cost to society from the last unit of paper (or gunk).

[11]Setting values for health benefits is particularly difficult. Epidemiological studies find a relationship between ozone concentrations and respiratory problems. Using surveys, economists ascertain individuals' willingness to pay to avoid these respiratory aliments. By combining these two types of information, researchers estimate the monetary value of reducing ozone to avoid respiratory trouble.

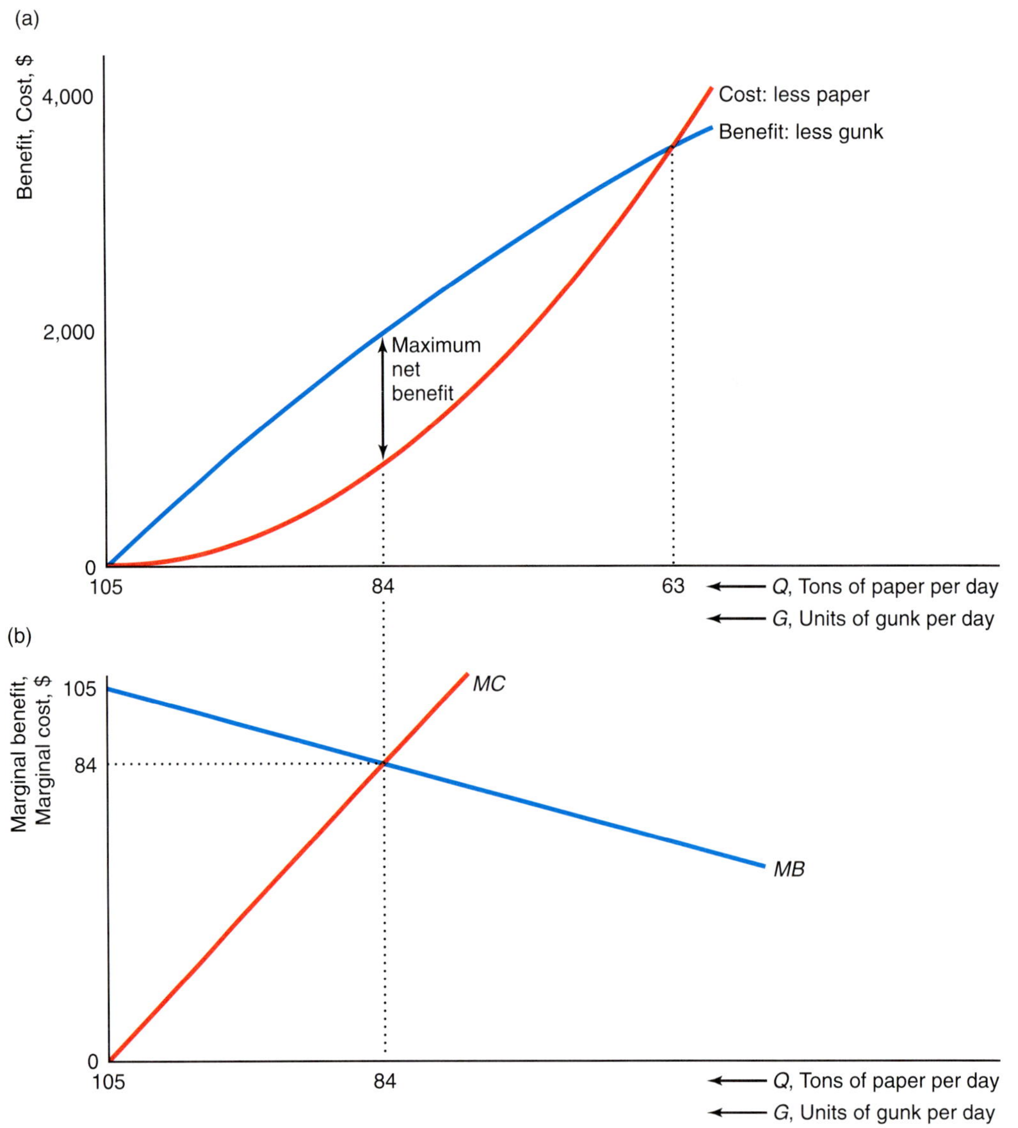

Figure 18.3 Cost-Benefit Analysis of Pollution. (a) The benefit curve reflects the reduction in harm from pollution as the amount of gunk falls from the competitive level. The cost of reducing the amount of gunk is the fall in output, which reduces consumer surplus and private producer surplus. Welfare is maximized at 84 tons of paper and 84 units of gunk, the quantities at which the difference between the benefit and cost curves, the net benefit, is greatest. (b) The net benefit is maximized where the marginal benefit, *MB*, which is the slope of the benefit curve, equals the marginal cost, *MC*, the slope of the cost curve.

populated areas, while the benefits of expanded agricultural yields occur in rural areas. Consequently, the optimal level of ozone differs in urban and agricultural areas.

The benefits of reducing the ozone level have outweighed the costs in Los Angeles over the last several decades. However, the new California standards may be too strict even in Los Angeles, which still has the worst air pollution problem in the country. Krupnick and Portney (1991) estimate that further reducing the ozone concentration in Los Angeles to the California standard has an annual benefit to human health and materials of about $4 billion, which is much less than the annual cost of about $13 billion.

Although the California standard appears to be too strict for an urban area such as Los Angeles, is it appropriate in an agricultural region? Ozone substantially damages crops. Crop losses due to high ozone levels range from 8.4% for alfalfa hay to 32% for oranges, according to the CARB. The CARB claims that production yields fall for ozone-sensitive crops such as beans, cotton, grapes, lemons, and oranges even at ozone levels as low as 0.09 ppm.

Kim, Helfand, and Howitt (1995) compare the benefits and costs of reducing ozone in the San Joaquin Valley, which produces 60% of California crops and 9% of total U.S. crops in terms of value. The San Joaquin Valley has the second-worst air quality in California, trailing only Los Angeles. The pollution in many San Joaquin Valley counties regularly exceeds both state and national standards. For example, in Kern County, the highest recorded ozone level in 1990 was 0.17 ppm, the 0.09 ppm state standard was surpassed on 120 days that year, and the 0.12 ppm national standard was exceeded on 37 days.

Kim, Helfand, and Howitt estimate that the health benefits from meeting California's 0.09 ppm standard range from $2.58 million to $51.58 million. Achieving the state standard would increase agricultural production, raising consumer surplus by $229 million to $270 million and producer surplus by $297 million to $348 million.

Panel a of Figure 18.4 shows Kim, Helfand, and Howitt's most conservative benefit estimates and their highest cost estimates from reducing ozone concentration levels. Panel b illustrates the corresponding marginal costs and benefits. Welfare is maximized at a concentration level slightly below 0.14 ppm, at which the gap between the benefit and cost curves in panel a is greatest and the marginal benefit equals the marginal cost in panel b.

Thus, given these conservative estimates, the state standards are too stringent in this agricultural area. According to the researchers' most likely (as opposed to most conservative) estimates, the federal standards are nearly optimal for this region. Even by these conservative estimates, however, society would benefit from substantially reducing ozone below current levels in many areas of the San Joaquin Valley. ■

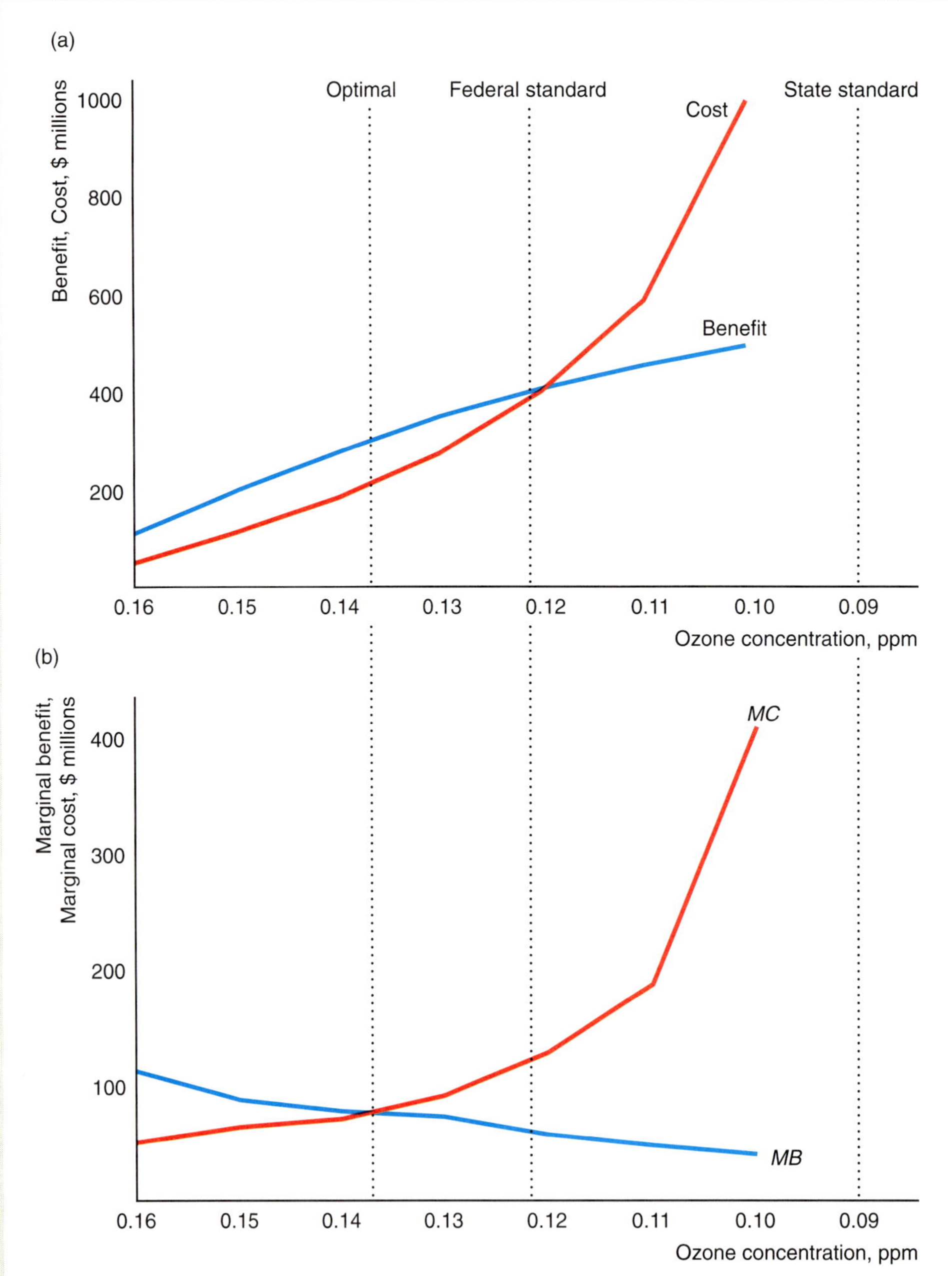

Figure 18.4 Ozone. (a) Welfare in the San Joaquin Valley is maximized at the ozone concentration level at which the gap between the benefit and cost curves is greatest. (b) Welfare is maximized at the ozone concentration level at which the marginal benefit equals the marginal cost. This figure is based on the most conservative (lowest benefit and highest cost) estimates from Kim, Helfand, and Howitt (1995).

18.3 MARKET STRUCTURE AND EXTERNALITIES

Two of our main results concerning competitive markets and negative externalities—that too much pollution is produced and that a tax equal to the marginal social cost of the externality solves the problem—do not hold for other market structures. Although a competitive market always produces too many negative externalities, a noncompetitive market may produce more or less than the optimal level of output and pollution. If a tax is set so that firms internalize the externalities, a competitive market produces the social optimum, whereas a noncompetitive market does not.

Monopoly and Externalities

We use the paper–gunk example to illustrate these results. In Figure 18.5, the monopoly equilibrium, e_m, is determined by the intersection of the marginal revenue, MR, and private marginal cost, MC^p, curves. Like the competitive firms, the monopoly ignores the harm its pollution causes, so it considers just its direct, private costs in making decisions.

Output is only 70 tons in the monopoly equilibrium, e_m, which is less than the 84 tons at the social optimum, e_s. Thus, this figure illustrates that *the monopoly outcome may be less than the social optimum even with an externality.*

Although the competitive market with an externality always produces more output than the social optimum, a monopoly may produce more than, the same as, or less than the social optimum. The reason that a monopoly may produce too little or too much is that it faces two offsetting effects. The monopoly tends to produce too little output because it sets its price above its marginal cost. But the monopoly tends to produce too much output because its decisions depend on its private marginal cost instead of the social marginal cost.

Which effect dominates depends on the elasticity of demand for the output and on the extent of the marginal damage the pollution causes. If the demand curve is very elastic, the monopoly markup is small. As a result, the monopoly equilibrium is close to the competitive equilibrium, e_c, and greater than the social optimum, e_s. If extra pollution causes little additional harm—MC^g is close to zero at the equilibrium—the social marginal cost essentially equals the private marginal cost, and the monopoly produces less than the social optimum.

Monopoly Versus Competitive Welfare with Externalities

In the absence of externalities, welfare is greater under competition than under monopoly (Chapter 11). With an externality, however, welfare may be greater with monopoly than with competition.

If both monopoly and competitive outputs are greater than the social optimum, welfare must be greater under monopoly because the competitive output is larger than the monopoly output. If the monopoly produces less than the social optimum, we need to check which distortion is greater: the monopoly's producing too little or the competitive market's producing too much.

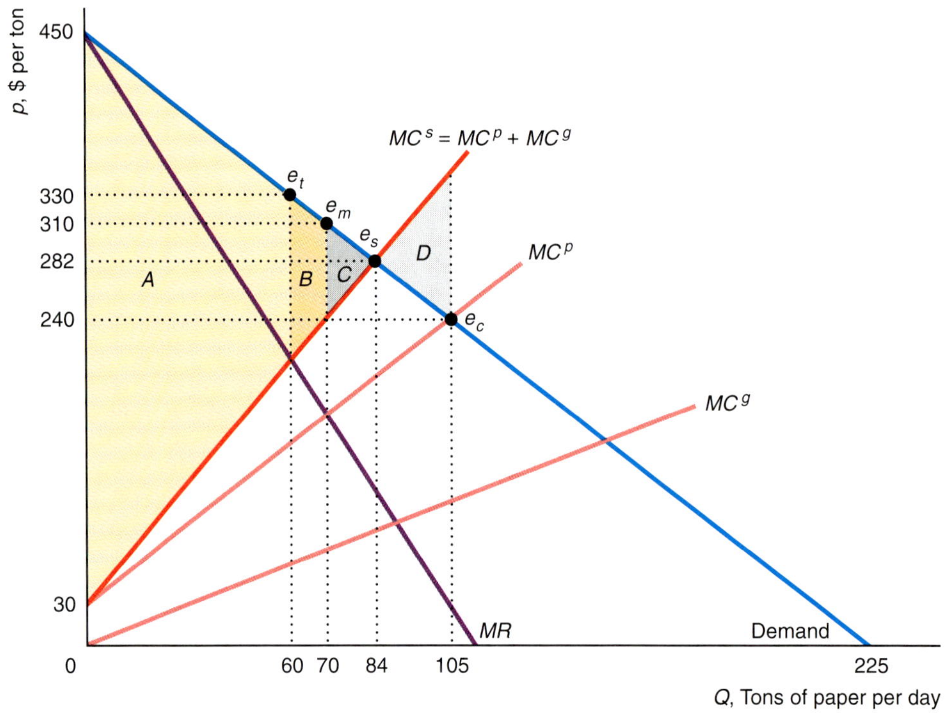

Figure 18.5 Monopoly, Competition, and Social Optimum with Pollution. At the competitive equilibrium, e_c, more is produced than at the social optimum, e_c. As a result, the deadweight loss in the competitive market is *D*. The monopoly equilibrium, e_m, is determined by the intersection of the marginal revenue and the private marginal cost, MC^p, curves. The social welfare (based on the marginal social cost, MC^s, curve) under monopoly is $A + B$. Here, the deadweight loss of monopoly, *C*, is less than the deadweight loss under competition, *D*.

Welfare is lower at monopoly equilibrium, areas $A + B$, than at the social optimum, $A + B + C$, in Figure 18.5.[12] The deadweight loss of monopoly, $-C$, results from the monopoly's producing less output than is socially optimal.

In the figure, the deadweight loss from monopoly, $-C$, is less than the deadweight loss from competition, $-D$, so welfare is greater under monopoly. The monopoly produces only slightly too little output, whereas competition produces excessive output—and hence far too much gunk.

[12]In this figure, we show only the welfare areas that we need to make our major points. Chapter 11 provides a full welfare analysis for a monopoly.

SOLVED PROBLEM 18.2

In Figure 18.5, what is the effect on output, price, and welfare of taxing the monopoly an amount equal to the marginal harm of the externality?

Answer

1. *Show how the monopoly equilibrium shifts if the firm is taxed*: A tax equal to the marginal cost of the pollution causes the monopoly to internalize the externality and to view the social marginal cost as its private cost. The intersection of the marginal revenue, *MR*, curve and the social marginal cost, MC^s, curve determines the taxed-monopoly equilibrium, e_t. The tax causes the equilibrium quantity to fall from 70 to 60 and the equilibrium price to rise from \$310 to \$330.
2. *Determine how this shift affects the deadweight loss of monopoly*: The sum of consumer and producer surplus is only *A* after the tax, compared to $A + B$ before the tax. Thus, welfare falls. The difference between *A* and welfare at the social optimum, $A + B + C$, is $-(B + C)$, which is the deadweight loss from the taxed monopoly. The tax exacerbates the monopoly's tendency to produce too little output. The deadweight loss increases from $-C$ to $-C - D$. The monopoly produced too little before the tax. The taxed monopoly produces even less. ■

Taxing Externalities in Noncompetitive Markets

Many people recommend that the government tax firms an amount equal to the marginal harm of pollution on the grounds that such a tax achieves the social optimum in a competitive market. Solved Problem 18.2 shows that such a tax may lower welfare if applied to a monopoly.[13]

If the government has enough information to determine the social optimum, it can force either a monopolized or a competitive market to produce it. If the social optimum is greater than the unregulated monopoly output, however, the government has to subsidize (rather than tax) the monopoly to get it to produce as much output as is desired.

In short, trying to solve a negative externality problem is more complex in a noncompetitive market than in a competitive market. To achieve a social optimum in a competitive market, the government only has to reduce the externality, possibly by decreasing output. In a noncompetitive market, the government must eliminate

[13]The tax definitely lowers welfare if the untaxed monopoly was producing less than the social optimum. If the untaxed monopoly was originally producing more than the social optimum, a tax may cause welfare to increase.

problems arising from both externalities *and* the exercise of market power. Thus, the government needs more information to regulate a noncompetitive market optimally and may also require more tools, such as a subsidy. To the degree that the problems arising from market power and pollution are offsetting, however, the failure to regulate a noncompetitive market is less harmful than the failure to regulate a competitive market.

18.4 ALLOCATING PROPERTY RIGHTS TO REDUCE EXTERNALITIES

Instead of controlling externalities directly through emissions fees and emissions standards, the government may take an indirect approach by assigning a **property right**: an exclusive privilege to use an asset. By owning this textbook, you have a property right to read it and to stop others from reading or taking it.

If no one holds a property right for a good or a bad, the good or bad is unlikely to have a price. If you had a property right that assured you of the right to be free from noise pollution, you could get the courts to stop your neighbor from playing loud music. Or you could sell your right, permitting your neighbor to play the music. If you did not have this property right, no one would be willing to pay you a positive price for it.

In earlier chapters, we implicitly assumed that property rights were clearly defined and that no harmful by-products were created, so externalities did not arise. In those chapters, all goods had prices.

For many bads, such as pollution, and for some goods, property rights are not clearly defined. No one has exclusive property rights to the air we breathe. Because of this lack of a price, a polluter's private marginal cost of production is less than the full social marginal cost.

Coase Theorem

According to the *Coase Theorem* (Coase 1960), the optimal levels of pollution and output can result from bargaining between polluters and their victims if property rights are clearly defined.[14] Coase's contribution is not so much a practical solution to the pollution problem as a demonstration that a lack of clearly defined property rights is the root of the externality problem.

To illustrate the Coase Theorem, we consider two firms, a chemical plant and a boat rental company, that share a small lake. The chemical manufacturer dumps its waste by-products, which smell bad but are otherwise harmless, into the lake. The chemical company can reduce pollution only by restricting its output; it has no other outlet for this waste. The resulting pollution damages the boat rental firm's business.

[14]See Libecap (1989) for a discussion of how property rights are assigned through contracting and other means.

There are other lakes nearby where people can rent boats. Therefore, because they dislike the smell of the chemicals, people rent from this firm only if it charges a low enough price to compensate them fully for the smell.

No Property Rights. These two firms won't negotiate with each other unless property rights are clearly defined. After all, why should the manufacturer reduce its pollution if the boat rental firm has no legal right to clean water? Why should the boat rental firm pay the chemical company not to pollute if the courts may declare that the rental company has a right to be free from pollution?

If the firms do not negotiate, the chemical firm produces the output level that maximizes its profit, ignoring the effect on the boat rental firm. The profit matrix in panel a of Table 18.2 shows that the chemical firm makes \$0 if it produces nothing, \$10 if it produces 1 ton, and \$15 if it produces 2 tons regardless of what the boat rental firm does. Thus, the chemical company has a dominant strategy: It produces 2 tons. Knowing that the chemical company will produce 2 tons, the boat rental firm maximizes its profit with 1 boat.

Because nobody else is directly affected by this pollution, we call an outcome *efficient* if it maximizes the sum of the profits of the two firms.[15] The firms maximize their joint profits at \$20 when the chemical company produces 1 ton and the boat rental firm rents 1 boat. Thus, the no-property-rights equilibrium, with joint profits of \$17, is inefficient: Too much pollution is produced.

Property Right to Be Free of Pollution. If a court or the government grants the boat rental firm the property right to be free of pollution, the firm can prevent the chemical company from dumping at all. With no pollution, the boat company rents 2 boats and makes \$15. Rather than shut down, the chemical company offers to pay the boat company for the right to dump. The boat rental firm is willing to permit dumping only if it makes at least \$15, and it may hold out for more. The largest "bribe" the chemical company is willing to offer for the right to dump is one that leaves it with a positive profit. Panel b of Table 18.2 shows one possible compensation agreement: The chemical company offers the boat rental firm \$7 per ton for the right to dump. If the firms agree to this deal, the chemical company's dominant strategy is to produce 1 ton, so the boat rental firm chooses to rent 1 boat. Both firms benefit. Indeed, in this equilibrium, their joint profits are maximized at \$20.

In general, the chemical firm pays the boat rental firm between \$5 and \$10. The boat rental firm wants at least \$5 so that its profit when both produce one unit is at least \$15—the amount that it makes with no pollution. Any payment larger than \$10 would leave the chemical company with a negative profit, so that's the most it is willing to pay. The exact payment outcome depends on the firms' bargaining skills. Because both parties benefit from a deal, they should be able to reach an agreement if transaction costs are low enough that it pays to negotiate.

---

[15]Because people who want to rent boats pay sufficiently less as compensation for putting up with the chemicals, they are not harmed by the pollution. Only the boat rental firm is harmed through lower prices.

Table 18.2 Property Rights and Bargaining

a) No Property Rights

Chemical Firm: Tons per Day	Boat Rental Firm: Boats Rented per Day 0	1	2
0	$0, $0	$0, $14	$0, $15
1	$10, $0	$10, $10	$10, $5
2	$15, $0	**$15**, **$2**	$15, –$3

b) Boat Rental Firm Has Property Right: Chemical company pays the boat rental firm $7 per ton for the right to dump

Chemical Firm: Tons per Day	Boat Rental Firm: Boats Rented per Day 0	1	2
0	$0, $0	$0, $14	$0, $15
1	$3, $7	**$3**, **$17**	$3, $12
2	$1, $14	$1, $16	$1, $11

c) Chemical Company Has Property Right: Boat rental firm pays the chemical company $6 for each ton by which it reduces its production below 2 tons

Chemical Firm: Tons per Day	Boat Rental Firm: Boats Rented per Day 0	1	2
0	$12, –$12	$12, $2	$12, $3
1	$16, –$6	**$16**, **$4**	$16, –$1
2	$15, $0	$15, $2	$15, –$3

Property Right to Pollute. Now suppose that the chemical company has the property right to dump in the lake.[16] Unless the boat rental company pays the chemical company not to pollute, the chemical company produces 2 tons, as in panel a of the table. The boat rental firm may bribe the chemical company to reduce its output so that both firms benefit. Again, the exact deal that is struck depends on their bargaining skills.

Panel c shows what happens if the boat rental firm pays the chemical company \$6 per ton for each ton less than 2 that it produces. The chemical company's dominant strategy is to produce 1 ton, and the boat rental firm rents 1 boat. The equilibrium is efficient as in the previous case. Now, however, the boat rental firm compensates the chemical company rather than the other way around.

To summarize the results from the Coase Theorem:

- If there are no impediments to bargaining, *assigning property rights results in the efficient outcome* at which joint profits are maximized.
- *Efficiency is achieved regardless of who receives the property rights.*
- Who gets the property rights affects the income distribution. *The property rights are valuable.* The party with the property rights may be compensated by the other party.

Problems with the Coase Approach. To achieve the efficient outcome, the two sides must bargain successfully with each other. However, the parties may not be able to bargain successfully for at least three important reasons (Polinsky 1979).

First, if transaction costs are very high, it might not pay for the two sides to meet. For example, if a manufacturing plant pollutes the air, thousands or even millions of people may be affected. The cost of getting them all together to bargain is prohibitive.

Second, if firms engage in strategic bargaining behavior, an agreement may not be reached. For instance, if one party says, "Give me everything I want" and will not budge, reaching an agreement may be impossible.

Third, if either side lacks information about the costs or benefits of reducing pollution, a nonefficient outcome may occur. It is difficult to know how much to offer the other party and to reach an agreement if you do not know how the polluting activity affects the other party.

For these reasons, Coasian bargaining is likely to occur in relatively few situations. Where bargaining cannot occur, the allocation of property rights affects the amount of pollution.

Markets for Pollution

If high transaction costs preclude bargaining, we may be able to overcome this problem by using a market, which facilitates exchanges between individuals. Starting in the early 1980s, governments experimented with issuing permits to pollute that could be exchanged in a market, often by means of an auction. Today,

[16]For example, a firm gains the right to pollute by paying a pollution tax.

many firms can buy the right to pollute—much as sinners bought indulgences in the Middle Ages.

Under this system, the government gives firms permits, each of which provides a firm with the property right to create a certain amount of pollution. Each firm may use its permits or sell them to another firm.

Firms whose products are worth a lot relative to the harm from pollution they create buy rights from other firms that have less valuable products. Suppose that the cost in terms of forgone output from eliminating each ton of pollution is $200 at one plant and $300 at another. If the government tells both plants to reduce pollution by 1 ton, the total cost is $500. With tradable permits, the first plant can reduce its pollution by 2 tons and sell its allowance to the second plant, so the total social cost is only $400. The trading maximizes the value of the output for a given amount of pollution damage, thus increasing efficiency.

If the government knew enough, it could assign the optimal amount of pollution to each firm, and no trading would be necessary. When it uses a market, the government does not have to collect this type of detailed information to achieve efficiency. Its only decision concerns what total amount of pollution to allow.

APPLICATION

Sulfur Dioxide Market

The Clean Air Act of 1990 created a market for sulfur dioxide pollution generated by power plants.[17] The program starts by setting emissions standards. The EPA issues permits, each of which allows a firm to produce 1 ton of emissions of sulfur dioxide annually. Initially, the 110 dirtiest coal-firing power plants in the United States received permits in proportion to the amount of fuel they used in 1985–1987. By the year 2000, all power plants—about another 800—will be in the program.

A firm producing more pollution than is permitted is fined $2,000 per ton of emissions above its allowance. But at the end of a year, if a company's emissions are less than its allowance, it may sell the remaining allowance to another firm, thus providing an incentive to reduce emissions. Permits are traded through the Chicago Board of Trade. The EPA holds an annual spot auction for permits that may be used in the current year and an advance auction for permits that will be effective in seven years.

Not just firms may buy the permits. Environmental groups may purchase and destroy them, thereby reducing pollution. In 1995, law students at several

[17]Sources for this discussion of the Clean Air Act are Burtraw (1996); Passell, Peter, "For Utilities, New Clean-Air Plan," *New York Times*, November 18, 1994:C1, C6; Wald, Matthew L., "Acid-Rain Pollution Credits Are Not Enticing Utilities," *New York Times*, June 5, 1995:C11; and Passell, Peter, "Economic Scene," *New York Times*, January 4, 1996:C2.

schools bid against corporate giants for pollution rights on the Chicago Board of Trade. They spent $3,256 on 18 of the 176,400 allowances (each for a ton of sulfur dioxide) auctioned, which they'll let expire unused. Similarly, Northeast Utilities and Niagara Mohawk Power donated some of their extra permits to the American Lung Association and an environmental group—thus preventing any other polluter from using them—to get a tax deduction equal to the permits' market value.

When the program first went into effect, annual emissions of sulfur dioxide fell by nearly 50%, at a cost between one-half and one-third that of the traditional standards approach.[18] The EPA estimates that trading saved utility rate payers $400 million to $600 million a year as of 1994. The U.S. Government Accounting Office projects that the cost of reducing sulfur dioxide emissions by 2001 with this method will be only $2.5 billion annually, compared to $7 billion if every utility had been required to install scrubbers or $4.3 billion if uniform emission rates had been applied to individual power plants. Canada, Mexico, and several European countries either have or are planning pollution markets. During international negotiations in 1997, the United States pushed hard (but unsuccessfully) for the international trading of pollution rights. ■

18.5 COMMON PROPERTY

So far, we've examined externalities that arise as an undesired by-product of a production or consumption activity. Another important externality arises with **common property**: resources to which everyone has free access. Unlike private property, for which the owner can *exclude* others from using the property, common property is not subject to such exclusion. For example, anyone can freely enter and enjoy urban parks such as Central Park in New York, Hyde Park in London, and the Boston Common.

Overuse of Common Property

Because people do not have to pay to use common property resources, they are overused. Parks with free entry often become crowded, an outcome that reduces everyone's enjoyment. Similarly, in less developed economies, the sharing of public lands for hunting, grazing, or growing crops results in the overuse of common

---

[18]The market has been less active and prices lower than expected, however. In the first trades in 1992, a 1-ton allowance sold for $250. The price fell each year thereafter. In early 1995, the price averaged $170 per ton, but it slumped to the low $100s by the end of the year. Two of the main reasons are the plunging price for low-sulfur coal and the introduction of new technologies, both of which made compliance with standards much easier than expected for power plants in some parts of the country. Another reason for not trading permits may be that utilities fear the reactions of other regulators that control the prices they set for power if they buy permits rather than installing pollution-control devices.

property. Other examples of common property problems involve common pools, the Internet, roads, and fisheries.

Common Pools. Petroleum, water, and other fluids and gases are often extracted from a common pool. Owners of wells drawing from a common pool compete to remove the substance most rapidly, thereby gaining ownership of the good. This competition creates an externality by lowering fluid pressure, which makes further pumping more difficult. Iraq justified its invasion of Kuwait, which led to the Gulf War in 1991, on the grounds that Kuwait was overexploiting common pools of oil underlying both countries.

The Internet. An important problem—one that may be inconveniencing you—is overcrowding on the Internet. Most users connect to the Internet for a flat fee that does not vary with the number of hours of use. Thus, the marginal cost for an extra minute of use (users' time aside) is zero. As a result, serious congestion occurs due to excessive use.[19] Often, gridlock prevents people from accessing Web pages—or at least slows use down to a crawl. Building greater capacity is not an efficient solution because Internet use is likely to continue to grow as long as marginal access is free. Until fees for marginal use are imposed, congestion is likely to persist.

Roads. If you own a car, you have a property right to drive that car. On the other hand, because you lack a property right to the highway on which you drive, you cannot exclude others from driving on the highway and must share it with them. Each driver, however, claims a temporary property right in a portion of the highway by occupying it (thereby preventing others from occupying the same space). Competition for space on the highway leads to congestion (a negative externality), which slows up every driver.

Fisheries. Many fisheries have common access such that anyone can fish and no one has a property right to a fish until it is caught. Each fisher wants to land a fish before others do to gain the property right to that fish. The lack of clearly defined property rights leads to overfishing. Fishers have an incentive to catch more fish than they would if the fishery were private property.

Suppose that each fisher owns a private lake. Because the property rights are clearly defined, there is no externality. Each owner is careful not to overfish in any one year so as to maintain the stock (or number) of fish in future years.[20]

In contrast, most ocean fisheries are common property. As with polluting manufacturers, ocean fishers look only at their private costs. In calculating these costs, fishers include the cost of boats, other equipment, a crew, and supplies. They do not include the cost that they impose on future generations by decreasing the stock of

---

[19]In February 1998, America Online, an Internet access provider, reported that average usage among its subscribers had tripled during the past year (to 23 hours a month) after it switched from metered rates to a flat rate for connection. (Swartz, Jon, "Is This the End of the Internet's Flat-Rate Buffet?" *San Francisco Chronicle*, February 12, 1998:B1, B6.)

[20]No: A stock of fish is not the same as a fish stock.

fish today, which reduces the number of fish in the sea next year. The fewer fish there are, the harder it is to catch any, so reducing the population today raises the cost of catching fish in the future. As a result, fishers do not forgo fishing now to leave fish for the future. The social cost is the private cost plus the externality cost from reduced future populations of fish.

APPLICATION

Extensive Overfishing

The tendency to overfish has diminished many fish populations dramatically because the rate at which fish are born has been lower than the rate at which they have been caught. According to the U.S. National Marine Fisheries Service in 1997, one-third of the 279 species in federal waters are overfished to the degree that their existence is threatened.[21] Endangered species include the Pacific salmon, bluefin tuna, and American lobster. The catch of Atlantic cod fell from about four million tons in the mid-1960s to about one million tons today due to overfishing.[22]

If the fishers overfish enough, they drive the fish population to extinction. Overfishing had gotten so severe by 1998 that the U.S. Secretary of Commerce slashed allowable catches of major Pacific Coast ocean fish (including black cod, ocean perch, lingcod, dover sole, and various rockfish) by as much as 65% to save these species.[23] The National Marine Fisheries Service estimates that overfishing of cod, haddock, and flounder there had already cost the economy $350 million a year in reduced catch because of the drop in the stock of fish. In 1998, federal officials imposed drastically lower catch limits on 83 Pacific species to help rebuild stocks, slashing some catches by 65%.

Unfortunately, many governments are exacerbating the problem rather than acting to solve it. The U.N. Food and Agriculture Organization estimates that the global fishing fleet cost $92 billion to operate in 1989 yet brought in only $70 billion in revenues.[24] The difference was made up by government subsidies to fishers and boat builders. The European Union, for instance, has annual subsidies of about $580 million. The Japanese government has extended $19 billion in credit to its fishing industry, much of which won't be paid back. ■

---

[21]"One-Third of Valuable U.S. Fish Species Depleted," *San Francisco Chronicle*, October 7, 1997:A5.

[22]"The Economics of the Sea," *The Economist*, 334(7906), March 18, 1995:48.

[23]Clifford, Frank, "Fishing Limits on Key Species Take Effect," *Los Angeles Times*, January 1, 1998:A29.

[24]Swardson, Anne, "Once Bountiful, the Seas Slowly Empty," *San Francisco Chronicle*, October 3, 1994:A10, A12.

Solving the Commons Problem

There are two approaches to ameliorating the commons problem. The first is direct government regulation through either taxation or restriction of access. The second is by clearly defining property rights.

Government Regulation of Commons. Overuse of a common resource occurs because individuals do not bear the full social cost. However, by applying a tax or fee equal to the externality harm that each individual imposes on others, a government forces each person to internalize the externality. For example, governments often charge an entrance fee to a park or a museum. However, if a government sets a tax or fee that is less than the marginal externality harm, it reduces but does not eliminate the externality problem.

Alternatively, the government can restrict access to the commons. One typical approach is to grant access on a first-come-first-served basis. With quotas, people who arrive early gain access. In contrast, with taxes or fees, people who most heavily value the resource or who are wealthier gain access.

APPLICATION

For Whom the Bridge Tolls

If anyone can drive across it, a bridge is a common property. Excessive use of a bridge leads to congestion.

The most congested bridge in the United States is the 8.5-mile Bay Bridge, which connects Oakland and Berkeley, California, to San Francisco.[25] Of the 275,000 vehicles that drive across the bridge in a day, 100,000 cross it westbound during the morning peak commuting hours, 6 to 10 A.M. The bridge can handle only about 10,000 commuters per hour in one direction without congestion.

The resulting extensive traffic jam during the morning commute is costly in terms of time, money, and pollution. Drivers frequently wait 20 minutes or more just to get on the bridge. More time is spent crawling across the bridge at low speed. Gasoline is wasted, and tailpipe pollution is 250% greater under these congested conditions than when cars drive at the speed limit.

From 1980 through 1997, a $1 toll was collected at all hours in only the westbound direction. Imposing a higher toll to cross the bridge during rush hour would reduce congestion by "tolling" some current drivers. Rather than drive across the bridge, these people would switch to car pools (three or more

---

[25]This section is based on Geoghegan (1995); Geoghegan, Kanninen, and Mohn (1996); Brazil, Eric, "$3 Bay Bridge Toll Faces Rough Ride," *San Francisco Examiner*, November 20, 1994:A1, A12; and Nolte, Carl, "Bay Bridge—All Grit, No Glory," *San Francisco Chronicle*, November 11, 1996:A1, A13.

people in a car may cross in a special lane and thus avoid a toll) or to public transit or would not cross at all.

What toll would maximize efficiency by optimally trading off the harm to some travelers versus the gain to other commuters and the reduced pollution? Economists used models employing survey and engineering data to calculate that the optimal peak-hour toll is \$3.60. Compared to no toll, the optimal toll would save commuters 20.6 minutes per day by decreasing trips by vehicles with one or two occupants by 9.5%. The benefit from time savings to people who continue to drive minus the loss to people who take other modes of travel is estimated at \$55,000 per day. There are additional savings from reduced pollution.

Why have authorities been reluctant to charge a higher toll during peak commuting hours? One explanation is that the travel-time gains from a steeper toll go to those who place a high value on their time and continue to drive across the bridge. But higher tolls harm poorer people, some of whom are discouraged from driving and others of whom continue to drive but value the time savings less than the toll increase. Although the gain to the wealthy is substantially larger than the loss to the poor, no transfer payments from one group to the other are likely. Politicians have hesitated to help wealthier commuters at the expense of harming poorer ones.

This situation has changed, however, as congestion has worsened. Traffic across the bridge rose 23% from 1980 through 1995, so the potential gains from a higher toll have increased over time. Recently, politicians have debated a \$3 toll. Estimates of the additional toll revenues from raising the toll from \$1 to \$3 are \$22 million per year above the \$40 million that is now collected. Despite these extra revenues, the politicians haven't had the nerve to raise the toll to \$3, though they did push it up to \$2 in 1998. ■

Assigning Property Rights. An alternative approach to resolving the commons problem is to assign private property rights. Converting common-access property to private property removes the incentive to overuse it.

In developing countries over the last century, common agricultural land has been broken up into smaller private farms. Similarly, fish farming on private land is increasingly used as common-access fisheries are depleted.

APPLICATION

Claiming Lobster Fisheries

The American lobster is overfished in both the United States and Canada common-property fisheries because fishers ignore the externalities they cause. If property rights were clearly allocated, individual fishers would take the true social costs (including the effect of today's catch on future supply) into account, thereby eliminating the excessive fishing problem. A test of this assertion is possible by using data from inshore lobster fisheries in Maine (Wilson 1977).

Some Maine harbors have been effectively (though not legally) appropriated by groups of fishers for their sole use. By preventing other fishers from "poaching," they create group property rights. In some cases, these fishers also limit the expansion of the group, thereby creating a large partnership.

Apparently, fishers in the controlled-access fisheries can prevent within-group externalities. Compared to hauls in controlled-access areas, lobster catches are lower in the open-access areas, where each fisher uses more traps and the stock of lobsters is smaller. Almost 61% more lobsters were caught per trap in a controlled-access fishery than in a public-access fishery: 0.98 versus 0.61. The average weight produced per trap haul is 69% greater with controlled access (0.54 kg versus 0.32 kg) because undersized lobsters are not harvested in the controlled areas. As a result of the larger stocks and less wasted effort due to crowding, fishers in the controlled-access areas have higher incomes than those in the open-access areas: $22,929 versus $16,449. Thus, by at least partially limiting entry to a fishery, fishers can gain substantially. ■

18.6 PUBLIC GOODS

We've seen that a competitive market produces too much output when a by-product creates a negative externality or when anyone can use a common property. That same competitive market may produce too little of a good in the presence of a positive externality. Positive externalities may arise with a **public good**—a commodity or service whose consumption by one person does not preclude others from also consuming it—if the producers cannot restrict access to that good.

Types of Goods

Previous chapters discussed only *private goods. Private goods have the properties of rivalry and exclusion. Rivalry* means that only one person can consume the good: The good is used up in consumption—it is *depletable*. If a second person is to consume a candy bar, the production of a second candy bar is required. *Exclusion* means that others can be prevented from consuming the good. Only the person who owns the candy bar may eat it.

Other types of goods lack either rivalry or exclusion or both, as Table 18.3 shows. *Public goods lack rivalry*. Your consumption of a public good does not preclude others from also consuming it. There is no need to ration a public good—Everyone can consume it. Indeed, excluding someone from consuming it harms that person without helping other consumers.

If no one can be prevented from consuming a public good, it is a **pure public good**: a commodity or service without rivalry—nondepletable—and without exclusion.

Table 18.3 Rivalry and Exclusion

	Exclusion	*No Exclusion*
Rivalry	*Pure private good*: candy bar, pencil, aluminum foil	*Common-access resource*: fishery, hunting, highway
No Rivalry	*Public good*: cable television, *club good* (concert, tennis club)	*Pure public good*: national defense, aerial spraying of pesticide, clean air

National defense is a pure public good. The cost of protecting an extra person is literally zero when all people are protected (no rivalry), and no one in the country can be left unprotected (no exclusion). Clean air is also a pure public good (and air pollution is a *pure public bad*). If the air is clean, we all benefit. If we clean up the air, we cannot prevent others who live nearby from benefiting from it. A *pure public good produces a positive externality*, and *excluding anyone from consuming a public good is inefficient*.

Other public goods are excludable but lack rivalry in consumption. Security guards prevent people who don't have a ticket from entering a concert hall. Until the concert hall is filled, the cost of providing the concert to one extra person is zero. Thus, a concert in a hall that is not filled has elements of both a private good (exclusion) and a public good (no rivalry).

Such a concert is a special type of public good, called a *club good*. Although the marginal cost of providing the concert to one more person is zero as long as attendance is less than the seating capacity of the hall, adding another person creates congestion or other externalities that harm concertgoers once the concert hall is filled. Similarly, allowing more people to join a swim club doesn't inflict extra costs until members start getting in each other's way.

In addition to private goods (rivalry, exclusion), pure public goods (no rivalry, no exclusion), and club goods (no rivalry, exclusion), there are resources with rivalry but without exclusion, such as a common. In an open-access fishery, anyone can fish (no exclusion), but once a fish is caught, no one else can catch it (rivalry).

Many goods differ in the degree to which they have rivalry and exclusion. Hence, many goods are hybrids, with properties of both private and public goods. Telling your friend about something that you learned in a textbook provides a positive externality. A textbook is often viewed as a private good; however, the information in it is a public good. Because the cost of excluding people from a toll road is less than that of excluding people from an ocean fishery, a toll road may more closely resemble a private good than a fishery does.

Markets for Public Goods

Markets for public goods exist only if nonpurchasers can be excluded from consuming them. Thus, markets do not exist for pure public goods because exclusion is impossible. Usually, if the government does not provide a pure public good, no one provides it.

Because computer software use is nonrival, computer software is a public good. At virtually no extra cost, a copy of the software program that you use can be supplied to another consumer.[26] In countries where exclusion is impossible, computer software is pirated and widely shared, so it is not profitable to produce and sell software. In countries where intellectual property rights to software are protected by preventing piracy, a company such as Microsoft can sell software (very) profitably.

Microsoft makes lots of money by selling its software at a price that is well above its marginal cost, so too few units are sold. Markets tend to produce too little of an excludable public good because of the lack of rivalry. In the absence of rivalry, the marginal cost of providing a public good to one extra person is (essentially) zero. Firms have no incentive to produce at a zero price. If firms set a price above zero, consumers buy too little of this public good.

Demand for Public Goods. The demand for a private good is different from that for a public good. The social marginal benefit of a private good is the same as the marginal benefit to the individual who consumes that good. The market demand, which is the social marginal benefit curve, for private goods is the *horizontal* sum of the demand curves of each individual (Chapter 2).

In contrast, the social marginal benefit of a public good is the sum of the marginal benefit to each person who consumes the good. Because a public good lacks rivalry, many people can get pleasure from the same unit of output. As a consequence, the *social demand curve* or *willingness-to-pay curve* for a public good is the *vertical* sum of the demand curves of each individual.

We illustrate this vertical summing by deriving the demand for guard services by stores in a mall that want to discourage theft. Guards patrolling the mall provide a service without rivalry: All the stores in the mall are simultaneously protected. Each store's demand for guards reflects its marginal benefit from a reduction in thefts due to the guards. The demand curve for the television store, which stands to lose a lot if thieves strike, is D^1 in Figure 18.6. The ice cream parlor, which loses less from a theft, demands fewer guards at any given price, D^2.

Because a guard patrolling the mall protects both stores at once, the marginal benefit to society of an additional guard is the sum of the benefit to each store. The social marginal benefit of a fifth guard, \$10, is the sum of the marginal benefit to the television store, \$8 (the height of D^1 at five guards per hour), and the marginal benefit to the ice cream store, \$2 (the height of D^2 at five guards per hour). Thus, the social demand is the vertical sum of the individual demand curves.

A competitive market supplies as many guards as the stores want at \$10 per hour per guard. At that price, the ice cream store would not hire any guards on its own. The television store would hire four. If the stores act independently, four guards are hired in the private equilibrium, e_p. The sum of the marginal benefit to the two stores from four guards is \$13, which is greater than the \$10 marginal cost of an

[26]Because there is some marginal cost (albeit a low one) to producing an extra copy of the software, some economists argue that software is not a public good.

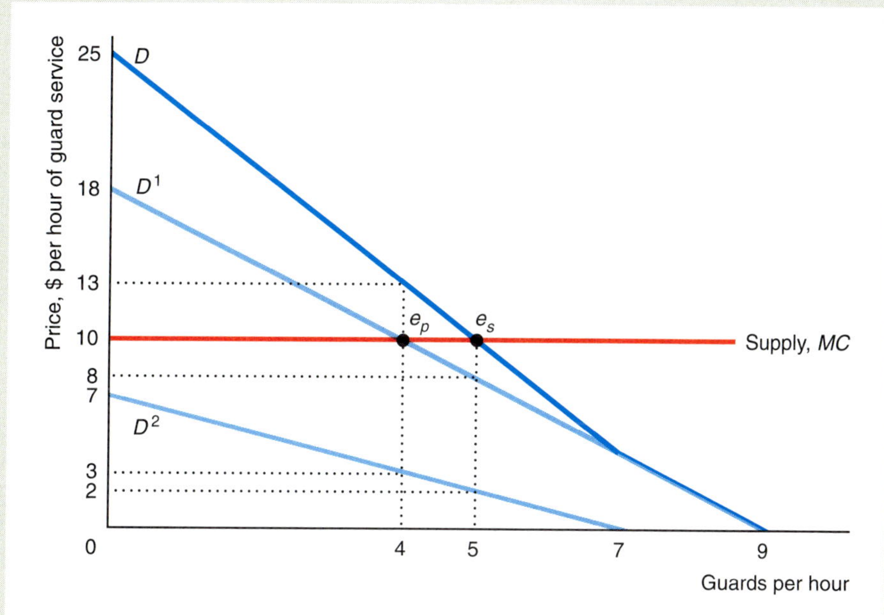

Figure 18.6 Inadequate Provision of a Public Good. Security guards protect both tenants of the mall. If each guard costs \$10 per hour, the television store, with demand D^1, is willing to hire four guards per hour. The ice cream parlor, with demand D^2, is not willing to hire any guards. Thus, if everyone acts independently, the equilibrium is e_p. The social demand for this public good is the vertical sum of the individual demand curves, D. Thus, the social optimum is e_s, at which five guards are hired.

additional guard. If a fifth guard is hired, the social marginal benefit, \$10, equals the marginal cost of the last guard. Thus, the social equilibrium, e_2, has five guards.

The ice cream store can get guard services without paying because the guard service is a public good. Acting alone, the television store hires fewer guards than are socially optimal because it ignores the positive externality provided to the ice cream store, which the television store does not capture. Thus, the competitive market for guard services provides too little of this public good.

Free Riding. Many people are unwilling to pay for their share of a public good. They try to get others to pay for it, so they can **free ride**: benefit from the actions of others without paying. That is, they want to benefit from a positive externality.

To illustrate the problem of free riding, we examine a game between two stores in a mall that are deciding whether to hire one guard or none. (For now, we assume that hiring two guards does no more good than hiring one.) The cost of hiring a guard is \$10 per hour. The benefit to each store is \$8. Because the collective benefit, \$16, is greater than the cost of hiring a guard, the optimal solution is to hire the guard.

If the stores act independently, however, they do not achieve this optimal solution. Table 18.4 shows two games. In panel a, each store acts independently and pays $10 to hire a guard on its own or does not hire a guard. If both decide to hire a guard, two guards are hired, but the benefit is still only $8 per store.

In panel b, the stores split the cost of a guard if both firms agree to hire one. If only one firm wants to hire the guard, it must bear the full cost.

In each of these games, the Nash equilibrium is for neither store to hire a guard because of free riding. Each store has a dominant strategy. Regardless of what the other store does, each store is always as well off or better off to not hire a guard. The nonoptimal outcome occurs for the same reason as in other prisoners' dilemma games (Chapter 12): The stores don't do what is best for them collectively when they act independently.

Reducing Free Riding

Governmental or other collective actions can reduce free riding. Methods that may be used include social pressure, mergers, compulsion, and privatization.

Sometimes, especially when the group is small, *social pressure* eliminates free riding. Social pressure results in at least minimal provision of some public goods. Such pressure may cause most firms at a mall to contribute "voluntarily" to a fund to hire security guards.

Table 18.4 Private Payments for a Public Good

a) Stores Independently Decide Whether to Hire a Guard

		Television Store	
		Hire Guard	*Do Hot Hire*
Stereo Store	*Hire Guard*	-$2, -$2	-$2, $8
	Do Not Hire	$8, -$2	$0, $0

b) Stores Voting to Hire a Guard Split the Cost

		Television Store	
		Hire Guard	*Do Hot Hire*
Stereo Store	*Hire Guard*	$3, $3	-$2, $8
	Do Not Hire	$8, -$2	$0, $0

A direct way to eliminate free riding by firms is for them to *merge* into a single firm and thereby internalize the positive externality. The sum of the benefit to the individual stores equals the benefit to the single firm, so an optimal decision is made to hire guards.

If the independent stores sign a contract that commits them to share the cost of the guards, they achieve the practical advantage from a merger. The question remains, however, as to why they would agree to sign the contract, given the prisoners' dilemma problem. One explanation is that firms are more likely to cooperate in a repeated prisoners' dilemma game (Chapter 12).

Another way to overcome free riding is through *compulsion*. Some outside entity such as the government may dictate a solution to a free-riding problem. For example, the management of a mall with many firms may require tenants to sign a rental contract committing them to pay "taxes" that are assessed through tenants' votes. If the majority votes to hire guards, all must share the cost. Although a firm might be unwilling to pay for the guard service if it has no guarantee that others will also pay, it may vote to assess everyone—including itself—to pay for the service.

With government enforcement—a form of compulsion—milk producers avoided free-rider problems by taxing themselves to produce the "Got Milk?" advertisements. In many cities, the restaurants and hotels tax themselves (or are taxed by the government) to advertise that their city is a place tourists should visit. Thus, actions by a group or government may overcome the free-rider problem so that a public service is provided.

Finally, privatization—exclusion—eliminates free riding. A good that would be a public good if anyone could use it becomes a private good if access to it is restricted. An example is water, the use of which is limited by individual meters.

APPLICATION

Free Riding on Water

Water is a private good for most households in Perth, Australia: They can consume it only if they pay the price for each unit. Others can be excluded from consuming the water because each household's consumption is individually metered. However, about 10% of the households share meters with one or more other households. Households in duplexes or apartments are likely to share meters. Perth's 20,545 flats have 1,800 meters between them, so on average, 11 households share each meter. Most group-metered households apportion the total bill equally among households.

How would you expect water consumption to vary between individually and collectively metered households? Because of free riding, you might expect households with individual meters to consume less water than households that draw from a common pool. Each member of the common pool has an incentive to free ride on the remaining members. As the household consumes a little more water, it receives all of the marginal benefits but only has to pay $1/n$ fraction of the marginal cost, where there are n households on a meter.

Moreover, you might expect that the incentive to free ride increases with the number of households sharing a meter. Not only is each household's share of the marginal cost smaller, but each household faces less effective social pressure to keep its free riding under control.

Grossman, Pirozzi, and Pope (1993) confirm these predictions. They find that collectively metered households consume 17% more water on average than households with private meters do.

The extra water consumption rises with the number of households sharing a meter. A household in a two-family duplex consumes only 0.05 kiloliter more per year than does an individually metered household. Even a household in a block of 10 housing units consumes only 1.3 kiloliters more. However, by the time the number in a housing block reaches 222 members (the largest in the sample), an extra household averages 640 extra kiloliters of water consumption. ■

Valuing Public Goods

To ensure that a pure public good is provided, a government usually produces it or compels others to do so. Issues that a government faces in providing pure public goods include whether to provide it at all and, if so, how much to provide. To grapple with these questions, the government needs to know the cost—usually the easy part—and the value of the public good to many individuals—the hard part.

The government may try to determine the value that consumers place on the pure public good through surveys or voting results. One major problem with these methods is that most people do not know how much a public good is worth to them. How much would you pay to maintain the National Archives? How much does reducing air pollution improve your health? How much better do you sleep at night knowing that the army stands ready to protect you?

Even if people know how much they value a public good, they have an incentive to lie on a survey. Those who value the good greatly and want the government to provide it may exaggerate the value of the benefit. Similarly, people who place a low value on it may report too low a value—possibly even a negative one—to discourage government action.

Rather than rely on surveys, a government may have citizens vote directly on public goods. Suppose that a separate, majority-rule vote is held on whether to install a traffic signal—a pure public good—at each of several street corners. If a signal is installed, all voters are taxed equally to pay for it. An individual will vote to install a signal if the value of the signal to that voter is at least as much as the tax each must pay for the signal.

Whether the majority votes for the signal depends on the preferences of the *median voter*: the person with respect to whom half the populace values the project less and half values the project more. If the median voter wants to install a signal, then at least half the voters agree, so the vote carries. Similarly, if the median voter is against the project, at least half the voters are against it, so the vote fails.

It is *efficient* to install the signal if the value of the signal to society is at least as great as its cost. Does majority voting result in efficiency? The following examples illustrate that efficiency is not ensured.

Each signal costs $300 to install. There are three voters, so each individual votes for the signal only if that person thinks that the signal is worth at least $100, which is the tax each person pays if the signal is installed. Table 18.5 shows the value that each voter places on installing a signal at each of three intersections.

For each of the proposed signals, Hayley is the median voter, so her views signal the outcome. If Hayley, the median voter, likes the signal, then she and Asa, a majority, vote for it. Otherwise, Nancy and Hayley vote against it. The majority favors installing a signal at Corners *A* and *C* and are against doing so at Corner *B*. It would be efficient to install the signal at Corner *A*, where the social value is $300, and at Corner *B*, where the social value is $375, because each value exceeds the cost of $300.

At Corner *A*, the citizens vote for the signal and that outcome is efficient. The other two votes lead to inefficient outcomes. No signal is installed at Corner *B*, where society values the signal at more than $300, but a signal is installed at Corner *C*, where voters value the signal at less than $300.

The problem with yes–no votes is that they ignore the intensity of preferences. A voter indicates only whether or not the project is worth more or less than a certain amount. Thus, such *majority voting fails to value the pure public good fully and hence does not guarantee that it is efficiently provided.*[27]

Table 18.5 Voting on $300 Traffic Signals

	Value to Each Voter			Value to Society	Outcome of Vote*
	Nancy	Hayley	Asa		
Signal at Corner *A*	$50	$100	$150	$300	Yes
Signal at Corner *B*	$50	$75	$250	$375	No
Signal at Corner *C*	$50	$100	$110	$260	Yes

*An individual votes to install a signal at a particular corner if and only if that person thinks that the signal is worth at least $100, the tax that individual must pay if the signal is installed.

[27]Although voting does not reveal how much a public good is worth, Tideman and Tullock (1976) and other economists have devised taxing methods that can sometimes induce people to reveal their true valuations. However, these methods are rarely used.

Summary

1. **Externalities:** An externality occurs when a consumer's well-being or a firm's production capabilities are directly affected by the actions of other consumers or firms, rather than indirectly affected through changes in prices. An externality that harms others is a negative externality, and one that helps others is a positive externality. Some externalities benefit one group while harming another.
2. **The inefficiency of competition with externalities:** Because producers do not pay for a negative externality such as pollution, the private costs are less than the social costs. As a consequence, competitive markets produce more negative externalities than are optimal. If the only way to cut externalities is to decrease output, the optimal solution is to set output where the marginal benefit from reducing the externality equals the marginal cost to consumers and producers from less output. It is usually optimal to have some negative externalities, because eliminating all of them requires eliminating desirable outputs and consumption activities as well. If the government has sufficient information about demand, production cost, and the harm from the externality, it can use taxes or quotas to force the competitive market to produce the social optimum. It may tax or limit the negative externality, or it may tax or limit output.
3. **Market structure and externalities:** Although a competitive market produces excessive output and negative externalities, a noncompetitive market may produce more or less than the optimal level. With a negative externality, a noncompetitive equilibrium may be closer to the social optimum than is a competitive equilibrium. A tax equal to the marginal social harm of a negative externality—which results in the social optimum when applied to a competitive market—may lower welfare when applied to a noncompetitive market.
4. **Allocating property rights to reduce externalities:** Externalities arise because property rights are not clearly defined. According to the Coase Theorem, allocating property rights to *either* of two parties results in an efficient outcome if the parties can bargain. The assignment of the property rights, however, affects income distribution, as the rights are valuable. Unfortunately, bargaining is usually not practical, especially when many people are involved. In such cases, markets for permits to produce externalities may overcome the externality problem.
5. **Common property:** Externalities are a problem with common property, which is a resource to which everyone has free access. Common property resources are overexploited. For example, if anyone can drive on a highway, too many people are likely to do so because they ignore the externality—delays due to congestion—that they impose on others. Taxes and quotas may reduce or eliminate overuse.
6. **Public goods:** Public goods lack rivalry. Once a public good is provided to anyone, it can be provided to others at no additional cost. Excluding anyone from consuming a public good is inefficient. If no one can be prevented from consuming a public good, it is a pure public good. Pure public goods provide a positive externality. Markets provide too little of a public good. A government faces challenges in providing the optimal amount because it is difficult to determine how much people value the public good.

Problems

1. Why is zero pollution not the best solution for society? Can there be too little pollution? Why or why not?
2. In the paper market example in the text, what is the optimal emissions fee and what is the optimal tax on output (assuming that only one fee or tax is applied)?
3. In Figure 18.2, the government may optimally regulate the paper market using either a tax or a quota on output. A technological change drives down the private marginal cost of production. Discuss the welfare implications if the output tax or quota is unchanged.

4. Suppose that the only way to reduce pollution from paper production is to reduce output. The government imposes a tax equal to the marginal harm from the pollution on the monopoly producer. Show that the tax may raise welfare.
5. Which allocation of property rights leads to the highest possible welfare level if firms cannot bargain with each other in Table 18.2?
6. Are broadcast television and cable television public goods? Is either a pure public good? If either is a public good, why is it privately provided?
7. Do publishers sell the optimal number of intermediate microeconomics textbooks? Discuss in terms of public goods, rivalry, and exclusion.
8. Analyze the following. Is garbage a positive or negative externality? Why is a market solution practical here?

   Garbage in Philadelphia is undesirable of course. Since the turn of the century, however, hog farmers in New Jersey have been feeding Philadelphia garbage to their pigs. Philadelphia saves $3 million a year and reduces its garbage mound by allowing New Jersey farmers to pick up leftover food scraps for their porcine recyclers. The city pays $1.9 million to the New Jersey pig farmers for picking up the waste each year, which is about $79 a ton. Otherwise, the city would have to pay $125 a ton for curbside recycling of the same food waste.[28]

9. In granting patents, governments give inventors monopoly rights to sell their invention for a fixed period of time. We know that monopolies set too high a price. Why, then, might a government reasonably grant patents? (*Hint*: Discuss in terms of the public good nature of information.)
10. In 1994, the state of Connecticut announced that commercial fleet operators would get a tax break if they converted vehicles from ozone-producing gasoline to what the state said were cleaner fuels such as natural gas and electricity. For every dollar spent on the conversion of their fleets or building alternative fueling stations, operators could deduct 50¢ from their corporate tax. Is this approach likely to be a cost-effective way to control pollution?

Math Problems

11. Using the numerical example in Appendix 18A, determine the social optimum if the marginal harm of gunk is $MC^g = \$84$ (instead of Equation 18A.3). Is there a short cut that would allow you to solve this problem without algebra?

★12. Using the numeric example of the model of the paper market in Appendix 18A, derive the equations for the benefit, cost, marginal benefit, and marginal cost curves in Figure 18.3.

13. Suppose that the inverse demand curve for paper is $p = 200 - Q$, the private marginal cost (unregulated competitive market supply) is $MC^p = 80 + Q$, and the marginal harm from gunk is $MC^g = Q$.
    A. What is the unregulated competitive equilibrium?
    B. What is the social optimum? What specific tax (per unit of output or gunk) results in the social optimum?
    C. What is the unregulated monopoly equilibrium?
    D. How would you optimally regulate the monopoly? What is the resulting equilibrium?
14. Let $H = \bar{G} - G$ be the amount that gunk, G, is reduced from the competitive level, $\bar{G}$. The benefit of reducing gunk is $B(H) = AH^{\alpha}$. The cost is $C(H) = H^{\beta}$. If the benefit is increasing but at a diminishing rate in H, and the cost is rising at an increasing rate, what are the possible ranges of values for A, α, and B?
15. Applying the model in the above problem, use calculus to determine the optimal level of H.
16. Two tenants of a mall are protected by the guard service, q. The number of guards per hour demanded by the television store is $q_1 = a_1 + b_1 p$, where p is the price of one hour of guard services. The ice cream store's demand is $q_2 = a_2 + b_2 p$. What is the social demand for this service?

[28]"What's for Dinner?" *San Francisco Chronicle*, May 1, 1994:A15.

CHAPTER 19

Asymmetric Information

The buyer needs a hundred eyes, the seller not one.
—George Herbert (1651)

So far, we've examined models in which everyone is equally knowledgeable or equally ignorant. In the competitive model, everyone knows all relevant facts. In the uncertainty models in Chapter 17, the companies that sell insurance and the people who buy it are equally uncertain about future events. In contrast, in this chapter's models, people have **asymmetric information**: One party to a transaction knows a material fact that the other party does not. For example, the seller knows the quality of a product and the buyer does not.

A more informed party may exploit a less informed party. Such *opportunistic* behavior due to asymmetric information leads to market failures, destroying many desirable properties of competitive markets. In a competitive market in which everyone has full information, consumers can buy whatever quality good they want at its marginal cost. In contrast, when firms have information that consumers do not—when information is asymmetric—firms may sell only the lowest-quality good, the price may be above marginal cost, or other problems may occur.

If consumers do not know the quality of a good they are considering buying, some firms may try to sell them a dud at the price of a superior good. However, knowing that the chance of buying schlock is high, consumers may be unwilling to pay much for goods of unknown quality. As a result, firms that make high-quality products may not be able to sell them at prices anywhere near their cost of production. In other words, *bad products drive good ones out of the market*. The market failure is that the market for a good-quality product is reduced or eliminated, even though (knowledgeable) consumers value the high-quality product at more than the cost of producing it.

If consumers (unlike sellers) do not know how prices vary across firms, *firms may gain market power and set prices above marginal cost*. Suppose that you go to Store A to buy a television set. If you know that a nearby store, Store B, is charging $299 for that set, you are willing to pay Store A at most $299 (or perhaps a little more to avoid having to go to Store B). *Knowledge is power*. On the other hand, if you don't know Store B's price for that set, Store A might sell you a television for much more than $299. *Ignorance costs*. This market failure results in a deadweight loss because price is set above marginal cost.

Market failures due to asymmetric information can be eliminated if consumers can inexpensively determine the quality of a product or learn the prices that various stores charge. In many markets, however, obtaining this information is prohibitively expensive.

In this chapter, we examine six main topics:

1. **Problems due to asymmetric information:** Informed people take advantage of uninformed people.
2. **Responses to adverse selection:** To reduce the harms from adverse selection—an informed person's benefiting from trading with an uninformed person who does not know about a characteristic of the informed person—government actions or contracts between involved parties may be used to prevent opportunistic behavior, or the information asymmetry may be reduced or eliminated.
3. **How ignorance about quality drives out high-quality goods:** If consumers cannot distinguish between good and bad products before purchase, it is possible that only bad products will be sold.
4. **Price discrimination due to false beliefs about quality:** If some consumers incorrectly think that quality varies across identical products, a firm may price discriminate.
5. **Market power from price ignorance:** Consumers' ignorance about the price that each firm charges gives firms market power.
6. **Problems arising from ignorance when hiring:** Attempts to eliminate information asymmetries in hiring may raise or lower social welfare.

19.1 PROBLEMS DUE TO ASYMMETRIC INFORMATION

When both parties to a transaction have equally limited information, neither has an advantage over the other. If a roadside vendor sells a box of oranges to a passing motorist and neither person knows the quality of the oranges, neither has an advantage because both are operating with equal uncertainty.

In contrast, asymmetric information leads to problems of *opportunism*, whereby the informed person benefits at the expense of the person with less information. If only the vendor knows that the oranges are of low quality, the vendor may allege that the oranges are of high quality and charge a premium price for them.

The two major types of opportunistic behavior are *adverse selection* and *moral hazard*. **Adverse selection** is opportunism characterized by an informed person's benefiting from trading or otherwise contracting with a less informed person who does not know about an *unobserved characteristic* of the informed person. For example, people who buy life insurance policies are better informed about their own health than are insurance companies. If an insurance company offers to insure people against death for 10 years at a fixed rate, a disproportionately large share of unhealthy people will buy this policy. Because of this adverse selection, the insurance company will pay off on more policies than it would pay if healthy and unhealthy people bought the policy in proportion to their share in the population.

Similarly, if one firm starts offering an unusually generous maternity leave to mothers of newborn children, a disproportionate number of women planning to become mothers in the near future will apply for employment with that firm. The intention to have children is known to potential employees but not to the firm. As a result, the cost of this benefit is greater to the firm than its cost would be if the employees were a random sample of the entire population.

Adverse selection creates a market failure by reducing the size of a market or eliminating it, thereby preventing desirable transactions. Insurance companies have to charge higher rates for insurance due to adverse selection or choose not to offer insurance at all. Very few older people, regardless of their health, buy term life insurance because the rates are extremely high because of adverse selection. A parental leave benefit's higher cost due to adverse selection may discourage firms from offering the benefit, a decision that hurts both employees who are new parents (because they lose the benefit) and the firm (because it cannot use a benefit that would otherwise allow it to pay a lower wage).

Moral hazard is opportunism characterized by an informed person's taking advantage of a less-informed person through an *unobserved action*. An employee may *shirk*—not work hard—if not monitored by the employer. An employer who observes shirking can prevent it. Similarly, insured people tend to take unobserved actions—engage in risky behaviors—that increase the probability of large claims against insurance companies, or they fail to take reasonable precautions that would reduce the likelihood of such claims. An insured homeowner may fail to remove fire hazards such as piles of old newspapers. Some insured motorists drive more recklessly than they would without insurance. Moral hazards such as shirking, failure to take care, and reckless behavior reduce output or increase accidents, which are market failures that harm society.

Not all moral hazards, despite the apparently pejorative term, are entirely harmful. Pregnant women with health insurance make more prenatal doctor visits. Although the extra cost from these visits is a moral hazard to insurance companies, society benefits from healthier mothers and babies.

The distinction between adverse selection and moral hazard—between unobserved characteristics and unobserved actions—is not always clear. A life insurance company may face unusually high risks if it insures George and Marge, who, unknown to the company, skydive. George will skydive whether or not he has life insurance. Knowing the risks of skydiving, he's more likely to buy life insurance than other, similar people are. His unobserved characteristic—his love of plunging toward the earth at high speed—leads to adverse selection. Marge will skydive only if she has life insurance. Her unobserved action is a moral hazard for the insurance company.

This chapter focuses on adverse selection and unobserved characteristics. We identify the problems that arise from adverse selection and discuss how they sometimes can be solved. The next chapter concentrates on moral hazard problems due to unobserved actions and on the use of contracts to deal with them.

19.2 RESPONSES TO ADVERSE SELECTION

Responses to adverse selection problems increase welfare in some markets, but they may do more harm than good in others. The two main methods for solving adverse selection problems are to *restrict opportunistic behavior* and to *equalize information*.

Controlling Opportunistic Behavior Through Universal Coverage

Adverse selection can be prevented if selection by informed people is eliminated. For example, a government can avoid adverse selection by providing insurance to everyone or by mandating that everyone buy insurance. Many states require that every driver carry auto insurance. They thereby reduce the adverse selection that would arise from having a disproportionate number of people who drive badly buy insurance.

Similarly, firms often provide health insurance to all employees as a benefit, rather than paying a higher wage and letting employees decide whether to buy such insurance on their own. By doing so, firms reduce adverse selection problems for their insurance carriers: Both healthy and unhealthy people are covered. As a result, firms can buy medical insurance for their workers at a lower cost per person than workers could obtain on their own (because relatively more unhealthy individuals buy insurance).

Equalizing Information

Either informed or uninformed parties can eliminate information asymmetries. **Screening** is an action taken by an uninformed person to determine the information possessed by informed people. A buyer may test-drive (screen) several used cars to determine which one starts and handles the best. **Signaling** is an action taken by an informed person to send information to a less informed person. A firm may send a signal—such as widely distributing a favorable report on its product by an independent testing agency—to try to convince buyers that its product is of high quality. In some markets, government agencies or nonprofit organizations such as Consumers Union also provide consumers with information.

"Good—very good! You qualify for our dental plan with no deductible whatsoever!"

Screening. Uninformed people may try to eliminate their disadvantage by screening to gather information on the hidden characteristics of informed people. If the originally uninformed people obtain better information, they may refuse to sign a contract or insist on changes in contract clauses or in the price of a good.

Insurance companies try to reduce adverse selection problems by learning the health history of their potential customers—for example, by requiring medical exams. A life insurance company uses such information to better estimate the probability that it will have to pay off on a policy. The firm can then decide not to insure high-risk individuals or can charge high-risk people a larger premium as compensation for the extra risk.

It is costly to collect information on how healthy a person is and on whether that individual has dangerous habits (such as smoking and drinking). As a result, insurance companies collect information only up to the point at which the marginal benefit from extra information equals the marginal cost of obtaining it. Over time, insurance companies have been increasingly likely to conclude that it pays to collect information about whether individuals exercise, have a family history of dying young, or engage in potentially life-threatening activities. If individuals but not insurance companies know about these characteristics, individuals can better predict whether they'll die young, and adverse selection occurs.

APPLICATION

Risky Occupations and Hobbies

To reduce the risk of adverse selection, life insurance companies no longer rely solely on information about age and general health in determining risk. They now also look into individuals' smoking and drinking habits, occupations, and hobbies.

The nature of an individual's occupation affects the likelihood of that person's being killed on the job. For example, workplace homicides range from 22.7 per 100,000 workers for taxicab drivers and chauffeurs to 10.7 for sheriffs and bailiffs, 5.9 for gas station or garage workers, 2.3 for bartenders or loggers, 2.0 for hotel clerks, and 1.3 for firefighters.[1] Similarly, some hobbies or activities greatly affect the probability that an individual will die from an accident. Various sports add $100 to $2,500 in annual premiums for each $100,000 of life insurance.

Steve Potter, a 40-year-old managing director at an executive recruiting firm, prepared to climb Mount Everest by buying a $2 million life insurance policy. His firm took out an additional $1 million on his life.[2] Although Prudential Insurance Company of America would offer a typical healthy 40-year-old a $1 million policy for $1,000, the company wanted $6,000 from a serious climber such as Mr. Potter. ■

Signaling. Signaling is used primarily by informed parties to try to eliminate adverse selection. If a buyer cannot tell a high-quality good or service from one of low quality, the buyer is unwilling to pay top dollar for the better good. Informed sellers of better goods and services may signal to potential buyers that their products are of high quality.

Likewise, potential employees use a variety of signals to convince firms of their abilities. For a job interview, candidates arrive on time, dress appropriately, don't

---

[1]National Institute for Occupational Safety and Health data for 1990–1992, as reported in "Cabbies Face Most Risk, Report Says," *San Francisco Chronicle*, July 9, 1996:A4.

[2]Cropper, Carol Marie, "Risk Takers Pay Dearly. It's the Danger of Living Fearlessly." *New York Times*, April 2, 1995:Section 3, p.11.

chew gum, document their training and achievements, and show that they worked for long periods at other firms. Similarly, an applicant for life insurance could have a physical examination and then present an insurance company with a written statement from the doctor to signal good health.

Only people who believe that they can show that they are better than others want to send a signal. Moreover, signaling solves an information problem only if the signals are accurate. For example, if it is easy for people to find an unscrupulous doctor who will report falsely that they are in good health, insurance companies won't rely on such signals. Here, screening may work better, and the insurance firms may require that potential customers go to a designated doctor for a checkup.

19.3 HOW IGNORANCE ABOUT QUALITY DRIVES OUT HIGH-QUALITY GOODS

We now examine some markets in which asymmetric information causes major problems due to adverse selection. In most of these situations, buyers know less than sellers.

Consumers often have trouble determining the quality of goods and services. Most people don't know how to judge the abilities of a professional such as a doctor, a lawyer, a plumber, an electrician, or an economist. Many of us have no reliable information about whether the processed foods we eat are safe. Are all the components in your computer of high quality? Is it safer to fly in a Boeing 747 than in a McDonnell Douglas DC-10?

Consumer ignorance about quality leads to a less efficient use of resources than would occur if everyone had perfect information. Here, we first show how limited consumer information leads to adverse selection. We demonstrate that adverse selection occurs whether or not a seller can alter the quality of the good. We then discuss how to ameliorate—though not necessarily eliminate—the adverse selection problem.

Lemons Market with Fixed Quality

When buyers cannot judge a product's quality before purchasing it, low-quality products—*lemons*—may drive high-quality products out of the market (Akerlof 1970). This situation is common in used-car markets: Owners of lemons are more likely to sell their cars, leading to adverse selection.

Cars that appear to be identical on the outside often differ substantially in the number of repairs they will need. Some cars—*lemons*—are cursed. They have a variety of insidious problems that become apparent to the owner only after the car has been driven for a while. In contrast, the seller of a used car knows from experience whether the car is a lemon. We assume that the seller cannot alter the quality of the used car—at least not practically.

Suppose that there are many potential buyers for used cars. All are willing to pay \$1,000 for a lemon and \$2,000 for a good used car: The demand curve for lemons, D^L, is horizontal at \$1,000 in panel a of Figure 19.1, and the demand curve for good cars, D^G, is horizontal at \$2,000 in panel b.

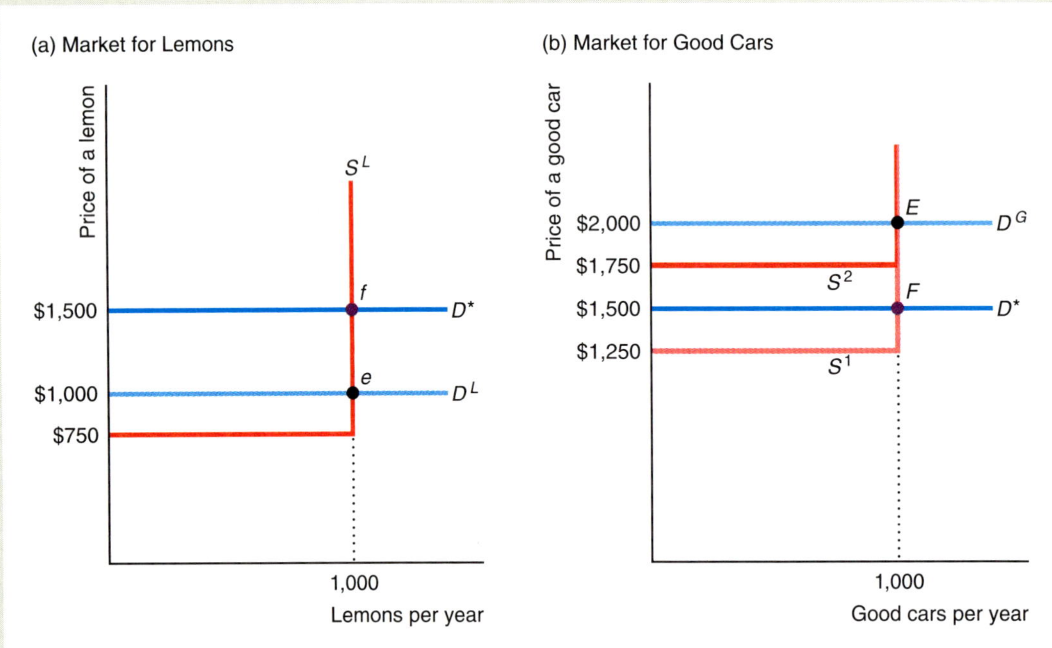

Figure 19.1 Markets for Lemons and Good Cars. If everyone has full information, the equilibrium in the lemons market is *e* (1,000 cars sold for $1,000 each), and the equilibrium in the good-car market is *E* (1,000 cars sold for $2,000 each). If buyers can't tell quality before buying but assume that equal numbers of the two types of cars are for sale, their demand in both markets is D^*, which is horizontal at $1,500. If the reservation price of the owners of good cars is $1,250, the supply curve for good cars is S^1, and 1,000 good cars (point *F*) and 1,000 lemons (point *f*) sell for $1,500 each. If the reservation price for good cars is $1,750, the supply curve is S^2. No good cars are sold; 1,000 lemons sell for $1,000 each (point *e*).

Although the number of potential buyers is virtually unlimited, only 1,000 owners of lemons and 1,000 owners of good cars are willing to sell. The *reservation price* of owners of lemons—the lowest price at which they will sell their cars—is $750. Consequently, the supply curve of lemons, S^L in panel a, is horizontal at $750 up to 1,000 cars, where it becomes vertical (no more cars are for sale at any price). The reservation price of owners of high-quality used cars is v, which is less than $2,000. Panel b shows two possible values of v. If v = $1,250, the supply curve of good cars, S^1, is horizontal at $1,250 up to 1,000 cars and then becomes vertical. If v = $1,750, the supply curve is S^2.

Symmetric Information. If both sellers and buyers know the quality of all the used cars before any sales take place, all the cars are sold and good cars sell for more than lemons. In panel a of Figure 19.1, the intersection of the lemons demand curve D^L

and the lemons supply curve S^L determines the equilibrium at e in the lemons market, where 1,000 lemons sell for \$1,000 each. Regardless of whether the supply curve of good cars is S^1 or S^2 in panel b, the equilibrium in the good-car market is E, where 1,000 good cars sell for \$2,000 each.

This market is efficient because goods go to people who value them the most. All current owners, who value the cars less than do the potential buyers, sell their cars.

More generally, all buyers and sellers may have symmetric information by being equally informed or equally uninformed. *All the cars are sold if everyone has the same information.* It does not matter whether they all have full information or all lack information—it's the equality of information that matters. However, *the amount of information they have affects the price at which the cars sell.* With full information, good cars sell for \$2,000 and lemons for \$1,000. If no one can tell a lemon from a good car at the time of purchase, both types of cars sell for the same price.

Suppose that everyone is risk neutral (Chapter 17) and no one can identify the lemons: Buyers *and* sellers are equally ignorant. A buyer has an equal chance of buying a lemon or a good car. The expected value (Chapter 17) of a used car is

$$\$1{,}500 = (\tfrac{1}{2} \times \$1{,}000) + (\tfrac{1}{2} \times \$2{,}000).$$

A risk-neutral buyer would pay \$1,500 for a car of unknown quality. Because sellers cannot distinguish between the cars either, sellers accept this amount and sell all the cars.[3] Thus, this market is efficient because the cars go to people who value them more than their original owners.

Sellers of good-quality cars are implicitly subsidizing sellers of lemons. If only lemons were sold, they would sell for \$1,000. The presence of good-quality cars raises the price received by sellers of lemons. Similarly, if only good cars were sold, their owners would obtain \$2,000. The presence of lemons lowers the price that sellers of good cars receive.

Asymmetric Information. If sellers know the quality but buyers do not, this market may be inefficient: The better-quality cars may not be sold even though buyers value good cars more than sellers do. The equilibrium in this market depends on whether the value that the owners of good cars place on their cars, v, is greater or less than the expected value of buyers, \$1,500. *There are two possible equilibria: All cars sell at the average price, or only lemons sell for a price equal to the value that buyers place on lemons.*

Initially, we assume that the sellers of good cars value their cars at $v = \$1{,}250$, which is less than buyers' expected value, so sellers are willing to sell their cars. The equilibrium in the good-car market is determined by the intersection of S^1 and D^G at F, where 1,000 good cars sell at \$1,500. Similarly, owners of lemons, who value their cars at only \$750, are happy to sell them for \$1,500 each. The new equilibrium in the lemons market is f.

---

[3]Risk-neutral sellers place an expected value of $(\tfrac{1}{2} \times \$750) + \tfrac{1}{2}v = \$375 + \tfrac{1}{2}v < \$1{,}375$ (because $v < \$2{,}000$) on a car of unknown quality, so they are willing to sell their cars for \$1,500.

Thus, all cars sell at the same price. Consequently, *asymmetric information does not cause an efficiency problem, but it does have equity implications*. Sellers of lemons benefit and sellers of good cars suffer from consumers' inability to distinguish quality. Consumers who buy the good cars get a bargain, and buyers of lemons are left with a sour taste in their mouths.

Now suppose that the sellers of good cars place a value of v = $1,750 on their cars and thus are unwilling to sell them for $1,500. As a result, the *lemons drive good cars out of the market*. Buyers realize that, at any price less than $1,750, they can buy only lemons. Consequently, in equilibrium, the 1,000 lemons sell for the expected (and actual) price of $1,000 and no good cars change hands. This equilibrium is inefficient because high-quality cars remain in the hands of people who value them less than potential buyers do.

In summary, if buyers have less information about product quality than sellers do, the result might be a lemons problem in which high-quality cars do not sell even though potential buyers value the cars more than their current owners do. If so, the asymmetric information causes a competitive market to lose its desirable efficiency and welfare properties. The lemons problem does not occur if the information is symmetric. If buyers and sellers of used cars know the quality of the cars, then each car sells for its true value in a perfectly competitive market. If, as with new cars, neither buyers nor sellers can identify lemons, both good cars and lemons sell at a price equal to the expected value rather than at their (unknown) true values.

SOLVED PROBLEM 19.1

Suppose that everyone in our used-car example is risk neutral, potential car buyers value lemons at $1,000 and good used cars at $2,000, the reservation price of lemon owners is $750, and the reservation price of owners of high-quality used cars is $1,750. The share of current owners who have lemons is θ (in our previous example, the share was $\theta = \frac{1}{2}$ = 1,000/[1,000 + 1,000]). For what values of θ do all the potential sellers sell their used cars? Describe the equilibrium.

Answer

1. *Determine how much buyers are willing to pay if all cars are sold*: Because buyers are risk neutral, if they believe that the probability of getting a lemon is θ, the most they are willing to pay for a car of unknown quality is

$$\begin{aligned} p &= [\$2{,}000 \times (1 - \theta)] + (\$1{,}000 \times \theta) \\ &= \$2{,}000 - (\$1{,}000 \times \theta). \end{aligned} \tag{19.1}$$

For example, p = $1,500 if $\theta = \frac{1}{2}$ and p = $1,750 if $\theta = \frac{1}{4}$.

2. *Solve for the values of θ such that all the cars are sold, and describe the equilibrium*: All owners are willing to sell if the market price is $1,750 or more. Using Equation 19.1, we know that the market (equilibrium) price is $1,750 or more if a quarter or fewer of the used cars are lemons, $\theta \le \frac{1}{4}$. Thus, for $\theta \le \frac{1}{4}$, all the cars are sold at the price given in Equation 19.1. ■

Lemons Market with Variable Quality

Many firms can vary the quality of their products. If consumers cannot identify high-quality goods before purchase, they pay the same for all goods regardless of quality. Because the price that firms receive for top-quality goods is no higher than the price for schlock, they do not produce top-quality goods. Such an outcome is inefficient if consumers are willing to pay sufficiently more for top-quality goods.

This unwillingness to produce high-quality products is due to an externality: *A firm does not completely capture the benefits from raising the quality of its product.* By selling a better product than what other firms offer, a seller raises the average quality in the market, so buyers are willing to pay more for all products. As a result, the high-quality seller shares the benefits from its high-quality product with sellers of low-quality products by raising the average price to all. *The social value of raising the quality*, as reflected by the increased revenues shared by all firms, *is greater than the private value*, which is only the higher revenue received by the firm with the good product.

To illustrate, suppose that it costs $10 to produce a low-quality book bag and $20 to produce a high-quality bag, consumers cannot distinguish between the products before purchase, there are no repeat purchases, and consumers value the bags at their cost of production. The 5 firms in the market produce 100 bags each. A firm produces only high-quality or only low-quality bags.

If all 5 firms make a low-quality bag, consumers pay $10 per bag. If one firm makes a high-quality bag and all the others make low-quality bags, the expected value per bag to consumers is

$$\$12 = [\$10 \times \tfrac{4}{5}] + [\$20 \times \tfrac{1}{5}].$$

Thus, if one firm raises the quality of its product, all firms benefit because the bags sell for $12 instead of $10. The high-quality firm receives only a fraction of the total benefit from raising quality. It gets $2 extra per high-quality bag sold, which is less than the extra $10 it costs to make the better bag. The other $8 is shared by the other firms. Because the high-quality firm incurs all the expenses of raising quality, $10 extra per bag, and reaps only a fraction, $2, of the benefits, it opts not to produce the high-quality bags. Thus, *due to asymmetric information, the firms do not produce high-quality goods even though consumers are willing to pay for the extra quality.*

Limiting Lemons

In some markets, it is possible to avoid problems stemming from consumer ignorance. Laws might provide protection against being sold a lemon, consumers might collect the information themselves, the government or another third party might supply reliable information, or sellers might send credible signals.

Laws to Prevent Opportunism. Product liability laws protect consumers from being stuck with nonfunctional or dangerous products. Moreover, many state supreme courts have concluded that products are sold with an implicit understanding that they will safely perform their intended function. If they do not, consumers can sue the seller even in the absence of product liability laws. If consumers can rely on explicit or implicit product liability laws to force a manufacturer to make good on defective products, they need not worry about adverse selection.

An inherent problem with legal recourse, however, is that the transaction costs of going to court are very high. Moreover, state laws may be less effective than federal regulations in protecting consumers with respect to cars that are lemons.

APPLICATION

Recycling Lemons

Daniel Garcia of Virginia bought a Dodge Caravan that leaked when it rained.[4] The Chrysler Corporation repurchased his minivan when he sued under his state's lemon law. Soon thereafter, Karen Melvin of Minneapolis, Minnesota, adopted the same unusual driving practice as Daniel Garcia: taking a towel along with the car keys on rainy days. That's not surprising, as she had bought Daniel Garcia's former Caravan. She too sued Chrysler and sold the company the minivan. Then Wade Wilson of Champaign, Illinois, purchased this lemon.

Cases such as these led consumer advocates to seek uniform laws to prevent cars that have been identified as lemons in one state from being sold without warning in another state. Today, all states have lemon laws, though they differ as to what they require dealers and manufacturers to do with returned vehicles.

In 12 states, firms are not required to tell a prospective car buyer that a car was previously returned as a lemon. Only Alabama, California, Connecticut, the District of Columbia, Florida, Indiana, Iowa, Louisiana, Maryland, New Jersey, New York, South Dakota, Utah, Vermont, Washington, and Wisconsin

[4] Adelson, Andrea, "Pushing Lemons over State Lines," *New York Times*, August 27, 1996:C1, C4.

require that a vehicle be labeled a lemon on its title. California, Idaho, and New Hampshire alone insist that titles be carried over from other states.[5]

Moreover, the enforcement of state laws is often lax. Florida, which requires reports on lemons, found that auto makers had reported only 12% of the 3,412 vehicles that were repurchased in the state between 1992 and 1994. In short: Buyer beware! ■

Consumer Screening. Consumers can avoid the lemon problem if they can obtain reliable information about quality. Consumers actively collect such information—screen—in some markets. When a consumer's cost of obtaining information is less than the private benefits, consumers obtain the information and markets function smoothly. However, if the cost exceeds the benefit, they do not gather the information and the market is inefficient. Consumers buy information from experts or infer product quality from sellers' reputations.

For many goods, consumers can buy reliable information from *objective experts*. For example, you can pay to have a mechanic appraise a used car. If the mechanic can reliably determine whether the car is a lemon, the information asymmetry is eliminated.

In some markets, consumers learn of a firm's *reputation* from other consumers or from observation. Consumers can avoid the adverse selection problem by buying only from firms that have reputations for providing high-quality goods. Consumers know that a used-car firm that expects repeat purchases has a strong incentive not to sell defective products.

You may have noticed that some firms have lavish offices or spend large sums on advertising that does not appear to be informative or persuasive. These firms may be trying to establish a reputation for high quality through their extravagant spending. Only firms that expect to be in business for a long time would sink such grand sums. In contrast, fly-by-night firms make minimal capital expenditures, sell a few bad-quality goods at high prices, and then disappear because they expect no repeat sales.

Generally, in markets in which the same consumers and firms trade regularly, a reputation is easy to establish. In markets in which consumers buy a good only once, such as in tourist areas, firms cannot establish reputations as easily.

Third-Party Comparisons. Some nonprofit organizations, such as consumer groups, and for-profit firms publish expert comparisons of brands. To the degree that this information is credible, it may reduce adverse selection by enabling consumers to avoid buying low-quality goods.

If an outside organization is to provide believable information, it must convince consumers that it is trustworthy and is not deceiving them. Consumers Union,

[5]For a $20 fee, however, consumers can track down a used vehicle's original title through Carfax at 1-888-422-7329 or on the World Wide Web at http://www.carfax.com to determine whether they are buying someone else's lemon.

which publishes the well-known product evaluation guide *Consumer Reports*, tries to establish its trustworthiness by refusing to accept advertising or other payments from firms.

Unfortunately, expert information is undersupplied because information is a *public good* (nonrival and only sometimes excludable—see Chapter 18). Consumers Union does not capture the full value of its information through sales of *Consumer Reports* because buyers lend their copies to friends, libraries stock the magazine, and newspapers report on its findings. As result, Consumers Union conducts less research than is socially optimal.

Standards and Certification. The government, consumer groups, industry groups, and others provide information based on a **standard**: a metric or scale for evaluating the quality of a particular product. For example, the R-value of insulation—a standard—tells how effectively insulation works. Consumers learn of a brand's quality through **certification**: a report that a particular product meets or exceeds a given standard level.

Many industry groups set their own standards and get an outside group or firm, such as Underwriters' Laboratories (UL) or Factory Mutual Engineering Corporation (FMEC), to certify that their products meet specified standard levels. For example, by setting standards for the size of the thread on a screw, we ensure that screws work in products across brands.

When standard and certification programs inexpensively and completely inform consumers about the relative quality of all goods in a market and do not restrict the goods available, the programs are socially desirable. Some of these programs have harmful effects, however.

Standard and certification programs that provide degraded information, for instance, may mislead consumers. Many standards use only a high- versus low-quality rating even though quality varies continuously. Such standards encourage the manufacture of products that have either the lowest-possible quality (and cost of production) or the minimum quality level necessary to obtain the top rating.

If standard and certification programs restrict goods that can be sold to those that are certified, such programs also may have anticompetitive effects. Many governments license only professionals and craftspeople who meet some minimum standards. People without a license are not allowed to practice their profession or craft. In most states, dozens, if not hundreds, of categories of professionals, craftspeople, and others are licensed, including electricians, plumbers, dentists, psychologists, contractors, and beauticians. In California, nearly one in four workers holds a professional license, including roughly 400,000 cosmetologists, 300,000 contractors, and 200,000 private investigators.

The restrictions raise the average quality in the industry by eliminating low-quality goods and services. They drive up prices to consumers for two reasons. First, the number of people providing services is reduced because the restrictions eliminate some potential suppliers. Second, consumers are unable to obtain lower-quality and less expensive goods or services. As a result, welfare may go up or down, depending on whether the increased-quality effect or the higher-price effect dominates. Whether such restrictions can be set properly and cost-effectively by government agencies is widely debated.

Moreover, licensing and mandatory standards and certification are often used for anticompetitive purposes such as erecting entry barriers to new firms and products. Doctors, lawyers, electricians, and other professionals establish their own licensing standards under government auspices. Frequently, these groups set standards that prevent entry of professionals from other states or those who have just finished their education so as to keep the wages of currently licensed professionals high. Such licensing is socially harmful because it excludes qualified professionals and raises consumers' costs.[6]

Signaling by Firms. Producers of high-quality goods often try to signal to consumers that their products are of better quality than those of their rivals. If consumers believe their signals, these firms can charge higher prices for their superior goods. But if the signals are to be effective, they must be credible.

Firms use brand names as a signal of quality. For example, some farms brand their produce, while rivals sell their produce without labels. Shoppers may rely on this signal and choose only fruits and vegetables with brand labels. Presumably, a firm uses a brand name to enable buyers to identify its product only if the item's quality is better than that of a typical, unbranded product.

Some firms provide guarantees or warranties as signals to convince consumers that their products are of high quality. Consumer durables such as cars and refrigerators commonly come with guarantees or warranties. Virtually all new cars have warranties. Moreover, one-third of used cars purchased from dealers include warranties, according to a Federal Trade Commission survey (Genesove 1993, p. 648).

Signals solve the adverse selection problem only when consumers view them as credible because only high-quality firms find their use profitable. Smart consumers may place little confidence in unsubstantiated claims by firms. Would you believe that a used car runs well just because an ad tells you so? Legally enforceable guarantees and warranties are more credible than advertising alone.

Signaling will not solve an adverse selection problem if it is unprofitable for high-quality firms to signal or if both high- and low-quality firms send the same signal. For example, if a firm's overhead costs are very high, it may not pay for a firm to provide a guarantee to signal the high quality of its product. Another possibility is that both low- and high-quality firms signal. If so, the signal is worthless to consumers. Both low-quality and high-quality fruit and vegetable firms can use trademarks in tourist areas, where there are few repeat purchases. Similarly, all firms may provide guarantees for inexpensive goods, for which transaction costs are usually too high for consumers to use guarantees.

---

[6]Unfortunately, economists have not been clever enough to get their profession licensed so that they can act anticompetitively to limit supply and raise their earnings.

APPLICATION

Wholesale Market for Cherries

From their study of the wholesale market for fresh cherries, Rosenman and Wilson (1991) concluded that cherries are not lemons. They found that seller characteristics signal quality to buyers and that buyers pay premiums to firms with these characteristics—thereby reducing the adverse selection problem.

Information is asymmetric at the time of sale. Because sellers have inspected their cherries, they know the fruit's quality—primarily size. By contrast, buyers, who may be making their purchases from across the country, cannot inspect the cherries.

Cherries are sold in 10 different size categories, the larger sizes being worth more. For seven of these categories, cherries are sorted into classes of narrowly defined sizes. Only the minimum size is specified for the other three categories, so the actual sizes of the unsorted cherries in these classes can differ substantially.

Because sorting is costly, a firm may decide not to sort and instead sell its high-quality (large) cherries mixed with smaller cherries at a lower minimum-size standard. *Sorting firms* sell in all 10 categories. *Nonsorting firms* sell their smallest cherries (13 cherries to a row) by themselves and sell all their other cherries in the lowest minimum-size, unsorted category (12 cherries or fewer to a row).

Buying cherries that are sorted by size reduces the potential lemons problem by providing useful information to buyers. An adverse selection problem is more likely for the 81% of cherries that are sold unsorted.

A buyer of this lowest minimum-size, unsorted category knows whether the seller sorts. As a result, a buyer pays nonsorting firms up to 11.6% ($1.24 per box) more than sorting firms. Boxes from nonsorting firms include valuable large cherries as well as small cherries, whereas those from sorting firms include almost exclusively minimum-size cherries because these firms sell their larger cherries separately. ■

19.4 PRICE DISCRIMINATION DUE TO FALSE BELIEFS ABOUT QUALITY

We've seen that bad products can drive out good products if consumers cannot distinguish lemons from good-quality products at the time of purchase. The market outcome also changes if consumers falsely believe that identical products differ in quality. Consumers pay more for a product that they believe is of higher quality.

If some consumers know that two products are identical while others believe that they differ in quality, a firm can profitably price discriminate. The firm takes advantage of the less informed customers by charging them a high price for the allegedly superior product. The firm does not want to charge informed customers this same high price. Doing so would reduce profit because the resulting fall in sales would be greater than the gain from the higher price on sales that are made.

Asymmetric information on the part of some, but not all, consumers makes price discrimination possible. However, if all customers are informed or all are uninformed about the quality of different products, firms charge a single price.

By intentionally increasing consumer uncertainty, a firm may be better able to exploit ignorant consumers and earn a higher profit (Salop 1977). One way in which firms confuse consumers is to create *noise* by selling virtually the same product under various different brand names. Similarly, firms sometimes sell a product under their own brand name at a relatively high price and supply grocery or discount stores with a virtually identical product that is sold at a lower price under a *private-label* (house or store) brand.

Brand proliferation pays if the cost of producing multiple brands is relatively low and the share of consumers who are willing to buy the higher-price product is relatively large. Otherwise, the firm makes a higher profit by selling a single product at a moderate price than by selling one brand at a low price and another at a high price.

Many stores sell national brand-name products and store-brand or generic products. The quality of these products may differ little if at all. For example, the same bakery produces Wonder Bread and similar house brands for various grocery stores.

Over time, as consumers have become familiar with private-label brands and recognized their quality, firms have reaped less advantage in maintaining multiple brands for many products.[7] Indeed, private-label products are rapidly gaining market share. Since 1991, the share of consumers who are familiar with store-brand products has risen from 86% to 91%, and the percentage of consumers who regularly buy the store brand has increased from 77% to 83%. Of consumers who have bought premium private-label items, 90% have rated the products equal to or better than national brands and plan to buy private-label products in the future. As a result of this trend, Wonder Bread is the only remaining national brand of white pan bread.

APPLICATION

Multiple Brand Names

By selling the same product under more than one brand name, firms can charge ignorant consumers higher prices. For decades, outside firms have manufactured products that Sears, Roebuck & Company sells under its house

[7]The following discussion is based on Krumrei, Doug, "Brand Ho! Bakery Industry Trends for 1996," *Bakery Production and Marketing*, May 15, 1996; and Palmer, Eric, "New Vigor in Bread," *Milling & Baking News*, December 5, 1995.

brand names, Kenmore, Die-Hard, and Craftsman. Amana refrigerators are sold under their own brand name and under the Kenmore brand name. Similarly, Whirlpool sells its own washers and driers, but Sears also markets these products under the Kenmore name.

Frequently, the Kenmore product is identical or superior to the brand-name product and available at a lower price. Knowledgeable consumers—those who realize that the two brands are identical except for the brand label—buy the Sears brand at the lower price. But customers who falsely believe that the name brand is better than the Kenmore product pay more for the name brand.

Similarly, a car manufacturer (or a group of manufacturers working collectively) sells cars that are nearly physically identical—at least in terms of their inner workings—under different brand names.[8] The Ford Taurus and Mercury Sable are automotive twins, as are the Toyota Camry and Lexus ES 300. Indeed, triplets and quadruplets are observed. For example, the Dodge Colt, Mitsubishi Mirage, Plymouth Colt, and Eagle Summit cars are virtual clones.

Twins often have very different prices. Consumers can save $1,124 by purchasing an Olds 98 Regency rather than its twin, the Buick Park Avenue. Even the rich can save a bundle if they don't mind a different grille and headlights: The $152,400 long-wheelbase Bentley Brookland costs $25,800 less than the $178,200 Rolls-Royce Silver Spur III. ■

19.5 MARKET POWER FROM PRICE IGNORANCE

We've just seen that consumer ignorance about quality can keep high-quality goods out of markets or lead to price discrimination. Consumer ignorance about how prices vary across firms has yet another effect: It gives firms market power. As a result, firms have an incentive to make it difficult for consumers to collect information about prices. For this reason, some stores won't quote prices over the phone.

We now examine why asymmetric information about prices leads to noncompetitive pricing in a market that would otherwise be competitive. Suppose that many stores in a town sell the same good. If consumers have *full information* about prices, all stores charge the full-information competitive price p^*. If one store were to raise its price above p^*, the store would lose all its business. Each store faces a residual demand curve that is horizontal at the going market price and has no market power.

In contrast, if consumers have *limited information* about the price that firms charge for a product, one store can charge more than others and not lose all its customers. Those customers who do not know that the product is available for less elsewhere

[8]According to the American Automobile Association, as discussed in Schuon, Marshall, "Twins, Triplets and Other Siblings," *New York Times*, November 7, 1993:Section 1, p. 27.

keep buying from the high-price store.[9] Thus, each store faces a downward-sloping residual demand curve and has some market power. In the following model, we show that, if there is a single price in such a market, it is higher than p^*.

Tourist-Trap Model

You arrive in a small town near the site of the discovery of gold in California. Souvenir shops crowd the street. Wandering by one of these stores, you see that it sells the town's distinctive snowy (or snow globe or snow dome): a plastic ball filled with water and imitation snow featuring a model of the Donner party. You instantly decide that you must buy at least one of these tasteful mementos—perhaps more if the price is low enough. Your bus will leave very soon, so you can't check the price at each shop to find the lowest price. Moreover, determining which shop has the lowest price won't be useful to you in the future because you do not intend to return anytime soon.

Let's assume that you and other tourists have a guidebook that reports how many souvenir shops charge each possible price for the snowy, but the guidebook does not state the price at any particular shop.[10] There are many tourists in your position, each with an identical demand function.

It costs each tourist c in time and expenses to visit a shop to check the price or buy a snowy. Thus, if the price is p, the cost of buying a snowy at the first shop you visit is $p + c$. If you go to two souvenir shops before buying at the second shop, the cost of the snowy is $p + 2c$.

When Price Is Not Competitive. Will all souvenir shops charge the same price? If so, what price will they charge? We start by considering whether each shop charges the full-information, competitive price, p^*.

The full-information, competitive price is the equilibrium price only if no firm has an incentive to charge a different price. No firm would charge less than p^*, which equals marginal cost, because it would lose money on each sale.

However, a firm could gain by charging a higher price than p^*, so p^* is *not* an equilibrium price. If all other shops charge p^*, a firm can profitably charge $p_1 = p^* + \varepsilon$, where ε, a small positive number, is the shop's price markup. Suppose that you walk into this shop and learn that it sells the snowy for p_1. You know from your guidebook that all other souvenir shops charge only p^*. You say to yourself, "How unfortunate [or other words to that effect], I've wandered into the only expensive

---

[9] A grave example concerns the ripping-off of the dying and the survivors of the dead. A cremation arranged through a memorial society—which typically charges a nominal enrollment fee of $10 to $25—costs $400 to $600, compared with $1,500 to $2,000 for the same service when it is arranged through a mortuary. Consumers who know about memorial societies—which get competitive bids from mortuaries—can obtain a relatively low price. The less knowledgeable people who deal directly with mortuaries pay more. Rowland, Mary, "Shedding Light on a Dark Subject," *New York Times*, July 24, 1994:13.

[10] We make this assumption about the guidebook to keep the presentation as simple as possible. This assumption is not necessary to obtain the following result.

shop in town." Annoyed, you consider going elsewhere. Nonetheless, you do not go to another shop if this shop's markup, $\varepsilon = p_1 - p^*$, is less than c, the cost of going to another shop.

As a result, it pays for this shop to raise its price by an amount that is just slightly less than the cost of an additional search, thereby deviating from the proposed equilibrium where all other shops charge p^*. Thus, *if consumers have limited information about price, an equilibrium in which all firms charge the full-information, competitive price is impossible.*

Monopoly Price. We've already seen that the market price cannot be lower than or equal to the full-information, competitive price. Can there be an equilibrium in which all stores charge the same price and that price is higher than the competitive price? In particular, can we have an equilibrium when all shops charge $p_1 = p^* + \varepsilon$? No, shops would deviate from this new proposed equilibrium for the same reason that they deviated from charging the competitive price. A shop can profitably raise its price to $p_2 = p_1 + \varepsilon = p^* + 2\varepsilon$. Again, it does not pay for a tourist who is unlucky enough to enter that shop to go to another shop as long as $\varepsilon < c$. Thus, p_1 is not the equilibrium price. By repeating this reasoning, we can reject other possible equilibrium prices that are above p^* and less than the monopoly price, p_m.

However, the monopoly price may be an equilibrium price. No firm wants to raise its price above the monopoly level because its profit would fall due to reduced sales. When tourists learn the price at a particular souvenir shop, they decide how many snowies to buy. If the price is set too high, the shop's lost sales more than offset the higher price, so its profit falls. Thus, although the shop can charge a higher price without losing all its sales, it chooses not to do so.

The only remaining question is whether a shop would like to charge a lower price than p_m if all other shops charge that price. If not, p_m is an equilibrium price.

Should a shop reduce its price below p_m by less than c? If it does so, it does not pay for consumers to search for this low-price firm. The shop makes less on each sale, so its profits must fall. Thus, a shop should not deviate by charging a price that is only slightly less than p_m.

Does it pay for a shop to drop its price below p_m by more than c? If there are few shops, consumers may search for this low-price shop. Although the shop makes less per sale than the high-price shops, its profits may be higher because of greater sales volume. If there are many shops, however, consumers do not search for the low-price shop because their chances of finding it are low.[11] As a result, when the presence of a large number of shops makes searching for a low-price shop impractical, no firm lowers its price, so p_m is the equilibrium price. Thus, *when consumers have asymmetric information and when search costs and the number of firms are large, the only possible single-price equilibrium is at the monopoly price.*

[11]It may be possible, however, for firms to advertise that they have low prices and thereby to overcome the high search-cost problem, as we discuss in the next section.

If the single-price equilibrium at p_m can be broken by a firm charging a low price, there is no single-price equilibrium. Either there is no equilibrium or there is an equilibrium in which prices vary across shops (see Stiglitz 1979 or Carlton and Perloff 1994). Multiple-price equilibria are common.

SOLVED PROBLEM 19.2

Initially, there are many souvenir shops, each of which charges p_m (because consumers do not know the shops' prices), and buyers' search costs are c. If the government pays for half of consumers' search costs, can there be a single-price equilibrium at a price less than p_m?

Answer:

Show that the argument we used above to reject a single-price equilibrium at any price except the monopoly price did not depend on the size of the search cost: If all other stores charge any single price p, where $p^* \le p < p_m$, a firm profits from raising its price. As long as it raises its price by no more than $c/2$ (the new cost of search to a consumer), unlucky consumers who stop at this deviant store do not search further. Although the price deviation is smaller than before, this profitable deviation shows that the proposed single-price equilibrium is not an equilibrium. Again, the only possible single-price equilibrium is at p_m.[12] ■

Advertising and Prices

The U.S. Federal Trade Commission (FTC), a consumer protection agency, opposes groups that want to forbid price advertising; the FTC argues that advertising about price benefits consumers. If a firm informs consumers about its unusually low price, it may be able to gain enough extra customers to more than offset its loss from the lower price. If low-price stores advertise their prices and attract many customers, they can break the monopoly-price equilibrium that occurs when consumers must search store by store for low prices. The more successful the advertising, the larger these stores grow and the lower is the average price in the market. If enough consumers become informed, all stores may charge the low price. Thus, without advertising, no store may find it profitable to charge low prices; but with advertising, all stores may charge low prices.

---

[12]Thus, with a positive search cost, no matter how small, the only possible single-price equilibrium is at p^m. If the search cost is low enough, however, the single-price equilibrium at p^m can be broken profitably by charging a low price so that only a multiple-price equilibrium is possible. If the search cost falls to zero, consumers have full information, so the only possible equilibrium is at the full-information competitive price.

APPLICATION

Advertising Lowers Prices

Many studies by FTC economists and other economists show that allowing stores to advertise their prices lowers the average price that consumers pay for products such as drugs, eyeglasses, liquor, toys, and retail gasoline. Years ago, some states banned the advertising of eyeglass prices. Benham (1972) found that banning all advertising raised prices by 28% relative to the prices in states that did not ban advertising. The price difference was negligible, however, between states that allowed advertising and those that banned only price advertising.

A subsequent FTC study (Bond et al. 1980) on eyeglass advertising found that prices were lower in cities that allowed advertising than in those that banned it. In cities without advertising bans, even optometrists who did not advertise charged an average of $20 less for an exam and glasses than did their counterparts in cities that banned advertising. Moreover, this study found that eyeglass quality was the same in cities with and without the ban.

Because advertising can lower prices in a market, professional groups try to ban it. Until Supreme Court decisions stopped them, medical, dental, and legal organizations blocked advertising, claiming that it was unprofessional. Today, many of these professionals advertise in newspapers and the Yellow Pages and on radio and television. Some law firms issue press releases after trial victories, mail brochures to prospective clients, and hire public relations firms to help penetrate the market. Schroeter, Smith, and Cox (1987) found that the cost of legal services for simple wills and uncontested bankruptcy proceedings fell with advertising. ■

19.6 PROBLEMS ARISING FROM IGNORANCE WHEN HIRING

Asymmetric information is frequently a problem in labor markets. Prospective employees may have less information about working conditions than firms do. Firms may have less information about potential employees' abilities than the workers do.

Information asymmetries in labor markets lower welfare below the full-information level. Workers may signal and firms may screen to reduce the asymmetry in information about workers' abilities. Signaling and screening may raise or lower welfare, as we now consider.

Information about Employment Risks

Firms typically have more information than workers about job safety. This asymmetric information may lead to less than optimal levels of safety (Viscusi 1979, pp. 119f).

Prospective employees who do not know the injury rate at individual firms may know the average injury rates in an industry because these data are reported by the U.S. Bureau of Labor Statistics. People will work in a risky industry only if they are paid more than they would earn in less risky industries.

Each firm must consider how safe to make its plant. Extra safety is costly. Safety investments—sprinkler systems, color-coded switches, fire extinguishers—by one firm provide an externality to other firms: That firm's lower incidence of accidents reduces the wage that all firms in the industry must pay. *Because each firm bears the full cost of its safety investments but derives only some of the benefits, the firms underinvest in safety.*

The prisoners' dilemma game in Table 19.1, which is played by the only two firms in an industry, illustrates this result. In the Nash equilibrium (upper left), neither firm invests and each earns $200.

An investment by only one firm raises safety levels at its plant. Workers in the industry do not know that safety has improved only at the plant of the investing firm. They realize only that it is safer to work in this industry, so both firms pay lower wages. The loss from the investment is greater than the wage savings, so the profit falls to $100 for the firm that invests. The wage savings causes its rival's profit to rise to $250.

If both firms invest (lower right), both earn $225, which is more than they would earn in the Nash equilibrium. However, investment by both firms is not an equilibrium, as each firm has an incentive to deviate.

This prisoners' dilemma would not occur if workers knew how safe each firm was. Only the firm that invested in safety would be able to pay a lower wage if workers knew the accident rate by firms. There would be no externality. Thus, a firm that can credibly convince workers that it is a relatively safe place to work can overcome this asymmetric information–externality problem.[13]

Table 19.1 Safety Investment Game

		Firm 2: *No Investment*	Firm 2: *Investment*
Firm 1	*No Investment*	Firm 1: $200; Firm 2: $200	Firm 1: $250; Firm 2: $100
	Investment	Firm 1: $100; Firm 2: $250	Firm 1: $225; Firm 2: $225

[13]Because this information is a pure public good, others may obtain this information if the firm provides it to employees. The cost to the firm of having others, such as government regulators, obtain this information may exceed the lower-wage benefit from providing it to workers.

In this example, the underinvestment problem could be avoided if the government provided the information, if the government set safety standards that would force both firms to invest, or if unions effectively lobbied both firms for higher levels of safety. For the government or unions to provide these useful functions practically, however, their cost of gathering the necessary information would have to be relatively low.

Cheap Talk

Honesty is the best policy—when there is money in it. —Mark Twain

We now consider situations in which workers have more information about their ability than firms do. We look first at inexpensive signals sent by workers, then at expensive signals sent by workers, and finally at screening by firms.

When an informed person voluntarily provides information to an uninformed person, the informed person engages in **cheap talk**: unsubstantiated claims or statements.[14] Even though such people may lie when it suits them, cheap talk sometimes helps everyone. One advantage of cheap talk, if it is effective, is that it is a lower-cost method of signaling ability to a potential employer than paying to have that ability tested.

Suppose that a firm plans to hire Cyndi to do one of two jobs. The demanding job requires someone with high ability. The undemanding job can be done better by someone of low ability because the job bores able people, who then perform badly.

Cyndi knows whether her ability level is high or low, but the firm is unsure. It initially thinks that either level is equally likely. Panel a of Table 19.2 shows the payoffs to Cyndi and the firm under various possibilities.[15] If Cyndi has high ability, she enjoys the demanding job: Her payoff is 3. If she has low ability, she finds the demanding job too stressful—her payoff is only 1—but she can handle the undemanding job. The payoff to the firm is greater if Cyndi is properly matched to the job: She is given the demanding job if she has high ability and the undemanding job if she has low ability.

We can view this example as a two-stage game. In the first stage, Cyndi tells the firm something. In the second stage, the firm decides which job she gets.

Cyndi could make many possible statements about her ability. For simplicity, though, we assume that she says either "My ability is high" or "My ability is low." This two-stage game has an equilibrium in which Cyndi tells the truth and the firm, believing her, assigns her to the appropriate job. If she claims to have high ability, the firm gives her the demanding job.

If the firm reacts to her cheap talk in this manner, Cyndi has no incentive to lie. If she did lie, the firm would make a mistake, and a mistake would be bad for both parties. Cyndi and the firm want the same outcomes, so cheap talk works.

---

[14]This section, which is based on Farrell and Rabin (1996), makes extensive use of their examples and insights. See their article and the others that they cite for more details. This topic is similar to incentive compatibility, which is discussed in the next chapter.

[15]Previously, we used a 2×2 matrix to show a simultaneous-move game (such as in Table 19.1), in which both parties choose an action at the same time. Here, only the firm can make a move. Cyndi does not take an action: She cannot choose her ability level.

Table 19.2 Employee-Employer Payoffs

a) Cheap Talk Works

Cyndi's Ability	*Job That the Firm Gives to Cyndi:* *Demanding*	*Undemanding*
High	3 / 2	1 / 1
Low	1 / 1	2 / 4

b) Cheap Talk Fails

Cyndi's Ability	*Job That the Firm Gives to Cyndi:* *Demanding*	*Undemanding*
High	3 / 2	1 / 1
Low	3 / 1	2 / 4

In many other situations, however, cheap talk does not work. Given the payoffs in panel b, Cyndi and the firm do not want the same outcomes. The firm still wants Cyndi in the demanding job if she has high ability and in the undemanding job otherwise. Here, Cyndi wants the demanding job regardless of her ability. Thus, she claims to have high ability regardless of the truth. Knowing her incentives, the firm views her statement as meaningless babbling—Her statement does not change the firm's view that her ability is equally likely to be high or low.

Given that belief, the firm gives her the undemanding job, for which its expected payoff is higher. The firm's expected payoff is $(\frac{1}{2} \times 1) + (\frac{1}{2} \times 4) = 2.5$ if it gives her the undemanding job and $(\frac{1}{2} \times 2) + (\frac{1}{2} \times 1) = 1.5$ if it assigns her to the demanding job. Thus, given the firm's asymmetric information, the outcome is inefficient if Cyndi has high ability.

When the interests of the firm and the individual diverge, cheap talk does not provide a credible signal. Here, an individual has to send a more expensive signal to be believed. We now examine such a signal.

Education as a Signal

No doubt you've been told that one good reason to go to college is to get a good job. Going to college may get you a better job because you obtain valuable training. Another possibility is that a college degree may land you a good job because it serves as a signal to employers about your ability. If high-ability people are more likely to go to college than low-ability people, schooling signals ability to employers (Spence 1974).

To illustrate how such signaling works, we'll make the extreme assumptions that graduating from an appropriate school serves as the signal and that schooling provides no training that is useful to firms.[16] High-ability workers are θ share of the work force, and low-ability workers are $1 - \theta$ share. The value of output that a high-ability worker produces for a firm is worth w_h, and that of a low-ability worker is w_l (over their careers). If competitive employers knew workers' ability levels, they would pay this value of the marginal product to each worker, so a high-ability worker receives w_h and a low-ability worker earns w_l.

We assume that employers cannot directly determine a worker's skill level. For example, when production is a group effort—such as in an assembly line—a firm cannot determine the productivity of a single employee.

Two types of equilibria are possible depending on whether or not employers can distinguish high-ability workers from others. If employers have no way of telling workers apart, the outcome is a **pooling equilibrium**: Dissimilar people are treated (paid) alike or behave alike. Employers pay all workers the average wage:

$$\bar{w} = \theta w_h + (1 - \theta)w_l. \tag{19.2}$$

Risk-neutral, competitive firms expect to break even because they underpay high-ability people by enough to offset the losses from overpaying low-ability workers.

We assume that high-ability individuals can get a degree by spending c to attend a school and that low-ability people cannot graduate from the school (or that the cost of doing so is prohibitively high). If high-ability people graduate and low-ability people do not, a degree is a signal of ability to employers. Given such a clear signal, the outcome is a **separating equilibrium**: One type of people takes actions (such as sending a signal) that allow them to be differentiated from other types of people. Here, a successful signal causes high-ability workers to receive w_h and the others to receive w_l, so wages vary with ability.

We now examine whether a pooling or a separating equilibrium is possible. We consider whether anyone would want to change behavior in an equilibrium. If no one wants to change, the equilibrium is feasible.

Separating Equilibrium. In a separating equilibrium, high-ability people pay c to get a degree and are employed at a wage of w_h, while low-ability individuals do not get a degree and work for a wage of w_l. The low-ability people have no choice, as they can't get a degree. High-ability individuals have the option of not going to school. Without a degree, however, they are viewed as low ability once hired, and they receive w_l. If they go to school, their net earnings are $w_h - c$. Thus, it pays for a high-ability person to go to school if

$$w_h - c > w_l.$$

[16]The following example is based on one in Stiglitz (1975).

Rearranging terms in this expression, we find that a high-ability person chooses to get a degree if

$$w_h - w_l > c. \tag{19.3}$$

Equation 19.3 says that the benefit from graduating, the extra pay $w_h - w_l$, exceeds the cost of schooling, c. If Equation 19.3 holds, no worker wants to change behavior, so a separating equilibrium is feasible.

Suppose that c = \$15,000 and that high-ability workers are twice as productive as others: w_h = \$40,000 and w_l = \$20,000. Here the benefit to a high-ability worker from graduating, $w_h - w_l$ = \$20,000, exceeds the cost by \$5,000. Thus, no one wants to change behavior in this separating equilibrium.

Pooling Equilibrium. In a pooling equilibrium, all workers are paid the average wage from Equation 19.2, $\bar{w}$. Again, because low-ability people cannot graduate, they have no choice. A high-ability person must choose whether or not to go to school. Without a degree, that individual is paid the average wage. With a degree, the worker is paid w_h. It does not pay for the high-ability person to graduate if the benefit from graduating, the extra pay $w_h - \bar{w}$, is less than the cost of schooling:

$$w_h - \bar{w} < c. \tag{19.4}$$

Thus, if Equation 19.4 holds, no worker wants to change behavior, so a pooling equilibrium persists.

For example, if w_h = \$40,000, w_l = \$20,000, and $\theta = \frac{1}{2}$, then

$$\bar{w} = (\tfrac{1}{2} \times \$40{,}000) + (\tfrac{1}{2} \times \$20{,}000) = \$30{,}000.$$

If the cost of going to school is c = \$15,000, the benefit to a high-ability person from graduating, $w_h - \bar{w}$ = \$10,000 is less than the cost, so a high-ability individual does not want to go school. As a result, there is a pooling equilibrium.

SOLVED PROBLEM 19.3

For what values of θ is a pooling equilibrium possible in general? In particular, if c = \$15,000, w_h = \$40,000, and w_l = \$20,000, for what values of θ is a pooling equilibrium possible?

Answer

1. *Determine the values of θ for which it pays for a high-ability person to go to school*: From Equation 19.4, we know that a high-ability individual does not go to school if $w_h - \bar{w} < c$. Using Equation 19.2, we substitute for $\bar{w}$ in Equation 19.4 and rearrange terms to find that high-ability people do not go to school if

$$w_h - [\theta w_h + (1 - \theta) w_l] < c,$$

or

$$\theta > 1 - \frac{c}{w_h - w_1}. \qquad (19.5)$$

If almost everyone has high ability, so θ is large, a high-ability person does not go to school. The intuition is that, as the share of high-ability workers, θ, gets large (close to 1), the average wage approaches w_h (Equation 19.2), so there is little benefit, $w_h - \bar{w}$, in going to school.

2. *Solve for the possible values of θ for the specific parameters*: If we substitute $c = \$15{,}000$, $w_h = \$40{,}000$, and $w_l = \$20{,}000$ into Equation 19.5, we find that high-ability people do not go to school—a pooling equilibrium is possible—if $\theta > \frac{1}{4}$. ■

Unique or Multiple Equilibria. Depending on differences in abilities, the cost of schooling, and the share of high-ability workers, only one type of equilibrium may be possible or both may be possible. In the following examples, using Figure 19.2, $w_h = \$40{,}000$ and $w_l = \$20{,}000$.

Only a pooling equilibrium is possible if schooling is very costly: $c > w_h - w_l = \$20{,}000$, so Equation 19.3 does not hold. A horizontal line in Figure 19.2 shows where $c = w_h - w_l = \$20{,}000$. Only a pooling equilibrium is feasible above that line, $c > \$20{,}000$, because it does not pay for high-ability workers to go to school.

Equation 19.5 shows that, if there are few high-ability people (relative to the cost and earnings differential), only a separating equilibrium is possible. The figure shows a sloped line where $\theta = 1 - c/(w_h - w_l)$. Below that line, $\theta < 1 - c/(w_h - w_l)$, relatively few people have high ability, so the average wage, $\bar{w}$, is low. A pooling equilibrium is not possible because high-ability workers would want to signal. Thus, below this line, only a separating equilibrium is possible. Above this line, Equation 19.5 holds, so a pooling equilibrium is possible. (The answer to Solved Problem 19.3 shows that no one wants to change behavior in a pooling equilibrium if $c = \$15{,}000$ and $\theta > \frac{1}{4}$, which are points to the right of x in the figure, such as y.)

Below the horizontal line where the cost of signaling is less than $20,000 and above the sloped line where there are relatively many high-ability workers, either equilibrium may occur. For example, where $c = \$15{,}000$ and $\theta = \frac{1}{2}$, Equations 19.3 and 19.4 (or equivalently, Equation 19.5) hold, so both a separating equilibrium and a pooling equilibrium are possible. In the pooling equilibrium, no one wants to change behavior, so this equilibrium is possible. Similarly, no one wants to change behavior in a separating equilibrium.

A government could ensure that one or the other of these equilibria occurs. It achieves a pooling equilibrium by banning schooling (and other possible signals). Alternatively, the government creates a separating equilibrium by subsidizing schooling for some high-ability people. Once some individuals start to signal, so firms pay either a low or high wage (not a pooling wage), it pays for other high-ability people to signal.

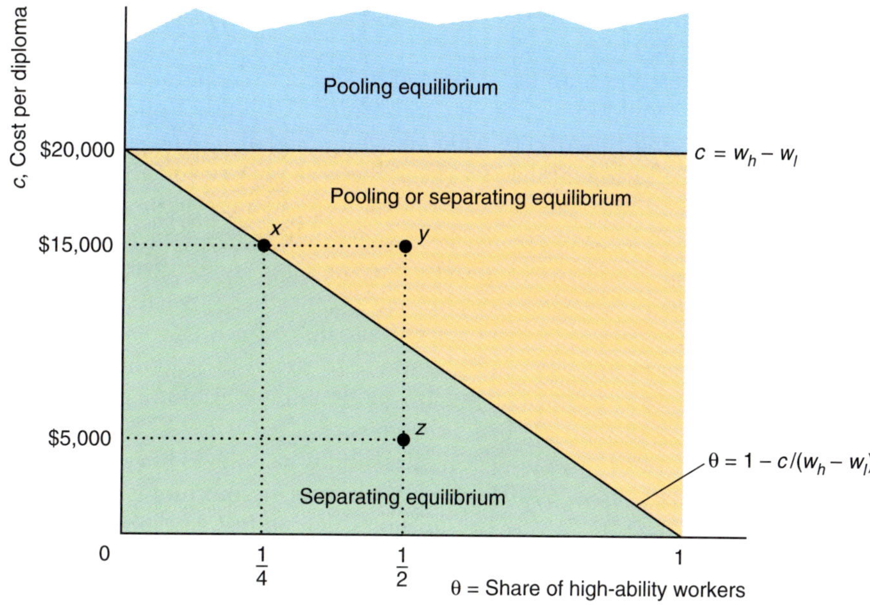

Figure 19.2 Pooling and Separating Equilibria. If firms know workers' abilities, high-ability workers are paid w_h = \$40,000 and low-ability workers get w_l = \$20,000. The type of equilibrium depends on the cost of schooling, c, and the share of high-ability workers, θ. If $c >$ \$20,000, only a pooling equilibrium, in which everyone gets the average wage, is possible. If there are relatively few high-ability people, $\theta < 1 - c/\$20{,}000$, only a separating equilibrium is possible. Between the horizontal and sloped lines, either type of equilibrium may occur.

Efficiency. In our example of a separating equilibrium, high-ability people get an otherwise useless education solely to show that they differ from low-ability people. An education is privately useful to the high-ability workers if it serves as a signal that gets them higher net pay. In our extreme example, education is socially inefficient because it is costly and provides no useful training.

Signaling changes the distribution of wages: Instead of everyone's getting the average wage, high-ability workers receive more pay than low-ability workers. Nonetheless, the total amount that firms pay is the same, so firms make zero expected profits in both equilibria.[17] Moreover, everyone is employed in both the pooling and the screening equilibrium, so total output is the same.

Everyone may be worse off in a separating equilibrium. At point y in Figure 19.2 (w_h = \$40,000, w_l = \$20,000, c = \$15,000, and $\theta = \frac{1}{2}$), either a pooling equilibrium

[17]Firms pay high-ability workers more than low-ability workers in a separating equilibrium, but the average amount they pay per worker is $\overline{w}$, the same as in a pooling equilibrium.

or a separating equilibrium is possible. In the pooling equilibrium, each worker is paid $\bar{w}$ = \$30,000 and there is no wasteful signaling. In the separating equilibrium, high-ability workers make $w_h - c$ = \$25,000 and low-ability workers make w_l = \$20,000.

Here, high-ability people earn less in the separating equilibrium, \$25,000, than they would in a pooling equilibrium, \$30,000. Nonetheless, if anyone signals, all high-ability workers want to send a signal to prevent their wage from falling to that of a low-ability worker. The reason why socially undesirable signaling happens is that the private return to signaling—high-ability workers net an extra \$5,000 (= $[w_h - c] - w_l$ = \$25,000 – \$20,000)—exceeds the net social return to signaling. The gross social return to the signal is zero—the signal changes only the distribution of wages—and the net social return is negative because the signal is costly.

This inefficient expenditure on education is due to asymmetric information and the desire of high-ability workers to signal their ability. Here, the government can increase total societal wealth by banning wasteful signaling. Both low-ability and high-ability people benefit from such a ban.

In other cases, however, high-ability people do not want a ban. At point z (where $\theta = \frac{1}{2}$ and c = \$5,000), only a separating equilibrium is possible without government intervention. In this equilibrium, high-ability workers earn $w_h - c$ = \$35,000 and low-ability workers make w_l = \$20,000. If the government bans signaling, both types of workers earn \$30,000 in the resulting pooling equilibrium, so high-ability workers are harmed, losing \$5,000 each. Thus, though the ban raises total output (wasteful signaling is eliminated), high-ability workers oppose the ban.

In this example, efficiency can always be increased by banning signaling because signaling is unproductive. However, some signaling is socially efficient because it increases total output. Education may raise output because its signal results in a better matching of workers and jobs or because it provides useful training as well as serving as a signal. Education also may make people better citizens. In conclusion, *total social output falls with signaling if signaling is socially unproductive but may rise with signaling if signaling also raises productivity or serves some other desirable purpose.*

APPLICATION

Wages Rise with Education

An implication of the *signaling model* is that workers with more education receive higher pay. According to this theory, schooling certifies a worker as being very intelligent or able. Firms use this signal to identify superior workers and pay them more.

There are other explanations for why workers with more education receive higher wages, however. One alternative theory attributes the higher pay to the greater productivity from schooling. According to the *training* or *human capital model*, schooling increases students' skills (human capital). Reading, writing, problem solving, knowledge of engineering or economics, and other skills and information that people are taught in school are valuable to firms. Wages rise with education because each year of education provides workers with additional useful skills.

Do the signaling and training models have different implications? If firms use years of schooling as the signal, both theories say that wages should rise with years of education. The implications differ, however, if an extreme version of the signaling model is used. In this *sheepskin model*, firms observe the signal of whether or not people get a degree (sheepskin) for graduating. If employers care only about the sheepskin signal, wages do not vary with the number of years of schooling, in contrast to the training model.

Economists have examined data in many countries to see whether people get higher wages if they have more years of schooling or if they have a degree. If wages do not increase with years of education, we can reject the training model. If receiving a degree does not increase a worker's wage, the sheepskin model is wrong. It is possible, of course, that both models are rejected by the evidence if schooling does not provide either training or a useful signal, so wages do not rise with education.

It is also possible that neither is rejected: Schooling provides useful training and serves as a signal. A sheepskin effect may be consistent with a training model even in the absence of signaling. Completing school may reflect superior aptitude or the ability to finish projects.

The evidence from around the world strongly indicates that wages rise with the years of education, a finding that is consistent with the training theory. But the evidence is not as clear as to whether people with degrees receive higher wages than people with nearly as many years of schooling who did not graduate.

Weiss (1988) concluded that the wages of American workers rise with schooling, a finding that is consistent with the training theory, and that workers get an additional increase in earnings with a degree, a finding that is consistent with the sheepskin hypothesis. He reported that the increase in wages from completing high school is more than three times as great as the increase in wages from completing eleventh grade.

In a study of Dutch workers, however, Groot and Oosterbeek (1994) found strong support for the training theory but not for the sheepskin effect. They rejected two screening hypotheses: that more rapid completion of a degree signals greater ability and should lead to higher earnings and that years spent in education without obtaining a degree should not increase earnings.

Grubb (1995) directly tested the sheepskin hypothesis and found support for the signaling hypothesis. He examined the return to education for Americans employed by others and for self-employed individuals, who have no need to signal an employer. After controlling for grades and other education, he found that salaried men with a college B.A. degree earn $5,563 more than men without a degree, compared to only a $2,843 difference for self-employed men. The comparable figures for women are $4,649 and $623 (though there were few self-employed women in his sample). ■

Screening by Employers

Firms try to screen workers in many ways. A firm may offer potential employees or consumers a choice and use their answer to screen. We examined examples of consumer screening and second-degree price discrimination in Chapter 13. Airlines give travelers a choice of high fares and no restrictions on travel or low fares and a requirement to stay over a Saturday night. Through self-selection, customers are screened between business travelers with relatively inelastic demand and vacationers with relatively elastic demand. Similarly, an employer may screen by observing whether a candidate for employment has a characteristic that the employer believes is correlated with ability, such as how the worker dresses or speaks.

Interviews and Tests. Employers pay attention to whether a candidate shows up on time for an interview, is well dressed and well spoken, and appears to be bright and alert. Firms may also give tests that they believe assess ability.

If such screening devices are accurate, they benefit the firm. As with signaling, however, these costly activities may be inefficient if they do not increase output. Such screening could lead to greater productivity if the result is a better match between workers and tasks.

These types of screening activities by firms are widely accepted in most societies. The use of interviews to hire is nearly universally accepted. In the United States, hiring tests are challenged in court only to the degree that they are not highly related to the actual activities or the needs of the firm's employees. We now turn to another type of screening that may be inefficient.

Statistical Discrimination. If employers think that people of a certain gender, race, religion, or ethnicity have higher ability on average than others, they may engage in *statistical discrimination* (Aigner and Cain 1977) and hire only people of a particular gender, race, or religion. Employers may engage in this practice even if they know that the correlation between gender or race and ability is imperfect.

Figure 19.3 illustrates one employer's belief that members of Race 1 have, on average, lower ability than members of Race 2. The figure shows that the employer believes that some members of the first race have higher ability than some members of the second race: Part of the Race 1 curve lies to the right of part of the Race 2 curve. Still, because the employer believes that a group characteristic, race, is an (imperfect) indicator of individual ability, the employer hires only people of Race 2 if enough of them are available.

The employer may claim not to be prejudiced but to be concerned only with maximizing profit.[18] Nonetheless, this employer's actions harm members of Race 1 as much as they would if they were due to racial hatred.

It may be very difficult to eliminate statistical discrimination even though ability distributions are identical across races. If all employers share the belief that members of Race 1 have such low ability that it is not worth hiring them, people of that race are never hired, so employers never learn that their beliefs are incorrect. Thus,

---

[18]Not all employment discrimination is due to statistical discrimination. Other common sources of discrimination are prejudice (Becker 1971) and the exercise of monopsony power (Madden 1973).

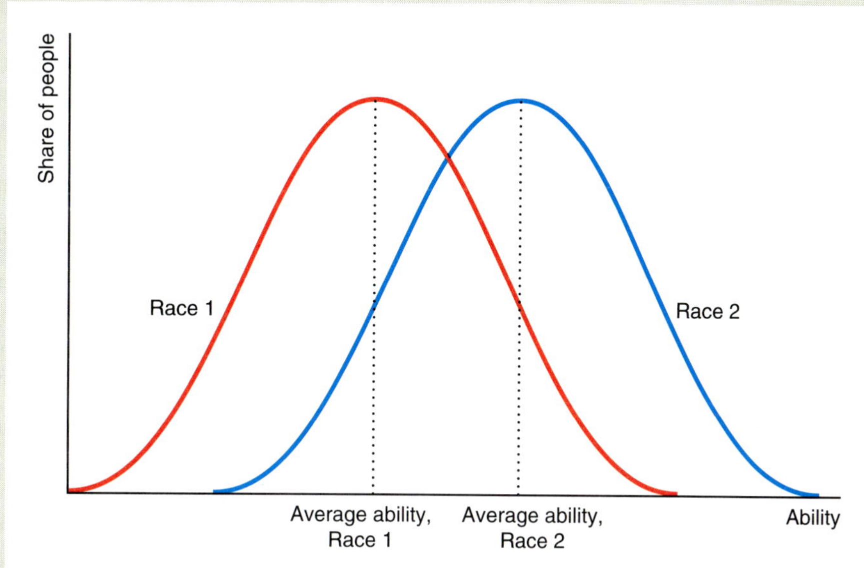

Figure 19.3 Statistical Discrimination. This figure shows the beliefs of an employer who thinks that people of Race 1 have less ability on average than people of Race 2. This employer hires only people of Race 2, even though the employer believes that some members of Race 1 have greater ability than some members of Race 2. Because this employer never employs members of Race 1, the employer may never learn that workers of both races have equal ability.

false beliefs can persist indefinitely. Such discrimination lowers social output if it keeps skilled members of Race 1 from performing certain jobs.

However, statistical discrimination may be based on true differences between groups. For example, insurance companies offer lower auto insurance rates to young women than to young men because young men are more likely, *on average*, to have an accident. The companies report that this practice lowers their costs of providing insurance by reducing moral hazard. Nonetheless, this practice penalizes young men who are unusually safe drivers and benefits young women who are unusually reckless drivers.

Summary

1. **Problems due to asymmetric information:** Asymmetric information causes market failures when informed parties engage in opportunistic behavior at the expense of uninformed parties. The resulting failures include the elimination of markets and pricing above marginal cost. Two types of problems arise from opportunism. Adverse selection is opportunism whereby only those informed parties who have an unobserved characteristic that allows them to benefit from a deal agree to it, to the detriment of a less informed party. Moral hazard is opportunism whereby an informed party takes advantage of a less informed party through an unobserved action.

2. **Responses to adverse selection:** Avoiding adverse selection problems requires restricting the opportunistic behavior or eliminating the information asymmetry. To prevent the opportunism that occurs when information is asymmetric, governments may intervene in markets or the people involved may write contracts that restrict the behavior of informed people. To eliminate or reduce information asymmetries, uninformed people screen to determine the information of informed people, informed people send signals to uninformed people, or third parties such as the government provide information.

3. **How ignorance about quality drives out high-quality goods:** If consumers cannot distinguish between good and bad products before purchase, bad products may drive good ones out of the market. This lemons problem is due to adverse selection. Methods of dealing with the lemons problem include laws limiting opportunism, consumer screening (such as by using experts or relying on firms' reputations), the provision of information by third parties such as government agencies or consumer groups, and signaling by firms (including establishing brand names and providing guarantees or warranties).

4. **Price discrimination due to false beliefs about quality:** Firms may price discriminate if some consumers incorrectly think that quality varies across identical products. Because only some consumers collect information about quality, only those consumers know whether the quality differs between products in some markets. Firms can exploit ignorant consumers by creating noise: selling the same good under two different brand names at different prices.

5. **Market power from price ignorance:** If consumers do not know how prices vary across firms, a firm can raise its price without losing all its customers. As a consequence, consumers' ignorance about price creates market power. In a market that would be competitive with full information, consumer ignorance about price may lead to a monopoly price or a distribution of prices.

6. **Problems arising from ignorance when hiring:** Companies use signaling and screening to try to eliminate information asymmetries in hiring. Where prospective employees and firms share common interests—such as assigning the right worker to the right task—everyone benefits from eliminating the information asymmetry by having informed job candidates honestly tell the firms—through *cheap talk*—about their abilities. When the two parties do not share common interests, cheap talk does not work. Potential employees may inform employers about their abilities by using expensive signals such as a college degree. If these signals are unproductive (as when education serves only as a signal and provides no training), they may be privately beneficial but socially harmful. If the signals are productive (as when education provides training or leads to greater output due to more fitting job assignments), they may be both privately and socially beneficial. Firms may also screen. Job interviews, objective tests, and other screening devices that lead to a better matching of workers and jobs may be socially beneficial. Screening by statistical discrimination, however, is harmful to discriminated-against groups. Employers who discriminate on the basis of a particular group characteristic may never learn that their discrimination is based on false beliefs because they never test these beliefs.

Problems

1. Some states prohibit insurance companies from using car owners' home addresses to set auto insurance rates. Why do insurance companies use home addresses? What are the efficiency and equity implications of forbidding such practices?

2. The state of California set up its own earthquake insurance program for home owners in 1997. The rates vary by zip code, depending on the proximity of the nearest fault line. However, critics claim that the people who set the rates ignored soil type. Some houses rest on bedrock; others sit on unstable soil. What are the implications of such rate setting?

3. You want to determine whether there is a lemons problem in the market for single-engine airplanes.

Can you use any of the following information to help answer this question? If so, how?

A. Repair rates for original-owner planes versus planes that have been resold.

B. The fraction of planes resold in each year after purchase.

4. Use Akerlof's lemons model to give one explanation for why the first-year depreciation of new cars is so high. (If you buy a new car and try to sell it in the first year—indeed, in the first few days after you buy it—the price that you get is substantially less than the original price.)

5. Use Akerlof's lemons model to explain why restaurants that serve only tourists are likely to serve low-quality meals. Tourists will not return to this area, and they have no information about the relative quality of the food at various restaurants, but they can determine the relative price by looking at menus posted outside each restaurant.

6. A firm spends a great deal of money in advertising to inform consumers of the brand name of its mushrooms. Should consumers conclude that its mushrooms are likely to be of higher quality than unbranded mushrooms? Why or why not?

7. Explain how a monopoly firm can act like a noisy monopoly by advertising sales in newspapers or magazines or through other media that only some of its customers see.

8. In the signaling model, suppose that firms can pay c^* to have a worker's ability determined through a test. Does it pay for a firm to make this expenditure?

9. When is statistical discrimination privately inefficient? When is it socially inefficient? Does it always harm members of the discriminated-against group?

10. For years, the University of California at Santa Cruz avoided giving letter grades. One rationale is that eliminating the letter-grade system reduces the pressure on students, thus enabling them to do better in school. Why might this policy help or hurt students?

11. Some firms are willing to hire only high school graduates. On the basis of past experience or statistical evidence, these companies believe that high school graduates perform better than nongraduates on average. How does this hiring behavior compare to statistical discrimination by employers on the basis of race or gender? Discuss the equity and efficiency implications of this practice.

Math Problems

12. There are many buyers who value high-quality used cars at the full-information market price of p_1 and lemons at p_2. There are a limited number of potential sellers who value high-quality cars at $v_1 \le p_1$ and lemons at $v_2 \le p_2$. Everyone is risk neutral. The share of lemons among all the used cars that might potentially be sold is θ. Under what conditions are all cars sold? When are only lemons sold? Are there any conditions under which no cars are sold?

13. Suppose that the buyers in Problem 12 incur a transaction cost of $200 to purchase a car. This transaction cost is the value of their time to find a car. What is the equilibrium? Is it possible that no cars are sold?

14. Suppose that you are given w_h, w_l, and θ in the signaling model in the chapter. For what value of c are both a pooling equilibrium and a separating equilibrium possible? For what value of c are both types of equilibria possible and high-ability workers have a higher net earnings in a separating equilibrium than in a pooling equilibrium?

15. Education is a continuous variable, where e_h is the years of schooling of a high-ability worker and e_l is the years of schooling of a lower-ability worker. The cost per period of education for these types of workers is c_h and c_l, respectively, where $c_l > c_h$. The wages they receive if employers can tell them apart are w_h and w_l. Under what conditions is a separating equilibrium possible? How much education will each type of worker get?

16. In Problem 15, under what conditions is a pooling equilibrium possible?

17. In Problems 15 and 16, describe the equilibrium if $c_l \le c_h$.

CHAPTER 20

Contracts and Moral Hazards

The contracts of at least 33 major league baseball players have incentive clauses providing a bonus if that player is named the Most Valuable Player in a Division Series. Unfortunately, no such award is given for a Division Series.[1]

An employee cruises the Internet for jokes instead of working when the boss is not watching. A driver of a rental car takes it off the highway and ruins the suspension. The dentist caps your tooth, not because you need it but because he wants a new stereo.

Each of these examples illustrates an inefficient use of resources due to a *moral hazard*, whereby an informed person takes advantage of a less informed person, often through an *unobserved action* (Chapter 19). In this chapter, we examine how to design contracts that *eliminate inefficiencies* due to moral hazard problems *without shifting risk to people who hate bearing it*—or contracts that at least reach a good compromise between these two goals.

For example, insurance companies face a trade-off between reducing moral hazards and increasing the risk of insurance buyers. Because an insurance company pools risks, it acts as though it is risk neutral (Chapter 17). The firm offers insurance contracts to risk-averse home owners so that they can reduce their exposure to risk. If home owners can buy full insurance so that they will suffer no loss if a fire occurs, some of them fail to take reasonable precautions. They store flammable liquids and old newspapers in their houses, increasing the chance of a catastrophic fire.

A contract that avoids this moral hazard problem specifies that the insurance company will not pay in the event of a fire if the company can show that the policy holders stored flammable materials in their home. If this approach is impractical, however, the insurance company might offer a contract that provides incomplete insurance, covering only a fraction of the damage from a fire. The less complete the coverage, the greater is the incentive for policy holders to avoid dangerous activities, but the greater is the risk that the risk-averse home owners must bear.

To illustrate methods of controlling moral hazards and the trade-off between moral hazards and risk, we focus in this chapter on contracts between a principal—such as an employer—and an agent—such as an employee. The *principal* contracts with the *agent* to take some *action* that benefits the principal. Until now, we have assumed that firms can produce efficiently. However, if a principal cannot practically monitor an agent all the time, the agent may steal, not work hard, or engage in other opportunistic behavior that lowers productivity.[2]

[1]FitzGerald, Tom, "Top of the Sixth," *San Francisco Chronicle*, January 31, 1997:C6.

[2]Sometimes, the principal's problem is not so much one of monitoring as one of legally verifying that opportunistic behavior occurred. For example, an insurance company (principal) might be able to determine that the home owner (agent) engaged in arson but might have trouble proving it.

Opportunistic behavior by an informed agent harms a less informed principal. Sometimes, the losses are so great that both parties would be better off if both had full information and opportunistic behavior were impossible.

In this chapter, we examine seven main topics:

1. **Principal-agent problem:** How an uninformed principal contracts with an informed agent determines whether moral hazards occur and how risks are shared.
2. **Production efficiency:** How much the agent produces depends on the type of contract used and the ability of the principal to monitor the agent's actions.
3. **Trade-off between efficiency in production and in risk bearing:** A principal and an agent may agree to a contract that does not eliminate moral hazards or optimally share risk but that strikes a balance between these two objectives.
4. **Payments linked to production or profit:** Employees work harder if they are rewarded for greater individual or group productivity.
5. **Monitoring:** Employees work harder if an employer monitors their behavior and makes it worthwhile for them to keep from being fired.
6. **Checks on principals:** As a restraint against taking advantage of employees, an employer may agree to contractual commitments that make it in the employer's best interest to tell employees the truth.
7. **Contract choice:** By observing which type of contract an agent picks when offered a choice, a principal may obtain enough information to reduce moral hazards.

20.1 PRINCIPAL-AGENT PROBLEM

When you contract with people whose actions you cannot observe or evaluate, they may take advantage of you. If you pay someone by the hour to prepare your tax return, you do not know whether that person worked all the hours billed. If you retain a lawyer to represent you in a suit arising from an accident, you do not know whether the settlement the lawyer recommends is in your best interest or the lawyer's.

Of course, many people behave honorably even if they have opportunities to exploit others. Many people also honestly believe that they are putting in a full day's work for their employer even when they are not working as hard as they might. Aiko, who manages Pat's printing shop, is paid an hourly wage. She works every hour she is supposed to and doesn't sit around reading novels or otherwise wasting time even though Pat rarely checks on her. Nonetheless, Aiko may not be spending her time as effectively as possible. She politely (but impersonally) asks everyone who enters the shop, "May I help you?" If she were to receive the appropriate financial incentives—say, a share of the shop's profit—she would memorize the names of her customers, greet them enthusiastically by name when they enter the store, and check with nearby businesses to find out whether they would be interested in new services.

A Model

We can describe many principal-agent interactions using the following model. This model stresses that the output or profit from this relationship and the risk borne by the two parties depend on the actions of the agent and the state of nature.

In a typical principal-agent relationship, the *p*rincipal, *P*aul, owns some property (such as a firm) or has a property right (such as the right to sue for damages from an injury). Paul hires or contracts with an *a*gent, *A*my, to take some action a that increases the value of his property or that produces profit, π, from using his property.

The principal and the agent need each other. If Paul hires Amy to run his ice cream shop, Amy needs Paul's shop and Paul needs Amy's efforts to sell ice cream. The profit from the ice cream sold, π, depends on the number of hours, a, that Amy works. The profit may also depend on the outcome of a random variable, θ, that represents the *state of nature*:

$$\pi = \pi(a, \theta).$$

For example, profit may depend on whether the ice cream machine breaks, $\theta = 1$, or does not break, $\theta = 0$. Or it may depend on whether it is a hot day, θ = the temperature.

In extreme cases, the profit function depends only on the agent's actions or only on the state of nature. At one extreme, profit depends only on the agent's action, $\pi = \pi(a)$, if there is only one state of nature: no uncertainty due to random events. In our example, the profit function has this form if demand does not vary with weather and if the ice cream machine is reliable.

At the other extreme, profit depends only on the state of nature, $\pi = \pi(\theta)$, such as in an insurance market in which profit or value depends only on the state of nature and not on the actions of an agent. For instance, a couple buys insurance against rain on the day of their marriage. The value they place on their outdoor wedding ceremony is $\pi(\theta)$, which depends only on the weather, θ, because no actions are involved.

Types of Contracts

A verbal contract isn't worth the paper it's written on. —Samuel Goldwyn

Where a formal market exists, the principal may deal impersonally with an anonymous agent by buying a good at the market price. In this chapter, we focus on situations for which either a formal market does not exist or a principal and an agent agree on a customized contract that is designed to reduce opportunism.

A contract between a principal and an agent determines how the outcome of their partnership (such as the profit or output) is split between them. Three common types of contracts are fixed-fee, hire, and contingent contracts.

In a *fixed-fee contract*, the payment to the agent, F, is independent of the agent's actions, a, the state of nature, θ, or the outcome, π. The principal keeps the *residual profit*, $\pi(a, \theta) - F$. Alternatively, the principal may get a fixed amount and the agent may receive the residual profit. For example, the agent may pay a fixed rent for the right to use the principal's property.

In a *hire contract*, the payment to the agent depends on the agent's actions as they are observed by the principal. Two common types of hire contracts pay employees an *hourly rate*—a wage per hour—or a *piece rate*—a payment per unit of output produced. If w is the wage per hour (or the price per piece of output) and Amy works a hours (or produces a units of output), then Paul pays Amy wa and keeps the residual profit $\pi(a, \theta) - wa$.

In a *contingent contract*, the payoff to each person depends on the state of nature, which may not be known to either party at the time they write the contract. For example, Penn agrees to pay Alexis a higher amount to fix his roof if it is raining than if it is not.

One type of contingent contract is a *splitting or sharing contract*, where the payoff to each person is a fraction of the total profit (which is observable). Alain sells Pamela's house for her for $\pi(a, \theta)$ for a commission of 7% on the sales price. He receives $0.07\pi(a, \theta)$, and she keeps $0.93\pi(a, \theta)$.

Efficiency

The type of contract selected depends on what the parties can observe. A principal is more likely to use a hire contract if the principal can easily monitor the agent's actions. A contingent contract may be chosen if the state of nature can be observed after the work is completed. A fixed-fee contract does not depend on observing anything, so it can always be used.

Ideally, the principal and agent agree to an **efficient contract**: an agreement with provisions that ensure that no party can be made better off without harming the other party. Using an efficient contract results in *efficiency in production* and *efficiency in risk sharing.*

Efficiency in production requires that the principal's and agent's combined value (profits, payoffs), π, is maximized. We say that production is efficient if Amy manages Paul's firm so that the sum of their profits cannot be increased. In our examples, the moral hazard hurts the principal by more than it helps the agent, so total profit falls. Thus, achieving efficiency in production requires preventing the moral hazard.

Efficiency in risk bearing requires that risk sharing is optimal in that the person who least minds facing risk—the risk-neutral or less risk-averse person—bears more of the risk. In Chapter 17, we saw that risk-averse people are willing to pay a risk premium to avoid risk, whereas risk-neutral people do not care if they face fair risk or not. Suppose that Arlene is risk averse and is willing to pay a risk premium of \$100 to avoid a particular risk. Peter is risk neutral and would bear the risk without a premium. Thus, Arlene and Peter can strike a deal whereby Peter agrees to bear *all* of Arlene's risk in exchange for a payment between \$0 and \$100. For simplicity, we concentrate on situations in which one party is risk averse and the other is risk neutral. (Generally, if both parties are risk averse, with one more risk averse than the other, both can be made better off if the less risk-averse person bears more but not all of the risk.)

If everyone has full information—there is no uncertainty and no asymmetric information—efficiency can be achieved. The principal contracts with the agent to perform a task for some specified reward and observes whether or not the agent completes the task properly before paying, so no moral hazard problem arises.

Throughout the rest of this chapter, we examine what happens when the parties do not have full information. Production inefficiency is more likely when either the agent has more information than the principal or both parties are uncertain about the state of nature.

When the agent has more information than the principal and there is no risk because there is only one state of nature, contracts are used to achieve efficiency in production by conveying adequate information to the principal to eliminate moral hazard problems. Alternatively, incentives in the contract may discourage the informed person from engaging in opportunistic behavior. The contracts do not have to address efficiency in risk bearing because there is no risk.

Given that they face both asymmetric information and risk, the parties try to contract to achieve efficiency in production and efficiency in risk bearing. Often, however, both objectives cannot be achieved, so the parties must trade off between them.

20.2 PRODUCTION EFFICIENCY

The contract that an agent and principal use affects production efficiency. In the following example, production efficiency is achieved by maximizing *total* or *joint profit*: the sum of the principal's and the agent's individual profits. To isolate the production issues from risk bearing, we initially assume that there is only one state of nature, so the parties face no risk due to random events: Total profit, $\pi(a)$, is solely a function of the agent's action, a.

Efficient Contract

To be efficient and to maximize joint profit, the contract that a principal offers to an agent must have two properties. First, the contract must provide a large enough payoff that the agent is willing to *participate* in the contract. We know that the principal's payoff is adequate to ensure the principal's participation because the principal offers the contract.

Second, the contract must be **incentive compatible** in that it provides inducements such that the agent wants to perform the assigned task rather than engage in opportunistic behavior. That is, it is in the agent's best interest to take an action that maximizes joint profit. If the contract is not incentive compatible—so the agent tries to maximize personal profit rather than joint profit—efficiency can be achieved only if the principal monitors the agent and forces the agent to act so as to maximize joint profit.

We use an example to illustrate why some types of contracts lead to efficiency and others do not. Paula, the principal, owns a store called Buy-A-Duck (located near a canal) that sells wood carvings of ducks. Arthur, the agent, manages the store. Paula and Arthur's joint profit is

$$\pi(a) = R(a) - 12a,$$

where $R(a)$ is the sales revenue from selling a carvings, and $12a$ is the cost of the carvings. It costs Arthur \$12 to obtain and sell each duck, including the amount he pays a local carver and the opportunity value of his time (best alternative use).

Because Arthur bears the full marginal cost of selling one more carving, he wants to sell the joint-profit-maximizing output only if he also gets the full marginal benefit from selling one more duck. To determine the joint-profit-maximizing solution, we can ask what Arthur would do if he owned the shop and received all the profit so that he would have an incentive to maximize total profit.

How many ducks must Arthur sell to maximize the parties' joint profit? As panel a of Figure 20.1 shows, he would maximize profit by selling 12 carvings, for which his marginal revenue curve, MR, intersects his marginal cost curve, MC = \$12, at the equilibrium point e.[3] Panel b shows that total profit, π, reaches a maximum of \$72 at point E.

Which types of contracts lead to production efficiency? To answer this question, we first examine which contracts yield that outcome when both parties have full information and then consider which contracts bring the desired result when the principal is relatively uninformed. It is important to remember that we are considering a special case: Contracts that work here may not work in some other settings, whereas contracts that do not work here may be effective elsewhere.

Full Information

Suppose that both Paula and Arthur have full information. Each knows the actions Arthur takes—the number of carvings sold—and the effect of those actions on profit. Because she has full information, Paula can dictate exactly what Arthur is to do. Are there incentive-compatible contracts that do not require such monitoring and supervision? To answer this question, we consider four kinds of contracts: a fixed-fee rental contract, a hire contract, and two types of contingent contracts.

Fixed-Fee Rental Contract. If Arthur contracts to rent the store from Paula for a fixed fee, F, joint profit is maximized. Arthur earns a residual profit equal to the joint profit minus the fixed rent he pays Paula, $\pi(a) - F$. Because the amount Paula makes is fixed, Arthur gets the entire marginal profit from selling one more duck. As a consequence, the amount, a, that maximizes Arthur's profit, $\pi(a) - F$, also maximizes joint profit, $\pi(a)$.

In Figure 20.1, Arthur pays Paula F = \$48 rent. This fixed payment does not affect his marginal cost. As a result, he maximizes his profit after paying the rent, π – \$48, by equating his marginal revenue to his marginal cost: $MR = MC = 12$ at point e in panel a.

Because Arthur pays the same fixed rent no matter how many units he sells, the agent's profit curve in panel b lies \$48 below the joint-profit curve at every quantity. As a result, Arthur's net profit curve peaks (at point E^*) at the same quantity, 12, where the joint profit curve peaks (at E). Thus, the fixed-fee rental contract is incentive compatible. Arthur participates in this contract because he earns \$24 after paying for the rent and the carvings (point E^*).[4]

---

[3]The demand curve is $p = 24 - \frac{1}{2}a$, where p is the price and a is the number of carved ducks sold. Revenue is $R = 24a - \frac{1}{2}a^2$, and marginal revenue is $MR = 24 - a$. Profit is maximized where $MR = 24 - a = 12 = MC$ or $a = 12$.

[4]Problem 1 at the end of this chapter asks you to analyze another fixed-fee contract by which Paula pays Arthur a fixed salary.

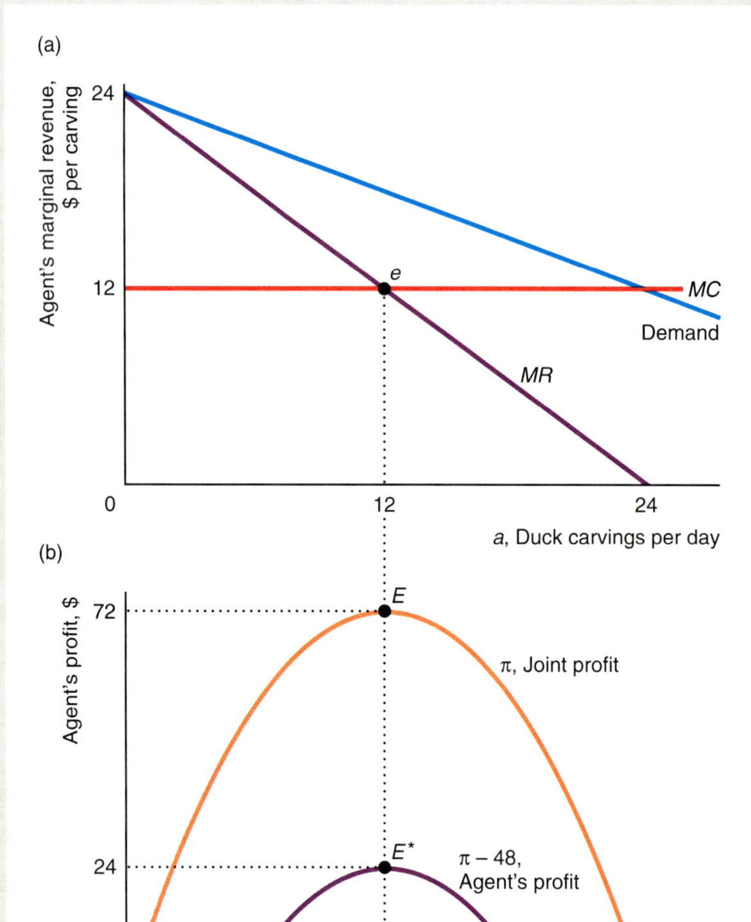

Figure 20.1 Joint Profit Is Maximized if the Agent Gets the Residual Profit. (a) If the agent, Arthur, gets all the joint profit, π, he maximizes his profit by selling 12 carvings at e, where the MR curve intersects his marginal cost curve: $MR = MC = 12$. If he pays the principal, Paula, a fixed rent of \$48, he maximizes his profit by selling 12 carvings. (A fixed rent does not affect either his marginal revenue or his marginal cost.) (b) Joint profit at 12 carvings is \$72, point E. If Arthur pays a rent of \$48 to Paula, Arthur's profit is π – \$48. By selling 12 carvings and maximizing joint profit, Arthur also maximizes his profit.

Hire Contract. Now suppose that Paula contracts to pay Arthur for each carving he sells. If she pays him \$12 per carving, Arthur just breaks even on each sale. He is indifferent between participating and not. Even if he chooses to participate, he does not sell the joint-profit-maximizing number of carvings unless Paula supervises him. If she does supervise him, she instructs him to sell 12 carvings, and she gets all the joint profit of \$72.

For Arthur to want to participate and to sell carvings without supervision, he must receive more than \$12 per carving. If Paula pays Arthur \$14 per carving, for example, he makes a profit of \$2 per carving. He now has an incentive to sell as many carvings as he can, which does not maximize joint profit, so this contract is not incentive compatible.

Even if the contract calls for Arthur to get \$14 per carving and for Paula to control how many carvings he sells, joint profit is not maximized. Paula keeps the revenue minus what she pays Arthur, \$14 times the number of carvings,

$$R(a) - 14a.$$

Thus, her objective differs from the joint-profit-maximizing objective, $\pi = R(a) - 12a$. Joint profit is maximized when marginal revenue equals the marginal cost of \$12. Because Paula's marginal cost, \$14, is larger, she directs Arthur to sell fewer than the optimal number of carvings.[5]

Revenue-Sharing Contract. If Paula and Arthur use a *contingent contract* whereby they share the *revenue*, joint profit is not maximized. Suppose that Arthur receives three-quarters of the revenue, $\frac{3}{4}R$, and Paula gets the rest, $\frac{1}{4}R$. Panel a of Figure 20.2 shows the marginal revenue that Arthur obtains from selling an extra carving, $MR^* = \frac{3}{4}MR$. He maximizes his profit at \$24 by selling 8 carvings, for which $MR^* = MC$ at e^*. Paula gets the remaining profit of \$40, which is the difference between their total profit from selling 8 ducks per day, π = \$64, and Arthur's profit.

Thus, their joint profit in panel b at $a = 8$ is \$64, which is \$8 less than the maximum possible profit of \$72 (point E). Arthur has an incentive to sell fewer than the optimal number of ducks because he bears the full marginal cost of each carving he sells, \$12, but gets only three-quarters of the marginal revenue.[6]

Profit-Sharing Contract. Paula and Arthur may instead use a *contingent contract* by which they divide the *economic profit*, π. If they can agree that the true marginal and average cost is \$12 per carving (which includes Arthur's opportunity cost of

---

[5]Paula maximizes $R - 14a = [24a - \frac{1}{2}a^2] - 14a = 10a - \frac{1}{2}a^2$. Setting the derivative with respect to a equal to zero, $10 - a = 0$, we find that she maximizes her profit by selling 10 carvings. Joint profit is only \$70 at 10 carvings, compared to \$72 at the optimal 12 carvings.

[6]Even if Paula controls how many carvings are sold, joint profit is not maximized. Because the amount she makes, $\frac{1}{4}R$, depends only on revenue and not on the cost of obtaining the carvings, she wants the revenue-maximizing quantity sold. Revenue is maximized where marginal revenue is zero at $a = 24$ (panel a). Arthur would not participate if the contract granted him only three-quarters of the revenue but required him to sell 24 carvings because he would lose money.

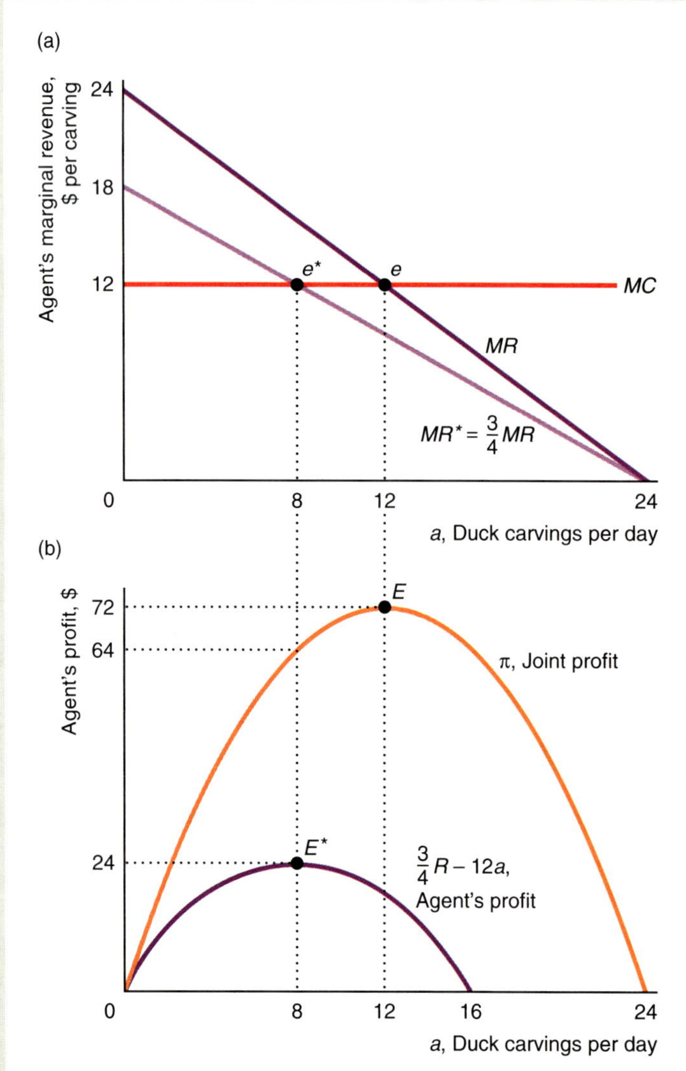

Figure 20.2 Revenue Sharing Reduces Agent's Efforts. (a) Joint profit is maximized at 12 carvings, where $MR = MC = 12$ at equilibrium point e. If Arthur gets three-quarters of the revenue and Paula gets the rest, Arthur maximizes his profit by selling 8 carvings, where his new marginal revenue curve $MR^* = \frac{3}{4}MR$ equals his marginal cost at point e^*. (b) Joint profit reaches a maximum of \$72 at E, where they sell 12 carvings per day. If they split the revenue, Arthur sells 8 ducks per day and gets \$24 at E^*, while Paula receives the residual, \$40 (= \$64 − \$24).

time), the contract is incentive compatible because Arthur wants to sell the optimal number of carvings. Only by maximizing total profit can he maximize his share of profit. As Figure 20.3 illustrates, Arthur receives one-third of the joint profit and chooses to produce the level of output, $a = 12$, that maximizes joint profit.[7] Arthur earns \$24, so he is willing to participate.

The second column of Table 20.1 summarizes our analysis. Whether efficiency in production is achieved depends on the type of contract the principal and the agent use. If the principal has full information (knows the agent's actions), she achieves production efficiency without having to supervise by using one of the incentive-compatible contracts: fixed-fee rental or profit-sharing.

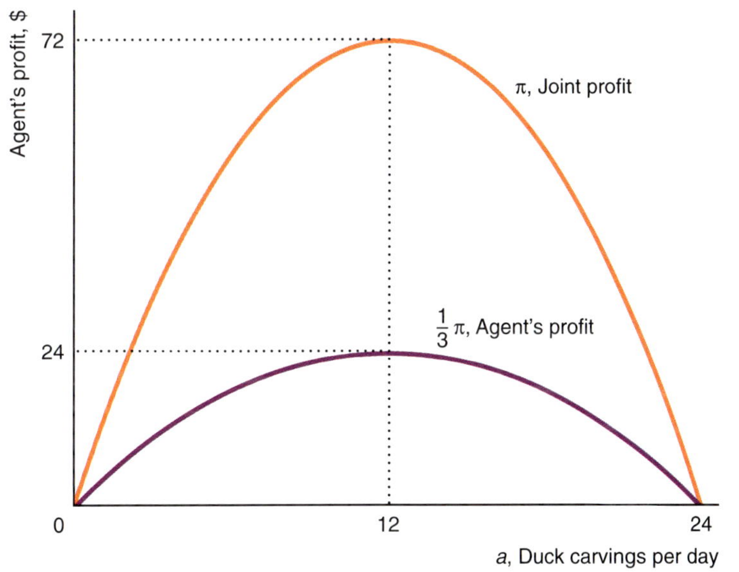

Figure 20.3 Profit Sharing Is Efficient. If the agent, Arthur, gets a third of the joint profit, he maximizes his profit, $\frac{1}{3}\pi$, by maximizing joint profit, π.

[7]Arthur gets one-third of profit, $\frac{1}{3}\pi = \frac{1}{3}(R - C) = \frac{1}{3}R - \frac{1}{3}C$, where R is revenue and C is cost. He maximizes his profit where $\frac{1}{3}MR = \frac{1}{3}MC$. Although he gets only one-third of the marginal revenue, $\frac{1}{3}MR$, he bears only one-third of the marginal cost. Dividing both sides of the equation by $\frac{1}{3}$, we find that this condition is the same as the one for maximizing total profit: $MR = MC$.

SOLVED PROBLEM 20.1

Zhihua and Pu are partners in a store in which they do all the work. They split the store's *business profit* equally (ignoring the opportunity cost of their own time in calculating this profit). Does their business profit-sharing contract give them an incentive to maximize their joint economic profit if neither can force the other to work? (*Hint:* Imagine Zhihua's thought process if it's late Saturday night and Zhihua, who is alone in the store, is debating whether to keep the store open a little later or go out on the town.)

Answer

Show that each partner has an incentive to work too few hours. A partner who works an extra hour bears the full opportunity cost of this extra hour but gets only half the marginal benefit from the extra business profit. The opportunity cost of extra time spent at the store is the partner's best alternative use of time. A partner could earn money working for someone else or use the time to have fun. Because a partner bears the full marginal cost but gets only half the marginal benefit (the extra business profit) from an extra hour of work, each partner works only up to the point at which the marginal cost equals half the marginal benefit. Thus, each has an incentive to put in less effort than the level that maximizes their joint profit, where the marginal cost equals the marginal benefit.[8] ■

Asymmetric Information

Now suppose that the principal, Paula, has less information than the agent, Arthur. She cannot observe the number of carvings he sells or the revenue. Due to this asymmetric information, Arthur can steal from Paula without her detecting the theft.

As Table 20.1 shows, with asymmetric information, *the only contract that results in production efficiency and no moral hazard problem is the one whereby the principal gets a fixed rent.* All the other contracts result in inefficiency, and Arthur has an opportunity to take advantage of Paula.

Fixed-Fee Rental Contract. Arthur pays Paula the fixed rent that she is due because Paula would know if she were paid less. Arthur receives the residual profit, joint profit minus the fixed rent, so he wants to sell the joint-profit-maximizing number of carvings.

---

[8]When I was in graduate school, I shared an apartment with a fellow who was madly in love with a woman who lived in another city. They agreed to split the costs of their long-distance phone calls equally, regardless of who placed the call. This agreement led to very long conversations. Late at night, whichever of them was enjoying the call the most apparently figured that he or she would get the full marginal benefit of one more minute of talking while having to pay only half the marginal cost. What I learned from this experience was not to open our phone bill so as to avoid being shocked by its size.

Table 20.1 Production Efficiency and Moral Hazard Problems for Buy-A-Duck

Contract	Full Information: *Production Efficiency*	Asymmetric Information: *Production Efficiency*	Asymmetric Information: *Moral Hazard Problem*
Fixed-fee rental contract			
Rent (to principal)	Yes	Yes	No
Hire contract, per unit pay			
Pay equals marginal cost	No[a]	No[b]	Yes
Pay is greater than marginal cost	No[c]	No	Yes
Contingent contract			
Share revenue	No	No[b]	Yes
Share profit	Yes	No[b]	Yes

[a]The agent may not participate and has no incentive to sell the optimal number of carvings. Efficiency can be achieved only if the principal supervises.
[b]Unless the agent steals all the revenue (or profit) from an extra sale, inefficiency results.
[c]The agent sells too many or the principal directs the agent to sell too few carvings.

Hire Contract. If Paula offers to pay Arthur the actual marginal cost of \$12 per carving and he is honest, he may refuse to participate in the contract because he makes no profit. Even if he participates, he has no incentive to sell the optimal number of carvings.

If he is dishonest, he may underreport sales and pocket some of the extra revenue. Unless he can steal all the extra revenue from an additional sale, he sells less than the joint-profit-maximizing quantity.

If Paula pays him more than the actual marginal cost per carving, he has an incentive to sell too many carvings, whether or not he steals. If he also steals, he has an even greater incentive to sell too many carvings.

Revenue-Sharing Contract. Even with full information, the revenue-sharing contract is inefficient. Asymmetric information adds a moral hazard problem: The agent may steal from the principal. If Arthur can steal a larger share of the revenues than the contract specifies, he has less of an incentive to underproduce than he does with full information. Indeed, if the agent can steal all the extra revenue from an additional sale, the agent acts efficiently to maximize joint profit, all of which the agent keeps.

Profit-Sharing Contract. If they use a contingent contract by which they agree to split the economic profit, Arthur has to report both the revenue and the cost to Paula so that they may calculate their shares. If he can overreport cost or underreport revenue, he has an incentive to produce a nonoptimal quantity. Only if Arthur can appropriate all the profit does he produce efficiently.

APPLICATION

Contracts and Productivity in Agriculture

In agriculture, landowners (principals) contract with farmers (agents) to work their land. Farmers may work on their own land (the principal and agent are the same person), work on land rented from a landowner (fixed-fee rental contract), work as employees for a time rate or a piece rate (hire contract), or sharecrop (contingent contract). A sharecropper splits the output (crop) with the landowner at the end of the growing season.[9]

Our analysis tells us that farmers' willingness to work hard depends on the type of contract that is used. Farmers who keep all the marginal profit from additional work—those who own the land or rent it for a fixed fee—work hard and maximize (joint) profit. Sharecroppers, who bear the full marginal cost of working an extra hour and get only a fraction of the extra revenue, put in too little effort. Hired farm workers who are paid by the hour may not work hard unless they are very carefully supervised. That is, they may engage in **shirking:** a moral hazard in which agents do not provide all the services they are paid to provide.

These predictions about contract type and agent effort were tested by using data on farmers in the Philippines. Foster and Rosenzweig (1994) could not directly monitor the work effort—any more than most landowners can. Rather, they ingeniously measured the effort indirectly. They contended that the harder people work, the more they eat and the more they use up body mass (defined as weight divided by height squared), holding calorie intake constant.

Foster and Rosenzweig estimated the effect of each compensation method on body mass and consumption (after adjusting for gender, age, type of activity, and other factors). They found that people who work for themselves or are paid by the piece use up 10% more body mass, holding calorie consumption constant, than time-rate workers do and 13% more

[9]If a farmer is someone who is out standing in his field, a sharecropper is someone who is out standing in someone else's field.

than sharecroppers. Foster and Rosenzweig also discovered that piece-rate workers consume 25% more calories per day and that people who work on their own farm consume 16% more than time-rate workers. ■

20.3 TRADE-OFF BETWEEN EFFICIENCY IN PRODUCTION AND IN RISK BEARING

Writing an efficient contract is extremely difficult if the agent knows more than the principal, the principal never learns the truth, and both face risk. Usually, a contract does not achieve efficiency in production *and* in risk bearing. Contract clauses that increase efficiency in production may reduce efficiency in risk bearing and vice versa. If these goals are incompatible, the parties may write imperfect contracts that reach a compromise between the two objectives. To illustrate the trade-offs involved, we consider a common situation in which it is difficult to achieve efficiency: contracting with an expert such as a lawyer.

We illustrate how contracts affect the outcome by using an example in which Pam, the principal, is injured in a traffic accident and is a plaintiff in a lawsuit, and Alfredo, the agent, is her lawyer. Pam faces uncertainty due to risk and to asymmetric information. The jury award at the conclusion of the trial, $\pi(a, \theta)$, depends on a, the number of hours Alfredo works before the trial, and θ, the state of nature due to the (unknown) attitudes of the jury. All else the same, the more time Alfredo spends working on the case, a, the larger the amount, π, that the jury is likely to award. Pam never learns the jury's attitudes, θ, so she cannot accurately judge Alfredo's efforts even after the trial. For example, if she loses the case, she doesn't know whether she lost because Alfredo didn't work hard (low a) or because the case was weak and the jury was prejudiced against her (bad θ).

Contracts and Efficiency

How hard Alfredo works depends on his attitudes toward risk and his knowledge of the payoff for his trial preparations. For any hour that he does not devote to Pam's case, Alfredo can work on other cases. The most lucrative of these forgone opportunities is his marginal cost of working on Pam's case.

The beneficiary of the extra payoff that results if Alfredo works harder depends on his contract with Pam. If Alfredo is risk neutral and gets the entire marginal benefit from any extra work, he puts in the optimal number of hours that maximizes their expected joint payoff. Alfredo collects the marginal benefit from the extra work and bears the marginal cost, so he sets his expected marginal benefit equal to his marginal cost, thus maximizing the expected joint payoff.

The choice of various possible contracts between Pam and Alfredo affects whether efficiency in production or in risk bearing is achieved. They choose among fixed-fee, hire (hourly wage), and contingent contracts. Table 20.2 summarizes the outcomes under each of these contracts.

Table 20.2 Efficiency of Client-Lawyer Contracts

Type of Contract	Fixed Fee to Lawyer	Fixed Fee to Client	Hire Lawyer (Wage per Hour)	Contingent Contract
Lawyer's payoff	F	$\pi(a, \theta) - F$	wa	$\alpha\pi(a, \theta)$
Client's payoff	$\pi(a, \theta) - F$	F	$\pi(a, \theta) - wa$	$(1 - \alpha)\pi(a, \theta)$
Production efficiency	No*	Yes	No*	No*
Who bears risk	Client	Lawyer	Client	Shared

* Production efficiency is possible if the client can effectively monitor and enforce optimal effort by the lawyer.

Lawyer Gets a Fixed Fee. If Pam pays Alfredo a fixed fee, F, he gets paid the same no matter how much he works. Thus, he has little incentive to work hard on this case, and production is inefficient.[10] Production efficiency could be achieved only if Pam could monitor Alfredo and force him to act optimally. Most individual plaintiffs, however, cannot monitor a lawyer and thus cannot determine whether the lawyer is behaving appropriately or not.

Whether the fixed-fee contract leads to efficiency in risk bearing depends on the attitudes toward risk on the part of the principal and the agent. Pam, the principal, bears all the risk. Alfredo's pay, F, is certain, while Pam's net payoff, $\pi(a, \theta) - F$, varies with the unknown state of nature, θ.

A lawyer who handles many similar cases may be less risk averse than an individual client whose financial future depends on a single case. If Alfredo has many cases like Pam's and if Pam's future rests on the outcome of this suit, their choice of this type of contract leads to inefficiency in both production and risk bearing. Not only is Alfredo not working hard enough, but Pam bears the risk even though she is more risk averse than Alfredo.

On the other hand, suppose that Alfredo is a self-employed lawyer working on a major case for Pam, who runs a large insurance company with many similar cases. Alfredo is risk averse and Pam is risk neutral (because she is able to pool many similar cases). Here, having the principal bear all the risk is efficient. If the insurance company can monitor Alfredo's behavior, it is even possible to achieve production efficiency. Indeed, many insurance companies employ lawyers in this manner.

Plaintiff Gets a Fixed Payment. Instead, the two parties could agree to a contract by which Alfredo could pay Pam a fixed amount of money, F, for the right to try the case and collect the entire verdict less the payment to Pam, $\pi(a, \theta) - F$. With such a contract, Alfredo has an incentive to put in the optimal number of hours. He works until his marginal cost—the opportunity cost of his time—equals the

[10]His main incentive to work hard is to establish a reputation as a good lawyer so as to attract future clients. For simplicity, we will ignore this effect, as it applies for all types of contracts.

marginal benefit—the extra amount he gets if he wins at trial. Because he has already paid Pam, all extra amounts earned at trial go to Alfredo.

Under this contract, Alfredo bears all the risk related to the outcome of the trial. No matter how risk averse Pam is, she may hesitate to agree to such a contract. Because she is not an expert on the law, she cannot easily predict the jury's likely verdict. Thus, she does not know how large a fixed fee she should insist on receiving. There is no practical way in which Alfredo's superior information about the likely outcome of the trial can be credibly revealed to her. She suspects that it is in his best interest to tell her that the likely payout is lower than he truly believes.[11]

Lawyer Is Hired by the Hour. In complicated cases, a lawyer's output is not easily measured, so it is not practical to pay the attorney by the piece. Pam could pay Alfredo a wage of w per hour for the a hours that he works. Doing so would create the potential for a serious moral hazard problem unless Pam could monitor Alfredo to determine how many hours he works. If she could not, Alfredo could bill her for more hours than he actually worked.[12] Even if Pam could observe how many hours he works, she would not know whether Alfredo worked effectively and whether the work was necessary. Thus, it would be difficult if not impossible for Pam to monitor Alfredo's work.

Here, Pam bears all the risk. Alfredo's earnings, wa, are determined before the outcome is known. Pam's return, $\pi(a, \theta) - wa$, varies with the state of nature and is unknown before the verdict.

Contingent Fee. Some lawyers offer plaintiffs a contract whereby the lawyer works for "free"—receiving no hourly payment—in exchange for splitting the compensation awarded in court or in a settlement before trial. The lawyer receives a **contingent fee**: a payment to a lawyer that is a share of the award in a court case (usually after legal expenses are deducted) if the client wins and nothing if the client loses. If the lawyer's share of the award is α and the jury awards $\pi(a, \theta)$, the lawyer receives $\alpha\pi(a, \theta)$ and the principal gets $(1 - \alpha)\pi(a, \theta)$. This approach is attractive to many plaintiffs because they cannot monitor how hard the lawyer works and are unable or unwilling to make payments before the trial is completed.

How they split the award affects the amount of risk each bears. If Alfredo gets one-quarter of the award, $\alpha = \frac{1}{4}$, and Pam gets three-quarters, Pam bears more risk than Alfredo does. Suppose that the award is either 0 or 40 with equal probability. Alfredo

---

[11]Alfredo may be hesitant to offer Pam a fixed fee. How well they do in court depends on the merits of her case. At least initially, Alfredo does not know how good a case she has. Initially, she has an incentive to try to convince him that the case is very strong. Moreover, a lawyer may worry that if he pays the plaintiff a fixed fee, she will not fully cooperate in preparing the case (an issue that we've ignored in our example, in which only the actions of the lawyer matter).

[12]A lawyer dies in an accident and goes to heaven. A host of angels greet him with a banner that reads, "Welcome Oldest Man!" The lawyer is puzzled: "Why do you think I'm the oldest man who ever lived? I was only 47 when I died." One of the angels replied, "You can't fool us; you were at least 152 when you died. We saw how many hours you billed!"

receives either 0 or 10, so his average award is 5. His variance (Chapter 17) is

$$\sigma_a^2 = \tfrac{1}{2}(0 - 5)^2 + \tfrac{1}{2}(10 - 5)^2 = 25.$$

Pam makes either 0 or 30, so her average award is 15 and her variance is

$$\sigma_p^2 = \tfrac{1}{2}(0 - 15)^2 + \tfrac{1}{2}(30 - 15)^2 = 225.$$

Thus, the variance in Pam's payoff is greater than Alfredo's.

Whether splitting the risk in this way is desirable turns on how risk averse each party is. If one is risk neutral and the other is risk averse, it is efficient for the risk-neutral person to bear all the risk. If they are equally risk averse, a splitting rule where $\alpha = \frac{1}{2}$ and they face equal risk may be optimal.[13]

A sharing contract encourages shirking: Alfredo is likely to put in too little effort. He bears the full cost of his labors—the forgone use of his time—but gets only α share of the returns from this effort. Thus, this contract results in production inefficiency and may or may not lead to inefficient risk bearing.

Choosing the Best Contract

Which contract is best depends on the parties' attitudes toward risk, the degree of risk, the difficulty in monitoring, and other factors. If Alfredo is risk neutral, they can achieve both efficiency goals if Alfredo gives Pam a fixed fee. He has the incentive to put in the optimal amount of work and does not mind bearing the risk.

However, if Alfredo is risk averse and Pam is risk neutral, they may not be able to achieve both objectives. Contracts by which Alfredo receives a fixed fee or a wage rate cause Pam to bear all the risk and lead to inefficiency in production because Alfredo has too little incentive to work hard.

Often, when the parties find that they cannot achieve both objectives, they choose a contract that attains neither goal. For example, they may use a contingent contract that certainly fails to achieve efficiency in production and may not achieve efficiency in risk bearing. The contingent contract strikes a compromise between the two goals. Alfredo has more of an incentive to work if he splits the payoff than he has if he receives a fixed fee. He is less likely to work excessive hours with the contingent fee than he would work if he were paid by the hour. Moreover, neither party has to bear all the risk—they share it under the contingent contract.

Lawyers usually work for a fixed fee only if the task or case is very simple, such as writing a will or handling an uncontested divorce. The client has some idea of whether the work is done satisfactorily, so monitoring is relatively easy and little risk is involved.

In riskier situations, the other types of contracts are more commonly used. When the lawyer is relatively risk averse or when the principal is very concerned that the lawyer works hard, an hourly wage may be used.

---

[13]If Pam and Alfredo split the award equally and each receives either 0 or 20, each has a variance of $\frac{1}{2}(0 - 10)^2 + \frac{1}{2}(20 - 10)^2 = 100$.

Contingent fee arrangements are particularly common for plaintiffs' lawyers who specialize in auto accidents, medical malpractice, product liability, and other *torts*: wrongful acts in which a person's body, property, or reputation is harmed and for which the injured party is entitled to compensation. Because these plaintiffs' lawyers can typically pool risks across clients, they are less concerned than their clients about risk. As a consequence, these attorneys are willing to accept contingent fees (and might agree to pay a fixed fee to the plaintiff). Moreover, accident victims often lack the resources to pay for a lawyer's time before winning at trial, so they often prefer contingent contracts.

Plaintiffs' lawyers receive contingent fees in most tort cases involving personal injury and medical malpractice in the United States. Kakalik and Pace (1986) report that most tort plaintiffs pay lawyers a contingent fee by which the lawyer gets a percentage of the compensation, usually after other legal expenses are deducted. Only 2% of individual plaintiffs in state courts and 6% in federal courts pay on an hourly basis, and only 1% pay on another basis such as a fixed fee. Most plaintiffs that are organizations also use contingent fees, but 12% of them in state courts and 15% in federal courts pay their lawyers by the hour. Lawyers' contingent fees usually range from 20% to 50%. Rates of 33% and 40% are particularly common.[14]

APPLICATION

Medical Partnerships

Doctors who form partnerships face a trade-off between moral hazards and risk bearing. The percentage of American physicians who are in a group practice has been rising and is currently over 61%.[15] Such partnerships allow doctors to share the fixed costs of maintaining an office and reduce risks through pooling, but they lower the incentive to work hard.

Doctors' incomes are risky. They rise or fall with the difficulty of collecting fees, malpractice suits, changes in insurance company practices, no-shows, and shifts in demand (as diseases pass through the community). If their incomes fluctuate independently to some extent, doctors can reduce their risk by sharing their earnings.

---

[14]Some jurisdictions restrict these fees. California limits medical malpractice contingent fees to 40% of the first $50,000 of compensation, one-third of the next $50,000, 25% of the next $100,000, and 10% of anything over $200,000. All provinces of Canada except Ontario permit contingent fees. Most European countries ban contingent fees. In England and Wales, American-style contingent fee contracts between lawyers and clients are unenforceable against the client (Gravelle and Waterson 1993). However, the Courts and Legal Services Act of 1990 permits contingent contracts whereby the lawyer receives no payment if the case is lost but is entitled to normal costs plus a percentage markup with a win.

[15]This discussion is based on Gaynor and Gertler (1995).

In a typical partnership of n doctors, the profit going to Doctor i is

$$y_i = \alpha R_i + (1/n)(1 - \alpha)R - (1/n)C,$$

where α is the proportion of his or her revenue that each doctor keeps, R_i is the revenue generated by Doctor i, R is the revenue generated by all doctors, and C is the common cost of running the office, including nonphysician labor. The doctor also has a personal opportunity cost of time.

For each extra dollar the doctor earns, the doctor keeps

$$\hat{\alpha} = \alpha + (1/n)(1 - \alpha).$$

The first term, α, is the share of the dollar that the doctor does not put into the common pool. The last term is the doctor's share of the pool of earnings. As the share that the doctors put into the common pool grows (α shrinks) and as the group increases (n rises), each doctor faces less risk.

The downside to this pooling arrangement is the reduced incentive for each doctor to work hard (see the related discussion of public goods in Chapter 18). Shirking is more likely, the more the doctors share profits (small α) and the larger the group (big n). An individual doctor bears the full marginal (opportunity) cost of working an extra hour. A fall in α reduces the doctor's resulting marginal revenue, so the doctor wants to work fewer hours. Similarly, as the number of partners, n, rises, the doctor's share of the revenue-sharing pool, $(1/n)(1 - \alpha)R$, falls, reducing marginal revenue, while the doctor's personal marginal opportunity cost is unchanged.

Gaynor and Gertler (1995) found that a 10% increase in a doctor's incentive to work, $\hat{\alpha}$, results in the doctor's seeing 3.8% more patients per year. As α goes from near 0 to near 1, a doctor in the average-size group of 21 doubles the number of patients seen per week, while a doctor in a small group of 3 sees 40% more patients.

Gaynor and Gertler measured risk by having doctors rank the importance they place on the regularity of income (lack of fluctuations). The more that doctors value regularity of income, the more they pool incomes and the less incentive they have to work hard. As their risk measure increases from 1 (doesn't mind risk) to 4 (hates risk), the number of annual office visits falls by 20% for the typical group. This reduced effort costs very risk-averse doctors $11,582 per year, or about 10% of the average salary. Thus, there is a significant trade-off between risk and moral hazard. ■

SOLVED PROBLEM 20.2

Gary's demand for medical services (visits to his doctor) depends on his health. Half the time his health is good and his demand is D^1 in Figure 20.4. When his health is less good, his demand is D^2. Without medical insurance, he pays

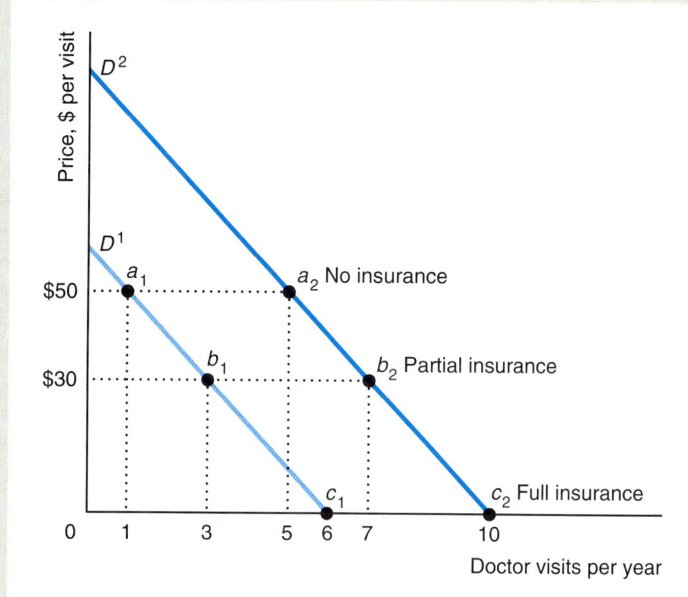

Figure 20.4 Trade-off Between Moral Hazard and Risk. Without medical insurance, Gary pays \$50 per visit and goes to the doctor once in a year, a_1, if his health is good, D^1; or he goes five times, a_2, if his health is bad, D^2. If his insurance pays the entire cost of the doctor's exam, he goes either 6 times, c_1, or 10 times, c_2, depending on his health. If the insurance pays only \$20, which is 40% of the expense, Gary pays \$30 and visits the doctor 3 times, b_1, or 7 times, b_2.

\$50 a visit. Because Gary is risk averse, he wants to buy medical insurance. With full insurance, Gary pays a fixed fee at the beginning of the year and the insurance company pays the full cost of any visit. Alternatively, with a contingent contract, Gary pays a smaller premium at the beginning of the year, and the insurance company covers only \$20 per visit and Gary pays the remaining \$30. How likely is a moral hazard problem to occur with each of these contracts? What is Gary's risk (variance of his medical costs) with each type of insurance? Compare the contracts in terms of the trade-offs between risk and moral hazards.

Answer

1. *Describe the moral hazard for each demand curve for each contract*: If Gary's health is good, he increases from one visit, a_1, with no insurance (where he pays \$50 a visit) to 6 visits, c_1, with full insurance (where he pays nothing per visit). Similarly, if his health is poor, he increases his

visits from 5, a_2, to 10, c_2. Thus, regardless of his health, he makes five extra visits a year with full insurance. These extra visits are the moral hazard. With a contingent contract whereby Gary pays $30 a visit, the moral hazard is less because he makes only two extra visits instead of five (the difference between the number of visits at b_1 and a_1 and between b_2 and a_2).

2. *Calculate the variance of Gary's medical expenses with each level of insurance*: Without insurance, his average number of visits is 3 ($= [\frac{1}{2} \times 1] + [\frac{1}{2} \times 5]$), so his average annual medical cost is $150. Thus, the variance of his medical expenses without insurance is

$$\sigma_n^2 = \tfrac{1}{2}([1 \times \$50] - \$150)^2 + \tfrac{1}{2}([5 \times 50] - \$150)^2$$
$$= \tfrac{1}{2}(\$50 - \$150)^2 + \tfrac{1}{2}(\$250 - \$150)^2$$
$$= \$10{,}000.$$

If he has full insurance, he makes a single fixed payment each year, so his payments do not vary with his health: His variance is $\sigma_f^2 = 0$. Finally, with partial insurance, he averages 5 visits with an average cost of $150, and his variance is

$$\sigma_p^2 = \tfrac{1}{2}(\$90 - \$150)^2 + \tfrac{1}{2}(\$210 - \$150)^2 = \$3{,}600.$$

Thus, $\sigma_n^2 > \sigma_p^2 > \sigma_f^2$.

3. *Discuss the trade-offs*: Because Gary is risk averse, efficiency in risk bearing requires that the insurance company bear all the risk, as with full insurance. Full insurance, however, results in the largest moral hazard. Without insurance, there is no moral hazard but Gary bears all the risk. The contingent contract is a compromise whereby both the moral hazard and the degree of risk lie between the extremes. ■

20.4 PAYMENTS LINKED TO PRODUCTION OR PROFIT

We now examine how additional clauses are added to a contract to eliminate or reduce moral hazards. For simplicity, we ignore risk bearing. We focus on employer-employee contracts. Under most such contracts, employees are paid by the hour or given a fixed salary. The problem with such agreements is that the workers are not directly rewarded for productive, profit-enhancing actions, so they tend to shirk. Here, rewarding agents for productive activities leads to greater efficiency.

There are two main ways to reward productive effort directly. One method is to link pay to a worker's individual output. Another is to link a worker's pay to the firm's output or profitability. Employers who cannot monitor workers, however, do not use incentive-compatible contracts.

Piece-Rate Hire Contracts

One direct approach to getting employees to work hard is to pay them by the *piece*—the output they produce—rather than by *time*—the number of hours they work. Piece rates are usually effective in increasing output, but they are not practical in all markets.

Greater Effort. Piece rates—by explicitly rewarding productivity—provide a greater incentive to employees to work hard than hourly wages do. For example, Billikopf (1995) found that employees who are paid by the piece prune a vineyard in only 19 hours of work per acre compared to 26 hours for employees paid by the hour.

The increase in joint profit due to this greater productivity may be shared between the firm and the employees. As the following application illustrates, many workers, because they earn more with piece rates than they would earn with hourly pay, are pleased to be paid by the piece.

APPLICATION

Pleased to Be Paid by the Piece

Mike Darrah sweeps up shards of broken glass from Safelite Glass's repair shop floor, lifts heavy replacement windshields onto car frames and wrestles them into position, and then carefully seals the rims.[16] He hardly pauses between tasks. He doesn't want to. He is an enthusiastic participant in Safelite's performance pay plan, which pays him in proportion to how much he accomplishes.

When Mr. Darrah started as a glass installer in 1994, he earned $7.50 an hour and could expect wage increases up to about $12 when he mastered the craft. In 1996, under the incentive system, he averaged $20 an hour. "I'd rather skip the coffee and get paid," he said. His annual take-home pay had roughly doubled without his working much overtime.

Safelite pays workers by the piece, with a guaranteed wage floor. In a typical month, two-thirds of the workers earn more than this guaranteed minimum, and in the long run, almost all do. Workers average 15% above the guaranteed minimum. That workers like this new program is shown by the drop in the absenteeism rate by 61%, which benefits Safelite, a firm that depends on timely, high-quality service.

According to Edward Lazear, a Stanford Business School economist who studied this transition to piecework from traditional wage-and-benefits compensation, the hourly output of glass installers rose 41% over the 18 months

[16]Passell, Peter, "Paid by the Widget, and Proud," *New York Times*, June 16, 1996:Section 3:1.

during the phase-in period for this program. The company received about half this gain in higher profits. The 41% increase is divided into two parts. Slightly more than half is due to increased productivity on the part of existing workers; the rest is due to the departure of less motivated workers, who were quickly replaced by eager beavers.

The workers who stayed, like Mr. Darrah, are pleased with their increased earnings. Likewise, Safelite relishes its higher profits, which stem from greater output per worker, lower turnover, and higher quality. Turnover in this industry can be 50–60% annually, but Safelite benefited from a disproportionate number of good workers staying.

By forcing employees to pay for making repairs for flawed installations, Safelite ensures that quality does not fall as employees rush to produce output. After jobs are completed, the company surveys 1 out of every 10 customers by phone, and each installer gets a monthly performance report. Before this performance pay system was instituted, the percentage of customers who were "very satisfied" was in the mid-80s; now this percentage is in the mid-90s. ■

Problems with Piece Rates. Piece rates are not always practical. There are three chief difficulties with this system: measuring output, eliciting the desired behavior, and persuading workers to accept piece rates.

Paying piece rates is practical only if the employer can easily measure the output produced, such as the number of pieces of fruit picked or windshields installed. Employers do not use piece rates to compensate teachers, managers, and others whose output is difficult to measure.

Thus, piece rates are more common for blue-collar jobs than for white-collar jobs. Roughly 15% of the labor force receives pay based on individual productivity, but most piecework is concentrated in a handful of low-paying industries such as agriculture (in which about a third of workers are paid by the piece) and apparel manufacturing or is confined to sales personnel, individual contractors, and other similar occupations.

Piece rates typically reward fast—but not necessarily careful—work. For this reason, farmers are more likely to pay piece rates to harvest relatively "tough" fruit than "delicate" fruit that can be easily bruised. Many strawberry growers pay harvesters by the hour rather than by the piece and tell them to be careful not to injure the fruit.

Similarly, piece rates backfire if they encourage harmful behavior. Sears, Roebuck & Company used to reward auto shop employees on the basis of the size of customers' repair bills. This system apparently led to overbilling of customers, which resulted in government actions and lawsuits.[17]

---

[17]Buchholz, Barbara B., "The Bonus Isn't Reserved for Big Shots Anymore," *New York Times*, October 27, 1996.

Some workers object to piece rates because they do not like to work hard or because they are concerned that firms will ratchet down workers' compensation after a while by lowering the pay per piece. In addition, piecework has a negative connotation in many people's minds because of its association with turn-of-the-century sweatshops, where workers toiled at repetitive tasks for 12 or more hours a day.[18]

Contingent Contract Rewards Linked to a Firm's Success

Although companies can use piece rates with workers who produce easily measured output, they need other incentive schemes for managers, corporate directors, and others whose productivity is difficult to quantify, especially those who work as part of a team. Such workers may be rewarded if their team or the firm does well in general. Frequently, year-end bonuses are based on increases in the firm's profit or the value of its stock.

Many firms reward both blue-collar and white-collar workers with lump-sum, year-end bonuses linked to the firm's performance that year. According to an annual survey by Buck Consultants, an employee benefits and compensation firm, the percentage of Fortune 1000 companies that offers bonus pay plans for hourly employees rose from 26% in 1993 to 37% in 1997.[19] Hourly employees' bonuses are typically 3–8% of their base salary. Middle managers receive 10–17%. Many executives receive 100% or more.

Managers (and increasingly other workers) may also receive a stock option, which gives them the opportunity to buy a certain number of shares of stock in the firm at a prespecified price. For example, in 1997, Intel, the leading computer chip firm, gave each of its 50,000 employees a stock option for at least 50 shares of Intel stock, which they could purchase at a specified price, the *exercise price*, during a ten-year period.[20] If the stock's market price exceeds the exercise price during that period, an employee can exercise the option—buy the stock—and then sell it at the market price, in this way making an immediate profit. But if the stock's price stays below the exercise price, the options are worthless. Beyond motivating employees to work hard, these incentives also are *golden handcuffs*: a deterrent to taking a job at a competing firm and forfeiting the stock option.

Today, about 5–10% of the biggest U.S. companies offer stock options to all their employees. However, most American firms reserve stock options for executives. The use of stock options as a part of executive compensation packages has grown sharply in many industries in recent years. The percentage of companies with executive stock option plans rose from 73% in 1986 to 98% in 1995 in retail trade,

---

[18]According to Harvard Professor Claudia Goldin, 40% of female workers were paid by the piece in the 1890s (Passell, Peter, "Paid by the Widget, and Proud," *New York Times*, June 16, 1996:Section 3:1).

[19]Buchholz, Barbara B., "The Bonus Isn't Reserved for Big Shots Anymore," *New York Times*, October 27, 1996.

[20]DeBare, Ilana, "Intel Options Go Companywide," *San Francisco Chronicle*, February 12, 1997:B1, B5.

from 82% to 93% in manufacturing, and from 24% to 61% in utilities.[21] According to a survey of 1996 pay packages of chief executives at 425 large companies, the average base salary was $450,000, while the average total pay, including bonus and options, was $609,300.

Apparently, firms benefit substantially from offering such bonuses. In one study of 70 companies, directors of firms rated in the top 25% in performance had $257,000 each in stock, while the directors of the worst 25% held just $49,000.[22]

APPLICATION

Australian Compensation

Australian firms use a wide variety of incentive schemes to induce workers to be productive. Over a third (34%) of the workplaces pay individual piece rates, about one in eight (12%) provides group incentives, a roughly equal fraction (11%) offers workplace-level incentives, 17% have higher-than-workplace incentives, and roughly one in twelve (8%) offers profit sharing (Drago and Heywood 1995). Workers who are paid either time rates or piece rates may also receive bonuses and stock options that are contingent on the success of their team, the output at their workplace, or the performance of the total firm, which may have facilities throughout the world. Nearly half the firms (44%) use at least one of these incentive plans, over a quarter (28%) employ exactly one of these schemes, 16% apply two or more, and 4% use three or more. ■

20.5 MONITORING

When using piece rates and rewarding workers for the success of the firm rather than individual output are not feasible, employers usually pay fixed-fee salaries or hourly wages. Employees who are paid a fixed salary have little incentive to work hard if the employer cannot observe shirking. If an employer pays employees by the hour but cannot observe how many hours they work, employees may inflate the number of hours they report working.

A firm can reduce such shirking by intensively supervising or monitoring its workers. Monitoring eliminates the asymmetric information problem: Both

[21]Dobrzynski, Judith H., "Top Post at Rock-Bottom Wage," *New York Times*, October 4, 1996:C1, C3.

[22]Stobaugh, Robert B., "More and More, Directors Are Owners," *New York Times*, January 1, 1995:Business, 9.

the employee and the employer know how hard the employee works. If the cost of monitoring workers is low enough, it pays to prevent shirking by carefully monitoring and firing employees who do not work hard.

Over the years, firms have experimented with a variety of means of lowering the cost of monitoring. Requiring employees to punch a time clock and installing videocameras to record the work effort are examples of firms' attempts to use capital to monitor job performance.[23] Similarly, by installing assembly lines that force employees to work at a pace dictated by the firm, employers can control employees' work rate.

According to a recent survey by the American Management Association, nearly two-thirds of employers record employees' voice mail, E-mail, or phone calls; review computer files; or videotape workers.[24] A quarter of the firms that use surveillance don't tell their employees. The most common types of surveillance are tallying phone numbers called and recording the duration of the calls (37%), videotaping employees' work (16%), storing and reviewing E-mail (15%), storing and reviewing computer files (14%), and taping and reviewing phone conversations (10%). Monitoring and surveillance are most common in the financial sector, in which 81% of firms use these techniques. Of course, few companies watch all employees all the time. Companies usually monitor selected workers using routine spot checks.

For some jobs, however, monitoring is counterproductive or not cost effective. Monitoring may lower employees' morale, in turn reducing productivity. Several years ago, Northwest Airlines took the doors off bathroom stalls to prevent workers from slacking off there.[25] When new management eliminated this policy (and made many other changes as well), productivity increased.

It is usually impractical for firms to monitor how hard salespeople work if they spend most of their time away from the main office. As telecommuting increases, monitoring workers may become increasingly difficult.

When direct monitoring is very costly, firms may use various financial incentives, which we now consider, to reduce the amount of monitoring that is necessary. Each of these incentives—bonding, deferred payments, and efficiency (unusually high) wages—acts as a *hostage* for good behavior (Williamson 1983). Workers who are caught shirking or engaging in other undesirable acts not only lose their jobs but give up the hostage too. The more valuable the hostage, the less monitoring the firm needs to use to deter bad behavior.

---

[23]In Australia, 100,000 Woolworth employees use optical fingerprint scanners instead of punching time cards. Using scanners eliminates "buddy punching" and reportedly reduces the company's payroll by 2%. Abate, Tom, "New Chip Verifies Fingerprints," *San Francisco Chronicle*, May 22, 1997:B3.

[24]Jackson, Maggie, "Most Firms Spy on Employees, Survey Finds," *San Francisco Chronicle*, May 23,1997:B1.

[25]Garcia, Kenneth J., "Multimillionaire's Run for His Money," *San Francisco Chronicle*, April 17, 1997:A1, A4.

Bonding

A direct approach to ensuring good behavior by agents is to require that they deposit funds guaranteeing their good behavior, just as a landlord requires tenants to post security deposits to ensure that they will not damage an apartment. An employer may require an employee to provide a performance *bond*, an amount of money that will be given to the principal if the agent fails to complete certain duties or achieve certain goals. Typically, the agent *posts* (leaves) this bond with the principal or another party, such as an insurance company, before starting the job.

Many couriers who transport valuable shipments (such as jewels and bearer bonds) or guards who watch over them have to post bonds against theft and other moral hazards. Similarly, bonds may be used to keep employees from quitting immediately after receiving costly training (Salop and Salop 1976). Academics who take a sabbatical—a leave of absence that is supposed to be devoted to training or other activities that increase their future productivity—typically must sign an agreement to pay the college or university a certain amount of money if they quit within a year after returning from their sabbatical. Most of the other approaches we examine below as strategies for controlling shirking can be viewed as a form of bonding.

Bonding to Prevent Shirking. Some employers require a worker to post a bond that is forfeited if the employee is discovered shirking. For example, a professional athlete faces a specified fine (the equivalent of a bond) for skipping a meeting or game. The higher the bond, the less frequently the employer needs to monitor to prevent shirking.

Suppose that the value that a worker puts on the gain from taking it easy on the job is G dollars. If a worker's only potential punishment for shirking is dismissal if caught, some workers will shirk.

Suppose, however, that the worker must post a *bond* of B dollars that the worker forfeits if caught not working. Given the firm's level of monitoring, the probability that a worker is caught is θ. Thus, a worker who shirks expects to lose θB.[26] A risk-neutral worker chooses not to shirk if the certain gain from shirking, G, is less than or equal to the expected penalty, θB, from forfeiting the bond if caught: $G \le \theta B$. Thus, the minimum bond that discourages stealing is

$$B = \frac{G}{\theta}. \qquad (20.1)$$

Equation 20.1 shows that the bond must be larger, the higher the value that the employee places on shirking and the lower the probability that the worker is caught.

Trade-off Between Bonds and Monitoring. Thus, the larger the bond, the less monitoring is necessary to prevent shirking. Suppose that a worker places a value

[26]The expected penalty is $\theta B + (1 - \theta)0 = \theta B$, where the first term on the left-hand side is the probability of being caught times the fine of B and the second term is the probability of not being caught and facing no fine.

of G = \$1,000 a year on shirking. A bond that is large enough to discourage shirking is \$1,000 if the probability of being caught is 100%, \$2,000 at 50%, \$5,000 at 20%, \$10,000 at 10%, and \$20,000 if the probability of being caught is only 5%.

SOLVED PROBLEM 20.3

Workers post bonds of B that are forfeited if they are caught stealing (but no other punishment is imposed). Each extra unit of monitoring, M, raises the probability that a firm catches a worker who steals, θ, by 5%. A unit of M costs \$10. A worker can steal a piece of equipment and resell it for its full value of G dollars. What is the optimal M that the firm uses if it believes that workers are risk neutral? In particular, if B = \$5,000 and G = \$500, what is the optimal M?

Answer

1. *Determine how many units of monitoring are necessary to deter stealing*: The least amount of monitoring that deters stealing is the amount at which a worker's gain from stealing equals the worker's expected loss if caught. A worker is just deterred from stealing when the gain, G, equals the expected penalty, θB. Thus, the worker is deterred when the probability of being caught is $\theta = G/B$. The number of units of monitoring effort is $M = \theta/0.05$, because each extra unit of monitoring raises θ by 5%.
2. *Determine whether monitoring is cost effective*: It pays for the firm to pay for M units of monitoring only if the expected benefit to the firm is greater than the cost of monitoring, \$10 × M. The expected benefit if stealing is prevented is G, so monitoring pays if G > \$10 × M, or G/M > \$10.
3. *Solve for the optimal monitoring in the special case*: The optimal level of monitoring is

$$M = \theta/0.05 = (G/B)/0.05 = (\$500/\$5{,}000)/0.05 = 0.1/0.05 = 2.$$

It pays to engage in this level of monitoring because G/M = \$500/2 = \$250 > \$10. ■

Problems with Bonding. Employers like the bond-posting solution because it reduces the amount of employee monitoring necessary to discourage moral hazards such as shirking and thievery. Nonetheless, firms use explicit bonding only occasionally to prevent stealing, and they rarely use it to prevent shirking.

Two major problems are inherent in posting bonds. First, to capture a bond, an unscrupulous employer might falsely accuse an employee of stealing. An employee who fears such employer opportunism might be unwilling to post a bond. One possible solution to this problem is for the firm to develop a reputation for not behaving in this manner. Another possible approach is for the firm to make the grounds for forfeiture of the bond objective and thus verifiable by others.

A second problem with bonds is that workers may not have enough wealth to post them. In our example, if the worker could steal \$10,000, and if the probability of being caught were only 5%, shirking would be deterred only if a risk-neutral worker were required to post a bond of at least \$200,000.

Principals and agents use bonds when these two problems are avoidable. Bonds are more common in contracts between firms than in those between an employer and employees. Moreover, firms have fewer problems than typical employees do in raising funds to post bonds.

Construction contractors sometimes post bonds to guarantee that they will satisfactorily finish their work by a given date. It is easy to verify whether the contract has been completed on time, so there is relatively little chance of opportunistic behavior by the principal.

Deferred Payments

Effectively, firms can post bonds for their employees through the use of deferred payments. For example, a firm pays new workers a low wage for some initial period of employment. Then, over time, workers who are caught shirking are fired, and those who remain get higher wages. In another form of deferred wages, the firm provides a pension that rewards only hard workers who stay with the firm until retirement. *Deferred payments serve the same function as bonds.* They raise the cost of being fired, so less monitoring is necessary to deter shirking.

Workers care about the present value (see Chapter 16) of their earnings stream over their lifetime. A firm may offer its workers one of two wage payment schemes. In the first, the firm pays w per year for each year that the worker is employed by the firm. In the second arrangement, the starting wage is less than w but rises over the years to a wage that exceeds w.

If employees can borrow against future earnings, those who work for one company for their entire career are indifferent between the two wage payment schemes if those plans have identical present values. The firm, however, prefers the second payment method because employees work harder to avoid being fired and losing the high future earnings.

Reduced shirking leads to greater output. If the employer and employee share the extra output in the form of higher profit and larger lifetime earnings, both the firm and workers prefer the deferred-payment scheme that lowers incentives to shirk.

A drawback of the deferred-payment approach is that, like bond posting, it can encourage employers to engage in opportunistic behavior. For example, an employer might fire nonshirking senior workers to avoid paying their higher wages and replace them with less expensive junior workers. However, if the firm can establish a reputation for not firing senior workers unjustifiably, the deferred-payment system can help prevent shirking.

Efficiency Wages

As we've seen, the use of bonds and deferred payments discourages shirking by raising an employee's cost of losing a job. An alternative is for the firm to pay an **efficiency wage**: an unusually high wage that a firm pays workers as an incentive to avoid shirking.[27] If a worker who is fired for shirking can immediately go to another firm and earn the same wage, the worker risks nothing by shirking. However, a high wage payment raises the cost of getting fired, so it discourages shirking.[28]

How Efficiency Wages Act Like Bonds. Suppose that a firm pays each worker an efficiency wage w, which is more than the *going wage* $\underline{w}$ that an employee would earn elsewhere after being fired for shirking. We now show that the less frequently the firm monitors workers, the greater the wage differential must be between w and $\underline{w}$ to prevent shirking.

A worker decides whether to shirk by comparing the expected loss of earnings from getting fired to the value, G, that the worker places on shirking. A shirking worker expects to lose $\theta(w - \underline{w})$, where θ is the probability that a shirking worker is caught and fired and the term in parentheses is the lost earnings from being fired. A risk-neutral worker does not shirk if the expected loss from being fired is greater than or equal to the gain from shirking:[29]

$$\theta(w - \underline{w}) \geq G.$$

The smallest amount by which w can exceed $\underline{w}$ and prevent shirking is determined where this expression holds with equality, $\theta(w - \underline{w}) = G$, or

$$w - \underline{w} = \frac{G}{\theta}. \tag{20.2}$$

The extra earnings, $w - \underline{w}$, in Equation 20.2 serve the same function as the bond, B, in Equation 20.1 in discouraging bad behavior.

---

[27]The following discussion is based on Yellen (1984), Stiglitz (1987), and especially Shapiro and Stiglitz (1984).

[28]There are other explanations for why efficiency wages lead to higher productivity. Some economists claim that, in less developed countries, employers pay an efficiency wage—more than they need to hire workers—to ensure that workers can afford to eat well enough that they can work hard. Other economists (such as Akerlof 1982) and management experts contend that the higher wage acts like a gift, making workers feel beholden or loyal to the firm, so that less (or no) monitoring is needed.

[29]To derive this result, we compare the earnings from shirking to those from not shirking. An employee who never shirks is not fired and earns w. A shirking employee expects to earn

$$(1 - \theta)w + \theta\underline{w} + G,$$

where the first term is the earnings if not caught times the probability of not being caught, the second term is the earnings elsewhere if caught and fired times the probability of being caught, and G dollars is the value that the worker places on shirking. Thus, the worker chooses not to shirk if the certain high wage from not shirking exceeds the expected return from shirking:

$$w \geq (1 - \theta)w + \theta\underline{w} + G,$$

which simplifies to $\theta(w - \underline{w}) \geq G$.

Suppose that the worker gets G = \$1,000 pleasure a year from not working hard and $\underline{w}$ is \$20,000 a year. If the probability that a shirking worker is caught is $\theta = 20\%$, then the efficiency wage w must be at least \$25,000 to prevent shirking. With greater monitoring, so that θ is 50%, the minimum w that prevents shirking is \$22,000.

Trade-off Between Efficiency Wage and Monitoring. From the possible pairs of monitoring levels and efficiency wages that deter shirking, the firm picks the combination that minimizes its labor cost. The greater the firm's monitoring cost, the higher the wage paid by the firm to prevent shirking.

The cost of employing a worker is

$$C = w + p_m M,$$

where w is the worker's efficiency wage, p_m is the cost per time spent monitoring, and M is the amount of time that supervisory personnel spend monitoring the worker. Figure 20.5 shows a typical isocost line with a slope of p_m. The figure also has an

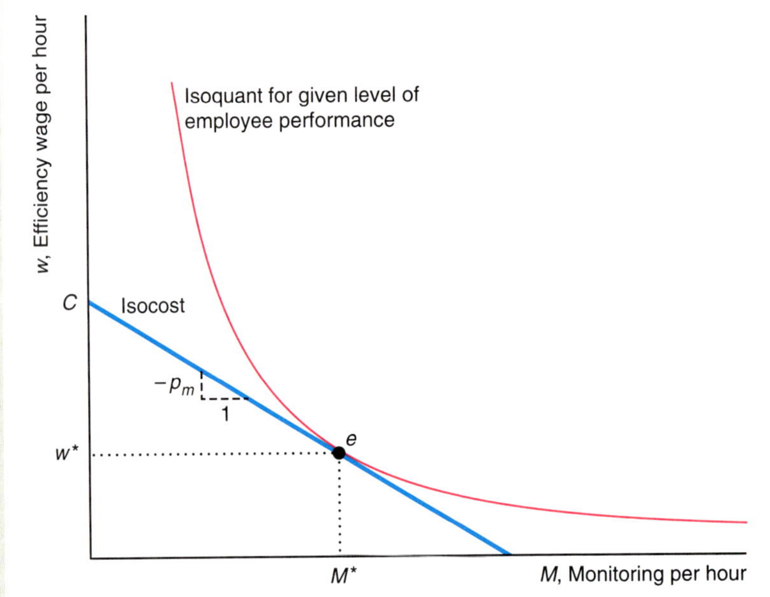

Figure 20.5 Trade-off Between Efficiency Wage and Monitoring. By paying an efficiency wage that is above a worker's best alternative, an employer can reduce its level of monitoring and still prevent shirking. The isoquant curve shows the combinations of efficiency wage, w, and monitoring, M, that produce a given level of employee performance. The employer sets the efficiency wage and the amount of monitoring to minimize its labor cost of producing where the straight-line isocost line is tangent to the isoquant.

isoquant that indicates the combinations of wage and monitoring that lead to a given level of employee performance. The firm picks the combination of efficiency wage, w^*, and monitoring, M^*, that minimizes its cost by operating at e at the tangency between the isoquant and the lowest isocost line that touches the isoquant.

Efficiency Wages and Unemployment. We've argued that it is in a firm's best interest to pay more than the "going wage" to discourage shirking. The problem with this conclusion is that, if it pays for one firm to raise its wage, it pays for all firms to do so. But if all firms raise their wages and pay the same amount, no one firm can discourage shirking by paying more than the others.

Nonetheless, the overall high wages do help prevent shirking. Because all firms are paying above the competitive wage, their labor demand falls, causing unemployment. Now if a worker is fired, the worker remains unemployed for a period of time while searching for a new job. Thus, the amount that the fired worker earns elsewhere, $\underline{w}$, is less than w because of this period of unemployment.[30] As a result, the (high) efficiency wages discourage shirking by creating unemployment.

One implication of this theory is that unemployment benefits provided by the government actually increase the unemployment rate. Such benefits raise $\underline{w}$, decrease the markup of w over $\underline{w}$, and thereby reduce the penalty of being fired. Thus, to discourage shirking, firms have to raise their efficiency wage even higher, and even more unemployment results.

APPLICATION

Deferred Payments Versus Efficiency Wages in Fast-Food Restaurants

Krueger (1991) investigated whether fast-food restaurants use deferred wages or efficiency wages to deter opportunism by employees. Inadequate monitoring in fast-food restaurants leads to absenteeism, high turnover, theft, poor service, waste, and neglect of equipment by workers. One study of first-time fast-food workers found that 62% gave away goods, falsely claimed to be sick, stole, worked while intoxicated, or damaged property during their initial nine months.

Some fast-food restaurants face particularly severe moral hazard difficulties. Shirking and other bad behavior are more likely to be a problem at restaurants that are owned by fast-food chains than at their franchised restaurants.

In a franchise arrangement, the chain or franchisor (such as McDonald's) sells a proven method of doing business and a brand name to an individual franchisee (the owner of a McDonald's outlet). The franchisee pays a start-up

[30] If γ is the share of time that the fired worker remains unemployed, the worker's expected earnings are $\underline{w} = (1 - \gamma)w + \gamma 0 = (1 - \gamma)w$.

cost of between $400,000 and $600,000 and then pays a monthly fixed fee and a royalty based on sales (usually 8%).

The share of company-owned fast-food restaurants is about 30% overall: 15% at Burger King, 18% at Kentucky Fried Chicken (KFC), 25% at McDonald's, and 35% at Wendy's. Company-owned outlets are more likely to be in large cities, where supervision by the chain may be easier.

If a restaurant manager is also the franchisee, the manager has a strong profit motive to work hard and to supervise employees closely. In contrast, at chain-owned restaurants, managers are employees who receive a fixed salary and do not get a bonus based on their performance or the restaurant's profit, so they are less likely to monitor other employees carefully. As Fred Turner, president and CEO of McDonald's, noted (Krueger 1991, p. 79), "[A]n owner-operator, with his personal interest and incentives, can inherently do a better job than a chain manager."

Because company-owned restaurants have the more severe monitoring problem, we would expect them to be more likely to use a financial incentive such as deferred wages or efficiency wages to prevent shirking. If such restaurants resort to deferred payments, they pay lower wages to new employees and higher wages to long-term employees than franchisees pay. In contrast, if company-owned restaurants use efficiency wages, all workers earn more—with the possibility that the pay differential will grow with time on the job as slackers are fired or quit.

Consistent with the efficiency-wage explanation, Krueger estimates that company-owned restaurants pay assistant and shift managers 8.7% more than franchise restaurants (after controlling for tasks performed, education, age, and other worker characteristics). The present value of this earnings differential is $1,250 at a 5% rate of interest. Full-time nonmanagement workers get 1.7% more; part-timers earn only 0.5% more. In addition, company-owned restaurants are 43 percentage points more likely to provide workers with free meals, 24 percentage points more likely to offer paid vacations, and 7 percentage points more likely to have paid holidays.

Inconsistent with the deferred-payment explanation, company-owned restaurants do not pay newly hired workers less than franchisee-owned restaurants pay. One explanation for why company-owned restaurants do not use deferred payments is that it is not practical to pay their workers very low rates initially because of minimum-wage laws. More than 90% of franchisee-owned and 60% of company-owned restaurants pay newly hired part-time workers the legal minimum wage; the rest pay more. ■

After-the-Fact Monitoring

So far, we've concentrated on monitoring by employers looking for bad behavior as it occurs. If shirking or other bad behavior is detected after the fact, the offending employee is fired or otherwise disciplined. This punishment discourages shirking in the future.

Punishment. It is often very difficult to monitor bad behavior when it occurs but relatively easy to determine it after the fact. As long as a contract holds off payment until after the principal checks for bad behavior, after-the-fact monitoring discourages bad behavior. For example, an employer can check the quality of an employee's work. If it is substandard, the employer can force the employee to make it right (as in the Safelite Glass example).

Insurance companies frequently use this approach in contracts with their customers. Insurance firms try to avoid extreme moral hazard problems by offering contracts that do not cover spectacularly reckless, stupid, or malicious behavior. If an insurance company determines after the fact that a claim is based on reckless behavior rather than chance, the firm refuses to pay.

For example, an insurance company will not pay damages for a traffic accident if the insured driver is shown to have been drunk at the time. A house insurance company disallows claims due to an explosion that is found to result from an illegal activity such as making crack cocaine. It will certainly disallow claims by arsonists who torch their own homes or businesses. Life insurance companies may refuse to pay benefits to the family of someone who commits suicide (as in the play *Death of a Salesman*).

APPLICATION

Abusing Leased Cars

Because drivers of fleet automobiles such as rental cars do not own them, they do not bear all the cost from neglecting or abusing the vehicles, resulting in a moral hazard problem. These vehicles are driven harder and farther and depreciate faster than owner-operated vehicles.

Using data from sales at used-car auctions, Dunham (1996), after controlling for mileage, found that fleet vehicles (not including taxis or police cars) depreciate 10–13% more rapidly than owner-driven vehicles.[31] The average auction price for a Pontiac 6000 is $5,200 for a fleet car and $6,500 for a non-fleet car. This $1,300 difference, which is one-fourth of the fleet car's price, reflects the increased depreciation of fleet cars.

To deal with this moral hazard, an automobile-leasing firm commonly writes contracts—open-ended leases—in which the driver's final payment for the vehicle depends on the sales price of the car. In this way, the contract makes the leasing driver responsible for at least some of the harm done to the car, to encourage the lessee to take greater care of the vehicle. Given the difference in auction prices, however, such leases apparently are not the full solution to this moral hazard. ■

[31]According to the National Public Radio show *Car Talk* (May 1997)—one of the world's most reliable sources of information—police cars have very few miles on them, but their engines are quickly shot because cops spend untold hours sitting in their cruisers in front of doughnut shops with the engine running and the air conditioner on high.

No Punishment. Finding out about moral hazards after they occur is too late if wrongdoers cannot be punished at that time. Indeed, there's no point in monitoring after the fact if punishment is then impossible or impractical. Although it's upsetting to find that you've been victimized, there's nothing you can do beyond trying to prevent the situation from happening again.

APPLICATION

Savings and Loans Moral Hazards

Moral hazard played an important role in causing the bankruptcies of many savings and loans (S&Ls) in the late 1980s and early 1990s. Individuals are willing to put their money into an S&L because they know that federal or state agencies insure their deposits against an S&L failure.

To prevent S&Ls from engaging in moral hazards that lead to bankruptcies, government agencies had traditionally required these institutions to invest primarily in relatively safe, local residential mortgage loans. In the early 1980s, however, government rules changed to allow S&Ls to make investments in other assets. It was hoped that giving S&Ls leeway to further diversify their portfolio of investments would reduce investment risks. With this change, the percentage of investments in nontraditional assets by federally insured S&Ls increased from 11.5% in 1982 to 20.2% in 1985.[32]

To keep S&Ls from engaging in extremely risky behavior or committing fraud, the government agencies examined their records. Unfortunately, just when S&Ls were given greater latitude in investment, such monitoring decreased. The number of examinations of S&Ls fell from 3,210 in 1980 to 2,347 in 1984, and the examinations per billion dollars of assets dropped from 5.4 to 2.4.

After the rules changed, many S&L managers started making extremely risky investments, including buying junk bonds. They reasoned that they'd make a lot of money if these investments paid off. If the investments failed and the S&L went bankrupt, the managers believed—correctly—that they could walk away with impunity. They anticipated that the federal government would make good on the losses and not punish them (unless fraud was involved—and apparently not always then). The combination of government insurance, greater freedom to invest, and slack monitoring created a moral hazard problem from bad investments.

The fastest-growing S&Ls tended to be those that took the largest risks. Whereas S&Ls that grew less than 15% in 1984 had 68% of their assets in traditional residential mortgages and mortgage-backed securities, only 53% of the assets in S&Ls growing at more than 50% were in traditional assets. Moreover, the investments of S&Ls that were soon to fail were different from

[32] This section is based on White (1991).

others. In 1985, soon-to-fail S&Ls had more commercial (rather than residential) mortgage loans, 13.4% versus 8.1%; more land loans, 7.7% versus 1.2%; more commercial loans (including junk bonds), 2.2% versus 1.3%; and more direct equity (stock) investments, 5.0% versus 1.7%. Many S&Ls that had invested heavily in these risky investments went into bankruptcy when the investments failed.

To bail out the failed S&Ls, the federal government made extremely large payouts—much larger than those of earlier periods. In 1979, the federal government had to dispose of only three failed S&Ls through liquidating their assets—about 0.1% of all S&L assets—or finding a new owner. In 1988, however, the federal government had to deal with 205 disposals, representing 7.45% of all S&L assets.

The present discounted value of the government's cost for 1988 alone was $38 billion. By 1990, a conservative estimate of the present value of costs for the financial disasters to date was about $150 billion, or nearly $600 for every man, woman, and child in the United States.

To minimize future moral hazard problems among S&Ls, the government insurers raised the capital requirements that govern how much money the owners and managers must provide. A capital requirement acts like an insurance deductible. It forces S&L managers and owners to put more of their own money (and less of account holders' money) at risk when making investments. As a consequence, S&L operators are likely to invest more conservatively. ■

20.6 CHECKS ON PRINCIPALS

To this point, we have concentrated on situations in which the employee knows more than the employer. Sometimes, however, the employer may have asymmetric information and engage in opportunistic behavior.

Because employers often pay employees after work is completed, employers have many opportunities to exploit workers. For example, a dishonest employer can underpay after falsely claiming that a worker took time off or that some of the worker's output was substandard. The employer can decrease piece rates over time, after employees are committed to this payment system. Employers who provide bonuses can underreport the firm's output or profit. An employer can dock earnings, claim that an employee bond was forfeited, or refuse to make deferred payments such as pensions after dishonestly claiming that a monitored worker engaged in bad behavior. Efficient contracts prevent or reduce such moral hazard problems created by employers as well as those caused by employees.

Requiring that a firm post a bond can be an effective method of deterring the firm's opportunistic behavior. For example, a firm may post bonds to ensure that it has the means of paying current wages and future pensions.

Another strategy for preventing a firm from acting opportunistically is to eliminate asymmetric information by requiring the employer to reveal relevant information to employees. For example, an employer can provide access to such information by allowing employee representatives to sit on the company board—from which vantage point they can monitor the firm's behavior. To induce workers to agree to profit sharing, a firm may provide workers with information about the company's profit by allowing them (or an independent auditor) to check its accounts. Alternatively, the firm may argue that its stock closely mirrors its profit and suggest that the known stock price be used for incentive payments.

As another means of conveying information to employees, firms may seek to establish a good reputation. For instance, a firm may publicize that it does not make a practice of firing senior employees to avoid paying pensions. The better the firm's reputation, the more likely workers are to accept a deferred payment scheme, which deters shirking.

When firms find these approaches infeasible, they may use inefficient contracts that might, for example, stipulate payments to employees on the basis of easily observed revenues rather than less reliable profit reports. The next application discusses a particularly damaging but common type of inefficient contract.

APPLICATION

Performance Termination Contracts

During economic downturns—recessions and depressions—demand for a firm's product falls. Many firms respond by laying off workers and reducing production rather than by lowering wages and keeping everyone employed (Hall and Lilien 1979). Figure 20.6 shows that real private U.S. hourly earnings remained relatively constant over the last decade even as the unemployment rate fluctuated substantially.

If both sides agreed to it, a wage reduction policy would benefit firms and workers alike. Workers would earn more than they would if they were laid off. Because the firm's costs would fall, it could sell more during the downturn than it otherwise could, so its profits would be higher than they would be if there were layoffs. Firms that provide relatively low wages and then profit share with employees achieve this type of wage flexibility.

Why then—as the figure shows—are wage reductions less common than layoffs? One explanation involves asymmetric information: Workers, unlike the firm, don't know whether the firm is actually facing a downturn, so they don't agree to wage cuts. In short, they don't trust the firm to tell them the truth. They fear that the firm will falsely claim that economic conditions are bad to justify a wage cut. If the firm has to lay off workers—an action that hurts the firm as well as the workers—the firm is more likely to be telling the truth about economic conditions.

We illustrate this reasoning in Table 20.3. Panel a shows the payoffs if wages are reduced during downturns. The value of output produced by each worker

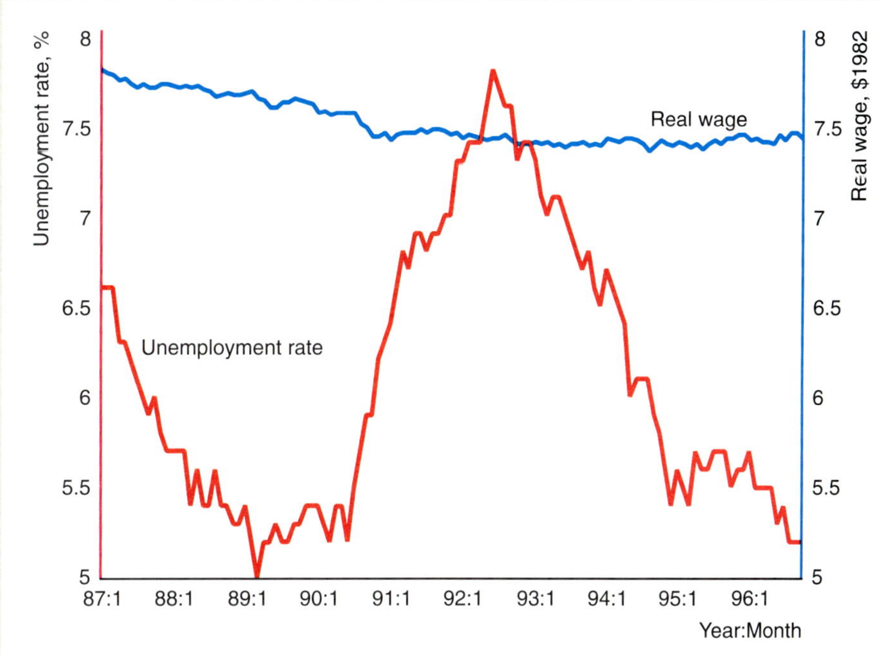

Figure 20.6 Wage and Unemployment Rates. Even though the unemployment rate fluctuated substantially from January 1987 through October 1996, the real wage (hourly earnings) measured in 1982 dollars remained relatively constant. *Source*: U.S. Bureau of Labor Statistics.

is $21 during good times and $15 during bad times. The firm pays employees $12 per hour if it reports that economic conditions are good and $8 if it says that conditions are bad. If economic conditions are bad, the firm earns more by reporting these bad conditions, $7, than it earns if it says that conditions are good, $3. Similarly, if conditions are good, the firm earns more if it claims that conditions are bad, $13, than if it says that they are good, $9. Thus, regardless of the true state, the firm always claims that conditions are bad.

To shield themselves from such systematic lying, employees may insist that the firm lay off workers whenever it says that conditions are bad. This requirement provides the firm with an incentive to report the true conditions. In panel b, the firm must lay off workers for half of each period if it announces that times are bad, causing the value of output to fall by one-third. Because they now work only half the time, workers earn only half as much, $6, as they earn during good times, $12. If conditions are bad, the firm makes more by telling the truth, $4, than by claiming that conditions are good, $3. In good times, the firm makes more by announcing that conditions are good, $9, than by claiming that they are bad, $8. Thus, the firm reports conditions truthfully.

Table 20.3 Payments over Business Cycles

a) Wage Cut

Conditions Are	Firm Claims That Conditions Are: Bad	Firm Claims That Conditions Are: Good
Bad	Worker 8, Firm 7	Worker 12, Firm 3
Good	Worker 8, Firm 13	Worker 12, Firm 9

b) Worker Layoff (for Half of Any Period the Firm Claims Is Bad)

Conditions Are	Firm Claims That Conditions Are: Bad	Firm Claims That Conditions Are: Good
Bad	Worker 6, Firm 4	Worker 12, Firm 3
Good	Worker 6, Firm 8	Worker 12, Firm 9

Note: The firm's payoff is in the upper-right corner of each cell, and the worker's payoff is in the lower-left corner. The total payoff is 21 during good times and 15 during downturns without layoffs. If workers are laid off for half of any period that the firm claims is bad, the respective total payoffs drop by a third to 10 and 14.

With the wage-cut contract in which the firm always says that conditions are bad, workers earn \$8 regardless of actual conditions. If economic conditions are good half the time, the firm earns an average of \$10 = ($\frac{1}{2}$ × \$7) + ($\frac{1}{2}$ × \$13). Under the contract that requires layoffs, the workers earn an average of \$9 = ($\frac{1}{2}$ × \$6) + ($\frac{1}{2}$ × \$12) and the firm earns an average of \$6.50 = ($\frac{1}{2}$ × \$4) + ($\frac{1}{2}$ × \$9).

Therefore, the firm prefers the wage-cut contract and the workers favor the layoff contract. However, if the workers could observe actual conditions, both parties would prefer the wage-cut contract. Workers would earn an average of \$10 = ($\frac{1}{2}$ × \$8) + ($\frac{1}{2}$ × \$12), and the firm would earn \$8 = ($\frac{1}{2}$ × \$7) + ($\frac{1}{2}$ × \$9). With the layoff contract, total payoffs are lower because of lost production. Thus, socially inefficient layoffs may be used because of the need to keep relatively well-informed firms honest. ■

20.7 CONTRACT CHOICE

We have examined how to construct a single contract so as to prevent moral hazards. Often, however, a principal gives an agent a choice of contract. By observing the agent's choice, the principal obtains enough information to prevent agent opportunism.

Firms want to avoid hiring workers who will shirk. Employers know that not all workers shirk, even when given an opportunity to do so. Thus, rather than focusing on stopping lazy workers from shirking, an employer may concentrate on hiring only industrious people. With this approach, the firm seeks to avoid *moral hazard* problems by preventing *adverse selection*, whereby lazy employees falsely assert that they are hardworking.

As discussed in Chapter 19, employees may *signal* to employers that they are productive. For example, if only nonshirking employees agree to work long hours, a commitment to work long hours serves as a reliable signal. In addition, employees can signal by developing a reputation as hard workers. To the degree that employers can rely on this reputation, sorting is achieved.

When workers cannot credibly signal, firms may try to *screen* out bad workers and keep only good workers. One way in which firms can determine which prospective employees will work hard and which will shirk is to give them a choice of contracts. If job candidates who are hard workers select a contingent contract whereby their pay depends on how hard they work and if job applicants who are lazy workers choose a fixed-fee contract, the firm can tell the applicants apart by their choices.

Suppose that a firm wants to hire a salesperson who will run its Cleveland office and that the potential employees are risk neutral. A hardworking salesperson can sell $100,000 worth of goods a year, but a lazy one can sell only $60,000 worth (Table 20.4). A hard worker can earn $30,000 from other firms, so the firm

Table 20.4 Firm's Spreadsheet

	Contingent Contract (30% of Sales)	Fixed-Fee Contract ($25,000 Salary)
Hard worker		
Sales	$100,000	$100,000
– Salesperson's pay	–$30,000	–$25,000
= Firm's net revenue	$70,000	$75,000
– Office expenses	–$50,000	–$50,000
= Firm's profit	$20,000	$25,000
Lazy worker		
Sales	$60,000	$60,000
– Salesperson's pay	–$18,000	–$25,000
= Firm's net revenue	$42,000	$35,000
– Office expenses	–$50,000	–$50,000
= Firm's profit	–$8,000	–$15,000

considers using a contingent contract that pays a salesperson a 30% commission on sales.

If the firm succeeds in hiring a hard worker, the salesperson makes $30,000 = $100,000 × 0.30. The firm's share of sales is $70,000. The firm has no costs of production (for simplicity), but maintaining this branch office costs the firm $50,000 a year. The firm's profit is therefore $20,000. If the firm hires a lazy salesperson under the same contract, the salesperson makes $18,000, the firm's share of sales is $42,000, and the firm loses $8,000 after paying for the office.

Thus, the firm wants to hire only a hard worker. Unfortunately, the firm does not know in advance whether a potential employee is a hard worker. To acquire this information, the firm offers a potential employee a choice of contracts:

- **Contingent contract:** No salary and 30% of sales.
- **Fixed-fee contract:** Annual salary of $25,000, regardless of sales.

A prospective employee who doesn't mind hard work would earn $5,000 more by choosing the contingent contract. In contrast, a lazy candidate would make $7,000 more from a salary than from commissions. If an applicant chooses the fixed-fee contract, the firm knows that person does not intend to work hard and decides not to hire that person.

The firm learns what it needs to know by offering this contract choice as long as the lazy applicant does not pretend to be a hard worker by choosing the contingent contract. Under the contingent contract, the lazy person makes only $18,000, but that offer may dominate others available in the market. If this pair of contracts fails to sort workers, the firm may try different pairs. If all these choices fail to sort, the firm must use other means to prevent shirking.

Summary

1. **Principal-agent problem:** A principal contracts with an agent to perform some task. The size of their joint profit depends on any assets that the principal contributes, the actions of the agent, and the state of nature. If the principal cannot observe the agent's actions, the agent may engage in opportunistic behavior. This moral hazard reduces the joint profit. An efficient contract leads to efficiency in production (joint profit is maximized by eliminating moral hazards) and efficiency in risk bearing (the less risk-averse party bears more of the risk). Three common types of contracts are *fixed-fee contracts*, whereby one party pays the other a fixed fee and the other keeps the rest of the profits; *hire contracts*, by which the principal pays the agent a wage or by the piece of output produced; and *contingent contracts*, wherein the payoffs vary with the amount of output produced or in some other way. Because a contract that reduces the moral hazard may increase the risk for a relatively risk-averse person, a contract is chosen to achieve the best trade-off between the twin goals of efficiency in production and in risk bearing.

2. **Production efficiency:** Whether efficiency in production is achieved depends on the contract that the principal and the agent use and the degree to which their information is asymmetric. For the agent to put forth the optimal level of effort in our example, the agent must get the full marginal profit from that effort or the principal must monitor the agent. When the parties have full information, an agent with a fixed-fee rental or profit-sharing contract gets the entire marginal profit and produces optimally without monitoring. If the principal cannot monitor the agent or does not observe profit and cost, only a fixed-fee

rental contract prevents moral hazard problems and achieves production efficiency.

3. **Trade-off between efficiency in production and in risk bearing:** A principal and an agent may agree to a contract that strikes a balance between reducing moral hazards and allocating risk optimally. Contracts that eliminate moral hazards require the agent to bear the risk. If the agent is more risk averse than the principal, the parties may trade off a reduction in production efficiency to lower risk for the agent.

4. **Payments linked to production or profit:** To reduce shirking, employers may reward employees for greater individual or group productivity. Piece rates, which reward faster individual work, are practical only when individual output can be easily measured and the quality of work is not critical. Bonuses and stock options that reward workers for increases in group effort provide less of an incentive than piece rates but still may reduce shirking.

5. **Monitoring:** Because of asymmetric information, an employer normally must monitor workers' efforts to prevent shirking. Less monitoring is necessary as the employee's interest in keeping the job increases. The employer may require the employee to post a large bond that is forfeited if the employee is caught shirking, stealing, or otherwise misbehaving. If an employee cannot afford to post a bond, the employer may use deferred payments or efficiency wages—unusually high wages—to make it worthwhile for the employee to keep the job. Employers may also be able to prevent shirking by engaging in after-the-fact monitoring. However, such monitoring works only if bad behavior can be punished after the fact.

6. **Checks on principals:** Often, both agents and principals can engage in opportunistic behavior. If a firm must reveal its actions to its employees, it is less likely to be able to take advantage of the employees. To convey information, an employer may let employees participate in decisionmaking meetings or audit the company's books. Alternatively, an employer may make commitments so that it is in the employer's best interest to tell employees the truth. These commitments, such as laying off workers rather than reducing wages during downturns, may reduce moral hazards but lead to nonoptimal production.

7. **Contract choice:** A principal may be able to obtain valuable information from an agent by offering a choice of contracts. Employers avoid moral hazard problems by preventing adverse selection. For example, they may present potential employees with a choice of contracts, prompting hardworking job applicants to choose one contract and lazy candidates to choose another.

Problems

1. In the duck-carving example with full information (which the second column of Table 20.1 summarizes), is a contract efficient if it requires that Paula give Arthur a fixed-fee salary of $168 and leaves all decisions to Arthur? If so, why? If not, are there any additional steps that Paula can take to ensure that Arthur sells the optimal number of carvings?

2. The state of California set up its own earthquake insurance program in 1997. Because the state agency in charge has few staff members, it will pay private insurance carriers to handle claims for earthquake damage. These insurance firms will receive 9% of each approved claim.[33] Is this compensation scheme likely to lead to opportunistic behavior by insurance companies? What would be a better way to handle the compensation?

3. Two students are given an assignment to produce a joint report for which they will both get the same grade. What problems, if any, are likely to arise?

4. In the duck-carving example with limited information (summarized in the second and third columns of Table 20.1), is a fixed-fee contract efficient? If

[33]Louis, Arthur M., "Insurance Aftershock," *San Francisco Chronicle*, May 3, 1997:B1, B2.

so, why? If not, are there any additional steps that Paula can take to ensure efficiency?

5. A health insurance company tries to prevent the moral hazard of "excessive" dentist visits by limiting the visits per person per year to a specific number. How does such a restriction affect moral hazard and risk bearing? Show in a graph.
6. Some companies offer to buy back the good they sell you now at some prespecified price. Why would a firm make such a commitment?
7. Traditionally, doctors have been paid on a fee-for-service basis. Now doctors are increasingly paid on a capitated basis (they get paid for treating a patient for a year, regardless of how much treatment is required). In this arrangement, a group of doctors typically sign a capitation contract whereby they take turns seeing a given patient. What are the implications of this change in compensation for moral hazards and for risk bearing? (*Hint*: Look at the application on doctor partnerships.)
8. Fourteen states have laws that limit a franchiser's ability to terminate a franchise agreement. What effects would such laws have on production efficiency and risk bearing?
9. A promoter arranges for many different restaurants to set up booths to sell Cajun/Creole food at a fair. Appropriate music and other entertainment are provided. Customers can buy food using only "Cajun Cash," which is scrip with the same denominations as actual cash sold by the promoter at the fair. Why aren't the food booths allowed to sell food directly for cash?
10. Many law firms consist of partners who share profits. On being made partner, a lawyer must effectively post a bond, that is, make a large payment to the firm that will be forfeited on bad behavior. Why?
11. According to a 1997 flyer from Schwab *Advisor-Source*, "Most personal investment managers base their fees on a percentage of assets managed. We believe this is in your best interest because your manager is paid for investment management, not solely on the basis of trading commissions charged to your account. You can be assured your manager's investment decisions are guided by one primary goal—increasing your assets." Is this policy in a customer's best interest?
12. Explain why full employment may be inconsistent with no shirking.

Math Problems

13. Suppose that a textbook author is paid a royalty of α share of the revenue from sales where the revenue is $R = pq$, p is the competitive market price for textbooks, and q is the number of copies of this textbook (which is similar to others on the market) sold. The publisher's cost of printing and distributing the book is $C(q)$. Determine the equilibrium, and compare it to the outcome that maximizes the sum of the payment to the author plus the firm's profit. Answer using both math and a graph.
14. Suppose now that the textbook publisher in Problem 13 faces a downward-sloping demand curve. The revenue is $R(Q)$, and the publisher's cost of printing and distributing the book is $C(Q)$. Compare the equilibria for the following compensation methods in which the author receives the same total compensation from each method: (a) the author is paid a lump sum, $\mathcal{L}$ (b) the author is paid α share of the revenue; (c) the author receives a lump-sum payment and a share of the revenue. Why do you think that authors are usually paid a share of revenue?
15. In Solved Problem 20.3, a firm calculated the optimal level of monitoring to prevent stealing. If G = \$500 and θ = 20%, what is the minimum bond that deters stealing?
16. In Problem 15, suppose that, for each extra \$1,000 of bonding that the firm requires a worker to post, the firm must pay that worker \$10 more per period to get the worker to work for the firm. What is the minimum bond that deters stealing?

Chapter Appendixes

Appendix 2A: Regressions

Economists use a *regression* to estimate economic relationships such as demand curves and supply curves. A regression analysis allows us to answer three types of questions:

- How can we best fit an economic relationship to actual data?
- How confident are we in our results?
- How can we determine the effect of a change in one variable on another if many other variables are changing at the same time?

Estimating Economic Relations

We use a demand curve example to illustrate how regressions can answer these questions. The points in Figure 2A.1 show eight years of data on Nancy's annual purchases of candy bars, q, and the prices, p, she paid.[1] For example, in the year when candy bars cost 20¢, Nancy bought q_2 candy bars.

Because we assume that Nancy's tastes and income did not change during this period, we write her demand for candy bars as a function of the price of candy bars and unobservable random effects. We believe that her demand curve is linear and want to estimate the demand function:

$$q = a + bp + e,$$

where a and b are coefficients we want to determine and e is an error term. This *error term* captures random effects that are not otherwise reflected in our function. For instance in one year, Nancy broke up with her long-time boyfriend and ate more candy bars than usual, resulting in a relatively large positive error term for that year.

The data points in the figure exhibit a generally downward-sloping relationship between quantity and price, but the points do not lie strictly on a line because of the error terms. There are many possible ways in which we could draw a line through these data points.

The way we fit the line in the figure is to use the standard criterion that our estimates *minimize the sum of squared residuals*, where a residual, $e = q - \hat{q}$, is the difference between an actual quantity, q, and the fitted or predicted quantity on the estimated line, $\hat{q}$. That is, we choose estimated coefficients $\hat{a}$ and $\hat{b}$ so that the

---

[1]We use a lowercase q for the quantity demanded for an individual instead of the uppercase Q that we use for a market. Notice that we violated the rule economists usually follow of putting quantity on the horizontal axis and price on the vertical axis. We are now looking at this relationship as statisticians who put the independent or explanatory variable, price, on the horizontal axis and the dependent variable, quantity, on the vertical axis.

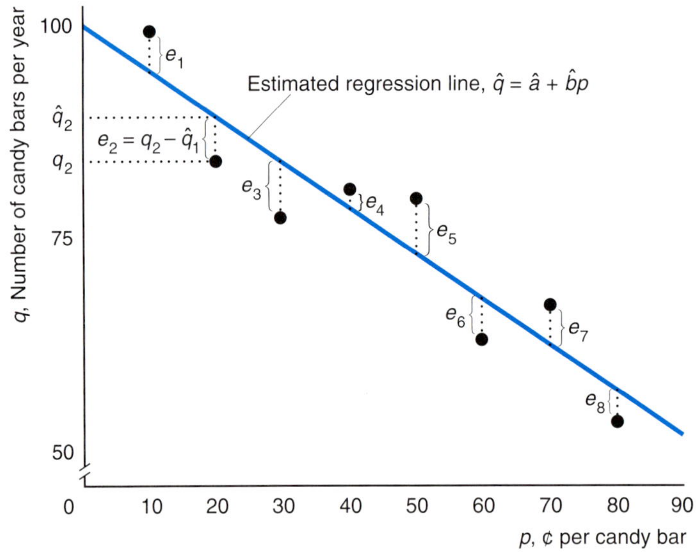

Figure 2A.1 Regression. The circles show data on how many candy bars Nancy bought in a year at several different prices. The regression line minimizes the sum of the squared residuals, e_1 through e_8.

estimated quantities from the regression line,

$$\hat{q} = \hat{a} + \hat{b}p,$$

make the sum of the squared residuals, $e_1^2 + e_2^2 + \ldots + e_8^2$, as small as possible. By summing the square of the residuals instead of the residuals themselves, we treat the effects of a positive or negative error symmetrically and give greater weight to large errors than to small ones.[2] In the figure, the regression line is

$$\hat{q} = 99.4 - 0.49p,$$

where $\hat{a} = 99.4$ is the intercept of the estimated line and $\hat{b} = -0.49$ is the slope of the line.

Confidence in Our Estimates

Because the data reflect random errors, so do the estimated coefficients. Our estimate of Nancy's demand curve depends on the *sample* of data we use. If we were to

[2]By using calculus, we can derive the $\hat{a}$ and $\hat{b}$ that minimize the sum of squared residuals. The estimate of the slope coefficient is a weighted average of the observed quantities, $\hat{b} = \Sigma_i w_i q_i$, where $w_i = (p_i - \bar{p})/ \Sigma_i(p_i - \bar{p})^2$, $\bar{p}$ is the average of the observed prices, and Σ_i means take the sum over each observation i. The estimate of the intercept, $\hat{a}$, is the average of the observed quantities.

use data from a different set of years, our estimates, $\hat{a}$ and $\hat{b}$, of the true coefficients, a and b, would differ.

If we had many estimates of the true parameter based on many samples, the estimates would be distributed around the true coefficient. These estimates are *unbiased* in the sense that the average of the estimates would equal the true coefficients.

Computer programs that calculate regression lines report a *standard error* for each coefficient, which is an estimate of the dispersion of the estimated coefficients around the true coefficient. In our example, a computer program reports

$$\hat{q} = \underset{(3.99)}{99.4} - \underset{(0.08)}{0.49}p,$$

where, below each estimated coefficient, its estimated standard error appears between parentheses.

The smaller the estimated standard error, the more precise is the estimate: The more likely it is to be close to the true value. As a rough rule of thumb, there is a 95% probability that the interval that is within two standard errors of the estimated coefficient contains the true coefficient.[3] Using this rule, the *confidence interval* for the slope coefficient, $\hat{b}$, ranges from $-0.49 - (2 \times 0.08) = -0.65$ to $-0.49 + (2 \times 0.08) = -0.33$.

If zero were to lie within the confidence interval for $\hat{b}$, we would conclude that we cannot reject the hypothesis that the price has no effect on the quantity demanded. In our case, however, the entire confidence interval contains negative values, so we are reasonably sure that the higher the price, the less Nancy demands.

Multiple Regression

We can also estimate relationships involving more than one explanatory variable using a *multiple regression*. For example, Moschini and Meilke (1992) estimate a pork demand function, Equation 2.2, in which the quantity demanded is a function of income, Y, and the prices of pork, p, beef, p_b, and chicken, p_c:

$$Q = 171 - 20p + 20p_b + 3p_c + 2Y.$$

The multiple regression is able to separate the effects of the various explanatory variables. The coefficient 20 on the p variable says that an increase in the price of pork by \$1 per kg lowers the quantity demanded by 20 million kg per year, holding the effects of the other prices and income constant.

Appendix 3A: Effects of a Specific Tax on Equilibrium

The government collects a specific or unit tax, τ, from sellers, so sellers receive $p - \tau$ when consumers pay p. We now determine the effect of the tax on the equilibrium.

In the new equilibrium, the price that consumers pay is determined by the intersection of supply and demand after taxes:

$$D(p) - S(p - \tau) = 0, \tag{3A.1}$$

[3] The confidence interval is the coefficient plus or minus 1.96 times its standard error for large samples (at least hundreds of observations) in which the coefficients are normally distributed. For smaller samples, the confidence interval tends to be larger.

where the supply equals demand equation is written in implicit function form (the right-hand side of the equation is zero).

We determine the effect of a small tax on price by totally differentiating Equation 3A.1 with respect to p and τ:

$$\frac{dS}{dp}d\tau + \left[\frac{dD}{dp} - \frac{dS}{dp}\right]dp = 0.$$

Rearranging terms, it follows that the change in the price that consumers pay with respect to a change in the tax is

$$\frac{dp}{d\tau} = \frac{\frac{dS}{dp}}{\frac{dS}{dp} - \frac{dD}{dp}}. \tag{3A.2}$$

We know that $dD/dp < 0$ from the Law of Demand. If the supply curve slopes up, $dS/dp > 0$, then $dp/d\tau > 0$. The price consumers pay is greater, the higher the tax is. If $dS/dp < 0$, the direction of change is ambiguous.

By multiplying both the numerator and denominator of the right-hand side of Equation 3A.2 by p/Q, we can express this derivative in terms of elasticities:

$$\frac{dp}{d\tau} = \frac{\frac{dS}{dp}\frac{p}{Q}}{\frac{dS}{dp}\frac{p}{Q} - \frac{dD}{dp}\frac{p}{Q}} = \frac{\eta}{\eta - \varepsilon},$$

where the last equality follows because dS/dp and dD/dp are the changes in the quantities supplied and demanded as price changes and the consumer and producer prices are identical when $\tau = 0$. The change in price, Δp, equals $[\eta/(\eta - \varepsilon)]\Delta\tau$. This expression holds for any size change in $\Delta\tau$ if both the demand and supply curves are linear or have constant elasticity at each point. The expression only holds for small changes $\Delta\tau$ for other curves.

To determine the effect on quantity, we can combine the price result from Equation 3A.2 with information from either the demand or supply curve. Differentiating the demand function with respect to τ, we know that

$$\frac{dQ}{d\tau} = \frac{dD}{dp}\frac{dp}{d\tau} = \frac{\frac{dD}{dp}\frac{dS}{dp}}{\frac{dS}{dp} - \frac{dD}{dp}},$$

which is negative if the supply curve is upward sloping.

Appendix 4A: Utility and Indifference Curves

We now use calculus to examine the relationship between utility and indifference curves and some properties of indifference curves. Suppose Lisa's utility function is $U(B, Z)$, where B is the number of burritos and Z is the number of pizzas. Lisa's marginal utility for burritos, MU_B, is the amount of extra pleasure she would get from extra burritos, holding her consumption of pizza constant. Formally, her marginal utility for burritos, B, is the partial derivative of utility, $U(B, Z)$, with respect to B holding Z constant:

$$MU_B(B, Z) = \lim_{\Delta B \to 0} \frac{U(B + \Delta B, Z) - U(B, Z)}{\Delta B} = \frac{\partial U(B, Z)}{\partial B}.$$

By assumption, marginal utility is always nonnegative: A little more of a good makes you better off or at least doesn't harm you. The marginal utility depends on the current level of B and Z.

Which combinations of B and Z leave Lisa with a given level of pleasure, say $\bar{U}$? We can write those combinations as

$$\bar{U} = U(B, Z). \qquad (4A.1)$$

Equation A4.1 is the equation for an indifference curve with utility level $\bar{U}$.

We can express the slope of an indifference curve—the marginal rate of substitution, *MRS*—in terms of the marginal utilities. The slope of the indifference curve is found by determining the changes in B and P that leave utility unchanged. Totally differentiating Equation 4A.1, we find that

$$\mathrm{d}\bar{U} = 0 = \frac{\partial U(B, Z)}{\partial B}\mathrm{d}B + \frac{\partial U(B, Z)}{\partial Z}\mathrm{d}Z \equiv MU_B\mathrm{d}B + MU_Z\mathrm{d}Z. \qquad (A4.2)$$

This equation says that a little extra utility, MU_B, times the change in B, $\mathrm{d}B$, plus the extra utility, MU_Z, times the change in Z, $\mathrm{d}Z$, must add to zero. If we increase one of the goods, we must decrease the other to hold utility constant so that we stay on the same indifference curve. In Equation 4A.2, $\mathrm{d}\bar{U} = 0$ because we are holding utility constant so that we stay on the same indifference curve. Rearranging the terms in Equation 4A.2, we find that

$$\frac{\mathrm{d}B}{\mathrm{d}Z} = -\frac{MU_Z}{MU_B}.$$

The slope of the indifference curve is the negative of the ratio of the marginal utilities.

Suppose Lisa has the following Cobb-Douglas utility function (named after its inventors):

$$U(B, Z) = AB^{\alpha}Z^{\beta}.$$

Her marginal utility of burritos is

$$MU_B(B, Z) = \alpha AB^{\alpha-1}Z^{\beta} = \alpha\frac{U(B, Z)}{B},$$

and her marginal utility of pizza is

$$MU_Z(B, Z) = \beta AB^{\alpha}Z^{\beta-1} = \beta\frac{U(B, Z)}{Z}.$$

Suppose that $\alpha = \beta = \frac{1}{2}$ and $A = 20$. If $B = Z = 4$, then $U(4, 4) = 80$ and $MU_B(4, 4) = MU_Z(4, 4) = 10$. If $B = 1$ and $Z = 4$, however, $U(1, 4) = 40$, $MU_B(1, 4) = 20$, and

$MU_Z(1, 4) = 5$. The extra pleasure that Lisa gets from an extra burrito is greater, the fewer burritos she initially has, all else the same.

The slope of her indifference curve is

$$MRS = \frac{dB}{dZ} = -\frac{MU_Z}{MU_B} = -\frac{\beta A B^{\alpha} Z^{\beta-1}}{\alpha A B^{\alpha-1} Z^{\beta}} = -\frac{\beta B}{\alpha Z}.$$

The slope of the indifference curve differs with the levels of B and Z. If $\alpha = \beta = \frac{1}{2}$, $B = 4$, and $Z = 1$, $MRS(4, 1) = -(\frac{1}{2} \times 4)/(\frac{1}{2} \times 1) = -4$. At $B = Z = 4$, $MRS(4, 4) = -1$.

Appendix 4B: Maximizing Utility

Lisa's objective is to maximize her utility, $U(B, Z)$, subject to (s.t.) a budget constraint:

$$\max_{B,Z} U(B, Z) \quad \text{s.t.} \quad Y = p_B B + p_Z Z, \tag{4B.1}$$

where B is the number of burritos she buys at price p_B, Z is the number of pizzas she buys at price p_Z, Y is her income, and $Y = p_B B + p_Z Z$ is her budget constraint (her spending on burritos and pizza can't exceed her income). The mathematical statement of her problem shows that her *control variables* (what she chooses) are B and Z, which appear under the "max" term in the equation. We assume that Lisa has no control over the prices she faces or her budget.

One way to solve this type of constrained maximization problem is to use the Lagrangian method, in which we convert the constrained problem in Equation 4B.1 into an unconstrained problem:

$$\underset{B,Z,\lambda}{\text{Maximize}}\ \mathcal{L} = U(B, Z) - \lambda(p_B B + p_Z Z - Y), \tag{4B.2}$$

where λ is called the Lagrange multiplier. With normal-shaped utility functions, the values of B, Z, and λ that maximize this unconstrained problem are the same as the values that maximize the original constrained problem.

The advantage of changing the problem to an unconstrained problem is that we know how to maximize it using standard calculus techniques. We need to derive first-order conditions of Equation 4B .2 with respect to the three control variables, B, Z, and λ:[4]

$$\frac{\partial \mathcal{L}}{\partial B} = MU_B(B, Z) - \lambda p_B = 0, \tag{4B.3a}$$

$$\frac{\partial \mathcal{L}}{\partial Z} = MU_Z(B, Z) - \lambda p_Z = 0, \tag{4B.3b}$$

$$\frac{\partial \mathcal{L}}{\partial \lambda} = Y - p_B B - p_Z Z = 0, \tag{4B.3c}$$

[4]To make our presentation as simple as possible, we assume that we have an interior solution, B and Z are infinitely divisible, and $U(B, Z)$ is continuously differentiable at least twice (so that the second-order condition is well defined). The first-order conditions give us the necessary conditions for an interior solution in which positive quantities of both goods are consumed.

where $MU_B(B, Z) \equiv \partial U(B, Z)/\partial B$ is the partial derivative of utility with respect to B (the marginal utility of B) and $MU_Z(B, Z)$ is the marginal utility of Z. Equation 4B.3c is the budget constraint. Equations 4B.3a and 4B.3b say that the marginal utility of each good equals its price times λ.

What is λ? If we equate Equations 4B.3a and 4B.3b and rearrange terms, we find that

$$\lambda = \frac{MU_B}{p_B} = \frac{MU_Z}{p_Z}. \tag{4B.4}$$

Because the Lagrangian multiplier, λ, equals the marginal utility of each good divided by its price, λ equals the extra pleasure one gets from one's last dollar of expenditures. Equivalently, λ is the value of loosening the budget constraint by one dollar.[5] Equation 4B.4 tells us that, to maximize her utility, Lisa should pick a B and Z so that, if she got one more dollar, spending that dollar on B or on Z would give her the same extra utility.

There is an alternative interpretation of this condition for maximizing utility. Taking the ratio of Equations 4B.3a and 4B.3b (or rearranging 4B.4), we find that

$$\frac{MU_Z}{MU_B} = \frac{p_Z}{p_B}. \tag{4B.5}$$

The left-hand side of 4B.5 is the absolute value of the marginal rate of substitution, $MRS = -MU_Z/MU_B$, and the right-hand side is the absolute value of the marginal rate of transformation, $MRT = -p_Z/p_B$. Thus, the calculus approach gives us the same condition for an optimum that we derived using graphs. The indifference curve should be tangent to the budget constraint: The slope of the indifference curve, MRS, should equal the slope of the budget constraint, MRT.

We assume that the second-order (sufficient) conditions hold, which is true if the utility function is quasiconcave or if the indifference curves are convex to the origin. That is, we assume that Lisa is maximizing rather than minimizing her utility when she chooses the levels of B and Z given by the first-order conditions.

[5]Differentiating utility with respect to Y, we find that

$$\frac{dU}{dY} = MU_B(B, Z)\frac{dB}{dY} + MU_Z(B, Z)\frac{dZ}{dY}.$$

Substituting from 4B.4 into this expression, we obtain

$$\frac{dU}{dY} = \lambda p_B \frac{dB}{dY} + \lambda p_Z \frac{dZ}{dY} = \lambda \frac{p_B dB + p_Z dZ}{dY}.$$

Totally differentiating the budget constraint, we learn that

$$dY = p_B dB + p_Z dZ.$$

Substituting this expression into the previous expression gives us

$$\frac{dU}{dY} = \frac{\lambda p_B dB + \lambda p_Z dZ}{p_B dB + p_Z dZ} = \lambda.$$

Thus, λ equals the extra utility one gets from one more dollar of income.

As an example, suppose that the utility is Cobb-Douglas as in Equation 4A.2: $U = AB^{\alpha}Z^{\beta}$. The first-order condition, Equation 4B.3c, the budget constraint, stays the same, and Equations 4B.3a and 4B.3b become

$$\frac{\partial \mathcal{L}}{\partial B} = \alpha \frac{U(B, Z)}{B} - \lambda p_B = 0, \tag{4B.6}$$

$$\frac{\partial \mathcal{L}}{\partial Z} = \beta \frac{U(B, Z)}{Z} - \lambda p_Z = 0. \tag{4B.7}$$

Using Equations 4B.6 and 4B.7, we can write Equation 4B.4 as

$$\lambda = \alpha \frac{U(B, Z)}{p_B B} = \beta \frac{U(B, Z)}{p_Z Z}.$$

Taking the ratio of Equations 4B.6 and 4B.7 and rearranging terms, we find that

$$\beta p_B B = \alpha p_Z Z. \tag{4B.8}$$

Substituting $Y - p_B B$ for $p_Z Z$, using Equation 4B.3c, into Equation 4B.8 and rearranging terms, we get

$$B = \frac{\alpha}{\alpha + \beta} \frac{Y}{p_B}. \tag{4B.9}$$

Similarly, by substituting Equation 4B.9 into Equation 4B.8 and using the budget constraint, we find that

$$Z = \frac{\beta}{\alpha + \beta} \frac{Y}{p_Z}. \tag{4.B10}$$

Thus, knowing the utility function, we can solve the expression for the *B* and *Z* that maximize utility in terms of income and prices.

Equations 4B.9 and 4B.10 are the consumer's demand curves for *B* and *Z*, respectively. (We derive demand curves using graphs in Chapter 5.)

If $\alpha = \beta = \frac{1}{2}$, $A = 20$, $Y = 80$, and $p_Z = p_B = 10$, then $B = Z = 4$ and the value of loosening the budget constraint is $\lambda = MU_B/p_B = MU_Z/p_Z = 10/10 = 1$. If p_B rises to 40, then $Z = 4$, $B = 1$, and $\lambda = 20/40 = 5/10 = \frac{1}{2}$.

Appendix 5A: Labor-Leisure Model

Jackie's utility, *U*, is a function,

$$U = U(Y, L), \tag{5A.1}$$

of her leisure, *L*, and her income, *Y*, which she uses to buy all other goods and services. Jackie maximizes her utility, Equation 5A.1, subject to two constraints. The first, imposed by the clock, is that the number of hours she works, *H*, equals her total hours in a day minus her hours of leisure:

$$H = 24 - L. \tag{5A.2}$$

The second constraint is that her earned income (earnings), Y, equals her wage, w, times the hours she works:

$$Y = wH, \tag{5A.3}$$

For now, we assume that her unearned income is zero.

Although we can maximize Equation 5A.1 subject to 5A.2 and 5A.3 using Lagrangian techniques, it is easier to do so by substitution. By substituting Equations 5A.2 and 5A.3 into 5A.1, we can convert this constrained problem into an unconstrained maximization problem:

$$\underset{H}{\text{Maximize}}\, U = U(wH, 24 - H). \tag{5A.4}$$

By using the chain rule of differentiation, we find that the first-order condition for an interior maximum to the problem in Equation 5A.4 is

$$\frac{dU}{dH} = MU_Y w - MU_L = 0,$$

where MU_Y, the marginal utility of goods or income, is the partial derivative of utility with respect to income, $\partial U/\partial Y$, and MU_L, the marginal utility of leisure, is the partial derivative with respect to leisure, $\partial U/\partial L$.[6] This expression can be rewritten as $w = MU_L/MU_Y$.

If we use the terminology from Chapter 4, to maximize her utility, Jackie must set her marginal rate of substitution of income for leisure, $MRS = -MU_L/MU_Y$, equal to her marginal rate of transformation of income for leisure, $MRT = -w$, in the market:

$$MRS = -\frac{MU_L}{MU_Y} = -w = MRT.$$

Suppose that Jackie's utility is

$$U = Y^{\alpha}L^{1-\alpha} = (wH)^{\alpha}(24 - H)^{1-\alpha},$$

which is a Cobb-Douglas utility function (Appendix 4A). Differentiating this utility function with respect to H, setting the derivative equal to zero, and rearranging terms, we find that $H = 24\alpha$. With this particular utility function, an individual works a fixed number of hours regardless of the wage. If $\alpha = \frac{1}{2}$, the individual works 12 hours a day whether the wage is 50¢ an hour or \$500 an hour.

Appendix 5B: The Slutsky Equation

In this appendix, we sketch the derivation of the Slutsky equation (for a more formal derivation, see a graduate microeconomics textbook such as Varian 1992). The chapter notes that the total effect on the quantity demanded when its price rises

[6]The second-order condition for an interior maximum is

$$\frac{d^2U}{dH^2} = \frac{\partial^2 U}{\partial Y^2}w^2 - 2\frac{\partial^2 U}{\partial Y \partial L}w + \frac{\partial^2 U}{\partial L^2} < 0.$$

equals the sum of the substitution and income effects. The total effect, $\Delta q/\Delta p$, is the change in the quantity demanded of a good, Δq, for a given change in the good's price, Δp. The substitution effect is the change in quantity demanded for a change in price, holding utility constant, which we label $(\Delta q/\Delta p)_{U\ constant}$.

A change in the price affects how much the consumer can buy and acts like a change in income. The income effect is the change in quantity as income changes times the change in income as price changes, $(\Delta q/\Delta Y)(\Delta Y/\Delta p)$, where ΔY is the change in income. The change in income from a change in price is $\Delta Y/\Delta p = -q$. For example, if price rises by \$1, income falls by the number of units purchased. From this last result, the income effect is $-q(\Delta q/\Delta Y)$.

Using these expressions, we write the identity that the total effect equals the substitution plus the income effect as

$$\Delta q/\Delta p = (\Delta q/\Delta p)_{U\ constant} - q(\Delta q/\Delta Y).$$

Multiplying this equation through by p/q, multiplying the last term by Y/Y, and rearranging terms, we obtain

$$\frac{\Delta q}{\Delta p}\frac{p}{q} = \left(\frac{\Delta q}{\Delta p}\right)_{U\ constant}\frac{p}{q} - \frac{\Delta q}{\Delta Y}\frac{Y}{q}\frac{pq}{Y}.$$

Substituting, $\varepsilon = (\Delta q/\Delta p)(p/q)$, $\varepsilon^* = (\Delta q/\Delta p)_{U\ constant}(p/q)$, $\xi = (\Delta q/\Delta Y)(Y/q)$, and $\theta = pq/Y$ into this last expression, we have the Slutsky Equation 5.1 in the text:

$$\varepsilon = \varepsilon^* - \theta\xi.$$

Appendix 6A: Cobb-Douglas Production Function

Economists frequently estimate production functions. The Cobb-Douglas production function (named after its inventors, Charles W. Cobb, a mathematician, and Paul H. Douglas, an economist and U.S. senator) is probably the most commonly estimated one. Examples of estimated Cobb-Douglas production functions include the Norwegian printing firm's production function (Griliches and Ringstad 1971) and the various Canadian manufacturing firms' production functions (Baldwin and Gorecki 1986) discussed in this chapter.

The Cobb-Douglas production function is

$$q = AL^{\alpha}K^{\beta}. \tag{6A.1}$$

Economists use statistical means to estimate A, α, and β, which determine the exact shape of the production function. The larger A is, the more output the firm gets from a given amount of labor and capital. A 1% increase in labor, holding capital constant, causes an α% increase in output. Similarly, a 1% increase in capital, holding labor constant, causes a β% increase in output.

For a Canadian thread mill (Table 6.3, based on Baldwin and Gorecki 1986), $\alpha = 0.64$ and $\beta = 0.18$. Thus, a 1% increase in labor, holding capital fixed, causes output to increase by 0.64%; and a 1% increase in capital causes only a 0.18% increase in output.

The α term tells us the relationship between the average product of labor and the marginal product of labor. By differentiating the Cobb-Douglas production function with respect to L, holding K constant, we find that the marginal product of labor is

$$MP_L = \frac{\partial q}{\partial L} = \alpha A L^{\alpha-1} K^{\beta} = \alpha \frac{A L^{\alpha} K^{\beta}}{L} = \alpha \frac{q}{L}.$$

The marginal product of labor equals α times the average product of labor, $AP_L = q/L$. Thus, a Canadian thread mill's marginal product of labor is about two-thirds, 0.64, of its average product of labor. Using similar reasoning, the marginal product of capital is $MP_K = \beta q/K$.

The marginal rate of technical substitution is $MRTS = MP_L/MP_K = (\alpha q/L)/(\beta q/K) = (\alpha/\beta)K/L$. For a Canadian thread mill, $MRTS = (0.64/0.18)K/L \approx 3.56K/L$.

Appendix 7A: Norwegian Printing Firm's SR Cost Curves

We can use math to derive the various short-run cost curves for a typical Norwegian printing firm. Based on the estimates of Griliches and Ringstad (1971), its production function is

$$q = 1.52L^{0.6}K^{0.4},$$

where labor, L, is measured in years of work (2,000 hours of work per year), K is the number of units of capital, and q is the amount of output that can be sold for 200 kronors (kr).

In the short run, the firm's capital is fixed at $\overline{K} = 100$. If the rental rate of a unit of capital is 8 kr, the fixed cost, F, is 800 kr. Figure 7.3 shows that the average fixed cost,

$$AFC = F/q = 800/q,$$

falls as output increases.

We can use the production function to derive the variable cost. First, we determine how output and labor are related. Setting capital, K, at 100 units in the production function, we find that the output produced in the short run is solely a function of labor:

$$q = 1.52L^{0.6}100^{0.4} \approx 9.59L^{0.6}.$$

Rearranging this expression, we can write the number of workers per year, L, needed to produce q units of output, as a function solely of output:

$$L(q) = \left(\frac{q}{1.52 \times 100^{0.4}}\right)^{\frac{1}{0.6}} \approx 0.023q^{1.67}. \quad (7A.1)$$

Now that we know how labor and output are related, we can calculate variable cost directly. The only variable input is labor, so if the wage is 24 kr, the firm's variable cost is

$$VC(q) = wL(q) = 24L(q).$$

Substituting for $L(q)$ using Equation 7A.1, we see how variable cost varies with output:

$$VC(q) = 24L(q) = 24\left(\frac{q}{1.52 \times 100^{0.4}}\right)^{\frac{1}{0.6}} \approx 0.55q^{1.67}. \quad (7A.2)$$

Using this expression for variable cost, we can construct the other cost measures.

We obtain the average variable cost as a function of output, $AVC(q)$, by dividing both sides of Equation 7A.2 by q:

$$AVC(q) = \frac{VC(q)}{q} = \frac{24L(q)}{q} \approx 24\left(\frac{0.023q^{1.67}}{q}\right) = 0.55q^{0.67}.$$

As Figure 7.3 shows, the average variable cost is strictly increasing.

To obtain the equation for marginal cost as a function of output, we differentiate the variable cost, $VC(q)$, with respect to output:

$$MC(q) = \frac{dVC(q)}{dq} \approx \frac{d(0.55q^{1.67})}{dq} = 1.67 \times 0.55q^{0.67} \approx 0.92q^{0.67}.$$

Thus, to construct all the cost measures of the printing firm, we need only the production function and the prices of the inputs.

Appendix 7B: Minimizing Cost

We can use calculus to derive the cost minimization conditions, Equations 7.6 and 7.7, discussed in the chapter. The problem the firm faces in the long run is to choose the level of labor, L, and capital, K, that will minimize the cost of producing a particular level of output, $\bar{q}$, given a wage of w and a rental rate of capital of r.

The relationship between inputs and output is summarized in the firm's production function: $q = f(L, K)$. The marginal product of labor, which is the extra output the firm produces from a little more labor, holding capital constant, is $MP_L(L, K) = \partial f(L, K)/\partial L$, which is positive. There are diminishing marginal returns to labor, however, so the marginal product of labor falls as labor increases: $\partial MP_L(L, K)/\partial L = \partial^2 f(L, K)/\partial L^2 < 0$. The marginal product of capital has the same properties: $\partial f(L, K)/\partial K > 0$ and $\partial MP_K(L, K)/\partial K < 0$.

The firm's problem is to minimize its cost, C, of production, through its choice of labor and capital,

$$\underset{L,K}{\text{Minimize}}\, C = wL + rK,$$

subject to the constraint that a given amount of output, $\bar{q}$, is to be produced:

$$f(L, K) = \bar{q}. \quad (7B.1)$$

Equation 7B.1 is the $\bar{q}$ isoquant.

We can change this constrained minimization problem into an unconstrained problem by using the Lagrangian technique. The firm's unconstrained problem is to minimize the Lagrangian, $\mathcal{L}$, through its choice of labor, capital, and the Lagrange multiplier, λ:

$$\underset{L,K,\lambda}{\text{Minimize}}\ \mathcal{L} = wL + rK - \lambda[f(L,K) - \bar{q}].$$

The necessary conditions for a minimum are obtained by differentiating $\mathcal{L}$ with respect to L, K, and λ and setting the derivatives equal to zero:

$$\partial\mathcal{L}/\partial L = w - \lambda MP_L(L, K) = 0, \tag{7B.2}$$

$$\partial\mathcal{L}/\partial K = r - \lambda MP_K(L, K) = 0, \tag{7B.3}$$

$$\partial\mathcal{L}/\partial\lambda = f(L, K) - \bar{q} = 0. \tag{7B.4}$$

We can rewrite Equations 7B.2 and 7B.3 as $w = \lambda MP_L(L, K)$ and $r = \lambda MP_K(L, K)$. Taking the ratio of these two expressions, we obtain

$$\frac{w}{r} = \frac{MP_L(L,K)}{MP_K(L,K)} = MRTS, \tag{7B.5}$$

which is the same as Equation 7.6. This condition states that cost is minimized when the rate at which firms can exchange capital for labor in the market, w/r, is the same as the rate at which capital can be substituted for labor along an isoquant. That is, the isocost line is tangent to the isoquant.

We can rewrite Equation 7B.5 to obtain the expression:

$$\frac{MP_L(L,K)}{w} = \frac{MP_K(L,K)}{r}.$$

This equation tells us that the last dollar spent on labor should produce as much extra output as the last dollar spent on capital; otherwise, the amount of factors used should be adjusted.

We can rearrange Equations 7B.2 and 7B.3 to obtain an expression for the Lagrangian multiplier:

$$\lambda = \frac{w}{MP_L(L,K)} = \frac{r}{MP_K(L,K)}. \tag{7B.6}$$

Equation 7B.6 says that the Lagrangian multiplier, λ, equals the ratio of the factor price to the marginal product for each factor. The marginal product for a factor is the extra amount of output one gets by increasing that factor slightly, so the reciprocal of the marginal product is the extra input it takes to produce an extra unit of output. By multiplying the reciprocal of the marginal product by the factor cost, we learn the extra cost of producing an extra unit of output by using more of this factor. Thus, the Lagrangian multiplier equals the marginal cost of production: It measures how much the cost increases if we produce one more unit of output.

If a firm has a Cobb-Douglas production function, $Q = AL^{\alpha}K^{\beta}$, the marginal product of capital is $MP_K = \beta q/K$ and the marginal product of labor is $MP_L = \alpha q/L$ (see Appendix 6A), so the $MRTS$ is $\alpha K/(\beta L)$. Thus, the tangency condition, Equation 7B.5, requires that

$$\frac{w}{r} = \frac{\alpha K}{\beta L}. \tag{7B.7}$$

Using algebra, we can rewrite Equation 7B.7 as

$$K = \frac{\beta w}{\alpha R} L, \tag{7B.8}$$

which is the expansion path for a Cobb-Douglas production function and given w and r. According to Equation 7B.8, the expansion path of a firm with a Cobb-Douglas production function is an upward-sloping straight line through the origin with a slope of $\beta w/(\alpha r)$.

Appendix 8A: A Competitive Firm's Demand Curve

As a practical matter, are the demand curves faced by individual competitive firms flat? To answer this question, we use a modified supply-and-demand diagram to derive the demand curve facing an individual firm.

The demand curve that an individual firm faces is called the *residual demand curve*: the market demand that is not met by other sellers at any given price. The firm's residual demand function, $D^r(p)$, shows the quantity demanded from the firm at a price p. A firm sells only to people who have not already purchased the good from another seller. We can determine how much demand is left for a particular firm at each possible price using the market demand curve and the supply curve for all *other* firms in the market. The quantity the market demands is a function of the price: $Q = D(p)$. The supply curve of other firms is $S^o(p)$. The residual demand function equals the market demand function, $D(p)$, minus the supply of all other firms:

$$D^r(p) = D(p) - S^o(p). \tag{8A.1}$$

At prices so high that $S^o(p)$ is greater than $D(p)$, the residual demand, $D^r(p)$, is zero.

In Figure 8A.1, we derive the residual demand for a Canadian manufacturing firm that produces metal chairs. Panel b shows the market demand curve, D, and the supply of all but one manufacturing firm, S^o.[7] At p = \$66 per chair, the supply of other firms, 500 units (one unit being a thousand metal chairs) per year, exactly equals the market demand (panel b), so the residual demand facing the remaining firm (panel a) is zero.

At prices below \$66, the other chair firms are not willing to supply as much as the market demands. At p = \$63, for example, the market demand is 527 units, but other firms want to supply only 434 units. As a result, the residual demand facing the individual firm at p = \$63 is 93 (= 527 – 434) units. Thus, the residual demand curve at any given price is the horizontal difference between the market demand curve and the supply of the other firms.

The residual demand curve facing the firm, panel a, is much flatter than the market demand curve, panel b. As a result, the elasticity of the residual demand curve is much higher than the market elasticity.

[7]The figure uses constant elasticity demand and supply curves. The elasticity of supply, 3.1, is based on the estimated cost function from Robidoux and Lester (1988) for Canadian office furniture manufacturers. I estimate that the elasticity of demand is –1.1, using data from Statistics Canada, *Office Furniture Manufacturers*.

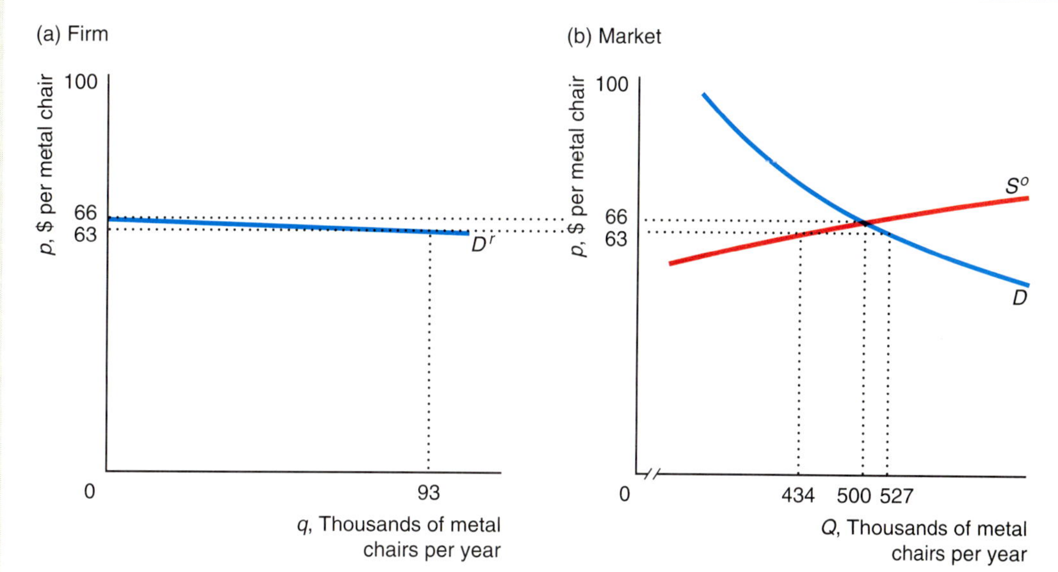

Figure 8A.1 Residual Demand Curve. The residual demand curve, $D^r(p)$, facing a single office furniture manufacturing firm is the market demand, $D(p)$, minus the supply of the other firms in the market, $S^o(p)$. The residual demand curve is much flatter than the market demand curve.

If there are n identical firms in the market, the elasticity of demand, ε_i, facing Firm i is

$$\varepsilon_i = n\varepsilon - (n - 1)\eta_o, \tag{8A.2}$$

where ε is the market elasticity of demand (a negative number), η_o is the elasticity of supply of each of the other firms (typically a positive number), and $(n - 1)$ is the number of other firms.[8]

---

[8]Differentiating the residual demand, $D^r(p)$, given in Equation 8A.1 with respect to p, we obtain

$$\frac{dD^r}{dp} = \frac{dD}{dp} - \frac{dS^o}{dp}.$$

Because the firms are identical, the quantity produced by each is $q = Q/n$ and the total quantity produced by all the other firms is $Q^o = (n - 1)q$. If we multiply both sides of the expression above by p/q and multiply and divide the first term on the right-hand side by Q/Q and the second term by Q^o/Q^o, this expression may be rewritten as

$$\frac{dD^r}{dp}\frac{p}{q} = \frac{dD}{dp}\frac{p}{Q}\frac{Q}{q} - \frac{dS^o}{dp}\frac{p}{Q_o}\frac{Q_o}{q},$$

where $q = D^r(p)$, $Q = D(p)$, and $Q_o = S^o(p)$. This expression in turn can be rewritten as Equation 8A.2 by noting that $Q/q = n$, $Q_o/q = (n - 1)$, $(dD^r/dp)(p/q) = \varepsilon_i$, $(dD/dp)(p/Q) = \varepsilon$, and $(dS^o/dp)(p/Q_o) = \eta_o$.

There are $n = 78$ firms manufacturing metal chairs in Canada. If they are identical, the elasticity of demand facing a single firm is

$$\begin{aligned}\varepsilon_i &= [n\varepsilon] \qquad -[(n-1)\eta_o]\\ &= [78 \times (-1.1)] - [77 \times 3.1]\\ &= -85.8 \qquad -238.7\\ &= -324.5.\end{aligned}$$

Thus, although the market demand elasticity is only −1.1, a typical firm faces a residual demand elasticity of −324.5. If a firm raises its price by one-tenth of a percent (about 0.7¢ per chair), the quantity it could sell would fall by nearly one-third. Thus, the competitive model assumption that this firm faces a horizontal demand curve with an infinite price elasticity is not much of an exaggeration.

As Equation 8A.2 shows, the residual demand curve facing a single firm is more elastic the more firms, n, are in the market, the more elastic is the market demand, ε, and the larger is the elasticity of supply of the other firms, η_o.

Appendix 8B: Profit Maximization

In general, a firm maximizes its profit, $\pi(q) = R(q) - C(q)$, by its choice of output q. A *necessary condition* for a maximum at a positive level of output is found by differentiating profit with respect to q and setting the derivative equal to zero:

$$\frac{d\pi}{dq} = \frac{dR(q^*)}{dq} - \frac{dC(q^*)}{dq} = 0. \tag{8B.1}$$

where q^* is the profit-maximizing output. Because $dR(q)/dq$ is the marginal revenue, $MR(q)$, and $dC(q)/dq$ is the marginal cost, $MC(q)$, Equation 8B.1 says that marginal revenue equals marginal cost at q^*:

$$MR(q^*) = MC(q^*). \tag{8B.2}$$

A *sufficient condition* for profit to be maximized at $q^* > 0$ is that the second-order condition holds:

$$\frac{d^2\pi}{dq^2} = \frac{d^2R(q^*)}{dq^2} - \frac{d^2C(q^*)}{dq^2} = \frac{dMR(q^*)}{dq} - \frac{dMC(q^*)}{dq} < 0. \tag{8B.3}$$

Equation 8B.3 can be rewritten as

$$\frac{dMR(q^*)}{dq} < \frac{dMC(q^*)}{dq}. \tag{8B.4}$$

Thus, a sufficient condition for a maximum is that the slope of the marginal revenue curve is less than that of the marginal cost curve, and that the MC curve cuts the MR curve from below at q^*.

For a competitive firm, $\pi(q) = pq - C(q)$, so the necessary condition for profit to be maximized, Equation 8B.1 or 8B.2, can be written as

$$p = MC(q^*). \tag{8B.5}$$

Equation 8B.5 says that a profit-maximizing, competitive firm sets its output at q^* where its marginal cost equals its price.

Because a competitive firm's marginal revenue, p, is a constant, $\mathrm{d}MR/\mathrm{d}q = \mathrm{d}p/\mathrm{d}q = 0$. Thus, the sufficient condition for profit to be maximized, Equation 8B.4, can be rewritten as

$$0 < \frac{\mathrm{d}MC(q^*)}{\mathrm{d}q}. \tag{8B.6}$$

for a competitive firm. Equation 8B.6 shows that a sufficient condition for a competitive firm to be maximizing its profit at q^* is that its marginal cost curve is upward sloping at the equilibrium quantity.

Appendix 12A: Cournot Equilibrium

In this appendix, we use calculus to determine the Cournot equilibrium for n identical oligopolistic firms. We first solve for the equilibrium using general demand and cost functions, which are identical for all firms. Then we apply this general solution to a linear example. Finally, using the linear example, we determine the equilibrium when two firms have different marginal costs.

General Model

Suppose that the market demand function is $p(Q)$ and each firm's cost function is the same $C(q_i)$. To analyze a Cournot market of identical firms, we first examine the behavior of a representative firm. Firm 1 tries to maximize its profits through its choice of q_1:

$$\underset{q_1}{\text{Maximize}}\ \pi_1(q_1, q_2, \ldots, q_n) = q_1 p(q_1 + q_2 + \ldots + q_n) - C(q_1), \tag{12A.1}$$

where $q_1 + q_2 + \ldots + q_n = Q$, the total market output. Firm 1 takes the outputs of the other firms as fixed. If Firm 1 changes its output by a small amount, the price changes by $(\mathrm{d}p(Q)/\mathrm{d}Q)(\mathrm{d}Q/\mathrm{d}q_1) = \mathrm{d}p(Q)/\mathrm{d}Q$. Its necessary condition to maximize profit (first-order condition) is found by differentiating profit in Equation 12A.1 and setting the result equal to zero. After we rearrange terms, this necessary condition is

$$MR = p(Q) + q_1 \frac{\mathrm{d}p(Q)}{\mathrm{d}Q} = \frac{\mathrm{d}C(q_1)}{\mathrm{d}q_1} = MC, \tag{12A.2}$$

or marginal revenue equals marginal cost. Equation 12A.2 specifies the firm's best-response function: the optimal q_1 for any given output of other firms.

The marginal revenue expression can be rewritten as $p(1 + [q_1/p][dp/dQ])$. Multiplying and dividing the last term by n, noting that $Q = nq_1$ (given that all firms are identical), and observing that ε, the market elasticity of demand, is $(dQ/dp)(p/Q)$, we can rewrite Equation 12A.2 as

$$p\left(1 + \frac{1}{n\varepsilon}\right) = \frac{dC(q_1)}{dq_1}. \tag{12A.3}$$

The left-hand side of Equation 12A.3 expresses Firm 1's marginal revenue in terms of the elasticity of demand of its residual demand curve, $n\varepsilon$, which is the number of firms, n, times the market demand elasticity, ε. Holding ε constant, the more firms, the more elastic is the residual demand curve, and hence the closer is a firm's marginal revenue to the price.

We can rearrange Equation 12A.3 to obtain an expression for the Lerner Index, $(p - MC)/p$, in terms of the market demand elasticity and the number of firms:

$$\frac{p - MC}{p} = -\frac{1}{n\varepsilon}. \tag{12A.4}$$

The larger the Lerner Index is, the greater is the firm's market power. As Equation 12A.4 shows, if we hold the market elasticity constant and increase the number of firms, the Lerner Index falls. As n approaches ∞, the elasticity facing any one firm approaches −∞, so the Lerner Index approaches 0 and the market is competitive.

Linear Example

Now suppose that the market demand is linear,

$$p = a - bQ,$$

and each firm's marginal cost is m, a constant, and it has no fixed cost. Firm 1, a typical firm, maximizes its profits through its choice of q_1:

$$\underset{q_1}{\text{Maximize}}\ \pi_1(q_1, q_2, \ldots, q_n) = q_1[a - b(q_1 + q_2 + \ldots + q_n)] - mq_1. \tag{12A.5}$$

Setting the derivative of profit with respect to q_1, holding the output levels of the other firms fixed, equal to zero, and rearranging terms, we find that the necessary condition for Firm 1 to maximize its profit is

$$MR = a - b(2q_1 + q_2 + \ldots + q_n) = m = MC. \tag{12A.6}$$

Because all firms have the same cost function, $q_2 = q_3 = \ldots = q_n \equiv q$ in equilibrium. Substituting this expression into Equation 12A.6, we find that the first firm's best-response function is

$$q_1 = R_1(q_2, \ldots, q_n) = \frac{a - m}{2b} - \frac{n - 1}{2}q. \tag{12A.7}$$

The other firms' best-response functions are derived similarly.

All these best-response functions must hold simultaneously. The intersection of the best-response functions determines the Cournot equilibrium. Setting $q_1 = q$ in

Equation 12A.7 and solving for q, we find that the Cournot equilibrium output for each firm is,

$$q = \frac{a - m}{(n + 1)b}. \tag{12A.8}$$

Total market output, $Q = nq$, equals $n(a - m)/[(n + 1)b]$. The corresponding price is obtained by substituting this expression for market output into the demand function:

$$p = \frac{a + nm}{n + 1}. \tag{12A.9}$$

Setting $n = 1$ in Equations 12A.8 and 12A.9 yields the monopoly quantity and price. As n becomes large, each firm's quantity approaches zero, total output approaches $(a - m)/b$, and price approaches m, which are the competitive levels. In Equation 12A.9, the Lerner Index is

$$(p - MC)/p = (a - m)/(a + nm).$$

As n grows large, the denominator goes to ∞, so the Lerner Index goes to 0, and there is no market power.

Different Costs

In the linear example with two firms, how does the equilibrium change if the firms have different marginal costs? The marginal cost of Firm 1 is m_1, and that of Firm 2 is m_2. Firm 1 chooses output to maximize its profit:

$$\underset{q_1}{\text{Maximize}}\, \pi_1(q_1, q_2) = q_1[a - b(q_1 + q_2)] - m_1 q_1. \tag{12A.10}$$

Setting the derivative of Firm 1's profit with respect to q_1, holding q_2 fixed, equal to zero, and rearranging terms, we find that the necessary condition for Firm 1 to maximize its profit is $MR_1 = a - b(2q_1 + q_2) = m_1 = MC$. Using algebra, we can rearrange this expression to obtain Firm 1's best-response function:

$$q_1 = \frac{q - m_1 - bq_2}{2b}. \tag{12A.11}$$

By similar reasoning, Firm 2's best-response function is

$$q_2 = \frac{a - m_2 - bq_1}{2b}. \tag{12A.12}$$

To determine the equilibrium, we solve Equations 12A.11 and 12A.12 simultaneously for q_1 and q_2:

$$q_1 = \frac{a - 2m_1 + m_2}{3b}, \tag{12A.13}$$

$$q_2 = \frac{a - 2m_2 + m_1}{3b}. \tag{12A.14}$$

By inspecting Equations 12A.13 and 12A.14, we find that the firm with the smaller marginal cost has the larger equilibrium output. Similarly, the low-cost firm has a higher profit. If m_1 is less than m_2, then

$$\pi_1 = \frac{(a + m_2 - 2m_1)^2}{9b} > \frac{(a + m_1 - 2m_2)^2}{9b} = \pi_2.$$

Appendix 12B: Stackelberg Equilibrium

We use calculus to derive the Stackelberg equilibrium for the linear example given in Appendix 12A with two firms that have the same marginal cost, m. Because Firm 1, the Stackelberg leader, chooses its output first, it knows that Firm 2, the follower, will choose its output using its best-response function, which is (see Equation 12A.7 where $n = 2$)

$$q_2 = R_2(q_1) = \frac{a - m}{2b} - \frac{1}{2}q_1. \tag{12B.1}$$

The Stackelberg leader's profit, $\pi_1(q_1 + q_2)$, can be written as $\pi_1(q_1 + R_2(q_1))$, where we've replaced the follower's output with its best-response function. The Stackelberg leader maximizes its profit taking the best-response function as given:

$$\underset{q_1}{\text{Maximize}}\, \pi_1(q_1, R_2(q_1)) = q_1\left[a - b\left(q_1 + \frac{a - m}{2b} - \frac{1}{2}q_1\right)\right] - mq_1. \tag{12B.2}$$

Setting the derivative of Firm 1's profit (in Equation 12B.2) with respect to q_1 equal to zero and solving for q_1, we find that the profit-maximizing output of the leader is

$$q_1 = \frac{a - m}{2b}. \tag{12B.3}$$

Substituting the expression for q_1 in Equation 12B.3 into Equation 12B.1, we obtain the equilibrium output of the follower:

$$q_2 = \frac{a - m}{4b}.$$

Appendix 13A: Perfect Price Discrimination

A perfectly price-discriminating monopoly charges each customer the reservation price $p = D(Q)$, where $D(Q)$ is the inverse demand function and Q is total output. The discriminating monopoly's revenue, R, is the area under the demand curve up to the quantity, Q, it sells:

$$R = \int_0^Q D(z)\,dz,$$

where z is a placeholder for quantity. Its objective is to maximize its profit through its choice of Q:

$$\underset{Q}{\text{Maximize}}\ \pi = \int_0^Q D(z)\,\mathrm{d}z - C(Q). \tag{13A.1}$$

Its first-order condition for a maximum is found by differentiating Equation 13A.1 to obtain

$$\frac{\mathrm{d}\pi}{\mathrm{d}Q} = D(Q) - \frac{\mathrm{d}C(Q)}{\mathrm{d}Q} = 0. \tag{13A.2}$$

According to Equation 13A.2, the discriminating monopoly sells units up to the quantity, Q, where the reservation price for the last unit, $D(Q)$, equals its marginal cost, $\mathrm{d}C(Q)/\mathrm{d}Q$. (This quantity is $Q_c = Q_d$ in Figure 13.4.)

For this solution to maximize profits, the second-order condition must hold: $\mathrm{d}^2\pi/\mathrm{d}Q^2 = \mathrm{d}D(Q)/\mathrm{d}Q - \mathrm{d}^2C(Q)/\mathrm{d}Q^2 < 0$. Thus, the second-order condition holds if the marginal cost curve has a nonnegative slope (because the demand curve has a negative slope). More generally, the second-order condition holds if the demand curve has a greater (absolute) slope than the marginal cost curve.

The perfectly price-discriminating monopoly's profit is

$$\pi = \int_0^Q D(z)\,\mathrm{d}z - C(Q).$$

For example, if $D(Q) = a - bQ$,

$$\pi = \int_0^Q (a - bz)\,\mathrm{d}z - C(Q) = aQ - \frac{b}{2}Q^2 - C(Q). \tag{13A.3}$$

The monopoly finds the output that maximizes the profit by setting the derivative of the profit in Equation 13A.3 equal to zero:

$$a - bQ - \frac{\mathrm{d}C(Q)}{\mathrm{d}Q} = 0.$$

By rearranging terms, we find that $D(Q) = a - bQ = \mathrm{d}C(Q)/\mathrm{d}Q = MC$, as in Equation 13A.2. Thus, the monopoly produces the quantity at which the demand curve hits the marginal cost curve.

Appendix 13B: Multimarket Price Discrimination

Suppose that a monopoly can divide its customers into two groups, as in Figure 13.7. It sells Q_1 to the first group and earns revenues of $R_1(Q_1)$, and it sells Q_2 units to the second group and earns $R_2(Q_2)$. Its cost of producing total output $Q = Q_1 + Q_2$ units is $C(Q)$. The monopoly can maximize its profit through its choice of prices or quantities to each group. We examine its problem when it chooses quantities:

$$\underset{Q_1, Q_2}{\text{Maximize}}\ \pi = R_1(Q_1) + R_2(Q_2) - C(Q_1 + Q_2). \tag{13B.1}$$

The first-order conditions corresponding to Equation 13B.1 are obtained by differentiating with respect to Q_1 and Q_2 and setting the partial derivative equal to zero:

$$\frac{\partial \pi}{\partial Q_1} = \frac{dR_1(Q_1)}{dQ_1} - \frac{dC(Q)}{dQ}\frac{\partial Q}{\partial Q_1} = 0, \tag{13B.2}$$

and

$$\frac{\partial \pi}{\partial Q_2} = \frac{dR_2(Q_2)}{dQ_2} - \frac{dC(Q)}{dQ}\frac{\partial Q}{\partial Q_2} = 0. \tag{13B.3}$$

Equation 13B.2 says that the marginal revenue from sales to the first group, $MR^1 = dR_1(Q_1)/dQ_1$, should equal the marginal cost of producing the last unit of total output, $MC = dC(Q)/dQ$, because $\partial Q/\partial Q_1 = 1$. Similarly, Equation 13B.3 says that the marginal revenue from the second group, MR^2, should also equal the marginal cost. By combining Equations 13B.2 and 13B.3, we find that the two marginal revenues are equal where the monopoly is profit maximizing:

$$MR^1 = MR^2 = MC.$$

Appendix 14A: Profit-Maximizing Advertising and Production

To maximize its profit, a monopoly must optimally set its advertising, A, and quantity, Q. Suppose that advertising affects only current sales, so the demand curve facing the monopoly is

$$p = p(Q, A).$$

As a result, the firm's revenue is

$$R = p(Q, A)Q = R(Q, A).$$

The firm's cost of production is the function $C(Q)$. It cost of advertising is A, because each unit of advertising costs $1 (because we chose the units of measure appropriately). Thus, its total cost is $C(Q) + A$.

The monopoly maximizes its profit through its choice of quantity and advertising:

$$\underset{Q,A}{\text{Maximize}}\ \pi = R(Q, A) - C(Q) - A. \tag{14A.1}$$

Its necessary conditions (first-order conditions) are found by differentiating the profit function in Equation 14A.1 with respect to Q and A in turn:

$$\frac{\partial \pi(Q, A)}{\partial Q} = \frac{\partial R(Q, A)}{\partial Q} - \frac{dC(Q)}{dQ} = 0, \tag{14A.2}$$

$$\frac{\partial \pi(Q, A)}{\partial A} = \frac{\partial R(Q, A)}{\partial A} - 1 = 0. \tag{14A.3}$$

The profit-maximizing output and advertising levels are the Q^* and A^* that simultaneously satisfy Equations 14A.2 and 14A.3. Equation 14A.2 says that output should be chosen so that the marginal revenue, $\partial R(Q,A)/(\partial Q)$, equals the marginal cost, $dC(Q)/(dQ)$. Equation 14A.3 says that the monopoly advertises to the point where its marginal revenue from the last unit of advertising, $\partial R(Q, A)/(\partial A)$, equals the marginal cost of the last unit of advertising, \$1.

Appendix 15A: Factor Demands

If a competitive firm hires L units of labor at a wage rate of w and K units of capital at a rental rate of r, it can produce $q = f(L, K)$ units of output. The firm sells its output at the market price of p. The firm picks L and K to maximize its profit:

$$\underset{L,K}{\text{Maximize}}\, \pi = pq - (wL + rK) = pf(L, K) - (wL + rK). \tag{15A.1}$$

Thus, the firm's revenues, pq, and costs both depend on L and K, so its profits depend on L and K.

Profit is maximized by setting the partial derivatives of profit (in Equation 15A.1) with respect to L and K equal to zero:

$$\frac{\partial \pi}{\partial L} = pMP_L - w = 0, \tag{15A.2}$$

$$\frac{\partial \pi}{\partial L} = pMP_K - r = 0, \tag{15A.3}$$

where $MP_L = \partial f(L, K)/\partial L$, the marginal product of labor, is the partial derivative of the production function with respect to L, and $MP_K = \partial f(L, K)/\partial K$ is the marginal product of capital. Solving Equations 15A.2 and 15A.3 simultaneously produces the factor demand equations.

Rearranging Equations 15A.2 and 15A.3, we can write these factor demand equations as

$$MRP_L \equiv pMP_L = w,$$

$$MRP_K \equiv pMP_K = r.$$

Thus, the firm maximizes its profit when it picks its inputs such that the marginal revenue product of labor equals the wage and the marginal revenue product of capital equals the rental rate of capital. For these conditions to produce a maximum, the second-order conditions must also hold. These second-order conditions say that the MRP_L and MRP_K curves slope downward.

If the production function is Cobb-Douglas, $q = AL^{\alpha}K^{\beta}$, then Equations 15A.2 and 15A.3 are

$$\frac{\partial \pi}{\partial L} = p\alpha AL^{\alpha-1}K^{\beta} - w = 0,$$

$$\frac{\partial \pi}{\partial K} = p\beta AL^{\alpha}K^{\beta-1} - r = 0.$$

Solving these equations for L and K, we find that the factor demand functions are

$$L = \left(\frac{\alpha}{w}\right)^{(1-\beta)/\delta}\left(\frac{\beta}{r}\right)^{\beta/\delta}(Ap)^{1/\delta}, \qquad (15A.4)$$

$$K = \left(\frac{\alpha}{w}\right)^{\alpha/\delta}\left(\frac{\beta}{r}\right)^{(1-\alpha)/\delta}(Ap)^{1/\delta}, \qquad (15A.5)$$

where $\delta = 1 - \alpha - \beta$. By differentiating Equations 15A.4 and 15A.5, we can show that the demand for each factor decreases with w or r and increases with p.

If the Cobb-Douglas production function has constant returns to scale, $\delta = 0$, then Equations 15A.4 and 15A.5 are not helpful. The problem is that, with constant returns to scale, a competitive firm with a Cobb-Douglas production function does not care how much it produces (and hence how many inputs it uses) as long as the market price and input prices are consistent with zero profit.

A competitive firm with a Cobb-Douglas production function pays labor the value of its marginal product, $w = p \times MP_L = p \times \alpha A L^{\alpha-1}K^{\beta} = \alpha pQ/L$. As a result, the share of the firm's revenues that is paid to labor is $\omega_L = wL/(pQ) = \alpha$. Similarly, $\omega_K = rK/(pQ) = \beta$. Thus, with a Cobb-Douglas production function, the shares of labor and of capital are fixed and independent of prices.

Appendix 15B: Monopsony

If only one firm can hire labor in a town, the firm is a monopsony. It chooses how much labor to hire to maximize its profit,

$$\pi = p(Q(L))Q(L) - w(L)L,$$

where $Q(L)$ is the production function, the amount of output produced using L hours of labor, and $w(L)$ is the labor supply curve, which shows how the wage varies with the amount of labor the firm hires. The firm maximizes its profit by setting the derivative of profit with respect to labor equal to zero (if the second-order condition holds):

$$\left(p + Q(L)\frac{dp}{dQ}\right)\frac{dQ}{dL} - w(L) - \frac{dw}{dL}L = 0. \qquad (15B.1)$$

Rearranging terms in Equation 15B.1, we find that the maximization condition is that the marginal revenue product of labor,

$$MRP_L = p \times MPL = \left(p + Q(L)\frac{dp}{dQ}\right)\frac{dQ}{dL} = p\left(1 + \frac{1}{\varepsilon}\right)\frac{dQ}{dL},$$

equals the marginal expenditure,

$$ME = w(L) + \frac{dw}{dL}L = w(L)\left(1 + \frac{w}{L}\frac{dw}{dL}\right) = w(L)\left(1 + \frac{1}{\eta}\right), \qquad (15B.2)$$

where η is the supply elasticity of labor.

If the supply curve is linear, $w(L) = g + hL$, the monopsony's expenditure is $E = w(L)L = gL + hL^2$, and the monopsony's marginal expenditure is $ME = \text{d}E/\text{d}L = g + 2hL$. Thus, the slope of the marginal expenditure curve, $2h$, is twice as great as that of the supply curve, h.

By rearranging the terms in Equation 15B.2, we find that

$$\frac{ME - w}{w} = \frac{1}{\eta}.$$

Thus, the markup of the marginal expenditure (and the value to the monopsony) to the wage, $(ME - w)/w$, is inversely proportional to the elasticity of supply. If the firm is a price taker, so η is infinite, the wage equals the marginal expenditure.

Appendix 18A: Welfare Effects of Pollution in a Competitive Market

We now show the welfare effects of a negative externality in a competitive market where demand and marginal costs are linear, as in Figure 18.1. The inverse demand curve is

$$p = a - bQ, \tag{18A.1}$$

where p is the price of the output and Q is the quantity. The private marginal cost is the competitive supply curve if pollution is an externality:

$$MC^p = c + dQ. \tag{18A.2}$$

The marginal cost to people exposed to the pollution, gunk, is

$$MC^g = eQ. \tag{18A.3}$$

Equation 18A.3 shows that there is no pollution harm if output is zero and that the marginal harm increases linearly with output. The social marginal cost is the sum of the private marginal cost and the marginal cost of the externality:

$$MC^s = c + (d + e)Q. \tag{18A.4}$$

The intersection of the demand curve, Equation 18A.1, and the supply curve, Equation 18A.2, determines the competitive equilibrium where pollution is an externality:

$$p_c = a - bQ_c = c + dQ_c = MC^p. \tag{18A.5}$$

If we solve Equation 18A.5 for Q, the competitive equilibrium quantity is

$$Q_c = \frac{a - c}{b + d}.$$

Substituting this quantity into the demand curve, we find that the competitive price is $p_c = a - b(a - c)/(b + d)$.

If the externality is taxed at a rate equal to its marginal cost, so the externality is internalized, the market produces the social optimum. We find the social optimum by setting p in Equation 18A.1 equal to MC^s in Equation 18A.4 and solving for the resulting quantity:

$$Q_s = \frac{a - c}{b + d + e}.$$

The corresponding price is $p_s = a - b(a - c)/(b + d + e)$.

If output is sold only by a monopoly, the monopoly's revenue is found by multiplying both sides of Equation 18A.1 by quantity: $R = aQ - bQ^2$. Differentiating with respect to quantity, we find that the monopoly's marginal revenue is

$$MR = a - 2bQ.$$

If the monopoly is unregulated, its equilibrium is found by setting MR, Equation 18A.6, equal to private marginal cost, Equation 18A.2, and solving for output:

$$Q_m = \frac{a - c}{2b + d}.$$

The corresponding price is $p_m = a - b(a - c)/(2b + d)$. If the monopoly internalizes the externality due to a tax equal to MC^g, the equilibrium quantity is

$$Q^*_m = \frac{a - c}{2b + d + e}.$$

The price is $p^*_m = a - b(a - c)/(2b + d + e)$.

In Figure 18.1, $a = 450$, $b = 2$, $c = 30$, $d = 2$, and $e = 1$. Substituting these values into the equations above, we solve for the following equilibrium values:

	Quantity	Price
Competition	105	240
Social optimum (competition with a tax)	84	282
Monopoly	70	310
Monopoly with a tax	60	330

Answers to Selected Problems

I know the answer! The answer lies within the heart of all mankind! The answer is twelve? I think I'm in the wrong building.

—Charles Schultz

Chapter 2

6. The law would create a price ceiling (at 110% of the pre-emergency price). Because the supply curve shifts substantially to the left during the emergency, the price control will create a shortage: A smaller quantity will be supplied at the ceiling price than will be demanded.

7. A ban has no effect if foreigners supply nothing at the pre-ban, equilibrium price. Thus, if imports occur only at prices above those actually observed, a ban has no practical effect.

12. The statement "Talk is cheap because supply exceeds demand" makes sense if we interpret it to mean that the *quantity supplied* of talk exceeds the *quantity demanded* at a price of zero. Imagine a downward-sloping demand curve that hits the horizontal, quantity axis to the left of where the upward-sloping supply curve hits the axis.

14. The demand curve for pork is $Q = 171 - 20p + 20p_b + 3p_c + 2Y$, where quantity is measured in millions of kg per year and income is measured in thousands of dollars per year. As a result, a ΔY change in income causes the quantity demanded to change by $\Delta Q = 2\Delta Y$. That is, a \$1,000 increase in income causes the quantity demanded to increase by 2 million kg per year, and a \$100 increase in income causes the quantity demanded to increase by a tenth as much, 0.2 million kg per year.

17. In equilibrium, the quantity demanded, $Q = a - bp$, equals the quantity supplied, $Q = c + ep$, so

$$a - bp = c + ep.$$

By solving this last equation for p, we find that the equilibrium price is $p = (a - c)/(b + e)$. By substituting this expression for p into either the demand curve or the supply curve, we find that the equilibrium quantity is $Q = (ae + bc)/(b + e)$.

Chapter 3

8. We showed that, in a competitive market, the effect of a specific tax is the same whether it is placed on suppliers or demanders. Thus, if the market for milk is competitive, consumers will pay the same price in equilibrium regardless of whether the government taxes consumers or stores.

10. A binding rent-control law results in excess demand in the short run and transfers wealth from landlords to renters by reducing the rent paid. In the long run, the supply curve of apartments shifts to the left and quality falls as landlords convert some existing apartments to condominiums, allow other units to deteriorate, and build fewer new units than they would without the law. As a consequence, the excess demand may be greater in the long run than in the short run.

12. The elasticity of demand is (slope)(p/Q) = $(\Delta Q/\Delta p)(p/Q)$ = (–9.5 thousand metric tons per year per cent)(45¢/1,275 thousand metric tons per year) ≈ –0.34. That is, for every 1% fall in the price, a third of a percent more coconut oil is demanded. The cross-price elasticity of demand for coconut oil with respect to the price of palm oil is $(\Delta Q/\Delta p_p)(p_p/Q) = 16.2 \times (31/1{,}275) \approx 0.39$.

14. Because the linear supply function is $Q = g + hp$, a change in price of Δp causes a $\Delta Q = h\Delta p$ change in quantity. Thus, $\Delta Q/\Delta p = h$, and the elasticity of supply is $\eta = (\Delta Q/\Delta p)(p/Q) = hp/Q$. By substituting for Q using the supply function, we find that $\eta = hp/(g + hp)$. Similarly, by using the supply function to substitute for p, we learn that $\eta = (Q - g)/Q$.

Chapter 4

5. If the neutral product is on the vertical axis, the indifference curves are parallel vertical lines.

9. Suppose that a consumer purchases two goods at prices p_1 and p_2. If the consumer's original income is Y, the intercept of the budget line on the Good 1 axis (where the consumer buys only Good 1) is Y/p_1. Similarly, the intercept is Y/p_2 on the Good 2 axis. A 50% income tax lowers income to half its original level, Y/2. As a result, the budget line shifts in toward the origin. The intercepts on the Good 1 and Good 2 axes are $Y/(2p_1)$ and $Y/(2p_2)$, respectively. The opportunity set shrinks by the area between the original budget line and the new line.

15. Using Equations 4B.9 and 4B.10, we find that the necessary conditions for a utility maximum are $B = \alpha Y/[2(\alpha + \beta)]$ and $Z = \beta Y/(\alpha + \beta)$.

Chapter 5

7. The CPI accurately reflects the true cost of living because Bessie does not substitute between the goods as the relative prices change.

9. In the figure, L^f is the budget line at the *f*actory store and L^o is the constraint at the outlet store. At the factory store, the consumer maximum occurs at e_f on indifference curve I^f. Suppose we increase the income of a consumer who shops at the outlet store to Y^*, so that the resulting budget line L^* is tangent to the indifference curve I^f. The consumer would buy the bundle e^*. That is, the pure substitution effect (the movement from e_f to e^*) causes the consumer to buy relatively more firsts. The total effect (the movement from e_f to e_o) reflects both the substitution effect (firsts are now relatively less expensive) and the income effect (the consumer is worse off after paying for shipping).

★22. The consumer's budget constraint is

$$p_1q_1 + p_2q_2 + \ldots + p_nq_n = Y,$$

where Y is income and p_i is the price and q_i is the quantity of Good *i*. Differentiating with respect to Y, we find that

$$p_1 \frac{dq_1}{dY} + p2 \frac{dq_2}{dY} + \ldots + p_n \frac{dq_n}{dY} = \frac{dY}{dY} = 1.$$

Multiplying and dividing each term by q_iY, we rewrite this last equation as

$$\frac{p_1q_1}{Y}\frac{dq_1}{dY}\frac{Y}{q_1} + \frac{p_2q_2}{Y}\frac{dq_2}{dY}\frac{Y}{q_2} + \ldots + \frac{p_nq_n}{Y}\frac{dq_n}{dY}\frac{Y}{q_n} = 1,$$

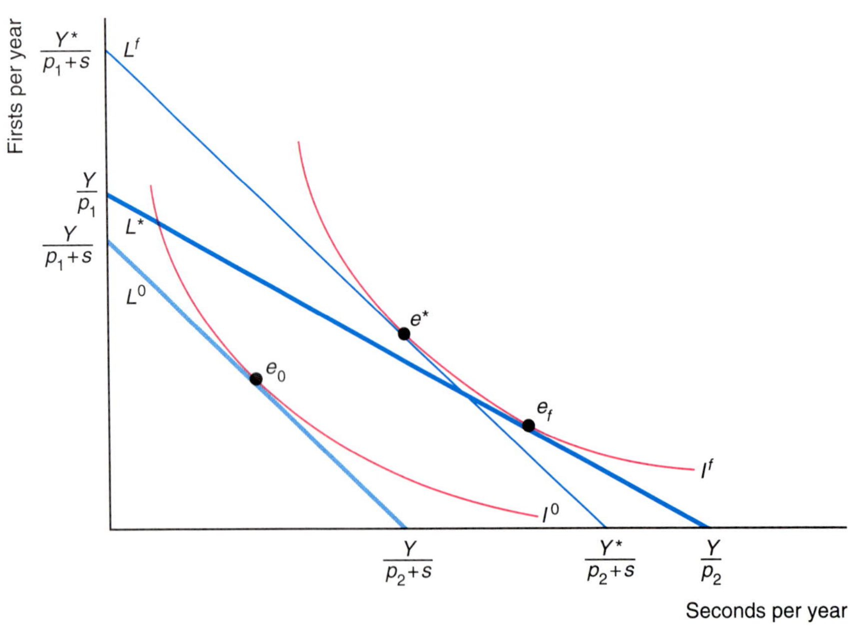

or

$$\omega_1\eta_1 + \omega_2\eta_2 + \ldots + \omega_n\eta_n = 1,$$

where η_i, the income elasticity for each Good i, equals $(dq_i/dY)(Y/q_i)$, and the budget share of Good i is $\omega_i = p_iq_i/Y$. That is, the weighted sum of the income elasticities equals 1. For this equation to hold, at least one of the goods must have a positive income elasticity; hence, not all the goods can be inferior.

Chapter 6

1. One worker produces one unit of output, two workers produce two units of output, and n workers produce n units of output. Thus, the total product of labor equals the number of workers: $q = L$. The total product of labor curve is a straight line with a slope of 1. Because we are told that each extra worker produces one more unit of output, we know that the marginal product of labor, $\Delta q/\Delta L$, is 1. By dividing both sides of the production function, $q = L$, by L, we find that the average product of labor, q/L, is 1.

11. Not enough information is given to answer this question. If we assume that Japanese and American firms have identical production functions and produce using the same ratio of factors during good times, Japanese firms will have a lower average product of labor during recessions because they are less likely to lay off workers. However, it is not clear how Japanese and American firms expand output during good times (do they hire the same number of extra workers?). As a result, we cannot predict which country has the highest average product of labor.

13. The production function is $q = L^{3/4}K^{1/4}$. (a) As a result, the average product of labor, holding capital fixed at $\overline{K}$, is $AP_L = q/L = L^{-1/4}\overline{K}^{1/4} = (\overline{K}/L)^{1/4}$. (b) The marginal product of labor is $MP_L = dq/dL = \frac{3}{4}(\overline{K}/L)^{1/4}$. (c) If we double both inputs, output doubles to $(2L)^{3/4}(2K)^{1/4} = 2L^{3/4}K^{1/4} = 2q$, where q is the original output level. Thus, this production function has constant returns to scale.

15. Using Equation 6.3, we know that the marginal rate of technical substitution is $MRTS = MP_L/MP_K = \frac{2}{3}$.

18. The marginal product of labor of Firm 1 is only 90% of the marginal product of labor of Firm 2 for a particular level of inputs. Using calculus, we find that the MP_L of Firm 1 is $\partial q_1/\partial L = 0.9\partial f(L, K)/\partial L = 0.9\partial q_2/\partial L$.

Chapter 7

1. If the plane cannot be resold, its purchase price is a sunk cost, which is unaffected by the number of times the plane is flown. Consequently, the average cost per flight falls with the number of flights, but the total cost of owning and operating the plane rises because of extra consumption of gasoline and maintenance. Thus, the more frequently someone has reason to fly, the more likely that flying one's own plane costs less per flight than a ticket on a commercial airline. However, by making extra ("unnecessary") trips, Mr. Agassi raises his total cost of owning and operating the airplane.

4. The total cost of building a 1 cubic foot crate is \$6. It costs four times as much to build an 8 cubic foot crate, \$24. In general, as the height of a cube increases, the total cost of building it rises with the square of the height, but the volume increases with the cube of the height. Thus, the cost per unit of volume falls.

5. You produce your output, exam points, using as inputs the time spent on Question 1, t_1, and the time spent on Question 2, t_2. If you have diminishing marginal returns to extra time on each problem, your isoquants have the usual shapes: They curve away from the origin. You face a constraint that you may spend no more than 60 minutes on the two questions: $60 = t_1 + t_2$. The slope of the 60-minute isocost curve is −1: For every extra minute you spend on Question 1, you have one less minute to spend on Question 2. To maximize your test score, given that you can spend no more than 60 minutes on the exam, you want to pick the highest isoquant that is tangent to your 60-minute isocost curve. At the tangency, the slope of your isocost curve, −1, equals the slope of your isoquant, $-MP_1/MP_2$. That is, your score on the exam is maximized when $MP_1 = MP_2$, where the last minute spent on Question 1 would increase your score by as much as spending it on Question 2 would. Therefore, you've allocated your time on the exam wisely if you are indifferent as to which question to work on during the last minute of the exam.

14. Let w be the cost of a unit of L and r be the cost of a unit of K. Because the two inputs are perfect substitutes in the production process, the firm uses

only the less expensive of the two inputs. Therefore, the long-run cost function is $C(q) = wq$ if $w \le r$; otherwise, it is $C(q) = rq$.

16. The average cost of producing one unit is α (regardless of the value of β). If $\beta = 0$, the average cost does not change with volume. If learning by doing increases with volume, $\beta < 0$, so the average cost falls with volume. Here, the average cost falls exponentially (a smooth curve that asymptotically approaches the quantity axis).

Chapter 8

2. Suppose a U-shaped marginal cost curve cuts a competitive firm's demand curve (price line) from above at q_1 and from below at q_2. By increasing output to $q_2 + 1$, the firm earns extra profit because the last unit sells for price p, which is greater than the marginal cost of that last unit. Indeed, the price exceeds the marginal cost of all units between q_1 and q_2, so it is more profitable to produce q_2 than q_1. Thus, the firm should either produce q_2 or shut down (if it is making a loss at q_2). (We can derive this result using calculus. The second-order condition, Equation 8B.3, for a competitive firm requires that marginal cost cut the demand line from below at q^*, the profit-maximizing quantity: $dMC(q^*)/dq > 0$.)

8. The shut-down notice reduces the firm's flexibility, which matters in an uncertain market. If conditions suddenly change, the firm may have to operate at a loss for six months before it can shut down. This potential extra expense of shutting down may discourage some firms from entering the market initially.

14. The competitive firm's marginal cost function is found by differentiating its cost function with respect to quantity: $dC(q)/dq = b + 2cq + 3dq^2$. The firm's necessary profit-maximizing condition is $p = MC = b + 2cq + 3dq^2$. The firm solves this equation for q for a specific price to determine its profit-maximizing output.

Chapter 9

4. If the tax is based on *economic* profit, the tax has no long-run effect because the firms make zero economic profit. If the tax is based on *business* profit and business profit is greater than economic profit, the profit tax raises firms' after-tax costs and results in fewer firms in the market. The exact effect of the tax depends on why business profit is less than economic profit. For example, if the government ignores opportunity labor cost but includes all capital cost in computing profit, firms will substitute toward labor and away from capital.

8. Solved Problem 8.3 and Figure 8.17 show the long-run effect of a lump-sum tax in a competitive market. Consumer surplus falls by more than tax revenue increases, and producer surplus remains zero, so welfare falls.

15. The consumer surplus at a price of 30 is $450 = \frac{1}{2}(30 \times 30)$.

Chapter 10

1. A tax is a negative subsidy. Thus, we can use the same analysis as in Solved Problem 10.1 to answer this question (reversing the signs of the effects).

15. Amos's marginal rate of substitution is $MRS_a = [\alpha/(1-\alpha)]H_a/G_a$ and Elise's is $MRS_e = [\beta/(1-\beta)]H_e/G_e$.

★16. Along the contract curve the two marginal rates of substitution are equal: $MRS_a = MRS_e$. Thus, to find the contract curve, we equate the right-hand sides of the expressions for MRS_a and MRS_e from the previous answer. Using the information about the endowments and some algebra, we can write the (quadratic) formula for the contract curve as

$$(\beta - \alpha)G_aH_a + \beta(\alpha - 1)50G_a + \alpha(1 - \beta)100H_a = 0.$$

Chapter 11

3. Because the government takes a percentage of before-tax economic profit, the quantity that maximizes the monopoly's before-tax profit also maximizes its after-tax profit. (Using calculus, we have the following: The before-profit is $\pi_B = R(Q) - C(Q)$, and the after-tax profit is $\pi_A = (1 - \gamma)[R(Q) - C(Q)]$. For both, the first-order condition is marginal revenue equals marginal cost: $R'(Q) = C'(Q)$.)

6. Yes. As the electric power utility application illustrates, the demand curve could cut the average cost curve only in its downward-sloping section. Consequently, the average cost is strictly downward sloping in the relevant region.

14. The figure shows that the dominant firm–competitive fringe equilibrium, e_{df}, lies between the competitive equilibrium, e_c, and the monopoly equilibrium, e_m. The supply of the fringe erodes but does not eliminate the dominant firm's market power. The dominant firm still faces a downward-sloping residual demand curve—hence, it retains some market power—but the residual demand curve lies below and is flatter than the market demand curve facing the monopoly. Because the residual demand curve is flatter, the dominant firm faces a more elastic demand than the monopoly; hence the dominant firm sets a lower price. At this lower price, consumers demand more and, collectively, the dominant firm and the fringe produce more than the monopoly did alone. Thus, consumers benefit from the entry of the fringe, and some but not all of the deadweight loss under monopoly is eliminated.

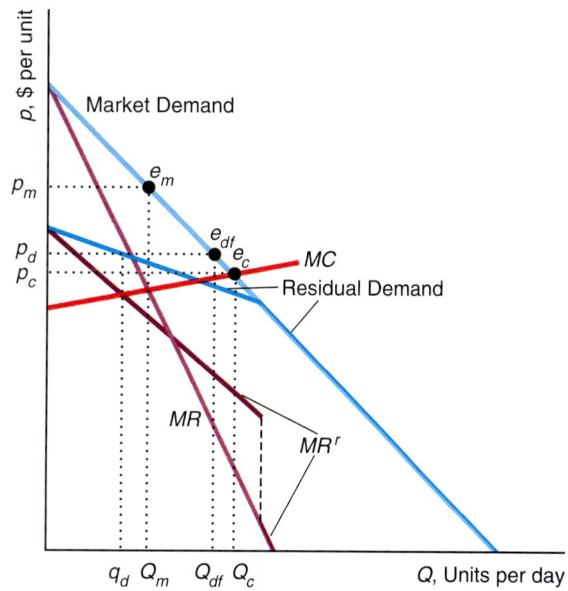

★15. Suppose that the monopoly faces a constant-elasticity demand curve, with elasticity ε, and has a constant marginal cost, m, and that the government imposes a specific tax of τ. The monopoly sets its price such that $p = (m + \tau)/(1 + 1/\varepsilon)$. Thus, $dp/d\tau = 1/(1 + 1/\varepsilon) > 1$.

Chapter 12

1. The payoff matrix in this prisoners' dilemma game is

		Duncan: Squeal	Duncan: Stay silent
Larry	Squeal	Larry: -2, Duncan: -2	Larry: 0, Duncan: –5
	Stay silent	Larry: –5, Duncan: 0	Larry: –1, Duncan: –1

If Duncan stays silent, Larry gets 0 if he squeals and –1 (a year in jail) if he stays silent. If Duncan confesses, Larry gets –2 if he squeals and –5 if he does not. Thus, Larry is better off squealing in either case, so squealing is his dominant strategy. By the same reasoning, squealing is also Duncan's dominant strategy. As a result, the Nash equilibrium is for both to confess.

5. The monopoly will make more profit than the duopoly will, so the monopoly is willing to pay the college more rent. Although granting monopoly rights may be attractive to the college in terms of higher rent, students will suffer (lose consumer surplus) because of the higher prices.

★6. Effectively, the government changes the domestic industry into a dominant firm facing a competitive fringe (as given by the supply curve in the other exporting country). The government sets the tax so that the domestic industry produces the same output level as a dominant firm would. (You can show this analysis using a graph similar to Figure 11.14.)

★7. Don't be silly: This problem is too difficult. For an answer to a slightly more complex problem, see Karp, Larry S., and Jeffrey M. Perloff, "The Failure of Strategic Industrial Policies Due to the Manipulation by Firms," *International Review of Economics and Finance*, 4(1), 1995:1–16.

13. The inverse demand curve is $p = 1 - 0.001Q$. The first firm's profit is $\pi_1 = [1 - 0.001(q_1 + q_2)]q_1 - 0.28q_1$. Its first-order condition is $d\pi_1/dq_1 = 1 - 0.001(2q_1 + q_2) - 0.28 = 0$. If we rearrange the terms, the first firm's best-response function is $q_1 = 360 - \frac{1}{2}q_2$. Similarly, the second firm's best-response function is $q_2 = 360 - \frac{1}{2}q_1$. By substituting one of these best-response functions into the other, we learn that the Cournot-Nash equilibrium occurs at $q_1 = q_2 = 240$, so the equilibrium price is 52¢.

17. Using Equations 12A.13 and 12A.14, we find that the equilibrium quantities are $q_1 = (a - 2m_1 + m_2)/3b = (90 + 30)/6 = 20$ and $q_2 = (90 - 60)/6 = 5$. As a result, the equilibrium price is $p = 90 - 20 - 5 = 65$.

Chapter 13

2. By differentiating its product, a firm makes the residual demand curve it faces less elastic everywhere. For example, no consumer will buy from that firm if its rival charges less and the goods are homogeneous. In contrast, some consumers who prefer this firm's product to that of its rival will still buy from this firm even if its rival charges less. As the chapter shows, a firm sets a higher price, the lower the elasticity of demand at the equilibrium.

10. This law delays entry by new firms. The patent holder has decided that it does not pay to sell both its name-brand drug and its own generic (otherwise, it would do so). Thus, the law delays the introduction of generics for several years. When entry occurs, the price of generics will fall below the current price of the name brand. The price of the name-brand drug may rise or fall (see the application in the chapter).

15. Firm 1 wants to maximize its profit:

$$\pi_1 = (p_1 - 10)q_1 = (p_1 - 10)(100 - 2p_1 + p_2).$$

Its first-order condition is $d\pi_1/dp_1 = 100 - 4p_1 + p_2 + 20 = 0$, so its best-response function is $p_1 = 30 + \frac{1}{4}p_2$. Similarly, Firm 2's best-response function is $p_2 = 30 + \frac{1}{4}p_1$. Solving, the Bertrand-Nash equilibrium prices are $p_1 = p_2 = 40$. Each firm produces 60 units.

Chapter 14

3. Allowing GM to enter first does not change the outcome of this game. Because Ford has a dominant strategy and enters regardless of GM's action, GM chooses not to enter even if it can act first.

★6. Let the probability that a firm sets a low price be α for Firm 1 and β for Firm 2. If the firms choose their prices independently, then $\alpha\beta$ is the probability that both set a low price, $(1 - \alpha)(1 - \beta)$ is the probability that both set a high price, $\alpha(1 - \beta)$ is the probability that Firm 1 prices low and Firm 2 prices high, and $(1 - \alpha)\beta$ is the probability that Firm 1 prices high and Firm 2 prices low. Firm 2's expected payoff, $E(\pi_2)$, is

$$\begin{aligned} E(\pi_2) &= 2\alpha\beta + (0)\alpha(1-\beta) \\ &\quad + (1-\alpha)\beta + 6(1-\alpha)(1-\beta) \\ &= (6 - 6\alpha) - (5 - 7\alpha)\beta. \end{aligned}$$

Similarly, Firm 1's expected payoff is

$$\begin{aligned} E(\pi_1) &= (0)\alpha\beta + 7\alpha(1-\beta) \\ &\quad + 2(1-\alpha)\beta + 6(1-\alpha)(1-\beta) \\ &= (6 - 4\beta) + (1 - 3\beta)\alpha. \end{aligned}$$

Each firm forms a belief about its rival's behavior. For example, suppose Firm 1 believes that Firm 2 will choose a low price with a probability $\hat{\beta}$. If $\hat{\beta}$ is less than $\frac{1}{3}$ (Firm 2 is relatively unlikely to choose a low price), it pays for Firm 1 to choose the low price because the second term in $E(\pi_1)$, $(1 - 3\hat{\beta})\alpha$, is positive, so that as α increases, $E(\pi_1)$ increases. Because the highest possible α is 1, Firm 1 chooses the low price with certainty. Similarly, if Firm 1 believes $\hat{\beta}$ is greater than $\frac{1}{3}$, it sets a high price with certainty ($\alpha = 0$).

If Firm 2 believes that Firm 1 thinks $\hat{\beta}$ is slightly below $\frac{1}{3}$, Firm 2 believes that Firm 1 will choose a low price with certainty, and hence, Firm 2 will also choose a low price. That outcome, $\beta = 1$, however, is not consistent with Firm 1's expectation that $\hat{\beta}$ is a fraction. Indeed, it is only rational for Firm 2 to believe that Firm 1 believes Firm 2 will use a mixed strategy if Firm 1's belief about Firm 2 makes Firm 1 unpredictable. That is, Firm 1 uses a mixed strategy only if it is *indifferent* between setting a high or a low price. It is only indifferent if it believes $\hat{\beta}$ is exactly $\frac{1}{3}$. By similar reasoning, Firm 2 will use a mixed strategy only if its belief is that Firm 1 chooses a low price with probability $\hat{\alpha} = \frac{5}{7}$. Thus, the only possible Nash equilibrium is $\alpha = \frac{5}{7}$ and $\beta = \frac{1}{3}$.

10. The firm's marginal revenue exceeded its marginal cost, so the firm should have increased its advertising.

12. In the Cournot equilibrium (see Chapter 12), $q_i = (a - m)/(3b) = (150 - 60)/3 = 30$, $Q = 60$, $p = 90$.

13. In the Stackelberg equilibrium (see Chapter 12) in which Firm 1 moves first, $q_1 = (a - m)/(2b) = (150 - 60)/2 = 45$, $q_2 = (a - m)/(4b) = (150 - 60)/4 = 22.5$, $Q = 45$, and $p = 82.5$.

Chapter 15

2. Before the tax, the competitive firm's labor demand was $p \times MP_L$. After the tax, the firm's effective price is $(1 - \alpha)p$, so its labor demand becomes $(1 - \alpha)p \times MP_L$.

17. The competitive firm's marginal revenue of labor is $\partial q/\partial L = 1 + 2K$, so its $MRP_L = p(1 + 2K)$.

19. The answer is given in Appendix 15A.

Chapter 16

3. An individual with a zero discount rate views current and future consumption as equally attractive. An individual with an infinite discount rate cares only about current consumption and puts no value on future consumption.

9. If the interest rate is set in real terms, putting \$2,000 in the bank today results in an annual flow of \$200 in real terms. If the interest rate is set in nominal terms, the real payment will shrink over time, so you cannot receive a real payment of \$200 annually. (If the nominal rate were set at 15.5%, an initial \$2,000 investment would ensure an annual flow of \$200 in real terms.)

16. The real payment this year is the same as the nominal payment: $f = \tilde{f}$. The real payment next year is obtained by adjusting the nominal payment for inflation: $f = \tilde{f}/(1 + \tau) = \tilde{f}/1.1$. Thus, the real present value of the two payments is this year's real payment plus next year's real payment discounted by the real interest rate: $f + f/(1 + i) = \tilde{f} + \tilde{f}/[(1 + \gamma)(1 + i)]$, which is less than $2\tilde{f}$ because nominal future payments are worth less than current ones because of both inflation and discounting.

17. *Hint*: Set profit equal to zero and solve for *rr*.

18. Solving for the *irr*, we find that the *irr* equals 1 or 9. Thus, this approach fails to give us a unique solution, so we should use the *NPV* approach instead.

Chapter 17

2. As the figure shows, Irma's expected utility of 133 at point *f* (where her expected wealth is \$64) is the same as her utility from a certain wealth of *Y*.

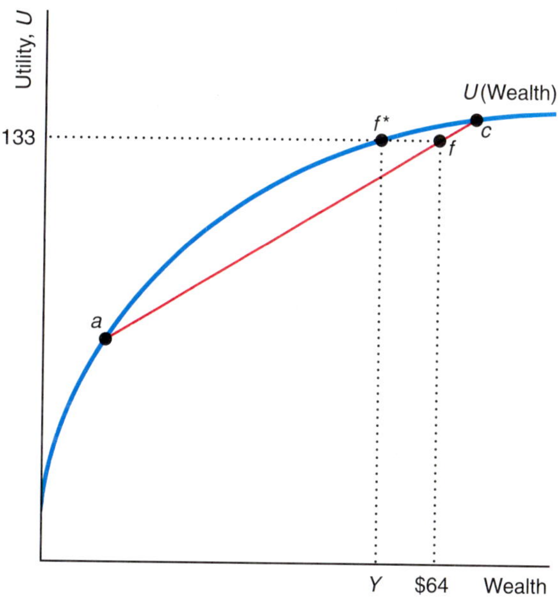

3. The expected punishment for violating traffic laws is θV, where θ is the probability of being caught and fined and V is the fine. If people care only about the expected punishment (there's no additional psychological pain from the experience), increasing the expected punishment by increasing θ or V works equally well in discouraging bad behavior. The government prefers to increase the fine, V, which is costless, rather than to raise θ, which is costly due to the extra police, district attorneys, and courts required.

11. Assuming that the painting is not insured against fire, its expected value is

$$\$550 = (0.2 \times \$1{,}000) + (0.1 \times \$0) + (0.7 \times \$500).$$

Chapter 18

2. A specific tax of \$64 per ton of output or per unit of emissions (gunk) leads to the social optimum.

5. Granting the chemical company the right to dump 1 ton per day results in that firm's dumping 1 ton and the boat company's maintaining one boat, which maximizes joint profit at \$20.

11. Using the paper market model in Appendix 18A, determine the equilibrium if the marginal harm of gunk is MC^g = \$84 (instead of Equation 18A.3). Is there a shortcut that would allow you to solve this problem without algebra?

    We care only about the marginal harm of gunk at the social optimum, which we know is MC^g = \$84 (because it is the same at every level of output). That is the same marginal cost as in the table at the end of Appendix 18A. Thus, the social optimum is the same as in that example (and no algebra is necessary). Using algebra, we set the demand curve equal to the new social marginal cost, $MC^2 = c + dQ + 84$ and find that the socially optimal quantity is $Q_s = (a - c - 84)/(b + d) = (450 - 30 - 84)/(2 + 2) = 84$.

Chapter 19

2. Because insurance costs do not vary with soil type, buying insurance is unattractive for houses on good soil and relatively attractive for houses on bad soil. These incentives create a moral hazard problem: Relatively more home owners with houses on poor soil buy insurance, so the state insurance agency will face disproportionately many bad outcomes in the next earthquake.

6. Brand names allow consumers to identify a particular company's product in the future. If a mushroom company expects to remain in business over time, it would be foolish to brand its product if its mushrooms are of inferior quality. (Just ask Babar's grandfather.) Thus, all else the same, we would expect branded mushrooms to be of higher quality than unbranded ones.

12. Because buyers are risk neutral, if they believe that the probability of getting a lemon is θ, the most they are willing to pay for a car of unknown quality is $p = p_1(1 - \theta) + p_2\theta$. If p is greater than both v_1 and v_2, all cars are sold. If $v_1 > p > v_2$, only lemons are sold. If p were less than both v_1 and v_2, no car would be sold. However, we know that $v_2 < p_2$ and $p_2 < p$, so owners of lemons are certainly willing to sell them. (If sellers bear a transaction cost of c and $p < v_2 + c$, no car is sold.)

Chapter 20

1. If Paula pays Arthur a fixed-fee salary of \$168, Arthur has no incentive to buy any carvings for resale, as the \$12 per carving cost comes out of his pocket. Thus, Arthur sells no carvings if he receives a fixed salary and can sell as many or as few carvings as he wants. The contract is not incentive compatible. For Arthur to behave efficiently, this fixed-fee contract must be modified. For example, the contract could specify that Arthur gets a salary of \$168 and that he must obtain and sell 12 carvings. Paula must monitor his behavior. (Paula's residual profit is the joint profit minus \$168, so she gets the marginal profit from each additional sale and wants to sell the joint-profit-maximizing number of carvings.) Arthur makes \$24 = \$168 – \$144, so he is willing to participate. Joint profit is maximized at \$72, and Paula gets the maximum possible residual profit of \$48.

6. By making this commitment, the company may be trying to assure customers who cannot judge how quickly the product will deteriorate that the product is durable enough to maintain at least a certain value in the future. The firm is trying to eliminate asymmetric information to increase the demand for its product.

9. Presumably, the promoter collects a percentage of the revenue at each restaurant. If customers can pay cash, the restaurants may lie to the promoter as to the amount of food they sold. The scrip makes such opportunistic behavior difficult.

15. The minimum bond that deters stealing is \$2,500.

Definitions

I hate definitions. —Benjamin Disraeli

adverse selection: opportunism characterized by an informed person's benefiting from trading or otherwise contracting with a less informed person who does not know about an unobserved characteristic of the informed person. (19)

asymmetric information: situation in which one party to a transaction knows a material fact that the other party does not. (19)

average cost (AC): the total cost divided by the units of output produced: $AC = C/q$. (7)

average fixed cost (AFC): the fixed cost divided by the units of output produced: $AFC = F/q$. (7)

average product of labor (AP_L): the ratio of output, q, to the number of workers, L, used to produce that output: $AP_L = q/L$. (6)

average variable cost (AVC): the variable cost divided by the units of output produced: $AVC = VC/q$. (7)

bad: something for which less is preferred to more, such as pollution. (4)

barrier to entry: an explicit restriction or a cost that applies only to potential new firms—existing firms are not subject to the restriction or do not bear the cost. (9)

Bertrand equilibrium: a *Nash equilibrium* in prices; a set of prices such that no firm can obtain a higher profit by choosing a different price if the other firms continue to charge these prices. (13)

best response: the strategy that maximizes a firm's profit, given its beliefs about its rivals' strategies. (12)

budget line (or *budget constraint*): the bundles of goods that can be bought if the entire budget is spent on those goods at given prices. (4)

bundling (*package tie-in sale*): a type of tie-in sale in which two goods are combined so that customers cannot buy either good separately. (13)

cartel: a group of firms that explicitly agree to coordinate their activities. (12)

certification: a report that a particular product meets or exceeds a given *standard* level. (19)

cheap talk: unsubstantiated claims or statements. (19)

common property: resources to which everyone has free access. (18)

comparative advantage: the ability to produce one good at a lower cost (giving up producing less of a second good) than someone else. (10)

competitive fringe (*or fringe*): small, price-taking firms that compete with a *dominant firm.* (11)

constant returns to scale (CRS): property of a production function whereby all inputs are increased by a certain percentage, output increases by that same percentage. (6)

consumer surplus (CS): the monetary difference between what a consumer is willing to pay for the quantity of the good purchased and what the good actually costs. (9)

contingent fee: a payment to a lawyer that is a share of the award in a court case (usually after legal expenses are deducted) if the client wins and nothing if the client loses. (20)

contract curve: the set of all Pareto-efficient bundles. (10)

cost (*total cost*, C): the sum of a firm's variable cost and fixed cost: $C = VC + F$. (7)

Cournot equilibrium: a *Nash equilibrium* in quantities; a set of quantities sold by firms such that, holding the quantities of all other firms constant, no firm can obtain a higher profit by choosing a different quantity. (12)

credible threat: an announcement that a firm will use a strategy harmful to its rival that the rivals believe because the firm's strategy is rational in the sense that it is in the firm's best interest to use it. (14)

cross-price elasticity of demand: the percentage change in the *quantity demanded* in response to a given percentage change in the price of another good. (3)

deadweight loss (*DWL*): the net reduction in welfare from losses of surplus by one group that are not offset by a gain to another group from an action that alters a market equilibrium. (9)

decreasing returns to scale (*DRS*): property of a production function whereby output increases less than in proportion to an equal percentage increase in all inputs. (6)

demand curve: the *quantity demanded* at each possible price, holding constant the other factors that influence purchases. (2)

discount rate: a rate reflecting the relative value an individual places on future consumption compared to current consumption. (16)

diseconomies of scale: property of a cost function whereby the average cost of production rises when output increases. (7).

dominant firm: a price-setting firm that competes with price-taking firms in a *competitive fringe*. (11)

dominant strategy: a strategy that strictly dominates (gives higher profits than) all other strategies, regardless of the actions chosen by rival firms. (12)

duopoly: an oligopoly with two firms. (12)

durable good: a product that is usable for years. (7)

economic cost (*opportunity cost*): the value of the best alternative use of a resource. (7)

economic profit: revenue minus *economic cost*. (8)

economically efficient: minimizing the cost of producing a specified amount of output. (7)

economies of scale: property of a cost function whereby the average cost of production falls as output expands. (7)

economies of scope: situation in which it is less expensive to produce goods jointly than separately. (7)

efficiency in production: situation in which the principal's and agent's combined value (profits, payoffs), π, is maximized. (20)

efficiency in risk bearing: a situation in which risk sharing is optimal in that the person who least minds facing risk—the risk-neutral or less risk-averse person—bears more of the risk. (20)

efficiency wage: an unusually high wage that a firm pays workers as an incentive to avoid shirking. (20)

efficient contract: an agreement with provisions that ensure that no party can be made better off without harming the other party. (20)

efficient production (*technological efficiency*): situation in which the current level of output cannot be produced with fewer inputs, given existing knowledge about technology and the organization of production. (6)

elasticity: the percentage change in a variable in response to a given percentage change in another variable. (3)

endowment: an initial allocation of goods. (10)

Engel curve: the relationship between the quantity demanded of a single good and income, holding prices constant. (5)

equilibrium: a situation in which no one wants to change his or her behavior. (2)

essential facility: a scarce resource that a rival must use to survive. (14)

excess demand: the amount by which the *quantity demanded* exceeds the *quantity supplied* at a specified price. (2)

excess supply: the amount by which the *quantity supplied* is greater than the *quantity demanded* at a specified price. (2)

exhaustible resources: nonrenewable natural assets that cannot be increased, only depleted. (16)

expansion path: the cost-minimizing combination of labor and capital for each output level. (7)

externality: the direct effect of the actions of a person or fim on another person's well-being or a firm's production capability rather than an indirect effect through changes in prices. (18)

fair bet: a wager with an expected value of zero. (17)

fair insurance: a bet between an insurer and a policyholder in which the value of the bet to the policyholder is zero. (17)

firm: an organization that converts inputs such as labor, materials, energy, and capital into outputs, the goods and services that it sells. (6)

fixed cost (*F*): a production expense that does not vary with output. (7)

fixed input: a factor of production that cannot be varied practically in the short run. (6)

flow: a quantity or value that is measured per unit of time. (16)

free ride: to benefit from the actions of others without paying. (18)

game: any competition between players (firms) in which strategic behavior plays a major role. (12)

game theory: a set of tools that economists, political scientists, military analysts, and others use to analyze decisionmaking by players that use strategies. (12)

general-equilibrium analysis: the study of how equilibrium is determined in all markets simultaneously. (10)
Giffen good: a commodity for which a decrease in its price causes the quantity demanded to fall. (5)
good: a commodity for which more is preferred to less, at least at some levels of consumption. (4)

incentive compatible: referring to a contract's provision of inducements such that the agent wants to perform the assigned task rather than engage in opportunistic behavior. (20)
incidence of a tax on consumers (ι): the share of the tax that falls on consumers. (3)
income effect: the change in the quantity of a good a consumer demands because of a change in income, holding prices constant. (5)
income elasticity of demand (or *income elasticity*): the percentage change in the *quantity demanded* in response to a given percentage change in income. (3)
increasing returns to scale (*IRS*): property of a production function whereby output rises more than in proportion to an equal increase in all inputs. (6)
indifference curve: the set of all bundles of goods that a consumer views as being equally desirable. (4)
indifference map (or *preference map*): a complete set of indifference curves that summarize a consumer's tastes or preferences. (4)
inferior good: a commodity of which less is demanded as income rises. (5)
interest rate: the percentage more that must be repaid to borrow money for a fixed period of time. (16)
internalize the externality: to bear the cost of the harm that one inflicts on others (or to capture the benefit that one provides to others). (18)
internal rate of return (*irr*): the discount rate that results in a net present value of an investment of zero. (16)
isocost line: all the combinations of inputs that require the same (*iso*) total expenditure (*cost*). (7)
isoquant: a curve that shows the efficient combinations of labor and capital that can produce a single (*iso*) level of output (*quant*ity). (6)

Law of Demand: consumers demand more of a good, the lower the price of a good, holding constant tastes, the prices of other goods, and other factors that influence the amount they consume. (2)
learning by doing: the productive skills and knowledge that workers and managers gain from experience. (7)
Lerner Index: the ratio of the difference between price and marginal cost to the price: $(p - MC)/p$. (11)
limited liability: condition whereby the personal assets of the owners of the corporation cannot be taken to pay a corporation's debts if it goes into bankruptcy. (6)
long run: a lengthy enough period of time that all inputs can be varied. (6)

marginal cost (*MC*): the amount by which a firm's cost changes if the firm produces one more unit of output. (7)
marginal product of labor (MP_L): the change in total output, Δq, resulting from using an extra unit of labor, ΔL, holding other factors constant: $MP_L = \Delta q/\Delta L$. (6)
marginal profit: the change in profit a firm gets from selling one more unit of output. (8)
marginal rate of substitution (*MRS*): the maximum amount of one good a consumer will sacrifice to obtain one more unit of another good. (4)
marginal rate of transformation (*MRT*): the trade-off the market imposes on the consumer in terms of the amount of one good the consumer must give up to obtain more of the other good. (4)
marginal revenue (*MR*): the change in revenue a firm gets from selling one more unit of output. (8)
marginal revenue product of labor (MRP_L): the extra revenue from hiring one more worker. (15)
marginal utility: the extra utility that a consumer gets from consuming the last unit of a good. (4)
market: an exchange mechanism that allows buyers to trade with sellers. (1)
market failure: inefficient production or consumption, often because a price exceeds marginal cost. (9)
market power: the ability of a firm to charge a price above marginal cost and earn a positive profit. (11)
market structure: the number of firms in the market, the ease with which firms can enter and leave the market, and the ability of firms to differentiate their products from those of their rivals. (8)
microeconomics: the study of how individuals and firms make themselves as well off as possible in a world of scarcity and the consequences of those individual decisions for markets and the entire economy. (1)

minimum efficient scale (full capacity): the smallest quantity at which the average cost curve reaches its minimum. (12)

model: a description of the relationship between two or more economic variables. (1)

monopolistic competition: a market structure in which firms have market power but no additional firm can enter and earn positive profits. (12)

monopoly: the only supplier of a good for which there is no close substitute. (11)

monopsony: the only buyer of a good in a market. (15)

moral hazard: opportunism characterized by an informed person's taking advantage of a less-informed person through an unobserved action. (19)

multimarket price discrimination (third-degree price discrimination): a situation in which a firm charges different groups of customers different prices, but charges a given customer the same price for every unit of output sold.

Nash equilibrium: a set of strategies such that, holding the strategies of all other firms constant, no firm can obtain a higher profit by choosing a different strategy. (12)

natural monopoly: situation in which one firm can produce the total output of the market at lower cost than several firms could. (11)

noncooperative strategic behavior: the set of actions taken by a profit-maximizing firm acting independently of other firms. (14)

nonuniform pricing: charging consumers different prices for the same product or charging a single customer a price that depends on the number of units the customer buys. (13)

normal good: a commodity of which as much or more is demanded as income rises. (5)

normative statement: a conclusion as to whether something is good or bad. (1)

oligopoly: a small group of firms in a market with substantial barriers to entry. (12)

opportunistic behavior: taking advantage of someone when circumstances permit. (15)

opportunity cost (*economic cost*): the value of the best alternative use of a resource. (7)

opportunity set: all the bundles a consumer can buy, including all the bundles inside the budget constraint and on the budget constraint. (4)

Pareto efficient: term referring to an allocation such that any reallocation harms at least one person. (10)

partial-equilibrium analysis: an examination of equilibrium and changes in equilibrium in one market in isolation. (10)

patent: an exclusive right granted to the inventor to sell a new and useful product, process, substance, or design for a fixed period of time. (11)

perfect complements: goods that a consumer is interested in consuming only simultaneously. (4)

perfect price discrimination (*first-degree price discrimination*): situation in which a firm sells each unit at the maximum amount any customer is willing to pay for it, so prices differ across customers and a given customer may pay more for some units than for others. (13)

perfect substitutes: goods that a consumer is completely indifferent as to which to consume. (4)

pooling equilibrium: an equilibrium in which dissimilar people are treated (paid) alike or behave alike. (19)

positive statement: a testable hypothesis about cause and effect. (1)

price discrimination: practice in which a firm charges consumers different prices for the same good. (13)

price elasticity of demand (or *elasticity of demand*, ε): the percentage change in the *quantity demanded* in response to a given percentage change in the price. (3)

price elasticity of supply (or *elasticity of supply*, η): the percentage change in the *quantity supplied* in response to a given percentage change in the price. (3)

prisoners' dilemma: a game in which all players have dominant strategies that result in profits (or other payoffs) that are inferior to what they could achieve if they used cooperative strategies. (12)

private cost: the cost of production only, not including externalities. (18)

producer surplus (*PS*): the difference between the amount for which a good sells and the minimum amount necessary for the seller to be willing to produce the good. (9)

production function: the relationship between the quantities of inputs used and the maximum quantity of output that can be produced, given current knowledge about technology and organization. (6)

production possibility frontier: the maximum amount of outputs that can be produced from a fixed amount of input. (7)

profit (π): the difference between revenues, R, and costs, C: $\pi = R - C$. (6)

property right: the exclusive privilege to use an asset. (18)

public good: a commodity or service whose consumption by one person does not preclude others from also consuming it. (18)

pure public good: a commodity or service without rivalry—nondepletable—and without exclusion. (18)

quantity demanded: the amount of a good that consumers are willing to buy at a given price, holding constant the other factors that influence purchases. (2)

quantity discrimination (a form of *second-degree price discrimination*): situation in which a firm charges a different price for large quantities than for small quantities but all customers who buy a given quantity pay the same price. (13)

quantity supplied: the amount of a good that firms *want* to sell at a given price, holding constant other factors that influence firms' supply decisions, such as costs and government actions. (2)

quota: the limit that a government sets on the quantity of a foreign-produced good that may be imported. (2)

rent: a payment to the owner of an input beyond the minimum necessary for the factor to be supplied. (8)

rent seeking: efforts and expenditures to gain a rent or a profit from government actions. (9)

requirements tie-in sale: a tie-in sale in which customers who buy one product from a firm are required to make all their purchases of another product from that firm. (13)

reservation price: the maximum amount a person would be willing to pay for a unit of output. (13)

residual supply curve: The market supply that is not met by demanders in other sectors at any given wage. (10)

risk: situation in which the likelihood of each possible outcome is known or can be estimated and no single possible outcome is certain to occur. (17)

risk averse: term for someone who does not want to make a fair bet. (17)

risk neutral: term for someone who is indifferent about making a fair bet. (17)

risk preferring: term for someone who may be willing to make a fair bet. (17)

risk premium: the amount that a risk-averse person would pay to avoid taking a risk. (17)

screening: an action taken by an uninformed person to determine the information possessed by informed people. (19)

separating equilibrium: an equilibrium in which one type of people takes actions (such as sending a *signal*) that allows them to be differentiated from other types of people. (19)

shirking: a *moral hazard* in which agents do not provide all the services they are paid to provide. (20)

shortage: a persistent excess demand. (2)

short run: a period of time so brief that at least one factor of production cannot be varied practically. (6)

signaling: an action taken by an informed person to send information to an uninformed person. (19)

social cost: the private cost plus the cost of the harms from *externalities*. (18)

standard: a metric or scale for evaluating the quality of a particular product. (19)

stock: a quantity or value that is measured independently of time. (16)

strategic behavior: a set of actions a firm takes to increase its profit, taking into account the possible actions of other firms. (14)

strategy: a battle plan of the actions a firm plans to take to compete with other firms. (12)

substitution effect: the change in the quantity of a good that a consumer demands when the good's price changes, holding other prices and the consumer's *utility* constant. (5)

supergame: a game that is played repeatedly, allowing players to devise strategies for one period that depend on rivals' actions in previous periods. (12)

sunk cost: an expenditure that cannot be recovered. (7)

supply curve: the *quantity supplied* at each possible price, holding constant the other factors that influence firms' supply decisions. (2)

tariff (*duty*): a tax on only imported goods. (9)

technical progress: an advance in knowledge that allows more output to be produced with the same level of inputs. (6)

technological efficiency (*efficient production*): property of a production function such that the current level of output cannot be produced with fewer inputs, given existing knowledge about technology and the organization of production. (6)

tie-in sale: a type of nonlinear pricing in which customers can buy one product only if they agree to buy another product as well. (13)

total product of labor: the amount of output (or total product) that can be produced by a given amount of labor. (6)

transaction costs: the expenses of finding a trading partner and making a trade for a good or service beyond the price paid for that good or service. (2)

two-part tariff: a pricing system in which the firm charges a consumer a lump-sum fee (the first tariff or price) for the right to buy as many units of the good as the consumer wants at a specified price (the second tariff). (13)

utility: a numerical value that reflects the relative rankings of various bundles of goods. (4)

utility function: the relationship between a *utility* measure and every possible bundle of goods. (4)

variable cost (*VC*)**:** a production expense that changes with the quantity of output produced. (7)

variable input: a factor of production whose quantity can be changed readily by the firm during the relevant time period. (6)

vertically integrated: term referring to a firm that participates in more than one successive stage of the production or distribution of goods or services. (15)

References

Adelaja, Adesoji O., "Price Changes, Supply Elasticities, Industry Organization, and Dairy Output Distribution," *American Journal of Agricultural Economics*, 73(1), February 1991:89–102.

Aigner, Dennis J., and Glen G. Cain, "Statistical Theories of Discrimination in Labor Markets," *Industrial and Labor Relations Review*, 30(2), January 1977:175–187.

Akerlof, George A., "The Market for 'Lemons': Quality Uncertainty and the Market Mechanism," *Quarterly Journal of Economics* 84(3), August 1970:488–500.

Akerlof, George A., "Labor Contacts as Partial Gift Exchanges," *Quarterly Journal of Economics*, 97(4), November 1982:543–569.

Akridge, Jay T., and Thomas W. Hertel, "Multiproduct Cost Relationship for Retail Fertilizer Plants," *American Journal of Agricultural Economics*, 68(4), November 1986:928–938.

Allingham, M. G., "Progression and Leisure," *American Economic Review*, 62(3), June 1972:447–450.

Anderson, Gordon J., and Richard W. Blundell, "Testing Restrictions in a Flexible Demand System: An Application to Consumers' Expenditure in Canada," *Review of Economic Studies*, 50(3), No. 162, July 1983:397–410.

Anderson, Keith B., and Michael R. Metzger, *Petroleum Tariffs as a Source of Government Revenues*. Bureau of Economics, Federal Trade Commission. Washington, D.C.: U.S. Government Printing Office, 1991.

Arrow, Kenneth, *Social Choice and Individual Values*. New York: Wiley, 1951.

Ayres, Ian, and Joel Waldfogel, "A Market Test for Race Discrimination in Bail Setting," *Stanford Law Review*, 46(5), May 1994:987–1047.

Baldwin, John R., and Paul K. Gorecki, *The Role of Scale in Canada/U.S. Productivity Differences in the Manufacturing Sector, 1970–1979*. Toronto: University of Toronto Press, 1986.

Baldwin, Robert E., and Paul R. Krugman, "Industrial Policy and International Competition in Wide Bodied Jet Aircraft," in Robert E. Baldwin, ed., *Trade Policy Issues and Empirical Analysis*. Chicago: University of Chicago Press, 1988.

Barlow, R., and G. R. Sparks, "A Note on Progression and Leisure," *American Economic Review*, 54(4), June 1964:372–377.

Battalio, Raymond, John H. Kagel, and Carl Kogut, "Experimental Confirmation of the Existence of a Giffen Good," *American Economic Review*, 81(3), September 1991:961–970.

Becker, Gary S., *The Economics of Discrimination*, 2nd edition. Chicago: University of Chicago Press, 1971.

Benham, Lee, "The Effect of Advertising on the Price of Eyeglasses," *Journal of Law and Economics*, 15(2), October 1972:337–352.

Berck, Peter, and William R. Bentley, "Hotelling's Theory, Enhancement, and the Taking of the Redwood National Park," *American Journal of Agricultural Economics*, 79(2), May 1997:287–298.

Berck, Peter, and Michael Roberts, "Natural Resource Prices: Will They Ever Turn Up?" *Journal of Environmental Economics and Management*, 31(1), July 1996:65–78.

Berndt, Ernst R., Linda T. Bui, David Reiley, and Glen L. Urban, *The Roles of Marketing, Product Quality and Price Competition in the Growth and Composition of the U.S. Anti-Ulcer Drug Industry*. Program on the Pharmaceutical Industry. WP 19–94, May 1994.

Berndt, Ernst R., Linda T. Bui, David Reiley, and Glen L. Urban, "Information, Marketing and Pricing in the U.S. Anti-Ulcer Drug Market." Unpublished manuscript, 1995.

Billikopf, Gregory Encina, "High Piece-Rate Wages Do Not Reduce Hours Worked," *California Agriculture*, 49(1), January–February 1995:17–18.

Blanciforti, Laura Ann, "The Almost Ideal Demand System Incorporating Habits: An Analysis of Expenditures on Food and Aggregate Commodity Groups." Ph.D. thesis, U.C. Davis 1982.

Bond, Ronald S., John E. Kwoka, Jr., John J. Phelan, and Ira Taylor Whitten, *Staff Report on Effects of Restrictions on Advertising and Commercial Practice in the Professions: The Case of Optometry*. Bureau of Economics, Federal Trade Commission. Washington, D.C.: U.S. Government Printing Office, 1980.

Bordley, Robert F., and James B. McDonald, "Estimating Aggregate Automotive Income Elasticities from the Population Income-Share Elasticity," *Journal of Business & Economic Statistics*, 11(2), April 1993:209–214.

Boskin, Michael J., Ellen R. Dulberger, Robert J. Gordon, Zvi Griliches, and Dale W. Jorgenson, "The CPI Commission: Findings and Recommendations," *American Economic Review*, 87(2), May 1997:78–93.

Boyd, Roy, and Barry J. Seldon, "Revenue and Land-Use Effects of Proposed Changes in Sin Taxes: A General Equilibrium Perspective," *Land Economics*, 67(3), August 1991:365–374.

Brander, James A., and Anming Zhang, "Market Conduct in the Airline Industry: An Empirical Investigation," *Rand Journal of Economics*, 21(4), Winter 1990:567–583.

Brown, Deborah J., and Lee F. Schrader, "Cholesterol Information and Shell Egg Consumption," *American Journal of Agricultural Economics*, 72(3), August 1990:548–555.

Brown, Robert W., "An Estimate of the Rent Generated by a Premium College Football Player," *Economic Inquiry*, 31(4), October 1993:671–684.

Brownlee, Oswald and George Perry, "The Effects of the 1965 Federal Excise Tax Reductions on Prices," *National Tax Journal*, 20(3), September 1967:235–249.

Brunk, Gregory G., "A Test of the Friedman-Savage Gambling Model," *Quarterly Journal of Economics*, 96(2), May 1981:341–348.

Burtraw, Dallas, "Trading Emissions to Clean the Air: Exchanges Few but Savings Many," *Resources*, 122, Winter 1996:3–6.

Buschena, David E., and Jeffrey M. Perloff, "The Creation of Dominant Firm Market Power in the Coconut Oil Export Market," *American Journal of Agricultural Economics*, 73(4), November, 1991:1000–1008.

Capps, Oral, Jr., and Rodolfo M. Nayga, Jr., "Effects of Length of Time on Measured Demand Elasticities: The Problem Revisited," *Canadian Journal of Agricultural Economics*, 38(3), November, 1990:499–512.

Carlson, Steven, "An Overview of Food Stamp Cashout Research in the Food and Nutrition Service," in Nancy Fasciano, Darryl Hall, and Harold Beebout, eds., *New Directions in Food Stamp Policy Research*. Alexandria, Va.: U.S. Department of Agriculture, Food and Nutrition Service, 1993.

Carlton, Dennis W., and Jeffrey M. Perloff, *Modern Industrial Organization*, 2nd edition. New York: HarperCollins, 1994.

Carter, Harold O., Lawrence E. Shepard, and Marilyn D. Whitney, *An Economic Analysis of the California Thoroughbred Racing Industry*. University of California, Giannini Research Report No. 342, October 1991.

Castillo-Freeman, Alida, and Richard B. Freeman, "When the Minimum Wage Really Bites: The Effect of the U.S.-Level Minimum on Puerto Rico," in George J. Borjas, and Richard B. Freeman, eds., *Immigration and the Work Force: Economic Consequences for the United States and Source Areas*. A National Bureau of Economic Research Project Report. Chicago and London: University of Chicago Press, 1992, pp. 177–211.

Caves, Richard E., and David R. Barton, *Technical Efficiency in U.S. Manufacturing Industries*, Cambridge, MA: MIT Press, 1990.

Caves, Richard E., Michael D. Whinston, and Mark A. Hurwitz, "Patent Expiration, Entry, and Competition in the U. S. Pharmaceutical Industry: An Exploratory Analysis," *Brookings Papers on Economic Activity*, Microeconomics, 1991:1–48.

Christensen, Laurits R., and William H. Greene, "Economies of Scale in U.S. Electric Power Generation," *Journal of Political Economy*, 84(4, pt. 1), August 1976:655–676.

Coase, Ronald H., "The Nature of the Firm." *Economica*, 4(16), November 1937:386–405.

Coase, Ronald H., "The Problem of Social Cost," *Journal of Law and Economics*, 3, October, 1960:1–44.

Crandall, Robert W., "The Effects of U.S. Trade Protection for Autos and Steel," *Brookings Papers on Economic Activity*, 1, 1987:271–288.

Davies, J. E., "Competition, Contestability and the Liner Shipping Market," *Journal of Transport Economics and Policy*, 20(3), September 1986:299–312.

Deacon, Robert T., and Jon Sonstelie, "The Welfare Costs of Rationing by Waiting," *Economic Inquiry*, 27(2), April 1989:179–196.

Deaton, Angus S., and John Muelbauer, "An Almost Ideal Demand System," *American Economic Review*, 70(3), June 1980:312–326.

de Melo, Jaime, and David Tarr, *A General Equilibrium Analysis of US Foreign Trade Policy*. Cambridge, MA: MIT Press, 1992.

Diewert, W. Edwin, and Alice O. Nakamura, eds., *Essays in Index Number Theory*, Vol. I. New York: North Holland, 1993.

Dixit, Avinash K., and Robert S. Pindyck, *Investment Under Uncertainty*, Princeton, N.J.: Princeton University Press, 1994.

Drago, Robert, and John S. Heywood, "The Choice of Payment Schemes: Australian Establishment Data," *Industrial Relations*, 34(4), October 1995:507–531.

Dunham, Wayne R., *Moral Hazard and the Market for Used Automobiles*. U.S. Department of Justice, Antitrust Division, Economic Analysis Group Discussion Paper 96–4, July 11, 1996.

Dunn, L. F., "Quantifying Nonpecuniary Returns," *Journal of Human Resources*, 2(3), Summer 1977:347–359.

Dunn, L. F., "An Empirical Indifference Function for Income and Leisure," *Review of Economics and Statistics*, 60(4), November 1978:533–540.

Dunn, L. F., "Measurement of Internal Income-Leisure Tradeoffs," *Quarterly Journal of Economics*, 93(3), August 1979:373–393.

Dunne, Timothy, Mark Roberts, and Larry Samuelson, "Patterns of Firm Entry and Exit in U.S. Manufacturing Industries," *Rand Journal of Economics*, 19(4), Winter 1988:495–515.

Eastwood, David B., and John A. Craven, "Food Demand and Savings in a Complete, Extended, Linear Expenditure System," *American Journal of Agricultural Economics*, 63(3), August 1981:544–549.

Exxon Company, U.S.A., *Competition in the Petroleum Industry*. Submission of Exxon Company, U.S.A. before the [U.S.] Senate Judiciary Subcommittee on Antitrust and Monopoly, January 21, 1975.

Farrell, Joseph, and Matthew Rabin, "Cheap Talk," *Journal of Economic Perspectives*, 10(3), Summer 1996:103–118.

Fasciano, Nancy, Daryl Hall, and Harold Beebout, eds., *New Directions in Food Stamp Policy Research*. Alexandria, Va.: U.S. Department of Agriculture, Food and Nutrition Service, 1993.

Fisher, Franklin M., "The Social Cost of Monopoly and Regulation: Posner Reconsidered," *Journal of Political Economy*, 93(2), April 1985:410–416.

Foster, Andrew D., and Mark R. Rosenzweig, "A Test for Moral Hazard in the Labor Market: Contractual Arrangements, Effort, and Health," *Review of Economics and Statistics*, 76(2), May 1994:213–227.

Fraker, Thomas M., "The Effects of Food Stamps on Food Consumption: A Review of the Literature," in Nancy Fasciano, Darryl Hall, and Harold Beebout, eds., *Current Perspectives on Food Stamp Program Participation*, Alexandria, Va.: U. S. Department of Agriculture, Food and Nutrition Service, 1990.

Frank, Richard G., and Davis S. Salkever, "Pricing, Patent Loss and the Market for Pharmaceuticals," *Southern Economic Journal*, 59(2), October 1992:165–179.

Frech, H. E., III, and William C. Lee, "The Welfare Cost of Rationing-by-Queuing across Markets: Theory and Estimates from the U.S. Gasoline Crisis," *Quarterly Journal of Economics*, 102(1), February 1987:97–108.

French, Ben C., and Gordon A. King, "Demand and Price-Markup Functions for Canned Cling Peaches and Fruit Cocktail," *Western Journal of Agricultural Economics*, 11(1), July 1986:8–18.

Friedlaender, Ann F., Clifford Winston, and Kung Wang, "Costs, Technology, and Productivity in the U.S. Automobile Industry," *Bell Journal of Economics and Management Science*, 14(1), Spring 1983:1–20.

Friedman, Milton, and Leonard J. Savage, "The Utility Analysis of Choices Involving Risk," *Journal of Political Economy*, 56(4), August 1948:279–304.

Fudenberg, Drew, and Jean Tirole, "A 'Signal-Jamming' Theory of Predation," *Rand Journal of Economics*, 17(3), Autumn 1986:366–376.

Fullerton, Don, "On the Possibility of an Inverse Relationship between Tax Rates and Government Revenues," *Journal of Public Economy*, 19(1), October 1982:3–22.

Gallini, Nancy T., "Demand for Gasoline in Canada," *Canadian Journal of Economics*, 16(2), May, 1983:299–324.

Gasmi, Farid, Jean Jacques Laffont, and Quang H. Vuong, "Econometric Analysis of Collusive Behavior in a Soft-Drink Market," *Journal of Economics & Management Strategy*, 1(2), Summer 1992, 277–311.

Gaynor, Martin, and Paul Gertler, "Moral Hazard and Risk Spreading in Partnerships," *Rand Journal of Economics*, 26(4), Winter 1995:591–613.

Genesove, David, "Adverse Selection in the Wholesale Used Car Market," *Journal of Political Economy*, 101(4), August 1993:644–665.

Geoghegan, Jacqueline M., "The Road Not Taken: Environmental Congestion Pricing on the San Francisco–Oakland Bay Bridge." Ph. D. dissertation, University of California, Berkeley, 1995.

Geoghegan, Jacqueline, Barbara Kanninen, and Craig Mohn, "The Bridge Not Taken: Optimal, Equilibrium Congestion Pricing for the San Francisco-Oakland Bay Bridge." Paper presented to the Association of Environmental and Resource Economists at the Allied Social Science Meetings, San Francisco, California, January 1996.

Gilbert, Richard J., "Patents, Sleeping Patents, and Entry Deterrence," in Steven C. Salop, ed., *Strategy, Predation, and Antitrust Analysis*. Washington, D.C.: Federal Trade Commission, 1979.

Globerman, Steven, "A Policy Analysis of Hospital Waiting Lists," *Journal of Policy Analysis and Management*, 10(2), Spring 1991:247–262.

Golec, Joseph, and Tamarkin, Maurry, "Do Bettors Prefer Long Shots Because They Are Risk Lovers, or Are They Just Overconfident?" *Journal of Risk and Uncertainty*, 11(1), July 1995:51–64.

Grabowski, Henry G., and John M. Vernon, "Brand Loyalty, Entry, and Price Competition in Pharmaceuticals after the 1984 Drug Act," *Journal of Law and Economics*, 35(2), October 1992:331–350.

Gravelle, Hugh, and Michael Waterson, "No Win, No Fee: Some Economics of Contingent Legal Fees," *Economic Journal*, 103(420), September 1993:1205–1220.

Griliches, Zvi, and Vidar Ringstad, *Economies of Scale and the Form of the Production Function: An Econometric Study of Norwegian Manufacturing Establishment Data*. Amsterdam: North Holland, 1971.

Groot, Wim, and Hessel Oosterbeek, "Earnings Effects of Different Components of Schooling: Human Capital Versus Screening," *Review of Economics and Statistics*, 76(2), May 1994:317–321.

Grossman, Philip J., Marco Pirozzi, and Jeff Pope, "An Empirical Test of Free-Rider Behaviour," *Australian Economic Papers*, 32(60), June 1993:152–160.

Grubb, W. Norton, "Postsecondary Education and the Sub-Baccalaureate Labor Market: Corrections and

Extensions," *Economics of Education Review*, 14(3), September 1995:285–299.

Gruber, Harald, "The Learning Curve in the Production of Semiconductor Memory Chips," *Applied Economics*, 24(8), August 1992:885–894.

Guillickson, William, and Michael J. Harper, "Multifactor Productivity in U.S. Manufacturing, 1949–83," *Monthly Labor Review*, 110(10), October 1987:18–28.

Hall, Robert E., and David M. Lilien, "Efficient Wage Bargains under Uncertain Supply and Demand," *American Economic Review*, 69(5), December 1979:868–879.

Hatton, T. J., G. R. Boyer, and R. E. Bailey, "The Union Wage Effect in Late Nineteenth Century Britain," *Economica*, 61(244), November 1994:435–456.

Hausman, Jerry A., *Valuation of New Goods under Perfect and Imperfect Competition*. MIT Working paper 94–21, June 1994.

Hausman, Jerry A., and Gregory K. Leonard, "Superstars in the NBA: Economic Value and Policy," *Journal of Labor Economics*, 14(4), October 1997:586–624.

Hay, George A., and Daniel Kelley, "An Empirical Survey of Price-Fixing Conspiracies," *Journal of Law and Economics*, 17(1), April 1974:13–38.

Head, J. G., "A Note on Progression and Leisure: Comment," *American Economic Review*, 56(1), March 1966:172–179.

Hennart, Jean-François, "Upstream Vertical Integration in the Aluminum and Tin Industries," *Journal of Economic Behavior and Organization*, 9(3), April 1988:281–299.

Hewitt, Julie A., and W. Michael Hanemann, "A Discrete/Continuous Choice Approach to Residential Water Demand under Block Rate Pricing," *Land Economics*, 72(2), May 1995:173–192.

Holmes, Thomas J., "Analyzing a Proposal to Ban State Tax Breaks to Businesses," *Quarterly Review, Federal Reserve Bank of Minneapolis*, 19(2), Spring 1995:29–39.

Holt, Matthew, "A Multimarket Bounded Price Variation Model under Rational Expectations: Corn and Soybeans in the United States," *American Journal of Agricultural Economics*, 74(1), February 1992:10–20.

Hotelling, Harold, "The Economics of Exhaustible Resources," *Journal of Political Economy*, 39(2), April 1931:137–175.

Jha, Raghbendra, M. N. Murty, Satya Paul, and Balbir S. Sahni, "Cost Structure of the Indian Cement Industry," *Journal of Economics Studies*, 8(4), 1991:59–67.

Kakalik, J.S, and N.M. Pace, *Costs and Compensation Paid in Tort Litigation*, The Institute for Civil Justice, RAND Corporation, Santa Monica, California, 1986.

Kalirajan, K.P., and M.B. Obwona, "Frontier Production Function: The Stochastic Coefficient Approach," *Oxford Bulletin of Economics and Statistics*, 56(1), 1994:87–96.

Keeler, Theodore E., Teh-Wei Hu, Paul G. Barnett, and Willard G. Manning, "Taxation, Regulation, and Addiction: A Demand Function for Cigarettes Based on Time-Series Evidence," *Journal of Health Economics*, 12(1), April 1993:1–18.

Kennickell, Arthur B., and R. Louise Woodburn, "Consistent Weight Design for 1989, 1992, and 1995 SCPs, and the Distribution of Wealth," Board of Governors of the Federal Reserve System working paper, August 1997.

Killingsworth, Mark R., *Labor Supply*. Cambridge, England: Cambridge University Press, 1983.

Kim, E. Han, and Vijay Singal, "Mergers and Market Power: Evidence from the Airline Industry," *American Economic Review*, 83(3), June 1993:549–569.

Kim, H. Youn, "Economies of Scale and Scope in Multiproduct Firms: Evidence from U.S. Railroads," *Applied Economics*, 19(6), June 1987:733–741.

Kim, Hongjin, Gloria E. Helfand, and Richard E. Howitt, *An Economic Analysis of Ozone Control in California's San Joaquin Valley*. University of California, Davis, Working Paper, December 1995.

Krattenmaker, Thomas G., and Steven C. Salop, "Antcompetitive Exclusion: Raising Rivals' Costs to Achieve Power over Price," *Yale Law Journal*, 96(2), December 1986:209–293.

Krueger, Alan B., "Ownership, Agency, and Wages: An Examination of Franchising in the Fast Food Industry," *Quarterly Journal of Economics*, 106(1), February 1991:75–101.

Krupnick, A. J., and Paul R. Portney, "Controlling Urban Air Pollution: A Benefit-Cost Assessment," *Science*, 252, April 1991:522–528.

Lenard, Thomas M., "The Efficiency Costs of the Postal Monopoly: The Case of Third-Class Mail," *Journal of Regulatory Economics*, 6(4), December 1994:421–431.

Levin, Richard C., Alvin K. Klevorick, Richard R. Nelson, and Sidney G. Winter, "Appropriating the Returns from Industrial Research and Development," *Brookings Papers on Economic Activity*, 3(Special Issue on Microeconomics), 1987:783–820.

Libecap, Gary, *Contracting for Property Rights*. New York: Cambridge University Press, 1989.

Lopez, Rigoberto A., and Emilio Pagoulatos, "Rent Seeking and the Welfare Cost of Trade Barriers," *Public Choice*, 79(1–2), April 1994:149–160.

MacAvoy, Paul W., "Tacit Collusion under Regulation in the Pricing of Interstate Long-Distance Services," *Journal of Economics & Management Strategy*, 4(2), Summer 1995:147–185.

MacCrimmon, Kenneth R., and M. Toda, "The Experimental Determination of Indifference Curves," *Review of Economic Studies*, 56(3), July 1969:433–451.

Machina, Mark, "Dynamic Consistency and Non-Expected Utility Models of Choice under Uncertainty," *Journal of Economic Literature*, 27(4), December 1989:1622–1668.

MacKie-Mason, Jeffrey K., and Robert S. Pindyck, "Cartel Theory and Cartel Experience in International Minerals Markets," in R. L. Gordon, H. D. Jacoby, and M. B. Zimmerman, eds., *Energy: Markets and Regulation: Essays in Honor of M. A. Adelman*. Cambridge, MA.: MIT Press, 1986.

MaCurdy, Thomas, David Green, and Harry Paarsch, "Assessing Empirical Approaches for Analyzing Taxes and Labor Supply," *Journal of Human Resources*, 25(3), Summer 1990:415–490.

Madden, Janice F., *The Economics of Sex Discrimination*. Lexington, MA: Heath, 1973.

Maddock, Rodney, Elkin Castano, Frank Vella, "Estimating Electricity Demand: The Cost of Linearizing the Budget Constraint," *Review of Economics and Statistics*, 74(2), May 1992:350–354.

Manser, Marilyn E., and Richard J. McDonald, "An Analysis of Substitution Bias in Measuring Inflation, 1959–85," *Econometrica*, 56(4), July 1988:909–930.

Mergos, George J., and George S. Donatos, "Consumer Behaviour in Greece: An Application of the Almost Ideal Demand System," *Applied Economics*, 21(7), July 1989:983–993.

Moffitt, Robert, "Estimating the Value of an In-Kind Transfer: The Case of Food Stamps," *Econometrica*, 57(2), March, 1989:385–409.

Moschini, Giancarlo, and Karl D. Meilke, "Production Subsidy and Countervailing Duties in Vertically Related Markets: The Hog-Pork Case between Canada and the United States," *American Journal of Agricultural Economics*, 74(4), November, 1992:951–961.

Nash, John F., "Equilibrium Points in *n*-Person Games," *Proceedings of the National Academy of Sciences*, 36, 1950:48–49.

Nash, John F., "Non-Cooperative Games," *Annals of Mathematics*, 54(2), July 1951:286–295.

Nemoto, Jiro, Yasuo Nakanishi, and Seishi Madono, "Scale Economies and Over-Capitalization in Japanese Electric Utilities," *International Economic Review*, 34(2), May 1993:431–440.

Norman, G., "Economies of Scale in the Cement Industry," *Journal of Industrial Economics*, 27(4), June 1979:317–337.

Panzar, John C., and Robert D. Willig, "Economies of Scale in Multi-Output Production," *Quarterly Journal of Economics*, 91(3), August 1977:481–493.

Panzar, John C., and Robert D. Willig, "Economies of Scope," *American Economic Review*, 71(2), May 1981:268–272.

Perloff, Harvey S., *Puerto Rico's Economic Future*. Chicago: University of Chicago Press, 1950. (Reprinted 1975; New York: Arno Press).

Perry, Martin K., "Forward Integration by Alcoa: 1888–1930," *Journal of Industrial Economics*, 29(1), September 1980:37–53.

Perry, Martin K., "Vertical Integration: Determinants and Effects," in Richard Schmalensee and Robert Willig, eds., *Handbook of Industrial Organization*. New York: North Holland, 1989.

Polinsky, A. Mitchell, "Controlling Externalities and Protecting Entitlements: Property Right, Liability Rule, and Tax-Subsidy Approaches," *Journal of Legal Studies*, 8(1), January 1979:1–48.

Pollak, Robert A., *The Theory of the Cost-of-Living Index*. New York: Oxford University Press, 1989.

Posner, Richard A., "The Social Cost of Monopoly and Regulation," *Journal of Political Economy*, 83(4), August 1975:807–827.

Pratten, Clifford F., "The Manufacture of Pins," *Journal of Economic Literature*, 18(1), March 1980:93–96.

Ransom, Michael R., "Seniority and Monopsony in the Academic Labor Market," *American Economic Review*, 83(1), March 1993:221–233.

Rawls, John, *A Theory of Justice*. New York: Oxford University Press, 1971.

Reynolds, Lloyd G., Peter Gregory, and Luz M. Torruellas, *Wages, Productivity, and Industrialization in Puerto Rico*. Homewood, Ill: Richard D. Irwin, 1965.

Ries, John C., "Windfall Profits and Vertical Relationships: Who Gained in the Japanese Auto Industry from VERs?" *Journal of Industrial Economics*, 41(3), September 1993:259–276.

Roberts, Mark J., and Larry Samuelson, "An Empirical Analysis of Dynamic Nonprice Competition in an Oligopolistic Industry," *Rand Journal of Economics*, 19(2) Summer 1988:200–220.

Robidoux, Benoît, and John Lester, "Econometric Estimates of Scale Economies in Canadian Manufacturing," Canadian Department of Finance Working Paper No. 88–4, 1988.

Robidoux, Benoît, and John Lester, "Econometric Estimates of Scale Economies in Canadian Manufacturing," *Applied Economics*, 24(1), January 1992:113–122.

Rosenman, Robert E., and Wesley W. Wilson, "Quality Differentials and Prices: Are Cherries Lemons?" *Journal of Industrial Economics*, 39(6), December 1991:649–658.

Ross, David R., and Klaus F. Zimmermann, "Evaluating Reported Determinants of Labor Demand," *Labour Economics*, 1(1), June 1993:71–84.

Rousseas, S.W., and A.G. Hart, "Experimental Verification of a Composite Indifference Map," *Journal of Political Economy*, 59(4), August 1951:288–318.

Salop, Steven C., "The Noisy Monopolist: Imperfect Information, Price Dispersion, and Price Discrimination,"

Review of Economic Studies, 44(3), October 1977:393–406.

Salop, Steven C., "Strategic Entry Deterrence," *American Economic Review*, 69(2), May 1979:335–338.

Salop, Joanne, and Steven Salop, "Self-Selection and Turnover in the Labor Market," *Quarterly Journal of Economics*, 90(4), November 1976:619–627.

Salop, Steven C., "Practices That (Credibly) Facilitate Oligopoly Coordination," in Joseph E. Stiglitz and G. Frank Mathewson, eds., *New Developments in the Analysis of Market Structure*. Cambridge, MA: MIT Press, 1986.

Salop, Steven C., and David T. Sheffman, "Cost-Raising Strategies," *Journal of Industrial Economics*, 36(1), September 1987:19–34.

Sazanami, Yoko, Shujiro Urata, and Hiroki Kawai, *Measuring the Costs of Protection in Japan*. Washington, D.C.: Institute for International Economics, 1995.

Schoemaker, Paul J. H., "The Expected Utility Model: Its Variants, Purposes, Evidence and Limitation," *Journal of Economic Literature*, 20(2), June 1982:529–563.

Schroeter, John R., Scott L. Smith, and Steven R. Cox, "Advertising and Competition in Routine Legal Service Markets: An Empirical Investigation, *Journal of Industrial Economics*, 36(1), September 1987:49–60.

Scott, Robert E., "The Effects of Protection on a Domestic Oligopoly: The Case of the U.S. Auto Market," *Journal of Policy Modeling*, 16(3), June 1994:299–325.

Shapiro, Carl, and Joseph E. Stiglitz, "Equilibrium Unemployment as a Worker Discipline Device," *American Economic Review*, 74(3), June 1984:434–444.

Shea, John, "Do Supply Curves Slope Up?" *Quarterly Journal of Economics*, 108(1), February 1993:1–32.

Shoesmith, Gary L. "Economies of Scale and Scope in Petroleum Refining," *Applied Economics*, 20(12), December 1988:1643–1652.

Slade, Margaret E., "Product Rivalry with Multiple Strategic Weapons: An Analysis of Price and Advertising Competition," *Journal of Economics & Management Strategy*," 4(3), Fall 1995:224–276.

Smiley, Robert, "Empirical Evidence on Strategic Entry Deterrence," *International Journal of Industrial Organization*, 6(2), June 1988:167–180.

Spence, A. Michael, "The Learning Curve and Competition," *Bell Journal of Economics and Management Science*, 12(1), 1981:49–70.

Spence, Michael, *Market Signaling*. Cambridge, MA: Harvard University Press, 1974.

Spencer, Barbara J., and James A. Brander, "International R&D Rivalry and Industrial Strategy," *Review of Economic Studies*, 50(4), October 1983:707–722.

Stewart, Mark B., "Union Wage Differentials in an Era of Declining Unionization," *Oxford Bulletin of Economics and Statistics*, 57(2), May 1995:143–166.

Stiglitz, Joseph E., "The Theory of 'Screening,' Education, and the Distribution of Income," *American Economic Review*, 65(3), June 1975:283–300.

Stiglitz, Joseph E., "Equilibrium in Product Markets with Imperfect Information," *American Economic Review*, 69(2), May 1979:339–345.

Stiglitz, Joseph E., "The Causes and Consequences of the Dependence of Quality on Price," *Journal of Economic Literature*, 25(1), March 1987:1–48.

Stuart, Charles, "Swedish Tax Rates, Labor Supply, and Tax Revenues," *Journal of Political Economy*, 89(5), October 1981:1020–1038.

Stuart, Charles, "Welfare Costs per Dollar of Additional Tax Revenue in the United States," *American Economic Review*, 74(3), June 1984:352–362.

Sullivan, Daniel, "Monopsony Power in the Market for Nurses," *Journal of Law and Economics*, 32(2, pt. 2) October 1989:S135–S178.

Suslow, Valerie Y., "Measuring Quality Change in Pharmaceutical Markets: Hedonic Price Indexes for Anti-Ulcer Drugs," in Robert B. Helms, ed., *Competitive Strategies in the Pharmaceutical Industry*. Washington, D.C.: AEI Press, 1996.

Tarr, David G., *A General Equilibrium Analysis of the Welfare and Employment Effects of US Quotas in Textiles, Autos and Steel*. Bureau of Economics Staff Report, Federal Trade Commission, February 1989.

Taube, Paul M., and Don N. MacDonald, "A Dynamic Almost Ideal Demand System Incorporating Consumer Expectations," *Managerial and Decision Economics*, 12(3), June 1991:197–206.

Terrell, Katherine, "Technical Change and Factor Bias in Polish Industry (1962–1983)," *Review of Economics and Statistics*, 75(4), November 1993:741–747.

Tideman, T. Nicholaus, and Gordon Tullock, "A New and Superior Process for Making Social Choices," *Journal of Political Economy*, 84(6), December 1976:1145–1159.

Timmer, C. Peter, "Choice of Technique in Rice Milling on Java," in Carl K. Eicher and John M. Staatz, eds., *Agricultural Development in the Third World*. Baltimore: Johns Hopkins University Press, 1984.

Tullock, G., "The Welfare Cost of Tariffs, Monopolies, and Theft," *Western Economic Journal*, 5(3), June 1967:224–232.

Tweeten, Luther, *Farm Policy Analysis*. Boulder, CO and London: Westview Press, 1989.

Urban, Glen L., Theresa Carter, and Steven Gaskin, "Market Share Rewards to Pioneering Brands: An Empirical Analysis and Strategic Implications," *Management Science*, 32(6), June 1986:645–659.

Vandermeulen, Daniel C., "Upward Sloping Demand Curves without the Giffen Paradox," *American Economic Review*, 62(3), June 1972:453–458.

Van Ravenstein, Ad, and Hans Vijlbrief, "Welfare Cost of Higher Tax Rates: An Empirical Laffer Curve for the Netherlands," *De Economist*, 136(2), 1988:205–219.

Varian, Hal R., "Measuring the Deadweight Cost of DUP and Rent-Seeking Activities," *Economics and Politics*, 1(1), Spring 1989:81–95.

Varian, Hal R., *Microeconomic Analysis*, 3rd edition. New York: W.W. Norton, 1992.

Villegas, Daniel J., "The Impact of Usury Ceilings on Consumer Credit," *Southern Economic Journal*, 56(1), July 1989:126–141.

Viscusi, W. Kip, *Employment Hazards*. Cambridge, MA: Harvard University Press, 1979.

Viscusi, W. Kip, *Pricing Environmental Risks*. Center for the Study of American Business, Washington University, Policy Study Number 112, June 1992.

von Neumann, John, and Oskar Morgenstern, *Theory of Games and Economic Behavior*. Princeton, N.J.: Princeton University Press, 1944.

Waldfogel, Joel, "The Deadweight Loss of Christmas," *American Economic Review*, 83(5), December 1993:1328–1336.

Walton, Clarence C., and Frederick W. Cleveland, *Corporations on Trial: The Electric Cases*. Belmont, Calif.: Wadsworth, 1964.

Weiss, Andrew, "High School Graduation, Performance, and Wages," *Journal of Political Economy*, 96(4), August, 1988:785–820.

Welsh, Finus, "Minimum Wage Legislation in the United States," *Economic Inquiry*, 12(3), September 1974:285–318.

Whinston, Michael D., and Scott C. Collins, "Entry and Competitive Structure in Deregulated Airline Markets: An Event Study Analysis of People Express," *Rand Journal of Economics*, 23(4), Winter 1992:445–462.

White, Lawrence J., *The S&L Debacle*. New York: Oxford University Press, 1991.

Williamson, Oliver E., *Markets and Hierarchies: Analysis and Antitrust Implications*. New York: The Free Press, 1975.

Williamson, Oliver E., "Credible Commitments: Using Hostages to Support Exchange," *American Economic Review*, 73(4), September 1983:519–540.

Willis, Robert J., "A New Approach to the Economic Theory of Fertility Behavior," *Journal of Political Economy*, 81(2, Part II), March–April 1973:S14–S64.

Wilson, James A., "A Test of the Tragedy of the Commons," in Garrett Hardin and John Baden, eds., *Managing the Commons*. San Francisco: W.H. Freeman, 1977, pp. 96–111.

Womer, N. Keith, and J. Wayne Patterson, "Estimation and Testing of Learning Curves," *Journal of Business & Economic Statistics*, 1(4), October 1983:265–272.

Yellen, Janet L., "Efficiency Wage Models of Unemployment," *American Economic Review*, 74(2), May 1984:200–205.

Credits

Chapter 2 p. 38: PhotoDisc; p. 41: UPI/Corbis-Bettmann

Chapter 3 p. 68: By Ruben Bolling/Quaternary Features. Cartoon originally appeared in Salon Magazine www.salonmagazine.com. Reprinted with permission.

Chapter 5 p. 149: Courtesy of Malden Mills

Chapter 6 p. 159: Courtesy of Ghirardelli Chocolate Co.; p. 191: Brown Brothers

Chapter 7 p. 237: PhotoDisc

Chapter 8 p. 269: PhotoDisc

Chapter 9 p. 306: Douglas Mason/Woodfin Camp & Associates

Chapter 10 p. 360 NYT Graphics/NYT Permissions; top left: Library of Congress; top right: Dorothea Lange/Library of Congress; middle left: U.S. Capitol Historical Society; middle right: Courtesy of The Ronald Reagan Presidential Library; bottom: The National Archives.

Chapter 11 p. 379: Courtesy of Lewis Galoob Toys, Inc.

Chapter 12 p. 449: Doug Wilson/Folio, Inc.

Chapter 13 p. 473: Courtesy of Jeffrey Perloff

Chapter 14 p. 528: *Better Homes and Gardens*, August 1946; p. 540: *Better Homes and Gardens*, March 1955

Chapter 15 p. 579: Courtesy of ALCOA

Chapter 16 p. 589: PhotoDisc

Chapter 17 p. 628: From William Cole and Mike Thaler, eds., *The Classic Cartoons* (Cleveland: The World Publishing Company, 1966).

Chapter 18 p. 657: AP/Wide World Photos

Chapter 19 p. 695: (c) 1998 Tribune Media Services. All Rights Reserved. Reprinted with permission.

Chapter 20 p. 738: PhotoDisc

Index

Selected World Wide Web Sites

Directories of basic economic, agricultural economics, and resource economics sites and data sources:

http://econwpa.wustl.edu/EconFAQ/EconFAQ.html

http://www.helsinki.fi/WebEc/

http://www.ncat.edu/~simkinss/econlinks.html

http://are.Berkeley.Edu/library/other.html

http://www.wisc.edu/aae/pointers.html#asites

http://kierkegaard.ifas.ufl.edu

http://dialspace.dial.pipex.com/geoff.riley

Government agencies (history, data, news):

http://www.ssa.gov/ *(Social Security Administration)*

http://www.usdoj.gov/ *(U.S. Department of Justice)*

http://www.ftc.gov/ *(Federal Trade Commission)*

http://www.sec.gov/ *(U.S. Securities and Exchange Commission)*

http://www.sec.gov/edgarha.htm *(information on specific firms)*

http://www.bls.gov *(Bureau of Labor Statistics)*

http://stats.bls.gov/eag.table.html *("Economy at a Glance" table)*

http://stats.bls.gov/top20.html *(Bureau of Labor Statistics most requested regional sites)*

http://www.stat-usa.gov/ *(Commerce Department)*

http://www.fdic.gov/ *(Federal Deposit Insurance Corporation)*

http://os.dhhs.gov/ *(Department of Health and Human Services)*

http://www.census.gov/ *(census)*

http://www.whitehouse.gov/ *(The White House)*

http://www.whitehouse.gov/fsbr/esbr.html/ *(economic statistics briefing room)*

http://lcweb.loc.gov *(Library of Congress)*

http://thomas.loc.gov *(Thomas Legislative Information on the Internet)*

http://www.libertynet.org/~fedresrv/ *(Federal Reserve Bank of Philadelphia)*

http://woodrow.mpls.frb.fed.us *(Federal Reserve Bank of Minneapolis)*

http://www.stls.frb.org/fred *(data from the St. Louis Federal Reserve Bank)*

http://www.statcan.ca/ *(Statistics Canada)*

http://europa.eu.int/index-en.htm/ *(European Commission)*

http://www2.echo.lu/ *[IM (International Market) Europe—European Commission]*

http://www.ons.gov.uk/ *(Office for National Statistics—U.K.)*

Other sources of data:

http://www.ntu.edu.sg/library/statdata.html

http://www.helsinki.fi/WebEc/webecc8d.html *(international data sources)*